W9-AYK-506

Psychology

Psychology

FIRST EDITION

David G. Myers

HOPE COLLEGE

WORTH PUBLISHERS, INC.

TO JACK, JANE, JOHN, TOM,
AND ALL PEOPLE OF HOPE

Psychology

Manufactured in the United States of America

Library of Congress Catalog Card Number 85-051770

ISBN: 0-87901-311-7

Third printing, March 1987

Editor: Anne Vinnicombe

Supplements editor: Betty Jane Shapiro

Production: George Touloumes and Patricia Lawson

Design: Malcolm Grear Designers

Art coordination and cover design: Demetrios Zangos

Picture editors: Elaine Bernstein and David Hinchman

Part- and chapter-opening picture research: Barbara Salz

Composition: York Graphic Services, Inc.

Printing and binding: Von Hoffmann Press

Illustration credits appear on p. 663, which constitutes an extension of the copyright page.

Worth Publishers, Inc.

33 Irving Place

New York, New York 10003

Preface

My goals in writing this book can be reduced to one overriding aim: *to merge rigorous science with a broad human perspective in a book that would engage both the mind and the heart*. I wanted this book to clearly set forth the principles and processes of psychology and at the same time to remain sensitive to students' capabilities and interests, and to their futures as individual human beings. Ideally, it would be a book that helped students to gain insight into the phenomena of their everyday lives, to feel a sense of wonder about seemingly ordinary human processes, and to see how psychology addresses deep intellectual issues that cross disciplines. I also wanted to produce a book that would convey to its readers the inquisitive, compassionate, and sometimes playful spirit in which psychology can be approached.

To achieve these goals, I established, and have steadfastly tried to follow, eight basic operating principles:

1. *To put facts in the service of concepts.* My intention has been not to fill students' intellectual file drawers with facts but to reveal psychology's major concepts. In each chapter I have placed the greater emphasis on the concepts that students should carry with them long after they have forgotten the details of what they have read.

2. *To exemplify the process of inquiry.* The student is shown, time and again, not just the outcome of research, but how the research process works—and how it sometimes doesn't work. Throughout, the book tries to excite the reader's curiosity. It invites readers to imagine themselves as participants in classic experiments. Several chapters introduce research stories as mysteries that are progressively unraveled, as one clue after another is put into place.

3. *To be as up-to-date as possible.* Few things dampen students' interest as quickly as the sense that they are reading stale news. I therefore sought to present the most recent developments in the discipline. Accordingly, 60 percent of the references in this text

are from the 1980s, and 60 percent of these were published between 1983 and 1986.

4. *To integrate principles and applications.* Throughout—by means of anecdotes, case histories, and the posing of hypothetical situations—I have tried to relate the findings of basic research to their applications and implications. Where psychology can help to illuminate pressing human issues—whether they be racism and sexism, health and happiness, or violence and war—I have let it do so.

5. *To enhance comprehension by providing continuity.* As I approached each chapter, I searched for a significant issue or theme that could link the subtopics, forming a thread through the chapter. The "Learning" chapter, for example, conveys the idea that bold thinkers (Pavlov, Skinner, Bandura) can serve as intellectual pioneers. The "Thinking and Language" chapter raises the issue of human rationality and irrationality. The "Gender" chapter reexamines from a new perspective the nature-nurture issue (which is introduced in Chapter 2 and reappears throughout the book).

6. *To teach critical thinking.* By presenting research as intellectual detective work, I have tried to help students to think more like research psychologists—with an inquiring, analytical mindset. The reader will discover how an empirical approach can help in evaluating claims for, among other things, such highly publicized phenomena as subliminal persuasion, ESP, and mother-infant bonding. And whether they are learning about memory, cognition, or statistics, students are led to see how what they are learning can help them to think more clearly.

7. *To reinforce learning at every step.* In addition to presenting material in a way that encourages students to process it actively, each chapter concludes with an organized narrative summary, a handy glossary of fully defined key terms, and reading suggestions that are attuned to students' interests and level of comprehension.

8. *To provide organizational flexibility.* I have chosen an organization in which developmental psychology is covered early because students usually find the material of particular interest and because it introduces themes and concepts that are used later in the text. Nevertheless, because many instructors have their own preferred sequence, the chapters were written in a way that anticipates other approaches to organizing the introductory course.

SUPPLEMENTS

Psychology is accompanied by a comprehensive teaching and learning package. For students, there is a *Study Guide,* prepared and class-tested by Richard Straub (University of Michigan, Dearborn). Using the SQ3R (study, question, read, recite, review) method, each chapter contains a topic guide, fill-in questions, progress tests, applications, and essay questions, along with student projects and sources for more information. Answers to the chapter review and progress tests (with page references) are provided.

To bring some of psychology's concepts and methods to life, Thomas Ludwig (Hope College) has created *PsychSim: Computer Simulations in Psychology*. These twelve interactive simulations (available for use on IBM PC and Apple II+/IIe/IIc) cover such topics as hemispheric specialization, visual illusions, and ELIZA, the computer therapist. Each provides an easy way to engage students in actively thinking about and responding to psychological procedures.

The *Instructor's Resource Manual,* created by Martin Bolt (Calvin College), provides an abundance of helpful resources in a loose-leaf case. The manual includes chapter objectives; suggestions for lecture/discussion topics, classroom exercises, student projects, and films; and ready-to-use handouts for student participation. There are also many slides and transparencies for overhead projection.

Finally, the *Test Bank,* coordinated, written, and edited by John Brink (Calvin College) with the able assistance of Martin Bolt (Calvin College), Nancy Campbell-Goymer (Birmingham-Southern College), James Eison (Southeast Missouri State University), and Anne Nowlin (Roane State Community College), provides 1200 multiple-choice questions. For each chapter, there are 20 definitional, 20 factual, and 20 conceptual questions, identified by topic and page number and keyed to objectives in the *Instructor's Resource Manual.* The *Test Bank* questions are available on a computerized test generation system.

IN APPRECIATION

A textbook may have one author's name on the cover, but in truth it is a team effort, a collaboration between the author, publisher, and, in my own case, a multitude of consultants and reviewers. It is a genuine pleasure, then, for me to acknowledge the fellow members of my team.

As Ralph Waldo Emerson once wrote, "Every man I meet is in some way my superior; and in that I can learn of him." My experience is that every consultant and reviewer of this book has, indeed, in some way been my superior, and I have learned from each of them. Our consultants helped me see how a new text might accurately portray the most current thinking in their specialties. The subsequent chapter drafts were each critiqued by some twenty subject matter experts and introductory psychology teachers and were class tested in four classes. The result is a book written by one author with a single voice, but a better book than one author alone (this author, at least) could have written. So, to the following consultants and reviewers I am indebted:

T. John Akamatsu, *Kent State University*
Harry H. Avis, *Sierra College*
Bernard J. Baars, *University of California-San Francisco*
John K. Bare, *Carleton College*
Jonathan Baron, *University of Pennsylvania*
Andrew Baum, *Uniformed Services University of the Health Sciences*
Les Beach, *Hope College*
Kathleen Stassen Berger, *Bronx Community College*
Allen E. Bergin, *Brigham Young University*
George Bishop, *University of Texas at San Antonio*
Douglas W. Bloomquist, *Framingham State College*
Kenneth S. Bowers, *University of Waterloo*
Robert M. Boynton, *University of California-San Diego*
Ross Buck, *University of Connecticut*
Timothy P. Carmody, *Oregon Health Sciences University*
Stanley Coren, *University of British Columbia*
Donald Cronkite, *Hope College*

Peter W. Culicover, *University of Arizona*
Richard B. Day, *McMaster University*
Edward L. Deci, *University of Rochester*
Timothy J. deVoogd, *Cornell University*
David Foulkes, *Georgia Mental Health Institute*
Larry H. Fujinaka, *University of Hawaii-Leeward Community College*
Robert J. Gatchel, *University of Texas Health Science Center at Dallas*
Mary Gauvain, *University of Pennsylvania*
Alan G. Glaros, *University of Florida*
Judith P. Goggin, *University of Texas at El Paso*
Marvin R. Goldfried, *State University of New York, Stony Brook*
Charles Green, *Hope College*
William T. Greenough, *University of Illinois at Urbana-Champaign*
J. H. Grosslight, *Florida State University*
James V. Hinrichs, *University of Iowa*
Douglas L. Hintzman, *University of Oregon*
Nils Hovik, *Lehigh County Community College*
Irene Hulicka, *State University of New York, Buffalo*
Janet Shibley Hyde, *Denison University*
Carroll E. Izard, *University of Delaware*
John Jung, *California State University-Long Beach*
John F. Kihlstrom, *University of Wisconsin*
Kathleen Kowal, *University of North Carolina at Wilmington*
Richard E. Mayer, *University of California-Santa Barbara*
Donald H. McBurney, *University of Pittsburgh*
Timothy P. McNamara, *Vanderbilt University*
Donald Meichenbaum, *University of Waterloo*
Donald H. Mershon, *North Carolina State University*
James Motiff, *Hope College*
Carol A. Nowak, *Center for the Study of Aging, State University of New York, Buffalo*
Anne Nowlin, *Roane State Community College*
Jacob L. Orlofsky, *University of Missouri-St. Louis*
Willis F. Overton, *Temple University*
Daniel J. Ozer, *Boston University*
Joseph J. Palladino, *University of Southern Indiana*
Herbert L. Petri, *Towson State University*
Robert Plutchik, *Albert Einstein College of Medicine*
Ovide F. Pomerleau, *School of Medicine at the University of Michigan-Ann Arbor*
Dennis R. Proffitt, *University of Virginia*
Judith Rodin, *Yale University*
Alexander J. Rosen, *University of Illinois at Chicago Circle*
Kay F. Schaffer, *University of Toledo*
Alexander W. Siegel, *University of Houston*
Ronald K. Siegel, *School of Medicine at the University of California-Los Angeles*
Aaron Smith, *University of Michigan-Ann Arbor*
Donald P. Spence, *School of Medicine at Rutgers The State University of New Jersey*
Richard A. Steffy, *University of Waterloo*
Leonard Stern, *Eastern Washington University*
Robert J. Sternberg, *Yale University*
George C. Stone, *University of California-San Francisco*
Fred D. Strider, *College of Medicine at the University of Nebraska Medical Center*
Don Tucker, *University of Oregon*
Rhoda K. Unger, *Montclair State College*
Phillip Van Eyl, *Hope College*
Richard D. Walk, *George Washington University*
George Weaver, *Florida State University*
Wilse B. Webb, *University of Florida*
Merold Westphal, *Hope College*
David A. Wilder, *Rutgers The State University of New Jersey*
Joan Wilterdink, *University of Wisconsin-Madison*
Jeffrey J. Wine, *Stanford University*
Joseph Wolpe, *The Medical College of Pennsylvania and School of Medicine at Temple University*
Gordon Wood, *Michigan State University*

Ten individuals read the whole manuscript and provided me not only with a critique of each chapter but also with their sense of the style and balance of the whole book. For their advice and warm encouragement, I am grateful to:

John Best, *Eastern Illinois University*
Cynthia J. Brandau, *Belleville Area College*
Sharon S. Brehm, *University of Kansas*
Steven L. Buck, *University of Washington*
Robert M. Levy, *Indiana State University*
G. William Lucker, *University of Texas at El Paso*
Angela P. McGlynn, *Mercer County Community College*
Bobby J. Poe, *Belleville Area College*
Catherine A. Riordan, *University of Missouri-Rolla*
Robert B. Wallace, *University of Hartford*

Five key people not only critically read every page in the early draft stages but also helped to nurture this project with their enthusiasm and wise advice. Martin Bolt (Calvin College) and Richard Straub (University of Michigan, Dearborn) contributed their sensitivities as successful teachers and knowledgeable psychologists. James Eison (Southeast Missouri State University) offered countless worthwhile suggestions. My wife, Carol Myers, not only reviewed the manuscript but inspired me to retain its spirit throughout all the revisions. Charles Brewer (Furman University) benefited me enormously with his meticulous attention to every sentence, his gentle, probing questions, and his constant encouragement.

At Worth Publishers—a company that lets nothing restrain its efforts to produce textbooks of the highest quality—a host of people played key supportive roles. I am particularly grateful to Alison Meersschaert, who commissioned this book, envisioned its goals and a process to fulfill them, and nurtured the book nearly to the end of its first draft. Without her vision and infectious enthusiasm, this book would not exist. I am also very indebted to Anne Vinnicombe, leader of a dedicated editorial team, for her prodigious effort in bringing this project to fulfillment and her commitment to ensuring the accuracy, logical flow, and clarity of every page, and to Amy Marsh, who supervised editorial details and maintained organization in an avalanche of paperwork. Thanks also go to Worth's production team, led by George Touloumes, for crafting a final product that exceeds my expectations.

At Hope College, the supporting team members include Jennifer Heitman, Beth Gunn, Julie Zuwerink, and Richard Burtt, who researched, checked, and proofed countless items; Betty Dolley, who efficiently xeroxed more than a quarter million pages for class testing and reviews; Kathy Adamski, who typed hundreds of dictated letters without ever losing her good cheer; and Phyllis and Richard Vandervelde, who processed some 15,000 pages of various chapter drafts with their customary excellence.

Finally, there are four very special people who for ten or more years now, and intensively throughout this project, have offered their friendship and support. Through his editing of this and two previous books, poet-essayist Jack Ridl has coached and encouraged this author's voice. Among my psychology department colleagues—all of whom have been supportive—John Shaughnessy, Jane Dickie, and Tom Ludwig played special roles in this book. Not only did they review every chapter, they have on hundreds of occasions been my sounding board. My dedication of the book is therefore a gesture of appreciation to the Hope College community, of which these four people are for me such an important part.

David G. Myers

Contents in Brief

Contents

Psychology

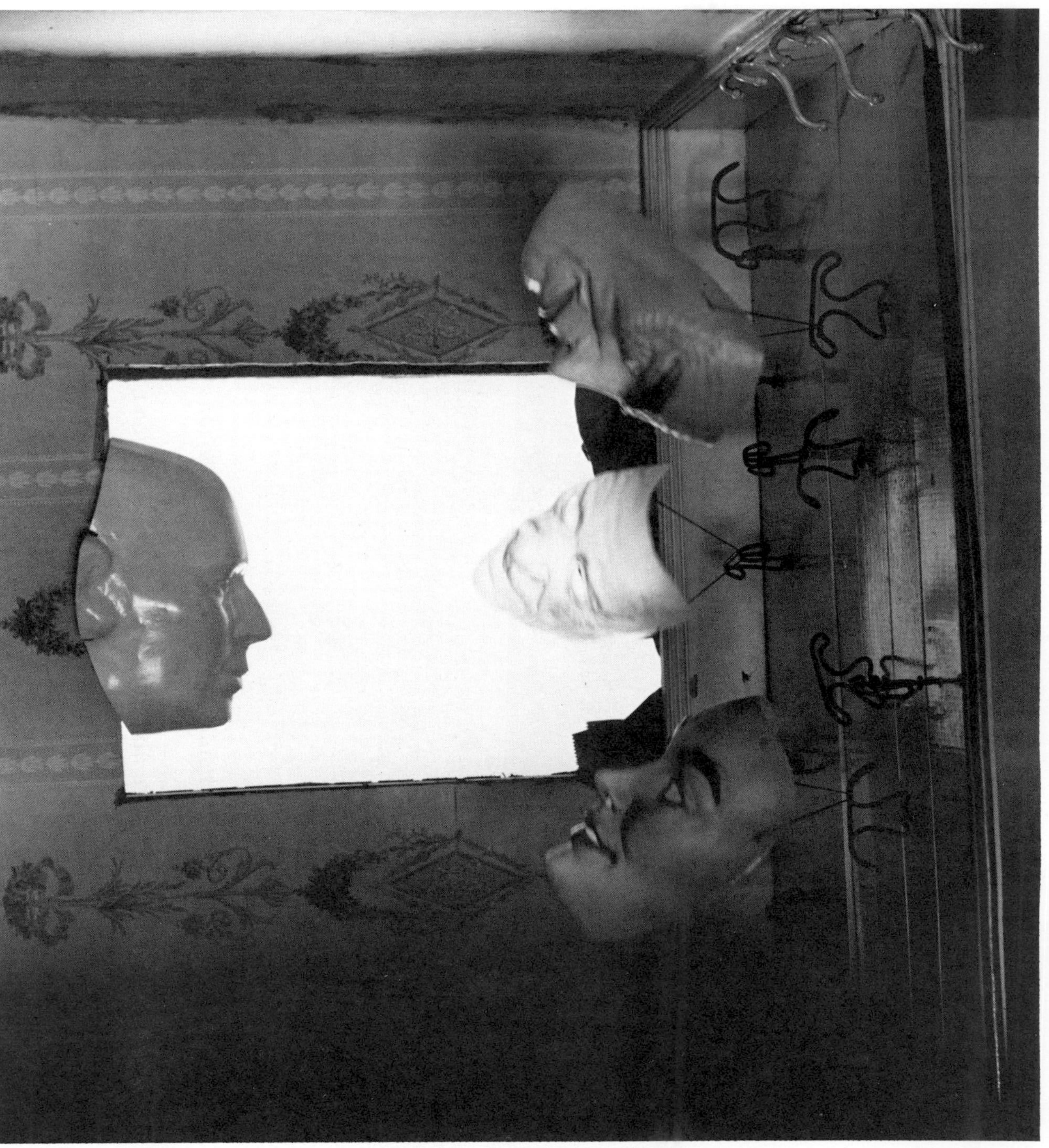

Ralph Eugene Meatyard

PART ONE

FOUNDATIONS OF PSYCHOLOGY

We begin by laying a foundation for our study of psychology. First, in Chapter 1, we consider what psychology is and how it is practiced. Understanding the nature of scientific inquiry in psychology will prepare us to understand research described in later chapters and to think more critically about events in everyday life. Then in Chapter 2 we consider the biological foundations of our behavior. We will see how our genes, nervous system, and body chemistry play a vital role in virtually everything else this book describes—our development as individuals, our abilities to perceive, learn, and think, and our normal and sometimes disordered behavior and emotions.

Jonathan Borofsky *Split Head at 2,723,117,* 1974 (painted 1981)

Collection of Jules and Barbara Farber

CHAPTER 1

Introducing Psychology

I was relaxing in the barber's black leather chair, enjoying my last haircut prior to leaving Seattle, when the barber struck up a conversation:

"What do you do?"

"Next week I'll be moving to Iowa to begin graduate school," I replied.

"What are you studying?"

"Psychology."

The haircutting ceased as the inquisitive barber took a step back, and then timidly wondered aloud:

"So what do you think of me?"

For this barber, as for many people whose exposure to psychology comes mostly from popular books and magazine articles, psychology is the assessment of personality, the analysis of motives, the practice of psychotherapy, the study of child-rearing. Is it? Yes, and much more.

Consider some of psychology's questions, questions that from time to time may be your questions, too:

> Have you ever found yourself reacting to something just as one of your parents would—perhaps in a way you've vowed you never would—and then wondered how much of your personality is inherited? To what degree are you really like your mother or your father? To what extent is their influence transmitted through their genes and to what extent through the environment they provided for you?
>
> Have you ever played peek-a-boo with a 6-month-old infant and wondered why the baby finds the game so delightful? The baby reacts as if, when you momentarily move behind a door, you disappear and then reappear out of thin air. What do babies actually perceive and think?
>
> Have you ever awakened from a nightmare and, with deep sighs of relief, wondered why we have such crazy dreams? How often do we dream? And what function is served by dreaming?

Have you ever been to a circus and wondered how the poodles were trained to dance, how the lions were taught to jump through hoops, how the chimps learned to ride bikes—and whether there are any constraints on what animals can be taught to do?

Have you ever suffered periods of depression, anxiety, or anger and wondered what triggers such emotions and how they might be alleviated?

Have you ever brooded over having lost an election or having not been invited to a party and wondered how you might better "win friends and influence people"? What makes some people so influential and socially attractive?

Such questions provide grist for psychology's mill, for psychology is a science that seeks to answer all sorts of questions about how we think, feel, and act.

WHAT IS PSYCHOLOGY?

Where, when, and how did psychology arise? What do psychologists study and do? From what perspectives do they analyze behavior? Let's see.

Psychology's Roots

Psychology is a young discipline, with roots in many disciplines, from physiology to philosophy. Wilhelm Wundt, who in 1879 at the University of Leipzig in Germany founded the first psychology laboratory, was both a physiologist and a philosopher. Ivan Pavlov, who pioneered the study of learning, was a Russian physiologist. Sigmund Freud, renowned personality theorist, was an Austrian physician. Jean Piaget, this century's most influential observer of children, was a Swiss biologist. William James, author of an influential 1890 psychology textbook, was an American philosopher.

As this list of pioneering psychologists illustrates (see also Figure 1-1), psychology has its origins not only in many disciplines but in many countries. In the last few decades, however, psychological research has flourished more in the United States than in any other country (Triandis, 1980). So it is not surprising that many of the discoveries we will encounter in later chapters have arisen from work done in the United States. Psychology is now growing rapidly in other countries (Rosenzweig, 1984b); more and more, psychology's researchers and students, like its historic pioneers, are citizens of many nations.

The membership of the American Psychological Association more than doubled during the 1950s, nearly doubled again during the 1960s, and has almost doubled again since 1970.

With current research that ranges from recording nerve cell activity to studying the effects of psychotherapy, and with perspectives that range from basic science to philosophy, psychology is a difficult field to define. In its early years, psychology was defined as the science of mental life. Its major focus was on the *internal* ("covert") experiences of consciousness—sensations, feelings, and thoughts. Psychologists of this era therefore relied upon people's reports of their conscious experiences in response to various stimuli. Then, from about 1920 to 1960, American psychologists redefined psychology as the science of *behavior*. After all, they said, science is rooted in observation. You cannot observe a sensation, a feeling, or a thought; but you *can* observe how people's *external* ("overt") behaviors are affected by external stimuli.

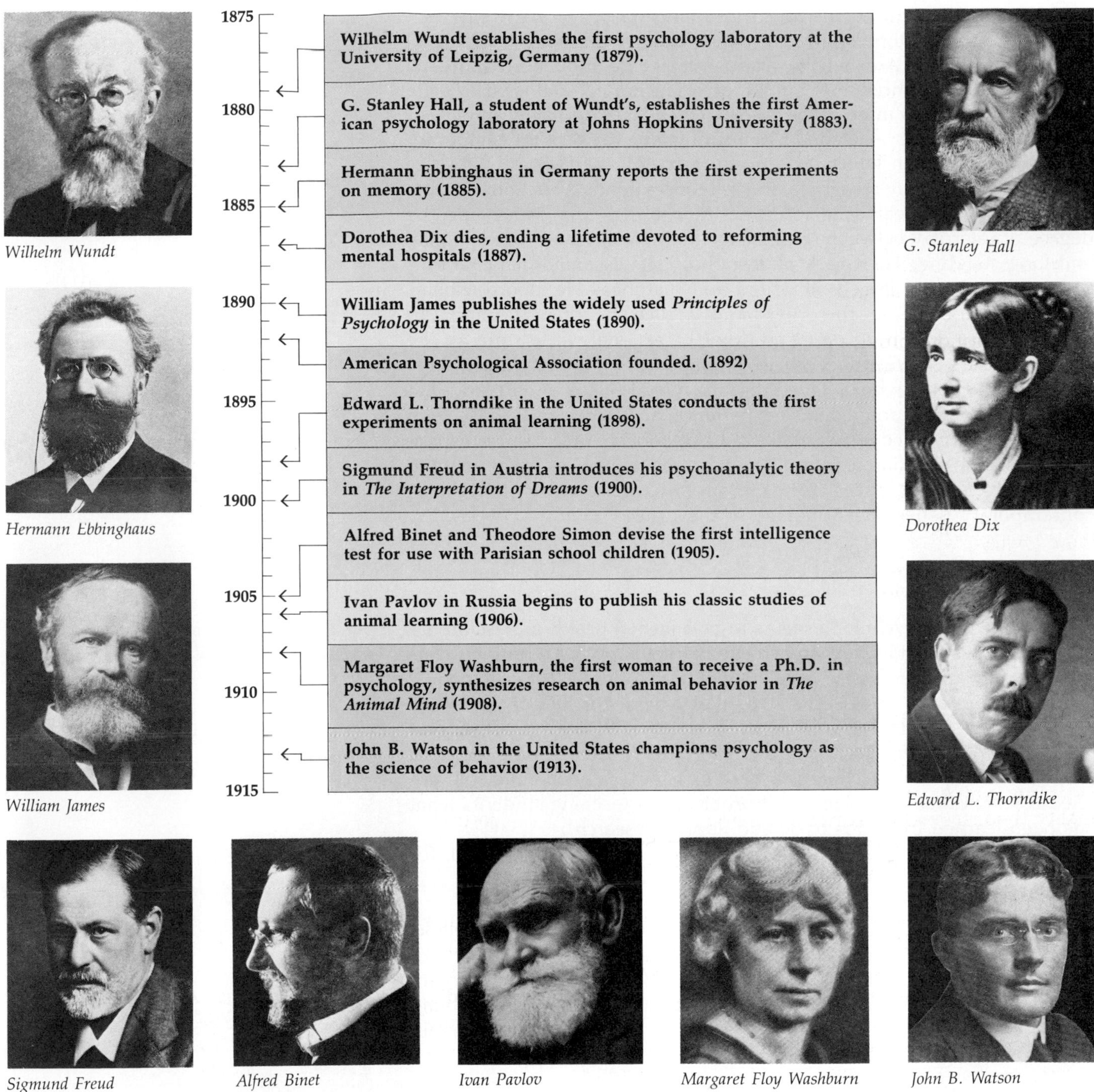

Figure 1-1 *A timeline of psychology's early history.*

Since the 1960s, psychology has recaptured its initial interest in conscious and unconscious mental processes. Today, many psychologists study how our minds process and retain information. To encompass psychology's historic concern with both internal and external factors, we can define ***psychology*** as the science of behavior and mental processes. The terms "behavior" and "mental processes" are meant to include just about every experience of humans and other animals—experiences that the ancient Greek philosopher Aristotle (who has been called the first psychologist) identified as growing, sensing, remembering, desiring, knowing, thinking, and reacting (Watson, 1978).

Throughout this book, important concepts will be set in boldface type. As a study aid, these terms are repeated with their definitions at the end of each chapter.

Whether human events are best understood by explanations that rely on internal factors or external ones remains an important issue in psychology today. Are behavior and intelligence influenced more by genes or by experiences? Are such motives as hunger and sexual desire mostly "pushed" by internal drives or "pulled" by external incentives? Is social behavior better explained by enduring inner traits or the temporary external situations in which we find ourselves?

As you probably recognize, the influences upon us are both internal and external. The real issue concerns their relative importance and the degree of interplay between them. This intellectual issue is fundamental and long-standing. The Greek philosopher Plato assumed that character and intelligence are largely inherited and that ideas are inborn (Robinson, 1981). Aristotle, on the other hand, argued that there is nothing in the mind that does not first come from the external world through the senses. In the seventeenth century, the issue was replayed by the philosophers John Locke, who believed that the mind is blank at birth and that knowledge comes through sense experience, and Gottfried Leibniz, who thought that knowledge is innate and not dependent on sense experience. Thus the question of internal and external influences forms an intellectual thread that weaves from the ancient past to some of the most contemporary issues of psychology in the 1980s.

Psychology's Subfields

To many people, psychology seems to be a mental health profession devoted to issues such as how to achieve marital happiness, how to overcome anxiety and depression, and how to raise children. For such people it often comes as a surprise to learn that only about half of America's professional psychologists work in the mental health fields (Stapp & Fulcher, 1983). What then are the other half doing? Most are doing the basic research that builds psychology's base of knowledge, or doing the applied research that tackles practical problems, or teaching students what has been learned from this basic and applied research.

For a more complete listing of psychology's specialties, see Appendix B.

Later chapters will introduce psychology's specialties. We will, for example, meet:

> ***Physiological psychologists***—psychologists who explore the links between biology and behavior. In Chapter 2, "Biological Roots of Behavior," we will see how such psychologists study hereditary influences on behavior, how they investigate the influence of brain chemistry on our moods and behavior, and how they go about identifying the psychological functions of various regions of the brain.
>
> ***Developmental psychologists***—psychologists who study the processes of physical, mental, and social changes throughout the life cycle. In Chapter 3, "Infancy and Childhood," and Chapter 4, "Adolescence and Adulthood," we will encounter one group of developmental psychologists who have used eye-tracking machines, pacifiers wired to electronic instruments, and other such devices to reveal the surprising abilities of newborn babies. We will find other developmental psychologists studying how young animals and humans become attached to their parents, and what happens when a closely attached parent and child are separated. We will see yet another group of developmentalists debating which aspects of intelligence change as we age.

A developmental psychologist, gathering data for research, records children's behavior in a classroom.

Experimental psychologists—research psychologists who study, among other things, sensation and perception, learning and memory, motivation and emotion. Peering over the shoulders of experimental psychologists at work in their laboratories, we will observe some of them flashing syllables, words, and faces on a screen to see how and how much people remember, and why they forget. We will find others studying the elements of learning by teaching animals to perform simple acts. We will see still others presenting various problems to people (such as that in Figure 1-2) and recording the speed and accuracy of their responses in order to discover how the mind processes information.

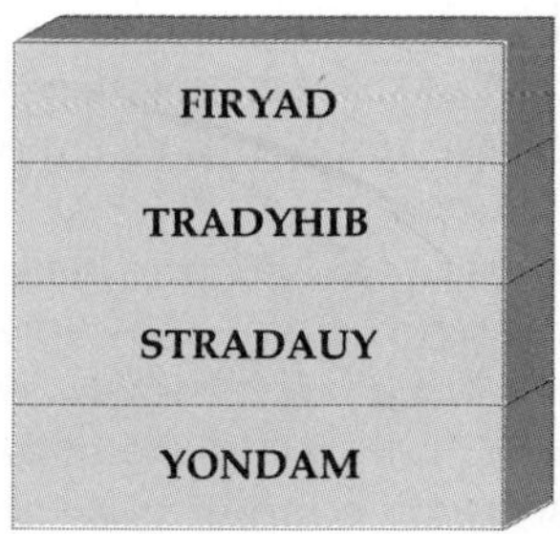

Figure 1-2 *Which one of these scrambled words does not belong with the others? (Answer is on the next page.)*

Personality and social psychologists—psychologists who study how individuals are influenced by enduring inner factors (personality psychology) and how they influence and are influenced by other people (social psychology). Such psychologists might be found observing people in a variety of situations to see whether their behavior reflects a consistent personality or whether it varies, depending on the people they are with and the situation.

Clinical psychologists—psychologists who study, assess, and treat people with psychological difficulties. Along with training in psychological research and theory leading to a graduate degree such as the Ph.D., clinical psychologists also receive several years of training and supervision in assessing and assisting those with psychological disorders. Unlike ***psychiatrists***, who have earned an M.D. degree and only then undertake a residency in psychiatry, clinical psychologists do not diagnose physical causes of psychological disorders and prescribe drugs. But they are trained to administer tests, provide psychotherapy, manage a mental health program, or do research and training.

A clinical psychologist counsels a patient. Each year millions of North Americans seek the help of professionals such as clinical psychologists who assess and assist people experiencing psychological difficulties.

Perspectives on Behavior and Mental Processes

Within these subfields of psychology there are differing perspectives. Each influences the questions psychologists ask and the kind of information they consider important.

The ***biological perspective*** helps us understand how the body and brain work to create emotions, memories, and sensory experiences. Biologically oriented psychologists may study hereditary influences on behavior, how messages are transmitted within the brain, or how blood chemistry is linked with moods and motives.

The ***psychoanalytic perspective*** assumes that behavior springs from unconscious drives and conflicts. Building on the ideas of Sigmund Freud, it analyzes personality traits and psychological disorders in terms of sexual and aggressive drives or the disguised effects of unfulfilled wishes and childhood traumas.

The ***behavioral perspective*** is not concerned with our inner biology or emotions. Rather, it studies the mechanisms by which observable responses are acquired and modified in particular environments.

The ***humanistic perspective*** arose as a reaction against the psychoanalytic view, which tends to see people as driven by unconscious inner forces, and the behavioristic view, which sees people as shaped by the environment. Humanistic psychologists emphasize our capacities to choose our life patterns and to grow to higher levels of maturity and fulfillment. They therefore seek to understand behavior more subjectively, in terms of its meaning to the individual.

The ***cognitive perspective*** explores how the mind processes, retains, and retrieves information. *Cognition* refers to thinking and knowing, both of which are important as aspects of our experience and as determinants of our actions.

Consider how from these perspectives we might view an emotion such as anger. Someone working from a biological perspective might study the brain circuits that trigger the physical state of being "red in the face" and "hot under the collar." Someone working from a psychoanalytic perspective might view an angry outburst as an outlet for pent-up, unconscious hostility. Someone working from a humanistic perspective might want to see anger from the individual's own perspective and to understand what it means to experience and express anger. Someone working from a behavioral perspective might study the facial expressions and bodily gestures that accompany anger, and might observe which external stimuli result in angry responses or aggressive acts. Someone working from a cognitive perspective might study how the different ways we perceive a frustrating situation may affect the intensity of our anger, and how an angry mood affects our thinking.

The biological, behavioral, psychoanalytic, humanistic, and cognitive perspectives describe and explain anger very differently. This does not mean that they contradict one another or that one is superior to the others. Rather, they are five useful ways of looking at the same psychological state. By using all five, we have a richer, fuller understanding of anger than that provided by any one perspective.

This important point—that different perspectives can complement one another—is also true of the different academic disciplines, each of which provides a different perspective on nature and our place in it. The basic sciences investigate nature's building blocks—atoms, molecules, and cells. The humanities address questions of meaning and value in human life and typically use a more subjective method. Psychology lies near the middle of this continuum; it uses scientific methods to seek principles that explain our thoughts and actions.

Each discipline, and each perspective within psychology, has its questions and its limits. They can be like different two-dimensional views of a three-dimensional object. Each two-dimensional view is a helpful perspective that can be compatible with the others; none by itself reveals the whole picture (see Figure 1-3). If you ignore psychology's limits and expect it to answer ultimate questions—Why am I here? How ought I to act? To what should I commit myself?—then you are destined for disappointment. If instead you hope psychology will help you better understand why people feel, think, and act as they do, and if you enjoy exploring such questions, then you should find the study of psychology fascinating and rewarding.

Answer for Figure 1-2: *The scrambled words are Friday,* birthday, *Saturday, and Monday.*

An emotion such as anger can be studied from several perspectives, each of which explores different aspects of the emotion in depth. Taken together these studies provide a fuller understanding of the emotion.

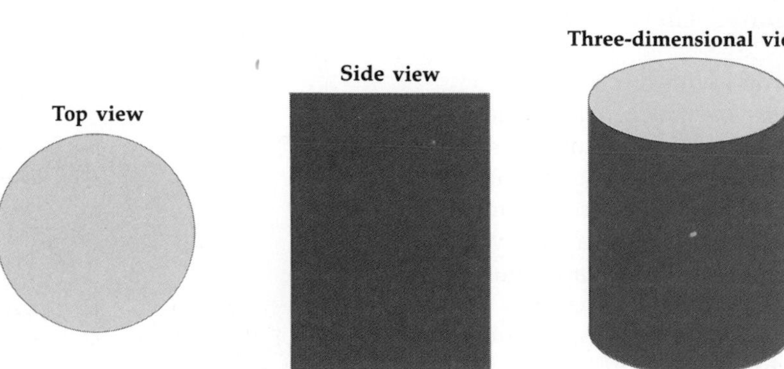

Figure 1-3 *What is this object? One person, looking down from the top, says it is a circular disk. Another person, looking at it from the side, says it is a rectangle. Their differing perspectives tell different stories that seem contradictory. In fact, they are complementary, for their respective images can be assembled into a more complete three-dimensional view of the object, a cup. So it often is with the views of behavior and mental processes offered by psychology's different perspectives.*

SCIENTIFIC ATTITUDES AND THEORIES

Scientific inquiry—psychological inquiry included—involves a set of *attitudes* and an effort to construct *theories* that organize, explain, and predict facts.

Skepticism and Humility

The first scientific attitude, skepticism, requires that ideas be checked against observable evidence. Many of our intuitive ideas about what might be true are actually false, so scientists typically approach them with an attitude of doubt until the evidence bears them out. Every claim—that mothers and infants "bond" with one another better if allowed to be together during the first hour after birth; that movie theater owners can motivate you to buy popcorn by flashing an imperceptible image of the words "Eat Popcorn" on the screen; that your handwriting provides clues to your personality—should be critically questioned. It is through careful testing of imaginative claims and ideas that we separate profound insights from believable mistakes. The scientist's attitude is like a detective's. As in sleuthing, a scientist checks various leads, dismissing most but verifying some.

"Truth is arrived at by the painstaking process of eliminating the untrue."
Arthur Conan Doyle's *Sherlock Holmes*

The scientific attitude is one of humility as well. Scientists know that their personal opinions and interpretations will not be accepted as the final authority. So they test their ideas and then report their procedures and findings precisely enough to allow other investigators to verify their observations. If it happens that nature does not conform to our ideas, then so much the worse for our ideas. If animals or people do not behave in accord with a psychological theory about how they should behave, then so much the worse for the theory. This attitude is expressed in psychology's most memorable motto: "The rat is always right."

This spirit of humility before nature is not always reflected in the pronouncements and behavior of scientists (who, like anyone else, can have big egos and may cling stubbornly to their own theories). Nevertheless, historians of science tell us that the attitudes of humility and skepticism are fundamental to science, that they in fact helped make modern science possible. Like Isaac Newton, many of the founders of modern science were people whose religious convictions assured them that the created material world was good and that, owing no ultimate allegiance to any human authority, they should humbly accept whatever truths it revealed (Hooykaas, 1972; Merton, 1938).

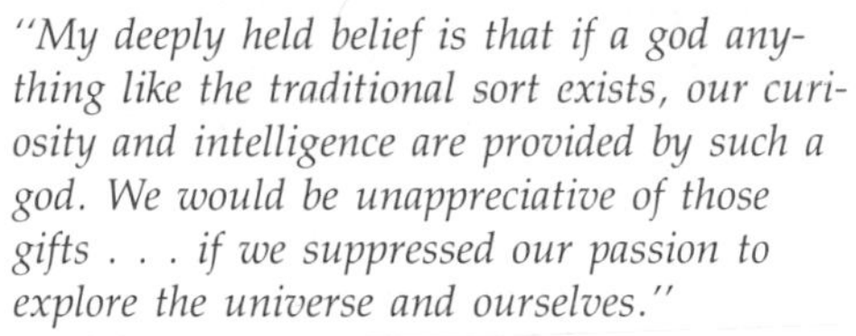

"My deeply held belief is that if a god anything like the traditional sort exists, our curiosity and intelligence are provided by such a god. We would be unappreciative of those gifts . . . if we suppressed our passion to explore the universe and ourselves."
Carl Sagan (1979a)

Fact and Theory

If psychology is to continue in this scientific spirit, how should it proceed? The scientific method is carried out by developing testable theories and critically evaluating them.

In everyday conversation, "theory" sometimes means "hunch"—a middle point on a continuum that runs from pure guess to sure fact. In science, "facts" and "theories" are quite different from each other. Facts are agreed-upon statements about what we observe. ***Theories*** are general ideas—integrated sets of principles—that explain and predict facts. "Science is built up with facts, as a house is with stones," wrote Jules-Henri Poincaré, "but a collection of facts is no more a science than a heap of stones is a house."

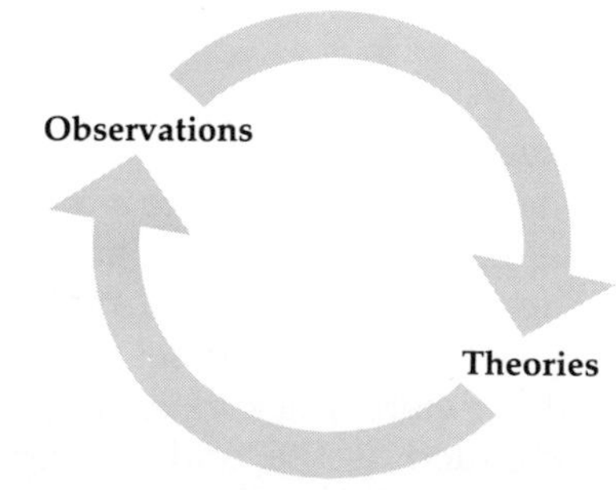

Theories are created to explain observations, but what we observe is influenced by our theoretical perspective.

A good theory, say a good theory of memory, must organize facts into a coherent structure. It also makes testable predictions, called

hypotheses, which can be used to check the theory and to suggest new explorations and applications. A good theory of memory would (1) organize and unify the many findings from studies of memory, and (2) make predictions that would allow us to test the theory and to suggest some practical tips for students who struggle to remember course material. Without a guiding theory, scientists lack direction; they haphazardly gather isolated facts. Charles Darwin put it more strongly: "Without the making of theories, I am convinced there would be no observations." With a theory to guide them—say, a set of ideas about how our memory system operates—scientists derive hypotheses and practical applications that might not have otherwise occurred to them.

"There is nothing so practical as a good theory."
Psychologist Kurt Lewin, 1890–1947

PSYCHOLOGY'S METHODS AND AIMS

We have seen that theories both explain and guide our observations, and that a good theory generates testable hypotheses. Psychologists test their theories and hypotheses with three basic methods—observation, correlation, and experimentation—that help achieve three aims—description, prediction, and explanation.

Observation and Description

The starting point of any science is careful observation that accurately describes events of interest. In psychology, too, all evidence involves some type of observation of perceivable events. In everyday life, we observe and describe people, often forming hunches about why they behave as they do. Professional psychologists are doing much the same, only much more systematically, by painstakingly recording behavior.

Psychologists use the case study method to explore individual cases in depth, often with the intent of understanding something that is typical of all of us.

The Case Study Method

Psychologists sometimes use a ***case study*** approach, in which individual cases are studied in great depth and detail and used to suggest what is true of us all. Much of our early knowledge about the function of different brain regions came from case studies of individuals who had suffered damage to a particular region of the brain and also had suffered a particular impairment. Sigmund Freud constructed a monumental theory of personality by studying individual cases in depth. The great developmental psychologist, Jean Piaget, taught us a great deal about children's thinking through the careful questioning and observation of his own three children.

The Survey

The ***survey*** method of observation studies more cases in less depth. In a survey a group of people are asked specific questions about their behavior or opinions. We will see in Chapter 13, "Motivation," how Alfred Kinsey used the survey method to describe the incidence of various sexual behaviors in the United States. The survey method, as Kinsey's use of it illustrated, sometimes reveals what many people never would have guessed, such as the finding that 37 percent of the adult males interviewed reported having had an adolescent or adult homosexual experience. Yet a survey has limitations. It must assume that questions are clear and unbiased, that the respondents will answer them honestly, and that the respondents are representative of the total population one is studying.

Like the Kinsey study, most surveys are taken of a sample of the population under study. If you wished to survey the students at your college you could question them all, but probably there are too many. So instead you survey a representative sample of the total student population. How do you make your sample representative of the whole? The best assurance you have is to make it a ***random sample***, one in which every person in the total group has an equal chance of being included. To randomly sample the students at your institution, you would *not* send them all a questionnaire, because the conscientious people who return it would not be a random sample. Rather, you would target a specific sample by selecting, say, every tenth person from an alphabetical listing and obtain responses from virtually all of them.

The random-sampling principle is also used in national surveys. If you had a giant barrel containing 60 million white beans that were thoroughly mixed with 40 million green beans, a scoop that randomly sampled 1500 of them would contain about 60 percent white and 40 percent green beans, give or take 2 or 3 percent. Sampling voters in a national election survey is like sampling those beans; 1500 randomly sampled people can provide a remarkably accurate snapshot of the opinions of a nation.

Following the Carter-Reagan presidential debate in 1980 (after 11 P.M. in the East, 8 P.M. in the more pro-Reagan West), ABC television invited viewers to place a 50 cent long distance call to indicate who they thought won the debate. Among the more than 700,000 callers, Mr. Reagan had a better than 2 to 1 edge. Other surveys of random samples of likely voters indicated the debate outcome was a virtual draw. Why might the ABC result have been misleading? (Are Republicans or Democrats more likely to own phones and make long distance calls? To be up after 11 P.M. Eastern time? To have been eager to voice support of their candidate in this election?)

Naturalistic Observation

Another type of observation is ***naturalistic observation,*** which involves watching and recording the behavior of organisms in their natural environment. Naturalistic observation ranges from the study of chimpanzee societies in the jungle to observations of parent-child interactions in different cultures to observations of students' self-seating patterns in the lunchrooms of desegregated schools.

Naturalistic observations do not explain behavior, they simply describe it. Nevertheless, the descriptions that naturalistic observation provides can be revealing. Some scientists have argued that "tool making" is a distinguishing feature of human behavior. However, naturalistic observation has revealed that chimpanzees sometimes use tools (for example, they have been observed to insert a stick in a termite mound and then withdraw it, eating the stick's load of termites). Through naturalistic observation we have also learned that American methods of child-rearing are not universally shared. And observation has shown that in many desegregated schools, students of different races tend not to mix much with each other outside the classroom. So unless special efforts are made to engage students in cooperative team efforts, school desegregation may not foster social integration.

One surprising finding of scientists using naturalistic observation is that tool use is not specific to humans. This otter is breaking open clams with a rock.

Correlation and Prediction

Describing events is a first step toward predicting them. When changes in one event are accompanied by changes in another, we say the two are ***correlated***. And if two events are correlated with (related to) one another, then the one can help predict the other. For example, if married people tend to be happier than unmarried people (which, on average, they do—see Chapter 14, "Emotion"), then marriage can serve as a modest predictor of happiness. If viewing a great deal of television violence is correlated with aggressive social behavior (which it is—see Chapter 20, "Social Relations"), then people's TV viewing habits will tend to be a predictor of their aggressiveness.

So, marriage promotes happiness and TV violence inspires aggression. Or do they? If, based on the correlational evidence, you agreed that

Correlation and other statistical tools of psychology are described in greater depth in Appendix A. A correlation *is a statistical measure of relationship. A positive correlation indicates a direct relationship, meaning that two factors tend to go up and down together (as in the positive correlation between height and weight). A negative correlation indicates an inverse relationship, meaning that as one factor goes up the other tends to go down (as in the negative correlation between mountain elevation and temperature).*

they do, you have much company. Perhaps the most irresistible thinking error made by both lay people and professional psychologists is assuming that correlation proves causation. If watching TV violence is correlated with aggressiveness, does that mean observing televised cruelty encourages cruel behavior? It may, but it may also be that aggressive people prefer violent programs. And what about the correlation between marriage and happiness? Perhaps marriage tends to make people happy, or perhaps instead happy people are more likely to be married. It is also possible that, though correlated, marriage and happiness might be causally unrelated; perhaps (as the third possibility in Figure 1-4 suggests) *both* are caused by an underlying third factor, such as good health or high income.

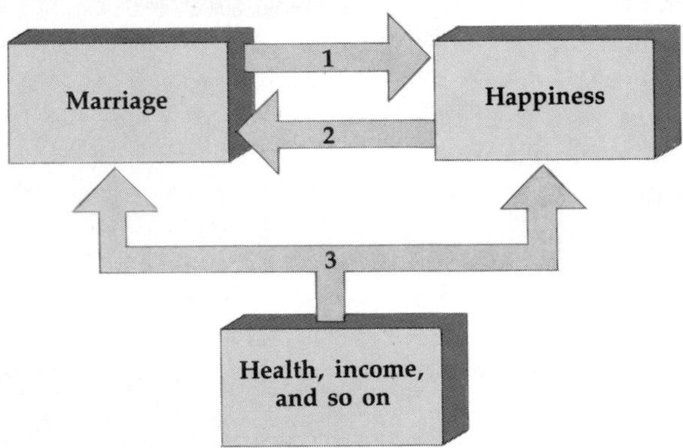

Figure 1-4 *Married adults tend to be happier than those unmarried. One possible explanation of this correlation is that marriage makes for a happier, more satisfied life. But, as the diagram indicates, any combination of three cause-effect relationships between these two factors is possible.*

Thus, although correlation provides the basis for prediction, it does not provide an explanation. Knowing that two events are related does not tell us what is causing what. Remember this principle and you will be the wiser as you read and hear reports of scientific studies in the news and in this book.

Experimentation and Explanation

To understand cause and effect, psychologists conduct ***experiments.*** Experiments enable a researcher to focus on the possible effects of a single factor or two *by holding constant those factors not being tested and manipulating the one or two being studied.* If behavior changes when the manipulated experimental factor is varied, while everything else remains the same, then the factor is having an effect. Note that unlike correlational studies, which discern naturally occurring relationships, experiments manipulate something, to see its effect. To illustrate, consider two experiments, a 200-year-old study on magnetism and mental health in which the experimental factor had no effect, and a modern experiment on exercise and mental health in which it did.

The need for the experimental method was anticipated by the work of an investigative team headed by Benjamin Franklin while he was the U.S. Ambassador to France. The Franklin Commission was established in 1784 by the king of France to investigate the claims of one Franz Anton Mesmer, a physician whose spectacular "magnetic" cures for various disorders had become the talk of Paris (Bowers, 1983). Within 2 years of Mesmer's arrival in the city, several thousand Parisians had applied for treatment. To handle the demand, Mesmer devised a form of the treatment for groups of people, in which they would touch special metal bars that would transfer "magnetism" to their bodies, thereby restoring their own "animal magnetism" to its proper balance.

Mesmer's procedure produced dramatic reactions, including convulsions and blackouts, followed by a relief of symptoms. Mesmerized patients who had lost feeling in a limb regained it; patients who had become paralyzed in some part of their bodies resumed normal functioning. The commission, however, found no magnetism or electricity in the metal apparatus when they tried to measure it. Moreover, the commissioners themselves were not noticeably affected by undergoing the treatments.

The commissioners, now more skeptical than ever, still had to account for the patients' dramatic reactions—or at least to rule out the effects of magnetism, which their tests had failed to detect. So, they undertook controlled experiments with five people who Mesmer's assistant had indicated were especially susceptible to the magnetism effect. In one experiment, a 12-year-old boy was taken to the garden of Benjamin Franklin's house where the assistant "magnetized" an apricot tree and claimed that anyone who touched it would be cured.

Parisians flocked to Franz Anton Mesmer to undertake his "magnetic" cure for a variety of ills. Scientific investigation by the Franklin Commission showed the popular success of Mesmer's treatment to be due to the powers of the human imagination rather than "animal magnetism."

Instead of bringing the boy to this "magnetized" fruit tree, the commissioners exposed him to what we today call ***control conditions.*** A control condition is identical to the ***experimental condition*** (the condition where subjects experience the experimental factor) in all respects except one: the treatment (in this case, contact with the "magnetized" apricot tree) is absent. The control condition of an experiment therefore provides a baseline against which one can compare the effect of the treatment found in the experimental condition. Blindfolded, the boy was led to a tree that was 27 feet from the "magnetized" apricot tree. Within a minute he was profusely perspiring and coughing. At a second tree, even farther away, he reported a headache. These symptoms grew stronger until at the fourth control tree the boy fainted. When tested, the other subjects similarly reacted as strongly to the unmagnetized control-condition trees as to the "magnetized" experimental tree. The commissioners had news for the king of France!

The effects of Mesmer's treatments, the commissioners reported, were due not to "animal magnetism," but to the powers of imagination. In solving one riddle, the Franklin Commission had created another: Today, 200 years later, these remarkable powers of imaginative involvement are still being explored in contemporary research on hypnosis (see Chapter 8, "States of Consciousness"). And so it frequently happens. Scientific inquiry is a voyage of discovery toward a horizon, beyond which yet another horizon often beckons.

"In solving one discovery we never fail to get an imperfect knowledge of others of which we had no idea before, so that we cannot solve one doubt without creating several new ones."
Joseph Priestley,
Experiments and Observations on Different Kinds of Air, 1775–1786

The Franklin Commission experiment was simple. It manipulated just one factor, "magnetism." This experimental factor is called the ***independent variable***, because its value can be varied independently of other factors. An experiment examines the effect of one or more independent variables on some ***dependent variable,*** so called because it can vary depending on one's experience during the experiment. In the Franklin Commission experiment, the dependent variable was the subjects' physical symptoms in response to the control (unmagnetized) and experimental ("magnetized") trees. A point to remember: Every experiment has at least two different conditions (a comparison or control condition and an experimental condition); in this way it tests the effect of at least one independent variable (what is manipulated) on a dependent variable (the response that is measured).

Summary of Experimental Design:

Independent Variable *The experimental factor you manipulate, the treatment itself.*

Dependent Variable *The behavior you are watching, the factor that might be changed by changes in the independent variable.*

Experimental Condition *Condition in which subjects are exposed to the independent variable.*

Control Condition *Identical to the experimental condition, except subjects are* not *exposed to the independent variable.*

Some experiments, including the Franklin Commission's, expose all the participants to all the conditions of an experiment, to see how they respond to each. Other experiments assign people to different conditions, but they do so using ***random assignment,*** which minimizes the chance that the results will be biased by preexisting differences between the groups. For example, if individuals of different ages and opinions are randomly assigned to two groups, the random assignment will make the two groups approximately equal in age, opinion, and every other characteristic that could possibly affect the results. With random assignment, we can therefore say with some confidence that if the two groups behave or feel differently at the end of the experiment, it must have something to do with the effect of the experiment's independent variable.

Let's review the elements of experimentation by looking at a modern experiment, reported recently by psychologists Lisa McCann and David Holmes (1984). McCann and Holmes were aware of dozens of studies that had linked regular exercise (such as jogging) with lower levels of depression and anxiety. People who exercise regularly are less depressed. But these researchers knew, as you do, that this correlation could be stated the other way around—people who are more depressed might simply exercise less.

To help resolve the ambiguity of cause and effect, McCann and Holmes studied mildly depressed women students at the University of Kansas. They randomly assigned some of them to an experimental condition of running and aerobic dancing, others to a no-treatment control condition. Remember that the experimental condition includes the treatment and that the control condition does not. Recall, too, that random assignment at the beginning of an experiment serves to equalize the experimental and control groups in every conceivable way (see Table 1-1). The two groups of women were also tested to measure their degree of depression before the experiment began. The final result? After 5 and again after 10 weeks of the exercise program, when the students in both groups again reported how depressed they felt, only those in the exercise group had become markedly less depressed. (Such conclusions must be supported by careful statistical analysis of the data, using procedures described in Appendix A.)

This experiment does not tell us *why* exercise affected depression (see p. 488 for several possibilities), but it does suggest that exercise can affect depression. By so doing, it illustrates what for some psychologists is a fourth aim of psychology—not only to describe, predict, and explain behavior and mental processes, but also to *control* them. By learning how behavior and mental processes can be controlled, these psychologists hope to help people overcome their psychological difficulties and enhance their functioning. If research can show that activities such as exercise contribute to well-being, then psychology can teach people how to exert more control over their lives.

Experiments linking regular exercise with reduced levels of depression and anxiety provide modern affirmation of Juvenal's (60–140 A.D.) dictum: Mens sana in corpore sano—*a sound mind in a sound body.*

Question: *In this experiment, what was the independent variable? The dependent variable?*

Table 1-1 **The design of the McCann and Holmes experiment.** (Most experiments are more complex than this, but the logic of the design remains the same.)

	Condition	Independent variable	Dependent variable
Random assignment of subjects	↗ Experimental condition	Exercise	Depression measure
	↘ Control condition	No exercise	Depression measure

COMMONLY ASKED QUESTIONS ABOUT PSYCHOLOGY

We have discussed psychology's historical roots and its current perspectives. We have seen how case studies, surveys, and naturalistic observations allow us to describe behavior. We have noted that correlational studies assess the extent of relationship between different factors, thus indicating how well we can predict one thing, knowing another. And we have examined the logic that underlies experimentation, which uses control conditions and random assignment to isolate whatever effects an independent variable will have on a dependent variable.

This is reasonable preparation for understanding what lies ahead. Yet, knowing this much, students often approach psychology with a mixture of curiosity and apprehension. So before we plunge into psychology's subject matters, let us address some of the typical questions and concerns.

Aren't Laboratory Experiments Artificial?

Perhaps when reading or hearing a report of psychological research you have wondered whether people's behavior in a contrived laboratory situation has anything to do with their behavior in real life. Does being able to detect the blink of a faint red light in a dark room have anything useful to say about the ability to fly planes at night? Does the fact that people remember best the first and last items in a list of unrelated words really tell us anything about our recall of the names of people we meet at a party? Does an angered man's increased willingness to push buttons that he thinks deliver electric shocks to a woman after he has seen a pornographic film really say anything about whether pornography makes men more prone to be abusive to women? Where on earth but a psychological laboratory does someone squint at red lights in a dark room, watch unrelated words flash on a video screen, or push buttons that supposedly deliver shock?

These questions reflect a misunderstanding of the intent of laboratory experiments. Far from considering artificiality to be a problem, the experimenter *intends* the laboratory environment to be a simplified reality where important features of everyday life can be simulated and controlled. Obviously, deciding whether to push a button that delivers shock is not literally the same as slapping someone in the face. But the point of the experiment is not to recreate the exact behavior that a person performs in everyday life; rather, it is to evaluate theoretical principles (Mook, 1983). *It is the resulting principles—not the specific findings—that help explain everyday behaviors.* When psychologists apply laboratory research on aggression to actual sexual violence, they are applying theoretical *principles* of aggressive behavior, principles that have been tested and refined in experiments. Likewise, it is the principles of the visual system, developed from countless experiments in artificial settings (such as looking at red lights in the dark), that we apply to night flying.

Said differently, it is the underlying *processes,* not the specific behaviors, that we assume can be generalized from one situation or culture to another. To check this assumption, psychologists attempt to ***replicate*** their findings: By repeating the essence of a study with new subjects in new situations, psychologists can see whether the process presumed to be at work generalizes to other people and circumstances. For example, when Warren Jones and his colleagues (1985) replicated loneliness research done on U.S. mainland collegians with college students in Puerto Rico, they found that the Puerto Rican students reported greater feelings of loneliness than did their counterparts on the mainland. Nevertheless, the processes that influenced loneliness were the same. In both cultures, people who were shy, uncertain about their purpose in life, and low in self-esteem reported feeling more loneliness. Much the same point could be made regarding racial attitudes, sexual behaviors, and other psychological attributes: Even when the specific attitudes and behaviors vary across cultures, as they often do, the underlying processes that form them may be much the same.

When a man has discovered why men in Bond Street wear black hats he will at the same moment have discovered why men in Timbuctoo wear red feathers."
G. K. Chesterton,
Heretics, 1909

Is It Ethical to Experiment on People—or on Animals?

If the image of people delivering what they think are electric shocks troubles you, you may find it reassuring that most psychological research involves no such stress. Blinking lights, flashing words, and pleasant social interactions are more the rule.

But, occasionally, researchers do temporarily stress or deceive people. Such procedures are used only when judged essential to achieving an important end, such as understanding and controlling violent behavior or studying the effects of mood swings. If the participants in such experiments knew all there was to know about the experiment beforehand, the procedures would be ineffective or the participants, wanting to be helpful, might try to confirm the researchers' predictions. Ethical principles developed by the American Psychological Association urge investigators to obtain the consent of potential participants, explaining enough for them to be able to make an informed decision about whether to take part, to protect participants from harm and discomfort, to treat information about individual participants confidentially, and to explain the research fully afterward.

Animals, too, are protected by professional and governmental guidelines. Nevertheless, in medicine, biology, and psychology advocates of animal rights question whether it is justifiable to cause suffering to laboratory-bred animals in hopes of alleviating human suffering. We will consider many examples of animal research throughout this book, and in Chapter 18 we will reflect on psychology's treatment of animals.

What Do Experiments with Animals Have to Do with People?

One reason psychologists study animals is that they find animals inherently interesting and want to discover what their behavior can tell us about them.

Psychologists also study animals because such studies can tell us about ourselves. The physiological systems, and often the processes that underlie behavior, are essentially similar in humans and many other animals. For example, the same processes by which humans see, exhibit emotion, and become obese operate in rats and monkeys. As we will see in Chapters 9 and 10, researchers are even adding to our understanding of simple human learning by studying learning in sea slugs. Human learning is far more complex, but it is precisely the simplicity of the sea slug that makes it suitable for discovering how the nervous system records simple forms of learning.

By experimenting, scientists have discovered and assessed the extent of certain animals' capabilities. This manatee, tested by University of Windsor psychologist Dale Woodyard, learns to discriminate between objects of different shapes, colors, and sizes for a food reward and remembers such lessons for as long as a year.

Aren't Psychology's Theories Mere Common Sense?

As we will note in a moment, psychology has sometimes been criticized as being dangerous. Ironically, it has also been criticized as merely documenting the obvious—as dressing in jargon what people know already.

In several experiments, psychologist Baruch Fischhoff and his colleagues (Fischhoff & Beyth, 1975; Slovic & Fischhoff, 1977) found that, actually, events seem far less obvious and predictable beforehand than in hindsight. Once people are told the outcome of an experiment, or of a historical episode, it suddenly seems less surprising to them than it is to people who are asked to guess the outcome. Finding out that something has happened makes it seem inevitable. Psychologists now call this 20/20 hindsight vision the ***I-knew-it-all-along phenomenon.***

Some readers may now be feeling that the I-knew-it-all-along phenomenon is obvious common sense.

The I-knew-it-all-along phenomenon can be demonstrated by giving half of a group some purported psychological finding and the other half an opposite result. For example, imagine that you were told that "Psychologists have found separation weakens romantic attraction. As the old adage says, 'Out of sight, out of mind.'" Could you imagine why this might be? Most people can, and nearly all of them will then report that the finding is unsurprising.

What if you were told that "Psychologists have found that separation intensifies romantic attraction. As the old adage says, 'Absence makes the heart grow fonder.'" People given this result can also easily explain it and overwhelmingly see *it* as unsurprising common sense. Obviously, when both a finding and its opposite can seem like common sense there is a problem with our sense of what is common sense.

Nevertheless, we should be surprised if many of the findings we will encounter had *not* been anticipated. As the English philosopher Alfred North Whitehead once remarked, "Everything important has been said before by someone who did not discover it." Regardless of whether psychological studies reveal that "You're never too old to learn" or that "You can't teach an old dog new tricks," their findings will have been anticipated. Should a psychologist discover that we are attracted to people whose traits are different from our own, someone is sure to chortle, "Of course! my grandmother could have told you that 'Opposites attract.'" Should it instead turn out that we are attracted to people whose traits are similar to our own, the same person may remind the psychologist that "Everyone knows 'Birds of a feather flock together.'" Thus the problem with common sense is not that it is necessarily wrong (25 centuries of casual observation are bound to have accumulated some wisdom), but that it is so often a judgment we make *after* we know the results.

"Life is lived forwards, but understood backwards."
Søren Kierkegaard, 1813–1855

Is Psychology Free of Hidden Values?

Psychology is definitely not value-free. Values influence our choice of research topics—whether to study worker productivity or worker morale, sex discrimination or sex differences, conformity or independence.

"Any concept has its cultural background, and so does any researcher. It is not possible to begin with a set of culture-free concepts."
Hiroshi Azuma (1984)

Values can also color "the facts." Our preconceptions can bias our observations and interpretations; sometimes we see what we are predisposed to see. Even the words we use to describe what we see can reflect

People interpret ambiguous information to fit their preconceptions.

our values. Whether we label sex acts we do not practice as "perversions" or "sexual variations" conveys a value judgment. "Conformity" is social responsiveness we disapprove of; "social sensitivity" is social responsiveness we admire. The same is true in everyday speech, as when one person's "terrorists" are another person's "freedom fighters." Both in and out of psychology, labels describe and labels evaluate.

Popular applications of psychology also contain hidden values. When people defer to "professional" advice that tells them how to live—how to raise their children, how to achieve self-fulfillment, how to get ahead at work—they are accepting more than objective information. Questions about life-style and goals are questions of values. A science of behavior may help us discover ways to reach our ultimate goals, but it cannot decide the goals themselves.

"It is doubtless impossible to approach any human problem with a mind free from bias."
Simone de Beauvoir,
The Second Sex, 1953

Isn't Psychology Potentially Dangerous?

Students often approach psychology with two apprehensions. First, they are concerned that psychology will reveal them as mere machines. Are we driven by forces beyond our control? Are we therefore devoid of real choice and able to evade responsibility for our actions? In fact, the human image that emerges from much of contemporary psychology is not that of a mindless robot; it is instead a picture of a highly evolved, self-conscious organism whose thoughts and perceptions include a sense of personal choice and control.

Second, students know that psychologists attempt to describe, predict, explain, and perhaps control behavior and mental processes. So they wonder, can psychology also be used to manipulate people? Might it become the tool of someone seeking to create a totalitarian *Brave New World* or *Nineteen Eighty-Four*?

Knowledge is a power that, like all powers, can be used for good or evil. Nuclear power has been used to light up cities, and to destroy them. Persuasive power has been used to educate people, and to deceive them. The power of mind-altering drugs has been used to restore sanity, and to destroy it.

Psychology's efforts to apply its principles have so far been mostly in directions that people usually consider constructive. Psychologists are exploring ways to enhance moral development, perceptual accuracy, learning, creativity, and compassion. What is more, psychology is an exciting field, both because it is so young and vigorous—barely a century old—and because it speaks to so many of the world's great problems—war, overpopulation, prejudice, and crime—all of which are problems of attitudes and behavior. It also speaks to humanity's deepest longings—for love, for happiness, even for food and water. Psychology cannot address all the great questions of life, but it speaks to some mighty important ones. So read on, and enjoy.

SUMMING UP

WHAT IS PSYCHOLOGY?

Psychology's Roots Beginning with the first psychological laboratory, founded in 1879 by German philosopher and physiologist Wilhelm Wundt, psychology's modern roots can be found in many disciplines and countries. Psychology's historic perspectives and current activities lead us to define the field as the science of behavior and mental processes.

Psychology's Subfields Psychologists' activities are widely varied, ranging from studies of the links between biology and behavior, to experimental studies of perception and memory, to the diagnoses and therapies of clinical psychology.

Perspectives on Behavior and Mental Processes There are many perspectives on human nature, of which psychology is one. Within psychology, the biological, behavioral, psychoanalytic, humanistic, and cognitive perspectives are complementary. Each has its own purposes, questions, and limits.

SCIENTIFIC ATTITUDES AND THEORIES

Skepticism and Humility Scientific inquiry requires a mixture of imagination, skepticism, and humility.

Fact and Theory Ideas are framed as theories, which organize facts and imply testable hypotheses that can be used to confirm or modify the theory, generate new exploration, and suggest practical applications.

PSYCHOLOGY'S METHODS AND AIMS

To describe, predict, and explain behavior and mental processes, psychologists use three basic methods: observation, correlation, and experimentation.

Observation and Description Through case studies, surveys, and naturalistic observations, psychologists observe and describe phenomena.

Correlation and Prediction Ascertaining the extent to which events are correlated with one another specifies the degree to which one event predicts another. Knowing that two things tend to be naturally correlated is valuable information, but such information does not indicate what is causing what.

Experimentation and Explanation To examine cause and effect relationships more directly, psychologists often do experiments. By constructing a miniature reality that is under their control, experimenters can vary one or two factors and discover how these things (called independent variables) affect a particular behavior (called the dependent variable). In many experiments, control is achieved by randomly assigning people either to be experimental subjects who receive treatment or control subjects who do not.

COMMONLY ASKED QUESTIONS ABOUT PSYCHOLOGY

Aren't Laboratory Experiments Artificial? By intentionally creating a controlled, artificial reality, experimenters aim to test theoretical principles. These principles, not the behaviors observed in the laboratory, help us to understand everyday behaviors.

Is It Ethical to Experiment on People—or on Animals? Occasionally (though not usually) researchers feel they must temporarily stress or deceive people in order to learn something important. Professional ethical standards provide guidelines concerning the treatment of both human and animal subjects.

What Do Experiments with Animals Have to Do with People? Some psychologists study animals out of an intrinsic fascination with animal behavior. Others do so because the physiological and psychological processes of animals enable them to understand, in a simpler form, processes that operate in humans.

Aren't Psychology's Theories Mere Common Sense? Experiments indicate an I-knew-it-all-along phenomenon: Finding out that something has happened can make it seem like obvious common sense.

Is Psychology Free of Hidden Values? Psychology is not value-free. Psychologists' values can influence their choice of research topics, their theories and observations, their labels for behavior, and their professional advice.

Isn't Psychology Potentially Dangerous? Knowledge is power that can be used for good or evil. Applications of psychology's discoveries have so far been mostly for the good, and psychology's potential is exciting.

TERMS AND CONCEPTS TO REMEMBER

Behavioral Perspective Emphasizes environmental influences upon observable behaviors.

Biological Perspective Emphasizes the influences of heredity and physiology upon our emotions, memories, and sensory experiences.

Case Study An observational technique in which one person is studied in depth.

Clinical Psychology A branch of psychology, usually practiced by people with a Ph.D. degree, involving the assessment and treatment of those with psychological disorders.

Cognitive Perspective Emphasizes how the mind processes and retains information.

Control Condition The condition of an experiment in which the experimental treatment of interest is absent; serves as a comparison for evaluating the effect of the treatment.

Correlation A statistical index that indicates the extent to which two things vary together and thus how well one measure can be predicted from knowing the other.

Dependent Variable The variable that is being measured; in an experiment, the variable that may change in response to manipulations of the independent variable.

Developmental Psychology The study of the process of physical, cognitive, and social changes throughout the life cycle.

Experiment A research method in which the investigator manipulates one or more independent variables to observe their effect upon some behavior (the dependent variable) while controlling other relevant factors.

Experimental Condition The condition of an experiment in which subjects are exposed to the treatment, that is, to the independent variable.

Experimental Psychology A branch of psychology that uses experimental methods to discover principles of behavior, such as those underlying sensation and perception, learning and memory, motivation and emotion.

Humanistic Perspective Emphasizes people's capacities for choice and growth; studies people's subjective experiences.

Hypothesis A testable proposition, often derived from a theory.

I-Knew-It-All-Along Phenomenon The tendency to exaggerate one's ability to have foreseen how something turned out, *after* learning the outcome. (Also known as the hindsight bias.)

Independent Variable The experimental factor, the variable whose effect is being studied. In an experiment, the independent variable is the variable manipulated by the investigator.

Naturalistic Observation Observing and recording behavior in naturally occurring situations, without trying to manipulate and control the situation.

Personality Psychology A branch of psychology that studies how individuals are influenced by relatively enduring inner factors.

Physiological Psychology A branch of psychology concerned with the links between biology and behavior.

Psychiatry A branch of medicine, practiced by physicians with an M.D. degree, and sometimes involving medical (for example, drug) treatments as well as psychological assistance.

Psychoanalytic Perspective Builds on Freud's ideas that behavior arises from unconscious drives and conflicts, some of which may stem from childhood experiences.

Psychology The science of behavior and mental processes.

Random Assignment Assigning subjects to experimental and control conditions by chance, thus minimizing preexisting differences between those assigned to the different groups.

Random Sample A sample that is representative of some larger group because every person has an equal chance of being included.

Replication Repeating the essence of an experiment with different subjects to see whether the basic finding is repeatable.

Social Psychology The study of how people influence and relate to one another.

Survey Ascertaining the self-reported attitudes or behaviors of people by questioning a representative (random) sample of them.

Theory An integrated set of principles that organizes, predicts, and explains observations.

FOR FURTHER READING

> The best effect of any book is that it excites the reader to self-activity.
>
> Thomas Carlyle, 1795–1881

At the conclusion of each chapter I suggest several books or articles you could explore for further information.

For many students, the most helpful supplementary source will be *Discovering Psychology* by Richard Straub, the innovative study guide that accompanies this text. It begins with a helpful summary of how best to study from this (or any other) textbook. For each text chapter, *Discovering Psychology* provides learning objectives, a programmed review of the chapter, multiple-choice practice quizzes, activities that will stretch your mind, and suggestions of where to go for more information.

For an informative free booklet that describes psychology's fields and careers, you can write the American Psychological Association, 1200 Seventeenth Street N.W., Washington, D.C. 20036, and request "Careers in Psychology."

The American Psychological Association also publishes *Psychology Today* magazine, an entertaining and readable source of information about current trends and research in psychology.

Constantin Brancusi *Vue d'atelier: L'écorché, Ecole des Beaux-Arts, Bucarest 1901* (View of the studio, Bucharest, 1901)

CHAPTER 2

Biological Roots of Behavior

The earliest fossils of our species, *Homo sapiens,* are estimated by anthropologists to be about 300,000 years old. On the time scale of human existence, the last 100 years are therefore only a few ticks of the clock. But it was not until that recently that a scientific understanding of the biological roots of our behavior began to emerge.

Consider that in the early nineteenth century, with more than 99.9 percent of our collective existence behind us, a German physician named Franz Gall invented an ill-fated theory, called ***phrenology,*** which contended that the bumps on one's skull could reveal one's mental faculties and character traits. Since then, in little more than a century, we have realized that the body is composed of cells, that among these are nerve cells that conduct electricity and "talk" to one another by sending chemical messengers across a tiny gap that separates them, that specific areas of the brain serve specific functions (though not the functions Gall supposed), and that our traits are influenced by chemical codes (genes) which come from both our parents. You and I are enormously privileged to be living at a time when our emergence from scientific ignorance is occurring at an exhilarating pace.

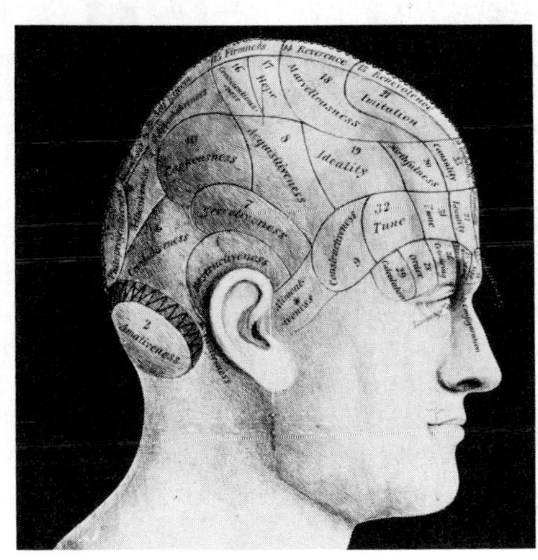

In his theory, called phrenology, *Gall speculated that the brain's functions were linked to various bumps on the skull. Despite its wrong-headedness, phrenology did help focus attention on the idea that various brain regions might have specific functions.*

In this chapter we will look at what this scientific explosion reveals concerning the biological bases of our behavior and mental processes. First, we will consider how the biological development of our *species* over eons of time has endowed us with a ***nervous system***—an electrochemical communication system—that underlies every idea, every mood, every urge that you or I have ever experienced. Understanding how our nervous system functions is fundamental to understanding how we think, feel, and act.

Although each of us is in many respects similar to all other members of our species, we are each in other respects unique. We will also look, therefore, at how our biological development as *individuals* differentiates us from other individuals. Specifically, how do our ***genes***—our biochemical units of heredity—interact with our environment to make us the unique individuals that we are?

NATURAL SELECTION

Among all the animal species, it is we, *Homo sapiens,* who are the most adaptable, the most intellectually capable, the most artistic, the most murderous of our own species. How did we come to be so? How did our collective history shape our bodies and behaviors?

Most scientists believe the answer lies in one of biology's unifying principles: ***natural selection.*** Through the process of natural selection, all of the millions of species of plants and animals have arisen from preexisting types by change across generations.

Charles Darwin proposed this process in his revolutionary 1859 book, *Origin of Species.* He recognized that in any given population, there are chance variations among individual organisms—in height, strength, susceptibility to disease, and so forth—and that some of these variations are inherited. He also recognized that all species tend to produce far more offspring than their environment can support. Imagine that a single pair of houseflies began breeding in April and that all their descendants survived to normal adulthood, each reproducing normally. It has been estimated that by August their 191,000,000,000,000,000,000 descendants would cover the earth to a depth of 47 feet! Yet the average number of houseflies generally remains the same over the years. So, although the average single breeding pair could have, over the summer, produced 191 million trillion offspring, it actually produced only 2. Why these particular 2?

Those who are troubled by an apparent conflict between scientific and religious accounts of human origins may find it helpful to recall (from Chapter 1) that different perspectives of life can be complementary. For example, the scientific account attempts to tell us when and how; religious creation stories usually aim to tell about an ultimate who and why.

Darwin proposed that which individuals survive and reproduce and which do not is influenced by their interactions with the environment. He saw that natural selection operates by favoring organisms that possess the inheritable variations that best equip them to survive and reproduce. And as certain offspring survive and reproduce from generation to generation and others die out, the characteristics of the survivors become more common in the species. If an insecticide such as DDT is introduced to control flies, and if some flies are resistant to it, the resistant flies will survive and reproduce more successfully and their offspring will soon outnumber those of nonresistant flies.

Darwin believed, as do most scientists today, that over countless generations the cumulative effect of natural selection enables different species to evolve, each adapted to its environment. Our world is now filled with adaptations that we never tire of admiring. One of the most dramatic examples was revealed when naturalists in the late 1800s noted that the light-colored peppered moth was being replaced in England's industrial areas by a formerly rare variant, the black peppered moth (Figure 2-1). This shift occurred as air pollution from the new industries killed the light-colored lichens that grew on rocks and tree trunks providing a natural camouflage for the light-colored moths. On the newly blackened tree trunks the light-colored moths became easily visible prey for birds, while the black moths became difficult to detect. In recent years, air pollution has been decreasing, lichens are returning, and the lighter moths are again becoming predominant. Clearly, natural selection is at work: Whichever moths possess the inheritable variations that best equip them to survive and reproduce in a particular environment become more common.

Figure 2-1 *As English trees became blackened with industrial soot, the formerly rare black peppered moth (shown at right) became a less easy prey for birds than the light-colored peppered moth. Thus the black moth, being better adapted to conditions created by industrial pollution, became more prevalent.*

Many psychologists are interested in natural selection because they believe that evolution's legacy resides in our behaviors as well as our bodies. Consider the controversial new field of sociobiology, which seeks to determine the ways in which evolutionary history may predispose our social behavior.

The adaptation that has been most responsible for the success of our species is our highly developed nervous system, including the brain. We

The more complex the nervous system, the more adaptable the organism. The weaver bird's construction skills are instinctual; the human's are learned.

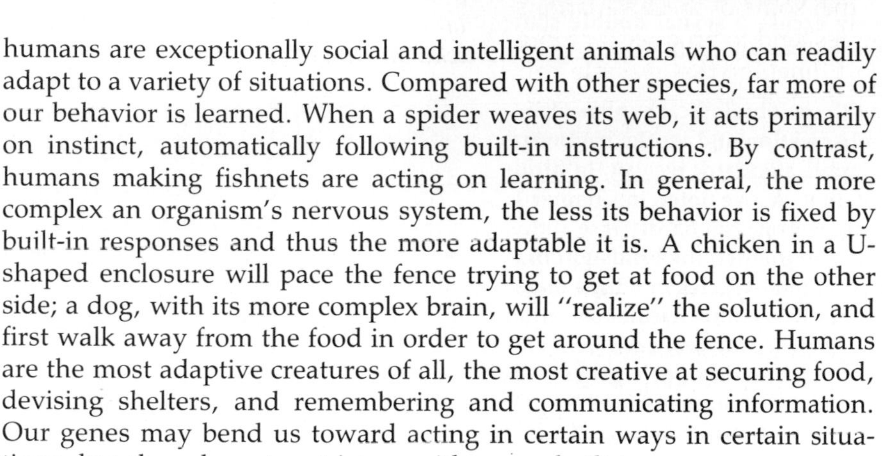

humans are exceptionally social and intelligent animals who can readily adapt to a variety of situations. Compared with other species, far more of our behavior is learned. When a spider weaves its web, it acts primarily on instinct, automatically following built-in instructions. By contrast, humans making fishnets are acting on learning. In general, the more complex an organism's nervous system, the less its behavior is fixed by built-in responses and thus the more adaptable it is. A chicken in a U-shaped enclosure will pace the fence trying to get at food on the other side; a dog, with its more complex brain, will "realize" the solution, and first walk away from the food in order to get around the fence. Humans are the most adaptive creatures of all, the most creative at securing food, devising shelters, and remembering and communicating information. Our genes may bend us toward acting in certain ways in certain situations, but they do not restrict us with many built-in responses.

Note that "adapt" is used here in two different ways—the evolutionary adaptations that occur over countless generations, and the ability of individuals to adapt their behavior to new situations. It is interesting that our chief evolutionary adaptation is our adaptability—our ability to adapt to the new by learning new behaviors.

Sociobiology: Doing What Comes Naturally

A century ago, the novelist Samuel Butler remarked that "A hen is only an egg's way of making another egg." In the same vein, the controversial new field of *sociobiology* views organisms as but their genes' way of making more genes. We are survival machines for our immortal genes: When we die, our genes live on in our biological relatives.

Sociobiologists study how natural selection may have predisposed social animals to behave in certain ways. Their underlying rationale is quite simple: If a behavioral tendency in ants or bees or any living thing is genetically determined and if it helps an organism to survive and spread its genes, then those genes will be favored in the competition for gene survival and so will become more common.

As an example of sociobiological explanation, consider why males of most species tend to initiate sexual relations more frequently and with more partners than do females—a pattern of social behavior that seems to be generally true of human societies (Hinde, 1984; Kenrick & Trost, in press). To insure the survival and spread of their genes, each male and female must maximize the number of their offspring that survive to reproduce. Sociobiologists suggest that to help achieve this end, natural selection has, over time, predisposed different behavior tendencies in males and females.

Because of their limited number of eggs and the reproductive time it takes to carry and nurse their young, female mammals have far fewer potential offspring than do males. Thus, to insure that a maximum number survive, females tend to be cautiously selective in their choice of a mate, looking for evidence of physical soundness and, in some species, a commitment of time and resources to helping raise their young.

On the other hand, sperm are an abundant resource, giving males a far higher ceiling on the number of their potential offspring. (Northern Dancer, the 1964 Kentucky Derby winner, has so far sired 487 offspring.) Because their reproductive success depends partly on how many females they fertilize, those males that most successfully seek out and compete for females should leave more offspring, thereby more successfully spreading their genes. And if, as sociobiologists suppose, social behaviors in humans are genetically predisposed, then the continued reproductive success of these individuals should, over time, predispose more sexual initiative in males than in females.

The idea that nature tends to select certain inheritable behavioral tendencies and thereby to contribute to the survival of the genes associated with those behaviors is not controversial, but the application of this idea to the complex social behaviors of human beings certainly is. In addition, critics of sociobiology fear that explaining human social behavior in terms of our genes may lead some people to assume, wrongly, that certain human behaviors are "natural" and so unchangeable—that, for example, someone may excuse a sexual double standard that tolerates male promiscuity with, "Men will be men—their male genes predispose philandering."

Critics contend that there are two problems with sociobiological explanations. First, evolutionary explanation starts with an observation and works backward to conjure up an explanation. Given a sexual double standard, we can, in hindsight, imagine how natural selection might explain it. As we noted in Chapter 1, after-the-fact explanations may sound convincing, but one can hardly lose at this game. When one begins by knowing what there is to predict, the hindsight bias assures an appealing "explanation." Given other animal species in which males mate with but one female, could we not just as easily see how natural selection might have favored males who are loyal to their mates? Ah, yes, such behavior helps protect and support one's young, thereby perpetuating one's genes. (Indeed, sociobiologists suggest that this helps explain why humans tend to pair off.) The moral: Unless they make testable predictions, all such after-the-fact explanations should be viewed with a healthy skepticism.

"There's a mighty big difference between good, sound reasons and reasons that sound good."
Burton Hillis

Second, some critics question whether genetic evolution really explains very much of human social behavior. Because all of us share the same evolutionary past, we do share certain universal behavioral tendencies: A smiling face can be read across cultural boundaries. But there is also great diversity in human behavior patterns. Marriage patterns vary from monogamy (one spouse) to serial monogamy (a succession of spouses) to polygamy (multiple wives) to polyandry (multiple husbands) to spouse-swapping. Our common evolutionary heritage

A universal behavior. You know the meaning of these facial expressions, and each of these people would understand the same expression on your face.

does not predict such diversity, nor does it explain rapid cultural changes in behavior. Our vast adaptability—our ability to learn and change—is our most crucial evolutionary trait.

In short, sociobiology offers a provocative evolutionary theory regarding how some of our characteristic human behaviors may have come to be. The jury is still out on how much these ideas will contribute to our understanding of human social behavior. But the ideas are intriguing.

THE NERVOUS SYSTEM

For scientists, it is a happy fact of nature that the nervous systems of humans and other animals operate similarly. The nervous system's elementary building block, the **neuron,** or nerve cell, is essentially identical in all animals. In closely related species of animals, these neurons are also organized in remarkably similar ways; small samples of brain tissue from a person and a monkey are indistinguishable. These facts allow researchers to study simple animals, such as squids and sea slugs, to discover how neurons operate and communicate, and to study brain functioning in various mammals in order to understand the organization of our own brains. Human brains are more complex, of course, but our nervous systems operate according to the same principles that govern the rest of the animal world.

To understand how this system makes possible our behavior and mental processes, let's first take a bird's-eye view of how the nervous system is organized, then look more closely at how its neurons transmit information, and then see how the brain governs nervous system activity.

Divisions of the Nervous System

The human nervous system is complex beyond comprehension; yet its basic organization is simple (Figure 2-2). It consists of two systems, the ***central nervous system*** (CNS), which includes all the neurons in the brain and spinal cord, and the ***peripheral nervous system*** (PNS), which connects the central nervous system to the rest of the body.

The peripheral nervous system consists of two components, the somatic and the autonomic nervous systems. The ***somatic nervous system*** directs the movements of our skeletal muscles, which are usually under our voluntary control. As you reach the bottom of this page, the somatic nervous system will report to your brain the current state of your skeletal muscles and will carry instructions back, enabling your hand to turn the page.

The ***autonomic nervous system*** controls the more autonomous (self-regulating) activities of our internal functioning, such as heartbeat, digestion, and glandular activity, which we usually think of as beyond our voluntary control (Figure 2-3). The autonomic nervous system is a dual system. One part, the ***sympathetic nervous system,*** arouses. If something alarms or enrages you, the sympathetic system will accelerate your heartbeat, slow your digestion, raise your blood sugar, dilate your arteries, and trigger perspiration to cool you, making you alert and ready for action. When the emergency is over, the other part, your ***parasympathetic nervous system,*** produces the opposite effects. In general, it calms you down, by decreasing your heartbeat, lowering your blood sugar, and so forth.

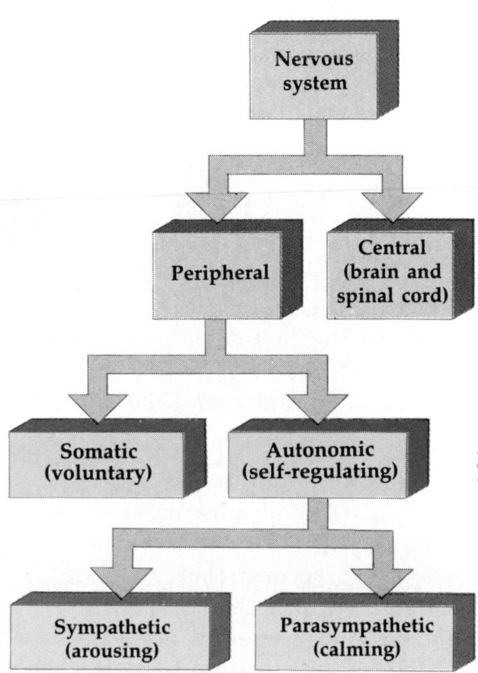

Figure 2-2 *The divisions of the human nervous system.*

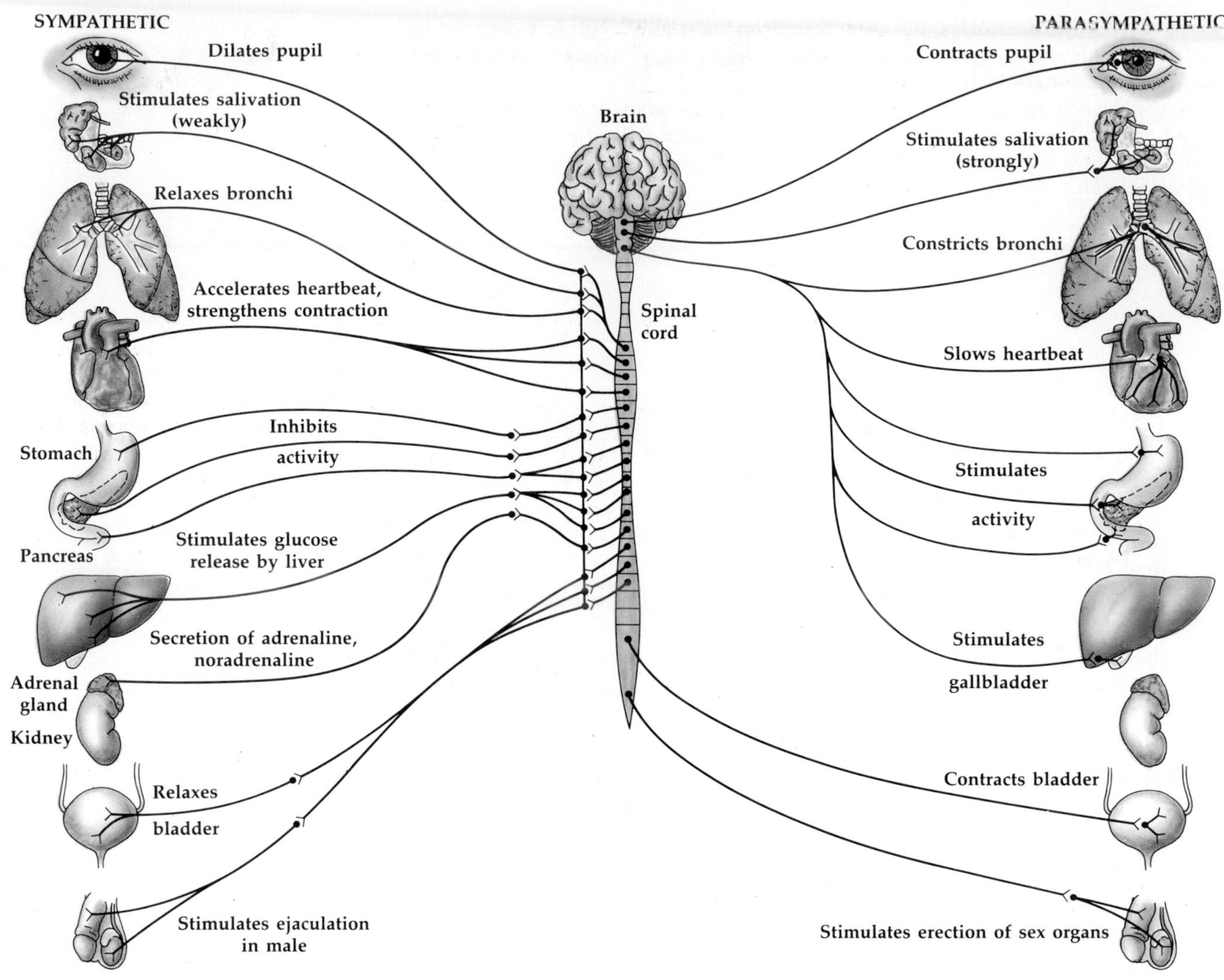

Figure 2-3 *The autonomic nervous system, which controls the more autonomous (or self-regulating) internal functions, consists of the sympathetic and parasympathetic divisions. The sympathetic system usually arouses and the parasympathetic system calms. Most organs are affected by both divisions, which usually function in opposition to each other. For example, sympathetic stimulation accelerates heartbeat while parasympathetic stimulation slows it.*

Having taken a look at the the nervous system's organization into its central and peripheral divisions, let us now examine its elementary components, the neural pathways and the neurons, which comprise them.

Neural Pathways and Their Components

There are three major classes of neurons involved in the pathways by which information travels in the nervous system. The ***sensory*** ("afferent") ***neurons*** transmit information from the body's tissues to the central nervous system, where the information is processed. This processing usually involves a second class of neurons, the ***interneurons*** of the brain and spinal cord. It is the complex activity of this incredible network of interneurons that somehow gives rise to a feeling of elation, a creative idea, or a memory of grandmother's freshly baked cookies. Instructions from the central nervous system are then relayed to the body's tissues via the ***motor*** ("efferent") ***neurons.***

The simplest neural pathways are those that govern our ***reflexes,*** our automatic responses to stimuli. A simple reflex pathway is composed of a single sensory neuron and single motor neuron whose communication is often through an interneuron. One such pathway is involved in the pain reflex (Figure 2-4). When you touch a hot stove, neural activity excited by the heat travels via sensory neurons to interneurons in the spinal cord. These interneurons respond by activating motor neurons to the muscles in your arm, causing you to jerk your hand away.

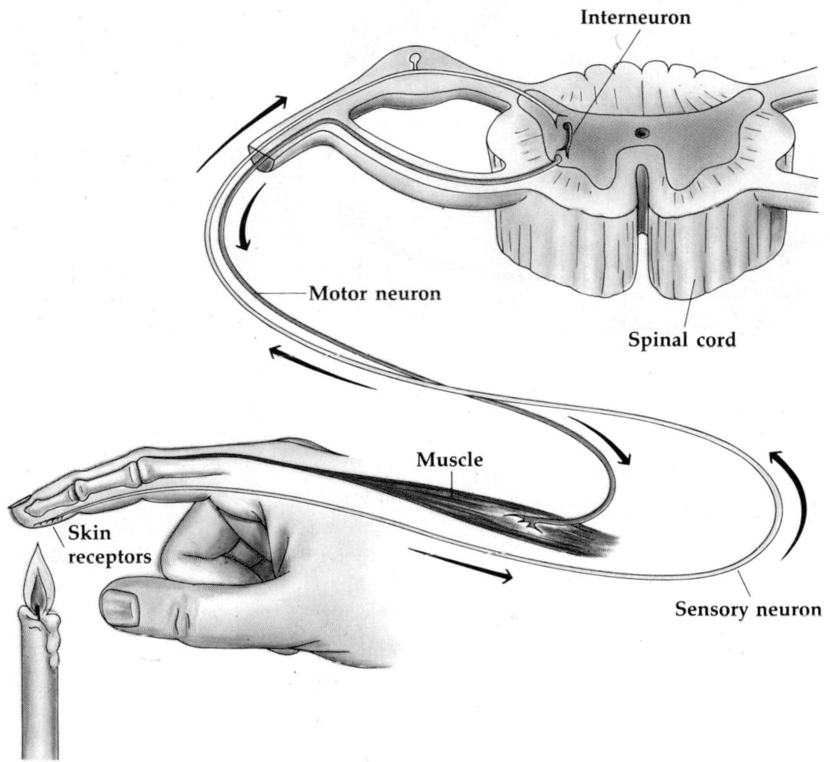

Figure 2-4 *In this simple reflex, information from the skin receptors travels via the sensory neurons to interneurons in the spinal cord, which send a signal to the muscles in the arm via the motor neurons. Because this reflex involves only the spinal cord, you would instantly jerk your hand away from the candle flame* before *your brain had received the information that caused you to experience pain.*

Because the simple pain reflex pathway runs through the spinal cord and out, you would instantly jerk your hand from the hot stove *before* your brain has received the information that causes you to feel pain. Information travels to and from the brain mostly by way of the spinal cord. Were the top of your spinal cord to be severed, you would not feel such pain. Or pleasure. If, as sometimes happens through injury, a person's spinal cord is severed, the individual loses all sensation and voluntary movement in the body regions whose sensory and motor neurons enter the spinal cord below the injury. (Because CNS neurons usually do not repair themselves, the effects are permanent.) Thus male paraplegics (whose legs are paralyzed) are usually capable of erection and ejaculation if their genitals are stimulated, but (depending on where the spinal cord is severed) they may have no genital feeling. To feel pain or pleasure, the sensory information must reach the brain.

"If the nervous system be cut off between the brain and other parts, the experiences of those other parts are non-existent for the mind. The eye is blind, the ear deaf, the hand insensible and motionless."
William James,
Principles of Psychology, 1890

Neurons and Their Messages

A neuron consists of a cell body and one or more branchlike outgrowths, or fibers, that extend away from it (Figure 2-5). These fibers are of two types, the ***dendrites,*** which receive information from sensory receptors or other neurons, and the ***axons,*** which transmit it to other neurons. The

"Dendrite" is derived from the Greek word dendron, *meaning tree.*

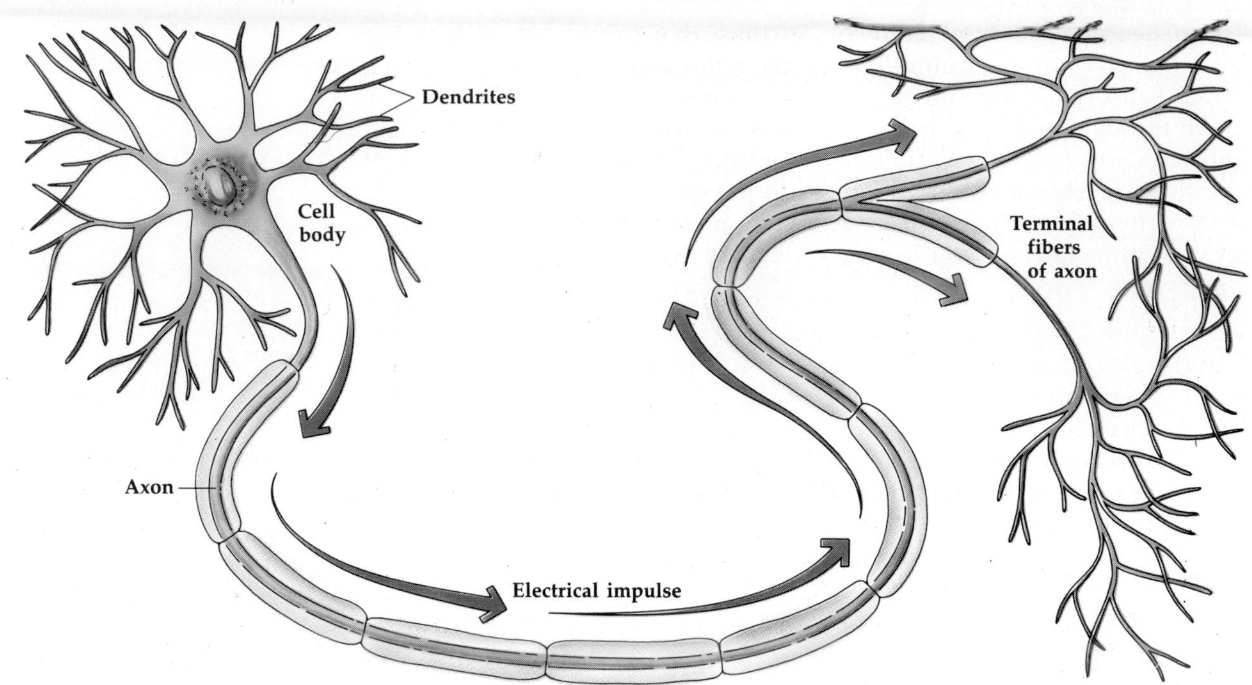

Figure 2-5 *A simplified diagram of a neuron. Each neuron consists of a cell body and one or more branchlike extensions or fibers. Information from sensory receptors or other neurons is received by the dendrites and is summed in the cell body, sometimes causing the neuron to fire an electrical impulse down its axon, which transmits this outgoing information to other neurons or to the body's muscles or glands.*

neuron is a miniature decision-making device. It receives signals to "fire" or "not fire" from hundreds or even thousands of other neurons on its dendrite receivers. These incoming signals are combined in the cell body, sometimes triggering the neuron to fire an electrical impulse down its axon, which branches into junctions with the body's muscles and glands or with the dendrites and cell bodies of hundreds or even thousands of other neurons. Unlike the short dendrites, axons may project up to several feet. The cell body and axon of a motor neuron can be roughly on the scale of a basketball attached to a rope four miles long.

Impulses travel through fibers at speeds ranging from a sluggish 2 miles per hour to a breakneck 200 miles or more per hour. But even this top speed is 3 million times *slower* than the speed at which electricity travels through a wire. That helps to explain why, unlike the nearly instantaneous reactions of a high-speed computer, it takes a quarter-second for you to react to a sudden stimulus, such as a child darting in front of your moving car.

Generating a Nerve Impulse

A sensory nerve impulse is generated when a nerve is stimulated in some way—by pressure, by heat, by light, or by any of a variety of other stimuli. To trigger an impulse, the stimulus must be above a certain intensity, called the ***threshold.*** Increasing the stimulus above this threshold will not increase the intensity or speed of the impulse generated. The neuron's reaction is therefore called an ***all-or-none response;*** neurons, like guns, either "fire" or they don't.

How then is information about the intensity of a stimulus transmitted? How do we distinguish between a gentle touch and a firm hug? Although a stronger stimulus cannot trigger a stronger or faster impulse in a neuron, it can initiate more frequent impulses. And since the same stimulus may affect many neurons, not all of which have the same thresholds, stimuli of differing intensities may trigger impulses in differing groups of neurons.

Transmission of Impulses Between Neurons

Neurons interweave so intricately that even with a microscope it is hard to see where one ends and another begins. At the end of the last century, many scientists believed that the branching axons of one cell were fused with the dendrites of another in an uninterrupted fabric of tissue. We now know this to be wrong. The axon terminal of one neuron is separated from the receiving neuron by a gap of about a millionth of an inch, called the ***synapse.*** To the pioneering Spanish neuroanatomist Santiago Ramon y Cajal (1917), these near-unions of neurons were one of nature's marvels—"protoplasmic kisses," he called them. How does the electrical impulse execute the protoplasmic kiss? How does it leap the tiny synaptic gap? The answer to this question has been one of the most exciting scientific discoveries of our age.

"All information processing in the brain involves neurons 'talking to' each other at synapses."
Solomon H. Snyder (1984a)

Surprisingly, the answer is chemically. By an elegant mechanism, the axon's knoblike terminals release chemical messengers, called ***neurotransmitters,*** into the synaptic gap (see Figure 2-6). Within 1/10,000th of a second, the neurotransmitter molecules cross the gap and combine with receptor molecules on the receiving neuron—as precisely as a key fits a lock. For an instant, tiny "gates" at the receiving site are unlocked, allowing certain ions (electrically charged atoms) to enter the neuron, thereby influencing its "decision" to fire.

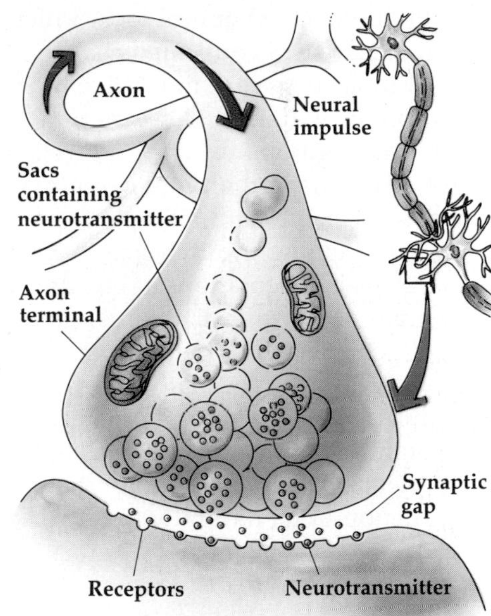

Figure 2-6 *Electrical impulses travel from one neuron to another across a junction known as the synaptic gap. When a signal reaches the axon terminal, it stimulates the release of neurotransmitter molecules. These molecules combine with receptor molecules on the receiving neuron. This allows electrically charged atoms to enter the receiving neuron, thereby influencing whether it will fire and its rate of firing.*

This influence may be either excitatory, increasing the likelihood of the neuron's firing, or inhibitory, decreasing the likelihood. Most neurons have a resting rate of firing that can be increased or decreased by excitatory or inhibitory input from other neurons. (Without inhibition our central nervous system would become turned on everywhere at once.) Roughly speaking, the neuron is democratic: If more excitatory than inhibitory messages are being received, the cell's rate of firing will increase.

The recent discovery of some fifty different neurotransmitters has created a neuropsychological revolution. Why are there so many neural messengers? Where in the nervous system are they found? What are their effects? Can they be increased or diminished through drugs or nutritional changes, thereby affecting our moods, memories, or mental abilities? These are questions that excite neuropsychological researchers and fascinate those of us who are their spectators.

We now know that a particular synapse generally uses only one neurotransmitter, that a particular neural pathway in the brain may use only one or two neurotransmitters, and that particular neurotransmitters may have particular effects on behavior and emotions. For example, one of the best understood neurotransmitters, ***acetylcholine (ACh),*** is found, among other places, at every synapse where a motor neuron from the spinal cord terminates at a skeletal muscle. With electron microscopes, neurobiologists can magnify thinly sliced specimens of the synaptic tissue enough to see the sacs that store and release the ACh molecules. When ACh is released to the muscle cells, the muscle contracts.

If the transmission of the ACh is blocked, the muscles cannot contract, a fact made dramatically clear by the effects of curare, a poison that South American Indians put on the tips of their blow darts. When introduced into the body, curare occupies and blocks the ACh receptor sites, leaving the neurotransmitter nowhere to go. The result: total paralysis. Botulin, a poison that can form in improperly canned food, causes paralysis by blocking the release of ACh. By contrast, the venom of the black widow spider releases a flood of ACh, causing violent muscle contractions.

The growing list of neurotransmitters lessens our amusement at the ancient Greek notion that emotions were affected by fluids or "humors" within the body. The modern list of "humors" includes serotonin, which is used by brain pathways that regulate sleep and temperature; norepinephrine, which affects mood and arousal; and dopamine, which affects attention and complex body movements. As we will see in Chapter 16, "Psychological Disorders," researchers are trying to determine if abnormalities in the level and use of these neurotransmitters might underlie depression and schizophrenia. If they do, then perhaps these disorders could be treated by drug and dietary therapies to help restore normal neurotransmitter production or functioning.

One of the most exciting discoveries concerning neurotransmitters occurred in 1973 at Johns Hopkins University, where Candace Pert and Solomon Snyder attached a radioactive tracer to morphine, allowing them to observe exactly where in an animal's brain it was taken up. Morphine, an opiate, elevates mood and eases pain, and, sure enough, Pert and Snyder discovered that the morphine was taken up by receptor sites in brain areas that have been linked to mood and pain sensations.

The increased release of pain-killing endorphins has been postulated as the basis of "runner's high," that feeling of increased emotional well-being that sometimes comes to long-distance joggers.

It was hard to imagine why the brain would contain these "opiate receptors" unless it had its own naturally occurring opiates. Why would the brain have a chemical lock, unless it also had a key that would fit it? Soon researchers confirmed that the brain does indeed have neurotransmitter molecules very much like morphine. Named ***endorphins*** (meaning "morphine within"), these natural opiates are released in response to pain and vigorous exercise (Farrell & others, 1982; Lagerweij & others, 1984). They have therefore been invoked to explain all sorts of good feelings, such as the pain-killing effects of acupuncture, the "runner's high," and the seeming indifference to pain in some badly injured people.

If such speculations about the endorphins are valid, could we flood the brain with artificial opiates, thereby magnifying the brain's own "feel good" chemistry? One problem seems to be that when the brain is flooded with such opiate drugs as heroin and morphine, it may stop producing its own natural opiates. Thus, when the drugs are withdrawn, the brain may be deprived of any form of opiate. The result, according to this theory, is pain and agony that persists either until the brain resumes production of its natural opiates, or until more of the drugs are administered.

This illustrates the risks inherent in trying to improve a person's mental state by altering the brain's chemistry. Alert to these dangers, researchers try to understand the effects of specific neurotransmitters by experimenting first with animals and only then by cautiously testing their conclusions on troubled people. In the meantime, those of us not afflicted with chemical abnormalities can marvel that our body's natural levels of various chemical messengers seem to be, for our functioning, just about ideal.

Physician Lewis Thomas on the endorphins:
"There it is, a biologically universal act of mercy. I cannot explain it, except to say that I would have put it in had I been around at the very beginning, sitting as a member of a planning committee."
The Youngest Science, 1983

THE BRAIN

In a bottle on a display shelf in Cornell University's psychology department there resides the well-preserved brain of Edward Titchener, a great turn-of-the-century experimental psychologist, founder of the Cornell University department, and proponent of the study of consciousness. Imagine yourself gazing at that wrinkled mass of gray tissue. Is there any sense in which Titchener is still in there?[1]

Perhaps you answer no, that without the living whir of electrochemical activity there could be nothing of Edward Titchener in there. Imagine

[1]Carl Sagan's *Broca's Brain* (1979a) inspired this question.

then an experiment of which perhaps even the inquisitive Titchener himself once dreamed. Imagine that before his death, Titchener's brain had been removed from his body and kept alive by pumping enriched blood through it as it floated in a tank of cerebral fluid. Would Titchener now still be in there? If, to carry our fantasy to its limit, the still-living brain were successfully transplanted into the body of a badly brain-damaged person, to whose home should the recovered patient return?

That we can imagine such questions illustrates how completely we have been convinced that we live in our heads. And for good reason. Earlier we noted that between the nervous system's sensory input and motor output there is everything else—mostly the brain's interneurons that enable the functions we attribute to the mind: seeing, hearing, remembering, thinking, feeling, speaking, dreaming. But precisely where and how are such mind functions tied to the brain? Let us first see how scientists explore such questions.

"The brain may be the originating power of the perceptions of hearing and sight and smell, and memory and opinion may come from them."
Plato, 428–348 B.C.

"Nature has contrived the brain as a counterpoise to the region of the heart with its contained heat. . . . The brain, then, tempers the heat and seething of the heart."
Aristotle, 384–322 B.C.

The Tools of Discovery

New discoveries are nearly always, as Santiago Ramon y Cajal recognized nearly a century ago, "a function of the methods used." The neuron is too small to study with the unaided eye, its electric signals too faint to record with ordinary electrodes. But as new generations of microscopes and microelectrodes were invented, it has become possible to observe neurons and to monitor or modify their activity. As often happens, a scientific revolution was triggered by new tools of discovery.

Clinical Observations

The oldest method of studying brain-mind connections is observing the effects of brain diseases and injuries. Although observations of the effects of brain damage were first recorded some 5000 years ago, it was not until the last two centuries that physicians began to record systematically the consequences of damage to specific brain areas. Some noted that damage to one side of the brain often caused numbness or paralysis on the body's opposite side. Others noticed that damage to the back of the brain disrupted vision, and that damage to the left front part of the brain produced speech difficulties. Gradually, the brain was being mapped.

"Disease is an experiment on the brain performed by nature."
John Hughlings Jackson

Manipulating the Brain

Rather than waiting for random brain injuries, scientists can surgically produce a brain *lesion* (destruction of tissue) or stimulate specific brain areas in animals. For example, in a rat, a lesion in one well-defined brain region diminishes eating, causing the rat to starve unless force-fed; a lesion in a nearby area unleashes overeating.

Recording the Brain's Electrical Activity

Researchers have also learned to eavesdrop on the brain. Modern microelectrodes have tips so small that they can detect the electrical activity in even a single neuron. As we will see, this technology has made possible some astonishingly precise findings: Researchers can now detect exactly where the information goes after a cat's whisker is stroked.

This electrical activity of the brain's approximately 100 billion neurons is orchestrated in regular waves that sweep across the brain's surface. In the 1920s, Hans Berger, a young German psychiatrist, discovered this when he placed electrically sensitive discs attached to a recording device on the head of his son,

Klaus. Berger observed that faint waves (changes in electrical activity in large portions of the brain) peaked about 10 times per second when Klaus was relaxed with his eyes closed. If Klaus opened his eyes and concentrated on a mental problem, the waves would speed up, indicating a more excited brain state. The *electroencephalogram (EEG)* is simply an amplified tracing of such waves by a machine called an electroencephalograph (Figure 2-7). This method for measuring the gross activity of the whole brain is roughly like studying the activity of a car engine by listening to the hum of its motor.

Now it is possible to detect by EEG the brain's response to specific stimuli, such as a sound, a flash of light, or even a thought. By presenting the stimulus repeatedly and having a computer filter out electrical activity unrelated to the stimulus, one can identify the electrical wave evoked by the stimulus. Observing such brain-wave responses—whether normal or abnormal—is an easy, painless way for physicians to diagnose certain forms of brain damage.

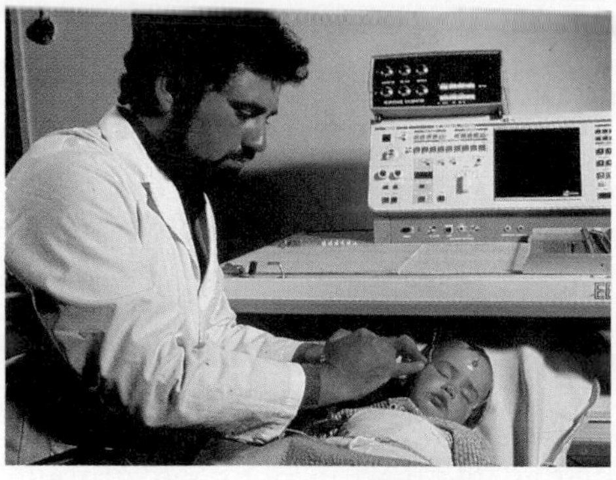

Figure 2-7 *An electroencephalograph provides amplified tracings of waves of electrical activity in the brain.*

Brain Scans

The newest window into the brain similarly allows researchers to scan the brain without lesioning or probing it. For example, the *CAT (computerized axial tomograph) scan* examines the brain by taking three-dimensional x-ray photographs that reveal hidden brain damage (Figure 2-8). Even more dramatic is the *PET (positron emission tomograph) scan,* which depicts the activity of different areas of the brain by picturing each area's consumption of its chemical fuel, glucose (Figure 2-9). The more active the neurons of a particular area, the more glucose they burn. If a person is given a temporarily radioactive form of glucose, the PET scan measures and locates the radioactivity, thereby detecting where this "food for thought" goes. In this way, researchers can see which areas are most active as the person performs mathematical calculations, listens to music, or daydreams (Phelps & Mazziotta, 1985).

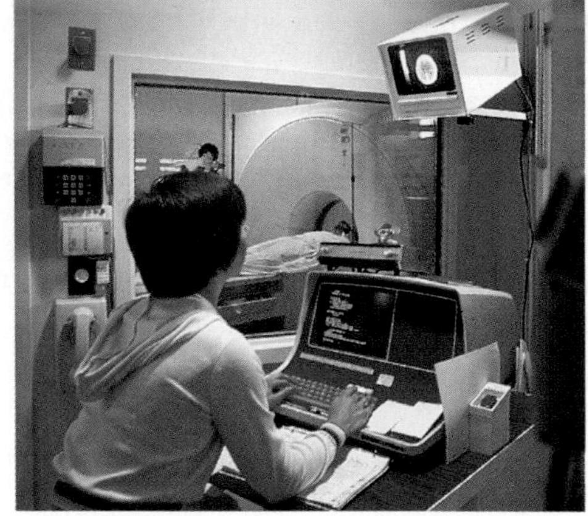

Figure 2-8 *The CAT scan examines the brain by taking three-dimensional X-ray photographs that reveal hidden brain damage.*

It is exciting to consider how fast and far the neurosciences have progressed within a lifetime. For centuries, the study of the human brain lay largely beyond the reach of science. We could feel bumps on the skull and dissect and analyze lifeless brains, but there were no tools gentle enough to explore the living brain. Now, that has all changed. Whether in the interests of science or medical practice, we can selectively destroy tiny clusters of normal or defective brain cells, leaving their surroundings unharmed. We can probe the brain with tiny electrical pulses. We can snoop on the messages of individual neurons and on the mass action of billions. We can see color representations of the brain's energy-consuming activity. Such are the tools and techniques that have enabled what can most certainly be called a scientific revolution.

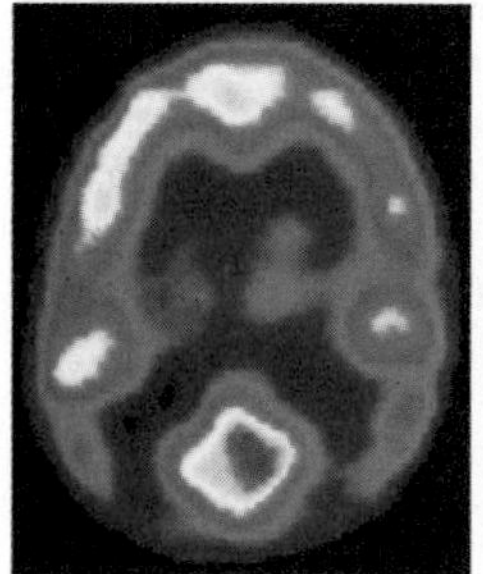

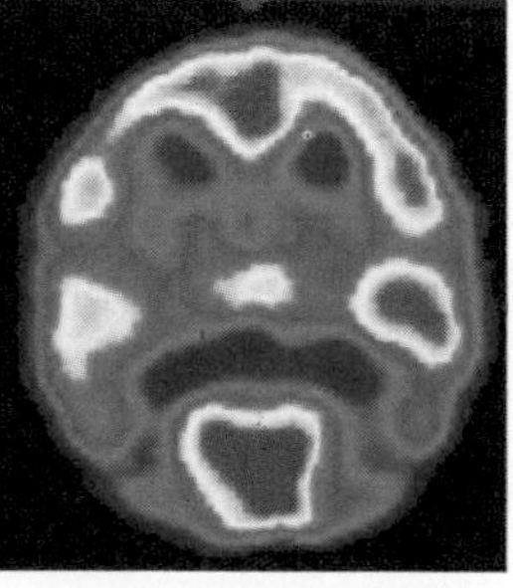

Figure 2-9 *The PET scan detects the activity of different areas of the brain by measuring their relative consumption of a special form of their normal fuel, glucose. A person is given a temporarily radioactive form of glucose, and then the PET scan visualizes how much of this radioactive glucose is consumed in different areas of the brain. In these scans, differences in glucose consumption patterns while resting (left) and while listening to music (right) are evident. Red blotches indicate where the brain is most rapidly consuming glucose.*

Bear in mind that the revolution is now in progress, most of its pioneers still living. It is like being able to study world geography at the time that Magellan was exploring the seas. Every year the explorers announce new discoveries, which also trigger new interpretations of old discoveries. Such times can be unsettling, but to those eager to learn the nature of things, they are never dull.

Organization of the Brain

We are ready to explore the brain's interior. Opening a human skull and exposing the brain, we would see its wrinkled, pinkish-gray tissue, shaped rather like the meat of an oversized walnut. The beauty of this organ lies not in its homely exterior but in its inner intricacy.

In primitive vertebrate animals, such as frogs, the brain is primarily involved with basic survival functions: breathing, sleeping, and feeding. In primitive mammals, the brain has expanded capacities for emotion and memory. In more advanced mammals the brain has an increased ability to process information and to act with foresight. Corresponding to these three stages of brain evolution, we can think of the brain as having three overlapping layers—the brainstem, the limbic system, and the cerebral cortex (Figure 2-10). With the addition of each succeeding layer, the tight control of the genes relaxes. Thus, lower vertebrates, such as fish, operate mostly on preprogrammed genetic instructions; higher mammals' increased capacities for learning and thinking enable them to be more versatile. However, brain evolution has not greatly altered the basic mechanisms of survival. Rather, as the English neurologist John Hughlings Jackson recognized a century ago, evolution has added new systems on top of the old, much as the earth's landscape covers the old with the new. Digging down, one discovers the fossil remnants of the past—brainstem components still performing much as they did in our distant ancestors.

Figure 2-10 *The structures of the human brain with a view of its three principal regions—the brainstem, the limbic system, and the cerebral cortex which covers the cerebral hemispheres. Each of these three overlapping layers of the brain can be thought of as representing a stage in brain evolution. The brainstem region is responsible for automatic survival functions. The limbic system is linked to emotion and behaviors that meet basic needs. The cerebral cortex receives and processes information, makes decisions, and directs voluntary actions.*

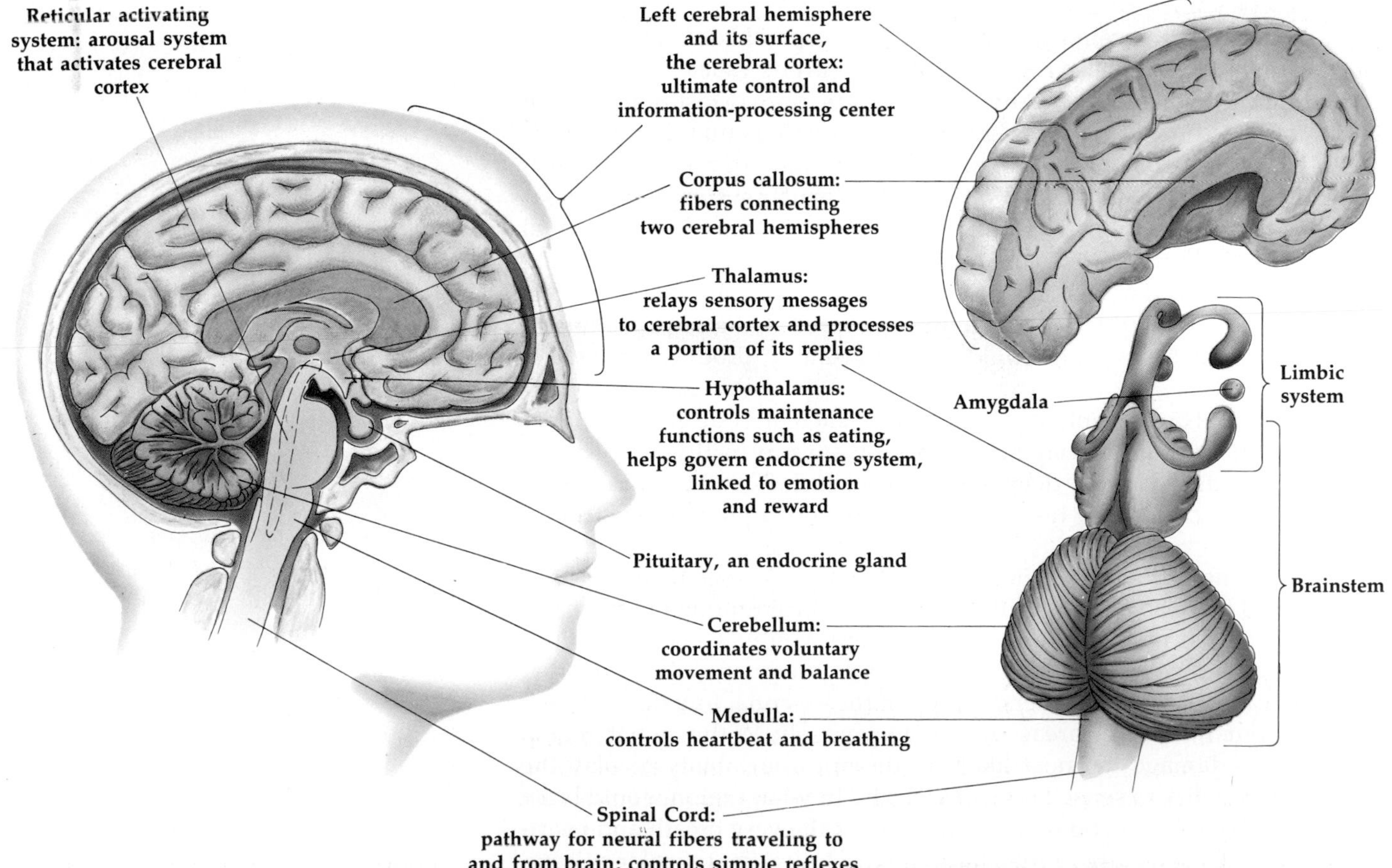

The Brainstem and Basic Survival

The ***brainstem*** is the brain's oldest and innermost region, and so is sometimes called the "old brain" or "central core." It begins where the spinal cord enters the skull and swells slightly, forming the ***medulla.*** Here lie the controls for heartbeat and breathing. Here also is the crossover point, at which nerves from the left side of the brain are mostly routed to the right half of the body, and from the right side of the brain to the left half of the body. This peculiar crosswiring is but one of many surprises the brain has to offer.

"No one has the remotest idea why there should be this amazing tendency for nervous-system pathways to cross."
David H. Hubel and Torsten N. Wiesel (1979)

Extending out from the rear of the brainstem is the ***cerebellum,*** which has two wrinkled hemispheres. Although the cerebellum has been linked to sensory experience, learning, memory, and emotion, its most obvious function is muscular control. On orders from the cortex, the cerebellum coordinates voluntary movement. If your cerebellum were injured, you would likely have difficulty walking, keeping your balance, or shaking hands.

The people who first dissected and labeled the brain used the language of scholars, Latin and Greek. Their words are actually attempts at graphic description: For example "cerebellum" means little brain, "thalamus" is inner chamber, and "cortex" is bark.

Atop the brainstem sit a joined pair of egg-shaped structures called the ***thalamus.*** This is the brain's sensory switchboard. It receives information from the sensory neurons and fans it out to the higher brain regions that deal with seeing, hearing, tasting, and touching. (Chapter 6, "Sensation," will describe some of these pathways—for example how information from the eye is transferred to the brain.) The thalamus also processes a portion of the higher brain's replies, which are then directed to the cerebellum and medulla.

To summarize, we can imagine looking up at the brain from the bottom. First, we see the spinal cord, which then swells to form a tube (the medulla), on which rest a pair of egg shapes (the thalamus), surrounding which, as we will see, are additional layers. Hanging at the back is the baseball-sized cerebellum (Figure 2-10).

Inside the brainstem, extending from the spinal cord right up into the thalamus, is a finger-sized network of neurons called the ***reticular activating system*** (also called the reticular formation). Most of the spinal cord axons of sensory neurons travel up to the thalamus (Figure 2-10). Along the way, some of them branch off to the adjacent reticular system. Thus, when sensory stimulation occurs, the reticular system is activated. The reticular system transmits information about its state to the cerebral cortex, which in turn arouses the brain. So, what do you suppose would happen if the reticular system of a sleeping cat were stimulated? In 1949 Giuseppe Moruzzi and H. W. Magoun discovered that electrical stimulation of the reticular system would almost instantly produce an awake, alert cat.

Magoun also was able to sever a cat's reticular system from higher brain regions without damaging the nearby sensory pathways. The effect? The cat lapsed into a deep sleep from which it could not be awakened. Magoun could clap his hands at its ear, even pinch it; still no response.

Under the influence of the cortex, the reticular system controls not only arousal but also attention. While you are concentrating on this paragraph (or for that matter when you are asleep), you may, thanks to your reticular system, be less sensitive to the sound of someone talking nearby.

You can check your understanding of the essential functions of each of these four brainstem areas by asking yourself: Within what region would brain damage be most likely to disrupt your ability to play the piano? Your ability to sense tastes or sounds? In what region would brain damage perhaps leave you in a coma? Without the very breath and heartbeat of life? (Answers: the cerebellum, the thalamus, the reticular system, and the medulla.) It is remarkable that such life-sustaining functions are so well managed by the brain that they require little or no conscious effort. Whether one is asleep or awake, the symphony of life plays on, freeing the higher brain regions to dream, to think, to talk, to savor a memory.

The Limbic System, Emotion, and Motivation

At the border (or "limbus") of the brainstem and the cerebral hemispheres is a doughnut-shaped neural structure called the ***limbic system.*** As we will see in Chapter 10, the limbic system plays a role in such mental functions as memory. Primarily, however, it has been linked to emotions such as fear and anger, and drives such as those for food and sex.

The Amygdala A pair of almond-shaped neural clusters in the limbic system, called the ***amygdala,*** is involved in both aggression and fear. In 1939, psychologist Heinrich Kluver and neurosurgeon Paul Bucy reported that a lesion in a part of the brain including the amygdala would transform a normally ill-tempered rhesus monkey into the most mellow of creatures. Poke it, pinch it, do virtually anything that would normally trigger a ferocious response, and still the animal would remain placid. In later studies with other wild animals, such as the lynx, wolverine, and wild rat, the same effect was observed. What then might be the effect of electrically stimulating the amygdala in a normally placid domestic animal, like a cat? Do so in one spot and the hissing cat prepares to attack, with its back arched, its pupils dilated, and its hair on end. Move the electrode only slightly to a nearby spot within the amygdala and the cat cowers in terror when caged with a small mouse.

Which division of the autonomic nervous system—sympathetic or parasympathetic—has been activated? (See p. 27.)

These experiments persuasively testify to the amygdala's role in such emotions as rage and fear. Still, we must be careful not to think of the amygdala as *the* control center for aggression and fear. The brain is not neatly organized into structures that correspond to our categories of behavior. Aggressive and fearful behavior involve neural activity in all levels of the brain—brainstem, limbic system, and cerebral cortex. Even within the limbic system, they can be evoked by stimulating neural structures other than the amygdala. Similarly, if you manipulate your car's carburetor, you can affect how the car runs but that does not mean that the carburetor by itself runs the car. It is merely one link in an integrated system.

"The incredible complexity of the brain is a cliché, but it is a fact."
David H. Hubel (1979)

However, given that amygdala lesions change violent monkeys into mellow monkeys, might amygdala lesions do the same in violent humans? Such "psychosurgery" experiments have been tried, with uneven results (Mark & Ervin, 1970; Valenstein, 1980). In a few cases involving patients who suffer brain abnormalities, fits of rage have been reduced, though sometimes with devastating side effects on the patient's ability to function in everyday life. For reasons of ethics as well as those of insufficient knowledge, psychosurgery is highly controversial and seldom used. Perhaps, though, as our knowledge about how the brain controls behavior becomes more precise, refinements in such surgery will increasingly be able to alleviate brain disorders without creating new ones.

Electrical stimulation of the amygdala provokes physical reactions in cats such as those shown here. However, in the natural environment, a cat's arousal involves more complex neural activity.

The Hypothalamus Another of the limbic system's fascinating structures lies below (*hypo*) the thalamus, and so is called the ***hypothalamus***. By making lesions and by stimulating different areas in the hypothalamus, neuroscientists have isolated groups of neurons within it that perform amazingly specific bodily maintenance duties. Some of these neural clusters influence hunger; still others regulate thirst, body temperature, and sexual behavior. The hypothalamus exerts its control both electrically, by triggering activity in the autonomic nervous system, and chemically, by secreting hormones that influence the nearby pituitary gland, the "master gland" of the body's other control system, the endocrine system (see p. 52).

Perhaps the most provocative discovery concerning the hypothalamus was reported in 1954. Its story illustrates how discoveries often are made—as curious, open-minded researchers confront an unexpected observation. Two young neuropsychologists working at McGill University in Montreal, James Olds and Peter Milner, were trying to implant stimulating electrodes in the reticular systems of white rats. One day they made a magnificent mistake. In one rat, an electrode went astray and ended up in what was later discovered to be the region of the hypothalamus (Olds, 1975).

Curiously, this rat kept returning to the place on its tabletop enclosure where it had previously been stimulated, as if it were seeking more of the stimulation. Upon discovering their mistake, the alert investigators recognized that they had stumbled upon a brain center that provided reward. In a painstaking series of experiments, Olds (1958) then went on to locate other "pleasure centers," as he called them. When rats were allowed to trigger their own stimulation in these areas by pressing a pedal, they would sometimes do so at a feverish pace—up to 7000 times per hour until they dropped from exhaustion. Moreover, they would do anything to obtain this stimulation, even crossing an electrified floor that a starving rat would not cross to reach food (Figure 2-11). Similar pleasure centers were later discovered in many other species, including goldfish, dolphins, and monkeys. In fact, animal research reveals that there are specific centers associated with the pleasures of eating, drinking, and sexual behavior.

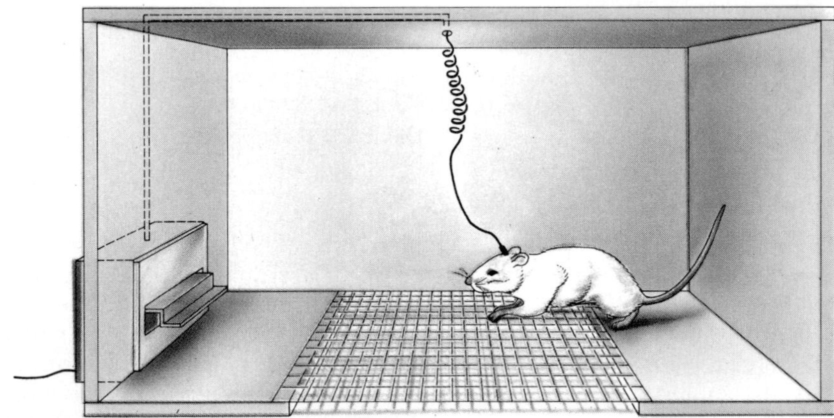

Figure 2-11 *James Olds' experiment. This rat willingly crosses an electrified grid, enduring the pain, in order to press a lever that activates electrical stimulation of certain regions of the hypothalamus, which Olds called "pleasure centers."*

These dramatic findings provoked people to wonder whether humans, too, might have hypothalamic centers for pleasure. Indeed they do. Humans receiving such stimulation find it mildly pleasurable, but unlike rats they are not driven to a frenzy by it (Deutsch, 1972).

The Cerebral Cortex and Information Processing

Roughly speaking, our brainstems are organized much like those of other vertebrates, and our limbic systems are similar to those of other mammals. Most of what defines our distinctive humanness is linked to the complex functions of our highly developed ***cerebral cortex.*** When the cortex ceases to function, a person can only vegetate in a deep coma, without voluntary movement; without the experiences of sight, sound, and touch; without consciousness.

Structure of the Cortex The cortex is a sheet of cells ¼-inch thick that covers the brain. This thin gray sheet is composed of billions of nerve cells and their countless interconnections. Being human takes a lot of nerve.

Glancing at the human cortex, the first thing we notice is its wrinkled appearance. These folds increase the surface area, enabling the skull to be packed with "lots of gray matter." In rats and other lower mammals the surface of the cortex is much smoother, which means there is less of this neural fabric.

Before considering what the cortex does, it helps to know its basic subdivisions. The cortex covers the left and right cerebral hemispheres. (The hemispheres, which account for four-fifths of the brain's weight, are filled with white, fat-covered axons that interconnect the neurons of the cortex with those of other brain regions.) Each hemisphere can be viewed as divided into four regions, or lobes (Figure 2-12). Starting at the front of your brain and going around over the top, these are the ***frontal lobes*** (behind your forehead), the ***parietal lobes*** (atop your head and to the rear), the ***occipital lobes*** (at the very back of your head), and the ***temporal lobes*** (just above your ears). These lobes are convenient geographic subdivisions rather than distinct operating units. As we will see, each lobe carries out many functions, and some functions require the interplay of several lobes.

Two-month-old Andrew, born in 1984, has a brainstem, but due to a cyst which formed over it, none of the higher brain regions. Andrew is therefore expected to be capable only of the basic survival functions automatically performed by the brainstem regions such as the medulla. Without a cortex, Andrew will lack even the perceptions of sight, sound, and touch common to all higher animals, let alone the consciousness specific to humans.

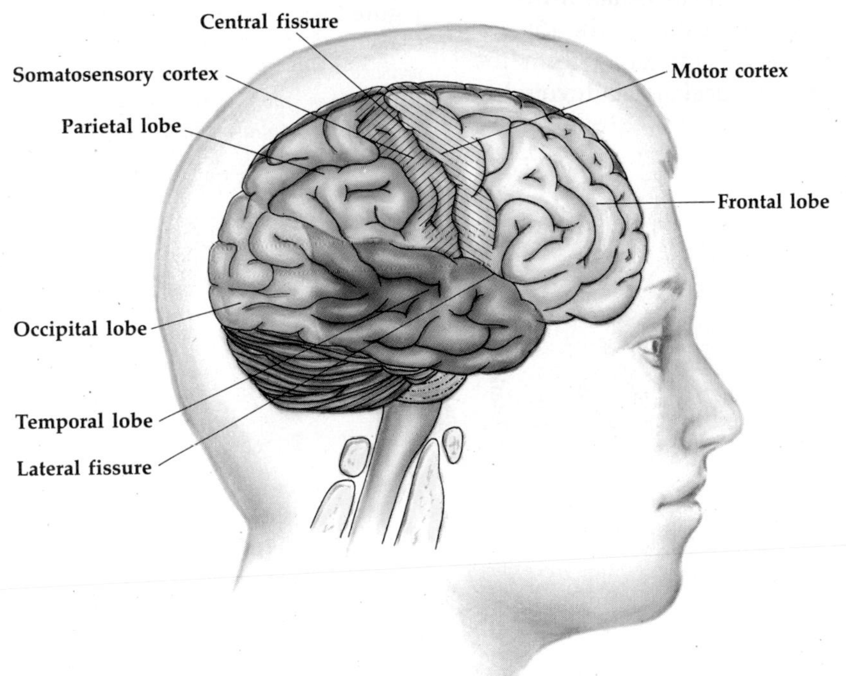

Figure 2-12 *The basic subdivisions of the cortex. The cortex can be viewed as divided into four lobes. The two principal fissures, or grooves, that separate these lobes are shown. The somatosensory cortex, which lies in back of the central fissure, specializes in receiving sensory information from receptors in the skin or from those for movement of body parts. The motor cortex, which lies in front of the central fissure, triggers movement in specific body parts.*

Functions of the Cortex More than a century ago, autopsies of individuals who had lost the ability to speak or to move certain parts of their bodies revealed damage to specific areas of the cortex. But this rather crude evidence did not convince everyone that specific parts of the cortex perform specific functions. After all, if control of speech and movement were diffused across the whole cortex, damage to almost any area might still produce the same effect. Likewise, if we were to cut a television's power cord it would cease functioning; but we would be deluding ourselves if we were to think we had "localized" the picture in the cord. This analogy hints at how easy it is to err when seeking to localize functions within the brain.

"We have to remember that what we observe is not nature herself, but nature exposed to our method of questioning."
Werner Heisenberg, 1901–1976

Sensory-Motor Functions In 1870, German physicians Gustav Fritsch and Eduard Hitzig published a landmark paper that shed light on the issue of whether functions are localized within the cortex. While applying mild electrical stimulation to the cortexes of dogs, they discovered that various body parts could be made to move. The effects were very selective: Only in what came to be called the ***motor cortex*** (Figure 2-12), an arch-shaped region at the back of the frontal lobe that runs roughly from ear to ear across the top of the brain, did stimulation cause movement. Moreover, stimulating specific parts of this region in the left or right hemisphere triggered movement in correspondingly specific body parts on the *opposite* side of the body.

In the 1940s, similar results were obtained in explorations of the human brain carried out on seizure patients by Montreal brain surgeon Wilder Penfield (1975). To relieve patients with severe seizures, Penfield would painlessly (the brain has no sensory receptors) remove the damaged cortical tissue that caused the disorder. To know the likely side effects of such surgery, he needed to find out what function the cortical areas to be removed played. So he mapped the cortex during surgery by giving hundreds of his wide-awake patients a local anesthesia and then stimulating different cortical areas and observing their responses. Like Fritsch and Hitzig, he found that when he stimulated different areas of the motor cortex at the back of the frontal lobe, different body parts moved. Penfield was therefore able to map the motor cortex according to the body parts it controlled (see Figure 2-13a). Interestingly, he discovered that those areas of the body requiring precise control, such as the fingers and mouth, had the greatest amount of cortical space devoted to them.

Figure 2-13 *A visual representation of the tissue in the (a) motor cortex and (b) somatosensory cortex devoted to each body part. As you can see, more of the cortex is devoted to sensitive areas and areas requiring precise control.*

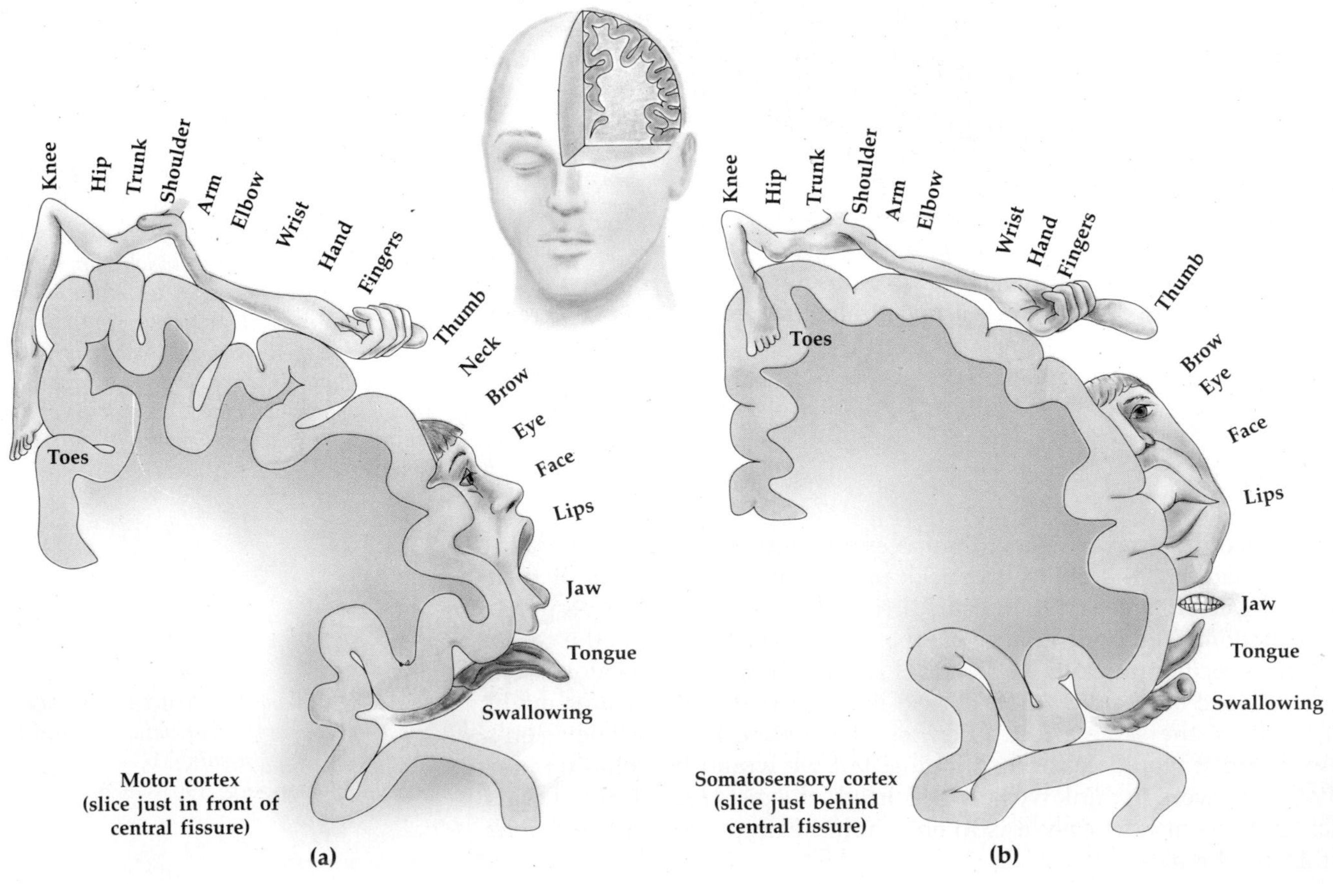

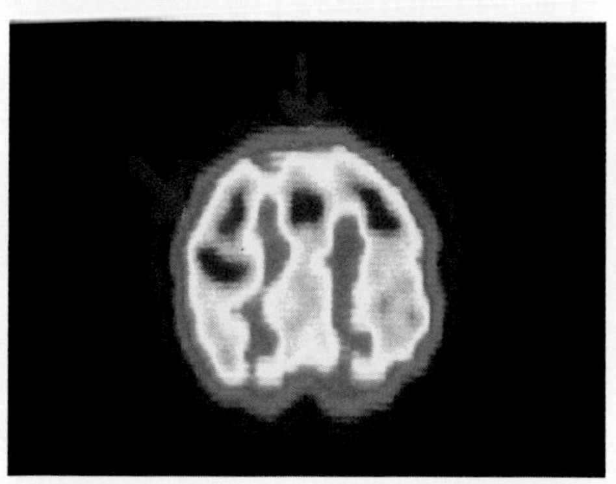

This PET scan shows areas of greatest brain activity as a person sequentially moves the fingers of the right hand. Not surprisingly, one of these areas is the left motor cortex (arrow on left).

More recently, José Delgado, a neuroscientist with a yen for showmanship, demonstrated that motor behavior can be controlled mechanically. In one monkey, he evoked a smiling response over 400,000 times. In one human patient, stimulation of a certain spot on the motor cortex of the left hemisphere made him close his right hand into a fist. Asked to keep his fingers open during the next stimulation, the fingers still closed, whereupon the patient remarked, "I guess, Doctor, that your electricity is stronger than my will" (Delgado, 1969, p. 114).

Penfield also identified a cortical area that specializes in receiving information from the skin senses and from the movement of body parts. This area, parallel to the motor cortex and just behind it at the front of the parietal lobe, we now call the ***somatosensory cortex*** (Figure 2-12). Stimulate the top of this strip, and the person may report being touched on the shoulder; stimulate some point on the side, and perhaps the person will feel something on the face. The more sensitive the body region, the greater the area of the somatosensory cortex devoted to it (Figure 2-13b). If a monkey or a human loses a finger, the region of the somatosensory cortex devoted to receiving input from that finger becomes available to receive sensory input from the adjacent fingers, which now become more sensitive (Fox, 1984).

Visual information is being received, right now, in the occipital lobes at the very back of your brain. Stimulated here, you might see flashes of light or dashes of color. So in a sense we *do* have eyes in the back of our heads. In fact, research is progressing on artificial visual systems that link the "eyes" of a computer-based video system to electrodes in the occipital lobes, thereby enabling a blind person to "see," at least crudely. In Chapter 6, we will look more closely at how this region of our occipital lobes manages to transform neural impulses into a visual perception.

Information from the ear travels to the auditory areas in the temporal lobes. Most of this auditory information travels a circuitous route from ear to the auditory receiving area above the opposite ear. Stimulated here, you might hear a sound.

Association Areas So far we have pinpointed small areas of the cortex that either receive sensory information or direct muscular responses. That leaves everything else—in humans some three-fourths of the cortex. Neurons in these ***association areas*** (the beige areas in Figure 2-14) communicate mainly with one another and with the cortical neurons of the sensory and motor areas. Since no observable response is triggered in these areas when electrically probed, their functions are not so easily specified as are those of the sensory and motor cortex areas. But from observations of lesioned animals and brain-damaged humans, it is clear that these vast areas somehow integrate and act upon information that has been received and processed by the sensory areas.

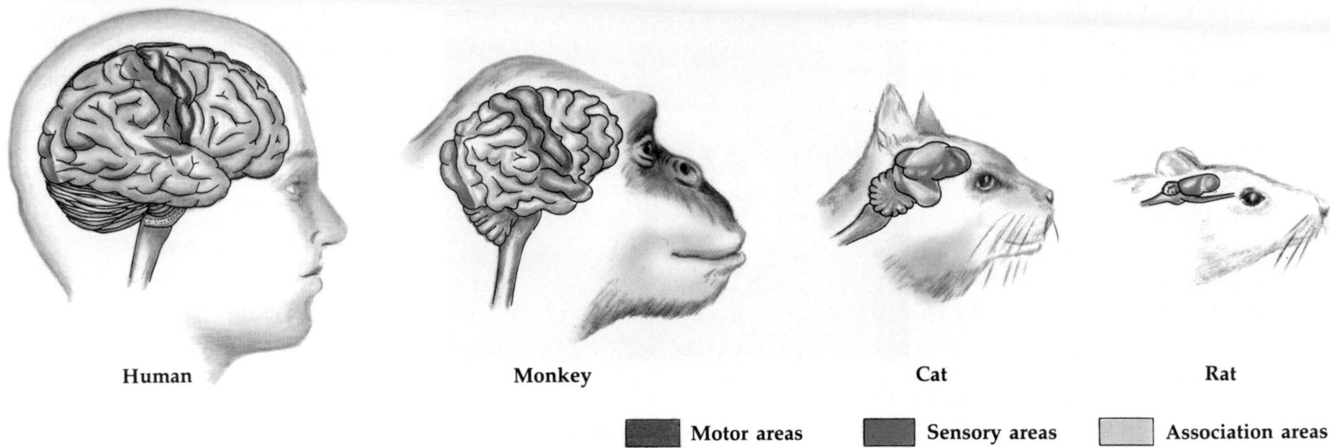

Figure 2-14 *As animals increase in complexity, there is an increase in the amount of "uncommitted" or association areas of the cortex. These vast areas of the brain seem to be responsible for integrating and acting on information received and processed by sensory areas.*

The frontal lobe association areas seem linked to making judgments and to forming and carrying out plans. People with damaged frontal lobes may have intact memories and high IQ test scores and be well able to bake a cake—yet they may be unable to plan ahead and thus to initiate baking a cake for an upcoming party.

Frontal lobe damage can also alter one's personality, leaving a person more uninhibited, profane, and even promiscuous. The classic case of such change is that of Phineas Gage, a 25-year-old railroad worker. One afternoon in 1848, Gage was packing gunpowder into a rock with a tamping iron. A spark ignited the gunpowder, shooting the rod through his left cheek and out the top of his skull, leaving his left frontal lobe massively damaged. To everyone's amazement, Gage was still able to sit up and speak, and after the wound healed he returned to work. His mental abilities and memories were preserved, but his personality was not. The affable, soft-spoken Phineas Gage was now an irritable, profane, capricious person who lost his job and ended up earning a living as a fairground exhibit. This person, said his friends, was "no longer Gage." Today we better understand the functions of the frontal lobes (Stuss & Benson, 1984). For example, we know that damage to them can separate knowledge from action, leaving a person able to explain the action required by some test but strangely unable to carry it out.

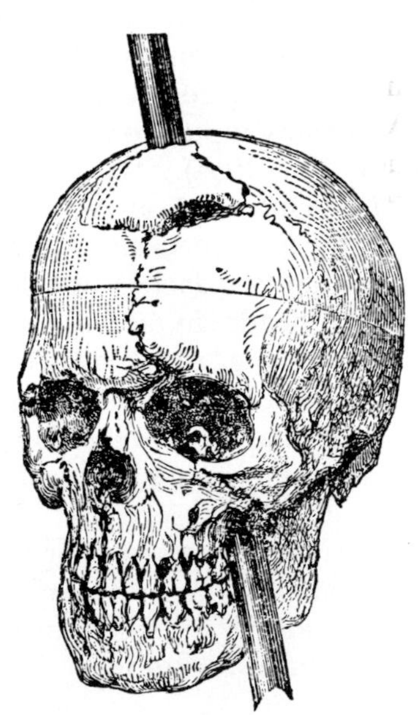

Phineas Gage's skull with the tamping rod passing through.

The association areas of the other lobes similarly participate in mental functions. For example, an area on the underside of the temporal lobes enables us to recognize faces. But by and large, complex mental functions such as learning and memory seem not to be localized in any one spot. For example, there is no one spot in a rat's association cortex that, when damaged, will obliterate its ability to learn or remember a maze. Such functions seem spread throughout much of the brain.

Language It is curious that ***aphasia***, an impairment of the ability to use language, can be caused by damage to any one of several cortical areas. It is even more curious that some aphasic people can speak fluently but (despite good vision) are unable to read, while others can comprehend what they read but are unable to speak. Still others are able to write but not to read, to read numbers but not letters, or to sing but not speak. These observations are puzzling because we tend to think of speaking and reading, or writing and reading, or singing and speaking, as merely different examples of the same general ability. The unraveling of the mystery of language illustrates clearly that such complex human abilities generally result from the intricate coordination of many brain areas. Consider the clues that led to the solving of this mystery:

Clue 1: In 1865, the French physician Paul Broca reported that damage to a specific area of the left frontal lobe, later called ***Broca's area,*** left a person struggling to form words, yet often able to sing familiar songs with ease.

Clue 2: In 1874 a German investigator, Carl Wernicke, discovered that damage to a specific area of the left temporal lobe (***Wernicke's area***), would leave people able to babble words but in a meaningless way without comprehending their meaning. Asked to describe a picture that showed two boys stealing cookies behind a woman's back, one patient replied that "Mother is away here working her work to get her better, but when she's looking the two boys looking the other part. She's working another time" (Geschwind, 1979).

Clue 3: It was later discovered that when we read, a third brain area, the angular gyrus, receives the visual information from the visual area and recodes it into the auditory form in which the word is understood in Wernicke's area.

Clue 4: These areas of the brain are interconnected by nerve fibers.

Norman Geschwind assembled these clues into an explanation of how we use language. When you read aloud, the words (1) register in the visual area, (2) are relayed to the angular gyrus, which translates the word into an auditory code that is (3) received and understood in the nearby Wernicke's area, and (4) transmitted to Broca's area, which (5) controls the adjacent motor cortex, creating the pronounced word (Figure 2-15). Depending on which link in this chain is damaged, a different form of aphasia occurs. Damage to the angular gyrus leaves the person able to speak and understand but unable to read. Damage to Wernicke's area disrupts understanding. Damage to Broca's area disrupts speaking.

Actually, normal conversation involves even more brain centers. The auditory receiving area transmits information directly to Wernicke's area, which passes it on to association areas to process and act upon.

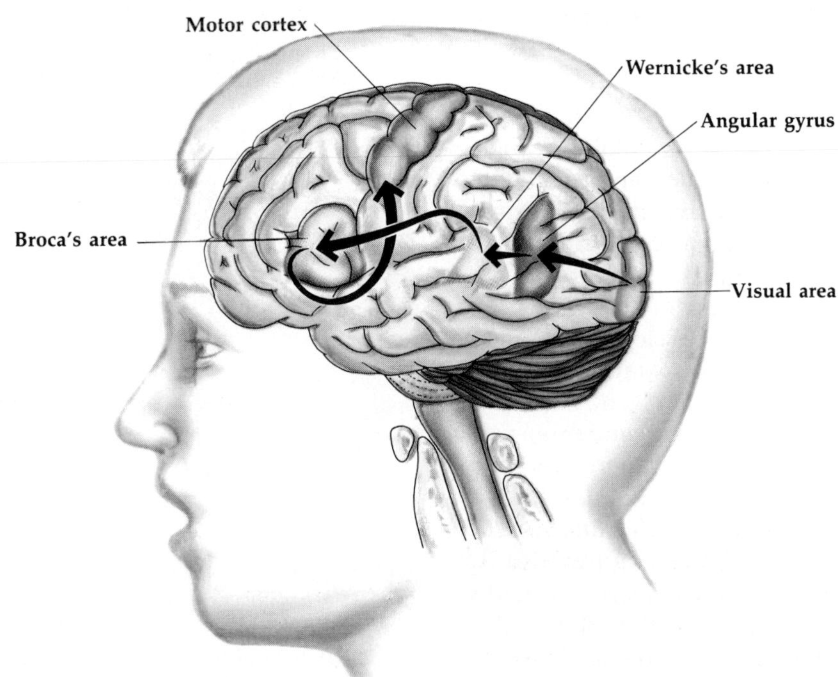

Figure 2-15 *Speaking a written word requires the coordination of a number of brain areas. The arrows show the movement of information in the brain from the time the word is read until it is spoken. (Adapted from "Specialization of the human brain" by N. Geschwind. Copyright © 1979 Scientific American, Inc. All rights reserved.)*

Moreover, these areas send directions to the motor cortex, which in turn transmits commands on down the brainstem to the mouth. Although the sequence of brain events quickly becomes overwhelming, this description is a simplified one. There is a continuous interplay of still other brain areas, and we have hardly begun to explore the internal operation of any one area. How does Wernicke's area squeeze meaning out of a sound? How does Broca's area play the keyboard of the motor cortex? More generally, how can we best describe the coordinated functioning of the whole brain? Mechanically, as a hierarchy of extremely sophisticated and unbelievably miniaturized computers? Artistically, as an "enchanted loom" of billions upon billions of interconnected neurons? Such images help us to think about the brain, but they do not diminish our sense of wonder.

"If the brain were so simple that we could understand it, we would be so simple that we couldn't."
Emerson M. Pugh

Our Divided Brains

We have seen that while certain attributes of mind such as language are localized in particular brain regions, the brain nevertheless acts as a unified whole. Both principles of brain functioning—specialization and integration—are apparent in some provocative research on how the two brain hemispheres work.

For more than a century, clinical evidence accumulated showing that the two sides of the brain serve differing functions. As we have seen, accidents, strokes, and tumors in the *left* hemisphere generally impair reading, writing, speaking, and understanding. Also linked to left-side damage are disorders of learned voluntary movement and of arithmetic reasoning ability. Similar lesions in the right hemisphere do not have comparably dramatic effects. Small wonder, then, that the left hemisphere came to be known as the "dominant" or "major" hemisphere, and its silent companion to the right as the "subordinate" or "minor" hemisphere. (With some people, especially some left-handers, this is reversed—see "Left-Handedness: Is Being a Lefty All Right?," page 50.)

The bullet from John Hinkley's gun that ripped through the right *frontal lobe of Presidential Press Secretary James Brady left him paralyzed on his left side, but able to talk, read, and write.*

By 1960, the assumption of left hemisphere superiority seemed well-established. But in science every understanding is best considered an approximation of truth that may in time be replaced by a fuller understanding. As if to illustrate this, scientists of the 1960s were surprised to discover that the "minor" right hemisphere was not so limited as was commonly thought (Sperry, 1982). The story of this discovery is one of the fascinating chapters in the history of psychology.

Splitting the Brain

More than a century ago, one of the fathers of experimental psychology, Gustav Fechner, imagined an impossible "thought experiment." Fechner (1860) wondered what would happen if it were possible to divide the brain. Would not the person be duplicated? "The two cerebral hemispheres," he wrote, "while beginning with the same moods, predispositions, knowledge, and memories, indeed the same consciousness generally, will thereafter develop differently according to the external relations into which each will enter."

During the 1950s, one of Fechner's intellectual descendants, psychologist Roger Sperry, made Fechner's imaginary experiment a reality. Working with Ronald Myers and Michael Gazzaniga, Sperry "divided the brains" of cats and monkeys by severing the ***corpus callosum,*** a wide band of nerve fibers that connects the two hemispheres (Figure 2-16). In these experiments, and in some prior surgical work with humans, the operation seemed not to be seriously incapacitating. (Recall that the brain's connections to the opposite side of the body cross over in the brainstem, and so are not injured by the operation.)

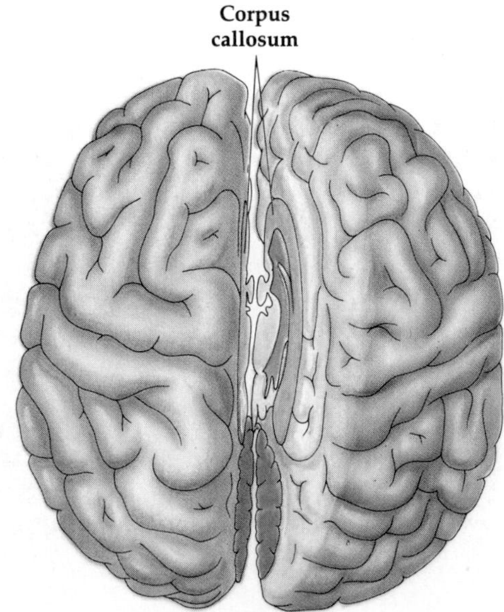

Figure 2-16 *The corpus callosum is a large band of neural fibers that connects the two brain hemispheres. In this top view of the brain, the hemispheres have been separated so that the corpus callosum is visible.*

In 1961, Los Angeles neurosurgeons Philip Vogel and Joseph Bogen speculated that major epileptic seizures were caused by an amplification of abnormal brain activity that reverberated back and forth across the corpus callosum. If true, epilepsy might be controlled by cutting communication between the two hemispheres. So they decided as a last resort to sever the corpus callosum in severely afflicted patients. The welcome results were that the seizures were nearly eliminated and the patients seemed surprisingly normal, their personalities and intellect hardly affected. Awakening from the surgery, one patient even managed to quip that he had a "splitting headache" (Gazzaniga, 1967). If you chatted with one of these ***split-brain*** patients over coffee, you would probably never notice anything out of the ordinary. Given this result, one can understand how only a decade earlier neuropsychologist Karl Lashley jested that maybe the corpus callosum served only "to keep the hemispheres from sagging." But surely a band of 200 million nerve fibers capable of transferring several billion bits of information per second between the hemispheres must have a more significant purpose.

It does, and the ingenious experiments of Sperry and Gazzaniga that revealed its purpose also provided a key to understanding the special functions of the two hemispheres. But first a word of caution: The more than 100 split-brain patients are a diverse and grossly atypical group (Gazzaniga, 1984). The disease that necessitated the operation to sever their hemispheres may have altered their brains in other ways that would help account for their behavior. Nevertheless, the testing of these patients has provided psychologists with hints as to what each hemisphere can do when pretty much on its own.

Shortly after one of these operations, it was noted that when an unseen object was placed in the patient's left hand he denied its presence. This came as no surprise to Sperry and Gazzaniga, who from their animal experiments expected that the right hemisphere (which, of course, receives the information from the left hand) would be unable to transmit this information to the speech-controlling areas of the left hemisphere. More extraordinary results came when Sperry and Gazzaniga conducted some perceptual tests.

Our eyes are connected to our brains in such a way that, when we look straight ahead the left half of our field of vision is received initially only by our right hemisphere and the right half of our field of vision only by our left hemisphere (Figure 2-17). In those of us with intact brains, a word that is flashed in this way to our right hemisphere is quickly transmitted over our corpus callosum to our left hemisphere, which names it. But what happens in a person whose corpus callosum has been severed? By asking the split-brain patient to look at a designated spot and then flashing information in the right or left half of the visual field, the experimenter can communicate solely with the right or left hemisphere.

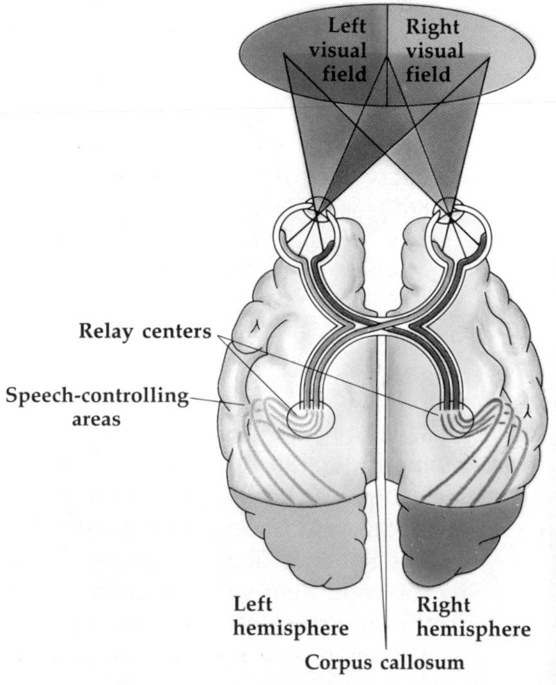

Figure 2-17 *The visual field is split down the middle, with the left half initially being received only by the right hemisphere, and the right half by the left hemisphere. The information received by either hemisphere is quickly transmitted to the other across the corpus callosum. In a split-brain patient, whose corpus callosum has been severed as shown, this sharing of information does not take place.*

See if you can guess the results of an experiment using this procedure (Gazzaniga, 1967), in which the word HEART was flashed across the visual field as H E • A R T. What did the patients *say* they saw? Asked to identify with their *left* hands what they had seen, HE or ART, which did they point to?

As Figure 2-18a shows, the patients said they saw ART, and so were surprised when their left hands pointed to HE. When given an opportunity to express itself, each hemisphere reported only what *it* had seen. Similarly, when a picture of a spoon was flashed to the right hemisphere, the patients could not say what they saw, but when asked to do so, they could, with their left hands, select a spoon from an assortment of objects hidden behind a screen (Figure 2-18b). It was as if the patients had "two separate inner visual worlds," noted Sperry (1968).

Figure 2-18 *Testing the divided brain.* *(a) When an experimenter flashes the word HEART across the visual field, the split-brain subject reports seeing the portion of the word transmitted to the left hemisphere, but points with the left hand to the portion of the word transmitted to the right hemisphere.* *(b) When a picture of a spoon is flashed to the right hemisphere, the split-brain patient cannot say what he has seen, because vocal naming is under left hemisphere control, but with his left hand he selects a spoon from an assortment of objects hidden behind the screen.*

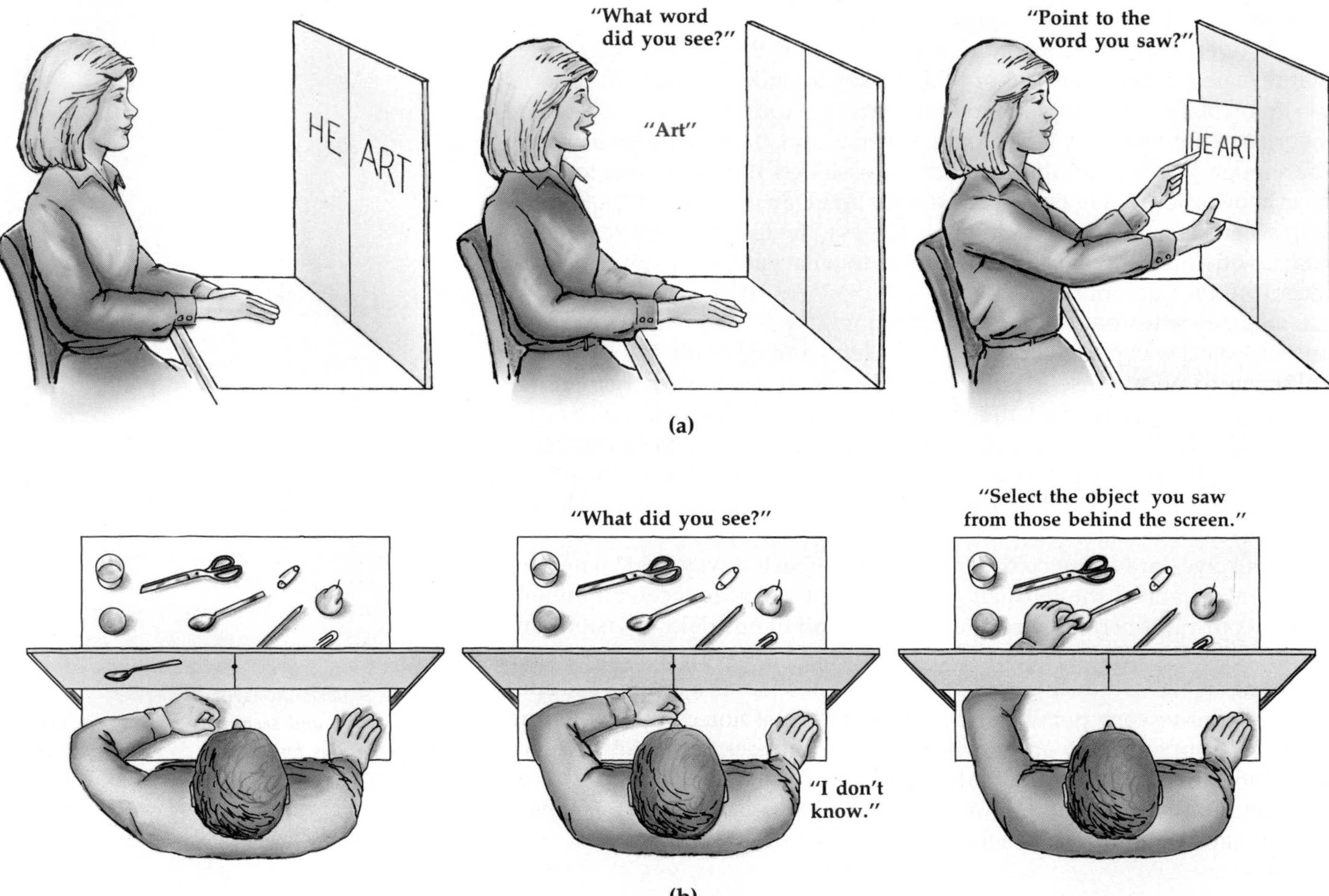

These experiments demonstrated that the right hemisphere can actually understand simple requests and can also easily perceive objects. In fact, the right hemisphere is superior to the left at copying drawings and at recognizing faces. Its perceptual superiority is also demonstrated in one of Sperry's films, in which a split-brain patient's left hand (directed by the right hemisphere) easily rearranges some blocks to match a drawing. When the right hand (directed by the left hemisphere) tries to perform the same perceptual task, it makes many errors. This apparently frustrates the right hemisphere, which is observing all this, triggering the left hand to interrupt the bumbling right hand. Outside of the laboratory, a few patients have occasionally been bothered by the unruly independence of their left hand, which may unbutton a shirt while the right hand buttons it. As this illustrates, split-brain surgery seems to leave people "with two separate minds" (Sperry, 1964).

"My suspicion is that the universe is not only queerer than we suppose, but queerer than we can suppose."

J. B. S. Haldane, 1892–1964, *Possible Worlds*

Figure 2-19 *When an experimenter flashes simple commands to the right hemisphere of split-brain patients, they comply. But when asked about their response, their left hemisphere, which controls speech and which is unaware of what the right hemisphere has seen, invents, and seemingly believes, plausible explanations for what it does not comprehend. Thus Michael Gazzaniga (1983) concludes that the left hemisphere has an "unrelenting need to explain actions."*

Hemispheric Specialization

Observations of split-brain patients have allowed us to glimpse the special functions of each hemisphere. As we have just noted, by presenting information to and then questioning each hemisphere separately, Sperry and others demonstrated that while the left is more verbal, the right excels at perceptual tasks. Perhaps because of its perceptual ability, the right hemisphere also helps us sense and express emotion (Tucker, 1981). When Sperry (1968) flashed a picture of a nude to the right hemisphere, split-brain patients would blush, grin, and giggle, yet could not correctly explain the emotion. (Patients would even sometimes invent incorrect explanations for their reactions—see Figure 2-19). In other tests, the right hemisphere would sometimes cause the patient to frown or wince upon hearing the left hemisphere speak a wrong answer (thus occasionally cuing the person to correct the answer). Moreover, right hemisphere damage may leave a person less able to express emotion and to recognize emotions in others. In Figure 2-20, which face is happier? Although the faces are mirror images, most people judge the happier face to be the one to the right: It projects its happy side to your right hemisphere where emotions are more easily recognized (Sackeim & others, 1978).

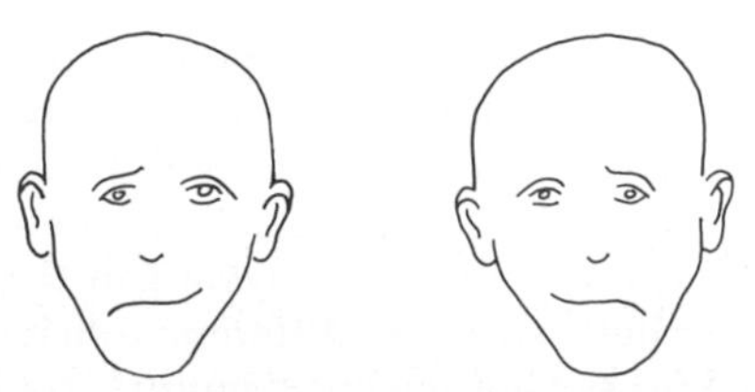

Figure 2-20 *These faces are mirror images of each other. Stare at the nose of each. Which face is happier?*

To say that the left hemisphere specializes in language and in the fine muscle control that enables us to speak and write, and that the right hemisphere specializes in perceptual and emotional tasks, does not mean that the right hemisphere is speechless or the left emotionless. Although controversy remains (see "Is the Right Hemisphere Intelligent?"), many neuropsychologists have concluded that the left hemisphere is usually more logical, rational, and able to deal with things in sequence, while the right is more intuitive, nonverbal, and able to deal with things all at once. But neuropsychologists also advise us to beware the fad of locating complex human capacities, such as abilities in science or art, in either hemisphere. Popularized descriptions of the left-right dichotomy have tended to run way ahead of the scientific findings. True, the cortex does have specialized regions for performing certain subtasks (Allen, 1983), but complex activities such as science or art emerge from the integration of the subprocesses of *both* hemispheres. Even when simply reading a story, both hemispheres are at work—the left in understanding the words and finding meaning, the right in appreciating humor, imagery, and emotional content (Levy, 1985).

"Foster here is the left side of my brain, and Mr. Hoagland is the right side of my brain."

"The left-right dichotomy in cognitive mode is an idea with which it is very easy to run wild."
Roger Sperry (1982)

Is the Right Hemisphere Intelligent?

Researchers who have studied split-brain patients concur on many findings: The function of the corpus callosum, the logical and linguistic superiority of the left hemisphere, and the superiority of the right hemisphere on at least some simple perceptual tasks. But on other issues, disagreement prevails. Does the right hemisphere possess language, too? No, concludes Michael Gazzaniga (1983): "Right hemisphere language is not common." Fellow researcher Jerre Levy (1983) partially disagrees; the right hemisphere often can grasp the meanings of words, she believes. Eran Zaidel (1983) even more strongly disputes the right hemisphere's alleged linguistic incompetence: "Evidence for right hemisphere involvement in normal language is becoming increasingly prominent."

Assuming that the right hemisphere is inferior to the left in language, is it correspondingly superior in other abilities? Again, the experts disagree. Gazzaniga (1983) states, "It could well be argued that the cognitive skills of a normal disconnected right hemisphere without language are vastly inferior to the cognitive skills of a chimpanzee." Here, Levy (1983) clearly parts company with Gazzaniga. She wonders, "Why is the right hemisphere so large if it is so stupid?" and from her research concludes that "the evidence is overpowering [that the right hemisphere] is active, responsive, highly intelligent, thinking, conscious, and fully human with respect to its cognitive depth and complexity."

What makes these disagreements so striking is that all three researchers have collaborated with Roger Sperry in the same laboratory, have observed many of the same patients, and have read the same research literature. Their clashing conclusions therefore sharply illustrate some of the observations made in Chapter 1 about the nature of science. Between the factual data and the interpretive conclusions there is always a gap that the theorist must leap. When different researchers arrive at different conclusions, their disagreements are a driving force for further scientific inquiry. Nevertheless, the researchers agree that their interpretive leaps must be consistent with the data and that their disagreements should be resolved not by opinion but by further research.

"Conciliatory smoothness is the lifeblood of diplomacy; it is the death of science. *Diplomacy consists of producing agreement. . . . Science consists of organizing controversy or, if need be, generating it."*
E. A. Murphy (1982)

Studying the Normal Brain

Perhaps you are wondering whether hemispheric specialization can be confirmed by studying how the hemispheres work in the 99.99+ percent of us with undivided brains. It indeed has been, by evidence from several different types of studies. For example, when a person performs a perceptual task, the brain waves, bloodflow, and glucose consumption of the right hemisphere indicate increased activity; when a person speaks or performs calculations, the same is true of the left hemisphere (Springer & Deutsch, 1985). These differences are not large—which confirms that at any given time the whole brain is active—but they do confirm the principle of hemispheric specialization.

"In the normal state, the two hemispheres appear to work closely together as a unit, rather than one being turned on while the other idles."
Roger Sperry (1982)

Hemispheric specialization has on occasion been even more dramatically demonstrated by briefly sedating an entire hemisphere. To check for the localization of language, a physician may administer a sedative to the neck artery that brings blood to the hemisphere on its side of the body. Just before the drug is administered the patient is lying down, arms in the air, conversing easily. When the drug is injected in the artery going to the left hemisphere, can you predict what happens? Within seconds, the right arm falls limp, and, assuming the person's left hemisphere controls language, the subject becomes speechless until the drug wears off. When the drug is administered to the artery going to the right hemisphere, the *left* arm falls limp, but conversation is still possible.

Hemispheric specialization has also been verified by tests in which most people recognize pictures faster and more accurately when they are flashed to the right hemisphere, but recognize words faster and more accurately when flashed to the left hemisphere. (If a word is flashed to your right hemisphere, perception takes a fraction of a second longer—which is how long it takes to transmit the information through the corpus callosum to the more verbal left hemisphere.)

Doreen Kimura (1973) refined a technique that further confirmed hemispheric specialization. As we noted earlier, input from the right ear goes mostly to the left hemisphere and vice versa. If a dual-track tape recorder were to simultaneously present the spoken number "one" to your left ear and "nine" to your right ear, which would you more likely hear? Kimura reported that with verbal information your right ear (left hemisphere) wins this "dichotic listening" contest, but that the left ear (right hemisphere) is superior at perceiving nonspeech sounds, such as melodies, laughing, and crying.

So, a variety of observations—both of split-brain subjects and of people with "normal" brains—converge beautifully. There is now little doubt that we have functionally integrated brains with specialized parts. From looking at the two hemispheres, which appear nearly identical to the naked eye, who would suppose that they contribute so uniquely to the harmony of the whole?

Brain Reorganization

If brain tissue is destroyed through injury or illness, are the special functions served by the now lesioned tissue forever lost? If you scrape your knee, new cells will be generated to repair the damage. Not so with the neurons of the CNS. If the spinal cord is severed or if brain tissue is destroyed, the injured neurons will normally not be replaced.

That is the bad news. The good news is that undamaged neurons nearby may in time partly compensate for the damage by making new connections that replace the lost tissue (Cotman & Nieto-Sampedro, 1982). These new connections are one way in which the brain struggles to recover from, say, a minor stroke.

Left-handedness: Is Being a Lefty All Right?

Judging by our talk, left-handedness is not all right. To be "coming from left-field," or to offer a "left-handed compliment" is hardly more complimentary than to be "sinister" or "gauche" (words derived from the Latin and French words for left). On the other hand, right is "right on," which any "righteous" "right-hand man" "in his right mind" usually is.

How Many People Are Left-handed?

Almost 10 percent (somewhat more among males, somewhat less among females) of the human population is left-handed. Judging from cave drawings and the tools of prehistoric humans, this veer to the right occurred a long way back in the development of our species.

Can One Predict at Birth Whether a Child Will Be Left- or Right-handed?

Observing 150 babies in the first 2 days after birth, George Michel (1981) found that two-thirds consistently preferred to lie with their heads turned to the right. When he restudied a sample of these babies at age 5 months, almost all of the "head right" babies reached for things with their right hands, and almost all of the "head left" babies reached with their left hands. Such findings, along with the universal prevalence of right-handers, suggest that handedness is genetically influenced.

Is the Brain Organization of Left-handers Opposite That of Right-handers?

Tests reveal that about 95 percent of right-handers process speech primarily in the left hemisphere (Springer & Deutsch, 1985). With left-handers it is not as clear-cut. More than half process speech in the left hemisphere, just as right-handers do. Of the remainder, about half process language in the right hemisphere and half use both hemispheres more or less equally. Researchers are currently debating and studying whether a lefty's writing posture—whether the hand is hooked over the pen or held straight—tells us which hemisphere processes language (Weber & Bradshaw, 1981).

So, Is It All Right to Be Left-handed?

There appears to be a disproportionate percentage of left-handers among those with reading disabilities, but left-handedness is also more common among musicians, mathematicians, and artists, including such luminaries as Michelangelo, Leonardo da Vinci, and Picasso. Generally, left- and right-handers do not differ discernibly in academic achievements (Hardyck & Petrinovich, 1977). If one can tolerate elbow jostling at dinner parties, right-handed desks, and awkward scissors, then apparently being left-handed matters little.

Could we augment the brain's own self-repair work by transplanting brain tissue? Even in this era of heart transplants and skin grafts, transplanting neural tissue still sounds like science fiction. But in experiments with animals, neuroscientists are now attempting, with some success, to mend the brain by replacing destroyed nerve cells with healthy ones (Sladek & Gash, 1984). For example, in one dramatic experiment, Randy Labbe and her colleagues (1983) removed a portion of the frontal lobes from a group of rats. A week later, some of these rats received replacement tissue from the frontal lobes of rat fetuses. Others, the controls, either received fetal brain tissue from cerebellums or else received no replacement tissue at all. After 4 more days, all the rats began learning to navigate a simple maze that rewarded them with water when they made the correct turns. Compared to rats that had not been brain-damaged, the rats with the transplanted frontal lobe tissue took longer to learn the maze, but they learned it twice as fast as the controls (Figure 2-21). So it seems that transplants of brain tissue may in some cases partially replace lost or damaged tissue.

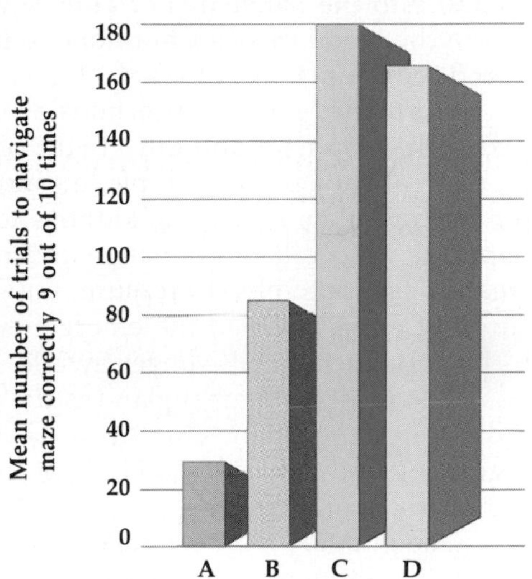

Figure 2-21 *Brain transplants and learning ability in rats. As the bar graph shows, rats with intact brains (A) require the least number of trials to navigate the maze at left correctly 9 out of 10 times. Of those with damaged frontal lobes, the group who received grafts of fetal frontal lobe tissue (B) learned more quickly than those who received fetal cerebellar tissue (C) or no replacement tissue (D).*

Already, there is much talk—and the beginnings of experimental surgery (Kolata, 1983)—suggesting that eventually, transplants of human brain tissue may enable neurosurgeons to repair the neural damage that underlies certain illnesses, such as the tremors of Parkinson's disease and the progressive senility of Alzheimer's disease, each of which involves a degeneration of brain tissue that normally produces vital neurotransmitters—dopamine in Parkinson's disease, acetylcholine in Alzheimer's. For both diseases, the hope is that tissue transplanted from elsewhere in the body, or from miscarried human fetuses, will release the needed neurotransmitters and thus halt the progress of the disease.

Perhaps the best news, though, concerns the brain's ***plasticity***. When one brain area is damaged, other areas may in time reorganize and take over its functions. Before the functions of their cortical regions become fixed, young children's brains are especially plastic. If the speech areas of an infant's left hemisphere are damaged, the right hemisphere will likely take over, with no noticeable impairment of language. Not until about age 8 does left hemisphere damage permanently disrupt language.

To take a drastic example, consider a 5-year-old boy whose severe seizures, caused by a progressively deteriorating left hemisphere, necessitate removal of the *entire* hemisphere. What hope for the future would such a child have? Is there any chance he might attend school and lead a normal life, or would he be permanently retarded?

This is an actual case, and, astonishingly, the individual is at last report a 35-year-old executive. Half his skull is filled with nothing but cerebrospinal fluid—for functional purposes it might as well be sawdust—yet he has scored well above average on intelligence tests, has completed college, and is now attending graduate school part time (Smith & Sugar, 1975; A. Smith, personal communication, April 1983). Although paralyzed on the right side, this individual (along with other such cases of "hemispherectomy") testifies to the brain's extraordinary powers of reorganization, especially when damaged before it is fully developed.

THE ENDOCRINE SYSTEM

We have seen that the nervous system is a relatively speedy communication system. Through its electrochemical activity, information can be transmitted directly from eyes to brain to hand in a fraction of a second. The ***endocrine system*** is the body's slower chemical communication system. Its glands (Figure 2-22) release their chemical messengers, the ***hormones,*** into the bloodstream. Thus several seconds or more may elapse before the blood carries a hormone to its target tissue, where it begins to affect body functions.

Hormones regulate functions as diverse as children's physical and sexual development and our "flight or fight" responses to danger. In a moment of danger, for example, the autonomic nervous system will order the ***adrenal*** glands atop the kidneys to release epinephrine and norepinephrine (also called adrenaline and noradrenaline), hormones that increase heart rate, blood pressure, and blood sugar, providing us with a surge of energy. When the emergency passes, the hormones—and the feelings of excitement—linger awhile.

Which division of the autonomic nervous system—sympathetic or parasympathetic—would trigger this effect? (See p. 27.)

The most influential gland is the ***pituitary,*** a pea-sized structure at the base of the brain. One of its hormones has the important task of regulating body growth. Too little of this hormone will produce a dwarf, too much, a giant.

The pituitary has been called the "master gland" because some of its secretions influence the release of hormones from other endocrine glands. But these other glands may also be influenced by the body's blood chemistry. For example, when we eat a candy bar the increase of sugar in the bloodstream triggers the pancreas to release the hormone insulin.

The secretions of the pituitary gland are themselves regulated by the hypothalamus, which as we noted earlier is a part of the brain that lies above the pituitary. The hypothalamus, in turn, monitors blood chemistry and receives information from other brain areas that regulate its secretions. This feedback system illustrates the close interaction of the nervous and endocrine systems. The nervous system directs the endocrine glands, and the secretions of these glands in turn affect neural activity. The maestro that conducts and coordinates this symphony is the brain. Understanding how the brain functions is therefore the ultimate scientific challenge: the mind seeking to understand the brain.

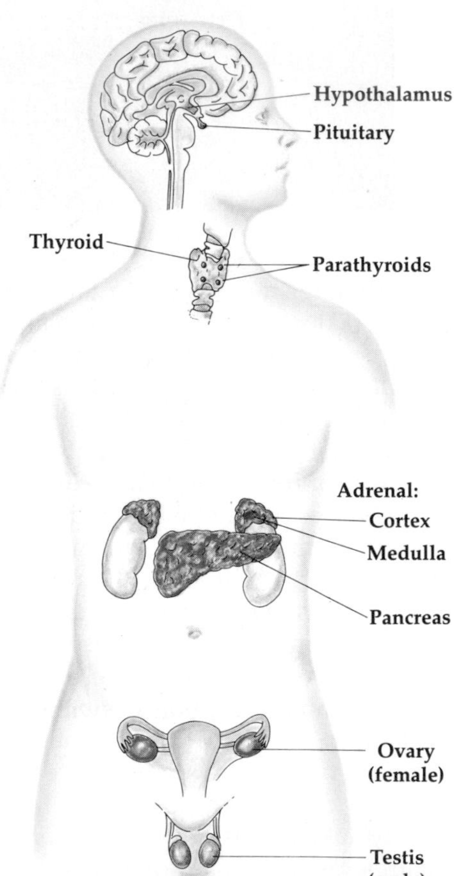

Figure 2-22 *The body's major endocrine glands. The pituitary releases hormones that, in turn, regulate the hormone secretions of the thyroid, the adrenal cortex, and the sex glands. The pituitary is itself under the regulatory control of the hypothalamus, which is sensitive to the concentration of circulating substances in the blood, including hormones. The hypothalamus thus is a major link between the nervous system and the endocrine system.*

GENES AND BEHAVIOR

Having so far considered our collective development—how we humans came to be who we are, and how our nervous and endocrine systems operate—we are prepared to understand better why we behave as we do. Yet, despite our commonalities, each of us is genetically unique. So let us conclude our discussion of the biology of behavior by considering the genetic determinants of our individuality.

Genes

What physical entity within you has controlled your growth with such exquisite exactness that your eyebrows (let us say) resemble your father's? When you are badly frightened, what within the cells of your adrenal glands makes them capable of producing epinephrine? What, in fact, contains the information necessary to make every digestive juice, every bone, every hair—every substance that is being simultaneously manufactured by each of the trillions of cells in your body? The answer to all of these questions is, of course, your genes (Figure 2-23).

These genes are contained in the 23 pairs of ***chromosomes*** that reside in nearly every cell in your body. You inherited one set of 23 chromosomes from your mother and one set from your father. The two sets form pairs that contain alternate genes for the same traits. Sometimes, as in the determination of the ability to roll the tongue, one gene rules (is "dominant"). More often our traits are the product of many pairs of genes working together.

Each chromosome is composed of long, exquisitely thin threads of a molecule called ***DNA*** (deoxyribonucleic acid). DNA is constructed in such a way that segments of it can form a template for the manufacture of proteins, some of which are important structural building blocks of cells and others of which are involved in regulating all the reactions that go on in cells. Any segment of DNA that is capable of synthesizing a specific protein is called a gene.

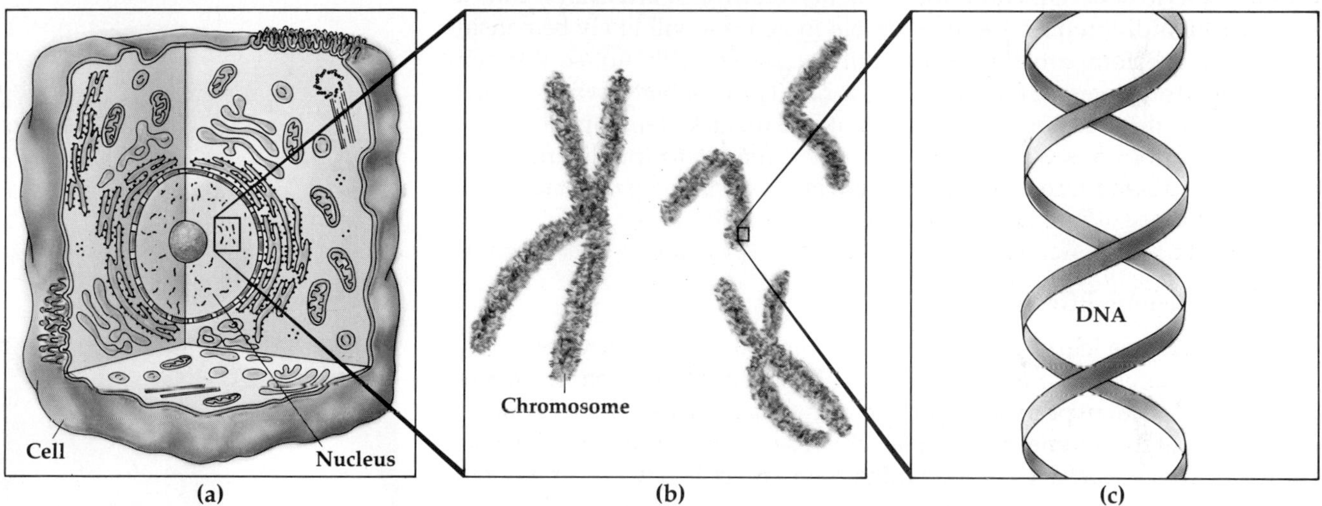

Figure 2-23 *The genes, their location and composition. Contained in each of the trillions of cells (a) in your body are chromosomes (b). Each chromosome is composed of the molecule DNA (c), segments of which, the genes, form templates for the production of proteins. By directing the manufacture of proteins, the genes determine our individual biological development. In turn, gene activity is influenced by the environment within each cell, which is affected by our overall environment.*

Statisticians tell us that when 23 chromosomes from a man and 23 from a woman meet they can form over 64 trillion different gene combinations. When one considers that combinations of genes are thereby produced that were not present in either parent, it is no wonder that no two people (with an exception we will get to in a minute) look, think, or act exactly alike.

Nature and Nurture

Do our genetic differences therefore help explain our psychological differences—why Bob is, say, outgoing but slow-witted, while Laurel is shy but smart? We know that such complex traits are not dictated by any single gene. Do they instead reflect the combined effect of many genes? Or is our life experience a more potent influence? This ***nature-nurture*** (or genes-experience) question has long been one of psychology's chief concerns. How we answer this question has important implications for our view of human nature—how changeable are we?—and for our beliefs in the effectiveness of certain social policies. If you presume people are the way they are entirely "by nature," you likely will not be optimistic about the potential benefits of programs of compensatory education, prisoner rehabilitation, or parent training. Given how fundamental the nature-nurture question is, the issue is understandably controversial.

In later chapters we will discuss genetic contributions to social development, intelligence, personality, and behavior disorders. To prepare for these discussions, let us consider how heredity and environment operate—and cooperate. On two principles nearly everyone—hereditarians and environmentalists alike—agrees. First, our behaviors are nearly always a product of the interaction of (1) our genes, (2) our past experience, and (3) the present situation to which we are responding. If an attractive, athletic teenage boy has been treated as a leader and is now much sought out by girls, shall we say his positive self-image is due to his genes or his environment? It is both. Because the effect of the environment depends on characteristics genetically endowed, we say the two factors *interact.* In such cases, asking which factor is more important would be like asking whether the area of a field is more due to its length or its width.

Second, apart from particular populations and particular environments it makes no sense to ask, "Precisely how much does heredity and environment each contribute to a given trait?"

If you compare people with very different heredities under not-so-different environmental conditions, the ***heritability*** of any trait—the extent to which differences are attributable to genes—will likely be considerable. If you compare this same trait in people with not-so-different heredities under very different conditions, its heritability will be much smaller. For this reason, we cannot make blanket statements about the precise contributions of heredity and environment to intelligence, personality, and other traits. *Heritability depends on the populations and environments studied.*

"This issue is not whether nature or nurture determines human behavior for they are truly inextricable, but the degree, intensity, and nature of the constraint exerted by biology."
Stephen Jay Gould (1983)

Studying Genetic Effects

How then can we learn whether, under a normal range of environmental conditions, hereditary influences are small or large? We noted in Chapter 1 that in the ideal experiment just one or two factors are varied, while all others are held the same; this enables the researcher to see how these one or two factors, separately or in combination, affect behavior. So by holding environment constant and varying heredity we could study the effect of heredity. And by holding heredity constant and varying environment, we could study the effect of environment. But, practically, are such experiments possible?

With humans, of course, the first of these experiments is out of the question. However, such experiments have been done with animals using ***selective breeding.*** This technique involves mating animals who share a given trait, and continuing to mate those among their descendants who best exemplify this trait. By selective breeding we have bred fast horses, highly aggressive gamecocks, ferociously protective German shepherds, and—in some psychological experiments—rats that learn a maze quickly or slowly (Tryon, 1940).

Such selective breeding experiments seek to vary heredity but not environment, thereby revealing an effect of heredity. Could we also do the reverse—vary environment but not heredity—to seek the effect of environment? Happily (for our purposes) in three or four human births out of every thousand, nature supplies us with a way to conduct this experiment. ***Identical twins*** develop from a single fertilized egg that splits into two genetically identical replicas, each of which becomes a person (Figure 2-24). When tested for certain psychological traits, such as intelligence, identical twins often score as similarly as would a person taking the same test twice. Moreover, they are more alike than are ***fraternal twins,*** who, having developed from different fertilized eggs, are no more genetically similar than any two nontwin siblings (brothers and sisters).

Through selective breeding, we have created both ferocious and gentle dogs.

Does this mean that genes are a major determinant of intelligence? Perhaps. (More on this in Chapter 12, "Intelligence.") But since identical twins look alike, are often dressed alike, and can be mistaken for each other, they are typically treated more alike than are fraternal twins. Maybe, then, they are similar because of their nearly identical environments. So, while twin studies can help us to study the influence of genes, their interpretation is often debated.

Adoption offers additional clues. For any given trait we can ask whether adopted children are more like their adoptive parents, who contribute a home environment, or their biological parents, who contribute their genes. Consider handedness. Does growing up in a right-handed world bias children toward right-handedness? If so, adoptive parents who are both left-handed should be more likely to have left-handed adoptive children. However, in a study of 700 adopted children, Louise Carter-Saltzman (1980) found that the rate of left-handedness among children was unaffected by the handedness of the adoptive parents. But if one of the adopted child's biological parents was left-handed, the likelihood of the child being left-handed doubled. So handedness seems to be inherited.

Figure 2-24 *Identical twins: 6 years ago these two people shared the same fertilized egg.*

In later chapters, we will consider whether in other ways, such as personality and intelligence, adoptive children similarly resemble their biological parents more than their adoptive parents. We will also consider new wrinkles in the research procedures—for example, by asking whether parents who are rearing both biological and adopted children are more like their biological children. For now, it is enough to appreciate that no one of these methods—selective breeding experiments, twin studies, or adoption studies—provides a simple answer to the nature-nurture question. It is by conducting all three types of studies and cross-checking the data from each that we can reasonably conjecture whether, for the people and the environments studied, the differences in any trait are more due to genes or to the environment.

SUMMING UP

As the first step in understanding our behavior and mental processes, we have examined our biological development, as a species and as genetically unique individuals.

NATURAL SELECTION

Those organisms with inheritable traits that best equip them to survive and reproduce leave more offspring. The genes associated with these traits will thus be naturally selected to persist. The controversial new field of sociobiology uses natural selection in an attempt to explain human social behaviors.

THE NERVOUS SYSTEM

Divisions of the Nervous System The body's circuitry, the nervous system, consists of billions of nerve cells, called neurons. These are organized into the central nervous system (CNS) neurons (many of them interneurons) in the brain and spinal cord, and the sensory and motor neurons of the peripheral nervous system (PNS). The PNS consists of the somatic nervous system, which directs voluntary movements and reflexes, and the autonomic nervous system, whose sympathetic and parasympathetic divisions control our involuntary and cardiac muscles and glands.

Neurons and Their Messages Neurons usually receive signals from other neurons through their dendrites, then combine these signals in the cell body, and transmit electrical impulses down their axons. When these signals reach the end of the axon, they stimulate the release of chemical messengers, called neurotransmitters, that traverse the tiny synaptic gap between neurons and combine with receptor sites on neighboring neurons, thus passing on their excitatory or inhibitory messages. Neurotransmitters are now being studied in hopes of understanding their importance for human thought and emotion.

THE BRAIN

Organization of the Brain The brain's three basic regions—the brainstem, the limbic system, and the cerebral cortex—each represent a stage of brain evolution.

The brainstem begins as the spinal cord swells to form the medulla, which controls heartbeat and breathing. The cerebellum, which is attached to the rear of the brainstem, coordinates muscle movement. Atop the brainstem is the thalamus, the brain's sensory switchboard. Within the brainstem, the reticular activating system controls arousal.

At the border of the brainstem and cerebral cortex is the limbic system, which has been linked primarily to emotions and drives. For example, one of its neural centers, the amygdala, is involved in aggressive and fearful responses. Another, the hypothalamus, has been linked to various bodily maintenance functions, to pleasurable rewards, and to the control of the pituitary gland.

The cerebral cortex can be viewed as having four geographical areas: the frontal, parietal, occipital, and temporal lobes. Small, well-defined regions within these lobes control muscle movement and receive information from the body senses. However, most of the cortex—its association areas—is uncommitted to such functions and is therefore free to process other information.

Some brain regions are known to serve specific functions. However, human emotions, thoughts, and behaviors generally result from the intricate coordination of many brain areas. For example, language depends on a chain of events in several brain regions.

Our Divided Brains Although clinical observations long ago revealed that the left cerebral hemisphere is crucial for language and certain other intellectual functions, experiments on split-brain patients have refined our knowledge of each hemisphere's special functions. By testing the two hemispheres separately, researchers have confirmed that for most people the left hemisphere is indeed the more verbal, but the right hemisphere excels in perceptual ability and the recognition of emotion. Controversy still exists regarding the capacities of the right hemisphere, but studies of normal people with intact brains generally confirm that the two hemispheres make unique contributions to the integrated functioning of the brain. Nevertheless, if one hemisphere is damaged early in life, the other will pick up many of its functions. This demonstrates the brain's plasticity.

THE ENDOCRINE SYSTEM

The body's slower but comprehensive chemical communication system is the endocrine system. Under the influence of the autonomic nervous system and the hypothalamus, endocrine glands, such as the adrenals and the pituitary, release hormones. Hormones travel through the bloodstream to various target organs, where they affect emotional states, growth, and other body functions.

GENES AND BEHAVIOR

Genes, our basic units of heredity, are segments of DNA molecules capable of synthesizing a protein. Genes make up the chromosomes found in each cell.

The enduring nature-nurture controversy addresses the relative importance of genes and experience to the person-to-person variations in psychological traits. Most scientists agree that our behaviors stem from the interaction of our genes, our past experience, and our current situation, and that one can specify the heritability of any trait differences only among individuals from a given population and from a given range of environments.

Genetic effects are studied through selective breeding experiments, twin studies, and adoption studies.

TERMS AND CONCEPTS TO REMEMBER

Acetylcholine (ah-seat-el-KO-leen) **(ACh)** A neurotransmitter that, among its functions, triggers muscle contraction.

Adrenal (ah-DREEN-el) **Glands** A pair of endocrine glands atop the kidneys. The adrenals secrete the hormones epinephrine (adrenaline) and norepinephrine (noradrenaline), which help to arouse the body in times of stress.

All-or-None Response The principle that, like a gun, at any moment a neuron either fires or does not.

Amygdala (a-MIG-dah-la) A neural center in the limbic system that is linked to emotion.

Aphasia Impairment of language, usually caused by left hemisphere damage either to Broca's area (impairing speaking) or to Wernicke's area (impairing understanding).

Association Areas Poorly understood brain areas that are involved not in primary motor or sensory functions, but rather in higher mental functions such as learning, remembering, thinking, and speaking.

Autonomic (awt-uh-NAHM-ik) **Nervous System** The part of the peripheral nervous system that controls the glands and the muscles of the internal organs (such as the heart). Its sympathetic division arouses; its parasympathetic division calms.

Axon The part of a neuron through which messages are sent to other neurons or to muscles or glands.

Brainstem The central core of the brain, beginning where the spinal cord swells as it enters the skull.

Broca's Area An area of the left frontal lobe that directs the muscle movements involved in speech.

CAT scan (Computerized Axial Tomograph) A three-dimensional X-ray photograph of a body structure such as the brain, which can reveal hidden damage or disease.

Central Nervous System (CNS) The brain and spinal cord.

Cerebellum (sehr-uh-BELL-um) The "little brain" attached to the rear of the brainstem that helps to coordinate voluntary movement and balance.

Cerebral (seh-REE-bruhl) **Cortex** The intricate fabric of interconnected neural cells that covers the cerebral hemispheres; the body's ultimate control and information-processing center.

Chromosomes Threadlike structures that contain the genes. A human cell has 23 pairs of chromosomes, one member of each pair coming from each parent.

Corpus Callosum (kah-LOW-sum) The largest bundle of nerve fibers connecting and carrying messages between the two brain hemispheres.

DNA (Deoxyribonucleic Acid) The complex molecules that contain the genetic information in cells.

Dendrite The bushy, branching extensions of a neuron that conduct impulses toward the cell body.

Electroencephalogram (EEG) An amplified recording of the waves of electrical activity that sweep across the brain's surface. These waves are measured by placing electrodes on the scalp.

Endocrine (EN-duh-krin) **System** The body's chemical communication system; a set of glands that secrete hormones into the bloodstream.

Endorphins (en-DOR-fins) "Morphine within"—natural, opiatelike neurotransmitters linked to pain control and pleasure.

Fraternal Twins Twins who develop from separate eggs and sperm cells, thus ordinary brothers and sisters who happen to be born only moments apart.

Frontal Lobes The portion of the cerebral cortex lying behind the forehead; involved in speaking and muscle movements and in making plans and judgments.

Genes The basic units of heredity that make up the chromosomes. A segment of DNA capable of synthesizing a protein.

Heritability The extent to which differences in a trait can be attributed to genes. Heritability of a trait may vary, depending on the populations and environments studied.

Hormones Chemical messengers manufactured by the endocrine glands and sent through the bloodstream.

Hypothalamus A neural structure lying below (*hypo*) the thalamus that directs several maintenance activities (eating, drinking, body temperature), helps govern the endocrine system via the pituitary gland, and is linked to emotion and reward.

Identical Twins Twins that develop from a single fertilized egg that splits in two, creating two genetic replicas. (Also called monozygotic twins.)

Interneurons Central nervous system neurons that intervene between the sensory inputs and motor outputs.

Lesion (LEE-zhuhn) Tissue destruction. A brain lesion is naturally or experimentally caused destruction of brain tissue.

Limbic System A doughnut-shaped system of neural structures at the border of the brainstem and cerebral hemispheres; associated with emotions such as fear and aggression and drives such as those for food and sex.

Medulla (muh-DUL-uh) The lowest part of the brainstem; controls heartbeat and breathing.

Motor Cortex An area at the rear of the frontal lobes that controls voluntary movements.

Motor Neurons The neurons that carry outgoing information from the CNS to the muscles and glands.

Natural Selection The process by which evolution favors organisms that, within a particular environment, are genetically best equipped to survive and reproduce.

Nature-Nurture Debate The long-standing controversy over the relative contributions of heredity and experience to psychological traits.

Nervous System The body's electrochemical communication system, consisting of all the nerve cells of the peripheral and central nervous systems.

Neuron A nerve cell; the basic building block of the nervous system.

Neurotransmitters Chemical messengers that traverse the synapses between neurons. When released by the sending neuron, neurotransmitters travel across the synapse and bind to receptor sites on the receiving neuron, thereby influencing whether it will fire.

Occipital (ahk-SIP-uht-uhl) **Lobes** The portion of the cerebral cortex lying at the back of the head, including the visual areas, each of which receives visual information, primarily from the opposite eye.

PET Scan (Positron Emission Tomograph) A visual display of brain activity that detects where a radioactive form of glucose goes while the brain performs a given task.

Parasympathetic Nervous System The division of the autonomic nervous system that calms the body, conserving its energy.

Parietal (puh-RYE-uh-tul) **Lobes** The portion of the cerebral cortex lying atop the head and toward the rear; includes the somatosensory cortex.

Peripheral Nervous System (PNS) The part of the nervous system that lies outside of the CNS. It consists of the sensory neurons, which carry messages to the CNS from the body's sense receptors, and motor neurons, which carry messages from the CNS to the muscles and glands.

Phrenology A discarded nineteenth-century theory that the conformation of the skull reveals one's abilities and character.

Pituitary Gland The endocrine system's master gland. Under the influence of the hypothalamus, the pituitary regulates growth and controls other endocrine glands.

Plasticity The brain's capacity for modification, as evident in brain reorganization following damage (especially in children) and in experiments on the effects of experience on brain development.

Reflex A simple, automatic, inborn response to a sensory input, such as the knee-jerk response.

Reticular Activating System A nerve network in the brainstem that plays an important role in controlling arousal and attention.

Selective Breeding A technique useful for studying genetic influences in which animals that display a particular trait are mated and those among their descendants that best express this trait are selected for further mating. If a trait is genetically influenced, continued selection should produce animals that strongly exhibit that trait.

Sensory Neurons Neurons that carry incoming information from the body's sense receptors to the CNS.

Sociobiology The study of the evolution of social behavior using the principles of natural selection. Social behaviors that are heritable and that contribute to the preservation and spread of one's genes are presumed to be favored by natural selection.

Somatic (so-MAT-ic) **Nervous System** The division of the peripheral nervous system that receives information from various sense receptors and that controls the skeletal muscles.

Somatosensory Cortex The area at the front of the parietal lobes that registers and processes body sensations.

Split-Brain A condition in which the two hemispheres of the brain are isolated by cutting the connecting fibers between them (mainly those of the corpus callosum).

Sympathetic Nervous System The division of the autonomic nervous system that arouses the body, mobilizing its energy in stressful situations.

Synapse (SIN-aps) The junction between the axon tip of the sending neuron and the dendrite or cell body of the receiving neuron.

Temporal Lobes The portion of the cerebral cortex lying roughly above the ears, including the auditory areas, each of which receives auditory information, primarily from the opposite ear.

Thalamus (THALL-uh-muss) The brain's sensory switchboard. Located atop the brainstem, the thalamus directs messages to the brain's sensory receiving areas and transmits replies to the cerebellum and medulla.

Threshold The level of stimulation required to trigger a response.

Wernicke's Area An area of the left hemisphere involved in language comprehension.

FOR FURTHER READING

The Brain, the September 1979 issue of *Scientific American* (also published in book form by Freeman in 1979).

An issue containing precisely illustrated research summaries by leading brain researchers.

Bloom, F. E., Lazerson, A., & Hofstadter, L. (1985). *Brain, mind, and behavior.* New York: Freeman.

A lavishly illustrated summary of recent brain research written to accompany the 1984 PBS television series "The Brain."

Barash, D. (1979). *The whisperings within: Evolution and the origin of human nature.* New York: Harper & Row. (Reprinted as a 1981 Penguin paperback.)

A provocative, readable explanation of the sociobiological perspective.

Lewontin, R. C., Rose, S., & Kamin, L. J. (1984). *Not in our genes.* New York: Pantheon.

A rebuttal of the hereditarian and sociobiological viewpoints.

Ornstein, R., & Thompson, R. F. (1984). *The amazing brain.* Boston: Houghton Mifflin.

An excellent introduction to recent brain research, written by two psychologists involved in it.

Plomin, R., DeFries, J. C., & McClearn, G. E. (1980). *Behavioral genetics: A primer.* San Francisco: Freeman.

A helpful introduction to research on genes and behavior.

Springer, S. P., & Deutsch, G. (1985). *Left brain, right brain* (2nd ed.). New York: Freeman.

An award-winning description of research on the two hemispheres of brain-damaged, split-brain, and normal subjects. Discusses handedness, gender differences, learning disabilities, and theories of consciousness.

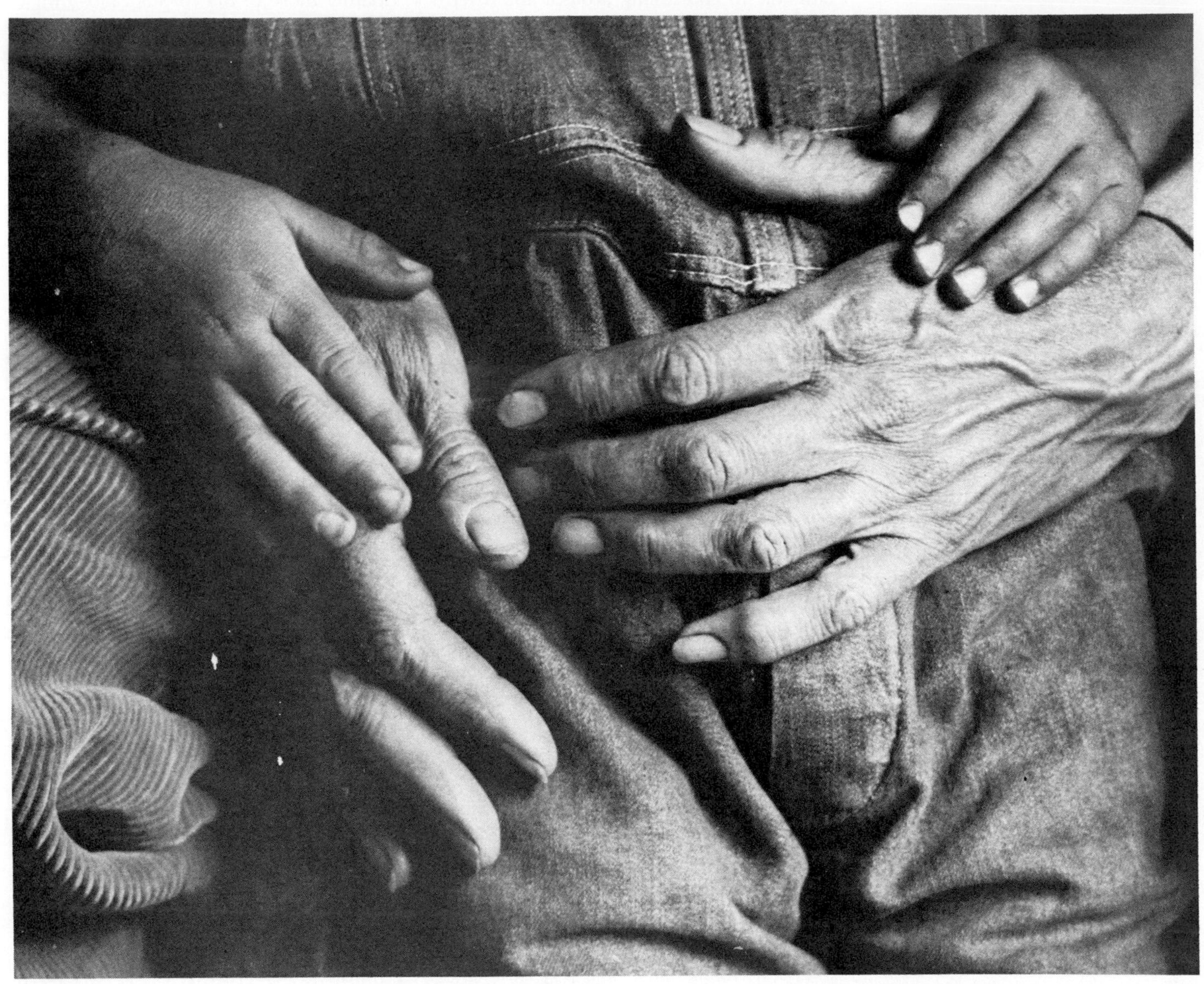

Dorothea Lange *Hands, Maynard and Dan Dixon, c. 1930*

PART TWO

DEVELOPMENT OVER THE LIFE-SPAN

How, over time, do we come to be the persons we are, and how might we expect to change in the future? In the next two chapters we consider how we develop—physically, mentally, and socially—during infancy and childhood (Chapter 3) and during adolescence, adulthood, and later life (Chapter 4). Then, in Chapter 5, we examine, in terms of both biological and social influences, how our development is affected by whether we are male or female.

Henry Moore *Rocking Chair No. 2,* 1950

Hirshhorn Museum and Sculpture Garden, Smithsonian Institution

Museum of Modern Art, New York

Marisol *The Family,* 1962

DEVELOPMENTAL ISSUES

Genes or Experience?

Continuity or Discontinuity?

PRENATAL DEVELOPMENT

INFANCY

Physical Development

Brain Development

Motor Development

Perceptual Development

Cognitive Development

How the Mind of an Infant Grows

The Effects of Early Experience

Social Development

Origins of Attachment

Effects of Attachment

CHILDHOOD

Physical Development

Cognitive Development

Social Development

Self-concept

Child-rearing Practices

CHAPTER 3

Infancy and Childhood

"What endless questions vex the thought, of
Whence and Whither. When and How."

Sir Richard Burton,
Kasidah, 1880

Male or female, young or old: Development is a process of physical, mental, and social growth that continues throughout the course of our lives.

Whence have we come to be who we are, and whither shall our future take us? As we journey through life, when and how do we change—physically, mentally, socially? Such are the questions that from antiquity to the present have vexed observers of the human life cycle.

Chapter 2 described how our nervous system and genes influence who we are. Developmental psychology, our focus in Chapters 3 and 4, draws on this understanding of neural and genetic underpinnings as it investigates how we grow and develop across the life-span.

As psychologists Clyde Kluckhohn and Henry Murray have noted (1956), each person develops in certain respects like all other persons, like some other persons, and like no other persons. Usually, our attention is drawn to the ways in which we are unique. But to developmental psychologists, our commonalities are as important as our uniquenesses. We are all human, and as such we travel some common paths. Virtually all of us—Michelangelo, Queen Elizabeth, Martin Luther King, Jr., you, me—began walking around age 1 and talking around age 2, and as children we engaged in social play in preparation for life's serious work. All of us smile and cry, love and hate, and occasionally ponder the fact that someday we will die. In Chapters 3 and 4 we will examine the human journey from conception to death, considering both the predictable developments in physical, mental, and social behavior and the influences that shape the unique course that each of us travels. For convenience, we divide the journey into seven phases: prenatal, infancy, and childhood in Chapter 3, and adolescence and young, middle, and late adulthood in Chapter 4. But first, let us confront two overriding developmental questions.

DEVELOPMENTAL ISSUES

Two major issues pervade developmental psychology: (1) How much is our development influenced by our genetic inheritance and how much by our experiences? (2) Is development a gradual, continuous process, or does it proceed through a sequence of discrete stages?

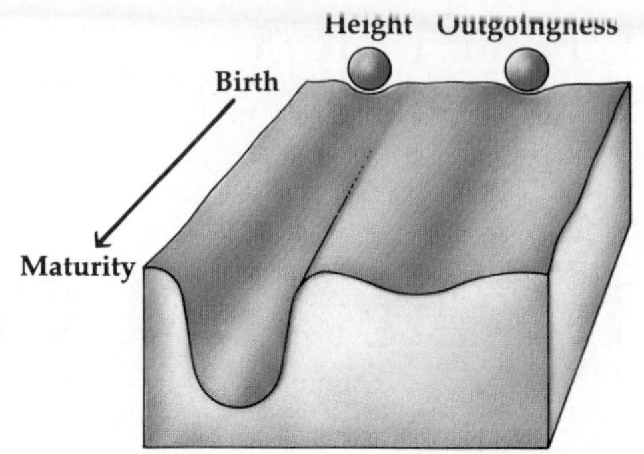

Figure 3-1 *A graphic analogy for the interaction of genes and experience in determining traits. The landscape represents the possibilities for a trait's development as determined by the individual's genes. The path of the ball represents the actual course of the trait's development. Such forces as winds constitute the environmental factors. With some traits, such as height, the path of development is largely determined by the narrow course defined by the genes. With others, such as outgoingness, the course defined by the genes is shallower and broader, allowing the environmental winds greater sway in determining the developmental path.*

Genes or Experience?

The first question is the familiar nature-nurture issue. In Chapter 2 we noted that genes and experience interact in determining how we develop, much as the length and width of a field together determine its area. The question, then, is not which one (genes or experience) influences any particular trait, but their relative influence. For some traits, such as height, the genetic controls are strong. Like the path of the ball on the left side of Figure 3-1, the development of height is constrained by the steep, narrow valley created by the genetic determinants. With other traits, such as outgoingness, the valley is shallower and wider, allowing environmental factors to have more influence. The issue is how much more influence? For which traits? And at what times in the life-span?

Some developmental psychologists have emphasized the influence of our genetic blueprints. Much as a flower unfolds in accord with its genetic instructions (unless squelched by a barren environment), so is human behavior said to unfold predictably. According to this view, the genetic blueprints program an orderly sequence of biological growth processes called ***maturation.*** Across a range of environments, maturation decrees our commonalities: crawling before walking, speaking nouns before adjectives. Although extreme deprivation or abuse will retard development, the growth tendencies are inherent.

Other developmentalists have emphasized external influences. Much as a potter shapes the clay, our experiences are presumed to shape us. This view was argued by the seventeenth-century philosopher John Locke, who proposed that at birth the child in some ways is a *tabula rasa*—a "blank slate" or "empty page"—on which experience writes its story. Although few today wholeheartedly support Locke's proposition, hundreds of researchers are now exploring the effects of nurture.

"Maturation (read the genetic program, largely) sets the course of development, which is modified by experience, especially if that experience is deviant from what is normal for the species."
Sandra Scarr (1982)

Continuity or Discontinuity?

Everyone agrees that adults are vastly different from infants. But do they differ as a giant redwood differs from its seedling—a difference created by gradual, cumulative growth? Or do they differ as a butterfly differs from a caterpillar—a difference of distinct stages? Generally speaking, researchers who emphasize experience and learning have tended to see development as a slow, continuous shaping process. Those who emphasize maturation have tended to see development as a sequence of predictable stages.

In this and the following chapter, we will look at stage theories of mental, moral, and social development. The sequence but not the timing of stages is presumed to be fixed. Depending on an individual's heredity and experiences, progress through the various stages may be quick or slow; but all individuals pass through the same stages in the same order.

Another version of the continuity question is whether development is characterized more by *stability* or by *change*. Will the cranky infant grow up to be an irritable adult, or is such a child as likely to become a placid, patient person? Do the differences among school classmates in, say, aggressiveness, aptitude, or strivings for achievement persist throughout

Nature or nurture? Stability or change? How much is this outgoing baby's temperament due to her heredity and how much to her upbringing? And how likely is it that she will be an outgoing adult? These questions raise two fundamental themes of developmental psychology.

the life-span? Is the class clown just as likely as the class president to become a community leader? In short, to what degree do we grow to be merely older versions of our early selves and to what degree can we develop into different persons than we once were?

Here in Chapter 3 we will look at physical, mental, and social development through childhood. Chapter 4 will examine adolescence through late adulthood and conclude by taking stock of current thinking on the underlying nature-nurture and continuity-discontinuity issues. Finally, Chapter 5 will apply developmental principles to an examination of the nature and extent of male-female differences.

PRENATAL DEVELOPMENT

Nothing is more natural than a species reproducing itself. Yet for those of us who are the beneficiaries of nature's creative work, nothing is more miraculous. Consider human reproduction: The process starts as a mature ***ovum*** (egg) is released by the female's ovary and some 300 million sperm begin their race upstream towards it. About half the sperm carry a ***Y sex chromosome,*** which when united with the egg's X sex chromosome produces a male; the other half carry an ***X sex chromosome,*** which when united with the egg's X sex chromosome produces a female. The relatively few sperm that make it to the egg release digestive enzymes that eat away the egg's protective coating, allowing one sperm to penetrate and fertilize the ovum. But even at that lucky moment, when a particular sperm cell has won the 1 in 300 million lottery, an individual's destiny is not assured, for fewer than half of fertilized eggs (called ***zygotes***) survive beyond the first week (Grobstein, 1979). If human life begins at conception, then most people die without being born.

But for you and me good fortune prevailed. Beginning as one cell, each of us became two cells, then four—each just like the first. Then, within the first week, when this cell division has produced a tiny ball of approximately 100 cells, the cells began to differentiate—to specialize in structure and function. Within 2 weeks, the newly formed ball of increasingly diverse cells became attached to the mother's uterine wall, beginning approximately 37 weeks of the closest human relationship (see Figure 3-2).

During the ensuing 6 weeks, the developing human is called an ***embryo.*** In this embryonic period the anatomical parts begin to form and may begin to function: The heart begins to beat and the liver begins to

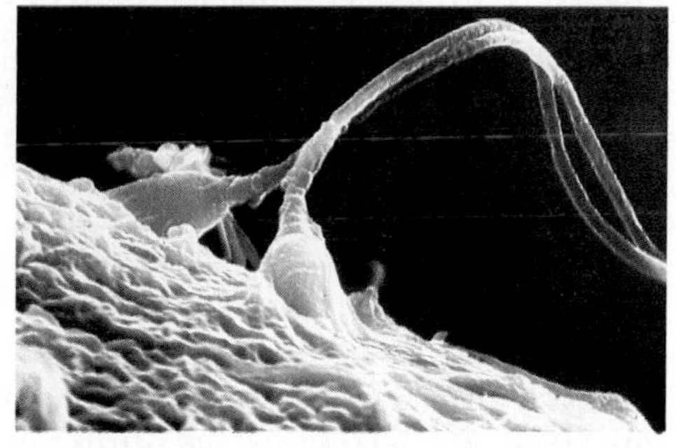

Figure 3-2 *Prenatal development begins when a single sperm fertilizes an egg. The resulting zygote journeys on to the uterus, where it implants. (a) The embryo grows and develops rapidly. At 40 days, the spine is visible and the arms and legs are beginning to grow. (b) Five days later the embryo's proportions have begun to change. The rest of the body is now bigger than the head, and the arms and legs have grown noticeably. (c) By the end of the second month, when the fetal period begins, the fetus has become recognizably human. Facial features, hands, and feet have formed. (d) As the fetus enters the third month, it weighs about 3 ounces. Until birth, it will be nourished through the umbilical cord.*

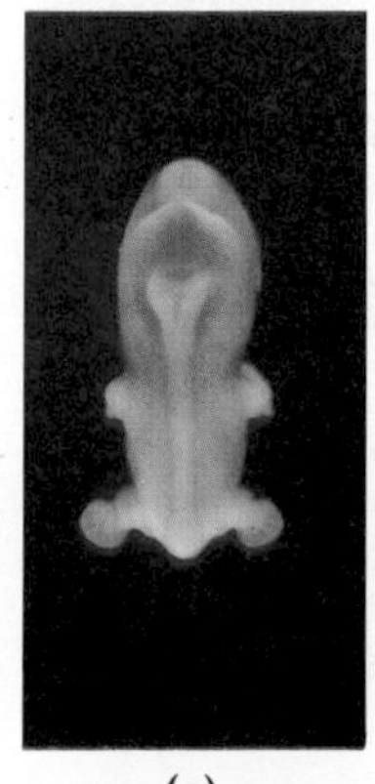

(a)

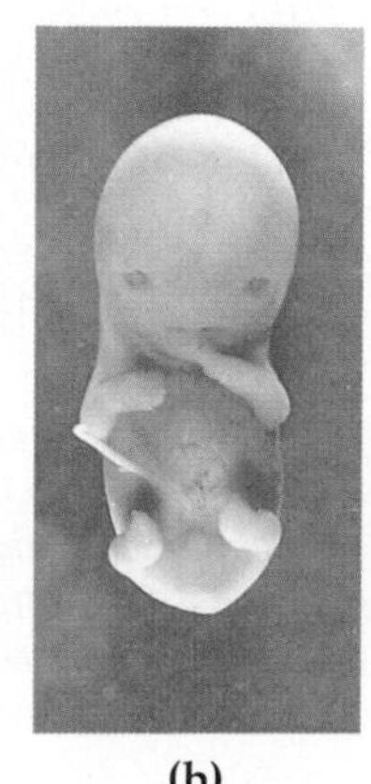

(b)

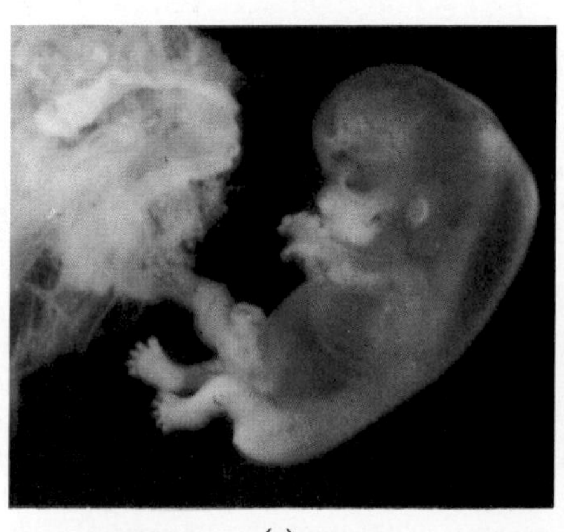

(c)

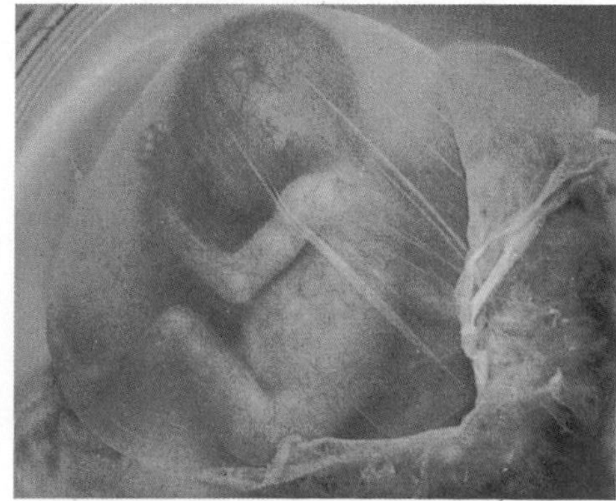

(d)

provide red blood cells. By the beginning of the third month, the embryo has become unmistakably human and is thereafter called a ***fetus.*** During the second of the three 3-month periods of prenatal development (called "trimesters"), internal organs such as the stomach become more fully formed and functional, enough so that by the beginning of the third trimester the fetus has a chance of survival if born prematurely.

Nutrients and oxygen in the mother's blood pass through the placenta into the blood of the fetus. If the mother is severely malnourished during the last third of the pregnancy, when the demand for nutrients peaks, the baby may be premature or even stillborn. Along with nourishment, certain harmful substances, called ***teratogens,*** can pass through the placenta with potentially tragic effects. If the mother is a heroin addict, her baby is born a heroin addict. If she is a heavy smoker, her newborn is likely to be underweight, sometimes dangerously so (U.S. Department of Health and Human Services, 1983a). If she drinks heavily, her baby is at greater risk for birth defects and mental retardation.

Tera *literally means "monster"; teratogens are "monstrous" agents, such as chemicals and viruses, that may harm the fetus.*

INFANCY

Until fairly recently, psychologists as well as parents tended to regard the newborn infant as a helpless, witless, and virtually senseless creature. This view has now given way to a growing appreciation of the newborn's physical, mental, and social competence. Ingenious new methods for observing and testing babies during the first weeks of life have revealed what marvelous creatures they actually are.

"One cannot love lumps of flesh, and little infants are nothing more."
Samuel Johnson, 1709–1784

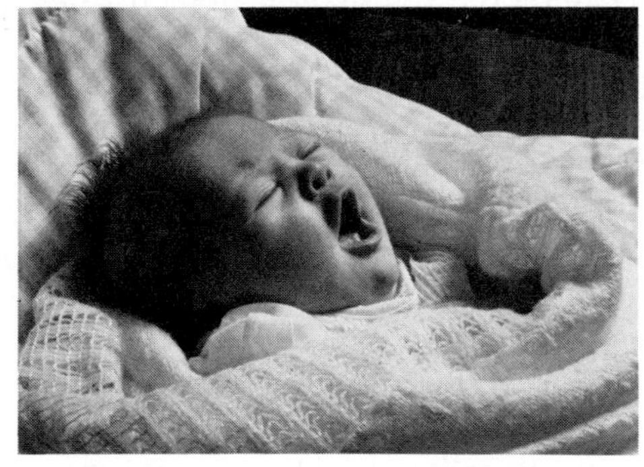

The newborn has been characterized in the past as everything from an empty slate awaiting instruction to a noble savage awaiting corruption. In reality, the newborn is a complex individual, with surprising inborn abilities to respond to environmental stimuli.

Physical Development

Brain Development

While you resided in your mother's womb, your body was forming nerve cells at the rate of about one-quarter million per *minute.* By the day you were born you had most of the brain cells you were ever going to have. But at birth the human nervous system is immature; the neural networks that enable us to walk, talk, and remember are only beginning to form. This helps to explain why most of us cannot retrieve childhood memories from the time before we were at least 2 years old (see Figure 3-3). Animals such as guinea pigs, whose brains *are* mature at birth, can form permanent memories from infancy, while animals with immature brains, such as rats, cannot (Campbell & Coulter, 1976). These findings cast doubt on the idea that people never forget their prenatal life or the trauma of their birth.

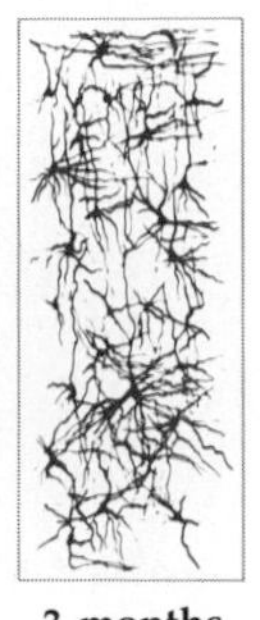

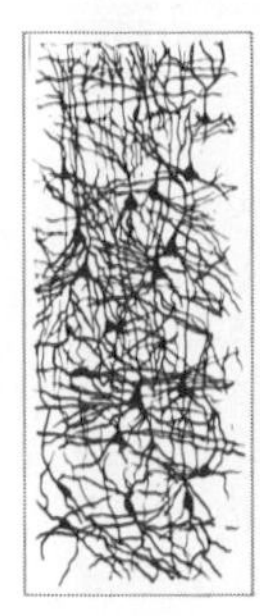

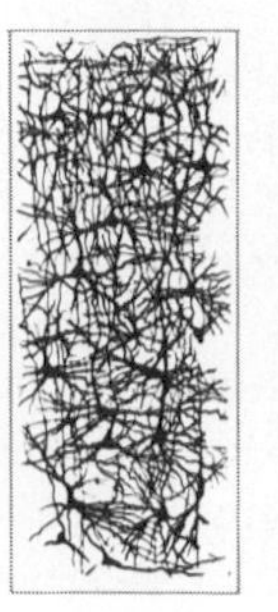

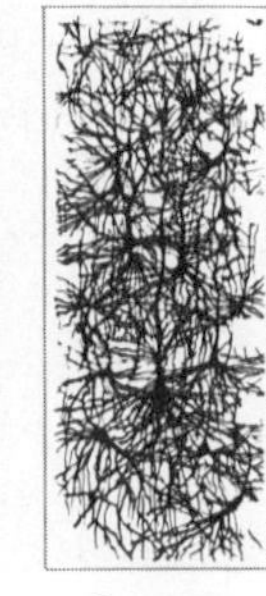

Figure 3-3 *In humans, the brain tissues mature rapidly after birth. These drawings of sections of brain tissue from the cerebral cortex illustrate the increasing complexity of the neural networks in the maturing human brain.*

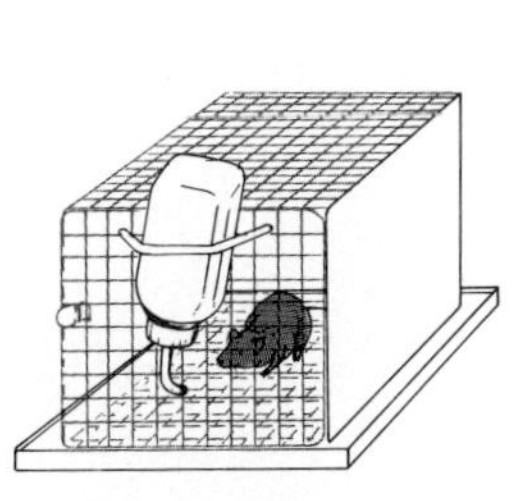

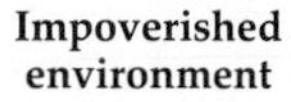

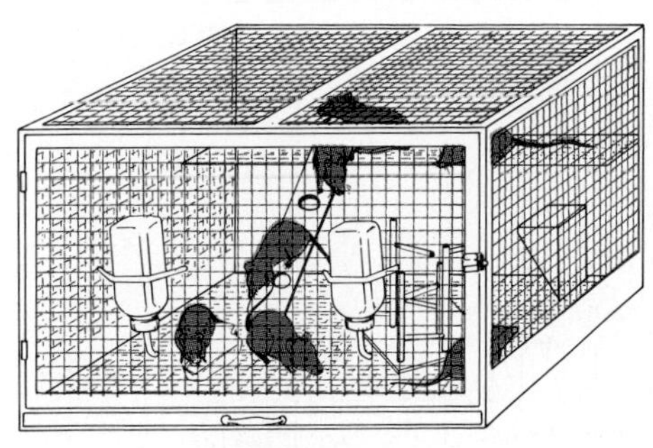

Figure 3-4 *In rats, experience affects the brain's development. In experiments pioneered by Mark Rosenzweig and David Krech, rats were reared either alone in an environment without playthings or with others in an environment enriched with playthings that were changed daily. In fourteen out of sixteen repetitions of this basic experiment, those placed in the enriched environment developed significantly more cerebral cortex relative to the rest of the brain's tissue than those in the impoverished environment. (From "Brain changes in response to experience" by M. R. Rosenzweig, E. L. Bennett, and M. C. Diamond. Copyright © 1972 Scientific American, Inc. All rights reserved.)*

Does experience, as well as biological maturation, help develop the brain's neural connections? Surely, our life's learning is somehow recorded "in there." If, indeed, our experiences affect us by leaving their "marks" in the brain, then it ought to be possible to detect evidence of this.

In the 1870s Paul Broca noted that male medical students had bigger heads than less educated male nurses. From this he concluded that the medical students' brains were expanding to accommodate their learning. When further studies refuted this, the search for the "marks" of experience was discontinued, until the modern tools of neuroscience enabled a closer look. Working at the University of California, Berkeley, Mark Rosenzweig and his colleagues (1972) caged some rats in solitary confinement, while others were caged in a communal playground (Figure 3-4). The rats living in the deprived environment usually developed a lighter and thinner cortex with smaller nerve cell bodies as well as fewer glial cells (the "glue cells" that support and nourish the brain's neurons). Rosenzweig (1984a) reported being so surprised by these effects of experience on brain tissue that he repeated the experiment several times before publishing his findings—findings that eventually led to improvements in the environments provided for laboratory and farm animals and for institutionalized children.

More recent studies have extended the findings. William Greenough and his University of Illinois co-workers (Greenough & Green, 1981) discovered that extended learning experiences seem to sculpt a rat's neural tissue—at the very spot where the experience is processed. This sculpting seems to work by preserving activated neural connections while allowing unused connections to degenerate. More and more, researchers are becoming convinced that the brain's neural connections are dynamic; from birth onward, our neural tissue is changing. Experience, it seems, helps nurture nature.

Motor Development

Newborn babies come equipped with reflexes that are ideally suited for survival and securing nourishment. Newborns will withdraw a limb to escape pain; if a cloth is put over their faces, interfering with their breathing, they will turn their heads from side to side and swipe at the offending cloth. New parents are often awed by the coordinated sequence of reflexes by which babies obtain food. The ***rooting reflex*** is one example: When their cheeks are touched, babies will open their mouths and vigorously "root" for a nipple. Finding one, they will automatically close on it and begin sucking—which itself requires a coordinated sequence of tonguing, swallowing, and breathing. Failing to find satisfaction, the hungry baby may cry—a behavior that parents are predisposed to find highly unpleasant, and very rewarding to relieve.

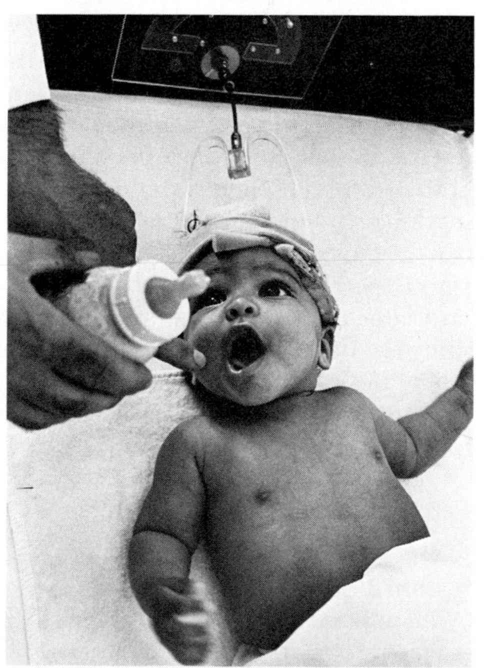

The rooting reflex. Babies respond to a stroke on the cheek or the corner of the mouth by turning toward the side that was stroked, seeking something to suck.

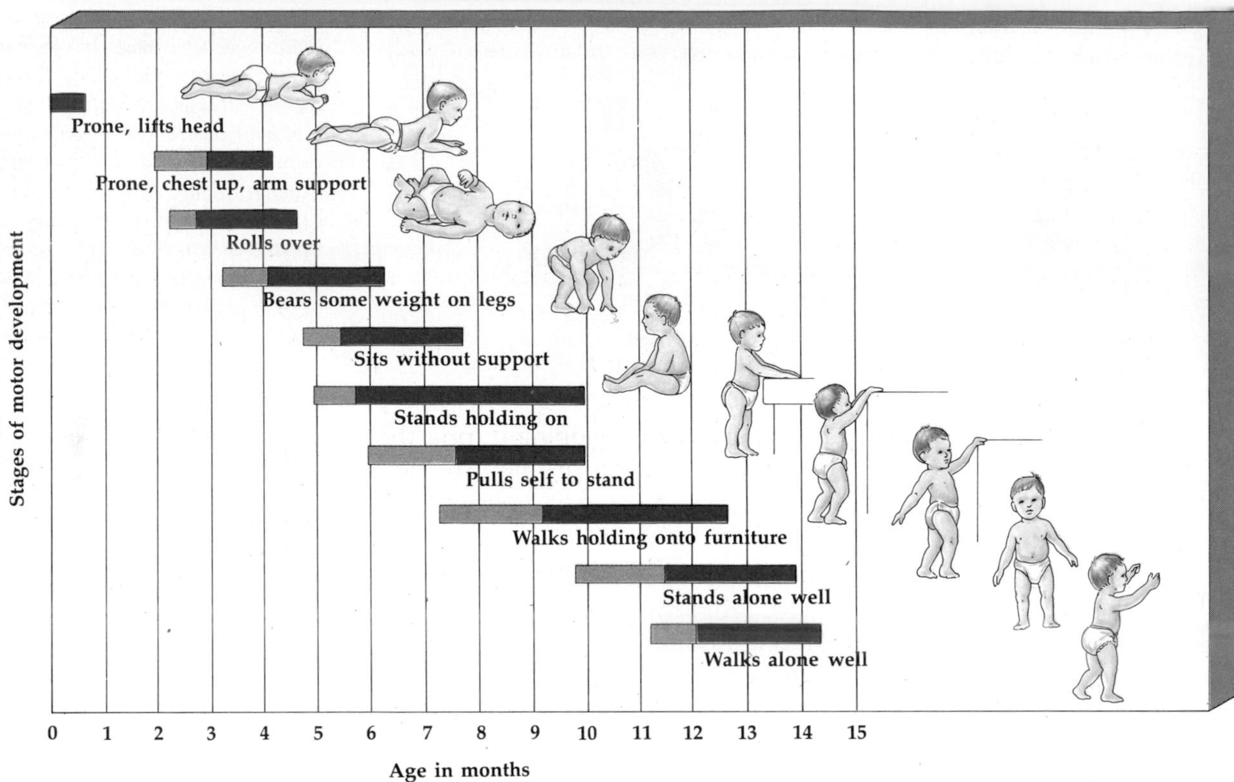

Figure 3-5 *Some stages of motor development in infants. Although some infants reach each stage ahead of others, the order of the stages is the same for all infants. The left side of the bar is the age by which 25 percent have mastered this movement; the right side is the age by which 90 percent have mastered it. The point on the bar where blue meets red is the age by which half of the infants have mastered the movement.*

As the infant's muscles and neural networks mature, more complicated skills emerge. Although the age at which infants sit, stand, and walk varies from child to child, the sequence in which these skills develop is universal. Different babies pass these developmental milestones (Figure 3-5) at different rates, but the basic order is predisposed.

Can experience retard or speed up the maturation of physical skills? If babies were bound to a cradleboard for much of their first year—the traditional practice among the Hopi Indians—would they walk later than unfettered infants? If allowed to spend an hour a day in a walker chair after age 4 months, would they walk earlier? Amazingly, in view of what we now know about the effects of experience on the brain, the answer to both questions seems to be no (Dennis, 1940; Ridenour, 1982). Biological maturation—including the rapid development of the cerebellum at the rear of the brain—creates a readiness to learn walking at about 1 year of age. Experience before that time has no more than a small effect (restriction later may, however, retard development [Super, 1981]). Much the same is true for other physical skills, including bowel and bladder control. Until the necessary muscular and neural maturation has occurred, no amount of pleading, harassment, or punishment can lead to successful toilet training.

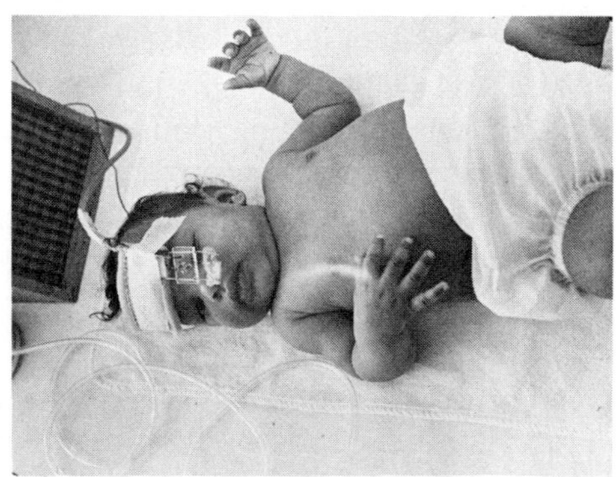

"It is a rare priviledge to watch the birth, growth, and first feeble struggles of a living human mind," said Helen Keller's teacher Annie Sullivan. Many researchers feel similarly. Because young infants cannot yet communicate, sophisticated techniques have been developed to discover what they can see, hear, and think. This photo shows an infant's visual reflexes being tested.

Perceptual Development

Is the newborn's sensory experience one of "blooming, buzzing confusion"? Such is what the turn-of-the-century philosopher-psychologist William James supposed. Until the 1960s few challenged that assessment. It was said that, apart from a blur of meaningless light and dark shades, newborns could not see. Then, much as the invention of new methods of inquiry led to a surge of progress in the neurosciences, so, too, did new investigative techniques enhance the study of infants. Scientists discovered babies can tell you a lot—if you know how to ask. To ask, you must capitalize on what the baby can do—gaze, suck, turn the head. So, equipped with eye-tracking machines, pacifiers wired to electronic gear, and other such devices, researchers set out to answer parents' age-old question: What can my baby see, hear, and think?

What they discovered was that a baby's sensory equipment is "wired" to facilitate social responsiveness. Newborns turn their heads in the direction of human voices, but not in response to artificial sounds. They gaze more at a drawing of a human face than at a bull's-eye pattern; yet they gaze more at a bull's-eye pattern—which has contrasts much like that of the human eye—than at a solid disk (Fantz, 1961). They focus best on objects about 9 inches away, which, wonder of wonders, just happens to be the typical distance between a nursing infant's eyes and the mother's. Newborns, it seems, arrive perfectly designed to see, first, their mothers' eyes.

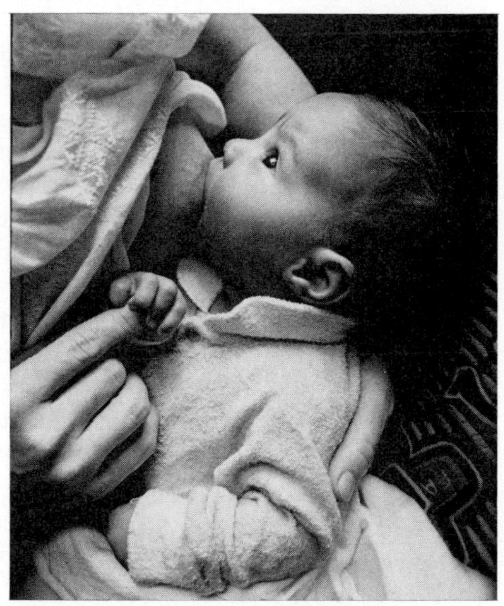

The ability to focus on their mothers' eyes is just one means by which newborns affect those important to their well-being. This baby's gaze will likely elicit a loving response from her mother.

Babies' perceptual abilities are continuously developing during the first months of life. Within days of birth, babies can distinguish their mothers' facial expression, odor, and voice. Two teams of investigators have reported the astonishing (and therefore controversial) finding that, in the second week or even the second day of life, infants tend to imitate facial expressions (Field & others, 1982; Meltzoff & Moore, 1977). Week-old nursing babies, placed between a gauze breast pad from their mothers' bra and another from another nursing mother, will generally turn toward the smell of their mothers' pad (MacFarlane, 1978). At 3 weeks of age, infants who are allowed to suck on a pacifier that sometimes turns on a recording of their mothers' voice, and sometimes that of a female stranger, will suck more vigorously when they hear their mothers' voice (Mills & Melhuish, 1974). So not only can babies see what they need to see, and smell and hear well, but they are already using their sensory equipment to learn. With the recent accumulation of such findings, the "incompetent" wet-behind-the-ears baby has become "the amazing newborn."

If they can be substantiated by further research, these findings will be a stunning tribute to the newborn's competence. For example, consider: Without seeing themselves, how do newborn babies know they have a mouth? Do they know that their mouth is like that of the stranger's? How are they able to coordinate the facial movements involved? The findings are controversial, since they suggest that the newborn's sensory and motor abilities may be beyond what has previously been suspected.

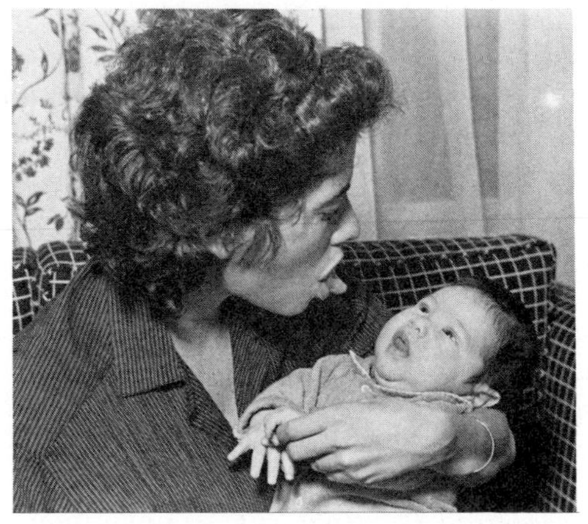

Imitation? Researchers have been surprised to see very young infants apparently copying adult facial expressions. In fact in one study, Tiffany Field and her colleagues (1982) found that on the second day of life, infants exhibited a rudimentary ability to imitate facial expressions. When a stranger made a pouting or surprised face, observers looking at the videotape of the infant could usually guess which face the stranger was making.

Cognitive Development

Cognition refers to all the mental activities associated with thinking and knowing. Few questions have intrigued developmentalists more than that of how cognition develops. Developmentalists ask: When can children begin to remember? See things from another's point of view? Reason logically? Think symbolically? Simply put, how does the child's mind grow? The most influential voice in answering these questions has been that of twentieth-century developmental psychologist Jean Piaget (pronounced Pea-ah-ZHAY).

How the Mind of an Infant Grows

"Who knows the thoughts of a child?" wondered the poet Nora Perry. As much as anyone of his generation, Piaget knew. Piaget's interest in children's cognitive processes began in 1920 in Paris, when he was working to develop questions for children's intelligence tests. In the course of administering sample tests to find out at what age children could answer certain questions correctly, Piaget became intrigued by children's *wrong* answers. Where others saw childish mistakes, Piaget saw intelligence at work. He observed that the errors made by children of a given age were often strikingly similar. The nature of these similarities suggested to Piaget that there is a developmental sequence to intellectual growth—that the *way* children think changes at different ages irrespective of *what* they are thinking about.

Piaget went on to describe cognitive development as occurring in four major stages (Table 3-1). Each of these stages is age-related and each one has distinctive characteristics that permit specific kinds of thinking. The differences between these kinds of thinking are qualitative: They involve changes in the way the child thinks, not just in the cumulative effect of having learned greater quantities of information.

In the first stage, which occurs between birth and approximately age 2, infants are limited to *sensorimotor intelligence:* Their understanding of the objects in their world is restricted to their interactions with them through their senses and motor abilities, that is, through looking, touching, sucking, grasping, and the like (Figure 3-6). Between the ages of 2 and 6 years most children demonstrate *preoperational intelligence.* They can think about objects independently of their actions on them, which means they can begin to think about them in a simplistically symbolic way.

Figure 3-6 *The sensorimotor stage of development begins in infancy and continues until about age 2. Very young children explore the world through their senses, enjoying the smell, feel, and taste of almost anything they can get their hands on.*

This new type of thinking is reflected in their ability to pretend, to think about past events and anticipate future ones, and to begin to use language (Figure 3-7). Children in the preoperational stage are not able, however, to think in a truly logical fashion; that is, they cannot perform the mental operations involved in relating facts to each other in a consistent way. Just because they can figure out that 5 plus 3 is 8 does not mean that they will automatically realize that 3 plus 5 is also 8. Beginning at about age 7, children demonstrate *concrete operational intelligence:* They are able to perform the mental operations that produce logical thought, but they are able to think logically only about concrete things. It is not until age 12 or so, when children enter the stage of *formal operational intelligence,* that they are able to begin to think hypothetically and to coordinate abstract ideas in a consistent way.

Table 3-1 **Piaget's cognitive development stages**

Approximate Age	Cognitive Development Stages
Birth–2 years	**Sensorimotor** Infant experiences the world through senses and actions.
2–6 years	**Preoperational** Child represents things with words and images, but cannot reason with logic.
7–12 years	**Concrete Operational** Child thinks logically about concrete events.
Teen years	**Formal Operational** Teenager becomes able to reason abstractly.

Figure 3-7 *An important sign that a child has moved into the preoperational stage is the ability to pretend. This delightful manifestation of cognitive development encompasses both the simple pretending of the toddler and the elaborate fantasy play of the older preschooler.*

Piaget arrived at these ideas of cognitive stages by questioning children and by playing games that might seem silly at first but that provided insight into the ways they understood their world. In one of his tests, he would show an infant an appealing toy and then flop his beret over it to see whether the infant searched for the toy. Infants whose cognition is still completely tied to their actions do not; they react as if there were no toy. If they cannot see the toy or touch it, for them it does not exist. With an older child, Piaget would roll one of two identical balls of clay into a rope shape and ask whether there was more clay in the rope or the ball. Children who are in the preoperational stage almost always say that the rope has more clay because they assume "longer is more." They cannot mentally reverse the clay-rolling process to see that the amount of clay is the same in both shapes. Children who are in the concrete-operational stage realize, on this and more complex tests, that a given quantity remains the same no matter how its shape changes. With adolescents, Piaget and his colleague Barbel Inhelder would often pose problems from chemistry and physics. For example, they might have provided some string and an assortment of weights and invited a teenager to use these to figure out what determines how fast a pendulum swings. By so doing, Piaget and Inhelder sought to discern when logic matures.

Jean Piaget (1930, p. 237): "If we examine the intellectual development of the individual or of the whole of humanity, we shall find that the human spirit goes through a certain number of stages, each different from the other . . ."

The more than 50 years Piaget spent in such informal activities with children convinced him that *the child's mind is not a miniature model of the adult's:* Young children actively construct their understandings of the world in radically different ways than adults do, a fact that we overlook when attempting to teach children by using our adult logic. Piaget further believed that the child's mind develops through a series of transformations, or stages, in an upward march from the sensorimotor simplicity of the newborn to the logical reasoning power of the adult. An 8-year-old child therefore comprehends things that a 3-year-old cannot. Thus while an 8-year-old might grasp the analogy—"getting an idea is like having a light turn on in your head"—trying to teach the same analogy to the 3-year-old would be fruitless.

"For everything there is a season, and a time for every matter under heaven."
Ecclesiastes 3:1

The driving force behind this intellectual progression is the unceasing struggle to make sense out of one's world. To achieve this goal, Piaget suggested, the maturing brain builds concepts, which he called ***schemas.*** Schemas are ways of looking at the world that organize past experience and provide a framework for understanding subsequent experience. We start out in life with the simplest of schemas—those that involve reflexes such as sucking and grasping. By adulthood we have built a seemingly limitless number of schemas that range from, say, how to tie a knot, to what the *Mona Lisa* looks like, to what it means to be in love.

The process of building schemas is an adaptive one in which our schemas are continually being refined as a result of our experiences. Piaget proposed two concepts to explain this adaptive process. First, we interpret our experience in terms of our current understandings; in Piaget's terms, we incorporate, or ***assimilate,*** new experiences into our existing schemas (see Figure 3-8). At the same time we adjust, or ***accommodate,*** our schemas to fit the particulars of each given experience. In other words, *assimilation* is interpreting new experiences in terms of one's schemas; when new experiences just will not fit our old schemas, then our schemas must change to *accommodate* the experiences.

Figure 3-8 *Can you find a man's head in this landscape? Lacking a schema to apply to this picture, you probably cannot. But once given a schema—give it a quarter-turn counterclockwise—you perhaps can return the book upright and still assimilate the image as a face.*

You might even say that science itself is a process of assimilation and accommodation. Scientists interpret nature using their preconceived theories to assimilate what would otherwise be a bewildering body of disconnected observations. Then, as new observations collide with these theories, the theories must be changed or replaced to accommodate the findings. New schemas—for example, a conception of the newborn as competent and active rather than incompetent and passive—replace old schemas. That, Piaget believed, is how children (and adults) construct reality using *both* assimilation and accommodation. What we know is never reality exactly as it is, but our constructions of reality.

Highly realistic art is easy to assimilate; it requires for interpretation only those schemas already available from observing the world. Highly abstract art is difficult to assimilate, which may explain the frustration it sometimes causes. Art often combines realism with abstraction, thereby allowing observers to impose meaning while stimulating them to stretch their schemas. For example, the grapes in the painting to the right retain a circular shape but are flat instead of rounded.

To better understand these concepts, let us look more closely at Piaget's first stage of cognitive development, the ***sensorimotor stage.*** As we have already seen, infants understand their world in terms of their senses and the effects of their actions; they are aware of only what they can see, smell, suck, taste, and grasp, and they seem to be unaware that things continue to exist apart from their perceptions. As we also noted, before the age of 8 months, infants lack ***object permanence***—the awareness that things continue to exist when not perceived (Figure 3-9). The infant lives completely in the here and now. What is out of sight is out of mind. By 8 months, infants begin to develop what psychologists now believe is a memory for things no longer seen. Hide the toy and the infant will momentarily look for it. Within another month or two, the infant will look for it, even after being restrained for several seconds.

"Children think not of what is past, nor what is to come, but enjoy the present time, which few of us do."
La Bruyère,
Les Caractères: De L'Homme

This flowering of recall occurs simultaneously with the emergence of a fear of strangers, called ***stranger anxiety.*** Beginning during the last third of the first year, infants who are handed over to a stranger will often cry and reach for their familiar caregivers. Is it a mere coincidence that object permanence and stranger anxiety develop together? Likely not. After about 8 months of age, the child can recall schemas for familiar faces; when a new face cannot be assimilated into these remembered schemas, the infant becomes distressed (Kagan, 1979). This link between cognitive development and social behavior illustrates the interplay of brain maturation, cognitive development, and social development. (It is occasionally useful to remind ourselves that, although it is convenient to discuss these dimensions of development separately, the child is actually a whole being!)

Piaget's stage theory is controversial. Do children's cognitive abilities really grow by leaps? Does object permanence in fact appear rather abruptly, much as a tulip blossoms in spring? As we will see, new evidence suggests that cognition unfolds more gradually than Piaget believed.

Figure 3-9 *Object permanence. Younger children lack the sense that things continue to exist when not in sight; but for this $8\frac{1}{2}$-month-old child, out of sight is not out of mind.*

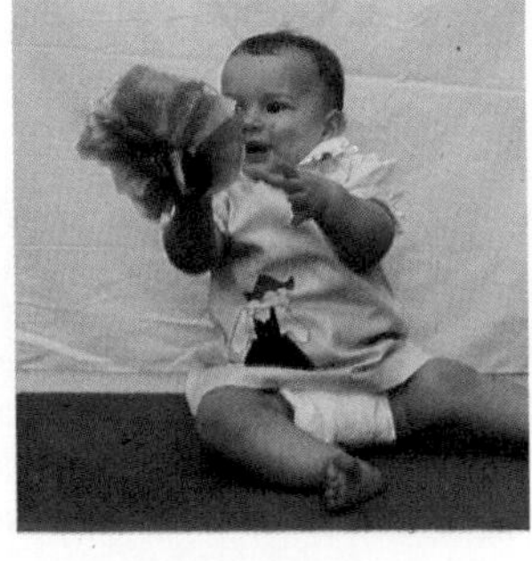

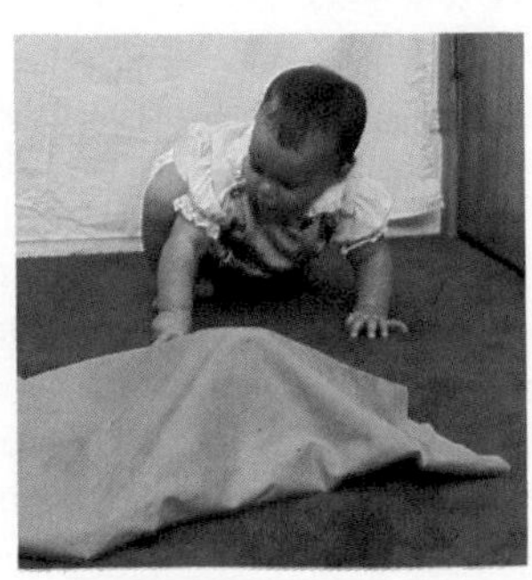

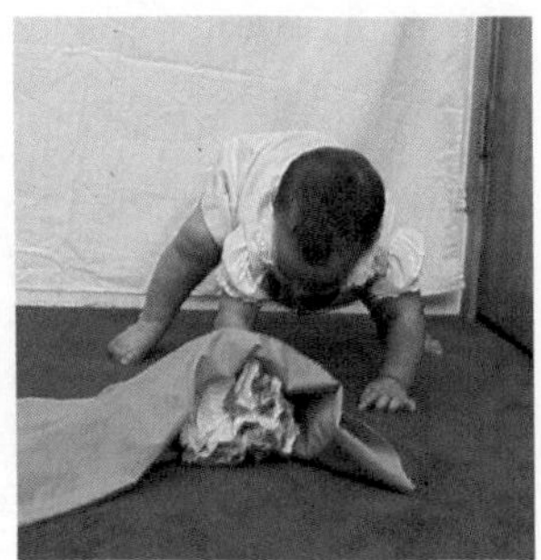

The Effects of Early Experience

One of the more striking facts about infancy is that we cannot recall it. The year-old infant's distress when his parents wave goodbye reveals that the infant well remembers who they are. But if the father then goes off to war and returns 2 years later, his 3-year-old will have forgotten him. For parents, this "infantile amnesia," as Freud called it, can be disconcerting: "After all the hours spent with my baby, after all the frolicking on the rug, after all the diapering, feeding, and rocking to sleep, if I died what would my baby later remember of me? Nothing!"

"Lord, I do not remember living this age of my infancy."
St. Augustine, 396–430

But if nothing is consciously recalled, something has still been gained. From birth (and even before), infants can learn. They can learn to turn their heads to make an adult "peek-a-boo" at them, or to pull a string to make a mobile turn (Bower, 1977; Lancioni, 1980). While there is little evidence that such learning persists (Campbell & Coulter, 1976), early learning may prepare us for those later experiences that we *do* remember. Moreover, some experiences during infancy have lasting effects. Consider the learning of language. Children who become deaf at age 2, after being exposed to speech, can later be trained much more easily in language than those deaf from birth (Lenneberg, 1967). It has been suggested that the first 2 years are a ***critical period*** for learning language. (Such a critical period—a restricted time for learning—is dramatically evident in certain birds, which learn to sing *if* they hear their species' song during a month-long period when their brains are primed to learn that skill; lacking this early experience, they can manage only crude vocalizations [Gould & Gould, 1981].) Potent demonstrations of the effects of early experience on cognitive development come also from studies of infants reared in orphanages where they received minimal custodial care—little more than being fed. Enriched later experiences can do much to reverse even severe deprivation during infancy (Kagan, 1976); nevertheless, compared with infants who are given more responsive care, the deprived infants may never realize their cognitive potential (see Chapter 12, "Intelligence").

The first 2 years are a critical period for language development. Most young children learn to speak easily and seemingly effortlessly. Case studies indicate that children deprived of contact with spoken language during these years never fully overcome their language deficiency.

Social Development

Babies are social creatures from birth. Right from the start, mothers and fathers have a two-way relationship with their babies. In subtle ways, including body language, they communicate with each other, each responding to the other in a ballet of movements. Close analysis reveals that newborns may even synchronize their movements in harmony with adult speech (Condon & Sander, 1974). Babies' perceptual, motor, and cognitive abilities work together to enable social behaviors that will promote their survival, so that they, too, may eventually pass the baton of life to the next generation.

In all cultures, infants develop an intense bond with those who care for them. Beginning with newborns' attraction to humans in general, infants soon come to prefer familiar faces and voices and then to coo and gurgle when given their mothers' or fathers' attention. By 8 months, they will crawl wherever mother or father goes and will become distressed when separated from them. At 18 months many infants cling tightly to a parent when frightened or anticipating separation and, when reunited, shower the parent with smiles and hugs. No social behavior is more striking than this intense infant love, called ***attachment.*** This powerful impulse keeping infants close to their parents helps our species survive. It is, therefore, not surprising that among the early social responses—love, fear, aggression—the first and greatest of these is the bond of love.

Origins of Attachment

Contact Might attachment be a matter of learning to love those who gratify our biological needs? As we will see in Chapter 9 ("Learning"), even neutral stimuli, such as the rustle of the dog food bag, can acquire value when associated with rewarding events. Since parents are associated with rewarding events, such as the satisfaction of the baby's basic needs for nourishment, perhaps babies learn to associate their parents with a sense of well-being and therefore want them close at hand.

Attachment—an intense and powerful bond between child and parent. This young child's love for her parents has survival value for the child and emotional value for everyone involved.

This analysis makes perfect sense, and for many years psychologists believed and taught it. But as an explanation of attachment it is incomplete. Interestingly, the best-known demonstration of its incompleteness began from an accidental finding. To study the development of learning abilities in monkeys, University of Wisconsin psychologist Harry Harlow needed to breed a large number of them. To equalize the infant monkeys' early experiences and to prevent the spread of contagious disease, he separated the monkeys from their mothers shortly after birth and raised them in sanitary, individual cages, each of which included a cheesecloth baby blanket (Harlow & others, 1971). Surprisingly, the infants became intensely attached to their blankets: When the blankets were taken to be laundered the monkeys were greatly distressed. They acted as if they had been separated from their mothers.

Harlow soon recognized that this attachment to the blanket contradicted the idea that attachment is derived from the association with nourishment. But could he demonstrate this more convincingly? Doing so required some way to pit the drawing power of a food source against the contact comfort of the blanket. Harlow's creative solution was two artificial mothers—one a bare wire cylinder with a wooden head, the other a similar cylinder wrapped with foam rubber and covered with terrycloth. Either could be associated with feeding through an attached bottle. When reared with a nourishing wire mother and a nonnourishing cloth mother, the monkeys overwhelmingly preferred the cloth mother (Figure 3-10). Much like human infants, they would cling to her when anxious and would use her as a base of security from which to venture out into the environment. Further studies with Margaret Harlow and others revealed that other qualities—rocking, warmth, and even feeding—could add small boosts to the magnetism of the comfortable cloth mother. In human infants, too, attachment usually grows from body contact with warm parents who rock, pat, and feed. But the fact remains—a fact that should reassure the fathers of nursing infants—that attachment does not depend on feeding.

Familiarity Another key to attachment is familiarity (Rheingold, 1985). Infants prefer faces and objects with which they have become familiar. In certain animals, such attachments are formed during a dramatic critical period shortly after birth. The first moving thing that a gosling, duckling, or chick is normally exposed to during the hours shortly after hatching is its mother, and the young fowl thereafter follows her, and her alone. This rigid attachment process, referred to as ***imprinting,*** was explored by Konrad Lorenz (1937), who wondered what ducklings would do if *he* were the first moving creature they observed. What they did, he discovered, was thereafter to follow him around. Further tests revealed that baby birds would imprint to a variety of moving objects—an animal of another species, a box on wheels, a bouncing ball—and that, once formed, this attachment was often difficult to reverse (Colombo, 1982).

Monkeys and humans (and other animals that cannot walk at birth) do not have such well-defined critical periods for attachment. But Harlow did find that monkeys that live their first 6 months in social isolation later have difficulty forming attachments; they become very disturbed when placed with other monkeys their age. The first 6 months of a monkey's life correspond to about the first 2 years of human development, during which, as we will see, deprivation of human contact can also have lasting impact.

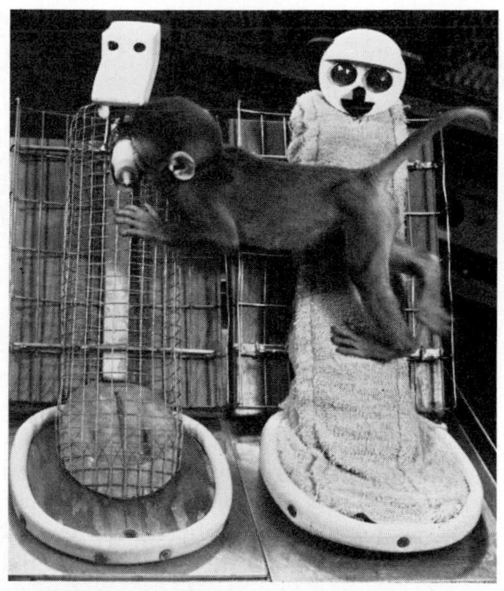

Figure 3-10 *When Harry Harlow reared monkeys with two artificial mothers—one a bare wire cylinder with a wooden head and an attached feeding bottle and the other a cylinder covered with foam rubber and wrapped with terrycloth but without a feeding bottle—they preferred the comfortable cloth "mother" to the nourishing wire "mother." It is interesting that monkeys also prefer the texture of terrycloth to the unmonkey-like smoothness of satins and silks, and that human infants are similarly more soothed by a textured than a smooth blanket (Maccoby, 1980).*

Responsive Parenting One aspect of the parent-child relationship that has greatly interested researchers is how children's attachments are linked with parental behavior. Placed in a strange situation (usually a laboratory playroom), some children show "secure attachment": In the mother's presence they play comfortably, happily exploring their new environment; when she leaves, they are distressed; when she returns, they seek contact with her. Other infants show "insecure attachment": They are less likely to explore their surroundings and may even cling to their mother; when the mother leaves, they cry loudly; and when she returns, they may be indifferent or even hostile toward her. What accounts for these differences?

Likely they are due partly to innate differences among infants. Some babies may be temperamentally more disposed to forming a secure attachment in the same way that, from birth, some babies are more easily held, cuddled, and comforted. But there is more to infant differences than biology. By observing mother-infant pairs at home during the first 6 months and then later observing the 1-year-old infants in a strange situation without their mother, Mary Ainsworth (1979) explored another influence upon attachment: the mother's behavior. Sensitive, responsive mothers—mothers who continually noticed what their babies were doing and responded appropriately—tended to have infants who became securely attached. Insensitive, unresponsive mothers—mothers who attended to their babies when they felt like doing so but ignored them at other times—tended to have infants who became less securely attached. The Harlows' monkey studies, in which artificial mothers were the ultimate unresponsive mothers, found even more striking consequences. Monkeys reared only with artificial mothers were, when put in strange situations without these mothers, not just distressed but terrified (Figure 3-11).

Konrad Lorenz (1966, p. 204): "Human behavior, and particularly human social behavior, far from being determined by reason and cultural tradition alone, is still subject to all the laws prevailing in . . . instinctive behavior."

Love at First Touch?

Attachments form not only from infants to their parents but from parents to their infants. Is there a critical period during which parents "bond" with their children? Does the pleasurable intimacy of breast-feeding enhance this bond and pay psychological dividends for the child?

Mother-Infant Bonding

Most mammals lick and groom their newborns during the first hours after birth and, if prevented from doing so, may later reject their offspring. Might there be, in humans, too, an optimal period during which contact triggers mother-infant attachment?

Pediatricians John Kennell and Marshall Klaus (1982) believe that the answer is yes, and that this optimal period may even be during the first hours after birth. Their widely publicized claim is that mothers who are allowed to have prolonged physical contact with their babies during the first hour after birth, and for several hours a day thereafter, form closer and more enduring attachments with them than do mothers denied this contact. Moreover, said Kennel and Klaus, the infants derive lasting physical, cognitive, and social benefits from this contact with the mother. Influenced by these claims, some medical societies now recommend allowing mothers and fathers more contact with their babies during the minutes and hours after birth.

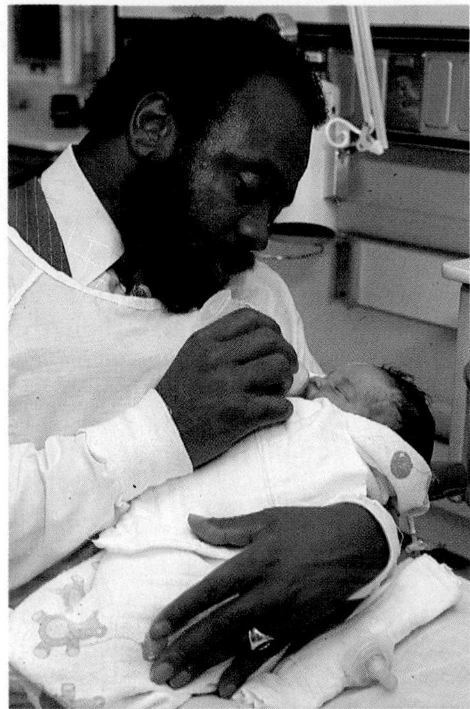

Does physical contact within the first hour after birth help parents form a bond with their newborns? Some pediatricians believe it does; though most researchers are skeptical.

Developmental psychologists Michael Lamb (1982), Susan Goldberg (1983), and Barbara Myers (1984a, 1984b) scrutinized the research on mother-infant bonding and were unconvinced. Either the studies were seriously flawed, they reported, or the effects of physical "bonding" are both minimal and temporary. Other critics have even mocked that "bonding" may become just another way for hospitals to institutionalize love: "The nurse gives the baby to the mother, notes the time, and returns one hour later, saying, 'Fine, you have bonded with your baby. Now give him back to me.'"

Most critics of the bonding notion nevertheless welcome the trend toward involving parents in the childbirth process. (What is more natural than immediately allowing parents the pleasure of getting to know their baby?) The danger, they suggest, comes in making parents who have not experienced early contact—including mothers who have had cesarean deliveries or parents who have adopted children—feel inadequate. They may be led by proponents of bonding to fear that they and their child have missed out on something terribly important. And that, say the critics, is simply not true.

Breast or Bottle?

Another controversy related to early parent-infant interaction is whether breast-feeding is more beneficial than bottle-feeding. Certainly breast milk has much to commend it: It is an inexpensive, sanitary, ready-to-serve, easily digestible nourishment that provides a baby with high-quality proteins, lipids (for brain development), a variety of hormones, and antibodies (for protection against diseases). The more researchers have analyzed breast milk, the more they have been struck by what an ideal food it is for babies—as ideal as cow's milk is for calves.

But does breast-feeding benefit the mother-infant relationship? For mothers, the experience of nursing often does heighten the sense of intimacy. (Interestingly, nursing stimulates the secretion of oxytocin, the same hormone that causes the nipples to become erect during lovemaking.) For infants, however, psychologists have been unable to verify any psychological benefits. Bottle-fed infants usually enjoy much the same cuddling, eye contact, and sensory experience as nursing infants. Thus, though breast-feeding is a pleasurable way to provide ideal nutrition, bottle-fed infants seem not to be psychologically handicapped.

There is no strong evidence that breast feeding is psychologically more advantageous to an infant than bottle feeding, but nursing can increase a mother's sense of intimacy with her infant.

By now perhaps you are wondering why the focus has been on mothers and not on fathers, too. The common assumption, long evident in court child-custody decisions, has been that fathers are less interested and less competent in child care. It is true that across the world mothers tend to assume more responsibility for infant care and that a breast-feeding mother and nursing infant have wonderfully coordinated biological systems that predispose their responsiveness to one another (Maccoby, 1980). Nevertheless, many modern fathers are becoming more involved in infant care, and researchers are becoming more interested in fathers.

One of the leading father-watchers, Ross Parke (1981), reported that fathers can be just as interested in, sensitive to, and affectionate toward their infants as mothers are; although mothers typically do most of the infant care, fathers are as capable (at least when researchers are watching). It also seems that although most infants prefer their mothers when anxious, when left alone in "the strange situation," they are as distressed by their fathers' departure as by their mothers'. Moreover, infants whose fathers have shared in their care, say by changing diapers, are more secure when left with a stranger.

Figure 3-11 *Monkeys raised by totally unresponsive artificial mothers were terrorized when placed in strange situations without their surrogate mothers.*

Always looking for differences, research psychologists have also uncovered several ways in which fathers and mothers are distinctive in their interactions with their infants. Fathers tend to smile less at their babies (males smile less at everyone), to spend more of their interaction in play rather than caretaking (especially with sons), and to play with more physical excitement. However, when fathers are the primary caregivers, they interact with their babies more as mothers typically do. This suggests that father-mother differences are not biologically fixed, but have social roots as well. (Monkey fathers also exhibit nurturant behaviors. When the Harlows caged mothers and fathers with their infants, the fathers were protective and affectionate toward their infants and more likely than mothers to engage in physical play.)

"Mothers and fathers can be equally effective as parents. They just have different styles."
Michael Lamb (1979)

Within two-parent families, both fathers and mothers have yet another gift to offer: their support of one another. Mothers and fathers who are observed to support one another and who sense one another's support and agreement in child rearing tend also to be more responsive to their infants and to feel more competent as parents (Dickie, 1986).

Research has shown that when fathers are primary caregivers, they interact with babies very much as mothers would. This suggests that mother-father parenting differences may be as much social as biological.

Effects of Attachment

Again, we confront the very important question: Do children's early experiences have a lasting impact? Some psychologists maintain that, if the child is sufficiently adaptive, positive later experiences can rectify all but the most severe early neglect. Others, such as Erik Erikson (1950), theorize that, depending on whether their caregivers are sensitive and responsive, infants form a lifelong attitude of either ***basic trust*** or of *mistrust* toward the world. Children whose needs are well met become trusting rather than fearful, Erikson believes.

Three types of research have shed light on the effects of early attachment: studies of the deprivation of social attachments, the disruption of social attachments, and the consequences of secure versus insecure attachments.

Deprivation of Social Attachments One way to study the benefits of positive early nurturing experiences is to observe the development of children denied such experiences. In all of psychology, few research literatures are more saddening. Children reared in institutions without the stimulation and attention of a regular caregiver, or locked away at home under conditions of extreme neglect, are frequently pathetic creatures—

"Out of the conflict between trust and mistrust, the infant develops hope, which is the earliest form of what gradually becomes faith in adults."
Erik Erikson (1983)

withdrawn, frightened, speechless. Adopted into a loving home, they usually progress rapidly, especially in their cognitive development and especially if they were in the company of other children while they were deprived of adult contact. Nevertheless, they often bear long-lasting scars from their early neglect (Rutter, 1979). Indeed, most abusive parents were themselves battered or neglected as children (Kempe & Kempe, 1978).

These findings were underscored by the Harlows. They reared monkeys not only with artificial mothers but also alone in barren cages or, worse, in total isolation from even the sight and sound of other monkeys. Regardless, those monkeys that were socially deprived 6 months or longer were socially devastated. They either cowered in fright or lashed out in aggression when placed with other monkeys their age (Figure 3-12). Upon reaching sexual maturity, most were incapable of mating. Females who were artificially impregnated often were neglectful, sadistically cruel, or even murderous toward their firstborn offspring. The unloved had become the unloving.

Figure 3-12 *Monkeys raised in total isolation from the sight or sound of other monkeys for more than 6 months were terrified of other monkeys and either lashed out aggressively or cowered in fright.*

The new generation of unloved animals would nevertheless persistently approach and cling to their abusive mothers. In fact, so powerful was the infant monkey's drive for attachment that even artificial "monster mothers"—mothers constructed to occasionally blast compressed air, fling their infant off, or even poke spikes through their terrycloth bodies—could only temporarily break their infant's attachment. When the monster mother "calmed down," the pitiful infant would return, clinging again, as if all were forgiven. Indeed, the distress of abuse seemed even to intensify the infant's clinging, a phenomenon sometimes observed among abused children.

Disruption of Attachment

What happens to an infant when a primary attachment is disrupted? Does being uprooted from one's primary caregiver—even from one's neglectful or abusive parents—predispose later emotional difficulties? The question bears on custody decisions in cases of child neglect or abuse.

Separated from their families, both monkey and human infants become agitated and, before long, withdrawn and even despairing (Bowlby, 1973; Mineka & Suomi, 1978). Fearing that such extreme stress might cause lasting damage (and when in doubt acting to protect parents' rights), the courts have generally been very reluctant to remove children from their homes. However, it seems that infants generally recover from this distress if placed in a more positive and stable environment. In studies of children placed for adoption, Leon Yarrow and his co-workers (1973) found that when children over 6 months of age were removed from their foster mothers they did for a time have difficulty eating, sleeping, and relating to their new mothers. But at 10 years of age there was little discernible difference in the adjustment of children who had been placed before the age of 6 months (with little accompanying distress) and those who had been adopted between 6 and 16 months (with much more distress). Although adoptions at later ages might more often be permanently disruptive, it seems that most year-old infants can form new attachments without permanent emotional scars. (Foster care with a series of foster families, or repeated removal from mother and then reunification with her, can be very disruptive, however.)

"We can hazard a tentative conclusion: The child's later adjustment will be primarily determined by the quality of the relationship with the new caretakers, not by the experience of separation."
Eleanor Maccoby (1980)

Secure Versus Insecure Attachments

If a trusting, secure attachment has lasting benefits, then the quality of an infant's attachments should predict the child's social competence in the years that follow. In research at the University of Minnesota, Alan Sroufe

(1978, 1983) and his co-workers confirmed that infants' attachments do predict their later social competence. Sroufe reported that infants who are securely attached at 12 to 18 months of age—those who use their mother as a base for comfortably exploring the world and as a haven when distressed—function more maturely as 2- to 3½-year-olds. Given challenging tasks, they are more enthusiastic and persistent. When with other children, they are more outgoing and responsive. Developmental theorist Erik Erikson would say they approach life with a sense of basic trust. These competent behaviors seem to reflect learned rather than innate temperamental differences among the children. However, some psychologists believe the child's competence reflects not so much the effects of the early parenting as it does the continued responsive parenting that these children are still receiving when retested (Lamb & others, 1984).

Whether raised entirely at home or also in a day care center, whether living in America, Guatemala, or the Kalahari Desert, anxiety over being separated from parents peaks in the first half of the second year and then gradually declines (Kagan, 1976; see Figure 3-13). With time, children become familiar with a wider and wider range of situations, and with the advent of language they communicate with strangers more freely. Does this mean that, as we develop, our need for and love of others fades away? Hardly. In other ways our capacity for love grows, and our pleasure in touching and holding those we love never dies. Yet, that powerful parental love gradually relaxes, allowing children to move into the world. One might even say that much of the life cycle story—from pregnancy and birth to infancy, to adolescence, to marriage and parenthood, to old age and death—boils down to but two poignant realities: attachment and separation.

Figure 3-13 *Infants' anxiety over separation from parents. In an experiment, groups of infants who had and had not experienced day care were left alone by their mothers in an unfamiliar room. In both groups, the percentage who cried when the mother left peaked at about 13 months.*

CHILDHOOD

Childhood as we think of it—roughly the years from toddler to teenager—is an astonishingly recent concept. For many centuries, particularly during the Middle Ages, children in the Western world were treated as miniature adults—smaller, weaker, dull-witted adults who would frequent the same taverns as adults, wear the same style clothes, sleep in the same

In some earlier eras, childhood was viewed as a less distinct phase of life than it is today; children were treated and dressed like adults.

rooms, and work the same long hours. Philippe Ariès (1962) reported that "in medieval society the idea of childhood did not exist. . . . As soon as the child could live without the constant solicitude of his mother, his nanny or his cradle-rocker, he belonged to adult society." Not until about a century ago did the idea of the "innocent" child in need of compulsory education and protection from labor abuses become codified in law, and not until this century did anyone establish a research center to study children.

Those of us who accept the "revolutionary" new concept of childhood must strain to comprehend how earlier generations could have so radically misunderstood and failed to protect their own children. Today we recognize that the decade of childhood is critically important not only for one's physical, cognitive, and social development (discussed in the next section) but, more specifically, for the development of one's gender identity, language, intelligence, and personality (as we will see in later chapters).

Physical Development

To predict a girl's adult height, double her height at eighteen months. To predict a boy's adult height, double his height at two years.

After a growth spurt during the first 2 years, growth settles down to a steady 2 to 3 inches per year. With all of the neurons and most of their interconnections in place, brain development after age 2 also proceeds at a slower pace. The sensory and motor cortex areas mature rapidly, enabling fine motor skills to develop further (Wilson, 1978). The last areas of the brain to develop are the cortex's association areas—the areas associated with thinking, memory, and language.

Despite these universal patterns of brain development, children diverge as they develop physically. Some of these differences are linked with their social functioning. For example, some children have more physical energy than others. To find out if physical energy level is correlated with social behavior, David Buss, Jeanne Block, and Jack Block (1980) placed a movement recording device on the wrists of 129 preschoolers for seven different 2-hour periods. They found that those most physically active were rated by their teachers as more socially assertive, aggressive, and competitive.

Cognitive Development

Viewed through the eyes of Piaget, preschool children are in some ways still inept. Although aware of themselves, of time, and of the permanence of objects, preschoolers, in Piaget's view, are *egocentric.* ***Egocentrism*** refers not to selfishness but to an inability to perceive things from another's point of view. The preschooler who blocks your view of the television while trying to see it herself and the one who asks a question while you are on the phone both assume that you see and hear what they see and hear. When relating to a young child, it may help to remember that such social behaviors reflect a cognitive limitation; the egocentric preschooler has difficulty taking another's viewpoint.

Preschoolers also find it more difficult to follow negative instructions ("Don't squeeze the guinea pig") than positive instructions ("Hold the guinea pig gently"). One characteristic of parents who abuse their children is their generally failing to understand these things. They tend to view their children as little adults who are in control of their behavior (Larrance & Twentyman, 1983). Thus children who stand in the way, spill food, disobey negative instructions, or cry may, unfortunately, be perceived as willfully malicious.

Piaget believed that during this preschool period and up to about age 7, children are ***preoperational***—still unable to perform mental operations such as reversing information. For a 5-year-old, the quantity of milk that is "too much" in a tall, narrow glass may become an acceptable amount if it is in a short, wide glass. This is because after transferring the milk from the tall glass to the wide one, the child is incapable of mentally pouring it back. The child lacks the concept of ***conservation***—the principle that the quantity of a substance remains the same despite changes in its shape (see Figure 3-14).

"Childhood is the sleep of reason."
Jean-Jacques Rousseau,
Emile, 1762

Children's conversations like this one with a young boy sometimes reveal this inability to reverse information (Phillips, 1969, p. 61):

> *"Do you have a brother?"*
>
> *"Yes."*
>
> *"What's his name?"*
>
> *"Jim."*
>
> *"Does Jim have a brother?"*
>
> *"No."*

My 6-year-old daughter, Laura, loves to be asked "math problems" at bedtime. Asked, "What is 8 plus 4?" she requires about 5 seconds to compute "12." If she is then immediately asked, "What is 12 minus 4?," can she answer "8" more quickly? To my astonishment—until considering Piaget—another 5 seconds are required. In Piaget's terms, she is unable to reverse the arithmetic operation she has already performed.

Figure 3-14 *The preoperational child cannot perform the mental operations essential to understanding conservation. The row of seven checkers seems to be "more" to this 6-year-old boy than the seven clustered checkers.*

But she should be able to soon. Piaget contended that during the stage of ***concrete operations*** (roughly ages 7 to 12) children acquire the mental operations needed to comprehend such things as mathematical transformations and conservation. The child is exhibiting logic, but the operations must involve concrete images of physical actions or objects, not abstract ideas. Eleven-year-olds can *mentally* pour the milk back and forth between different-shaped glasses, and roll a clay rope into a ball, and so they realize that the quantity and volume of the substance are unchanged. They also enjoy jokes that allow them to utilize their recently acquired concepts, such as conservation:

> Mr. Jones went into a restaurant and ordered a whole pizza for his dinner. When the waiter asked if he wanted it cut into 6 or 8 pieces, Mr. Jones said, "Oh, you'd better make it 6, I could never eat 8 pieces!" (McGhee, 1976)

If Piaget was correct that children construct their understandings through assimilation and accommodation, and that in early childhood their thinking is radically different from adult thinking, then what implications are there for preschool and elementary school teachers? Since children actively construct their own understandings, Piaget contended, teachers should strive to "create the possibilities for a child to invent and discover." Don't just talk *at* the children; rather, build on what children already know, allow them to touch and see, to witness concrete demonstrations, to think for themselves. Since the young child is incapable of adult logic, a second implication is that it pays to know the mind of the child, to know that what is simple and obvious to you and me—that subtraction is the reverse of addition—may be incomprehensible to a 6-year-old.

"When I was a child, I spoke as a child, I thought as a child, I reasoned as a child; when I became a man, I gave up childish ways."
St. Paul,
I Corinthians 13:11

"The better you know something yourself, the greater the risk of not noticing that children find it bewildering."
Margaret Donaldson (1979)

But is the young child as incapable as Piaget presumed? Increasingly, researchers contend that we have underestimated the competence of young children. Given very simple tasks, preschoolers are *not* purely egocentric; they will adjust their explanations to make them more clear to

Piaget's writings have influenced many educators to provide children with situations and encouragement that will prompt them to do their own exploring and discovering. For younger children, especially, direct observation has proved an effective learning tool, augmenting or even replacing traditional lecturing and "book learning."

a listener who is blindfolded, and will show a toy or picture with the front side facing the viewer (Gelman, 1979; Siegel & Hodkin, 1982). If questioned in a way that makes sense to them, 5- and 6-year-olds will exhibit some understanding of conservation (Donaldson, 1979). It seems, then, that the abilities to take another's perspective and to perform mental operations are not utterly absent (in the preoperational stage) and then suddenly present. Rather, these abilities begin earlier than Piaget believed and develop more gradually.

What, then, remains of Piaget's ideas about the mind of the child? Plenty. For it was Piaget who helped identify and name the important cognitive phenomena and who helped stimulate interest in studying how the mind develops. If we today are adapting his ideas to accommodate new findings, he would not be surprised.

Social Development

One of the more important achievements of childhood is the construction of a sense of self. By the end of childhood most children have developed a clear sense of their own personal worth and social identity. Let's consider two questions: When and how does a child's sense of self develop? And how can parents help foster a child's self-esteem?

Self-concept

"Is my baby aware of herself—does she know that she is a person distinct from others?" How might we answer such a question? The baby cannot talk, so we cannot ask her. Perhaps, however, the infant's *behavior* could provide clues to the beginnings of her self-awareness. But what sorts of behavior? In 1877 Charles Darwin published one idea: Maybe her self-awareness begins when she recognizes herself in a mirror. By this indicator, self-recognition emerges gradually over about a year, starting in roughly the sixth month, when the child reaches toward the mirror to touch her image as if it were another child (Damon & Hart, 1982).

How can we know when the infant recognizes that the girl in the mirror is indeed herself and not just an agreeable playmate? In a simple variation of the mirror procedure, researchers have surreptitiously dabbed a bit of rouge on their subjects' noses before placing them in front of the mirror. Beginning at about 18 months, children, upon seeing the red spot, will touch their noses (Damon & Hart, 1982). Apparently, 18-month-olds have a schema of how their faces should look; it is as if they wonder, "What is that spot doing on *my* face?"

Mirror images are fascinating to infants from the age of about 6 months, but the recognition that the child in the mirror is "me" does not happen until about 18 months.

Beginning with this simple self-awareness, the child's sense of self gradually becomes stronger. By school age, children begin to describe themselves in terms of their gender, their group memberships, and their psychological traits. They come to see themselves as good and skillful in some ways, but not others. They form a concept of which traits, ideally, they would like to have, and by age 8 or 10 their self-image has become quite stable.

How children view themselves may affect how they act. Children who have formed a positive self-image tend to be more confident, independent, optimistic, assertive, and sociable (Maccoby, 1980). All this raises a profoundly important question: How can parents encourage a positive self-image?

Child-rearing Practices

Some parents spank, some parents reason; some parents are strict, some parents are lax; some parents seem indifferent to their children, some parents liberally hug and kiss them. Whether such differences in parenting affect children's behavior has been the subject of a good deal of research. The most heavily researched aspect of parenting has been how, and to what extent, parents seek to control their children. Some investigators have identified three specific styles of child management: (1) permissive, (2) authoritarian, and (3) firmly controlling. *Permissive* parents tend to submit to their children's desires, make few demands, and use little punishment. *Authoritarian* parents impose rules and expect obedience: "Don't interrupt." "Don't leave your room a mess." "Don't stay out late or you'll be grounded." "Why? Because I said so." *Firmly controlling* parents exert control by establishing rules and enforcing them, but they also explain the reasons for rules and, especially with older children, encourage open discussion when making the rules. Studies by Stanley Coopersmith (1967), Diana Baumrind (1973), and others found that the children of firmly controlling parents have the highest self-esteem and are the most self-reliant.

What might account for this finding? As Chapters 15, "Personality," and 19, "Social Influence," will explain, many experiments indicate that people become more motivated and self-confident if they have experienced some control over their own lives; those who experience little control tend to see themselves as somewhat helpless and incompetent. Moreover, children who sense enough control to be able to attribute their behaviors to their own choices ("I obey because I am a good boy") tend to internalize their behaviors more than do children who comply solely because they are intimidated ("I obey or I get in bad trouble").

Although no child enjoys being disciplined, and most will at times rebel against family rules, both rules and discipline are necessary for the child's welfare. Studies suggest that consistency in enforcing rules, when combined with discussion and explanation, helps the child achieve self-control and self-reliance.

Of the three parenting styles studied, it seems that the firmly controlling one provides children with the greatest sense of control over their own lives. There seem to be at least two reasons for this. First, because firmly controlling parents openly discuss family rules, explaining them to younger children and reasoning about them with older children, such rules seem not so much imposed as negotiated. Especially for older children, this approach may foster a sense that they have at least some control over the rules to which they comply (Baumrind, 1983; Lewis, 1981). Second, when parents enforce rules with consistent, predictable consequences, the child controls the outcome. (Recall that infants become more attached to parents who sensitively and predictably respond to their behaviors. Such infants experience control.) It is when the consequences become extreme—perhaps a coercive threat for noncompliance—that the child of authoritarian parents is left with no feeling of choice. So it seems, concluded Eleanor Maccoby (1980, p. 389), that "skillful parents must operate within a very delicate balance of forces. They need to obtain compliance to reasonable demands—for the child's, the parents', and the family's sake—without . . . destroying their children's sense of [choice].''

Before jumping to any conclusions about the consequences of different parenting styles, we must heed a caution. The evidence here is correlational. It tells us that certain child-rearing styles (say, being firm but open) are associated with certain childhood outcomes (say, social competence). But as we have seen before, correlation does not necessarily reveal cause and effect. Firm parenting may, in fact, lead to social competence. But there may be other possible explanations (see Figure 3-15). Perhaps socially mature, agreeable children *elicit* greater trust and more reasonable treatment from their parents than do less competent and less cooperative children. Or perhaps it is some other unnoted characteristic of firmly controlling parents that encourages their children's competence. For example, such parents are less likely to be enduring the stresses of poverty or recent divorce (Hetherington, 1979), and they are more likely to be well educated—factors that might also be linked with children's competence. Or maybe competent parents and their competent children share genes that predispose social competence. In short, knowing that parents' behavior is related to their children's behavior hints at, but does not prove, causation.

When considering ''expert'' child-rearing advice—of which there seems to be no shortage—we should also remember that child-rearing advice inevitably reflects the advice-giver's values. Even if we knew exactly how to encourage the development of any given trait in children, we could not advise parents without assuming that some traits are to be preferred over others. But which? Should the chief end of childhood be unquestioning obedience? Then an authoritarian style could be commended. Are sociability and self-reliance a higher end? Then firm but open parenting is advisable. Different ''experts'' have different values. And that, along with the uncertainties of cause and effect, helps explain their disagreements.

Parents struggle with conflicting advice and with the other stresses of child rearing. Indeed, the tens of thousands of dollars it costs to raise a child buys 20 years of not only joy and love but also worry and irritation. Yet for most parents, a child is a personal investment in the human future. To paraphrase the psychiatrist Carl Jung, we reach backward into our parents and forward into our children, and through their children into a future that we will never see, but about which we must therefore care.

For both child and parent, childhood can be a joy.

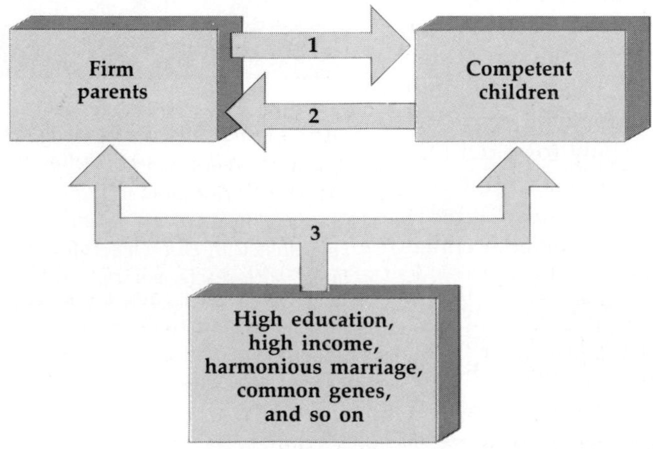

Figure 3-15 *Three possible explanations of the correlation between parental firmness and social competence in children.*

SUMMING UP

Developmental psychologists study the human life cycle, from conception to death, examining how we develop physically, cognitively, and socially.

DEVELOPMENTAL ISSUES

Two issues pervade developmental psychology. First, to what extent is each of our traits—from physical ones such as height to personality traits like outgoingness—influenced by our genes and to what extent by our experiences? Second, is development a gradual, continuous process, or do we develop by leaps and bounds through distinct stages?

PRENATAL DEVELOPMENT

The life cycle begins as 1 sperm out of the some 300 million ejaculated penetrates and fertilizes the egg. Two weeks later, the already developing embryo attaches to the mother's uterine wall, and after 2 months is a recognizably human fetus. Along with nutrients, teratogens ingested by the mother can reach the developing child and possibly place it at risk.

INFANCY

Physical Development Within the brain, nerve cells form before birth and, sculpted by experience, their interconnections continue to multiply after birth. With the aid of new methods for studying babies, researchers have discovered that newborns are surprisingly competent. They are born with sensory equipment and reflexes that facilitate their interacting with people and securing nourishment; they quickly learn to discriminate the smell and sound of their mothers; and they may even be capable of imitating simple gestures. Infants' more complex physical skills—sitting, standing, walking—develop in a predictable sequence that is strongly influenced by maturation.

Cognitive Development Jean Piaget's observations of children convinced him—and most everyone else—that the mind of the child is not that of a miniature adult. Piaget theorized that the mind develops by forming schemas that help us assimilate our experiences and that must occasionally be adapted to accommodate new information. In this way, children progress from the sensorimotor simplicity of the infant to the more complex preoperational, concrete operational, and formal operational stages of thinking. For example, at about 8 months, an infant becomes aware that things still exist even when not perceived. This sense of object permanence coincides with the development of stranger anxiety, which requires remembering who is familiar and who is not. While the experiences of infancy are not for long consciously remembered and their effects may even be largely reversed by later experiences of a different sort, they can nevertheless have a lasting influence upon thinking, language, and personality. This is evident in the critical period for language learning during the first 2 years.

Social Development The primary social response of infancy is attachment. Infants become attached to their mothers and fathers not simply because mothers and fathers gratify biological needs, but, more importantly, because they are comfortable, familiar, and responsive. If denied such care during their infancy, both monkey and human infants may become pathetically withdrawn, anxious, and eventually abusive. Once an attachment forms, infants who are separated from their caregiver will, for a time, be distressed. Infants who display secure attachment to their mothers generally become socially competent preschoolers.

CHILDHOOD

Physical Development Childhood—from toddlerhood to the teen years—is a period of slow, steady physical development. During this time, individual differences in children's physical development (for example, in activity level) are linked to differences in their social functioning (for example, their aggressiveness).

Cognitive Development Piaget believed preschool children to be egocentric (unable to take another's perspective) and preoperational (unable to perform simple logical operations). However, he believed that at about age 7 children become capable of performing concrete operations, such as those required to comprehend the principle of conservation. Recently, some researchers have questioned whether young children are as incapable as Piaget presumed. It seems that at each age children already possess the rudiments of the cognitive abilities that Piaget saw fully developed at a later age.

Social Development As with cognitive abilities, self-concept develops gradually. At about age 18 months, infants will recognize themselves in a mirror, as indicated by their curiosity over a conspicuous red spot placed on the face. By age 10, children's self-images are quite stable, and are linked to their independence, optimism, and sociability. Children who develop a positive self-image and a happy, self-reliant manner tend to have been reared by parents who are neither permissive nor authoritarian, but firmly controlling without depriving their children of a sense of control over their own lives. However, knowing how best to rear children requires making value assumptions about what traits in children should be encouraged.

TERMS AND CONCEPTS TO REMEMBER

Accommodation Adapting one's current understandings (schemas) to incorporate new information.

Assimilation Interpreting one's experience in terms of one's existing schemas.

Attachment An emotional tie with another person; evidenced in children by their seeking closeness to the caregiver and their showing distress on separation.

Basic Trust According to Erik Erikson, a sense that the world is predictable and trustworthy; said to be formed during infancy by experiences with responsive caregivers.

Cognition All the mental activities associated with thinking and knowing.

Concrete Operational Stage In Piaget's theory, the stage of cognitive development (from about 7 to 12 years of age) during which children acquire the mental operations that enable them to think logically about concrete events.

Conservation The principle (which Piaget believed comes to be understood during the concrete operational period) that properties such as mass, volume, and number remain the same despite changes in the appearance of objects.

Critical Period A restricted period of development during which an organism is especially susceptible to certain influences, such as the formation of attachments or the learning of language.

Egocentrism In Piaget's theory, the inability of the preoperational child to take another's point of view.

Embryo The early developmental stage of an organism after fertilization; in human development, the prenatal stage from about 2 weeks to 2 months.

Fetus The developing human organism from 8 weeks after conception to birth.

Imprinting The process by which certain birds and mammals form attachments during a critical period early in life.

Maturation Biological growth processes that, relatively uninfluenced by experience, enable orderly changes in behavior.

Object Permanence The awareness that things continue to exist even when not perceived.

Ovum The female reproductive cell, which after fertilization develops into a new individual.

Preoperational Stage In Piaget's theory, the stage (from about 2 to 7 years of age) during which a child learns to use language but does not yet comprehend the mental operations of concrete logic.

Rooting Reflex A baby's tendency, when touched on the cheek, to open the mouth and search for the nipple.

Schema A concept or framework that organizes and interprets information.

Sensorimotor Stage In Piaget's theory, the stage (from birth to about 2 years of age) during which infants know the world mostly in terms of their sensory impressions and motor activities.

Stranger Anxiety The fear of strangers that infants commonly display for a few months beginning at about 8 months of age.

Teratogens Agents, such as chemicals and viruses, that sometimes cross the placenta from mother to fetus, causing harm.

X Sex Chromosome The chromosome (from the father) that, when paired with the mother's X sex chromosome, will produce a female. (For definition of chromosome, see Chapter 2.)

Y Sex Chromosome The chromosome (which only comes from the father) that, when paired with an X sex chromosome from the mother, will produce a male.

Zygote The one-celled organism created by the union of sperm and ovum.

FOR FURTHER READING

Berger, K. (1986). *The developing child* (2nd ed.). New York: Worth.

A comprehensive, current, and readable textbook summary of what we know about infancy, childhood, and adolescence.

Flavell, J. H. (1985). *Cognitive development* (2nd ed.). Englewood Cliffs, NJ: Prentice-Hall.

A comprehensive overview of intellectual growth from infancy through adolescence. Includes discussions of the development of perception, memory, and language.

Kagan, J. (1984). *The nature of the child.* New York: Basic Books.

A prominent developmental psychologist reviews research on child development.

Maccoby, E. (1980). *Social development: Psychological growth and the parent-child relationship.* San Diego: Harcourt Brace Jovanovich.

An authoritative but not intimidating review of the development of children's attachments, aggressiveness, impulse control, self-concept, and moral thinking, and of research on parent's effects on children.

Mussen, P. (Ed.) (1983). *Handbook of child psychology* (4th ed.; Vols. 1–4). New York: Wiley.

Authoritative summaries of research on major aspects of child development written by leading experts.

Parke, R. D. (1981). *Fathers.* Cambridge, MA: Harvard University Press.

A prominent developmental psychologist describes his own and others' studies of fathering.

Hirshhorn Museum and Sculpture Garden, Smithsonian Institution

Giacomo Manzu *Young Girl on a Chair*, 1955

CHAPTER 4

Adolescence and Adulthood

For much of the past century psychologists echoed William Wordsworth's sentiment that "the child is father of the man." In this view, by the end of childhood one's traits have nearly set like clay. Although it remains for life experiences to smooth the rough edges of one's character, the really pliable period of development is over. The heritage of infancy and childhood will reach decades into the future, for the course of development has been set.

So long as psychologists tended to hold this point of view, they focused their attention on the "critical" early years. Now, among a new generation of developmentalists, this popular belief that there are no important changes in personality after childhood is giving way to a growing sense that the development of the individual is *lifelong*. Yes, we are shaped during infancy and childhood, but the shaping continues during adolescence and well beyond. At a 5-year high school reunion, friends may be astonished at the divergence of their paths. A decade after college, two former soul mates may have trouble communicating. Always, we are in the process of becoming.

Not until this century were young teenagers routinely spared the demands of adult labor. Adolescents were expected to work as soon as they were physically able; the young miner shown here looks distinctly proud of his adult status.

ADOLESCENCE

Adolescence extends from the beginnings of sexual maturity to the achievement of independent adult status. In preindustrial societies, there is typically no adolescence; adult status and responsibilities are bestowed rather abruptly at the time of sexual maturation, often marked by an initiation ceremony. In pre-20th-century North America, young teenagers often labored as adults but until marriage were expected to behave as obedient children (Kett, 1977). Not until this century, when schooling extended the period of dependence and postponed adult labor until well past biological maturity, was the concept of adolescence as a distinct period of life invented.

What are the teen years like? Let's let three writers describe them. To St. Augustine, these years were a time of fiery passions involving

> the hot imagination of puberty. . . . Both love and lust boiled within me and swept my youthful immaturity over the precipice of evil desires to leave me half drowned in a whirlpool of abominable sins.

In Leo Tolstoy's *Anna Karenina*, the teenage years were not turmoil, but rather,

> that blissful time when childhood is just coming to an end, and out of that vast circle, happy and gay, a path takes shape.

In her diary, written as a teenager while she hid from the Nazis with her family, Anne Frank observed that

> My treatment varies so much. One day Anne is so sensible and is allowed to know everything; and the next day I hear that Anne is just a silly little goat who doesn't know anything at all and imagines that she's learned a wonderful lot from books. . . . Oh, so many things bubble up inside me as I lie in bed, having to put up with people I'm fed up with, who always misinterpret my intentions.

To G. Stanley Hall (1904), the first American psychologist to describe it, adolescence was, as it sometimes was for Anne Frank—a period of "storm and stress," of emotional turbulence caused by the tension between biological maturity and enforced dependence. Indeed, after age 30, many people look back on their teenage years as a time they would not like to relive (Macfarlane, 1964). They recall those years as a period in which the social approval of peers was imperative; when pressures for achievement were nerve-racking; when the sense of one's direction in life was in flux; when the alienation from one's parents was deepest.

"When I was a boy of 14 my father was so ignorant I could hardly stand to have the old man around. But when I got to be 21, I was astonished at how much he had learnt in 7 years."
Mark Twain, 1835–1910

Other psychologists have noted that for many, adolescence is much as Tolstoy described it—a time of vitality without the cares of adulthood, a time of congenial family relationships punctuated by only occasional tensions, a time of rewarding friendships, a time of heightened idealism and a growing sense of life's exciting possibilities (Coleman, 1980). With such conflicting observations, what can we say adolescents are like? We must ask in return, which adolescent? In which culture? On what day? Nevertheless, we can describe the adolescent years in terms of their most common physical, cognitive, and social changes.

Physical Development

Adolescence starts with ***puberty,*** the time of rapid growth and developing sexual maturity. This period commences with a surge of hormones, which triggers a growth spurt, a 2-year period of rapid development that begins in girls at about age 11 and in boys at about age 13. The male growth spurt is more intense—boys grow as much as 5 inches a year, compared to some 3 inches for girls—propelling the average male, for the first time in his life, noticeably higher than the average female (Figure 4-1). During the growth spurt, not only are there rapid gains in height and weight, there are also dramatic developments of the ***primary sex characteristics*** (the reproductive organs) and the ***secondary sex characteristics*** (the nonreproductive traits of sex, such as enlarging female breasts and hips, male body hair and voice change, and the growth of pubic hair in both sexes), as noted in Figure 4-2.

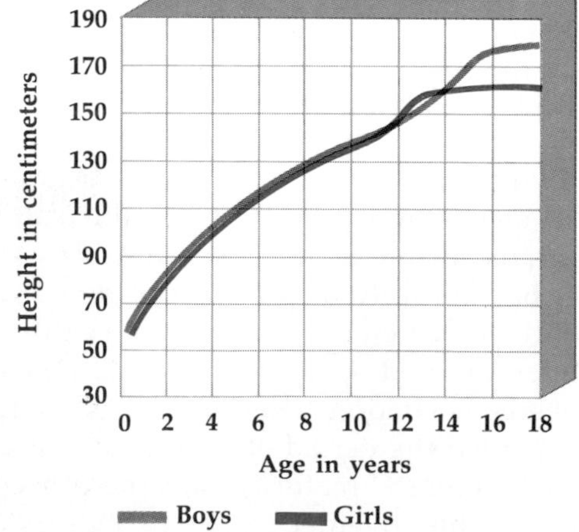

Figure 4-1 *Throughout childhood, boys and girls are similar in height. At puberty, girls surge ahead, but then boys overtake them at about age 14.*

Among the many pubertal changes that take place, the events that are true landmarks are the first ejaculation in boys, which usually occurs in a wet dream or through masturbation at about age 14, and the first menstrual period in girls, at about age 13. (These events do not necessarily signify fertility; it may be another year or more before ejaculations contain abundant live sperm and the menstrual cycle includes ovulation [Tanner, 1978].) The first menstrual period, called ***menarche,*** is an especially memorable event, one that is recalled by nearly all adult women.

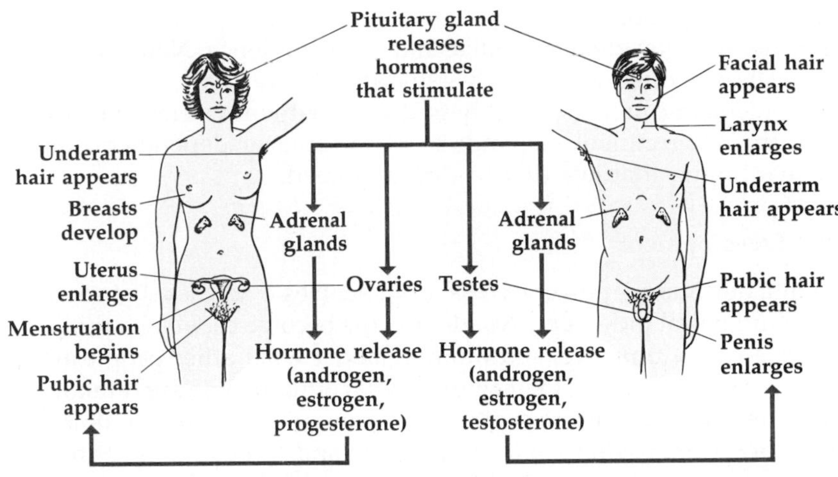

Figure 4-2 *Puberty commences with a surge of hormones that trigger a variety of physical changes.*

Most recall it with a mixture of feelings—pride, excitement, embarrassment, and apprehension (Greif & Ulman, 1982; Woods & others, 1983). Girls who are well prepared for menarche, and know what to expect, are more likely than those not prepared to experience it as a positive life transition. And a transition it is: Regardless of the age at which their menarche occurs, girls often begin soon after to see and present themselves as increasingly different from boys and to function more independently of their parents (Golub, 1983).

As in the earlier life stages, the *sequence* of physical changes (for example, breast buds before visible pubic hair before menarche) is far more predictable than their *timing.* Some girls start their growth spurt at age 9, some boys as late as age 16. Such variations have little effect on ultimate height. However, they may have psychological consequences. Studies performed in the 1950s by Mary Cover Jones and her colleagues revealed that for boys early maturation pays dividends. Early-maturing boys, being stronger and more athletic during their early teen years and seemingly less childlike, tend to be more popular, self-assured, and independent, and some of their greater sociability may continue into early adulthood (Jones, 1957). For girls, early maturation is less advantageous (Brooks-Gunn & Petersen, 1983). The 11-year-old who towers over her classmates and becomes sexually attractive before her peers do may temporarily suffer embarrassment and be the object of teasing. But as her

Girls often begin their "ascent" into puberty earlier than boys. This can lead to social embarrassment for early and late bloomers alike.

peers catch up, in junior and senior high school, her postpubertal experience helps her to enjoy greater prestige and self-confidence. Note that the psychological consequences of early versus late physical maturation again illustrate a recurring theme: heredity and environment interact. In this case, how the environment responds to the youngster depends on the maturational timing that heredity has programmed.

Cognitive Development

Adolescents' developing power of reasoning enables a new level of social awareness and moral judgment. As adolescents become capable of thinking about their own thinking, and thinking about what other people are thinking, they become prone to imagining what other people are thinking about *them.* As their cognitive abilities continue to grow, many adolescents begin to ponder what is ideally possible and to be critical of their society, their parents, and even of themselves for falling short.

Formal Operations

Piaget theorized that these developing reasoning skills define a final stage of cognitive growth, which he called ***formal operations.*** According to Piaget, preadolescents are restricted to reasoning about the concrete, but adolescents become capable of thinking logically about abstract propositions. They can reason hypothetically and deduce consequences: *if* this, *then* that. Unlike preadolescents, the adolescent can deduce that when an investigator hides a poker chip and says, "Either this chip is green or it is not green," the statement must be true (Osherson & Markman, 1974–1975).

"The principal novelty of this period is the capacity to reason in terms of verbally stated hypotheses and no longer merely in terms of concrete objects and their manipulation."
Jean Piaget (1972)

Formal operations are the summit of intellectual development. Early adolescents may already have enough command of formal operations to, say, learn algebra. But their capacity to reason systematically, the way a scientist might do in testing hypotheses and deducing conclusions, awaits the full development of their capacity for reasoning in terms of formal operations (Inhelder & Piaget, 1958).

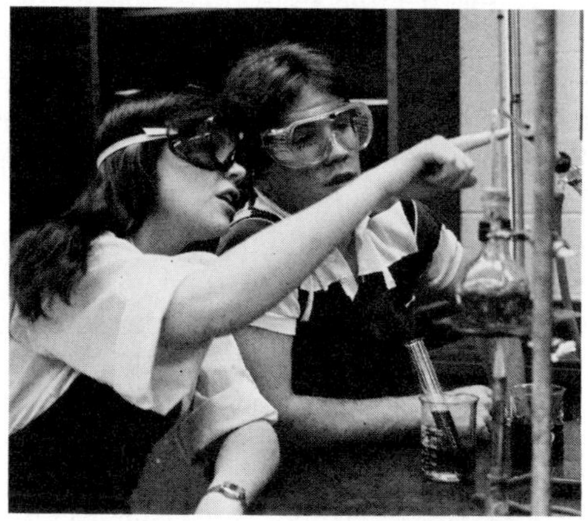

The adolescent's growing ability to think logically about abstract propositions is evidence of the achievement of Piaget's final stage of cognitive growth, formal operations.

Piaget's critics have raised a number of objections to his depiction of formal-operational intelligence. For one thing, they maintain, the rudiments of logic can begin earlier than Piaget believed. It is just that the nature of Piaget's tests often obscured this fact. Given a simple problem such as, "If John is in school, then Mary is in school. John is in school. What can you say about Mary?," many 7-year-olds would have no trouble answering correctly (Patrick Suppes, cited by Ennis, 1982).

Piaget's critics also object that the attainment of formal logic is *not* inevitable. Not only do many adolescents never achieve formal-operational reasoning, many adults never do either, particularly if they are unschooled in the logic of science and mathematics. An example of this is offered in a conversation between researcher Sylvia Scribner (1977) and an illiterate Kpelle farmer in a Liberian village:

> ***Sylvia Scribner:*** *All Kpelle men are rice farmers. Mr. Smith is not a rice farmer. Is he a Kpelle man?*
>
> ***Kpelle farmer:*** *I don't know the man. I have not laid eyes on the man myself.*

Other Kpelle villagers—those who had been to school—could answer logically.

Finally, new research in cognitive psychology reveals that even if we do develop the capacity for formal reasoning, we do not employ it regularly. Much of the time our thinking is nonlogical or even illogical (see Chapter 11, "Thinking and Language").

Nevertheless, it seems fair to conclude that formal logic is far more likely to be found in adolescents than preadolescents. One of the ways this new cognitive power manifests itself most frequently is in adolescents' pondering and debating such topics as human nature, good and evil, and how to raise children. Adolescents' logical powers enable them to detect logical inconsistencies in others' reasoning. As Roger Brown (1965, pp. 232–233) observed, it may seem to the adolescent that socialism follows

Adolescents' new ability to reason formally manifests itself in bull sessions about the problems of their worlds.

> inevitably from Christian axioms, that discrimination against minorities cannot possibly coexist with democratic principles, that Cold War tensions would necessarily be eased if we would set an example of trustfulness, that a rational society must exercise economic controls. . . . Whatever the conclusions of the adolescent's reasoning on social issues may be, the reasoning itself seems to him to be perfectly rigorous, and rigorous thought, he believes, will compel social change. There is a powerful emotional attachment to abstract ideas. As an adolescent one is amazed at adults who do not seem to realize the logical implications of their own ideas and who, still more unaccountably, do not make their actions consistent with their beliefs. The adolescent vows that he will never get to be like that; he will fight off whatever it is that clouds the adult intelligence. And suddenly he is ten years older, uncertain about everything and thoroughly compromised, trying to recall what it was he vowed to preserve.

Moral Thinking

As any parent will tell you, one chief task of childhood is learning right from wrong. How do our notions of right and wrong develop?

Following Piaget's (1932) contention that children's moral development is tied to their cognitive development, Lawrence Kohlberg (1981, 1984) proposed that moral thought develops in specific ways in a set sequence. To study people's moral thinking, Kohlberg (1981, p. 12) posed stories to children, adolescents, and adults in which the characters face a moral dilemma. Ponder for a moment his best-known dilemma:

> In Europe, a woman was near death from a very bad disease, a special kind of cancer. There was one drug that the doctors thought might save her. It was a form of radium that a druggist in the same town had recently discovered. The drug was expensive to make, but the druggist was charging ten times what the drug cost him to make. He paid $200 for the radium and charged $2,000 for a small dose of the drug. The sick woman's husband, Heinz, went to everyone he knew to borrow the money, but he could get together only about $1000, which was half of what it cost. He told the druggist that his wife was dying and asked him to sell it cheaper or let him pay later. But the druggist said, "No, I discovered the drug and I'm going to make money from it." Heinz got desperate and broke into the man's store to steal the drug for his wife.

What do you think: Should Heinz have stolen the drug? Why was what he did right or wrong? Kohlberg would not be interested in whether you judged Heinz's behavior as right or wrong—either answer could be justified—but rather in the reasoning process by which you arrived at your judgment. We all are moral philosophers, Kohlberg proposed, and our moral reasoning helps guide our behavior.

On the basis of his research, Kohlberg postulated that as we develop intellectually we pass through as many as six stages of moral reasoning (see Table 4-1) that are divided into three basic levels: preconventional, conventional, and postconventional. The term *conventional* refers to reasoning that upholds laws and conventions simply because they are the laws and conventions. Before age 9, most children have a "preconventional" morality of self-interest: One obeys to avoid punishment (Stage 1) or gain concrete rewards (Stage 2). By early adolescence, morality usually matures to a more conventional level. Being able to take others' perspectives, adolescents may approve actions that will gain others' approval (Stage 3) or that do a duty that helps maintain the social order (Stage 4). A few of those who become sophisticated in the abstract reasoning of formal operational thought may finally progress, usually after age 20, to a "postconventional" morality that affirms people's socially agreed-upon rights (Stage 5) or follows what their individual conscience perceives as universal ethical principles that may sometimes conflict with society's rules (Stage 6).

Table 4-1 **Kohlberg's levels and stages of moral development**

Stage description	Examples of moral reasoning in support of Heinz's stealing	Examples of moral reasoning against Heinz's stealing
Preconventional Morality		
1. Avoids punishment	"If you let your wife die, you will get in trouble."	"You shouldn't steal the drug because you'll get caught and sent to jail if you do."
2. Gains concrete rewards	"If you do happen to get caught you could give the drug back and you wouldn't get much of a sentence."	"He may not get much of a jail term if he steals the drug, but his wife will probably die before he gets out."
Conventional Morality		
3. Gains approval/ avoids disapproval	"Your family will think you're an inhuman husband if you don't."	"It isn't just the druggist who will think you're a criminal, everyone else will, too."
4. Does duty to society/avoids dishonor or guilt	"If you have any sense of honor, you won't let your wife die because you're afraid to do the only thing that will save her."	"You'll always feel guilty for your dishonesty and lawbreaking."
Postconventional Morality		
5. Affirms agreed-upon rights	"If you let your wife die, it would be out of fear, not out of reasoning it out."	"You'd lose respect for yourself if you're carried away by emotion and forget the long-range point of view."
6. Affirms own ethical principles	"If you don't steal the drug you would have lived up to the outside rule of the law but you wouldn't have lived up to your own standards of conscience."	"If you stole the drug, you wouldn't be blamed by other people but you'd condemn yourself because you wouldn't have lived up to your own conscience and standards of honesty."

Source: Second and third columns adapted from Kohlberg (1984).

Kohlberg's controversial claim is that these six stages form a moral ladder that extends from the immature, preconventional morality typical of the 7-year-old to, at its top rung, a recognition of what the individual perceives to be fundamental ethical principles. The sequence is said to be unvarying. People begin at the bottom rung and ascend to varying heights. The rungs above are always shrouded in fog; that is, one cannot see and comprehend moral stages much above one's own level. Thus Stage 4 thinkers are not able to tolerate the civil disobedience of such leaders as Martin Luther King, Jr., who, arguing from a postconventional morality of human rights, maintain that basic human rights take precedence over the laws of the state (Kohlberg, 1981).

Kohlberg's theory of moral development is unquestionably provocative. It spells out some of the ways by which people know right from wrong. It suggests why people who operate from different levels of moral thinking often clash in their political and social judgments. And it implies

Those who conform to a society's rules often do not take kindly to those who seek to change those rules. Kohlberg contends that Stage 6 moral thinking, embodied here by Martin Luther King, Jr., may be rejected by those who, not comprehending, feel threatened by it.

a program for moral education. In the tradition of Piaget, Kohlberg believes that moral thinking matures as children's minds actively confront moral challenges. Moral education is therefore consciousness-raising—raising a person's moral consciousness to a higher stage through dialogue concerning rules and moral issues.

Provocative, yes. But is the theory valid? Does it accurately and helpfully describe moral development? Kohlberg's detractors offer two criticisms. The first emphasizes that, while our moral reasoning may largely determine our moral *talk,* it is but one of several influences upon our *actions.* Morality, some critics say, involves what you *do* as well as what you think. And what we do is powerfully influenced by the social situation as well as by our inner attitudes (see Chapter 19, "Social Influences"). Many of the guards in the Nazi concentration camps were rather ordinary people who were corrupted by a powerfully evil situation (Arendt, 1963). Given the imperfect link between moral reasoning and moral action (Blasi, 1980), say the critics, we should also concentrate on instructing children how to *act* morally in given situations and on modeling such behavior ourselves.

The second criticism is one of cultural bias. Granted, say the critics, children in various cultures do seem to progress sequentially through the first three or four of Kohlberg's stages (Edwards, 1981; Snarey, 1985). But the postconventional stages are generally found only in educated, middle-class people in industrialized countries such as the United States, Britain, and Israel (Edwards, 1982). Moreover, who is to say that the nonconformity of what Kohlberg calls the "highest" and most "mature" postconventional level is indeed morally preferable? And what would happen to society if everyone adopted Stage 6 moral reasoning and acted in accord with their individual convictions with little regard for society's conventions?

To psychologist Richard Shweder (1982) the Stage 6 morality of self-chosen principles is actually the morality "of an articulate liberal secular humanist" masquerading as objective truth. As Shweder would expect, when political conservatives are asked to respond to a test of moral reasoning as they imagine a liberal person might, they score much higher than when responding on the basis of their own views (Emler & others, 1983).

To Kohlberg's friend and Harvard colleague, Carol Gilligan (1982), Stage 6 is morality from a male perspective—based on studies by and of males. For women, she argues, moral maturity is less an impersonal morality of abstract ethical principles and more a morality of responsible relationships. Gilligan believes that women's moral reasoning regarding the dilemma of Heinz and the druggist reveals their concern for the whole network of human relationships and feelings among the people involved. This tends to place them at the conventional (socially concerned) level of moral reasoning rather than at the postconventional level (Blake & Cohen, 1985). Thus, measured by a male yardstick, women's moral differences become moral deficits. Actually, contends Gilligan (1982, p. 173), women's concern for social responsibilities is a moral strength that complements men's concern with rights: "In the different voice of women lies the truth of an ethic of care."

"It is obvious that the values of women differ very often from the values which have been made by the other sex."
Virginia Woolf,
A Room of One's Own, 1929

So, while Kohlberg's critics agree that moral reasoning is linked with cognitive development, they suggest, first, that moral reasoning is but one determinant of moral action, and also that Kohlberg's postconventional moral stages are those of a liberal, Western male.

By trying out different roles, adolescents try out different "selves." Although some of their roles are uncomfortable for both the adolescents and their parents, most teenagers eventually forge a consistent and comfortable identity.

Social Development

Adolescents have a sense of what they were as children (or at least of what others said they were), a sense of the person they might be becoming, and a sense of the expectations others have of them and they have of themselves. Theorist Erik Erikson (1963) contended that each stage of life has its own task, which for adolescents is to synthesize their past, their present, and their future possibilities into a clear sense of self. This attempt to establish a sense of self is the adolescent's search for ***identity.***

Forming an Identity

Basically, the adolescent's search for identity is a search for the answers to such questions as "Who am I as an individual? What do I want to do with my life? What values should I live by? What do I believe in?" In a modern, open society like our own, the answers lie in a maze of possibilities. Yet, according to Erikson, arriving at answers that provide a stable and consistent identity is essential to the adolescent's being able to find a meaningful place in society.

To gain this sense of identity, adolescents usually try out different "selves" in different situations—perhaps acting out one self at home, another with friends, and still another at school and work. If two of these situations overlap and the self one is in one situation differs considerably from the self one is in the other—as when a teenager brings home friends with whom he is Joe Cool—the discomfort can be considerable. The teen

asks, "Which self should I be? Which is the real me?" Ideally, and often, this role confusion gets resolved by the gradual forging of a self-definition that unifies the various selves into a consistent and comfortable sense of who one is.

But not always. Erikson believes that some adolescents form their identity early, simply by taking on their parents' values and expectations. Others may form a negative identity, one that defines itself in opposition to parents and society. Still others never quite seem to find themselves or to develop strong commitments. For most, the struggle for identity continues throughout the teen years (and reappears at turning points during adult life).

"I am becoming still more independent of my parents; young as I am, I face life with more courage than Mummy; my feeling for justice is immovable, and truer than hers. I know what I want, I have a goal, an opinion, I have a religion, and love. Let me be myself and then I am satisfied. I know that I'm a woman, a woman with inward strength and plenty of courage."
Anne Frank,
Diary of a Young Girl, 1947

The late teen years, when many people begin attending college, provide new opportunities to try out possible roles. By the senior year many students—though by no means all—have achieved a clearer identity than they had as freshmen (Waterman & others, 1974). This identity tends to incorporate a more positive self-concept than existed before. In several nationwide studies, researchers have given young Americans tests of self-esteem (sample item: "I am able to do things as well as most other people"). Between ages 13 and 23, the sense of self tends to become more positive (O'Malley & Bachman, 1983). A clearer, more self-affirming identity is forming.

To Carol Gilligan (1982), the "normal" struggle to create one's separate identity characterizes the individualistic male more than the relationship-oriented female. Gilligan believes that females are less concerned than males with viewing themselves as separate individuals, and more concerned with intimate relationships. Erikson himself (1968) acknowledged that in adolescent females intimacy is important; yet in his theory the male norm of forming identity (in adolescence) before intimacy (in young adulthood) remains the assumed human standard, from which females are a departure.

Relationships with Parents and Peers

Are adolescents indeed preoccupied with separating themselves from their parents in order to form their own identities? Is adolescence a time of undeclared war between restrictive parents and their rebellious, independence-seeking, identity-craving offspring? Everyone agrees that in Western cultures adolescence is typically a time of growing peer influence and shrinking parental influence, especially on matters of personal taste and life-style (music, dress, recreation). For example, the best predictor of whether a high school student smokes marijuana is simply how many of the student's friends smoke it (Andrews & Kandel, 1979). After high school, those who continue to live with their parents show little change in drug use, while those who move in with peers become more likely to use drugs (Bachman & others, 1984). So, as peer influences grow, parental influences diminish.

Although adolescents are susceptible to peer pressure, most still report that they get along at least "fairly well" with their parents. The teenagers in this merged family seem to enjoy the company of both their siblings and their parents, as together they plan a vacation.

Does this mean that parents and their adolescents are estranged? For a small minority, it does. But for most families the generation gap is easily bridged, chiefly because it is rather narrow. In a 1977 Gallup poll that asked adolescents how they got along with their parents, 56 percent indicated they got along with them "very well," 41 percent indicated "fairly well," and only 2 percent indicated they got along "not at all well" (Gallup, 1977). Indeed, researchers have been surprised at how closely most adolescents reflect the social, political, and religious views of their parents (Gallatin, 1980). As often as not, what "generation gaps" there were on such issues merely involved differences in the strength with which adolescents and their parents held their shared opinions.

ADULTHOOD

Until recently, adulthood, the center-of-life years between adolescence and old age—the longest period of the life-span—was commonly viewed as one long plateau. No longer. As we will see, contemporary developmentalists who have closely followed the unfolding of people's adult lives have been impressed by the degree to which change continues during adulthood. Physically, cognitively, and (especially) socially, people at age 50 are not the same as they were at age 25. The fact of change has prompted developmental theorists to propose various stages of adult development, with transition points between. As people become independent of their parents and assume work roles, a transition from adolescence to adulthood occurs—at about age 20, give or take a few years depending on the culture and the individual. Early adulthood extends to about age 40, at which time a transition to middle adulthood is said to occur. Within the later adult years, many developmentalists distinguish the "young-old" post-retirement years (65 to 75) from the "old-old" years (after 75) of more rapid physical decline.

Such life phases are convenient ways to organize the adult years. But they are somewhat arbitrary, and their transition points are fuzzy. Moreover, it is important to remember that age per se causes nothing. People do not get wiser with age; they get wiser with experience. People do not die because of old age; they die because of physical deterioration accompanying aging. For that matter, during the adult years age only modestly predicts people's traits. If you know that Maria is a 1-year-old and Meredith is a 10-year-old, you could say a great deal about each. But not so with adults of similarly differing ages. In Western societies not highly structured by seniority, the boss may be 30 or 60; the marathon runner may be 20 or 50; the reader of this book may be a teenager or a grandparent.

"I am still learning."
Michelangelo's motto, 1560, at age 85

The unpredictability of adult lives reflects the increasing importance of individual experiences. As we move through the first 2 years of life, maturation narrowly restricts our course. The infant who is strapped on a cradleboard and the one who moves freely about will both walk and talk at about the same age. As the years pass, we sail a widening channel, allowing the environmental winds to diverge our courses more and more.

The growing recognition of the importance of individual experience makes it much more difficult to generalize about adulthood than about life's early years. Yet in some underlying ways our life courses are often similar. Our bodies, our minds, and our social relationships undergo many of the same changes experienced by those childhood friends who in other ways now seem so different.

Physical Development

Although few of us are aware of it at the time, our physical abilities peak in early adulthood. Muscular strength, reaction time, sensory acuity, and cardiac output all crest by the mid-twenties. Like the declining daylight after the summer solstice, the decline in physical prowess begins imperceptibly. Athletes are often the first to notice. World-class sprinters and swimmers generally peak in their teens or early twenties, with women (who mature earlier) peaking earlier than men. But most people—especially those whose daily lives do not require physical peak performance—hardly perceive the early signs of decline.

In middle adulthood, physical decline gradually begins to accelerate (Figure 4-3), but even diminished vigor is sufficient for the normal activities of middle age. Moreover, during early and middle adulthood a per-

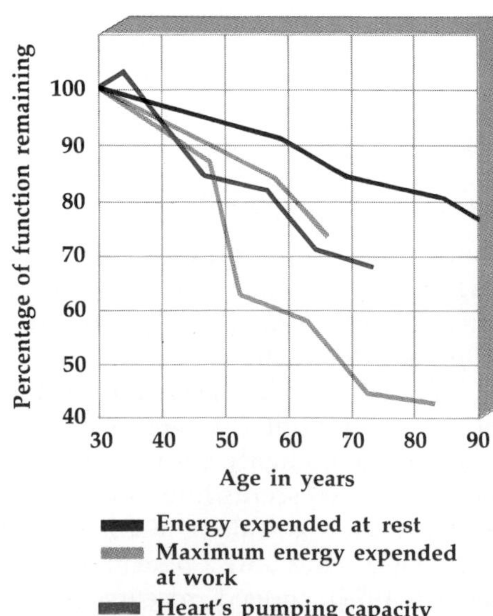

Figure 4-3 *The body's physical capacities decline slowly during adulthood.*

son's health and exercise habits have more to say about physical vigor than does aging. Many of today's physically fit 40-year-olds can run several miles with ease, while sedentary 25-year-olds find themselves huffing and puffing on a jog around the block.

The physical changes of adult life can trigger psychological responses, depending on how one views growing older. In some Eastern cultures where respect and power come with age, outward signs of one's advancing years are generally accepted, even welcomed. In Western cultures where the perceived ideal, particularly for women, is smooth skin and a slim torso, the wrinkles and bulges that frequently accompany middle age can be a threat to self-esteem—something to work to avoid. But nature will not be defeated; inevitably the lines appear, the youthful form begins to change its shape.

The rate of physical decline in middle adulthood depends more on individual health and exercise habits than on chronological age. Forty-four-year-old Pete Rose is probably in better physical condition than most readers of this text.

For women, the most definite biological change related to aging is ***menopause,*** the cessation of the menstrual cycle, within a few years of age 50. This change, which is caused by a reduction in the levels of the hormone estrogen, is, in some women, accompanied by physical symptoms such as hot flashes and sweating. Some women also experience periods of anxiety, emotional instability, or depression. But like the stereotype of adolescent storm and stress, the image of menopausal upheaval is giving way to a recognition that, on the whole, menopause does not create significant psychological problems for women, nor does it greatly diminish sexual appetite or appeal (Newman, 1982).

What seems crucial in determining the emotional impact of menopause is the woman's attitude toward it. Does she see menopause as involving a loss of femininity and sexual attractiveness, the beginning of growing old? Or does she look on it as a form of liberation—from contraceptives, periods, fears of pregnancy, and the demands of mothering children? To ascertain women's attitudes toward menopause, Bernice Neugarten and her colleagues (1963) did what, amazingly, no one had bothered to do earlier: They asked questions of a sample of women whose experience of menopause had not led them to seek treatment. When asked, for example, whether it is true that after menopause "women generally feel better than they have for years" only one-fourth of the premenopausal women under age 45 guessed yes, whereas two-thirds of the older women who had experienced menopause *agreed* with the statement. As one woman said, "I can remember my mother saying that after her menopause she really got her vigor, and I can say the same thing myself."

Cognitive Development

One of the most controversial questions in the study of development is whether cognitive abilities such as learning and memory, problem solving, and creativity follow a similar course of gradually accelerating decline during adulthood. We do know that early adulthood provides the peak years for some types of learning and remembering (Craik, 1977). For example, David Schonfield and Betty-Anne Robertson (1966) asked adults of various ages to learn a list of 24 words. Some were then asked, without being given any clues, to *recall* as many words as they could from the list. As Figure 4-4 indicates, younger adults had better recall. Others were given multiple-choice questions that asked them simply to *recognize* which words they had seen. In this test there was no significant change in ability with age. So it seems that our ability to recall new learning gradually declines during adulthood; but until very late in life (beyond the years depicted in Figure 4-4) our ability to recognize what we have learned remains strong.

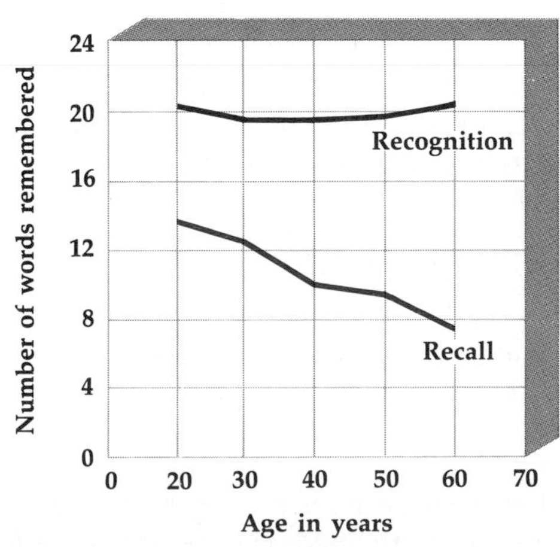

Figure 4-4 *In this experiment of recall and recognition in adulthood, the ability to* recall *new information declined during early and middle adulthood while the ability to* recognize *new information showed little decline.*

The proficiency of adults in retaining newly acquired learning is also evident in classrooms. In recent years, American adults have returned to school in rising numbers. During the last half of the 1970s, the college enrollment of post-35-year-olds rose 37 percent (National Center for Education Statistics, 1982). By 1980, one-third of college students were age 25 and older (American Council on Education, 1983). Despite occasional difficulties in adjusting to the demands of coursework and testing, older students, on the whole, are successful in their academic efforts. In fact, most older students do better than the typical 18-year-old, perhaps because they have clearer goals and greater motivation (Badenhoop & Johansen, 1980).

College enrollments of post–35 year olds are rising. Despite occasional adjustment problems, older students usually do better than the typical 18-year-old.

Social Development

Most of the differences between early and middle adulthood are created not by the physical and cognitive changes linked to aging but by life events—events often associated with work, marriage, and parenting. A new job means new relationships, new expectations, and new demands. A marriage bears the potential for both the joy of intimacy and the stress of merging one's life with another's. The birth of children introduces a new depth of responsibility for the parents and significantly alters the focus of their lives. A sudden shift in economic fortune may turn a person's world upside down, for better or for worse. The death of a loved one creates a sense of irreplaceable loss, and eventually the need to reaffirm one's own life. Each such life event represents a challenge, which may result in significant change in the person facing it.

"Perhaps middle-age is, or should be, a period of shedding shells; the shell of ambition, the shell of material accumulations and possessions, the shell of the ego."
Anne Morrow Lindbergh,
Gift from the Sea, 1955

Stages of Adulthood

To the extent that these major events of adult life are common to many, say some developmentalists, we may expect their influence to shape a predictable sequence of life changes.

Erik Erikson (1963) theorized that in young adulthood the individual is faced with the challenge of achieving intimacy with others, by forming close relationships and growing in one's capacity for love. In middle age, the challenge is to achieve ***generativity***—to become less self-absorbed, more productive, more caring for the world and its future generations.

Other developmentalists have attempted to describe in a more detailed way how people feel and act at various ages. In the best known of these investigations, psychiatrist Daniel Levinson and his associates (1978) spent 10 to 20 hours talking with each of forty 35- to 45-year-old men, three-fourths of whom were sophisticated executives, novelists, or university professors. On the basis of the subjects' recollections and his impressions of their recollections, Levinson proposed a series of distinct stages of adult development (see Figure 4-5).

In brief, Levinson's view is that after a transitional time of breaking away from their preadult world, men devote most of their twenties to entering and exploring the adult world and "to creating a stable life structure" by embarking on careers and beginning a family. At the end of their twenties most men begin a stressful transitional period in which they take stock of their lives and seek to restructure them in more satisfying ways. This accomplished, they settle down for most of their thirties, tending to family life and seeking advancement in their careers. Then the cycle of stability and turbulence repeats. As men enter their forties they undergo a transition to middle adulthood, which for most is a crisis, a time of great struggle or even of feeling struck down. The dream of becoming rich and famous—or the illusion that fame and fortune guarantee happiness—is

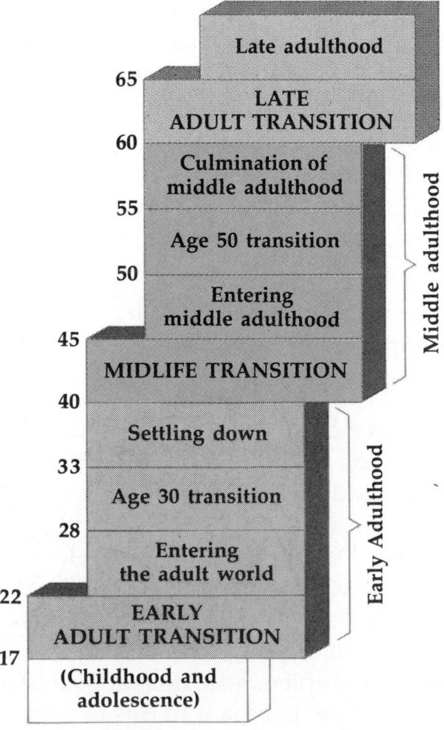

Figure 4-5 *Developmental periods in early and middle male adulthood as proposed by Levinson.*

given up; work and family commitments are called into question; and turmoil and despair result. When this painful growth period is concluded, at about age 45, men again settle into new or deepened attachments and to completing their careers. The basic idea, then, is that life's progression is a predictable cycle of stability and crisis.

"How many of us older persons have really been . . . prepared for the second half of life, for old age, death and eternity?"
Carl Jung,
Modern Man in Search of a Soul, 1933

Two other psychiatrists, George Vaillant (1977) and Roger Gould (1978), reported somewhat similar findings based on their observations of adults—Vaillant from a follow-up study of 94 Harvard alumni who were interviewed as undergraduates and reinterviewed in their early thirties and late forties, and Gould from 524 respondents to a questionnaire survey of 16- to 50-year-olds. Although Vaillant and Gould define stages that differ somewhat from each other's and from Levinson's, and that encompass different ages, they agree that the early forties are a time of turbulence and transition to the more settled life of middle age. However, whereas Gould sees the midlife crisis as agonizing, and Levinson sees it as dramatic, Vaillant maintains that it is relatively mild.

"The term midlife crisis *brings to mind some variation of the renegade minister who leaves behind four children and the congregation that loved him in order to drive off in a magenta Porsche with a twenty-five-year-old striptease artiste. . . . As with adolescent turmoil, [such] mid-life crises are much rarer in* community *samples than in* clinical *samples."*
George Vaillant (1977, pp. 222–223)

Other researchers are skeptical about any attempt to define adult life in neatly packaged stages, especially those based merely on Levinson's and Vaillant's interviews with a select few people, most of whom were high achievers and all of whom were males. To generalize from their career-oriented lives and to use their "midlife crises" to explain or justify the renouncing of old relationships would be both misleading and dangerous (Gilligan, 1982). Contrary to the new stereotype, job dissatisfaction, marital dissatisfaction, divorce, anxiety, and suicide do not—and certainly need not—surge during the early forties (Costa & McCrae, 1980; Scanzoni & Scanzoni, 1981; Schaie & Geiwitz, 1982). Moreover, the ***social clock***—the cultural prescription of "the right age" to leave home, get a job, marry, have children, and retire—varies from culture to culture and era to era. In Turkey, 76 percent of brides are in their teens; in Belgium, only 35 percent are (United Nations, 1980). In Western nations, contemporary women, with their smaller families and raised self-expectations, are increasingly entering the workplace and classroom during middle adulthood, if not before. In earlier times, such ventures outside the home were often frowned upon.

"Goodbye, Alice. I've got to get this California thing out of my system."

Life Events

Given the variations in the social clock, the critics suspect that any proposed timetable of ages and stages will have limited generality. More important than age per se are one's historical and cultural setting (being divorced in 1985 does not mean what it meant in 1955) and one's life events, regardless of age. Retirement marks a transition to a new life stage whenever it occurs.

Graduation from college often marks the entrance into the world of work, and retirement, the passage from it. Such significant life events mark transitions in adult development much as physical and cognitive changes due to maturing do in infancy, childhood, and adolescence.

Even chance encounters can have lasting significance, deflecting us down one road rather than another (Bandura, 1982). The actress Nancy Davis might never have met her future husband had she not, through a mix-up, begun to receive announcements of communist meetings intended for another person of the same name. Fearing that her career might be jeopardized by this mistaken identity, she went to see the president of the Screen Actors Guild. Before long she and this man, Ronald Reagan, were wed (Reagan & Libby, 1980). Given the impact of "chance" encounters, it is small wonder that one of the most experienced researchers of adult development, Bernice Neugarten (1980), concludes that "adults change far more, and far less predictably, than the oversimplified stage theories suggest." Nevertheless, we can credit theories of adult life stages with sensitizing us to the principle that development is indeed lifelong.

"Two roads diverged in a wood, and I—
I took the one less traveled by,
And that has made all the difference."
Robert Frost,
The Road Not Taken, 1916

"That power which erring men call chance."
John Milton,
Comus, 1634

Summing up the case against a stage view of adulthood, Neugarten (1979) writes:

> It is a truism, even though it sometimes goes unmentioned, that the psychological preoccupations of adults are recurrent. They appear and reappear in new forms over long periods of time. This being so, it is something of a distortion to describe adulthood as a series of discrete and neatly bounded stages, as if adult life were a staircase.

Let's now look at some of the psychological preoccupations that do, in fact, recur throughout adulthood.

Commitments of Adulthood

Theorists of adulthood from a variety of perspectives have called our attention to two basic adult needs. Erik Erikson called them intimacy and generativity. Personality theorist Abraham Maslow (1968) described them as a need to love and belong, which, when met, triggers a need for success and esteem. Contemporary researchers have chosen other terms—affiliation and achievement, attachment and productivity, commitment and competence. But Sigmund Freud (1935) put it most simply: The healthy adult, he said, is one who can love and work. For most adults, *love* is centered on family commitments toward spouse, parents, and children. *Work* is one's other productive activities, including one's career.

"Happiness, I have discovered, is nearly always a rebound from hard work."
David Grayson, 1870–1946

Marriage and Family "Traditional" families—father, mother, and children under 18—compose only 30 percent of American households (Bureau of the Census, 1982). Who are the other 70 percent? They are the divorced and their children, the widowed, the older couples with an empty nest, the singles, the cohabiting men and women, and the childless (or voluntarily "child-free") married people. Despite the alternatives to marriage, and the celebration of single life, most young adults marry and most who get divorced remarry. Indeed, 95 percent of Americans age 35 and over have been married, and among the women of this group 92 percent have had a child (Bureau of the Census, 1982).

The number of single-parent families has risen. Although single parents often experience more stress than do parents in traditional families, most function effectively.

Having a child is usually a happy event, and one that often makes people feel more mature. However, as children begin to absorb one's time, money, and emotional energy, satisfaction with the marriage itself tends to decline (Rollins & Galligan, 1978). Whether the decline is due to children or to other factors linked to aging and years of marriage is difficult to discern.

An equally significant event in family life is when the children leave home. Consider your parents' experience: If you still live with your parents, in what ways will their lives change when you leave? If you have left home, did your parents suffer an "empty nest syndrome"—were either

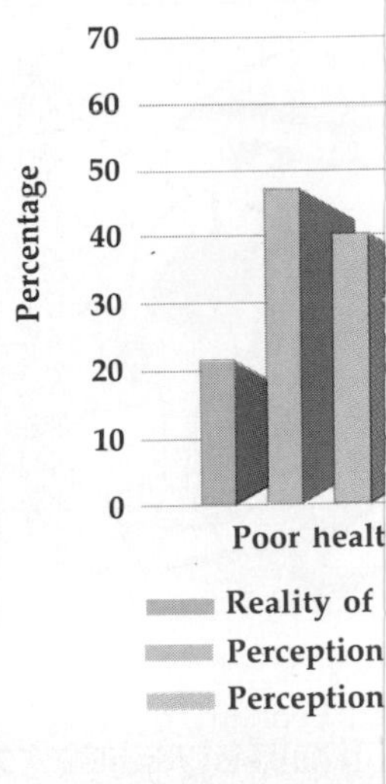

of your parents distressed by a loss of purpose and relationship? Or did your parents discover renewed freedom, relaxation, and satisfaction with their own relationship? If you have children, how did you or will you feel upon their leaving home?

Contrary to the myth of the empty nest syndrome, the empty nest for most couples is a happy place. As Neugarten (1974, p. 38) commented,

> Just as the major problem of middle-aged women is not the menopause, it is also not the empty nest. Most women are glad to see their children grow up, leave home, marry, and have their careers. The notion that they mourn the loss of their reproductive ability and their mother role does not seem to fit modern reality. No matter what the stereotypes tell us, it is not the way women talk when you listen.

"Appearances notwithstanding, for women, at least, midlife is not a stage tied to chronological age. Rather, it belongs to that point in the life cycle of the family when the children are grown and gone, or nearly so—when, perhaps for the first time in her adult life, a woman can attend to her own needs, her own desires, her own development as a separate and autonomous being."
Lillian B. Rubin (1979)

Work A large part of the answer to "Who are you?" is the answer to "What do you do?" Much of what adults do (to fulfill their need to feel productive and competent) is (1) to raise children and (2) to undertake a career. Predicting people's career choices and guiding them toward satisfying vocations is a complex matter. Because it often takes time for people to settle into one vocation and because of the impact of chance encounters, there will always remain a large element of unpredictability. For example, during the first 2 years of college most students cannot accurately predict their later career path. Most students shift from their initially intended majors while in college, many find their postcollege employment in fields not directly related to their majors, and most will change careers at least once (Astin & Panos, 1969). To many career counselors, this means that the best education is not a narrow vocational training, but rather a broad liberal education that prepares one for the varied demands of an uncertain future.

For men—and increasingly for women—careers are a major focus of adulthood.

However, some adults do eventually suffer a tragic loss of brain neurons. A series of small strokes, a brain tumor, or alcoholism can result in progressive brain damage causing senility. One of the most feared diseases of aging, Alzheimer's disease, strikes even more people—5 to 10 percent—causing a relentlessly progressive senility that can steal even the brightest minds. Memory, thinking, and language gradually deteriorate, and delusions creep in. Often the situation is worsened by others who mistakenly believe the condition represents some form of mental laziness. The tragedy of Alzheimer's disease was captured by Robert Sayre's (1979) account of his father shouting at his afflicted mother to "think harder" when she could not remember where she had put something, and of his mother, confused, embarrassed, on the verge of tears, randomly searching the house to find whatever she had misplaced. In 1983, researchers reported that the disease is linked to an unexplained deterioration of specific neurons that produce acetylcholine, an important neurotransmitter. The brain's neural pathways are still present, but without this neurotransmitter some of them go dead. Combined with developments in brain transplants (see Chapter 2), this finding has raised hopes that someday treatment of Alzheimer's disease may become possible.

"What is it, Leonard?
What happened to your lust for life?"

Cognitive Development

What should society do with its elderly? Retire them? Or capitalize on their experience? Does a 75-year-old person retain the agility of mind, the flexibility of thought, and the judgment required to lead a nation? More personally, for what tasks are our minds especially well suited during early, middle, and later adulthood?

"It is always in season for the old to learn."
Aeschylus, 525–456 B.C.,
Fragments

Assessing the cognitive abilities of older people is complicated. For example, how well do they learn and remember? As we noted earlier, it depends: Are they being asked simply to *recognize* what they have tried to memorize (little decline), or to *recall* it without clues (more decline). Actually, the truth is even more complicated. If the information being recalled is meaningless—remembering nonsense syllables, saying five digits backward—then the older you are, the more errors you may make. But the elderly's rich web of existing knowledge aids their catching of meaningful information; thus their capacity to learn and remember meaningful material shows little decline with age (Labouvie-Vief & Schell, 1982; Perlmutter, 1983).

The ability to learn is one aspect of intelligence (see Chapter 12, "Intelligence"). So, in the twilight years do people tend to become less intelligent? The evolving answer to this question makes an interesting research story, one that illustrates science's self-correcting process. At any stage of scientific inquiry, conclusions may be reached that seem sound, that meet ready social acceptance, and that shape social policy. But then an awareness grows of shortcomings in the research, and new studies must be done. This particular research story has progressed through three phases.

Phase I: Cross-sectional Evidence for Intellectual Decline

In ***cross-sectional studies,*** people of various ages are tested at the same time. When administering intelligence tests to representative samples of people, researchers consistently found that older adults gave fewer correct answers than younger adults (see Figure 4-9). The growth and decline of intelligence bore out the adage, it seemed, that whatever goes up must come down. As David Wechsler (1972, p. 30), creator of the widely used adult intelligence test, put it, "the decline of mental ability with age is part of the general [aging] process of the organism as a whole."

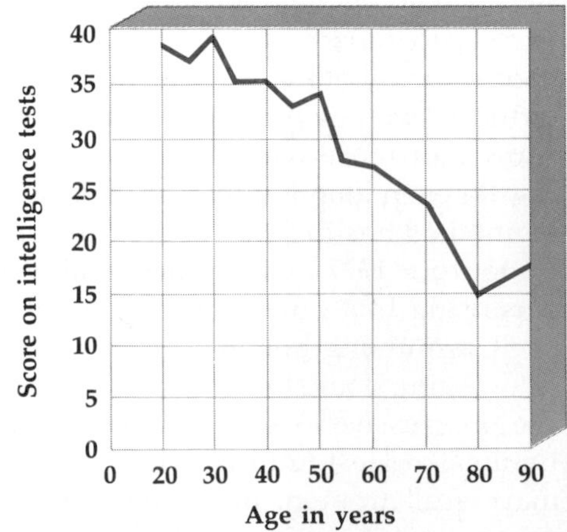

Figure 4-9 *When intelligence tests were administered to representative samples of adults of various ages, older adults consistently got fewer questions correct than younger adults. But see Figure 4-10.*

Until the 1950s, this rather dismal view of intelligence declining with age remained essentially unchallenged. During this period, many corporations were establishing mandatory retirement policies under the presumption that the company would benefit by replacing aging workers with younger, presumably more capable, employees. As everyone "knew," you cannot teach an old dog new tricks.

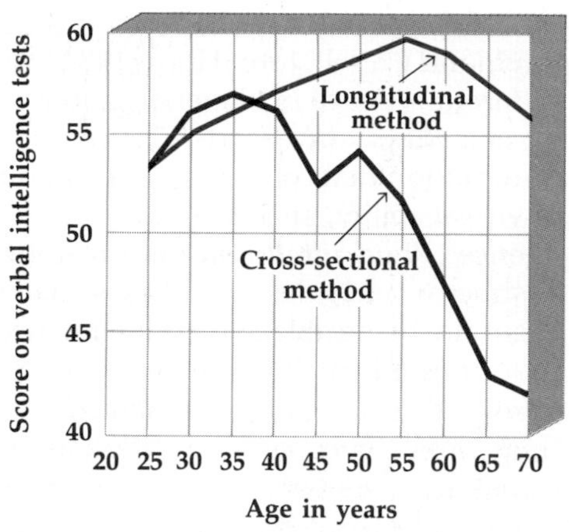

Figure 4-10 *In this test of verbal intelligence, when the cross-sectional method was used (the same method as in the Figure 4-9 studies), scores were observed to drop with age. But when the longitudinal method was used (in which the same people were retested over a period of years) scores rose until late adulthood.*

Phase II: Longitudinal Evidence for Intellectual Stability

Colleges began administering intelligence tests to freshmen about 1920. So by the 1950s it was possible to find 50-year-olds who had taken an intelligence test 30 years earlier. Several psychologists saw their chance to study intelligence ***longitudinally*** by retesting the same people over a period of years. What they expected to find was the usual decrease in intelligence after about age 30 (Schaie & Geiwitz, 1982). What they actually found was a surprise (Figure 4-10): Intelligence remained stable, and on some tests even increased!

How then are we to account for the previous findings from the cross-sectional studies? In retrospect, researchers saw the problem. Whenever a cross-sectional study compares people of different ages, age is not the only factor that influences the result. There is also something called the cohort, or generation, factor at work. In this case the average 70-year-old and the average 30-year-old who were tested in 1950 were born and raised in different eras, offering different opportunities. So when comparing 70- and 30-year-olds, one compares not only people of two different ages, but also less educated people with more educated people, people raised in large families with people raised in smaller families, and so forth.

"Ah, nothing is too late
'Til the tired heart shall cease to palpitate.
Cato learned Greek at eighty, Sophocles
Wrote his grand Oedipus, and Simonides
Bore off the prize of verse from his compeers
When each had numbered more than
fourscore years."
Henry Wadsworth Longfellow,
1807–1882, at age 68

According to this new, more optimistic view, the "old myth" that intelligence sharply declines with age had been laid to rest. As everyone "knows," you're never too old to learn. Dr. John Rock, who at age 70 developed the birth control pill, Grandma Moses, who at age 76 took up painting, and architect Frank Lloyd Wright, who at age 89 designed New York's Guggenheim Museum, are only a few whose activities lend support to the view of psychologist David Krech that, "He who lives by his wits, dies *with* his wits" (quoted by Diamond, 1978).

Phase III: It All Depends

But the controversy was not, and still is not, over. First, longitudinal studies have their own pitfalls. If more intelligent people live longer (which they do), and if they suffer less decline in intelligence with age (which also tends to be true), then the longitudinal studies may be selecting the very people whose intelligence is least likely to decline.

Recognizing the value of their experience, the Small Business Administration engages retired executives in offering the wisdom of their crystallized intelligence to younger business people.

Psychologists are increasingly convinced that intelligence is not a single trait (see Chapter 12). Intelligence tests that were designed to assess school abilities—including speed of thinking—may place older adults at a disadvantage, since their neural mechanisms for processing information are slower than those of younger people. And, in fact, some researchers find that on tests involving speed of response, senior citizens do perform relatively poorly (Cerella, 1985; Woodruff, 1983). A 70-year-old is probably no match for a 20-year-old at Pac-Man. But slower need not mean less intelligent. Given other tests that assess general vocabulary, knowledge, and ability to integrate information, older adults generally hold their own. Researcher Paul Baltes (1983) proposes a test of "wisdom"—one that would assess traits such as expertise and sound judgment. His informed hunch is that, on such a test, older adults might more than hold their own.

"In youth we learn, in age we understand."
Marie Ebner von Eschenbach,
Aphorism, 1905

Building on a distinction originally suggested by intelligence expert Raymond Cattell, John Horn (1982) proposes that we all possess two quite different types of intelligence, and that these are quite differently affected by age. ***Crystallized intelligence*** is basically the accumulation of stored information that comes with education and experience. For example, tests of verbal ability, such as vocabulary tests, tend to reflect crystallized intelligence. ***Fluid intelligence*** is presumed to reflect one's ability to reason abstractly, and is less closely associated with one's stored knowledge. For example, being able to identify the next letter in the series d f i m r x e ___ reflects fluid intelligence (Horn, 1982). When these are assessed separately, it turns out that crystallized intelligence *increases* with age, while fluid intelligence *decreases*. Perhaps this helps explain why mathematicians and scientists often do their most notable work during their late twenties or early thirties, while those in literature, history, and philosophy tend to produce their best work later—in their forties, fifties, and beyond, after more knowledge has accumulated (Denney, 1982). So, while the controversy is not yet resolved, it seems that whether intelligence increases or decreases with age depends partly on what type of intellectual performance is measured.

"I used to be old, too, but it wasn't my cup of tea."

Social Development

Life Satisfaction

Although few grow old gratefully, many do so gracefully. Not only does marital satisfaction rise during the retirement years, but satisfaction with life in general is relatively high (Figure 4-11). Contrary to the stereotyped image of crotchety old people, national surveys have repeatedly found that feelings of happiness and well-being tend to be higher among today's elderly than among younger adults (Herzog & others, 1982). Particularly for those older adults not yet facing serious health problems, life tends to seem less burdensome, less trying, and freer than it does to younger adults.

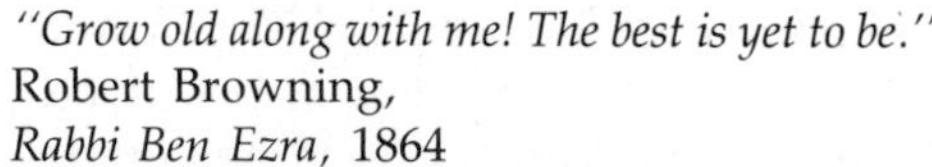

"Grow old along with me! The best is yet to be."
Robert Browning,
Rabbi Ben Ezra, 1864

Among the elderly, the happiest tend to be those who are married, financially secure, religiously devout, close to friends, and, especially, in good health (Herzog & others, 1982; Dickie & others, 1979). In fact, when asked what makes them happy or unhappy, older adults mention "health" far more frequently than any other factor.

With the tasks of the earlier adult years behind them, many older adults have more time to enjoy pursuing their personal interests. No wonder their satisfaction with life is generally high, especially if they are relatively healthy.

According to Erikson (Table 4-2), the final task, or crisis, of adulthood is achieving a sense of ***integrity***—that is, arriving at a feeling that

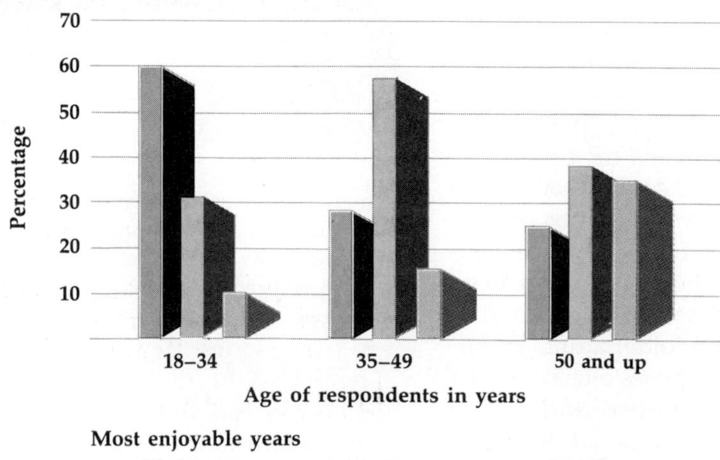

Figure 4-11 *Which time of adult life is most enjoyable? Most young adults think young adulthood is. But even better times may lie ahead. Three-fourths of those 35 or older think life's most enjoyable years are during middle or late adulthood.*

Table 4-2 **Erickson's psychological stages (postchildhood)**

Approximate age	Stage descriptions
Adolescence (teen years)	**Identity vs. Role Confusion** Teenager works at developing a sense of self by integrating roles into one identity.
Young Adulthood (20–40 years)	**Intimacy vs. Isolation** Young adult struggles to form close relationships, gaining a capacity for intimate love.
Middle Adulthood (40–65 years)	**Generativity vs. Stagnation** Middle-aged person seeks a sense of contributing to the world, through, for example, raising children.
Late Adulthood (65 years and up)	**Integrity vs. Despair** Reflecting on life, the elderly person may experience satisfaction or a sense of failure.

one's life has been meaningful. Those who cannot do this—who feel that they have failed to realize their goals or to make a contribution to others' well-being—are likely to approach their final days with a sense of despair. Those who do achieve integrity look back on their lives with a sense of completion. Keenly aware of their mortality, they review their relationships and accomplishments and judge that, yes, life has been good.

"He is the happiest man who can trace an unbroken connection between the end of his life and the beginning."
Goethe, 1749–1832,
Maxims and Reflections

Death and Dying

Those who live to old age must suffer and cope with the deaths of relatives and friends. Usually, the most difficult separation is that from one's spouse—a loss suffered by five times more women than men. Grief is especially severe when the death of a loved one comes before its expected time on the social clock. The accidental death of a teenage child, or the sudden heart attack that claims a 45-year-old husband-father, may trigger mourning that lasts a year or more, and mild depression that sometimes continues for several additional years (Lehman & others, 1985). Although the sense of separation and loss may continue to life's end, most emerge from the vale of tears, turning their attention outward again and regaining a more positive view of life (Glick & others, 1974).

For survivors such as this grieving widow on Memorial Day, death is especially tragic when it comes before its appointed time on the social clock.

Those who die gradually due to a terminal illness usually are obliged to cope with the realization of their impending death. In looking at dying, we see that once again the stage theorists have arrived ahead of us. From her interviews with dying patients, Elizabeth Kübler-Ross (1969) proposed that these patients pass through a sequence of five stages in this coping process: *denial* of the terminal condition, *anger* and resentment ("Why me?"), *bargaining* with God or physicians for more time, *depression* stemming from the impending loss of everything and everyone, and, finally, peaceful *acceptance* of one's fate.

The critics of Kübler-Ross's proposal first question the generality of the stages, stressing that each dying person's experience is unique (Kastenbaum & Costa, 1977). Moreover, they argue, the simplified stages ignore many important factors; for example, people who are old tend to view death with less expressed fear and resentment (Wass & others, 1978–1979). Critics also express concern about the eagerness with which the death-and-dying formula has been popularized in courses and books. The danger, they fear, is that rather than having their feelings respected, dying people may be analyzed or manipulated in terms of the stereotyped stages: "She's just going through the anger stage."

*"Do not go gentle into that good night,
Old age should burn and rave at close of day;
Rage, rage against the dying of the light."*
Dylan Thomas,
Do Not Go Gentle into That Good Night,
1952, a poem written to his father
as he lay peacefully dying

Nevertheless, the death-education movement has enabled us to deal more openly and humanely with death and grief. A growing number of individuals are now helped to die with dignity by the ***hospice*** movement, whose staff and volunteers work in special facilities and in people's homes to support the dying and their families. We can be grateful that death-denying practices are being dislodged. For when death is faced with dignity and openness, it helps a person to complete the life cycle with a sense of the meaningfulness and unity of life—that one's existence has been good and that one's life and death have their place in the ongoing cycle of life. Although death may be unwelcome, life itself can be affirmed even at death.

If our attitudes toward death are sometimes contradictory, it is because death itself contains a contradiction: It is both the enemy of life—to be dreaded and avoided—and the completion of life—to be accepted with peace and dignity. It is as much a part of the life cycle as birth and growth. In the end death always wins, and yet it always loses: Life goes on.

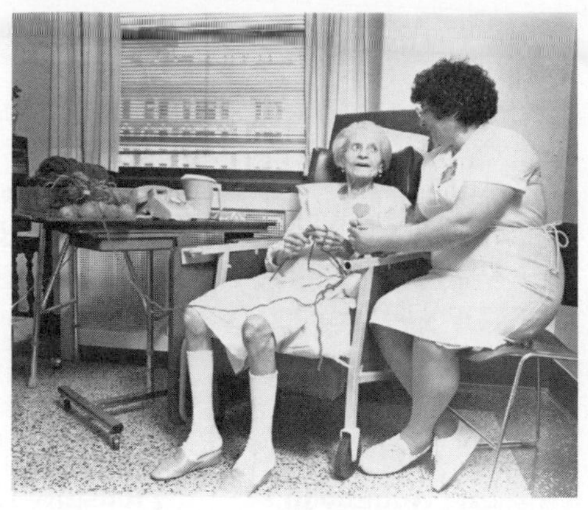

Hospice workers seek to enable dying persons to live and die with dignity and to aid their families in dealing with the impending loss. The hospice movement is but one sign of the more open and understanding attitudes toward death and grief in America today.

REFLECTIONS ON THE DEVELOPMENTAL ISSUES

Our journey through developmental psychology began in Chapter 3 by identifying two pervasive issues: (1) whether development is steered more by genes or experience and (2) whether development is a gradual, continuous process or a discontinuous one. It is time now to step back and take stock of current thinking on each issue.

Genes and Experience

Everyone agrees: Each of us is influenced by genes *and* experience working together. The real question is: How important is each? For physical attributes such as height, the genetic factor predominates. For psychological attributes, the answer is less obvious. In Chapter 12, we will examine the thorny issue of genetic versus environmental determinants of intelligence. For now, let us consider the provocative findings of several recent investigations into the inheritance of personal and social traits.

Separated at birth, the Mallifert twins meet accidentally.

Twin Studies

Do identical twins, being genetic replicas of one another, develop more similar personalities than fraternal twins, who are no more alike genetically than any other siblings? To find out, Birgitta Floderus-Myrhed and her colleagues (1980) administered tests of extraversion (outgoingness) and neuroticism (psychological instability) to nearly 13,000 pairs of Swedish identical and fraternal twins. Their finding: On both personality dimensions identical twins were much more similar than fraternal twins were, suggesting that there is substantial genetic influence on both traits.

To see if similar findings would be obtained on other dimensions of personality, John Loehlin and Robert Nichols (1976) gave a battery of questionnaires to 850 identical and fraternal twin pairs who were identified while competing for National Merit scholarships. Once again, identical twins were substantially more similar, and in a variety of ways—in abilities, personality, and even interests. However, the identical twins also reported being treated more alike than did fraternal twins, raising the possibility that their rearing rather than their genes accounts for their similarity. Not so, said Loehlin and Nichols, because identical twins

"The best explanation for the twin data in our study and in the literature is that about half of the variation among people in a broad spectrum of psychological traits is due to differences among the people in genetic characteristics."
Robert Nichols (1978)

whose parents treated them very similarly were *not* psychologically more alike than identical twins who were treated less similarly.

Better than studying identical twins who *recall* being reared differently would be to study identical twins who were actually reared in different environments. As we noted in Chapter 2, to the extent that such twins differ from one another, one could only credit their differing environments. Thus in 1979 when University of Minnesota psychologist Thomas Bouchard read a newspaper account of the reuniting of 39-year-old twins who had been separated from infancy, he seized the opportunity and flew them to Minneapolis for extensive tests. What Bouchard was looking for were differences; what "the Jim twins," Jim Lewis and Jim Springer, presented were amazing similarities (Holden, 1980a, 1980b). Both had married women named Linda, divorced, and married women named Betty. One had a son James Alan, the other a son James Allan. Both had dogs named Toy, chain-smoked Salems, served as sheriff's deputies, drove Chevrolets, chewed their fingernails to the nub, enjoyed stock car racing, had basement workshops, and had built circular white benches around trees in their yards. They also had similar medical histories: Both had gained 10 pounds at about the same time and then lost it; both had suffered what they mistakenly believed were heart attacks, and both had begun having late-afternoon headaches at age 18.

Equally striking similarities were presented by twins Oskar Stohr and Jack Yufe, one of whom was raised by his grandmother in Germany as a Catholic and a Nazi, while the other was raised by his father in the Caribbean as a Jew. Nevertheless, they share peculiarities galore: They like spicy foods and sweet liqueurs, have a habit of falling asleep in front of the television, flush the toilet before using it, store rubber bands on their wrists, and dip buttered toast in their coffee. Stohr is domineering toward women and yells at his wife, as did Yufe before he was separated.

Aided by the publicity of magazine and newspaper stories, Bouchard and his team of 16 colleagues have located and studied some 3 dozen identical twins reared apart. They continue to be impressed by the similarities not only of tastes and physical attributes but also of test measurements of personality, abilities, and even fears. The more bizarre similarities—such as flushing the toilet before using it—exist not because we have genes for specific behaviors, contends Bouchard, but because, presented with a similar range of options, similarly disposed people tend to make similar choices.

The cute stories do not impress Bouchard's critics. They contend that if any two strangers of the same sex and age were to spend hours comparing their behaviors and life histories, they would likely discover a string of coincidental similarities. Even the more impressive data from the personality measurements (Bouchard, 1984) are clouded by the fact that many of the separated twins were actually together for several months before adoption, or had been reunited for some years after reunion before being tested. Moreover, as we noted in Chapter 2, adoption agencies tend to place separated twins in similar homes. Nevertheless, the Swedish, National Merit, and Minnesota twin studies are an improvement over earlier twin studies, and they illustrate why scientific opinion is shifting toward a greater appreciation of genetic influences, and why further research is needed.

"The Jim twins." Despite having been separated at birth, these identical twins have remarkable similarities. Here each is shown in his basement carpentry workshop, only one of the "coincidences" psychologist Thomas Bouchard discovered.

"In some domains it looks as though our identical twins reared apart are . . . just as similar as identical twins reared together. Now that's an amazing finding and I can assure you none of us would have expected that degree of similarity."
Thomas Bouchard (1981)

Coincidences are not unique to twins. Patricia Kern of Colorado was born March 13, 1941 and named Patricia Ann Campbell. Patricia DiBiasi of Oregon also was born March 13, 1941 and named Patricia Ann Campbell. Both had fathers named Robert, worked as bookkeepers, and have children ages 21 and 19. Both studied cosmetology, enjoy oil painting as a hobby, and married military men—within eleven days of each other—in 1959. Patricia and Patricia are not genetically related.
Adapted from an Associated Press report, May 2, 1983

Adoption Studies

Do other methods of assessing the genetic factor confirm the heritability of personality? Sandra Scarr (Scarr, 1982; Scarr & Weinberg, 1983) and John Loehlin and his colleagues (1981, 1982, 1985) sought an answer by studying several hundred adoptive families in Minnesota and Texas, respectively. The most striking finding of these studies is that people who grow up together do *not* much resemble one another in personality, whether they are biologically related or not. Moreover, in many studies of ordinary families the personalities of parents have been astonishingly unrelated to the personalities of their children. Sandra Scarr (1981, p. 889) summarized the findings vividly:

> It would have to be concluded that upper-middle class brothers who attended the same school and whose parents took them to the same plays, sporting events, music lessons, and therapists and used similar child-rearing practices on them would be found to be only slightly more similar to each other in personality measures than to working-class or farm boys, whose lives would be totally different.

"Shared genes plus *shared environments do not seem to make family members much alike."*
John C. Loehlin, Joseph M. Horn, and Lee Willerman (1981)

"Our studies suggest that there's virtually no family environmental effect on personality. . . . These data say that in any reasonable environment, people will become what they will become."
Sandra Scarr (1984)

It remains for future research to explain why identical twins are so much alike in personality when biological parent-child and sibling pairs are so little alike. Is it because identical twins share not only the same individual genes but also the same combinations of genes? Is it because they tend not only to be treated alike by parents and friends but, being the same age, also to experience the same cultural influences simultaneously? And why the lack of resemblance among ordinary family members? Is it because even though siblings share genes, each sibling has a very different combination of genes? Is it because personality is shaped by unmeasurable differences in the environments (including differing peer influences, birth orders, and so forth) experienced by the different siblings of a family? Might sibling differences be triggered by brothers and sisters comparing and contrasting themselves with one another, perhaps unconsciously distancing themselves in an effort to create their own identities? All these possibilities have been suggested.

Studies of adopted families have provided new clues to hereditary and environmental influences on development. How similar would you expect these children to be to their adoptive parents and siblings? To their biological parents and siblings?

While the personalities of adopted children do not much resemble those of their adoptive parents, these studies have shown adoption to have many positive effects. First, in ways such as their values and social attitudes, the children were demonstrably influenced by their home environments. Second, the adoptive homes studied were nearly all good homes, in which child neglect and abuse were virtually unheard of. So it is not surprising that nearly all the adoptive children thrived. They developed higher IQs than their biological parents, and they almost surely became happier and more stable people than they would have become had they remained in a neglectful environment. Such benefits—shared by nearly all adoptive children—are real. Children need not resemble their adoptive parents to have benefited greatly from adoption.

Temperament

Infants and young children cannot take personality tests. So investigators have instead observed their actual behavior and inferred from it the infant's temperament. ***Temperament*** is a catchall term for the rudiments of personality and generally refers to the child's emotional excitability—that is, whether the child is reactive, intense, and fidgety, or easygoing, quiet, and placid.

From the first weeks of life, some—easy—babies are cheerful, relaxed, and predictable in feeding and sleeping. Other—difficult—babies are more irritable, intense, and unpredictable (Thomas & Chess, 1977, 1981). Infant monkeys also vary in temperament. From birth, some are fearful, and others are more relaxed (Suomi, 1983). Are such temperamental differences hereditary?

"All parents are environmentalists . . . until they have their second child."
Child psychiatrist Stella Chess (quoted by Lerner, 1983)

Several lines of evidence point to the heritability of temperament. Various animal species have been selectively bred to be either highly reactive or easygoing. In one such study, Kirsti Lagerspetz (1979), a Finnish psychologist, took normal albino mice and bred the most aggressive ones with one another and the least aggressive ones with one another. After repeating this for 26 generations, she had one set of fierce mice and one of placid mice.

Judging from the greater temperamental similarity of identical than fraternal twins, genes seem to help determine human temperament, too (Buss & Plomin, 1975; Goldsmith, 1983). This conclusion also seems supported by the finding that newborns of different ethnic groups (and with slightly differing genetic heritages) exhibit differing temperaments. Chinese and American Indian babies (who share a common Asian descent) tend to be less reactive and irritable than Caucasian and black babies. If restrained, undressed, or covered with a cloth, Caucasian babies will typically respond more intensely (Freedman, 1979).

Even the father of modern environmentalism, philosopher John Locke, was something of a hereditarian when it came to temperament: "Few of *Adam's* Children are so happy, as not to be born with some [bias] in their natural Temper" (quoted by Loehlin, 1983).

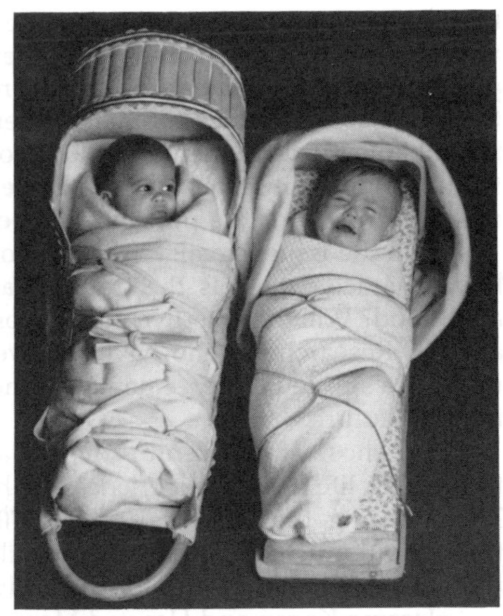

Most Navajo babies calmly accept the cradleboard; Caucasian babies protest vigorously. Findings like these suggest that the rudiments of personality are to some extent genetically influenced.

To say, as we do, that genes and experience are *both* important is true. But it is still oversimplified. More precisely, their effects are intertwined, partly because genes direct experience (Scarr & McCartney, 1983). Imagine two babies, one genetically predisposed to be attractive, sociable, and easygoing, the other less so. Assume further that the first baby attracts more affectionate and stimulating care than the second, and so develops into a warmer and more outgoing person. Moreover, as the two children grow older, the more naturally outgoing one seeks out activities and friends that encourage further social confidence. What has caused their resulting personality difference? One cannot truthfully say that their personalities are formed of *X* percent genes and *Y* percent experience, for the gene-experience effect is combined. As in our imaginary example, one's genetically influenced traits may *evoke* significant responses in others. Moreover, as we grow older we *select environments* well suited to our natures. In such ways, our genes influence the experiences that shape us.

Physically punitive parents tend to have physically aggressive children. How might genes and environment interact *to explain this effect?*

Continuity and Discontinuity

The issue of continuity in development comes in two forms—the question of whether development occurs as a gradual, cumulative process or through discrete stages, and the question of whether development is more characterized by stability over time or by change.

Chapters 3 and 4 described three major stage theories: Jean Piaget's theory of cognitive development, Lawrence Kohlberg's theory of moral development, and Erik Erikson's theory of psychosocial development. As we have seen, these stage theories have been vigorously criticized as failing to recognize the early rudiments of later abilities (Piaget), as biased by a liberal worldview characteristic of educated males in Western cultures (Kohlberg), or as contradicted by research demonstrating that adult life does not progress up a fixed series of steps (Erikson and Levinson). Nevertheless, stage theories have served to encourage a developmental perspective on the whole life-span by suggesting how people at one age think and act differently when they arrive at a later age.

This leads us to the second question: Over time, are people's personalities consistent, or do they change? If reunited with a long-lost grade school friend, would you instantly recognize that "It's the same old Andy"? Or is a person at one period of life likely to be quite different at a

On some occasions, your identity is your gender.

As we grow up, we also learn our assigned ***gender roles***, the set of social expectations that prescribes how we, as males or females, should act. These roles—the behaviors *expected* of males and females—often strongly influence how we behave. Since they arise partly from the behaviors that we *perceive* to characterize males and females, it is vital for us to ask, *how* males and females differ and *why*. For example, do males and females differ in abilities? In social sensitivities? In social power and aggressiveness? If so, *why?* One's sex is a biological fact. Does that mean that gender differences are predisposed by genes? By hormones? By brain differences? One's sex—hereafter called "gender" to distinguish it from the purely biological connotations of "sex"—is also a social fact. So, are gender differences shaped by one's rearing? By the larger culture? By one's own thinking? Chapters 2, 3, and 4 indicated that the course of human development is directed by the interplay of biological and experiential factors. By pondering the puzzle of the genders, we can better appreciate how nature and nurture intertwine, and how difficult it is to disentangle them.

GENDER DIFFERENCES

How different are boys from girls? Young men from young women? Older men from older women? Note how the phrasing of the questions immediately draws our attention to the ways in which the genders differ, not to their similarities. In many ways—the age of first sitting up, teething, and walking, and in generosity, helpfulness, and overall intelligence, to name a few—males and females are not noticeably different (Maccoby, 1980). But because our attention is so invariably drawn to how we *differ* from others, these gender similarities are seldom mentioned. Similarities tend not to require explanation; differences do. In science, as in everyday life, differences provoke interest.

Between 1967 and June 1985, Psychological Abstracts, *the "reader's guide" to psychological research, indexed 16,416 articles on "human sex differences."*

It is also important to remember that "differences" are only differences between averages. Even in many demanding physical tasks, such as swimming and marathon running, the overlap between the sexes is considerable. The winner of the 1932 men's Olympic marathon in Los Angeles would have finished tenth in the 1984 women's Olympic marathon run in the same city. Tiffany Cohen's winning time in the 1984 women's Olympic 400-meter freestyle swim would have beaten that of the 1964 men's winner by more than 5 seconds.

Tiffany Cohen about to win the 1984 women's Olympic 400-meter freestyle. Don Schollander, the 1964 men's winner, though he set a world record, would have finished almost 10 meters behind her.

For the psychological traits we are about to consider, the overlap between women and men is even greater; the variations among women and among men far exceed those between the average woman and the average man. And that is why judgments about the suitability of people for particular roles and occupations are best made on an individual basis, without prejudgments based on gender. Could you become a competent engineer? Or child-care worker? Knowing that you are a man or a woman tells us little; knowing you as an individual would tell us much more.

We often exaggerate the number and the extent of differences between the sexes because we treat as real both the differences that actually exist and those we believe exist based on our perceptions (Unger, 1979). Just knowing that you are male or female triggers certain perceptions of you in people's minds. That perceived gender differences need not reflect actual gender differences is most obvious in infancy, where differences between the sexes in appearance and behavior are negligible. Without the obvious clues of pink or blue, people will struggle over whether to call the new baby a "he" or a "she." Nevertheless, fathers have been found to rate their day-old daughters as softer, smaller, and more beautiful, and their sons as firmer, stronger, and better coordinated (Rubin & others, 1974). And when John and Sandra Condry (1976) showed people a videotape of a 9-month-old infant reacting strongly to a jack-in-the-box, those told the child was a boy, "David," perceived "his" emotion as mostly anger; those told "she" was "Dana" perceived the identical reaction as mostly fear. So some gender differences exist not in the genders, but rather in the eyes of their beholders.

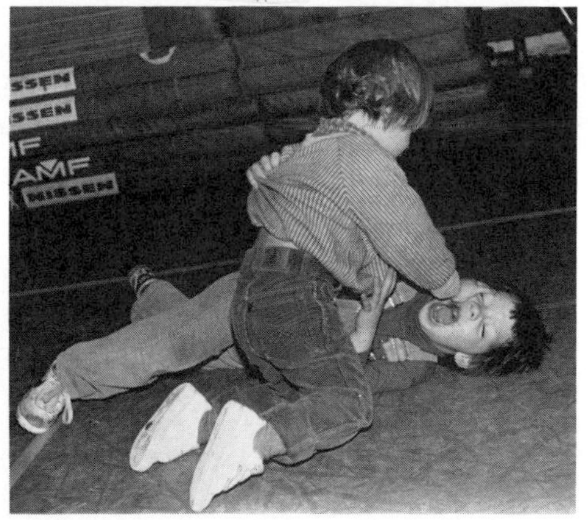

"Boys will be boys."

How Do Males and Females Differ?

Among the few differences in psychological traits and social behavior that seem actually to exist between males and females are the following:

Aggression

By ***aggression***, psychologists refer not to assertive, ambitious behavior (as in "Claire is an aggressive saleswoman") but rather to physical or verbal behavior that intends to hurt someone. In surveys, men admit to considerably more hostility and aggression than do women. To some extent, such admissions may simply reflect people's acceptance of the common perception that males are more aggressive. But in laboratory experiments, men are indeed somewhat more likely actually to behave aggressively by administering what they think are higher levels of hurtful electric shock (Hyde, 1984b). And in everyday American life, men are arrested for violent crimes eight times more often than women (FBI, 1984). Moreover, throughout the world, hunting, fighting, and warring are primarily men's activities. Eleanor Maccoby's review of research (1980, p. 216) leaves little doubt: "The tendency of males to be more aggressive than females is perhaps the most firmly established sex difference and is a characteristic that transcends cultures."

"There is little doubt that we would all be safer if the world's weapon systems were controlled by average women instead of by average men."
Melvin Konner (1982)

"This feels *terrific,* Henry."

Social Power

In every known society, men are socially dominant. When groups are formed, leadership tends to go to males. When political leaders are elected, they are usually men. When salaries are paid, those in traditionally male occupations are judged more deserving. Although these differences in social power are decided by groups, they are often reinforced by the behavior of individual men and women. In everyday behavior, men are more likely to act as powerful people do—to talk more assertively, to interrupt more, to smile less (Mayo & Henley, 1981).

"When rewards are distributed, the woman gets one half the pay that a man does, and if disgrace is given out she bears it all."
Elbert Hubbard,
The Philistine, 1897

Empathy

To have ***empathy*** is to understand and feel what another feels—to rejoice with those who rejoice, and weep with those who weep. When surveyed, women are far more likely to describe themselves as empathic than are men. But are they? In the laboratory, the empathy difference is smaller. Females are more likely to cry and to report feeling distressed at another's distress, perhaps partly because they are also slightly better than males at reading other people's nonverbal emotional cues (Eisenberg & Lennon,

Do women feel more empathy, or is it just that our society has granted them more freedom to recognize and express it?

1983). Yet physiological measures, such as heart rate, taken while someone observes another's emotional distress indicate that women do not consistently exhibit more distress. Similarly, when rating their reactions to pictures or videotapes of babies, women *report* much stronger reactions than men do. But measures of heart rate and perspiration failed to confirm that women actually respond more strongly (Berman, 1980). Perhaps women respond much as men do but are more aware of their emotional reactions or more willing to report them. If so, the self-report studies may simply demonstrate this greater awareness in women. So, women report and express more empathy, but this gender difference is difficult to demonstrate physiologically.

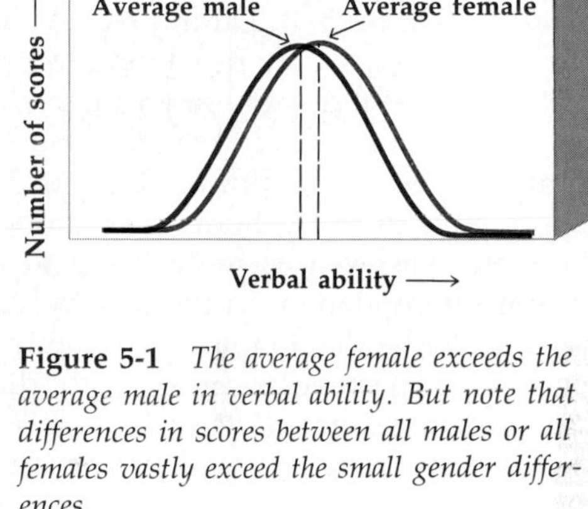

Figure 5-1 *The average female exceeds the average male in verbal ability. But note that differences in scores between all males or all females vastly exceed the small gender differences.*

Verbal and Spatial Abilities

Although the evidence is somewhat contradictory, females tend to average slightly higher than males on tests of verbal abilities such as spelling and comprehending difficult material (See Figure 5-1). This difference is most obvious among those who are especially slow to develop language; in remedial reading classes, boys outnumber girls by 3 to 1 (Finucci & Childs, 1981). Speech defects such as stuttering are also predominantly boys' problems.

On spatial tasks, such as the speed with which one can mentally rotate objects in space, males tend to surpass females (Linn & Peterson, 1986). (See Figure 5-2.) Spatial abilities are advantageous when playing chess, mentally rotating suitcases to see how they might fit in the car's trunk, and doing geometry problems. This may help to explain why annual results of the College Board's Scholastic Aptitude Test (SAT) show that males average about 50 points higher (on a scale of 200 to 800) on the mathematical aptitude portion. However, in spatial abilities, too, the overlap between the sexes is considerable, with the difference being most obvious among the mathematically superior. Among mathematically precocious seventh-graders (those scoring above 700 on the SAT mathematics test in nationwide talent searches), boys have outnumbered girls by 13 to 1 (Benbow & Stanley, 1983).

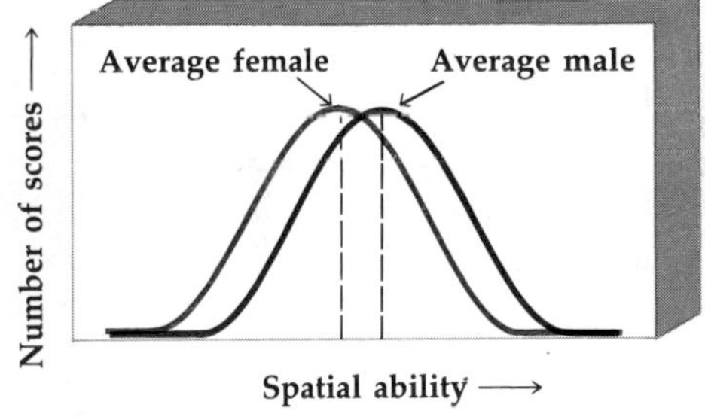

Figure 5-2 *The average male's spatial abilities surpass those of the average female. However, given the overlap of scores between the sexes, the small average differences cannot explain why 96 percent of American architects are men.*

Gender Differences Across the Life-Span

When do these average differences between men and women appear? Once developed, are they lifelong? By studying *when* gender differences emerge and whether they remain constant or change over the life-span, we can hope to gain more clues as to their origins, both biological and social.

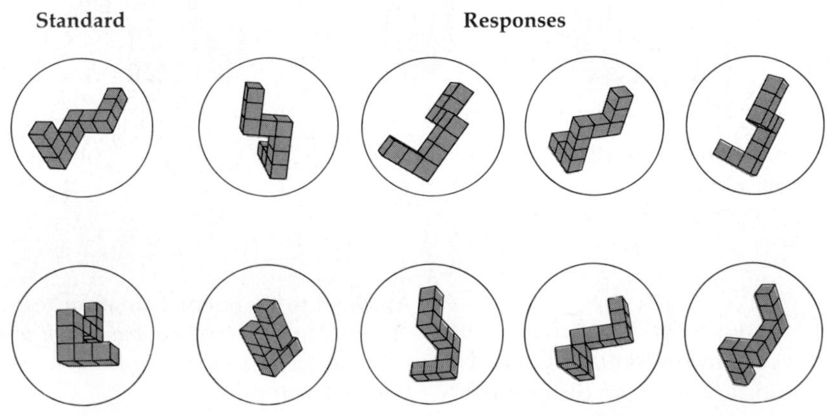

A test of spatial abilities: the mental rotation test. Which two responses show a different view of the standard? Answers on next page.

Early Development

The game and toy choices of boys and girls begin to diverge even during infancy. When Peter Smith and Linda Daglish (1977) observed 1- to 2-year-old British infants in their own homes, they found that, already, the boys were far more likely to prefer trucks and cars and the girls to prefer dolls and soft toys. By nursery school age, most boys and girls segregate themselves into same-sex play groups. Carol Jacklin and Eleanor Maccoby (1978) dressed unacquainted 3-year-olds in unisex clothing, often making it impossible for adults to identify the sex of the individual child. But the children could still tell; they interacted much more with playmates of their own sex (Figure 5-3). During elementary school, the sex segregation in play continues, with girls coming to prefer small-group play with a best friend or two, and boys preferring play in larger groups (Maccoby, 1980).

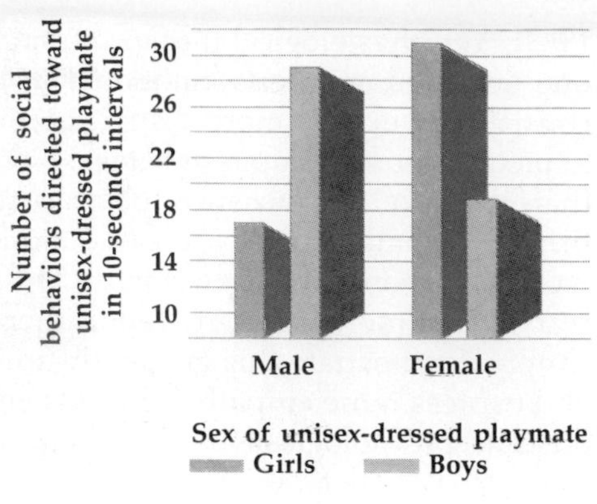

Figure 5-3 *At about 3 years old, unacquainted children dressed in unisex clothing direct more social behaviors toward playmates of their own sex.*

Gender differences in aggression and social power appear as soon as aggressive behavior appears, by 2 or 3 years of age (Hyde, 1984b). Preschool boys in many cultures are noticeably more rough-and-tumble in their play, as well as more likely to attempt to dominate their peers through intimidation. In the Jacklin-Maccoby study, girls placed with a boy partner tended to retreat or quietly watch the boy play with the toys; given a girl partner, the girls rarely did so. Moreover, girls often made cooperative gestures ("Let's do . . . "), and they were more eager than boys to share rewards equally rather than maximize their own gain (Maccoby, 1980). Such behaviors may be the rudiments of what developmental psychologist Carol Gilligan (see Chapter 4) believes to be a greater social concern among adult women.

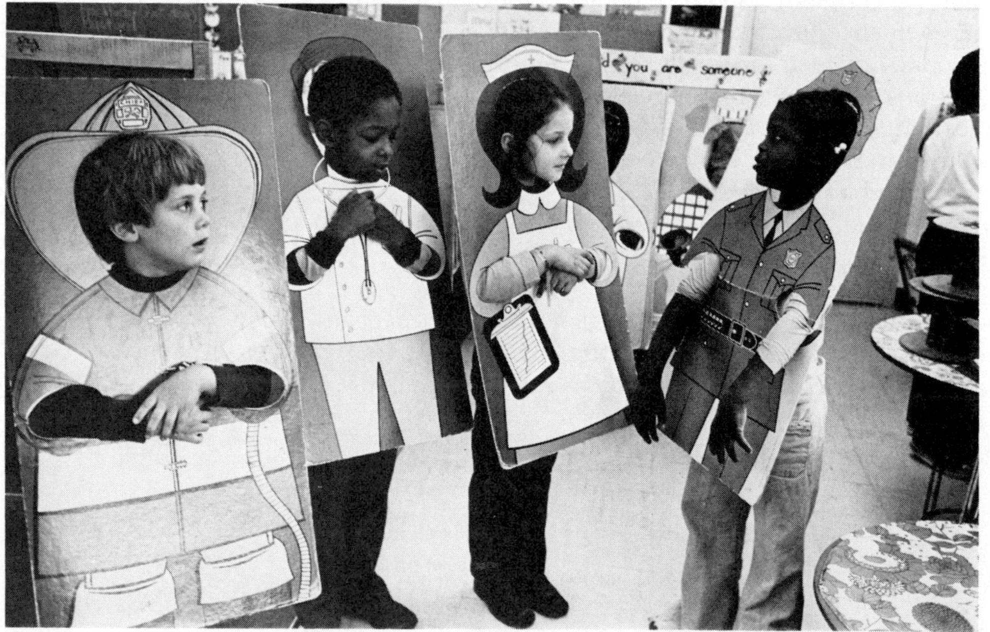

Gender differences show in children's play; adults reinforce these differences.

Although the gender difference in spatial abilities appears before puberty (Linn & Peterson, 1986), that in verbal abilities is not apparent until adolescence (Shepherd-Look, 1982).

Later Development

Personality differences between males and females seem to peak in late adolescence and early adulthood—the very years most commonly studied. Several studies have found that during middle age these differences

Answers to the mental rotation test: *For the top standard, the first and fourth alternatives; for the bottom standard, the second and third alternatives.*

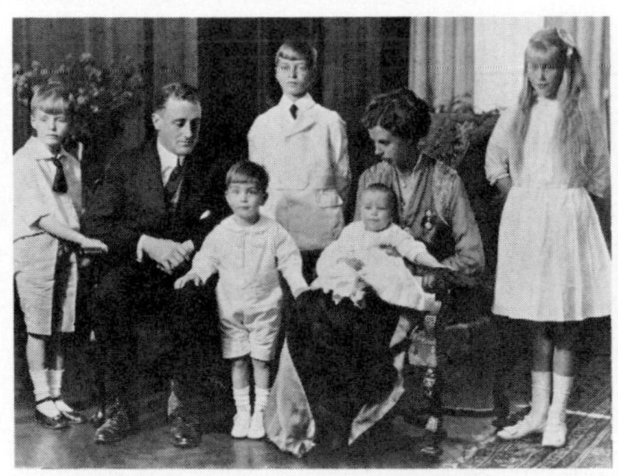

A shy and private mother of five young children, Eleanor Roosevelt was forced by the circumstances of her husband's political career and his polio to become a public figure. Eventually, she took on the role of the nation's moral gadfly and conscience, a persona she could not, as a young woman, have imagined assuming.

diminish; women become more assertive and self-confident and men more emotionally expressive and less domineering (Turner, 1982). For example, Florine Livson (1976) studied the evolving gender differences among 40 females and 40 males as young teenagers in Oakland, California, and periodically thereafter up to age 50. During the teen years the girls became progressively less assertive and more flirtatious, while the boys became more domineering and unexpressive. But by age 50, these differences had diminished; the men were expressing more warm feelings for others, and many of the women had become more assertive. When M. F. Lowenthal and his colleagues (1975) asked married couples "Who's the boss in your family?," both husbands and wives were, with age, progressively less likely to single out the husband. Even trivial behaviors such as the customary masculine and feminine ways of carrying books (Figure 5-4) become less predictable in middle age (Jenni & Jenni, 1976).

Why do gender differences first increase and then decrease as life progresses? Personality theorist Carl Jung (1933) speculated that both masculine and feminine tendencies exist in everyone, and that during the second half of life people develop their previously repressed feminine or masculine aspects. Others have speculated that during courtship and early parenthood social expectations have traditionally led each sex to deemphasize traits that interfere with their roles at that time. So long as men are expected to provide and protect, they forgo their more dependent and tender sides (Gutmann, 1977), and so long as women are expected to nurture, they forgo their impulses to be self-assertive and independent. When they graduate from these early adult roles, men and women then become freer to develop and express their previously inhibited tendencies.

Figure 5-4 *The customary masculine and feminine ways of carrying books.*

*"In the long years liker must they grow;
The man be more of woman, she of man."*
Alfred, Lord Tennyson,
The Princess, 1847

WHY DO THE GENDERS DIFFER?

As we noted earlier, one's gender is both a biological and a social fact. Are the modest gender differences therefore ordained by biology? By culture? By an intricate interplay between biology and culture? The reality of gender differences poses one of the most fundamental and fascinating riddles of human life.

Biological Roots

In Chapter 2 we saw how our genes can influence us by directing the development of our endocrine and nervous systems. So, is it possible that men's and women's genes, hormones, and brains differ in ways that might help explain their differing behaviors?

Genes

Sociobiologists E. O. Wilson (1978) and David Barash (1979) suggested that natural selection might help to explain gender differences. They proposed that we carry the heritage of the division of labor in primitive societies, where men were hunters and warriors and women were food gatherers who bore and nursed children. They argued that gender differences exist today partly because those males and females who were well-suited to performing their complementary functions in our distant past survived and reproduced more successfully. Thus natural selection predisposed traits such as aggressiveness and a keen spatial sense in males and nurturance in females. Over time, culture may have exaggerated these genetic predispositions, by creating gender roles that *prescribe* such behaviors.

In today's industrial societies, where most men no longer hunt nor women gather, these gender differences nevertheless persist as relics of our evolutionary and cultural past. So it is not surprising that in every one of the twenty-five scattered countries surveyed in one recent study, males were characterized as the more aggressive and dominant sex, females as the more nurturant and submissive sex (Hinde, 1984; Williams & Best, 1982).

As we have seen in Chapter 2, sociobiology has been criticized (1) for rationalizing traditional gender differences as natural and therefore inevitable, and (2) for offering after-the-fact explanations of these differences. When one begins by knowing what there is to explain—males are more aggressive—it usually is easy to speculate about a plausible explanation. Had it turned out that females were more aggressive, might not sociobiologists have conjectured that natural selection favored tough females who could aggressively protect their infants?

Still, in the mammalian kingdom females generally do perform most of the parental care. A sociobiologist might say, "Of course! A female can be certain that her offspring bear her genes; the male(s) with whom she mates cannot. Thus males, especially in polygamous groups, invest less in parental care, because their genetic relatedness to offspring is less certain." And it is true that among mammals, including humans, males *are* less invested in caring for the young if they live in a polygamous society (Redican & Taub, 1981). However, this sociobiological explanation cannot account for the fact that in both monkey and human societies fatherly involvement in infant care varies widely. As we move up the evolutionary scale, the genetic control of behavior loosens. By providing us with a capacity for learning, nature enables us to flexibly adapt to varying situations.

"Throughout their evolutionary history, males have generally been ill advised to devote themselves too strongly to the care of children, since the undertaking might turn out to be [in terms of genetic investment] a wasted effort."
Sociobiologist David Barash (1979)

Hormones

As noted in Chapter 2, the genes direct the development of biological sex, which includes both primary and secondary sex characteristics. A pair of XX sex chromosomes directs development of a female and a pair of XY sex chromosomes, a male.

In a male, once the primitive internal sex organs are formed in the embryo, they begin to secrete ***testosterone***, the principal male sex hormone. Its presence causes the development of the external male sex organs. In its absence or when the embryo does not respond to it, external female sex organs develop. What, then, do you suppose will be the effect on a female embryo that is exposed to excess testosterone, either because her embryonic hormone-secreting glands malfunction and overproduce it or because during pregnancy her mother received injections of a miscarriage-averting hormone at the time when the fetus's external sex organs were developing? These girls often are born with masculine-appearing genitals, which can be corrected surgically. As children, they nevertheless tend to act in more aggressively "tomboyish" ways than do most girls, and to play in a manner more typical of boys than girls (Ehrhardt & Money, 1967). They usually prefer sports and masculine clothing over dolls and dresses. As women, they tend to be less interested in marriage and motherhood (Hines, 1982). In general, then, they exhibit more masculine behavior.

Does this indicate that prenatal exposure to male hormones causes masculine behavior? Given just this case-study evidence, we cannot be sure. Since at birth these girls frequently looked masculine, perhaps their parents treated them like boys or expected them to be more active.

With animals, experiments can be conducted that remove the ambiguities of the human case studies. In many species, from rats to monkeys, females that are given male hormones before birth develop a masculine appearance and masculine behaviors. Their play is rough-and-tumble. In rats, even their learning of spatial mazes is like that of proficient males (Hines, 1982).

So, can we conclude that, as has been mockingly suggested, "macho" behavior in males is caused by "testosterone poisoning"? Perhaps. But we must be cautious in generalizing from animals to humans as hormonal controls over behavior are much stronger in animals than in humans.

As often happens, no single line of evidence is completely convincing, but the *convergence* of different findings is. Consider the gender difference in aggression: In humans, violent criminals have tended to have higher than normal testosterone levels (Rubin & others, 1980). In some animals, aggressiveness can be increased by administering male hormones. Moreover, the gender difference in aggression appears very early in life, across a variety of human cultures and animal species. Together, these lines of evidence, each inconclusive by itself, point to a hormonal contribution to the greater aggressiveness of males.

Some scientists believe that excess testosterone during pregnancy may also contribute to the exceptional characteristics of those junior high whiz kids who score above 700 on the SAT mathematics test. These children are more likely than others their age to be left-handed, suffer allergies or asthma, and be near-sighted—characteristics that brain scientists Norman Geschwind and Peter Behan (1984) believe are linked with the presence of excess male hormone during prenatal development.

Brain Differences

Our genes influence which sex hormones predominate in our bodies. Hormones in turn help affect the development of the brain. Researchers have therefore begun searching for evidence that under hormonal influence, the brain is "masculinized" or "feminized." With rats and birds, the evidence is clear: Brain regions that play an important role in sexual behavior, maternal behavior, and aggression are discernibly different (for example, in size) in males and females (Arnold, 1980).

In humans, too, there are detectable differences between males' and females' brains. As we saw in Chapter 2, the two hemispheres of the human brain have some specialized functions. For example, the left hemisphere usually exhibits higher verbal intelligence than the right. Damage to a man's left hemisphere tends to impair verbal intelligence more than does damage to a woman's. Such findings suggest that the left hemisphere's specialization for language is more pronounced in men than women (Inglis & Lawson, 1982). Other methods of measuring hemispheric specialization yield mixed results: In some respects, male brains tend to function more unsymmetrically (Kimura & Harshman, 1984; McGlone, in press; Springer & Deutsch, 1985).

Why this gender difference in left hemisphere language specialization? Theories abound. Some attribute it to biology—to natural selection of more specialized hemisphere functioning in males and more integrated hemispheric functioning in females (Levy, 1978, 1980), or to males' slower physical maturation, which gives their developing hemispheres longer to become specialized (Waber, 1976). Others have wondered whether it might be environmentally caused—whether the differing childhood experiences of males and females might lead to the differing development of their brains. Recall from Chapter 2 that experiences help to form the neural connections of the brain. The traffic between biology and psychology is two-way.

For some, the idea of a biological basis for gender differences may seem to threaten the ideal of social equality. The oppression of women has historically been bolstered by theories that men and women are "naturally" different.

"There is no female mind. The brain is not an organ of sex."
Charlotte Perkins Gilman,
Women in Economics, 1898

But does social equality require biological sameness? The connotation of any biological difference is given by the words used to describe it. Can you feel a difference between saying that females' brains are "less specialized" versus saying they are "more integrative"? Such gender differences, whether biologically based or not, have no direct bearing on social equality; it is the value we place on them that does. So let us remember: Biological differences need not be regarded as deficits.

"Men and women are different. *What needs to be made equal is the value placed upon these differences."*
Diane McGuinness and Karl Pribram (1978)

Social Roots

Children's biological sex dictates their assignment to the social category of male or female. Without question, this social assignment—and all the expectations that accompany it—mold the experience of maleness or femaleness. And when social expectations vary, so do behaviors. Small biological differences may trigger big social differences. What biology initiates, culture accentuates.

Drawing by Sidney Harris

"Gilmore speaking. Anatomy isn't destiny."

Gender Assignment

Recall the cases of the females who, having received extra male hormones while in the womb, are born with some of the appearances of a male. In earlier decades, when such infants were of uncertain genetic sex, the physician and parents were forced to choose the baby's socially assumed sex. (Note that even when one's biological sex is ambiguous, human beings can only tolerate two categories—you must be considered either male *or* female.) What then do you suppose would typically become the child's gender identity (sense of being male or female)? Would the self-image as boy or girl be in accord with the genetic sex? The socially assigned gender? Or would the child more likely have a confused gender identity?

Most such children comfortably accepted whatever gender they were assigned, whether genetically correct or not (Ehrhardt & Money, 1967; Money & others, 1957). Like other children, by age 3 they knew whether they were a boy or a girl, and this gender identity was thereafter difficult to reverse. Our gender identity, it seems, is socially determined.

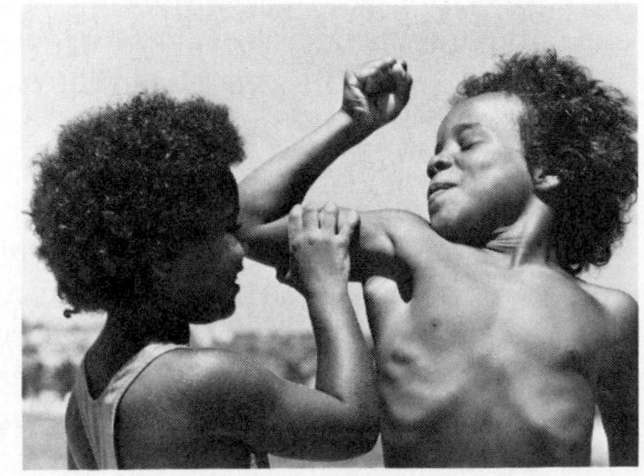

"Me Tarzan, you Jane." Boys still strut and girls still admire.

Gender-Typing

During childhood we acquire not only our gender identity but also many masculine or feminine behaviors and attitudes. Although nearly everyone has a biologically appropriate gender identity, some children become more strongly ***gender-typed*** than others. Some boys exhibit more strictly masculine interests than other boys, and some girls become more distinctly feminine than other girls. By what process do girls become feminine and boys masculine? Four theories of gender-typing have been proposed.

Gender identity: *One's sense of being male or female.*
Gender-typing: *How masculine a boy is, how feminine a girl is.*
Gender roles: *Expected behaviors for males and females.*

Identification Theory The best-known theory is also the oldest: Sigmund Freud's (1933) theory of ***identification***. Freud proposed that, at about age 5 or 6, children become unable to cope with their sexual longing for the parent of the other sex, so they renounce these feelings by identifying with the same-sex parent, unconsciously adopting his or her characteristics.

For further information on Freud's theory of personality, see Chapter 15.

Although historically influential and still well known outside of psychology, this theory is now disputed by most research psychologists as well as many clinical practitioners. Children become gender-typed well before age 5 or 6 and may become strongly so even in the absence of a same-sex parent (Frieze & others, 1978). Moreover, young children do not seem biased toward imitating their same-sex parent. Rather, children tend to imitate familiar people who are powerful yet warm—which generally includes both parents.

Social Learning Theory Another well-known theory explains gender-typing by applying principles of learning that (as we will see in Chapter 9, "Learning") explain a multitude of human behaviors. The basic idea is simple: Bit by bit, children *learn* the behaviors deemed appropriate for their sex. Through rewards and punishments, parents teach their daughters to be feminine ("You're such a good mommy to your dolls!"), and their sons to be masculine ("Don't cry like a baby, Dick"). Children are also rewarded for imitating people of their own sex. When Dick dresses up in Daddy's clothes, his parents are more amused than when he dons Mommy's dress and shoes. But more must be going on than this, for children exhibit all sorts of gender-typed behaviors for which they have not been directly rewarded. By observing others in the home, the neighborhood, and on television, children learn the consequences of various behaviors without having to experience them.

If it was the girl who fell in love with the motorcycle and the boy who adored strutting down the runway, their parents and other adults might not have found their behavior so charming. As it is, they are rewarded by their society for gender-typed behaviors, which they learn by observation and imitation.

In contrast to the assumption of Freud's identification theory that gender-typing comes from within the child (as the child identifies with the same-sex parent), social learning theory assumes that children are molded (or socialized, as psychologists and sociologists say) by their social worlds. Researchers generally concur that children learn behaviors associated with their gender by observation, by imitation, and by being rewarded and punished. But critics complain that children are not so passive as social learning theory assumes. Whether their social worlds encourage or discourage traditional gender-typing, children inevitably seem to know that "boys are boys and girls are girls," to organize their worlds accordingly, and to create and enforce their own rules for what boys and girls should do.

Are these children identifying with the same-sex parent? Are they being socialized into traditional gender-typed behaviors? Or both?

Cognitive-Developmental Theory To account for the child's active participation in the gender-typing process, Lawrence Kohlberg (1966) proposed a theory of gender-typing that applied Piaget's principles of cognitive development. As children struggle to comprehend themselves and their worlds, one of the first concepts they form is that of their own gender. Having identified themselves as male or female, they soon begin to organize their worlds on the basis of gender—even in the absence of any external pressure to do so. As their cognitive machinery matures, so do their understandings of what defines the genders. To a preschool girl, short hair may define a man and long hair a woman, in which case the girl may insist on having long hair, or may think she can change her gender with a haircut. But by the concrete operational stage, when a child knows that the amount of milk remains constant after being poured from a tall, narrow glass into a short, wide glass, the child also knows that a woman remains a woman whether she wears her hair long or short (Tavris & Wade, 1984). Once children's understanding of gender identity is firmly established, they know to use members of their own sex as models for their behavior.

Critics of cognitive-developmental theory generally agree that what children think *is* important. But why among all the possible ways of categorizing people do children so consistently do so in terms of gender? Why not eye color? Or religion? Or, in another culture, caste? Is it because sex is a more visible category? Then why even in multiracial societies are children more gender-typed than race-typed (S. L. Bem, 1985)? And why do preschoolers begin to exhibit gender-appropriate behaviors before they fully understand gender constancy?

Gender Schema Theory To answer these questions, Sandra Bem (1985) proposed a new theory, ***gender schema theory***, that combines aspects of both the social learning and cognitive-developmental theories. Gender schema theory proposes that the *process* of gender-typing is best explained with Piaget's concepts of cognitive development, and that the *content*—the behaviors considered appropriate for males and females—is provided by social learning.

Bem builds on Piaget's idea that children make sense out of their experiences by forming concepts called schemas: These, she argues, include powerful schemas for maleness and femaleness. Once formed, these schemas help children assimilate their experiences—by recognizing boys with varying haircuts as males, for example. And from time to time their schemas must be adapted to accommodate new information—as when a child comes to realize that being "female" need not entail wearing long hair or skirts but does entail having a particular anatomy. Using their far-reaching schemas for maleness and femaleness, children can sort incoming information into masculine categories ("strong," "hawk") and feminine categories ("gentle," "robin"). Many languages, including the European languages, broaden gender schemas by classifying objects as either masculine (in French, "*le* train") or feminine ("*la* table"). Pronouns, too, require classifying people by gender. To speak, even a 3-year-old must learn the difference between he and she, his and hers.

Even the child's own self-concept gets assimilated into a gender schema: "I am male—thus masculine, strong, aggressive," or "I am female—therefore feminine, sweet, and helpful" (or whatever are the socially learned associations with one's sex). Gender-typing occurs as children learn what it means to be male or female, compare themselves to their schema, and evaluate themselves accordingly. This motivates them to adjust their behaviors to conform to their gender concept, and so to become more strongly gender-typed.

Gender Roles

According to Bem's gender schema theory, then, our gender-typing is very much affected by the society's ***gender roles.*** Like a theatrical role, a social role is a set of prescriptions concerning how those who occupy the role should talk, act, dress, and so forth. Knowing someone's role—as professor, student, parent, or whatever—tells us, in general terms, how others believe that person ought to behave, which usually strongly influences how that person does behave. Traditional gender roles similarly prescribe behavior, indicating, for example, that men are the ones who are expected to initiate dates, drive the car, and pick up the check.

Such social prescriptions serve to grease the social machinery. They free us from self-conscious preoccupation with awkward little decisions, such as who reaches for the check. When we already know how we are to act, our attention is freed for other matters. But these benefits come at a price: Roles also constrain and shape us. When we deviate from them—as in some settings when a woman initiates a formal date with a man—we may feel anxious.

"Civilization advances by extending the number of operations which we can perform without thinking about them."
Alfred North Whitehead, 1861–1947

Several experiments show that contemporary men and women do adjust their behavior to fulfill others' gender-role expectations. In one, Mark Zanna and Susan Pack (1975) had college women answer a questionnaire in which they described themselves to a tall, unattached, senior classman they expected to meet. Those led to believe that the man had traditional gender-role expectations described themselves as more traditionally feminine than did those who expected to meet a man who liked nontraditional women. Moreover, when given an aptitude test, those who expected to meet the traditional man solved 15 percent fewer problems. This illustrates how our gender-role expectations—and our perceptions of others' expectations—can be self-fulfilling; expectations help create gender differences.

Cultural Variations in Gender Roles Gender roles often vary from society to society. In almost all primitive societies, men predominate in fighting wars and hunting large game, women in gathering food and caring for infants. In agricultural societies, women are generally restricted to home and child care, while men roam freely; nomadic societies have less distinct gender roles (Van Leeuwen, 1978). Even among industrialized societies, the roles assigned men and women vary enormously from country to country. In the United States, medicine and dentistry are predominantly male occupations; in Russia, most doctors are women, as are most dentists in Denmark.

Marcia Guttentag and Paul Secord (1983) analyzed societies from classical Athens to modern America and found that gender roles vary across time as well. In times when marriageable women are in short supply, women are protected and marital fidelity is strong. When migration, war, or adult mortality put marriageable men in short supply, men become more sexually promiscuous and women become more self-reliant—more likely to become employed and to organize social movements to improve their status. So, the behaviors expected of males and females vary across cultures and over time, while the biological differences between males and females do not. Clearly, then, social rather than biological factors must explain these cultural variations.

Changing Gender Roles Consider the changing role of women. Gender roles that may have been adaptive in past eras when women were pregnant or nursing for much of their adult lives may be less adaptive now that most women live longer, bear fewer children, and are employed.

In the United States, gender expectations have shifted dramatically. The change is evident first in people's expressed attitudes (*Public Opinion*, 1978, 1980). In 1937, 1 in 3 Americans said they would be willing to vote for a qualified woman whom their party nominated for President; in 1984, 4 in 5 said they would. In 1938, 1 in 5 approved "of a married woman earning money in business or industry if she has a husband capable of supporting her"; in 1978, 3 out of 4 approved. In 1970, Americans were split 50-50 on whether they favored or opposed "efforts to strengthen women's status." By 1979 such efforts were approved by a 2 to 1 margin. In 1984, a *Gallup Report* indicated that 63 percent of Americans supported the Equal Rights Amendment. A 1981 Gallup poll found that even more—80 percent—agreed that "Equality of Rights under the law shall not be denied or abridged by the United States, or by any state on account of sex"—which *was* the ERA.

The changing role of women is also evident—though less dramatically—in their changing behavior. Most obvious is the increase in the rate of women's employment, as noted in Chapter 4. Changes are also evident in the nature of women's employment. When America's class of 1988 began college in the fall of 1984, 44 percent of the women were intending to pursue careers in law, business, medicine, or engineering—double the percentage in 1970 (Green, 1985).

Joseph Pleck (1981) reports that a more "subtle revolution" has also been occurring in men's roles. Compared to the mid-1960s, men are now devoting more time to family work. Increasingly, men have pressing engagements at the ironing board, in front of the stove, behind the vacuum cleaner, and over the diaper changing table. Still, even in countries that have sought to equalize the roles of women and men, the distinctions persist. Whether in Russia, China, or Sweden, answers to "Who works in the child-care nurseries?," "Who cooks dinner?," and "Who runs the country?" remain nearly as predictable as in the United States and Canada.

"Sometimes I miss the old days, when men were ashamed to cry in public."

Should There Be Gender Roles? Social scientists' personal concerns motivate their interest in topics such as gender roles, and many share Sandra Bem's (1985) conviction that "Human behaviors and personality attributes should no longer be linked with gender." Unlike some parents who are timid about "imposing" their values and beliefs on their children, Bem feels that parents who have deep social, political, or religious convictions should not be bashful about transmitting their convictions to their children. Children are going to absorb an ideology from somewhere—from the culture if not from the home. So she suggests how those who share her values might raise children who are freer of gender schemas: At home, make gender irrelevant to who cooks and does dishes and to what toys are available; when children are young, censor their books and television programs and teach them that one's sex entails anatomical and reproductive traits and not much else; to help them process what their culture tries to tell them about gender, teach them alternative schemas (concepts such as how individuals differ, how gender roles vary, and how sex discrimination is practiced).

In Bem's ideal world, gender roles would cease to exist. In our world they still do. Gender role researchers have therefore wondered: Are people who are less gender-typed and more androgynous healthier and happier? ***Androgyny*** is the possession of both masculine and feminine qualities. In research studies, those classified as androgynous describe themselves with both traditionally masculine adjectives (independent, assertive, competitive) and traditionally feminine adjectives (warm, tender, compassionate). So, do such people in fact feel better about themselves than do gender-typed (masculine) men and (feminine) women? Initial reports suggested they do.

But analysis of more than 100 such studies by Marylee Taylor and Judith Hall (1982) revealed that androgynous people do not consistently exhibit higher self-esteem or better adjustment. Rather, in both men and women, positive self-feelings are linked to masculine traits. People who describe themselves as independent, assertive, and so forth also express high self-regard. This has led psychologists to question the ideal of androgyny. (It has also offered ammunition to those who contest the assumption that a traditionally feminine woman is a happy woman.) Moreover it hints at a masculine cultural bias. Perhaps the entire culture measures people against a male yardstick by valuing masculine traits more than feminine traits.

However, when it comes to relationships, feminine qualities may be an asset. In a study of 108 Australian married couples, John Antill (1983) found that when either the wife or husband possessed feminine traits such as gentleness, sensitivity, or affectionateness—or better yet, when *both* did— marital satisfaction was higher. Although masculine traits may boost self-esteem, says Antill, "they are apparently not the qualities that hold the key to a happy, long-term relationship."

Should gender roles be preserved? Some say that men's and women's biological differences make their social differences—to some extent at least—both desirable and inevitable. Yes, they say, the sexes share traits and abilities in common, but each sex also bears special gifts. To distinguish between two wines, composers, or genders is to appreciate each, by discerning their virtues. So, equality and freedom of individual choice, yes; sameness, no. Others say the biological differences are socially trivial. Human beings—both women *and* men—should be unshackled from all that constrains their being complete human beings: assertive and nurturant, self-confident and tender, independent and compassionate. Should gender roles be preserved? Science informs the debate, but personal convictions decide it.

Those who advocate raising their children without traditional gender schemas believe gender should be irrelevant to who plays with which toys and who does which household tasks.

"I was a better man as a woman with a woman than I've ever been as a man with a woman."
An out-of-work actor (Dustin Hoffman), who masquerades as a woman to land a job, finds his transformation has some surprising consequences for his relationship with a real woman (Jessica Lange) in the movie "Tootsie."

"In sex, as in race, there are no separate but equal social categories."
Rhonda Unger (1979)

Nature-Nurture Interaction

Our discussion has proceeded as if the biological and social sources of gender differences were two opponents in a fencing match. The biological factor scores points for observed hormonal and brain differences; the social factor responds with points scored for the social sources of cultural variations, gender identity, gender-typing, and gender roles.

But surely we create a false dichotomy by trying to partition gender differences neatly into nature and nurture, for biological and social factors interact. Biological factors that create male and female physical characteristics may predispose different cultural influences on males and females (Harris, 1978). If hormones predispose males to be slightly more aggressive, society may then amplify this difference by encouraging males to be tough and females to be gentle. Such a gender difference would be both a biological and a social effect: culture developing what biology has initiated.

We can conclude by restating the principle in general terms: Biological factors always operate within a social context, and social effects operate upon what is biologically given. In the weaving of the human fabric, the biological and social threads act as warp and woof.

It comes as little surprise today when the "man of the house" is also the chef. Perhaps it won't be long before no eyebrows are raised by the telephone lineman being a woman.

SUMMING UP

Few aspects of our lives are more central to our existence than our being born male or female. Examining the development of our maleness and femaleness, and of the behaviors *expected* of males and females, enables us to see at work some of the important biological and social factors (previously discussed in Chapters 2, 3, and 4) and to appreciate how intertwined such factors are.

GENDER DIFFERENCES

Differences—even small average differences between overlapping groups of people—catch the eye of layperson and scientist alike, causing us sometimes to be more impressed by small differences than by large similarities. In the few ways in which men and women do differ, individual variations within each sex far exceed the variation between the sexes. Moreover, the mere fact of knowing someone is male or female often triggers an exaggerated perception of gender differences.

How Do Males and Females Differ? Research studies have shown that males have tended to behave more aggressively, to exert more social power, and to exhibit greater spatial ability. Women have tended to evidence somewhat greater sensitivity to others' nonverbal messages, to report more empathy, and to exhibit slightly greater verbal ability. In general, men and women differ more in their reports on their social behaviors than is observed in their actual behaviors.

Gender Differences Across the Life-Span The gender differences in aggression and spatial ability appear very early. Gender differences in social behavior peak in adolescence and early adulthood, and diminish by midlife.

WHY DO THE GENDERS DIFFER?

Biological Roots Might biological sex differences create behavioral gender differences? Sociobiologists speculate that the sexual division of labor in prehistoric times may have favored the evolution of certain traits in males, others in females. The evidence is clearer that hormonal differences contribute at least to the gender difference in aggression. There also exists a puzzling male-female difference in brain functioning: The tendency for the two hemispheres to serve differing functions is more pronounced in men than in women.

Social Roots The social sources of gender differences are striking. The social definition of gender identity, the social and cognitive sources of gender-typing, and the extent to which varying social expectations influence gender roles all testify to the social roots of "manhood" and "womanhood." Gender roles have been converging, yet in no culture have they been eliminated. Whether they can or should be eliminated is a debate that science can inform, but not decide.

TERMS AND CONCEPTS TO REMEMBER

Aggression Physical or verbal behavior intended to hurt someone.

Androgyny (*andros*, man, + *gyne*, woman) Possession of both masculine and feminine psychological traits.

Empathy To be able to understand and feel what another feels.

Gender Identity One's sense of being a male or a female. Note: One's gender identity is distinct from one's sexual orientation (as heterosexual or homosexual—see p. 356) and from the strength of one's *gender-typing* (see later definition).

Gender Role A set of expected behaviors for males and for females.

Gender Schema Theory The theory that the process of gender-typing is explained by children's developing schemas for maleness and femaleness, the content of which is determined by social learning.

Gender-Typing The extent to which a male displays traditionally masculine traits or a female displays traditionally feminine traits.

Identification Freud's term for the presumed process by which a child adopts the characteristics of the same-sex parent. More generally, the process by which people associate themselves with and copy the behavior of significant others.

Testosterone The most important of the male sex hormones (androgens). Both males and females have it, but the additional testosterone in males stimulates the growth of the male sex organs before birth and the development of the male sex characteristics during puberty.

FOR FURTHER READING

Bleier, R. (1984). *Science and gender: A critique of biology and its theories on women.* New York: Pergamon Press.

Provides a feminist scientist's critique of biological explanations of gender differences.

Doyle, J. A. (1983). *The male experience.* Dubuque, IA: W. C. Brown.

An unusual book about the male sex role.

Hyde, J. (1985). *Half the human experience: The psychology of women* (3rd ed.). Lexington, MA: Heath.

One of several textbooks that provide a comprehensive discussion of the psychology of women.

Tavris, C., & Wade, C. (1984). *The longest war: Sex differences in perspective* (2nd ed.). San Diego, CA: Harcourt Brace Jovanovich.

A provocative and delightfully readable discussion of gender.

Charles Harbutt

PART THREE

EXPERIENCING THE WORLD

To experience the world around us, we must take in, process, and selectively interpret the myriad of messages that that world is constantly emitting. In the first step, various stimuli that strike our bodies must first be received and transformed into neural messages that reach the brain (a process we investigate in Chapter 6, "Sensation"). These messages must then be organized and interpreted in meaningful ways (ways we consider in Chapter 7, "Perception"). As we examine the processes by which we experience the world, we will touch on such fascinating issues as: Can we be affected by stimuli that are too faint to be consciously perceived? What happens when a person is deprived of sensory input? What does the evidence tell us about extrasensory perception? Conscious experience also occurs in altered states—states induced by sleep, hypnosis, and drugs, the topics of Chapter 8, "States of Consciousness."

Ralph Eugene Meatyard

CHAPTER 6

Sensation

In a silent, cushioned inner world of utter darkness floats your brain. In the outer world a myriad of sounds and colors continually surround your body. These facts raise a fundamental question, one that predates psychology by over 2000 years, one that helped inspire the beginnings of modern psychology some 100 years ago: *How does the world out there get in?*

How do we manage to discern the world's form and texture, its motion and temperature, its aroma and beauty? And can we be sure that our experiences of sight, sound, touch, taste, and smell really do correspond to what is out there? Some people are able to see a bearded face in Figure 6-1; others are not. So, *is* there a face in the drawing? Whose experience best represents the real drawing "out there"? Such questions have intrigued human beings since at least the time of the ancient Greek philosophers Plato and Aristotle.

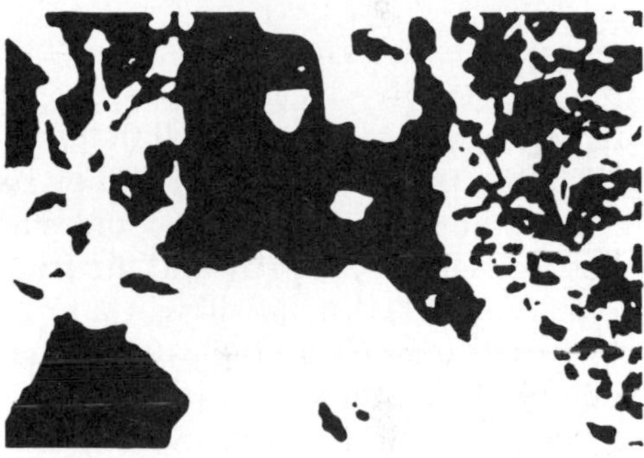

Figure 6-1 *Everyone* senses *an array of black and white here, but most people require a few minutes before they can* perceive *anything meaningful.*

To grasp an overview of how the world out there gets in, three computer concepts are useful: input, information processing, and output. As Figure 6-2 illustrates, physical objects emit or reflect energies: Our sensory organs detect these stimuli (input) and encode them into neural information that our brains organize and interpret (processing) as a per-

Figure 6-2 *How sensory input is processed.*

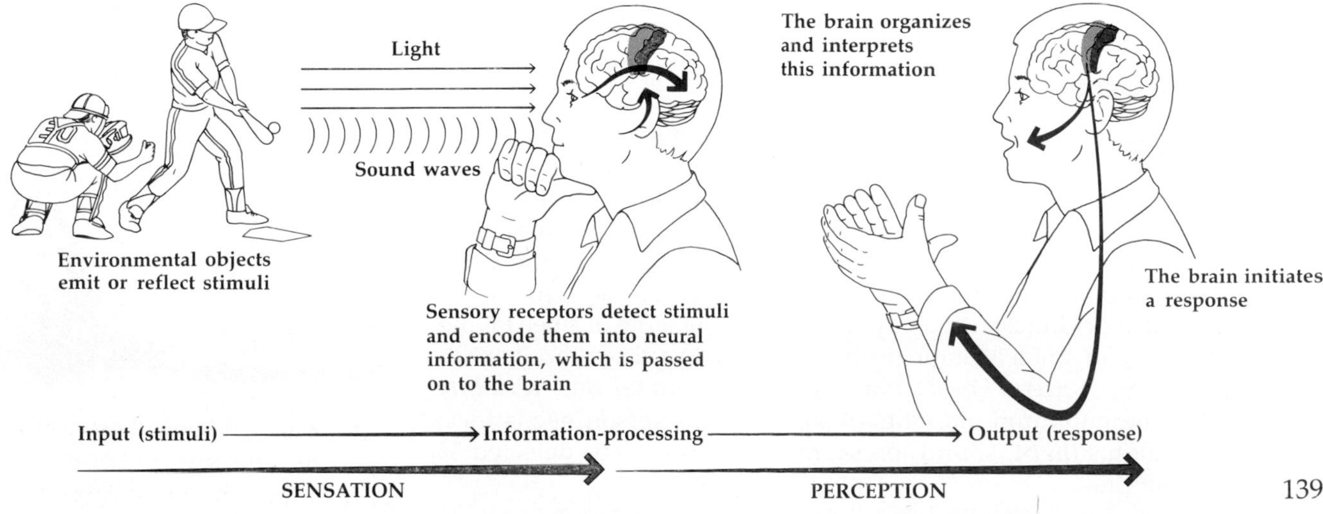

ceptual experience (output). As we will see later, our resulting perceptual experiences may affect our actions, which may in turn modify our perceptions. The inexperienced baseball outfielder who runs in too far to catch fly balls soon learns to judge them better.

Perception and sensation are difficult to separate. Nevertheless, we can think of ***sensation*** as the process by which stimuli are detected and encoded, enabling us to experience a baseball as a moving white object. To study sensation is therefore to study how stimuli that strike our bodies are transformed into neural messages received by the brain. ***Perception*** (our topic in Chapter 7) is the mental process of organizing and interpreting our sensations, enabling us to see not just moving whiteness, but a baseball. Roughly speaking, perception takes up where sensation leaves off. So, to recognize, say an A and an A as **A**'s, and not **H**'s or **R**'s, we must be capable both of sensing (detecting, encoding) and perceiving (organizing, interpreting) information.

"Only mind has sight and hearing; all things else are deaf and blind."
Epicharmus,
Fragments, 550 B.C.

"What thin partitions Sense from Thought divide!"
Alexander Pope,
Essay on Man, 1734

SENSING THE WORLD: SOME BASIC PRINCIPLES

Sensation enables an organism to obtain the information it needs to function and survive. A frog, which feeds on flying insects, has eyes that include a type of receptor cell that fires only in response to small, moving dark objects—"bug detectors" they have been called (Barlow, 1972; Lettvin & others, 1959). A frog could starve while knee deep in motionless flies, but let one zoom by and the frog's "bug detectors" are triggered. So sensitive are the male silkworm's receptors for the odor of the female sex-attractant that a single female silkworm moth need only release a billionth of an ounce of attractant per second to attract every male silkworm moth within a mile (Sagan, 1979a). And that is why there continue to be silkworms. Humans, as we will see, are similarly designed to detect what for them are the important features of their environments. Nature's gifts, it seems, are suited to their recipient's needs.

Thresholds

We exist in a sea of energy. At this moment, you and I are being bombarded with x-rays and radio waves, with ultraviolet and infrared light, with very high and very low frequency sound waves. But to all of them we are blind and deaf. Our senses, our windows on the world, are open just a crack, allowing us only a restricted awareness of this vast sea.

Absolute Thresholds

Each organism comes equipped with its special sensitivities. Pigeons navigate by magnetic fields. Dogs can hear a high-pitched whistle that is undetectable by the human ear. To those stimuli to which we humans are sensitive, we are exquisitely sensitive. For those of us with normal senses: Standing atop a mountain on an utterly dark, clear night, we can see a candle flame atop another mountain 30 miles away. In a silent room, we can hear a watch ticking 20 feet away. We can feel the wing of a bee falling on our cheeks, and smell a single drop of perfume in a three-room apartment (Galanter, 1962). These faint stimuli illustrate our ***absolute thresholds***—the minimum amounts of stimulation a person needs for a particular stimulus (light, sound, pressure, odor, taste) to be detected 50 percent of the time.

"And you know those whistles that only dogs can hear . . . ? I can't *hear* them."

To test our absolute thresholds for sounds, a hearing specialist presents low-, medium-, and high-pitched sounds to each ear, sometimes so weakly that we never hear them, sometimes so strongly that we never miss them. In between is a zone of uncertainty for each pitch, where half the time we will correctly detect the sound and half the time not. For each of the senses, that fifty-fifty point defines our absolute threshold.

Researchers who study ***signal detection*** are learning how to predict people's ability to detect faint stimuli. Signal-detection theory assumes that our detecting a weak signal depends not only on the strength of the signal (such as a tone on a hearing test), but also on our psychological state—our experience, expectations, and motivation. Thus there is no single absolute threshold for detecting a stimulus. In a horror-filled wartime situation where a failure to detect an intruder may mean death, a sentry standing guard alone at night may notice (and fire at) an almost imperceptible noise; but in peacetime, when this need to be alert is not as crucial, and when a mistake in judgment may endanger others, the same sentry will require a stronger signal before detecting danger. Such variations in one's threshold for deciding whether a signal is present affect one's performance in important tasks such as detecting blips on a radar screen.

Subliminal Stimulation

In 1957 a storm of controversy erupted over a report that some New Jersey movie audiences were unwittingly influenced by imperceptible messages to "drink Coca-Cola" and "eat popcorn" flashed on the screen. A quarter-century later the controversy has erupted anew. Advertisers are said to be manipulating us by imperceptibly printing the word "sex" on crackers and embedding erotic images in liquor ads. Rock recordings are said to contain "Satanic messages" that are consciously discernible if the recordings are played backward and unconsciously persuasive when played normally. Entrepreneurs are offering to help us lose weight, stop smoking, or improve our memories by selling taped sounds of the ocean that contain messages "below your conscious hearing." These claims all assume that we can unconsciously perceive ***subliminal*** (literally, "below threshold") stimuli.

Do we, in fact, ever perceive stimuli that are below the absolute threshold for awareness? In one sense the answer is clearly yes. Remember that the "absolute" threshold is really just a statistically defined point at which we detect a stimulus only half the time. Slightly below this threshold we will still detect the stimulus some of the time. The answer is yes in another sense, too. People who plead total ignorance when asked to make some perceptual judgment (for example, when having to decide which of two very similar weights is heavier) may nevertheless do better than random guessing when forced to *guess*. Sometimes the mind knows more than it thinks it does.

Now the question is, can we be affected by stimuli that are too subliminal for us ever to notice? Recent experiments hint that under certain conditions the answer may be yes. For example, a group of University of Michigan students was repeatedly shown a series of geometric figures, one at a time, each for 0.001 second—long enough to perceive only a flash of light (Kunst-Wilson & Zajonc, 1980). Later the students expressed greater liking for these figures than for other figures that they were viewing for the first time, even though they had no idea which was which. When John Seamon and his colleagues (1983) repeated this experiment with Wesleyan University students, they obtained similar results. Sometimes, it seems, we feel what we cannot know or describe.

Moreover, sometimes we are more knowing than we are aware. Researchers have found that when words are flashed so briefly that they are invisible, some meaning from the unseen words may nevertheless be retained (Marcel, 1983). For instance, Carol Fowler and her associates (1981) flashed words on a screen so briefly that their Dartmouth College students could not even guess whether the flash of light contained a word or not. They then showed the students two words (such as "penny" and "rabbit") and asked which was closest to the invisible word (such as "cent"). Typically, the subjects guessed whichever of the two words "felt right." Remarkably, they were more often right than wrong.

In hindsight, we can surmise how this might be. Stimuli too weak to cross our thresholds for conscious awareness may nevertheless trigger a small response in our sense receptors, a response that may even be transmitted to the brain and cross some threshold for feeling or meaning, though not for conscious awareness. Experiments such as these have convinced researchers that our brains process much information without our awareness.

Why is it, then, that subliminal persuasion is probably a myth? Perhaps you can detect a difference between the conditions under which subliminal advertising might occur and the conditions of these last two experiments. In the experiments, the people's undivided attention was focused on the subliminal stimuli; they were straining to glimpse the imperceptible forms or words. When watching a movie, viewing an advertisement, or listening to a record, our attention is focused not on any subliminal stimuli that might be present but on the images and sounds of which we are *consciously* aware. There is every reason to suppose that stimuli strong enough to command our attention will overpower any effect of subliminal stimuli. To summarize, we do process sensory information without conscious awareness. But so far, at least, the research on subliminal persuasion indicates that what you see is what you get (Moore, 1982; Tisdell, 1983).

"Secret attempts to manipulate people's minds have yielded results as subliminal as the stimuli used."
James V. McConnell (1977, p. 31)

Difference Thresholds

Recall that sensation enables an organism to get the information needed to function effectively in the environment. This requires absolute thresholds low enough to allow the organism to detect important sights, sounds, tastes, and textures. It also requires the ability to detect small differences among stimuli. An orchestra member must be able to detect small discrepancies in an instrument's tuning. A wine taster must be able to detect the slight difference in flavor between two vintage wines.

For their jobs, these performers and this specialist have learned to detect slight variations in pitch or taste.

The ***difference threshold*** is the minimum difference a person requires to experience a ***just noticeable difference*** (nicknamed the jnd) between any two stimuli 50 percent of the time. The difference threshold increases with the magnitude of the stimulus. Add 1 ounce to a 10-ounce weight and you could detect the difference; add 1 ounce to a 10-pound weight and you could not, because the difference threshold has increased. More than a century ago, Ernst Weber noted that regardless of their magnitude, two stimuli must differ by a constant proportion for their difference to be perceived. This principle—that the threshold is not a constant amount but some constant proportion of the stimulus—is so simple and so widely applicable that we still refer to it as ***Weber's law.*** The exact proportion varies, depending on the stimulus (see Table 6-1). For their differences to be perceived by the average person, two objects need differ in weight by only 2 percent and two tones in frequency by only 0.3 percent.

Table 6-1 **Some common difference thresholds**

To be experienced by the average person as a just noticeable difference,

two ______	must vary in ______	by ___
solutions	saltiness	8%
lights	brightness	8%
sounds	intensity	5%
objects	weight	2%
sounds	frequency	0.3%

Source: Adapted from Teghtsoonian, 1971.

Weber's law is a rough approximation that works well for nonextreme sensory stimuli. It also approximates many of our life experiences. A $5 per hour worker may require a pay raise to $5.25 to notice the difference; a $10 per hour worker may require a 50 cent raise to notice. Weber's principle: Difference thresholds (measured as amount of increased stimulation) are a constant proportion of the magnitude of the stimulus.

Sensory Adaptation

Upon entering someone's room, you are hit with an unpleasant odor; you wonder how the person tolerates it, but within minutes you no longer notice it yourself. When the refrigerator motor turns on you may notice how noisy it is, but only for a moment or two. Jumping into a swimming pool, you shiver and complain how cold it is; a short while later a friend arrives and you exclaim, "C'mon in. Water's warm!" These examples illustrate ***sensory adaptation***—our diminishing sensitivity to a prolonged unchanging stimulus. (To experience this phenomenon right now, move your watch up your wrist an inch: You will feel it—but only for a few moments.) After constant exposure to a stimulus, the receptor cells of any of our senses will begin to fire less vigorously. This makes our senses less accurate than they would otherwise be. But adaptation is nevertheless adaptive: It enables us to focus our attention on informative changes in our environment without being distracted by the uninformative constant stimulation of garments, odors, and street noise. This reinforces a fundamental lesson of our study of sensation and perception: We perceive the world not exactly as it is out there, but as it is useful for us to perceive it.

"We need above all to know about changes; no one wants or needs to be reminded 16 hours a day that his shoes are on."
David Hubel (1979)

These principles of absolute threshold, difference threshold, and adaptation are not the only commonalities among the senses. The senses also share a common task of receiving sensory stimulation, transforming it into neural information, and delivering that information to the brain. How do they do it? Let us find out, beginning with vision, the most thoroughly studied of our windows on the world.

SEEING

Our sensory processing model (Figure 6-2) suggested that the study of any sensory system begins with (1) the analysis of its triggering stimuli, and (2) the process—called ***transduction***—by which these stimulus energies are converted into neural messages. A phonograph needle is a transducer: It receives energy in the form of minute vibrations and transforms, or transduces, this energy into electrical activity. Give it another form of energy—shine a light on it, warm it up, put perfume on it—and nothing happens. Like each of our sensory receptors, those of the eye transduce a specific form of energy into neural activity.

The Stimulus Input: Light Energy

The pulses of electromagnetic energy that we know as light waves provide the stimulus energy for vision. What we humans see as visible light is actually but a thin slice of the whole spectrum of electromagnetic waves. As Figure 6-3 illustrates, the electromagnetic spectrum varies from the relatively slow pulses, or waves, of radio transmission to the narrow band of the spectrum that is visible to the extremely fast waves of cosmic rays. Other organisms are sensitive to slightly different portions of the spectrum. Bees, for example, cannot see red, but can see ultraviolet light, the part of the spectrum that causes sunburn in humans.

Three physical characteristics of light determine our sensory experience of it. Its ***wavelength***—the distance from one wave peak to the next—determines its ***hue***, the color that we experience, such as blue or green.

Figure 6-3 *The spectrum of electromagnetic energy ranges from long-range radio waves to gamma rays. The narrow band of wavelengths visible to the human eye (shown enlarged) extends from the longer waves of red light to the shorter waves of violet light and are measured, like all electromagnetic waves, in nanometers—billionths of a meter.*

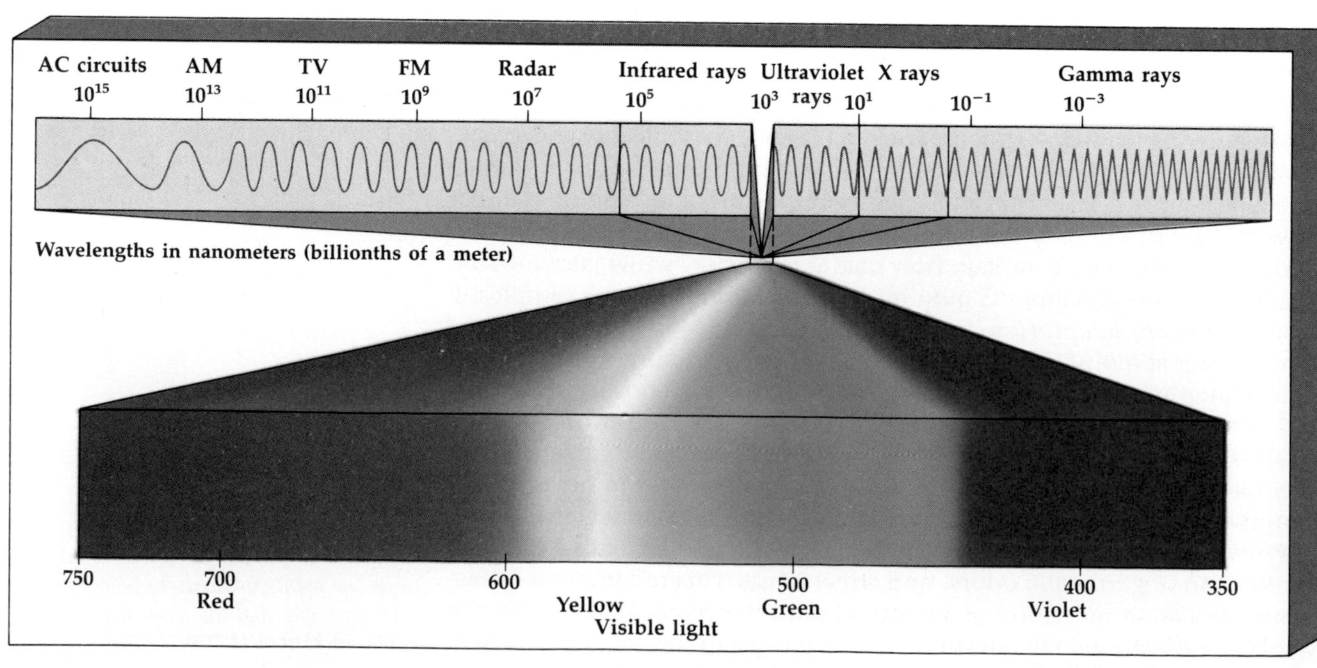

The *intensity,* or amount of energy in light waves, helps determine its *brightness.* (Brightness is also influenced by wavelength; a given intensity of light will seem brighter if it represents a color such as yellow near the middle of the visible spectrum.) The *complexity,* or mixture of wavelengths, determines its *saturation* or colorfulness. Pure wavelengths, such as those in Figure 6-3, have little complexity and therefore are highly saturated, vivid colors.

The spectrum of light is a continuum of wavelengths. Strangely, however, we tend to see it not as a continuum but as divided into four basic colors: blue-violet, yellow, green, and red (Lumsden & Wilson, 1983). To understand why this is so, and, more generally, how it is that we manage to see at all, we need first to understand the structure of the visual system.

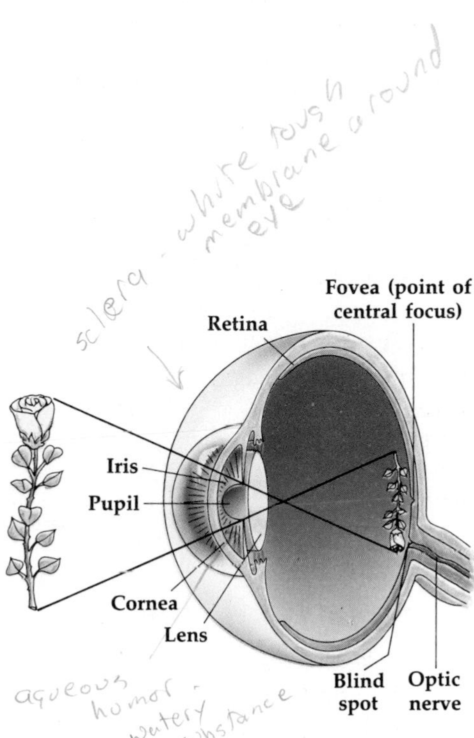

Figure 6-4 *The eye. Light rays reflected from the rose pass through the cornea, pupil, and lens. Changes in the curvature of the lens allow it to focus the image of both near and distant objects on the retina. Because light rays travel in straight lines, rays from the top of the rose strike the bottom of the retina and those from the bottom of the rose strike the top of the retina. They therefore form an upside-down and reversed image on the retina.*

The Eye

In some ways, the eye functions like a camera (or, more exactly, the camera functions like the nineteenth-century understanding of the eye). In both the eye and camera, light is admitted through a small opening, behind which is a lens that focuses the incoming rays into an image on a light-sensitive surface. The eye's small opening is the *pupil.* Its size, and therefore the amount of light entering the eye, are regulated by the dilations and contractions of the *iris,* the colored muscular tissue that surrounds the pupil. The *lens* focuses the incoming rays by changing its curvature in a process referred to as *accommodation.* The light-sensitive surface onto which the rays are focused is the *retina,* which lines the inside of the back of the eyeball.

Long before 1600, it was known that when the image of a candle passed through a small opening, it appeared inverted on a dark wall behind. Like that image, the one which falls on the retina is upside down (Figure 6-4). But how then can we see the world right side up if the image the retina receives is upside down? The assumption was we could not. Students of vision therefore struggled to conceive how the eye received an upright image (Crombie, 1964). One idea was that the eye's sensing device is the lens. Realizing that this was not so, the ever curious Leonardo da Vinci theorized that light rays were refracted (bent) by the eye's watery fluids in such a way that the inverted image was reinverted to the upright position as it reached the retina. Not until the astronomer Johannes Kepler applied the science of optics to the eye in 1604 was it shown that the eye was indeed receiving the world upside down. And how could we make sense of such a world? "I leave it," said the befuddled Kepler, "to natural philosophers."

"Vision is brought about by a picture of the thing seen being formed on the white concave surface of the retina. That which is to the right outside is depicted on the left on the retina . . . that above below."
Johannes Kepler,
Ad Vitellionem Paralipomena, 1604

The "natural philosophers" eventually included research psychologists who helped discover that the retina is a layer of millions of receptor nerve cells that convert light energy into neural impulses that are sent to the brain and reassembled there to create a coherent perceived image (Figure 6-5).

If we were to follow a single particle of light energy into the eye we would see that it first is absorbed by the retina's receptor cells, the *rods* and *cones.* When struck by light energy, the rods and cones generate a neural signal that activates neighboring bipolar cells, which in turn activate their neighboring ganglion cells (see Figure 6-6). The axons from the network of ganglion cells converge to form the *optic nerve* that carries information to the brain. Where the optic nerve leaves the eye, there are no receptor cells—creating a *blind spot* (see Figure 6-7). Nearly a million messages can be transmitted up the optic nerve at once, through the nearly 1 million ganglion fibers.

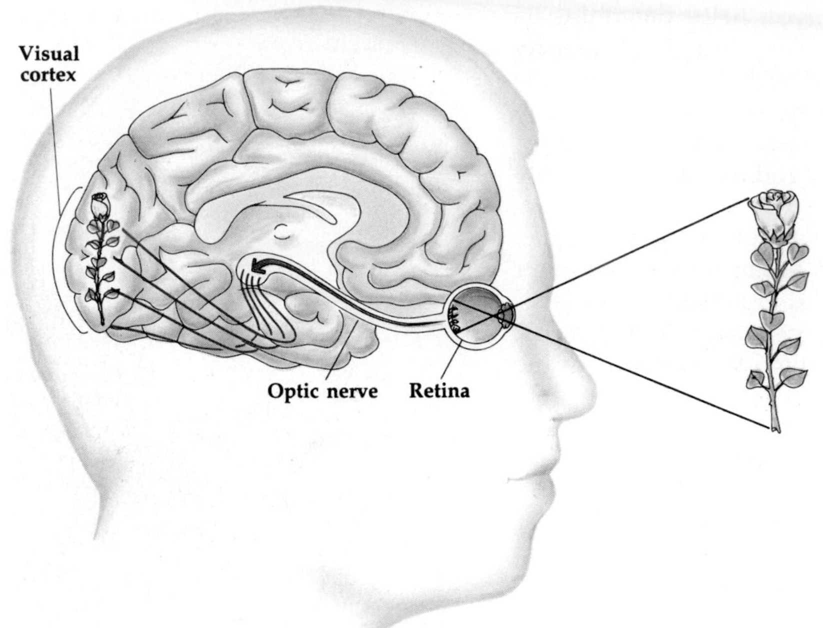

Figure 6-5 *How the brain's visual cortex receives images detected by the eye. Light rays reflected by the rose strike the retina's millions of receptor nerve cells triggering nerve impulses. These signals travel along a nerve pathway to the visual cortex at the back of the brain.*

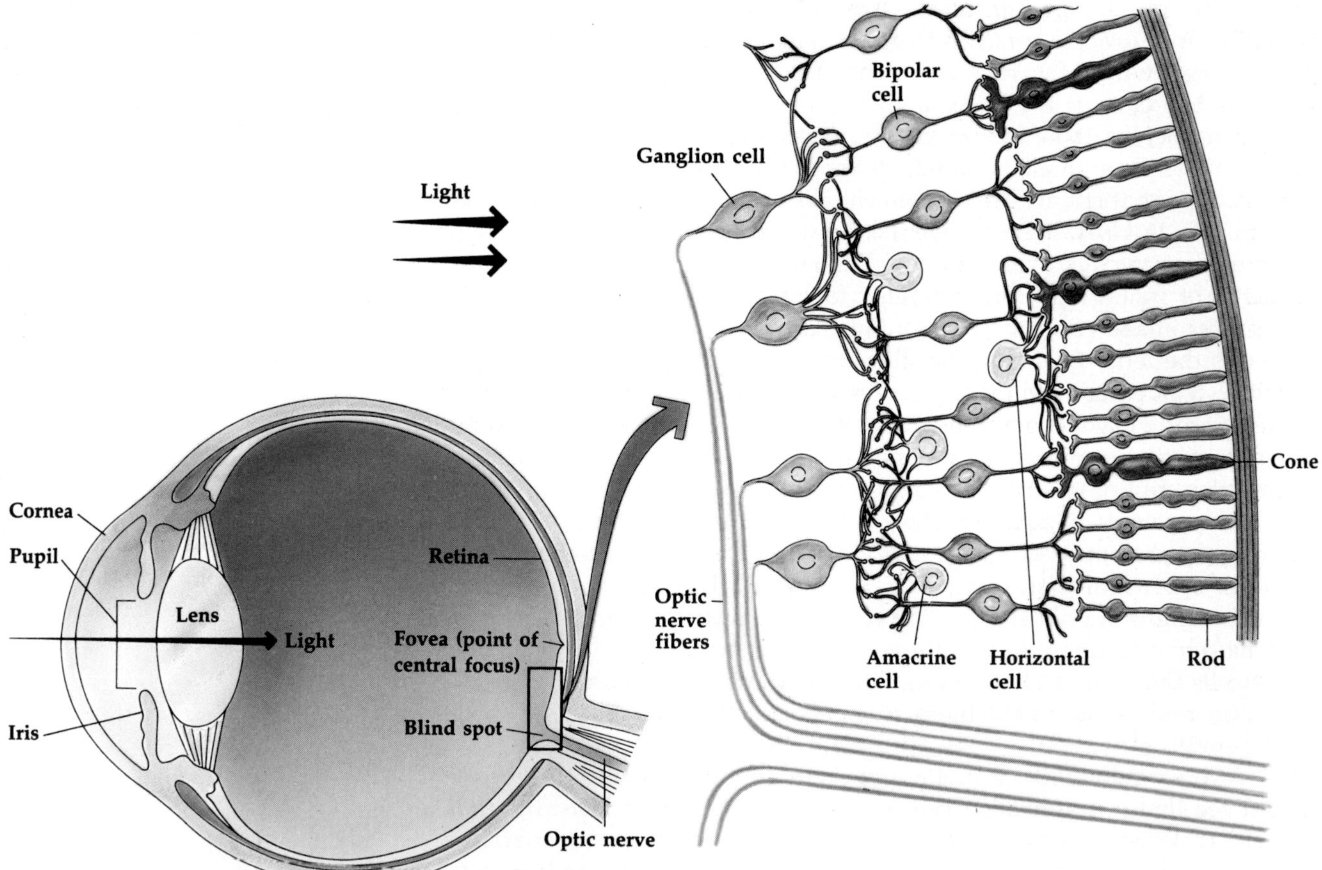

Figure 6-6 *How the retina processes visual information. Before signals from the retina reach the brain, they are transformed by a switchboard of neural cells. A photochemical reaction in the rods and cones (which are at the back of the retina behind the other neural layers) triggers the bipolar cells, which activate the ganglion cells, which converge to form the optic nerve.*

Figure 6-7 *The blind spot. Where the optic nerve leaves the eye (see Figure 6-5), there are no receptor cells. This creates a blind spot in our vision. To demonstrate, close your left eye, look at the spot, and move the page to a distance from your face (about 9 inches) where the oncoming car disappears.*

Most of the 6 million cones are clustered around the fovea, the point of central focus in the retina. In fact, the fovea contains only cones, no rods. Unlike rods, many cones have their own bipolar cells to help relay their individual messages to the cortex. This preserving of their precise information makes them more sensitive to fine detail. (Rods share bipolar cells with other rods, so their individual messages get combined.) If you pick a word in this sentence and stare directly at it, thereby focusing its image on the cones in your fovea, you will see that words a few inches off to the side appear blurred. This is because their image is striking the outer region of your retina, where the 120 million rods predominate.

It is only cones that enable you to see color. That is why you cannot distinguish colors in dim light, where the more light-sensitive rods do most of your seeing.

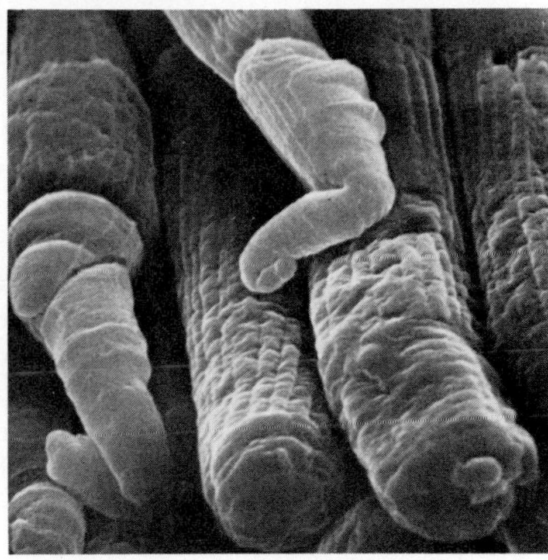

Rods and cones as shown by the scanning electron microscope. Rods, which are responsible for black-and-white vision, are more light sensitive than cones, which is why the world becomes colorless to us at night. Some nocturnal animals such as toads, mice, rats, and bats, have retinas made up almost entirely of rods. Cones, in addition to being responsible for color vision, provide a greater degree of resolution than rods and are concentrated at the fovea.

Visual Information Processing

Our visual processing system is made up of a series of levels, with each higher level dealing with more abstracted versions of reality. At the entry level, the retina—which turns out actually to be a piece of the brain that split off during early fetal development—processes information before routing it to the cortex. The retina's neural layers are not just passing along electrical impulses, they are involved in encoding and analyzing the sensory information.

In simple animals, in fact, much of the important processing of visual information takes place in the retina's neural tissues. By the third neural layer in a frog's eye there already exist cells that fire only in response to specific types of stimulation hitting the receptors—recall the "bug detector" cells. In more complex animals, too, information is processed by the retina's interconnected cells. In human eyes, for example, the raw information from the retina's 130 million receptor rods and cones converge onto the million or so ganglion cells whose fibers make up the optic nerve. But most of the information processing occurs in the brain. Any given area of the retina relays its information via the optic nerve through the thalamus to a corresponding location in the visual cortex at the back of the brain (see Figure 6-5). Each of the cortical neurons to which these messages are relayed specializes in recognizing certain types of visual information.

If we wish to see a particular dim star at night, should we look straight at it? Why or why not?

By measuring the response of these neurons singly to flashes of light in a cat's or monkey's eye, Nobel Prize winners David Hubel and Torsten Wiesel (1979) identified what seemed to be the precise stimuli that most strongly activate neurons at various levels in the visual cortex. Individual ganglion cells send signals to the visual cortex when they register a spot of a particular size in their region of the visual field. Hubel and Wiesel believe that when the cortical neurons—which they call ***feature detectors***—receive this information, they respond only to specific features of what is viewed.

And what features do these receiving cells of the visual cortex detect? According to Hubel and Wiesel, the brain first detects particular bars, edges, and lines, and from these elements assembles the perceived image. They report that a given brain cell might respond maximally to a line flashed at a particular tilt. If the line is tilted further—say from a 2 o'clock to a 3 o'clock or 1 o'clock position—the cell's response will likely decrease or stop (see Figure 6-8). Thus the feature detector cells seem to record amazingly specific features that are abstracted from the visual information taken in by the eye. These cells pass on this information to other cells that only signal when a more complex pattern, such as a particular angle formed by two lines, is present.

The precise nature of the features and patterns that brain cells detect is currently being debated. New research suggests that the actual building blocks of perception may not only be individual bars of light and dark, but also, or instead, more complicated patterns of changes in light intensity (DeValois & DeValois, 1980). Nevertheless, Hubel, Wiesel, and other researchers agree that visual information is broken down into millions of neural impulses, then step by step reassembled into its component features, and finally—in some as yet mysterious way—composed into the consciously perceived image, which is then compared with previously stored images and recognized as, for example, one's grandmother. The whole process (see Figure 6-9) is as complex as taking a house apart, splinter by splinter, transporting it to a different location, and then having millions of specialized workers reconstruct it. That all of this happens in a fraction of a second, and that it continuously transpires in motion, in three dimensions, and in color, is truly awesome.

Figure 6-8 *Electrodes record the responses of individual cells in this monkey's visual cortex to different visual stimuli. Hubel and Wiesel won the Nobel Prize for their discovery that most cells in the visual cortex respond only to particular features —for example, to the edge of a surface. Other more complex detector cells might respond only to a line at a 30-degree angle from the horizontal in the upper right part of the field of vision or to a horizontal bar in the lower left part of the field of vision. Higher-level detector cells, which integrate information from these simpler ones, are triggered only by even more complex features.*

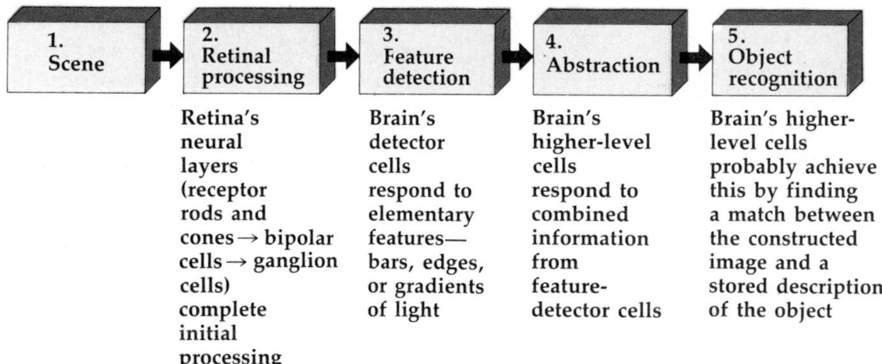

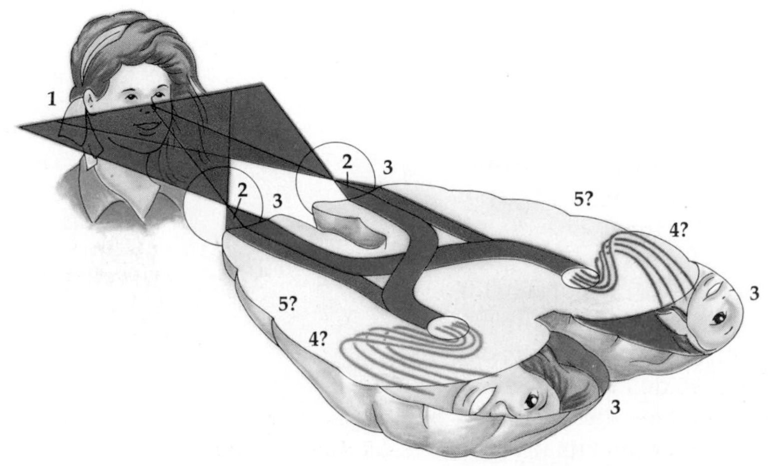

Figure 6-9 *A simplified summary of visual information processing. The drawing depicts the different levels of processing identified in the flowchart. A question mark indicates a level of processing that is thought (but not known with certainty) to occur in that location in the brain.*

Visual Sensitivity

Acuity

Acuity, or sharpness, of sight can be affected by small distortions in the shape of the eye (see Figure 6-10). Normally the eye focuses the image of any object on the retina. But if an eyeball is longer than normal in relation to its lens, the image of distant objects gets focused in front of the retina rather than on it. The result is ***nearsightedness,*** in which perception of near objects is clear but that of distant objects is blurred. Correspondingly, if an eyeball is shorter than normal in relation to its lens, the image of near objects gets focused behind the retina, producing ***farsightedness,*** in which perception of distant objects is clear, but that of near objects is blurred.

When viewing an eye chart, people with normal 20/20 vision can read material of a certain size from a distance of 20 feet. If standing 20 feet away you can discriminate only what people with normal vision can see at 50 feet, then you have 20/50 vision.

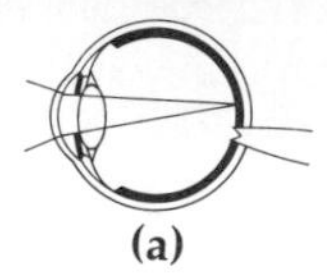
(a)
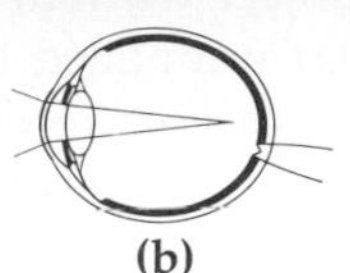
(b)
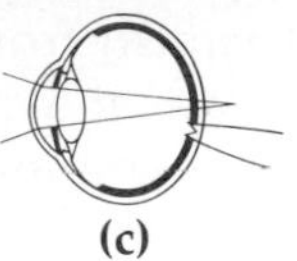
(c)

Figure 6-10 *(a) Normal vision. Andrea Parker, 16, floats in a neighbor's pool in Arlington, Virginia. To a person with normal vision, both the boat in front of Andrea and the flowerpots behind her look clear and sharp. As the diagram below shows, rays of light come to a point on the retina of a normal eye. When this occurs, both nearby and faraway objects appear in focus. (b) Nearsighted vision. To a near-sighted person, Andrea and the flowers behind her appear as a blur; the boat, however, is clear. The diagram below shows that in a nearsighted eyeball, which is longer than normal, the light rays from distant objects are focused in front of the retina. When their image reaches the retina, the rays are spreading out and the image is blurred. (c) Farsighted vision. A farsighted person also sees a blurred image of Andrea. The toy boat looks out of focus but the flowers are distinct. As the diagram shows, light rays from nearby objects come into focus behind the retina in the farsighted eyeball, which is shorter than normal, resulting in blurred images. Only far-away objects are clearly seen.*

In later life the lens hardens, losing some of its ability to thicken for focusing on near objects. With age the diameter of the pupil also shrinks and the lens becomes less transparent, reducing the retina's access to light. In fact, the 65-year-old retina receives only about one-third as much light as its 20-year-old counterpart (Kline & Schieber, 1985). To have a similar visual experience when reading, a 65-year-old will therefore require three times as much light as a 20-year-old.

Dark Adaptation

The 65-year-old's threefold loss of sensitivity seems less handicapping when we consider the enormous range of illumination to which the human eye can adapt. Sunlight illuminates objects with 1 million times more light than moonlight, but we can see under both conditions (McBurney & Collings, 1984). When viewing a white piece of paper in direct sunlight, your eye receives 10 billion times the light it receives at your absolute threshold when you detect a candle flickering 30 miles away—yet your eyes can adjust to both conditions (Riggs, 1975).

As illumination diminishes, the cones quickly become more sensitive. The rods reach maximum sensitivity much more slowly. However, the rods are keenly sensitive in dim light, to which the cones do not respond (see Figure 6-11). Thus when we enter a darkened theater or turn off the light at night, the pupil dilates to allow more light to reach the rods in the retina's periphery. In such conditions of sudden light change, it typically takes 20 minutes or more before our eyes are maximally sensitive. This period of dark adaptation seems to be yet another instance of the remarkable adaptiveness of our sensory systems, for it corresponds to the natural twilight transition period between the sun's setting and darkness.

How might older people's generally smaller pupil diameters affect their night vision?

Figure 6-11 *As the light on this brick gateway fades, we can still see the structure but the details of the brickwork and its color are vanishing. In dim light, it is the rods in our retinas that do most of our seeing.*

Eye Movements

We noted earlier that under conditions of constant stimulation our sense receptors undergo another form of adaptation—diminished sensitivity. Within minutes of our entering a room that has a distinct odor, that odor seems to vanish. Why then, if we stare at an object without flinching, does it not vanish from sight? The answer is that unnoticed by us, our eyes are always moving, quivering just enough to guarantee that the retinal image is continually changing. But what if we could stop our eyes from moving? Then would sights vanish like odors? To answer this question, psychologists have devised several ingenious instruments for maintaining a constant image on the retina. Imagine that we fitted a subject, Mary, with one of these instruments—a miniature projector mounted on a contact lens (see Figure 6-12a). When Mary's eye moves, the image from the projector moves as well. Thus everywhere that Mary looks the light is sure to go.

If an image of, say, the profile of a face is projected from such an instrument, what will Mary see? At first she will see the complete profile. But then within a few seconds, as the receptors begin to fatigue, a strange phenomenon will occur. Bit by bit, the image will vanish, only later to reappear and then disappear—in recognizable fragments or in whole (see Figure 6-12b). Interestingly, the disappearance and reappearance of an image occurs in meaningful units. Whole portions of the face come and go. If a person is shown a word containing other words, the projected word will disappear and new words made up of parts of it will appear and then vanish. This phenomenon anticipates a major conclusion about perception that we will come to in Chapter 7: Our perceptions are organized by the meanings that our minds impose.

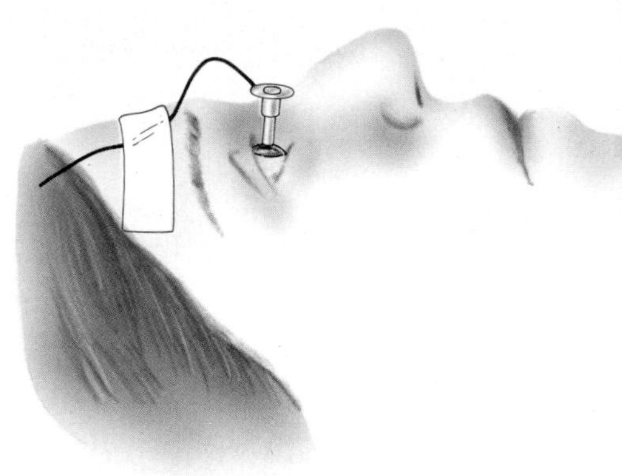

(a)

BEER PEER PEEP BEE BE

(b)

Figure 6-12 *A stabilized image experiment. (a) A subject wears a projector mounted on a contact lens; whenever her eye moves so does the projected image. (b) As these sample progressions illustrate, when first projected, the stabilized image is clear, but soon it fades. It reappears in meaningful fragments or as a whole, only to fade and reappear, perhaps in different fragments, again and again. (From "Stabilized images on the retina" by R. M. Pritchard. Copyright © 1961 Scientific American, Inc. All rights reserved.)*

Color Vision

In the study of vision, one of the most fundamental and intriguing mysteries is, how do we manage to see the world in color—and in such a multitude of colors? Our difference threshold for colors is so low that we can discriminate some 7 million differing shades and brightnesses (Geldard, 1972)!

Modern detective work on the mystery of color vision began in the nineteenth century when a German physiologist, Hermann von Helmholtz, built on the insights of an English physicist, Thomas Young. Recog-

Figure 6-13 *The three basic colors can be mixed to create other colors. For example, red and green combine to create yellow. All three basic colors combine to create white.*

nizing a clue in the fact that any color can be arrived at through some combinations of the three basic colors (see Figure 6-13)—red, green, and blue—Young and Helmholtz inferred that the eye must therefore have three types of receptors, one for each of these three basic colors. A century later, researchers measured the response of various cones to different colors and confirmed the ***Young-Helmholtz three-color theory,*** which simply states that the retina has three types of color receptors, each especially sensitive to one of three colors: red, green, or blue. When combinations of these cones are stimulated, other colors are perceived. For example, there are no receptors for yellow, yet when both red- and green-sensitive cones are stimulated, we see yellow.

As physiologist Ewald Hering soon pointed out, however, the Young-Helmholtz three-color theory left other parts of the color vision mystery unsolved. For example, if we see yellow as a result of stimulation of red- and green-sensitive receptors, how is it that people who are color blind to red and green see yellow? And why does yellow appear to be a pure color and not a mixture of red and green, as purple does of red and blue? Hering found his clue to the answers in the well-known occurrence of afterimages. When you stare at a green square for a while and then look at a white sheet of paper, you will see red, green's "opponent color." Stare at a yellow square and you will later see its opponent color, blue, on the white paper (as in the demonstration of Figure 6-14). Hering surmised that there were two types of color receptors: one responsible for red versus green perception, and one for yellow versus blue.

A century later, researchers also confirmed Hering's ***opponent-process theory,*** with one exception. The modern theory assumes that it is *after* visual information leaves the receptor cells that it is analyzed in terms of the opponent colors, red and green, blue and yellow, and black and white. So if you detect one of these colors at a particular point on the retina you cannot simultaneously detect the opposing color at the same point; you therefore cannot see a greenish-red. Psychologist Russell DeValois (DeValois & DeValois, 1975) discovered this in research with

Figure 6-14 *After-image effect. Stare at the center of the flag for a minute and then shift your eyes to a white surface. What do you see?*

monkeys, whose visual system is similar to our own. DeValois measured the activity of single neurons in a portion of the thalamus (where impulses from the retina are relayed to the visual cortex) and found that some are turned "on" by red, but turned "off" by green. Others are turned on by green, but off by red. Still other cells show the same opposing reactions to yellow and blue.

If you have grasped the basic idea, then you should be able to follow the reasoning by which opponent processes explain afterimages. White light is a mixture of all colors. Thus if your green "on"/red "off" neurons are fatigued by your having stared at green, your red "on"/green "off" neurons will still detect the red in white light. If after staring at the green-striped flag you look at something white, you therefore see a red afterimage. (It is interesting that the four opponent colors are the same four colors into which our brains divide the continuum of colors in the color spectrum.)

Our understanding of color vision is incomplete, and is complicated by other puzzling phenomena. But it seems that the solution to the mystery of color vision will include both the three types of color-sensitive receptors of the eye (for red, green, or blue) and the two types of opponent process cells (for red versus green, and for blue versus yellow) that receive and process information from the eye on its way to the visual cortex.

HEARING

Like all our senses, our hearing, or ***audition,*** is highly adaptive. We hear a wide range of sounds, but we best hear sounds whose pitch lies within a range that corresponds to the usual range of human voices. We are also remarkably sensitive to faint sounds, an obvious boon to survival if one is hunting or being hunted. (Were our ears any more sensitive we would hear a constant hiss from the movement of air molecules.) Moreover, we are acutely sensitive to differences in sounds. We can easily detect differences among thousands of human voices and so instantly recognize the voice of almost anyone we know. For hearing as for seeing, the fundamental question is, how do we do it? How do we transduce the energy of auditory stimuli into neural messages that the brain then interprets as a particular sound coming from a particular place?

The Stimulus Input: Sound Waves

The stimulus energy for hearing is sound waves, air-pressure waves composed of moving bands of compressed and expanded air. (We can think of these pressure waves as something like the ripples on a pond circling out from where a tossed stone broke the water.) The length and therefore the *frequency* of these waves determines their *pitch:* the longer and slower the waves, the lower the pitch; the shorter and faster the waves, the higher the pitch. A piccolo produces much shorter, faster waves than a kettle drum. The size, or *amplitude,* of the waves determines their *loudness;* the greater the amplitude, the louder the sound. But rather than being of one pure frequency, most sound waves are a complex mixture of many frequencies. A piano and a clarinet can both produce a pitch of middle C, but neither is pure middle C. It is the *complexity* of mixing in those "other frequencies" that provides the ***timbre,*** or tone color, of a sound and that enables you to tell that one middle C has come from the piano, the other from the clarinet.

The pitch of a sound corresponds to the hue of light (both being determined by wavelength and frequency), loudness corresponds to brightness (both being determined by amplitude), and timbre corresponds to saturation (both being determined by complexity).

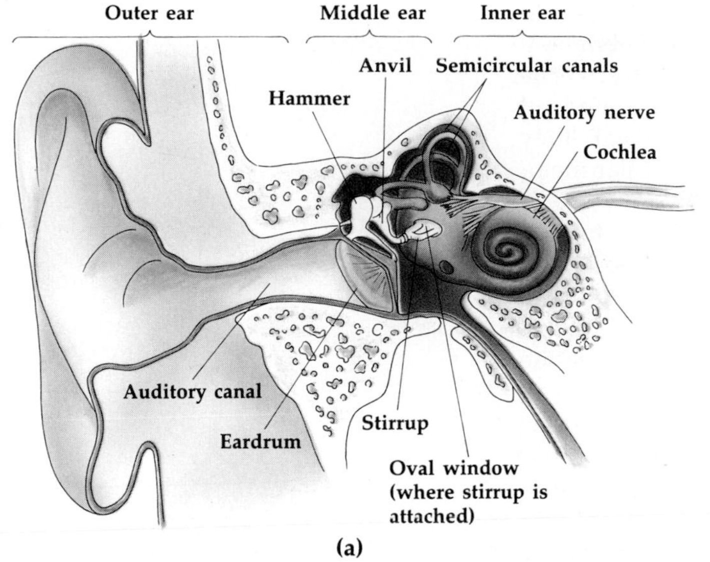

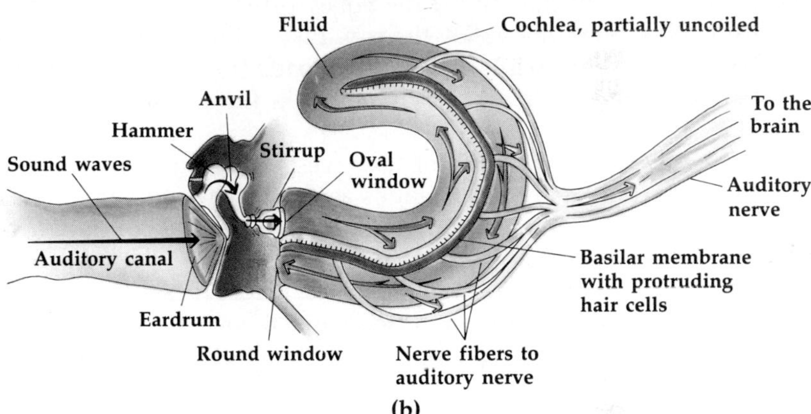

Figure 6-15 *How sound waves are transformed into nerve impulses in the ear. (a) Sound waves are funneled by the outer ear to the eardrum. The bones of the middle ear amplify and relay the eardrum's vibrations through the oval window into the fluid-filled cochlea. (b) The resulting waves in the cochlear fluid cause the basilar membrane to ripple, bending the hair cells on its surface. This sets off impulses in the nerve cells at their bases, whose fibers converge to form the auditory nerve. (For clarity the cochlea is shown partially uncoiled.)*

The Ears

How Does the Brain Get Information from the Ears?

To hear, we must somehow convert sound waves into neural messages. The human ear accomplishes this feat through an intricate mechanical chain reaction. First, the visible outer ear (see Figure 6-15) channels the sound waves toward the eardrum, a tight membrane that vibrates in step with the waves. The ***middle ear*** then amplifies the eardrum's vibrations by transmitting them via a piston made of three tiny bones (the hammer, anvil, and stirrup) to a coiled tube in the ***inner ear*** called the ***cochlea.*** The incoming vibrations cause the cochlea's outer membrane (the oval window) to vibrate, triggering waves within this fluid-filled tube. These waves cause ripples in the basilar membrane, which is lined with hair cells. The rippling of the basilar membrane in turn bends these hair cells, triggering impulses in the nerve fibers attached to the hair cells. Through this mechanical chain of events, sound waves cause the hair cells of the inner ear to send neural messages up to the brain (see Figure 6-16).

The ear's exquisite sensitivity allows us to detect vibrations of the eardrum as tiny as 0.0000000000003 meters, which is roughly the diameter of a hydrogen molecule (Kaufman, 1979).

How Do We Perceive Pitch?

How do we know whether a sound is the high-pitched chirp of a bird or the low-pitched roar of a truck? ***Place theory*** presumes that we hear different pitches because sound waves of various frequencies trigger activity at different places on the cochlea's basilar membrane. Thus the brain can determine the pitch of a sound by recognizing the place on the membrane from which it receives neural signals. When Georg von Bekesy (1957) cut holes in the cochleas of guinea pigs and human cadavers and looked

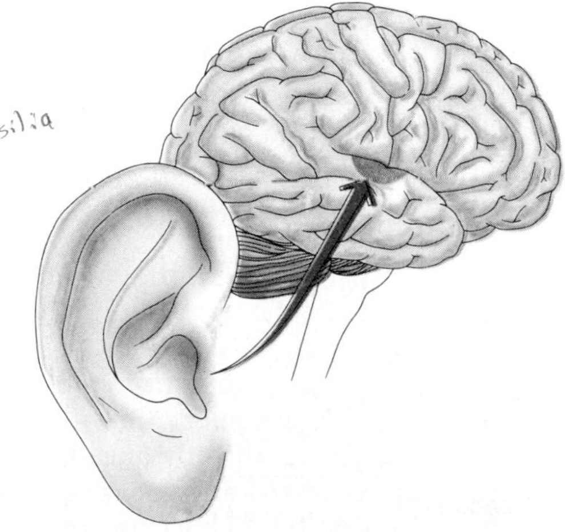

Figure 6-16 *Information from the ears travels first to the auditory areas in the temporal lobe.*

inside with a microscope, he discovered that high-frequency waves triggered activity mostly near the beginning of the cochlea's membrane, a discovery that contributed to his receiving the 1961 Nobel Prize. While place theory could therefore explain how we hear high-pitched sounds, it had trouble with low-pitched sounds, because the neural signals they generated were not so neatly localized to one place on the basilar membrane.

Frequency theory suggests an equally simple mechanism for the brain's ability to determine pitch. The whole basilar membrane vibrates in step with the incoming sound wave, thus triggering neural impulses to the brain at the same frequency as the sound wave. If the sound wave has only 100 waves per second, then 100 impulses per second travel up the auditory nerve. Thus the brain can determine pitch from the frequency of these impulses. Unlike place theory, this theory can explain how we perceive low pitches. But individual neurons cannot fire faster than 1000 times per second, so how could it explain our sensation of sounds with frequencies above 1000 waves per second (roughly the upper third of a piano keyboard)? It does so by the volley principle (hence the frequency theory is also called the volley theory). Like soldiers who alternate firing so that one can fire while the other reloads, neural cells can alternate firing and thereby can achieve a combined firing rate well above 1000 times per second.

The current explanation of how we discriminate pitch, like that of how we discriminate color, includes aspects of two theories. With color vision the three-color theory describes the retinal receptors and the opponent-process theory describes the neural processing between the retina and the visual cortex. With pitch, place theory best explains how we sense the very high pitches, and frequency theory the lower pitches. But some combination of the two apparently handles the intermediate range pitches.

How Do We Locate Sounds?

The fact that we have two ears allows us to enjoy stereophonic ("three-dimensional") hearing. The slightly different messages sensed by the two microphones used in creating a stereophonic recording mimics the slightly different sound messages received by our two ears. If a car to our right honks its horn, our right ear will receive a louder sound slightly sooner than the left ear. Given that sound travels 750 miles per hour and our ears are but a half-foot apart, the loudness difference and time lag are extremely small. But the sensitivity of our auditory system is such that our two ears can detect extremely small differences (Brown & Deffenbacher, 1979). A just noticeable difference in the direction from which two sounds come corresponds to a time difference of just 0.000027 second!

So how well do you suppose we do at locating a sound that is equidistant from our two ears, such as those that come from directly ahead, behind, overhead, or beneath us? The answer is not very well, because such sounds strike the two ears simultaneously. You can demonstrate this by having a friend sit with eyes closed while you snap your figures at various locations around your friend's head. Your friend will easily point to the sound when it comes from either side, but will likely make mistakes when it comes from directly ahead, behind, below, or above. Similarly, when you make mistakes in locating a sound in an everyday situation, the mislocated sound has likely come from a location where it strikes the ears the same as would a sound from a different location. And that is why when trying to pinpoint a sound you find it helpful to turn your head, ensuring that your two ears receive different messages.

Hearing Loss

The ear's intricate and delicate structure makes it vulnerable to damage. Problems with the mechanical system by which sound wave vibrations reach the cochlea cause ***conduction deafness.*** For example, if the eardrum is punctured or if the tiny bones of the middle ear lose their flexibility, the ear's conduction of vibrations diminishes. However, a hearing aid may restore hearing by amplifying the vibrations.

Problems with the cochlea's receptors or with the auditory nerve can cause ***nerve deafness.*** Once neural tissue is destroyed, no hearing aid can restore its functioning. This type of deafness has three causes—prolonged exposure to ear-splitting noise or music (see "Noise," p. 156), diseases, and biological changes linked with aging (Figure 6-17). Hearing losses with age are especially pronounced in the higher frequencies. In later adulthood, birds appear to chirp more softly and whispered conversation becomes frustratingly unintelligible.

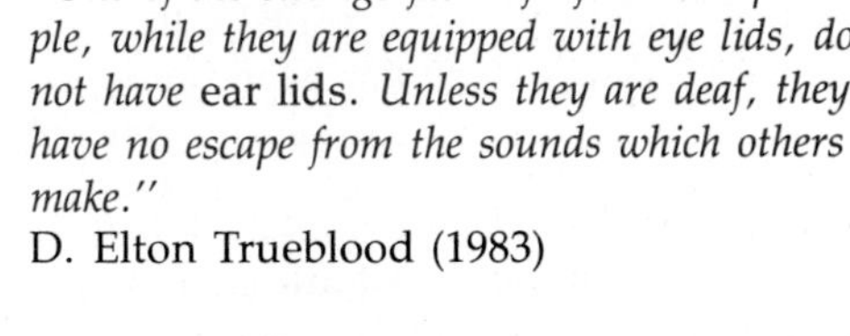

"One of the strange facts of life is that people, while they are equipped with eye lids, do not have ear lids. *Unless they are deaf, they have no escape from the sounds which others make."*
D. Elton Trueblood (1983)

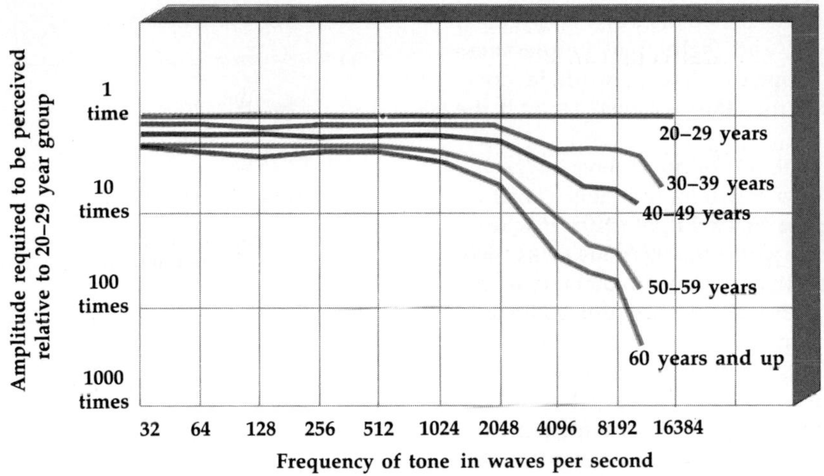

Figure 6-17 *Elderly people tend to hear low frequencies well but suffer hearing loss for high frequencies. This high-frequency loss has been linked to nerve degeneration near the beginning of the basilar membrane. Which explanation of hearing does this confirm, place or frequency theory?*

THE OTHER SENSES

For humans, seeing and hearing are the major senses. We depend upon them most, particularly for communication. Our cortexes give these two senses priority in the allocation of its sense-related tissue. For other animals, the priorities among the senses differ. Sharks and dogs rely on their extraordinary senses of smell, which are facilitated by the proportionately large amount of their cortexes devoted to them. Nevertheless, without our sense of touch, our senses of taste and smell, and our senses of body motion and position, we humans would be seriously handicapped, and our capacities for enjoying the world would certainly be diminished.

If you had to give up one sense, which would it be? If you could retain but one sense, which would it be?

Touch

Our "sense of touch" is actually a mix of at least four distinct skin senses—pressure, warmth, cold, and pain. Touching various spots on the skin with a soft hair, a warm or cooled wire, and a pin point, reveals that some spots are especially sensitive to pressure (from the hair), others to warmth, others to cold, and still others to pain. Within the skin there are different types of specialized nerve endings. Does that mean that each type is a receptor for one of the basic skin senses, much as the cone receptors of the eye correspond to the basic colors of light?

The word "touch" is so rich with meaning that in the Oxford English Dictionary *its definition runs the longest of any entry.*

Noise

Urban life is noisy. Traffic roars. Factory machines clatter. Jackhammers tear up pavement. Escaping to more pleasant sounds, joggers are driven by the beat of intense music over their portable headphones.

But the intensity of that sound may, in the long run, cause a serious problem. Brief exposure to extremely intense sounds, such as gunfire near one's ear, and prolonged exposure to intense sounds, such as amplified music, can alter or destroy the receptor cells and auditory nerves for sound (Backus 1977). For some rock musicians, the sad truth is that while rock and roll is here to stay their hearing may not be. It has been found that prolonged exposure to sounds above 85 *decibels* produces hearing loss (see Figure 6-18). (The absolute threshold for hearing is arbitrarily defined as 0 decibels. Every 10 decibel increase, say from 60 to 70 decibels, doubles the perceived loudness.)

Noise may affect not only our hearing, but our behavior as well. On tasks requiring alert performance, many experiments have shown that people in noisy surroundings work less efficiently and make more errors (Broadbent, 1978). People who live with continual noise in factories, in homes near airports, and in apartments adjacent to trains and highways suffer elevated rates of stress-related disorders such as high blood pressure, anxiety, and feelings of helplessness (Cohen & others, 1980). Might people who happen to live or work in noisy environments be susceptible to these problems for other reasons? Or is it the noise per se that causes the stress?

Laboratory experiments on the psychological effects of noise have suggested an answer. In one such experiment, David Glass and Jerome Singer (1972) recreated the noise of city life by tape recording the chattering of office machines and of people speaking foreign languages. While working at various tasks, people heard this noise, played either loudly or softly, at either predictable or unpredictable intervals. Regardless of these conditions, the people soon adapted to the noise and on most tasks performed well. However, having coped with the noise, those who had been exposed to the *unpredictable* loud noise later made more errors on a proofreading task and reacted more quickly to frustration. Results such as these suggest that noise is most stressful when it is unanticipated or uncontrollable. Don't you, after all, find the unpredictable and uncontrollable blaring of someone else's stereo more upsetting than the same decibels from your own?

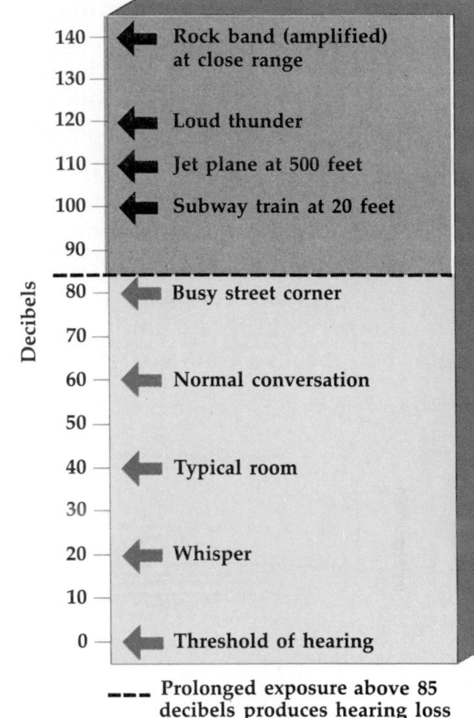

Figure 6-18 *The intensity of some common sounds, measured in decibels. The absolute threshold for hearing is arbitrarily defined as zero decibels. Perceived loudness increases geometrically with decibels: a 10 decibel increase from 60 to 70 decibels doubles perceived loudness.*

(a)

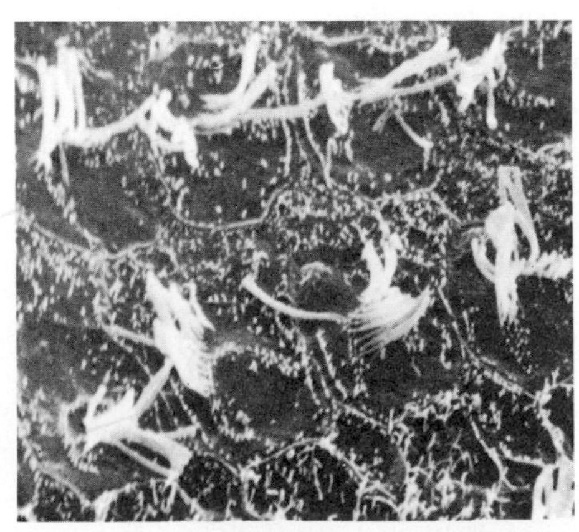

(b)

These scanning electron micrographs of the hair cells of a guinea pig before (a) and after (b) exposure to 24 hours of loud noise (comparable to that of a loud rock concert) testify to the destructive effects of such noise.

To answer this question, researchers have compared different sensitive spots on the skin with the particular receptors located at those spots. Surprisingly, there is no simple relationship between what we feel at a given spot and the type of specialized nerve ending found there. Except for pressure, which does have identifiable receptors, the relationship between warmth, cold, and pain and receptors that respond to them remains a mystery. Some investigators even believe that pain does not have specialized receptors, but rather results from the overstimulation of any receptor.

Other skin sensations are variations on the basic sensations. Stroking adjacent pressure spots creates a tickle. Repeated gentle stroking of a pain spot will create an itching sensation. Touching adjacent cold and pressure spots triggers a sensation of wetness (which can therefore be experienced by touching dry but cold metal). Stimulating nearby cold and warmth spots produces a feeling of "hot" (see Figure 6-19). (Cold spots respond either to very low or very high temperatures. Thus we sense hot when a high temperature activates both warm and cold spots. We have no special "hot spots.")

Warm water

Cold water

Figure 6-19 *Warm + Cold = Hot. When ice-cold water is passed through one coil and comfortably warm water through another, the combined sensation is perceived as burning hot.*

Taste

Our sense of taste operates much like that of touch (McBurney & Gent, 1979). We experience four basic taste sensations—sweet, sour, salty, and bitter—with all other tastes being varying mixtures of these. Investigators have been frustrated in their search for specialized nerve fibers for each of the four basic taste sensations, but they have found spots on the surface of the tongue that have special sensitivities—the tip of the tongue for sweet and salty tastes, the back of the tongue for bitter (see Figure 6-20).

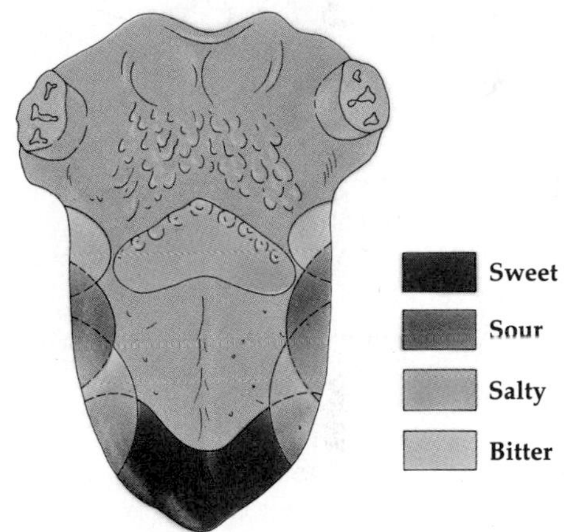

Figure 6-20 *Different parts of the tongue have different sensitivities to the four basic taste sensations—sweet, sour, salty, and bitter.*

Inside each of the little bumps on the top and sides of your tongue are more than 200 taste buds, each a cluster of 15 to 20 taste receptors. Some of these receptors respond mostly to sweet-tasting molecules, others to salty-, sour-, or bitter-tasting ones. And it doesn't take much to trigger a response. When a stream of water is pumped across the tongue, the addition of a concentrated salty or sweet taste for but 1/10th of a second can usually be detected (Kelling & Halpern, 1983). When a friend asks for "just a taste" of your soft drink, you can squeeze off the straw after a fraction of a second and have fulfilled the request.

Taste receptors reproduce themselves every week, so if you burn your tongue with hot food it matters little. However, as you grow older, the receptors change; their number declines because the number of taste buds decreases, and so taste sensitivity declines as well (Cowart, 1981). (This is one reason why adults enjoy strong-tasting foods that children resist.) The decline in taste sensitivities might be due to aging, but it might also be due to behaviors, such as smoking or alcohol use, that could deaden the taste buds.

Although taste buds are essential for taste, there is more to taste than meets the tongue. Hold your nose, close your eyes, and have someone feed you various foods. A piece of apple may then be indistinguishable from a piece of raw potato; a piece of steak may taste like cardboard. To savor a taste, we normally exhale the aroma through the nose—which is why eating is not much fun when you have a bad cold. What the tongue cannot know, the nose knows (Figure 6-21). This is ***sensory interaction*** at work—the principle that one sense may be influenced by another. The sense of taste is influenced by smell. Similarly, we correctly perceive the location of the voice directly in front of us because we *see* that the person is in front of us, not behind, above, or beneath us.

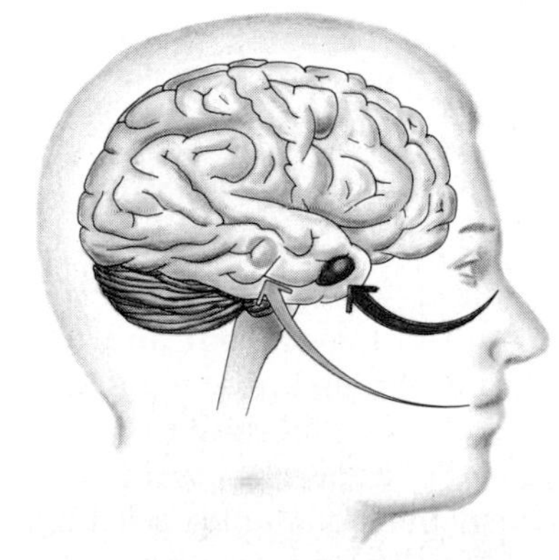

Figure 6-21 *Information from the taste buds travels to an area of the temporal lobe not far from that where olfactory information is received.*

Smell

Like taste, smell is a chemical sense. To smell something, molecules of a substance must be carried by air to a tiny cluster of 5 million receptor cells atop each of our nasal cavities (Figure 6-22). Other animals, which may have many more receptors located more centrally in the nose, often communicate and navigate through their sense of smell. Long before the shark can see its prey, or the moth its mate, odors direct the way.

Unlike taste, there appears to be no simple set of basic smells. Nevertheless, sensitivity to certain smells, such as the musky odor emitted by the males of some mammalian species, is exquisite—as little as 1 trillionth of an ounce present in a pint of air can be detected. Near the time of ovulation women are especially sensitive to such odors, which are also present in some men's colognes (Parlee, 1983).

Our olfactory powers are paltry in comparison to a bloodhound's. Bloodhounds, who have relatively poor eyesight, have followed a person's trail for over 100 miles and can detect someone's scent for as long as 3 or 4 days after they have passed by. Judging by their olfactory nerve endings, bloodhounds are thought to be about 2 million times as sensitive to odors as human beings.

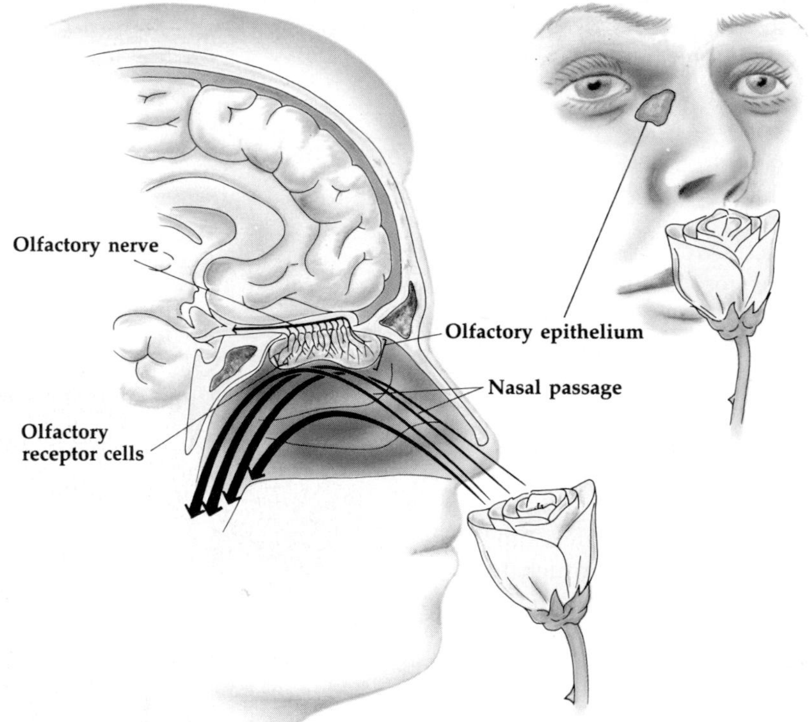

Figure 6-22 *The sense of smell. To smell a rose, molecules of its fragrance must reach receptors at the top of the nose. Sniffing swirls air up to the receptors, enhancing the aroma.*

Body Movement and Position

With only the sensory capabilities we have so far considered, we would be helpless. We could not put food in our mouth. We could not stand up. We could not reach out and touch someone. To perform such acts we must at all times know what we are doing, so we can know what to do next. To know just how to move our arms to grasp someone's hand, we first need to know the current position of our arms and hands and then be aware of their changing positions as we move them.

Humans come equipped with millions of such position and motion sensors. They are all over our bodies—in the muscles, tendons, and joints—and they are continually providing our brains with information. If we twist our wrists 1 degree, the sensors immediately report it. This sense of the position and movement of body parts is called ***kinesthesis.***

Olympic gold medalist Mary Lou Retton demonstrates on the balance beam her exquisite kinesthetic sense and sense of equilibrium.

A companion sense of ***equilibrium*** monitors the position and movement of the whole body. The receptors for our sense of equilibrium are in the inner ear. The ***semicircular canals***, which look rather like a three-dimensional pretzel, and the ***vestibular sacs***, which connect the canals with the cochlea, each contain substances that move when the head rotates or tilts. This movement stimulates hairlike receptors in these organs of the inner ear, which trigger messages to the brain that enable us continually to sense our body position and thereby maintain our balance.

Those who lose one sensory input generally become more attentive to input from their other senses.

SENSORY RESTRICTION

Imagine that one or more of your sensory windows on the world was closed. Would your other senses partially make up for the loss? People with sensory handicaps show us the rich potential of the senses. Blind people cope by making greater use of their sense of hearing. For example, they attend more to echoes bouncing off obstacles in their path in order to determine their location and size. (Close your eyes and immediately you will notice your attention being drawn to extraneous sounds.) Struck blind and deaf, Helen Keller nevertheless learned to speak, read, and write by becoming very attentive to information available through her sense of touch.

"Ears are eyes to the blind."
Sophocles, *Oedipus at Colonus*, 407 B.C.

The loss of a sense is but one type of a restricted sensory input. Another is sensory monotony—the relatively unchanging sensory input experienced by prisoners in solitary confinement, nighttime truck drivers and pilots, and animals in barren zoos. In experiments, several thousand people have temporarily experienced simulations of such restrictions. Some have spent several days in monotonous environments—small rooms where light and sound are unchanging. Others have passed time in dark, silent rooms, deprived of normal sensory input. The first such experiments, conducted in the early 1950s, produced some rather bizarre and widely publicized findings (Heron, 1957). The subjects, lying on beds and wearing translucent goggles to diffuse the light, typically began the experiment in good spirits. Here was a chance to make some easy money while enjoying relaxation and a time for creative thinking. However, before long they became somewhat disoriented, most experienced hallucinations, and many became susceptible to piped-in tape recorded messages arguing for the reality of ghosts.

Sensory deprivation can, in small doses, provide a welcome time-out. But it can become a source of anguish if extended too long, as is obvious in this photograph of a subject in a sensory-deprivation experiment.

As often happens in science, manipulating one factor may simultaneously manipulate other hidden factors. Are the effects of spending a day or two in a monotonous environment in fact due to the sensory restriction, or might they have been the result of the social isolation, the confinement, or the stressful procedures? The dramatic reports from early experiments prompted many more such investigations, most of which produced less newsworthy results (Suedfeld & Kristeller, 1982). Researchers have found that while most people are not dramatically affected by sensory restriction, the experience does seem to reduce stress and to help people become more suggestible.

How might the principle of sensory adaptation explain this sensitivity?

In experiments at the University of British Columbia with smokers and overweight people, Peter Suedfeld (1980) and his colleagues found that reduced sensory input can help people modify their behavior. Suedfeld (1975) emphasized that during voluntary sensory deprivation persuasion does "not reach the awesome proportions which many fiction writers (and some scientists who are writing fiction without knowing it) have indicated." But he also reported that people who wanted to alter their behavior often were able to gain increased self-control after 24 hours of what he aptly called REST—Restricted Environmental Stimulation Therapy. In one such experiment conducted by Suedfeld and Allan Best (1982), smokers attended antismoking instructional classes and also listened to messages concerning smoking while spending 24 hours lying on beds in quiet, dark rooms (rising only to drink a liquid diet available through tubes or to use toilets next to the beds). In the week that followed, none relapsed to smoking. A year later, two-thirds were still abstaining—double the number among those who received the instruction without the day of REST.

In other times and places, periods of solitude and sensory restriction have similarly been judged important for human fulfillment. Sensory restriction is an essential component of the "quiet therapies" of Japan (Reynolds, 1982); for example, Morita therapy for depressed or anxious people begins with a week of bed rest and meditation and progresses to assigned light tasks. The religious visions of Moses, Mohammed, and Buddha are believed to have occurred during times of solitude and contemplation. Jesus is reported to have begun his public ministry after 40 days alone in the wilderness. As social creatures we need the support and stimulation we provide one another, but there are also times we can benefit from the peace and relaxation of restricted stimulation.

SUMMING UP

To study sensation is to study an ageless question: How does the world out there get in? For example, how are the external stimuli that strike our bodies transformed into messages that our brains comprehend?

SENSING THE WORLD: SOME BASIC PRINCIPLES

Thresholds Each species comes equipped with sensitivities that enable it to survive and thrive. We sense only a portion of the sea of energy that surrounds us, but to most of this portion we are exquisitely sensitive. Our absolute threshold for any stimulus is the minimum amount that is detectable 50 percent of the time. Do we ever react to stimuli that are not only subthreshold (subliminal), but so weak that we could never consciously perceive them? Although some recent experiments reveal that people can process some information from stimuli that are too weak to be recognized, the restricted conditions under which this occurs would not enable advertisers to exploit us with hidden persuasive messages.

To survive and thrive, an organism must also have difference thresholds low enough to detect minute changes in important stimuli. In humans, difference thresholds (also called just noticeable differences, or jnd's) increase with the magnitude of the stimulus—a principle known as Weber's Law.

Sensory Adaptation The phenomenon of sensory adaptation helps focus our sensitivities on changing stimulation, by diminishing our sensitivities to constant odors, sounds, and so forth.

Our senses must all receive stimulation, transduce (transform) it into neural signals, and transmit the neural signals to the cortex. How does each sense do this?

SEEING

The Stimulus Input: Light Energy The energies we experience as light are a slice from a broad spectrum of electromagnetic waves. After being admitted into the eye through a camera-like mechanism, light waves strike the retina. The retina's rods and cones convert the light energy to neural impulses, which are coded by the retina before being transmitted by the optic nerve to the brain. In the cortex, individual feature detector cells respond to specific features of the visual stimulus, and their information is apparently pooled by higher-level brain cells.

Visual Sensitivity Visual acuity is often diminished by distortions in the shape of the eyeball (which cause the focusing problems of nearsightedness and farsightedness) and by other changes linked to aging. Despite such problems, our eyes are able to adapt to an enormous range of stimulation.

Color Vision Research on how we see color points to the validity of two old theories. First, as the Young-Helmholtz three-color theory suggests, the retina contains three types of cones, each of which is most sensitive to one of the three basic colors (red, green, or blue). Second, the nervous system codes the color-related information from the cones into pairs of opponent colors, as demonstrated by the phenomenon of afterimages and as confirmed by measuring opponent processes within visual neurons.

HEARING

The Stimulus Input: Sound Waves The pressure waves we experience as sound vary in frequency and amplitude, and correspondingly in perceived pitch and loudness.

The Ears Through a mechanical chain of events, minuscule vibrations in the eardrum are transmitted via the bones of the middle ear to the fluid-filled cochlea, where the movement of tiny hair cells triggers neural messages to the brain. Research on how we hear pitch has provided evidence for both the place theory, which best explains the sensation of high-pitched sounds, and frequency theory, which best explains the sensation of low pitches.

We localize sound by detecting miniscule differences in the loudness and timing of the sounds received by our two ears.

Hearing Loss Hearing losses linked to conduction and nerve disorders can be caused by prolonged exposure to loud noise and by diseases and age-related changes. Exposure to unpredictable loud noises may also produce stress-related disorders.

THE OTHER SENSES

Touch Our sense of touch is actually four senses—pressure, warmth, cold, and pain—that combine to produce other sensations, such as "hot."

Taste Taste is likewise a composite of four basic sensations—sweet, sour, salty, and bitter—and of the aromas that interact with information from the taste buds.

Smell Like taste, smell is a chemical sense, but there are no basic sensations for smell, as there are for touch and taste.

Body Position and Movement Finally, our effective functioning requires a kinesthetic sense (of the position and movement of body parts), and a sense of equilibrium (of the position and movement of the whole body).

SENSORY RESTRICTION

People temporarily or permanently deprived of one of their senses typically compensate by becoming more acutely aware of information from the other senses. Temporary experiences of sensory monotony or sensory deprivation have somewhat unpredictable effects. However, the loss of sensory input often evokes a heightened sensitivity to all forms of sensation, and under supervision may provide a therapeutic boost for those seeking control over problems such as smoking.

TERMS AND CONCEPTS TO REMEMBER

Absolute Threshold The minimum stimulation that a subject can detect 50 percent of the time.

Accommodation The process by which the lens of the eye changes shape to focus the image of near or distant objects on the retina.

Acuity The sharpness of sight.

Audition The sense of hearing.

Blind Spot The insensitive area of the retina (without rods and cones) where the optic nerve leaves the eye.

Brightness The psychological dimension of color (its brilliance) that is determined mostly by the intensity of light, but also by its nearness to the middle of the visible spectrum.

Cochlea (COCK-lee-a) A coiled, bony, fluid-filled tube in the inner ear in which sound waves trigger nerve impulses.

Complexity The mixture of different wavelengths of light or sound. Complexity determines the saturation of light and the timbre of sounds (low complexity = purity).

Conduction Deafness Hearing loss caused by damage to the mechanical system that conducts sound waves to the cochlea.

Cones Receptor cells concentrated near the center of the retina that operate in daylight. The cones detect fine detail and give rise to color sensations.

Decibel A unit of measure that specifies sound intensity.

Difference Threshold The minimum difference in stimulation that a subject can detect 50 percent of the time. We experience the difference threshold as a just noticeable difference (jnd).

Equilibrium The sense of body movement and position, including the sense of balance.

Farsightedness A condition in which faraway objects are seen clearly, but near objects are blurred because the lens focuses the image behind the retina.

Feature Detectors Nerve cells in the brain that respond to specific features of the stimulus, such as movement or shape.

Frequency Theory In hearing, the theory that the rate of pulses traveling up the auditory nerve matches the frequency of a tone, thus enabling us to sense its pitch.

Hue The dimension of color that we know as the color names (blue, green, and so forth) and that is determined by the wavelength of light.

Inner Ear The innermost part of the ear, containing the cochlea, semicircular canals, and vestibular sacs.

Intensity The amount of energy in a light or sound wave.

Iris A ring of tissue that forms the colored portion of the eye around the pupil and controls the size of the pupil opening.

Just Noticeable Difference See **Difference Threshold.**

Kinesthesis The system for sensing the position and movement of muscles, tendons, and joints.

Lens The transparent structure behind the pupil that changes shape to focus images on the retina.

Middle Ear The chamber between the eardrum and cochlea containing three tiny bones (hammer, anvil, and stirrup) that concentrate the vibrations of the eardrum on the cochlea.

Nearsightedness A condition in which nearby objects are seen clearly, but distant objects are blurred because the lens focuses the image in front of the retina.

Nerve Deafness Hearing loss caused by damage to the cochlea's receptor cells or to the auditory nerves.

Opponent-Process Theory In visual sensation, the theory that color vision depends on pairs of opposing retinal processes (red-green, yellow-blue, and white-black). For example, some cells are stimulated by green and inhibited by red, while others are stimulated by red and inhibited by green.

Optic Nerve The nerve that carries neural impulses from the eye to the brain.

Perception The process of organizing and interpreting sensory information, enabling us to recognize meaningful objects and events.

Place Theory In hearing, the theory that links the pitch we hear with the place where the cochlea's membrane is stimulated.

Pupil The adjustable opening in the center of the eye through which light enters.

Retina The light-sensitive inner surface of the eye, containing the receptor rods and cones plus layers of neurons that begin the processing of visual information.

Rods Retinal receptors that detect black, white, and gray, especially in peripheral and nighttime vision.

Saturation The purity of color, which is greater when complexity (the number of other wavelengths mixed in) is low.

Semicircular Canals Three curved, fluid-filled structures of the inner ear with receptors that detect body motion.

Sensation The process by which certain stimulus energies are detected and experienced.

Sensory Adaptation Diminished sensitivity with constant stimulation.

Sensory Interaction The principle that one sense may influence another, as when the smell of food influences its taste.

Signal Detection Theory A theory that assumes that there is no single absolute threshold, because the detection of a weak signal depends partly on a person's experience, expectation, and motivation.

Subliminal Below threshold.

Timbre The tone color of a sound that distinguishes it from other sounds of the same pitch and loudness.

Transduction Conversion of one form of energy into another. In sensation, the transforming of stimulus energies into neural firings.

Vestibular Sacs Two structures of the inner ear with receptors that provide the sense of upright body position.

Wavelength The distance from the peak of one light or sound wave to the peak of the next. Waves vary from long and slow to short and fast.

Weber's Law The principle that two stimuli must differ by a constant minimum percentage (rather than a constant amount) for their difference to be perceived.

Young-Helmholtz Three-Color Theory The theory that the retina contains three different color receptors—one most sensitive to red, one to green, one to blue—which in combination can produce the perception of any color.

FOR FURTHER READING

Frisby, J. P. (1980). *Seeing: Illusion, brain and mind.* Oxford: Oxford University Press.

A wonderfully illustrated introduction to the visual system.

Gregory, R. L. (1978). *Eye and brain: The psychology of seeing* (3rd ed.). New York: McGraw-Hill.

The classic popular introduction to vision. An informative and easily readable book.

McBurney, D. H., & Collings, V. B. (1984). *Introduction to sensation perception* (2nd ed.). Englewood Cliffs, NJ: Prentice-Hall.

A crisp survey, with many everyday examples of how we process sensory information.

Robert Doisneau *Picasso and the Loaves, 1952*

Zeke Berman *Table Study 1982*

CHAPTER 7

Perception

In Chapter 6 we examined the processes by which we sense sights and sounds, tastes and smells. Here in Chapter 7 our central question is, how do we see not just shapes and colors, but a rose in bloom, a familiar face, a sunset? How do we hear not just a mix of pitches and rhythms, but a child's cry of pain, the hum of distant traffic, a symphony? In short, how do we organize and interpret our sensations as meaningful perceptions?

BASIC ISSUES IN PERCEPTION

Puzzling Perceptions

During the late 1800s—about the time that psychology was emerging as a distinct discipline—scientists became fascinated with perceptual illusions. These illusions, we now know, provide valuable clues to the ordinary mechanisms of perception. They mislead us by playing on the ways we organize and interpret our sensations. Before we look at the process of perception and misperception, let's look at a few of the perceptual puzzles that tease the mind, and then discover what their solutions tell us about our normal perceptual processes.

Puzzle 1 Consider the classic illusion created in 1889 by Franz Müller-Lyer. Does either line segment, AB or BC, appear longer?

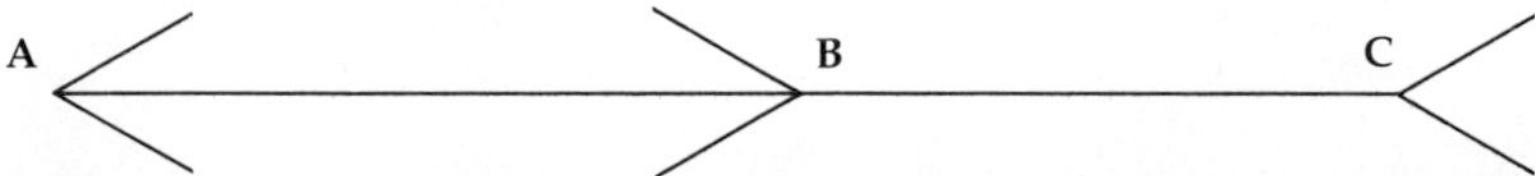

To most people the two segments appear to be the same length. Surprise, they are not. As your ruler can verify, line AB is a full one-third longer than line BC. Why do our eyes deceive us? (On page 173 we will discover one explanation.)

Puzzle 2 Here we have two unretouched photos of the same boy and dog, in the same room. You perceive these two scenes here much as you would if you were viewing them through a peephole with one eye. Why do the boy and dog seem to change size? (Page 174 will reveal why.)

Puzzle 3 Is the Gateway Arch in St. Louis taller or wider? To most it appears taller. In truth, its height and width are equal. Once again, seeing is deceiving. Why? (On page 172, we will meet this phenomenon again.)

Puzzle 4 Aircraft pilots, ship captains, and car drivers must judge distances under varying conditions of visibility. To simulate such judgments, psychologist Helen Ross (1975) asked passersby to estimate the distances of white disks she had placed on the lawn at Britain's Hull University. Those who judged the distance in the thick morning fog perceived the disks to be farther away than did those who made their estimates in the brilliant midday sunshine. What does this suggest about how we normally judge distances? (Page 171 will discuss distance perception.)

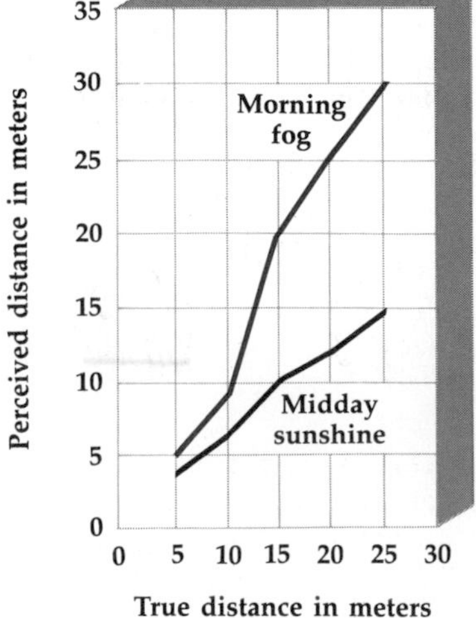

Morning fog

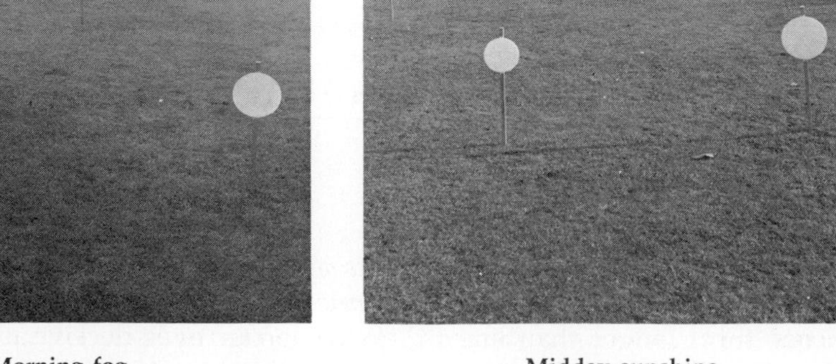

Midday sunshine

Illusions occur with the other senses, too. More than a century ago, the psychologist Wilhelm Wundt was puzzled by the fact that people hear the steady beat of a metronome or clock as if it were a repeating rhythm of two, three, or four beats—not as an unaccented click-click-click-click, which it is, but as, say, CLICK-click CLICK-click CLICK-click. From the steady beat that strikes the ear, each listener unconsciously shapes an auditory pattern. What perceptual principle is at work here? (On page 175 we will see.)

Nativism and Empiricism: Nature-Nurture Revisited

The philosopher Plato argued some 2400 years ago that we perceive objects through the senses with the mind. As it turns out, he was right. The question is, *how* does the mind work to create our perceptions, both accurate and illusory? And how do these perceptual processes originate—through biological maturation or through experience? On this latter question there has been a long-standing debate.

The debate is another version of the now familiar nature-nurture debate. On one side were the ***nativists,*** such as the German philosopher Immanuel Kant (1724–1804), who maintained that knowledge comes from our innate ways of organizing sensory experiences. On the other side were the ***empiricists,*** such as the British philosopher John Locke (1632–1704), who argued that we learn how to perceive the world through our experiences of it. In keeping with the emerging democratic spirit of his time, Locke believed that at birth all people's minds were equally blank. If the mind is blank at birth, then all knowledge, including perceptual knowledge, comes through experience. Today, it is generally accepted that perception depends both upon nature's endowments (recall from Chapter 6 the brain's built-in feature detectors) and the experiences that influence what we *make* of our sensations.

"Let us then suppose the mind to be, as we say, white paper void of all characters, without any ideas:—How comes it to be furnished? . . . To this I answer, in one word, from EXPERIENCE."
John Locke, *An Essay Concerning Human Understanding* (1690)

So, what exactly are the contributions of each? Which aspects of our perception are innately endowed and which are learned? The perennial nativism-empiricism issue will occasionally surface as we consider how we organize and interpret the input from our senses. As we will see, many of our ways of *organizing* our sensations seem native to our species; when *interpreting* our sensations, our past experiences seem more crucial.

PERCEPTUAL ORGANIZATION

Early in this century, a number of German psychologists became intrigued with the mind's apparent power of organization. Given a cluster of sensations, the human perceiver tends to organize them into a ***gestalt,*** a German word meaning a "form" or a "whole." The Gestalt psychologists provided many compelling demonstrations of how we do this. Look at Figure 7-1. Note that the individual elements of the figure are really nothing but red circles with three white lines on them. But when we view them all together, is that what we see? Perhaps for a moment. But soon we see a *whole* form, a "Necker cube." As the Gestalt psychologists were fond of saying, in perception the whole is different from the sum of its parts. There is more to perception than meets the senses.

There is more in the so-called Necker cube, too. With a little patience you may see several cubes to which these eight segmented circles can give rise. At first you will see the X on the front edge of a cube, but after a few moments the cube will reverse and the X will go to the back. Perhaps you see the cube floating in front of the page with the red circles behind it

Figure 7-1 *What do you see: red circles with white lines or a cube? (From D. R. Bradley, S. T. Dumais, H. M. Petry, "Reply to Cavonius," Nature, vol. 268, p. 78, 1976.)*

(Figure 7-2a). But if you look again, the circles may become holes in the page, through which the cube can be glimpsed floating behind it (Figure 7-2b). Either way, the position of the cube reverses every few moments. We are looking at eight segmented circles, but organizing them into several coherent images. Because the several coherent images into which the circles can be organized are equally plausible, the brain does not adopt one organization over another, but rather switches from one to the next.

Figure 7-2 *The Necker cube. Sometimes you perceive the cube in front, with the red circles behind it (a). At other times, the cube is floating behind the red circles (b). (From D. R. Bradley, S. T. Dumais, and H. M. Petry, "Reply to Cavonius," Nature, vol. 261, p. 78, 1976.)*

This and similar demonstrations led the Gestalt psychologists to describe some of the principles by which we organize our sensations into perceptions. As you read about these organizational principles, keep in mind the fundamental truth that is illustrated by them all: Our minds do more than merely register information about the world. Always, we are filtering sensory information and structuring our perceptions of it in ways that make sense to us.

Form Perception

To structure incoming sensory information our minds must perceive objects as separate from other stimuli and as having a meaningful form.

Figure and Ground

When confronted with an object, our perceptual task is to recognize it. To do so we must first perceive the object, called the *figure,* as distinct from its surroundings, called the *ground.* Among the voices you hear at a party, the one you attend to becomes the figure, all others part of the ground. As you read, the words are the figure, the white page the ground. In the classic illustration of Figure 7-3, the ***figure-ground*** relationship continually reverses—but always the stimulus is organized into a figure seen against a ground (either a white vase on a black background or two black profiles on a white background). This demonstrates once more that the same stimulus can trigger more than one perception.

Various artists, including the Dutch graphic artist M. C. Escher, have studied Gestalt psychology's analysis of the organizational principle of figure and ground and applied it in their art (Teuber, 1974). For example, Escher's "Day and Night" (Figure 7-4) depicts a slow transformation of ground into figure and figure into ground. Note that in the middle of the picture the same cluster of sensations may be organized in different ways, giving rise to an image of white birds on a black landscape or black birds on a white landscape.

Figure 7-3 *The reversible figure-ground relationship. In this vase, created for the 1977 Silver Jubilee of Britain's Queen Elizabeth II, either the vase or the profiles of the Queen and Prince Philip (which greet each other from opposite sides of the vase) can be the figure transforming the other element into the background.*

Figure 7-4 *The transformation of figure into ground. Moving from left to right in M.C. Escher's 1938 woodcut* Day and Night, *the figure, the black birds, gradually becomes the ground, the landscape.*

Grouping

Having discriminated figure from ground, we next organize the figure into a meaningful form. To bring order to what we sense and give it form, our minds seem to follow certain rules for ***grouping*** stimuli together. These rules, which were identified by the Gestalt psychologists, illustrate the underlying Gestalt principle that the perceived whole is different from the mere sum of its parts. For example, consider four of the Gestalt principles of perceptual organization:

Proximity If figures are near each other, we tend to group them together. We see not six separate lines, but three sets of two lines.

Similarity If figures are similar to each other, we tend to group them together. We see the triangles and circles as columns of similar shapes, not as rows of dissimilar shapes.

Closure If a figure has gaps, we tend to complete it, filling in the gaps to create a complete, whole object. By filling the gaps we see a whole shell.

Continuity We tend to perceive smooth, continuous patterns rather than discontinuous ones. This pattern could be an alternating series of semicircles, but we tend to perceive it as a wavy line and a straight line.

Usually the grouping principles help us see reality as it is. Sometimes, as in viewing the impossible doghouse in Figure 7-5, they can lead us astray.

Figure 7-5 *You probably perceive this doghouse as a gestalt—a whole (though impossible) structure. Actually, as the photo on p. 181 indicates, Gestalt principles such as closure lead us to perceive interrupted boards as continuous.*

Relative height We perceive higher objects as farther away. This may contribute to the illusion that vertical dimensions are longer than identical horizontal dimensions (as in the St. Louis Gateway Arch). Is the vertical line here longer, shorter, or equal to the horizontal? (Measure and see.)

Relative motion As we move, objects in our environment appear to move relative to us as when we look out a train window. We perceive those that appear to move the greatest distance relative to us as closest, with those appearing to move less and less as farther and farther away.

Linear perspective We perceive the convergence of what we know to be parallel lines as indicating increasing distance.

(a)

(b)

Figure 7-8 *(a) This ancient Egyptian wall painting, depicting the wine harvest, lacks any of the monocular cues that artists now use to portray depth. (b) By the time that Canaletto (1697–1768) painted this scene of Venice, the techniques for showing perspective were well established. Note the effective use of distance cues such as texture and gradient, overlap, and relative size and height.*

To convey depth on a flat canvas artists use such cues (Figure 7-8). They also are relied upon by people who must gauge depth with but one eye. In 1960 the University of Washington football team won the Rose Bowl, thanks partly to the throwing of star quarterback Bob Schloredt, who was obviously skilled at judging the distance of his pass receivers, although blind in his left eye. Schloredt must have been extremely sensitive to monocular cues for distance.

Perceptual Constancies

Having perceived an object as a coherent form (not just a disorganized cluster of sensations) and located it in space, our next task is to recognize it without being deceived by changes in its size, shape, brightness, or color of its image. Although we commonly take it for granted, this perceptual feat—to perceive as unchanging the changing pattern of stimuli from an object—has intrigued perception researchers for decades.

Size and Shape Constancies

Two of the features that contribute to perceptual constancy are the ability to perceive objects as having a constant shape, regardless of viewing angle, and a constant size, regardless of distance.

Shape constancy is the perception of a familiar object as having a constant form, even while our retinal images of it change. When a door opens (Figure 7-9), it casts a changing shape on our retinas, yet we manage to perceive the door as having a constant doorlike shape.

Figure 7-9 *Shape constancy. A door casts an increasingly trapezoidal image on our retinas as it opens, yet we continue to perceive it as rectangular.*

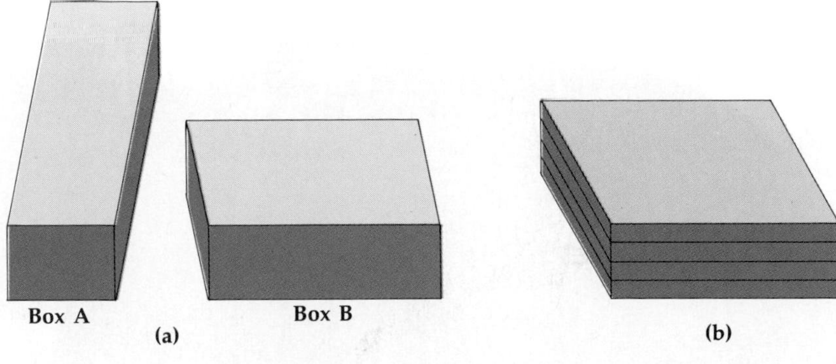

Perceiving shape. (a) Do the tops of boxes A and B have different dimensions? They appear to. But if you measure, you will see that they are, in fact, identical. With both boxes we adjust our perceptions in terms of what we take our viewing angle to be. (b) Will a dime fit in this box? Most people think so; they make a shape constancy correction in order to perceive this familiar shape as a square. But try placing a dime in the box and you will see that the top surface is actually a parallelogram with longer horizontal sides.

Size constancy—the tendency to perceive an object as having a constant size—allows us to perceive an airplane as large enough to carry hundreds of people, even when it appears as just a speck in the sky. This illustrates the close connection between an object's perceived *distance* and perceived *size*. Correctly perceiving an object's distance provides clues to its size; likewise, knowing its size—that the object is, say, an airplane—provides clues to its distance.

The marvel of size perception is how effortlessly it occurs. Given the perceived distance of an object and the size of its retinal image, we instantly and unconsciously infer the object's size. Although the cylinders in Figure 7-10 cast the same retinal images, the texture gradient cues us that the upper cylinder is more distant, and we therefore perceive it as larger. It is this interplay between perceived size and perceived distance that explains several well-known illusions. For example, can you imagine why the moon looks larger—up to 50 percent larger—near the horizon than when high in the sky? One reason for this "moon illusion" is that distance cues at the horizon make the moon seem farther away and therefore larger (like the distant cylinder in Figure 7-10). Take away these distance cues—by looking at the horizon moon through a paper tube—and it immediately shrinks.

The size-distance relationship helps us understand two illusions we experienced at the start of this chapter—the Müller-Lyer illusion (of distances between arrow tips) and the elastic boy and dog. One explanation for the Müller-Lyer illusion is that experience has taught us to interpret converging lines with these configurations as cues to distance and therefore to the length of the center line. From our experience with the corners of rooms or buildings (see Figure 7-11), we interpret the center line to the left to be closer to us and therefore shorter, and the center line to the right to be farther away and so longer. Further support for this explanation

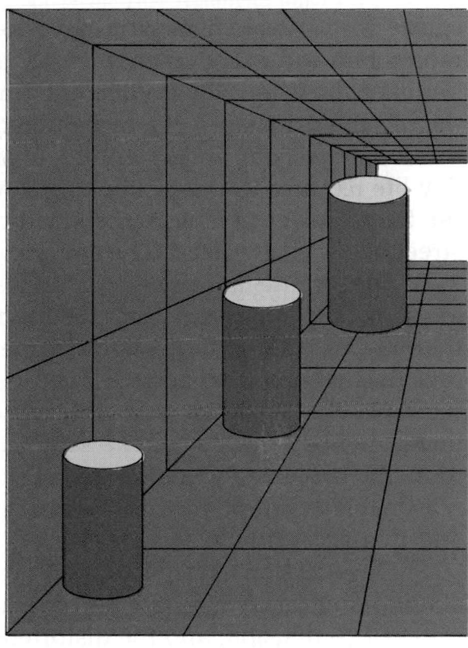

Figure 7-10 *The interplay between perceived size and distance. The monocular cues for distance make the "farthest away" cylinder look larger. But it isn't.*

(a)

(b)

Figure 7-11 *The Müller-Lyer illusion. Richard L. Gregory (1968) suggests that the (a) outer and (b) inner corners in our rectangularly carpentered world have taught us to interpret "outward" or "inward" pointing arrowheads on a line as a cue to the line's distance from us and so to its length. The outer corner to the left is perceived as shorter than the inner corner to the right, but if you measure them you will see that both are the same length.*

tinguish the two. Locke's answer was no, because the man would never have *learned* to see.

Molyneux's hypothetical case has since been put to the test in dozens of instances in which adults blind from birth have gained sight (Gregory, 1978; Senden, 1932). Most were patients with cataracts, whose clouded lenses had enabled them to see only diffused light, rather as you or I might see the world if looking through half a ping pong ball. When the cataracts were surgically removed, the patients could distinguish figures from ground and could sense colors—suggesting that these aspects of perception are innate. But, much as Locke supposed, the patients often could not recognize objects with which they were tactually familiar. Learning to perceive shape and form visually was so difficult that some of the patients gave up and returned to living as blind persons.

It is of course possible in these cases that after surgery the patients' visual mechanisms were not completely intact. Seeking to gain more control than can be provided by such clinical cases, researchers conducted Molyneux's imaginary experiment with animals. They wondered whether altering a young animal's normal visual experience would permanently alter its perceptual abilities. Researchers gave infant kittens and monkeys simulated cataracts by sewing their eyelids closed or by outfitting them with goggles through which only diffuse, unpatterned light could be seen (Wiesel, 1982). After infancy, when their visual impairments were removed, these animals exhibited perceptual limitations much like those of human cataract patients; they could distinguish colors and brightness, but not the form of a circle from that of a square. Their eyes had not degenerated, their retinas still relayed signals to their visual cortex; but functionally these animals were permanently blind.

In both humans and animals, a similar period of sensory restriction occurring later in life is not permanently disruptive. If the eye of an adult animal is covered for several months, vision will be unaffected later. If cataracts that develop *after* early childhood are later removed, a human will enjoy normal perception. So in cats, monkeys, and humans, visual experiences during infancy seem critical for normal perceptual development. As we noted on p. 67, experience helps sculpt the brain's neural connections.

The profound effects of early experience on perception are also apparent in other experiments in which young animals were reared with severely restricted visual input. In one such study, two Cambridge University researchers, Colin Blakemore and Grahame Cooper (1970), reared kittens in darkness, except for 5 hours each day, during which they were in an environment of all horizontal stripes or all vertical stripes (as in Figure 7-15). Remarkably, those raised without exposure to horizontal lines later had difficulty perceiving horizontal rods, and those raised without vertical lines had similar difficulty seeing vertical rods. When two of these kittens were playing in a room and one of the researchers playfully shook a long black rod, the kitten reared in a world of vertical lines would play with it only when it was held upright. When the rod was held flat, that kitten would ignore it while a companion reared in a world of horizontal lines would run to play with it.

To determine how the kittens' restricted visual experience had affected those cells of the visual cortex that detect specific features, such as horizontal or vertical lines, Blakemore and Cooper sampled the electrical activity of those neurons. There did not seem to be any unresponsive neurons. Rather, the cortical neurons of the kittens reared with horizontal lines now seemed mostly attuned to horizontal stimuli, while the neurons of the kittens reared with only vertical lines responded mostly to vertical stimuli. So it seemed that the kittens' restricted visual environment had

Figure 7-15 *The experimental apparatus for the Blakemore and Cooper studies. From the time their eyes first opened to age 5 months, these kittens were removed from darkness each day to spend 5 hours alone in a black and white striped cylinder with a clear glass floor. A stiff collar prevented the kittens from seeing anything else, even their own bodies. The perceptual consequences of these sensory restrictions were profound: these kittens were forever afterward insensitive to horizontal forms.*

"Innate mechanisms endow the visual system with highly specific connections, but visual experience early in life is necessary for their maintenance and full development."
Torsten N. Wiesel (1982)

not caused any feature-detector cells to degenerate, but had simply determined the features to which most would be responsive. The neural circuits for feature detection are present at or soon after birth but only become fully developed through experience.

This research provides a partial answer to one of the questions debated in Chapter 4, "Adolescence and Adulthood." Does the imprint of early experience last a lifetime? Or, can we be reshaped by later experiences? For visual perception, the answer seems clear. Even if an animal that grew up with one eye sewn shut is now forced to use that eye, it never regains normal vision. The imprint of the infant's visual experiences—or lack of them—is retained far into the future.

(a)

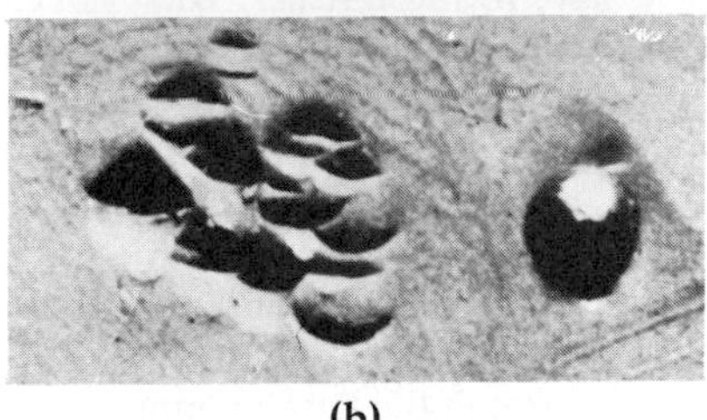

(b)

Figure 7-16 *The effects of visual distortion on chicks. When chicks were fitted with prisms that visually displaced objects to the left (a), they could not adapt. They would persistently peck to the left of objects, such as this food grain (b) embedded at the right of the pecking marks made in modeling clay.*

Perceptual Adaptation

The visual imprint remains, but in humans, the most adaptable of creatures, perception can be modified. Given a new pair of glasses, we may find ourselves slightly disoriented and dizzy. But within a day or two we adapt, and the world seems normal again. Now imagine a far more dramatic new pair of prescription glasses—one that shifts the apparent location of objects 20 degrees to the left. When you first put them on and toss a ball to someone, it sails off about 20 degrees to the left. Walking forward to shake hands with the person, you veer to the left.

Could you satisfactorily adapt to this distorted world? Chicks cannot. When fitted with such lenses, they will thereafter peck where food grains *seem* to be (Hess, 1956; Rossi, 1968) (see Figure 7-16). But humans wearing such distorting lenses can quickly adapt. Before long you would adjust your behavior. Your throws would again be accurate, your stride on target. Remove the lenses and you would experience an aftereffect: At first your throws would err in the *opposite* direction, sailing off to the right; but within minutes you would readapt.

Now imagine an even more radical pair of new glasses—one that literally turns the world upside down. The ground is up, the sky is down. Could you adapt? Fish, frogs, and salamanders cannot. When Roger Sperry (1956) surgically turned their eyes upside down, they thereafter reacted to objects by moving in the wrong direction. But, believe it or not, kittens, monkeys, and humans can adapt to an inverted world. The turn-of-the-century psychologist George Stratton (1896) experienced this when he invented and wore for 8 days optical headgear that flipped left to right *and* up to down, making him the first known person on earth to experience a right-side-up retinal image.

At the outset, Stratton was disoriented. When he wanted to walk, he had to search for his feet, which were now up. Eating was nearly impossible. He became somewhat nauseated and depressed. But Stratton persisted and gradually began to adapt. By the end of the 8 days, he could comfortably reach in the right direction for something and walk without bumping into objects. (When the headgear was finally removed it did not take Stratton long to readapt.)

Subsequent experiments have removed any doubts about Stratton's experience (Dolezal, 1982; Kohler, 1962). After a period of adjustment, people wearing the optical gear have even been able to ride a motorcycle, ski the Alps, and fly an airplane. Is this because with experience they perceptually reinverted their upside-down world to an upright position? No, the street, ski slopes, and runway were still above their heads. But by moving about in this topsy-turvy world, they had learned the new relationships between the actual and perceived locations of objects. This learning enabled them to coordinate their movements without being very conscious of the inversion.

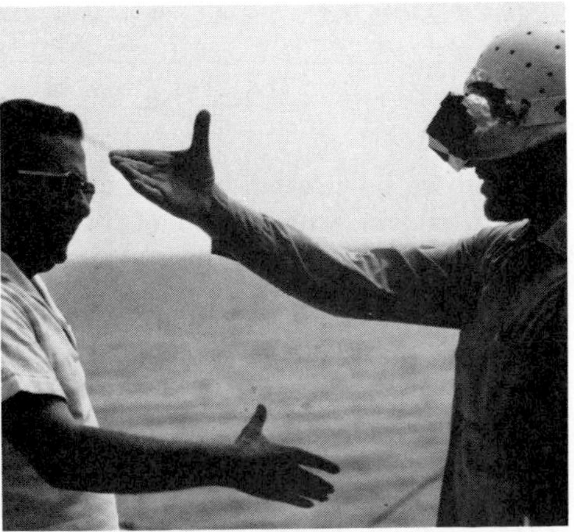

Dr. Hubert Dolezal views the world through inverted lenses. Remarkably, people can learn to adapt to an upside-down world.

Selective Attention

Note that with the young-woman–old-woman illustration, as with the Necker cube and figure-ground demonstrations (Figures 7-1 and 7-3), you can *know* that two interpretations are possible, yet at any moment you can consciously experience only one of them. This illustrates an important principle: Our conscious attention is selective; always, it is focused on some very limited aspect of all that we are capable of experiencing at a given moment. Are we ever affected by stimuli of which we are unaware? Right now, you are unaware of many perceptible stimuli entering your sensory system. Until reading this sentence you have been unaware of your shoes pressed against your feet or of the fact that while reading your nose is in your line of vision. Now, suddenly, your feet feel encased, your nose stubbornly intrudes on the page before you.

The ability to attend to only one conversation at a time—the cocktail party phenomenon—enables those who work at the stock exchange to converse coherently in the midst of auditory chaos.

Even when exposed to readily detectable messages, people whose attention is directed elsewhere remember little of a message to which they were not attending. Psychological experiments have captured this *cocktail party effect*—the ability to attend selectively to but one voice—by exposing subjects to two conversations, one in each ear (Kahneman, 1973). When the person's attention is drawn, say, to the left ear, what is said in the right ear generally goes unperceived. At the level of conscious awareness, whatever has our attention has our undivided attention.

Can you listen to two people at once? Try it. Your attention will switch back and forth between the two.

Similarly, among the immense array of visual stimuli before us, only a few are selected for consciousness. Ulric Neisser (1979) and Robert Becklen and Daniel Cervone (1983) demonstrated this by showing people a 1-minute videotape of three young men in black shirts passing a basketball; this tape was superimposed over the image of three other men in white shirts doing the same thing. Midway through the tape a young woman carrying an umbrella saunters through the game (see Figure 7-17). With their attention focused on the basketball game (they had been asked to press a key every time the black-shirted players passed the ball) most viewers failed to notice the intruder. When the researchers replayed the tape for them, they were astonished to see her. They had selectively attended to the relevant ball tossing, and missed perceiving the woman.

Figure 7-17 *In this experiment on selective attention, viewers were shown a videotape of three black-shirted men playing basketball superimposed over a tape of three men in white shirts doing the same. Midway through the game a woman with an umbrella saunters through. When viewers were paying careful attention to the basketball being tossed among the dark-shirted players, they usually failed to notice this incongruous event.*

Could we be affected by such unattended-to stimuli? The answer is yes. In one experiment, women students listened to a prose passage presented through headphones to one ear (Wilson, 1979). While doing so, they repeated the words out loud and compared them to a written transcript, checking for errors. Meanwhile, some simple, novel melodies were played to the other ear. But with their attention so focused on the passage, the women were no more aware of the tunes than you normally are of your shoes encasing your feet. Thus when they later heard these tunes interspersed among similar ones that had not been played, they could not recognize the tunes to which they had been exposed (much as people cannot recall a conversation to which they did not pay attention). Nevertheless, when asked to rate their fondness for each tune, they preferred the ones that were previously played. Their preferences revealed what their conscious memories could not.

Perceptual Set

As everyone knows, to see is to believe. As many people also know, but do not fully appreciate, to believe is to see. Our assumptions and expectations may give us a ***perceptual set,*** or mental predisposition, that greatly influences what we perceive. Is the woman in Figure 7-18 young or old? Which we see can be influenced by our first viewing one of the two unambiguous versions of this drawing shown, that of an attractive young woman or an ugly old woman (Boring, 1930).

Figure 7-18 *Which do you see in the center picture: the old woman or the young woman? Viewing one of the two unambiguous versions of this picture first often influences what you see.*

Everyday examples of the effects of perceptual set abound. Dr. Peter Thompson at the University of York in England experimented with our fixation on the eyes and the mouth when we perceive a human face. Using Prime Minister Margaret Thatcher as a model, Thompson turned 2 photographs upside down and made some alterations in one of them (Figure 7-19). The distortion is surprisingly easy to overlook. In 1972, a British newspaper published genuine, unretouched photographs of a "monster" in Scotland's Loch Ness—"the most amazing pictures ever taken" stated the paper. If this information creates the same perceptual set in you as it did in most of the paper's readers, you, too, will see the monster in the photo reproduced in Figure 7-20. But when Steuart Campbell (1982–1983) approached the photos with a different perceptual set, he saw a curved tree trunk—very likely the same tree trunk others had seen in the lake the day the photo was shot (just after some heavy rains had, most likely, washed it down the flooded river to the lake). Moreover, with this perceptual set, you may now notice that the object is floating motionless, without any water disturbance or wake around it—hardly what one would expect of a lively monster.

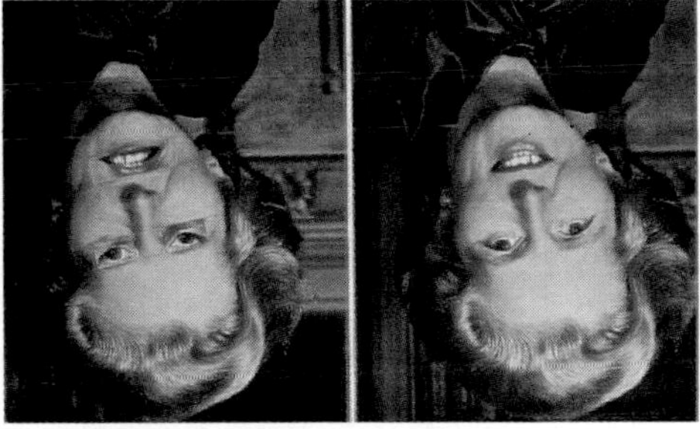

Figure 7-19 *When we look at faces, we focus so strongly on the eyes and the mouth that we can easily overlook facial distortions, if the eyes and mouth conform to our perceptual set. Turn the book upside down for an unexpected view of Mrs. Thatcher.*

Our perceptual set can also influence what we hear. This principle was painfully learned by the kindly airline pilot who, on the takeoff run, looked over at his depressed copilot and said "cheer up." The copilot heard the usual "gear-up" and promptly raised the wheels—before they had left the ground (Reason & Mycielska, 1982).

Figure 7-20 *Is this the Loch Ness monster or a log? We often see what we expect to see.*

What is it that determines our perceptual set? As you may recall from Chapter 3, "Infancy and Childhood," our experiences help us develop and elaborate schemas, concepts that we use to organize and interpret information. In order to interpret unfamiliar information, we compare it with our schemas, which are stored in our memories. Our preexisting schemas for young woman and old woman, for monsters and tree trunks, for airplane lights and UFOs are all available to help us interpret ambiguous sensations. Confronted with an ambiguous moving object in the sky, different people may therefore apply different schemas: "It's a bird." "It's a plane." "It's Superman!"

Children's drawings allow us to glimpse the development of their perceptual schemas. A 4-year-old can draw circles and angled lines, but cannot combine these to create an elaborate human figure. Why not? The child's problem is not just clumsiness. A right-handed adult who draws with the left hand will create an awkward drawing, but it will be unlike the child's drawing in Figure 7-21. Although it is true that part of the difference lies in the difficulty that children (and nonartistic adults as well) have representing what they know, the fundamental difference lies in the child's simplified concept of essential human characteristics. For a 4-year-old, a face is a more essential human feature than a body. From ages 4 to 8, children's schemas for bodies become elaborated, and so in turn do their drawings of bodies. The same principle of schema-guided drawings operates with adults. If you doubt it, look at the impossible object in Figure 7-22 and then—still lacking a schema for this object—turn away and try to reproduce it.

In different people a given stimulus may trigger radically different perceptions, partly because of the differing schemas people develop from their past experiences, but also partly because of the immediate context. Whether the speaker is concerned about "cults and sects" or "cults and sex" must be discerned from the context surrounding the words.

The combined effects of perceptual set and context sometimes work to our benefit. In the hospital where I was once employed as an orderly, we occasionally faced the task of transporting a dead body through crowded hallways without alarming any of the patients or their visitors. Our solution was to create a context that matched people's schemas for sleeping and sedated patients: With face uncovered, and the sheet turned down in normal fashion, an apparently "sleeping" corpse could be wheeled past any number of unsuspecting perceivers.

Figure 7-21 *Children's drawings seem to reflect their perceptual schemas, as well as their abilities to represent what they know. This drawing by a 3-year-old illustrates the vastly greater importance of the face than the body in young children's simplified schemas of essential human characteristics.*

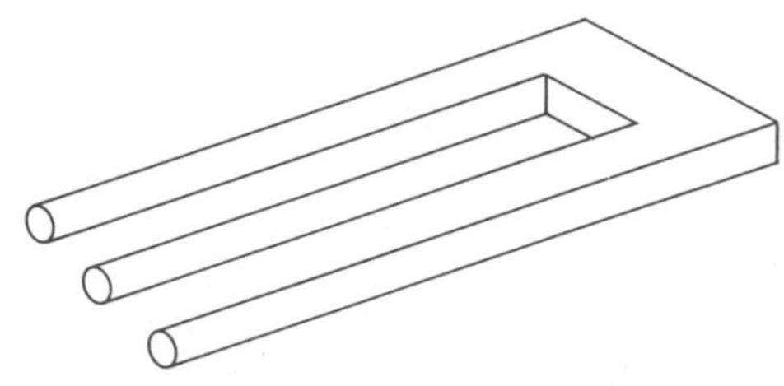

Figure 7-22 *Since we lack a schema for this impossible figure, few people can reproduce it without looking. People without formal education have fewer schemas for three-dimensional graphic representations and so can more easily perceive and reproduce this as a pattern of lines.*

What is above the woman's head? In an experiment, nearly all the participants from East Africa thought she was balancing a metal box or can on her head. In an environment and culture with few angular visual cues, the family is seen to be sitting under a tree. Westerners, to whom corners and boxlike architecture are more common, were more likely to perceive the family as being indoors with the woman sitting under a window through which plants can be seen.

Expectations predispose perceptions in science as well as in everyday life. Confronted with ambiguous information, a scientist will propose a *theory* that serves to organize and interpret the available data, such as when the so-called canals on Mars were first perceived through telescopes and presumed by some to be the product of intelligent creatures, rather than simply natural landforms. The theory acts as a schema, making it more difficult to see things any other way, until someone offers a convincing new way of interpreting the facts. Thus the canals that were so often "seen" on Mars turned out indeed to be the product of intelligent life—but an intelligence on the viewing end of the telescope.

The effects of learned schemas, or perceptual sets, are further evidence that experience influences how we perceive the world. So, to return to our original question—Is perception innate or learned?—we can answer: Our innate sensory equipment makes possible our elementary sensations, and our experiences in infancy and later help us to construct meaningful perceptions from them.

Another view of the impossible doghouse in Figure 7-5 reveals the secrets of this illusion.

IS THERE PERCEPTION WITHOUT SENSATION?

Can we perceive only what we take in through our senses or are some of us capable of ***extrasensory perception*** (ESP)—able to read minds, see through walls, or foretell the future? Certainly most Americans, including most collegians, believe in the reality of ESP (Frazier, 1984–85; Gallup Poll, 1978; Jones & others, 1977). And the media are full of reports of psychic wonders. Psychics are said to solve police cases that have dumbfounded detectives. Ordinary people are reported to have spontaneous dreams of dreaded events—only to discover their dreams fulfilled. In laboratory experiments, ***parapsychologists*** (those who study paranormal—literally, beyond the normal—happenings) have sometimes been astonished at psychics who seem capable of discerning the contents of sealed envelopes, influencing the roll of a die, or drawing a picture of what someone else is viewing at an unknown remote location.

If these things are true, the scientific understanding of human nature—that we are creatures whose minds are tied to our physical brains and whose perceptual experiences of the world are built of sensations—might have to be modified. For this reason—but not for this reason alone—research psychologists and prominent scientists are overwhelmingly skeptical of such claims (McClenon, 1982). Let us first take a look at some of the phenomena of ESP and then see why the skeptics are so dubious.

Many religions, including Judaism and Christianity, similarly assume that we are finite creatures, not little gods.

Claims of ESP

Among the acclaimed paranormal phenomena—including astrological predictions, psychic healings, reincarnation, communication with the dead, and out-of-body travel—the most respectable, testable, and (for a chapter on perception) relevant claims are for the following varieties of ESP:

1. *Telepathy*, or mind-to-mind communication—one person sending thoughts to another, or perceiving another's thoughts.
2. *Clairvoyance*, or perceiving remote events, such as sensing that a friend's house is on fire.
3. *Precognition*, or perceiving future events, such as the fate of a political leader.

Closely linked with the claims of ESP is *psychokinesis,* or "mind over matter" actions, such as levitating a table or influencing the roll of a die.

Most people's beliefs about these ESP phenomena are based on stage or television performances of psychics, which are quite different from the controlled situation necessary for a researcher to test for ESP. On stage, the psychic controls what the audience sees and hears. In the laboratory, the experimenter controls what the psychic sees and hears. It is therefore no surprise that the results reported by parapsychologists who test for ESP in the laboratory are modest by comparison to the stage feats of so-called psychics.

"A psychic is an actor playing the role of a psychic."
Daryl Bem (1984)

However, "modest" does not necessarily mean statistically insignificant. As an example, consider a clairvoyance experiment conducted by Bruce Layton and Bill Turnbull (1975). They had a computer generate a randomized 100-item list of the digits 1, 2, 3, 4, and 5 for each of their 179 University of North Carolina student participants. Each of the students was given a sealed envelope containing a list and was asked to guess which number was in each of the 100 positions. By chance, about 1 guess in 5, or 20 guesses out of the 100, was expected to be correct. However, the average number of correct guesses was 20.66 out of 100 when it was suggested beforehand that ESP was beneficial to people, and only 19.49 when it was said that ESP was harmful. Although such a difference might seem insignificant—indeed you would never have noticed so small an effect had you been observing the experiment—a statistical analysis indicated that a difference that large (from so many participants) would seldom occur by chance. So the investigators concluded that an ESP effect had occurred.

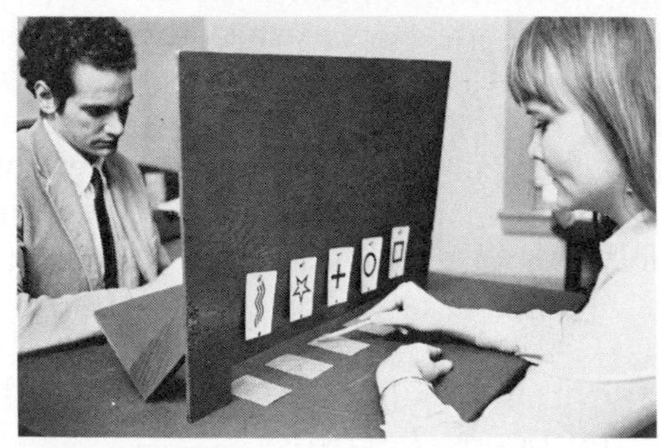

An ESP experiment. As the man touches the face-down card on the top of a pile, the woman indicates which of the five cards she believes it to be. When the series of cards is completed, the percentage of "hits" is compared with the 1 in 5 (20 percent) rate expected.

In the face of such experiments, believers in ESP accuse research psychologists of the same sort of skepticism that led eighteenth-century scientists to scoff at the idea that meteorites came from outer space. Novelist Arthur Koestler, who in 1983 left more than $700,000 to fund a British professorship in parapsychology, once complained that today's skeptical scientists resemble the Italian philosophers who refused to look at Jupiter's moons through Galileo's telescope—because they "knew" that such moons did not exist. Skepticism sometimes blinds people to important truths.

"A man does not attain the status of Galileo merely because he is persecuted; he must also be right."
Stephen Jay Gould,
Ever Since Darwin, 1973

Skepticism about ESP

The skeptics reply that the uncritical mind is a gullible mind. They point to the fact that, time and again, so-called psychics have exploited unquestioning audiences with amazing performances in which they appeared to communicate with the spirits of the dead, read minds, or levitate objects—only to have it revealed later that their acts were a hoax, nothing more than the illusions created by stage magicians. Indeed, many psychic deceptions have been exposed by magicians, who resent the exploitation of their arts in the name of psychic powers.

"The most eminent scientist, untrained in magic, is putty in the hands of a clever charlatan."
Martin Gardner (1983)

Skeptics are quick to point out that even scientists are vulnerable to being hoodwinked. Perhaps the most notable case involved two teenage magicians, Steve Shaw and Michael Edwards (Randi, 1983a, 1983b). In 1979, this young pair approached Washington University's new parapsychological laboratory, offering to demonstrate their psychic powers. Over the next 3 years, the two pretended to defy the laws of nature by projecting mental images onto film, causing clocks to slide across a table, effortlessly bending metal objects, affecting objects in sealed jars, and performing other wondrous feats. Although the director of the laboratory had been forewarned by an adviser to the two magicians against trickery, he ignored the warnings and for a time proclaimed that "these two kids are the most reliable of the people that we've studied" (*Psychic Abscam,* 1983).

Every belief system can be exploited. The existence of frauds and the gullibility of some parapsychologists does not discredit the possibility that somewhere there is a genuine psychic. But when one impressive "psychic" after another is debunked, skeptics do begin to wonder if anyone has ESP.

The skeptics are equally critical of psychics who claim to see into the future. Those who have taken the trouble to go back and tally the unfiltered past forecasts of "leading psychics" report meager predictive accuracy. For example, between 1978 and 1984 the New Year's predictions by the *National Enquirer*'s favorite psychics yielded 2 accurate predictions out of 425 (Strentz, 1984). During these years, none of the significant unexpected events—that a woman would run for Vice-President of the United States, that famine would devastate Ethiopia, and so forth—were foreseen by any of the psychics. *The People's Almanac*'s favorite psychics have fared slightly better; among 85 predictions 5 were accurate, such as the prediction that Russia and the United States would "remain as leading world powers" (Donnelly, 1983). Checks on the predictions of "police psychics" revealed that these, too, are no more accurate than guesses made by others (Reiser, 1982). Police psychics do, however, generate dozens or even hundreds of predictions; this increases the odds of an occasional correct guess, which can then be reported to the media.

Magicians Shaw and Edwards with adviser Randi after revealing their hoax at a news conference. A few months before, a newspaper article about their "psychic powers" triggered what Edwards described as "tons of mail, people asking for lucky numbers, lost children. People were basically asking me to help them guide their lives."

Are the spontaneous "visions" of ordinary people any more accurate? Consider our dreams. Do they foretell the future? Or do they only seem to because we are more likely to recall or reconstruct dreams that seem to have come true? A test of the prophetic power of dreams was conducted a half-century ago, after the Lindbergh baby was kidnapped and murdered but before the body was discovered. Two Harvard psychologists (Murray & Wheeler, 1937) invited the public to send in their dream reports concerning the whereabouts of the child. Of the 1300 dream reports received—all spontaneously experienced by people who felt they might have significance—how many accurately perceived that the child was dead? A mere 5 percent.

So why do so many people believe that dreams and premonitions foretell the future? The skeptics say that after the fact we selectively recall past predictions and adjust them to fit the facts. As later chapters will reveal, people often tend to notice and recall events that confirm their expectations, to be overly persuaded by misleading but vivid anecdotes, and to be unaware that among the billions of events in the world each day some astonishing coincidences are bound to occur. As the sixteenth-century French psychic Nostradamus explained in an unguarded moment, his ambiguous prophecies "could not possibly be understood till they were interpreted after the event and by it."

Finally, and most important, say the skeptics, is the fact that *there has never been a reproducible ESP phenomenon, nor any individual who could convincingly demonstrate psychic ability.* As British psychologist Mark Hansel (1980, p. 314) observed, "After a hundred years of research, not a single individual has been found who can demonstrate ESP to the satisfaction of independent investigators." One skeptic, magician James Randi, has offered $10,000 to anyone who can demonstrate "*any* paranormal ability" before a group of competent experts. The offer has been well publicized for two decades and dozens of people have been tested, sometimes under the scrutiny of an independent panel of judges. As yet, no one has exhibited any such power.

This most basic issue was highlighted at the 1981 convention of the American Psychological Association at which two symposia examined the "case for" and the "case against" ESP. Ironically, nearly the same conclusions were expressed at each. Both believers and skeptics agreed that what parapsychology needs to give it credibility is a reproducible phenomenon and a theory to explain it.

Could the Layton and Turnbull clairvoyance experiment provide such a reproducible phenomenon? The skeptical editor of the *Journal of Experimental Social Psychology,* to which Layton and Turnbull submitted their results for publication, wondered. So he made an unusual offer. If they would repeat their experiment, the journal would then publish the results of both experiments, regardless of the outcome. Layton and Turnbull accepted. (As this illustrates, both ESP researchers and skeptics genuinely seek truth and are therefore usually willing to accept valid evidence, no matter which viewpoint it supports.) The result of the second experiment? Layton and Turnbull summarized succinctly: "no [statistically] significant effects were present." And when the data from *both* experiments were combined, the results were nearly identical to what one would expect by chance (Greenwald, 1975).

"ESP in the laboratory generally shows up weakly or inconsistently, so it has been hard to study its nature."
Parapsychologist Charles Tart (1983)

To refute those who say there is no ESP, it is enough to produce a single reproducible ESP phenomenon. So far, the promoters of ESP have failed to find one.

For all these reasons, most research psychologists are skeptical of those who claim the powers of ESP and are dismayed at the numbers of books and magazines published on paranormal and occult topics. Should we share their skepticism and dismay? Should we agree that our own perceptual gifts equal those of any would-be *psychic?* Can we acknowledge that perception requires sensation without deciding that humans are mere machines?

"Mankind is poised midway between the gods and the beasts."
Plotinus, 205–270

A personal answer: We surely can be skeptical of human pretensions of ESP without being closed to all unprovable claims. We can be open to new ideas without being gullible, critical without being cynical. Indeed, the skeptical testing of claims that violate our current understanding enables us to separate mere nonsense from genuine natural phenomena. Knowing that our understanding of nature is incomplete and subject to revision, we can be critical thinkers yet sympathize with Shakespeare's Hamlet that "There are more things in heaven and earth, Horatio, than are dreamt of in your philosophy." Some things that we assume to be true—the reality of another's love, the existence or nonexistence of God, the finality of death or the reality of life after death—are beyond science. That is but one reason why, after clearing the decks of tested and rejected pseudomysteries, we can still retain a humble sense of wonder regarding life's untestable mysteries.

Drawing by Sidney Harris

Why, then, if one can be skeptical of ESP while retaining a sense of wonder, are so many people predisposed to believe that ESP exists? In part, such beliefs may stem from understandable mistakes of perception, interpretation, and memory. But it also seems that for some people there exists an unsatisfied hunger for wonderment, an itch to be brought face to face with the nearly magical. To be awestruck we need look no further than our own perceptual system and its capacity for organizing formless nerve impulses into colorful sights and vivid sounds. Within our ordinary moment-to-moment experiences of seeing and hearing lies much that is truly extraordinary—surely much more than has so far been dreamt of in our psychology. A century of research has revealed many of the secrets of sensation and perception, but for future generations of researchers there remain profound and genuine mysteries.

SUMMING UP

BASIC ISSUES IN PERCEPTION

Puzzling Perceptions A century ago, as psychology was emerging as a distinct discipline, scientists became fascinated with visual and auditory illusions. Explaining illusions required a deeper knowledge of how we transform sensory information into meaningful perceptions. Thus the study of perception became one of the first items on psychology's agenda.

Nativism and Empiricism: Nature-Nurture Revisited Historically, the basic debate in perception was between the nativists, who emphasized innate mechanisms for organizing sensory information, and the empiricists, who argued that we learn to perceive the world through our experiences in it.

PERCEPTUAL ORGANIZATION

The early Gestalt psychologists were impressed with the seemingly innate ways in which we organize sensory data. Our minds structure the information that comes to us in several demonstrable ways:

Form Perception To recognize an object, we must first perceive it (see it as a figure) as distinct from surrounding stimuli (the ground). We must also organize the figure into a meaningful form. Several Gestalt principles—proximity, similarity, closure, and continuation—describe how we organize an otherwise chaotic set of stimuli into simpler groups.

Depth Perception Research on the visual cliff suggests that in various species the ability to perceive the world in three dimensions is present at, or very shortly after, birth. We transform two-dimensional retinal images into three-dimensional perceptions by use of both binocular cues, such as retinal disparity, and various monocular cues, such as the relative sizes of objects.

Perceptual Constancies Having perceived an object as a coherent figure and located it in space, how then do we recognize it—despite the varying images that it may cast upon our retinas? The phenomena of size, shape, whiteness, and color constancy describe how objects appear to have constant characteristics regardless of their distance, shape, and so forth. These constancies also explain several of the well-known visual illusions.

INTERPRETATION: DO WE LEARN TO PERCEIVE?

The most direct tests of the nativism-empiricism issue come from experiments on the modification of human perceptions.

Sensory Restriction and Restored Vision If adults blind from birth are made to see (through the removal of their cataracts), they are unable to perceive the world normally. Generally, they can distinguish figure from ground and perceive colors, but even with much effort they are unable to distinguish shapes and forms. In better-controlled experiments, infant kittens and monkeys have been reared with goggles or with an eyelid sewn closed, or with eyes open but with severely restricted visual input. Later, when their visual exposure is returned to normal they, too, suffer permanent visual handicaps. Since sensory restriction later in life has little permanent effect, it appears that infancy is a critical period, during which the brain's innate visual mechanism must be activated through experience.

Perceptual Adaptation Human vision is nevertheless remarkably adaptable. If given glasses that shift the world slightly to the left or right, or even invert the world 180 degrees, people manage to adapt their movements and, with practice, to move about with ease.

Perceptual Set Clear evidence that perception is influenced by our assumptions and beliefs in addition to being based on sensory input comes from the many demonstrations of perceptual set. The schemas we have stored in memory help us to interpret otherwise ambiguous stimuli, a fact that helps explain why some people "see" monsters, ghosts, and UFOs that other people do not.

IS THERE PERCEPTION WITHOUT SENSATION?

Many people believe in, and even claim to have experienced, extrasensory perception. Parapsychologists have attempted to document several forms of ESP—telepathy, clairvoyance, and precognition. But for a number of reasons, such as the apparent lack of a reproducible ESP phenomenon, most research psychologists are skeptical.

TERMS AND CONCEPTS TO REMEMBER

Aerial Perspective A monocular cue for perceiving distance; distant objects appear less distinct than nearby objects.

Binocular Cues Depth cues that depend on the use of two eyes.

Closure The perceptual tendency to fill in gaps, thus enabling one to perceive disconnected parts as a whole object.

Cocktail Party Effect The ability to attend selectively to but one voice among many.

Color Constancy Perceiving familiar objects as having consistent color, even if their actual color is altered by changing illumination.

Continuity A perceptual tendency to group stimuli into smooth, continuous patterns.

Convergence A binocular depth cue; the extent to which the eyes converge inward when looking at an object.

Depth Perception The ability to see objects in three dimensions although the images that strike the retina are two-dimensional.

Empiricism The view that ideas and perceptions are learned through experience.

Extrasensory Perception (ESP) The controversial claim that valid perceptions of the environment can occur apart from sensory input. Said to include telepathy, clairvoyance, and precognition.

Figure-Ground The organization of the visual field into objects (the figure) that stand out from the background (the ground).

Gestalt An organized whole. Gestalt psychologists emphasize our tendency to integrate pieces of information into meaningful wholes.

Grouping The tendency, emphasized by Gestalt psychologists, to organize stimuli into coherent groups.

Linear Perspective A monocular cue for perceiving distance; we perceive the convergence of what we know to be parallel lines as indicating increasing distance.

Monocular Cues Depth cues available to either eye alone.

Nativism The view that important aspects of perception are innate, and thus do not have to be learned through experience.

Overlap A monocular cue for perceiving distance; nearby objects partially block our view of more distant objects. (Also called interposition, because nearby objects are interposed between our eyes and more distant objects.)

Parapsychology The study of paranormal phenomena such as ESP.

Perceptual Adaptation In vision, the ability to adjust to an artificially displaced or even inverted visual world.

Perceptual Set A mental predisposition to perceive one thing and not another.

Proximity A perceptual tendency to group together things that are near each other.

Relative Height A monocular cue for perceiving distance; we perceive higher objects as farther away.

Relative Motion A monocular cue for perceiving distance; when we move, objects at different distances change their relative positions in our visual image with those closest moving most. (Also called motion parallax.)

Relative Size A monocular cue for perceiving distance; when two objects are assumed to be the same size, the one that produces the smaller image appears to be more distant.

Retinal Disparity A binocular cue for perceiving depth; the more the disparity (difference) between the two images the retina receives of an object, the closer to us the object is. (Also called binocular disparity.)

Shape Constancy Perceiving familiar objects as having a constant shape, even while their retinal image changes with viewing angle.

Similarity A perceptual tendency to group together similar elements.

Size Constancy Perceiving an object as having a constant size, despite variations in its retinal image.

Texture Gradient A monocular cue for perceiving distance; a gradual change to a less distinct texture suggests increasing distance.

Visual Cliff A laboratory device for testing depth perception.

Whiteness Constancy Perceiving objects as having consistent whiteness even when their illumination varies.

FOR FURTHER READING

Coren, S., & Girgus, J. S. (1978). *Seeing is deceiving: The psychology of visual illusions.* Hillsdale, NJ: Erlbaum.

This intriguing book presents visual illusions and the perception principles which explain them.

Fineman, M. (1981) *The inquisitive eye.* New York: Oxford University Press.

Written for students in psychology, art, design, and photography, this entertaining book discusses and demonstrates many perceptual phenomena.

Rock, I. (1984). *Perception.* New York: Scientific American Books. (Distributed by Freeman.)

A beautifully illustrated treatment of many of the classic concerns of perception.

ESP

Alcock, J. E. (1981). *Parapsychology: Science or magic? A psychological perspective.* Oxford: Pergamon Press.

A critical analysis of parapsychology that provides psychological explanations of why so many people continue to believe in paranormal phenomena.

Marks, D., & Kammann, R. (1980). *The psychology of the psychic.* Buffalo, NY: Prometheus Books.

Uses painstaking detective work to uncover the secrets of several well-known psychic performers, such as Uri Geller, and to reveal the scientific bungling that lay behind some famous parapsychology experiments.

Wolman, B. B., Dale, L. A., Schmeidler, G. R., & Ullman, M. (Eds.). (1985) *Handbook of parapsychology.* New York: Van Nostrand Reinhold.

This book, written by parapsychologists, provides summaries of research they have undertaken.

Jonathan Borofsky *Installation at Paula Cooper Gallery,* November 5–December 3, 1983.

CHAPTER 8

States of Consciousness

Most sciences have concepts so fundamental that they are nearly impossible to define. In biology, the science of life, biologists generally agree on what is alive and what isn't, but they do not agree on precisely what life is. In physics, matter and energy are fundamental concepts, yet they elude simple definition. For psychology, mind and consciousness are similarly fundamental yet slippery concepts. What is consciousness? Is it an awareness of the world? An awareness of one's thoughts? An awareness of one's awareness?

STUDYING CONSCIOUSNESS

In its beginning, psychology was sometimes defined as "the description and explanation of states of consciousness" (Ladd, 1887). But the difficulty of studying such an elusive concept led most psychologists during the first half of this century to abandon the study of consciousness in favor of direct observations of behavior—a tendency encouraged by an emerging school of psychology called behaviorism. Under the influence of behaviorism (see p. 224), psychology by midcentury was no longer defined as the study of consciousness (or of "mental life"), but rather as the science of behavior. Psychology had nearly lost consciousness.

"Psychology must discard all references to consciousness."
Behaviorist John B. Watson (1913)

By 1960, mental concepts began to reenter psychology. Advances in neuroscience made it possible to relate various kinds of brain activity to various mental states—waking, sleeping, dreaming. Researchers were beginning to study what seemed to be altered states of consciousness induced by hypnosis, meditation, and drugs. In many other areas of psychology, the importance of mental processes (cognition) was being recognized. Psychology was regaining consciousness.

"People are often not even aware of what they do. . . . How do you turn right on a bicycle? Most people will say something like the following: 'First lean right and then turn the wheel to the right.' This is not how one turns right on a bicycle. It is actually a prescription for how to fall off a bicycle (to the left)."
Donald McBurney and Virginia Collings (1984)

Although there still is no agreed-upon definition of ***consciousness,*** we can think of it as *selective attention to ongoing perceptions, thoughts, and feelings.* When learning a complex concept or behavior—say, when learning to drive—consciousness focuses our attention on the mechanical tasks of controlling the car and on the traffic conditions around us. With practice, driving becomes automatic, freeing our consciousness to focus on other things.

Many of our past and future chapter topics (perception, thinking and language, learning, memory, emotion) involve the study of consciousness—normal waking consciousness. But research in each of these areas also reveals that we process much information outside of conscious awareness: We can type proficiently without conscious attention to the placement of letters on the keyboard. We may change our attitudes or reconstruct our memories with no awareness of having done so. We register and react to stimuli we do not consciously perceive. After a driving lesson we may find ourselves whistling a particular tune and wondering why, not realizing that it was playing on the car radio while we were learning to parallel park. Unlike *un*conscious information processing (that occurs without our awareness), consciousness processes things in succession (not simultaneously), is relatively slow, and has a limited capacity. Consciousness, it seems, is like the small, visible top of a plant, whose hidden activity below ground both feeds and is fed by what happens above the surface.

With experience, many tasks, such as driving, become mostly automatic, freeing our conscious attention for other matters.

Psychologists may be unsure exactly what consciousness is, but they recognize that it occurs in varied states. Thus we have not only alert seeing and hearing, reasoning and remembering, but also the alternate states that are our focus in this chapter—daydreams and sleep dreams, trances and meditative states, hallucinations and mystical visions.

DAYDREAMING

In James Thurber's classic story "The Secret Life of Walter Mitty," the bland existence of mild-mannered Walter Mitty is spiced with gratifying fantasies. As he drives past a hospital, Mitty imagines himself as Dr. Mitty, rushing to an operating room where two renowned specialists are pleading for his help. The patient saved, the bumbling real-life Walter Mitty again and again relieves the tedium of his existence by imagining himself as the triumphant Walter Mitty—now the world's greatest marksman, now a heroic pilot.

André Derain's (1880–1954) painting La Tasse de Thé *captures the charm of a reflective moment of quiet. The pleasure and relaxation afforded by such moments are part of the adaptive value of daydreams.*

The story became a classic because most people can identify with Walter Mitty's fantasizing. From interviews and questionnaire studies with hundreds of adults, clinical psychologist Jerome L. Singer (1975) reported that nearly everyone has daydreams or waking fantasies, every day—on the job, in the classroom, walking down the street—in fact, almost anywhere at any time. Not all daydreaming is as overtly escapist or dramatic as Walter Mitty's. Much of it involves the homelier details of our lives—perhaps imagining an alternative approach to a task we are performing, or picturing ourselves explaining to the course instructor why a paper will be late, or replaying in our minds personal encounters that we particularly enjoyed or wish had gone differently. Compared to older adults, young adults spend more time daydreaming and they admit to more sexual fantasies (Cameron & Biber, 1973; Giambra, 1974).

Are the hours we spend in fantasy merely a way of escaping rather than facing reality? At times, they are. However, there are hints that daydreaming may also be adaptive. Some daydreams help us prepare for future events, by keeping us aware of unfinished business and serving as mental rehearsals. Playful fantasies have enhanced the creativity of scientists, artists, and writers. For children, daydreaming in the form of imaginative play is important to social and cognitive development. Daydreams may also be of some benefit by substituting for impulsive behavior or by providing relaxation. This possibility is suggested by the fact that people prone to delinquency and violent behavior, or to seeking the artificial highs of dangerous drugs, tend to have fewer vivid fantasies (Singer,

"When I examined myself, and my methods of thought, I came to the conclusion that the gift of fantasy has meant more to me than my talent for absorbing positive knowledge."
Albert Einstein

1976). So it may be that Walter Mitty's imaginative reveries not only rescue him from boredom, but also may allow him to indulge his impulses within the safety of his inner world.

"The art of living requires us to steer a course between the two extremes of external and internal stimulation."
Jerome L. Singer (1976)

SLEEP AND DREAMS

Sleep—sweet, renewing, mysterious sleep. Sleep—the irresistible tempter to whom we must all succumb. Sleep—that for a time steals us away from our cares and sorrows. What is it? Why do we need it? How does the lack of it affect us?

Such questions have intrigued humans for centuries. Now, in our own time, some of the age-old mysteries of sleep have begun to be solved. In laboratories across the world, thousands have slept, attached to modern gadgetry, while others have observed. By recording sleepers' brain waves and muscle movements, by observing and awakening people at different times in their night's sleep, the sleep-watchers have glimpsed things that a thousand years of common sense never told us. Perhaps you can anticipate some of their discoveries—are the following statements true or false?

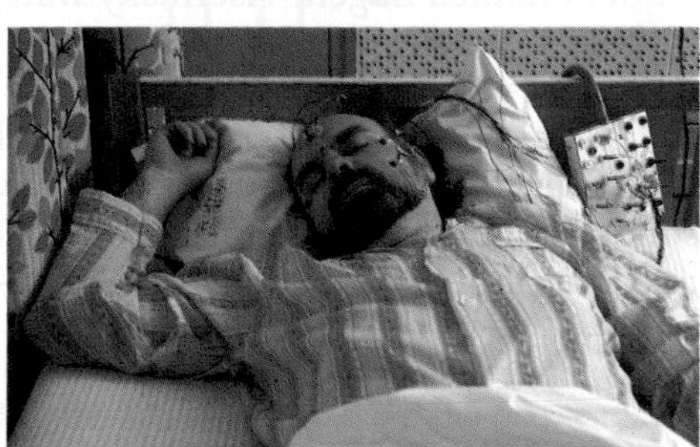

In this modern sleep laboratory, a researcher electronically monitors and records a sleeping subject's bodily state. This information together with observations made of the sleeper's activities and his reports when awakened at different points in his sleep cycle provide clues to the mysteries of sleep.

1. When people dream of performing some activity, their limbs often move in concert with the dream.
2. Older adults sleep more than young adults.
3. After going without sleep for 2 or 3 days, a person's performance on a brief but demanding intellectual task will suffer.
4. Highly creative people, such as Albert Einstein, have tended to sleep less than average.
5. Sleepwalkers are acting out their dreams.
6. Sleep experts recommend an occasional sleeping pill to break a pattern of insomnia.
7. The dreams we have before awakening in the morning tend to be quite similar to those we have soon after falling asleep.
8. Some people dream every night; others seldom dream at all.

Research has shown all these statements (adapted from Palladino & Carducci, 1983) to be false. How have these and other such conclusions been reached?

The Rhythm of Sleep

The rhythm of each day has been likened to the rhythm of life—from the birth of a new day to our nightly succumbing to what Shakespeare called "death's counterfeit." Our bodies time the daily pattern with a biological clock known as ***circadian rhythm*** (from the Latin *circa*, "approximately," and *dies*, "day"). For example, synchronized with the 24-hour cycle of day and night, body temperature rises as morning approaches, peaks during the day, and then begins descending before sleep. After a transoceanic or cross-country flight our circadian rhythm is disrupted and we may experience jet lag, because now we are awake at a time when our biological clock predisposes us to sleep. Radically altering one's sleeping schedule from weekdays to weekends can similarly throw the biological clock

Mysteriously, when research volunteers are isolated without clocks or daylight, they tend to adopt a 25-hour day.

Why We Sleep

Sleep commands one-third of our lives. Deprived of it, we begin to feel terrible; our bodies yearn to be taken by it. Obviously, we need sleep. But why?

"Sleep, dear Sleep, sweet harlot of the senses,
Delilah of the spirit, you unnerve
The strong man's knees, depose his laughing brain,
And make him a mere mass of steady breathing."
Christopher Morley, 1890–1957, "Sleep"

One might think this question could be answered easily: Just keep people awake for several days and note how they deteriorate. If you were a subject in such an experiment, how do you think it would affect your body and mind? At times, you would, of course, become terribly drowsy—especially during the hours when your biological clock programs you to be asleep. Would you be physically damaged? Would your biochemistry or bodily organs be noticeably altered? Would you become emotionally out of control, intellectually disoriented?

Surprisingly, the major effect of sleep deprivation is merely sleepiness. The other effects are more subtle: diminished immunity to disease (Palmblad & others, 1979), a slight hand tremor, minor irritability, and occasional inattentions or misperceptions, especially on slow, monotonous tasks (Webb, 1982a). (Of course, with some monotonous tasks, such as driving, such effects are potentially devastating.) On short, highly motivating tasks, sleep deprivation has little effect. When 17-year-old Randy Gardner temporarily made his way into the *Guinness Book of World Records* by staying awake for 11 days, he at times had to keep moving to stay awake. Nevertheless, during his final night of sleeplessness, Gardner managed to beat researcher William Dement 100 straight times on a pinball game. He then slept for 15 hours and awoke feeling fine (Gulevich & others, 1966).

The current record holder, Maureen Weston of England, reportedly stayed awake for 18 days, 17 hours in a rocking chair marathon. She suffered some hallucinations, but no long-term damage.

So the simple question stubbornly persists: Why do we sleep? There is indirect evidence that sleep helps restore bodily tissues. In one study of runners in a 92-kilometer (57-mile) marathon, the competitors averaged 7 hours sleep on nights before the race, and 8½ hours on the two nights following the race. The night after the run, deep Stage 4 sleep doubled (Shapiro & others, 1981).

Sleep may also play a role in the growth process. During deep sleep, the pituitary gland releases a growth hormone. As adults grow older, they release less of this hormone; they also sleep less, especially in the deepest stage (Pekkanen, 1982). Perhaps such clues will someday be assembled into an understanding of the mechanism that creates our need to sleep, and that is satisfied by sleep. For now, the riddle of sleep—and the quest to solve it—continues. As researcher Dement (1978, p. 83) deadpanned, "We have miles to go before we sleep."

"This concludes the conscious part of your day. Good night."

Sleep Disorders

The maxim "Everyone needs 8 hours sleep" is untrue. Age-related differences in sleep (newborns spend at least two-thirds of their day asleep, the elderly barely more than one-fourth) are rivaled by differences among individuals at any age. Some people thrive with less than 6 hours per night; others regularly sleep 9 hours or more. Although these sleep differences are not accompanied by striking personality differences (Webb, 1979), sleep patterns may be genetically influenced. When Wilse Webb and Scott Campbell (1983) monitored the pattern and duration of sleep among fraternal and identical twins, only the genetic replicas were strikingly similar.

Horses and cows sleep but 3 to 4 hours per day; rats and cats sleep 14 to 15 hours. (Webb, 1982b).

Whatever their normal need for sleep, some 15 percent of adults complain of ***insomnia***—recurring problems in falling or staying asleep. The emphasis in this definition is on "recurring." True insomnia is not the occasional inability to sleep that we may experience when we are feeling anxious or excited. Alertness is a natural and adaptive response to stress. (However, because sleep is less easily remembered than wakefulness, we commonly underestimate the amount of sleep we get on such nights and may think we have insomnia.)

"The lion and the lamb shall lie down together, but the lamb will not be very sleepy."
Woody Allen in the movie "Love and Death," 1975

The two most common quick fixes for insomnia, sleeping pills and alcohol, can worsen the problem. Both tend to reduce needed REM sleep, and when their use is discontinued, insomnia may worsen. Sleep experts instead advise (1) relaxing before bed; (2) avoiding rich foods around bedtime (milk is better, since it aids in the manufacture of serotonin, a neurotransmitter that facilitates sleep); (3) sleeping on a regular schedule (rising at the same time even after a restless night and avoiding naps); and (4) reassuring oneself that a temporary loss of sleep causes no great harm.

Rarer but more severe sleep disorders include ***narcolepsy*** and ***sleep apnea.*** Narcoleptics suffer periodic overwhelming sleepiness, sometimes at the most inopportune times—perhaps just after taking a terrific swing at a softball or when laughing loudly or shouting angrily (Dement, 1978). The person collapses directly into a brief period of REM sleep, with its accompanying loss of muscular tension. The estimated 100,000 or more Americans who suffer from narcolepsy must live with extra caution, lest they, for example, fall asleep while driving.

Those who suffer from sleep apnea intermittently stop breathing while sleeping (*apnea* means "cessation of respiration"). After an airless minute or so, the diminishing of oxygen in the blood arouses the sleeper to snort in air for a few seconds. The process is repeated hundreds of times during a night's sleep. Apart from their being sleepy during the daytime—and receiving complaints from their mates about their loud "snoring"—apnea sufferers are often not aware of their disorder. Yet, were they not to become aroused and resume breathing, they would suffocate, which some scientists speculate is what happens to sleeping babies who mysteriously die of Sudden Infant Death Syndrome (crib death).

This baby, who suffers sleep apnea, is attached to a monitor that sounds an alarm if he stops breathing.

Still other sleepers are afflicted with ***night terrors.*** The person—often, but not always, a child—might sit up or walk around, talk incoherently, experience a doubling of heart and breathing rates, and appear terrified (Hartmann, 1981). Unlike those who experience a nightmare, the night-terror sufferer seldom awakens fully and the next morning recalls little or nothing—at most a fleeting frightening image. Unlike nightmares, which typically occur toward morning during REM sleep, but *like* sleepwalking, night terrors usually occur during the first 2 or 3 hours of sleep and during Stage 4 sleep.

Dreams

The discovery of the linkage between REM sleep and dreaming opened a new era of dream research. Now, instead of having to trust someone's hazy recall of a dream hours afterward, it became possible to catch dreams as they happen. Researchers could awaken someone during one of the REM sleep periods, or within 5 minutes afterward, and be given a vivid account of anything that was being dreamed.

What Do We Dream?

Compared to daydreams, REM dreams are more colorful, emotional, and bizarre. In the dream world, events frequently occur in a jumbled sequence, scenes change suddenly, people appear and disappear, physical laws, such as the law of gravity, may be violated. Yet dreams are so vivid that we may take them for reality. (Upon awakening from a vivid dream, we may even wonder whether our waking existence, too, is but a dream.)

"Why does the eye see a thing more clearly in dreams than the imagination when awake?"
Leonardo da Vinci, 1452–1519

Occasionally, during the course of a dream, we may be sufficiently lucid that we wonder whether, in fact, we are dreaming. When experiencing such "lucid dreams," some people are able to test their state of consciousness. If they can perform some absurd act, such as floating in the air, then they know they are dreaming.

"Is this a dream? Oh, if it be a dream, Let me sleep on, and do not wake me yet!"
Henry Wadsworth Longfellow, "Spanish Student," 1843

Although we are more likely to be awakened by, and thus to remember, our most emotional dreams, many of our dreams are rather ordinary. When awakened during REM sleep, people report dreams with sexual imagery less often than you might think—in one study some 1 in 10 dreams among young men and 1 in 30 among young women had sexual overtones (Hall & Van de Castle, 1966). (Thus, assuming we can trust the dreamers' reports, the genital arousal that tends to accompany REM sleep is usually *not* a consequence of obviously sexual dreams.) More commonly we dream of events related to our daily lives, such as taking exams or experiencing an incident at work. Although it has been said that "dreaming is better than parties," most dreams are not notably sweet. People commonly dream of repeatedly failing in an attempt to do something, of being attacked, pursued, or rejected, or of experiencing misfortune (Hall & others, 1982).

"For what one has dwelt on by day, these things are seen in visions of the night."
Menander of Athens, 342–292 B.C., *Fragments*

Across the world, people of all ages show a curious gender difference in dream content. The average female dreams of males and females equally often, but the average male's dream characters are about 65 percent male. Why this is so, no one is sure. But whatever its significance, dream researcher Calvin Hall (1984) believed this fact could be added to the short list (see Chapter 5, "Gender") of apparently universal gender differences.

The surface story line of our dreams—what Sigmund Freud called their ***manifest content***—often incorporates experiences and preoccupations from our day's events, especially in our first dreams of the night. The sensory stimuli of our sleeping environment may also influence dream content. The ringing of an alarm clock or telephone, or a particular odor, may be instantly and ingeniously woven into the dream story. In one experiment, William Dement and Edward Wolpert (1958) lightly sprayed cold water on dreamers' faces. Compared to sleepers who did not get the cold water treatment, these subjects were more likely to dream about water—about waterfalls, leaky roofs, or even about being sprayed by someone.

Drawing by Sidney Harris

"Dreams are the true interpreters of our inclinations, but art is required to sort and understand them."
Montaigne, *Essays*, 1580

Why Do We Dream?

In his landmark book *The Interpretation of Dreams* (1900), Freud argued that dreams are a psychic safety valve that provide a harmless expression of otherwise inexpressible feelings. According to Freud, a dream's manifest content is but a censored, symbolic version of its deeper ***latent content,*** which consists of drives and wishes that would be threatening if expressed directly. Although most dreams do not have overt sexual imagery, Freud nevertheless believed that "most of the dreams of adults are traced back by analysis to *erotic wishes.*" In Freud's view, a gun, for example, might actually be a disguised representation of the penis, and a dream in which a person is being robbed at gunpoint might be seen as expressing a wish for sexual surrender.

Freud attached such significance to the meaning of dreams that he considered them the key to understanding the individual's inner conflicts. However, many of Freud's critics believe that dream interpretation is little more than a blind alley. Some contend that even if dreams are symbolic, they can be read almost any way one wishes. Others maintain that there is nothing hidden in dreams. A dream about a gun is, they say,

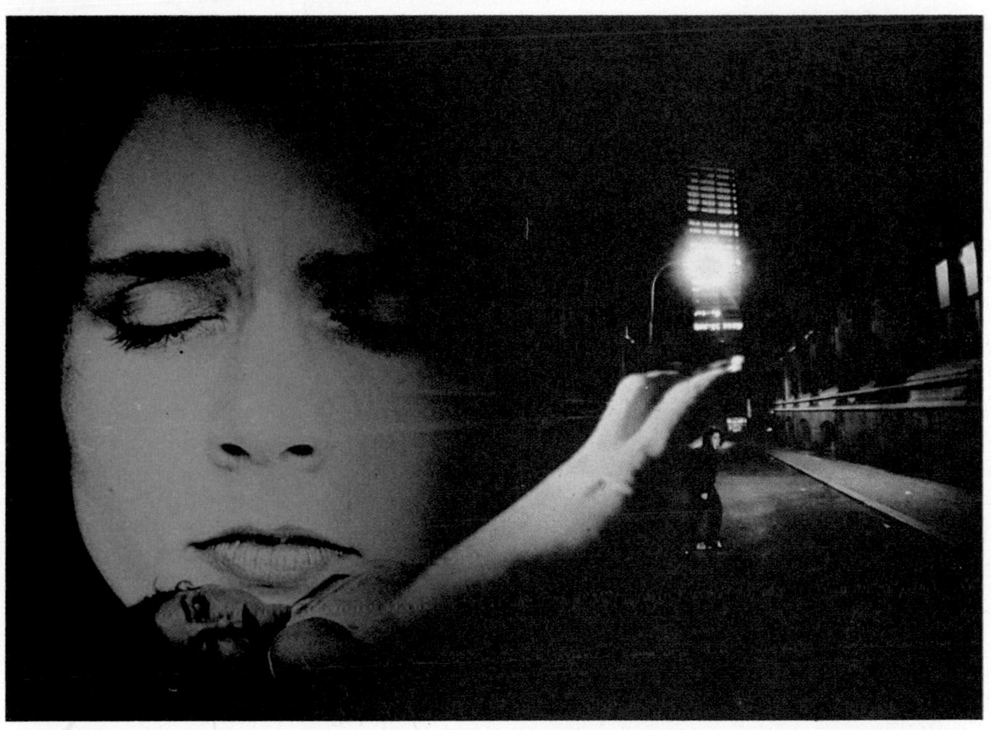

Freud held that a dream's manifest content—what the dreamer experiences and perhaps recalls—is a symbolic version of its hidden latent content.

a dream about a gun. Dreams tell us about little except the dreamer's current preoccupations.

Several alternatives to Freud's theory of dreams have recently been offered. One of these sees dreams in terms of an information processing function: Dreams may help sift, sort, and fix in memory our day's experiences; following stressful experiences or intense learning periods, REM sleep tends to increase (Palumbo, 1978). What is more, a whole series of experiments has produced "consistent and compelling evidence" that REM sleep facilitates memory for unusual or anxiety-arousing material (McGrath & Cohen, 1978). For example, after hearing unusual phrases before bedtime, people the next morning remembered fewer phrases if they had been awakened every time they began REM sleep than if awakened during other sleep stages (Empson & Clarke, 1970). A solid night's sleep does, it seems, have a justifiable place in a student's life.

Dreams sometimes may also involve more creative cognitive activity (Lindzey & others, 1978). Robert Louis Stevenson credits his dreams for the plot of "Dr. Jekyll and Mr. Hyde." Handel claimed that the last movements of his *Messiah* were dream-inspired. Artists Salvador Dali and Paul Klee drew heavily upon their dreams. In all these cases, the cognitive activity of the dream simply reorganized ideas from the dreamer's ongoing waking concerns.

Another proposed explanation of dreams is compatible with the information processing theory: Dreams may serve a physiological function. Perhaps dreams—or the associated physiological activity of REM sleep—provide the sleeping brain with periodic stimulation. As you may recall from Chapter 2, "Biological Roots of Behavior," stimulating experiences both preserve and develop the brain's neural pathways. Certainly this theory makes sense from a developmental point of view, since infants, whose neural networks are just developing, spend the most time in REM sleep (about half their sleep), and as people age they gradually spend less and less time in REM sleep (Figure 8-5).

Paul Klee (1879–1940) often painted images that he first experienced in dreams. His painting entitled The Mount of the Sacred Cat *suggests the fantastical visions of dreams.*

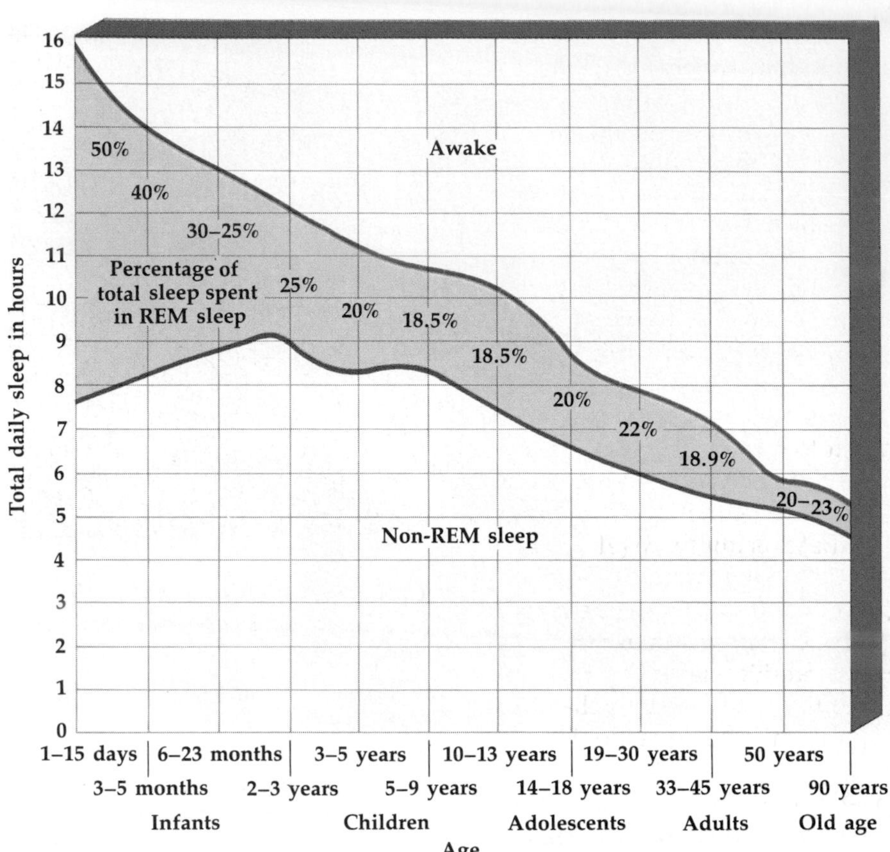

Figure 8-5 *With age, we spend less time sleeping, and proportionately less time in REM sleep.*

Still other physiological theories propose that dreams are triggered by neural activity that spreads upward from the brainstem. According to one version, this neural activity is random, and dreams are the brain's attempt to make sense out of it (McCarley & Hobson, 1981). The result is bizarre scenes that are forgotten unless mentally rehearsed upon awakening.

While the function of our dreams is currently a topic of vigorous debate, the disputants do agree that we need REM sleep. Deprived of it by repeated awakenings, people return more and more quickly to the REM stage after falling back to sleep. When finally allowed to sleep undisturbed, they literally sleep like babies—with increased REM sleep. This ***REM rebound*** effect occurs in other mammals as well (most of which share our REM sleep stage). And their need for REM sleep is consistent with the physiological explanation of REM. The fact that REM occurs in mammals (but not in animals such as fish whose behavior is less influenced by learning) also is consistent with the information processing theory of dreams. All of which serves to remind us of a fundamental and familiar lesson: Biological and psychological explanations of behavior are partners, not competitors.

This beagle, like his master, needs REM sleep. If deprived of it, he will, when allowed to sleep undisturbed, experience increased REM sleep.

HYPNOSIS

Imagine yourself about to be hypnotized. The hypnotist invites you to sit back, fix your gaze on a spot on the ceiling, and relax. In a quiet, low voice the hypnotist suggests, "Your eyes are growing tired. . . . Your eyelids are becoming heavy . . . now heavier and heavier. . . . They are beginning to close. . . . You are becoming ever more deeply relaxed. . . . Your breathing is now deep and regular. . . . Your muscles are becoming more and more relaxed. Your whole body is beginning to feel like lead."

After a few minutes of this hypnotic induction, your eyes are likely closed (anyone's eyes will get tired after staring at the ceiling) and you may, in fact, have become hypnotized. If so, you are now in a state of ***hypnosis***—of heightened suggestibility that enables the hypnotist's coaxings and directions to trigger changed behaviors, perceptions, and memories. When it is suggested to you that "your eyelids are shutting tight . . . tighter . . . so tight that you cannot open them even if you try," your eyes will in fact remain closed—seemingly beyond your control. Told to forget the number 6, you will appear puzzled when you count eleven fingers on your hands. Invited to smell a sensual perfume that is actually ammonia, you will linger delightedly over the acrid odor. Asked to describe a nonexistent picture the hypnotist claims to be holding, you will talk about it in detail. Told that you cannot see a certain object such as a chair, you will indeed report that it is not there (although curiously, you will manage to avoid it when walking around). And if instructed to forget all these happenings when brought out of the hypnotic state, you will later experience ***posthypnotic amnesia,*** an experience rather like being temporarily unable to recall a familiar name. (The "forgotten" material is nevertheless "in there," for it can affect later behavior and can be recalled at a prearranged signal or upon subtle questioning—Kihlstrom, 1985; Spanos & others, 1985.)

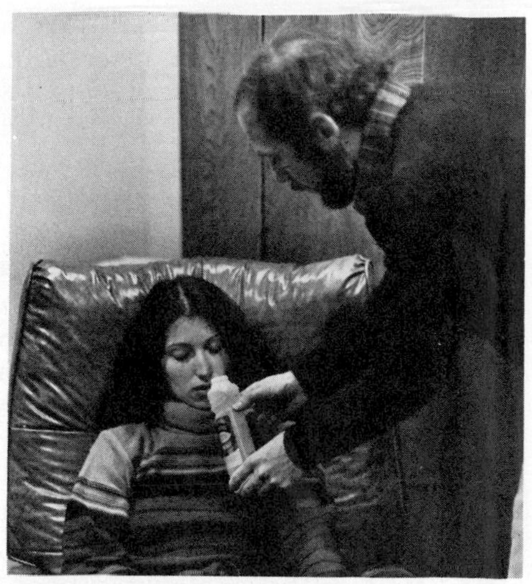

In response to suggestion, this hypnotized subject is outwardly unresponsive to the smell of ammonia.

Although hypnotic techniques have been in use since antiquity, the "discovery" of hypnosis is commonly credited to an Austrian physician, Anton Mesmer (1734–1815), who mistakenly thought he had discovered a universal principle of body magnetism. With great flourish Mesmer passed magnets over the bodies of ailing people, some of whom would lapse into a trancelike ("mesmerized") state and awaken much improved. As we noted in Chapter 1, scientists found no evidence of body magnetism and instead attributed the "cures" to "mere imagination." Thus, hypnosis—or mesmerism as it was then called—became linked with quackery and bizarre claims. This archaic linkage can still be seen in the Library of Congress classification scheme: books on hypnosis are grouped with parapsychology—just after the books on phrenology and just before the books on ghosts and witchcraft.

Recently, research on hypnosis has gained more respectability. But, as we will see, hypnosis researchers are far from agreement on whether the hypnotic state is actually a special state of consciousness. They do agree, however, that the hypnotic state is real; that some people can enter the hypnotic state more readily than others; and that some claims for hypnotic effects are real and others grossly exaggerated. So let us first consider these areas of general agreement. With the facts of hypnosis in mind, we can then step back to ponder the more fundamental and perplexing question: What is hypnosis, and what does it tell us about human consciousness?

"We are presently in something like a golden age of hypnosis research."
Kenneth S. Bowers (1984)

Facts and Falsehoods

Can Anyone Be Hypnotized?

Those who study hypnosis agree that its power resides not in the hypnotist but in the subject's capacity to be open to suggestion (Bowers, 1984). To some extent, nearly everyone is suggestible. When standing upright with eyes closed and told repeatedly that they are swaying back and forth, most people will sway a little. Interestingly, those who sway most tend to be most easily and deeply hypnotized. And, in fact, postural sway is one of several items on a standardized scale that is used to assess a person's hypnotizability (see Figure 8-6). The person is given a brief hypnotic induction and then presented with a graded series of suggestions ranging from "easy"—such as that one's extended arms will move together—to "difficult"—such as that the subject, with eyes open, will see a nonexistent person.

Among a group of people, those who can be deeply hypnotized today will likely still be the most hypnotizable if retested in 1996 (Morgan & others, 1974). These hypnotizable people are likely to have the capability of becoming deeply absorbed in imaginative activities. Typically, they have rich fantasy lives and can easily give themselves over to imaginary events such as those in a novel or movie. In many ways the ability to become deeply absorbed is beneficial; it underlies both hypnotic responsiveness and creativity (Bowers & Bowers, 1979). Consequently, many researchers today refer to hypnotic "susceptibility" as hypnotic *ability*. Note how the label one gives a phenomenon dictates its connotations. Few of us would care to be "susceptible" to hypnosis; who wants to be a puppet under someone else's control? Yet most of us would be glad to have the "ability" to focus our attention totally on a task, to become imaginatively absorbed in it, to entertain fanciful possibilities. And that is what the person with hypnotic ability can do.

"You certainly may *not* try to hypnotize me."

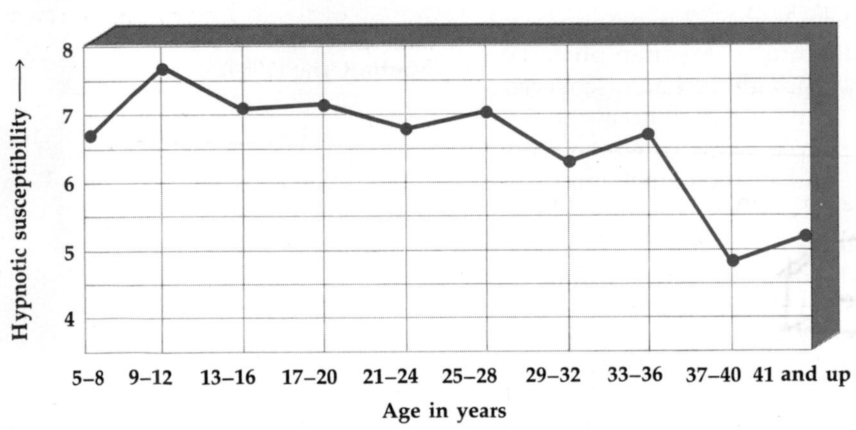

Figure 8-6 *Hypnotic responsiveness (as measured by the Stanford hypnotic susceptibility scale) tends to decrease with age, as does the time spent in daydreaming. This is consistent with the idea that hypnosis is experienced through the same psychological processes that produce spontaneous fantasy.*

Can a Hypnotized Person Perform Otherwise Impossible Feats?

During the nineteenth century, mesmerized people were said to surpass their waking potentials in strength and perceptiveness. They could supposedly see with the back of their heads, perceive others' internal organs, or communicate with the dead (Spanos, 1982). Today, there is agreement that hypnotized persons cannot perform such feats.

Hypnotized people can, however, do some seemingly amazing things. Some can become a "human plank," with body so rigid that the head and shoulders can be placed on one chair, the calves on another, and a person can stand on the unsupported stomach (Figure 8-7). Some may even be induced to perform perilous acts. In one investigation of the power of hypnosis, five of six hypnotized individuals were induced to pick up with their fingers a coin that was dissolving in fuming acid and then to throw the acid in a research assistant's face (Orne & Evans, 1965). (The subject's unharmed hand was immediately washed after the coin was plucked out, and before the liquid was thrown a harmless but identically colored liquid was substituted for the acid.)

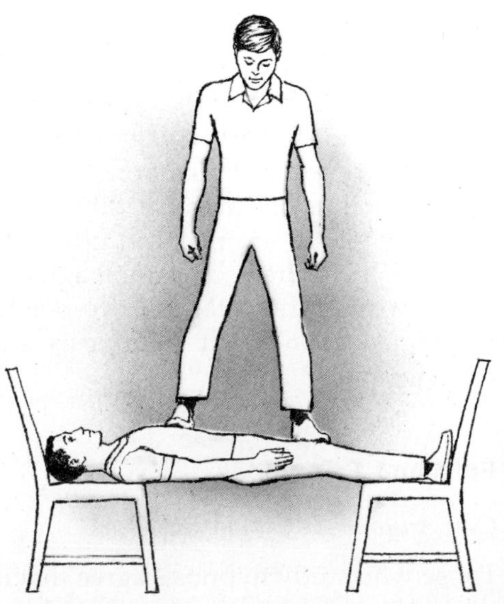

Figure 8-7 *The "amazing" hypnotized "human plank." Actually, nonhypnotized people can do the same.*

Does this mean that hypnosis can trigger special powers? And atypical behaviors? Might it be exploited by inducing a subject to, say, commit a heinous crime? No. Hypnotized subjects perform only such acts as they might do normally, if the situation were right. If motivated, almost anyone could become a human plank. Hypnotized subjects can extend their arms for about 6 minutes, but so can unhypnotized people. But without being hypnotized, would people ever plunge their hands in acid and throw acid in a bystander's face? Interviewed the day after the experiments, the acid-throwers denied the possibility that they would follow orders to perform such behaviors. This might suggest that hypnosis had given the hypnotist a unique power to control people. But, in fact, this experiment had intermingled the hypnotized subjects with six unhypnotized control subjects who were asked merely to pretend to be hypnotized. The experimenter who gave the orders did not know which subjects were hypnotized and which were faking, so he treated everyone in the same persuasive way. The result? In this situation—under orders from an authoritative experimenter operating within a legitimate scientific laboratory—all six of the *un*hypnotized subjects performed the same acts. Such experiments as this have led hypnosis researcher Nicholas P. Spanos (1982) to conclude that "the overt behaviors of hypnotic subjects are well within normal limits."

So, hypnosis does not endow us with special abilities, nor does it surpass other techniques for controlling people. Its uniqueness lies rather in the subject's inner experience of those compelling and subjectively real fantasies—of altered feelings, of seeing what is not there and not seeing what is, of posthypnotic amnesia.

"Hypnosis turns out to be a powerful way to alter experience, but not a powerful way to alter behavior."
Martin Orne (1984)

Can Hypnosis Enhance Recall of Forgotten Events?

Can hypnosis enable people to relive earlier experiences? To recall kindergarten classmates? To retrieve suppressed or forgotten details of a crime? Should testimony obtained under hypnosis be admissible in court?

Most people believe that your past experience is all " in there," that everything that has happened to you is recorded in your brain, even if you are unaware of it, and that it could be recalled if only you could break through your own defenses (Loftus, 1980). Testimonies to this come from ***age regression,*** in which subjects supposedly relive their earlier experiences. When Freud asked his hypnotized patients to relive traumatic events from their childhood, they did so with intense emotion and in astonishingly vivid detail, often recalling even trivial matters such as a crooked picture on the wall or a stain on the table. Such descriptions were seductively convincing. So much so that it was not until years later that Freud came to believe that these memories, though sincere, were nevertheless fantasies, not recollections of actual events.

In criminal investigations, the relaxed, focused state of hypnosis has on a few occasions enabled witnesses to produce important leads. On July 15, 1977, twenty-six children and their bus driver, Ed Ray, were kidnapped and forced into an abandoned trailer truck buried 6 feet underground. After their rescue, Ray was put under hypnosis and was able to recall all but one digit of the kidnapper's license plate. With this crucial information, the abductors were tracked down. Although the ancedote is atypical, most hypnosis researchers agree that hypnosis may have value—or at least can do little harm—when used as an investigative tool.

Nevertheless, because of the unreliability of hypnotically influenced memories, perils arise when attempts are made to put a previously hypnotized person on the witness stand. Researchers have time and again found that "hypnotically refreshed" memories tend to combine fact with fiction—a finding that is causing a growing list of state court systems to curtail testimonies derived from hypnosis. Hypnosis typically either fails to boost recall of information that was previously learned or, worse, contaminates one's memory (Dywan & Bowers, 1983; Orne, 1982; Smith, 1983). When pressed under hypnosis to recall details, perhaps to "zoom in on your visual screen," people begin to incorporate more and more of their imaginations into their memories. Thus they may end up testifying confidently to events that, apart from the hypnotist's leading questions ("Did you hear loud noises?"), they never experienced (Laurence & Perry, 1983). Without either person being aware of what is going on, the hypnotist's hints become the subject's memory.

A True Story

What shall we make of a clever study by Robert True (1949)? He regressed hypnotized volunteers back to their birthday parties and Christmases at ages 10, 7, and 4. In each case he asked them what day of the week it was. Without hypnosis, the odds that one could name the correct day are hardly better than 1 in 7. Remarkably, the hypnotized subjects' answers were 82 percent correct.

With hypnosis could we, too, retrieve the days? Since other investigators had been unsuccessful in replicating True's study, hypnosis researcher Martin Orne (1982) asked Dr. True why. True replied that *Science,* the journal in which his paper was published, had shortened his key question to: "What day is this?" Actually, he had asked his age-regressed subjects, "Is it Monday, Is it Tuesday?," and so forth until the subject would stop him with a yes. When Orne asked if True himself knew the actual day of the week while posing the questions, True granted that he did, but was puzzled as to why Orne would ask.

Can you see why? The experiment appears to be a beautiful example of how hypnotists can subtly influence the memories of their subjects (and more generally, of how experimenters can subtly communicate their expectations to their subjects). "Given the eagerness of the hypnotized subject to fulfill the demands placed upon him," surmised Orne, "it takes only the slightest change of inflection for him to respond, 'It's Wednesday.'" The final blow to True's experiment came when Orne simply asked ten 4-year-olds what day of the week it was. To his surprise, none knew. If 4-year-olds do not know the day of the week, then True's adults were reporting information that they likely never knew when they were age 4.

If people's hypnotic regressions to childhood are fabricated, then how believable are claims of "regression to past lives"?

Can Hypnosis Help Solve Problems or Break Bad Habits?

Recently, the clinical use of hypnosis has mushroomed. Under the direction of a professional psychologist or physician, ***posthypnotic suggestions*** (suggestions to be carried out after the hypnotic session has ended) have at least temporarily reinforced a person's own efforts to diet and give up smoking, and have alleviated headaches, asthma, and skin disorders. One woman, who for more than 20 years had suffered open sores all over her body, was asked to imagine herself swimming in shimmering, sunlit liquids that would cleanse her skin and to experience her skin as smooth and unblemished. Within 3 months her sores were gone and remained so (Bowers, 1984). Just how the hypnotic treatment achieves these effects is unclear. In some studies where hypnosis has helped, it has *not* given more help to those who could be deeply hypnotized than to those who could not. This suggests that the treatment benefits may sometimes be due to something other than hypnotic suggestion.

Can Hypnosis Alleviate Pain?

Yes. Even light hypnosis can reduce fear, and thus hypersensitivity to the pain of, say, dental treatment. Some 10 percent of people can become so deeply hypnotized that childbirth or even major surgery is possible without anesthesia.

That pain can be relieved through hypnosis has been well-established experimentally (Kihlstrom, 1985). Hypnotized subjects report far less pain than others when their arms are placed in ice water. Moreover, their reports have a consistency that would be hard to fake. For example, if low-level pain is reduced by half through hypnotic suggestion, then a pain twice as strong will also be reduced by about half through the same suggestion (Hilgard, 1983).

The explanation of hypnotic pain relief is still being debated. A possibility that has recently been eliminated is the involvement of endorphins, the pain-reducing neurotransmitters (see p. 32). When endorphin production is chemically prevented, hypnotic pain relief still occurs (Watkins & Mayer, 1982). Why?

The experience of pain is reduced, even eliminated, at times when one's attention is strongly diverted toward something else.

One theory of hypnotic pain relief is that hypnosis dissociates, or separates, the sensation of the pain stimulus—of which both hypnotized and unhypnotized subjects are aware—from the emotional suffering that defines our experience of pain. The ice water may be experienced as cold, but without pain. Another theory proposes that hypnotic pain relief resembles the pain relief that commonly occurs when our attention is refocused away from the painful experience, as when an injured athlete, caught up in the heat of competition, feels little pain until the game has ended. Unanswered as it is, the question of whether hypnosis relieves pain by splitting the experience of pain off from our conscious awareness of the stimulus, or merely by exercising normal cognitive processes such as concentrating on other things, brings us to a fundamental issue: *whether or not hypnosis is a special state of consciousness.*

Is Hypnosis a Unique State of Consciousness?

So far we have seen that while hypnosis does not endow a person with special powers, it can sometimes enhance recall of past events, aid in overcoming undesirable habits, and help alleviate pain. We have also seen that hypnosis involves a heightened state of suggestibility. The question now is whether hypnosis is a genuinely altered state. Just what hypnosis is has been a subject of debate since Mesmer's time. The word *hypnosis* is derived from the Greek word for sleep. However, if we recorded the brain waves of hypnotized subjects, we would see that they are like those of a person relaxed and awake. Unlike dreaming, which is accompanied by brain activity unlike that of waking consciousness, hypnosis shows no distinct physiological patterns. To some psychologists, this suggests that hypnosis is actually *not* a special state of consciousness.

Hypnosis as a Social Phenomenon

Not only is the physiology of hypnotized subjects indistinctive, their behavior is largely indistinctive as well. The fact that a wide range of hypnotic phenomena can be produced without hypnosis hints that the phenomena may be nothing more than the workings of ordinary consciousness (Barber & others, 1974).

We saw in Chapter 7, "Perception," how powerfully our ordinary perceptions are influenced by our interpretations. Especially in the case of pain, where the effects of hypnosis seem most dramatic, what we perceive depends on where our attention is directed. As we have seen, imaginative people can manufacture vivid perceptions without hypnosis. Perhaps, then, when people become "hypnotized," they are in actuality enacting the role of "good hypnotic subject," and are simply allowing the hypnotist to direct their fantasies. The idea is not that people are consciously faking hypnosis. Rather, like actors who get caught up in their parts, they may begin to feel and behave in ways appropriate to the hypnotic role. Thus, this first point of view contends that the hypnotic phenomena are *not* unique to hypnosis.

Hypnosis as Divided Consciousness

The majority of hypnosis researchers grant that normal social and cognitive processes play a part in hypnosis, but they believe that hypnosis is more than the imaginative acting of a social role. For one thing, hypnotized subjects will carry out suggested behaviors on cue even when they believe no one is watching. This suggests that more may be at work than merely trying to be a "good subject." Moreover, researchers remain convinced that certain phenomena *are* unique to hypnosis, and that a special state of consciousness is required to explain hypnotic experiences—such as the reduction of pain, the compelling hallucinations, the seemingly automatic behaviors.

Is Meditation a Hypnotic State?

The meditation practices of both Eastern and Western religions are in some ways similar to hypnosis. They encourage meditators to assume a comfortable position in a quiet environment and to adopt a receptive, inwardly still attitude. They focus meditators' attention—on their breathing, on a word (in Eastern meditation, a mantra such as *Om*), or a phrase (in Christianity, perhaps a short prayer). And, also like hypnosis, meditation is finding clinical uses, such as in the control of pain and stress (see Chapter 18, "Health").

But unlike hypnotized subjects, who are influenced by the hypnotist's suggestions, meditators are self-controlled. Also unlike hypnotized subjects, experienced meditators exhibit rapidly decreased metabolism and changed blood pressure, heart rate, and brain waves, all of which suggest a deeply relaxed state (Wallace & Benson, 1972). Although meditation is therefore *not* a hypnotic state, its bodily changes are not unique; merely resting can produce similar effects (Holmes, 1984). And as we noted in Chapter 6, "Sensation," rest (or, at least, REST—Restricted Environmental Stimulation Therapy) can also be therapeutic.

"Sit down alone and in silence. Lower your head, shut your eyes, breathe out gently, and imagine yourself looking into your own heart. . . . As you breathe out, say 'Lord Jesus Christ, have mercy on me.' . . . Try to put all other thoughts aside. Be calm, be patient and repeat the process very frequently."
Gregory of Sinai, died 1346

Drawing by Frascino; © 1975 The Saturday Review of Literature

To veteran hypnosis researcher Ernest Hilgard (1977), what is at work is a split or ***dissociation*** between different levels of consciousness (such as the dissociation proposed on p. 203 to explain pain relief). Hilgard regards dissociation during hypnosis as simply a more extreme form of the everyday divisions that occur in our information processing—the kind that sometimes cause us to drive for miles through familiar surroundings and then suddenly realize that we recall almost nothing of the trip, though we can recall what we were thinking or talking about while driving. Putting a child to bed, we might read *Cinderella* for the fourteenth time while mentally organizing a busy schedule for the next day. Dreaming, too, is consciousness that is split off from waking consciousness.

"The so-called unity of consciousness is an illusion. . . . We like to think that we are one but we are not."
Carl G. Jung,
Tavistock Lectures, 1935

The modern rediscovery of hypnotic dissociation occurred dramatically. In a class demonstration of hypnosis, Hilgard induced deafness in a subject and then showed the class that the person was now utterly unresponsive to questions, taunts, and even to sudden loud sounds. When a student asked whether some part of the subject might still be able to hear, Hilgard decided to demonstrate that the answer was no. So he quietly asked the subject to raise his right index finger if some part of him could still hear. To everyone's surprise—including the subject's—the finger rose. When the subject's hearing was restored, he explained that, "It was a little boring just sitting here . . . when I suddenly felt my finger lift; that is what I want you to explain to me."

From this moment of discovery sprang other inquiries into this passive ***hidden observer.*** When unhypnotized subjects put their arms in an ice bath, they feel intense pain within 25 seconds. When hypnotized subjects do the same thing after being given suggestions that they will feel no pain, they report feeling little pain. But when asked to press a key if "some part" of them does feel the pain, they press the key. To Hilgard, this suggests that there is a second consciousness that is passively aware of what is happening.

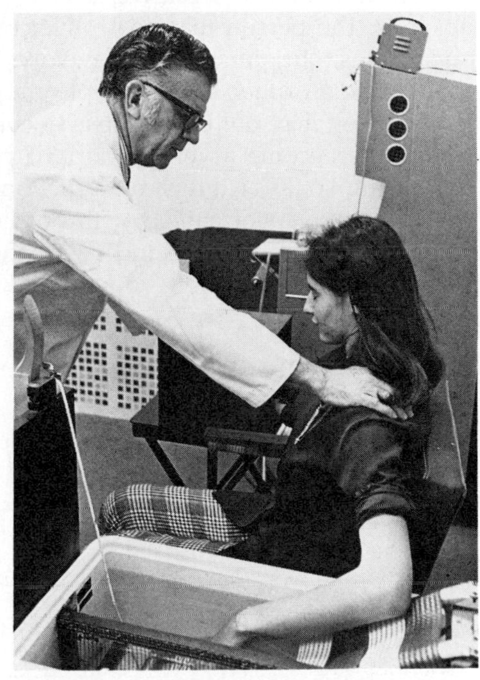

A hypnotized subject being tested by Ernest Hilgard exhibits no pain response (as non-hypnotized people typically do) when her arm is placed in an ice bath. But when asked to press a key if some part of her felt the pain, she did so.

In other studies, subjects have written answers to questions on one topic while talking or reading on a different topic. This is perhaps a more extreme form of the mild dissociation you experience when doodling while sitting in class, or that I experience as my fingers finish typing a sentence while I begin conversing with someone who has just entered my office.

The divided-consciousness theory of hypnosis remains controversial, yet this much seems clear: You and I process much information without being consciously aware of our doing so. We met this principle of nonconscious information processing in the chapters on sensation and perception and we will meet it again in our ensuing chapters on learning, memory, and cognition. Without doubt, there is more to thinking than we are aware of.

DRUGS AND CONSCIOUSNESS

Of the states of consciousness we have so far examined, none is more markedly altered than that induced by ***psychoactive*** drugs, drugs (both legal and illegal) that can often dramatically alter one's perceptions and moods. The widespread use of legal psychoactive drugs can be dramatized by an imaginary drug user's day: The day begins with a cup of strong coffee to get going. By midday several cigarettes and a tranquilizer have helped calm the nerves. Leaving work early, a happy hour cocktail provides a relaxing and sociable prelude to a dental appointment, where nitrous oxide makes an otherwise painful experience mildly pleasurable.

Drawing by Sidney Harris

"Just tell me where you kids got the idea to take so many drugs?"

An amphetamine diet pill before dinner helps stem the appetite and can later be partially offset with a sleeping pill. Before drifting off into REM-depressed sleep, our mythical drug user is dismayed by news of "rising drug abuse."

With many psychoactive drugs, continued usage produces a ***tolerance*** for the drug—that is, the user requires higher and higher doses before experiencing the drug's effect. A person who has never had alcohol before might get tipsy on one can of beer, but with continued, regular experience at drinking might not get tipsy until the second six-pack. After stopping a psychoactive drug, people may experience ***withdrawal***—undesirable effects of ceasing use. As the body responds to the drug's absence, the person may feel physical pain and an intense craving. In such cases, the person has developed an ***addiction,*** that is, a *physical dependence.* In other cases, people may develop a ***psychological dependence.*** They may not be addicted to (physically dependent on) the drug, but it has become a very important part of their lives, particularly for alleviating stress. A physical addiction and a psychological dependence may affect behavior similarly: In both cases, the person's primary focus tends to be on obtaining and using the drug.

For our purposes it simplifies things to discuss three broad categories of drugs: ***depressants*** ("downers"), which tend to calm neural activity and slow down body functions; ***stimulants*** ("uppers"), which tend, at least temporarily, to excite neural activity and arouse body functions; and ***hallucinogens,*** which tend to alter perceptions (see Table 8-1). All three categories have one thing in common: They do their work at the synapses, by stimulating, inhibiting, or mimicking the activity of the brain's chemical messengers, the neurotransmitters. By studying how drugs affect consciousness, researchers hope to understand better how the brain's own chemistry affects consciousness.

Depressants

Let us look first at some drugs that tend to slow down body functions.

Alcohol

True or false: In large amounts, alcohol is a depressant; in small amounts, it is a stimulant.

False. Small doses of "spirits" may seem to liven a person, but they do so by slowing activity in brain centers that control judgment and inhibitions. Because alcohol lowers inhibitions, it most affects urges that the

Table 8-1 **Effects of selected psychoactive drugs†**

	Possible immediate effects	**Effects of overdose**	**Withdrawal symptoms**
Depressants			
Alcohol	Slurred speech, disorientation, drunken behavior	Shallow respiration, cold and clammy skin, dilated pupils, weak and rapid pulse, coma, possible death	Anxiety, insomnia, tremors, delirium, convulsions, possible death
Barbiturates and sedatives	Slurred speech, disorientation, drunken behavior	Shallow respiration, cold and clammy skin, dilated pupils, weak and rapid pulse, coma, possible death	Anxiety, insomnia, tremors, delirium, convulsions, possible death
Opiates (morphine, heroin)	Euphoria, drowsiness, shallow respiration, constricted pupils, nausea	Shallow respiration, clammy skin, convulsions, coma, possible death	Watery eyes, runny nose, yawning, loss of appetite, irritability, tremors, panic, fever, cramps, nausea
Stimulants			
Amphetamines	Increased alertness, pulse rate, and blood pressure; euphoria; insomnia; loss of appetite	Agitation, increase in body temperature, hallucinations, convulsions, possible death	Apathy, long periods of sleep, irritability, depression, disorientation
Cocaine	Increased alertness, pulse rate, and blood pressure; euphoria; insomnia; loss of appetite	Agitation, increase in body temperature, hallucinations, convulsions, possible death	Apathy, long periods of sleep, irritability, depression, disorientation
Hallucinogens			
LSD	Delusions, hallucinations, distorted perceptions of time and space	Longer, more intense "trip" episodes, psychosis, possible death	Withdrawal symptoms not reported
Marijuana	Euphoria, relaxed inhibitions, increased appetite, disoriented behavior	Fatigue, paranoia, possible psychosis	Insomnia? Hyperactivity?

Source: Adapted from "Drugs of abuse," *Drug Enforcement*, July 1979, vol. 6(2), and from the American Psychiatric Association (1980).
†For most psychoactive drugs, substance abuse is defined as a month-long (or more) drug-related disturbance involving impaired social or occupational functioning, intoxication, and an inability to stop.

individual might otherwise resist (Steele and others, 1985; Steele & Southwick, 1985). A provoked person will behave more aggressively if under the influence of alcohol; an unprovoked person will not. A strong appeal to help with an unpleasant task gets a more positive response from those under the influence (when there is an urge to help, alcohol diminishes inhibitions against helping). Thus alcohol seems to make us more aggressive or helpful—or self-disclosing, sexually daring, and so forth—only when such tendencies are present but restrained in the absence of alcohol.

In common with the barbiturates and anxiety-reducing tranquilizers, alcohol has several other effects, too. Low doses relax a person by minimizing arousal from the sympathetic nervous system. With higher doses, alcohol can become a staggering problem: reactions slow, speech slurs, skilled performance deteriorates. Such effects, combined with the lowering of inhibitions, contribute to alcohol's worst consequences—severe car accidents, spouse abuse, and other violent crimes (Taylor & Leonard, 1983).

"If merely 'feeling good' could decide, drunkenness would be the supremely valid human experience."
William James,
Varieties of Religious Experience, 1902

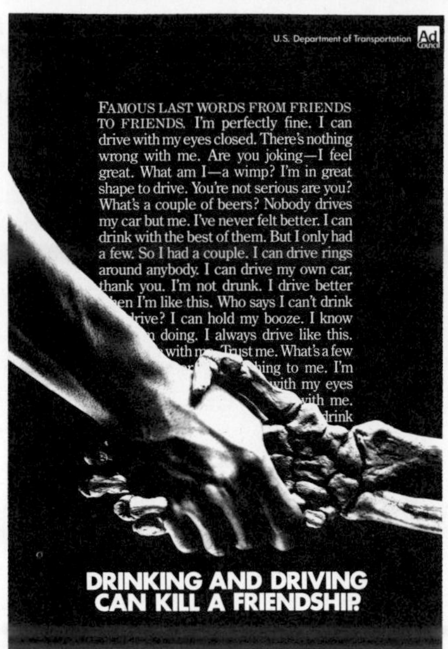

This celebration could abruptly turn tragic if the lowered inhibitions (evident here) and slower reactions that result from drinking were to contribute to an accident. Our society's tolerance for this particular brand of high jinks has sharply diminished as drinking-related fatalities have mounted.

Alcohol has an intriguing effect on memory. It impairs neither one's recall for what has just been said nor one's established long-term memories. But it can disrupt the processing of recent experiences into long-term memories. Thus the day after being intoxicated, heavy drinkers may not recall whom they met or what they said the night before. This stems partly from an inability to transfer memories from one emotional state (intoxicated) to another (sober) (Eich, 1980). Memory blackout after drinking may also result from the suppression of REM sleep. (Recall that people deprived of REM sleep seem to have difficulty fixing their day's experiences into permanent memories.)

Fact: *Adopted individuals are more susceptible to alcoholism if they had an alcoholic biological parent (Holden, 1985).*

As with other psychoactive drugs, the effects of alcohol stem not only from its alteration of brain chemistry but also from the user's expectations. For example, many studies have found that when people *believe*, rightly or wrongly, that they have been drinking alcohol, they become less anxious, more aggressive, and more sexually uninhibited. In one experiment by David Abrams and Terence Wilson (1983), Rutgers University men who had volunteered for a study on "alcohol and sexual stimulation" were given either an alcoholic or a nonalcoholic drink. In each group, half the subjects thought they were drinking alcohol, half thought they were not. Regardless of what they drank, after being shown an erotic movie clip, the men who *thought* they had consumed alcohol were the more likely to report having strong sexual fantasies and feeling unembarrassed over their sexual arousal. Apparently, being able to attribute their sexual responses to alcohol enabled them to become more uninhibited—whether they actually had drunk alcohol or not. This illustrates an important principle—that a drug's psychological effects are powerfully influenced by the user's psychological state.

Fact: *More than 9 in 10 alcoholics are cigarette smokers (Istvan & Matarazzo, 1984).*

Fact: *Binge drinking—defined as the consumption of five or more drinks on some occasion during the last month—is reported by 22 percent of American adults. The highest rate of binge drinking—52 percent—is among 18- to 24-year-old males (Center for Disease Control, 1983).*

Opiates

The ***opiates***, opium and its derivatives morphine and heroin, similarly depress neural functioning. The pupils constrict, the breathing slows, the user becomes lethargic. For a few hours, pain and anxiety are replaced by blissful pleasure. But for pleasure one pays a price, which for the heroin user is the gnawing craving for another fix, the need for progressively larger doses, and the anguish of withdrawal if use is discontinued.

"Soma, *delicious* soma, *half a gramme for a half-holiday, a gramme for a week-end, two grammes for a trip to the gorgeous East, three for a dark eternity on the moon. . . .*"
Aldous Huxley,
Brave New World, 1932

The withdrawal symptoms occur because, as you may recall from Chapter 2, when flooded with artificial opiates the brain stops producing its own, the endorphins. When the drug is withdrawn, the brain lacks the normal amounts of these painkilling neurotransmitters, and pain and agony result.

Stimulants

Stimulants "speed" up body functions. With strong stimulants, heart and breathing rates increase, the pupils dilate, appetite diminishes (because blood sugar rises), and energy and self-confidence rise. For these reasons stimulants are used in hopes of staying awake, losing weight, or boosting athletic performance or mood. For "speed freaks," as for other drug users, the benefits come with a price tag. When the drug stimulation ends, the user may crash into tiredness, headaches, irritability, and depression. And like the depressants, stimulants can be habit-forming.

The most widely used stimulants are caffeine, nicotine, the more powerful ***amphetamines,*** and cocaine. Amphetamines, such as Desoxyn and Dexedrine, are believed to stimulate the nervous system by triggering the release of neurotransmitters such as norepinephrine. Cocaine seems to trigger a similar flooding of norepinephrine by blocking the absorption of excess norepinephrine by the synaptic tissues. The psychological consequences of snorting or injecting cocaine include a rush of pleasurable sensations that last for 15 to 30 minutes, followed by a "crash" of depression after the effect wears off and the norepinephrine supply has been left depleted. In regular users, cocaine can become powerfully addictive and can cause emotional disturbance, tissue damage, and even convulsions or respiratory failure. As with all psychoactive drugs, cocaine's effects on conscious experience also depend on a complex mix of factors, including not only the dosage and form in which the drug is taken but also the expectations and personality of the user. Given an inert substance called a ***placebo,*** cocaine users who think they are taking cocaine often have a cocaine-like experience (Van Dyke & Byck, 1982).

In the alcohol study described on p. 208, which drink was the placebo?

Hallucinogens

Hallucinogens are powerful consciousness-altering drugs. Hallucinogens can distort perceptions and evoke vivid images in the absence of sensory input (which is why they are also called psychedelics, meaning "mind-manifesting").

LSD

The first "acid trip" was taken in 1943 by the creator of ***LSD (lysergic acid diethylamide),*** chemist Albert Hoffman. After accidentally ingesting some of the chemical, Hoffman reported that he "perceived an uninterrupted stream of fantastic pictures, extraordinary shapes with intense, kaleidoscopic play of colors" (Siegel, 1984). LSD is chemically similar to, and therefore may displace and disrupt, the neurotransmitter serotonin, which has quieting effects. The emotions that accompany an LSD trip vary from euphoria to detachment to panic. Again, the drug experience may be colored by the person's current mood and expectations.

Despite the emotional variations, people's hallucinations do share certain commonalities. Research psychologist Ronald Siegel (1982) reported that whether the brain is provoked to hallucinate by loss of oxygen, sensory deprivation, or drugs, "it will hallucinate in basically the same way." The experience typically begins with simple geometric forms,

Drawing by Sidney Harris

"You didn't serve any hallucinogenics for dinner, did you, dear?"

such as a lattice, a cobweb, a tunnel, or a spiral (see Figure 8-8). The next phase consists of more meaningful images; some may be superimposed on a tunnel or funnel, others may be flashbacks to childhood or past emotional experiences. When the hallucinogenic experience reaches its peak, people frequently feel dissociated from their bodies and experience dreamlike scenes as if they were real.

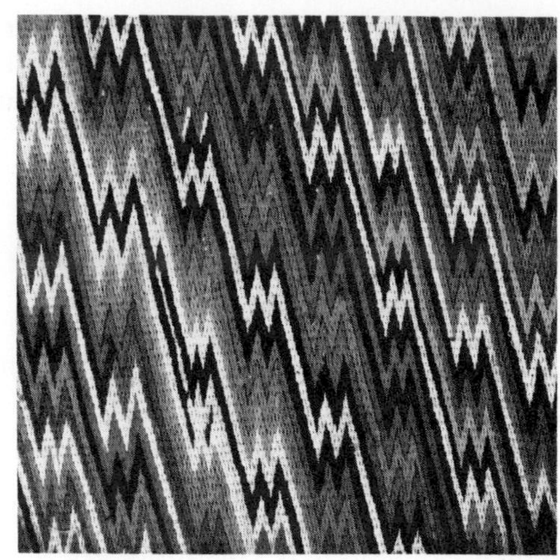

Figure 8-8 *Lattice forms, such as those reported by drug users during drug-induced hallucinations, can be seen in the embroidery of the Huichol, Mexican Indians who use peyote, an hallucinogenic substance.*

Marijuana

Marijuana is one of the oldest drugs (having been cultivated for some 5000 years), the most widely used illegal drug, and one of the most popular of psychoactive drugs. By the time marijuana usage peaked near the end of the 1970s, some 50 million Americans had tried it at least once.

Marijuana's active ingredient is ***delta-9-tetrahydrocannabinol,*** known more simply as ***THC.*** Whether smoked or eaten in such foods as brownies, THC triggers a mixture of effects that makes the drug difficult to classify. Like alcohol, marijuana relaxes, disinhibits, and may produce a euphoric "high." But marijuana is also a mild hallucinogen that can slow the perceived passage of time and amplify one's sensitivity to colors, sounds, tastes, and smells. With marijuana, too, the drug user's experience can vary, depending on the situation in which it is taken. If the person is anxious or depressed, taking the drug may intensify such feelings.

In other situations, using marijuana can be not only pleasurable but even therapeutic. For those who suffer the pain of glaucoma (caused by pressure within the eyeball) or the severe nausea of cancer chemotherapy, marijuana may offer relief. In acknowledging such benefits, a 1982 review of marijuana research published by the National Academy of Sciences also identified some not-so-pleasant consequences. Like alcohol, marijuana impairs the motor coordination and perceptual skills necessary for safe driving and machine operation. Also like alcohol, marijuana disrupts the transfer of one's experiences into permanent memories and with high doses may even interfere with immediate recall. Clearly, being stoned is not conducive to learning.

"Memory impairment is the single most consistently reported psychological deficit produced by [marijuana]."
Loren Miller & Roland Branconnier (1983)

Unlike alcohol, which is rapidly eliminated from the body, THC remains in the body for days. Although much uncertainty persists about marijuana's physical effects, medical research hints that long-term marijuana use may depress male sex hormone levels. It also can be as damaging to the lungs as cigarette smoking. Taking all the unanswered questions about marijuana's effects on health into consideration, the National Academy's report concluded that what we do know and what we suspect "justifies serious national concern."

And such concern appears to be growing among teenagers. The American Council on Education's annual survey of college freshmen reveals that support for the legalization of marijuana dropped from 53 percent in 1977 to 33 percent in 1984. The University of Michigan's annual survey of American high school seniors likewise revealed that the proportion who disapproved of regular marijuana use rose from 65 percent in 1977 to 85 percent in 1984 (Johnston & others, 1985). Consistent with this growing concern, daily marijuana use declined from 11 percent of all seniors in 1978 to 5 percent in 1984. Similar attitude and usage changes are evident in Gallup Organization surveys of Canadian teenagers (*Behavior Today*, 1984).

For those who suffer severe pain or nausea, marijuana may spell relief. But the National Academy of Sciences reports that marijuana also impairs coordination, perception, and memory, and with prolonged use may damage lungs and depress male sex hormone levels.

Developmental psychologist Diana Baumrind (1984) reported that teenagers who experimented with light marijuana use were not socially deficient; if anything, they tended to be more outgoing, self-confident, and intelligent than those who never experimented. (The exception to this finding is "rational abstainers," who refrain from experimenting because they see through the conformity to peer pressures that influences some adolescents to smoke.) But she suspected that becoming more seriously involved in marijuana use often led to "lower achievement motivation, greater passivity, dependence on artificial substances to attain a sense of well-being, withdrawal from intense, committed love relationships, and adoption of an external locus of control."

NEAR-DEATH EXPERIENCES

> A man is dying and . . . hears himself pronounced dead by his doctor. He begins to hear an uncomfortable noise, a loud ringing or buzzing, and at the same time feels himself moving very rapidly through a long dark tunnel. After this, he suddenly finds himself outside of his own physical body . . . and sees his own body from a distance, as though he is a spectator. . . . Soon other things begin to happen. Others come to meet and to help him. He glimpses the spirits of relatives and friends who have already died, and a loving, warm spirit of a kind he has never encountered before—a being of light—appears before him. . . . He is overwhelmed by intense feelings of joy, love, and peace. Despite his attitude, though, he somehow reunites with his physical body and lives. (Moody, 1976, pp. 23, 24)

This passage from Raymond Moody's best-selling book, *Life After Life,* represents an idealized account of what is popularly known as the ***near-death experience.*** Because the reports of these experiences are nearly all warmly positive (upon being revived, people seldom recall having teetered on the brink of hell), the reports have been devoured by those eager for "proof" that there is happiness after death. What should we make of these reports? Do they prove that we can anticipate bliss on the other side of death? Do they confirm Plato's doctrine that mind—or soul—is separable from body? Do such experiences reliably occur to those who face death?

Although some of these people may have been thought by someone to have been "dead," none had suffered true brain death. If they had, they would not have survived to recall their experience—hence the label near-death.

Although Moody's description is idealized, interviews with patients who have come close to death through physical traumas such as cardiac arrest confirm that many people do indeed experience an altered state of consciousness. Several investigators each interviewed a hundred or more such people; in every study, one-third to two-fifths of the patients recalled some sort of conscious near-death experience (Ring, 1980; Sebom, 1982; Schnaper, 1980). And when George Gallup, Jr. (1982) interviewed a national sample of Americans, 15 percent reported having experienced a close brush with death, and one-third of these people reported having had a mystical experience in connection with it.

The other side of these studies is that most people who have been resuscitated from near death do not recall having experienced any kind of altered consciousness. Skeptics suggest that the unreliability of the experience poses a problem for those who want to infer some universal truth about what happens at death. But as we have seen, the fact that most people do not recall dreaming during their last night's sleep does not mean they failed to dream. The dream experience is real, whether remembered or not.

Figure 8-9 *A near-death vision or an hallucination? Psychologist Ronald Siegel (1977) reports that under the influence of hallucinogenic drugs, people often see "a bright light in the center of the field of vision. . . . The location of this point of light create[s] a tunnel-like perspective."*

Did Moody's description of the "complete" near-death experience have a familiar ring? The parallels between it and Ronald Siegel's (1977) descriptions of the typical hallucinogenic experience are striking: the visions of tunnels or funnels and bright lights (Figure 8-9), the memory flashbacks, the out-of-body sensations. Moreover, since the setting in which hallucinations occur is known to affect their content, and since oxygen deprivation and other insults to the brain are known to produce hallucinations, it is difficult to resist wondering whether near-death experiences are manufactured by the brain under stress. Siegel (1980) in fact concluded that the near-death experience is best understood "as a dissociative hallucinatory activity of the brain." In Siegel's view, when external input dims, the brain's own interior activity becomes perceivable. He illustrated with an analogy: When gazing out a window at dusk, we begin to see the reflected interior of the room as if it were outside, either because the light from outside is dimming (as in the near-death experience) or because the inside light is amplified (as with LSD).

*"**Joan [of Arc]:** I hear voices telling me what to do. They come from God.*
***Robert:** They come from your imagination.*
***Joan:** Of course. That is how the messages of God come to us."*
George Bernard Shaw, *St. Joan,* 1924

The controversy over interpreting near-death experiences raises the fundamental mind-body issue: Is the mind immaterial? Can it exist separate from body? ***Dualists*** answer yes. They believe that the mind and body are two distinct entities—the mind nonphysical, the body physical—that somehow manage to interact with each other. As Socrates expressed it in Plato's *Phaedo,* "Does not death mean that the body comes to exist by itself, separated from the soul, and that the soul exists by herself, separated from the body? What is death but that?"

"The mind seems to act independently of the brain in the same sense that a programmer acts independently of his computer."
Wilder Penfield (1975, p. 79)

Note that for Socrates as for those today who believe that near-death experiences are proof of immortality, death is not really the death of the person but merely the liberation of that person from the bodily prison. In this sense, death is viewed as an occasion for rejoicing. (Carried to its extreme, this dualistic view has given rise to glorifications of the afterlife trip under such titles as "The Thrill of Dying" and "The Wonderful World of Death.")

Monists (who answer "no" to the above questions) have their doubts. They argue that mind and body are different aspects of the same thing. Whether they are scientists who assume the inseparability of mind and brain, or theologians who hold to an afterlife as some form of bodily resurrection, monists generally believe that death is real and that without bodies we truly are nobodies.

"It may be implausible to say that consciousness consists of a biochemical activity of a multitude of nerve impulses traversing pathways in the brain but it nevertheless begins to look very much as though the proposition is true."
D. O. Hebb (1980)

As these debates over the significance of dreams, hypnotic states, drug-induced hallucinations, and near-death experiences illustrate, science informs our wonderings about human consciousness and human nature. Although there remain questions that it cannot answer, science nevertheless helps fashion our image of who we are, of our human potentials, and our human limits.

SUMMING UP

STUDYING CONSCIOUSNESS

Psychology began as the study of consciousness, then turned to the study of observable behavior, and now is again investigating states of mind. Consciousness can be experienced in various states, all of which involve a focused awareness of perceptions, thoughts, and feelings as they occur. This chapter has considered several alternatives to normal waking consciousness.

DAYDREAMING

Virtually everyone daydreams, especially in times when attention can be freed from the tasks at hand. Daydreaming can be adaptive; it can help us prepare for future events and may substitute for impulsive behavior.

SLEEP AND DREAMS

The Rhythm of Sleep Our daily schedule of waking and sleeping is timed with a bodily clock known as circadian rhythm. Each night's sleep also has a rhythm of its own, running from transitional Stage 1 sleep to deep Stage 4 sleep and back up to the more active REM sleep stage. This cycle is repeated several times during a normal night's sleep, with the Stage 4 sleep stages progressively shortening and REM sleep lengthening.

Why We Sleep Depriving people of sleep has failed to reveal why, physiologically, we need sleep. Nevertheless, it is believed that sleep is linked with the release of pituitary growth hormone and that it helps to restore exhausted tissues.

Sleep Disorders The disorders of sleep include insomnia (wakefulness), narcolepsy (uncontrollable lapsing into REM sleep), and sleep apnea (the cessation of breathing while sleeping).

Dreams Although conscious thoughts can occur during any sleep stage, awakening people during REM sleep yields predictable "dreamlike" reports; awakening during other sleep stages yields more occasional "thoughtlike" reports. Our dreams are mostly rather ordinary; they often relate to everyday experiences and more frequently involve anxiety or misfortune than triumphant achievements.

Freud believed that a dream's manifest content is a censored version of its latent content, which gratifies our unconscious wishes. Newer explanations of why we dream suggest that dreams help process information from the day and fix it in memory, and that dreams serve a physiological function (either by stimulating the sleeping brain or as a means of coping with random activity initiated in the brainstem). Despite their differences, most theorists agree that REM sleep and its associated dreams serve an important function, as is hinted at by the REM rebound that occurs following REM deprivation.

HYPNOSIS

Although hypnosis has historically been linked with quackery, it has more recently become the subject of serious research. It is now widely agreed that hypnosis is a state of heightened suggestibility; that neither the hypnotist nor the subject acquires magical powers; that hypnosis can at least temporarily boost people's efforts to overcome certain problems; that hypnotizable people can enjoy significant pain relief; that hypnosis can be distinguished from meditative states; and that while hypnosis may help someone recall something, the hypnotist's beliefs also frequently work their way into the subject's memories.

There is debate, however, on whether hypnosis is a byproduct of normal social and cognitive processes or whether it is a unique state of consciousness, perhaps involving a dissociation between levels of consciousness.

DRUGS AND CONSCIOUSNESS

Another route to altered consciousness is through psychoactive drugs, including depressants, stimulants, and hallucinogens.

Depressants Alcohol and the opiates act by depressing neural functioning. Each offers its pleasures, but at the cost of impaired memory or other physical consequences.

Stimulants Caffeine, nicotine, the amphetamines, and cocaine all act by stimulating neural functioning. As with nearly all psychoactive drugs, they act at the synapses by influencing the brain's neurotransmitters, and their effects depend both on dosage and on the user's personality and expectations.

Hallucinogens LSD and marijuana both can distort one's judgments of time and, depending on the setting in which they are taken, can alter one's sensations and perceptions.

NEAR-DEATH EXPERIENCES

Some one-third of those who have approached death, such as through cardiac arrest, later recall visionary experiences. Such experiences have been interpreted by some as evidence of human immortality, although the reports of such experiences closely parallel reports of hallucinations.

TERMS AND CONCEPTS TO REMEMBER

Addiction A physical dependence or need for a drug, with accompanying withdrawal symptoms if discontinued.

Age Regression In hypnosis, the supposed reliving of earlier experiences, such as in early childhood; has been found to be greatly susceptible to false recollections.

Alpha Waves The relatively slow brain waves of a relaxed but awake state.

Amphetamines Drugs that stimulate neural activity, causing speeded-up body functions and associated energy and mood changes.

Circadian Rhythm Regular bodily rhythms (for example, of temperature and wakefulness) that occur on a 24-hour schedule.

Consciousness Selective attention to ongoing perceptions, thoughts, and feelings.

Delta Waves The large, slow brain waves associated with deep sleep.

Depressants Drugs (such as alcohol, barbiturates, and opiates) that reduce neural activity and slow down body functions.

Dissociation A split in consciousness, allowing some thoughts and behaviors to occur simultaneously with others.

Dualism The presumption that mind and body are two distinct entities that interact with each other.

Hallucinations False sensory experiences, such as seeing something in the absence of any external visual stimulus.

Hallucinogens Psychedelic ("mind-manifesting") drugs, such as LSD, that distort perceptions and evoke sensory images in the absence of sensory input.

Hidden Observer Hilgard's term describing a hypnotized subject's awareness of experiences, such as pain, that go unreported during hypnosis.

Hypnosis A temporary state of heightened suggestibility in which some people narrow their focus of attention and experience imaginary happenings as if they were real.

Insomnia Difficulty in falling or staying asleep.

Latent Content According to Freud, the underlying but censored meaning of a dream (as distinct from its manifest content). Freud believed that a dream's latent content serves a safety valve function.

LSD (Lysergic Acid Diethylamide) A powerful hallucinogenic drug, also known as "acid."

Manifest Content According to Freud, the remembered story line of a dream (as distinct from its latent content).

Monism The presumption that mind and body are different aspects of the same thing.

Narcolepsy A sleep disorder characterized by uncontrollable sleep attacks in which the sufferer lapses directly into REM sleep, often at inopportune times.

Near-Death Experience An altered state of consciousness reported after a close brush with death (such as through cardiac arrest); often similar to drug-induced hallucinations.

Night Terrors A sleep disorder characterized by high arousal and an appearance of being terrified; unlike nightmares, night terrors occur during Stage 4 sleep, within 2 or 3 hours of falling asleep, and are seldom remembered.

Opiates Opium and its derivatives, such as morphine and heroin, which depress neural activity, temporarily alleviating pain and anxiety.

Placebo An inert substance that may, in an experiment, be administered in place of an active drug; it may trigger the effects that the user believes the actual drug has.

Posthypnotic Amnesia A condition, sometimes suggested during hypnosis, in which a subject appears unable to recall what happened during hypnosis. Recall may, however, be established if a prearranged signal is given to remember.

Posthypnotic Suggestion A suggestion, made during a hypnotic session, that is to be carried out afterward when the subject is no longer hypnotized; it is used by some clinicians as a boost to controlling undesired symptoms and behaviors.

Psychoactive Drugs Drugs that alter mood and perceptions.

Psychological Dependence A psychological need to use a drug, such as to relieve stress.

REM Rebound The tendency for REM sleep to increase following REM sleep deprivation (created by repeated awakenings during REM sleep).

REM Sleep Rapid eye movement sleep, a recurring sleep stage during which vivid dreams commonly occur. Also known as paradoxical sleep, because the muscles are relaxed (except for minor twitches) but the brain and eyes are active.

Sleep Apnea A sleep disorder characterized by temporary cessation of breathing when the person is asleep, and consequent momentary reawakenings.

Sleep Spindles Rhythmic bursts of brain activity occurring during Stage 2 sleep.

Stimulants Drugs (such as caffeine, nicotine, and the more powerful amphetamines and cocaine) that excite neural activity and arouse body functions.

THC (Delta-9-Tetrahydrocannabinol) The active ingredient in marijuana that triggers a variety of effects, including mild hallucinations.

Tolerance Requiring larger and larger doses before experiencing a drug's effect, or a diminishing of the drug's effect with regular use of the same dose.

Withdrawal The distressing physical and psychological symptoms that follow the discontinued use of certain drugs.

FOR FURTHER READING

Sleep and Dreams

Cartwright, R. D. (1978). *A primer on sleep and dreaming*. Reading, MA: Addison-Wesley.

A helpful introduction to what we do and do not know about sleep and dreams.

Dement, W. C. (1978). *Some must watch while some must sleep*. New York: Norton.

An easily readable paperback that surveys sleep disorders as well as normal sleeping and dreaming.

Faraday, A. (1984). *Dream power*. New York: Berkley.

One sleep expert reports that this book helps college students "get close to their dreams."

Hypnosis

Bowers, K. S. (1983). *Hypnosis for the seriously curious*. New York: Norton.

An authoritative, even-handed introduction to hypnosis—its nature, its phenomena, and its clinical applications.

Hilgard, E. R. (1977). *Divided consciousness: Multiple controls in human thought and action*. New York: Wiley.

An intriguing, provocative introduction to a host of phenomena (possession states, multiple personalities, and hypnotic events) that suggest that consciousness can be divided.

Drugs

Ray, O. (1983). *Drugs, society, and human behavior* (3rd ed.). St. Louis: Mosby.

A thorough textbook introduction to the physical and psychological effects of psychoactive drugs.

David Hockney *The Scrabble Game, January 1, 1983,* Photographic Collage, 39 × 58″

PART FOUR

LEARNING AND THINKING

At the center of psychology is the question of how we learn, retain, and use information. Chapter 9, "Learning," describes three fundamental types of learning and suggests how they mold our emotions and behavior and how we can use them to our benefit. Chapter 10, "Memory," examines the process by which memories are formed, stored, and retrieved, and the factors that sometimes cause us to forget. Chapter 11, "Thinking and Language," explores how we reason with, and communicate, the information we have retained, and points out the efficient but sometimes error-prone ways in which we make judgments and decisions. Finally, Chapter 12, "Intelligence," describes historical and current attempts to measure individual differences in learning and thinking ability.

Alfred Eisenstaedt *Children at Puppet Show at the Tuilleries, Paris,* 1963

Bill Witt

CHAPTER 9

Learning

When a chinook salmon first emerges from its egg in the gravel bed of a stream, it has in its genes and its developing nervous system virtually all the behavioral instructions it needs for life. It instinctively knows how to swim, how to navigate, what to eat and what not to eat, how to protect itself from predators. Following this built-in plan, the young salmon soon begins a trek to the sea. After some 4 years in the ocean, the mature salmon undertakes a genetically predetermined return to its birthplace. Having learned the scent of its home stream, it navigates hundreds of miles back to the mouth of its home river and then begins an upstream odyssey that will take it back to its precise ancestral spawning ground. Once there, the salmon seeks out the exact conditions of temperature, gravel, and waterflow that will maximize the success of its breeding, and then performs its appointed reproductive functions.

Drawing by Sidney Harris

"Actually, sex just isn't that important to me."

Unlike the salmon, we are not born with a blueprint for life. We must learn almost everything, and therein lie the seeds of our uniqueness. For though we must struggle to acquire the life directions that a salmon is born with, our learning gives us vastly greater flexibility. We can learn how to build igloos, or grass huts, or underwater air chambers and thereby adapt to almost any environment. Indeed, nature's most important gift to us may well be our capacity to be nurtured—to learn behaviors that enable us to cope with our circumstances.

No topic is closer to the heart of psychology than ***learning,*** a change in an organism, due to experience, that can affect the organism's behavior (Hintzman, 1978). In earlier chapters, we considered the learning of moral ideas, of gender roles, of visual perceptions. In future chapters we will consider how learning shapes our thought and language, our motivations and emotions, our personalities and attitudes. The importance of learning in all such realms breeds hope. What is learnable can potentially be taught—an assumption that encourages animal trainers, athletic coaches, parents, and educators. What has been learned can potentially be replaced by new learning—an assumption that is fundamental to counseling, psychotherapy, and rehabilitation training. Thus, people in all such vocations, as well as psychologists of every sort, are eager to learn about learning.

"Learning is the eye of the mind."
Thomas Drake,
Bibliotheca Scholastica Instructissima, 1633

Simple animals can learn simple associations. If disturbed by a squirt of water, the sea snail *Aplysia* will protectively withdraw its gill. If this disturbance is continually repeated, as happens naturally in choppy water, the response diminishes. But if an *Aplysia* is repeatedly given a shock just after being squirted, its withdrawal response to the squirt alone becomes stronger. Somehow the animal has learned to associate the squirt with the impending shock. More complex animals can learn more complicated associations, especially those that bring favorable consequences. Sea lions in an aquarium will repeat behaviors, such as slapping and barking, that prompt people to toss them food. Still more complex animals, such as chimpanzees, can learn behaviors by merely observing others perform them. We humans can learn in all these ways, and through language we can learn things we have neither experienced nor observed.

This elephant has learned to associate standing on its hind legs with a food reward, just as its trainer has learned to associate having trained the elephant successfully with a salary reward.

These varieties of learning enable us to adapt to our environments. As this chapter will explain, we learn to anticipate and prepare for significant events such as getting food or avoiding pain—an elementary type of learning studied in experiments on ***classical conditioning.*** We also tend to repeat acts that bring good results and avoid acts that bring bad results—a type of learning studied in experiments on ***operant conditioning.*** And by watching others we learn valuable information about our environment—a phenomenon studied in research on ***observational learning.***

The study of how we learn has revealed many facts. It has also stimulated several ongoing controversies: First, how distinct are these three types of learning? Second, do animals other than primates and humans have cognitive (thinking) abilities? For example, do rats learn to *expect* predictable events? Do they *remember* their experiences and the layout of their environments? Third, is one set of learning principles universally applicable to all species? If so, studying any one species would tell us about the others, much as studying the nervous system of one species has revealed principles of nervous system functioning common to all species, including our own.

To prepare us to consider these questions, let us first review some key discoveries from twentieth century research on learning.

CLASSICAL CONDITIONING

During the seventeenth and eighteenth centuries, British philosophers such as John Locke and David Hume argued that a key ingredient in learning is association: Our minds naturally assume that events occurring in sequence are connected; we associate them. If, after seeing and smelling freshly baked bread, we eat some of it and feel satisfied, then the next time we see and smell a loaf of bread our previous experience will lead us to expect that eating some of this loaf will likewise be satisfying. Similarly, if we experience certain sounds in conjunction with frightening consequences, then we may be made fearful of the sounds themselves. As one 4-year-old exclaimed after watching a TV character get mugged, "If I had heard that music I wouldn't have gone around the corner!" (Wells, 1981).

Although the philosophers' idea of learning by association generated much discussion, it was not until the twentieth century that it was captured in some of the most famous research in psychology. For many people, the name Ivan Pavlov rings a bell. His experiments are classics, which is why the phenomenon he explored is today called *classical* (or Pavlovian) *conditioning.*

Pavlov's Experiments

After obtaining a medical degree at age 33, Pavlov, driven by a passion for research, spent the next two decades studying the digestive system, work that would in 1904 make him Russia's first Nobel Prize winner. But it was the next three decades of work, up to his death at age 86, that earned the feisty Pavlov his place in scientific history.

Pavlov's new direction came when his creative mind seized on an incidental occurrence. Pavlov had been studying salivary secretion in dogs and had already determined that when food was put in a dog's mouth, the animal would reflexively salivate. Pavlov also noticed that when he used the same dog repeatedly, the dog would salivate at a number of stimuli that had come to be associated with its food—the mere sight of the food, of the food dish, of the person who regularly brought the food, or even of the sound of that person's approaching footsteps. Because these "psychic secretions" interfered with his experiments on digestion, Pavlov considered them an annoyance—until he saw that they represented a simple but important form of learning. From that point forward, Pavlov devoted his efforts to the study of learning, which he hoped might enable him to understand better the workings of the brain.

Ivan Pavlov (1927, p. 4): "Experimental investigation . . . should lay a solid foundation for a future true science of psychology."

The basic premise of Pavlov's work on learning arose from his initial distinction between salivation in response to food in the mouth and salivation in response to stimuli that had become associated with food. Pavlov called the salivation in response to the food in the mouth an ***unconditioned response (UCR)*** because its occurrence was not conditional upon the dog's previous experience: It automatically triggered the dog's salivary reflex. Salivation in response to something that was associated with food, on the other hand, did not occur automatically: Its occurrence was conditional upon the dog's developing a connection between food in the mouth and, say, the sight of the food. This learned response is therefore called the ***conditioned response (CR).***

Remember:
UCS = Unconditioned Stimulus
UCR = Unconditioned Response
CS = Conditioned Stimulus
CR = Conditioned Response

Pavlov similarly distinguished between the stimuli that triggered these two kinds of responses. The stimulus (in this case food in the mouth) that triggered the unconditioned response Pavlov called the ***unconditioned stimulus (UCS).*** The stimulus (in this case, the sight of the food) that became associated with the UCS and thereby gained the power to elicit the conditioned responses Pavlov called the ***conditioned stimulus (CS).*** (It might help you to distinguish between these two kinds of stimuli and responses by remembering that *un*conditioned = *un*learned, and conditioned = learned.)

Pavlov and his assistants tried to imagine what the dog was thinking and feeling as it drooled in anticipation of the food. This only got them into fruitless debates. So to attack the phenomenon more objectively, Pavlov decided to experiment by pairing various neutral stimuli with food in the mouth to see if—and to what degree—dogs would eventually begin salivating to the neutral stimuli alone. To eliminate the possible influence of extraneous stimuli, he isolated the dog in a small room, where it was held securely in place by a harness and attached to a device that diverted its saliva to a measuring instrument (Figure 9-1). From an adjacent room Pavlov could present food—at first by sliding in a food bowl, later by blowing meat powder into the dog's mouth at a precise moment (Gormezano & Kehoe, 1975). If a neutral stimulus—anything that the dog could see or hear—now regularly signaled the arrival of food, would the dog eventually begin salivating to the neutral stimulus alone?

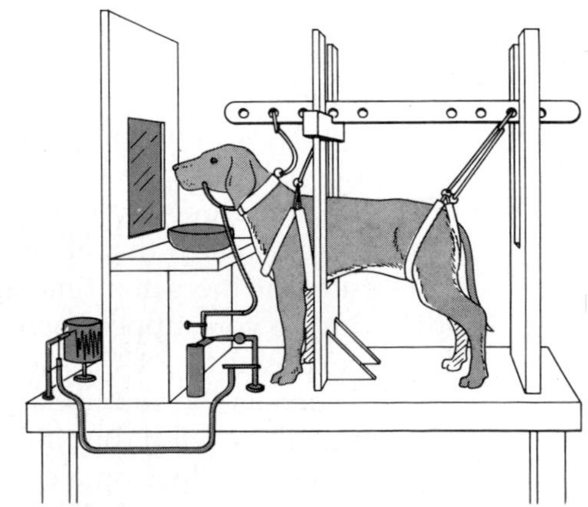

Figure 9-1 *Pavlov's device for recording salivation. The dog's saliva is collected drop by drop in a tube as it is secreted. The number of drops is recorded on a revolving cylinder outside the chamber. Food is delivered by remote control and, through the window, the experimenter can observe the dog.*

The answer proved to be yes, and it led to Pavlov's famous procedure for conditioning (Figure 9-2). Just before placing food (the UCS) in

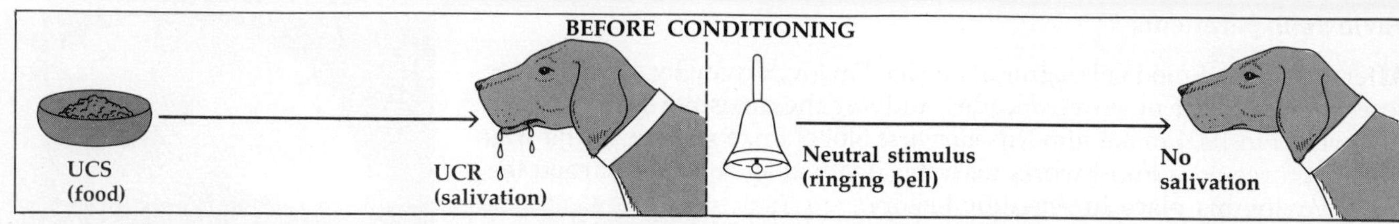

An unconditioned stimulus (UCS) produces an unconditioned response (UCR). A neutral stimulus produces no response.

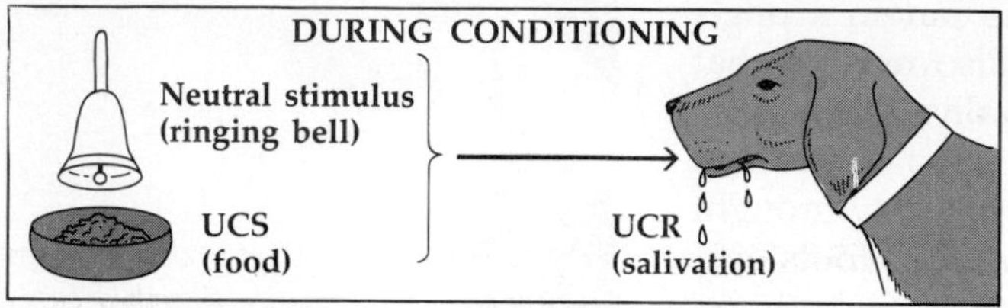

The unconditioned stimulus is presented just after a neutral stimulus. The unconditioned stimulus continues to produce an unconditioned response.

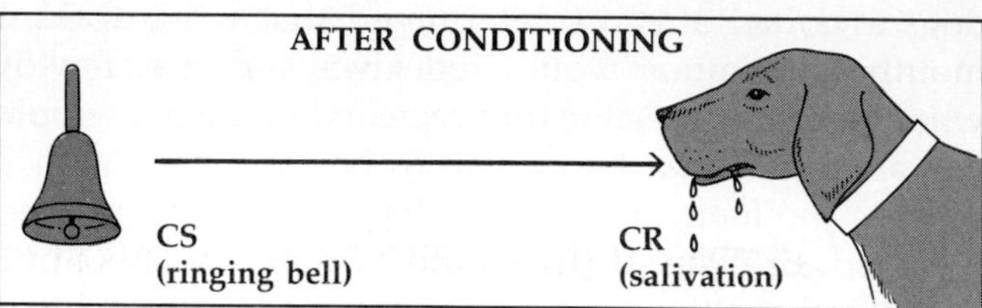

The neutral stimulus becomes a conditioned stimulus (CS), now producing a conditioned response (CR).

Figure 9-2 *Pavlov's classic experiment. By presenting a neutral stimulus, the ringing of a bell, just before an unconditioned stimulus, food, the neutral stimulus became a conditioned stimulus (CS). The CS now triggers a conditioned response (CR), salivation. The CR is a response similar to (though often less intense than) the unconditioned response (UCR) previously produced by the unconditioned stimulus (UCS).*

the dog's mouth to produce salivation (the UCR), Pavlov would sound a bell (the CS). After several pairings of the sounding of the bell and the food, the sounding of the bell alone caused salivation.

Note that the conditioned response is similar to the unconditioned response, except that it occurs in reaction to the conditioned stimulus. If the sound of bacon crackling sets your mouth to watering, then the sound has become a conditioned stimulus; by association with the taste of bacon (UCS), the sound triggers a conditioned response. Using the same procedure, Pavlov was able to condition a dog to salivate to a buzzer, a light, a touch on the leg. In each case, the CR was the same as the UCR except that it was somewhat less intense.

If the experiment was so simple, what did Pavlov do for the next three decades? He explored the determinants and implications of classical conditioning. In the course of his research he distinguished four major conditioning processes: acquisition, extinction, generalization, and discrimination.

Acquisition

Regarding the ***acquisition,*** or learning, of the response there was first a question of timing: How much time should elapse between the presentation of the conditioned stimulus (the bell, light, touch, or whatever) and the unconditioned stimulus? Not much. Later work with a variety of species and procedures revealed that about $\frac{1}{2}$ second is frequently optimal. If the CS is presented at the same time as the UCS or even after it, how much conditioning do you suppose occurs? Usually none. If, for example, the organism is exposed to a UCS such as an electric shock and then is exposed to a CS such as the sound of a bell, no conditioned response to the bell sounding will develop. But if the shock *follows* the sounding of a bell, then the animal will develop a conditioned fear response to it. This finding fits the presumption that classical conditioning is biologically adaptive by helping organisms *prepare* for good or bad events that are about to occur. Since there is no need to prepare for events that have already occurred, little conditioning occurs when the UCS comes before the CS. However, when the CS is presented first, signaling that something significant is coming—say when a loving (or angry) tone of voice repeatedly precedes rewarding (or painful) behavior—then we begin to respond emotionally in preparation for what usually follows.

Extinction

What happens if, after conditioning has occurred, the prepared-for stimulus no longer occurs? In other words, will the CS continue to elicit the CR even in the absence of the UCS? Pavlov found that when he rang the bell again and again without presenting food, the dogs would salivate less and less. Pavlov called this fading of the conditioned response in the absence of a UCS ***extinction.*** Extinction, as Pavlov soon discovered, is actually inhibition of the CR rather than elimination of it. If he allowed several hours to elapse before ringing the bell again, the conditioned response to the bell ringing would reappear (Figure 9-3). Pavlov called this reappearance of the response after a rest pause ***spontaneous recovery.***

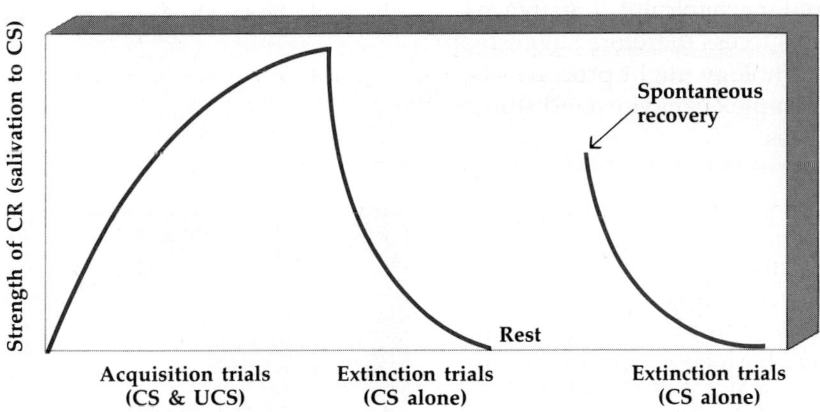

Figure 9-3 *Acquisition, extinc n, and spontaneous recovery. A smoothed curve indicates that the CR grows stronger as the CS and UCS are repeatedly paired (acquisition), then wanes as the CS is repeatedly presented alone (extinction), but spontaneously recovers after a rest pause.*

Generalization

Pavlov noticed that after a dog was conditioned to the ringing of the bell, it would also respond somewhat to a bell with a different tone, or even to a buzzer (Figure 9-4). This tendency to respond to stimuli similar to the CS as though they were the CS Pavlov called ***generalization.*** Generalization can be adaptive, as when toddlers are taught to fear the cars in the street in front of their home, and then respond similarly to other cars.

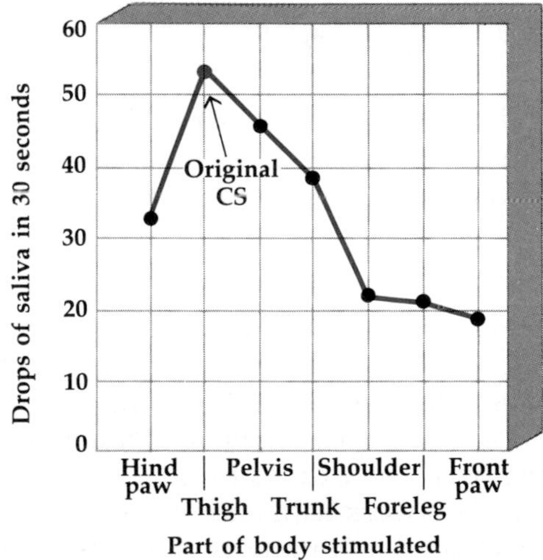

Figure 9-4 *Generalization was demonstrated in an experiment in which miniature vibrators were attached to various parts of a dog's body. After salivation had been conditioned to stimulation of the thigh, other areas of the body were stimulated. The closer they were to the original site of stimulation, the stronger the conditioned response.*

Discrimination

The dogs could also learn *not* to respond to other stimuli, such as the sound of a different bell. This learned ability to distinguish between conditioned stimuli and similar but irrelevant stimuli he called ***discrimination.*** Like the ability to generalize, the ability to discriminate also has survival value. Sometimes different stimuli are followed by different consequences. To be able to recognize these differences would clearly be adaptive. Thus, children learn to walk across the street with minimal fear when a light facing them is green but to fear crossing when the light is red.

Discrimination training has become a way of determining what a nonverbal organism can perceive. Can a dog distinguish between shapes? Can a baby distinguish between different sounds? If they can be conditioned to respond to one stimulus and not to the other, then obviously they can.

Why has all this been considered so important? If Pavlov had only taught us that old dogs can learn new tricks, his experiments would long ago have been forgotten. Who cares that a dog can be conditioned to drool at the sound of a bell, the touch of a leg, or even the sight of a circle? The importance lies in the fact that many other responses to many other stimuli have subsequently been classically conditioned in many other organisms—in fact, in every species tested, from worms to fish to dogs to monkeys to people (Schwartz, 1984). For example, Gregory Razran (1940), a psychologist who helped translate Pavlov's writings into English, found that when political slogans (a CS) were associated with the eating of food (UCS), people became more approving of them. When slogans were linked with putrid odors piped into the room where the experiments were being conducted, people became less approving of them.

Pavlov's work was additionally important as an example of how a significant internal process such as learning could be studied objectively. Pavlov was proud that his method involved virtually no subjective judgments or guesses about the dogs' mental events. The salivary response was an overt behavior that could be measured mechanically—as so many drops or cubic centimeters of saliva. Pavlov's success therefore suggested a model for how the young discipline of psychology might proceed—by isolating the elementary building blocks of complex behaviors and studying these with objective laboratory procedures.

Drawing by Sidney Harris

"Perhaps, Dr. Pavlov, he could be taught to seal envelopes."

Behaviorism

Pavlov's work added momentum to arguments made by the American psychologist John B. Watson, who in 1913 began to urge that psychology should discard references to thoughts, feelings, and hidden motives and should instead become a science of *behavior*. Its focus should be on an organism's response to its environment. Forget the mind, said Watson, psychology's goal is "to be able, given the stimulus, to predict the response."

John Watson (1924, p. 104): "Give me a dozen healthy infants, well-formed, and my own specified world to bring them up in and I'll guarantee to take any one at random and train him to become any type of specialist I might select—doctor, lawyer, artist, merchant-chief and, yes, even beggar-man and thief, regardless of his talents, penchants, tendencies, abilities, vocations, and race of his ancestors."

As we noted in Chapter 8, "States of Consciousness," Watson's position, called ***behaviorism,*** prevailed over much of psychology during the first half of this century. It was particularly influential in promoting the idea that human behavior could be understood in terms of conditioned responses. In one famous study, Watson and Rosalie Rayner (1920; Harris, 1979) showed how specific fears might be conditioned in humans. Their subject, an 11-month-old infant named Albert, was known to fear loud noises but not white rats. So they presented "Little Albert" with a white rat and, as he reached to touch it, struck a hammer against a steel bar just behind his head. After seven repetitions of seeing the rat and hearing the frightening noise, Albert burst into tears at the mere sight of the rat. What is more, 5 days later Albert showed generalization of his conditioned response to the rat when he reacted with some fear when presented with a rabbit, a dog, and a sealskin coat. Although some psychologists had difficulty repeating these findings with other children, Watson's work with Little Albert has had legendary significance for many psychologists, a number of whom have wondered if each of us might not be a walking museum of conditioned emotions. Correspondingly, they have wondered if our more unproductive emotions might be controlled by an application of extinction procedures or by conditioning new responses to emotion-arousing stimuli. In Chapter 17, "Therapy," we will see how such procedures are being used to treat emotional disorders.

Question: *In Watson's experiment, what was the UCS? The CS? The UCR? The CR?*

Behaviorism Reconsidered

The use of scientific methodology advocated by behaviorists continues to this day in all areas of psychological research. But behaviorists' disdain for mentalistic concepts such as consciousness has given way to a growing sense that (1) cognitive processes—thoughts, perceptions, expectations—have an important place in the science of psychology, and that (2) the power of conditioning is constrained by the biological predispositions of the organism being conditioned.

Psychology's "factual and theoretical developments in this century—which have changed the study of mind and behavior as radically as genetics changed the study of heredity—have all been the product of objective analysis—that is to say, behavioristic analysis."
D. O. Hebb (1980)

Cognitive Processes

As we have seen, the early behaviorists believed that the learned behavior of various organisms could be reduced to simple universal stimulus-response mechanisms. When the issue of the universality of learning principles was raised earlier, perhaps it occurred to you, as it has to contemporary learning psychologists, that the growing brain power of complex animals likely enables new ways of learning. Animals with minimal cortex (such as reptiles) do seem to learn solely by having stimulus-response associations gradually stamped in, much as Pavlov supposed. With more complex animals, some very simple stimulus-response associations are learned in much the same way. Rats can be conditioned to fear a noise that is paired with shock to their leg even while they sleep under general anesthesia (Weinberger & others, 1984).

Although simple stimulus-response associations may be learned without any cognitive awareness, the study of more complicated behaviors in complex animals eventually forced psychologists to revise the "mindless" behaviorism of Pavlov and Watson. For example, once having learned to *swim* a maze, rats can (when the water level is lowered) *wade* through it correctly. More significantly, they can learn a maze while passively riding through it in a wire basket. Cats, too, can learn without responding. When cats are repeatedly given shocks on a foreleg just after a tone is sounded, they will later jerk in response to the tone—even if during the conditioning they had been immobilized by a paralyzing drug that left them awake and aware. In all these animal experiments (Hintzman, 1978), something more is learned than a mechanical association between stimulus and response.

Drawing by Miller; © 1984 The New Yorker Magazine, Inc.

Thirty years ago, the idea that animals as lowly as rats exhibit a cognitive form of learning struck many psychologists as silly. No longer. Classical conditioning experiments by Robert Rescorla and Allan Wagner (1972) revealed that animals act as if they know how to calculate the likelihood that the UCS will occur just after the CS. If a UCS such as electric shock occurs randomly while an animal is repeatedly exposed to a CS such as a tone, then the UCS will by chance occasionally follow the CS. Do such chance pairings serve to "stamp in" an association between conditioned stimulus and response? If conditioning depends on how *often* the CS and UCS are associated, then eventually enough chance associations of the tone and shock should have occurred to make the animals become fearful of the tone. But they do not. The animal becomes conditioned only when the tone begins to *predict* the shock. The more predictable the association, the stronger the conditioned response. It is as if what gets "stamped in" is an *expectation,* an awareness, of how likely it is that the UCS will follow the CS.

The role of awareness may help explain why classical conditioning treatments that ignore cognition are often not completely successful. When alcoholics are given a drug that makes them sick after drinking, will they thereafter associate alcohol with sickness? If classical conditioning were merely a matter of stamping in stimulus-response associations, we might hope so. And, to some extent, this does occur (as we will see in Chapter 17). However, alcoholics who have received this treatment can blame their misery on the drug, not the alcohol. This cognition tends to weaken the association between alcohol and sickness. To summarize, in classical conditioning it is not only the simple stimulus-response association, but also the thought that counts.

Biological Constraints

The early behaviorists were highly optimistic about the power and generality of conditioning principles. Because the basic laws of learning were believed to be essentially similar in all animals, it was thought to make little difference whether one studied rats, pigeons, or people. Moreover, it seemed that any natural response could be conditioned to any neutral stimulus. As learning researcher Gregory Kimble (1956, p. 195) proclaimed, "just about any activity of which the organism is capable can be conditioned and . . . these responses can be conditioned to any stimulus that the organism can perceive."

Twenty-five years later, Kimble (1981) humbly acknowledged that "half a thousand" scientific reports had proven his pronouncement wrong. Particular animals are predisposed to learn certain associations—those that will enhance their survival—and not others.

The person most responsible for challenging the prevailing view was John Garcia, a child of California farm workers who went on to receive the American Psychological Association's (1980) Distinguished Scientific Contribution award. While researching the effects of nuclear radiation on laboratory animals, Garcia noted that rats began to avoid drinking water from the plastic bottles in the radiation chambers. He wondered, might this be a result of classical conditioning? Might the sickness (UCR) induced by the radiation (UCS) have been linked to the plastic-tasting water (a CS)?

To test his hunch, Garcia undertook a number of experiments in which rats were sickened by radiation or drugs some time after experiencing an assortment of tastes, sights, and sounds. Two startling findings emerged: First, the rats developed an aversion only to the tastes (not to the sights and sounds), thus contradicting the idea that any perceivable neutral stimulus can be conditioned. (Conversely, rats would associate electric shock with the sights and sounds, but not with the tastes.) Second, even if sickened more than an hour after tasting a particular flavor, the rats would thereafter avoid that flavor. This violated the notion that the UCS must immediately follow the CS (usually by about ½ second) for conditioning to occur.

Have you ever developed an aversion to something you ate that made you sick?

"Not everything which is incredible is untrue."
Cardinal De Retz,
Memoirs, 1673–1676

Garcia's findings on taste aversion were initially aversive to other investigators. At first, the leading journals refused to publish his work. The findings were impossible, said some of the critics. But as often happens in science, the provocative findings stimulated new research, which in this case confirmed and extended the initial findings. Other animal species also seemed disposed to learn certain aversions. For example, when coyotes are tempted into eating sheep carcasses laced with a sickening poison, they will develop an aversion to sheep (Gustavson & others, 1974). Such findings suggest that predators and agricultural pests might be humanely controlled through taste-aversion experiences. (This is but one instance where psychological research that necessitated the suffering of some laboratory animals has contributed to the welfare of many more animals—in this case animals that might otherwise be slaughtered by ranchers and farmers.)

Saving coyotes by making them sick. When coyotes were fed poisoned lamb meat, the poison (UCS) made them sick (UCR). As a result, they developed an aversion (CR) to the lamb (CS) and returned to feeding on their natural prey. With their livestock no longer endangered, ranchers were less adamant about destroying the coyotes.

Have such results compelled researchers to abandon the search for principles of learning that generalize across species? No, the principles seem not so much wrong as they are "constrained" by biological predispositions. Each organism is better prepared to learn some associations than others. This is true of humans, too. A child can more readily be conditioned to fear animals (as Little Albert was) than to fear flowers (Kimble, 1981).

Although these results challenge some of Pavlov's principles of classical conditioning, they also affirm the deeper principle that learning processes enable animals to adapt to their environments. This adaptation principle helps us understand why animals would be responsive to stimuli that help them anticipate significant events, such as food or pain. Animals are generally predisposed to associate a CS with a UCS that immediately follows because, as a rule, causes *immediately* precede effects. The adaptation principle also helps explain the exceptions, such as the taste-aversion findings. In these cases, causes need not precede effects immediately—sometimes bad food causes sickness 1 or 2 hours after it has been consumed. The familiar principle that nature has selected traits that favor survival and reproduction therefore holds: Each organism comes prepared to learn those things crucial to its survival.

What, then, remains of Pavlov's ideas about conditioning? A great deal. All the researchers we have met so far in this chapter concur with Pavlov that theories of learning should be tested objectively. And they agree that classical conditioning is an important kind of learning, although one that is constrained by cognitive processes and biological predispositions. Judged by today's knowledge, Pavlov's ideas may seem incomplete. But if we see farther than Pavlov did, it is partly because we stand on his shoulders.

OPERANT CONDITIONING

We have seen that classical conditioning links simple, involuntary responses with neutral stimuli. How then do we learn more complex voluntary behaviors? It is one thing to teach an animal to salivate or become anxious in response to a novel stimulus, and quite another to teach a pigeon to walk a figure 8, a child to learn arithmetic, or a disturbed adult to behave more appropriately. The behaviorist would reply that another type of conditioning—what B. F. Skinner called *operant conditioning*—can explain and train such behaviors.

Superficially at least, it is easy to distinguish classical from operant conditioning. Classical conditioning occurs with what Skinner calls ***respondent behavior***—behavior that occurs as an automatic *response* to some stimulus. ***Operant behavior*** is more voluntary and is influenced by its consequences; operant behavior *operates* on the environment to produce rewards and avoid punishments. Usually, you can distinguish classical from operant conditioning by simply asking yourself whether the behavior being conditioned is involuntary (such as salivation or a fear response) or a voluntary effort to produce a desirable consequence (such as an animal's performing a trick to obtain food).

Operant conditioning experiments with pigeons often involve shaping their natural pecking response.

As everyone knows, behavior that is rewarded is likely to recur. Using that simple fact of life as a starting point, Skinner developed a "behavioral technology" that enabled him to teach pigeons such unpigeonlike behaviors as walking in a figure 8, playing ping pong, and even keeping a "guided missile" on course by pecking at a moving target displayed on a screen.

Skinner's Experiments

B. F. Skinner was a college literature major and aspiring writer who, discouraged by lack of success, entered graduate school in psychology and went on to become the most visible representative of modern behaviorism. For his pioneering studies with rats and later with pigeons, Skinner designed the now famous ***Skinner box*** (Figure 9-5). The "box" is typically a chamber with metal ends and glass side walls, a bar or key that can be manipulated to release a food or water reward, and devices that electronically record the animal's rate of bar pressing or key pecking.

(a)

(b)

Figure 9-5 *(a) Inside the Skinner box, the rat presses a bar for a food reward. (b) Outside, a device attached to the bar records the animal's accumulated responses. Figure 9-6 shows four such recordings of pigeon key pecks superimposed on the same recording paper.*

Shaping

In his experiments, Skinner used a procedure called ***shaping,*** in which an animal's natural behavior is, with the aid of rewards, gradually guided toward a desired behavior. Say Skinner wanted to condition a rat to push a bar. After observing how the animal naturally behaves before training, Skinner would then begin to build upon its existing behaviors. He might, for example, give the rat a food reward each time it approached the bar. Once the rat was doing so regularly, he would then require it to move closer, then closer still, and finally to touch the bar before giving it the reward. With this method of ***successive approximations,*** acceptable responses that represent steps in the desired direction are rewarded and all other responses are ignored. In this way, the researcher or animal trainer gradually shapes complex behaviors. Similarly, a parent may use rewards to shape desired behavior, such as by rewarding requests made courteously while ignoring those that are not.

The procedure sounds simple. But let's compare its essential features to what often happens in homes, schools, and the workplace. In the operant conditioning procedure, the trainer builds upon the individual's existing behaviors by immediately rewarding small steps in the desired direction. In everyday life, we are continually rewarding and shaping the behavior of others, says Skinner, often unintentionally. Sometimes we even reward behaviors that are offensive to us. Billy's parents, for example, are annoyed and mystified by his loud whining, without realizing how they actually encourage it:

> ***Billy:*** *"Could you tie my shoes?"*
>
> ***Father:*** *(Continues reading paper.)*
>
> ***Billy:*** *"Dad, I need my shoes tied."*
>
> ***Father:*** *"Uh, yeh, just a minute."*
>
> ***Billy:*** *"DAAAAD! TIE MY SHOES!"*
>
> ***Father:*** *"How many times have I told you not to yell? Now which shoe shall we do first?"*

Or compare the way learning psychologists shape behavior (by continually rewarding small improvements) to the way rewards are administered in some schoolrooms. On the spelling chart the teacher may record stars only after the names of those scoring 100 percent. All children take the same test. As everyone can then see, some children are academic all-stars and others, no matter how hard they try, are not.

As important as the principle of shaping by successive approximations is, the experiments of Skinner and other operant researchers did far more than teach us how to pull habits out of a rat. They went on to explore the precise conditions that foster efficient and enduring learning.

The goose won the prize, but it's obviously the boy who has been positively reinforced.

Principles of Reinforcement

The Concept of Reinforcement So far we have referred rather loosely to the power of "rewards." This idea is given a more precise meaning in Skinner's concept of ***reinforcement,*** which is any event that increases the likelihood of a response that it follows. Some stimuli, such as food, are usually ***positive reinforcers;*** *presenting* them after a response will strengthen the response. For most people, attention, approval, and money are positive reinforcers that will strengthen behaviors that trigger them. Other stimuli, such as electric shock, create ***negative reinforcers;*** *terminating* them after a response will strengthen the response. The child who is allowed to leave the chair in the corner after calming down is being negatively reinforced. (Remember: Whether it works by delivering something positive or withdrawing something negative, a reinforcer strengthens behavior.)

Note that "positive" means presenting a stimulus, and "negative" means withdrawing one. Since reinforcers always reward, the withdrawal of an aversive stimulus (such as shock) is a negative reinforcer.

Reinforcers can be further differentiated as either ***primary*** (innate) or ***secondary*** (conditioned). Primary reinforcers, such as food and the termination of shock, are unlearned. Their power to strengthen behavior is automatic. Secondary reinforcers, on the other hand, ultimately get their power through association with primary reinforcers. If a buzzer in a Skinner box has reliably signaled that food is coming, a rat will work to turn on the buzzer; the buzzer has become a secondary reinforcer. Our lives are filled with secondary reinforcers—money, good grades, a tone of voice, a gesture of praise, a word of promise—each of which has been linked with desirable consequences. These and other secondary reinforcers greatly enhance our power to nurture one another.

The third-grader will be negatively reinforced as soon as he is allowed to rejoin the class.

Another important distinction is between *immediate* and *delayed* reinforcement. In a typical experiment, an animal will engage in a whole sequence of "unwanted" behaviors—scratching, sniffing, walking about—before performing a "wanted" behavior such as pressing the bar. Whichever of these behaviors immediately precedes the reinforcement is more likely to occur again. Thus if the reinforcement for bar pressing is delayed as long as $\frac{1}{2}$ minute, allowing other behaviors to intervene, virtually no learning of the bar pressing occurs. Human cognitive abilities—our abilities to reflect on our past and project into our future—enable us to be responsive to reinforcers that are greatly delayed: the paycheck at the end of the week, the grade at the end of the semester, the trophy at the end of the season. Nevertheless, many of our behaviors, too, are influenced by the immediacy of reinforcement. Smokers, alcoholics, and other drug users may know that the immediate reinforcements of their consumption are more than offset by the dangers and punishments that lie in the future. Still, the immediate reinforcements prevail.

Schedules of Reinforcement So far, our examples have mostly assumed ***continuous reinforcement:*** Every time the desired response occurs, it gets reinforced. Under such conditions, learning occurs rapidly; but when the reinforcement terminates—when the food delivery mechanism is disconnected—extinction also occurs rapidly. The rat stops pressing the bar. If a normally dependable candy machine twice in a row fails to deliver a candy bar, chances are you will stop putting money into it (although a week later you may exhibit spontaneous recovery by trying it again).

In real life, continuous reinforcement is a rare phenomenon. A saleswoman does not make a sale with every pitch, nor does a fisherman get a bite with every cast. But they keep on trying because every now and then they are rewarded for their efforts. In experiments, researchers have explored a number of ***partial reinforcement*** schedules, in which responses are sometimes reinforced, sometimes not. Partial reinforcement typically slows learning (making continuous reinforcement preferable until a behavior is mastered.) But it does produce persistence—a resistance to extinction that is not found with continuous reinforcement. If a pigeon that has mastered pecking a key to obtain food is placed on a reinforcement schedule where reinforcement gradually fades out until it occurs only very occasionally, the pigeon may peck 10,000 times or more without a reward. With partial reinforcement, hope springs eternal.

Again, human counterparts to the animal experiments come readily to mind. Gamblers who play the slot machines are rewarded occasionally and unpredictably and this partial reinforcement affects them very much the way it does pigeons: It keeps them trying. There is a valuable lesson here to parents of children prone to throwing tantrums: Occasionally giving in to such behavior for the sake of peace and quiet puts the child, in effect, on a partial reinforcement schedule—the very best procedure for making the tantrums persist.

Skinner (1961) and his collaborators compared various schedules of partial reinforcement. Some of the schedules were rigidly fixed; some were unpredictably variable. ***Fixed-interval schedules*** provide no reinforcements during a set period of time, but then reinforce the first response after a fixed, or specified, interval is over. Like people checking more frequently for the mail as the time for mail delivery approaches, pigeons on a fixed-interval schedule peck a key more frequently as the time for reward draws near (Figure 9-6).

With the ***variable-interval schedule,*** a response is reinforced after a varying amount of time has elapsed. Like the unpredictable pop quiz that reinforces your study, or the "hello?" that finally rewards your persistence in calling back a busy number, variable-interval schedules tend to produce steady responding (Figure 9-6). This makes sense, since there is no way of knowing when the waiting interval will be over. Should the pop quiz become somewhat predictable, students will begin the stop-start work pattern that characterizes fixed-interval schedules.

The ***fixed-ratio schedule*** reinforces behavior after a set number of responses. Like people paid on a "piecework" basis, say for every thirty pieces of work, laboratory animals may be reinforced on a fixed ratio of, say, one reinforcement to every thirty responses. Typically, the animal will pause after receiving a reinforcement and then return to a high rate of responding (Figure 9-6). Because resting while on a fixed-ratio schedule results in reduced rewards, humans have found piecework so exhausting that unions have pressured employers to adopt hourly wage schedules.

Finally, ***variable-ratio schedules*** provide reinforcement after an unpredictable number of responses. This is the reinforcement schedule that gamblers experience. Like the fixed-ratio schedule, it produces high rates of responding and like the equally unpredictable variable-interval schedule, this schedule creates great resistance to extinction (Figure 9-6).

"[The child should] gain no request by anger; when he is quiet let him be offered what was refused when he wept."
Seneca (4 B.C.–A.D. 65).

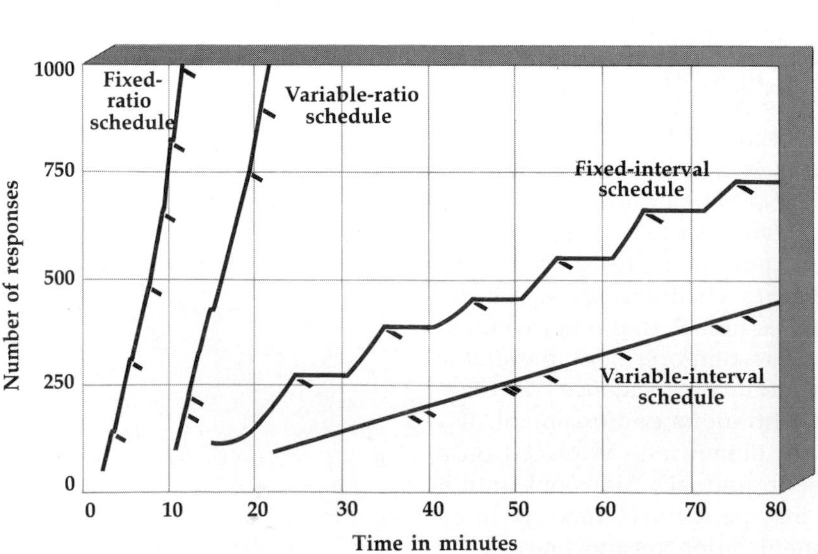

Figure 9-6 *Pigeon response curves to differing partial reinforcement schedules. Each curve is a cumulative record of pigeon key pecks. The slash marks indicate the points at which the reinforcers were given. The fixed-interval schedule produces increased responding as the time for the reinforcer nears. The variable-interval schedule produces a steady rate of responding. The fixed-ratio and variable-ratio schedules produce a high rate of responding. (From "Teaching machines" by B. F. Skinner. Copyright © 1961 Scientific American, Inc. All rights reserved.)*

Skinner's (1956) behavioristic conviction is that these principles of learning are universal. It matters little, he said, what response, what reinforcer, or what species you use; the effect of a given reinforcement schedule is pretty much the same: "Pigeon, rat, monkey, which is which? It doesn't matter. . . . Behavior shows astonishingly similar properties."

Punishment

Punishment is the opposite of reinforcement: It is an aversive (unpleasant) consequence that tends to *decrease* the recurrence of behaviors that precede it. There is no question that punishment can be a powerful instrument for restraining unwanted behavior—at least under conditions similar to those that make reinforcement effective. Of particular importance is the strength, timing, and consistency of the punishment. Strong, immediate, consistent consequences affect behavior more rapidly than do weak, delayed, inconsistent consequences (Schwartz, 1984). The rat that is shocked after touching the forbidden object, and the child who is disciplined after running into the street, will more quickly learn to avoid repeating their behaviors if their punishments are swift and sure.

Note: Punishment is the delivery *of an aversive stimulus. Negative reinforcement is the* withdrawal *of an aversive stimulus.*

As powerful as punishment can be, there is much controversy over whether it is a desirable means of controlling behavior. First, punished behavior is not forgotten; it is suppressed. This temporary suppression of "bad" behavior may reinforce people for using punishment. But if the punishment is discontinued or avoidable, the punished behavior may reappear. The child who learns through spankings not to swear around the house, may do so freely elsewhere. The driver who has been hit with a couple of tickets for speeding may buy a "fuzz buster" and speed freely when no radar patrol is in the area. Teenagers who have been punished for telling the truth regarding their whereabouts may begin lying. What punishment often teaches, says Skinner, is how to avoid punishment.

Punishment is most effective when strong, immediate, and consistent, but it can also have undesirable side effects. This boy's anger at his father's scolding might, if this were to become their principal mode of communication, translate into a resistance to listening to his father.

Second, punishing stimuli can create fear. Picture the following experimental procedure (Solomon & others, 1953): A dog is placed in a box that is divided into two compartments by a low barrier. Shortly after a light comes on, a powerful shock delivered through an electrified floor sends the dog leaping over the barrier. Because the other compartment is not electrified, the escape behavior is reinforced. (This learning to escape an aversive stimulus is, naturally enough, called ***escape learning.***) On succeeding trials, the dog is again shocked soon after the light comes on, unless it learns to quickly leap the barrier and is reinforced by avoiding the feared shock altogether (called ***avoidance learning***). Note that in these ways, both classical and operant conditioning can occur in the same learning situation: The dog is classically conditioned to fear shock once the light comes on, and operantly conditioned to avoid it by being reinforced for jumping into the "safe" half.

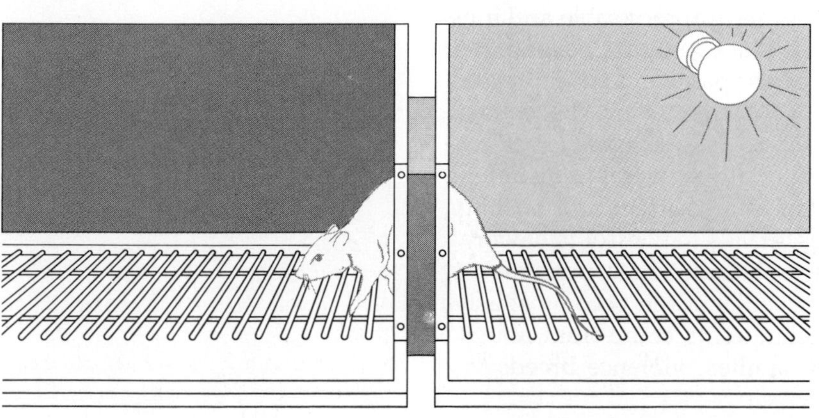

Escape and avoidance learning are often studied using a "shuttle box" with two compartments. When an electric current is transmitted to one compartment, the animal can escape to the other compartment after being shocked. Or it may avoid the shock completely by responding to a cue such as a light going on that signals the shock's impending arrival. In this shuttle box, escape is through an opening between the two compartments just large enough for this rat to squeeze through.

Rape as Traumatic Fear Conditioning

Experiments with dogs reveal that if a painful stimulus is sufficiently powerful, a single experience may be sufficient to traumatize the animal when it again faces the same situation. What follows is a human counterpart—one woman's experience of traumatic fear learning. Her fear is most powerfully associated with particular locations and persons, but generalizes to other places and people. Note how this traumatic experience has robbed the woman of her normal, relaxing associations with stimuli such as home and bed.

> Four months ago I was raped. In the middle of the night I awoke to the sound of someone outside my bedroom. Thinking my housemate was coming home, I called out her name. Someone began walking slowly toward me, and then I realized. I screamed and fought, but there were two of them. One held my legs, while the other put a hand over my mouth and a knife to my throat and said, "Shut up bitch, or we'll kill you." Never have I been so terrified and helpless. They both raped me, one brutally. As they then searched my room for money and valuables, my housemate came home. They brought her into my room, raped her, and left us both tied up on my bed.
>
> We never slept another night in that apartment, for we were too terrified there. Still, when I go to bed at night—always with the bedroom light left on—the memory of them entering my room repeats itself endlessly. I was an independent person who had lived alone or with other women for 4 years; now I can't even think about spending a night alone. When I drive by our old apartment, or when I have to go into an empty house, my heart pounds and I sweat. I am afraid of strangers, especially men, and the more they resemble my attackers the more I fear them. My housemate shares many of my fears, and is frightened when entering our new apartment. I'm afraid to stay in the same town, I'm afraid it will happen again, I'm afraid to go to bed. I dread falling asleep.

Experiments on escape and avoidance learning provide a laboratory counterpart to everyday situations in which we learn to escape or avoid punishment—be it a spanking, a deprivation of privilege, a fine, an imprisonment, or simply social disapproval. In everyday life, a person may associate the punishment not only with the undesirable behavior, but also with the person who administers it or the situation in which it is administered. Thus a child may come to fear the punitive teacher and want to avoid school. Worse yet, when punishments are unpredictable and inescapable, both animals and people may sense that events are beyond their control. As a result, they may become helpless, passive, and depressed. (More on this in Chapter 15, "Personality," and Chapter 16, "Psychological Disorders.")

A third way in which punishment, especially physical punishment, is problematic, is that, being painful, it can arouse anger and hostility. Moreover, since physical punishment uses attacks to control behavior, it models aggression as a way to cope with problems. The combination of these factors may explain why so many abused children become abusive parents, and why so many aggressive delinquents come from abusive families (Strauss & Gelles, 1980). Within families, violence breeds violence.

Finally, even when punishment successfully suppresses unwanted behavior, it usually does not guide one toward more desirable behavior. Punishment tells you what *not* to do; reinforcement tells you what to do. Punishment in combination with reinforcement is therefore generally more effective than punishment alone. The dogs in the avoidance learning experiments were both punished for inaction and reinforced for correct action, and so learned quickly. The teacher whose feedback on a paper says not only, "No, not that!" but, more often, "Yes, that's it!," is eliminating unwanted behavior by reinforcing alternative behaviors.

To sum up, punishment is sometimes effective, and may on occasion cause less pain than does the behavior it suppresses. However, punished behavior may reappear if the threat of punishment can be avoided. Punishment can also have undesirable side effects, such as fear and hostility; and it often fails to teach how to act positively. Thus most psychologists join Skinner in favoring an emphasis on positive reinforcement rather than punishment; catch people doing something right and affirm them for it. When you stop to think about it, many of our threats of punishment could be just as forceful, and perhaps more effective, if rephrased positively: "Johnny, if your room is not cleaned you may not go outside," could become "Johnny, when your room is cleaned you may go outside." "Maria, if you don't get your homework done, there'll be no TV, " could become ". . . ."

Applications of Operant Conditioning

Already we have seen numerous everyday applications of operant conditioning principles, and in later chapters we will see how the principles are being applied in the treatment of human problems (as in the discussion of behavior therapy in Chapter 17, "Therapy," and the discussion of biofeedback in Chapter 18, "Health"). Operant learning principles have also been applied in "behavior technologies" devised for schools, hospitals, businesses, and homes.

Computer Assisted Instruction

Imagine two mathematics teachers. Faced with an academically diverse class of students, Teacher A gives the whole class the same math lesson, knowing well that some students already understand the concepts being taught while others are frustrated by their inability to comprehend. When test time comes, the whiz kids breeze through, unchallenged, while the slower learners once again experience failure. Faced with a similar class, Teacher B paces the material according to each student's rate of learning and provides prompt feedback with much positive reinforcement to both slow and fast learners.

Computer Assisted Instruction (CAI) can provide individualized instruction with immediate reinforcement for correct responses.

Does the individualized instruction of Teacher B sound like an impossible ideal? A generation ago, Skinner and others advocated teaching machines and textbooks that would apply operant principles by shaping learning in small steps with immediate reinforcement for correct responses. These machines and texts, it was said, would revolutionize education and free teachers for closer relationships with their students.

The predicted revolution never occurred. But by the 1980s the availability and economy of computers began to make the impossible ideal more realistic, and Skinner (1984) remains hopeful. For some types of educational tasks, such as the teaching of reading and math, the computer can be Teacher B: engaging the student actively, pacing material according to the student's rate of learning, quizzing the student to find gaps in understanding, providing immediate feedback, and keeping flawless records for the supervising teacher. Experiments comparing ***computer assisted instruction (CAI)*** with traditional instruction suggest that for some "drill and practice" types of tasks the computer can indeed be more effective (Kulik & others, 1980, 1985). As microcomputers have become more widely available, so too have new techniques of CAI, such as educational games and simulations that entice students to explore and discover principles on their own (Lepper, 1982).

Drawing by Sidney Harris

"You mene I've bin spending this whol term with a defektiv reeding machin?"

Business and Economic Behavior

Believing that people's productivity and economic behavior are influenced by reinforcers much as are their other behaviors, some economists are now beginning to capitalize upon psychological research. In their best-selling book, *In Search of Excellence,* Thomas Peters and Robert Waterman, Jr. (1982, pp. 68–69) described the new managerial emphasis on positive reinforcement rather than punishment:

> The most important lesson from Skinner is the role of positive reinforcement, of rewards for jobs well done. . . . Positive reinforcement . . . not only shapes behavior but also teaches and in the process enhances our own self-image. . . . Positive reinforcement . . . nudges good things onto the agenda instead of ripping things off the agenda.

Economists and psychologists tend to view people's spending behavior, like other behaviors, as controlled by its consequences, or what economists call its costs and benefits. On that much the capitalist economist Adam Smith and the psychologist Skinner could probably agree. Neither would be surprised that people in master-metered apartment buildings (with energy costs paid by the landlord) use about 25 percent more energy than those living in comparable buildings with individually metered apartments (in which people reap the rewards of their own energy savings), or that home electricity users on an "energy diet" are helped by frequent feedback that shows their current usage compared with their past consumption (Darley & others, 1979). In homes, as in the learning laboratory, behavior is most effectively modified when linked with immediate consequences.

Self-Control

A spate of recent books and articles offers advice on how we can use operant learning principles to control our own behavior by strengthening desired actions. First, we are advised to state our goals in measurable terms—whether they are to stop smoking, lose weight, study more, or get more exercise. Next, we should record how often we engage in the behaviors we wish to promote, and note how these behaviors are currently being reinforced. Then we can begin systematically to reinforce the desired behaviors. To increase study time, allow yourself to eat a snack (or whatever other activity you find reinforcing) only after specified periods of study. By helping people bring their own behavior under systematic control, such procedures are intended to help them become more self-directed.

Further Reconsideration of Behaviorism

B. F. Skinner has been one of the more controversial intellectual figures of our time. The controversy stems not from his research on operant conditioning, but rather from his proposals that operant principles be used to control people's behavior in families, schools, and businesses, and from his insistence that external influences, not internal thoughts and feelings, are what shape behavior. To manage people effectively, he says, we should worry less about people's freedom and dignity. Recognizing that behavior is shaped by its consequences, we should administer rewards in ways that promote more desirable behavior.

B. F. Skinner (1983, p. 25): "I am sometimes asked, 'Do you think of yourself as you think of the organisms you study?' The answer is yes. So far as I know, my behavior at any given moment has been nothing more than the product of my genetic endowment, my personal history, and the current setting."

Critics outside of psychology object that Skinner dehumanizes people by neglecting their personal freedom and by seeking to control their actions. Skinner and his defenders reply that if people's behavior is already controlled by external reinforcers, then why not manipulate those controls for human betterment? Furthermore, in place of the widespread use of punishment in homes, schools, and prisons, would not the use of positive reinforcers be more humanitarian? They also suggest that even if it is humbling to think that we are shaped by our histories, the very idea also creates the hope that we may in turn shape the future.

Within psychology, Skinner has been widely faulted for not recognizing the importance of cognitive processes and for underappreciating the extent to which our biological predispositions constrain the environment's power to shape behavior.

Cognitive Processes

We have seen several hints that cognitive processes may be involved in operant learning. If partially reinforced for a behavior, animals may develop an expectation that repeating the behavior will eventually trigger the reward. If previously placed in a situation where they were unable to terminate a negative reinforcer, such as shock, animals may continue to act helpless—expecting that events are still beyond their control. Rats that explore a learning maze are like people who drive around a new town; they develop a ***cognitive map,*** a mental representation, of it. If offered a reward for solving the maze, they seem to do so rather suddenly after a period of exploration, as if in a flash of insight. Indeed, research by Edward Tolman (1948) showed that if the short route through a well-learned maze was blocked, the rats would choose a sensible detour as if they had a map of the maze in mind.

The rats would even develop a cognitive map *without* reinforcement. When, after thoroughly exploring a maze, a reward was then made available in the goal box, the rats would have little trouble finding it. As Figure

9-7 indicates, the animals had experienced some sort of ***latent learning,*** that is, learning that does not become apparent until there is some incentive to demonstrate it.

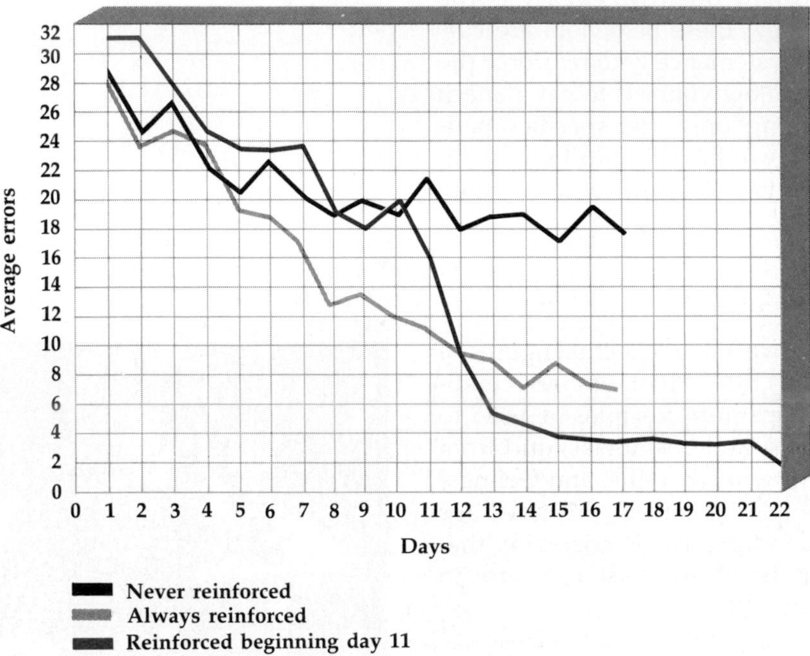

Figure 9-7 *Latent learning. Animals learn whatever they experience, with or without reinforcement. When rats that had explored a maze for 10 days were then offered a food reward at the end of the maze, they quickly demonstrated their prior learning of the maze—by immediately doing as well as rats that had been reinforced after running the maze. This suggests that reinforcement may be more important for triggering performance than for learning.*

The cognitive perspective has also led to an important qualification concerning the power of rewards: Unnecessary rewards carry a hidden cost. Promising people a reward for doing a task they already enjoy can lead them to see the reward as the motivation for performing the task, thus undermining their intrinsic enjoyment of the task. The phenomenon is called the ***overjustification effect,*** because an already justifiable activity becomes overjustified by the promise of added reward. It is as if the person thinks, "If I have to be bribed or coerced into doing this, then I must not enjoy doing it for its own sake."

The overjustification effect has been demonstrated in dozens of experiments. For example, people who are promised and receive payment for playing with enjoyable puzzles will later play with the puzzles less than people who played without pay (Deci, 1980; Lepper & Greene, 1979). Likewise, children who are rewarded for playing with an interesting toy later exhibit less interest in the toy than do children who are not rewarded (Newman & Layton, 1984). Why? It seems that the promise of reward leads people to view their actions as externally rather than internally controlled—which has the effect of turning play into work.

When the first-grade teacher offers candy each day to all who do their homework, how might this affect their natural eagerness to do schoolwork?

Biological Constraints

Accumulating evidence indicates that, as with classical conditioning, operant conditioning principles are constrained by each organism's natural predispositions. For example, when reinforced with food, the golden hamster can easily be conditioned to dig or to rear up, because these actions are among the animal's natural behaviors when deprived of food. Hamster behaviors not normally associated with food or hunger, such as face washing, are difficult to shape with reinforcement (Shettleworth,

1973). Two former associates of Skinner, Keller and Marian Breland (1961), came to appreciate biological constraints while applying operant principles in the training of animal acts for circuses, TV shows, and movies—principles that have since been applied in most trained animal shows (Bailey & Bailey, 1980). They had originally assumed that the principles could be generalized to almost any response that any animal could make. But after training some 6000 animals of thirty-eight different species, from chickens to whales, they concluded that biological predispositions were more important than they had initially supposed. For example, pigs were trained to pick up large wooden "dollars" and deposit them in a piggy bank. After learning the behavior, however, the animals began to revert to their natural ways; they would drop the coin, push it with their snouts as pigs are prone to do, pick it up again, and then repeat the sequence—despite the fact that this delayed their food reinforcement. As this illustrates, animal misbehaviors usually occurred as they would drift back to their biologically predisposed patterns.

Animals can most easily learn and retain behaviors that draw upon their biological predispositions, such as a raccoon's natural tendency to use its paws.

LEARNING BY OBSERVATION

From drooling dogs, running rats, and pecking pigeons we have learned much about the basic processes of learning. However, these animals have not told us the whole story of learning. Among higher animals—we humans, especially—learning occurs not only by direct experience but also through observation. By observing and imitating others, we learn gender roles, problem-solving strategies, and athletic skills.

We also learn specific social behaviors. Picture this scene from a famous experiment devised by Albert Bandura, the pioneering researcher of ***observational learning*** (Bandura & others, 1961). A nursery school child is at work on an interesting art activity. An adult in another part of the room is working with some Tinker Toys. The adult then gets up and for nearly 10 minutes pounds, kicks, and throws a large inflated Bobo doll, all the while yelling such remarks as "Sock him in the nose. . . . Hit him down. . . . Kick him."

After observing this outburst, the child is taken to another room where there are many appealing toys. But soon the experimenter interrupts the child's play and explains that she had decided to save these best toys "for the other children." The frustrated child is now taken to an adjacent room containing a variety of toys, including a Bobo doll. Left alone, what does the child do? Compared to other children who were not exposed to the adult model, children who had observed the aggressive outburst were many times more likely to lash out at the doll. Apparently, their inhibitions were lowered by observing the adult model lashing out. But something more than lowered inhibitions was occurring, for the children also imitated the very acts, using the identical words, that they had previously observed. Their latent learning had become manifest.

The bad news from such studies is that antisocial models—in one's family, one's neighborhood, one's TV programs—may have antisocial effects (see Chapter 20, "Social Relations"). This further helps us understand how abusive parents might have aggressive children, and why men who batter their wives often had fathers who did the same (Roy, 1977).

The good news is that ***prosocial*** (positive, helpful) models can have prosocial effects. In life both in and out of the psychological laboratory, people who exemplify nonviolent, helpful behavior can trigger similar behavior in others. Gandhi and Martin Luther King, Jr. both drew on the power of modeling nonviolent action. Separate studies of European Christians who risked their lives to rescue Jews from the Nazis, and of the civil rights activists of the late 1950s, have revealed that such individuals tended to have had a close relationship with at least one parent who modeled a strong moral or humanitarian concern (London, 1970; Rosenhan, 1970).

Sometimes models preach one thing and do another. Many parents, in fact, seem to operate according to the principle "Do as I say, not as I do." But experiments suggest that children learn both (Rice & Grusec, 1975; Rushton, 1975). When exposed to hypocrites, they tend later to imitate their hypocrisy, by doing what the model did and saying what the model said.

Why this tendency to imitate models? Bandura (1977) believes that reinforcements and punishments—those received by the model as well as by the imitator—help determine whether people will perform a behavior they have observed. We look and learn. By looking, we (cognitively) learn to anticipate what consequences a behavior might bring. By watching certain TV programs, for example, we may "learn" that physical intimidation is an effective way to control others, that sexual promiscuity brings pleasure without misery, or that it is okay for a man to say and do some things and for a woman to say and do other things.

Although our knowledge of learning principles is built upon the work of thousands of investigators, this chapter has focused on the ideas of a few pioneers, such as Pavlov, Watson, Skinner, and Bandura. It has done so partly to illustrate the impact that can result from single-minded devotion to a few well-defined problems and ideas. Bandura, and especially Pavlov, Watson, and Skinner, were perhaps prone to overenthusiasm for the power of their ideas. But it was they who defined the issues and impressed on us the importance of learning phenomena. As their legacy demonstrates, intellectual history often is made by people who, at the risk of overstatement, pursue an idea to its limits.

Albert Bandura (1977, p. 22): "Learning would be exceedingly laborious, not to mention hazardous, if people had to rely solely on the effects of their own actions to inform them what to do."

"The imitativeness of our early years makes us acquire the passions of our parents, even when those passions poison our lives."
Stendhal,
Love, 1822

"Children need models more than they need critics."
Joseph Joubert,
Pensées, 1842

"We are, in truth, more than half what we are by imitation. The great point is, to choose good models and to study them with care."
Lord Chesterfield,
Letters, January 18, 1750

SUMMING UP

All animals, but humans especially, adapt to their environments aided by learning. Through classical conditioning they learn to anticipate events such as being fed or experiencing pain. Through operant conditioning they learn to repeat acts that bring desired results and avoid acts that bring punishment. Through observational learning they learn from the experience and example of others.

CLASSICAL CONDITIONING

Pavlov's Experiments Although the idea of learning by association had been discussed for two centuries, it remained for Ivan Pavlov to capture the phenomenon in his classic experiments on conditioning. A neutral stimulus (such as a bell) was repeatedly presented just before an unconditioned stimulus (food), which triggered an unconditioned response (salivation). After several repetitions, the neutral stimulus alone (now the conditioned stimulus) began triggering a conditioned response (salivation). Experiments by Pavlov and others revealed that conditioning was usually greatest when the conditioned stimulus was presented just before the unconditioned stimulus, thus preparing the organism for what was coming. Further experiments explored the phenomena of extinction, spontaneous recovery, generalization, and discrimination.

Behaviorism Pavlov's work supported John B. Watson's emerging belief that psychology should study overt behavior scientifically, without recourse to considering unobservable mental activity, a position called behaviorism.

Behaviorism Reconsidered The behaviorists' discounting of the importance of mental processes has been strongly challenged by experiments suggesting that even for animals, cognition is important for learning. Animals appear capable of learning without responding and learning when to "expect" an unconditioned stimulus. The behaviorists' optimism that learning principles would generalize from one response to another and from one species to another has been tempered by research indicating that conditioning principles are constrained by an animal's biological predispositions. For example, rats are biologically prepared to learn associations between taste and illness.

OPERANT CONDITIONING

Unlike classical conditioning, operant conditioning occurs with behavior that actively operates upon the environment to produce rewards and avoid punishments.

Skinner's Experiments When rats or pigeons are placed in a Skinner box, their behavior can be shaped by successive approximations. The procedure has been used to study the effects of positive and negative reinforcers, primary and secondary reinforcers, and immediate and delayed reinforcers. Partial reinforcement schedules (fixed-interval, fixed-ratio, variable-interval, and variable-ratio) produce slower acquisition than does continuous reinforcement; but much more resistance to extinction. Like reinforcement, punishment is most effective when strong, immediate, and consistent. However, punishment is not simply the logical opposite of reinforcement, for it can have several undesirable side effects.

Applications of Operant Conditioning Operant principles are being applied in schools, in businesses, and at home. Computer assisted instruction embodies the operant ideal of individualized shaping and immediate positive reinforcement. Reinforcement principles are also being applied in management, in analyses of people's consumption patterns, and to self-management.

Further Reconsideration of Behaviorism Many psychologists have criticized behaviorists, such as Skinner, for underestimating the importance of cognitive and biological processes in operant conditioning. Research on cognitive mapping, latent learning, and the overjustification effect points to the importance of cognitive processes in learning. Attempts at operantly conditioning many responses in various animals make clear that biological predispositions constrain what an animal can be taught.

LEARNING BY OBSERVATION

An important type of human learning is observational learning, in which people learn from watching others' behavior. In experiments, children tend to imitate both what a model does and says, whether the behavior is prosocial or antisocial.

TERMS AND CONCEPTS TO REMEMBER

Acquisition The initial stage of classical conditioning during which a response to a neutral stimulus is established and gradually strengthened.

Avoidance Learning Learning to avoid an aversive stimulus or to prevent it from occurring.

Behaviorism The view that psychology should (1) be an objective science, that (2) studies only overt behavior without reference to mental processes. Most research psychologists today agree with (1) but not (2).

Classical Conditioning A type of learning in which a neutral stimulus, after being paired with an unconditioned stimulus, begins to trigger a response similar to that normally triggered by the unconditioned stimulus. (Also known as Pavlovian or respondent conditioning.)

Cognitive Map A mental representation of the layout of one's environment. For example, rats, once they have learned a maze, act as if they have acquired a cognitive map of the maze.

Computer Assisted Instruction (CAI) Computer tutored teaching featuring self-paced, individualized instruction and immediate feedback.

Conditioned Response (CR) In classical conditioning, the learned response to a conditioned stimulus.

Conditioned Stimulus (CS) In classical conditioning, an originally neutral stimulus that, after association with an unconditioned stimulus, comes to trigger a conditioned response.

Continuous Reinforcement Reinforcing a response every time it occurs.

Discrimination The ability to distinguish between a conditioned stimulus and similar stimuli that do not signal an unconditioned stimulus.

Escape Learning Learning to terminate an aversive stimulus.

Extinction The fading of a response when a conditioned stimulus is not followed by an unconditioned stimulus or when a response is not reinforced.

Fixed-Interval Schedule In operant conditioning, a schedule of reinforcement in which a response is reinforced only after a specified time interval has elapsed.

Fixed-Ratio Schedule In operant conditioning, a schedule of reinforcement in which a response is reinforced only after a specified number of responses.

Generalization The tendency, once a response has been conditioned, for stimuli similar to the conditioned stimulus to evoke the response.

Latent Learning Learning that occurs but is not apparent until there is an incentive to demonstrate it.

Learning A change in an organism, due to experience, that can affect the organism's behavior.

Negative Reinforcer The withdrawal of an aversive stimulus, such as shock; as with all reinforcers, negative reinforcers strengthen behaviors that trigger them.

Observational Learning Learning by observing and imitating the behavior of others.

Operant Behavior Behavior that operates upon environment to produce consequences.

Operant Conditioning A type of learning in which behavior is strengthened if followed by reinforcement, or suppressed if followed by punishment.

Overjustification Effect The effect of promising a reward for doing what one already likes doing: The person may now see the reward, rather than intrinsic interest, as the motivation for performing the task.

Partial Reinforcement Reinforcing a response only part of the time; results in less rapid acquisition of response but much greater resistance to extinction than does continuous reinforcement.

Positive Reinforcer A rewarding stimulus, such as food, which, when presented after a response, strengthens the response.

Primary Reinforcer An innately reinforcing stimulus, such as one that satisfies a biological need.

Prosocial Behavior Positive, constructive, helpful behavior. The opposite of antisocial behavior.

Punishment An aversive stimulus that, when presented, suppresses prior behavior.

Reinforcement In operant conditioning, any event that increases the likelihood of a response that it follows.

Respondent Behavior Behavior that occurs as an automatic response to some stimulus.

Secondary Reinforcer A conditioned reinforcer; a stimulus that acquires its reinforcing power by association with another reinforcer, such as a primary reinforcer.

Shaping A procedure in operant conditioning that starts with some existing behavior and reinforces closer and closer approximations to a desired behavior.

Skinner Box An operant conditioning chamber containing a bar or key that an animal can manipulate to obtain a food or water reinforcer and devices to record the animal's rate of bar pressing or key pecking.

Spontaneous Recovery The reappearance, after a rest period, of an extinguished conditioned response.

Successive Approximations In operant conditioning, the small steps by which some existing behavior is shaped toward a desired behavior.

Unconditioned Response (UCR) In classical conditioning, the unlearned response to the unconditioned stimulus.

Unconditioned Stimulus In classical conditioning, a stimulus that naturally triggers a response without conditioning.

Variable-Interval Schedule In operant conditioning, a schedule of reinforcement in which a response is reinforced after unpredictable time intervals.

Variable-Ratio Schedule In operant conditioning, a schedule of reinforcement in which a response is reinforced after an unpredictable number of responses.

FOR FURTHER READING

Bower, G. H., & Hilgard, E. R. (1981). *Theories of learning* (5th ed.). Englewood Cliffs, NJ: Prentice-Hall.

A classic textbook that offers individual chapters on selected theories of learning, including those of Pavlov and Skinner.

Hintzman, D. L. (1978). *The psychology of learning and memory.* San Francisco: Freeman.

A readable introduction to research on animal learning and human learning and memory.

Schwartz, B. (1984). *Psychology of learning and behavior* (2nd ed.). New York: Norton.

A current and comprehensive textbook summary of research on conditioning.

Skinner, B. F. (1948). *Walden Two.* New York: Macmillan.

A controversial novel by the noted behavioral psychologist, presenting his view of a utopian world guided by an intelligent application of the principles of operant learning.

Williams, R. L., & Long, J. D. (1982). *Toward a self-managed life style* (3rd ed.). Boston: Houghton Mifflin.

This book suggest how learning principles can be applied to one's own life, thereby enhancing self-control.

W. Eugene Smith *Sculptures by Elie Nadelman, As I Found Them in His Home After His Death, 1949*

CHAPTER 10

Memory

Your memory is your mind's storehouse, the reservoir of your accumulated learning. To Cicero, memory was "the treasury and guardian of all things." To a psychologist, ***memory*** is any indication that learning has persisted over time.

Imagine life without your memory. There would be no savoring the remembrances of joy-filled moments, no guilt or misery over painful recollections. Each moment would be a fresh experience. And each person would be a stranger, each task—dressing, cooking, biking—a novel challenge, every language a foreign language.

The range of human memory is evident in some fascinating cases:

Conversing with John you would be impressed by his wit, his intelligence (he might tell you the title of his master's thesis in physics), and his skill at tasks such as typing. It might be some time before you noticed that John suffers a tragic defect, caused by a brain injury suffered in a motorcyle accident. John has great difficulty forming new memories. Each morning when his rehabilitation therapist greets him she must reintroduce herself. She must listen patiently as over and over he retells anecdotes from his life before the accident. Each time the need arises, he must inquire, "Where is the bathroom?" and be told anew.

Berenice Abbott *Shop, Christopher Street*

At the other extreme are some special people who likely would have been medal winners in a memory Olympics. One woman, whom psychologist Ulric Neisser (1982) calls MZ, would have been the envy of every student. Until suffering a severe illness at age 29, MZ could recall verbatim anything her teachers wrote on the board and whole sections from her textbooks. When she later worked as a biology technician, the researcher for whom she worked would begin each day by giving her detailed instructions on the exact order in which to mount some 150 insects, which MZ would then do without writing anything down.

In 1917, George Stratton (whom we met in Chapter 7, "Perception," wearing glasses that inverted the visual world) described the memory prowess of some Polish Hebrew scholars. Not only had they committed the entire multivolume Talmud (the authoritative body of scriptural commentary in Judaism) to memory, but they also knew the exact placement of every word on every page. When a volume of the Talmud would be thrown open, say at page 10, and a pin driven through the book, say at the fourth word in the eighth line, these experts could name the word from a glance at the location of the pin, and could even identify the corresponding word through which the pin was driven on any other page. It was as if all the pages of the Talmud existed as photographs in their brains.

The winner of our memory Olympics would probably be the Russian, Shereshevskii, or S as he was more simply called by the distinguished Soviet psychologist Alexander Luria (1968). S's memory has earned him a place in virtually every modern book on memory. You and I can repeat back a string of about 7 digits—almost surely no more than 9. S could repeat 30, 50, or even 70 digits or words, provided they were read about 3 seconds apart in an otherwise silent room. Moreover, he could recall them as easily backwards as forwards. And his accuracy was unerring even when asked to recall a list as much as 15 years later, after having memorized hundreds of other lists. "Yes, yes," he might recall. "This was a series you gave me once when we were in your apartment. . . . You were sitting at the table and I in the rocking chair. . . . You were wearing a gray suit and you looked at me like this. . . ."

"Many a man fails to become a thinker for the sole reason that his memory is too good."
Nietzsche, 1844–1900,
Maxims

Do these memory feats make your own memory seem feeble? If so, consider your capacity for remembering countless voices, sounds, and songs; tastes, smells, and textures; faces, places, and happenings. Ralph Haber (1970) demonstrated the enormous capacity of our memories in an experiment involving more than 2500 slides of faces and places. The painstaking efforts of the researcher was exceeded only by the patience of his subjects, who over 2 to 4 days viewed each slide once, for 10 seconds. Afterward, the subjects were shown 280 of the pictures again; this time each slide was paired with a previously unseen picture, and the subjects were asked to identify which slide they had seen before. Nine times in ten they could.

How are such memory feats accomplished? How can we remember things we have not thought of for years, yet forget the name of someone we were introduced to a minute ago? How are memories stored in our brains? Does what we know about how memory works give us clues to how we could improve our memories? These will be among the questions we try to answer as we review some of the insights gleaned from a century of research on memory.

"The memory is sometimes so retentive, so serviceable, so obedient; at others, so bewildered and so weak; and at others again, so tyrannic, so beyond control! We are, to be sure, a miracle every way; but our powers of recollecting and forgetting do seem peculiarly past finding out."
Jane Austen,
Mansfield Park, 1814

FORMING MEMORIES

History is often determined by what people can remember about events. On June 17, 1972, five men were caught trying to tap the telephones of the Democratic National Committee in the Watergate Office Building in Washington, D.C. In 1973, when President Nixon's legal counselor, John Dean, testified before a U.S. Senate Committee investigating White House involvement in the Watergate scandal, his recall of conversations with the President was so impressive that some writers called him "the human tape recorder." Ironically, it was later revealed that an actual tape recorder had secretly recorded the conversations that Dean was remembering, providing a rare opportunity to compare an eyewitness's recollections with the actual event. Dean's recollection concerning essentials was proven correct; the highest ranking members of the White House staff went to prison for doing what John Dean said they had done, and the President was forced to resign.

However, when Ulric Neisser (1981) compared the details in the tapes to the testimony, it became evident that John Dean was far from a human tape recorder. For example, Dean recalled that entering a September 15th meeting, he

> found Haldeman and the President. The President asked me to sit down. Both men appeared to be in very good spirits and my reception was very warm and cordial. The President then told me that Bob—referring to Haldeman—had kept him posted on my handling of the Watergate case. The President told me I had done a good job and he appreciated how difficult a task it had been and the President was pleased that the case had stopped with Liddy.

John Dean testifying before the Senate Watergate Committee. When compared to the White House tapes, John Dean's memory was found to be accurate for the substance but not for the details of most conversations.

But virtually everything Dean said was wrong. The tape of the meeting revealed that the President did not ask Dean to sit down, he did not say Dean had done a good job, he did not say anything about Liddy or the indictments.

Dean's memory was better for a March 15th conversation at which he delivered a well-prepared report to the President on the unraveling of the cover-up of White House involvement. The tape caught Dean saying that "We have a cancer within, close to the presidency, that is growing. It is growing daily . . . because (1) we are being blackmailed; (2) people are going to start perjuring themselves. . . ." In his later testimony, Dean recalled "telling the president that there was a cancer growing on the presidency and . . . that it was important that this cancer be removed immediately because it was growing more deadly every day."

How could John Dean have been so right in his basic understanding of the Watergate discussions yet, except for the March 15th conversation, so wrong in recalling the details of most conversations? To understand Dean's memory (and our own) better, we need a model that can help us to organize the many research findings regarding memory. In this age, the most helpful model of memory is that of a dynamic information-processing system such as the computer.

Memory as Information Processing

Although the ordinary human memory stores more information and is more complex than any computer, both systems can be viewed as processing information in three steps. First, information must be ***encoded*** or translated into some form that enables it to get into the system. Material to be entered is transformed into electronic signals that the computer memory will accept, or into images or meaningful units that the human memory can process. Next, information must be ***stored*** or retained by the system over time. A computer might store information magnetically on a disk; a person stores information within the brain. Finally, there must be a method in which information can be ***retrieved,*** or located and gotten out when needed. Computers can search their memory stores and present the retrieved information on a screen or in a printout; people retrieve memories less exactly, by combining their stored information with what they currently believe. These three tasks—*encoding, storage, retrieval*—are the tasks not only of human memory and computer systems, but of other information processing systems as well: A library, for example, must have some way of getting information in, retaining it, and making it available to users.

Bear in mind that the danger in using any model of memory is that we may take it too literally. A model can help us to organize and simplify a great many observations by summarizing what we know so far. But as we learn more, any model is likely to be altered or replaced by another that more accurately reflects how the memory system works. A hundred years from now, most of the current facts and observations about memory will almost surely have survived, but our explanations of them will likely have changed.

Figure 10-1 summarizes the information-processing model for memory. It illustrates that information coming in from the senses must be processed (either automatically or with conscious effort), stored away, and retrieved when needed. First, however, the sensory information must be registered.

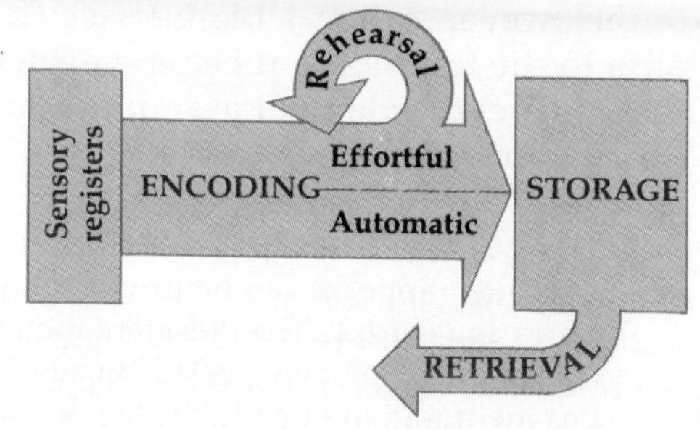

Figure 10-1 *A simplified information-processing model of memory. To be remembered, information must be encoded, stored, and retrieved.*

Sensory Registers

Consider what one intriguing memory experiment revealed about how sensory information initially enters the memory system. As part of his doctoral research, George Sperling (1960) showed people three rows of three letters each for only 1/20th of a second (see Figure 10-2). It was like trying to read by the flashes of a lightning storm. After the nine letters had disappeared from the screen, the subjects could recall only about half of them.

Figure 10-2 *Momentary photographic memory. When groups of letters similar to this were flashed for 1/20th of a second, people could recall only about half of the letters. But when signaled immediately after the letters had disappeared to recall any particular row, they could do so with near-perfect accuracy.*

Why? Was it because they had insufficient time to see them? No, Sperling cleverly demonstrated that even at such lightning-flash speed, people actually *can* see and recall all the letters, but only momentarily. Rather than ask subjects to recall all nine letters at once, Sperling instead would sound a high, medium, or low tone, immediately *after* the nine letters were flashed. This cue directed the subject to report only the letters of the top, middle, or bottom row, respectively. Now the subjects rarely missed a letter. Because they did not know in advance which row would be requested, all nine letters must have been momentarily available for recall.

What this revealed is that we do, in a sense, have photographic or ***iconic memory.*** For a moment, we retain an exact representation of a scene, and can recall any part of it in amazing detail. But only for a moment. If Sperling delayed the tone signal by as much as a second, the iconic memory was gone and the subjects once again recalled only about half of the letters. The visual screen clears quickly, as it must, lest new images be superimposed over old images. With sound, the sensory image, called ***echoic memory,*** disappears more slowly. The last few words spoken seem to linger for 3 or 4 seconds; sometimes just as you ask, "What did you say?," you can hear in your mind the echo of what was said.

Icon *A picture image. Iconic memory is therefore picture image memory.*

Psychologists have extensively studied our ability to remember simple verbal material—letters, numbers, and syllables. Increasingly, memory researchers are also studying our memories for more complex information—for words, for the meanings of sentences (such as, "The angry rioter threw the rock at the window"), for scenes and complex events. Their questions are both theoretical (how do we encode, store, and retrieve information?) and practical (how can we get the most from time spent studying?).

Encoding

How does sensory information, once registered, get encoded and transferred into the memory system? In your reading of the previous sentence, how did the information get encoded? Did the *image* of the words enter your memory, a process called ***visual encoding?*** Did you enter the *sound* of the words, a process called ***acoustic encoding?*** Or was the sentence coded by its *meaning*, a process called ***semantic encoding?*** Some combination of these seems to occur depending upon the timing of retrieval. If I were to show you a string of letters and then were immediately to ask you to repeat them, your occasional errors would be revealing (Baddeley, 1982). Though you had seen the letters, your errors would be less often visual (confusing a p with a q) than acoustic (confusing a b with a v), indicating that you had encoded the list acoustically rather than visually. An hour later, your errors would tend to be semantic rather than acoustic; if you had learned a list of words including the word "labor," it would more likely be misrecalled as "work" rather than as "later," indicating that semantic encoding had been retained. Some psychologists believe this reflects two very different types of memory storage—(1) a ***short-term memory,*** where items are often stored by sound, before being transferred to (2) a ***long-term memory,*** where they are more often stored by meaning. Short-term memory has a very limited capacity; except for what is consciously rehearsed, it holds information only very briefly. Long-term memory has an essentially unlimited capacity, and it holds information more permanently.

How many F's are in this sentence: FINISHED FILES ARE THE RESULTS OF YEARS OF SCIENTIFIC STUDY COMBINED WITH THE EXPERIENCE OF YEARS. Answer on p. 248.

The short- versus long-term memory distinction is an example of a memory model that to some psychologists no longer seems as useful as it once did. For one thing, even in the short run, we encode meaning as well as sound (we instantly hear "eye-screem" either as "ice cream" or "I scream"), and in the long run, memory of a poem may be enhanced by its acoustical rhythms and rhymes in addition to its meaning. So equating short-term memory with acoustic encoding and long-term memory with semantic encoding does not always work.

However, a useful distinction can be made between memory processing that tends either to be ***automatic*** (your memory for your dinner last night) or ***effortful*** (your processing of this chapter's concepts). Some memory researchers find it helpful to think of our memory systems being managed by a "central executive." To be effective, business executives must delegate routine activities to subordinates, freeing the executives to give their attention to more important problems. The same is true of your memory executive; it delegates some memory processing to subordinate systems, which function automatically, so that the executive's attention and effort can be devoted to other novel or long-range problems.

"The matters about which I'm being questioned, Your Honor, are all things I should have included in my long-term memory but which I mistakenly inserted in my short-term memory."

Automatic Processing

With little or no effort, you encode an enormous amount of information about space, time, and frequency: Your occasional recall of the place on the page where the material you are looking for appears, your recreating a sequence of the day's events in order to guess where you left your coat, and your realizing that "This is the third time I've run into you this afternoon," are all memories that you formed automatically. In fact, not only does automatic processing occur effortlessly, but it is also difficult to shut off. When you hear or read a word in your native language, it is virtually impossible not to register automatically its meaning.

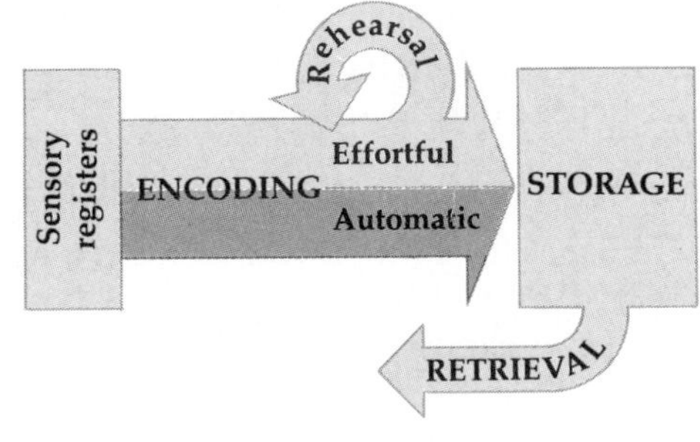

Some types of automatic processing, such as your encoding of space, time, and frequency, seem innate to the human information-processing system. But other automatic processes, such as your encoding of word meanings, are learned. Researchers have explored how, through learning, effortful processing can become more automatic. For example, they have trained people to search for a target letter, such as J, among a group of letters (Schneider & Shiffrin, 1977; Shiffrin & Schneider, 1977).

With practice, subjects find that the processing becomes automatic; the target letter seems to pop out. Similarly, reading reversed sentences requires effort:

.citamotua emoceb nac gnissecorp luftroffE

After practice, it begins to be less effortful, much as reading right to left becomes easy for any student of the Hebrew language (Kolers, 1975).

So far we have seen that automatic processing seems to occur with little or no effort, without our being aware we are doing it and without interfering with our efforts to think about and remember other things. If, indeed, such processing requires no special attention, then asking people to pay special attention to information they automatically encode (say, to how frequently different words appear among a group of words) should be of no benefit. That is just what Lynn Hasher and Rose Zacks (1979) found. In their experiment, one group was told that they would be asked to recall how many times a word occurred in a long list of words. Another group was not forewarned. Both groups did equally well. Moreover, reported Hasher and Zacks, not only is people's memory for space, time, and frequency information unaffected by effort, it also matters little how old people are, how depressed they are, or how much they practice. Our automatic processing is genuinely automatic: It is difficult to switch it off and on at will.

How many F's were there in the sentence on p. 247? Partly because your initial processing of the letters was primarily acoustic rather than visual, you probably missed some of the six F's, especially those that sound like a V rather than an F.

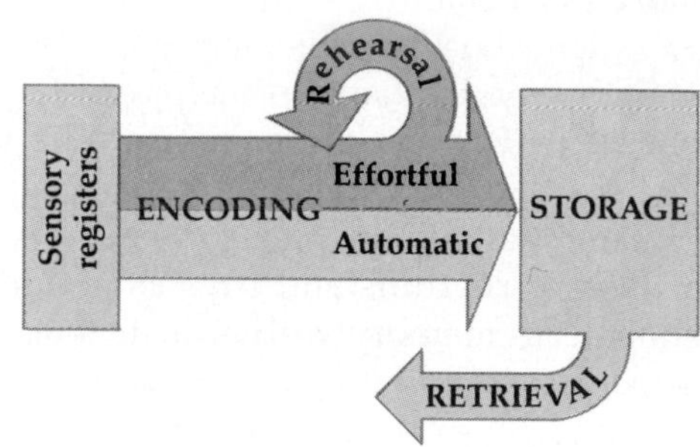

Effortful Processing

We encode and retain other types of information only with effort and attention. Between the phone book and the phone, your memory of a telephone number will disappear, unless you work to keep it in consciousness. To find out how quickly it will disappear, Lloyd Peterson and Margaret Peterson (1959) gave people three letters to remember, such as CHJ. To prevent their rehearsing the syllable, the subjects were asked to begin immediately counting aloud backward by threes from some number. As Figure 10-3 indicates (and as you can demonstrate with the help of a friend), after 3 seconds the letters were recalled about half the time; after 10 seconds they were seldom recalled.

The importance of ***rehearsal*** (conscious repetition) was demonstrated long ago by the pioneering researcher of verbal memory, German philosopher Hermann Ebbinghaus (1850–1909). Ebbinghaus helped do for the study of memory what his contemporary Ivan Pavlov did for the study of learning. Impatient with philosophical speculations about memory, Ebbinghaus wanted to study memory scientifically. To do so, he decided to study his own learning and forgetting of novel verbal materials.

Where could Ebbinghaus find verbal material that was not already familiar? His solution was to form a list of all possible nonsense syllables created by sandwiching a vowel between two consonants; then, for a particular experiment, he would more or less randomly select a sample of these. To get a feel for how Ebbinghaus experimented on himself, try rapidly reading aloud, eight times over, the following list and then recalling the items (from Baddeley, 1982): JIH, BAZ, FUB, YOX, SUJ, XIR, DAX, LEQ, VUM, PID, KEL, WAV, TUV, ZOF, GEK, HIW.

After learning the list, Ebbinghaus could recall few of the syllables a day later. But were they entirely forgotten? As Figure 10-4 portrays, the more times he had repeated the list aloud on day 1, the fewer repetitions were required to relearn the list on day 2. Here, then, was a simple beginning principle: *The amount remembered depends on the time spent learning.*

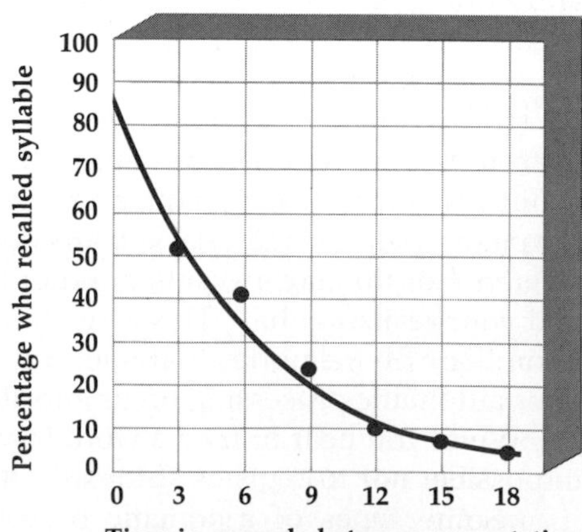

Figure 10-3 *Information that is not automatically processed may be quickly forgotten unless rehearsed. When people were prevented from rehearsing three-letter syllables, they usually forgot them within 10 seconds.*

Even after material has been learned, additional repetition or "overlearning" increases retention. Thus John Dean recalled almost perfectly his "cancer on the presidency" remarks, which he had rehearsed several times before uttering them to the President. Harry Bahrick (1984a) also illustrated Ebbinghaus's principle when he found that teachers at a small college soon forgot the names and faces of most of their former students, whom they saw for only a term. In contrast, the college classmates saw each other repeatedly for 4 years; this overlearning helps explain why a quarter-century later they could still recognize one another's names and yearbook pictures.

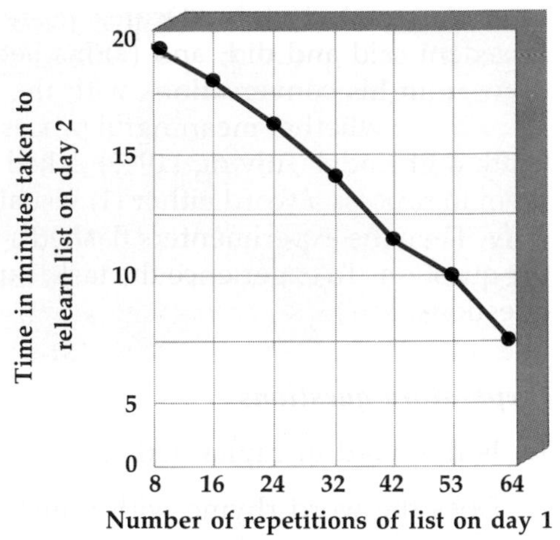

Figure 10-4 *Ebbinghaus's retention curve. Ebbinghaus observed that the more time he devoted to practicing a list of nonsense syllables on day 1, the fewer repetitions he required to relearn it on day 2, or, more simply, the more time spent learning novel information, the more that is retained.*

The benefits of rehearsal can also be seen in a phenomenon that you have likely experienced. Many experiments have found that when people are shown a list of items (words, names, dates) and then immediately are asked to recall the items in any order, they tend to remember the last and first items most often and the middle items least. This phenomenon is known as the ***serial position effect*** (Figure 10-5). But after a delay, only the first items tend to be better recalled. As an everyday parallel, imagine that while you are introduced to a string of people you rehearsed all the names as each successive person was introduced. By the end you will have spent more time thinking about (rehearsing) the earlier names than the later names; thus even the next day you will probably recall the earlier names better.

Rehearsal will not encode all information equally effectively, however. Sometimes merely repeating information, as with the phone number we are about to dial, is not the most efficient way to get it into memory storage. In an experiment on the serial position effect, Fergus Craik and Michael Watkins (1973) demonstrated that mere repetition need not lead to encoding. They had people keep the last four words of a list in consciousness until being tested 20 seconds later. By repeating these words aloud, the subjects usually remembered not only the list's first word but also these last four words, just as if they had been tested immediately. After doing the same on several more lists, they were then surprised with a request to recall as many words as possible from all the lists. How many of the final words of each list do you suppose they now remembered? Practically none, though they could still recall half of the first words. Consider: Only a few minutes earlier they had repeated these last four words over and over to keep them on their mental screen, but it now seemed that this "maintenance rehearsal" had done nothing to encode the words for more permanent storage. The finding is an important one for students who struggle to learn facts for tests: Merely repeating information may be insufficient to encode it for memory.

"The mind is slow in unlearning what it has been long in learning."
Seneca, 4 B.C.–A.D. 65
Troades

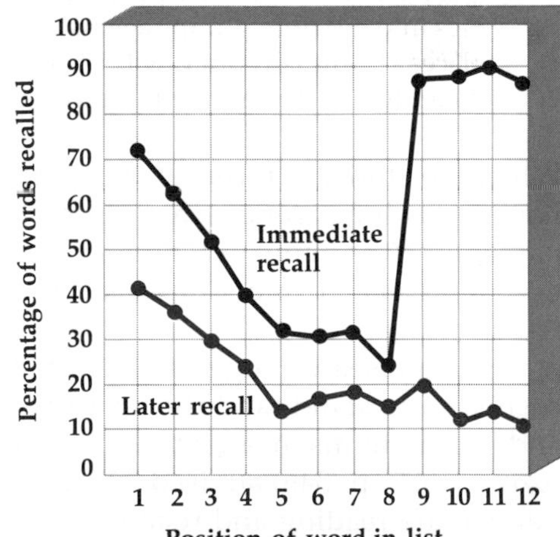

Figure 10-5 *The serial position effect. After being presented with a list of words, people immediately recall the last and first items most accurately. But later they recall only the first items most accurately—even if they had repeated the last items for a few moments to keep them in their consciousness.*

How then do we get information into permanent storage? We must somehow process it. Nothing processed, nothing stored. But what types of effortful processing pay the most dividends?

Meaning Do you recall (from page 246) the sentence about the rioter? Imagine that as an eyewitness you had to recall it as exactly as possible. What was it: "The angry rioter threw. . . ."?

When we process verbal information for storage we usually encode its meaning by associating it with what we already know or can imagine. Perhaps, then, like the subjects in an experiment by William Brewer (1977), you recalled the rioter sentence not as written ("The angry rioter threw the rock at the window"), but rather the meaning you encoded when you read it, such as, "The angry rioter threw the rock *through* the window." As such recall indicates, we do not remember exactly what is out there, but how we encode it, much as after studying for an exam you may remember your lecture notes rather than the lecture itself. This helps and try to reproduce the line segments. It's nearly impossible, yet you can easily reproduce the line segments of the second row, which are no less complex. Similarly, the fourth row is much easier to remember than the third, though both contain the same letters, and the sixth cluster is more easily remembered than the fifth, though both contain the same words. In each case, the more easily remembered information is processed as familiar units, or ***chunks.***

Chunking information into familiar units occurs so naturally that we take it for granted. Consider your ability to reproduce perfectly the 150 or so line segments that make up the sixth cluster of phrases. Surely it would astonish an illiterate person, especially one unfamiliar with the alphabet. Such admiration would be the same as you or I might feel at the ability of someone literate in Chinese to glance at the ideographs in Figure 10-10 and then to reproduce all the stokes. Or the awe we might have for a chess master, who, after a 5-second glance at the board during a game, can recall the exact positions of most of the pieces (Chase & Simon, 1973). For the Chinese reader and the chess master, as for you when reading English, the to-be-remembered information is chunked into familiar units.

Chunking also can aid our recall of unfamiliar material by organizing it into a more familiar form. One such mnemonic technique forms words (called acronyms) from the first letters of words to be remembered. Should you ever need to recall the names of the five Great Lakes, just remember HOMES (*H*uron, *O*ntario, *M*ichigan, *E*rie, *S*uperior). Like to remember the colors of the rainbow in order? Think of ROY G. BIV (*R*ed, *O*range, *Y*ellow, *G*reen, *B*lue, *I*ndigo, *V*iolet).

By chunking digits, you can increase your recall. An impossible string of sixteen numbers—1-4-9-2-1-7-7-6-1-8-1-2-1-9-4-1—becomes easy when chunked into 1492,1776,1812,1941. Two Carnegie Mellon University students even managed—after more than 200 hours of practice in the laboratory of Anders Ericsson and William Chase (1982)—to increase their memory span from the typical seven digits to more than eighty. In one testing session, Dario Donatelli heard the researcher read one digit per second in a monotonous voice: "151859376550215784166585061209-4885686772731418186105462974801294974965928." Motionless while the numbers were read, Donatelli then sprang alive. He whispered numbers, rubbed his chin, tapped his feet, counted on his fingers, and ran his hands through his hair. "Okay," he announced almost 2 minutes later. "The first set is 1518. Then 5937. . . ." He repeated all seventy-three digits, in groups of three and four.

How did he do it? By chunking. "First set was a 3-mile time," reported Donatelli, an All-American cross-country runner. "Second set was a 10-mile time. Then a mile. Half-mile. Two-mile time. An age. . . . Two mile. Age. Age. Age. Two-mile" (Wells, 1983).

As people develop expertise in an area, they process information as Donatelli did in this example, not only in chunks, but also in hierarchies composed of a few broad concepts divided into lesser concepts and facts, which are divided into still smaller categories. By organizing their knowledge in such ways, experts can retrieve information efficiently. This chapter therefore aims not only to teach you the elementary facts of memory, but also to help you organize these facts around broad principles (such as encoding), subprinciples (such as automatic and effortful processing), and still more specific concepts (such as meaning, imagery, and organization).

Gordon Bower and his colleagues (1969) demonstrated the benefits of hierarchical organization by presenting words either randomly or grouped into categories such as shown in Figure 10-11. When the infor-

1.

2. K L C I S N E

3. KLCISNE NVESE YNA NI CSTTIH TNDO
4. NICKELS SEVEN ANY IN STITCH DONT

5. NICKELS SEVEN ANY IN STITCH DONT
SAVES AGO A SCORE TIME AND
NINE WOODEN FOUR YEARS TAKE

6. DONT TAKE ANY WOODEN NICKELS
FOUR SCORE AND SEVEN YEARS AGO
A STITCH IN TIME SAVES NINE

Figure 10-9 *Effects of chunking on memory. When information is organized into familiar units, such as letters, words, and phrases, we recall it more easily.*

Figure 10-10 *After looking at these ideographs, can you reproduce them exactly? If so, you are almost certainly literate in Chinese.*

mation was hierarchically organized, recall was better; in fact it was two to three times better. Such results hint at the benefits of organizing what you study—of giving special attention to chapter outlines, headings, topic sentences, and summary paragraphs. If you can master not only the individual concepts of this chapter, but also the organization of the whole chapter, or if you can fit the information into what you already know, the odds are that come test time your recall will be good. Taking lecture and text notes in outline form—a type of hierarchical organization—may help.

Figure 10-11 *Effects of organization on memory. When people saw words organized into hierarchical categories (as illustrated here), they remembered them far better than when the same words were presented randomly.*

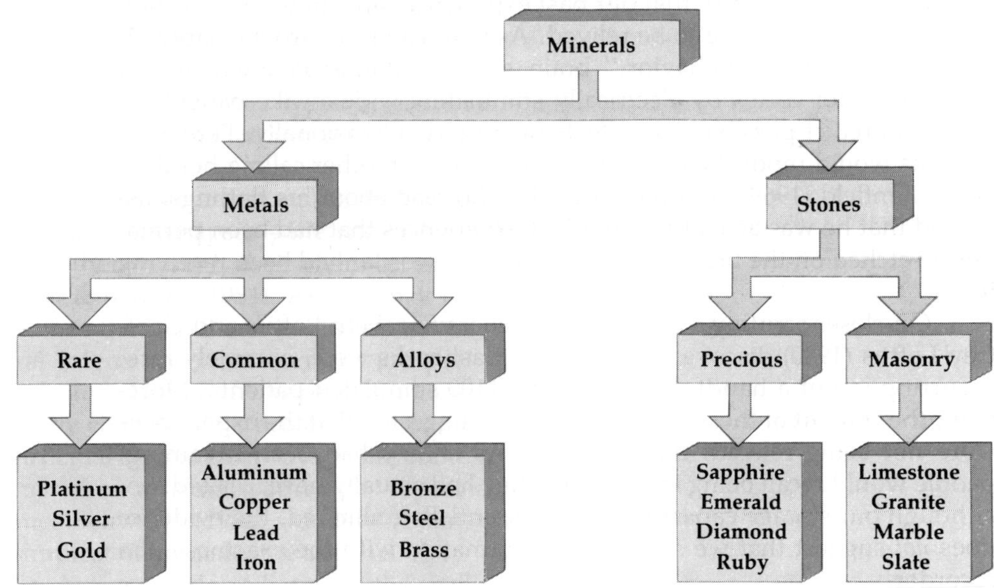

Storage

If an event occurs that you encode and later retrieve, we infer that you must, somehow, have stored it. What is stored lies dormant, waiting to be reawakened by a cue. Storage is difficult to isolate and describe; we cannot see stored memories, but we infer that they exist. What is our storage capacity? And just how and where are memories stored in our brains?

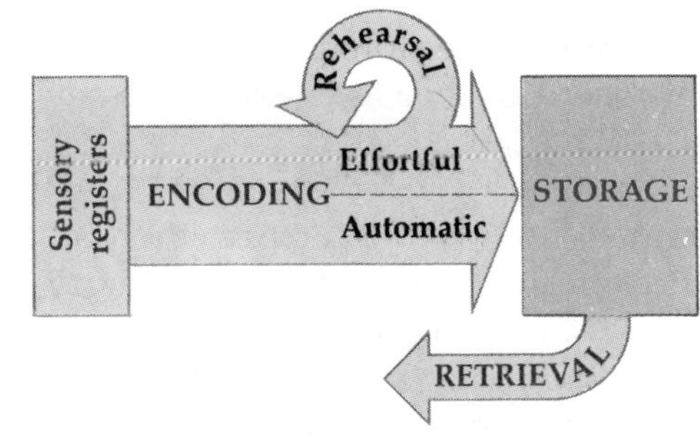

Memory Capacity

Our short-term memory for new information is very limited. As we noted earlier, we can immediately recall roughly seven items of information (give or take two), a recall capacity that has been enshrined in psychology as "the Magical Number Seven, plus or minus two" (Miller, 1956). Actually, people's short-term memory spans—the quantity of information they can immediately recall correctly 50 percent of the time—may vary from seven items. Recall is slightly better for random digits (such as those of a phone number) than for random letters, which sometimes have similar sounds. It is slightly better for information we hear rather than see (recall that echoic memory lasts somewhat longer than iconic memory). And adults have greater memory spans than children (Chi, 1976). Still, the basic principle holds true: At any given moment, we can process but a very limited amount of information.

Our capacity for storing long-term memories is essentially limitless. Our brains are not like warehouses, which once filled can be added to only by discarding old items. Indeed, the more expertise we have, and therefore the better we can organize and form meaningful associations with new information, the easier it often is both to learn and remember.

Probably you were able to recall exactly what you ordered, and maybe even the color of the tablecloth. Is retrieval therefore merely "reading" the information stored in our brain's library? We do have an enormous capacity for storing and reproducing the incidental details of our daily experience (Alba & Hasher, 1983). But as we have seen, often we construct our memories as we encode them, and we may also alter our memories as we draw them out from the memory bank. Like a scientist inferring the appearance of a dinosaur from its remains, we may infer our past, based on stored information plus what we now assume. Did the waiter give you a menu? Not in the paragraph given (from Hyde, 1983). Nevertheless, many people answer "yes." Why? Their schema for restaurants directs their memory construction, by filtering information and filling in missing pieces.

This process of memory construction explains why John Dean's recollections of the Watergate conversations were a mixture of real and imagined events. It also explains why "hypnotically refreshed" memories of crimes (see Chapter 8) so easily incorporate errors, some of which originate with the hypnotist's leading questions ("Did you hear loud noises?").

Memory researcher Elizabeth Loftus has repeatedly shown how eyewitnesses similarly construct memories when asked to retrieve information. In one experiment with John Palmer, Loftus showed a film of a traffic accident and then quizzed the viewers about what they saw (Loftus & Palmer, 1973). Those asked "How fast were the cars going when they *smashed* into each other?" gave higher estimates than those asked "How fast were the cars going when they *hit* each other?" A week later, when asked if they recalled seeing any broken glass, those who had been asked the question with "smashed" were more than twice as likely as those asked the question with "hit" to recall broken glass (Figure 10-14). In fact, the subjects had unwittingly reconstructed their memories: There was no broken glass. After being questioned, the subjects were like computer programmers who call up a file, edit it, then store only the *revised* file. Summarizing this and other experiments, Loftus (1983) reported that

> when exposed to misleading post-event information, subjects have misrecalled the colour of a car that was green as being blue, a yield sign as a stop sign, broken glass or tape recorders that never existed, and even recalled something as large and conspicuous as a barn when no barn was ever seen. . . . These experiments . . . show that people will pick up information, whether it is true or false, and integrate it into their memory.

"Memory is a great betrayer."
Anais Nin,
The Diary of Anais Nin, 1974

"Imagination and memory are but one thing which for divers[e] considerations hath divers[e] names."
Thomas Hobbes,
Leviathan, 1651

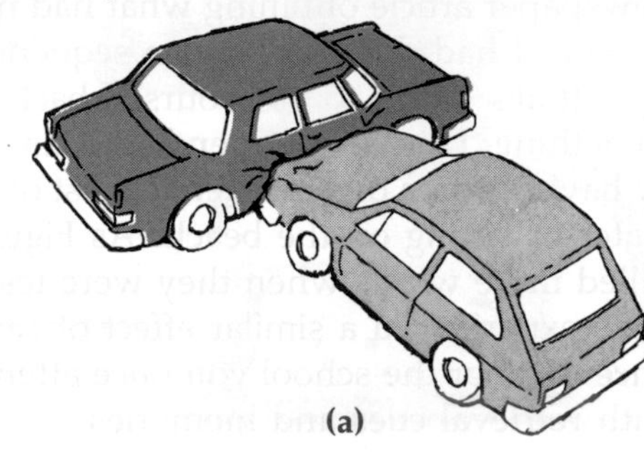

(a)

"About how fast were the cars going when they *smashed* into each other?"

(b)

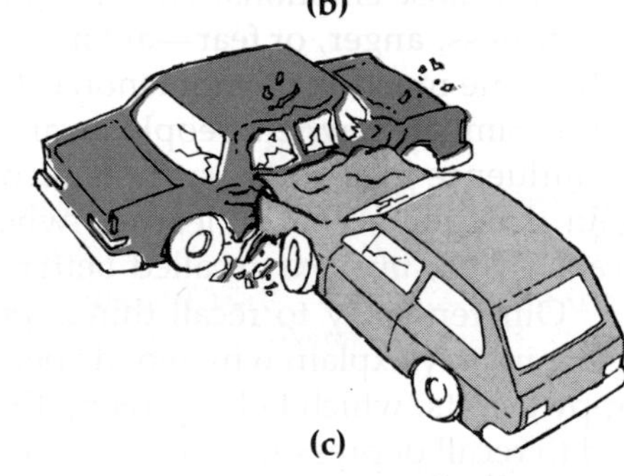

(c)

Figure 10-14 *Memory construction. When people who viewed a filmed car accident (a) were then asked a leading question (b), they integrated the old and new information and "remembered" a more serious accident (c) than they had witnessed.*

Knowing What We Know

Sometimes we know more than we are aware that we know. Other times—perhaps when taking an exam—we discover that we do not know something as well as we thought we knew it. The difficulties of knowing what one knows are strikingly evident in the special cases of some amnesiac patients, patients similar to the one described at the beginning of this chapter. These patients are incapable of learning new facts or recalling anything they have recently done. Nevertheless, in experiments they can be classically conditioned, and with practice they can learn to read mirror-image writing, do a jigsaw puzzle, or even solve a complicated block-stacking brainteaser (Squire, 1982; Weiskrantz & Warrington, 1979). All this they do with absolutely no memory of having learned the skill; indeed, when presented with a block-stacking problem they will deny they have ever before seen it, insist it is silly for them to try it, and then proceed to solve it like a practiced expert (Figure 10-15). Mysteriously, they know *how* to do these things without knowing *that* they know. (The

Drawing by Cheney; © 1983 *Omni* Magazine.

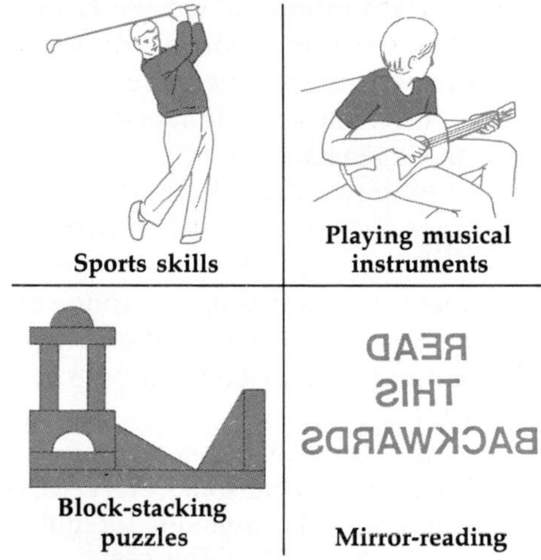

Figure 10-15 *The ability of some brain-injured patients to learn and remember skills but not facts suggests that skill and fact memory involve different brain mechanisms.*

parallel to learning during infancy is intriguing: We recall nothing, yet the reactions and skills we learned reach far into our future.)

How accurate are we at assessing our own knowledge? John Shaughnessy and Eugene Zechmeister (1979) explored this question in an experiment with college students. One group of students was (1) repeatedly shown dozens of factual statements, (2) asked to judge the likelihood of their later remembering each fact, and then (3) actually tested on their recall. Students in this group tended—even on the questions they later missed—to feel fairly confident of their knowledge.

Instead of repeatedly reading the statements, students in a second group spent much of their time answering practice test questions that helped them evaluate their knowledge. These students learned the facts just as well as did the first group. This was true despite their having seen the statements fewer times. Better yet, compared to the mere-repetition group, the practice-test group could better discriminate what they knew from what they did not. So, self-testing not only encourages active rehearsal, it also can help you to know what you know—and thus to focus your study time on what you do not yet know. As the British statesman Benjamin Disraeli once noted, "To be conscious that you are ignorant is a great step to knowledge."

"When you know a thing, to hold that you know it; and when you do not know a thing, to allow that you do not know it; this is knowledge."
Confucius, 551–479 B.C.,
Analects

FORGETTING

In implicit praise of memory, we seek to understand its mysteries, we read books and articles on how to improve it, we are dismayed at our memory lapses. Amidst all the applause for memory, have any voices been heard in praise of forgetting? The philosopher-psychologist William James (1890, p. 680) was one: "If we remembered everything, we should on most occasions be as ill off as if we remembered nothing." To discard the clutter of useless or out-of-date information—where we parked the car yesterday, a friend's old phone number, restaurant orders already cooked and served—is surely a blessing (Bjork, 1978). The Russian memory whiz, S, whom we met at the beginning of the chapter, was haunted by his junk heap of memories, which continually dominated his consciousness. He found it more difficult than did others with lesser memories to think abstractly—to generalize, to organize, to evaluate. A good memory is beneficial, but so is the ability to forget.

"It is indeed exasperating to have a memory that begins too young and continues long . . . . There are some things I would like to forget. But I never forget."
Pearl S. Buck,
China, Past and Present, 1972

"Child of Nature, learn to unlearn."
Benjamin Disraeli,
Contarini Fleming, 1832

What causes forgetting? When we forget something do we fail to *encode* the information? Do we have difficulty *storing* it? Is the memory stored but for some reason *irretrievable?* Much as you may fail to find a book in your library—because it was never acquired, was discarded from storage, or is currently inaccessible—memory failure can occur at each of these three stages.

Encoding

Most memory failures are simply explained: The information never gets into the memory system. The English novelist-critic C. S. Lewis (1967, p. 107) vividly described why we remember "next to nothing":

> Each of us finds that in his own life every moment of time is completely filled. He is bombarded every second by sensations, emotions, thoughts, which he cannot attend to for multitude, and nine-tenths of which he must simply ignore. . . . The past . . . was a roaring cataract of billions upon billions of such moments: any one of them too complex to grasp in its entirety, and the aggregate beyond all imagination. . . . At every tick of the clock, in every inhabited part of the world, an unimaginable richness and variety of "history" falls off the world into total oblivion.

Drawing by Sidney Harris

Much of what we are exposed to we never notice. For example, if you live in the United States, you have probably looked at thousands of pennies in your lifetime. Can you recall what the side with Lincoln's head looks like? If not, let's make the memory test easier: Can you *recognize* the real thing in Figure 10-16? Raymond Nickerson and Marilyn Adams (1979) reported that most people cannot. The details of a penny are not very meaningful (nor are they essential for distinguishing pennies from other coins) and few of us have made the effort to encode them.

Figure 10-16 *One of these pennies is the real thing. Which one?*

Storage

Even after knowing something well, we sometimes forget it. In one experiment on himself, Ebbinghaus (1885) learned lists of nonsense syllables, and then measured how much less time it took to relearn each list, from 20 minutes to 30 days later. His famous "forgetting curve" (Figure 10-17) indicates that much of what we learn we quickly forget.

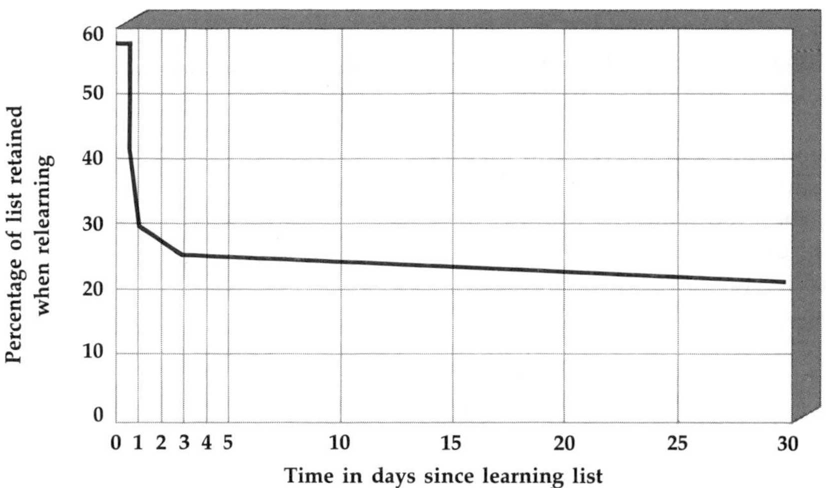

Figure 10-17 *Ebbinghaus's forgetting curve. After learning lists of nonsense syllables, Ebbinghaus studied how long it took to relearn each list from 20 minutes to 30 days later. He found that retention of this novel information drops quickly, then levels out.*

A modern-day descendant of the Ebbinghaus tradition, Harry Bahrick (1984b), examined the forgetting curve for Spanish learned in school. Bahrick used the cross-sectional method (see p. 106), by comparing the knowledge of Spanish among people who had just taken Spanish with that of those who had studied Spanish up to 50 years previously. Compared to those just completing a high school or college Spanish course, those who had been out of school for 3 years had forgotten much of what they had learned (Figure 10-18). However, after about 3 to 5 years, forgetting stopped; what people remembered at that point they still remembered a quarter-century later, even if they had not used their Spanish at all.

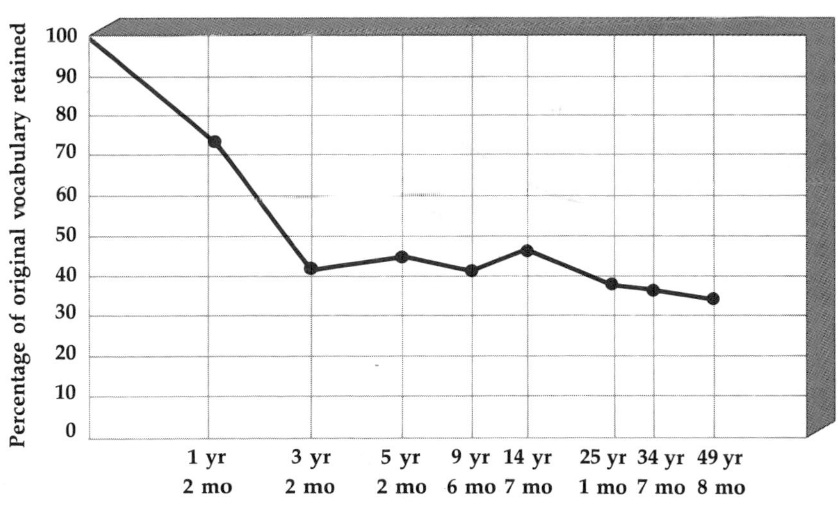

Figure 10-18 *The forgetting curve for Spanish vocabulary. Compared to people just completing a Spanish course, those 3 years out of the course remember much less. Compared to the 3-year group, however, those who studied Spanish even longer ago exhibit little more forgetting.*

Decay

One possible explanation for these forgetting curves is that a physical memory trace gradually fades for a time. Earlier we noted the decay of iconic memory, a decay that occurs so rapidly that by the time the letters of one row of an array are read the rest have vanished. Too little is known about the physical basis of memory to evaluate the physical ***decay*** of memory. But what we do know suggests that memories fade, not merely because the trace fades as time passes, but because of other disruptions that happen with time.

Another type of fixation, referred to by the appropriate but awkward label ***functional fixedness,*** is our tendency to perceive the functions of objects as fixed and unchanging. A person may see a dime as a coin, and not as a needed screwdriver. You may have experienced functional fixedness when you tried to solve the candle problem. If you thought of the matchbox as having only the function of holding matches, you may have overlooked its potential for serving as a platform for the candle, as shown in Figure 11-8. Indeed, perceiving and relating familiar things in new ways is an important aspect of creative thinking, a topic we will discuss in Chapter 12, "Intelligence."

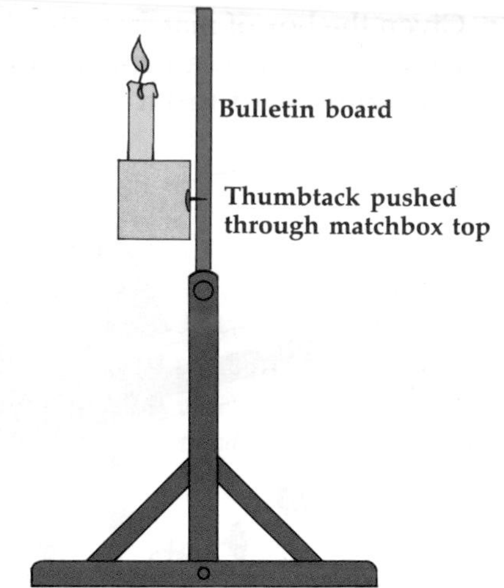

Figure 11-8 *Solving the candle-mounting problem requires recognizing that a box need not always serve as a container.*

Insight

Having now learned about some of the simple but powerful obstacles to thinking logically, you may be beginning to have some doubts about our species' reasoning abilities. Despite these obstacles, we do pretty well at solving problems. In fact, we can all recall times when we have puzzled over a problem for some time and then, suddenly, everything fit together and we perceived the solution. This facility for sudden flashes of inspiration that allow us to solve problems, often in novel ways, is commonly referred to as ***insight.***

Occasional examples of insight have been documented in animals. One notable instance was recorded by the German Gestalt psychologist Wolfgang Köhler (1925). During World War I, Köhler found himself on a remote African island and turned to studying the resident chimpanzees. In one experiment with a chimp named Sultan, he placed a piece of fruit and a long stick outside the chimp's cage, well beyond the chimp's reach, and placed a short stick inside the cage. Spying the short stick, Sultan grabbed it and tried to reach the fruit with it. But the stick, by design, was too short. After several unsuccessful attempts, the chimp dropped the stick and paused to survey the whole situation. Then suddenly, as if thinking, "Aha!," Sultan jumped up, seized the short stick again and this time used it to pull in the longer stick—which he then used to reach the fruit (Figure 11-9). Sultan's actions were stunning proof of animal cognition, claimed Köhler, as well as further evidence that there is more to learning than mindless conditioning.

Figure 11-9 *Chimpanzee problem-solving. In a moment of apparent insight, the chimpanzee uses a shorter stick to reach a stick long enough to reach the fruit.*

Even pigeons appear to be capable of insight. Robert Epstein and his associates (1984) trained some pigeons to perform three separate acts—

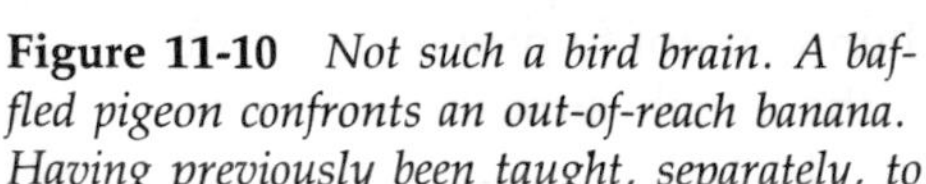

Figure 11-10 *Not such a bird brain. A baffled pigeon confronts an out-of-reach banana. Having previously been taught, separately, to push boxes, climb on boxes, and peck bananas, the pigeon suddenly solves the problem by integrating the three behaviors.*

pecking a banana, moving a box, and climbing up on the box. When these pigeons were later confronted with a banana that had been placed out of reach, they initially appeared to be confused. Then, after looking back and forth from the banana to the box several times, they suddenly pushed the box under the banana, climbed up on the box, and pecked the banana (see Figure 11-10).

What makes for an occasional anecdote about the animal world is fairly commonplace in human experience. Köhler described insight as the sense of satisfaction that accompanies such flashes of inspiration. Satisfying insights are familiar to you from moments when you have solved a difficult math problem, realized how you could organize a term paper, or even hit upon the solutions to some of the problems posed in this chapter.

The joy of a joke may similarly lie in our capacity for insight—in our suddenly comprehending an unexpected ending or a double meaning, as in the story of Professor Smith, who complained to his colleagues that student interruptions had become a problem. "The minute I get up to speak," he explained, "some fool begins to talk."

Making Decisions and Forming Judgments

Our lives are shaped by our everyday decisions—whom to date, where to go to school, what career to work toward, how to vote, where to live. Likewise, the judgments we make and the opinions we hold color our lives and lead us to seek out or avoid particular people and experiences.

If we were perfectly rational and had limitless time we might make decisions as professional gamblers do, by weighing the value of each possible outcome after adjusting for its likelihood. Mathematically, at least, a 50 percent chance of winning $10 has the same value as a sure $5.

Making Sound Decisions

Psychologists Daniel Wheeler and Irving Janis (1980) studied how people arrive at good and bad decisions and devised a system for making a wise decision when faced with a challenge. They recommend proceeding systematically through five stages:

1. **Accept the challenge. If the opportunity or the problem is genuine, do not ignore it, do not rationalize ("It can't happen to me"), do not procrastinate (I'll deal with it later"), do not buck-pass ("let George do it"), and do not panic.**
2. **Search for alternatives. Specify your goals and think up ways to achieve them.**
3. **Evaluate the alternatives. For each reasonable alternative, fill out a balance sheet, such as the one in Figure 11-11. List positive and negative considerations in several categories. Wheeler and Janis reported that people who do so tend later to express fewer regrets and to remain more strongly committed to their choice.**
4. **Make a commitment. Choose the alternative that gives you maximum benefits at minimum costs.**
5. **Adhere to the decision. Anticipate likely difficulties and prepare to deal with them. Assess the consequences and begin the next decision cycle, by accepting the challenge of new problems and opportunities.**

Pros	Cons
1. Gains for self:	1. Losses for self:
2. Gains for others:	2. Losses for others:
3. Self-approval:	3. Self-disapproval:
4. Social approval:	4. Social disapproval:

Figure 11-11 *Wheeler and Janis's balance sheet for decision making. Filling in the boxes helps people to think through important decisions, evaluating alternatives more logically.*

When making very important decisions, such as what career to prepare for or where to live, it may indeed pay to systematically list and weigh the pros and cons, perhaps using the sort of procedure described in "Making Sound Decisions." But for dozens of decisions we face every day, we need to react more swiftly.

Using and Misusing Heuristics

When making each day's hundreds of tiny judgments and decisions—Is it worth the bother to buckle my seat belt? Who's the smartest person in my psychology class? Should I study tonight or go to a movie?—we seldom pause to reason systematically. Usually, we follow our intuition. So, just how trustworthy is our intuition? Usually it is pretty good, as we saw in our consideration of those rules of thumb that we called heuristics. Although heuristics often enable us to make reasonably accurate snap judgments, the price we pay for their cognitive efficiency can sometimes be costly bad judgments. To gain a sense of how heuristics determine our intuitive judgments—and how they can lead us astray—consider two heuristics that were identified by cognitive psychologists Amos Tversky and Daniel Kahneman (1974): the *representativeness heuristic* and the *availability heuristic.*

The representativeness heuristic To experience the representativeness heuristic, answer the following question (adapted from Nisbett & Ross, 1980):

> A stranger tells you about a person who is short, slim, and likes to read poetry, and then asks you to guess whether this person is more likely to be a professor of classics at an Ivy League university or a truck driver. Which would be the better guess?

If you are like most people, you answered a professor because the description is more *representative* of your image of the typical Ivy League scholar than it is of a truck driver. To judge the likelihood of things in terms of how well they represent particular prototypes, such as professor and truck driver, is to use the ***representativeness heuristic.*** The heuristic is a quick and easy way to make a snap judgment. But it does ignore other relevant information, such as the total number of classics professors and truck drivers. When I talk with people about this question and invite them to consider other such information, their own reasoning usually leads them to an answer that contradicts their intuition. The typical conversation goes something like this:

> ***Questioner:*** *First, let's figure out how many professors fit the description. How many Ivy League universities do you suppose there are?*
>
> ***Answerer:*** *Oh, about ten, I suppose.*
>
> ***Questioner:*** *How many classics professors would you guess there are at each?*
>
> ***Answerer:*** *Maybe four.*
>
> ***Questioner:*** *Okay, that's forty Ivy League classics professors. What fraction of these are short and slim?*
>
> ***Answerer:*** *Let's say half.*
>
> ***Questioner:*** *And, of these twenty, how many like to read poetry?*
>
> ***Answerer:*** *I'd say half—ten professors.*
>
> ***Questioner:*** *Okay, now let's figure how many truck drivers fit the description. How many truck drivers do you suppose there are?*

"The information-processing shortcuts—called heuristics—which are normally both highly efficient and immensely time-saving in day-to-day situations, work systematically against us in the marketplace . . . The tendency to underestimate or altogether ignore past probabilities in making a decision is undoubtedly the most significant problem of intuitive prediction in fields as diverse as financial analysis, accounting, geography, engineering, and military intelligence. The implications of such consistent errors and cognitive biases are enormous, not only in economics, management, and investments, but in virtually every area where such decision-making comes into play."
David Dreman,
Contrarian Investment Strategy: The Psychology of Stock Market Success, 1979

Answerer: *Maybe 400,000.*

Questioner: *What fraction are short and slim?*

Answerer: *Not many—perhaps 1 in 8.*

Questioner: *Of these 50,000, what percent like to read poetry?*

Answerer: *Truck drivers who like poetry? Maybe 1 in 100—oh, oh, I can see where this is going—that leaves me with 500 short, slim, poetry-reading truck drivers.*

Questioner: *Yup. So we see that though the person I described may be much more representative of classics professors than of truck drivers, this person is still (even accepting your stereotypes) fifty times more likely to be a truck driver.*

Had the question explicitly reminded you to consider the number of classics professors and truck drivers, would you have responded differently? Probably not. To see why, consider the question that Tversky and Kahneman (1980) asked a group of college students:

> A panel of psychologists interviewed a sample of 30 engineers and 70 lawyers, and summarized their impressions in thumbnail descriptions of those individuals. The following description has been drawn at random from the sample of 30 engineers and 70 lawyers.
>
> "John is a 39-year-old man. He is married and has two children. He is active in local politics. The hobby that he most enjoys is rare book collection. He is competitive, argumentative, and articulate." *Question:* What is the probability that this is a lawyer rather than an engineer?

Most students said the odds were better than 90 percent that this argumentative, political person was a lawyer. How do you think the estimates changed when the question was changed to say that 70 percent of the sample were engineers? Not at all. In the students' minds, John was more representative of lawyers than engineers, and that was all that seemed to matter. Given an opportunity to use the representativeness heuristic, people usually disregard other relevant information.

To sense the power of the representativeness heuristic consider one more of Tversky and Kahneman's (1983) experiments. College students were told that "Bill is 34 years old. He is intelligent, but unimaginative, compulsive, and generally lifeless. In school, he was strong in mathematics but weak in social studies and humanities." Based on this description, the students judged that there was virtually no chance that "Bill plays jazz for a hobby." But 87 percent thought there was a somewhat better chance that "Bill is an accountant who plays jazz for a hobby" (because Bill seemed more representative of accountants). If that seems logical, think about it—is there a better chance that Bill *both* plays jazz *and* is an accountant than that he plays jazz?

"In creating these problems, we didn't set out to fool people. All our problems fooled us, too."
Amos Tversky (1985)

These examples all point to the power of the representativeness heuristic. To judge the likelihood of something we intuitively compare it to our mental representation of a prototype of that category—of, say, what a truck driver, engineer, or accountant is like. If the two match, then that fact usually overrides any other consideration of statistics or logic.

The Availability Heuristic A similar vulnerability to error stems from our use of the ***availability heuristic,*** which leads us to base our judgments on the availability of information in our memories. If instances of something come to mind readily, we tend to presume that the event is commonplace. Usually it is—but not always. To see this, guess—or ask someone else to guess—whether the letter "k" appears more often as the first letter of words or as the third letter.

Because words beginning with "k" come to mind more easily than words having "k" as their third letter, most people guess that "k" occurs more frequently as the first letter. In fact, though, "k" is three times more likely to appear as the third letter. So far in this chapter, words such as "know," "kingdoms," and "kin" are outnumbered more than 2 to 1 by words such as "make," "likely," "asked," and "acknowledged."

The judgmental errors caused by the availability heuristic are usually harmless, but occasionally they are not. Many important decisions involve judgments of risk. For instance, the decision whether to produce energy with nuclear power or by burning coal depends in part on our judgments of the risks associated with each. Our support for, or opposition to, spending tax dollars on social services is influenced by our judgment of the frequency of welfare fraud. Our efforts to cure or prevent various deadly diseases depend on our judgments of the likelihood of their occurrence.

"Numerous studies show that people (including experts) have great difficulty judging probabilities, making predictions, and otherwise attempting to cope with uncertainty. Frequently these difficulties can be traced to the use of judgmental heuristics, which serve as general strategies for simplifying complex tasks."
Paul Slovic, Baruch Fischoff, and Sarah Lichtenstein (1985)

Those who sell life, health, and theft insurance sometimes exploit our tendency to presume that such events are more likely if we can readily picture them (Cialdini & Carpenter, 1981). By having people imagine their families without them, their cars totaled, or their possessions stolen, sellers of insurance may cause the images of these disasters to linger in people's memories, making them seem more likely to occur and therefore worth insuring against.

The availability heuristic can also affect our social judgments. In one study (Hamill & others, 1980), people were presented with a single, vivid case of the misuse of welfare. The case involved a ne'er-do-well woman who had a number of unruly children fathered by different men. The subjects of the study were more persuaded by this single memorable case than by statistics indicating that the case was the exception—that in fact, in the 10 years from 1969 to 1979, more than 9 in 10 Americans who received welfare assistance were *not* persistently dependent on welfare income for more than 7 of the 10 years (Duncan, 1984).

Likewise, in choosing courses, students have been found to be more influenced by two or three in-person testimonials about a course than by the statistically summarized evaluations of a large number of students (Borgida & Nisbett, 1977). An anecdote, it almost seems, is worth a thousand factual statistics.

"The human understanding is most excited by that which strikes and enters the mind at once and suddenly, and by which the imagination is immediately filled and inflated. It then begins almost imperceptibly to conceive and suppose that everything is similar to the few objects which have taken possession of the mind."
Francis Bacon,
Novum Organum, 1620

Overconfidence

Our tendencies to use quick and easy heuristics when forming judgments and to seek confirmation rather than refutation of our hypotheses can give rise to the ***overconfidence phenomenon,*** an overestimation of the accuracy of our current knowledge.

Kahneman and Tversky (1979) asked people to answer factual questions similar to the following: "I feel 98 percent certain that the number of nuclear power plants operating in the world in 1980 was more than _____ but less than _____." Nearly a third of the time, the correct answer to such questions (189 nuclear power plants for this question) lies outside the range about which people feel 98 percent confident. This finding suggests that we often fail to recognize the extent of our susceptibility to errors.

Similarly, people tend to underestimate their potential for errors when answering such questions as "Is absinthe a liqueur or a precious stone?" On a question where their answers to a question are only 60 percent correct, people will typically feel 75 percent confident of those answers. (In case you are wondering, absinthe is a licorice-flavored liqueur.) Even when people feel 100 percent sure of an answer, they still err about 15 percent of the time (Fischoff & others, 1977).

"What do you mean 'Your guess is as good as mine'? My guess is a hell of a lot *better* than your guess!"

The human tendency to feel more confident than warranted is commonplace in both the scientific laboratory and in everyday life. However, like all of the cognitive limitations we have studied so far, it probably has adaptive value. People's failure to appreciate their potential for error when making military, economic, or political judgments can have devastating consequences, but so too can the lack of self-confidence. People who doubt their own capacities may shrink from speaking up or making tough decisions. Moreover, when people are given prompt and clear feedback on the accuracy of their judgments—as weather forecasters are after each day's prediction—they soon learn to estimate the accuracy of their judgments more realistically (Fischhoff, 1982). The wisdom to know when we know a thing and when we do not is born of experience.

Framing Decisions

A further test of rationality in making decisions and forming judgments is whether the same question, posed in two different but obviously equal ways, will trigger the same answer. For example, when we are told either that 10 percent will die or that 90 percent will live as a result of a particular medical treatment, the information is the same. But the effect is not. The risk seems greater when we hear that 10 percent will die. This effect of the way a decision is posed is known as ***framing.***

Kahneman and Tversky (1984) explored the effects of framing. In one study, they set up situations such as the following:

> Imagine that the United States is preparing for the outbreak of an unusual Asian disease which is expected to kill 600 people. Two alternative programs to combat the disease have been proposed.

They then presented their subjects with these two alternatives:

> If Program A is adopted, 200 people will be saved.
>
> If Program B is adopted, there is ⅓ probability that 600 people will be saved, and ⅔ probability that no people will be saved.

The subjects favored Program A by about 3 to 1, reasoning that it is better to save those lives that can be saved than to choose the ⅔ chance that no one will be saved. The researchers then rephrased the alternatives for another group of subjects:

> If Program A is adopted, 400 people will die.
>
> If Program B is adopted, there is ⅓ probability that nobody will die, and ⅔ probability that 600 people will die.

This time, the subjects favored Program B by 3 to 1, reasoning that it is better to gamble on saving everyone than to consign 400 people to certain death.

Similarly, if our dentist offers a 5 percent discount for immediate cash payment, we do not feel particularly unhappy if we have to pay the full fee when making a late payment. However, if the basic fee were to be lowered by 5 percent and an equivalent surcharge were to be added for later payment, we would probably feel irritated, even though the late payment would result in exactly the same fee as in the first case. The way a situation is framed can make an enormous difference in the way we react. The fact that people's judgments flip-flop so dramatically, even on problems involving life and death, is a bit scary. It suggests that our judgments and the decisions based on them may not be well-reasoned, and that those who understand the power of framing might use it to influence our decisions.

Reasoning

In order to solve problems, make decisions, and form judgments, we must first be able to reason. How, and how well, do we do so? Let us consider the ways humans reason, and some reasons for unreason.

The skills involved in playing chess include a well-practiced ability to reason deductively (from the rules of the game) and inductively (generalizing from past experiences).

Deductive and Inductive Reasoning

Our reasoning takes two forms: deductive reasoning and inductive reasoning. In ***deductive reasoning,*** we begin with assumptions or general truths that we know or believe to be true and then use them to arrive at particular conclusions. For instance, we know as a general truth that all cats meow. We are therefore justified in concluding that Cinder, a cat we do not know, will meow. If the assumptions we begin with are indeed true and if our reasoning is valid, then our conclusions must be true. Mathematics, some forms of theology, and law are mostly deductive.

In ***inductive reasoning,*** we arrive at a conclusion based on our observations. Inductive reasoning works from the "bottom up," by *generalizing from instances.* For instance, if every cat we have ever seen meows, then we can reasonably conclude that Cinder, our friend's new cat, will meow, too. However, with inductive reasoning, we can never be completely sure that our conclusion is correct. There is always the chance that we will meet a cat that does not meow. Furthermore, if that ever happens, we will then know that our conclusion was wrong. Basically, then, inductive reasoning is hypothesis testing.

As Diane Halpern (1984) has pointed out, in real life we switch back and forth between the two constantly. Furthermore, our beliefs (our general assumptions) influence what we observe, and our observations, in turn, influence what we believe.

The Belief Perseverance Phenomenon

Our beliefs have a tremendous impact on our reasoning abilities. Indeed, a major source of irrationality in our reasoning is our tendency, called the ***belief perseverance phenomenon,*** to cling to our beliefs even in the face of contrary evidence.

In both science and everyday experience, our beliefs operate like a telescope that selectively brings certain parts of the world into view. Thus, they can powerfully affect what we notice, how we interpret what we notice, and what we remember. In earlier chapters, for instance, we noted how our preconceptions can bias (or "set") our visual perceptions. We also saw that believers in paranormal phenomena tend to notice and remember incidents that support their beliefs—a dream that comes true, perhaps—and to ignore and forget incidents that refute them—all those dreams that do not come true.

The perseverance of our beliefs often fuels social conflict. Charles Lord and his colleagues (1979) demonstrated how this can happen. To two groups of college students, one that favored capital punishment and one that opposed it, they showed two purportedly new research studies. One of the studies supported and the other refuted the crime-deterring effectiveness of the death penalty. Each side positively evaluated the study that supported its beliefs but disputed the study that contradicted them. Showing the two groups the *identical* body of mixed evidence therefore did not narrow their disagreement but actually *increased* it.

For those who wish to restrain the irrational effects of the belief perseverance phenomenon, a simple remedy exists: *Consider the opposite.* When Charles Lord and his colleagues (1984) repeated the capital punishment study, they added a couple of variations. They asked some of their

"Once you have a belief, it influences how you perceive all other relevant information. Once you see a country as hostile, you are likely to interpret ambiguous actions on their part as signifying their hostility. A more neutral observer might see many other possible explanations.

In the political arena, people don't realize how their opinions shape their conclusions. They see all information as independent confirmations of their view, not realizing—as cognitive psychologists have shown—that their bias preselects the information they notice and determines how they will construe it."

Political scientist Robert Jervis (1985)

subjects to be "as *objective* and *unbiased* as possible." The people who received this plea turned out to be every bit as biased in their evaluation of the evidence as those who did not. A third group, however, was asked to consider the opposite—to ask themselves "whether you would have made the same high or low evaluations had exactly the same study produced results on the *other* side of the issue." Having considered the possibility of opposite findings, these people were much less likely to be biased in their evaluations of the evidence for and against their own views.

If ambiguous evidence gets interpreted as supporting a person's preexisting belief, would the belief be demolished by information that clearly discredits its premises? Not necessarily. In some provocative experiments, Craig Anderson and Lee Ross discovered that it can be surprisingly difficult to change a false belief once a person has in mind some ideas in support of it. In one such study with Mark Lepper (1980), the researchers asked subjects to consider whether risk-prone people or cautious people make better fire fighters. Half of the subjects were shown a case about a risk-taker who was an excellent fire fighter and a case about a cautious person who was a poor fire fighter. From these cases, the subjects surmised that risk-prone people tend to make better fire fighters. When they were asked to explain the reason for their belief, a typical response was, "Risk-takers are braver." The other subjects were shown two cases suggesting the opposite conclusion, that cautious people make better fire fighters. They typically reasoned, "Cautious people think before they act, and so are less likely to make foolish mistakes."

The researchers then totally discredited the foundation for the beliefs of both groups by truthfully informing them that the cases were simply made up for the experiment. How much do you suppose this information undermined the subjects' newly formed beliefs? Not much. The subjects tended to hold on to their explanations for *why* these new beliefs made sense. Paradoxically, then, the more we come to appreciate why our beliefs *might* be true, the more tightly we cling to them. Once people have explained to themselves why they believe that a child is "gifted" or "learning disabled," that presidential candidate X or Y will be more likely to preserve peace or start a war, or that women are naturally superior or inferior, they tend to ignore evidence that undermines that belief.

The point of this discussion of the belief perseverance phenomenon is not that people never change their beliefs. Rather, it is simply that once beliefs are formed and justified, it may take more compelling evidence to change them than it did to create them.

Do risk-prone or cautious people make better fire fighters? Once you have been persuaded to have an opinion on such a question, and can cite some reasons for your view, you are likely to be reluctant to change it, even if shown that the information on which you formed your opinion is invalid.

"To begin with it was only tentatively that I put forward the views I have developed . . . but in the course of time they have gained such a hold upon me that I can no longer think in any other way."
Sigmund Freud,
Civilization and Its Discontents, 1930

Formal Deductive Reasoning

We have seen that part of the new thinking about thinking emphasizes our susceptibility to bias. We search for information that would support our hunches (confirmation bias) and we cling to our beliefs even when confronted with mixed evidence or discrediting information (belief perseverance). By reasoning with the tools of formal logic, can we escape the effects of our beliefs on our reasoning? Let us see.

In philosophy, the ***syllogism***—an argument in which two presumably true statements, called premises, lead to a third statement, the conclusion—is the basis of formal deductive reasoning. For instance, consider the following famous syllogism:

All humans are mortal.
Socrates is human.
Therefore, Socrates is mortal.

"Marry me, Sandra, and share my preconceptions."

Most all of us are rational enough to realize that the conclusion of this syllogism logically follows from the premises.

Sometimes, however, our preexisting knowledge and beliefs interfere with our ability to think logically. For example, take a look at the following syllogism (adapted from Hunt, 1982a):

> Those who believe in democracy believe in free speech.
> Communists do not believe in democracy.
> Therefore, Communists do not believe in free speech.

Does the conclusion sound logical? If so, consider another syllogism with the same form and logic:

> Robins have feathers.
> Chickens are not robins.
> Therefore, chickens do not have feathers.

In both cases the reasoning is invalid; the conclusion does not follow from the premises. Now, try this syllogism:

> Whatever makes for full employment is socially beneficial.
> War makes for full employment.
> Therefore, war is socially beneficial.

In this case, the conclusion does logically follow from the premises. What is wrong is not the reasoning but the false assumption of the first premise.

The syllogisms we have just examined illustrate some of the ways our knowledge and beliefs can bias our reasoning. We tend to accept as logical those conclusions that may agree with our opinions, such as the idea that communism restricts freedom. But we have a harder time accepting conclusions that run counter to our opinions, such as the idea that war is beneficial. This belief bias can cause serious problems, particularly when we are facing challenging issues that involve our beliefs.

The perils of invalid reasoning are apparent in the argument that has frequently been advanced to "prove" the intellectual inferiority of blacks and other ethnic groups. This argument can be stated as the following syllogism:

> If blacks are mentally inferior to whites, they will have lower average IQ scores than whites.
> Blacks do have lower average IQ scores than whites.
> Therefore, blacks are mentally inferior to whites.

Although the reasoning in this syllogism is no more valid than in the "chickens do not have feathers" example (blacks could have lower scores for other reasons, such as poorer schooling), the widespread acceptance of this false syllogism has encouraged the very discriminatory practices that have tended to put blacks at a disadvantage on traditional intelligence tests. (We will examine this issue more closely in the next chapter, which deals with intelligence.)

In Defense of Our Thinking Abilities

We have seen how our irrationality, our lapses in logic, can foil our attempts at solving problems, making decisions, forming judgments, and even reasoning correctly. From this we might be tempted to conclude that our headpieces are indeed filled with straw. All in all, the findings we have reviewed—and many more that we have not—suggest "bleak implications for human rationality" (Nisbett & Borgida, 1975). Since it may be shocking to realize our capacity for error, what can we say in defense of our thinking abilities? How is it that we generally cope so well? Our cognitive processes have, after all, functioned efficiently and effectively enough to have enabled our survival and given us control over the earth.

One reason we function as well as we do is that flawed reasoning does not always result in false conclusions. Despite the illogic of one syllogistic argument we examined earlier, for instance, communist countries do tend to restrict free speech.

Another reason we thrive despite some flaws in our logic is that we can usually tolerate some inconsistency and uncertainty in our reasoning in exchange for the utility and efficiency of quick, plausible intuitive judgments. Physicians, for example, do not have the time to diagnose by systematic deduction. Instead, they recognize the similarity between a patient's symptoms and those typical of a particular disease and then proceed to check out their hunch. In effect, their reasoning goes like this (Hunt, 1982a):

> Disease X is indicated by symptoms A, B, and C.
> This patient has symptoms A, B, and C.
> Therefore, I presume this patient has disease X.

The physician's conclusion may not be accurate. Yet it is plausible, perhaps even probable. As long as the doctor recognizes that the conclusion might be wrong, it offers an efficient way to proceed. We reason, then, not so much by perfectly rigorous logic as by simplified, speedy ways, such as, "This situation reminds me of similar situations I have faced before, so what was true in those situations ought to be true here." Human reasoning is efficient and normally adaptive.

Still, we should not underestimate the importance of rational reasoning. When engaged in such pursuits as deriving scientific hypotheses, playing chess, or debating political issues, it helps to have the powers of reason at our disposal. This is why one of the most important aspects of a college education is learning how to think logically and critically. It is also the reason psychologists study obstacles to problem solving and biases in reasoning. By learning what our irrationality reveals about how we normally process information, we hope to discover how we might learn to reason more accurately. When necessary, we can solve arithmetic problems efficiently *and* rationally—because we have been taught to do so. Perhaps we could also teach people how to think through other sorts of problems more efficiently and rationally. Indeed, this is one of the goals of Appendix A, which explains some common flaws in people's statistical intuition and suggests some correctives.

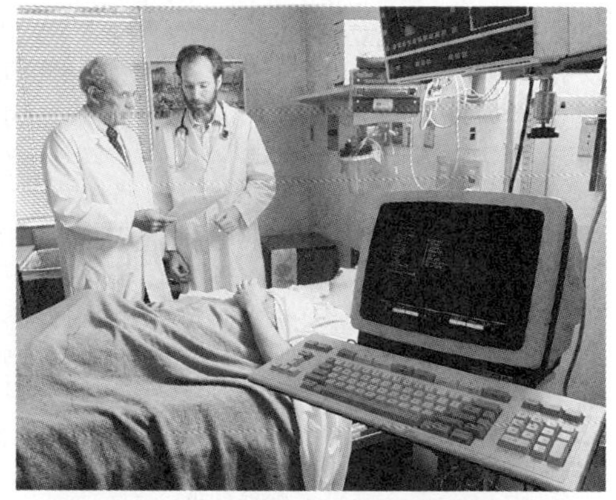

Artificial intelligence is being applied in new expert systems, such as this medical system (dubbed HELP) that tracks patient data and suggests possible diagnoses and treatments. Industrial robots designed to perform routine but often dangerous industrial tasks illustrate another use of artificial intelligence.

Artificial Intelligence

A rather ironic tribute to human cognitive powers comes from using computers to think about thinking. ***Artificial intelligence*** (AI) is the science of making computers perform operations that appear intelligent. A hybrid of cognitive psychology and computer science, AI has moved in two directions, one practical, the other theoretical. The practical efforts have given us chess programs that can beat all but the masters, industrial robots that can sense their environment, and "expert systems" that (thanks to a massive amount of stored information and rules for retrieving it) can carry out chemical analyses and help physicians diagnose their patients' diseases. The theoretical efforts, pioneered by the Nobel Prize winning psychologist Herbert Simon, have involved studying the way humans think, by, for example, attempting to mimic human problem-solving strategies.

Simon's basic assumption is not that the mind is a computer or that computers have minds but rather that, as we noted in the preceding chapter, both are information processors. Both receive the input of information from the environment: The computer uses keyboards, disks, tapes, and the like; our minds use our eyes, our ears, and our other senses. Both store this information in memory, selectively retrieve the stored information as it is needed, and manipulate the information in order to perform specific tasks. And both express the results of their information processing in some type of output: The computer displays output on a screen or printout; we talk and write.

"The computer is claiming *its* intelligence is real, and *ours* is artificial."

Computers can even be programmed to use heuristics, which are in large part responsible for our own cognitive efficiency. For instance, a computer programmed to simulate how a human might solve anagrams—remember the CINERAMA puzzle—can be instructed not to consider letter combinations that begin with, say, "nc" or "rc" since English words never start with these letters. Putting a human problem-solving strategy in the form of a computer program forces the theorist to be extremely precise. If there is any vagueness in the steps included or if any necessary step is left out, the computer will balk.

So, can computers match our thinking powers? In those areas where we seem to have the most difficulty—manipulating large amounts of numerical data or retrieving specific detailed facts from memory, for instance—the computer shines. Indeed, the proficiency of computers in areas such as these has made them almost indispensable to banks, the space program, and even libraries. Ironically, though, the most ordinary human mental abilities—recognizing objects or faces, knowing whether the word "line" refers to a rope or a fragment of poetry or a social come-on, and exercising common sense—dwarf those of the most sophisticated computer. Moreover, notes Donald Griffin (1984), "Human minds do more than process information; they think and feel. We experience beliefs, desires, fears, expectations, and many other subjective mental states."

Imagine a relatively simple task—instructing a computer to discern the difference between these two ads (from Schnitzer, 1984):

1. *Car for sale. A classic! Lemon yellow coupe. Exterior is completely rust-proof. Can be delivered upon request. No engine runs better. If the sun is out, you can remove the roof for the feel of the wind in your hair. Go ahead and kick the tires.*
2. *Car for sale. A classic lemon. Yellow coupe exterior is completely rust. Proof can be delivered upon request! No engine. Runs better if the sun is out. You can remove the roof. For the feel of the wind in your hair, go ahead and kick the tires.*

Consider also the respective modes of operation of the computer and the brain. Electricity races through the computer's microchips millions of times faster than our neurons can transmit information. Yet virtually all computers must process information serially—one step at a time. Serial processing can be likened to a society in which work can be done only by one person at a time. By contrast, the human brain can process millions of different bits of information simultaneously. Here, too, the brain has the computer hopelessly outclassed. Thus the hope for artificial intelligence in the future lies in a new generation of computers that function more like the brain does, by using parallel processing, in which multiple operations can be performed at once (Kurzweil, 1985).

Despite all the amazing things computers can do, what they have done best so far is reaffirm the magnificence of the human mind. Computers provide us with an amazing but narrowly focused intelligence. Their abilities exceed our own at tasks that utilize their unique strengths such as vast memory and precise logic. But they are far from duplicating the wide-ranging intelligence of a human mind, a mind that can *all at once* converse naturally, perceive the environment, use common sense, experience emotion, and consciously reflect on its own existence.

LANGUAGE

Perhaps the most tangible indication of the power of human thinking, and definitely one of our species' greatest achievements, is language. Since antiquity, humans have proudly proclaimed that the ability to speak is what sets us above all other animals. "When we study human language," asserted linguist Noam Chomsky (1972), "we are approaching what some might call the 'human essence,' the distinctive qualities of mind that are, so far as we know, unique to man." Whether spoken, written, or signed, language enables us to communicate complex ideas from person to person and to transmit civilization's accumulated knowledge from generation to generation.

Language enables the transmission of cultural knowledge and lore from generation to generation.

Language Structure

A good way to begin looking at language is to consider how we might go about inventing a language. First, we would need a set of basic sounds, which linguists refer to as ***phonemes.*** These sounds correspond roughly to the letters of the alphabet. For instance, the "b," the "a," and the "t" sounds that we put together to say the word "bat" are all phonemes. So are the "ch" sound in "chat" and the "th" sound in "that." Different languages have different numbers of phonemes. English has about forty; other languages have anywhere from half to twice that many.

Changes in phonemes result in changes in meaning. For example, variations in the vowel sound between a "b" and a "t" can create eleven different meanings: bat, beat, bit, bait, bet, bite, boot, but, boat, bought, and bout (Fromkin & Rodman, 1983). Generally, though, consonant phonemes carry more information than do vowel phonemes: THE TRETH EF THES STETEMENT SHED BE EVEDENT FREM THES BREF DEMENSTRESHEN.

People who grow up learning one set of phonemes may later have difficulty pronouncing the phonemes of another language. Thus, the native English speaker may smile at the native German speaker's difficulties with the "th" sound, which often makes "this" sound like "dis" and "them" like "dem." But the German speaker can smile in turn at the problems English speakers have rolling the German "r" or pronouncing the breathy "ch" in "Ich," the German word for "I."

The next building block of our new language will be ***morphemes,*** which are the smallest units of speech that carry meaning. In English, a very few morphemes are also phonemes—the personal pronoun "I" and the article "a," for instance—but most are combinations of two or more phonemes. "Bat," for example, is a morpheme made up of the phonemes "b," "a," and "t." Most morphemes are words, but some are only parts of words, such as prefixes, suffixes, the "-ed" that shows past tense, or the "-s" that shows plurals. The word "undesirables," for example, has four morphemes—"un," "desire," "able," and "s." As you can see, each of these morphemes adds to the total meaning of the word.

Question: *How many morphemes are in the word "cats"?*
Answer: *Two—"cat," and "s."*

Lastly, our new language must have a ***grammar,*** a system of rules that enables us to use our language to speak to and understand others. Two important aspects of grammar are semantics and syntax. ***Semantics*** refers to the system of rules we use to derive meaning from morphemes, words, and even sentences. These rules tell us that our barking household pet is a "dog" or that adding "-ed" to "laugh" means that it happened in the past. ***Syntax*** is the system of rules we use to string words together into proper sentences. For example, one of the rules of English syntax says that adjectives normally come before nouns, so we say "white house." In Spanish, the rule is different; adjectives normally come after nouns, so a Spanish speaker says "casa blanca." Another rule of English syntax says that subjects normally precede verbs and objects normally follow verbs, as in the sentence, "Mary (the subject) sees (the verb) the dog (the object)."

For a better sense of the importance of grammar, consider the following sentence: "They are hunting dogs." The English rules of syntax tells us that the sentence is a proper one. And, given the context in which the sentence was spoken, semantics tells us whether it refers to people who are looking for some dogs or to dogs that like to look for rabbits.

While we were looking at the building blocks of our language, you probably noticed that language becomes more complex at each succeeding level. In English, the relatively small number of forty or so phonemes can be combined to form more than 100,000 morphemes, which alone or in combination can give us more than half a million words. These words can then be used to create an infinite number of sentences, most of which, like this one, are original. Like the brain that conceives it, language is complexity built of simplicity.

You probably know 50,000 or more words, but you use only 150 words for about half of what you say.

Language Development

What human achievement is more remarkable than the acquisition of language? Before children can add 2 plus 2, they are already creating their own original and grammatically appropriate sentences, and they understand more complex sentences than they can yet speak. Furthermore, the typical 6-year-old's ability to recognize some 8000 or more root words is evidence of a remarkable facility for learning words (Carey, 1977). Indeed, it has been estimated that 3-year-olds acquire several new words every day! How does this facility for language unfold, and how can we explain it?

Describing Language Development

The way a child's language develops mirrors our conception of how language itself is constructed—by moving from simplicity to complexity. Beginning at about 3 or 4 months of age, babies enter a ***babbling stage,*** in which they spontaneously utter a variety of sounds. Babbling is not the imitation of adult speech, for it includes phonemes of various languages, even phonemes that do not occur in the language of the household. From this early babbling, a listener could not identify an infant as being, say, French, Russian, or British. Moreover, deaf infants also babble, even though they obviously cannot be imitating speech they have heard (Fromkin & Rodman, 1983). This suggests that the playful babble may be preprogrammed into the brain.

Babbling is responsive to input from the environment, however. Increasingly, it comes to resemble the characteristic sounds and intonations of the household language. By 10 months of age, an infant's babbling will be identifiably French, Russian, or English, and those phonemes that are foreign to the infant's native tongue will have begun to disappear.

The tendency of babbling infants to begin selectively reproducing the sounds they hear parallels the development of song in birds. By depriving white-crowned sparrows of exposure to normal song during different periods after hatching, psychologist Peter Marler (1970) observed that 10 to 50 days of age is a critical period for song development. The birds are born with a predisposition to make the sounds of their species, but it is during this critical period that they learn their local dialect. Although Marler does not equate bird song with human language, he suspects their early development has similarities: Young sparrows and humans are both genetically predisposed to attend to and produce their species' sounds, and both seem to learn the specific sounds of their local dialect by matching the sounds they make to those they hear and remember.

About the time of the first birthday (the exact age varies from child to child and is not closely linked with the child's later intelligence), most children enter the ***one-word stage.*** Having already learned that sounds can be linked with meanings, they begin to use sounds to communicate meaning. Their first words usually contain but one syllable—"ma" or "da," for instance—and may be barely recognizable. But family members quickly learn to understand the infant's language, and gradually the infant's language conforms more and more to the family's.

Children have a remarkable ability first to reproduce the sounds they hear and then to learn words and grammatical rules.

Most of the child's first words refer to things that move or can be played with—things such as a ball or a dog, rather than the table or crib that just sits there (Nelson, 1973). At this one-word stage, a word may equal a sentence. "Doggy!" may mean "Look at the dog out there!"

Although some children *begin* speaking in phrases (Nelson, 1981), most children accumulate more and more single words during the second year, until finally, at about the second birthday (again, this varies), they rather abruptly start uttering two-word sentences. This ***two-word stage*** exemplifies ***telegraphic speech,*** because, like telegrams (TERMS ACCEPTED. SEND MONEY.), it contains mostly nouns and verbs ("More juice"). Also like telegrams, there is already syntax; the words are in a sensible order. For instance, they will typically say "big doggie" instead of "doggie big," indicating that they already know that adjectives come before rather than after nouns.

There seems to be no "three-word stage." Once children—after another half year or so—move out of the two-word stage, they quickly begin uttering three, four, five, or even more words together (Fromkin & Rodman, 1983). Although the sentences may still sound like a Western Union message, they continue to follow the rules of syntax, such as putting subjects in front of verbs and objects after verbs: "Mommy get ball." The remarkable explosion of complexity has begun, and by early elementary school the child is comprehending complex sentences and beginning to enjoy the humor conveyed by double meanings: "You never starve in the desert because of all the sand-which-is there."

Explaining Language Development

Those who study children's acquisition of language inevitably wonder how they do it. The question is not an easy one to answer, and the attempts that have been made have sparked a spirited intellectual controversy. Basically, this controversy parallels the debate we noted in Chapter 9, "Learning," over the behaviorist's view of the malleable organism versus the contrasting view that each organism is biologically prepared to learn certain associations.

According to behaviorists such as B. F. Skinner (1957), the acquisition of language can be explained by such familiar learning principles as association (of the sights of things with the sounds of words), imitation (of the words and syntax modeled by others), and reinforcement (with success, smiles, and hugs when saying something right). Thus, the behaviorists argue, babies learn to talk in many of the same ways that animals learn to peck keys and press bars.

"Verbal behavior evidently came into existence when, through a critical step in the evolution of the human species, the vocal musculature became susceptible to operant conditioning."
B. F. Skinner (1985)

To linguist Noam Chomsky (1959, 1975), this view of language learning is simplistic and naive. Granted, children do learn the language of their environment. But the feats of language acquisition are far too extraordinary to be explained by learning principles alone. For instance, children create all sorts of sentences they have never before heard, and many of their errors tend to result from the application of logical, though still somewhat inaccurate, grammatical rules. The child who says, "She swimmed across the pool," is not imitating anyone. Rather, the child is overgeneralizing the grammatical rule that says the past tense is normally formed by adding -ed to the verb. Indeed, when one thinks about it, this mistake is really testimony to children's amazing facility for language. Most parents could not state the intricate rules of grammar, yet their children quickly learn to use them without any formal training. Chomsky argues that the ease with which children soak up complex language, even while still unable to tie their shoelaces, suggests that we are biologically prepared to learn language.

Drawing by Glenn Bernhardt

"No, Timmy, not 'I sawed the chair.' It's 'I saw the chair' or 'I have seen the chair.'"

Although most language experts agree that our brains are prepared to learn language, not even Chomsky contends that language is innate. Children who are raised in isolation from language do not spontaneously speak words and sentences. Consider Genie, a 13-year-old who had spent most of her life tied to a chair without being spoken to. When she was discovered by Los Angeles authorities, she was mute and uncomprehending (Curtiss, 1977). Since being found, Genie has learned some aspects of language, but still cannot construct elaborate sentences. This may be because she did not learn language during the critical years for language development.

To recapitulate, children are biologically prepared to learn language as they and their caregivers interact. The behaviorists' emphasis on learning principles helps to explain why infants acquire their parents' language and how they add new words to their vocabularies. Chomsky's emphasis on our built-in readiness to learn grammatical rules helps explain why preschoolers acquire language so readily and use grammar so well. Once again we see biology and experience working together.

Returning to our debate about humanity's intellectual powers, we might pause to issue a midterm report card with imaginary grades that suggest researchers' impressions of our relative strengths and weaknesses. On reasoning, both deductive and inductive, our error-prone species might receive a C+. In problem solving, where humans are inventive yet vulnerable to fixation, the researchers would probably award better marks, perhaps a B+. On cognitive efficiency, our "good guess" heuristics earn us an A. And when it comes to learning and using language, the awestruck experts would surely award the human species an A+.

Animal Language

If in our use of language we humans are, as the psalmist rhapsodized, "little less than God," where do other animals fit in the scheme of things? Are they "little less than human"? For many, the answer lies in the extent to which animals share the human capacity for language. Without a doubt, animals communicate with one another. But do they have language?

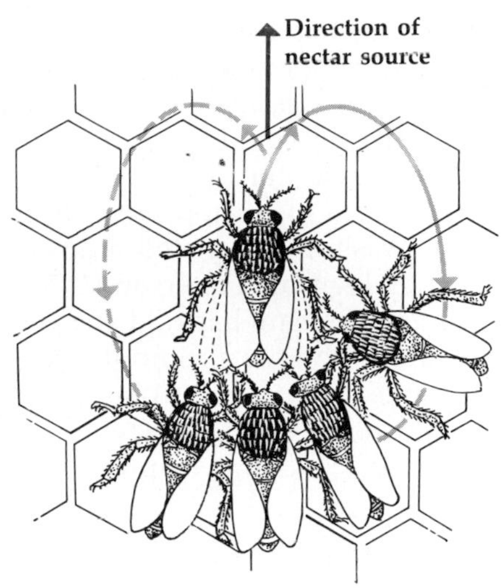

Figure 11-12 *The dance of the honeybee. The straight-line part of the dance points in the direction of a nectar source relative to the sun, and its duration indicates the distance. The other bees, who cannot see the dance in the dark hive, huddle close in order to feel what is going on.*

The Case of the Honeybee

Consider the humble honeybee. More than 2000 years ago, the Greek philosopher Aristotle observed that once a lone honeybee discovers a source of nectar, other bees soon head out of the hive and straight to the newfound food source. Aristotle surmised that the original explorer must return to the hive and recruit other bees to follow it back to the food. But, surprising as it may seem, Aristotle was wrong. In 1901, a clever German researcher followed the explorer bee back to the hive and trapped it as it left the hive to return to the food source. Although deprived of their guide, the new recruits still flew straight to the nectar.

How did the bees know where to go? This question intrigued Austrian biologist Karl von Frisch (1974) so he undertook some experiments for which he ultimately won the Nobel Prize. The experiments revealed that the explorer bee communicates with the other worker bees by means of an intricate dance. The direction and duration of the dance, he discovered, inform other bees of the direction and distance of the food source (see Figure 11-12).

Impressive as it is, the dance of the honeybee hardly challenges the complexity, flexibility, and power of human language. The honeybee communicates, but not with the words and rules for combining them that make up a language.

The Case of the Apes

A greater challenge to humanity's claim to be the only language-using species has come from recent reports of apes that "talk" with people. One of the earliest studies of the language potential of apes was conducted by psychologists W. N. and L. A. Kellogg (1933). The Kelloggs tried to teach a chimpanzee named Gua to talk by raising him with their son Donald. Donald learned to talk but Gua did not, so Gua was soon sent back to the primate station. Some two decades later, Cathy Hayes (1951) and her husband Keith began a more intensive effort when they adopted a 3-day-old chimp named Viki. After 3 years, Viki could say "Mama," "Papa," "cup," and "up" (at the correct times). Disappointingly, she never learned a fifth word.

Not content with these dismal results, University of Nevada researchers Allen and Beatrice Gardner (1969) wondered whether the chimps' vocal apparatus might have hampered their ability to communicate words. They therefore undertook a study of chimpanzee language potential by attempting to teach a chimp named Washoe sign language, as though she were a deaf human child. After 4 years, Washoe could use 132 signs. The Gardners' announcement that their efforts had succeeded aroused enormous public interest and triggered new investigations of the language potential of apes. One reporter for *The New York Times*, whose first language was sign language because he had been raised by deaf parents, visited Washoe and reported, "Suddenly I realized I was conversing with a member of another species in my native tongue."

Although Donald and the chimpanzee Gua (shown here ready for bed) were raised from infancy together, Gua never learned to speak more than four words.

During the 1970s, further evidence of "ape language" was even more disturbing to those who believed that the capacity for language set the human species apart from all other creatures. Not only could apes use words, but they could also string words together to form intelligible sentences. Washoe, for instance, was quoted as signing, "You me go out, please." Apes even appeared to be capable of combining words creatively. Washoe designated a swan as a "water bird." Koko, a gorilla trained by Francine Patterson (1978) in California, described a Pinocchio doll as an "elephant baby." Lana, a chimpanzee who "talked" by punching buttons wired to a computer that translated her punchings into English, wanted her trainer's orange one day, but she had no word for orange. However, she did know her colors and the word for apple, so she improvised: "? Tim give apple which-is orange" (Rumbaugh, 1977).

The result of studies with Washoe, who was taught sign language, aroused new interest in the language capabilities of chimpanzees.

Lana, another chimpanzee, has learned to "speak" by punching word symbols on a computer console in a coherent order.

But Can Apes Really Talk?

As reports of the language abilities of apes accumulated, it began to seem that they might indeed be "little less than human." Although their vocabularies and sentences were simple compared to human language—corresponding roughly to the capacities of a 2-year-old—apes did seem to share what we humans have considered our unique ability.

But did they? By the late 1970s, the claims of "talking apes" had begun to trigger a chorus of skeptical and sometimes caustic reactions. The ape language researchers were making monkeys out of themselves, said the skeptics. Consider some of their stronger arguments:

"Language is a property of humans. If any other animal had a language capacity, they'd be using it. It's like thinking humans have an undiscovered capacity to fly."
Noam Chomsky (quoted by Wyman, 1983)

> The apes have acquired their limited vocabularies only with great difficulty. They can hardly be compared to human children, who effortlessly soak up dozens of new words each week.
>
> Chimps can make signs or push buttons in sequence to get a reward, but so can pigeons (by pecking a sequence of keys to get grain—Straub & others, 1979), and no one says that the pigeon is "talking."

"If a lion could talk, we could not understand him."
Ludwig Wittgenstein, 1889–1951

While apes can certainly use symbols meaningfully, the evidence is far from convincing that they can equal even a 3-year-old's ability to order words with proper syntax. To a child, "you tickle" and "tickle you" communicate different ideas, but a chimp might use the phrases interchangeably.

After training a chimp whom he named Nim Chimpsky, Herbert Terrace (1979) concluded that much of chimpanzees' signing is nothing more than their imitating their trainer's signs.

Presented with ambiguous information, people tend to see what they want or expect to see. (Recall the demonstrations of perceptual set in Chapter 7, "Perception.") Interpreting chimpanzee signs as language may therefore be little more than wishful thinking on the parts of their trainers, claims Terrace. When Washoe signed "water bird," she was probably just separately naming "water" and "bird," he suggests.

Drawing by Sidney Harris

"Although humans make sounds with their mouths and occasionally look at each other, there is no solid evidence that they actually communicate with each other."

In science as in politics, controversy is the stimulus for progress. The provocative claim that "apes share our capacity for language" and the skeptical rejoinder that "apes no use language" (as Washoe might have put it) have moved psychologists toward a greater appreciation of the remarkable capabilities of the apes on the one hand and of our own genius at using words on the other. Most psychologists agree that, so far as we know, humans alone possess language, if by the term we mean the ability to do all the things humans can do with words. If we mean, more simply, the ability to communicate meaning through the use of symbols (such as spoken words or gestured signs), then apes are capable of it.

On reflection, one of chimpanzee Lana's trainers, Duane Rumbaugh (1983) stated that it is too simplistic to ask, "Do the apes have the capacity for human language—or don't they?" The question allows no in-between answer. Chimpanzees may not use language as well as humans do, but their thinking and communicating abilities continue to impress their trainers. Washoe herself managed to teach 55 words of her sign language vocabulary, which at last report was up to 240 signs, to her foster son Loulis before he received any training from humans. Moreover, Washoe, Loulis, and three other chimps who were trained in sign language now use it spontaneously when communicating with one another (Fouts & others, 1984). Lana's instructors have trained two new chimps, Sherman and Austin, to use computer keyboards to communicate with each other. The chimps will ask one another for a specific food (as shown in Figure 11-13) or even for a tool that can be used to obtain food (Savage-Rumbaugh & others, 1978). And Koko the gorilla not only makes most of her signs spontaneously, she has also been reported to use her sign language to swear, joke, and even lie (Patterson, 1978).

"Man's egocentric view that he is distinctively unique from all other forms of animal life is being jarred to the core."
Duane Rumbaugh and Sue Savage-Rumbaugh (1978)

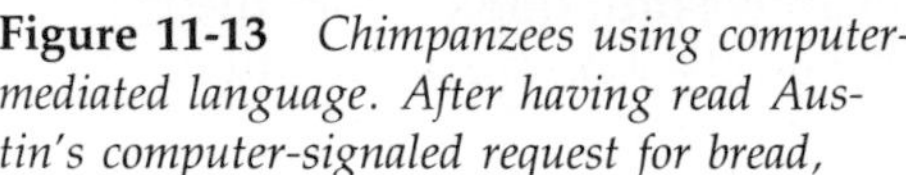

Figure 11-13 *Chimpanzees using computer-mediated language. After having read Austin's computer-signaled request for bread, Sherman selects the correct food from a tray (left). He then hands the food to Austin (center) and licks his fingers (right).*

So, though trained apes have small vocabularies and modest abilities to order words correctly, their language potential seems far greater than we once supposed. However, it would be too much to say that their abilities make apes "little less than human."

THINKING AND LANGUAGE

Thinking and language share the same chapter because they are intricately intertwined. Asking which comes first has become one of psychology's chicken-and-egg questions. Do our ideas come first, and wait for words to name them? Or are our thoughts conceived in words and unthinkable without them?

Linguistic Influences on Thinking

In this century, one advocate of the position that language shapes thought has been linguist Benjamin Lee Whorf, who contended that language determines the way we think. According to Whorf's (1956) ***linguistic relativity hypothesis,*** "Language itself shapes a man's basic ideas." Different languages impose different conceptions of reality, Whorf believed.

Whorf's view of the linkage between language and thought can be seen at the level of individual words. For example, English has only one word for snow, whereas the Eskimo language has a variety of terms that denote various conditions of snow and ice. This, said Whorf, allows the Eskimos to perceive differences in snow that would go unnoticed by people who speak English. The linkage can also be seen at the level of grammar. The Hopi, for instance, have no past tense for their verbs. Therefore, Whorf contended, the Hopi cannot so readily think about the past.

Critics of the idea that language determines thought claim that words reflect rather than create distinctions in the way we think. The Eskimos' very lives depend on their ability to recognize different conditions of snow and ice, so they need different words for these conditions (like skiers who use such terms as "sticky snow" or "powder" to describe the slopes). Just because you lack the Eskimos' rich vocabulary for describing snow does not mean that you are incapable of perceiving these differences, too. Likewise, people who lack our words for shapes and colors nevertheless seem to perceive them much as we do (Rosch, 1974).

Although it may be too strong to say that language determines the very way we think, our words do influence what we think. We therefore do well to choose our words carefully. When people refer to women as "girls"—as in "the girls at the office"—it perpetuates a view of women's status as being menial, does it not? Or consider the generic pronoun "he." Does it make any difference whether we write "A child learns language as *he* interacts with *his* caregivers" or "Children learn language as *they* interact with *their* caregivers"? It is often argued that it makes no difference because every reader knows that "the masculine gender shall be deemed and taken to include females" (as the British Parliament declared in 1850). Besides, gender-linked connotations can be either positive ("A doctor finds his work rewarding") or negative ("A criminal must pay for his crimes").

"All words are pegs to hang ideas on."
Henry Ward Beecher, 1813–1887,
Proverbs from Plymouth Pulpit

But is the generic "he" always taken to include females? Several researchers have concluded that it is not. Janet Hyde (1984), for example, reached this conclusion after she asked children to finish stories for which they were given a first line such as, "When a kid goes to school, _____ often feels excited on the first day." When the blank was filled in with the pronoun "he," the image reflected in the children's stories was nearly always male, whereas "he or she" in the blank resulted in female images about one-third of the time. Studies with adults (for example, Martyna, 1978) have found similar effects of the generic "he."

In addition, people tend to use the generic pronouns selectively, as in "the doctor . . . he" and "the secretary . . . she" (MacKay, 1983). If the generic masculine pronouns were truly gender-free, it should not startle us to hear that "a nurse must answer his calls" or that "man, like other mammals, nurses his young." That we are startled indicates that the "his" carries a gender connotation that clashes with our idea of "nurse."

The power of language to influence thinking is one reason why the enlargement of vocabulary is such a crucial part of education. To expand language is to expand the ability to think. David Premack (1983) reported that language training enhances the ability to think abstractly and to reason by analogy even among chimpanzees. For example, shown a cylinder half-filled with water, a chimp that had not been language trained had difficulty recognizing that half of an apple was more like it than three-fourths of an apple. Chimps could more readily grasp the analogy if they were language-trained. What is true for chimpanzees is more true for humans: *It pays to increase your word power.* This is the reason why most textbooks, including this one, cannot teach new ideas and new ways of thinking without introducing new words to denote them.

Thinking Without Language

So, is thinking simply conversing with ourselves? Without a doubt, putting our ideas into spoken or written words can sharpen them. But are there not times when ideas precede words? To turn the cold water on in your bathroom, in which direction do you turn the handle? To answer this question, you probably thought not in words but with a mental picture. Indeed, when we consider it, thinking in images is not at all uncommon. Artists painting pictures think in images. So do composers, poets, mathematicians, and scientists. Albert Einstein, for instance, reported that he achieved some of his greatest insights in the form of visual images. Only later did he put them into words. Words were the containers for the ideas, containers that then shaped the thoughts poured into them.

"Words are but the signs of ideas."
Samuel Johnson, 1709–1784,
Preface to his *English Dictionary*

Drawing by Henry Miller; © 1984 The New Yorker Magazine, Inc.

Many athletes are now being advised to prepare for contests by imagining themselves performing their events (Weinberg, 1981). The wisdom of this advice was demonstrated in a laboratory test of mental practice conducted by Georgia Nigro (Neisser, 1984). The researchers had their subjects make 24 dart throws at a target. They then had half of the subjects think through 24 throws. Finally, they had all of the subjects again make 24 throws. Only those who had mentally practiced showed any improvement.

What, then, should we say about the relationship between thinking and language? We noted earlier that language influences thinking. But if thinking did not affect language, there would never be any new words. Obviously, though, words are invented to express new ideas and new actions all the time. In basketball, the term "slam dunk" was coined after the act itself had become fairly common. So, let us simply say that *thinking shapes our language, which then shapes our thought.*

"The way men usually are, it takes a name to make something visible for them. Those with originality have for the most part also assigned names."
Nietzche,
The Gay Science, 1882–1887

To return to the philosophical issue of human rationality, psychological research on thinking and language mirrors the mixed reviews given our species in literature and religion. The human mind is simultaneously capable of striking intellectual failures and of vast intellectual power. On the one hand, our deductive reasoning is often flawed and our inductive reasoning sometimes warps our perceptions of reality. In an age when misjudgments can have disastrous consequences, it is well that we appreciate that our headpieces are indeed sometimes filled with straw. On the other hand, our "good guess" heuristics usually serve us well, and they certainly are efficient. Moreover, our ingenuity at problem solving and our extraordinary power of language do surely, among the animals, rank our species as almost "infinite in faculties"!

SUMMING UP

THINKING

Concepts One of the building blocks of thinking is our concepts, which serve to simplify and order the world by organizing it into a hierarchy of categories. Concepts often form around prototypes, or best examples of a category.

Problem Solving When faced with novel situations for which no well-learned response suffices, we may use any of several strategies—trial and error, hypothesis testing, methodical algorithms, and rule-of-thumb heuristics. We do, however, face certain obstacles to successful problem solving. The confirmation bias predisposes us to verify rather than challenge our hypotheses. And fixations, such as mental set and functional fixedness, may prevent our taking a needed fresh perspective on the problem.

Making Decisions and Forming Judgments Our use of heuristics, such as the representativeness and availability heuristics, provide highly efficient but occasionally misleading guides for making quick decisions and forming intuitive judgments. Our tendencies to seek confirmation of our hypotheses and to use quick and easy heuristics sometimes blind us to our vulnerability to error, a phenomenon known as the overconfidence phenomenon. Also, the way a question is posed, or framed, can significantly affect our responses.

Reasoning Deductive reasoning begins with assumptions or general truths and uses them to derive certain conclusions. Even when reasoning with formal syllogisms, people tend to accept as more logical those conclusions that agree with their beliefs. Inductive reasoning is the process of generalizing from observed instances. As the belief perseverance phenomenon indicates, we often are not impartial in our use of evidence.

In Defense of Our Thinking Abilities Despite our capacity for error and susceptibility to bias, our cognitive mechanisms are remarkably efficient and adaptive.

Artificial Intelligence Scientists have created computers and robots that perform operations previously thought to require human intelligence. The most notable successes have focused the computer's capacities for memory and precise logic on specific tasks, such as playing chess or diagnosing illnesses. For now, however, the brain's capacity for processing millions of bits of information simultaneously and the wide range of its abilities dwarf those of the most sophisticated computer.

LANGUAGE

Language Structure Language is built of basic speech sounds, called phonemes; elementary units of meaning, called morphemes; words; and the semantics and syntax that make up grammar.

Language Development Among the greatest marvels of nature is a child's ability to acquire language. The ease with which children progress from the babbling stage through the one-word stage to the telegraphic speech of the two-word stage and beyond has sparked a lively debate concerning how they do it. The behaviorist's explanation is that language is learned by the familiar principles of association, imitation, and reinforcement. This has been challenged by indications that children are biologically prepared to learn words and to organize them according to an inborn readiness to use grammar.

Animal Language Another vigorously debated issue is whether language is a uniquely human ability. It has been known for some time that bees communicate the location of food through an intricate dance. More recently, several teams of psychologists provoked enormous interest by teaching various apes, including a number of chimpanzees, to communicate with humans, either by using sign language or by pushing buttons wired to a computer. The animals have developed considerable vocabularies and are able to string words together to express meaning and requests. Skeptics point out significant differences between apes and humans in their facility with language, especially in their respective abilities to order words using proper syntax. Nevertheless, these studies have revealed that apes possess surprising cognitive abilities.

THINKING AND LANGUAGE

We have considered thinking and language within the same chapter because they are so difficult to disentangle.

Linguistic Influences on Thinking There is no disputing that ideas are associated with words, and that different languages embody different ideas and world views. According to the linguistic relativity hypothesis, language not only mirrors thought, it determines it. Although this may be stating the relationship a bit too strongly, our words do influence what we think. Research on the effects of masculine generic pronouns and on the ability of vocabulary enrichment to enhance thinking support this.

Thinking Without Language Nevertheless, there is evidence that some ideas, such as the ability to perceive and remember different colors, do not depend on one's having the relevant vocabulary. Moreover, we sometimes think in images rather than in words, and we invent new words to contain new ideas. So we might say that our thinking shapes our language, which then shapes our thought.

TERMS AND CONCEPTS TO REMEMBER

Algorithm A methodical, logical rule or procedure for solving a particular problem. May be contrasted with the more efficient, but also more error-prone use of *heuristics.*

Artificial Intelligence (AI) The science of making computers do things that appear intelligent; includes both practical applications (chess playing robots, expert systems) and theoretically inspired efforts at modeling thinking.

Availability Heuristic Judges the likelihood of things in terms of their availability in memory; if instances of something come readily to mind (perhaps because of their vividness), we presume the thing to be more likely.

Babbling Stage The stage in speech development, beginning at about 3 or 4 months, in which the infant spontaneously utters a variety of sounds (which at first are unrelated to the household language).

Belief Perseverance Clinging to one's initial conceptions after the basis on which they were formed has been discredited.

Concept A mental grouping of similar things, events, and people.

Confirmation Bias A tendency to search for information that confirms one's preconceptions.

Deductive Reasoning The deriving of conclusions, given certain assumptions.

Fixation The inability to take a new perspective on a problem.

Framing The way an issue to be decided is posed; can significantly affect judgments.

Functional Fixedness The tendency to think of things only in terms of their usual functions; an impediment to problem solving.

Grammar A system of rules that enables us to use our language to speak to and understand others.

Heuristic A rule-of-thumb strategy that enables efficient judgments and problem solutions.

Hypothesis Testing A problem-solving process in which a tentative assumption is made about how to solve the problem and then tested to see if it works.

Inductive Reasoning The inferring of a general truth from particular examples.

Insight A sudden and often novel realization of the solution to a problem; contrasts with trial-and-error solutions.

Linguistic Relativity Whorf's hypothesis that language determines the way we think.

Mental Set A tendency to approach a problem in a particular way, especially a way that has been successful in the past but may or may not be helpful in solving a new problem.

Morphemes The smallest speech units that carry meaning; may be words or parts of words (such as a prefix).

One-Word Stage The stage in speech development, from about age 1 to 2 years, during which a child speaks mostly in single words.

Overconfidence Phenomenon The tendency to be more confident than correct—to overestimate the accuracy of one's beliefs and judgments.

Phonemes A language's smallest distinctive sound units.

Prototype The best example of a category; matching new items to the prototype provides a quick and easy method for including items in a category (for example, comparing feathered creatures to a prototypical bird such as a robin).

Representativeness Heuristic Judging the likelihood of things in terms of how well they seem to represent, or match, particular prototypes; may lead one to ignore other relevant information.

Semantics The study of meaning, as derived from morphemes, words, and sentences.

Syllogism An argument in which two presumably true statements, called premises, lead to a third statement, the conclusion; the basis of formal deductive reasoning.

Syntax Rules for combining words into grammatically correct sentences.

Telegraphic Speech An early speech stage in which the child speaks like a telegram—using mostly nouns and verbs and omitting prepositions and other auxiliary words.

Trial and Error A problem-solving process in which one solution after another is tried until success is achieved.

Two-Word Stage The stage in speech development, beginning about age 2, during which a child speaks mostly two-word utterances.

FOR FURTHER READING

Bransford, J. D., & Stein, B. S. (1984). *The IDEAL problem solver.* New York: Freeman.

Offers concrete strategies organized into an IDEAL system for attacking problems, including academic problems: Identify problem; Define it; Explore strategies for solving it; Act on those strategies; Look at the effects of your efforts.

Griffin, D. R. (1984). Animal thinking. *American Scientist, 72,* 456–464.

A fascinating, illustrated description of the remarkable thinking and problem-solving abilities of animals, from insects to chimpanzees.

Halpern, D. F. (1984). *Thought and knowledge: An introduction to critical thinking.* Hillsdale, NJ.: Erlbaum.

A marvelous book that shows how the findings of psychological research can help us to think more rationally and critically.

Hunt, M. (1982). *The universe within: A new science explores the human mind.* New York: Simon & Schuster.

Science journalist Morton Hunt has been thinking about thinking, and the result is perhaps the most engaging and informative book ever written on the subject. Hunt draws upon interviews with scores of researchers in presenting his well-documented summary of recent discoveries.

Kahneman, D., Slovic, P., & Tversky, A. (Eds.). (1982). *Judgment under uncertainty: Heuristics and biases.* New York: Cambridge University Press.

Here, many of the researchers whom Morton Hunt discusses in The universe within *(1982) speak for themselves, describing various ways in which people's intuitions, predictions, and diagnoses depart from the laws of probability and statistics.*

Nisbett, R., & Ross, L. (1980). *Human inference: Strategies and shortcomings of social judgment.* Englewood Cliffs, NJ: Prentice-Hall.

Is it possible for a book that summarizes psychological research to tickle your funny bone? This book will, as it reveals the pitfalls of human inductive reasoning.

Wood, G. (1982). *Cognitive psychology: A skills approach.* Monterey, CA: Brooks/Cole.

An authoritative, yet practical and accessible textbook introduction to human thinking, decision making, and problem solving.

Werner Bischof *Frank Lloyd Wright*

The Solomon R. Guggenheim Museum

Frank Lloyd Wright *Solomon R. Guggenheim Museum*

CHAPTER 12

Intelligence

Scott, an energetic kindergartner, acts bored and restless in class. Concerned that he might have a learning disability, Scott's teacher asks the school psychologist to evaluate him. The psychologist's testing reveals that Scott is actually an extraordinarily capable boy who can read like a third grader and add numbers like a second grader. Little wonder that he acts bored; Scott needs activities better suited to his abilities.

Larry and six other California children were also tested by school psychologists; they were then assigned to special education classes for the mentally retarded. Their parents and the San Francisco Bay Area Black Psychology Association were not convinced by the psychologists' judgments. They suspected that the tests used might have been biased against the children, all of whom were black. Federal District Court Judge Robert Peckham agreed: Intelligence tests, he ruled, are "racially and culturally biased, have a discriminatory impact on black children, and have not been validated for the purpose of [putting] black children into educationally dead-end, isolated, and stigmatizing classes" (Opton, 1979).

Jennifer and Maria have been close friends throughout high school. Both have grade averages near the top of the class and both hope to be pre-med students in college. "Wouldn't it be fun to go to the same school," they wistfully dream. Then they spend a morning taking the Scholastic Aptitude Test. Jennifer does very well on the SAT and is subsequently admitted to the school she and Maria have chosen. Maria does rather poorly and, despite her excellent high school record, is rejected. "How awful!," they moan. "After three years of making A's in the same classes, a 150-minute test separates us."

Of all psychology's controversies, none has been more heated than that provoked by the idea that there exists in each person a general mental capacity and that this capacity can be measured and quantified as a number. The controversy is further fueled by the fact that these numbers are often used to rank individuals and to determine whether or not they will be allowed to pursue various educational and vocational opportunities. Indeed, concern with this topic has spilled over into the public arena as school boards, courts, and journalists debate the fairness of intelligence and aptitude tests.

In this chapter, we will explore the controversy surrounding tests of intelligence and other abilities by examining such questions as:

What is intelligence?

How are intelligence tests used? How are they abused?

Is intelligence more a product of nature or of nurture?

What do differences in test scores among individuals and groups tell us about those individuals and groups?

By the end of the chapter, we should be able to examine objectively the usefulness and the fairness of intelligence testing. Is it society's best means of identifying those who would benefit from special opportunities? Or is the very idea of testing for intelligence a potent discriminatory weapon that is camouflaged as science?

THE MEASUREMENT OF INTELLIGENCE

To understand the concept of intelligence and the impact of intelligence tests, we first need to know something about the origins and purposes of these tests. The story of the testing movement sheds light on the current controversy about testing. In addition, it reminds us of an important lesson—namely, that although science strives for objectivity, it is carried out by people who see and interpret evidence through the spectacles of their own assumptions and values. Scientists can be led astray by their biases just as easily as the rest of us.

The Origins of Intelligence Tests

Many people in the world—the inhabitants of China, for instance—appear to be more concerned with the values of the society, the community, and the family than they are with those of the individual. They seem to be less concerned than those of us in Western societies with encouraging individual uniqueness. Another tradition, which emphasizes the individual over the group, can be traced to Plato, who more than 2000 years ago wrote in the *Republic* that "No two persons are born exactly alike; but each differs from the other in natural endowments, one being suited for one occupation and another for another." As heirs to Plato's emphasis on individualism, people in Western societies consider questions about how and why individuals differ to be of fundamental importance. It may therefore be surprising that attempts to measure individual differences began in earnest only about a century ago, thanks to the efforts of three quite different people—Sir Francis Galton, Alfred Binet, and Lewis Terman.

Sir Francis Galton: Quantifying Superiority

In the history of the testing movement, no one has been more preoccupied with measuring and ranking people than the brilliant English scientist Sir Francis Galton (1822–1911). While a student at Cambridge University, Galton's letters home revealed a constant concern with how examinations ranked him relative to his fellow students (Fancher, 1979). In time, his fascination with quantification led him to invent methods for measuring boredom, even-temperedness, the beauty of British women, the effects of prayer, and much else besides.

When his cousin Charles Darwin proposed that nature "selects" successful traits through the "survival of the fittest," Galton concluded that similar dynamics could be applied to people. If human traits could be measured, he reasoned, these measurements could be used as the basis for selectively breeding people who possessed superior traits. Those with the greatest "natural ability" should be encouraged to mate with each other, he argued, while those not so well endowed should be discouraged or prevented from reproducing. To promote this plan for what in his eyes was human betterment, Galton founded the "eugenics" movement (taking its name from the Greek word *eugenes,* which means "well-born").

Galton assumed that important human traits are inherited. He supported this assumption by noting that, like height, social eminence tended to run in families. Unsurprisingly, Galton himself was an eminent child of an eminent upper-class family. Furthermore, although he popularized the phrase "nature and nurture," he was smugly insensitive to the implications of the cultural and environmental advantages enjoyed by the upper class in Victorian England (Fancher, 1979). A British male, he also believed in the natural superiority of Caucasian men.

Sir Francis Galton (1892, p. 89): "I have no patience with the hypothesis occasionally expressed, and often implied, especially in tales written to teach children to be good, that babies are born pretty much alike, and that the sole agencies in creating differences between boy and boy, and man and man, are steady application and moral effort. It is in the most unqualified manner that I object to pretensions of natural equality."

Beginning with his commitment to quantifying human superiority and his belief in its inheritability, Galton set about trying to measure innate mental capacity. In his 1869 book, *Hereditary Genius,* he toyed with the idea of assessing intelligence by measuring head size, and over the next few years, he developed various measures of what he presumed were the biological underpinnings of genius. Galton put his ideas to the test at London's 1884 International Exposition. Over 10,000 visitors to the exposition paid to receive his assessment of their abilities based on his tests of "intellectual strengths," which precisely measured such things as reaction time, sensory acuity, muscular power, and body proportions.

So, how did the tests turn out? Did "superior" individuals (eminent adults and excellent students) outscore those supposedly not-so-bright? Did they, for instance, process information more swiftly on the tests of reaction time? They did not. Nor did the various measures correlate with one another. Nor did men consistently outscore women.

Although Galton had failed in his efforts to invent simple measures of general mental ability, he was an innovative researcher who pioneered some basic statistical techniques. More important, he was an influential proponent of the idea that people's mental abilities can be quantitatively measured.

Alfred Binet: Predicting School Achievement

The modern intelligence testing movement began when the pioneering French psychologist Alfred Binet (1857–1911) applied Galton's idea of measuring intellectual abilities to a more humanitarian goal. When the French government passed a law requiring all children to attend school, teachers soon found themselves coping with a wider range of individual differences than they could reasonably handle. Some of the children seemed to be incapable of benefiting from the regular school curriculum and appeared to need special classes. But how could the schools identify children with these special needs?

The government was reluctant to trust teachers' judgments of children's learning potential. Academic slowness might merely reflect inadequate prior education. Also, teachers might tend to prejudge children on the basis of their social and racial backgrounds. To solve this problem, the minister of public education commissioned Binet to develop an objective test that would identify those children who were likely to have difficulty in the regular classes.

Binet and his collaborator, Theodore Simon, began by assuming that all children follow the same course of intellectual development but that some develop more rapidly than others. "Dull" children, they presumed, were merely "retarded" in their development. On tests, therefore, a dull child should perform like a normal child of a younger age, and a "bright" child like a normal child of an older age.

Binet and Simon's task, then, was to figure out a way to measure a child's ***mental age,*** which they defined as the chronological (calendar) age that most typically corresponds to a given level of performance. By comparing a child's mental age with his or her chronological age, the researchers reasoned that it should be possible to assess the child's ability to handle normal schoolwork. (Although it did not affect their findings, one of Binet and Simon's assumptions was incorrect. We now know, thanks to cognitive psychologists, that an 11-year-old with a mental age of 9 thinks somewhat differently than a 7-year-old with a mental age of 9.)

Alfred Binet (Binet & Simon, 1905): "The scale, properly speaking, does not permit the measure of intelligence, because intellectual qualities . . . cannot be measured as linear surfaces are measured."

In attempting to devise a method for measuring mental age, Binet and Simon theorized that intelligence, like athletic ability, is a general capacity that shows up in various ways. They therefore set about developing various reasoning and problem-solving questions, the answers to which would allow them to predict school achievement better than did Galton's measures of physical and sensory skills. By testing "bright" and "backward" Parisian school children on these questions, Binet and Simon succeeded in identifying those items that did indeed seem to predict how successful the children were in regular schoolwork.

Note that Binet and Simon made no assumptions concerning *why* a particular child was slow, average, or precocious. Binet personally leaned toward an environmental explanation. He believed that the capacities indicated by the test were not fixed, and to raise the capacities of children who had low scores he recommended "mental orthopedics" that would train children how to develop their attention and self-discipline. Binet refused to speculate regarding what the test was actually measuring. It did not measure inborn intelligence in the way that a yardstick measures height, he insisted. Rather, it had a single practical purpose: to predict which children would be likely not to succeed in the Paris school system of the early 1900s. Binet was not completely at ease with the test he had devised, though. His hope was that it would be used to help children improve. His fear was that it would be used to label children and limit their opportunities (Gould, 1981).

"The IQ test was invented to predict academic performance, nothing else. If we wanted something that would predict life success, we'd have to invent another test completely."
Robert Zajonc (1984)

Lewis Terman: The Innate IQ

What Binet viewed as merely a practical guide for identifying slow learners who needed special help was soon seen by others to be what Galton had been searching for: a numerical estimate of inherited intelligence. After Binet's death in 1911, a Stanford University professor named Lewis Terman decided to import Binet's test. He soon found, however, that the Paris-developed age norms did not work very well with California school children. So Terman revised the test. He selected some of Binet's original items (translated, of course), added others, established new age norms, and extended the upper end of the test's range from teenagers to "superior adults." Terman gave his revision the name that through numerous later revisions it retains today—the ***Stanford-Binet.***

It was not until World War II that the IQ test became fashionable in France—under the name of Terman, not Binet! (Miller, 1962)

Terman's test yielded the famous ***intelligence quotient*** or ***IQ.*** The IQ was simply mental age divided by chronological age and multiplied by 100 to get rid of the decimal point:

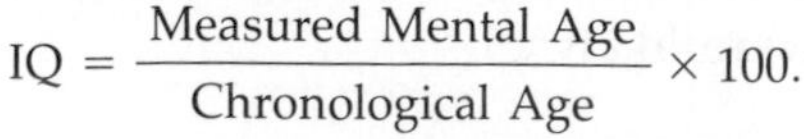

$$IQ = \frac{\text{Measured Mental Age}}{\text{Chronological Age}} \times 100.$$

Thus an 8-year-old who answered questions with the proficiency typical of a 10-year-old was said to have an IQ of 125. Note that, by definition, an average child would have the same measured mental age and chronological age, and so an IQ of 100.

On current intelligence tests, including the Stanford-Binet itself, the IQ is no longer computed in this manner. Although the original IQ formula worked fairly well for children, it was not appropriate for adults. Consider: If a 20-year-old does as well on the test as the average 40-year-old, is it reasonable to say the person has an IQ of 200? Obviously, something is out of whack. For this reason, today's intelligence tests result in an "IQ score" based on the test-taker's performance relative to the average performance of others the same age.

If this 8-year-old girl taking the Stanford-Binet test responds at a level typical of the average 8-year-old, her IQ score will be 100.

Drawing by Sidney Harris

"You did very well on your IQ test. You're a man of 49 with the intelligence of a man of 53."

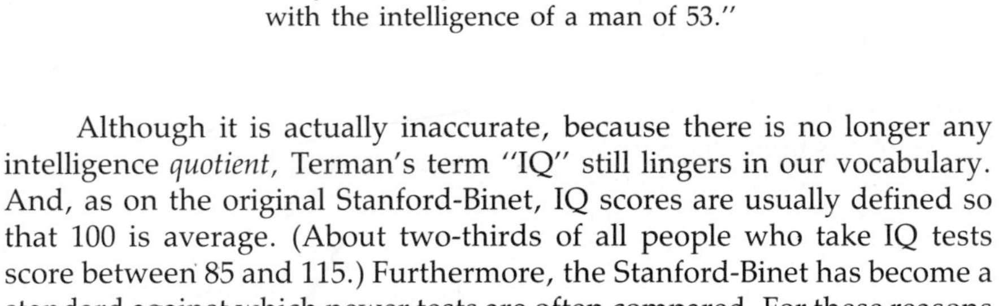

Although it is actually inaccurate, because there is no longer any intelligence *quotient*, Terman's term "IQ" still lingers in our vocabulary. And, as on the original Stanford-Binet, IQ scores are usually defined so that 100 is average. (About two-thirds of all people who take IQ tests score between 85 and 115.) Furthermore, the Stanford-Binet has become a standard against which newer tests are often compared. For these reasons and others, Terman's influence reaches into the present.

Terman promoted the widespread use of intelligence testing. His motive was to "take account of the inequalities of children in original endowment" by assessing their "vocational fitness" (Terman, 1916). Terman also sympathized with the eugenics movement. He lamented what he considered to be the low level of intelligence that he saw as

> very, very common among Spanish-Indian and Mexican families of the Southwest and also among negroes. Their dullness seems to be racial. . . . There is no possibility at present of convincing society that they should not be allowed to reproduce, although from a eugenic point of view they constitute a grave problem because of their unusually prolific breeding. (Terman, 1916, pp. 91–92)

Terman envisioned that the use of intelligence tests would "ultimately result in curtailing the reproduction of feeble-mindedness and in the elimination of an enormous amount of crime, pauperism, and industrial inefficiency" (p. 7).

Lewis Terman (1916, p. 115): "The children of successful and cultured parents test higher than children from wretched and ignorant homes for the simple reason that their heredity is better."

When given intelligence tests in the early 1900's, immigrants arriving in the United States from non-English-speaking countries tended to score poorly, leading some psychologists to conclude that they were intellectually inferior.

During the same era, adaptations of Binet's and Terman's tests were used to evaluate World War I army recruits and newly arriving immigrants. The results of the tests were interpreted by some as documenting the inferiority of people not of Anglo-Saxon descent. For instance, following his study of European immigrants arriving at Ellis Island (many of them not English speaking), psychologist Henry Goddard claimed that 83 percent of the Jewish immigrants, 80 percent of the Hungarians, 79 percent of the Italians, and 87 percent of the Russians were "feebleminded" (Eysenck & Kamin, 1981).

These conclusions might have pleased Galton, but they would surely have horrified Binet. Indeed, they eventually became an embarrassment to most test authors, including Terman, who came to appreciate that the test scores could reflect not only people's innate mental abilities but also their education, their familiarity with the culture assumed by the test, and so forth. Furthermore, there was little scientific information at the time about whether intelligence actually was or was not an inherited trait, or whether different ethnic groups differ in innate abilities. (Such questions can be studied objectively, as we will see.) But abuses of the early intelligence tests do remind us that scholarship can be value-laden. Behind the screen of science, ideology sometimes hides.

"The primary concerns of researchers should be to discover . . . the realities that prevail despite shifting politics and policies."
Arthur R. Jensen (1984)

"Science must be understood as a social phenomenon, a gutsy, human enterprise, not the work of robots programmed to collect pure information."
Stephen Jay Gould,
The Mismeasure of Man, 1981

Modern Tests of Intelligence

By this point in your life, your abilities have undoubtedly been measured by dozens of different tests: elementary school tests of basic reading and math skills, course examinations, IQ tests, driver's license examinations, and college entrance examinations to mention just a few. Traditionally, tests such as these are classified as either ***aptitude tests,*** which are intended to predict your ability to learn a new skill, or ***achievement tests,*** which are intended to measure what you have learned. Thus, a college entrance exam, which seeks to predict how you will do in college, would be called an aptitude test, whereas a final exam covering what you should have learned in this course would be an achievement test.

Actually, the differences between aptitude tests and achievement tests are not as clear-cut as their definitions imply. Your score on an aptitude test, such as the Stanford-Binet, depends to some extent on your vocabulary achievement. Similarly, your grades on the achievement exams given in this course reflect not only how effectively you have stud-

Drawing by Sidney Harris

"What with the primary mental ability test and the differential aptitude test and the reading readiness test and the basic skills test and the IQ test and the sequential tests of educational progress and the mental maturity test, we haven't been learning *anything* at school."

ied but also your aptitude for learning. Thus the best approach might be to think of aptitude and achievement as the two ends of a continuum. Most tests, whether labeled aptitude or achievement tests, measure to some extent both ability and how far that ability has been developed, so they fall somewhere in between. Distinguishing between them is therefore mainly a matter of practicality: Aptitude tests are used to predict future performance, achievement tests to assess current competence.

Though primarily intended to measure what a child has learned, achievement tests may also reflect one's aptitude for learning.

Tests can also be distinguished on the basis of whether they assess general or specific abilities. An intelligence test is designed to evaluate general aptitude by sampling a fairly broad array of abilities. Conversely, a test to predict the ease with which an individual can learn mechanical tasks assesses a specific aptitude. A typing test given to a prospective employee assesses a specific achievement, whereas a high school competency examination tests for general achievement. Tests also vary in the procedure by which they are administered. Group tests are very efficient. Individual testing allows the examiner to adjust the difficulty of the questions and to use more varied materials, such as puzzles.

To get a better feel for modern intelligence-related tests and some of the differences among them, let's look at three tests that are widely used today. We can then refer to these examples as we consider what makes an effective test and how test scores can be used and abused.

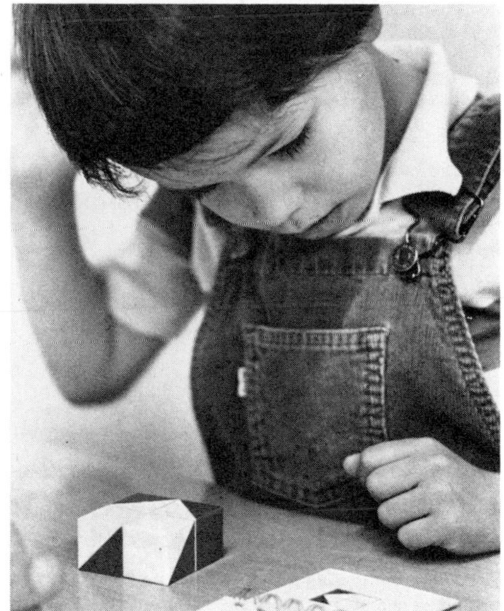

The Wechsler intelligence test comes in forms suited for adults (WAIS) and for children (WISC).

An Individual Test of General Ability: The WAIS

During the 1930s, psychologist David Wechsler created a test of adult abilities that he called the ***Wechsler Adult Intelligence Scale (WAIS).*** Later he developed a similar test for children called the Wechsler Intelligence Scale for Children (WISC). The WAIS, which is individually administered, consists of 11 subtests, as illustrated in Figure 12-1 on p. 308. It yields not only an overall IQ score, as does the Stanford-Binet, but also separate "verbal" and "performance" (nonverbal) IQ scores. Striking differences between the two scores may alert the examiner to possible learning problems. For example, a much lower verbal than performance IQ might indicate a reading disability.

The Wechsler scales are among the most popular and most respected intelligence tests. More than 3000 books and articles have been published about them (Anastasi, 1982), and the WAIS is used by more psychologists than any other psychological test (Lubin & others, 1984).

VERBAL

General Information
What day of the year is Independence Day?

Similarities
In what way are *wool* and *cotton* alike?

Arithmetic Reasoning
If eggs cost 60 cents a dozen, what does 1 egg cost?

Vocabulary
Tell me the meaning of corrupt.

Comprehension
Why do people buy fire insurance?

Digit Span
Listen carefully, and when I am through, say the numbers right after me.

7 3 4 1 8 6

Now I am going to say some more numbers, but I want you to say them backward.

3 8 4 1 6

PERFORMANCE

Picture Completion
I am going to show you a picture with an important part missing. Tell me what is missing.

'85

SUN	MON	TUE	WED	THU	FRI	SAT
1	2	3	4	5	6	7
8	9	10	11	12	13	14
15	16	17	18	19	20	21
22	23	24	25	26	27	28
29	30					

Picture Arrangement
The pictures below tell a story. Put them in the right order to tell the story.

Block Design
Using the four blocks, make one just like this.

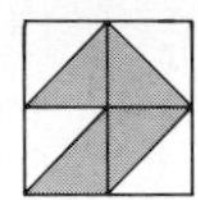

Object Assembly
If these pieces are put together correctly, they will make something. Go ahead and put them together as quickly as you can.

Digit-Symbol Substitution

Code

△	○	▱	×	8
1	2	3	4	5

Test

△	8	×	○	△	▱	8	×	△	8

etc.

Figure 12-1 *Sample items from the Wechsler Adult Intelligence Scale subtests.*

A Group Test of General Ability: The SAT

Large-scale testing is now efficiently accomplished through the use of multiple-choice tests such as the well-known Scholastic Aptitude Test (SAT), which is taken annually by nearly 1 million college-bound high school seniors. As with the original Binet test, the SAT aims to predict academic performance. Unlike the Stanford-Binet and Wechsler tests, however, the SAT yields no overall intelligence score. Rather, it measures verbal and mathematical abilities separately.

Do you suppose that "intelligence" tests would be less controversial had Binet and his followers named them "academic aptitude" tests?

The SAT is a good example of an aptitude test that falls somewhere in the middle of the aptitude-achievement continuum, as can be seen from the sample items in Figure 12-2. More than half of its 60 mathematical questions, for example, presume a basic knowledge of either algebra or geometry.

A Group Test of Specific Abilities: The DAT

The Differential Aptitude Test (DAT) is widely used as an aid to counseling junior and senior high school students. As the sample items in Figure 12-3 on p. 310 illustrate, the DAT evaluates not only such academi-

VERBAL

Choose the word or phrase that is most nearly *opposite* in meaning to the word in capital letters.

WILT: (A) prevent (B) drain (C) expose (D) revive (E) stick
(93 percent correctly answered D)

GARNER: (A) disfigure (B) hedge (C) connect (D) forget (E) disperse
(26 percent correctly answered E)

Each question below consists of a related pair of words or phrases, followed by five lettered pairs of words or phrases. Select the lettered pair that best expresses a relationship similar to that expressed in the original pair.

PAINTING : CANVAS (A) drawing : lottery (B) fishing : pond (C) writing : paper (D) shading : crayon (E) sculpting : design
(92 percent correctly answered C)

SCOFF : DERISION (A) soothe : mollification (B) slander : repression (C) swear : precision (D) stimulate : appearance (E) startle : speediness
(21 percent correctly answered A)

MATHEMATICAL

If $x^3 + y = x^3 + 5$, then $y =$
(A) -5 (B) $-\sqrt[3]{5}$ (C) $\sqrt[3]{5}$ (D) 5 (E) 5^3
(93 percent correctly answered D)

In a race, if Bob's running speed was $\frac{4}{5}$ Alice's, and Chris's speed was $\frac{3}{4}$ Bob's, then Alice's speed was how many times the average (arithmetic mean) of the other two runners' speeds?
(A) $\frac{3}{5}$ (B) $\frac{7}{10}$ (C) $\frac{40}{31}$ (D) $\frac{10}{7}$ (E) $\frac{5}{3}$
(10 percent correctly answered D)

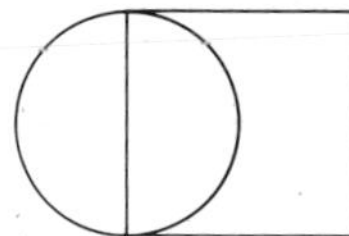

In the figure above, one side of the square is a diameter of the circle. If the area of the circle is p and the area of the square is s, which of the following must be true?

I. $s > p$
II. $s \geqq 2p$
III. $s < p$

(A) None (B) I only (C) II only (D) III only (E) I and II
(45 percent correctly answered B)

Figure 12-2 *Sample items from the Scholastic Aptitude Test of November 6, 1982.*

cally related abilities as verbal reasoning, spelling, and language usage but also such vocational abilities as clerical speed and mechanical reasoning. Thus, like the SAT, it is an "aptitude" test that also reflects achievement. Combined with other available information, such as the students' interests, DAT scores are frequently used by school counselors to help guide students toward appropriate courses and careers.

Principles of Test Construction

We can use the three tests just discussed to illustrate three requirements of any good test—standardization, reliability, and validity.

VERBAL REASONING

Choose the correct pair of words to fill the blanks. The first word of the pair goes in the blank space at the beginning of the sentence; the second word of the pair goes in the blank at the end of the sentence.

. . . . . . is to night as breakfast is to . . . . . .

A. supper —— corner
B. gentle —— morning
C. door —— corner
D. flow —— enjoy
E. supper —— morning

The correct answer is E.

NUMERICAL ABILITY

Choose the correct answer for each problem.

Add	13	A. 14	Subtract	30	A. 15
	12	B. 25		20	B. 26
		C. 16			C. 16
		D. 59			D. 8
		N. none of these			N. none of these

The correct answer for the first problem is B and for the second is N.

ABSTRACT REASONING

The four "problem figures" in each row make a series. Find the one among the "answer figures" that would be next in the series.

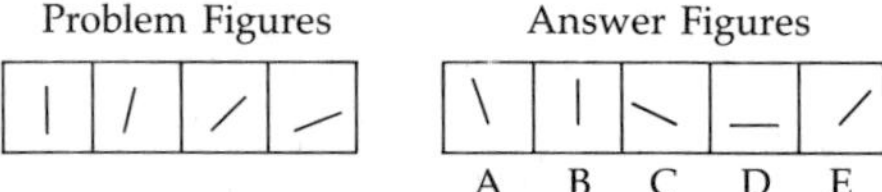

The correct answer is D

MECHANICAL REASONING

Which man has the heavier load? (If equal, mark C.)

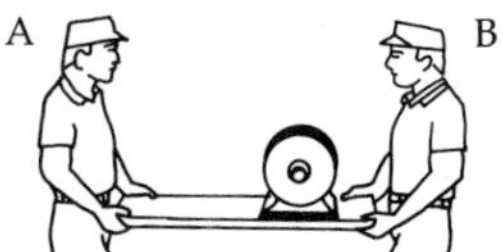

The correct answer is B.

CLERICAL SPEED AND ACCURACY

In each test item, one of the five combinations is underlined. Find the same combination on the answer sheet and mark it.

Test Items

V.	AB	AC	AD	AE	AF
W.	aA	aB	BA	Ba	Bb
X.	A7	7A	B7	7B	AB
Y.	Aa	Ba	bA	BA	bB
Z.	3A	3B	33	B3	BB

Sample of Answer Sheet

V.	AC	AE	AF	AB	AD
W.	BA	Ba	Bb	aA	aB
X.	7B	B7	AB	7A	A7
Y.	Aa	bA	bB	Ba	BA
Z.	BB	3B	B3	3A	33

SPACE RELATIONS

Which one of the following figures could be made by folding the pattern at the left? The pattern always shows the outside of the figure. Note the gray surfaces.

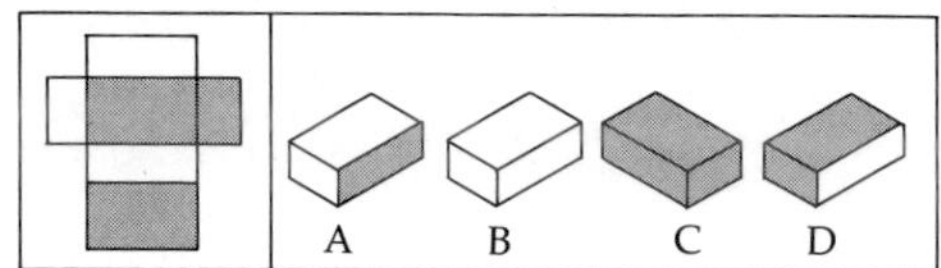

The correct answer is D.

SPELLING

Indicate whether each word is spelled right or wrong.

W. man X. gurl

The correct answer for W is right and for X is wrong.

LANGUAGE USAGE

Decide which of the lettered parts of the sentence contains an error and mark the corresponding letter on the answer sheet. If there is no error, mark N.

X. Ain't we / going to / the office / next week?
A B C D

The correct answer is A.

Figure 12-3 *Sample items from the Differential Aptitude Test.*

Standardization

Knowing how many questions someone answers correctly on an intelligence test does not tell us whether the person's performance is low, high, or average. To assign a meaningful score to an individual's test performance, we must be able to compare performance to some sort of standard or norm. So before an intelligence-related test can be used, the creators of the test must administer it to a large sample of people who are representative of those with whom the later test-takers will be compared. This process of defining meaningful scores relative to a pretested group is called ***standardization.***

For instance, when Terman realized that the test Binet had created in France did not work so well with California school children, he revised the test and then standardized the new version by administering it to 2300 white, native-born Americans of all socioeconomic levels. Thereafter, this sample of people comprised the norm against which subsequent takers of the test were compared. (Terman and his colleagues recognized that a scale standardized on Parisians did not provide a satisfactory standard for evaluating Americans. But, ironically, they then proceeded to evaluate nonwhite and immigrant groups in comparison to the native-born white American standard [Van Leeuwen, 1982].)

On both the Stanford-Binet and the Wechsler scales, the average score for any age group has been arbitrarily set at 100. Other IQ scores are then assigned according to how much the test-taker's performance deviates above or below this average. For example, a raw score that is higher than 97 percent of all the scores is assigned an IQ score of 130. Similarly, a raw score that is comparably below average—that is, one that is below 97 percent of all the scores—is assigned an IQ score of 70. This method of assigning scores is based on the concept of a ***normal distribution,*** a bell-shaped distribution of scores that forms what is called the ***normal curve*** (Figure 12-4). Whether we are measuring people's heights, weights, or mental abilities, this distribution is common: Most of the values we obtain will tend to cluster around the average. As we move away from the average toward the extreme in either direction, we will find fewer and fewer values.

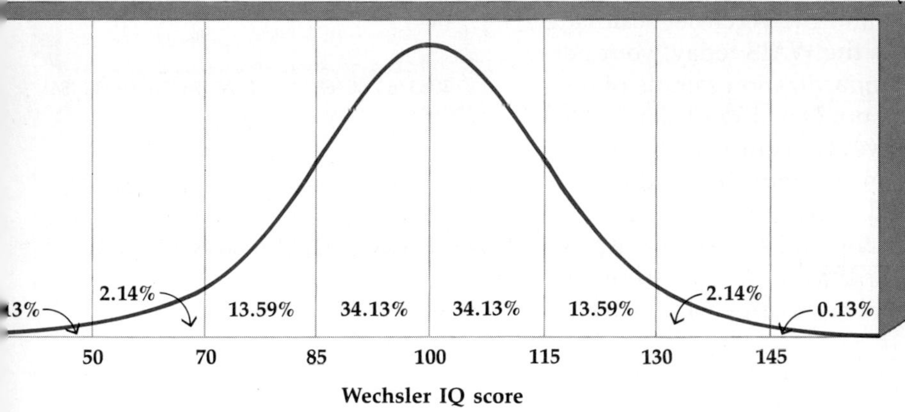

Figure 12-4 *The normal curve. When many scores on a test are compiled, they tend to be distributed in a normal or bell-shaped curve. On an IQ test, such as the Wechsler scale, the average score is assigned an IQ of 100. The percentages under the curve indicate that about 68 percent of the scores normally fall within about 15 IQ points above or below 100 and about 95 percent within 30 IQ points above and below 100. (Any individual's score can be expressed in terms of its deviation from the average. The statistical measures of this deviation and of the average, or "mean," score are described in Appendix A.)*

The SAT was initially standardized using a group of 10,654 students who took the test in April, 1941 (Carroll, 1982). The average performance of these students on both the verbal and math portions of the SAT was assigned a score of 500 (rather than 100 as on most IQ tests). The points above and below the average that encompassed 68 percent of all the raw scores were assigned SAT scores of 600 and 400, respectively (see Figure 12-5). Because all of the students in the SAT standardization sample were college bound and were thus a somewhat select group, especially back in 1941, this sample is not equivalent to the one used for the Stanford-Binet or the Wechsler scales. A person whose scores average 500 on the two parts of the SAT would probably score well above 100 on an IQ test.

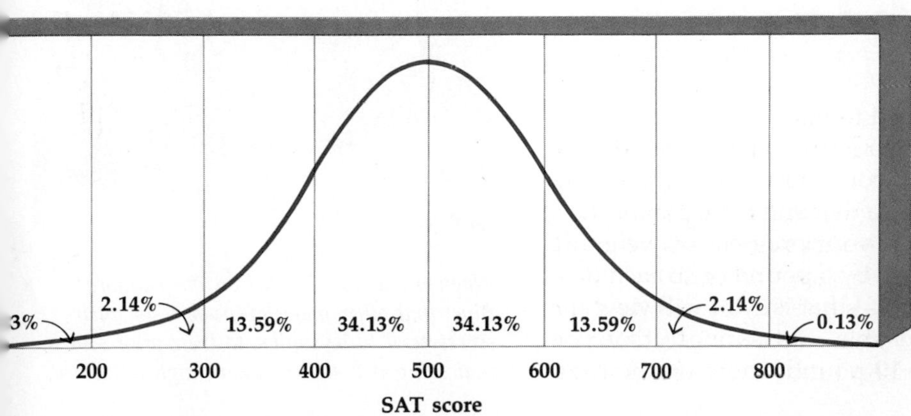

Figure 12-5 *When the SAT test was standardized on a normal distribution curve in 1941, the average score was assigned a value of 500. The percentages under the curve point out that about 68 percent of the scores normally fall within about 100 points above and below 500. Note, however, that an IQ score of 115 on the WAIS is not the equivalent of an SAT score of 600: the academic ability of the groups on which the tests were standardized was not the same.*

If you took the SAT in the past year or so—40-plus years after those first 10,654 students set the standard, you answered different questions than they did. However, the items on the test you were given had been statistically equated to those that appeared on all previous versions of the test. Thus your performance could be—and was—measured with the 1941 yardstick. Because of this comparability, the SAT has become something of an educational barometer. Between 1963 and 1980, scores on the SAT dropped steadily (see Figure 12-6). Of those who took the test in 1981, only the upper 30 percent did better than the average test-taker in 1963. Part of this decline can be attributed to the fact that during the 1960s the number of aspiring college students taking the test grew to include more people with modest academic achievements (Astin & Garber, 1982). But what else might explain the decline? The displacement of reading by the spread of television? A decline in the effectiveness of schools? Changes in the courses required or offered by schools? This issue has been the subject of much controversy.

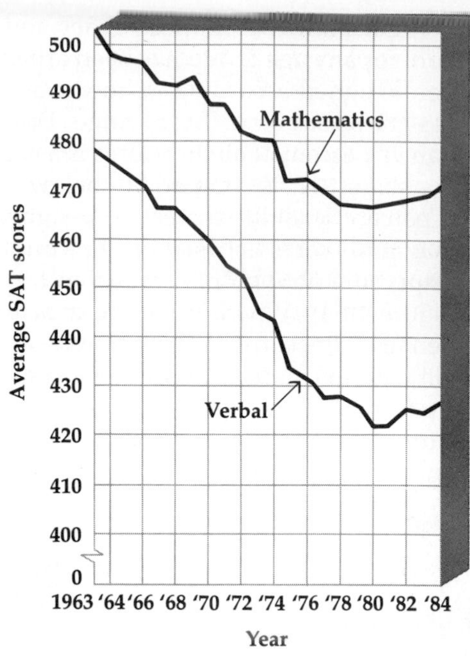

Figure 12-6 *Between 1963 and 1980, average SAT scores dropped significantly, with a slight recovery in recent years.*

Unlike the SAT, the Stanford-Binet test and the Wechsler scales are periodically restandardized. Were you to take the WAIS today, your performance would be compared to that of a standardization sample of people who took the test between 1976 and 1980, not David Wechsler's initial 1930s standardization sample. We can, however, compare the performance of the most recent standardization sample with that of the 1930s sample. If we did, do you suppose we would find rising or declining IQ test performance? Amazingly—given the decline in SAT scores—IQ test performance has actually improved (Flynn, 1984b). A raw score that would earn you an IQ score of 100 today would have earned a score of 114 in the 1930s!

How can this be? Are the aptitudes of Americans decreasing, as some have inferred from the decline in SAT scores, or are they rising, as the IQ data suggest? Although these conflicting trends have been called a "baffling" mystery, we can speculate about some partial explanations. First, remember that the decline in SAT scores can be partly attributed to the greater academic diversity of the students who began taking the test during the 1960s. Conversely, the group of people who take the WAIS, and who are broadly representative of Americans in general, has always been diverse in abilities, much more so than those taking the SAT are even today. Americans—and therefore the IQ standardization group—have become more literate, better educated, and more experienced at taking tests since the 1930s. These facts help explain why the scores on the more academically advanced SAT dropped while those on the academically simpler WAIS rose, at least initially (Flynn, 1984a). What it does not explain is why the SAT scores continued to decline after 1970 (when the sample of students taking the SAT stabilized), while IQ performance continued to rise.

Reliability

A good test must measure what it is designed to measure with dependable consistency. This characteristic of a test is referred to as its ***reliability.*** To understand the importance of reliability, consider the following analogy: Suppose that you have decided to go on a diet and have purchased a bathroom scale so that you can keep track of your progress by weighing yourself every morning. If your weight varies by a pound or so each day, you will probably believe what the scale says—that is, you will view the scale's measurement of your weight as reliable. But suppose that you weigh 5 pounds less on one morning and 10 pounds more on the next.

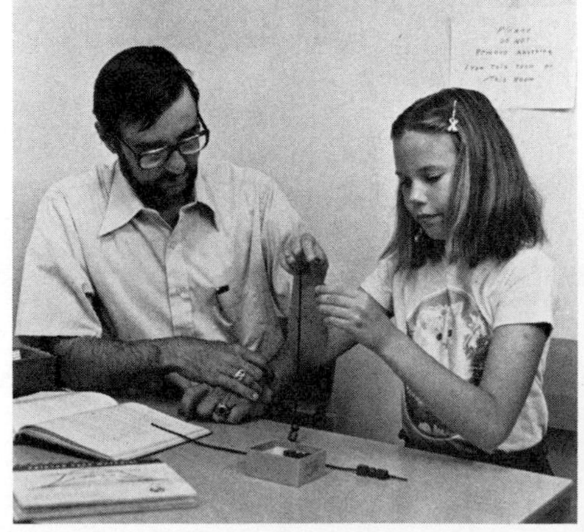

When people are retested on the Stanford-Binet and other major aptitude tests, their scores tend to be similar to their prior scores, indicating that the tests have high reliability.

After the initial shock, you will probably decide to take the scale back and get a replacement, because it isn't reliable.

When psychologists construct tests, they are very concerned that the tests be reliable. They need to know that two people who are essentially the same with regard to whatever it is the test measures will achieve essentially similar scores. Likewise, a person who takes the test twice within a relatively short period should achieve similar scores. Two common methods for evaluating the reliability of tests are the test-retest procedure and the split-half technique. To check ***test-retest reliability,*** subjects are retested either on the same test (which is commonly done with the WAIS or WISC) or on an alternate form of the test (which is commonly done with the SAT). To check ***split-half reliability,*** scores for the odd and even questions can be compared. If the two scores obtained by either method generally agree (are correlated), the test is said to be reliable. The higher the correlation between the scores, the higher the reliability of the test. The tests we have considered so far—the Stanford-Binet, the WAIS and WISC, the SAT, and the DAT—all have reliabilities of about +.90, which means that they are very reliable.

A correlation scale can vary from −1.0 (which would be perfect disagreement *between two scores—as one goes up, the other goes down) to 0 (no consistency) to +1.0 (perfect consistency).*

Coaching Effects

Suppose that after taking the SAT, the Law School Aptitude Test (LSAT), the Medical College Admission Test (MCAT), or the Graduate Record Examination (GRE), you feel you did not do very well. By enrolling in one of the widely advertised test-preparation courses, could you count on increasing your score if you were to take the test again? Or is your score on the test likely to be unvarying?

Being familiar with a test and knowing how to pace yourself on it does help. But this much you can get from spending an evening with the sample test that is available to anyone who registers for one of these tests. Beyond this, does it pay to sign up for a crash test-preparation course? These courses can allow people to brush up on their academic knowledge, especially in mathematics. They may also provide a few useful tips about how to take the test. For instance, on the initial questions in a section of one of these tests, which 80 percent or more of those taking the test typically get right, the most obvious answer is usually correct; however, on the final questions, which 75 percent or more typically get wrong, the "obvious" answer is often incorrect.

Despite the test-relevant teaching and the test-taking clues that SAT-preparation courses provide, two recent research reviews found that the courses increased scores by an average of only 15 points on the 200 to 800 scale (Kulik & others, 1984; Messick & Jungeblut, 1981). This small boost is probably the effect of disciplined study—a miniature version of the greater benefit that comes from taking high school courses in English, algebra, and geometry.

Validity

High reliability does not ensure that a test has ***validity***—that it measures what it is supposed to measure or predicts what it is supposed to predict. For instance, if you use your bathroom scale to estimate height, you would obtain values with high reliability but modest validity. How, then, can we determine whether a test is valid? For some tests, it is sufficient that they have ***content validity,*** which means that they do indeed tap the behavior they were designed to measure. The road test for a driver's license has content validity because it samples those tasks a driver routinely faces. Similarly, your classroom course exams have content validity if they adequately measure your mastery of course material.

Drawing by Sidney Harris

"I'm studying for my IQ test."

Other tests, such as the aptitude tests we have considered, must have ***predictive validity,*** which is assessed by determining the extent to which the tests predict the future achievements they are intended to predict. Some aptitude tests are created by selecting items that best predict the ***criterion*** (the behavior the test is designed to predict). During World War II, psychologist John Flanagan (1947) gave men who were entering pilot training twenty different tests that seemed to sample the requirements of successful piloting. Later, knowing which men successfully completed the training (the criterion) and which did not, Flanagan could adapt and score his test so that it gave the best possible estimate of success. When the test was then actually used to admit people to the training program, the failure rate was cut by more than half.

Is the predictive validity of general aptitude tests as high as their reliability? As critics of aptitude tests are fond of noting, the answer to this question is plainly no. For example, the predictive power of aptitude tests starts out fairly strong in the early grades, but later it weakens. IQ scores are reasonably good predictors of achievement in elementary school, the correlation between IQ and achievement being about +.60 (Jensen, 1980). The SAT is less successful in predicting the grades of college freshmen; here, the correlation is only about +.40 (Linn, 1982). By the time we get to the Graduate Record Examination (GRE) aptitude test, the correlation between it and graduate school grades is, at best, modest. Why does the predictive power of aptitude scores diminish as students move up the educational ladder? Understanding the answer to this question will also help us to understand one reason why the predictive validity of tests is often so much lower than their reliability.

In general, the best predictor of future grades is past grades, which reflect both aptitude and motivation. Even more generally, the best predictor of future behavior is a large sample of past behaviors of the same sort.

Suppose that you are a racehorse owner about to hire some jockeys and you wish to know whether body weight predicts a jockey's success at horse racing. To find out, you have a large sample of jockeys, whose weights range from a slight 98 pounds to a husky 227, race comparable horses. Sure enough, weight does have predictive validity; the lighter jockeys have the faster times. Based on this research, you set a 105-pound cutoff for your hiring. The Association of Big Jockeys hears about your hiring practices and claims that your test of body weight and racing speed unfairly discriminates against heavier jockeys. Convinced that your test proves that lighter jockeys do better, you correlate the new jockeys' weights, which range between 100 and 105 pounds, with their racing times. You are surprised and embarrassed because body weight no longer predicts racing speed.

Can you figure out what went wrong? When you conducted the first test, you had a wide range of weights. Given this range, body weight did have predictive validity. With the second test, however, the range of body weights had been greatly restricted. Within this very narrow range, body weight completely lost its predictive power.

A similar narrowing of range explains why the GRE is only a modest predictor of graduate school grades. If a graduate school rejects people with low aptitude scores and receives few applications from people with high aptitude scores, the students that are admitted will have aptitude scores that fall within a narrow range. So it is hardly surprising that their aptitude scores will not be highly correlated with their grades. This will be true even if the test is a good predictor given a full spectrum of student abilities. Thus, when a test is validated using a wide range of people but is then used with a restricted range of people, there is no guarantee that this use of the test will have predictive validity.

The sport of horse racing actually adjusts for the body weight of jockeys by requiring that all horses in a race carry a specified total weight.

THE NATURE OF INTELLIGENCE

So far in this chapter, we have used the term "intelligence" as though we all naturally agreed upon what it means. In reality, though, defining intelligence is a controversial issue. During the last century, psychologists have debated whether intelligence should be defined as an inherent brain capacity, as an achieved level of intellectual functioning, or as an ascribed quality that, like beauty, is in the eye of the beholder.

The popular trend toward identifying, labeling, and grouping together children who are "gifted" is a current example of how arbitrary our definitions can be. To one person, gifted might imply being precocious at mathematics; to another, at playing the violin; to someone else, at athletics. Some 3 to 5 percent of all children are said to be gifted and therefore deserving of special educational opportunities both in and after school. The implication is that the other 95 to 97 percent of all children are "not gifted" and can therefore be excluded from the special educational opportunities. (Actually, as we will see, even children who score very low on IQ tests may have some remarkable gifts.)

"Alpha children wear grey. They work much harder than we do, because they're so frightfully clever. I'm really awfully glad I'm a Beta, because I don't work so hard. And then we are much better than the Gammas and Deltas. Gammas are stupid."
Aldous Huxley,
Brave New World, 1932

In labeling children as "gifted" or "not gifted," rather than calling attention to their specific abilities, we may be committing a common logical error called ***reification***—regarding an abstract concept as though it were a real, concrete thing. In other words, we tend to develop a concept, give it a name, and then convince ourselves that such a thing objectively exists in the world. Once we develop the idea of "giftedness," we begin thinking that children are naturally clustered into two well-defined groups, the "gifted" and "not gifted." Newspaper and magazine articles appear advising parents how to spot "the signs of giftedness" in their children, as if giftedness were an objective quality, like red hair, that a child either has or does not. We forget that "gifted" is a label of our own devising and, moreover, that we select which "gifts" will qualify for this label. Similarly, virtually all the experts agree that intelligence is not a "thing." Rather, it is a concept that we have invented to explain why some people perform more effectively than others, especially on cognitive tasks. In the *Handbook of Human Intelligence* Robert Sternberg and William Salter (1982, p. 3) report that most experts view ***intelligence*** as a person's capacity for "goal-directed adaptive behavior"—behavior that successfully meets challenges and achieves its aims. This definition of intelligence is general enough to be acceptable to many researchers and to leave room for their differences.

"The tendency has always been strong to believe that whatever received a name must be an entity or being, having an independent existence of its own."
John Stuart Mill, 1806–1873

"Intelligence is the particular facility a person has to cope with any given situation."
M. S. Michel,
Sweet Murder, 1943

Precisely what are the controversies regarding the nature of intelligence? As we will see, they concern whether intelligence should be considered as culturally defined or as a general ability to solve problems, and whether intelligence is best considered as overall mental ability or as many specific abilities.

"I'm a gifted child."

Intelligence as Culturally Defined or as a Problem-Solving Ability

One view of intelligence emphasizes the importance of the environment. According to this view, behavior that is adaptive varies with the people and the situation involved. For Binet, it meant children's adapting successfully in Parisian schools. For islanders in the South Pacific, it might be the ability to fish and to "read" the ocean. For a manager or salesperson in our society, it might be competence in interpersonal relations.

Those who view intelligence as people's successful adaptation to their environments tend to be skeptical about the prospects for a "culture-free" test of intelligence—a test that is uninfluenced by the culture to which one has adapted. They feel that those who hope for such a test fail to understand that intelligence tends to be defined within the cultural context. It might make sense to talk about a "culture-free" measure of height, but not of intelligence. To say that someone is intelligent necessarily requires making a judgment about what qualities are adaptive.

Others view intelligence as those cognitive abilities, whatever they may be, that help people to solve problems effectively and to achieve their rationally chosen goals, regardless of their cultural environment (Baron, 1985). The abstract and novel questions asked on intelligence tests provide miniature challenges that are intended to evaluate people's abilities to solve a variety of problems effectively, no matter what their cultural backgrounds may be. The assumption is that people who on the WAIS can remember a long string of digits and then report them backward, or can find the missing element in a picture, will likely have an edge at solving a variety of other problems, be it taking tests in school or growing corn.

According to one view, intelligence is successful adaptation to the challenges of one's environment. Environments vary, so this view implies that what it means to be intelligent varies.

Intelligence as General Versus Specific

We are all aware of the fact that some people are talented in mathematics, others in creative writing, and still others in art or music. We might therefore begin to wonder whether people's mental abilities are just too diverse for us to be justified in assigning them the single label "intelligence" or qualifying them with a single IQ score. Should we think of intelligence as a single dimension of general intellectual ability or as a collection of specific abilities?

The Factor Analysis Approach

The question we just asked about intelligence might also be asked of athletic ability. Is there a general trait—let us call it athleticism—that runs through all the more specific aspects of athletic ability, such as reaction time, speed, strength, and so forth? Or are these aspects distinct and independent?

If we test the specific aspects and discover that they are independent skills—if, for example, there is no correlation between being strong and being quick, or between endurance and coordination—then we would not be justified in assuming that a general athleticism underlies them. Suppose, though, that our tests of reaction time, speed, and strength reveal that people who score high on one tend to score high on the others. We could then statistically extract the common factor that runs through all the skills and call it general athleticism. Of course, there would still be those components of the specific skills that are unique to each of them. Thus, your potential to excel at a particular sport would depend on both your general athleticism and the specific skills you bring to the sport.

With intelligence, as with athletic ability, virtually everyone agrees that there are certain specific abilities. Recall that intelligence tests, such as the WAIS, often distinguish between verbal and performance intelligence; that aptitude tests, such as the SAT, typically discriminate between verbal and mathematical aptitude; and that the discussion of adult development in Chapter 4 describes changes in fluid versus crystallized intelligence. In your own experience, you may have known a talented artist who was dumfounded by the simplest mathematical problems or a brilliant mathematician who seemed to have little aptitude for philosophical discussion. (Of course, you may also have encountered a mathematically skilled artist or a philosophically minded mathematician.)

But are there some common factors that run through our specific mental abilities? In attempts to find out, psychologists have given people many different kinds of tests and have then correlated their answers to different questions to see which items were related to one another.

A statistical procedure called ***factor analysis*** allows researchers to identify clusters of test items that seem to tap a common ability. For example, people who do well on vocabulary items often do well on paragraph comprehension. This cluster, which might also include other items that pertain to language usage, might define a verbal intelligence factor. Indeed, psychologists have identified clusters that do point to a verbal intelligence factor, a spatial ability factor, and a reasoning ability factor, among others (Hunt, 1983).

Charles Spearman (1863–1945), who helped to develop the factor analysis concept and procedure, believed that there was also a ***general intelligence,*** or ***g,*** factor that, like our presumed trait of general athleticism, underlies each of the specific factors. People often have special abilities that stand out, Spearman allowed, but there is also some tendency for people who score high on one factor, such as verbal intelligence, to score high on other factors such as spatial or reasoning ability. Spearman believed that this commonality, the g factor, underlies all of our intelligent behavior.

The idea that, in addition to specific mental abilities, there is also a general mental capacity that can be characterized by a single IQ score was controversial in Spearman's day, and it remains so in our own. Opposing Spearman, fellow British psychologist Godfrey Thomson (1881–1955) argued that intelligence is not one thing but many things, including habits, knowledge, and various mental processes. Another of Spearman's contemporaries, L. L. Thurstone (1887–1955), also believed that each individual has a unique profile of abilities. In conducting his research, Thurstone administered fifty-six different tests to people and analyzed the results mathematically. From these analyses, he was able to identify eight different clusters of abilities that he believed were distinguishable. Thurstone did not rank his subjects on a single scale of general ability. But when other investigators studied the profiles of his subjects they detected at least a small tendency for those who excelled in one of the eight clusters of abilities to score well on the others also. So they concluded that there was still some evidence of a g factor.

More recently, psychologist Howard Gardner (1983) has reaffirmed and expanded upon Thurstone's view. Gardner argued that we do not have *an* intelligence, but, rather, *multiple* intelligences, each independent of the others. In addition to the verbal and mathematical intelligences assessed by the standard tests, Gardner identified distinct aptitudes for musical accomplishment, for spatially analyzing the visual world, for mastering movement skills such as those characteristic of dance, and for insightfully understanding ourselves and others.

Indications of these special intelligences come not from mathematical analyses of the sort that Thurstone performed, but from such sources as studies of people who excel in one area but not in others. ***Idiot savants,*** for instance, are otherwise retarded people who possess incredible specific skills, such as drawing ability, memory for music, or computing ability (see Figure 12-7). Idiot savants may have virtually no language ability, yet they may be able to compute numbers as quickly and accurately as an electronic calculator or identify almost instantaneously the day of the week that corresponds to any given date in history.

Figure 12-7 *Although lacking in language ability, a severely subnormal English girl named Nadia could draw scenes she had witnessed with remarkable skill and accuracy. Nadia drew this horse and rider at age 5.*

The abilities of the idiot savants are extreme instances of what virtually everyone now agrees is the multidimensional nature of intelligent behavior. As we noted earlier, IQ scores validly predict academic achievement. However, what is too often lost sight of when we speak of intelligence and giftedness is the realization that different people have different gifts. Mozart, for instance, was a genius at composing music, as was Einstein at physics, but there is little reason to think that either of them would have excelled in poetry, painting, or politics. And yet the main issue stubbornly persists: Is there or is there not a general intelligence factor that underlies all these distinct mental abilities?

Drawing by Sidney Harris

"Gifted class, indeed! One is gifted in science, but can't read; one is gifted in reading, but won't even try math. . . ."

The Information-Processing Approach

Recently, a wholly different approach to identifying the components of intelligence has begun to emerge. Instead of deriving a theory of intelligence from the existing measures, why not derive the measures from a theory of how people process information? This approach asks whether differences in people's performance on intelligence tests can be traced to differences in their more fundamental capacities for processing sensory input, learning, memory, and problem solving.

To identify the components of the information-processing procedures that people use when taking intelligence tests, psychologist Robert Sternberg (1982) conducted experiments to study the steps that people go through when solving problems like those typically found on intelligence tests. For example, Sternberg presented a subject with the question portion of a multiple-choice analogy, such as "lawyer is to client as doctor is to ______," and then measured the amount of time that elapsed until the person signaled that he or she understood the question. Then he would show the subject the answer choices (such as [a] patient, or [b] medicine) and measure the time it took for the subject to select an answer. Sternberg found that people who scored as highly intelligent tend to spend *more* time analyzing the question than do those who scored lower, but the high scorers were then able to recognize the correct answer more quickly. Sternberg (1984) noted that his research findings put a qualification on the common-sense maxim that "smart is fast." High scorers are apparently "quick-witted" only after they have taken sufficient time to reflect upon and comprehend a problem.

Working at a more elementary level of cognitive processing, Earl Hunt (1983) and his colleagues found that verbal intelligence scores are modestly related to the speed with which people retrieve information from memory. Those who score high in verbal ability tend to be quicker than low scorers in recognizing, for example, that "SINK" and "wink" are different words, or that "A" and "a" share the same name.

At a still more elementary level, Philip Vernon (1983) and Hans Eysenck (1982) found that people with high IQ scores react faster than people with low IQ scores on various tests that measure the speed with which they process sensory information. Vernon allowed that intelligence tests contain items that measure acquired information, but speculated that high scorers may know more because "faster cognitive processing may allow more information to be acquired."

Do Vernon's and Eysenck's attempts to link IQ scores to information-processing speed sound familiar? A century after Galton's futile attempts to gauge intelligence in terms of people's reaction times and sensory abilities, his ideas still live. Will the new efforts be more successful? Will they achieve Galton's aim of reducing what we now call the g factor to a neurological basis? Or are these efforts totally wrongheaded because what we call intelligence is not a single general trait but a multiplicity of culturally defined adaptive skills? As you can see, the controversies surrounding intelligence are a long way from being resolved.

"'Intelligence test' is an unfortunate label. It is too easily misunderstood to mean that intelligence is a unitary ability, fixed in amount, unchanged over time, and for which individuals can be ranked on a single scale."
National Research Council (Wigdor & Garner, 1982)

Dynamics of Intelligence

Although researchers still debate their perspectives on intelligence, their studies have provided much information about the stability and significance of test scores. Let's see what they have found.

Stability Versus Change in IQ

Here we again consider an issue first raised in our examination of developmental psychology: How consistent are people's traits over time? If we were to test people periodically throughout their lives, would their IQ scores be stable? Would their earlier performance predict their later performance?

The question is especially interesting to new parents, who may eagerly seek signs indicating whether their baby is bright or not-so-bright. Parents who are anxious about their baby seeming a little "slower" than other babies can relax. As developmental psychologist Robert McCall (1981) reported, "Nearly 50 years of research shows that prediction coefficients from infant behavior to later I.Q. are sufficiently low to be conceptually uninteresting and clinically useless." Sophisticated new methods for measuring infants' attention to novel stimuli do help to predict later intelligence (Fagan, 1984). But except for extreme cases of retardation caused by physical defects, there is currently no practical way, apart from knowing something about their own intelligence, for parents to predict a baby's later aptitude. By periodically testing children over a number of years, McCall and his colleagues (1973) found that there is an average difference of about 30 points between a child's IQ at $2\frac{1}{2}$ years of age and his or her score at 17.

After age 3, however, children's performances on IQ tests begin to predict their adult IQ scores, and after about age 7 and throughout adulthood the stability in IQ scores becomes noteworthy (Bloom, 1964). So, the consistency over time of IQ scores increases with the age of the child. Although there are anecdotal reports to the contrary—Einstein, for instance, was slow in learning to talk (Quasha, 1980)—precocious adolescents tend to have been precocious preschoolers. One study surveyed the parents of 187 seventh and eighth graders who had taken the SAT as part of a seven-state talent search and had scored considerably higher than most high school seniors. When the parents were asked when their precocious adolescents had begun reading, more than half said by age 4 and more than 80 percent recalled their children reading by age 5 (VanTassel-Baska, 1983).

Extremes of IQ

One way to glimpse the validity and significance of any test is to compare people who score at the two extremes. The two groups should differ noticeably, and on IQ tests they do. In one famous study begun in 1921, Lewis Terman tested more than 1500 California school children with IQs over 135. Contrary to Seneca's widely accepted maxim that "There is no great genius without some touch of madness," these high-IQ children were found to be unusually healthy, well adjusted, and academically successful. When restudied over the next 6 decades (Goleman, 1980), many were found to have attained high levels of education. While their vocational success was varied, the group included many doctors, lawyers, professors, scientists, and authors of numerous books and articles. Such findings lend credence to the idea that the IQ test is at least somewhat predictive of later academically related achievements.

At the other extreme are people who score below 70 on an IQ test, many of whom are labeled ***mentally retarded.*** To be so labeled today, a child must have both a low IQ *and* difficulty adapting to the normal demands of life. Only about 1 percent of the population meets these two criteria, with males outnumbering females by 2 to 1 (American Psychiatric Association, 1980). As Table 12-1 indicates, most of them are mildly retarded individuals who suffer no obvious physical defect and who, with support, can be socially and vocationally successful. More severe retardation usually results from known physical causes, such as ***Down's syndrome*** (formerly and inappropriately called "mongolism" because of the victims' typically round faces and almond-shaped eyes). Down's syndrome is a defect caused by an extra chromosome in the person's genetic makeup.

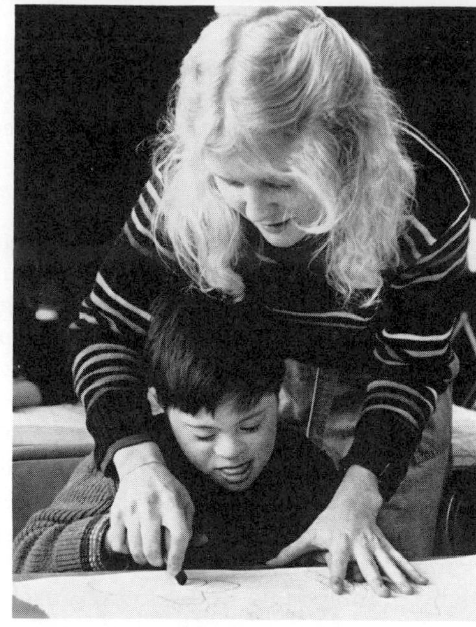

About 1 baby in every 600 is born with Down's syndrome. In addition to mental retardation, such children usually have rounder faces and shorter limbs than normal children, and suffer heart, eye, or ear problems. With today's better medical care, however, and with sufficient love and education, some Down's syndrome children can become self-sufficient adults.

Table 12-1 **Descriptions of mental retardation**

Level of retardation	Percent of the retarded	IQ levels	Characteristics
Mild	80%	50–70	May learn academic skills up to sixth-grade level. As adults, may, with assistance, achieve self-supporting social and vocational skills.
Moderate	12%	35–49	May progress to second-grade level. As adults, may contribute to own support by labor in sheltered workshops.
Severe	7%	20–34	May learn to talk and to perform simple work tasks under close supervision, but generally are unable to profit from vocational training.
Profound	1%	Below 20	Require constant aid and supervision.

Source: Adapted from the American Psychiatric Association (1980, p. 36).

Moderately retarded individuals may live satisfying lives when given support, such as provided by this group home for retarded women.

Intelligence and Creativity

Creativity is the ability to produce ideas that are both novel and valuable. Psychologists have had difficulty constructing tests of creativity that agree with one another or that predict actual creativity in science, inventions, and the arts (Jensen, 1980). What these tests commonly do is assess people's capacity for generating unusual responses to questions such as, "How many uses can you think of for a brick?"

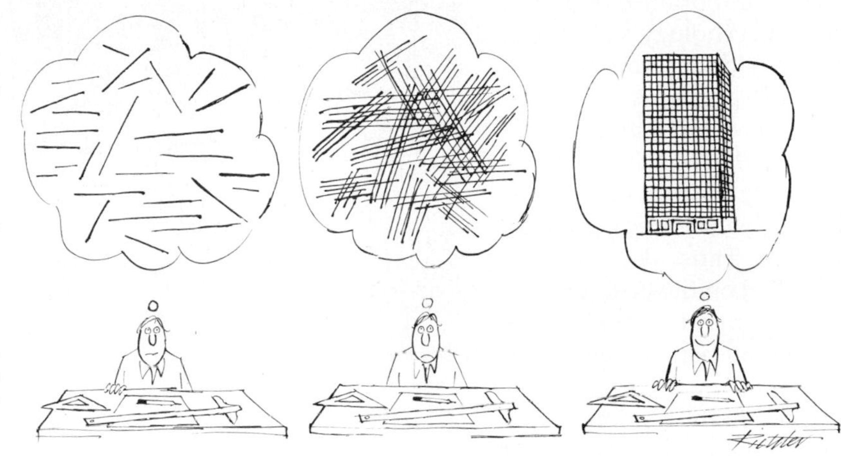

Results from tests of intelligence and creativity suggest that a certain level of intelligence is necessary but not sufficient for creativity. In general, people with high IQ scores tend to be more creative on tests and in their vocations than people with low IQ scores. But beyond a certain threshold—an IQ score of about 120—there appears to be little correlation between IQ scores and creativity. To some extent, this may reflect the tendency we noted earlier for correlations to diminish when one of the measures being correlated is restricted to a narrow range (in this case, to IQs above 120). Nevertheless, exceptionally creative architects, mathematicians, scientists, and engineers usually score no higher on intelligence tests than their less creative peers (MacKinnon & Hall, 1972).

The fact that people with high IQ scores can be more or less creative than others hints that intelligence is but one component of creativity. Studies of creative people suggest that other components include a high level of intrinsic curiosity and motivation and a low level of concern about what other people think. The most creative people, it appears, focus primarily on their work, not on such rewards as social approval.

Social conditions that foster little worry about social approval apparently enhance creativity. In an experiment conducted by Teresa Amabile (1983a, 1983b), college students were asked to make paper collages. Half of the students were told beforehand that their work would be evaluated by experts and half were not told this. The students who were *not* made to worry about what the experts would think produced collages that judges later rated as more creative. In another experiment, Amabile (1985) studied young creative writers. Half of the subjects were asked to rank intrinsic motives for writing, such as "you enjoy the opportunity for self-expression" and "you achieve new insights through your writing." The other half were asked to rank extrinsic motives, such as "you enjoy public recognition of your work" and "you know that many of the best jobs require good writing skills." The subjects were then asked to write poems. Sure enough, those whose attention had been focused on intrinsic motives wrote poems that were judged to be significantly more creative than those who had been reminded of extrinsic motives.

GENES, ENVIRONMENT, AND INTELLIGENCE

Determinants of Intelligence

As Sir Francis Galton recognized, intelligence seems to run in families. But why? Is it because intellectual abilities are inherited? Or is it because children's intellectual abilities are molded by the environment that the parents provide? These questions about the relative importance of nature and nurture to intelligence have generated one of psychology's stormiest debates. To understand why, consider how people with differing political views have often used the "nature" and "nurture" positions.

If, on the one hand, differences in mental abilities are mainly inherited, and if socioeconomic success tends to reflect those abilities (especially in societies where social position depends more on individual merit than on one's social connections), then people's socioeconomic standings will correspond to inborn differences among them. Thus, those on top may tend to feel that their social positions are justified on the basis of their innate superiority. They may even be tempted to remind us that it was only Thomas Jefferson, not God, who insisted that all persons were created equal.

If, on the other hand, mental abilities are determined primarily by nurture—by the environment in which individuals are raised and schooled—then children from disadvantaged environments will tend to lead disadvantaged lives because their intellectual abilities will not have had the chance to develop fully. In this case, people's socioeconomic standings will be the result of unequal opportunities, a situation that many regard as basically unjust.

Not surprisingly, those on the political right often tend to favor the nature position, whereas those on the left tend to find the nurture position closer to their views. Virtually everyone, though, now admits that both genes and the environment have some influence on IQ scores. The unresolved question is, "How much?"

Enter the scientists who say that dispassionate research can shed light on this question. As we saw in Chapter 2, "The Biological Roots of Behavior," there are objective methods for weighing the impact of genetic and environmental factors within a given range of individuals and situations. And, as behavioral geneticist Robert Plomin (1984) recently reported:

> The relative importance of both nature and nurture in the development of mental ability [is] the oldest continually researched question in the behavioral sciences. IQ tests have been administered to more than 4,000 individuals in adoptive relationships, to more than 4,500 twin pairs, and to more than 24,000 family members in pursuit of an answer to this question. If anything, the pace of research on the topic has picked up in recent years: Nearly as much data have been reported in the past 5 years as in the previous 50 years combined.

Let us see what these studies have revealed about genetic and environmental influence on intelligence.

Genetic Determinants

We begin our examination of the influence of heredity on intelligence by studying whether similarities in the IQs of any two individuals can be predicted from their genetic relatedness.

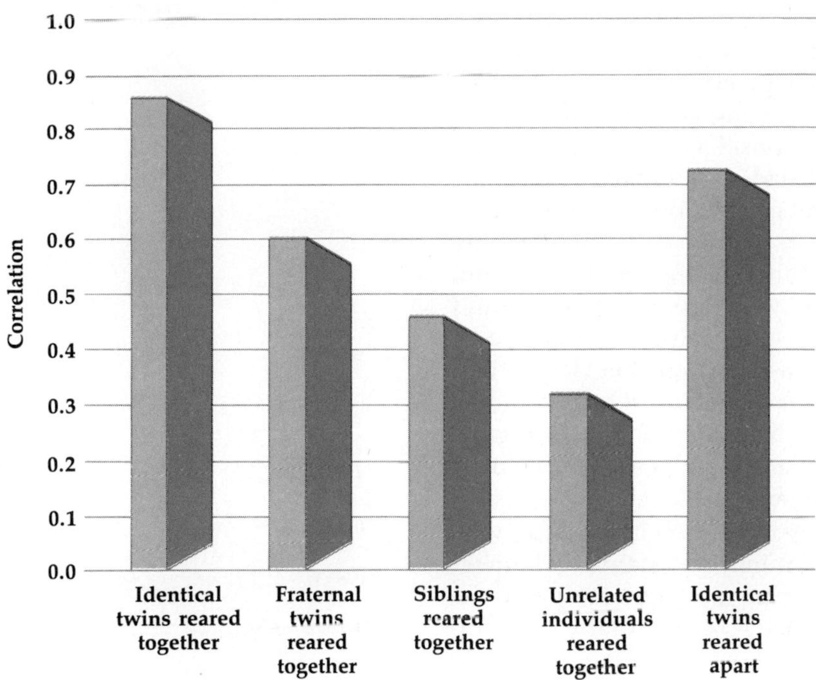

Figure 12-8 *The correlations of IQ test scores between identical twins, fraternal twins, siblings, and unrelated individuals raised together and identical twins raised apart. A score of 1 indicates a perfect correlation; a score of 0 indicates no correlation at all.*

Twin Studies Do people who share the same genes tend also to share mental abilities? As you can see from Figure 12-8, which summarizes the world's accumulated data (as reported by Bouchard & McGue, 1981), the answer clearly is yes. For example, identical twins score more similarly on IQ tests than do fraternal twins. What shall we make of these results? Let's eavesdrop on an imaginary conversation between two people—one who believes that heredity powerfully influences intelligence test performance, and one who does not.

Hereditarian: *Identical twins have IQ scores virtually as similar as those of the same person taking the test twice. In mental ability, as well as in genes, they are carbon copies of one another. By contrast, fraternal twins and other siblings share but half their genes. And, sure enough, they are less similar in IQ.*

Environmentalist: *Ah, but the identical twins are similar because they are treated similarly. Look at the data again and you'll see that fraternal twins, who are genetically no more alike than any other siblings, nevertheless tend to score more alike. And as John Loehlin and Robert Nichols documented in their 1976 study of hundreds of twins, identical twins are even more likely than fraternal twins to be dressed alike, to sleep in the same room, to have the same friends and teachers, and so forth. So their greater IQ similarity may be environmental.*

Hereditarian: *But Loehlin and Nichols also found that identical twins whose parents treated them alike were only slightly more similar than those whose parents did not. Furthermore, note that even when identical twins are reared separately, they still have IQs more alike than fraternal twins and other siblings reared together. Having the same genes has more effect than having the same environment.*

Environmentalist: *Psychologist Leon Kamin analyzed the studies of separated identical twins and he reported that the separated twins often were selectively placed in similar environments. Moreover, as new data accumulate, behavior geneticists are dropping their estimates of the extent to which variation in IQ scores can be attributed to heredity—from earlier estimates of around 80 percent to newer estimates of about 50 percent (Plomin & DeFries, 1980). As this illustrates, studies of the genetic determinants of behavior can tell us as much about the importance of the environment as about the importance of genes.*

As our imaginary conversation illustrates, the issue persists to the present day because of a stubbornly persistent problem: As long as genes and environment vary together, we cannot precisely disentangle their relative influences. But other methods of studying genetic and environmental influences can shed additional light. Consider one variation on the basic twin-study method: If your mother had an identical twin, your mother and your aunt would have the same genes. You would therefore be as genetically similar to your aunt as to your mother because you would share half of your genes with both of them. You would also share, on average, this same degree of relatedness with your full brothers and sisters. Furthermore, your aunt's children, your cousins, would be as genetically similar to you as half brothers or sisters would be. Half of their genes would be those of your aunt (and your mother) and half would be those of their father. Now, the question is, does this rather complicated family tree tell us anything about how similar in intelligence you would probably be to these various relatives? The answer is yes.

Richard Rose and his associates (1979) located 65 individuals who had a parent who was an identical twin, administered nonverbal intelligence tests to them and to their extended families, and then compared the scores. They found no relationship between the IQ scores of the individuals and their aunt or uncle by marriage (with whom they were genetically unrelated). However, their scores were as similar to those of their parent's twin as they were to their full siblings, with whom they shared the same environment. Moreover, the individuals were more similar to their cousins (who, remember, were the genetic equivalents of half siblings) than is normally the case. All in all, the results were consistent with those from the earlier twin studies: Among these people, one-half the variation in the intelligence scores could be attributed to genetic factors.

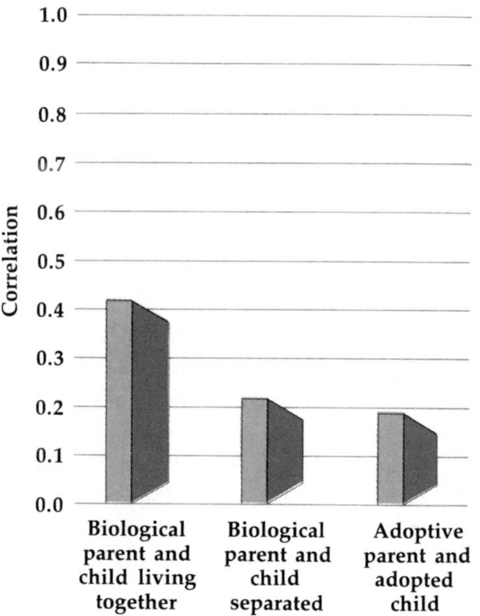

Figure 12-9 *The correlations of IQ test scores between children and their adoptive and biological parents.*

Adoption Studies Further evidence of the genetic influence on intellectual abilities is made possible by the fact of adoption. We might, for example, ascertain whether adopted children have IQ scores more like their biological parents, from whom they receive their genes, or their adoptive parents, who provide their home environment.

Several researchers have asked just this question, and their findings are summarized in Figure 12-9. As the figure shows, the magnitudes of the correlations are fairly low. One reason for this is the fact that adoptive parents tend mostly to be quite bright, so there is less than the usual variation in their IQ scores. (As we saw when we looked at predicting horse-racing times among lightweight jockeys, narrowing the range of possible variations tends to lessen the observed correlations.)

When a statistical adjustment is made for the similarities in the IQs of adoptive parents, the correlations rise, but the conclusions remain the same. Adopted children are somewhat more similar in IQ to their biological parents than to their adoptive parents, though there are definite similarities to both sets of parents. As with the other evidence we have so far considered, these findings indicate that both genes and the environment are important.

Clues to possible biological foundations of intelligence are also being sought in animals. It is possible to breed animals who show special talents at learning new behaviors or solving problems. For instance, rats bred so that an area of the brain called the hippocampus is larger than usual tend also to be more skilled at learning than rats usually are (Gardner & Dudai, 1985).

Environmental Determinants

We have seen that our genes have a significant effect on our intellectual abilities. But we have also seen that heredity doesn't tell the whole story. Within the limits dictated by our genes, we are shaped by our life experiences. As you may recall from Chapter 3, experience can literally leave its mark on the brain: Rats reared in impoverished environments tend to develop lighter and thinner brain cortexes than are normal, and specific learning experiences have very specific effects on their brains' neural connections. Among humans, brain lesions that occur very early in life may, thanks partly to the formative powers of early experience, not be terribly disruptive.

Impoverished human environments may also leave marks on a person's tested mental abilities. In his classic study begun in the 1930s, H. M. Skeels (1966) followed the development of a number of young, supposedly retarded children living in an Iowa orphanage. Some of the children were soon thereafter transferred to a more spacious home for the mentally retarded. Each of these children was provided with enriching environmental experiences by being placed in the loving care of a retarded young woman, who devoted much of her time to caring for and playing with her foster child. Four years later, these children had gained, on the average, some 30 points in IQ. Over the same period their counterparts who remained in the overcrowded orphanage had lost more than 20 IQ points.

When Skeels tested the children again more than 20 years later, the differences between the two groups were even more dramatic. Most of the group raised by the foster mothers had completed high school, were married, and were self-supporting. Sadly, most of the orphanage-reared children had dropped out of school by third grade and were either still institutionalized or were not fully self-supporting.

More recently, psychologist J. McVicker Hunt (1982) examined the effects of introducing similar environmental improvements in an Iranian orphanage in Tehran (prior to the Khomeini revolution). The typical child could not sit up unassisted at age 2 nor walk at age 4. What care infants in the orphanage did receive was not in response to their crying, cooing, or other behaviors. The infants were therefore not developing any sense of personal control over their environment, and so were becoming passive "glum lumps" (Figure 12-10a).

Hunt was well aware of research on the positive benefits of responsive caregiving (see Chapter 3, "Infancy and Childhood"). So he proceeded to put the principle into action by instituting a program he called "tutored human enrichment." For instance, the caregivers were trained to play vocal games with the infants. First, they imitated the babies' babbling; then they led the babies in vocal follow-the leader by shifting from one familiar sound to another; and then they began to concentrate on sounds from the Persian language.

The results were dramatic. Without exception, all eleven infants who received these language-fostering experiences and whose signs of distress were promptly responded to could name more than fifty objects and parts of the body by the age of 22 months (Figure 12-10b). In fact, so charming had the infants become that most of them were chosen for adoption—an unprecedented success for the orphanage.

Skeels's and Hunt's findings are impressive testimonials to the importance of environmental factors in the development of mental abilities. But do such findings provide clues as to how you can "give your child a superior intelligence"? Some popular books claim that this is possible, but many experts are not so sure (Detterman & Sternberg, 1982). For example, developmental psychologist Sandra Scarr (1984) agrees that neglectful upbringing can have grave long-term consequences for children. However, she also believes that "as long as an infant has normal human contact and normal exposure to sights, sounds, human speech and so forth, the baby will thrive." So far as intelligence is concerned, "Parents who are very concerned about providing special educational lessons for their babies are wasting their time."

Although Hunt would probably agree with Scarr that extra instruc-

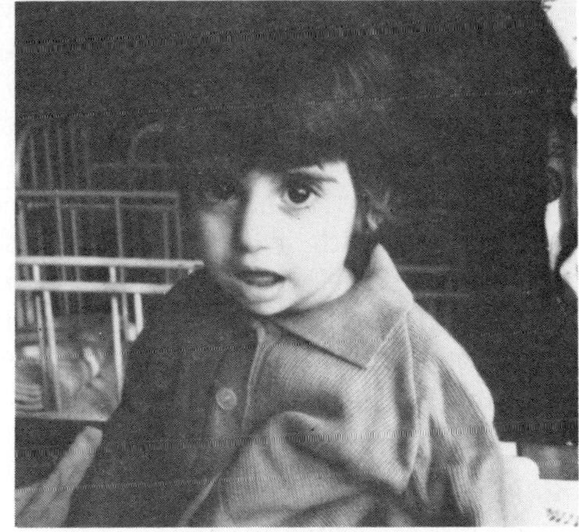

(a)

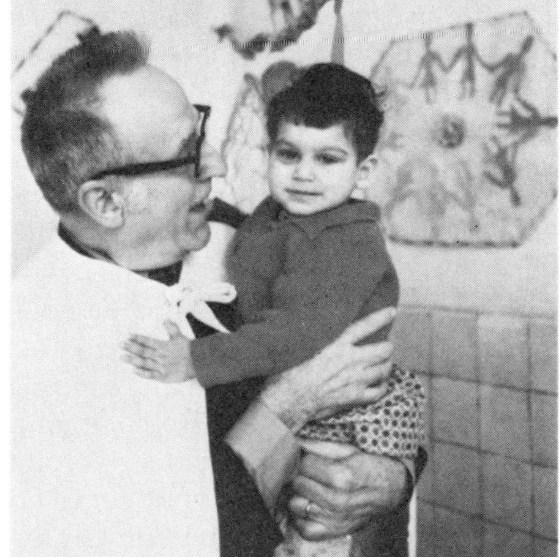

(b)

Figure 12-10 *The Iranian orphanage study. (a) This child's vacant expression was typical of those receiving the customary unresponsive care. (b) But after experiencing "tutored human enrichment," this child, similar in age to the one above, showed the benefits of positive caregiving.*

tion has little effect on the development of the intellectual abilities of children from "normal" environments, he is optimistic when it comes to children from disadvantaged environments. Indeed, his views, as expressed in his 1961 book *Intelligence and Experience,* helped launch Project Head Start in 1965.

Head Start is a family of preschool programs designed for children from disadvantaged environments and funded by the U.S. government. All of these programs "share a commitment to enhancing the quality of life for children and families," and more specifically, to improving children's cognitive and social-emotional maturity (Zigler & Berman, 1983). In 1984, Head Start was serving 430,000 children and their families in over 1200 communities (Collins, 1984). Research studies on its effects initially triggered euphoria over the short-term IQ gains that resulted, and then pessimism because of the lack of longer-term gains. Now, 20 years and 1500 studies later, there appears to be a growing consensus that Head Start has been a qualified success. In the words of the Reagan administration official responsible for distilling the accumulated research, "compensatory education has been tried, and it works" (Collins, 1983).

Although Head Start children do not show large, enduring gains in IQ, they do on other measures surpass disadvantaged children who have not participated. They are less likely to repeat grades or require special education classes, for example, and they are more likely to enjoy positive self-esteem and to adjust well to school. These benefits appear to be greatest for children from the most disadvantaged families and for those who participate in racially integrated rather than all-minority programs.

As Hunt (1982), in a reflective vein, stated:

> Project Head Start . . . failed to achieve the unrealistic hopes for it, but we learned . . . that the younger the children involved, the greater the effects attained. Second, we learned that it is difficult, if not impossible, to make up in a year or two of compensatory education, beginning at an age of four years, for the damage that is often done in the first four years. . . . From what I know today, I believe that the focus should be preventive, that the effort should start at birth for the children, and that it should be carried out by the parents with the help of tutelage such as we employed with our caregivers at the [Tehran orphanage].

Conclusions

From studies of family relations, twin studies, and adoption studies, we have seen evidence indicating that intelligence test performance is linked with heredity (see Figure 12-11). These same studies, plus others that compare neglectful and enriched environments, also indicate that intelligence test performance is linked with life experiences. All these findings, taken together, have led many investigators to conclude that the heritability of intelligence—that is, the amount of variation in intelligence that is attributable to genetic factors—is roughly 50 percent. If true, this conclusion does *not* mean that your genes are responsible for 50 percent of your intelligence and your environment for the rest. (Likewise, saying that the heritability of height is 90 percent does not mean that a 60-inch tall woman can credit her genes for 54 inches and her environment for the other 6 inches.) Rather, it means that, *of the variation in intelligence among individuals,* 50 percent can be attributed to heredity.

This conclusion must be qualified, however. First, the apparent heritability of any trait depends on the context in which that trait is being studied. As we noted in Chapter 2, "Biological Roots of Behavior," the heritability of a trait will appear to be low when we compare people with not-so-different heredities in drastically different environments. Con-

"There is no such thing as the *heritability of IQ, since heritability of a trait is different in different populations at different times."*
Richard Lewontin (1976)

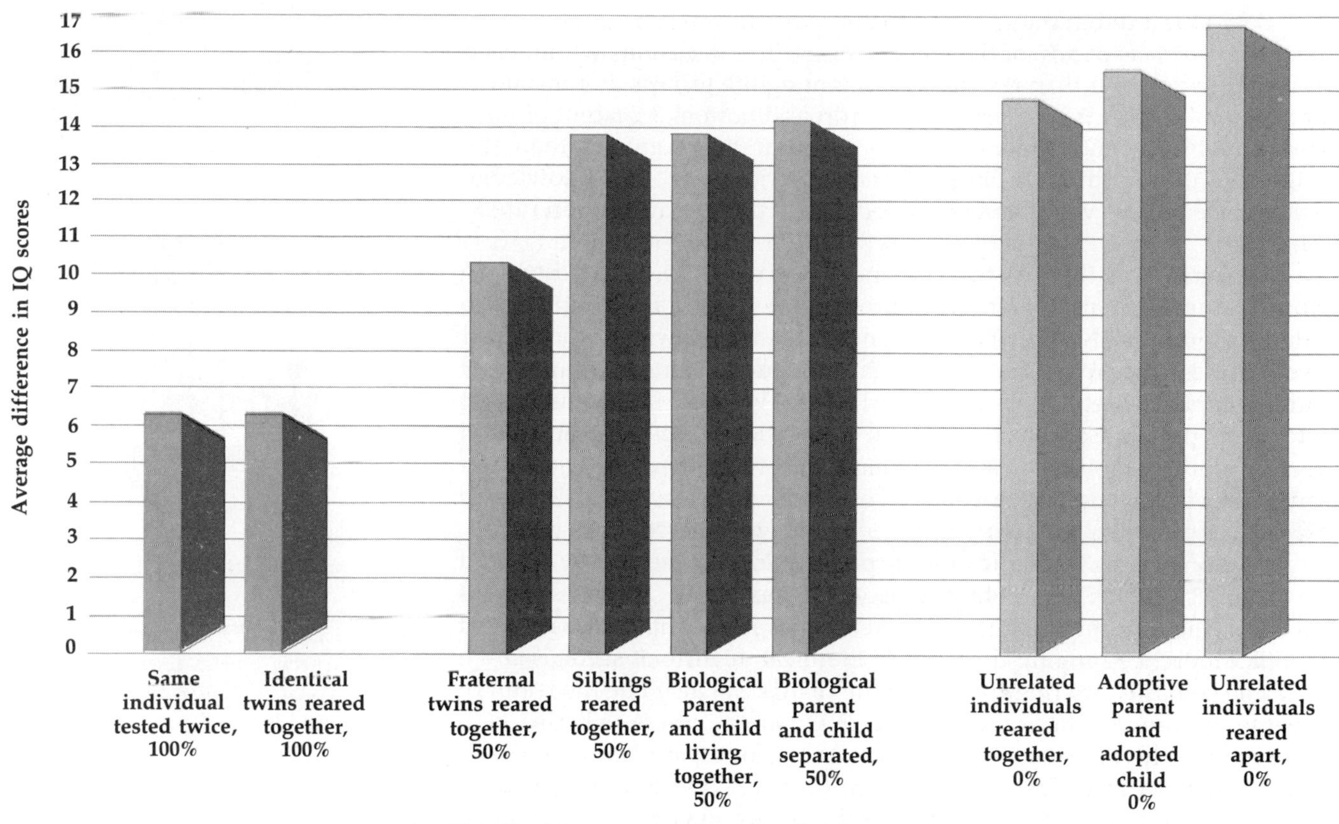

Figure 12-11 *The average difference in IQ test scores for nine different levels of genetic and environmental relatedness.*

versely, heritability will appear to be high when we compare people with very different heredities in basically similar environments.

Second, we must always remember that genes and environment are intertwined, not separate. Our genetically influenced traits may trigger responses that encourage us to develop our natural gifts, and may lead us to select particular environments. For instance, students with a natural aptitude for mathematics are more likely to select math courses in high school, and subsequently to score well on the SAT math test. Thus, the truth of the matter is that our genes shape the experiences that, in turn, shape us.

Race and Intelligence

The issue of hereditary versus environmental determinants of intelligence would not be debated so passionately were there no differences in the average IQ scores among various racial and ethnic groups. But there are. When American blacks have been compared to American whites (neither of which is a random sample of blacks and whites worldwide), blacks have been found to average about 15 points lower than whites on IQ tests and a comparable 100 points lower on the SAT verbal and math tests (Loehlin & others, 1975; "Racial gap," 1982). Similarly, recent comparisons have found that Japanese school children have a slightly higher average than American children on nonverbal items from the WISC (Lynn, 1982, 1983) and on mathematics achievement tests (Stevenson, 1983). Asian-Americans comprise less than 2 percent of the U.S. population, but they won 30 percent of the top 40 spots in the Westinghouse Science Talent Search in 1983 and 23 percent in both 1984 and 1985 (Doerner, 1985; McGrath, 1983; Williams, 1984).

In mathematics, Japanese school children outperform their American counterparts. What, if anything, does this tell us about the math aptitude of youngsters in the United States relative to those in Japan?

Bear in mind that these *average* differences may tell us nothing about specific *individuals* in any of the racial groups. The variations within each group are far greater than the variations among the groups. For instance, the 60 or so IQ points that separate the top and bottom 3 percent of both American blacks and American whites is four times greater than the roughly 15 percent difference between the two groups. Thus, knowledge of your race tells us very little about your likely performance on an intelligence test.

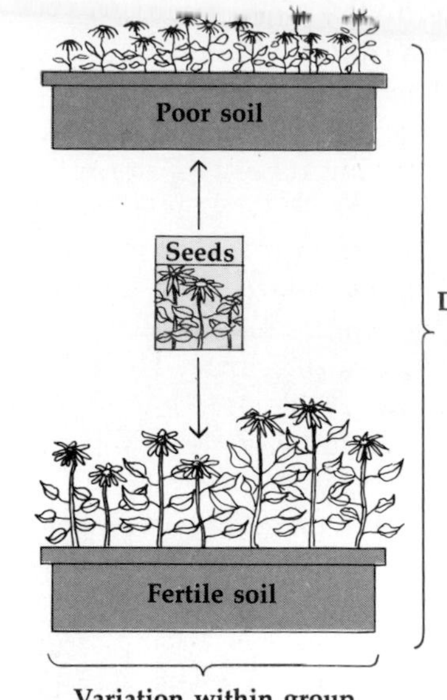

Figure 12-12 *Even if the variation within a group reflects genetic differences (differences between seeds), the average difference between groups may be wholly due to the environment.*

Nevertheless, the differences demand explanation. If heredity contributes to individual differences in intelligence, does it also contribute to group differences? Not necessarily. Consider the following hypothetical case. Suppose that we were to study math aptitude in an American school and in a Japanese school. Suppose further that we were somehow able to determine that the differences among the children within each school were entirely due to heredity. If we then found that the Japanese children had higher scores than the American children, could we also attribute the differences between the two groups of children to heredity?

The answer to this question is plainly no, and geneticist Richard Lewontin (1976) has demonstrated why. If a mixture of seeds is sown on poor soil, the differing heights of the resulting plants will be the result of genetic differences among them. If an identical mixture of seeds is sown on fertile soil, the differing heights of the plants will again be the result of genetic differences. But, as Figure 12-12 illustrates, there will also be a difference in the average heights of the two groups of plants. Since we know that both mixtures of seeds were identical, we obviously cannot attribute the greater average heights of the plants sown in fertile soil to a genetic difference between the two mixtures. The difference in average height is due to differences in the soil in which the plants grew. Thus, even if the heritability of a trait is high within a particular group, differences in that trait between groups may have environmental causes.

Among psychologists, the prevailing opinion is that differences in intelligence and related test scores among various racial and ethnic groups are environmental. Consider the following findings, each of which points to an environmental explanation.

"Most scholars accept a significant role for genes in the creation of individual differences in IQ. Race differences are another matter."
Joseph M. Horn (1982)

1. In the past, the average white person in the United States has grown up and been educated under conditions more advantageous than those experienced by the average black person. One attempt at equalizing the conditions experienced by blacks and whites, desegregation, has generally had only slight effects on the school achievements of black children. The benefits, though, have been the most notable when desegregation began in kindergarten or the first grade and extended over a number of years (Cook, 1984). As conditions for blacks improve in general, the IQ gap between blacks and whites should begin to disappear. And there are indications that it is indeed beginning to shrink (Jones, 1984).

While the IQ gap between blacks and whites appears to be decreasing, the gap in math scores between Japanese and American students appears to be growing. Psychologist Harold Stevenson (1983), who closely studied elementary school children in two comparable cities—Sendai in Japan and Minneapolis in the United States—believes that this gap is attributable to the more fertile academic soil in Japan. In comparison to American students, Japanese elementary school students attend school 30 percent more days a year, spend substantially more of their school day studying math, and do perhaps twice the homework, especially in the early grades.

2. Further evidence of environmental impact on intelligence scores comes from adoption studies. Consider: If black children were raised in privileged, white middle-class homes, would their average IQ score be

closer to the average score for black children or for white children? Sandra Scarr and Richard Weinberg (1976) studied 99 such children in Minneapolis. The average IQ of these children was 110, which is comparable to the average IQ of white children adopted into similar advantaged families. Thus, being reared as a privileged middle-class child appears to produce middle-class IQ scores.

3. Scarr and her co-workers (1977) also found that having more or less African ancestry bears no relation to scores on cognitive tests within the black population. (The extent of a black person's African ancestry is not necessarily detectable from skin color; for a better estimate, researchers may run blood tests.) Similarly, children who were fathered by black or by white American servicemen stationed in Germany after World War II and who were reared in similar German environments had nearly identical average IQ scores (MacKenzie, 1984).

4. At different times in history, different ethnic groups have experienced "golden ages," periods of remarkable achievement—2500 years ago it was the Greeks and then the Romans of southern Europe, in the eighth and ninth centuries the Arab world, five hundred years ago the Aztec Indians, and, starting somewhat earlier, the peoples of northern Europe and their descendants. Cultures rise and fall over centuries; genes do not. That fact makes it difficult to attribute any ethnic group's past (or current) achievements to its "natural" superiority.

Whether black or white, children raised in privileged middle-class homes tend to have IQ scores typical of the middle class.

Despite all the evidence supporting environmental explanations for racial score differences in intelligence, suppose that genetic differences do play some role. Would it, should it, matter? Not to any individual, for group averages are essentially irrelevant when considering a particular person. Not to any potential employer, for knowing a person's race tells the employer nothing about the person's potential. And not to social policy, for the impact of environmental disadvantages would nevertheless unquestionably remain significant.

Finally, we must remember that IQ is a measure of only one important domain of personal competence. As we have seen, there are other domains that are also important: motivation, character, social skills, sensitivity, emotional maturity, artistic talent, athletic ability. Said differently, the competence that is sampled by intelligence tests is important, but far from all-important.

The Question of Bias

How we answer the question of whether or not intelligence tests are biased depends on what we mean by the term "bias." One meaning is that the tests are sensitive not only to innate differences in intelligence but also to differences caused by cultural experiences. In this sense, virtually everyone agrees that the tests are biased. No one claims that heritability is 100 percent responsible for the score obtained on any test. An intelligence test measures a person's developed abilities at a particular moment in time, and these abilities necessarily reflect that person's experiences and environmental background. If people's experiences and backgrounds are unequal, those inequalities will be reflected in the test's results.

No doubt you have read examples of intelligence test items that make middle-class assumptions (for example, that a cup goes with a saucer or, as we noted in one of the examples from the WAIS in Figure 12-1 on page 308, that people buy fire insurance to protect the value of their homes and possessions). Does the presence of such items bias the test against those who do not use saucers and whose meager possessions and income hardly warrant the cost of fire insurance? Could such test questions explain the racial differences in test performance? If so, are tests therefore a discriminatory vehicle that could be used to consign potentially capable children to dead-end classes and jobs (as the judge argued in the case of Larry and the six other black California children noted at the beginning of this chapter)?

The defenders of aptitude testing report that racial group differences have been reported on nonverbal items, such as counting digits backwards, as well as on verbal items, such as vocabulary knowledge (Jensen, 1983). Moreover, they say that to blame the test for a group's lower scores is comparable to blaming a messenger for bringing the bad news—that the culture provides unequal experiences and opportunities to different people. If because of malnutrition the people in country X were to suffer stunted growth, would one blame the measuring stick that reveals it? To the extent that unequal past experiences predict unequal future achievements, a valid aptitude test will detect such inequalities. Moreover, to say that a test should not reflect the effects of a person's experiences and environmental background makes the questionable assumption that there is some hidden "real intelligence" that lies waiting for an unbiased test that will measure it fairly.

Another meaning of "bias" hinges on whether or not a test is less valid for some groups than for others. If the SAT accurately predicts the college achievement of whites but is irrelevant to that of blacks, then the test would be biased. The near consensus among psychologists today, as summarized by the National Research Council's Committee on Ability Testing (Wigdor & Garner, 1982), is that the major aptitude tests are *not* biased with regard to this meaning of the term. The predictive validity of the SAT, for example, is roughly the same for blacks and whites, and the SAT does not generally underestimate minority students' college grades.

So, it is possible for aptitude tests to be biased in one sense and not in another. For example, if a college's courses and teachers share a particular vocabulary and set of assumptions that make it difficult for people from a foreign culture to excel there, then scores on a test that accurately predicts success in that school will be influenced by a person's cultural background. The test would therefore be culturally biased, because it mirrors the school's cultural bias. Yet the test might be an equally valid predictor of performance for all those who take it, and so, in the second sense, not be biased.

Are tests discriminatory? Again, the answer can be yes or no. In one sense, yes, their purpose is to discriminate—to distinguish among individuals. In another sense, their purpose is to reduce discrimination by reducing reliance on the irrelevant criteria that were once more crucial for school and job placement—criteria such as who you know, what you look like, or how much the interviewer happens to like your kind of person. Civil service tests were devised to discriminate among individuals, but to do so more fairly, by reducing the political discrimination that preceded their use. Perhaps, then, our aim should be to realize the benefits that Alfred Binet foresaw for intelligence tests—to guide individuals toward opportunities for which they are especially well-suited—while being wary of what Binet feared, that test scores might be misinterpreted as measures of a person's worth and fixed potential.

Tests assess one's developed ability, which is influenced by one's life experience. To the extent that a particular environment has hampered or enhanced intellectual growth, a valid test will reflect this effect.

SUMMING UP

THE MEASUREMENT OF INTELLIGENCE

The Origins of Intelligence Tests The measurement of individual mental abilities was first undertaken more than a century ago by Sir Francis Galton. Although Galton failed in his efforts to invent simple, quantifiable measures of mental ability, his idea of measuring intellectual capacity was applied by Alfred Binet, who developed questions that helped to predict a child's future progress in the Paris schools. Like Galton, Lewis Terman of Stanford University was convinced that intelligence was inherited, and, like Binet, he believed his test (called the Stanford-Binet) could help steer people into appropriate roles. During the early part of this century, intelligence tests were sometimes used in ways that, in hindsight, seemed regrettable even to their designers—to "document" the presumed innate inferiority of certain ethnic and immigrant groups.

Modern Tests of Intelligence Tests are commonly classified as either aptitude tests (designed to predict learning ability) or achievement tests (designed to assess current competence), and as assessing either general abilities (as do the Wechsler scales and the SAT) or more specific abilities (as does the DAT).

Principles of Test Construction A good test must be standardized, so that a person's performance can be meaningfully compared to others'; reliable, so that it yields dependably consistent scores (over the short run); and valid, so that it measures what it is supposed to measure. Test scores tend to fall into a normal distribution, with the average score given some arbitrary number (such as 100 on an IQ test). Despite small coaching effects, aptitude tests tend to be highly reliable. Their predictive validity is fairly strong in the early grades but weakens for predicting grades in college and even more so in graduate school, as the range of student abilities becomes restricted.

THE NATURE OF INTELLIGENCE

Intelligence as Culturally Defined or as a Problem-Solving Ability It is tempting but misleading to reify concepts such as "intelligence" and "giftedness"—to regard these abstract concepts as if they were real, concrete things. Intelligence is most commonly defined by experts as "goal-directed adaptive behavior." Some psychologists argue that this makes its precise definition (as, say, a person's ability to successfully adapt to the demands of school or work) culturally relative; others contend that intelligence can be viewed as a general ability to solve problems.

Intelligence as General Versus Specific Psychologists agree that people possess specific abilities, such as verbal and mathematical aptitudes, but they debate whether a general intelligence (g) factor runs through them all. Factor analysis and studies of special people such as idiot savants have been used to identify people's clusters of abilities. More recently, psychologists have linked people's intelligence to their more fundamental capacities for processing information.

Dynamics of Intelligence The stability of intelligence test scores increases with age, with predictive value beginning at about age 3. Comparing those who score extremely high (the "gifted") or low (the "retarded") will magnify a test's apparent validity. Intelligence appears to have a "threshold relationship" with creativity; increases in intelligence beyond a necessary threshold level are not associated with increased creativity.

GENES, ENVIRONMENT, AND INTELLIGENCE

Determinants of Intelligence Because of its political and racial overtones, the nature-nurture debate with regard to intelligence has been vehement. Twin studies, studies of family relations, and adoption studies all are controversial, yet together point to a significant hereditary contribution to IQ scores. These same studies, plus others that compare children reared in neglectful or enriched environments, indicate that life experiences also significantly influence test performance.

Race and Intelligence Like individuals, groups may vary in intelligence. The existence of hereditary variation within a group does not necessitate a hereditary explanation of the differences between groups. In the case of the gap between black and white Americans in average IQ, the evidence suggests that environmental differences are largely, perhaps entirely, responsible.

The Question of Bias If by "biased" one means sensitive to differences caused by cultural experiences, then aptitude tests are necessarily biased. If by biased one means what psychologists commonly mean—that a test predicts less validly for one group than for another—then the major tests we have considered seem not to be biased.

TERMS AND CONCEPTS TO REMEMBER

Achievement Tests Tests designed to assess what a person has already learned.

Aptitude Tests Aptitude is the capacity to learn. Thus aptitude tests are designed to predict a person's future performance.

Content Validity The extent to which a test samples the behavior that is of interest (such as a driving test that samples driving tasks).

Creativity The ability to produce ideas that are both novel and valuable.

Criterion The behavior (such as obtained college grades) that a test (such as the SAT) is designed to predict; thus the measure used in defining whether the test has predictive validity.

Down's Syndrome A condition of retardation and associated physical disorders caused by an extra chromosome in one's genetic makeup.

Factor Analysis A statistical procedure that identifies clusters of related items (called factors) on a test; used to identify different dimensions of performance that underlie one's total score.

General Intelligence (g) A general underlying intelligence factor that was believed by Spearman and others to be measured by every task on an intelligence test.

Idiot Savant A retarded person who possesses an amazing specific skill, such as in computation or drawing.

Intelligence The capacity for goal-directed adaptive behavior (behavior that successfully meets challenges and achieves its aims). Involves the abilities to profit from experience, solve problems, reason, remember, and so forth.

Intelligence Quotient (IQ) An intelligence measure that was originally defined as the ratio of mental age to chronological age multiplied by 100 (thus IQ = MA/CA × 100). Contemporary tests compute IQ by giving the average performance for a given age a score of 100, with other IQ scores defined in terms of their deviation from the average.

Mental Age A measure of intelligence test performance devised by Binet; the chronological age that most typically corresponds to a given level of performance. Thus a child who does as well as the average 8-year-old is said to have a mental age of 8.

Mental Retardation A condition of low IQ (such as below 70) plus difficulty adapting to the demands of life; varies from mild to profound.

Normal Curve (or **Normal Distribution**) The symmetrical bell-shaped curve that describes the distribution of many physical and psychological attributes (including IQ scores), with most scores falling near the average and fewer and fewer near the extremes.

Predictive Validity The success with which a test predicts the behavior it is designed to predict; assessed by computing the correlation between test scores and the criterion behavior.

Reification To regard an abstract concept (such as giftedness) as if it were a real, concrete thing.

Reliability The extent to which a test yields consistent results (as assessed by the consistency of scores on two halves of the test, on alternate forms of the test, or on retesting). See *split-half* and *test-retest reliability*.

Split-half Reliability A measure of the internal consistency of a test; typically assessed by correlating total scores obtained on the odd and even items.

Standardization Defining meaningful scores by comparison with the performance of a representative "standardization group" that has been pretested.

Stanford-Binet The widely used American revision (by Terman at Stanford University) of Binet's original intelligence test.

Test-Retest Reliability A measure of the consistency of test scores obtained by retesting people.

Validity The extent to which a test measures or predicts what it is supposed to measure (or predict). (See also *content* and *predictive validity*.)

Wechsler Adult Intelligence Scale (WAIS) The most widely used intelligence test; contains a variety of verbal and nonverbal (performance) subtests.

FOR FURTHER READING

The Consortium for Longitudinal Studies (1983). *As the twig is bent . . . : Lasting effects of early education.* Hillsdale, NJ: Erlbaum.

Can research-based early intervention programs such as Head Start make a difference? Provides the accumulated evidence and answers yes.

Eysenck, H. J. (1981). *The intelligence controversy: H. J. Eysenck vs. Leon Kamin.* New York: Wiley.

Provides a spirited debate between a well-known hereditarian (Eysenck) and environmentalist (Kamin).

Gould, S. J. (1981). *The mismeasure of man.* New York: Norton.

Offers a provocative, engaging, and sharply critical look at the history of the intelligence testing movement and its abuses.

Sternberg, R. (1986). *Intelligence applied: Understanding and increasing your intelligence.* San Diego: Harcourt Brace Jovanovich.

A leading researcher presents his theory of intelligence to a general audience and offers "how to" suggestions for increasing one's practical intelligence.

White, J. L. (1984). *The psychology of blacks: An Afro-American perspective.* Englewood Cliffs, NJ: Prentice-Hall.

A black psychologist looks at racial differences in intelligence and other traits and behaviors.

Wigdor, A. K., & Garner, W. R. (1982). *Ability testing: Uses, consequences, and controversies.* Washington, DC: National Academic Press.

A blue-ribbon panel of the U.S. National Research Council offers its analysis of ability testing. An authoritative source of prevailing professional opinion on the major issues.

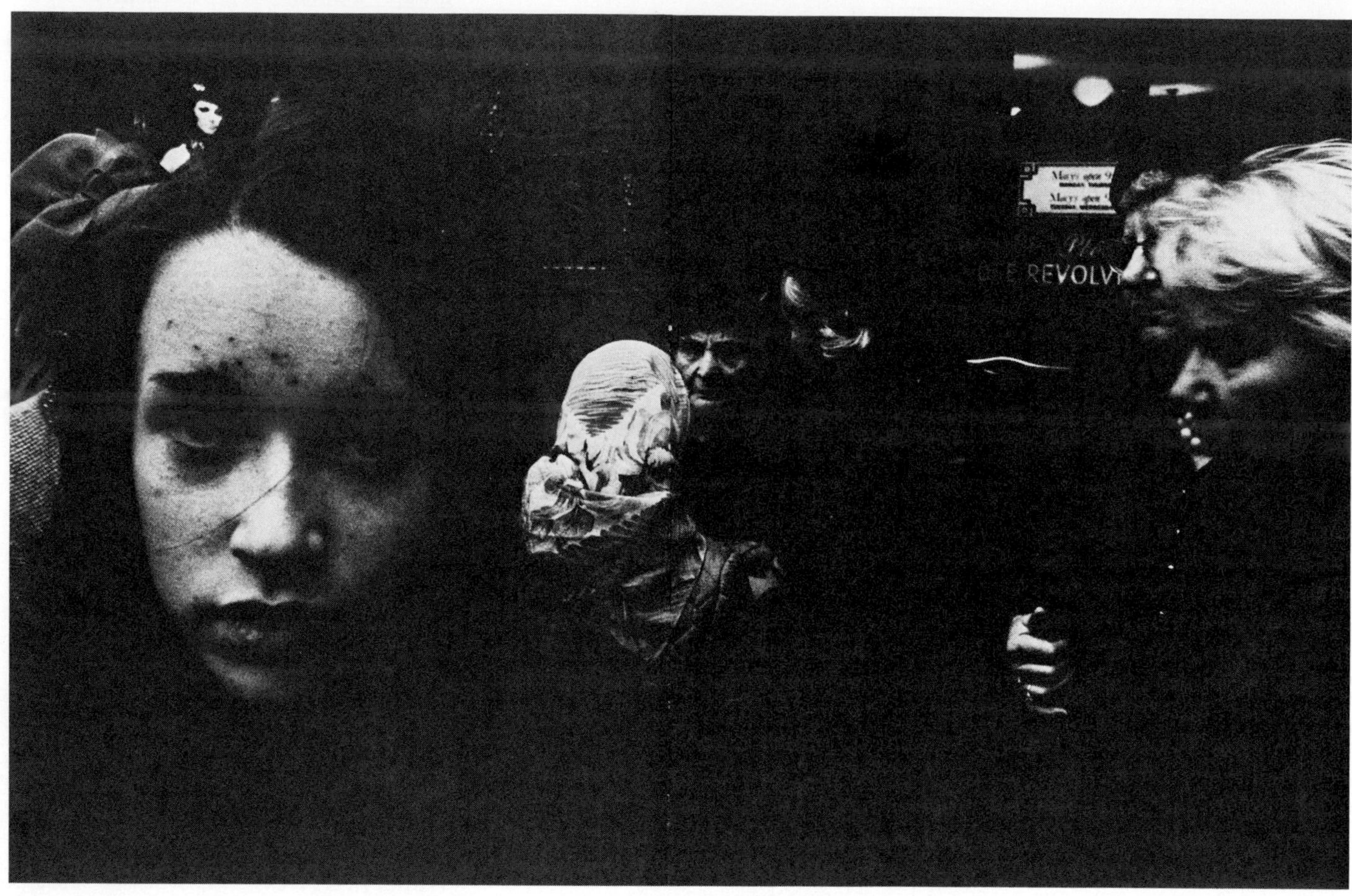

William Klein

PART FIVE

MOTIVATION AND EMOTION

Our behavior is energized and directed by a complex mixture of motives and emotions. In Chapter 13, "Motivation," we consider the nature of motivation and look closely at the workings of three specific motives—hunger, sexuality, and the need to achieve. Chapter 14, "Emotion," examines emotions such as fear, anger, and happiness that add color to our lives, and suggests how each is composed of a mixture of physiological arousal, expressive behaviors, and experienced thoughts and feelings.

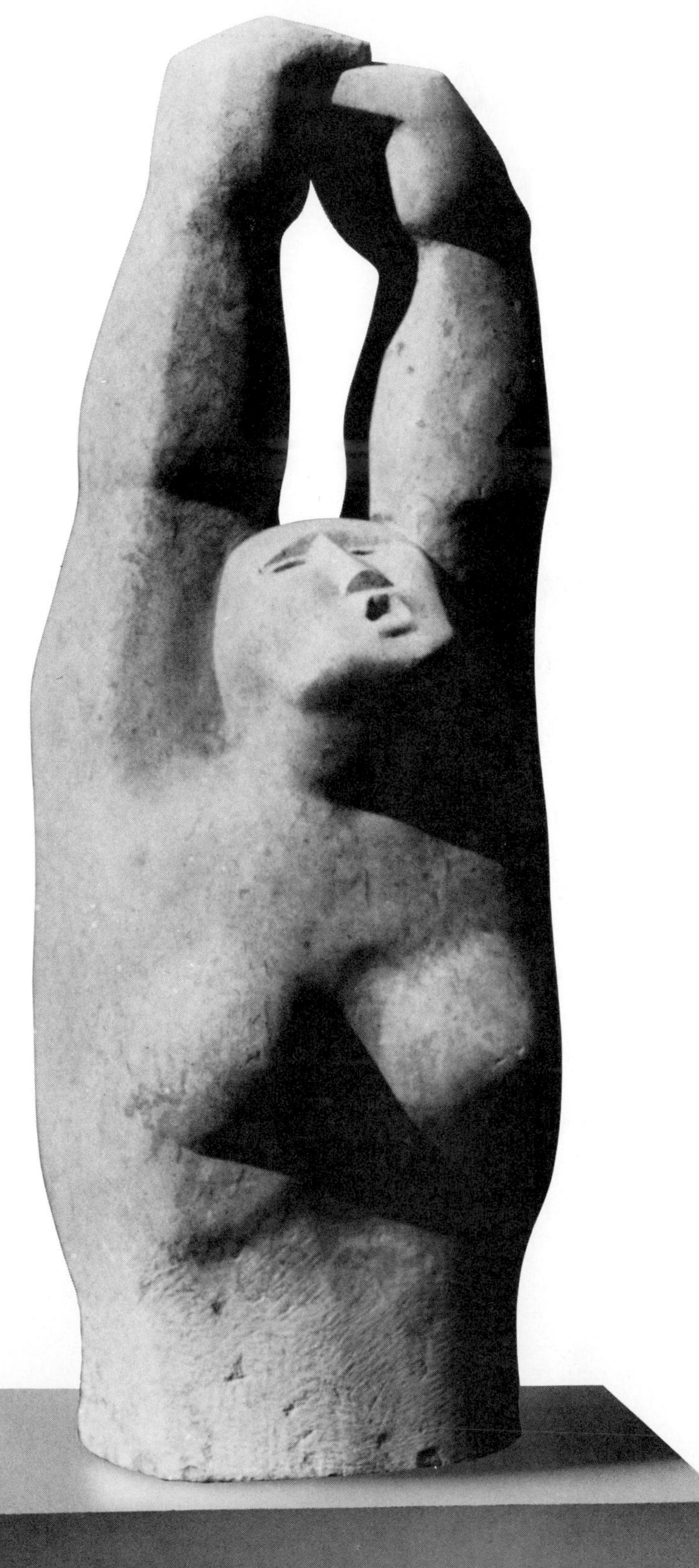

Henry Moore *Woman with Upraised Arms,* 1924–25

CHAPTER 13

Motivation

In everyday conversation, the question "What motivated them to do that?" is a way of asking "What *caused* them to do that? *Why* did they act that way?" To psychologists—whose entire discipline aims to reveal the causes of behavior—the word ***motivation*** has a more specific meaning. To motivate is to *energize* (literally, to move) behavior and to *direct* it toward goals. Like intelligence, motivation is a hypothetical concept that we infer from behaviors as varied as the following:

The yearning for food—

> In the Nazi concentration camps . . . we would get up early, about 4 or 4:30 in the morning, and stand in line. They would give us a hot tea or a coffee which was hot water boiled with some kind of grassy substance. There was no sugar or anything else to put in it. It was just something hot. We downed it and that was our breakfast. . . .
>
> I was so glad I wasn't with my father or brother during this time. You have no idea how a father and son would fight over a piece of bread. Like dogs.
>
> One man in my barracks was about 45. He was dignified in spite of his emaciated state. He had a son about 20 who also lived in the barracks.
>
> One evening the son ate his own bread while the father placed his under a piece of cloth he used as a pillow. The next morning I heard the father scream—his bread was gone. His son had eaten it during the night.
>
> The father went into a deep depression. He kept asking how his son could do such a thing to him. I guess the father lost his will to live, because the next day he was dead. . . .
>
> Hunger does something to you that's hard to describe. I can't believe it myself today, so how can I expect anyone else to understand it?
>
> David Mandel (1983)

The longing for sexual intimacy—

> I am sick with love.
> O that his left hand were under my head,
> and that his right hand embraced me! . . .

Your lips distill nectar, my bride;
honey and milk are under your tongue;
the scent of your garments is like the
scent of Lebanon. . . .
How fair and pleasant you are,
O loved one, delectable maiden!
You are stately as a palm tree,
and your breasts are like its clusters.
I say I will climb the palm tree
and lay hold of its branches.
Oh, may your breasts be like clusters of the vine,
and the scent of your breath like apples,
And your kisses like the best wine
that goes down smoothly,
gliding over lips and teeth. . . .

Eat, O friends, and drink:
drink deeply, O lovers!

Song of Solomon (Old Testament)

The need to achieve—

Alfredo Gonzales, winner of his community's "man of the year" award and three-time chairperson of Michigan's Commission on the Spanish-speaking, is now a successful 35-year-old college administrator with a master's degree from the University of Michigan.

Although born in the United States, Alfredo Gonzales as a 14-year-old would have been found where he had spent all but the first year of his life—on his grandparents' primitive farm in Mexico, tilling the land with a team of oxen, planting and picking crops, and hauling water from a canal several miles away. Later that year, after Alfredo rejoined his parents in Texas, a school truant officer discovered him picking fruit and ordered him off to the local junior high school.

There, for the first time in his life, Alfredo saw the inside of a school classroom and heard the English language. "I walked into a room filled mostly with other Mexican-Americans," recalls Gonzales, "all of whom were prohibited from speaking Spanish. Several times I was caught trying to ask a question in Spanish—for which the 'cure' was being beaten with a paddle."

How did the shy illiterate child of migrant farm workers achieve his present status? Although placed at the lowest skill level by his schools and discouraged from high aspirations, he began to sense, as he still does, that "I could do better. I don't know as much as I could know."

So, while working as a city human relations officer after his release from the army, he completed his college education part time, and then became director of a college Upward Bound program for disadvantaged youth. Its aim, he says, is to motivate students by giving them what he obviously developed in himself—"an awareness of their own potential and a desire to achieve it."

Alfredo Gonzales. What is it that drives a shy, illiterate 14-year-old migrant laborer to complete graduate school and become a college administrator?

In this chapter we will explore motivation by focusing on these three heavily researched motives—hunger, sexuality, and achievement. Although many more identifiable motives exist (thirst, curiosity, need for approval), a close look at just these three will reveal some important principles of motivation, such as the interplay between internal biological influences and external stimuli. We will see that hunger, sexuality, and achievement each combine biological and cognitive factors in a distinct mix, and that each motive depends to a varying extent on learning. Along the way, we will discover answers to some intriguing questions: What is the source of gnawing hunger or ardent sexual desire? Why is the arousal provided by these motives directed toward some targets rather than others, say toward a person of one sex rather than another? What motivates someone such as an Alfredo Gonzales to achieve—is it purely an inner quest to excel, or also a desire for rewards such as social recognition? First, however, let us look at a few historic insights into motivation.

CONCEPTS OF MOTIVATION

As the influence of Darwin's theory of evolution grew, people began viewing human behavior less as a product of rational choices, and more as a product of biological forces. Sigmund Freud theorized that biologically based sexual and aggressive urges motivated a wide variety of behaviors. (Freud's ideas will be explored further in Chapter 15, "Personality.") Other theorists focused on the instinctive behavior of animals and wondered whether humans might similarly be governed by biological instincts. To qualify as an ***instinct,*** a behavior must be rigid in form and be characteristic of the whole species, occur in organisms reared in isolation from one another, and develop without practice (Tinbergen, 1951). Thus to be considered instinctive, a human behavior would have to occur in all people, regardless of differing cultures and opportunities for learning. Apart from simple behaviors such as breathing, few human behaviors are sufficiently automatic to meet these criteria.

Nevertheless, during the early part of this century it became fashionable to classify all sorts of behaviors as instincts. If people criticized themselves, it was because of their "self-abasement instinct"; if they boasted, it reflected their "self-assertion instinct." One sociologist compiled a list of 5759 supposed human instincts! Before long, the instinct-naming fad collapsed under its own weight. What the instinct theorists were doing was not explaining human behaviors, but naming them.

There is an important lesson to be learned here. What the instinct theorists did is what we are still sometimes tempted to do: *explain* a behavior by *naming* it. "Why do we humans spend $2 billion per *day* for arms and armies, while hundreds of millions of people must subsist without adequate food and shelter?" "It's because of our aggression instinct." "How do you know we have an aggression instinct?" "Just look at how much the world spends on preparing for war—more than $100 per year for every person on earth, millions of whom will never receive $100 in a year!" While we might agree that the world's spending habits are tragic, this circular explanation of them is no explanation at all. It is like "explaining" a bright child's low grades by saying he or she is an "underachiever." Descriptive labels are an essential part of every science. Nevertheless, to name a behavior, as a supposed instinct or with a diagnostic label, is *not* to explain it.

Drives: The Internal Pushes

When the instinct theory collapsed, it was replaced by the idea that a biological need creates an aroused state, driving an organism to satisfy the need. To psychologists, a ***need*** is a deprivation, such as a physiological need for food or water. Food or water deprivation will arouse an organism to replenish its stores. This aroused or activated state is called a ***drive,*** and it prompts the organism to reduce the drive by, in this case, eating or drinking. Because the purpose of motivated behavior was presumed to be the reduction of drives, the theory was called ***drive-reduction theory.***

Our underlying biological needs and the resultant drives we experience are usually synchronized. If a need increases, its psychological consequence, a drive, normally increases. But not always. Five hours after lunch, your hunger drive may peak. With additional hours of food deprivation your need for food will continue to increase, but your hunger may not. So needs and drives are often, but not always, linked.

The physiologic aim of drive reduction is ***homeostasis***—which literally means "staying the same"—the maintenance of a balanced or constant (homeostatic) internal bodily state. An example of this is the body's temperature-regulation system, which works much as a thermostat works to keep room temperature at a constant level. Both systems operate through feedback loops, with adjustments based on information that is continually fed back into the system. Sensors detect the temperature of the room or body and feed this information to a control device, which notes any deviations from the desired state and sends instructions that help adjust the temperature (Figure 13-1). If the room is too cool the furnace comes on. If body temperature cools, blood vessels constrict to conserve warmth and we may feel driven to put on more clothes or seek a warmer environment. Similarly, if our cellular water level drops, sensors will detect this and thirst will drive us to drink.

Figure 13-1 *To maintain a constant desired temperature, both your home-heating system and your body's temperature-regulation system utilize feedback loops. In your home, a thermostat senses the temperature and compares it to that desired. Then it acts, turning the furnace on or off to reach the desired level. Your body's "thermostat" is in the hypothalamus and is set at 98.6°F except when you have a fever. It directly monitors not only the temperature of your skin but also that of your blood and can initiate a variety of responses to changing body temperature, some of which are voluntary (putting on or taking off covers) and some of which are involuntary (shivering or perspiring).*

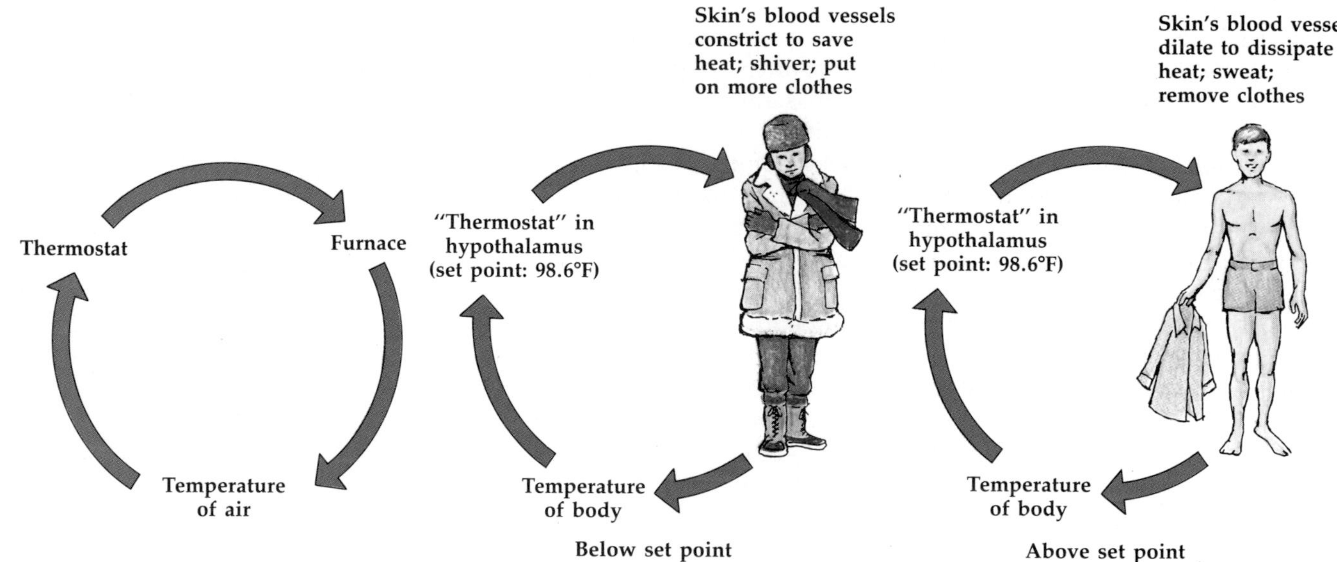

Incentives: The External Pulls

As the cognitive perspective gained prominence, psychologists began to appreciate that we are not only pushed by our needs, but pulled by incentives in the environment. An ***incentive*** is anything that is perceived as having positive or negative value in motivating behavior. The aroma of food, the sight of one's lover, and the threat of a punishment all motivate behaviors. Behavior is energized and directed by these external incentives, as well as by our internal needs. When there is both a need and an incentive, the experienced drive can be strong. The food-deprived person who smells a sizzling steak may feel famished.

For people who crave the stimulation of ever-increasing tests of their courage or mastery, physical and mental challenges are powerful incentives.

Some motives are triggered more by incentives than by a definable biological need. The sex drive has certain biological components, but it usually is aroused by sexual stimuli. The "need" to achieve is not primarily a biological need, but rather a drive to attain some incentive. Thus the extent to which behavior is motivated by the push of our biological needs and the pull of external incentives varies from motive to motive.

A Hierarchy of Motives

You don't need to read this book to know that some needs take priority over others. At this moment, your needs for air and water are probably satisfied, so other motives—such as your need to achieve—may be energizing and directing your behavior. Let your need for water go unsatisfied, and your thirst will become a preoccupation. Deprive yourself of air, and your thirst will be temporarily forgotten.

As these examples hint, the particular needs that motivate our behavior depend on which needs are unmet and, among those, which are the more fundamental. Abraham Maslow (1970) proposed a ***hierarchy of needs*** (Figure 13-2), at the base of which are our physiological needs, such as for food, water, and shelter. Only if these needs are met are people prompted to meet their need for physical safety, and then further to meet the uniquely human needs to give and receive love, to enjoy self-esteem, and to actualize their full potential. (More on self-esteem and self-actualization in Chapter 15.)

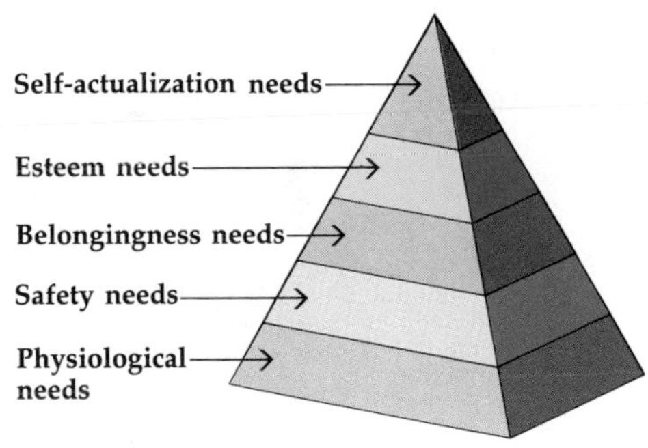

Figure 13-2 *Maslow's hierarchy of needs. We are not prompted to satisfy our higher-level needs, Maslow believed, until our more fundamental, lower-level needs are met.*

Maslow's hierarchy can be criticized: It is somewhat arbitrary, and the order is not universally fixed (people have sometimes starved themselves to make a political statement). Nevertheless, the idea that some motives are more compelling than others—until they are satisfied—is appealing. Let us now consider three representative motives, beginning with the most basic of the three.

"Nobody wants to kiss when they are hungry."
Dorothea Dix, 1802–1887

HUNGER

Concern for the starving populations of World War II Europe led scientist Ancel Keys and his colleagues (1950) to undertake a study of starvation's effects. Aware of the war-related hunger, thirty-six compassionate conscientious objectors, many of them Quakers or Mennonites, agreed to undergo semistarvation. First, the men were fed just enough to maintain their initial weight. Then, for six months, this food level was cut in half.

The physical effects were visible. Soon, without thinking about it, the men began conserving energy; they appeared listless and apathetic. Their body weights dropped rapidly, eventually stabilizing at about 25 percent below their starting weights. The psychological effects were even more dramatic. Consistent with Maslow's idea of a need hierarchy, the subjects became obsessed with food (Figure 13-3). They talked about food. They daydreamed about food. They collected recipes, read cookbooks, and feasted their eyes on delectable forbidden foods. Meanwhile, they lost their former interests in such things as sex and social activities. They had become preoccupied with their unfulfilled needs. As one subject reported, "If we see a show, the most interesting part of it is contained in scenes where people are eating. I couldn't laugh at the funniest picture in the world, and love scenes are completely dull."

"One cannot hide from hunger."
George Herzog,
Jabo Proverbs, 1936

What triggered the gnawing hunger? For that matter, what drives you and me to eat three or four times a day?

Figure 13-3 *During Keys' semistarvation experiment with conscientious objectors, food became an obsession.*

The Internal Physiology of Hunger

The hunger of Keys' semistarved subjects was the response of a homeostatic system designed to maintain normal body weight and adequate supplies of nutrients for our tissues. But precisely what is it that triggers hunger? Is it the pangs of an empty stomach? So it feels, and so it seemed after A. L. Washburn, working with Walter Cannon (Cannon & Washburn, 1912), intentionally swallowed a balloon, which, when inflated in his stomach, could transmit his stomach contractions to a recording device (Figure 13-4). While his stomach was being monitored, Washburn would press a key each time he felt hungry. This, too, was transmitted to the recording device, which revealed that Washburn was having powerful contractions of the stomach whenever he said he was hungry.

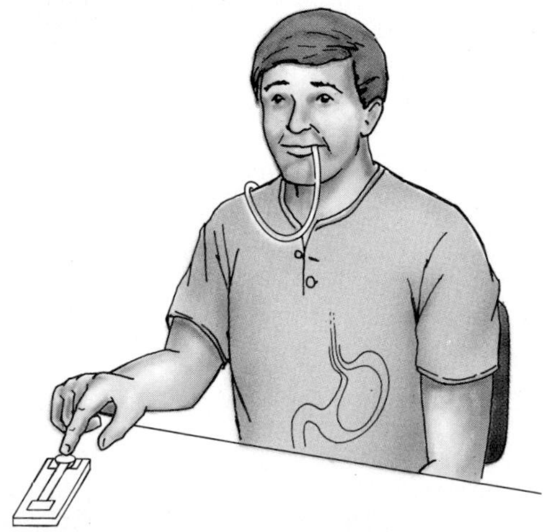

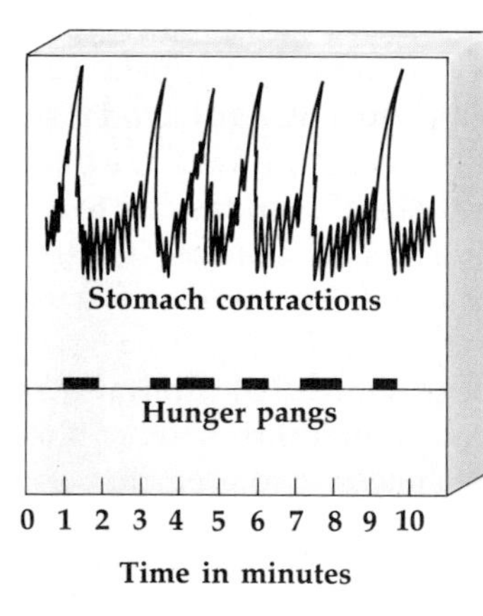

Figure 13-4 *A diagram of the experiment by which Washburn showed that our feelings of hunger (as indicated by a key press) are accompanied by contractions of the stomach (as transmitted through the stomach balloon).*

And so the hunger experience seemed explained, until several decades later when hunger researchers removed some rats' stomachs and attached their esophagi to their small intestines (Tsang, 1938). Without stomach pangs, did hunger persist—did the rats continue to eat regularly? Indeed they did. Hunger persists similarly in humans whose ulcerated or cancerous stomachs have been removed. In fact even a full stomach will not necessarily prevent hunger. Animals that fill their stomachs by eating low-calorie food will nevertheless eat more than animals that consume a less filling, high-calorie diet (McHugh & Moran, 1978). If the pangs of an empty stomach are not the only source of our hunger, what else is?

Blood Chemistry

Hunger is also affected by changes in blood chemistry. The fact that people and other animals automatically regulate their caloric intake to maintain a stable body weight suggests that the body is somehow keeping tabs on its available resources. One such resource is blood ***glucose*** (a type of sugar). We know from experiments that when glucose is injected into the bloodstream, hunger decreases. When the hormone ***insulin*** is injected, diminishing blood glucose partly by converting it to stored fat, hunger increases.

New experiments by Judith Rodin (1985) and others indicate that blood insulin levels may also affect hunger directly, and not just by decreasing blood glucose levels. Rodin reports that insulin injections will trigger hunger even when blood glucose levels are held steady by ongoing infusions. When insulin levels are artificially raised, people report feeling hungrier, they find sweets more tasty, and they eat more.

"The hungry think any food sweet."
Menicus,
Discourses, 300 B.C.

The Hypothalamus

Low blood glucose and high blood insulin are each a source of hunger. But we do not consciously feel our blood chemistry. Rather, information on our body's state is routed to the brain for evaluation. During the 1940s and 1950s, researchers attempted to locate the precise part of the brain where this occurs. They located hunger controls within the hypothalamus, a small but complex neural traffic intersection buried deep in the brain. The hypothalamus, as was mentioned in Chapter 2, performs various bodily maintenance functions and influences the endocrine system via the pituitary gland. The hypothalamus is also richly supplied with blood vessels, enabling it to respond to blood chemistry as well as to incoming neural information about the body's state.

Experiments suggest that there may be not one but two distinct hypothalamic centers that control eating—one that activates hunger, another that activates satiety (Grossman, 1979). The side areas of the hypothalamus, known as the ***lateral hypothalamus,*** or ***LH,*** seem to regulate hunger. When electrically stimulated there, a well-fed animal will begin to eat; when the area is destroyed, even a food-deprived animal will lose interest in food. An area near the bottom and middle of the hypothalamus, known as the ***ventromedial hypothalamus,*** or ***VMH,*** seems to regulate satiety separately. Stimulate this area and an animal will stop eating; destroy it and the animal will eat voraciously and become grossly fat (Figure 13-5).

Figure 13-5 *Lesioning the ventromedial hypothalamus (VMH) caused this mouse to triple its weight.*

Can we therefore say that the LH is a simple "hunger on" switch, and the VMH a "hunger off" switch? No, because even animals whose LH has been destroyed will start eating once their body weight drops low enough. To biopsychologist Richard Keesey (Keesey & Corbett, 1983), this suggests that the LH helps to set the body's "weight thermostat" at a particular weight level, called its ***set point.*** As the body weight of semistarved rats falls below the set point, changes in their hunger and energy expenditure act to restore the lost weight; as soon as they are given free access to food, their weight returns to normal. When body weight rises above the set point, the same homeostatic processes tend to return the body to its normal set point; force-fed rats gain weight, but as soon as the force feeding ends, their weight drops to normal.

External Incentives to Hunger

Our eagerness to eat is not only pushed by our bodily state—our blood chemistry and hypothalamic activity—but pulled by external stimuli. Like Pavlov's dogs, people learn to salivate in anticipation of appealing foods (Wooley & Wooley, 1973). When such foods are in abundant supply, those who are especially responsive to external food stimuli tend to gain the most weight. Consider the 9- to 15-year-old girls at one 8-week summer camp studied by Judith Rodin and Joyce Slochower (1976). When tested during the first week of camp, some girls could not resist munching readily visible M&Ms even after a full meal. Such people, whose eating is triggered more by the presence of food stimuli than by internal factors such as time elapsed since the last meal, are called *externals*. In the 7 weeks that followed, these "external" girls gained the most weight.

As those who are involved in preparing, displaying, selling, or advertising food know, few of us are immune to food cues.

In a delicious demonstration of how biological needs and external incentives interact, Rodin (1984) invited people to her laboratory for lunch after they had endured 18 hours without food. While blood samples were being taken, a large, juicy steak was brought in, crackling as it finished grilling. As the hungry subjects sat watching, hearing, and smelling the soon-to-be-eaten steak, Rodin observed their rising blood insulin levels, which were accompanied by increases in their reported feelings of hunger. Moreover, those subjects who in prior testing were found to be "externals" had the greatest insulin response to the sight and aroma of the steak. This illustrates how our psychological experience of an incentive (the steak) can affect our inner biological state.

Obesity

Are some people motivated to overeat until they are obese? Recent insights into hunger help us to understand obesity. Let's preview the new research with a quiz. Are the following statements true or false?

1. Exercise and other physical activities consume only a fraction of the calories most people burn; two-thirds of all the energy we expend would be expended even if we lay in bed all day.
2. Compared to other body tissues, fat tissue can be maintained with fewer calories.
3. Once we acquire fat cells, we never lose them, no matter how severely we diet.
4. It is possible for one person to be overweight while another person of the same height is thin, even when both eat the same amount of food and are equally active.
5. To maintain a significant weight loss, formerly overweight people usually must forever remain either on an exercise program or a restricted food intake.
6. Most researchers today discount the idea that obese people are obese because they lack normal willpower or turn to food as a substitute for other satisfactions.

See if you can spot the answers to these questions in what follows.

Why are some people fat and others not? Why do some eat moderately and gain weight, while others eat all they want and do not? What hope is there for the 30 million Americans who are somewhat ***obese***—have a surplus of body fat—and who for reasons of health, vitality, or appearance wish to reduce? To understand the puzzling problem of obe-

Note that one can be over normal weight—due to large muscle and bone mass—and not be even slightly obese. One can also be obese (having excess fat) without being overweight (U.S. Department of Health and Human Services, 1983b).

sity, we must fit together a number of pieces: heredity, blood chemistry, set points, fat cells, and environment.

First, the good news about fat: Being just a few pounds overweight seems not to contribute to serious health problems. Moreover, fat is an ideal form of stored energy, offering the body a high caloric fuel reserve to carry it through periods when food is scarce—a common occurrence in the feast-or-famine existence of our prehistoric ancestors. Eating three meals each and every day is a relatively recent phenomenon—a luxury that hundreds of millions of people still do not enjoy. In circumstances of alternating feast and famine, having one's hunger turned on by external food cues is adaptive; overeating when food is abundant prepares the body to withstand periods of starvation.

The bad news, however, is that in those parts of the world where food and sweets are now abundantly available, this adaptive tendency has become maladaptive. For example, Americans consume some 100 pounds of sugar per person every year, ingest 40 percent of their calories in fats, and rank fifth in the world in the consumption of calorie-laden liquors (Langone, 1981). Such eating patterns contribute to obesity, which, according to a 1985 report of the National Institutes of Health, increases one's risk of diabetes, high blood pressure (which increases the risk of stroke or heart attack), gallstones, arthritis, and certain types of cancer (Kolata, 1985a).

Obesity is not just a threat to physical health; it may also affect how obese people feel about themselves. Many people think that fat people are gluttons. They see obesity either as a personality problem (a means of reducing anxiety, of dealing with guilt, or of gratifying an "oral fixation"), or as a matter of choice. If, indeed, fat people "choose to overeat," then their obesity might be considered the natural consequence of a failure of willpower. If being obese signifies either a personality problem or a lack of self-discipline, then who would want to hire, date, or associate with such a person? And if obese people believe such things about themselves, how could they themselves feel anything but unworthy and undesirable?

New research is exploding these myths about the obese. It is true that the only way people get fat is by consuming more calories than they expend. It is also true that 3500 calories of food contain the energy equivalent of a pound of fat. Does it therefore follow that, assuming a person's activity level remains unchanged, a pound will be lost for every 3500-calorie reduction in diet? That is what dieters have been told for years. Surprisingly, as we will see, it turns out to be untrue.

Recent research on obesity has exploded certain myths about its causes.

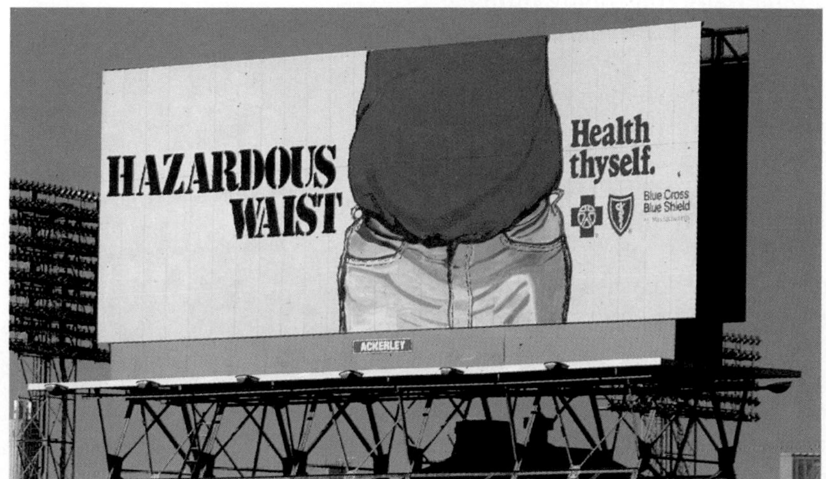

During the 1960s and 1970s the average weight of women under 30 increased. Meanwhile—to judge from the decreasing body measurements of Miss America contestants and Playboy *centerfolds—the beauty ideal was becoming thinner (Rodin & others, 1984).*

Fat Cells

The immediate determinant of our body fat is the size and number of our fat cells. A typical adult has about 30 billion of these miniature fuel tanks, only about half of which lie near the skin's surface. A fat cell can vary from relatively empty to full. In the obese, fat cells may enlarge two or three times their normal size, and then multiply. Once fat cell numbers increase—due to genetic predisposition, early childhood eating patterns, or later overeating—they never decrease (Sjostrom, 1980). On a sustained diet, fat cells may shrink, but they do not die.

"No change in the number of fat cells has been observed during short-term (less than 1 year) weight r. luction programs. The result seems to be a biological trap. Each time body weight is elevated over previous levels, new fat cells may be formed. Comparatively short periods of weight reduction, however, do not reduce the number of fat cells. The result is a mechanism for continuous increases in weight in middle age."
Lars Sjöstrom (1980)

The unyielding nature of our fat cells is but one way in which, once we become fat, our bodies work to keep us fat. Another has to do with the fact that the ***metabolic rate***—the rate of energy expenditure—is lower in fat than in other tissue: fat tissue takes less food energy to maintain. Thus, once we become fat it takes less food to maintain the weight than it did to attain it, because more of the weight is now composed of fat.

For the would-be dieter there is more bad news. Earlier we noted that a short-term determinant of hunger, insulin, (1) helps convert blood sugar to fat, (2) triggers hunger, and (3) is secreted in response to tempting food stimuli, particularly in people who are most responsive to external food cues. Because they are often dieting, obese people tend to be somewhat more responsive to external food cues, such as a waitress's appetizing description of a dessert (Herman, Olmsted, and Polivy, 1983). After a meal, obese people also secrete more insulin (Rodin, 1985). These are more reasons why, as obesity researcher Judith Rodin says, "being fat works to keep someone fat."

Set Points and Metabolism

There is still another reason why those who are fat find it so difficult to become and stay thin. Their bodies are "set" to maintain a higher weight. Given the day-to-day variations in our eating patterns, our bodies are astonishingly good at regulating weight, much better than we could be through conscious efforts to control food intake precisely. If today you weigh within a pound of what you weighed a year ago, you have managed to keep your average energy intake and expenditure within 10 calories a day of one another. Keep everything the same and add a single carrot per day of caloric input and within a decade you will have gained 30 pounds! This remarkable weight regulation/energy balance system is yet another example of the wonders that lie concealed within the most ordinary aspects of human experience.

"To marvel is the beginning of knowledge."
Sir Ernst Hans Gombrich, 1909–

How do our bodies do it? For a long time it was thought that weight regulation was accomplished simply by automatically controlling hunger and consequently food intake. If body weight rises above the set point (the weight at which the body's "weight thermostat" is set), we eat less; if weight drops below, we eat more. But the body's defense of its set-point weight also turns out to be metabolic. By the end of their 24 weeks of semistarvation, the subjects in the World War II experiment had stabilized at three-quarters of their normal weight—while eating half what they previously did. This resulted from a corresponding reduction in energy expenditure, achieved partly by physical lethargy. But physical activity accounts for only about one-third of our energy use. The other two-thirds is consumed by the maintenance processes that keep us alive even while we rest. And, sure enough, the resting energy expenditure of the semistarving men had dropped 29 percent.

As many a dieter can testify, this drop in resting metabolic rate can be frustrating. After rapid weight losses during the initial 3 weeks or so of a diet, further drops in weight come slowly. In one experiment (Bray,

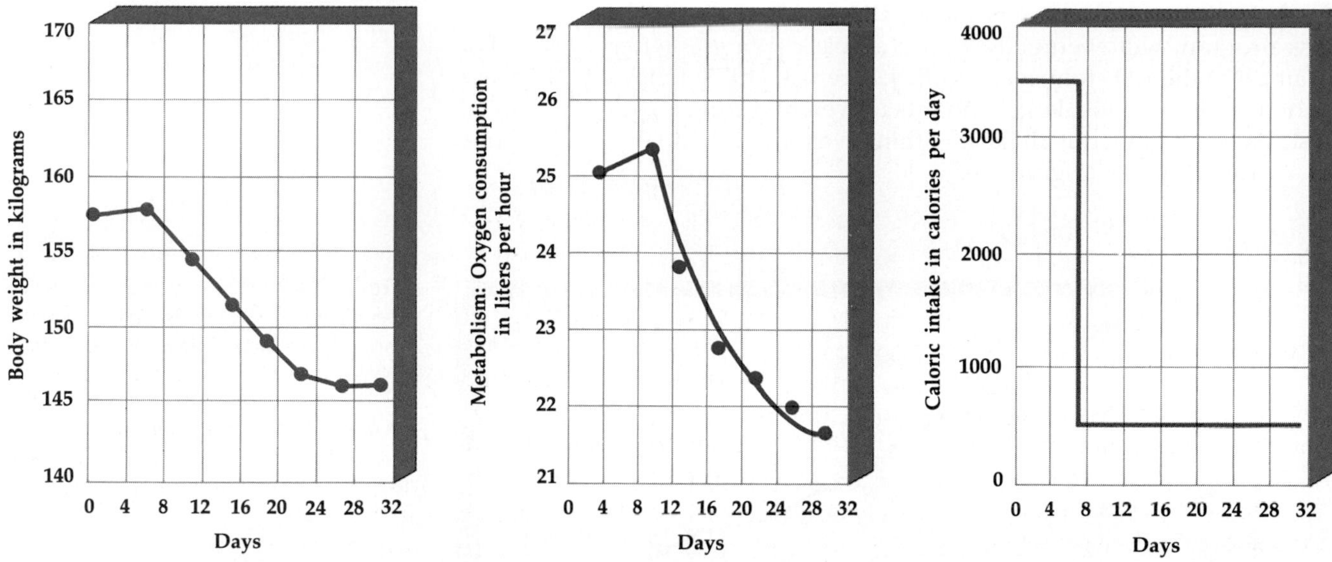

Figure 13-6 *The effects of a severe diet on obese patients' body weight and metabolism. After seven days on a 3500 calorie diet, six obese patients were allowed only 450 calories a day for the next 24 days. Body weight declined only 6 percent and then leveled off, because metabolism dropped 15 percent.*

1969), obese patients whose daily intake was reduced from 3500 to 450 calories lost only 6 percent of their weight—partly because their metabolic rates dropped 15 percent (see Figure 13-6). Thus, the body adapts to starvation by burning off fewer calories, and adapts to extra calories by burning off more. That is why reducing your food intake by 3500 calories may not reduce your weight by 1 pound. And that is why when a diet is over, previously sustaining amounts of food may now be fattening.

Person-to-person differences in set points and resting metabolism explain why—contrary to the stereotype of the overweight glutton—it is possible for two people of the same height and age to maintain the same weight and activity level, while one of them eats *twice* what the other does, or why it is possible for a person to eat less than another similarly active person, yet weigh more (Rose & Williams, 1961).

A genetic contribution to one's body weight set point is apparent from studies of twins and adoptees. For example, identical twins reared apart have much more similar weights than nonidentical twins reared together (Bray, 1981). Experiments on rats also suggest a genetic tendency toward obesity. For example, adult "Zucker fatties," as one strain of genetically obese rats is called, eat little more than other Zucker rats that are genetically predisposed to normal weight. But their metabolism per gram of body weight is lower, and, as with normal weight rats, it shows the expected energy-conserving drop when they are put on a diet. Thus psychologist Richard Keesey (1978) surmised that "the same metabolic adjustments that serve to maintain lean Zuckers at a normal body weight also operate in fatties to sustain them at obese levels." There is good reason to presume that a similar genetic influence operates in humans.

Losing Weight

Perhaps you are shaking your head in sympathy with obese people: "Slim chance they (or we) have of becoming and staying thin; if they lose weight on a diet, their metabolism slows and their hungry fat cells cry out 'feed me!'" Indeed, the condition of an overweight person reduced to normal weight is often like that of a normal weight person who has been semi-starved; when both bodies are held under their normal set point, each may "think" it is starving. Having lost weight, formerly obese people look normal, but their fat cells may be abnormally small, their caloric consumption 25 percent below normal, and their minds obsessed with food. And that explains why most patients who lose weight on a weight loss program will eventually gain it all back (Wing & Jeffery, 1979). For example, when D. Johnson and E. J. Drenick (1977) followed 207 obese patients who had lost large amounts of weight during a 2-month hospital fast, half had gained it all back within 3 years, and virtually all had done so within 10 years (Figure 13-7).

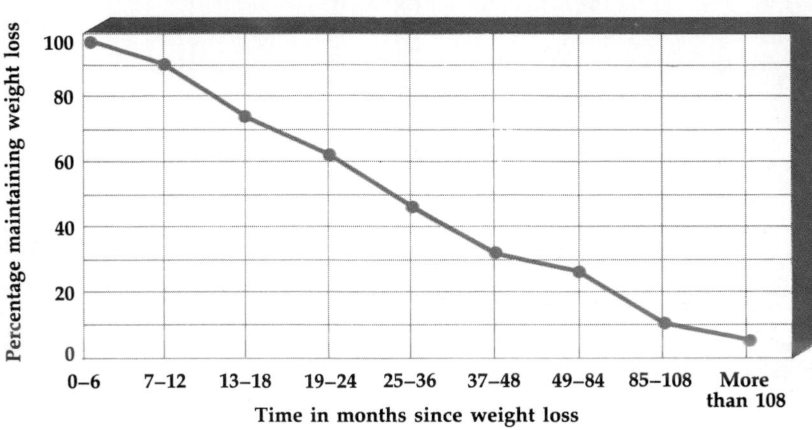

Figure 13-7 *Obese patients successfully lost weight on a hospital fast, but few were able to maintain their weight loss permanently.*

The evidence regarding set points and dieting failure rates becomes poignant when viewed through the experiences of individuals. Consider Ray Goldsmith (WGBH, 1983), a 5′ 6½″ man who dropped from 300 to 170 pounds:

> When I lost the weight, I was just obsessed about the fact of not putting it back on. So I literally did just about everything: I went into behavior modification, I tried slowing down my eating patterns, and that kind of thing. And then, at one point, where I saw myself still binging and still eating, I actually fasted a couple days a week, just to try to keep it off. I would sit there and eat six apples to try to, to try to make it work. I mean I got really fanatic and very scared about putting the weight back on. I was very, very nervous about that, but I also found that I was not in control. . . . I even went to a hypnotist to try to stop eating. And that worked for three days.
>
> It took me about a year and a half to put the 130 pounds back on. I mean, I fought it. I tried to fight it like a son of a gun. I mean, I did it. I lost 130 pounds. I was able to do it. So clearly, it can be done. And I probably could have kept it off somehow, but I never found out the way to.

What advice, then, can we offer to those who have gained weight and wish to lose it? We might advise them first to assess the cost. There are no easy routes to permanent weight loss. Maintaining weight loss will be difficult, and the more your weight fluctuates up and down from going on and off a diet, the more quickly your body will begin its energy-saving metabolic slowdown each time you diet (Wooley & others, 1979). It's as if the body learns from previous diets how to combat more rapidly the deprivation of yet another one. So begin a diet only if you are determined to succeed permanently.

For those who are determined, research on hunger and obesity suggests some helpful hints: First, minimize exposure to tempting food cues. All of us to some extent, and some of us to a great extent, have our hunger accentuated by tempting food cues. Our insulin responses to food cues motivate our eating and enable us to convert the food to fat. So keep tempting foods out of the house, or at least stored out of sight.

Second, remembering that the only way to lose weight is to burn more calories than you take in, you can take steps to boost your metabolism. The most effective way is through the one-third of your energy expenditure over which you have some control: exercise. Sustained exercise, such as running and swimming, not only empties fat cells, builds muscle, and makes us feel better, it also temporarily suppresses appetite (apparently by reducing insulin level) and speeds up metabolism. Thus lack of exercise can contribute to obesity (see Figure 13-8), while sustained exercise can be a major weapon against the body's normal metabolic slowdown while dieting (Thompson & others, 1982).

The statements in the obesity quiz on page 344 are all true.

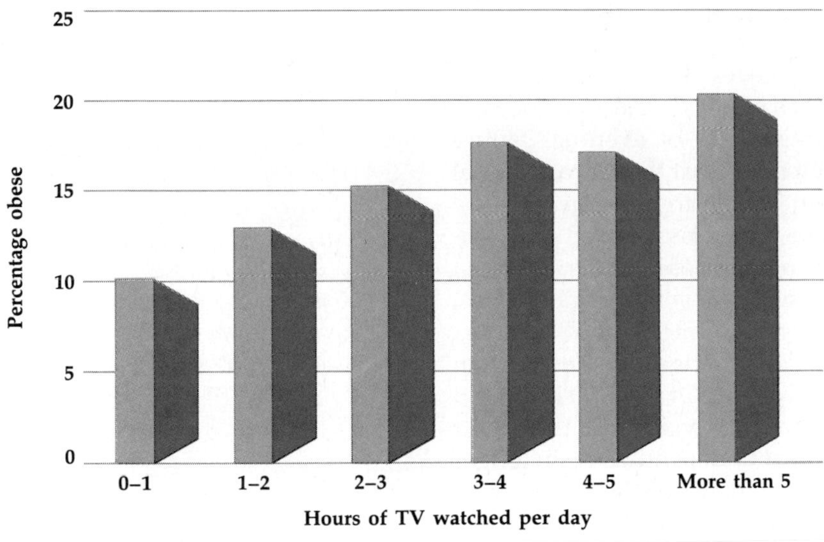

Figure 13-8 *TV watching and obesity. In one study of 6,671 12- to 17-year-olds, obesity was more common among those who watched the most television. The TV-obesity correlation remained when many other factors were controlled, suggesting to the researchers that the inactivity of TV-watching contributes to obesity.*

Third, you can modify both your hunger and metabolic rate by changing the food you eat (Rodin, 1979, 1985). New findings suggest that eating carbohydrates triggers a greater increase in metabolism than does eating fats. Among the fats, saturated fats (those, like animal fat and butter, that turn hard when left standing) seem to produce the most weight gain. Also, some foods do more than others to boost postmeal insulin levels, and thus to renew hunger sooner and stronger. After ingesting a sugar drink, insulin levels rise, causing blood sugar levels to fall within 2 or 3 hours. When the ingested sugar is glucose (such as is found in pancake syrup), the rise in insulin and the resulting fall in blood sugar is especially steep, causing the average subject in one experiment to wolf down 1400 calories from a buffet of foods offered little more than 2 hours later. After ingesting an equal number of calories in the form of fructose, the sugar found in fruits, the insulin rise is smaller, and the average subject was content after eating only 869 calories (Spitzer, 1983). Table sugar, sucrose, has effects more like those of glucose. Other foods, such as potatoes and rice, seem to trigger less of the hunger-producing insulin jump. So how hungry you are by lunchtime will depend not just on how much, but on *what* you had for breakfast.

Fourth, avoid starving all day and eating one big meal—an eating pattern common to overweight people. This eating pattern slows down metabolism.

Finally, beware of the binge. Among people who consciously restrain their eating (as overweight people often do), drinking alcohol or feeling either anxious or depressed can unleash eating (Herman & Polivy, 1980). Stress may break down one's normal restraints. Temporarily going

Judith Rodin: "The worst possible diet is one that is high in fats and low in carbohydrates, although these diets are very popular."

off a diet, by eating just a little of a forbidden food, can do the same. In several "taste testing" experiments, Peter Herman and his colleagues (Herman & Mack, 1975) asked Northwestern University students to drink zero, one, or two milkshakes, and then to taste test ice cream, helping themselves to as much as they wished. As Figure 13-9 indicates, those who normally restrained their eating ate less ice cream than the unrestrained eaters, *if* their restraint was not first broken with the milkshakes. But restrained eaters who first drank the milkshakes ate much more ice cream. They consumed more than did the unrestrained eaters (whose eating dropped if they had previously been fed milkshakes) and much more than restrained eaters who had not previously broken their diet. Thus dieting is often self-defeating, because by making the person more responsive to external food cues it may trigger binging (Polivy & Herman, 1985).

Figure 13-9 *A laboratory eating binge. Normally unrestrained eaters (nondieters) ate* less *ice cream if they had first consumed one or two milkshakes. Restrained eaters (dieters) ate* more *ice cream after having their restraint broken with a milkshake or two, a tendency that has been dubbed the "what-the-hell phenomenon."*

Although preserving weight loss will forever challenge those who wish to do it, Stanley Schachter (1982) is not as pessimistic as most obesity researchers. He recognizes the overwhelming rate of eventual failure among patients in weight loss programs, but notes that these are a special group of people, most of whom have been unable to help themselves. Moreover, the failure rate recorded for these programs is based on a single attempt at weight loss. Perhaps when other people make repeated attempts to lose weight, they—despite the negative consequences of repeated dieting—eventually succeed. When he interviewed people, Schachter found that one-fourth of them had at one time been more than 15 percent overweight and had tried to lose weight. Of these, 6 in 10 had *succeeded,* in that they now weighed more than 10 percent less than their maximum pre-diet weight (average loss = 35 pounds) and were no longer obese. These findings must be interpreted cautiously, for they come from a limited sample of people. (One other study found that 30 percent of formerly overweight people were no longer overweight [Jeffery & Wing, 1983].) But they do hint that prospects for losing weight may be brighter than the dismal conclusions indicated by follow-up studies of patients undergoing a single weight loss program.

Society's increasing obsession with thinness defines an ideal that many people cannot achieve.

There is, however, another option for overweight people, the one chosen by 13 percent of Schachter's interviewees. That is simply to accept, not fight, one's weight. The new research on obesity can perhaps encourage overweight people to accept themselves, and others to feel less negative about them. Note what researchers have not identified as causes of obesity: guilt, hostility, oral fixation, or any such personality maladjustment. If obese people are more likely to binge when under stress or after breaking their diets, this may be more a consequence of their constant dieting than a cause of their obesity. So "fat is not a four-letter word," proclaims the National Association to Aid Fat Americans. Although this motto neglects the health risks linked with significant obesity, it does convey a valid point: It may be better to accept oneself as a little chubby and encourage society to do likewise than to diet and binge, feeling continually out of control and guilty.

SEXUALITY

"I lose my respect for the man who can make the mystery of sex the subject of a coarse jest," wrote Henry David Thoreau, "yet, when you speak earnestly and seriously on the subject, is silent." Let us speak earnestly and seriously, by seeking to understand sexual motivation. Before looking at what energizes and directs our sexual arousal, let us digress for a moment to describe the sexual behavior patterns that a theory of sexual motivation must explain.

Describing Sexual Behavior

Psychologist Donn Byrne (1982, p. 212), whose summaries of sex research inform much of what follows, has noted that for many years sexuality was a scientifically acceptable topic so long as it "avoided the 'normal' sexual practices of Caucasian human beings residing in Europe or North America. Thus, research interest was largely focused on 'crazy sex, animal sex, and native sex.'"

"Abnormal" Sexual Behavior

Scientific research on sexuality began in the late 1800s with reports by Richard von Krafft-Ebing and Henry Havelock Ellis that included descriptions of what were considered abnormal ways of obtaining sexual gratification. However, before long it was realized that what is "abnormal" in one time and place may not be in another. To Krafft-Ebing (1886), mouth-genital contact was a "horrible sexual act." To many married couples who respond to sex surveys, it seems to be a quite normal aspect of sexual relations (Hunt, 1974). To William Walling (1912), masturbation was "shameful and criminal." Today, the practice is not only widely accepted, but often prescribed for women seeking to become orgasmic. Recognizing the variety of accepted sexual practices, most sex researchers today limit their definitions of abnormal sexuality to behaviors that emotionally or physically hurt someone, or that are considered bizarre, such as activities involving animals, corpses, or inanimate objects.

(a)

(b)

The rigidly patterned, instinctive courtship displays of the male blue-footed booby (a) differs from the more flexible, learned human behaviors (b), but their purpose is remarkably similar.

Animal Sexual Behavior

In the animal world, sexual behavior is varied. Bees mate in midair, rats mount and dismount several times during mating, and a bull may complete the act in a single thrust as the cow placidly munches grass. Relationships vary from promiscuous random matings (dogs) to polygamy of a male with his harem (seals) to lifelong companionship (grey-necked geese). Animals have been observed engaging in sexual violence, masturbation, exposure of engorged genitals to strangers, oral sex, and homosexuality.

Cross-cultural Comparisons

Studies of sexual practices around the world also confirm that there is considerable variety in human sexual practice. When anthropologist Clellan Ford and psychologist Frank Beach (1951) reviewed research on 190 premodern societies from all regions of the world, they discovered enormous variation in sexual behaviors, in stimuli considered arousing, and in the context in which sexual interaction occurred. Anthropologists have reported on societies ranging from the Mangaia of the South Pacific, where young adolescents were given sexual instruction and by age 18 claimed to be having nightly intercourse and experiencing multiple orgasms (Marshall, 1971), to an island off the Irish coast, where married partners remained partially clothed while engaging in sex and where female orgasm was virtually unknown (Messenger, 1971).

Despite this great diversity in sexual practices, there are also commonalities. Mouth-to-mouth kissing, caressing of the woman's breasts, and stroking of the partner's sexual organs are widespread elements of foreplay, reported Ford and Beach (1951). Most humans favor some variation on the face-to-face position for intercourse, which apparently reflects the anatomical fact that the vaginal opening of our upright species is farther forward than that of other mammals. Moreover, such a position generally enables more effective stimulation of the woman's most sensitive sexual organ, the clitoris.

American Sexual Behavior

The Kinsey Reports Unable to answer his students' questions about people's sexual practices, Indiana University biologist Alfred Kinsey and his colleagues (1948, 1953) set out to find some answers. Kinsey's confidential interviews with more than 5000 men and nearly 6000 women made history. Although social scientists were quick to point out what Kinsey readily acknowledged—that his nonrandom sample contained an overrepresentation of well-educated, white, urban people from Indiana, Illinois, and several eastern states—his statistics-laden volumes nevertheless became best sellers. Here one could learn the then surprising news that, among Kinsey's sample at least, most men and nearly half of the women reported having premarital sexual intercourse, that most women and virtually all men reported they had masturbated, and that women who reported masturbating to orgasm before marriage seldom had difficulties experiencing orgasm after marriage. One could also find more evidence that sexual behavior is enormously varied. Kinsey found some men and women who said they never had orgasms, and others of each sex who said they had four or more a day. For those who evaluate themselves by comparisons with others, Kinsey's findings have been reassuring; given the variety of sexual behaviors and the range of sex drives (from disinterest in sex to preoccupation with it), one's own sexual interest and activities probably fall within the range of "normal."

Kinsey and his colleagues did not begin their interviews with such questions. Rather, they first helped people feel at ease by asking less threatening questions about family background, health, and education.

Because we do not know whether Kinsey's sample accurately represented the nation's sexual practices in the 1940s, let alone the 1980s, it can be misleading to report his precise findings. But Kinsey's surveys were probably less misleading than some of the haphazard sexual surveys that have been reported more recently in the popular press. When in a national survey of American sexual practices only 20 percent of the people approached agreed to participate (Hunt, 1974), and when popular "sex reports" (such as the best-selling *Hite Report*) begin with a biased sample of people (such as the subscribers to selected magazines) and receive replies from only 3 percent of them, there is every reason to doubt the generality of their findings. For example, we may wonder whether those who choose to participate are more likely to be sexually uninhibited people. (The answer appears to be yes [Hyde, 1986].) We may further wonder how honestly and accurately participants recall their own experiences.

The Masters and Johnson Studies The headlines created by Kinsey's 1940s surveys were recreated by some 1960s studies in which scientists carefully observed the bodily responses of volunteers who masturbated or had intercourse. With the help of 382 female and 312 male volunteers, gynecologist-obstetrician William Masters and Virginia Johnson (1966) monitored or filmed over 10,000 sexual cycles of arousal and orgasm.

"The psychologist-asker averages up all the lies . . . and everybody in America feels inferior."
Sol Gordon, 1923–

Their description of the sexual response cycle identified four stages, which are essentially similar in men and women (Figure 13-10). During the initial ***excitement phase,*** the genital areas become engorged with blood, causing the man's penis to become partially erect and the woman's clitoris to swell and the inner lips covering her vagina to open up. Her vagina also expands and secretes lubricant and her breasts and nipples may enlarge.

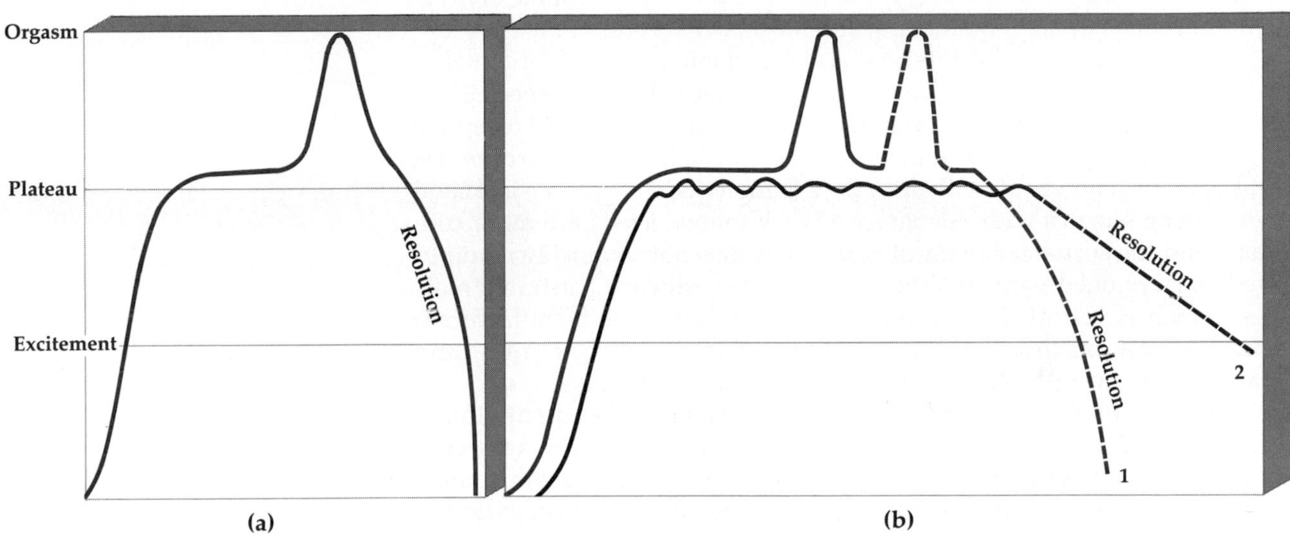

Figure 13-10 *The sexual response cycle in males (a) and in females (b) with orgasm (1) and without (2).*

In the ***plateau phase,*** excitement peaks as breathing, pulse, and blood pressure rates continue to increase. The penis becomes fully engorged and some fluid (possibly containing live sperm) may appear at the tip of the penis. Vaginal secretion continues to increase, the clitoris retracts, and orgasm feels imminent.

During ***orgasm,*** Masters and Johnson observed muscle contractions all over the body, and even further increases in breathing, pulse, and blood pressure rates. In the excitement of the moment, men and women are hardly aware of all this, but are more aware of their rhythmic genital contractions that create a pleasurable feeling of sexual release. The feeling apparently is much the same for both sexes; in one study, a panel of experts could not reliably distinguish descriptions of orgasm written by men from those written by women (Vance & Wagner, 1976).

After orgasm, the body gradually returns to its unaroused state as the engorged genital blood vessels release their accumulated blood—relatively quickly if orgasm has occurred, relatively slowly otherwise. (It is like the nasal tickle that goes away rapidly if you have sneezed, slowly otherwise.) During this ***resolution phase,*** a male enters a ***refractory period,*** lasting from a few minutes to 24 hours, during which he is incapable of being aroused to another orgasm. A woman does not have a refractory period, which may make it possible for her to have another orgasm if restimulated during resolution.

Understanding Sexual Motivation

Having described sexual behavior patterns, we are ready to ask how such behavior is energized and directed. Like hunger, sexual arousal depends on the interplay of internal and external stimuli. To understand sexual motivation, we must consider both.

Hormones and Sexual Behavior

Sex hormones have two effects (Feder, 1984). First, as we noted in the discussion of gender in Chapter 5, the genes determine the sexes by initiating, in male embryos, the secretion of the male sex hormone testosterone. With sufficient testosterone, the embryo develops male sex glands and organs. Otherwise, the embryo develops female sex glands and organs. In humans, the hormonal surge at puberty further triggers the development of the male or female secondary sex characteristics; in women, hormone production also controls the menstrual cycle, the course of pregnancy, and menopause. So the first and most obvious effect of the sex hormones is to direct our development and functioning as males or females.

Second, sex hormones help activate sexual behavior, especially in nonhuman animals. In most mammals, the female is sexually receptive ("in heat") if and only if production of the female hormone ***estrogen*** has peaked, which occurs at ovulation. (In experiments, this can be simulated by injecting females with estrogen.) Male hormone levels are more constant, and the sexual behavior of male animals is not so quickly manipulated by hormone treatments (Feder, 1984). Nevertheless, castrated male rats (which have lost their testes, where testosterone is manufactured) gradually lose much of their former interest in receptive females, and gradually regain it if injected with testosterone.

So far, our discussion of sexuality parallels our earlier discussion of hunger: Blood chemistry helps trigger arousal, but how? The answer is again the same: primarily through the activity of the hypothalamus, which both detects variations in blood hormone levels and activates the neural circuits involved in arousal. For example, in rats, destroying a key area of the hypothalamus may eliminate sexual activity; stimulating this area, either electrically or by directly inserting minute quantities of hormones, may activate sexual behavior.

Compared to animal sexual behavior, human sexual behavior is less strictly controlled by hormones. On the one hand, a person's interests in dating, in sexual play, and in sexual stimuli usually increase with the pubertal surge in sex hormones. Later in life, as sex hormone levels begin to diminish, so too does the typical frequency of sexual intercourse (Hunt, 1974; Kinsey & others, 1953). Moreover, John Money and his colleagues (1983) have reported that male sex offenders who are given Depo-Provera, a drug that inhibits the release of testosterone, experience a decrease in their sexual urges as the drug reduces their testosterone level to that of a normal prepubertal boy. Unlike nonhuman females, women's sexual interests have been linked with their testosterone levels rather than their estrogen levels; testosterone increases sometimes trigger increased sexual appetite in women (Kaplan, 1979; Meyer-Bahlburg, 1980).

On the other hand, normal daily and monthly fluctuations in hormones seem not to affect sexual desire greatly. Research efforts attempting to link women's sexual desire with the phase of their menstrual cycles have produced weak results; for example, female-initiated intercourse is only slightly higher at ovulation (Adams & others, 1978). Normal fluctuations in men's testosterone levels, from man to man and from hour to hour, have little effect on their sexual drives (Byrne, 1982).

To summarize, we might compare the sex hormones, especially testosterone, to the fuel in a car. Lacking fuel, the car will not run, but if the fuel level is minimally adequate, adding more fuel to the gas tank will not change the way it runs. The analogy is imperfect, partly because the interaction between hormones and sexual motivation is two-way. Like the effect of the sizzling steak on insulin level, being sexually stimulated is as much a cause of increased testosterone levels as it is an effect (Pirke &

others, 1974). The analogy correctly suggests, however, that the biological contribution is a necessary but insufficient explanation of human sexual behavior. The biological fuel is essential, but so are the stimuli that will turn on the engine.

External Stimuli

There are, as we have seen, certain similarities between hunger and sexual motivation. And there are differences. One key difference is that sexual motivation is triggered to a greater extent by external stimuli.

In many species of animals, the members of one sex are aroused automatically by odors emitted by the other sex. Are humans, also? Despite the millions of dollars spent on advertising scents that are supposed to attract the other sex, attempts to identify unlearned human sexual responses to particular odors have been generally unsuccessful (Morris & Udry, 1978). The only unlearned stimulus for human sexual arousal appears to be touch—the pleasurable genital caresses that are a component of foreplay worldwide (Byrne, 1982).

"Ours is a society which stimulates interest in sex by constant titillation. . . . Cinema, television, and all the formidable array of our marketing technology project our very effective forms of titillation and our prejudices about man as a sexy animal into every corner of every hovel in the world."
Germaine Greer (1984)

Many studies reveal that men become aroused when they see, hear, or read erotic stimuli. More surprising (in view of the fact that sexually explicit materials are sold mostly to men) is that most of these studies also reveal that women are similarly aroused by the same stimuli.

A study by psychologist Julia Heiman (1975) illustrates both the power of such external stimuli and the methods that researchers have used to measure sexual arousal. Much as hunger researchers have developed multiple measures of hunger-related changes (stomach contractions, blood chemistry changes, self-reported hunger, and eating behavior), so sex researchers such as Heiman have developed multiple measures of changes in sexual arousal. These include self-ratings of arousal and direct measures of males' erections and of females' vaginal blood volumes.

Sexually explicit materials arouse, but they also may lead to a devaluing of one's romantic or marital partner and, as Chapter 20 will explain, distorted perceptions of sexual reality.

In Heiman's experiment, instruments that detected changes in the penis circumference or in vaginal color were attached to sexually experienced university volunteers. Then the students listened to either a sexually explicit erotic tape, a romantic tape (of a couple expressing love, without any indication of physical contact), a combined erotic-romantic tape, or a neutral control tape. Which do you suppose the men were most aroused by? And the women?

Both the men and the women found the tape of explicit sex most arousing, especially when the sex depicted was initiated by a female and when the depiction centered on her responses. However, the men's verbal reports of arousal tended to correspond more closely to their actual physical arousal, which was easily noticed. The women's sexual responses were more hidden, even to themselves.

Sexually explicit materials arouse, and may therefore be either pleasant or distracting. (If the arousal is distracting, those wishing to control it can limit their exposure to external sexual stimuli, just as those wishing to control hunger are advised to limit their exposure to external food stimuli.) Certain kinds of sexual materials can also have two additional effects that seem not so harmless. First, depictions of women being sexually overpowered—and enjoying it—tend to increase viewers' acceptance of the myth that many women would enjoy being raped, and tend to increase men's willingness to hurt women (see Chapter 20, "Social Relations").

"There is no difference between being raped and being run over by a truck except that afterward men ask if you enjoyed it."
Marge Piercy,
Rape Poem, 1976

Second, exposure to sexually explicit material may lead people to devalue their partners and relationships. Several studies (Gutierres & others, 1985; Kenrick & Gutierres, 1980; Weaver & others, 1984) have found that after male college students viewed depictions of sexually attractive women, they rated an average woman, or their own girlfriends or wives, as less attractive than did men who had not experienced this "contrast effect." Similarly, some sex researchers fear that reading erotic literature can create expectations that few men and women can hope to attain. Sex therapists are sometimes sought out by otherwise normal and satisfied people for the treatment of "problems" such as an inability to have multiple orgasms, or ejaculation after "only" 30 minutes of intercourse (LoPiccolo, 1983).

Imaginative Stimuli

The stimuli inside our heads—our images—also influence our sexual arousal. One example is our dreams. As noted in Chapter 8, "States of Consciousness," most dreams do not have overt sexual content, and genital arousal accompanies all types of dreams. But dreams do sometimes contain sexual imagery that leads to orgasm. In men, these nocturnal emissions ("wet dreams") are more likely when orgasm has not occurred recently during the waking hours.

When awake, people may become sexually aroused not only by memories of previous sexual interactions but also by fantasies. Fantasies need not correspond to actual behavior. Men sometimes imagine themselves forcing sex on their partners. Women sometimes fantasize themselves being sexually overpowered, perhaps even being raped by a handsome captor (Byrne, 1982). These images may be cultivated by unrealistic film and literature portrayals of women who seem to enjoy being taken. But a woman's having such fantasies does not mean she actually wishes that such attacks would happen, or, moreover, that if they did they would be anything but horrid and terrifying.

Sexual motivation, then, arises from the interplay of biological factors and external and imaginative stimuli (Figure 13-11). When all the ingredients are present, the sexual chemistry creates arousal.

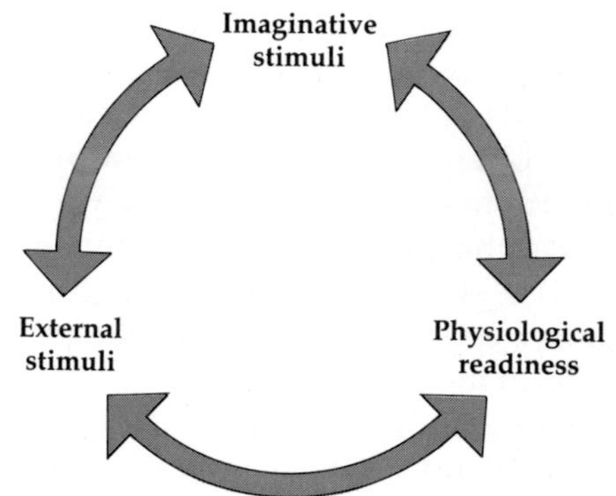

Figure 13-11 *Sexual arousal results from the interplay of physiological readiness and external and imaginative stimuli.*

Sexual Orientation

To motivate is to energize and direct behavior. So far, we have considered the energizing of sexuality but not its direction. The direction of our sexual interest is expressed in our ***sexual orientation***—our sexual attraction toward, and responsiveness to, erotic stimuli associated with members of a particular sex (Storms, 1980).

Describing Sexual Orientation

First, it may help to distinguish a person's sexual orientation from what Chapter 5 referred to as the person's gender identity and sex-typing. Gender identity is the awareness and acceptance of one's biological sex. Sex-typing is the extent to which males display traditionally masculine traits and females display traditionally feminine traits. Whether their sexual orientation is heterosexual or homosexual, people nearly always have a clear gender identity—they know whether they are male or female. Likewise, researchers have found—contrary to media stereotypes of effeminate gay men and masculine lesbian women—that people of either sexual orientation may or may not be strongly sex-typed.

So far as we know, virtually all cultures in all times have been predominantly heterosexual (Ford & Beach, 1951). Whether homosexuality is condemned and punished or viewed as an acceptable alternative, homosexuality survives, but heterosexuality prevails.

How many people are exclusively homosexual? In both Europe and the United States, studies suggest about 2 to 4 percent of men and 1

"Since we have admitted no substantial change in man's nature during historic times, all technological advances will have to be written off as merely new means of achieving old ends—the acquisition of goods, the pursuit of one sex by the other (or by the same), the overcoming of competition, the fighting of wars."
Will and Ariel Durant,
The Lessons of History, 1968

percent of women. But many more adults—perhaps 25 percent of men and 15 percent of women—have had some homosexual experience (Hyde, 1986), and most people have had occasional homosexual fantasies such as those described by Anne Frank in *The Diary of a Young Girl:*

> I remember that once when I slept with a girl friend I had a strong desire to kiss her, and that I did so. I could not help being terribly inquisitive over her body, for she had always kept it hidden from me. . . . I go into ecstasies every time I see the naked figure of a woman. . . . It strikes me as so wonderful and exquisite that I have difficulty in stopping the tears rolling down my cheeks. If only I had a girl friend!

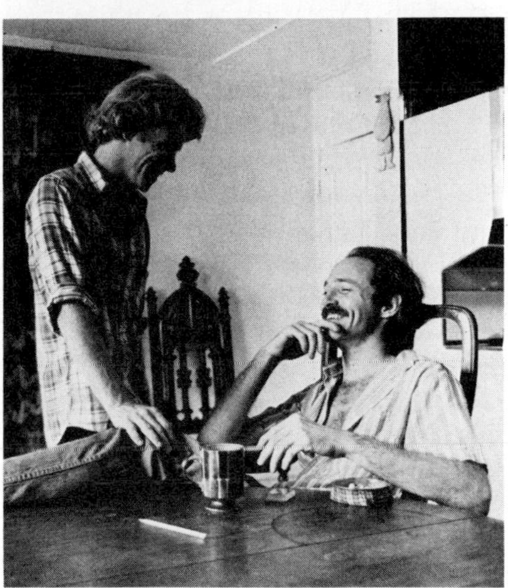

As with heterosexuals, homosexual couples can progress from romantic love to the deep affectionate attachment of companionate love as the relationship matures.

What does it feel like to be homosexual in a heterosexual culture? One way for heterosexual people to attempt to understand is to imagine how they would feel if they were to be ostracized or fired for openly admitting or publicly displaying their feelings toward someone of the other sex, to imagine that people made crude jokes about heterosexual people, or to imagine that family members were pleading with them to change their heterosexual feelings and to enter into a homosexual marriage.

Facing such reactions, homosexual people often struggle with their sexual desires. At first, they may try to ignore or deny such desires, hoping they will go away; but they don't. Then they may try to change them, through psychotherapy, willpower, or prayer; but the feelings typically remain as persistent as those of most heterosexual people—who are similarly incapable of becoming reoriented to homosexuality. Eventually, they may therefore accept their orientation—by electing celibacy (as do some heterosexuals), by engaging in promiscuous sex (a choice more commonly made by men than women), or by entering into a committed, loving, long-term relationship (a choice more often made by women than men) [Peplau, 1982; Weinberg & Williams, 1974].

There is a growing agreement that one's sexual orientation seems neither willfully chosen nor easily changed. Nor is sexual orientation linked with psychological disorder or being a child molester. Some homosexuals do abuse children, but so do some heterosexuals (Gonsiorek, 1982). These conclusions led the American Psychiatric Association in 1973 to eliminate homosexuality from its list of "mental illnesses," thus providing yet another example of how our definitions of "abnormal sexual behavior" can change with place or time.

Understanding Sexual Orientation

If our sexual orientation is something we do not choose and cannot change, then from where do these preferences come? When and how do we diverge toward either a heterosexual or homosexual orientation? See if you can anticipate the consensus that has emerged from hundreds of research studies by responding yes or no to the following questions:

1. Is homosexuality linked with problems in a child's relationships with parents, such as with a domineering mother and a weak, ineffective father, or a possessive, "seductive" mother and a hostile father?
2. Does homosexuality involve a fear or hatred of the other sex, which leads people to direct their sexual desires toward members of their own sex?
3. Is homosexuality linked with a known chemical imbalance in the individual's sex hormones?
4. As children, were many homosexuals molested, seduced by an adult homosexual, or otherwise sexually victimized?

Contrary to widely held ideas about homosexuality the answers are all no (Storms, 1983). Just as many popular explanations of obesity have been refuted by research, so have many explanations of homosexuality. For example, consider the findings of lengthy interviews with nearly 1000 homosexuals and 500 heterosexuals conducted by the Kinsey Institute (Bell & others, 1981; Hammersmith, 1982). The investigators assessed every possible psychological cause of homosexuality they could think of—parental relationships, childhood sexual experiences, peer relationships, dating experiences, and number of brothers and sisters. Their findings: Apart from homosexual feelings and somewhat greater nonconformity, the backgrounds of homosexuals were not discernibly different from those of heterosexuals.

Given these findings, the Kinsey Institute investigators wondered whether sexual orientation might have a biological cause. But efforts to link sexual orientation with biological factors have thus far been unproductive. A subtle difference between homosexual and heterosexual men has been observed in their responses to injection of the female hormone estrogen (Gladue & others, 1984). But sex hormone levels are not consistently linked with sexual orientation (Gartrell, 1982). Moreover, although sexual appetite may increase with injections of male hormones, its direction remains unchanged.

One controversial new theory proposes that sexual orientation is determined at puberty, as sexual desire emerges (Storms, 1981). It has long been recognized that objects, smells, and sights that are associated with early experiences of sexual pleasure can become conditioned cues for arousal. This helps to explain why some people develop a sexual response to objects that once were associated with sexual arousal or orgasm, and why sexually arousing stimuli are so varied. In laboratory experiments, even a geometric figure can become sexually arousing if it is repeatedly associated with an erotic stimulus (Byrne, 1982). (Note that in this case the geometric figure is a conditioned stimulus, which acquires its power to arouse by repeated pairing with a naturally erotic stimulus.) Perhaps, then, the time when the sex drive matures is a critical period for developing erotic associations with homosexual or heterosexual cues. As their sexual urges intensify, early maturing individuals are likely to be segregated with others of their own sex. For example, as seventh graders, boys are still associating almost exclusively with other boys. So perhaps a boy who matures early is more likely to associate his developing feelings with other boys, an association that becomes a lifelong preference.

Donn Byrne (Kelley & Byrne, 1983): "A large proportion of the variability in human sexuality can be attributed to learned behavior sequences."

It is a simple and logical idea. But the Kinsey researchers doubt it. For example, sexual precocity (as measured by the age at which a person could recall first masturbating, having an orgasm in sleep, and ejaculating) was unrelated to sexual orientation. Moreover, their homosexual sample usually recalled having homosexual feelings *before* engaging in any homosexual behavior. One member of the Kinsey team even proposed a theory that is very nearly the opposite of Storms' theory of erotic attachment. Alan Bell (1982) believes that people develop romantic attachments to those who are *different* from, and thus more fascinating than, the sex they have mostly associated with while growing up. So he speculates that boys who have grown up in a male peer group will find it "virtually impossible" to be fascinated by other males when they reach adolescence.

The bottom line of such conflicting theories is that after 100 years of research on human sexuality, we remain ignorant as to why some people become heterosexual, others homosexual. Indeed, the wonder of it all is that after so much research, the determinants of sexual orientation remain a mystery.

Sexual Dysfunction and Therapy

Sexual dysfunctions are problems that consistently impair sexual functioning. Some, but not all, of these dysfunctions are problems in sexual motivation, especially in one's sexual energy and arousability. A man, for example, may experience premature ejaculation (before he or his partner wishes) or impotence (the inability to have or maintain an erection). A woman may experience orgasmic dysfunction (infrequently or never experiencing orgasm) or low sexual desire.

What causes such problems? Once again, the old idea that personality disorders are to blame has been largely discounted. Men who complain of premature ejaculation seem essentially similar, even in their sexual arousal patterns, to men who do not; they simply ejaculate at lower levels of sexual arousal, which often occur because they have longer periods of sexual abstinence (Spiess & others, 1984). When Barbara Andersen (1983) reviewed research on the diagnosis and treatment of orgasmic dysfunction in women, she could find no personality dimension that was involved. Furthermore, she reported that attempts to treat orgasmic dysfunction through traditional psychotherapy (as though there were a personality disorder) have been unsuccessful. On the other hand, she reported a nearly 100 percent success rate with a new treatment that trains women to enjoy their bodies and give themselves orgasms, with a vibrator if necessary; most of these women can then be trained to transfer their new sexual responsiveness to interactions with their mates.

Success has also been reported in training men to control their ejaculations by repeatedly stimulating the penis and then stopping stimulation (or even firmly squeezing the head of the penis) when the urge to ejaculate arises. In Chapter 17, "Therapy," we will see similar indications that specific treatments for specific behavior problems are more successful than are attempts to change deep-seated emotional disorders.

Sex and Human Values

Questions of how we ought to act, of what choices we should make, of what ends are desirable, are questions of human values. Recognizing that values are a personal and cultural matter, most sex researchers and educators prefer not to express moral values in their writings on sexuality. As scientists and teachers, their primary aim is simply to help us understand sexual behavior and what motivates it.

Can the study of sex be free of values? Should it be? Critics think not. First, they note that the words we use to describe behavior often reflect our values. When sex researchers label sexually restrained individuals as "erotophobic" and as having "high sex guilt" they express a value judgment. Whether we label sexual acts we do not practice as "perversions," "deviations," or part of an "alternative sexual life-style" depends on our attitude toward the behaviors. As we noted in Chapter 1, labels both describe and evaluate.

Second, the critics suspect that when information about sexual behavior and motivation is taught apart from a context of human values, the message some students may get is that sexual intercourse is merely recreational activity, or a biological act that is nothing more than "the depositing of seminal fluid, like squirting jam in a doughnut" (Greer, 1984). Diana Baumrind (1982), a University of California child-rearing expert, suspects that adolescents interpret sex education that pretends to be "value-free" as meaning that adults are neutral about adolescent sexual activity. She feels that such an implication would be unfortunate, because "promiscuous recreational sex poses certain psychological, social, health, and moral problems that must be faced realistically."

For most adults, sexuality is not only a biological motive but also a social one—a sharing of love and intimacy.

Several investigators have reported that the number of premarital sexual partners is correlated with marital unhappiness. One explanation of this is that premarital sexual behavior is sometimes predictive of extramarital sexual behavior, which tends to disrupt a marriage (Newcomb & Bentler, 1981).

On the other hand, some sex researchers have found that teenagers who have had formal sex education are actually no more likely to engage in premarital sex than those who have not (Zelnik & Kim, 1982). Moreover, consider the benefits we have gained from sex research and education. By knowing ourselves, by realizing that our feelings are shared by others, by understanding what is likely to please or displease our loved one, our lives are enriched. Witness the crumbling of falsehoods about homosexuality. Witness the growing realization that some forms of erotic stimuli can lead us to devalue or hurt other people.

Perhaps we can agree that the knowledge provided by sex research is preferable to ignorance, yet also agree that hidden values should be stated openly, enabling us to debate them and to reflect upon our own values. We might also remember that while scientific research on sex has answered important questions, it does not aim to define the personal meaning of sex for our lives as men and women. One can know every available fact about sex—that the initial spasms of male and female orgasm come at 0.8-second intervals, that the female nipples expand 10 millimeters at the peak of sexual arousal, and so forth—but fail to understand the human significance of sexual intimacy.

Surely one significance of sexual intimacy is its expression of our social nature. Sex is a social as well as a biological motive. Men and women can have orgasms just as strongly and surely when alone. Yet, given the relationship, opportunities, and social approval provided by marriage, most people find greater satisfaction in joining themselves in the embrace of their loved one. Although the yearning for closeness was not part of our description of sexuality, this social motive is part of the whole sexual experience. For our predominantly monogamous species, sex can be not merely the mutual stimulation of two bodies but a life-uniting and love-renewing act.

"Let us say with all possible emphasis that human sexuality is a very good thing. . . . It is tied in with and expressive of the urgent desire to love, which is deepest and highest in the universe."
Norman Pittenger,
Making Sexuality Human, 1970

ACHIEVEMENT MOTIVATION

So far we have seen two examples of why the drive theory of motivation—the idea that biological needs drive us to satisfy those needs—is only a partial explanation of what energizes and directs our behavior: First, although it is true that food deprivation creates a need for food that drives us to satisfy that need, it is also true that external food stimuli can trigger or amplify the hunger drive. Second, sexual motivation is triggered even less by biology and more by external incentives.

There are other motives that do not seem to satisfy any biologically based needs, and that may even serve to increase rather than reduce arousal. Monkeys will monkey around trying to figure out how to unlock a latch that opens nothing or will attempt to open a window that allows them to see outside their room (Butler, 1954). The 9-month-old infant who investigates every accessible corner of the house, the scientists whose work we have been discussing, and the adventurers who first crossed the ocean from Europe were all motivated to explore. Asked why he wanted to climb Mt. Everest, George Mallory answered, "Because it is there." Recall, too, the experiments on sensory restriction described in Chapter 6. The peace and quiet of sensory monotony was worse than boring; it was disturbing, and it motivated the subjects to seek any available stimulation. As these examples indicate, despite having all our biological needs satisfied we may be driven by curiosity or by a seeming "need" for some optimum level of stimulation. If arousal falls below this point, we may be driven to increase stimulation.

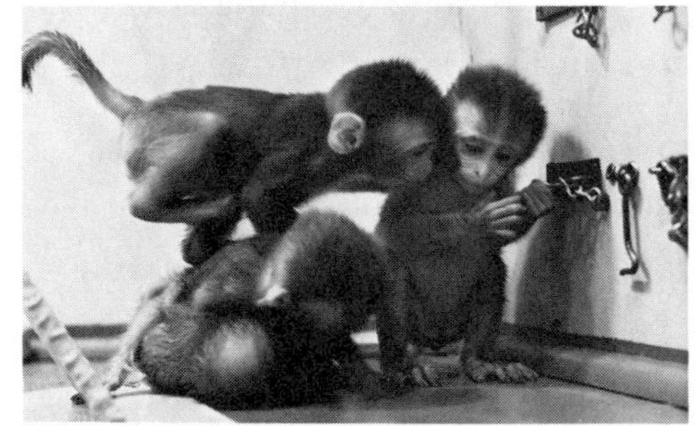

The activities of these young monkeys and this child powerfully demonstrate the early presence of an insatiable drive to explore—one of the many intrinsic motives that does not fulfill a physiologic need.

Moreover, there are some motives that, unlike hunger and sex, are hard to satisfy. Millionaires may be motivated to make ever more money, movie stars to become ever more famous, politicians to achieve ever more power, daredevils to seek ever greater thrills. Such motives seem not to diminish when they are fed. The more we achieve, the more we may need to achieve.

"No man is ever full fed with success."
Herodotus,
History, 445 B.C.

Describing Achievement Motivation

From among your friends, think of two people, one who strives to succeed by excelling at any task where evaluation is possible, and one who seems unconcerned about success. Psychologist Henry Murray (1938) defined the first person's high ***need for achievement*** as a desire for significant accomplishment; for mastering things, people, or ideas; for rapidly attaining a high standard.

If we were to study this motive, our first step would probably be to measure it. But how? Recall from the semistarvation studies that people driven by hunger begin to fantasize about food. Recall, too, that the strength and direction of our sexual motivation is reflected in our sexual fantasies. Do these examples suggest one way to assess a person's need to achieve?

Murray and investigators David McClelland and John Atkinson presumed that the strength of people's need for achievement would similarly be reflected in their fantasies. So the researchers asked subjects to invent stories about ambiguous pictures. For example, if when shown the daydreaming boy of Figure 13-12, a subject commented that the boy was preoccupied with his pursuit of a goal, that he imagined himself performing a heroic act, or that he was feeling pride in some success, the subject's story was scored as indicating achievement concerns. People whose stories consistently include achievement themes are regarded as having a high need for achievement.

Figure 13-12 *What is this boy daydreaming about? By analyzing responses to ambiguous photos like this, motivation researchers seek clues to people's levels of intrinsic motivation.*

In dozens of studies, investigators have compared people whose stories indicate a high need for achievement with other people whose stories seldom exhibit concern with achievement. The results are intriguing. Would you expect people whose stories express a high need for achievement to prefer tasks that are easy, moderately challenging, or very difficult? People whose stories suggest a low need for achievement tend to choose either very easy or very difficult tasks, where failure is either unlikely or unembarrassing (Geen, 1984). Those whose need for achievement is high tend to prefer moderately difficult tasks, for which success is attainable yet attributable to their own skill and effort. In a ring toss game, for instance, they often choose to stand at an intermediate distance from the stake on which the ring is to be tossed; this allows them some successes, yet provides a suitable challenge. People with a strong need to achieve also are more likely to persist on a task when things get difficult (Cooper, 1983).

As you might expect from their persistence and eagerness for realistic challenge, people with high needs for achievement do tend to achieve more. For example, compared with others whose ability is equal to theirs, they tend to be more successful in business. And when achievement motivation is raised, it can promote greater achievement. McClelland (1978) reported that by training the businessmen of a village in India to think, talk, and act like achivement-motivated people, he and his colleagues were able to boost the villagers' business successes. Compared to other businessmen from a comparable nearby town, those trained in achievement motivation started more new businesses and employed over twice as many new people during the ensuing 2 years.

Origins of Achievement Motivation

Parental Influences

Why, despite similar potentials, does one person become more motivated to achieve than another? Researchers have observed that children whose parents encourage their independence from an early age and who are praised and rewarded for their successes tend to become more achievement motivated (Teevan & McGhee, 1972). Such parents encourage their children to dress and feed themselves and to do well in school, and they express their delight when their children do well. Theorists speculate that the high achievement motivation displayed by such children has both *emotional* roots, as children learn to associate achievement with positive emotions, and *cognitive* roots, as they learn to attribute their achievements to their own competence and effort, and so to develop higher expectations of themselves (Dweck & Elliott, 1983).

"They can because they think they can."
Virgil,
Aeneid, 19 B.C.

These parental influences may also help explain a fascinating finding—that birth order is linked with achievement. In separate studies of children from two-child families who went on to achieve eminence, 64 percent of "distinguished Americans" were firstborn, as were 61 percent of Rhodes Scholars, 66 percent of National Merit Scholars, and 64 percent of those in *Who's Who.* Among the *Who's Who* designates and National Merit Scholars who came from three-child families, 52 percent of both groups were firstborn (Altus, 1966). Firstborn children also tend to do slightly better in school and on intelligence tests, and are more likely to achieve admission to prestigious colleges than are their later-born brothers and sisters. Why?

Remember the two friends you chose, one who consistently strives to succeed, the other who seems less concerned with achievement? Is either a firstborn (or only) child?

It is fun to speculate about differences between the experiences of firstborn and later-born children. One difference seems to be the greater parental attention given firstborn children during their years as solo children. Perhaps parents of firstborn children expect more and affirm their children's achievements more than do the more distracted parents of later-born children. On the other hand, researchers have found that later-born individuals often have strengths of their own, such as being more socially relaxed and popular. Having less power than one's older and stronger siblings apparently fosters more effective social skills (Miller & Maruyama, 1976).

Situational Influences

At every moment, our behavior is a product not only of our personal dispositions (such as our need to achieve) but also of the immediate situation. Researchers have therefore studied how certain situations nurture achievement. For example, in nine out of ten studies of the effects of setting a goal, those who were given specific, challenging goals achieved more than did those who were given no goals or urged simply to "do your best" (Locke & others, 1981). Clear, specific goals, such as those you might set in planning your coursework, serve to direct one's attention, to boost effort and persistence, and to stimulate creative strategies for achieving the goals.

Chrysler Board Chairman Lee Iacocca's high intrinsic need for achievement has driven him to continually seek out new and more difficult challenges.

Intrinsic Motivation and Achievement

Even more research has been done on the conditions that breed intrinsic motivation for achievement—in the classroom, at the workplace, on the athletic field. ***Intrinsic motivation*** is the desire to be effective and to perform a behavior for its own sake; ***extrinsic motivation*** is being moved by external rewards and punishments.

To sense the difference between extrinsic and intrinsic motivation, you might reflect on your own current experience in this course. Are you feeling pressured to get the reading finished before a deadline? Worried about your course grade? Eager for rewards that depend on your doing well? If your answers are yes, then you are extrinsically motivated (as to some extent students nearly always are). Are you also finding the course material interesting? Does learning it enable you to feel more competent? If there were no grade at stake, might you be curious enough to want to learn the material for its own sake? If your answers are yes, you are also intrinsically motivated.

After studying the motivations and achievements of thousands of college students, scientists, pilots, business people, and athletes, Janet Spence and Robert Helmreich (1983) concluded that intrinsic motivation fuels achievement, while extrinsic motivation (such as a desire for a high-paying career) often does not. But what sort of intrinsic motivation? Spence and Helmreich separately measured people's quests for *mastery* (for example, as indicated by their strongly agreeing that "If I am not good at something, I would rather keep struggling to master it than move on to something I may be good at"), their drives to *work* ("I like to work hard"), and their *competitiveness* ("I really enjoy working in situations involving skill and competition"). How do you suppose the mastery, work, and competitiveness orientations were related to achievement?

Despite similar abilities, people oriented toward mastery and hard work tended to achieve more. If students, they tended to get better grades; if MBA graduates, they tended to earn more money; if scientists, their work was more likely to be cited by other scientists. No surprise there. But, surprisingly, those who were most competitive (which is a more extrinsic orientation) often tended to achieve less. As Figure 13-13 illustrates, this was especially true among people who scored high on the mastery and work orientations. These results illustrate what psychologists call an ***interaction effect;*** two factors are said to interact if the effect of one depends on the other. In this case, the effect of competitiveness depends on the degree of work-mastery orientation. Among people who do not intrinsically enjoy mastery and hard work, it pays to be highly competitive; among those who are oriented toward mastery and hard work, it pays to be less competitive.

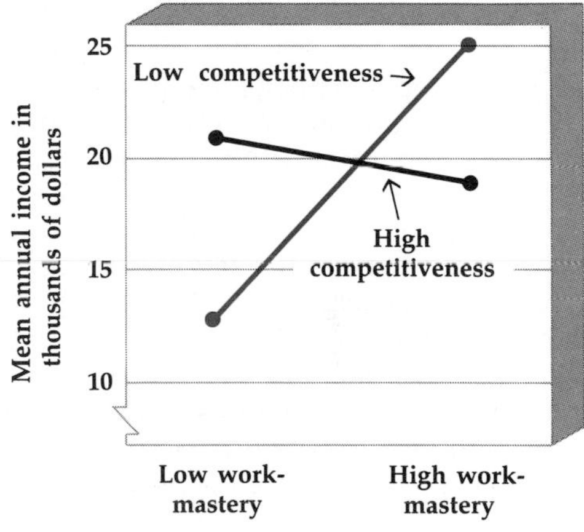

Figure 13-13 *Among the MBA graduates with a high work-mastery orientation, less competitive people tend to achieve the highest earnings. Among the low work-mastery group, the more competitive did better. The effect of competitiveness thus depends on ("interacts with") the effect of work and mastery.*

If intrinsic motivation stimulates achievement, especially in situations where people work independently (as students, executives, and scientists often do), then how might we encourage it? The consistent answer, from hundreds of studies, is first by providing tasks that challenge and trigger curiosity (Malone & Lepper, in press) and second by not snuffing out people's sense of self-determination with an overuse of extrinsic rewards (Deci & Ryan, 1985). Note that rewards can be used in two ways: to *control* us ("If you clean up your room you can have some ice cream") or to *inform* us of our successes ("That was outstanding—we owe you a tribute"). Researchers have repeatedly observed that attempts to influence people's behaviors through rewards, deadlines, and surveillance may be successful as long as these controls are present; but if they are taken away, interest in the activity often drops. Ironically, when teachers try hardest to boost their students' achievements on competency tests, they tend to become most controlling, thus undermining their students' intrinsic eagerness for challenge and mastery. (This is similar to the earlier finding that the children of parents who discourage independence tend to have lower achievement motivation.)

On the other hand, verbal or monetary rewards that inform people when they are doing well can boost their feelings of competence and intrinsic motivation. In one experiment, Thane Pittman and his co-researchers (1980) asked college students to work on puzzles. Those who received informative compliments ("Compared to most of my subjects, you're doing really well") were much more likely to continue playing with the puzzles when left alone later than were those who did not receive such praise. So, depending on whether rewards are used to control or inform, they can either lower or raise intrinsic motivation.

Intrinsic motivation researchers believe there is an important practical principle here (Deci, 1984). Given that the controlling use of rewards has so widely been shown to undermine intrinsic motivation (and creativity—see Chapter 12, "Intelligence"), parents, teachers, and managers should take care not to be overcontrolling. It is important to expect, support, challenge, and inform; but if you want to encourage internally motivated, self-directed achievements, do not control.

Intrinsic Motivation and Sports Enjoyment

For most people, participation in sports activities is its own reward. The 20 million American youngsters who participate in organized sports do so not so much for extrinsic rewards as for enjoyment and for the sense of accomplishment. In fact, motivation researchers Edward Deci and Richard Ryan (1985) reported that rewarding children for participating in physical activities makes them *less* likely to participate again after the rewards are removed.

Another researcher, Dean Ryan (1980), studied football players and found that those on athletic scholarships (who were, in a sense, playing for pay) enjoyed their play less than did nonscholarship players. Apparently, pay and pressure turn play into work. But as in other studies of intrinsic motivation, rewards could also increase intrinsic motivation *if* their effect was to inform the players of their athletic competence (as with a "most improved player" award) rather than to control their participation (as when playing for pay).

Researchers have also found that enjoyment of sports is greatest when the activity is neither too easy (and therefore boring) nor too demanding (causing us to worry about our performance). When the challenge is optimally suited to our skills, we experience "flow"; without feeling anxious or self-conscious, we become totally involved in the challenge (Csikszentmihalyi, 1975).

In sports as in other activities, excessive external pressures and incentives can undermine intrinsic enjoyment. Many children who participate in organized sports find their enjoyment lessened by excessive pressure to win.

Does a competitive orientation enhance or diminish the intrinsic love of sport activity? It all depends, say Deci and Ryan (1985). Like other extrinsic incentives, the lure of victory can be very motivating. Moreover, winning makes us feel competent. So as long as we are winning, we will likely still enjoy the activity. Yet in the long run, especially if we begin losing, a competitive orientation may undermine our love of the activity for its own sake.

So, should coaches emphasize extrinsic pressures, rewards, and competition? It depends on what the goal is, report Deci and Ryan. If, as professional football coach Vince Lombardi once said, "Winning isn't everything; it's the only thing," then it may pay to control the players with pressures and rewards for winning. But if the goal is—as it should be for most programs of physical education, fitness, and amateur sports—the promotion of an enduring interest and participation in physical activity, then "external pressures, competitive emphasis, and evaluative feedback are in contradiction to this goal." Thus if Little League coaches want their players to continue playing baseball after Little League, they had best focus not on the urgency of winning, but on the joy of playing well.

Lateral Hypothalamus (LH) The side areas of the hypothalamus that, when stimulated, trigger eating and, when destroyed, cause an animal to stop eating.

Metabolic Rate The body's rate of energy expenditure.

Motivation The forces that energize and direct behavior.

Need A deprivation that usually triggers a drive to reduce or eliminate itself.

Need for Achievement A desire for significant accomplishment; for mastery of things, people, or ideas; for rapidly attaining a high standard.

Obesity Having a surplus of body fat. Obesity is not defined simply as weighing more than normal, which may also be caused by large muscle mass.

Orgasm An intense sensation experienced at the peak of the sexual response cycle; involves rhythmic muscle contractions, increases in breathing, pulse, and blood pressure rates, and pleasurable feelings of sexual release.

Plateau Phase The second phase of the sexual response cycle, occurring just before orgasm, in which excitement peaks and breathing, pulse and blood pressure rates continue to rise.

Refractory Period A resting period after orgasm during which a male cannot be aroused to another orgasm.

Resolution Phase The last phase in the sexual response cycle, during which the body gradually returns to its unaroused state.

Set Point The point at which an individual's weight "thermostat" is set. When the body falls below this weight, changes in hunger and metabolic rate act to restore the lost weight.

Sexual Dysfunctions Problems that consistently impair sexual functioning.

Sexual Orientation One's sexual attraction toward and responsiveness to erotic stimuli associated with members of either one's own sex (homosexual orientation) or the other sex (heterosexual orientation).

Ventromedial Hypothalamus (VMH) The bottom and middle areas of the hypothalamus that, when stimulated, trigger the cessation of eating and, when destroyed, cause an animal to overeat.

FOR FURTHER READING

Hunger and Obesity

Chernin, K. (1981). *The obsession: Reflections on the tyranny of slenderness.* New York: Harper & Row.

A thought-provoking analysis of society's demand that women be thin, rather than accept their body's natural dimensions.

Polivy, J., & Herman, C. P. (1983, paperback 1985). *Breaking the diet habit: The natural weight alternative.* New York: Basic Books.

This book, by two psychologists who are obesity researchers, questions the practice of dieting and instead recommends realizing one's "natural weight" with an "undiet" that meets needs but discourages eating when hunger is satisfied.

Sexuality

Hyde, J. S. (1986). *Understanding human sexuality* (3rd ed.). New York: McGraw-Hill.

A comprehensive overview of every aspect of human sexuality, including sexual orientation and sexual disorders.

Kilmann, P. R., & Mills, K. H. (1983). *All about sex therapy.* New York: Plenum Press.

This is not a self-help book, but is instead a gentle introduction to the available methods of treating male and female sexual disorders.

Szasz, T. (1980). *Sex by prescription.* New York: Anchor/Doubleday.

A critical look at the values implicit in the diagnosis and treatment of sexual disorders.

Other Motivational Topics

Petri, H. L. (1985). *Motivation: Theory and research (2nd ed.).* Belmont, CA: Wadsworth.

Provides an up-to-date overview of the major topics in motivation.

SUMMING UP

Motivation is the energizing and directing of our behavior, as exemplified in our yearning for food, our longing for sexual intimacy, and our need to achieve.

CONCEPTS OF MOTIVATION

Under Darwin's influence, behavior came to be viewed as being controlled by biological forces, such as instincts. But when it became clear that people were merely naming various behaviors as instincts, psychologists turned to a drive theory of motivation.

Drives: The Internal Pushes Most (but not all) physiological needs create psychological drives that motivate need satisfaction. The aim of drive reduction is a stable state of internal homeostasis.

Incentives: The External Pull Not only are we pushed by our drives, we are pulled by positive or negative incentives.

A Hierarchy of Motives Maslow's hierarchy of needs expresses the idea that, until satisfied, some motives are more compelling than others.

HUNGER

The Internal Physiology of Hunger The inner push of hunger originates not primarily from the stomach's pangs of hunger, but from variations in blood chemistry. For example, we are likely to feel hungry when our glucose levels are low and our insulin levels are high. This information is monitored by the lateral and ventromedial areas of the hypothalamus, which regulate the body's weight by influencing felt hunger or satiety.

External Incentives to Hunger Especially in "external" people, food stimuli can trigger hunger and eating, partly by stimulating a rise in insulin level.

Obesity Fat is a concentrated fuel reserve that is stored in fat cells. The number and size of these cells determine one's body fat. Obese people find it difficult to lose weight permanently because the number of fat cells is not reduced by a diet, because the rate of energy expenditure necessary for tissue maintenance is lower in fat than in other tissues, and because the overall metabolic rate decreases when body weight drops below the set point. Those who nevertheless wish to diet are advised to minimize exposure to food cues, boost energy expenditure through exercise, and modify eating patterns.

SEXUALITY

Describing Sexual Behavior Studies of "abnormal" sexual behaviors, animal sexual behaviors, sexual practices in different cultures, and sexual surveys by Kinsey and others, all indicate that sexual behaviors vary enormously. Nevertheless, the human sexual response cycle seems to follow a common pattern of excitement, plateau, orgasm, and resolution.

Understanding Sexual Motivation Sex hormones help our bodies develop and function as either male or female. In nonhuman animals, they also help to activate sexual activity, but in humans, they influence sexual behavior more loosely, especially once minimally sufficient levels are present. External stimuli can trigger sexual arousal in both men and women, although women may be less likely to notice their physiological responses. Erotic materials may also lead people to devalue their comparatively less appealing partners and relationships. In combi-

This comparison phenomenon helps us understand why the middle and upper income people in a given country do tend to be slightly more satisfied with life than the relatively poor, with whom they can compare themselves (Diener, 1984). Nevertheless, even within a country, once a person reaches a moderate income level, further increases do little to increase happiness. Why? Because as people climb the ladder of success they tend mostly to compare themselves with those who are at or above their current level (Gruder, 1977; Suls & Tesch, 1978). The result is rising expectations and therefore little rise in satisfaction.

"I have also learned why people work so hard to succeed: it is because they envy the things their neighbors have. But it is useless. It is like chasing the wind. . . . It is better to have only a little, with peace of mind, than be busy all the time with both hands, trying to catch the wind."
Ecclesiastes 4:4

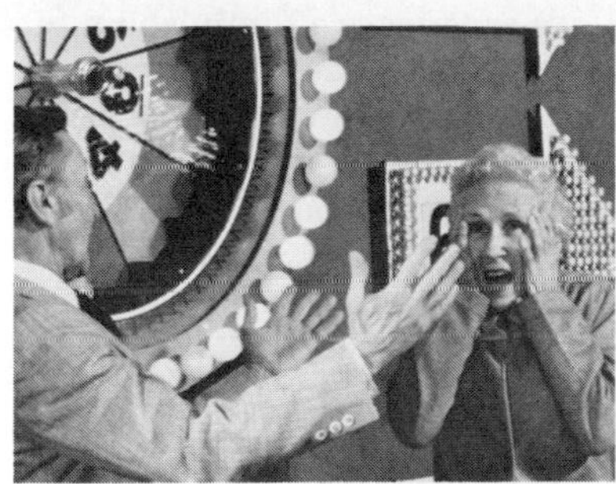

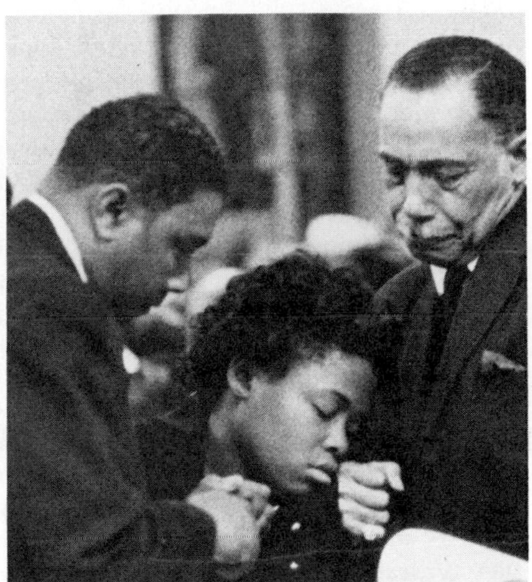

People have the need both to identify and explain their emotions and to share them with others.

The bad news of the adaptation level and relative deprivation principles is that seeking happiness through material achievement requires an ever-increasing abundance of things. At the end of his *Chronicles of Narnia,* novelist C. S. Lewis depicts heaven as such a place, a place where good things do continually increase, an existence "which goes on for ever: in which every chapter is better than the one before." Here on earth, however, the ups and downs of life preclude such perpetual happiness.

The good news is that should we in the affluent nations choose or be forced to simplify our ways of life, we would likely adapt. At first, there would be unhappiness, but eventually we would probably recover life's normal balance of joy and sorrow, pleasure and pain. Moreover, by remembering our own low points and by "counting our blessings" when comparing ourselves with those less fortunate, we can increase our contentment. Marshall Dermer and his colleagues (1979) demonstrated this by having University of Wisconsin-Milwaukee women imagine others' deprivation and suffering. After viewing vivid depictions of how grim life was in Milwaukee in 1900, or after imagining and then writing about various personal tragedies such as being burned and disfigured, the women expressed greater satisfaction with their own lives. If comparing ourselves with those who have more than we do creates envy, then, it seems, comparing ourselves with those who have less brings contentment.

This effect of comparison with others helps us understand why students of a given level of academic ability tend to have a higher academic self-concept if they attend a school where most other students are not highly able (Marsh & Parker, 1984). If many of your classmates are brilliant, the comparison may leave you feeling intellectually deprived.

Opponent-Process Theory of Emotion

> How strange would appear to be this thing that men call pleasure! And how curiously it is related to what is thought to be its opposite, pain! . . . Wherever the one is found, the other follows up behind.
>
> Plato,
> *Phaedo*

Adaptation-level theory helps explain why, in the long run, our emotional ups and downs tend to balance. University of Pennsylvania psychologist Richard Solomon (1980) believes that the same is true in the short run as well, and he has developed a theory to explain why. Like Plato, Solomon was intrigued by the emotional price tag that seems to follow pleasure, and the emotional dividends that sometimes compensate for suffering. For the pleasure of a drug high, one pays the price of discomfort when the drug wears off. For the pain of jogging or a hot sauna bath, one afterward receives the dividend of a pleasurable feeling of well-being.

Why? Solomon proposes, with support from laboratory studies of human and animal emotions, that *every emotion triggers an opposing emotion* that lingers after the first emotion is switched off. He calls this *opponent-process theory.* Because the opposing emotion develops in response to the primary emotion, our most intense emotional experiences—of terror or delight—occur immediately after an emotion-arousing event. Once the opposing emotion is activated, perhaps to keep the initial emotion under control, we experience a diminishing of our initial emotion's intensity. After the initial emotion subsides, the opposing emotion lingers and we experience it (Figure 14-10a). For example, after parachutists survive their first free-fall, which for many is a terrifying experience, they typically feel elated. And for those who experience the labor of childbirth, the after-reaction may be euphoria.

Repetitions of the emotion-arousing event have little effect on the primary emotion, but tend to strengthen the opposing emotion. The net result is that the primary emotional experience, such as the high from drug use or the fear aroused by parachuting, lessens with repetitions, while the after-reaction, such as the pain of drug withdrawal or the exhilaration after landing, remains strong or even becomes stronger (Figure 14-10b). As a result first-time blood donors—especially those who are initially most anxious—report feeling relaxed and warmhearted afterward; with repeated donations the initial jitters subside but the postdonation warm glow remains (Piliavin & others, 1982).

Figure 14-10 *Opponent processes in emotion. (a) A primary emotional response to a stimulus triggers an opposing emotion. We experience the difference between the two. (b) But with repeated stimulations, the opponent emotion becomes stronger, weakening the experience of the primary emotion and, after the primary emotion subsides, providing a strengthened aftereffect.*

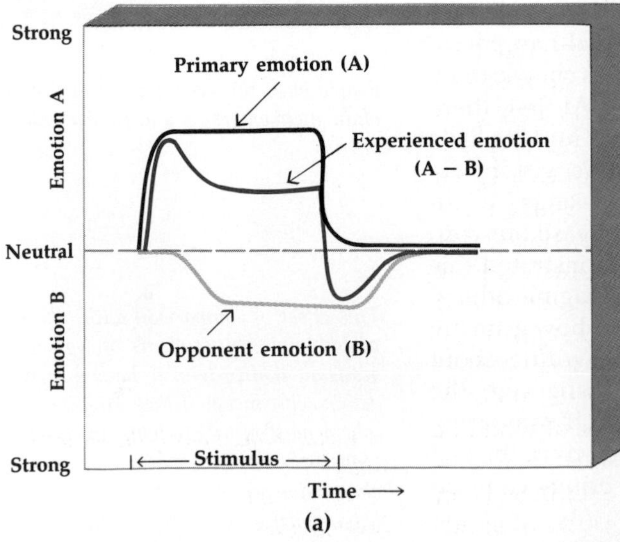

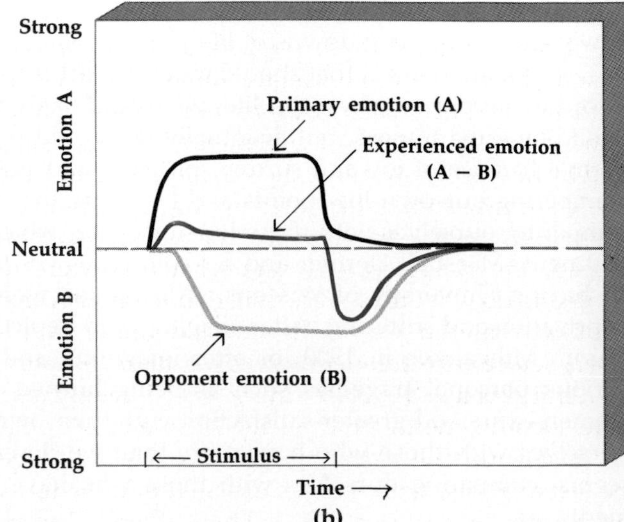

As Solomon wisely notes, opponent-process theory and the research that supports it are good news for puritans, not hedonists. The theory suggests that those who seek pleasure pay for it later and that with repetition their pleasures lose much of their intensity; moreover, those who suffer will receive their reward and will find that with repetition their suffering will become more tolerable.

If, as the adaptation-level and opponent-process theories imply, our emotions tend to balance around normal, then day after day why do some people seem so filled with joy and others so gloomy? What makes one person normally happy and another depressed? In reviewing research on people's feelings of general happiness and well-being, Ed Diener (1984) spotted several predictors of life satisfaction. For example, people who are happy with themselves (who express high self-esteem) tend to be happy with life in general, as are people who are happily married or in love. While intriguing, these predictors of happiness may or may not be the causes of happiness. Table 14-1 indicates that sleeping well is correlated with happiness. So are people happier if they sleep well, or do they sleep better if they are happier? Just knowing that the two variables are correlated does not tell us.

Table 14-1 **Happiness is . . .**

Researchers have found that happy people tend to:	*However, other factors seem unrelated to happiness:*
Have high self-esteem	Age
Have a satisfying marriage or other love relationship	Race
Have a meaningful religious faith	Gender (women are more often depressed but also more often joyful)
Be socially outgoing	Educational level
Sleep well	Intelligence
Exercise	Parenthood (having children or not)
Be employed	

(*Source:* From Diener, 1984.)

Even when all these predictors of happiness are taken together, most of the person-to-person variations in general happiness remain unpredictable. That is partly because our random day-to-day fluctuations in mood color our reports of general well-being. Our feelings are also colored by how we view our daily activities. Ronald Graef and his colleagues (1983) surmised this after interrupting more than 100 Chicagoans eight times a day with an electronic paging device. Whenever they were beeped, the people would note what they were doing, whether they wanted to do what they were doing, and whether they wished they could be doing something else. (How would you answer such questions right now?) Those who frequently enjoyed doing whatever they were doing, even if it was a routine activity, reported being happier overall. Yet they were spending neither more nor less time in leisure activities, at work, or in housework. The lesson from this, concluded the researchers, is that in the last analysis, happiness is usually not to be found in ever-increasing leisure time or even in a different type of work, but in one's state of mind.

"He that thinks himself the happiest man, really is so."
C. C. Colton,
Lacon, 1820

THEORIES OF EMOTION

We have seen that emotions are built from the interplay of physiological arousal, outer expressions, and experienced thoughts and feelings. But precisely how? We can glimpse some possible answers by looking at two controversies, one long-standing and one fairly new, both of which concern the sequence of the basic aspects of emotion.

The James-Lange and Cannon-Bard Theories

Let us first evaluate the oldest controversy among theories of emotion. Simply put, does your heart pound and your body quiver *while* you are afraid, or are you afraid *because* your heart pounds and your body quivers?

To most people in the nineteenth century, as well as in our own, we cry because we are sad, lash out because we are angry, tremble because we are afraid. To the pioneering American psychologist William James (who once said, "The first lecture on psychology I ever heard was the first I ever gave"), the common-sense view was 180 degrees out of line. Instead, wrote James, "we feel sorry *because* we cry, angry *because* we strike, afraid *because* we tremble" (1890, p. 1066). If an oncoming car is in your lane, you will swerve sharply to avoid it, and *then* notice your racing heart and feel shaken with fright. Your feeling of fear thus seems to follow your body's response (see Figure 14-11).

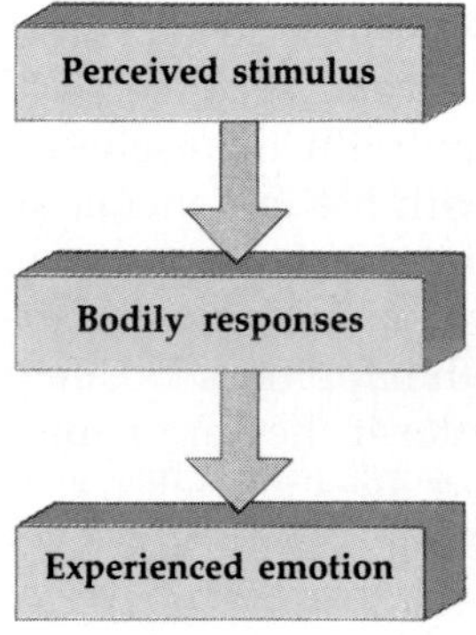

Figure 14-11 *A summary of the James-Lange theory of emotion.*

This idea, which was independently proposed by Danish physiologist Carl Lange and thus is called the ***James-Lange*** theory, struck American physiologist Walter Cannon as implausible. For one thing, the body's responses did not seem distinct enough to trigger the different emotions. Does a racing heart indicate fear, anger, or love? For another, changes in heart rate, perspiration, and body temperature seemed to occur too slowly to trigger sudden emotion. Cannon, and later another American physiologist, Philip Bard, therefore concluded that bodily arousal and experienced emotion occur simultaneously: The emotion-arousing stimulus is simultaneously routed (1) to the cortex, causing the subjective awareness of emotion, and (2) to the sympathetic nervous system, causing the bodily arousal. Thus, said Cannon and Bard in what came to be known as the ***Cannon-Bard*** theory, your heart begins pounding at the same time you experience fear, but the one does not cause the other (see Figure 14-12).

So long as the evidence seemed to indicate that one emotion is much the same as another in terms of arousal, the James-Lange assumption that we experience our emotions through differing bodily states seemed impossible. But now that new evidence indicates there are indeed some subtle but distinct physiological differences among the emotions, the James-Lange theory has become more plausible. Moreover, effects like those of facial expression on felt emotion are precisely what James might have predicted. As he struggled with his own feelings of depression and grief, James came to believe that emotions could be controlled by going "through the outward motions." "To feel cheerful," he advised, "sit up cheerfully, look around cheerfully and act as if cheerfulness were already there." According to a recent theory (Zajonc, 1985) the muscle movements involved in such expressions may even influence bloodflow through the face to the brain, thereby affecting feelings.

Let's now check your understanding of the James-Lange and Cannon-Bard theories. Imagine that your brain was unable to sense your heart pounding or your stomach churning. According to each theory, what effect would this have on your experiencing of emotions?

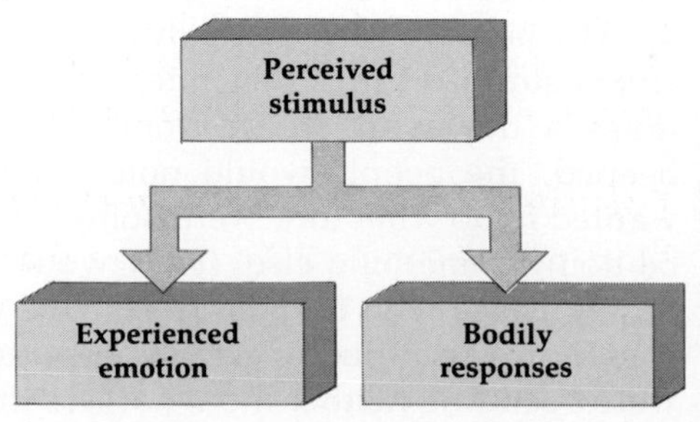

Figure 14-12 *A summary of the Cannon-Bard theory of emotion.*

Cannon and Bard would expect you to experience emotions normally, because they believed that the experiencing of emotions occurs separately from (though simultaneous with) the bodily responses. James and Lange would expect greatly diminished emotions, because to feel emotion you must perceive your bodily responses. The situation we have imagined actually exists in individuals with severed spinal cords. Psychologist George Hohmann (1966) interviewed twenty-five such persons (soldiers who were injured in World War II) and asked them to recall emotion-arousing incidents that occurred before and after their spinal cords were severed. Those with injuries in the lower part of the spine, who lost sensation only in their legs, reported little change in their emotions. But those with injuries at neck level, who could feel nothing below the neck, reported (just as James and Lange would have expected) a considerable decrease in emotions. These victims said they might act much the same in emotion-arousing situations, but as one said about his anger, "It just doesn't have the heat to it that it used to. It's a mental kind of anger." On the other hand, emotions that are expressed mostly in body areas above the neck were intensified. Virtually all the men experienced an increase in weeping, lumps in the throat, and getting choked up when saying good-bye, worshipping, or watching a touching movie.

While such evidence has revived the James-Lange theory, many researchers agree with Cannon and Bard that our experience of emotions also involves the cognitive activity of the cortex. Whether or not we fear the man in the dark alley depends entirely on whether we interpret his actions as hostile or friendly. So with James and Lange we can say that our bodily responses are an important ingredient of emotion, and with Cannon and Bard we can also say there is more to the experience of emotion than that.

Cognition and Emotion

During the 1980s, the biggest controversy among emotion researchers has concerned the relationship of thought and emotion. Put simply, what is the connection between what we *think* and how we *feel?*

We have already noted that emotions affect thinking; our mood helps trigger memories of events associated with the mood. This partly explains why our moods also color our perceptions of life. When we feel like singing "Oh what a beautiful morning!" we recall the world and the people around us as wonderful; if the following day we feel crabby, we may remember the same people as less wonderful.

Does our thinking also affect our emotions? Or can we experience emotion apart from thinking? This fundamental issue has practical implications. If our emotions are always a reaction to our thoughts, then by consciously altering our thinking patterns we could change our emotions. As we will see in Chapter 17, this is what some therapists seek to help people to do. On the other hand, if our emotions need not arise from our conscious thoughts, then therapists may need to explore or condition people's emotional responses directly.

Schachter's Two-Factor Theory of Emotion

Most psychologists today believe that our cognitions—our perceptions, memories, and interpretations—are indeed an essential ingredient of emotion. One such theorist is Stanley Schachter, whose influential ***two-factor*** theory proposes that emotions have two ingredients: physical arousal plus a cognitive label (Figure 14-13). Like James and Lange, Schachter presumed that our experience of emotion grows from our awareness of our bodily state. Like Cannon and Bard, he believed that an

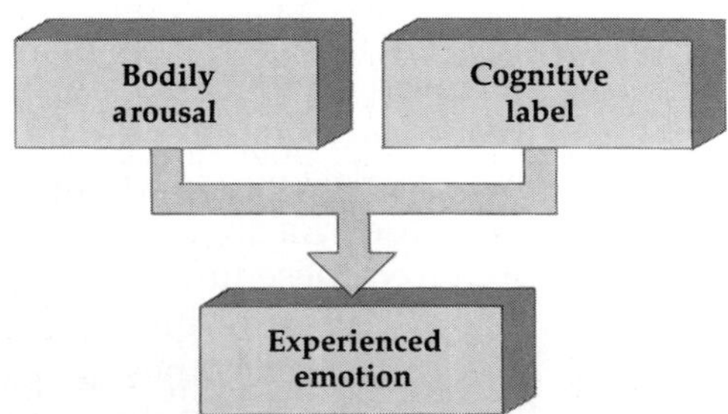

Figure 14-13 *A summary of the two-factor theory of emotion. To experience emotion, one must be aroused and label the arousal.*

emotional experience requires a conscious interpretation of the event as well.

Usually, it is hard to disentangle our arousal in response to an event from our interpretation of the event. But imagine that you were aroused and were not sure why, or that you attributed some of your arousal to the wrong source. Perhaps after an invigorating run you arrive home to find a message that you got the job for which you applied. Might you feel more elated (because you are more aroused, but attribute your arousal entirely to the news) than if you received the same news after awakening from a nap?

To find out, Schachter and Jerome Singer (1962) aroused some college men with injections of epinephrine. Picture yourself as a subject: After receiving the injection, you are taken to a waiting room, where you find yourself with another person (actually an accomplice of the experimenter) who is acting either euphoric or irritated. As you observe this person, you begin to feel your heart race, your body flush, and your breathing becoming more rapid. If you were told to expect such effects from the injection, what would you feel? Schachter and Singer's subjects felt little emotion—because they cognitively attributed their arousal to the drug. If you were led to think the injection would produce no effects, what would you feel? Perhaps you would have reacted as many of the subjects did, by catching the emotion of the person you were with—becoming happy if with the euphoric accomplice and testy if with the irritated accomplice.

This discovery that a stirred-up state can be experienced as one emotion or another, depending on how we interpret and label it, has been tested in dozens of subsequent experiments. Later experiments indicate that arousal is not as emotionally undifferentiated as Schachter believed. Nevertheless, the experiments do generally confirm that being physically stirred up can intensify just about any emotion (Reisenzein, 1983). For example, if people who have been aroused by pumping an exercise bike or watching a rock concert film are then insulted, they find it easy to misattribute their arousal to the provocation. Thus they typically feel angrier than do similarly provoked people who were not previously aroused (Zillmann, 1979).

Must Cognition Precede Emotion?

So can we say that we really do not have an emotion until we put a label on our arousal? Robert Zajonc (1980, 1984) contends the answer is no, that some emotions we feel *before* we think. He suggests that sometimes our emotions are more instantaneous than our interpretations of a situation. (Can you recall immediately liking something or someone without at first knowing why?) Consider the evidence for this:

1. In Chapter 6, "Sensation," and Chapter 7, "Perception," we reviewed experiments in which people had musical tunes piped to one ear while attending to something read into the other ear, or were flashed visual shapes for too short a time to perceive them consciously as anything but flashes of light. Later, they preferred these tunes or shapes over others—despite being unable to recognize them. The subjects felt a preference for the stimuli to which they had been previously exposed, despite being unaware that they had been exposed to them. Cognition did not precede their emotional preference.
2. Although the brain functions as an integrated whole, some of its neural pathways involved in emotion can be distinguished from

those for cognitive processes. Emotional processes are more likely to involve the right hemisphere of the brain. Moreover, Zajonc reports, there is a pathway directly from the eye to one of the brain's emotional control centers, the hypothalamus. Thus visual stimuli, such as startling flashes of light, could trigger instant emotional responses, such as fear, without involving the cognitive pathways.

3. As we have seen, changes in facial expression may affect people's feelings and bodily states directly, apparently without conscious thought being involved.

Such evidence convinces Zajonc that *some* of our emotional reactions involve no deliberate rational thinking. Cognition, he believes, is not necessary for emotion. The heart is not always subject to the mind.

"The heart has its reasons which reason does not know."
Blaise Pascal, 1623–1662

Emotion researcher Richard Lazarus (1982, 1984) disagrees. Granted, he says, that some emotional responses do not require conscious thinking. Still, most of the important emotions, such as anger, guilt, happiness, and love, do arise from our interpretations, memories, and inferences. And those more instant emotions that do not, still require some cognitive appraisal of the situation. The appraisal may be effortless—like the automatic encoding processes we discussed in Chapter 10 on memory—but it is still a function of the mind (see Figure 14-14).

Ultimately, the controversy reduces to a matter of definition. Should the instantaneous information processing required to appraise a stimulus—to at least sense the stimulus—always be considered cognition? Lazarus says yes; Zajonc says that sometimes the processing requires so little mental work, with no awareness, that cognition is not involved.

For us, the important conclusion concerns what Lazarus and Zajonc seem to agree on: Some emotional responses—especially simple likes, dislikes, and fears—involve no conscious thinking. We may instantly fear the spider, even if we think it harmless. After conditioning, Little Albert exhibited an instantaneous fear of furry objects. Such emotions are hard to alter by changing thinking.

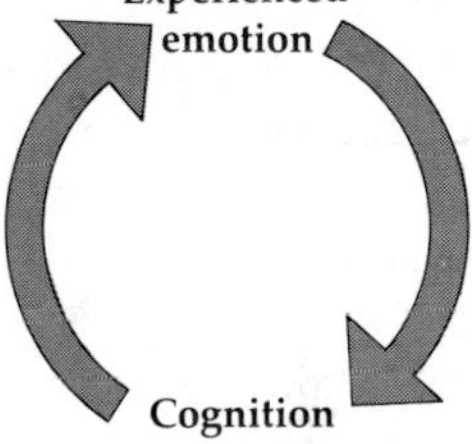

Figure 14-14 *Emotion and cognition feed each other. But which is the chicken and which the egg? Lazarus believes that cognition always precedes emotion. Zajonc contends that some of our emotional reactions occur prior to any cognitive processing.*

Other emotions—including moods such as depression and complex feelings such as hatred and love—are greatly affected by our interpretations, memories, and expectations. For these, as we will see in Chapter 17, new ways of thinking may enable new states of feeling.

SUMMING UP

Emotions are psychological responses of the whole organism that involve an interplay among (1) physiological arousal, (2) expressive reactions, and (3) conscious feelings and thoughts.

THE PHYSIOLOGY OF EMOTION

Arousal According to the Yerkes-Dodson law, our performance on a task is usually best when arousal is moderate, though this varies with the difficulty of the task.

Physiological States Accompanying Specific Emotions The physical arousal that occurs with one emotion is in some ways the same as that with another. However, scientists have discovered subtle differences in the brain pathways and hormones associated with different emotions.

Lie Detection The polygraph measures several physiological indicators of emotion. Can it therefore detect lies by revealing the tension that one might feel while lying? The polygraph does better than chance, but many experts believe not nearly well enough to justify its spreading use in business and government.

THE EXPRESSION OF EMOTION

Nonverbal Communication Much of our communication is through the silent language of the body. Is such language universal? Gestures appear to be culturally determined, but facial expressions, such as those of happiness and fear, are common the world over.

The Effects of Facial Expressions Expressions not only communicate emotion, they both amplify the felt emotion and signal the body to respond accordingly.

THE EXPERIENCING OF EMOTION

Among the various emotions, we looked closely at three: fear, anger, and happiness.

Fear Fear is a traumatic but also an adaptive emotion. Although we seem biologically predisposed to acquire some fears, the enormous variety of human fears is best explained by learning.

Anger Anger is most often aroused by events that are not only frustrating or insulting but also interpreted as willful and unjustified. Contrary to the catharsis hypothesis, blowing off steam does not, in the long run, reduce anger and aggression.

Happiness A good mood boosts people's perceptions of the world and their willingness to help others. The moods triggered by the day's good or bad events seldom last more than a day. Even seemingly significant good events, such as a substantial raise in income, seem not to increase happiness for long. The apparent relativity of happiness can be explained by the adaptation-level and relative-deprivation principles. Nevertheless, some people are normally happier than others, and researchers have identified factors that predict such happiness.

THEORIES OF EMOTION

The James-Lange and Cannon-Bard Theories One of the oldest theoretical controversies regarding emotion is whether we feel emotion after we notice our bodily responses (as James and Lange proposed) or while our bodies respond (as Cannon and Bard believed).

Cognition and Emotion Today's number one controversy among emotion researchers concerns whether human emotions can be experienced apart from cognition. Can we feel before we think? Stanley Schachter's two-factor theory of emotion contends that the cognitive labels we put on our states of arousal are an essential ingredient of emotion. Richard Lazarus agrees that cognition is essential: Many important emotions are rooted in our interpretations and inferences, while other emotions require only a simple cognitive appraisal of the emotion-arousing situation. But Robert Zajonc believes that some simple emotional responses occur instantly, outside of conscious awareness and before any cognitive processing could occur. The issue has practical implications, for to the extent that emotions are rooted in thinking, we can hope to change our emotions by changing our thinking.

TERMS AND CONCEPTS TO REMEMBER

Adaptation-Level Phenomenon The tendency for our judgments (of sounds, of lights, of income, and so forth) to be relative to a neutral "adaptation level" that is defined by our prior experience.

Cannon-Bard Theory The theory that an emotion-arousing stimulus simultaneously triggers (1) physiological responses, and (2) the subjective experience of emotion.

Catharsis Emotional release. In psychology, the catharsis hypothesis maintains that aggressive urges are relieved by "releasing" aggressive energy (through action or fantasy).

Emotion A response of the whole organism, involving (1) physical arousal, (2) expressive reactions, and (3) conscious experience.

Guilty Knowledge Test A lie detection procedure that assesses a suspect's responses to details of a crime known only to the guilty person.

James-Lange Theory The theory stating that to experience emotion is to be aware of one's physiological responses to emotion-arousing stimuli.

Opponent-Process Theory The theory that every emotion triggers an opposing emotion that fights it and lingers after the first emotion is extinguished.

Polygraph A machine, commonly used in attempts to detect lies, that measures several of the physiological responses that accompany emotion (such as perspiration, heart rate, and breathing changes).

Relative Deprivation The sense that one is worse off relative to those with whom one compares oneself.

Two-Factor Theory The theory that to experience emotion one must (1) be physically aroused and (2) cognitively label the arousal.

Yerkes-Dodson Law The principle that, in general, moderate arousal enables optimal performance. But for different tasks the optimal level of arousal varies; the easier the task, the higher the optimum arousal.

FOR FURTHER READING

Darwin, C. (1872/1965). *Expression of the emotions in man and animals.* Chicago: University of Chicago Press.

The classic description of emotional expressions and their adaptive functions.

Ekman, P. (1985). *Telling lies: Clues to deceit in the marketplace, politics, and marriage.* New York: Norton.

A fascinating book about how our faces and gestures communicate emotion and betray actual feelings.

Izard, C. E., Kagan, J., & Zajonc, R. B. (1984). *Emotions, cognition and behavior.* New York: Cambridge University Press.

Straight from the horses' mouths—leading emotion scholars explain current issues and summarize recent findings.

Lykken, D. T. (1981). *A tremor in the blood: Uses and abuses of the lie detector.* New York: McGraw-Hill.

The foremost scholar of lie detection discusses the potential and limits of polygraph testing.

Tavris, C. (1984). *Anger: The misunderstood emotion.* New York: Simon & Schuster.

A provocative, beautifully written summary of research on anger that points to the dangers of letting it all hang out.

André Kertesz *Self-Portrait with Life Masks, New York, 1976*

PART SIX

PERSONALITY, DISORDER, AND WELL-BEING

Each of us is a unique individual—someone with a characteristic personality and with our own physical and psychological ups and downs that are influenced by particular experiences. In Chapter 15, "Personality," we explore four important theoretical perspectives on how we come to be the unique individuals we are and on how best to understand and describe the workings of personality. Sometimes, a person's uniqueness shades into a "Psychological Disorder," the topic of Chapter 16. There we delve into how and why disordered people are labeled as such, and we consider the symptoms and known causes of major disorders such as depression and schizophrenia. Chapter 17, "Therapy," reviews the major approaches to treating psychological disorders and takes a hardheaded look at their effectiveness. Finally, Chapter 18, "Health," describes new research on how our behavior and emotions can affect our health and what steps we can take to promote our own health and well-being.

Collection of Mr. and Mrs. Joseph R. Shapiro

Joseph Cornell *Untitled (Medici Prince)*, c. 1952

THE PSYCHOANALYTIC PERSPECTIVE

- **Personality Structure**
- **Personality Development**
- **Personality Dynamics**
- **Freud's Descendants and Dissenters**
- **Assessing the Unconscious**
- **Evaluating the Psychoanalytic Perspective**

THE TRAIT PERSPECTIVE

- **Describing Traits**
- **Assessing Traits**
- **Evaluating the Trait Perspective: How Consistent Are We?**

THE HUMANISTIC PERSPECTIVE

- **Abraham Maslow's Self-Actualizing Person**
- **Carl Rogers' Person-Centered Perspective**
- **Assessing the Self**
- **Evaluating the Humanistic Perspective**
  - *Criticisms of Humanistic Psychology*
  - *Research on the Self*

THE SOCIAL-COGNITIVE PERSPECTIVE

- **Reciprocal Influences**
- **Personal Control**
  - *Locus of Control*
  - *Learned Helplessness Versus Control*
- **Assessing Behavior in Situations**
- **Evaluating the Social-Cognitive Perspective**

CHAPTER 15

Personality

The novelist William Faulkner was a master at creating characters with vivid personalities, personalities so real they are capable of casting shadows. One of his creations, Ike McCaslin, appears at various ages in over a dozen novels and short stories. Ike is highly principled, and consistently so. At age 10 he senses within himself a deep reverence for the wilderness and its creatures. At 21 he forfeits what he perceives as a "tainted" inheritance. In his late seventies he counsels his nephew to use his land responsibly. Ike the adult is an extension of Ike the child. Another Faulkner character, Jason Compson, is a selfish, whining 4-year-old in the opening section of *The Sound and the Fury,* and a selfish, screaming 34-year-old as the novel closes. Head of the Compson household, he verbally abuses his doting mother, his retarded brother, his niece, and the household servants; through blackmail he prevents his sister, Caddy, from seeing her daughter. He regularly misappropriates funds Caddy sends to support the child and fosters his mother's estrangement from Caddy. Lying, threatening, conniving, he is a self-centered adult who developed from a self-centered child.

Faulkner's characters, as they appear and reappear throughout his fiction, exhibit the distinctiveness and consistency that define personality. Having emphasized in the preceding chapters of this book how we are similar—how we develop, perceive, learn, remember, think, and feel, and how our bodies accomplish all this—we now acknowledge that each of us is in some ways unique. This distinctiveness helps define our individual personalities. ***Personality*** consists of "an individual's enduring response patterns across a variety of situations" (Harre & Lamb, 1983). To put it differently, your personality is defined by your relatively distinctive and consistent ways of thinking, feeling, and acting. If your response patterns are unusually distinctive and consistent—if, say, you are always outgoing, whether at a party or in a classroom—people are likely to say that you have a "strong" personality.

Not just this chapter but much of this book has to do with personality. We have considered biological influences on personality, personality across the life-span, and aspects of personality related to processes of learning, motivation, and emotion. In later chapters we will consider personality disorders, personal well-being, and social influences on personality.

In this chapter we will focus upon four major perspectives on personality and upon research that is relevant to their assumptions: first, Sigmund Freud's *psychoanalytic* theory, with its emphasis on the origins of personality in childhood sexuality and the driving force of unconscious motivations; second, the efforts of the *trait* theorists to identify specific dimensions of our distinctiveness and consistency; third, the focus of *humanistic* psychologists on our capacities for growth and self-fulfillment; and fourth, the concern of *social-cognitive* psychologists with how we are shaped by interaction with our environment. Each perspective offers a distinctive view of personality that provides valuable insights and, in doing so, reveals some limitations of the other perspectives. Let us, therefore, appraise each critically yet sympathetically by asking of each—What does it offer us? How can we make use of it?

THE PSYCHOANALYTIC PERSPECTIVE

According to Freud, all facets of human personality—all emotions, strivings, and ideas—arise from a basic conflict between our aggressive and pleasure-seeking biological impulses and the social restraints against them. In Freud's view, individual personality is the result of each person's attempt to resolve this conflict, to express these impulses in ways that bring satisfaction without also bringing guilt or punishment.

Underlying Freud's conception of personality was his belief that the mind is like an iceberg—mostly hidden. Our conscious thoughts are the part of the iceberg above the surface. Below that is a much larger ***unconscious*** region, a whole reservoir of thoughts, wishes, feelings, and memories of which we are unaware. Some of these thoughts are merely temporarily out of mind in a ***preconscious*** area, from which they can be retrieved at will into conscious awareness. Of more interest to Freud was the balance of the unconscious, a mass of unacceptable, threatening passions and thoughts that are repressed—forcibly blocked from consciousness because they would be overwhelming if they were recognized. Though we are unaware of these troublesome feelings and ideas, they are powerful shapers of our personalities, said Freud, because they push to be expressed in disguised forms—in the work we do, in the beliefs we hold, in our daily habits, in our troubling symptoms.

Freud explained these views, which evolved during his treatment of patients, in twenty-four volumes published between 1888 and 1939. Although his first solo book, *The Interpretation of Dreams,* sold but 600 copies in its first 8 years, his ideas gradually began to attract many followers—and intense criticism.

For now, let us reserve judgment on Freud's theory and instead try to see things as Freud did. Though it is difficult to summarize twenty-four volumes in a few pages, we can understand some of the highlights of Freud's theory—the first comprehensive theory of personality.

For most of his life, Freud lived in Vienna, where he earned a medical degree in 1881 and went into private practice, specializing in nervous disorders. He became interested in the hidden aspects of personality when he found himself confronted with certain patients whose apparent neurological disorders made no neurological sense. For example, a patient might have lost all feeling in her hand, or have become deaf or blind, with no evidence of neurological impairment. (There is no sensory nerve that when damaged would destroy feeling in the entire hand and nothing

Sigmund Freud: "I was the only worker in a new field."

else.) Noting that such symptoms could also be produced through hypnosis, Freud became intrigued with the idea that they might be psychological rather than physiological in nature. Accordingly, he spent several months in Paris studying with Jean Charcot, a French neurologist who was using hypnosis to treat such disorders.

When he returned to Vienna, Freud began to use hypnosis with his own patients, encouraging them while in the hypnotic trance to talk freely about themselves and the circumstances surrounding the onset of their symptoms. Typically the patients responded by discussing themselves quite openly and becoming agitated during the hypnotic experience, and sometimes they would later find their symptoms removed or at least much relieved.

It was in this way that Freud "discovered" the unconscious. Piecing together his patients' accounts of themselves, he determined that anesthesia of the hand might be caused by, say, the fear of touching one's genitals; that blindness or deafness might be caused by not wanting to see or hear something that aroused intense anxiety. In time Freud began to see patients with a wide variety of symptoms and abandoned hypnosis in favor of ***free association***—in which the patient merely relaxed and said whatever came to mind, no matter how embarrassing or trivial. He believed this procedure would produce a chain of thought leading into the patient's unconscious thereby allowing retrieval and release of the suppressed energy of painful unconscious memories. The analysis of these unconscious tensions, Freud called ***psychoanalysis;*** thus the theory of personality that he created to explain his observations is called psychoanalytic theory.

Freud believed he caught glimpses of the unconscious not only in people's free associations and in their symptoms, but also in their everyday dreams and slips of the tongue and pen. Dreams, he contended, are a major outlet for people's unconscious wishes. The remembered content (the "manifest content"—see Chapter 8, "States of Consciousness") he believed to be a censored expression of those wishes (the dream's "latent content"). In Freud's view, dreams are the "royal road to the unconscious." By analyzing people's dreams, Freud believed he could help reveal the nature of their inner conflicts and release their troublesome tensions. Slips in reading, writing, and speaking further suggested that what we say and do may reflect the workings of our unconscious minds (as in Freud's example of the man who, meaning to attribute his nervous state to worries about the effects of a frigid cold *wave* on his crops, referred to his frigid *wife* instead).

"Good morning, beheaded—uh, I mean beloved."

Personality Structure

For Freud, personality was composed of three interacting systems: the id, ego, and superego. Like other psychological concepts such as intelligence and memory, id, ego, and superego cannot be directly observed; they are, Freud said, "useful aids to understanding" that he invented to help explain things that can be observed.

The ***id*** is a reservoir of unconscious psychic energy that constantly strives to satisfy our instinctual drives for survival (such as hunger, thirst, and sex) and for aggression. The id operates on the ***pleasure principle:*** It seeks immediate gratification, totally unconstrained by reality. The most straightforward example of the id's functioning is the newborn infant, who, totally governed by the id, cries out for satisfaction the moment a need is felt, with no recognition of the conditions and demands that may exist in the outside world.

The ***ego*** develops gradually as the infant learns to cope with the real world. It operates on the ***reality principle,*** which seeks to gratify the id's impulses in realistic ways that will bring true pleasure rather than pain or destruction. Imagine what would happen if we expressed our sexual or hostile impulses whenever we felt them, no matter when or where, rather than restraining ourselves. The ego, which contains our mostly conscious perceptions, thoughts, judgments, and memories, is said to be the "executive" of personality because it decides our actions as it mediates between the impulsive demands of the id and those of the external world. In addition, beginning at around age 4 or 5, the ego also mediates the demands of a newly emerging psychic system, the superego.

The ***superego*** is like a voice of conscience that forces the ego to consider not just the real, but the ideal: Its sole focus is on how one *ought* to behave. Developing as the individual internalizes the morals and values of parents and society, the superego provides both our sense of right and wrong and our ideal standards; it strives for perfection and judges our actions with accompanying feelings of guilt or pride. An individual with an exceptionally strong superego may be continually upright or guilt-ridden, while one with a weak superego may be wantonly self-indulgent.

"The Incredible Hulk" in the background is a TV writer's personification of the id impulses of a mild-mannered physicist, David Banner. When Banner gets angry, he is physically transformed into the "Hulk" and his normally restrained and unconscious impulses are unleashed.

Personality Development

Freud's analysis of his patients' problems and memories convinced him that personality is decisively shaped in the first few years of life. Again and again his patients' symptoms appeared to him to be rooted in unresolved conflicts that originated in early childhood. He concluded that children pass through a series of ***psychosexual stages*** of development—stages during which the id's pleasure-seeking energies are focused on different pleasure-sensitive areas of the body called "erogenous zones."

The first of these stages, the ***oral stage,*** centers on the mouth. During this stage, which lasts throughout the first 18 months of life, the infant's sensual pleasures focus on sucking, biting, and chewing.

During the ***anal stage,*** from about age 18 months to 3 years, stimulation of the bowels and bladder, through retention and elimination, becomes a source of gratification.

The ***phallic stage,*** from roughly ages 3 to 6 years, occurs as the pleasure zone shifts to the genitals. During this stage, Freud believed, children seek genital stimulation and develop both unconscious sexual desires for the parent of the other sex and feelings of jealousy and hatred for the rival parent of the same sex. They also develop feelings of guilt and a fear that the rival parent will punish them horribly. This collection of feelings he called the ***Oedipus complex*** (after the Greek legend of Oedipus, who unknowingly killed his father and married his mother). Children eventually cope with these threatening feelings by repressing them and identifying with—that is, by trying to become like—the rival parent. It is through this ***identification*** process, in which children incorporate many of their parents' values, that the superego begins to develop.

With their sexual feelings repressed, children enter a ***latency period,*** during which sexuality is dormant and children play mostly with peers of the same sex. At puberty, this period gives way to the final stage, the ***genital stage,*** as youths begin to experience mature sexual feelings toward others.

In Freud's view, maladaptive behavior in the adult results from unresolved conflicts that originated during the course of these psychosexual stages. At any point in these stages, strong conflict could lock, or ***fixate,*** the person's pleasure-seeking energies in that stage. Thus, people who were deprived of sufficient oral gratification might be *fixated* at the oral stage as adults, exhibiting either passive dependence (like that of a nursing infant) or an exaggerated denial of this dependence—perhaps through acting tough and indulging in biting sarcasm. They might also continually seek oral gratification through excessive smoking, eating, and the like. Those who never quite resolve the anal conflict between the desire to eliminate at will and the demands of toilet training may as adults become either messy and disorganized or highly controlled and compulsively neat. In such ways, believed Freud, the twig of personality is bent.

Personality Dynamics

To live in social groups, we cannot act out our sexual and aggressive impulses willy-nilly. We must control them. When the ego fears losing control of the inner war between the demands of the id and the superego, the result is anxiety. Anxiety, said Freud, is the price we pay for civilization.

Unlike the specific fears discussed in Chapter 14, "Emotion," the dark cloud of anxiety is not focused on any specific object. It is therefore hard to cope with, as when you have an unsettled feeling but are unsure why. Freud proposed that the ego protects itself against anxiety with what he called ego ***defense mechanisms.*** Defense mechanisms reduce anxiety by unconsciously distorting reality.

"I'm sorry, I'm not speaking to anyone tonight. My defense mechanisms seem to be out of order."

Because ***repression*** banishes anxiety-arousing thoughts and feelings from consciousness, it underlies the other defense mechanisms, all of which serve to disguise threatening impulses and keep them from reaching consciousness. Freud believed that repression explains why we do not remember our childhood lust for our parent of the other sex. However, he also believed that often the repression is not complete and the repressed urges leak through in dream symbols and slips of the tongue.

Another means of coping with anxiety is through ***regression***—retreating to an earlier, more infantile stage of development where some of our psychic energies are still fixated. Thus, when facing the anxious first days of school, a child may regress to the oral comfort of thumb sucking or nail biting.

In ***reaction formation,*** the ego unconsciously transforms unacceptable impulses into their opposites. Hatred becomes love. Timidity becomes daring. Feelings of inadequacy become bravado. According to the principle of this defense mechanism, vehement social crusaders, such as those who rail against gay rights, may be motivated by the very sexual desires against which they are crusading.

"The lady doth protest too much, methinks."
William Shakespeare,
Hamlet, 1600

Projection disguises threatening impulses by imputing them to others. Thus "He hates me" may be a projection of the actual feeling "I hate him" (Hall & Lindzey, 1978). According to Freudian theory, racial prejudice may be the result of projecting one's own unacceptable impulses onto members of another racial group.

The common mechanism of ***rationalization*** offers self-justifying explanations in place of what, unknown to us, are the real reasons for our actions. Thus habitual drinkers may explain that they drink with their friends "just to be sociable," and students who fail to study may rationalize that "All work and no play makes Jack (or Jill) a dull person."

Displacement diverts one's sexual or aggressive impulses toward a more socially acceptable object than the one that aroused them. Thus children who do not feel free to express anger against their parents will sometimes displace their anger onto the family pet. ***Sublimation*** is displacing impulses into socially valued achievements. Sublimation is therefore socially adaptive. In fact, it may even be a wellspring for great cultural and artistic achievements. Freud suggested that Leonardo da Vinci's painting of Madonnas was a sublimation of his longing for intimacy with his mother, from whom he had been separated at an early age.

Note that all these defense mechanisms are thought to be indirect and unconscious methods of reducing anxiety by disguising one's threatening impulses. We never say, "I'm feeling anxious; I'd better project my sexual or hostile feelings onto someone else." Defense mechanisms would not work were we to recognize them as such.

Freud's Descendants and Dissenters

Although controversial, Freud's writings soon attracted a group of followers, some of whom later broke away to establish their own versions of psychoanalytic theory. These "neo-Freudians," as they are called, generally accepted Freud's basic ideas about the importance of the unconscious; the personality structures of id, ego, and superego; the shaping of personality in childhood; and the dynamics of anxiety and the defense mechanisms. Yet they viewed these concepts differently, placing somewhat more emphasis on the role of the conscious mind in interpreting experience and coping with the environment. Moreover, they doubted that sex and aggression were all-consuming instincts, and they placed more emphasis on social relationships.

Alfred Adler and Karen Horney agreed with Freud that childhood is important. But they believed that the social, not the sexual, tensions of childhood were crucial for personality formation. Adler, who himself struggled to overcome childhood illnesses and accidents, said that behind much of our behavior lies an attempt to vanquish childhood feelings of inferiority, feelings that trigger strivings for superiority and power. Horney said that childhood anxiety caused by a sense of helplessness triggers desires for love and security.

Erich Fromm agreed with Freud that the ego is important. But in deemphasizing the role of sexual and aggressive impulses, he viewed the ego as more than a mediator between id and superego. The ego, he said, strives for unity and love, for truth and freedom; such conscious strivings are not merely a sublimation of baser motives.

Erik Erikson agreed with Freud that development proceeds through a series of critical stages. But he believed these were psycho*social*, not psychosexual, stages. As we noted in Chapter 4, "Adolescence and Adulthood," Erikson also believed that life's developmental stages encompass the whole life-span. Just as Erikson maintained that infancy was a time for establishing basic trust, and adolescence for establishing identity, he proposed that in adulthood people strive first for intimacy, then for generativity (through family and work), and then for integrity, a sense that their lives have been meaningful.

Unlike these neo-Freudians, Freud's disciple-turned-dissenter, Carl Jung, placed less emphasis on social factors and agreed with Freud that the unconscious exerts a powerful influence. But he contended that the unconscious contains more than a person's repressed thoughts and feelings. There is also a collective unconscious, he believed, a reservoir of images derived from our early ancestors' universal experiences. This inherited unconscious was said to include deep-rooted spiritual concerns and to explain why people in different cultures share certain myths and images, such as that of mother to symbolize nurturance.

Assessing the Unconscious

Researchers who study personality and mental health workers who provide therapy for troubled persons need methods for measuring personality characteristics. Each theory of personality implies a particular method for describing and assessing personality.

Psychoanalytic theory maintains that the most significant influences on our personalities arise from the unconscious, which contains residues or memories from early childhood experiences. Thus, practitioners of this perspective have tended to dismiss agree-disagree or true-false questionnaires as merely tapping the conscious surface. Needed is a sort of psychological x-ray—a test that can see through our surface pretensions and reveal our hidden conflicts and impulses.

One type of test that is designed to provide such a view is the ***projective test,*** in which a person is presented with an ambiguous stimulus and then asked to describe it or tell a story about it. Since the stimulus contains no inherent meaning, it is assumed that whatever meaning people read into it will reflect their interests, biases, and conflicts. Henry Murray (1933) demonstrated a possible basis for such a test at a house party hosted by his 11-year-old daughter. Murray engaged the children in playing a frightening game called "Murder." When he showed the children some photographs after the game, Murray found that the children perceived the photos as more malicious than they had before the game. The children, it seemed to Murray, had *projected* their inner feelings into the

Drawing by Sidney Harris

"The forward thrust of the antlers shows a determined personality, yet the small sun indicates a lack of self-confidence . . . "

pictures. A few years later, Murray introduced the Thematic Apperception Test (TAT)—ambiguous pictures about which people are asked to make up stories (Figure 15-1). As you may recall from Chapter 13, "Motivation," one use of the TAT has been to assess the extent to which people "read into" the pictures their own achievement strivings. Shown a daydreaming boy, those who imagine him fantasizing or thinking about some achievement are presumed to be projecting their own achievement concerns.

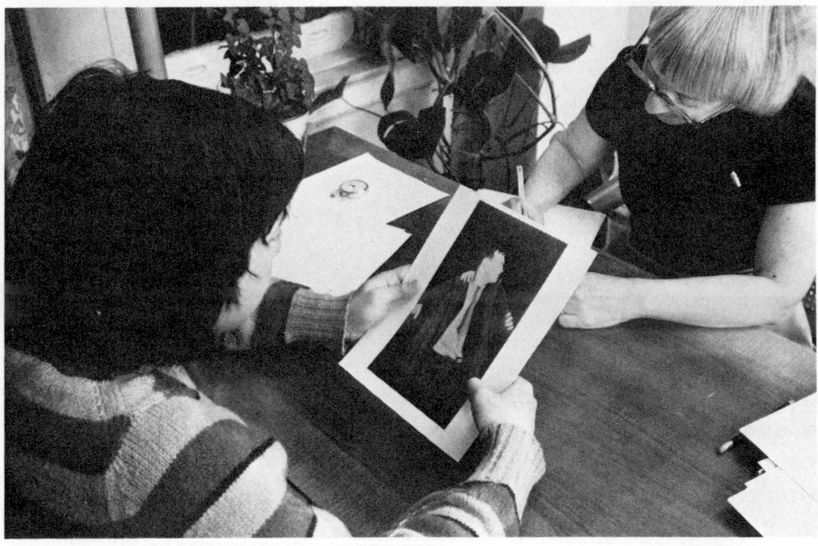

Figure 15-1 *The hopes, fears, interests, and biases revealed in this young's man's descriptions of a series of ambiguous pictures in the Thematic Apperception Test (TAT) are presumed to be projections of his inner feelings. As such, they provide valuable leads to the psychologist assessing him.*

There are now a variety of other projective tests. One test asks subjects to draw a person, another to complete sentences ("My mother . . ."), another to provide the first word that comes to mind after the examiner says a test word. More widely used than any of these is the famous inkblot test, introduced by Swiss psychiatrist Hermann Rorschach in 1921. The ***Rorschach*** test provides ten such blots (Figure 15-2). Those who use the inkblots assume that what we see in them is a projection of our inner feelings and conflicts. For example, if we see fierce animals or weapons in the blot, the examiner may infer that we have aggressive tendencies.

Figure 15-2 *This girl is taking the most familiar projective test for personality, the Rorschach. Although its reliability and validity are questioned, the Rorschach test is still widely used.*

Is this a reasonable assumption? If so, can the psychologist who administers the test use the Rorschach to understand one's personality and help diagnose any emotional disorder? Recall from our discussion of intelligence tests (Chapter 12) the two primary criteria of a good test: reliability and validity. On these criteria, how good is the Rorschach?

Not very good. There is no one accepted system for scoring the test, so unless two raters have been trained in the same scoring system, their agreement on the results of any given test may be modest. There is also no set system for interpretation. So, in effect, a subject's inkblot interpretations are themselves ambiguous stimuli, which different examiners may interpret differently. Nor is the test very successful at predicting behavior (who is likely to attempt suicide and who is not) or at discriminating between groups (who is homosexual and who is heterosexual). Writing in *The Eighth Mental Measurements Yearbook*, Rolf Peterson (1978) summed up 50 years of research and 5000 articles and books by concluding that "the general lack of predictive validity for the Rorschach raises serious questions about its continued use in clinical practice."

Although now declining in use, the test nevertheless remains one of the most widely used psychological instruments (Lubin & others, 1984). Some clinicians continue to be confident of the test's validity—not as a device that by itself can provide a diagnosis, but as a source of suggestive leads that can be supplemented with other information. Other clinicians believe that even if the Rorschach scoring systems have no validity, the test is still a revealing interview technique. Freud himself would probably have been uncomfortable with attempts to test patients, and more interested in the therapist-patient interactions triggered by the test.

Evaluating the Psychoanalytic Perspective

Having sought to understand Freud's ideas, let us now listen to his critics. Bear in mind that we do so from the perspective of the 1980s, a perspective that is itself subject to revision. Freud died half a century ago, without the benefit of all that we have since learned about human development, thinking, and emotion, and without today's tools for research. To criticize Freud in comparison with the concepts of the 1980s is rather like criticizing Henry Ford's Model T in comparison with a late model Corvette.

The criticisms occur at two levels. First, many of Freud's specific ideas are contradicted by more recent theory and research. His idea that conscience and gender identity are formed by the child's resolving the Oedipus complex at age 5 or 6 is questioned by newer work in developmental psychology. Developmental research (see Chapters 3 to 5) indicates that human development is lifelong, not fixed in childhood.

Freud's idea that dreams are disguised wish fulfillments that can be interpreted by skilled analysts has been disputed by newer conceptions of dreams (see pp. 197–198). His belief that forgetting is a function of repression is somewhat supported by reports of memory loss among victims of war trauma and sexual abuse, but the evidence indicates that other mechanisms of forgetting account for most memory loss (see pp. 260–264). Freud's idea that people project their own undesirable traits onto others and thereby protect themselves against painful self-knowledge has generally not been supported by research (Holmes, 1978, 1981).

History has been kinder to Freud's "iceberg" view of the mind, at least in part. Research findings confirm that our access to what goes on in our minds is very limited. However, the iceberg view of the mind held by today's research psychologists is not that of Freud. As we saw in earlier chapters, many researchers today think of the unconscious not in terms of seething passions and repressive censoring but of information processing that occurs without our awareness. To them, the unconscious involves such things as the schemas that automatically control our perceptions and interpretations; the processing of stimuli to which we have not consciously attended; the functioning in the right hemisphere that enables the split-brain patient's left hand to carry out an instruction the patient cannot verbalize. This understanding of unconscious information processing is more like the pre-Freudian view of the unconscious—in which spontaneous creative ideas were viewed as the surfacing of an underground stream of thought.

"Two passengers leaned against the ship's rail and stared at the sea. 'There sure is a lot of water in the ocean,' said one. 'Yes,' answered his friend, 'and we've only seen the top of it.'"
George A. Miller (1962)

The second level at which the theory is criticized concerns not its specific concepts, but its shortcomings as a theory. As we noted in Chapter 1 good scientific theories make sense of observations and can be tested in terms of their hypotheses. Freud's theory, say the critics, rests upon few objective observations and offers few testable hypotheses that would allow one to verify or falsify it. (For Freud, his own interpretations of patients' free associations, dreams, and slips were evidence enough.)

The most serious problem with Freud's theory, according to critics, is that it offers after-the-fact explanations of any characteristic (of one person's smoking, another's fear of horses, another's sexual orientation), yet it fails to predict such behavior and traits in advance. If you feel angry at your mother's death, you support the theory because it can be said that your unresolved childhood dependency needs are threatened. If you do not feel angry, you also support the theory because it can be said that you are repressing your anger. This "explains" behavior as a historian might retrospectively speculate about the causes of the Vietnam war. And that, said Calvin Hall and Gardner Lindzey (1978, p. 68), "is like betting on a horse after the race has been run." After-the-fact interpretation is perfectly appropriate for historical and literary scholarship (which helps explain Freud's currently greater influence on literary criticism than on psychological research), but in science a good theory enables prediction.

Such criticisms of Freud's specific concepts and after-the-fact interpretations have led some modern critics to scorn his theory. Peter Medawar (1982, pp. 71–72) compared it to "a dinosaur . . . one of the saddest and strangest of all landmarks in the history of twentieth-century thought." Perhaps we can evaluate Freud less harshly, for three reasons.

First, to criticize Freudian theory for failing to satisfy the criteria of predictive science is like criticizing baseball for not being an aerobic exercise. Is it fair to fault something for not being what it was never intended to be? As Freudian sociologist Phillip Rieff explains (1979, p. 130):

> Freud never made for psychoanalysis the fundamental claim of modern science: the power of prediction. Psychoanalysis, he maintained, is a retrospective science, never a predictive one. . . . Neurotic states of mind are systematically meaningful—which is what Freud meant by causation—whether we can predict them or not.

Second, some of Freud's ideas appear to be enduring. It was Freud who drew our attention to the unconscious and the irrational, to anxiety and our struggle to cope with it, to the importance of human sexuality, and to the tension between our individual impulses and our social well-being. It was Freud who challenged our self-righteousness, punctured our pretensions, and reminded us of our potential for evil. No one disputes that Freud's ideas were creative, courageous, and comprehensive.

Third, correctly or incorrectly, Freud influenced our view of human nature. Some things that we today assume to be true—that childhood experiences mold personality, that many behaviors have disguised motives, that dreams do have symbolic meaning—are partly Freud's legacy, which lives on in our own ideas. As Peter Drucker (1982) remarked, "[Many] psychologists have no use for Freud, and I have some grave doubts about him, but he is the only one who created vision and insight and changed our view of ourselves and of the world." And for that, Sigmund Freud ranks as one of the towering intellectual figures of modern history.

THE TRAIT PERSPECTIVE

Psychoanalytic theory defines personality in terms of emotional dynamics that underlie behavior. It is always looking beneath the surface to find hidden motives. *Trait theory,* on the other hand, defines personality in terms of the behaviors themselves. It takes behavior more or less at face value.

In 1919, Gordon Allport (1967, pp. 7–8), a curious, ambitious, 22-year-old psychology student, discovered how preoccupied Freud was with finding hidden motives for behavior when he interviewed him in Vienna:

> Soon after I had entered the famous red burlap room with pictures of dreams on the wall, he summoned me to his inner office. He did not speak to me but sat in expectant silence, for me to state my mission. I was not prepared for silence and had to think fast to find a suitable conversational gambit. I told him of an episode on the tram car on my way to his office. A small boy about four years of age had displayed a conspicuous dirt phobia. He kept saying to his mother, 'I don't want to sit there . . . don't let that dirty man sit beside me.' To him everything was *schmutzig* (filthy). His mother was a well-starched *Hausfrau,* so dominant and purposive looking that I thought the cause and effect apparent.
>
> When I finished my story Freud fixed his kindly therapeutic eyes upon me and said, 'And was that little boy you?' Flabbergasted and feeling a bit guilty, I contrived to change the subject. While Freud's misunderstanding of my motivation was amusing, it also started a deep train of thought.

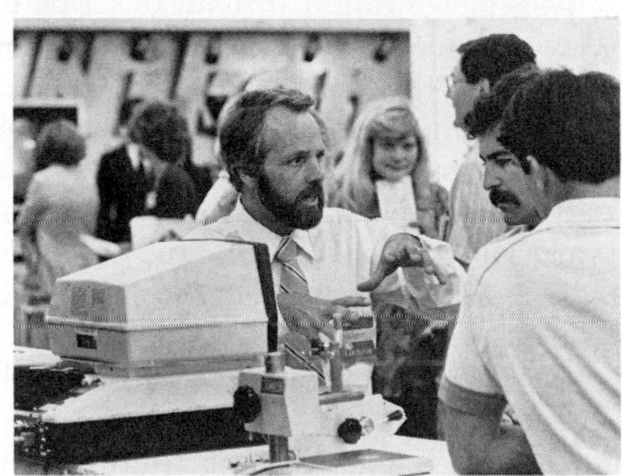

Personality traits can be fundamental to job performance. The gregariousness so vital to being a persuasive salesman would not be necessary to a scientist doing research. Some corporations, well aware of the desirability of certain traits for specific jobs, make personality evaluations an important part of their hiring processs.

That train of thought ultimately led Allport to do what Freud did not—to describe personality in terms of people's characteristic behaviors and conscious motives (such as the professional curiosity that actually motivated Allport's coming to see Freud). "This experience," said Allport, "taught me that depth psychology, for all its merits, may plunge too deep, and that psychologists would do well to give full recognition to manifest motives before probing the unconscious." Allport therefore became a trait theorist, a theorist somewhat less concerned with *explaining why* we differ from one another, and more concerned with *describing how* we differ.

In our consideration of intelligence in Chapter 12, we confronted a similar distinction between psychologists who seek to explain intelligence (in terms of genes and experience) and those who seek to describe the components or dimensions of intelligence.

It is important to remember the distinction between explanation and description. To say that someone is generally talkative *because* he or she has an outgoing personality is merely to describe behavior with a trait name, not to explain it.

Description is, however, an important starting point for any science. So how do psychologists set about describing and classifying personalities? An analogy may help. Imagine that we wished to describe and classify apples. Someone might correctly say that every apple is unique. Still, we might find it useful to begin by classifying apples by *types*—Delicious, Jonathan, McIntosh, and so forth.

That is how the ancient Greeks described personality—by classifying people according to four types. Depending on which of one's bodily "humors," or fluids, was believed to predominate, people were said to be either melancholic (depressed), sanguine (cheerful), phlegmatic (unemotional), or choleric (irritable). Although this attempt to classify may today seem humorous, there have been more recent efforts to classify people according to their body types. Santa Claus typifies what psychologist William Sheldon (1954) called the plump "endomorphic" type: relaxed and jolly. Superman typifies the muscular "mesomorphic" type: bold and physically active. Sherlock Holmes typifies the thin "ectomorphic" type: high strung and solitary.

Are different body types actually associated with different personalities? It is conceivable. However, when people's body types and personalities are separately assessed, the actual linkage is modest. The stereotypes of the chubby, happy-go-lucky person and of the muscular, confident person turn out to be just that—stereotypes that exaggerate a kernel of truth (Tucker, 1983).

"Forget it, pal. I thought I recognized you, but, as it turns out, it was just your type that I recognized."

Describing Traits

If classifying people as one type or another fails to capture their individuality, how else might we describe their personalities? To return to our analogy, we might instead describe each apple in terms of several trait dimensions—as relatively large or small, red or yellow, sweet or sour. Similarly, the trait perspective seeks to describe and classify people in terms of their fundamental ***traits***—their predispositions to behave in certain ways. By viewing people on several dimensions simultaneously, trait psychologists can describe countless individual variations. If this seems surprising, recall that the hundreds of thousands of color variations we can distinguish may each be described on just three color dimensions (hue, saturation, and brightness).

But on what trait dimensions shall we describe personality? Trait theorist Gordon Allport and his associate H. S. Odbert (1936) noted the possibilities by recording from an unabridged dictionary all the words that could be used to describe people. The list numbered almost 18,000 words! How, then, can we condense the list to a manageable number of basic traits?

One way has been to propose traits, such as anxiety, that appear to be basic according to clinical judgment or to a particular psychological theory. A newer technique is factor analysis. This is the statistical procedure we saw used in Chapter 12, to identify clusters of test items that tap basic components of intelligence (such as spatial ability, reasoning ability, and so forth). Imagine that we find that people who describe themselves as outgoing also tend to say that they like excitement and practical jokes, but that they do not like quiet reading. Such a statistically correlated cluster of behaviors might be viewed as reflecting a basic trait, or factor. In this particular case, the identified items are part of a cluster that make up a trait that has been called extraversion.

Raymond Cattell (1973) used factor analysis to reveal sixteen distinct personality traits—traits such as outgoingness, assertiveness, and stability. The degree to which a person embodies each of the sixteen basic traits is seen as forming a unique pattern, called a personality profile. Hans Eysenck (1981), a British psychologist, believes that many of our individual variations can be reduced to but two important dimensions: extraversion-introversion, and emotional stability-instability. Eysenck notes that the four combinations of these two trait dimensions resemble the ancient personality types of the Greeks (see Figure 15-3).

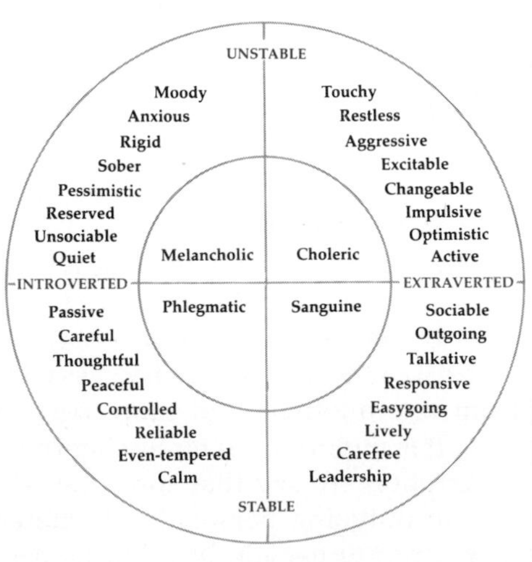

Figure 15-3 *In this chart, various combinations of Eysenck's two primary personality factors—extraversion-introversion and stability-instability—are used to define other, more specific traits. The four basic combinations of the two factors curiously resemble the personality types proposed by the ancient Greeks, which are noted in the center of the chart.*

Assessing Traits

Assessment techniques derived from trait theory aim not to reveal hidden dynamics, as do projective tests, but to provide a profile of a person's characteristic traits. When administering ***personality inventories***—questionnaires on which people report their feelings and behaviors—psychologists do not presume to measure personality as a whole; rather, they seek to measure important aspects of personality.

Some inventories have been developed with the aid of factor analysis. For example, Raymond Cattell has developed a lengthy questionnaire that assesses the extent to which people describe themselves as possessing each of the sixteen personality factors identified by his factor analyses. These analyses identified 184 items that, when answered yes or no, score points toward one end or another of each factor scale. These trait scores can then be visually depicted as a personality profile, such as in Figure 15-4.

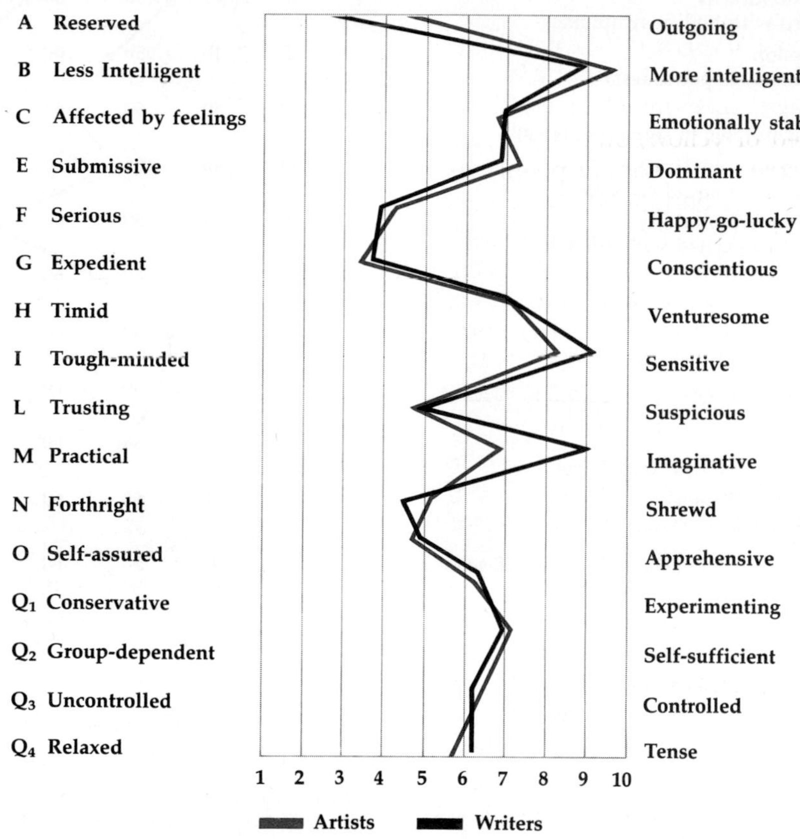

Figure 15-4 *These personality profiles developed from responses to Raymond Cattell's Sixteen Personality Factor Questionnaire show the average scores of a group of writers and a group of artists. The extremes for each factor are labeled with trait names, which are shown to the left and right of the graph. (From the* Handbook for the Sixteen PF *by Cattell, Eber, and Tatsuoka. Copyright © 1970 by the Institute for Personality and Ability Testing, Inc. Adapted and reproduced by permission.)*

A second way to develop a personality inventory is illustrated by the most extensively researched and widely used of all personality tests, the ***Minnesota Multiphasic Personality Inventory (MMPI).*** One of the creators of the test, Starke Hathaway (1960), likened his effort to that of Alfred Binet, who, as described in Chapter 12, developed the first intelligence test by selecting items that successfully discriminated between children who were and were not progressing in Paris schools. Likewise, the MMPI items were ***empirically derived***—that is, they were arrived at by selecting from a large pool of items those that were found to differentiate particular groups. Hathaway and his collaborators initially administered hundreds of true-false items ("No one seems to understand me," "I get all the sympathy I should," "I like poetry") to different groups of psychologically disordered patients and to "normal" people. Those items that a patient group answered differently were retained for the test. Depressed people, for example, were more likely than nondepressed people to agree with the statement "I feel weak all over much of the time," and to disagree with the statement "My memory seems to be all right."

The MMPI that resulted contains ten such "clinical scales" (see Figure 15-5). Also included are several "validity scales," including a "lie scale" that assesses the extent to which a person is faking a good impression (by responding "false" to statements such as "I do not like everyone I know").

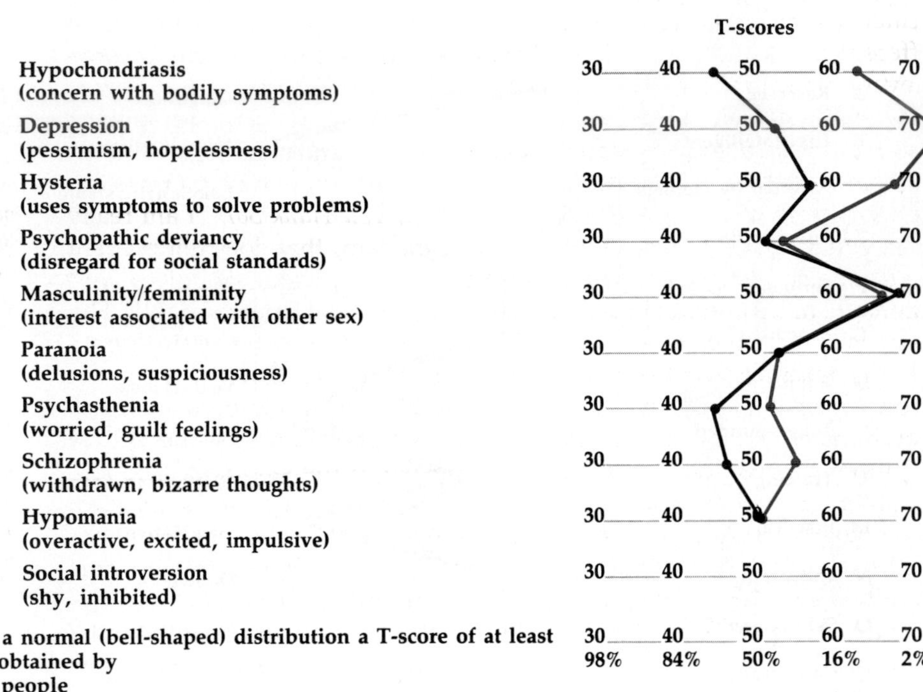

Figure 15-5 *These personality profiles developed from responses to the Minnesota Multiphasic Personality Inventory (MMPI) were obtained from the thirty-two conscientious objectors who participated in the World War II hunger study described in Chapter 13 (Schiele & Bozek, 1956). Note that after semistarvation the men expressed considerably more physical complaints and depression (scales 1, 2, and 3). (Technical note: Scores on the MMPI scales are not distributed in perfect bell-shaped curves, so these percentages are only approximate.)*

Other investigators have administered the 550 revised MMPI items to countless other clearly differentiated groups (for example, successful and unsuccessful nurses) in hopes of empirically deriving a scale for use in selecting or evaluating people. Hundreds of such MMPI scales now exist. However, most experts believe that the test is more appropriately used for its original purpose—assessing emotionally troubled people by comparing their test profile with those of thousands of other troubled persons.

In contrast to the subjectivity of projective tests, these personality inventories are objective—so objective that they can be administered, scored, and evaluated by a computer. (The computer simply reports descriptions of people who have previously responded similarly.) Objectivity does not, however, guarantee validity; it is possible, for example, for sophisticated test takers to fake a good impression if taking the MMPI for employment purposes (by answering in socially desirable ways, except on the items where nearly anyone would admit to being imperfect). Moreover, the ease of computerized testing tempts untrained administrators, including many employers, educational admissions officers, physicians, and others, to use the test for purposes for which it has not been validated (Matarazzo, 1983). Nevertheless, for better or for worse, the objectivity of the MMPI has contributed to its rising popularity (Lubin & others, 1984) and to its translation into dozens of languages.

Evaluating the Trait Perspective: How Consistent Are We?

Do we indeed possess stable and enduring traits? Or, does our behavior depend on where we are and whom we are with at the time? As we noted earlier, William Faulkner, who strove to reconstruct reality in his fiction, created characters whose personal traits were consistently expressed at different times and places. Jason Compson, for example, is self-centered at every turn. The Italian playwright Luigi Pirandello had a quite different view of the nature and consistency of personality. For him, personality was ever-changing, tailored to the particular roles and situations in which we find ourselves. As Lamberto Laudisi says, in summarizing himself to Signora Sirelli in Pirandello's play *It Is So! (If You Think So)*, "I am really what you take me to be; though, my dear madam, that does not prevent me from also being really what your husband, my sister, my niece, and Signora Cini take me to be—because they also are absolutely right!" She responds, "In other words you are a different person for each of us."

"There is as much difference between us and ourselves, as between us and others."
Michel de Montaigne,
"Of the Inconsistency of Our Actions,"
Essays, Book II, 1588

So who best represents human personality, Faulkner's consistent Jason Compson or Pirandello's inconsistent Laudisi? Everyone agrees that this is not strictly an either/or question: Our behavior is influenced by our inner dispositions, and is also responsive to the situation. The real question—one of the most important and long-standing questions in all psychology—is which is *more* important? Are we *more* like what Faulkner or like what Pirandello imagines us to be? Forced to choose, most people would likely side with Faulkner. (Until recently, most psychologists would have too.) After all, isn't it obvious that some people are dependably conscientious and others unreliable, some cheerful and others dour, some outgoing and others shy?

Roughly speaking, the temporary, external influences on behavior are the focus of social psychology, and the enduring, inner influences are the focus of personality psychology.

Remember that to be a genuine personality trait a characteristic must *both* endure over time and persist across situations. If friendliness is a trait, friendly people must act friendly in different times and places. Do they? In Chapter 4, we considered the research of those who have followed lives through time. We noted that while some researchers have been most impressed with personality change (especially those who have begun by studying infants), others have been struck by the stability of important traits from adolescence through adulthood. For example, if people's temperaments are rated in young adulthood and then rated again several decades later, their basic temperamental traits seem to persist. Faulkner would not have been surprised.

Can you predict whether neatness is characteristic of each of these workers just by looking at their desks? Most personality researchers would say no, that people's behavior often varies with the situation. However, it is possible to predict someone's average behavior over many situations.

The consistency of behavior from one situation to the next is another matter, however. As Walter Mischel (1968, 1984) points out, people seem not to act with predictable consistency from one situation to the next. One of the first studies to suggest this, noted Mischel, was one in which Hugh Hartshorne and Mark May (1928) gave thousands of children a variety of opportunities to lie, cheat, and steal, at home, at play, and in the classroom. Were some children consistently honest, others dishonest? Generally not. "Most children will deceive in certain situations and not in others," the researchers reported. "Lying, cheating, and stealing as measured by the test situations used in these studies are only very loosely related" (p. 411). More than a half century later, Mischel's studies of college students' conscientiousness revealed a similar finding. There was virtually no relationship between a student's being conscientious on one occasion (say, showing up for class on time) and being similarly conscientious on another occasion (say, turning in assignments on time). Pirandello would have guessed as much.

"I find nothing more difficult to believe than man's consistency, and nothing more easy than his inconsistency. If we examine him in detail and judge each of his actions separately, bit by bit, we shall most often find this true."
Michel de Montaigne,
"Of the Inconsistency of Our Actions,"
Essays, Book II, 1588

Mischel also points to the fact that people's scores on personality tests generally predict only 10 percent or less of the variation among their behaviors in a given situation. For example, people's scores on an extraversion test are not closely related to how sociable they actually are on any given day. If we remember such results, says Mischel, we will be more cautious about trying to label and pigeon-hole individuals. We will be more restrained when asked to predict if someone is likely to violate parole, commit suicide, or be an effective employee. Years in advance, science can tell us the phase of the moon for any given date, but it is a long way from being able to predict how you will feel and act tomorrow.

"Every man is more the man of the day than a regular and consequential character."
Lord Chesterfield, 1694–1773

In defense of the importance of traits, personality psychologist Seymour Epstein (1983a, 1983b) notes that trying to predict a specific act on the basis of either a previous behavior or a personality test is like trying to predict your answer to a single test question on the basis of either your answer to another question or your score on an intelligence test. Your answer to any given question is largely unpredictable, because it depends on so many things (your reading of the question, your understanding of the subject in question, your concentration level at the moment, luck). But your accuracy rate over many questions on several tests *is* somewhat predictable. Likewise, says Epstein, people's outgoingness, happiness, or carelessness on any given occasion varies with the situation. But their *average* outgoingness, happiness, or carelessness over *many* situations is more predictable. This fact enables people who know a person well to agree when rating the person's behavioral traits, such as how shy the person is (Kenrick & Stringfield, 1980). As our best friends can verify, we *do* have personality traits.

What is more, each of us is more consistent in some ways than others. Do you pride yourself on being especially consistent in some ways? Are you nearly always sincere, or helpful, or friendly? Daryl Bem (1983; Bem & Allen, 1974) reports that people are fairly consistent—but only in the ways they perceive themselves as consistent. In his research he found that some people saw themselves as consistently conscientious, others saw themselves as consistently friendly. When rated or observed by others, these self-assessments were generally confirmed.

Significantly, people who perceive themselves as self-directed ("My behavior is usually an expression of my true inner feelings, attitudes, and beliefs") tend to act more consistently across different situations than do people who perceive themselves as adjusting their behavior to fit specific situations ("In different situations and with different people, I often act like very different persons") (Snyder, 1983). People who describe themselves as self-directed also show more consistency between their private attitudes and public actions.

To sum up, we can say that at any moment a person's behavior is powerfully influenced by the immediate situation. Nevertheless, by averaging people's behavior across different situations and by focusing on their strongest traits, we see evidence of distinctive and consistent personalities.

THE HUMANISTIC PERSPECTIVE

By 1960, several prominent personality psychologists became discontented both with the determinism and negativity of Freud's views and with the seeming irrelevance of what was derisively termed behavioristic "rat psychology." In place of Freud's emphasis on the unconscious sexual and aggressive impulses of "sick" people, these "humanistic psychologists" proposed a perspective that emphasized the strivings of "healthy" people for self-determination and self-realization. In place of behaviorism's mechanistic analysis, which seemed to belittle the role of subjective experience and reduce human behavior to animal-level conditioning, they proposed to study what they regarded as the whole of personality, including personal experiences of sorrow and joy, alienation and intimacy, frustration and fulfillment. These emphases on positive human potential and on seeing the world through the person's (not the experimenter's) eyes are illustrated in the views of two influential theorists, Abraham Maslow (1908–1970) and Carl Rogers (1902–).

Abraham Maslow's Self-Actualizing Person

As you may recall from Chapter 13, Maslow proposed that humans are motivated by a hierarchy of needs. If our physiological needs are met we become concerned with personal safety; if we achieve a sense of security, we then are motivated to love and be loved and to experience self-esteem; and if all these needs continue to be met, we ultimately experience a quest for ***self-actualization***, the process of fulfilling one's potential, of becoming the self one is capable of becoming.

Abraham Maslow (1970, p. 33): "Any theory of motivation that is worthy of attention must deal with the highest capacities of the healthy and strong person as well as with the defensive maneuvers of crippled spirits."

Unlike many theorists before him, Maslow (1970) developed his ideas from the study of healthy, creative people rather than clinical cases. His description of self-actualization was based on a study of acquaintances and historical figures—Abraham Lincoln, Thomas Jefferson, and Eleanor Roosevelt among them—who seemed notable for the richness and productiveness of their lives. These people seemed to share a number of characteristics. Maslow reported they were self-aware and self-accepting, open and spontaneous, loving and caring, yet not paralyzed by others' opinions. Being secure in their sense of who they were as individuals, they tended to be problem-centered rather than self-centered. Often their energies were focused on a particular task that they regarded as their mission in life. Many had been moved by peak mystical or spiritual experiences. Most enjoyed a few deep relationships rather than many superficial ones.

These are adult qualities, said Maslow, ones not likely to be found in those too young to have learned enough about life to be compassionate, to have outgrown their mixed feelings toward their parents, to have found their calling, to have "acquired enough courage to be unpopular, to be unashamed about being openly virtuous, etc." His work with college students led him to speculate that those likely to become self-actualizing adults tended to be likable, caring, "privately affectionate to those of their elders who deserve it," and "secretly uneasy about the cruelty, meanness, and mob spirit so often found in young people."

Carl Rogers' Person-Centered Perspective

Fellow humanistic psychologist Carl Rogers agrees with much of Maslow's thinking. Rogers believes that people are basically good and are endowed with inherent self-actualizing tendencies: Each of us is like the seed of an oak tree, containing within the potential for tremendous growth and fulfillment, unless thwarted by a climate that inhibits growth.

Rogers (1980) believes that a "growth-promoting" climate requires three conditions—genuineness, acceptance, and empathy. (Although Rogers' recognition of these conditions for nurturing growth arose from his counseling experience, he believes they are also applicable to relations between parent and child, leader and group, teacher and student, administrator and staff, or any two human beings.)

"You sprang that question on me quite unexpectedly, Karen. Could you give me a few minutes to get in touch with my feelings?"

According to Rogers, people nurture our growth, first, by being *genuine*—by being open to their own feelings, by dropping their facades, by being transparent or self-disclosing. They nurture our growth, second, by being *accepting*—by offering us what Rogers called ***unconditional positive regard.*** This is an attitude of grace, an attitude that allows them to value us, even though they know our failings. Perhaps you have experienced the relief of being able to drop your pretenses, to confess your worst feelings, and discover that you are still accepted. This is the gratifying experience we sometimes enjoy in a good marriage or an intimate friendship in which we no longer feel the need to justify and explain ourselves and are free to be spontaneous without fear of losing the other's esteem.

People nurture our growth, third, by being *empathic*—by sensing and nonjudgmentally reflecting our feelings and meanings. "Rarely do we listen with real understanding, true empathy," says Rogers. "Yet listening, of this very special kind, is one of the most potent forces for change that I know." These three conditions—genuineness, acceptance, and empathy—are the water, the sun, and the nutrients that enable people to grow like strong, vigorous oak trees. For "as persons are accepted and prized, they tend to develop a more caring attitude toward themselves." As persons are empathically heard, "it becomes possible for them to listen more accurately to the flow of inner experiencings" (1980, p. 116).

Being open and sharing confidences is easy when you have an empathic listener. The listener in turn benefits from the good feelings of helping and the pleasures of trust.

For Maslow, and even more so for Rogers, a central feature of personality is one's self-concept. ***Self-concept*** is all the thoughts and feelings we have in response to the question, "Who am I?" If our self-concept is positive, we tend to act and perceive the world accordingly. If negative—if in our own eyes we fall far short of our "ideal self"—then we feel dissatisfied and unhappy. Thus a goal for parents, teachers, and other helpers is to help people know, accept, and be true to themselves.

Assessing the Self

Humanistic psychologists sometimes assess personality with questionnaires that measure people's self-concepts. For example, humanistic psychologist Everett Shostrom (1966) created an inventory that assesses self-actualization (see Table 15-1). Another questionnaire, inspired by Carl Rogers, asks people to describe themselves both as they ideally would like to be and as they actually are. When the ideal and the actual self are nearly alike, the self-concept is considered positive. Thus Rogers used the similarity of rated actual and ideal self as a way to assess personal growth during therapy.

Other humanistic psychologists believe that any type of formal, objective assessment of personality tends to be depersonalizing. Even a questionnaire detaches the psychologist from the living human being being studied. Rather than forcing the person to respond to the psychologist's categories, these humanistic psychologists believe it is better to get close to the person's own thoughts, perceptions, and feelings—and thus to understand better the person's unique experiences.

Table 15-1 **The Personal Orientation Inventory**

From the text description of self-actualization, can you anticipate for each of these sample items whether answer a or b is considered the more self-actualized response?

1. a. I often feel it is necessary to defend my past actions.
   b. I do not feel it is necessary to defend my past actions.
2. a. It is better to be yourself.
   b. It is better to be popular.
3. a. I have had moments of intense happiness when I felt as if I was experiencing a kind of ecstasy or bliss.
   b. I have not had moments of intense happiness when I felt as if I was experiencing a kind of bliss.
4. a. I often make my decisions spontaneously.
   b. I seldom make my decisions spontaneously.
5. a. I blame my parents for a lot of my troubles.
   b. I do not blame my parents for my troubles.

The self-actualized answers are: b, a, a, a, b.

Source: From E. L. Shostrom, *EdITS Manual for the Personal Orientation Inventory*. Copyright © 1966 by Educational and Industrial Testing Service, P.O. Box 7234, San Diego, CA 92107. Reprinted with permission.

Evaluating the Humanistic Perspective

One thing said of Freud can also be said of the humanistic psychologists: Their impact has been, to use Rogers' word, "pervasive." Their ideas have reached into counseling, education, child-rearing, and management. They have also influenced—sometimes in ways they did not intend—much of the popular psychology proclaimed in recent best-selling books. Many of us have absorbed some of what Maslow and Rogers have so effectively taught; it is partially due to their influence that so many people assume that a positive self-concept is a key to happiness and success, that acceptance and empathy help nurture positive self feelings, and that people are basically good and capable of self-improvement.

Criticisms of Humanistic Psychology

The prominence of these ideas has also helped to trigger an avalanche of criticism. First, say the critics, the concepts are vague and subjective. For example, consider the description of self-actualizing people as open, spontaneous, loving, self-accepting, and productive. Is this really a scientific description of human fulfillment? Or is it merely a description of Maslow's personal values and ideals? What Maslow did, noted M. Brewster Smith (1978), was to pick his own personal heroes and offer his impressions of them. Had some other theorist (with different values) begun with a different set of heroes—perhaps people like Napoleon, Alexander the Great, and John D. Rockefeller, Sr.—the resulting picture of the self-actualizing person would have probably included descriptives such as "undeterred by the needs of others," "motivated to achieve," and "obsessed with power."

Second, some critics object to the idea that, as Carl Rogers has said, "The only question which matters is, 'Am I living in a way which is deeply satisfying to me, and which truly expresses me?'" (quoted by Wallach & Wallach, 1985). They fear that the priorities encouraged by humanistic psychology—self-fulfillment, trusting and acting on one's feelings, being true to oneself—have encouraged self-indulgence, selfishness, and an erosion of moral restraints (Campbell & Specht, 1985; Wallach & Wallach, 1983). Humanistic psychologists reject such objections. They insist that belligerence, hostility, and insensitivity are often traceable to a poor self-concept and that self-love is actually the first step toward loving others. The critics respond that self-fulfillment comes as we focus not on ourselves but beyond ourselves. Compared to people who are self-preoccupied, those who exhibit a high level of concern for others tend to receive more social support, enjoy life more, and be less upset by stressful experiences (Crandall, 1984).

"Man is not a solitary animal, and so long as social life survives, self-realization cannot be the supreme principle of ethics."
Bertrand Russell, 1872–1970

Third, the humanistic psychologists have been accused of failing to appreciate the reality and perils of the human capacity for evil. When faced with the assaults on the environment, overpopulation, and threats of nuclear war, there are at least two rationalizations for apathy. One is a naive optimism that denies the threat ("People are basically good; everything will work out"). The other is a dark despair ("It's hopeless; why try?"). Action requires enough pessimism to trigger concern and enough optimism to provide hope. Humanistic psychology, say the critics, encourages the needed hope, but not the pessimism.

Mini-Debate

Does Human Nature Contain Evil? Two Humanistic Psychologists Debate

Carl Rogers: NO

Though I am very well aware of the incredible amount of destructive, cruel, malevolent behavior in today's world—from the threats of war to the senseless violence in the streets—I do not find that this evil is inherent in human nature. In a psychological climate which is nurturant of growth and choice, I have never known an individual to choose the cruel or destructive path. Choice always seems to be in the direction of greater socialization, improved relationships with others. So my experience leads me to believe that it is cultural influences which are the major factor in our evil behaviors. The rough manner of childbirth, the infant's mixed experience with the parents, the constricting, destructive influence of our educational system, the injustice of our distribution of wealth, our cultivated prejudices against individuals who are different—all these elements and many others warp the human organism in directions which are antisocial. So I see members of the human species, like members of other species, as essentially constructive in their fundamental nature, but damaged by their experience. (From Rogers [1981]. Reprinted with permission.)

Rollo May: YES

The culture admittedly has powerful effects upon us. But it could not have these effects were these tendencies not already present in us. Who makes up the culture except persons like you and me? The culture is evil as well as good because we, the human beings who constitute it, are evil as well as good. We are bundles of both evil and good potentialities.

Some people who join and lead the humanistic movement do so in order to find a haven, a port in the storm, a community of like-minded persons who also are playing possum to the evils about us. Life, to me, is not a requirement to live out a preordained pattern of goodness, but a challenge coming down through the centuries out of the fact that each of us can throw the lever toward good or toward evil. This seems to me to require the age-old religious truths of mercy and forgiveness and it leaves no place for self-righteousness. (Excerpted from May [1982]. Reprinted with permission.)

Research on the Self

Psychology's concern with people's sense of self dates back at least to William James, who devoted more than 100 pages of his 1890 *Principles of Psychology* to the topic. Nevertheless, in 1943 Gordon Allport lamented that the self had become "lost to view." Although humanistic psychology's emphasis on the self did not trigger much experimental research, it did help renew the concept and keep it alive. Now, in the 1980s, the self has become one of psychology's most vigorously researched topics. Studies are being conducted on many different aspects of the self—"self-esteem," "self-disclosure," "self-awareness," "self-schemas," "self-monitoring," and so forth. During 1984 the word "self" appeared in 4233, or 14 percent, of all the article and book summaries appearing in *Psychological Abstracts*, the "reader's guide" to psychological research—double the number and almost double the percentage appearing in 1974.

The assumption underlying all these research topics is also an assumption of humanistic psychologists—that the self, as organizer of our thoughts, feelings, and actions, is a pivotal aspect of personality (Greenwald & Pratkanis, 1984). How we think and feel about ourselves is crucially important. To illustrate, consider research studies that testify to the benefits of positive self-esteem, and other studies that point to the pervasiveness of self-serving pride.

"What you think of yourself is much more important than what others think of you."
Seneca,
Ad Lucilium, A.D. 64

The Benefits of Self-Esteem High *self-esteem*—a feeling of self-worth—seems to pay dividends. People who feel good about themselves tend to be less depressed, freer of ulcers and insomnia, less prone to drug addictions, more independent of conformity pressures, and more persistent at difficult tasks (Brockner & Hulton, 1978; Greenwald & Pratkanis, 1984).

Low self-esteem seems to exact costs. Psychotherapy researcher Hans Strupp (1982, pp. 64–65) reflected that

> As soon as one listens to a patient's story, one encounters unhappiness, frustration, and despair which find expression in diverse forms of psychopathology including psychosomatic symptoms, neurotic symptoms, and maladaptive character styles. . . . Basic to all these difficulties are impairments in self-acceptance and self-esteem.

These correlational links between low self-esteem and life problems have other possible interpretations (for instance, maybe life problems cause low self-esteem). However, the effect of low self-esteem is more clearly demonstrated in experiments. People whose self-image is temporarily deflated (say, by being told they did poorly on an aptitude test or by receiving a negative evaluation of their personality) are, at such a time, more likely to disparage other people, or even to express heightened racial prejudice. More generally, people who are negative about themselves also tend to be negative about others (Crocker & Schwartz, 1985; Willis, 1981). Low self-esteem can feed contemptuous attitudes.

In some related experiments, Teresa Amabile (1983a; Amabile & Glazebrook, 1982) captured a happening she had noticed in everyday life. Insecure people, it seemed to her, were often excessively critical, as if to impress others with their own brilliance. When Amabile asked college students to assess the intellect of someone who was interviewed on videotape, who do you suppose were the more scathing in their judgments—the students who were made to feel *insecure* (compared to the experimenter who they thought was a doctoral student), or those who were made to feel *secure* (by having the experimenter declare herself to be merely a fellow undergraduate)? Amabile reported that the first group—those who thought their opinions would be judged by a person of higher status—were the more critical.

Although few of these researchers would call themselves humanistic psychologists, their findings—for example, that people who feel positive and secure about themselves tend to be more compassionate—are consistent with Maslow's and Rogers' presumption that a "healthy" self-image is beneficial. This apparent truth, however, is complemented by another one: that the most common error in people's self-image is not unrealistically low self-esteem, but rather a self-serving bias that, though often adaptive for the individual, can lead to problems.

The Pervasiveness of Self-Serving Bias Carl Rogers (1958) once objected to the religious doctrine that humanity's problems originate in excessive self-love, or pride, by noting that most people he had known "despise themselves, regard themselves as worthless and unlovable." Actually, researchers find that although some people express low self-esteem, most of us have a good reputation with ourselves. Furthermore, suggests social psychologist John Darley (1983), we have several strategies for protecting our self-esteem even when we fail on a task. We can deny that our poor performance reflects our ability ("I had an off day," "I hadn't had time to study"). We can say the ability is irrelevant ("Who cares about sports, anyway?"). We can even reverse the scale, so that to be good at that would be bad ("Everyone knows the best doctors have the worst handwriting"). Only when we are trapped in an environment that insists on telling us we are no good does self-esteem become chronically low, suggests Darley.

"To love oneself is the beginning of a life-long romance."
Oscar Wilde,
An Ideal Husband, 1895

Social psychologists have also discovered a powerful phenomenon called ***self-serving bias***—a tendency to judge ourselves favorably (Myers, 1983). Consider:

1. People typically accept more responsibility for success than for failure, for good deeds than for bad. Time and again, experimenters have found that people readily accept credit when told they have succeeded (attributing the success to their own ability and effort), yet attribute failure to such uncontrollable factors as bad luck or the "impossibility" of the task. Athletes, too, often privately credit their victories to themselves, but are more likely to attribute losses to bad breaks, bad officiating, or the other team's exceptional effort. And who do you suppose are quickest to spot flaws in an exam—the highest scoring students who presumably know best? No, a half dozen recent studies have found that after receiving an exam grade, students tend to judge the exam as a good test of their competence if they did well and as a poor test if they did not. "What have I done to deserve this?" is a question we ask of our troubles, not our successes—those we assume we deserve.

Drawing by Sidney Harris

"Actually this way of life is just my way of covering up a severe superiority complex."

2. Most people see themselves as relatively superior on nearly any dimension that is both subjective and socially desirable. For example, most American business people see themselves as more ethical than the average American business person. Most community residents see themselves as less prejudiced than others in their communities. Most drivers—even those drivers who have been hospitalized as a result of accidents—believe themselves to be more skillful than the average driver. Most high school seniors rate themselves in the top 10 percent of seniors in their "ability to get along with others."

"People experience life through a self-centered filter."
Anthony Greenwald (1984)

These two observations are joined by others:

We tend to justify our past actions.

We have an inflated confidence in the accuracy of our beliefs and judgments.

We overestimate how desirably we would act in situations in which most people are known to behave less than admirably.

"Without self-confidence we are babes in the cradle. And how can we generate this imponderable quality, which is yet so invaluable, most quickly? By thinking that other people are inferior to oneself."
Virginia Woolf,
A Room of One's Own, 1929

We are quicker to believe flattering descriptions of ourselves than unflattering ones.

We "remember" our own past in self-enhancing ways.

We exhibit a Pollyanna-ish optimism about our personal futures.

We guess that physically attractive people have personalities more like our own than do unattractive people.

"Self-love is the greatest of all the flatterers."
La Rochefoucauld,
Maxims, 1665

The reasons for this self-serving bias can be debated, and may vary, but the phenomenon certainly exists.

Many of us resist these findings: Like Carl Rogers, we know people who seem to despise themselves, who feel depressed and inadequate. Indeed, all of us some of the time, and some of us most of the time, *do* feel inferior—especially when comparing ourselves to those who are a step or two higher on the ladder of status, grades, looks, income, agility, or whatever. And some people—especially depressed and oppressed people—*do* suffer the costs of chronic low self-esteem.

So it is important to recognize what humanistic psychologists have emphasized—that for the individual, self-affirming thinking is generally adaptive; such thinking maintains self-confidence and minimizes depression. But it is also important to recognize the reality of self-serving bias and the harm that self-righteousness can wreak upon relationships. The question is, therefore, how we can encourage self-acceptance, while not encouraging the pretensions of self-serving pride.

"It seems that Nature, which has so wisely constructed our bodies for our welfare, gave us pride to spare us the painful knowledge of our shortcomings."
La Rochefoucauld,
Maxims, 1665

"A Man may have a just Esteem of himself, without being proud."
Thomas Fuller,
Gnomologia, 1732

THE SOCIAL-COGNITIVE PERSPECTIVE

Our fourth major perspective on personality is derived from the principles of social learning and cognition. In Chapter 9, "Learning," we considered behaviorism, its basic tenet being that external events, in the form of rewards and punishments, influence behavior through conditioning. Pigeons can learn to play ping pong and children to behave less aggressively when their behavior is shaped by reinforcements. Contemporary ***social-cognitive*** theorists agree that external events are important, and therefore emphasize how situations affect behavior. Some of our emotions are indeed acquired by conditioning and by observing models as well. At the same time, however, social-cognitive theorists propose that internal events—what we think and feel—are also important. Instead of emphasizing how the environment controls us (behaviorism), they focus on how we and our environment interact: How do we interpret and respond to external events? How do our schemas, our memories, and our expectations influence our responses?

Reciprocal Influences

Albert Bandura (1978, 1983) believes this interaction involves ***reciprocal determinism***—in which "behavior, internal personal factors, and environmental influences all operate as interlocking determinants of each other" (see Figure 15-6). For example, children's behavior is influenced by television (an environmental factor), which is influenced by their personal preferences (an internal factor), which are influenced by their past viewing behaviors. The influences are all mutual. Thus the social-cognitive perspective (as Bandura [1986] has labeled it) directs our attention to *environmental* factors, to *personal-cognitive* factors, and to their *interaction*.

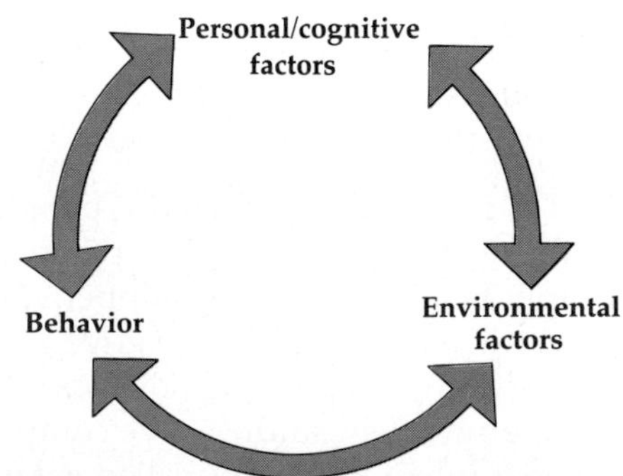

Figure 15-6 *The social-cognitive perspective proposes that our personalities are shaped by reciprocal determinism—the interaction of our situations, our thoughts and feelings, and our behaviors.*

Consider some of the ways in which environmental and personal factors interact. First, our individual personality shapes how we interpret, and thus how we react to, specific events. Whether we perceive a difficult situation as an unbearable crisis or an exhilarating challenge depends partly on personal traits, and this perception, in turn, influences how we respond—whether we duck out or dig in. Second, different people choose to be a part of different environments. The college you attend, the areas of interest you pursue, the neighborhood in which you live, are all environmental influences that you, to some extent, have chosen, partly on the basis of your personal traits. Third, our own personalities help create the environments to which we react. Our expectations and actions—how we treat our families when we next see them, for example—may trigger reactions that then influence our own behavior.

If all this has a familiar ring, it may be because it parallels, and reinforces, what may be psychology's greatest lesson: Behavior is best understood in terms of the interplay of internal and external influences. *At every moment,* our behavior is determined by our genes *and* our experiences, our personalities *and* our environments.

This interactive perspective has inspired researchers to study how the environment shapes personal factors such as self-control and self-concept, and how these in turn influence behavior. Unlike some humanistic psychologists, social-cognitive theorists do not assume that one's "self" is innate, waiting to be "discovered" or "actualized." Rather, they assume that self-related cognitions are shaped by the environment.

Unbearable crisis or exhilarating challenge? Our individual personalities are expressed in the distinctive ways we react to situations.

Personal Control

One important way people differ in their self-concepts, say some theorists, is in whether they see themselves as in control of, or controlled by, their environments. Numerous studies of people's sense of ***personal control*** have demonstrated that behavior is affected by whether people perceive the control of their lives as internal, in themselves, or external, in the forces of the outside world. Unlike the feelings of control that come from adjusting one's behavior to fit the environment—a type of control more valued in Japan, say, than in North America (Weiss & others, 1984)—personal control refers to the individual's perceived power to change the environment. As with most personality factors, there are two ways to study personal control: (1) by *measuring individual differences* in the extent to which people feel in control and then *correlating* these measurements with their behaviors and achievements; and (2) by *experimenting*—by raising or lowering people's perceptions of control and observing the effects of doing so.

Locus of Control

Do you feel that the direction of your life is beyond your control? That the world is run by a few powerful people? That getting a good job depends mainly on being in the right place at the right time? Or do you more strongly believe that what happens to you is your own doing? That the average person can influence government decisions? That being a success is a matter of hard work, not luck?

Hundreds of studies have compared people who perceive what psychologist Julian Rotter has called ***external locus of control***—that their fate is determined by chance or by outside forces—with those who perceive ***internal locus of control***—that to a great extent they control their own destinies. In study after study, "internals" have been observed to achieve more in school (Findley & Cooper, 1983), and to be more independent, better able to delay gratification, and better able to cope with various stresses and problems (Lefcourt, 1982).

Learned Helplessness Versus Control

If indeed the person-environment relationship is reciprocal, then people's perceptions of control may both affect and be affected by their environments. Helpless, oppressed people may perceive that control is external, and this perception may deepen their feelings of resignation. Those who experience their actions as making a difference may perceive that control is internal, and this perception may strengthen their persistence and assertiveness.

"If my mind can conceive it and my heart can believe it, I know I can achieve it."
Jesse Jackson,
Civil rights march on Washington, 1983

This is precisely what researcher Martin Seligman (1975) and others found in experiments with both animals and people. When dogs are strapped in a harness and given repeated shocks, with no opportunity to avoid them, they learn a sense of helplessness. When later they are placed in another situation where they *could* escape the punishment by merely leaping a hurdle, they do not attempt to do so. This passive resignation is called ***learned helplessness.*** In contrast, animals that are able to escape the shocks in the first situation learn personal control and are easily able to escape the shocks in the new situation.

In research on personal control in humans, Ellen Langer (1983) and her associates found that when the aged, the infirm, and those facing stress are led to think they can influence and control the happenings around them (often by actually giving them more control), they become more alert, effective, and happy. For example, when nursing-home patients—normally the passive recipients of staff care—were given responsibilities for their own care and made aware of opportunities to change their environments, they showed improved health during the ensuing 3 weeks. Those who continued to receive the usual kind-hearted care, over which they had no control, continued to decline. "Perceived control is basic to human functioning," Langer concluded. Thus, "we must create environments, for the young and old alike, that foster feelings of mastery" (p. 291).

Nursing home patients who take an active part in their care and pursue their interests are more alert and happy than those who do not.

Assessing Behavior in Situations

True to their concern with how persons and situations interact, social cognition researchers have studied personality by observing and rating people's behavior or by measuring their attitudes and intended behaviors in different situations.

An ambitious example that predates the theory is the U.S. Army's World War II strategy for assessing candidates for spy missions. Rather than assess the candidates' stress-tolerance and problem-solving ability with personality tests, the Army psychologists subjected the candidates to simulated undercover conditions that tested their ability to handle stress, solve problems, maintain leadership, and withstand intense interrogation without blowing their covers. Although time consuming and expensive, the assessment of behavior in a realistic situation helped predict later success on real spy missions (OSS Assessment Staff, 1948). This confirms that one of the best ways to predict a person's future behavior is to observe the person's past behavior in similar situations (Mischel, 1981).

Pseudo-Assessment: How to Be a "Successful" Astrologer or Palm Reader

Some personality assessment techniques have minimal validity, yet are widely believed in by their devotees. Ray Hyman (1981), palm reader turned research psychologist, helps us to see why as he reveals the methods by which astrologers, palm readers, and crystal-ball gazers can persuade so many people that they can accurately assess their personalities and problems.

The first technique, the "stock spiel," builds on the truth of the observation that each of us is in some ways like no other person and in other ways like all other persons. The fact that some things are true of nearly all of us enables the "seer" to offer statements that seem impressively accurate: "I sense that you're nursing a grudge against someone; you really ought to let that go." "You worry about things more than you let on, even to your best friends." "You are adaptable to social situations and your interests are wide-ranging."

Such generally true statements can be combined into a personality description. Imagine yourself taking a personality test and then receiving back the following character sketch:

> **You have a strong need for other people to like you and for them to admire you. You have a tendency to be critical of yourself. . . . You pride yourself on being an independent thinker and do not accept other opinions without satisfactory proof. You have found it unwise to be too frank in revealing yourself to others. At times you are extraverted, affable, sociable, while at other times you are introverted, wary, and reserved. Some of your aspirations tend to be pretty unrealistic.**

In a number of experiments college students have received assessments like the one above. What they did not know was that they had all received the same profile. Nevertheless, when they thought the bogus feedback was prepared just for them and when, like the above statements, it was generally favorable, they nearly always rated the description as either "good" or "excellent." This acceptance is called the *Barnum effect,* named in honor of master showman P. T. Barnum's dictum that "There's a sucker born every minute." So powerful is the Barnum effect that when given a choice between this stock spiel and a personality description actually based on an established test, most people choose the phony description as the more accurate. Astrologers and palm readers sprinkle their assessments with stock spiel statements. (Indeed, the description just quoted was drawn from a newsstand astrology book.)

The second technique is to "read" the person's clothing, physical features, nonverbal gestures, and reactions to what you are saying. Imagine yourself as the character reader who was visited by a young woman in her late twenties or early thirties. Hyman describes the woman as "wearing expensive jewelry, a

"Ah-ha! You are not happy."

French psychologist Michel Gauguelin placed an ad in a Paris newspaper offering a free personal horoscope. Ninety-four percent of those receiving the horoscope later praised the description as accurate. Actually, all had received the horoscope of France's Dr. Petiot, a notorious mass murderer (Kurtz, 1983).

wedding band, and a black dress of cheap material. The observant reader noted that she was wearing shoes which were currently being advertised for people with foot trouble." Do these clues suggest anything?

By means of just these observations the character reader proceeded to amaze his client with his insights. He assumed that this client had come to see him, as did most of his female customers, because of a love or financial problem. The black dress and the wedding band led him to reason that her husband had died recently. The expensive jewelry suggested that she had been financially comfortable during marriage, but the cheap dress indicated that her husband's death had left her penniless. The therapeutic shoes signified that she was now standing on her feet more than she was used to, implying that she was working to support herself since her husband's death (Hyman, 1981, pp. 85–86).

If you are not so shrewd as this character reader (who correctly guessed that the woman was wondering if she should marry in order to end her economic hardship), no matter, says Hyman. Just tell people what they want to hear. Memorize some Barnum statements (which you can get from astrology and fortune-telling manuals) and use them liberally. Tell them it is their responsibility to cooperate by relating your message to their specific experiences, and later they will recall that you predicted the specifics. Phrase statements as questions, and when you detect a positive response assert the statement strongly. Be a good listener, and later, in different words, reveal to people what they earlier revealed to you.

Better yet, beware of those who exploit people by using such techniques.

Evaluating the Social-Cognitive Perspective

The social-cognitive perspective has sensitized those who study personality to how situations affect, and are affected by, individuals. More than the other perspectives, it can also be credited with building upon the broad base of psychological research on learning and cognition.

One criticism is that the theory works too well, after the fact. In hindsight, anything can be "explained" as a product of cognition and the social environment. Another criticism is that the theory has focused so much on the situation that the inner traits of the person are not fully appreciated. Granted, the situation guides our behavior. But so, too, do unconscious motives and pervasive traits, say the critics. And so, also, do genetic influences. Twin and adoption studies indicate that some personality traits, such as extraversion, are hereditarily predisposed (Hewitt, 1984).

And that brings us back to the thought with which we began our review of the major personality theories—that each offers a perspective that can teach us something. The psychoanalytic perspective has drawn our attention to the unconscious and irrational aspects of human existence. The trait perspective has systematically described and measured important components of personality. The humanistic perspective has reminded us of the pivotal importance of our sense of self and of our healthy potential. The social-cognitive perspective has applied some of psychology's basic concepts to the study of personality and has taught us that we always act in the context of situations, situations that we often help to create.

Seldom in life does one perspective give us the complete picture. Certainly our subject matter—the workings of human personality—is mysterious and complex enough to reveal different aspects when viewed from different perspectives. Thus we can do as most psychologists do today and allow each perspective to enlarge our vision.

SUMMING UP

Personality is one's relatively distinctive and consistent pattern of thinking, feeling, and acting. This chapter examines four major perspectives on personality.

THE PSYCHOANALYTIC PERSPECTIVE

Sigmund Freud's treatment of emotional disorders led him to see unconscious psychological dynamics at work, which he sought to analyze through patients' free associations and dreams.

Personality Structure Freud saw personality as composed of a reservoir of pleasure-seeking psychic impulses (the id), a reality-oriented executive (the ego), and an internalized set of ideals (the superego).

Personality Development Freud believed that children develop through several formative psychosexual stages—the oral, anal, phallic, latency, and genital stages. He suggested that people's later personalities were influenced by how they resolved conflicts associated with these stages, and whether they remained fixated at any stage.

Personality Dynamics To cope with anxiety stemming from the tensions between the demands of id and superego, the ego has protective defense mechanisms, of which repression is the most basic.

Freud's Descendants and Dissenters Neo-Freudians Alfred Adler, Karen Horney, Erich Fromm, and Erik Erikson accepted many of Freud's ideas, as did Carl Jung, but have argued that sex and aggression are not the only important motives.

Assessing the Unconscious Psychoanalytic assessment techniques attempt to reveal aspects of personality that are thought to be hidden in the unconscious. However, projective tests such as the Rorschach ink blots have generally not exhibited much reliability or validity.

Evaluating the Psychoanalytic Perspective Many of Freud's specific ideas have been criticized as implausible or have not been validated. His theory has also been faulted for offering after-the-fact explanations. Nevertheless, Freud drew psychology's attention to the unconscious, to the struggle to cope with anxiety and sexuality, and to the conflict between individual impulses and social restraints. Moreover, his cultural impact has been enormous.

THE TRAIT PERSPECTIVE

Describing Traits Rather than explain the hidden aspects of personality, trait theorists have described the predispositions that underlie our actions. For example, through factor analysis, these theorists have isolated distinct dimensions of personality.

Assessing Traits To assess traits, psychologists have devised personality inventories such as the empirically derived MMPI.

Evaluating the Trait Perspective: How Consistent Are We? Critics of trait theory question the consistency with which traits are expressed. Although people's traits do seem to persist through time, human behavior varies widely from situation to situation. Despite these variations, people's average behavior (across different situations) is fairly consistent, especially on those traits they deem their strongest.

THE HUMANISTIC PERSPECTIVE

Humanistic psychologists have sought to turn psychology's attention to the growth potential of healthy people, as seen through the individual's own experiences.

Abraham Maslow's Self-Actualizing Person Maslow believed that if more basic human needs are fulfilled, people will strive to actualize what they have the potential to become. To describe self-actualization, he studied some exemplary personalities and summarized his impressions of their qualities.

Carl Rogers' Person-Centered Perspective To nurture growth in others, Rogers advises being genuine, accepting, and empathic. Such a climate is said to enable people to get in touch with themselves and to develop a more realistic and positive self-concept.

Assessing the Self Humanistic psychologists assess personality through questionaire measures of self-concept and through seeking to understand others' unique personal experiences.

Evaluating the Humanistic Perspective Humanistic psychology's critics complain that its concepts are vague and subjective, its values self-centered, and its assumptions naively optimistic. Nevertheless, humanistic psychology has helped to renew psychology's interest in the concept of self, which is now being vigorously researched through studies of phenomena such as self-esteem and self-serving bias.

THE SOCIAL-COGNITIVE PERSPECTIVE

The social-cognitive perspective applies principles of social learning and cognition to personality.

Reciprocal Influences This perspective also emphasizes the reciprocal influence of persons and situations, and of people's expectations regarding their situations.

Personal Control By studying variations among people in their perceived locus of control and in their experiences of learned helplessness or control, researchers have found that perceived control helps people to cope with trying situations.

Assessing Behavior in Situations Social-cognitive researchers study how people's behavior and beliefs both affect and are affected by their situations. They believe that the best way to predict someone's behavior is to observe that person's behavior in similar situations.

Evaluating the Social-Cognitive Perspective This theory has been faulted for underemphasizing the importance of unconscious dynamics and inner traits. Nevertheless, like each of the other major theories, the social-cognitive perspective is valuable; it builds on psychology's well-established concepts of learning and cognition and has reminded us of the power of social situations.

TERMS AND CONCEPTS TO REMEMBER

Anal Stage The second of Freud's psychosexual stages, during which pleasure is focused on bowel and bladder elimination and retention.

Barnum Effect The tendency to accept as valid descriptions of one's personality that are generally true of everyone (such as those found in astrology books).

Collective Unconscious Carl Jung's concept of memory traces from our species' history.

Defense Mechanisms In psychoanalytic theory, the ego's methods of reducing anxiety by unconsciously distorting reality.

Displacement The shifting of one's impulses toward a more acceptable or less threatening object or person, as when redirecting anger toward a safer outlet.

Ego The largely conscious executive part of personality that, according to Freud, mediates between the demands of the id and superego and the reality of the external world.

Empirically Derived Test An inventory (such as the MMPI) that is developed by testing a pool of items and then selecting those that differentiate groups of interest.

External Locus of Control The belief that one's fate is determined by chance or outside forces that are beyond one's control.

Fixation According to Freud, a lingering focus of pleasure-seeking energies at an earlier psychosexual stage.

Free Association A psychoanalytic method of exploring the unconscious in which the person relaxes and says whatever comes to mind, no matter how trivial or embarrassing.

Genital Stage The final of Freud's psychosexual stages, beginning in puberty, during which pleasure is sought through sexual contact with others.

Id The instinctual drives that, according to Freud, supply psychic energy to personality.

Identification The process by which, according to Freud, children incorporate their parents' values into their superegos.

Internal Locus of Control The belief that one can control one's own fate.

Latency Period The fourth of Freud's psychosexual stages, from about age 6 to puberty, during which sexual impulses are repressed.

Learned Helplessness A condition of passive resignation that is learned when an animal or human has been unable to avoid repeated aversive events.

Minnesota Multiphasic Personality Inventory (MMPI) The most widely researched and used of all personality inventories, containing ten scales of clinical dimensions and other validity scales and subscales.

Oedipus Complex According to Freud, the 3- to 5- or 6-year-old child's sexual desires toward the parent of the other sex and feelings of jealousy and hatred for the rival parent of the same sex.

Oral Stage The first of Freud's psychosexual stages, during which pleasure centers on the mouth.

Personal Control People's perception that they can control their environment.

Personality An individual's relatively distinctive and consistent pattern of thinking, feeling, and acting.

Personality Inventories Questionnaires (often with true-false or agree-disagree items) on which people report their customary feelings and behaviors; used to assess personality traits.

Phallic Stage The third of Freud's psychosexual stages, during which the pleasure zone is the genitals and sexual feelings arise toward the parent of the other sex.

Pleasure Principle The id's demand for immediate gratification.

Preconscious The region of the unconscious that, according to Freud, contains nonthreatening material that can be retrieved into conscious awareness.

Projection In psychoanalytic theory, the defense mechanism by which people disguise threatening impulses by imputing them to others.

Projective Tests Personality tests, such as the Rorschach and TAT, that provide ambiguous stimuli designed to trigger projection of one's inner dynamics.

Psychoanalysis The technique of treating disorders by analyzing unconscious tensions. Freud's psychoanalytic theory of personality sought to explain what he observed during psychoanalysis.

Psychosexual Stages The developmental stages (oral, anal, phallic, latency, genital) during which, according to Freud, the id's pleasure-seeking energies are focused on different erogenous zones.

Rationalization In psychoanalytic theory, a defense mechanism in which self-justifying explanations are offered in place of the real, more threatening, unconscious reasons for one's actions.

Reaction Formation In psychoanalytic theory, the ego's unconscious switching of unacceptable impulses into their opposites. Thus people may express feelings that are the opposite of their anxiety-arousing unconscious feelings.

Reality Principle The ego's tendency to satisfy the id's desires in ways that will realistically bring pleasure rather than pain.

Reciprocal Determinism The two-way influences among personal factors, environmental factors, and behavior.

Regression In psychoanalytic theory, an individual's retreat, when faced with anxiety, to an earlier, more comfortable stage of development.

Repression In psychoanalytic theory, the basic defense mechanism that banishes anxiety-arousing thoughts and feelings from consciousness.

Rorschach A projective test designed by Hermann Rorschach that uses people's interpretation of inkblots in an attempt to identify their projected feelings.

Self-Actualization According to Maslow, the final psychological need that arises when basic physical and psychological needs are met; the process of fulfilling one's potential as one achieves qualities such as self-acceptance, spontaneity, love, mastery, and creativity.

Self-Concept All our thoughts and feelings about ourselves in answer to the question, "Who am I?"

Self-Esteem One's feelings of high or low self-worth.

Self-Serving Bias The bias of perceiving oneself favorably.

Social-Cognitive Perspective Applies principles of social learning and cognition to personality.

Sublimation In psychoanalytic theory, the defense mechanism by which people rechannel their unacceptable impulses into socially approved activities.

Superego The part of personality that, according to Freud, represents internalized ideals, thus providing standards for judgment (conscience) and for future aspirations.

Trait Perspective Describes personality in terms of scores on various scales, each of which represents a personality dimension.

Traits Our predispositions to behave in given ways, measured by personality inventories.

Unconditional Positive Regard According to Rogers, an attitude of total acceptance toward another person.

Unconscious According to Freud, a reservoir of mostly unacceptable thoughts, wishes, feelings, and memories. According to contemporary research psychologists, information processing of which we are unaware.

FOR FURTHER READING

Bandura, A. (1986). *Social foundations of thought and action. A social-cognitive theory.* Englewood Cliffs, NJ: Prentice-Hall.

The definitive introduction to the social-cognitive perspective.

Freud, S. (1933). *Introductory lectures on psychoanalysis.* Published separately in 1966, J. Strachey (Ed. & trans.). New York: Liveright. Also published in 1963, in J. Strachey (Ed. & trans.), *The standard edition of the complete psychological works of Sigmund Freud.* London: Hogarth.

One of Freud's most popular works, introducing his ideas about human motivation, dream interpretation, slips of the tongue, and psychoanalytic therapy.

Hall, C. S., Lindzey, G., Loehlin, J. C., & Manosevitz, M. (1985). *Introduction to theories of personality.* New York: Wiley.

A revision of the classic text summary of personality theories, from Freud to the modern social-cognitive perspective.

Rogers, C. R. (1961). *On becoming a person.* Boston: Houghton Mifflin.

A warm and readable introduction to Carl Rogers' view of the person and of how to nurture personal growth.

Reg Butler *Manipulator*, 1956

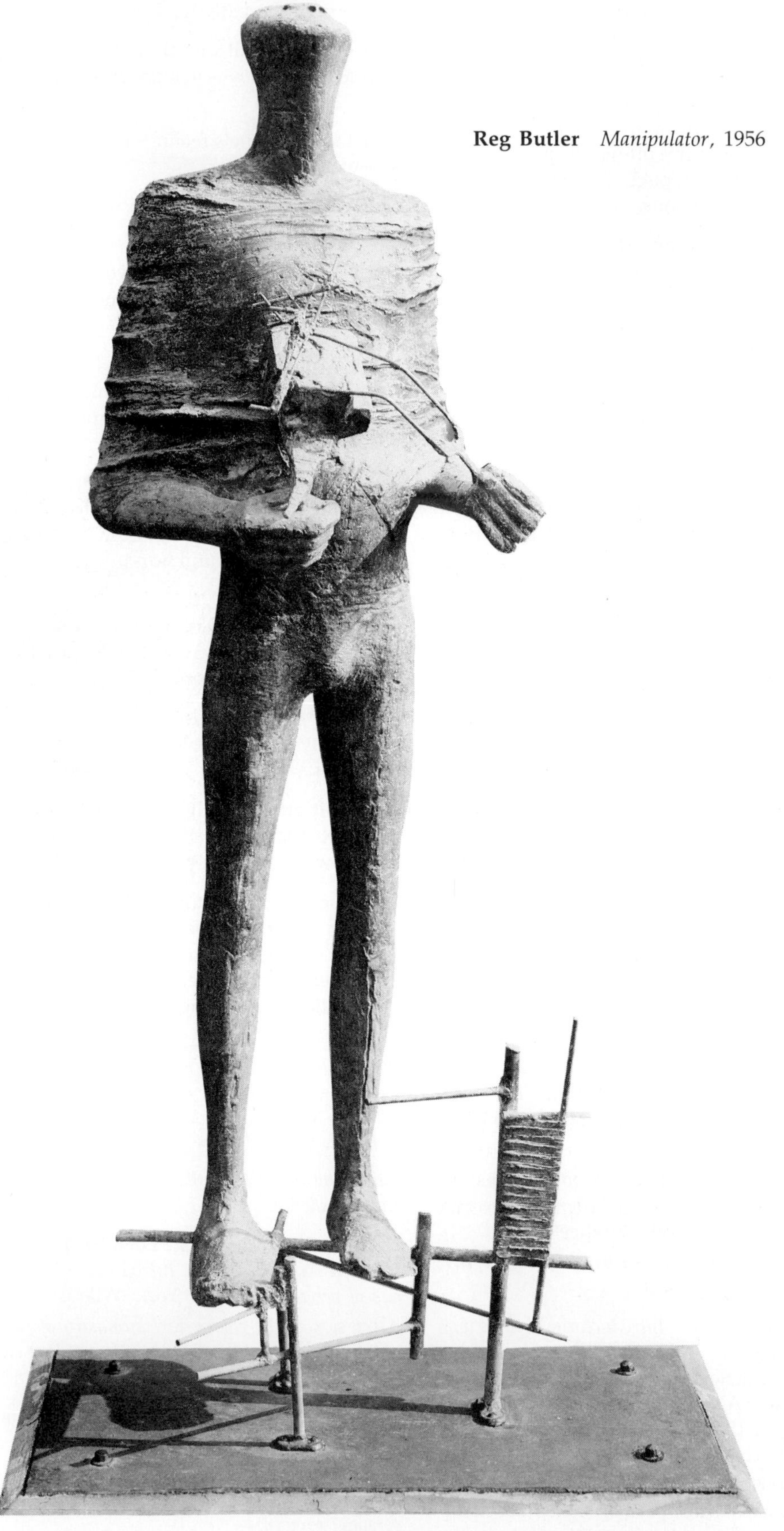

Hirshhorn Museum and Sculpture Garden, Smithsonian Institution

CHAPTER 16

Psychological Disorders

Algimantas Kezys

"It is a common calamity; we are all mad at some time or another."
Battista Mantuanus,
Eclogues, 1500

Many people, it seems, are as curious about abnormal behavior as about normal behavior. Indeed, Ralph Waldo Emerson thought people were *more* curious about the out-of-the-ordinary: "The sun shines and warms and lights us and we have no curiosity to know why this is so; but we ask the reason of all evil, of pain, and hunger, and mosquitoes and silly people."

In books such as this, many students are drawn to the descriptions of psychologically disturbed people. They turn immediately to the pages on depression, or read with consuming interest an account of the inner world of the schizophrenic. One reason for this fascination with disturbed people is that in them we may see something of ourselves. All of us, at some time, feel, think, or act as disturbed people do much of the time: We, too, may at times be anxious, depressed, withdrawn, suspicious, deluded, or antisocial. "Abnormal" people are in such ways like "normal" people—only more so and for greater periods of time. Perhaps, then, studying psychological disorders will illuminate our own personality dynamics.

Another reason for our curiosity may be that so many of us have been touched, either personally or through friends or family members, by the bewilderment and pain of a psychological disorder. In all likelihood, you, or someone you care about deeply, has at some time been disabled by unexplained physical symptoms, overwhelmed by irrational fears, or paralyzed by the feeling that life was not worth living. Each year there are more than a million admissions to U.S. mental hospitals and psychiatric units; more than double that number are served by outpatient clinics and community mental health centers (*Statistical Abstract of the U.S.: 1984*); still others seek out private counseling; and even more are judged to need it (Dohrenwend, 1980; Robins & others, 1984). Few of us go through life unacquainted with the reality of psychological disturbances.

PERSPECTIVES ON PSYCHOLOGICAL DISORDERS

Most people would agree that a person who is too depressed to get out of bed for weeks at a time is suffering from a psychological disorder. But what about people who, having experienced a loss, are unable to take up their usual round of social activities? Where should we draw the line between normality and abnormality? In other words, how should we *define* psychological disorders? Equally important, how should we *understand* disorders—as sicknesses that need to be diagnosed and cured or as adaptive responses to a troubling environment? Finally, how should we describe and *classify* disordered personalities? Can we do so in a way that allows us to help disturbed people and not merely label them?

Defining Psychological Disorders

James Oliver Huberty had been hearing voices. He "talked with God," his wife reported. Although he had never been to Vietnam, he strode into a San Ysidro, California, McDonald's restaurant one summer day in 1984 screaming "I've killed a thousand in Vietnam and I'll kill a thousand more." In the next few minutes, before being gunned down by police, Huberty proceeded to slaughter twenty-one children, women, and men.

At the end of World War II, James Forrestal, the first U.S. Secretary of Defense, became convinced that Israeli secret agents were following him. His suspiciousness struck his physicians as bizarre, so they diagnosed him as mentally ill and confined him to an upper floor of Walter Reed Army Hospital. From there he plunged to his death. Although Forrestal had other problems, it was later discovered that he had indeed been followed by Israeli agents, who were worried that he might secretly negotiate with representatives of Arab nations (Sagan, 1979b).

"I don't know how you and I would be rated by the psychiatrists in the Soviet Union, but I'd say we're fairly sane by New York standards."

Both Huberty's hearing voices and Forrestal's suspicion that people were following him were deviations from statistical norms. These were "ab-normal" (different from normal) perceptions. Being different from most other people is *part* of what it takes to be defined as disordered. In the Soviet Union, for example, outspoken political opponents of the government are more atypical than in Western democracies and, partly for this reason, they are more likely to be labeled and confined as mentally disordered (Reich, 1983). As the poet Emily Dickinson observed in 1862

Much Madness is divinest Sense—
To a discerning Eye—
Much Sense—the starkest Madness—
'Tis the Majority
In this, as All, prevail—
Assent—and you are sane—
Demure—you're straightway dangerous—
And handled with a Chain.

Dickinson suggests that simply being different from the majority can make one seem dangerous and in need of being "handled with a chain." But there is more to being disordered than being different. Those who win Olympic gold medals are abnormal, and they are heroes; Albert Einstein was atypical in his intellect, and is acclaimed as one of the great minds of our century; Picasso's atypical creativity contributed to his artistic renown. To be considered disordered, the atypical behavior must also be *disapproved* of by a person's culture. In virtually all times and places the atypical behavior of a James Oliver Huberty would be disapproved. But standards of acceptability for other behaviors vary. They vary from culture to culture and from time to time. Thus in the latest revision of the American Psychiatric Association's manual on psychological disorders, some disorders were added and some eliminated, reflecting changes in our standards of acceptability. For example, heavy smoking has become less fashionable now that it is known to cause certain health problems.

"If a man is in a minority of one we lock him up."
Oliver Wendell Holmes

Thus, smokers who have these health problems or who have tried unsuccessfully to stop smoking are now diagnosed as suffering tobacco dependence, a psychological disorder. On the other hand, homosexuality has been eliminated as a psychological disorder (unless the person feels distressed by it).

As these examples suggest, atypical and undesirable behaviors are more likely to be considered disordered when they bring harm or distress. Indeed, many clinicians define disorders as behaviors that are *maladaptive*—as tobacco dependence is, for example, when it results in physical damage or emotional distress. According to this reasoning, even typical behaviors, such as the despondency that college students sometimes feel, may be viewed as psychological disorders if they begin to cause serious harm.

Finally, strange behaviors are most likely to be considered disordered when others find it hard to justify them rationally. Forrestal's suspicions were attributed to his imagination—and he was declared disordered. Had he managed to convince people that his suspicions were based upon real events, he might not have been so labeled. James Oliver Huberty claimed to hear voices and talk with God, and we presume he was mad. When the late Episcopal Bishop James Pike reported that he had had conversations with his dead son, enough people took him seriously (after all, he was a bishop) that he was not considered disordered. It is acceptable to be different from others only if both you and they can justify the difference.

In practice, it is when all these criteria are met that we are most likely to define behavior as ***psychologically disordered.*** James Oliver Huberty's behavior was *atypical, undesirable, maladaptive,* and *unjustifiable,* and so we have few doubts about our judgments of the man.

The Insanity Defense on Trial

You perhaps have noticed that in discussing what psychological disorders are, we have made no mention of insanity. That is because *insanity* and sanity are legal terms, ones that must be judged either/or. You can be a little depressed or greatly depressed, but you cannot be judged a little bit insane.

The "not guilty by reason of insanity" defense was formally established in 1843 when a deluded Scotsman, Daniel M'Naghten, tried to shoot the British Prime Minister (who he thought was persecuting him) and killed the Prime Minister's secretary by mistake. A national furor erupted after M'Naghten was acquitted as insane and sent to a mental hospital rather than a prison. The written insanity rule that resulted from the upholding of the M'Naghten verdict limited the insanity defense to cases where the persons were judged not to have known what they were doing or not to have known that it was wrong.

By the time John Hinckley came to trial in 1982 for shooting President Reagan and his press secretary, the insanity defense in U.S. federal courts and most state courts had been broadened. The prosecution was required to prove that Hinckley was sane, which under the Model Penal Code meant his having "a substantial capacity" not merely to "know" his act was wrong, but to "appreciate" its wrongfulness and "to conform his conduct to the requirements of law."

The prosecution was unable to prove sanity to the jurors' satisfaction, and so Hinckley, like M'Naghten, was sent to a mental hospital. As in the first insanity case, the public verdict on the trial was outrage (Hans & Slater, 1983). One newspaper headlined "Hinckley insane, public mad." The outrage stemmed partly from the fact that, like others declared not guilty by reason of insanity, Hinckley will be released when declared sane and no longer dangerous—conceivably earlier, though possibly later, than his release from a prison would have been.

A posed self-portrait of John W. Hinckley, Jr., President Reagan's would-be assassin.

In the U.S. Congress a flurry of bills was introduced to abolish the insanity defense. Some news commentators complained that the heinousness of a crime had become the very basis for evading responsibility for it, "like the person who kills his parents and demands mercy because he is an orphan." Are "sick crimes" necessarily the products of sick minds that need treatment, not punishment? Must the genuinely bad be truly mad? If so, said one commentator, then modern society has become like Aldous Huxley's nightmarish *Brave New World,* where when someone commits a crime the response is, "I did not know he was ill."

In defense of the insanity plea, psychologist David Rosenhan (1983a, 1983b) pointed out that the vivid Hinckley case distorted our impressions of how often the plea is used. Only about 2 times in every 1000 felony cases is such a plea entered, and in 85 percent of these cases all parties—mental health experts, prosecutor, and defense attorney—agree that the sadly deranged person was not in a responsible state of mind. Thus the most important issues that involve psychology and law deal not with the rare disputes over insanity but with the far more frequent cases concerning child custody (judging who will be the better parent), involuntary commitment to mental hospitals, and predictions about future criminal behavior made at the time of sentencing or parole.

On the strength of recommendations from the American Bar Association and the American Psychiatric Association, the insanity defense has survived in the United States, but, under a 1984 law, in a narrowed form that shifts the burden of proving insanity to the defense (as it is in Canada). Now defendants must establish that they did not understand the wrongfulness of their acts.

When psychiatrists and psychologists have predicted violence they have been wrong more often than they have been right (Monahan, 1983). Thus even the American Psychiatric Association has argued that predictions of dangerousness should be barred from court, because such predictions give "the appearance of being based on expert medical judgment, when in fact no such expertise exists" (Tierney, 1982).

Understanding Psychological Disorders

Psychological disorders existed long before there were psychologists to name and explain them. Imagine yourself living hundreds or thousands of years ago. How might you have accounted for the behavior of a James Oliver Huberty? To explain puzzling behavior, our early ancestors often presumed that strange forces—the movements of the stars, god-like forces, or evil spirits—were at work. "The devil made him do it," you might have said. Believing such, the cure might have been to get rid of the evil force—by exorcising the demon, or perhaps even by chipping a hole in the skull to allow the evil spirit to escape (Figure 16-1). In Europe, until the last two centuries, "mad" people were sometimes caged under zoo-like conditions or given "therapies" appropriate to a demon, including:

> beatings, whippings, blistering the shaved head, burning, and scarring fingers. Surgically, the mentally disordered have had lengths of intestines removed and teeth pulled, they have been castrated, hysterectomies have been performed, the clitoris has been cauterized, they have had animal blood transfused into their veins, and their own blood has been removed . . . . (Farina, 1982, p. 306)

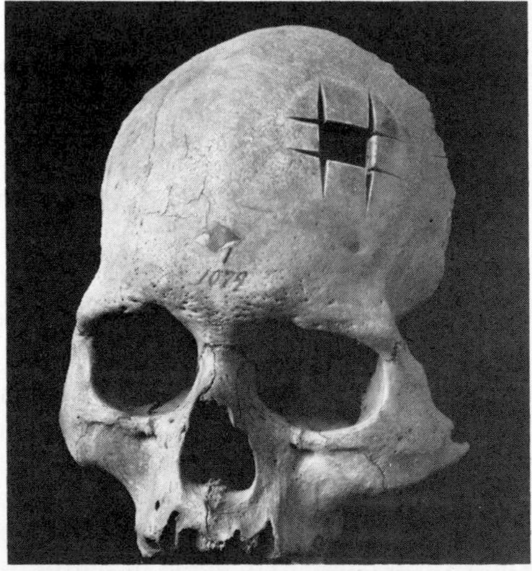

Figure 16-1 *A skull found in Peru, showing a hole chipped through the person's head to allow evil spirits to escape. One wonders whether this patient survived the cure.*

The Medical Perspective

In response to such conditions, reformers such as Philippe Pinel (1745–1826) insisted that madness was not demon-possession but a disease that, like other diseases, could be treated and cured. For Pinel, treatment meant boosting patients' morale by talking with them and by providing humane living conditions. Later, when it was discovered that an infectious disease, syphilis, produced a psychological disorder, people came to believe in physical causes for such disorders and to search for medical treatments.

Today, the medical perspective of Pinel and his followers is familiar to us in the terminology of the mental *health* movement: A mental *illness* (also called a psycho*pathology*) needs to be *diagnosed* on the basis of its *symptoms* and *cured* through *therapy*, which may include *treatment* in a psychiatric *hospital*. The assumption of this ***medical model***—that psychological disorders are sicknesses—provided the impetus for much needed reforms. The "sick" were unchained and asylums were replaced by hospitals.

But the medical model has its critics, among them psychiatrist Thomas Szasz, who, beginning with his 1961 book, *The Myth of Mental Illness*, has argued that "problems in living" are not diseases, as are cancer and tuberculosis. Szasz believes that mental illnesses are socially, not medically, defined. When some psychiatrists judged 1964 Republican presidential candidate Barry Goldwater as having "paranoid" tendencies and when Soviet psychiatrists diagnose dissident citizens as "psychotic," they were and are using medical terminology to disguise their contempt for people's unusual political ideas. Szasz (1984) concludes that psychiatrists and other mental health practitioners have assumed too much authority in today's society. This can be harmful, for when people are demeaned with the label "mentally ill" they may begin to view themselves as "sick" and therefore become unable to take responsibility for coping with their problems.

"It's no measure of health to be well adjusted to a profoundly sick society."
Krishnamurti, 1895–1986.

Despite such criticisms, the medical perspective has survived and even gained renewed credibility from recent discoveries. As we will see, genetically influenced disorders in brain biochemistry have been linked with two of the most prevalent and troubling psychological disorders, depression and schizophrenia, both of which are sometimes treated medically, with drugs.

Psychological Perspectives

Some psychologists, such as those who adopt Freud's psychoanalytic perspective, agree that disorders are sicknesses that have diagnosable and treatable causes. However, they insist that these causes may include psychological as well as physical factors.

Other psychologists find the "sickness" idea, and the terminology that has grown up around it, unnecessary and misleading. They contend that *all* behavior, whether labeled normal or disordered, can be viewed as arising from the interaction of (1) genetic and physiological factors and (2) past and present experiences. To presume that a person is "mentally ill" attributes the condition to an internal problem—to a "sickness" that must be found and cured. Maybe, though, there is no deep, internal problem, but rather a growth-blocking difficulty in the person's environment, in the person's current interpretations of events, or in the person's bad habits and poor social skills. When native Americans were banished from their lands, put on reservations to live in poverty and unemployment, and deprived of the feelings of personal control that their ancestors enjoyed, the result was a high rate of alcoholism. Noting that only some native Americans become alcoholic, those who adopt the medical model might attribute such alcoholism to an individual Indian's "sickness." Those who reject the medical model would attribute the problem to the interaction between the individual and the environment.

Should the high incidence of alcoholism among native Americans be viewed primarily as an individual's sickness to be treated by therapy or is it also a social problem that can be dealt with only by environmental changes?

Classifying Psychological Disorders

In psychology, as in biology and the other sciences, classification creates order. To classify an animal as a mammal says a great deal—that its young are nourished by milk, that its skin has hair or fur, that it has a relatively high body temperature, and so forth. In psychiatry and psychology, too, classification provides a way of ordering and describing clusters of symptoms. To classify a person's disorder as "schizophrenic" suggests that the person talks incoherently, has hallucinations or delusions (bizarre beliefs), shows either little emotion or inappropriate emotion, and is socially withdrawn. Thus the diagnostic label provides a handy shorthand for describing a complex disorder.

In both medicine and psychology, diagnostic classification seeks not only to describe a disorder and to predict its future course, but also to facilitate research on its causes and treatment. Indeed, naming and describing a disorder is the first step in studying it. In the United States, the authoritative scheme for classifying disorders is the American Psychiatric Association's *Diagnostic and Statistical Manual of Mental Disorders (Third Edition),* nicknamed ***DSM-III***. This volume and the book of case illustrations that accompanies it (Spitzer & others, 1981) provide the basis for much of the material in this chapter. The World Health Organization's international classification of mental disorders is generally compatible with the newer DSM-III diagnostic categories.

Although the task force that prepared DSM-III included not only psychiatrists (who are medical doctors) but clinical psychologists as well, DSM-III was nevertheless influenced by the medical model. The very idea of "diagnosing" people's problems in terms of their "symptoms" seems to assume the existence of "mental diseases." Most clinical psychologists are not enthralled with this medical terminology (Smith & Kraft, 1983). But most health insurance companies require a "diagnosis" before paying for therapy, so even those who question the diagnostic system usually comply with it.

Drawing by Sidney Harris

"I'm always like this, and my family was wondering if you could prescribe a mild depressant."

All told, there are more than 200 specific psychological disorders and conditions, most of which are grouped into fifteen major categories of "mental disorders." There are diagnoses for almost any conceivable complaint. In fact, some critics fault DSM-III for bringing "almost any kind of behavior within the compass of psychiatry" (Eysenck & others, 1983)—from irrational fear of humiliation and embarrassment (social phobia) to persistently breaking rules at home or school (conduct disorder) to a grandiose sense of one's self-importance (narcissistic personality disorder). The range of human problems that can be fit into DSM-III is evident in a recent National Institute of Mental Health survey of 10,000 Americans, which revealed that 1 in 5 adults suffers a recognizable psychological disorder (Myers, 1984).

"Saying one out of every five people has a mental disorder is like saying the average person is crazy. The average person isn't crazy. He or she may act crazy sometimes but that's all part of being normal."
Andy Rooney,
Tribune Media Series,
October 10, 1984 column

The most important concern with DSM-III categories, however, is with their reliability. If one psychologist or psychiatrist diagnoses someone as having, say, a "catatonic schizophrenic disorder," what are the chances that another psychologist or psychiatrist would independently give the same diagnosis? With previous diagnostic schemes, reliability has been modest. For broad diagnostic groupings, such as "schizophrenic disorders," the agreement has averaged 70 percent or better in most studies. But for more specific diagnoses, such as "catatonic schizophrenia," agreement has not been much above 50 percent (Eysenck & others, 1983).

In evaluating the reliability of psychological diagnoses, we should bear in mind that medical diagnoses are hardly more reliable (diagnoses of cause of death agree with autopsy results only about half the time!). Moreover, the DSM-III's new system for classifying disorders has been designed to improve reliability. Instead of requiring a subjective assessment of the patient's condition, it bases diagnoses on observable behaviors. By asking clinicians a series of questions with yes or no answers (such as, "Is the person afraid to leave home?"), it attempts to guide them to diagnoses that can be reached with greater consensus.

Let us now consider a few of the most prevalent and perplexing disorders, remembering that the people we will meet are not curiosities in a mental ward, but our human brothers and sisters. These are real people—people who are troubled, and whose loved ones are troubled for them.

Two other categories of disorder were discussed earlier—substance abuse in Chapter 8 and sexual dysfunctions in Chapter 13.

ANXIETY DISORDERS

When speaking in front of a class, when peering down from a ledge, when waiting for a big game to begin, any one of us might feel anxious. At one time or another most of us feel enough anxiety in some social situation that we fail to make eye contact or we avoid talking to someone—"shyness," we call our social anxiety. But for about 1 in 12 people, according to the recent report of the National Institute of Mental Health (Regier & others, 1984), anxiety becomes so distressing and persistent that they are said to suffer an ***anxiety disorder.*** Anxiety disorders are examples of ***neurotic disorders***—psychological disorders that are distressing, but which allow one to think rationally and function socially. Under the influence of Freud, neurotic disorders were previously labeled *neuroses*—Freud's term for the process by which he believed unconscious conflicts caused anxiety. The newer term "neurotic disorder" describes distressing symptoms without assuming Freud's theoretical explanation for them. Because it is vague enough to include many distressing disorders, some psychologists follow DSM-III in making minimal use of the term "neurotic." Others still use the term as a contrast to the more serious "psychotic" disorders, which involve bizarre behavior and thinking (see p. 448).

"You may tell the waiter he can take his time. I've conquered my neurotic need to be served immediately."

Anxiety is a part of our everyday experiences. But it does not entail the intense suffering endured by those with anxiety disorders. There are three important types of anxiety disorder: the ***generalized anxiety disorder,*** in which a person, for no apparent reason, feels uncontrollably tense and uneasy; the ***phobic disorder,*** in which the person feels irrationally afraid of a specific object or situation; and the ***obsessive-compulsive disorder,*** in which the person is troubled by repetitive thoughts and actions.

Generalized Anxiety Disorder

Tom, a 27-year-old electrician, seeks help, complaining of dizziness, sweating palms, heart palpitations, and ringing in the ears. He feels edgy, and sometimes finds himself shaking. With reasonable success he tries to hide his symptoms from his family and co-workers. Nevertheless, he has had few social contacts since the symptoms began 2 years previously. Worse yet, he has sometimes had to leave work. His family doctor and neurologist can find no physical problem, and a special diet for those with low blood sugar has not helped.

Tom's chronic, unfocused anxiety suggests a generalized anxiety disorder. The symptoms of this disorder are commonplace; their persistence is not. The sufferers are continually tense and jittery, apprehensive and worrying about bad things that might happen, and experiencing all the symptoms of autonomic nervous system arousal (racing heart, clammy hands, butterflies in the stomach, and such). The tension and apprehension may be apparent to others through a furrowed brow, an eyelid twitch, or fidgeting.

One of the worst characteristics of a generalized anxiety disorder is that the person cannot identify, and therefore cannot avoid, its cause. To use Freud's term, the anxiety is "free-floating." Indeed, for no apparent reason the anxiety may at times suddenly escalate into a terrifying ***panic attack***—an episode of intense dread, several minutes long, that is typically accompanied by chest pain, choking or smothering sensations, trembling, dizziness, or fainting. The experience is unpredictable, and so frightening that the sufferer may then avoid situations where attacks have previously occurred.

We can only speculate about the causes of anxiety disorder. Psychoanalysts believe it illustrates what happens when the ego's defense mechanisms are weak and the ego is therefore unable to cope with the demands of the id, the reprimands of the superego, and the pressures of living in a complex world.

Learning researchers suggest that anxiety is a response to helplessness. Drawing on animal research, they note that one can create the disorder in the laboratory by giving rats unpredictable electric shocks (Schwartz, 1984). After experiencing such aversive events without forewarning, the animals become chronically anxious and often develop ulcers. Never knowing when something bad will happen, they seem apprehensive whenever they are in their laboratory environment. (They are in some ways like the rape victim described on p. 232, who reported being terrified of her old apartment and anxious about approaching the neighborhood where she was attacked.) On the other hand, when similar shocks are preceded by a conditioned stimulus, the animals become fearful of only *that stimulus* and can relax in its absence. They are more like people who suffer phobic disorders.

Phobic Disorders

In some people, anxiety may be focused in a phobic disorder—an unreasonable fear of some specific object, activity, or situation. (See Figure 16-2 for a list of some common fears.) Next to alcohol abuse, phobias are the most common psychological disorders (Robins & others, 1984). Marilyn, a 28-year-old homemaker, is so frightened of thunderstorms that she feels anxious as soon as a weather forecaster mentions the possibility of storms later in the week. If her husband is away and a storm is forecast, she sometimes stays with a close relative. During a storm, she hides from windows and buries her head to avoid seeing the lightning. She is otherwise healthy and happy.

Figure 16-2 *This 1984 national survey shows the extent to which Americans are fearful of some common sources of anxiety.*

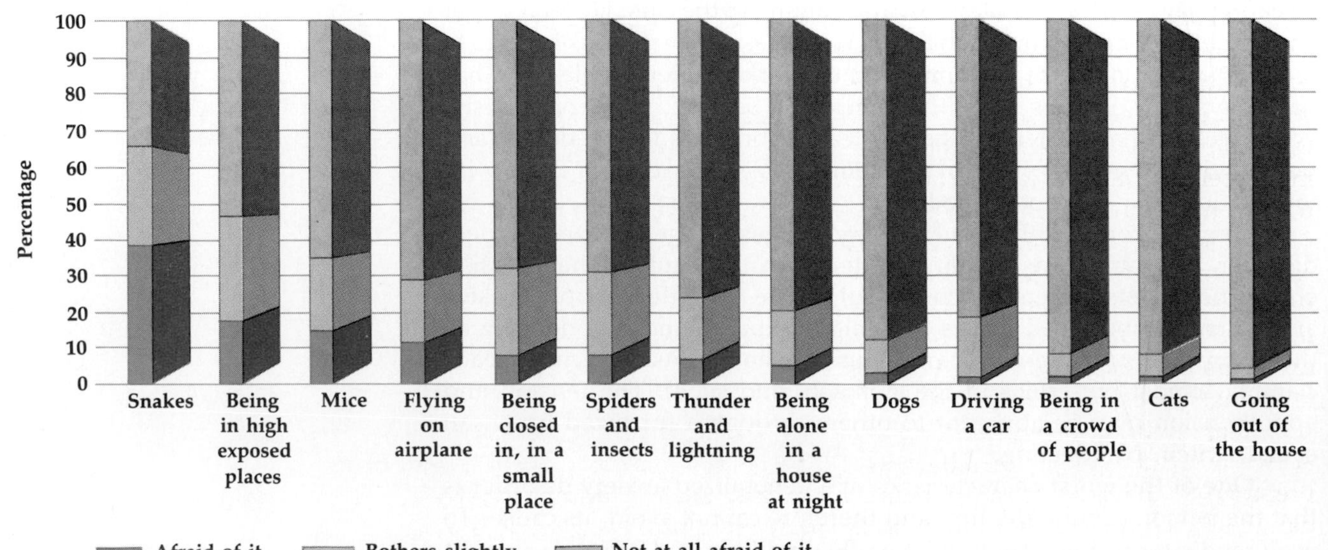

Marilyn suffers from an irrational and debilitating fear—a phobia. Other people with phobic disorders suffer from irrational fears of specific animals, or airplanes, or elevators, or even public places such as department stores. Sometimes it is possible to avoid the fear-arousing stimulus; one can hide during thunderstorms or avoid airplanes. However, if one suffers from a fear of open, public places (as is true of those who suffer from "agoraphobia"), avoiding the fear-arousing stimulus may dictate never leaving home.

Many people are uneasy when looking down from a great height and few enjoy being in a crowded elevator. But only people suffering from severe phobias are incapacitated, their lives crippled by their attempts to avoid terrifying situations.

There are several theories as to the causes of phobic disorders. The psychoanalytic explanation is that phobia sufferers are actually afraid of their own impulses. When repression of these impulses is incomplete, anxiety surfaces and becomes attached to a harmless stimulus. One of Freud's classic cases concerned a 5-year-old boy known as Little Hans, whose phobia of horses prevented, in those days before automobiles, his going outdoors. Freud concluded that Little Hans' fear of horses was but an expression of his underlying fear of his father, whom Hans perceived as his rival for his mother's affections.

The learning explanation is that phobias are conditioned fears—or at least are fears that can (as we will see in the next chapter, "Therapy") be *un*learned through extinction or counterconditioning. Recently, my car was struck by another whose driver failed to notice a stop sign. Now, every time I see a car approaching a stop sign on a cross street ahead of me, I feel a twinge of fear. Perhaps Marilyn had some more terrifying or painful experience during a thunderstorm. But often, those who complain of such fears report no such frightening past experiences. A person can be afraid of airplanes without ever having flown. Perhaps the fear response has generalized from, say, a fear of heights (due to a fall) to a fear of flying. Or perhaps the fear has been learned from observing others' fears and frightening experiences; for example, parents often unknowingly *transmit their fears* to their children.

Biological predispositions may also contribute to phobic disorders. As we noted in Chapter 14, "Emotion," human beings seem biologically prepared to develop fears of heights, storms, snakes, and insects—dangers that our ancestors surely faced. Some psychologists even believe that our individual genetic makeup can help predispose particular fears.

Identical twins who have been raised separately sometimes develop identical phobias (Eckert & others, 1981). One pair of 35-year-old female twins, for example, independently developed claustrophobia and also became so fearful of water that they would gingerly wade backward into the ocean, and even then, only up to their knees.

Obsessive-Compulsive Disorder

As with the generalized anxiety and phobic disorders, we can recognize images of ourselves in the obsessive-compulsive disorder. We may at times be obsessed with senseless or offensive thoughts that will not go away. Or we may engage in compulsive, rigid behavior—checking several times to see if the door is locked, stepping over the cracks in the sidewalk, or lining up our books and pencils "just so" before studying.

Obsessive thoughts and compulsive behaviors cross the fine line between normality and disorder when they become so persistent that they interfere with living or cause great distress. Checking to see that the doors are locked is normal; checking the doors five times is disordered. Hand washing is normal; hand washing so often that one's skin becomes raw is disordered. Consider Julius, a college junior whose obsessive-compulsive behaviors are clearly maladaptive. He is so preoccupied with unwanted thoughts that he is unable to study. He spends hours each night rehashing the day's interactions, and mentally correcting any behavior that he regrets. He says it is like replaying a videotape of each interaction, over and over. After a period of such rumination he might look up and discover that 2 or 3 hours have gone by. What is more, before going out with friends he must go through a 2-hour ritual of shaving, showering, and grooming to perfection. To have second thoughts about one's actions and to find comfort in familiar routines is normal; to act as Julius does is to experience an obsessive-compulsive disorder.

Again, the psychoanalytic and learning perspectives offer differing explanations for the disorder. In the Freudian view, obsessive thoughts may be a thinly disguised expression of forbidden impulses (which often have violent or sexual content). These thoughts may prompt the person to perform compulsive acts that counter the forbidden impulse. Repetitive hand washing, for example, may help to suppress anxiety over one's "dirty" urges.

"He always times '60 Minutes.'"

In the learning view, obsessive thoughts and compulsive behaviors are a learned response to anxiety. Obsessive behavior temporarily reduces anxiety, which then reinforces and maintains the behavior. If the hand washing relieves the anxiety, the person may repeat this behavior when again feeling anxious.

The anxiety of the obsessive-compulsive disorder is measurable as a biological state of overarousal (Turner & others, 1985). Twin studies suggest that a genetic predisposition to an anxious, aroused state may lead the obsessive-compulsive person to be overreactive to threatening stimuli and therefore to take actions that control perceived threats.

Eating Disorders

Mary is a 5′3″ 15-year-old who, having reached 100 pounds, decided that she needed to lose weight to enhance her attractiveness. After gradually reducing her diet to a few vegetables a day and then adding a vigorous exercise program, she dropped to 80 pounds. Mary remains discontented about her weight. Moreover, she has been having difficulty sleeping, has at times been depressed, and no longer has regular menstrual periods. Although she is socially inactive and seldom dates, Mary is successful academically; she is a very conscientious student who studies hard and obtains high grades. She does not regard herself as ill or in need of treatment.

Alice is a 5′9″, 160 pound 17-year-old who says she has always been tall and a little chubby. For the last 5 years, her eating has been characterized by binges followed by vomiting. She will eat a quart of ice cream or an entire pie and then, to control her weight, make herself vomit. She wants to date, but she is ashamed of her looks. She has at times taken pills to try to lose weight.

Mary's condition is diagnosed as *anorexia nervosa,* a disorder in which a person loses 25 percent or more of her normal weight, yet feels fat and is fearful of becoming obese. Even when emaciated, the person continues to restrict food intake. The disorder usually develops in adolescence, and is nine times more common in females than in males.

Alice's condition, which is more common, is diagnosed as *bulimia*—a disorder characterized by repeated "binge-purge" episodes of overeating high caloric foods followed by vomiting or laxative use. Most bulimic individuals are women in their late teens or twenties who, like those with anorexia, are preoccupied with food, fearful of becoming overweight, and often experiencing depression or anxiety (Schlesier-Stropp, 1984). About 50 percent of those with anorexia also display the binge-purge symptoms of bulimia. But most bulimics fluctuate within or above normal weight range, which enables them to keep the condition hidden (Polivy & Herman, 1985).

Researchers report that the families of bulimia patients have a higher than usual incidence of alcoholism, obesity, and depression. Anorexia patients often come from families that are high-achieving and protective. Nevertheless, the origins of these disorders are, for now, a mystery.

A cultural explanation would suggest that the "sickness" lies not just within the young woman but within her weight-obsessed culture—a culture that in countless ways says "fat is bad," that motivates millions of young women to be "always dieting," and that therefore encourages the eating binges by semistarvation. Anorexia nervosa always begins as a weight-loss diet, and the self-induced vomiting of bulimics nearly always begins after one has broken diet restrictions and gorged. Obesity researchers Susan Wooley and Orland Wooley (1983) concluded that "an increasingly stringent cultural standard of thinness for women has been accompanied by a steadily increasing incidence of serious eating disorders in women."

Singer Karen Carpenter's death of cardiac arrest at age 32 was believed to be related to her long struggle with anorexia nervosa.

Consistent with this explanation, it appears that the extremely thin women one sees in today's fashion magazines and advertisements appear to have distorted women's perceptions of what men find attractive. In one study of nearly

500 University of Pennsylvania men and women students, April Fallon and Paul Rozin (1985) found that women tended to rate both their ideal body weight and the weight they thought men preferred as lighter than the weight men actually preferred (see Figure 16-3). For men—who are far less likely than women to suffer eating disorders—researchers found no such discrepancies. They tended to rate their current weight, their ideal weight, and the man's weight they thought women preferred as all quite similar.

"Women, like men, come in all shapes, sizes and ages. The media would have us believe that women are acceptable only in one shape, size or age."
YWCA of Winnipeg, Canada

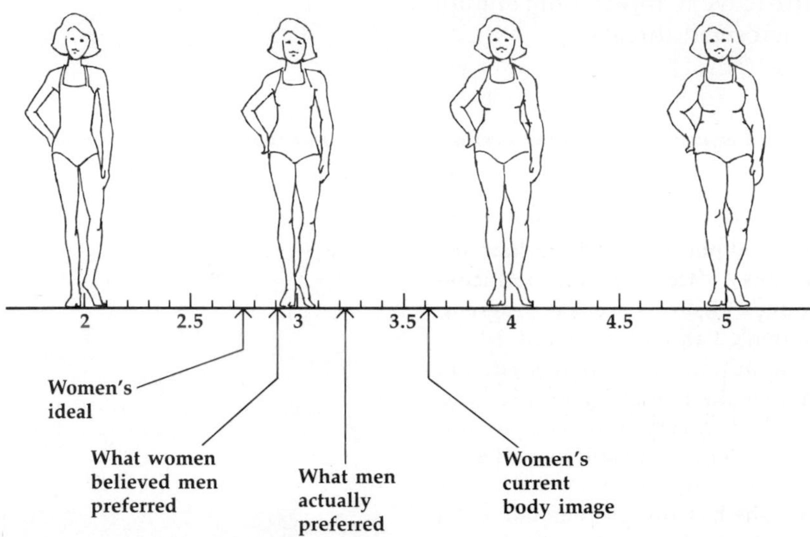

Figure 16-3 *Many women tend to idealize, and misperceive men as idealizing, a body shape considerably thinner than their own.*

SOMATOFORM DISORDERS

Ellen becomes dizzy and nauseated in the late afternoon—shortly before her husband is expected home. Neither her family doctor nor a neurologist has been able to identify a physical cause for her dizzy spells, and it seems likely that they have a psychological origin, in her feelings about her husband, for example. In ***somatoform disorders,*** such as Ellen's, the distressing symptoms take a somatic (bodily) form, even though there seem to be no physical causes. One person may have a variety of complaints—vomiting, dizziness, blurred vision, difficulty in swallowing, and so forth. Another may experience severe and prolonged pain. The problem is familiar to us; for to a lesser and briefer extent, we have all experienced inexplicable physical symptoms, especially when we are under stress. It is little comfort to be told that the problem is "all in your head"; although it may be psychological in origin, the symptoms are nevertheless genuinely felt.

One type of somatoform disorder, more common in Freud's day than ours, is the ***conversion disorder,*** so called because anxiety was presumed to be converted into a specific physical symptom. As we noted in Chapter 15, "Personality," Freud's whole effort to treat and understand psychological disorders stemmed from his puzzlement over ailments for which no physiological basis could be found. For example, a patient would lose sensation in a way that made no neurological sense. Yet, the symptoms were real; one could stick pins in the affected area without triggering a response. Other persons experienced unexplained paralysis, blindness, or an inability to swallow.

"He was a dreadful hypochondriac."

As you can imagine, somatoform disorders send people not to a psychologist or psychiatrist but to a physician. This is especially true of those who experience ***hypochondriasis.*** In this relatively common disorder, the person interprets normal sensations (a stomach cramp today, a headache tomorrow) as symptoms of a dreaded disease. Moreover, no amount of reassurance by the physician convinces the patient not to worry, so the patient may move on to another physician, seeking more medical attention.

DISSOCIATIVE DISORDERS

Among the most uncommon and most intriguing of the psychological disorders are the ***dissociative disorders,*** in which the patient experiences a sudden loss of memory or change in identity. Under extreme stress, conscious awareness becomes *dissociated,* or separated, from previous memories, thoughts, and feelings.

Amnesia

Amnesia, or failure to recall important events, can be caused by head injuries or alcoholic intoxication. However, psychogenic amnesia—a dissociative disorder—usually begins as a response to intolerable psychological stress. For example, one 18-year-old victim was rescued from his sailboat by the Coast Guard and brought to a hospital. He knew he had gone sailing with friends and that he was a college student, but he could not recall what had happened to his friends. Moreover, he kept forgetting that he was in the hospital; each time he was reminded, he seemed surprised. Later, with the aid of a relaxing drug, he was able to recall that a ferocious storm had washed his companions overboard.

As this case illustrates, the forgetfulness of amnesia tends to be selective; the young man forgot what was intolerably painful. Those with amnesia may be somewhat disoriented and may forget who they are, but will remember how to drive, count, and talk. Typically, the amnesia vanishes as abruptly as it began and rarely recurs.

Fugue

Like amnesia, ***fugue*** (meaning "flight") involves forgetting; but it also involves fleeing one's home and identity for days, months, or years. When suddenly awakening from a fugue state, people will remember their old identities but will have no memory for what transpired during the fugue. Such was the self-reported experience of Steven Kubacki, a college senior who, on a cold February afternoon in 1978, went hiking on the ice over Lake Michigan and failed to return. His parents presumed him dead and his college awarded him a posthumous degree. The next thing he knew he was awakening in a field in Massachusetts on a warm spring day. Beside him was a backpack with someone's running shoes, swimming goggles, and glasses. "What the hell's going on here?," he reports wondering. Fourteen months of his life had vanished.

Multiple Personality

Even more mysterious is the massive dissociation of self from ordinary consciousness in those with ***multiple personality disorder.*** Such people have two or more distinct personalities. The first is usually rather restrained and dull, the second more impulsive and uninhibited. The person may be prim and proper one moment and loud and flirtatious the next. Each personality has its own voice and mannerisms, and the original one is typically unaware of the other.

Individuals with multiple personality are thought to be quite rare. Although they are usually nonviolent, there have been cases in which the person reportedly became dissociated into a "good" and a "bad" or aggressive personality—a Dr. Jekyll/Mr. Hyde split of the sort immortalized in Robert Louis Stevenson's story. Freud would say that without the original "good" personality's awareness, the wanton second personality is free to discharge forbidden impulses. One unusual case that for a time seemed to support this interpretation involved Kenneth Bianchi, who was implicated in the "Hillside Strangler" rapes and murders of ten California women. Bianchi revealed a sadistic second personality during a hypnosis session with psychologist John Watkins (1984).

"Hillside Strangler" Kenneth Bianchi at his trial. One frightening aspect of Bianchi's extreme emotional disturbance is that it was disguised by his pleasant appearance and manner.

Watkins first told Bianchi that hypnosis is a tool for uncovering hidden aspects of personality. He then "called forth" a hidden personality:

> I've talked a bit to Ken, but I think that perhaps there might be another part of Ken that I haven't talked to, another part that maybe feels somewhat differently from the part that I've talked to . . . Would you talk with me, Part, by saying, "I'm here"? (Watkins, 1984)

Bianchi answered "yes" to this question and engaged with the psychologist in the following interchange:

> ***Psychologist:*** *Part, are you the same thing as Ken, or are you different in any way?*
>
> ***Bianchi:*** *I'm not him.*
>
> ***Psychologist:*** *You're not him? Who are you? Do you have a name?*
>
> ***Bianchi:*** *Steve. You can call me Steve.*

While speaking as Steve, Bianchi stated that he hated Ken because Ken was nice and that he (Steve), with the help of a cousin, had murdered a number of women. He also claimed that Ken knew nothing about his existence and that Ken was innocent of the murders.

Was Bianchi's second personality a ruse, simply a way of disavowing responsibility for his actions? The psychologist who diagnosed Bianchi believes he is a genuine case of multiple personality. Others doubt the diagnosis. They believe either that Bianchi, a consistent rule-breaker and liar since childhood, was consciously faking it to save his own skin (Orne, 1984), or that to dissociate himself from his impulses and actions he unconsciously created the multiple personality during the hypnotic session (Allison, 1984).

To see if normal people might act as if they had a multiple personality, skeptic Nicholas Spanos (1984) asked college students to pretend they were an accused murderer being examined by a psychiatrist. When given the same hypnotic treatment that Bianchi received, most spontaneously expressed a second personality. Spanos wonders, are clinicians who discover multiple personalities perhaps merely triggering people to enact a role, whether consciously or unconsciously? If so, can such people then be convinced of the authenticity of their own role enactments? You may recall from Chapter 8, "States of Consciousness," a similar question as to whether hypnosis is a unique state of consciousness or a social phenomenon. People diagnosed as multiple personality typically are able to drift spontaneously into a hypnotic state, and they may have distinct brain states associated with each of their personalities (Goleman, 1985). As yet, however, the issue of whether most diagnosed cases of multiple personalities are genuine is unresolved.

"Pretense may become reality."
Chinese proverb

With the dissociative disorders as with the anxiety and somatoform disorders, the psychoanalytic and learning perspectives both view the symptoms as ways of dealing with anxiety—as defenses against the eruption of anxiety that stems from the threat of unacceptable impulses (as Freud would say), or as behaviors that have been reinforced by anxiety reduction (as a learning theorist would say). Maladaptive as they may be, such psychological disorders are expressions of our human struggle to cope with and survive the stresses of life.

"Though this be madness, yet there is method in 't."
William Shakespeare,
Hamlet, 1600

AFFECTIVE DISORDERS

A major class of psychological disorders, the ***affective disorders,*** are characterized by emotional extremes. There are two principal forms of affective disorder, both of which are disturbances of moods: (1) ***major depression,*** in which the person experiences the hopelessness and lethargy of prolonged depression until eventually rebounding to normalcy, and (2) ***bipolar disorder,*** in which the person alternates between depression and ***mania,*** an overexcited, hyperactive, wildly optimistic phase.

Major Depression

Probably you already know something about what depression feels like. If you are like most of the college students studied by Aaron Beck and Jeffrey Young (1978), at some time during this year you will probably experience a few of the symptoms of depression—by feeling deeply discouraged about the future, dissatisfied with your life, isolated from people, sad, lacking energy; by having little appetite; by being unable to concentrate; by wondering if you would be better off dead. Perhaps academic success came easily to you in high school, but now you find that disappointing grades jeopardize your career goals. Maybe conflicting parental and peer pressures seem almost intolerable. Perhaps social difficulties such as loneliness or the breakup of a romantic relationship have plunged you into despair. And maybe your self-torment has at times only worsened the very problems you were brooding over.

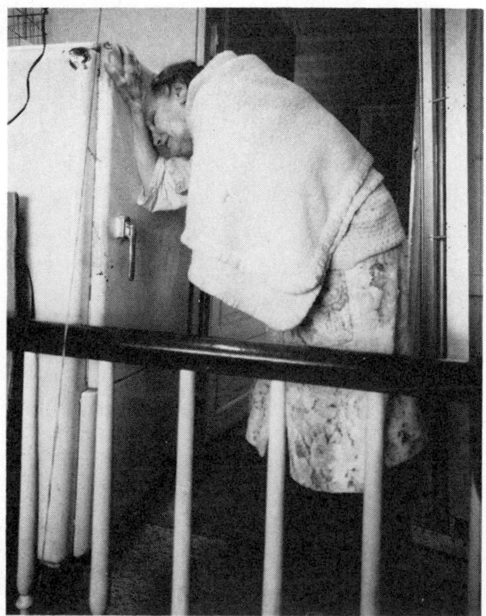

The attitude of this woman's body eloquently testifies to the loss of energy and sense of isolation that accompany a major depression.

If so, you are not alone. Depression has been called "the common cold" of psychological disorders—an expression that well states its pervasiveness, but not its seriousness. Studies in the United States and Europe suggest that at some time during their lives 5 to 10 percent of men and twice that many women will suffer a major depressive episode. The line between life's normal ups and downs and major depression is difficult to define. Joy, contentment, sadness, and despair are different points on a continuum, points at which any of us may be found at any given moment. Depression can be an appropriate response to profoundly sad events, such as to a significant loss or bereavement. It is when signs of depression (poor appetite, insomnia, lethargy, feelings of worthlessness, or loss of interest in family, friends, and fun activities) last two weeks or more without there being any discernible cause that the depressed mood is likely to be diagnosed as major depression.

"My life had come to a sudden stop. I was able to breathe, to eat, to drink, to sleep. I could not, indeed, help doing so; but there was no real life in me."
Leo Tolstoy,
My Confession, 1887

Suicide

> But life, being weary of these worldly bars, Never lacks power to dismiss itself.
>
> William Shakespeare,
> *Julius Caesar*, 1599

This year in the United States, some 25 to 30 thousand wearied, despairing, and sometimes angry people will say no to life. In retrospect, their family and friends may recall signs that they believe should have forewarned them—the suicidal talk, the giving away of possessions, or the withdrawal and preoccupation with death. Perhaps a third will have already tried suicide before.

Preventing suicide is difficult; suicidal people often do not give unambiguous warnings of their intentions. But for those who do seek help in a moment of crisis, the suicide hotline worker can often mean the difference between life and death.

Actually, few of those who think suicidal thoughts actually attempt suicide, and few of these succeed in killing themselves. But some do. To see who commits suicide, researchers have compared the suicide rates of different groups (see Figure 16-4). National differences are puzzling: The suicide rates of Ireland and Israel are half that in the United States; those of Austria, Denmark, and Switzerland are nearly double (*Statistical Abstract of the United States: 1985*). Racial differences are intriguing: In the United States whites kill themselves twice as often as blacks. Personal differences are suggestive: Suicide rates have tended to be higher among the rich, the irreligious, and the unmarried (including the widowed and divorced—Stengel, 1981). Gender differences are dramatic: Women are much more likely than men to attempt suicide, but, depending on the country, men are two to three times more likely to succeed. (Men are more likely to use methods sure to succeed, such as putting a bullet into the brain.)

Bear in mind that all these links with suicide are correlations, for which cause and effect is uncertain.

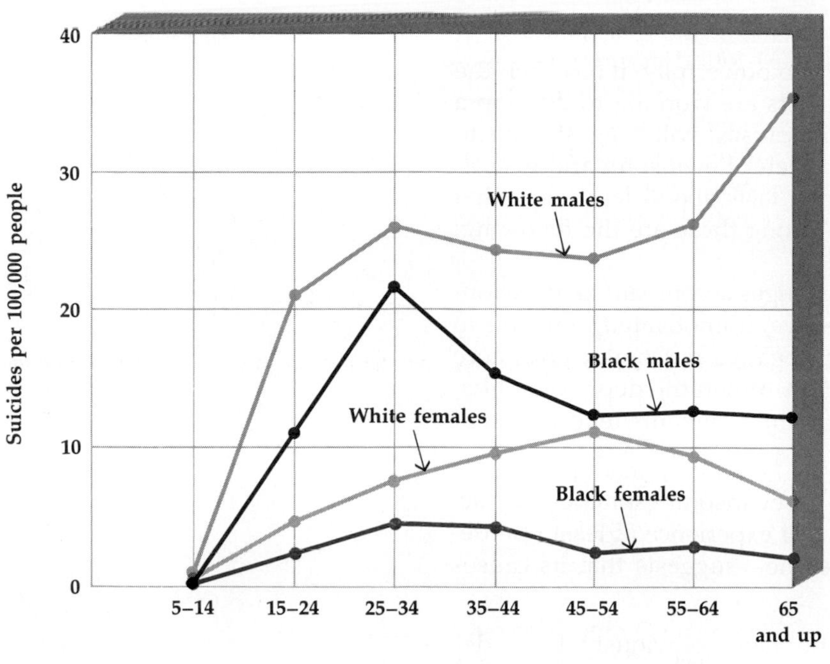

Figure 16-4 *In the United States, suicide rates are higher among whites than blacks, and males than females.*

It is important to know that suicide often occurs not in the depths of depression, when the person may lack energy and initiative, but rather when the person begins to rebound. In the elderly, it is sometimes chosen as an alternative to future suffering. Social suggestion may also play a role: Known suicides as well as fatal auto "accidents" and private airplane crashes increase following highly publicized suicides, even those on soap operas (Phillips, 1982).

Bipolar Disorder

After days, weeks, or months, depressive episodes usually are self-terminating. Depressed people nearly always rebound—usually by returning to normal. However, some people rebound to the opposite emotional extreme—to a euphoric, hyperactive state called mania. People who alternate between depression and mania are said to suffer from bipolar disorder. If the depression they experience is like living in slow motion, the mania is like a speeded-up movie. During the mania phase of a bipolar disorder, the person is typically overtalkative, elated (except easily irritated if crossed), needing little sleep, and sexually uninhibited. Speech is loud, flighty, and hard to interrupt. One of the most maladaptive symptoms of mania is that the person's grandiose optimism and inflated self-esteem may lead to reckless spending and investment sprees. Thus, like other disordered people, manic individuals may need to be protected from the consequences of their own poor judgments; yet they will be irritated at those who try to provide guidance or advice.

It is true of emotions as of other things: what goes up generally comes down. Before long, the mood either returns to normal or plunges into a brief depression. Though equally as maladaptive as depression, bipolar disorder is much less common, occurring in about 1 percent of both men and women.

Explaining Depression

Because depression affects so many people so powerfully, it has been the subject of thousands of studies. Psychologists are working to develop a theory of depression that, by explaining its causes, will suggest ways to treat or prevent it. Depression researchers Peter Lewinsohn and his colleagues (1985) have summarized the known facts about depression that any theory of depression must explain. Among these are the following:

1. Many behavioral and cognitive changes accompany depression. Depressed people tend to be inactive, unmotivated, sensitive to negative happenings, expecting negative outcomes, and more likely to recall negative information. When the depression lifts, these behavioral and cognitive accompaniments tend to disappear.
2. The commonality of depression—Lewinsohn estimates that actually 25 percent or more of us will experience at least one depressive episode during our lifetime—suggests that its causes must be common.
3. Females, especially females who have previously been depressed, are at greatest risk for depression.
4. Most depressive episodes last less than 3 months, and most people return to normal without professional assistance.
5. Stressful events related to work, marriage, and close relationships tend to precede depression.

As might be expected, researchers understand and interpret these facts in ways that reflect their different perspectives.

The Psychoanalytic Perspective

As we noted in Chapter 15, Freud assumed the importance of early childhood experiences and of unconscious feelings and impulses. The psychoanalytic theory of depression applies these assumptions. It suggests that depression in adulthood can be triggered by significant losses that evoke feelings associated with earlier losses experienced in childhood. For example, loss of a romantic relationship or job might evoke feelings associated with the loss of the intimate relationship with one's mother. Unresolved anger toward one's parents is also a factor, Freud believed. Some losses, such as the death of a loved one, may evoke the anger once felt toward parents who were similarly "abandoning" or "rejecting." Since such anger is unacceptable to the superego, the emotion may be turned inward against the self. The net result of this reaction to loss and internalized anger is said to be depression.

"Pain of mind is worse than pain of body."
Publius Syrus,
Sententiae, 43 B.C.

The Biological Perspective

Some of the most exciting new research on psychological disorders explores their possible physiological bases. It has long been known that the affective disorders run in families. The available data suggest that if an identical twin is diagnosed as having a bipolar disorder, the chances are nearly 3 in 4 that the other twin will at some point be similarly diagnosed; if an identical twin is diagnosed as suffering a major depression, the chances are about 40 percent that sometime the other twin will be, too. Among fraternal twins, the corresponding odds are not greater than 10 to

15 percent (Allen, 1976). We must remember the familiar cautions about interpreting twin similarities, since identical twins tend also to share quite similar environments. Nevertheless, the twin studies hint that genetic influences contribute to a risk of depression.

As we noted in Chapter 2, "Biological Roots of Behavior," genes act by directing biochemical events that, down the line, influence behavior. Through what biochemical processes might genes predispose affective disorders? Recall that some of the body's most important biochemicals are the mind's messenger molecules—the neurotransmitters that shuttle signals between nerve cells. These biochemicals have been implicated in depression. For example, norepinephrine, a neurotransmitter that increases arousal and boosts mood, appears to be overabundant during mania and in short supply during depression. Drugs that alleviate mania tend to reduce norepinephrine; drugs that relieve depression tend to increase norepinephrine (Bootzin & Acocella, 1984). This hints that keeping norepinephrine within normal bounds might be one way to alleviate depression.

Other biochemical links with depression are emerging. For example, researchers are studying the role of the neurotransmitters serotonin and acetylcholine. The hope is that it may soon be possible to identify people likely to experience affective disorders and to take steps to reduce that risk by psychological interventions or by counteracting the disorder's biological underpinnings.

Drawings by Charles Shultz; © 1956 United Feature Syndicate, Inc.

The Cognitive-Learning Perspective

Biological factors do not operate in a vacuum; they are correlated with psychological reactions to particular experiences. In recent years some of the most exciting research in the psychology of depression has come from psychologists of the cognitive-learning perspective. Cognitive psychologists claim that depression is linked with negative perceptions, beliefs, and thoughts. For example, psychiatrist Aaron Beck's (1982) work with depressed patients convinced him that depression is linked with *self-defeating beliefs*. Depressed people view life as if through dark-colored glasses. Their intensely negative assumptions about themselves, their situations, and their futures lead them to magnify bad experiences and minimize good ones. As one occasionally depressed young woman put it (Burns, 1980, pp. 28–29):

> My thoughts become negative and pessimistic. As I look into the past, I become convinced that everything that I've ever done is worthless. Any happy period seems like an illusion. My accomplishments appear as genuine as the false facade of a Western movie. I become convinced that the real me is worthless and inadequate. I can't move forward with my work because I become frozen with doubt.

Self-defeating beliefs may arise from *learned helplessness*. As we saw in Chapter 15, both dogs and humans act depressed, passive, and withdrawn after experiencing uncontrollable events that persuade them that their actions are futile. Society has more often rendered women helpless to control their lives than men, which helps to explain why women—especially traditional, "feminine" women—have been twice as vulnerable to depression as men (Baucom & Danker-Brown, 1984).

"He is desperate that thinks himself so."
Thomas Fuller,
Gnomologia, 1732

But why do life's unavoidable failures lead some people to become depressed—and not others? The difference lies partly with people's *attributions* of blame (Abramson & others, 1978). The fact is that we have some choice in whom or what we blame for our failures. If you fail a test and blame it on yourself, you may conclude that you are stupid and feel very depressed. However, if you attribute your failure to an unfair test, you are more likely to feel angry. In study after study, depressed people have been more likely to blame themselves for failures and negative experiences (Coyne & Gotlib, 1983). When something goes wrong they are more likely to overgeneralize—to doubt their ability to do well at anything or to disparage themselves after making a single mistake (Carver & Ganellen, 1983). Moreover, unlike most people (who tend to exhibit the "self-serving bias"—see Chapter 15), the depressed do not overestimate others' judgments of them or their own successes at controlling events (Martin & others, 1984). They have fewer illusions. As researchers Lauren Alloy and Lyn Abramson (1979) put it, they are "sadder but wiser."

"I have learned to accept my mistakes by referring them to a personal history which was not of my making."
B. F. Skinner (1983)

"A key to avoiding depression is to see oneself less stringently and more favorably than others see one."
Peter M. Lewinsohn and others (1980)

There is, however, a chicken-and-egg problem with the cognitive explanation of depression. Self-blame and negative attributions surely do support depression, but do they cause it? Depression researcher Peter Lewinsohn and his colleagues (1985) noted that such cognitions are *indicators,* not predictors, of depression. Depressing thoughts coincide with, but do not precede, a depressed mood; before or after being depressed, people's thoughts are normal. Perhaps this is because, as we noted in earlier chapters, a depressed mood triggers negative thoughts. If you temporarily put people in a bad or sad mood, their memories, judgments, and expectations are suddenly more pessimistic. This is strikingly illustrated in one recent experiment (Forgas & others, 1984). After being put in a temporary good or bad mood via hypnosis, the subjects watched a videotape of themselves (made the day before) in which they interacted with someone. The happy subjects detected in themselves more instances of positive than negative behavior; the depressed subjects, on the other hand, more often saw themselves behaving negatively (see Figure 16-5). Thus even when viewing themselves on videotape, people judge themselves more negatively when they are feeling depressed.

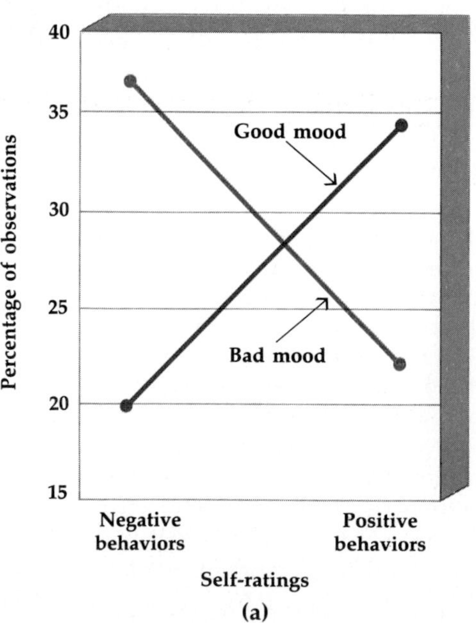

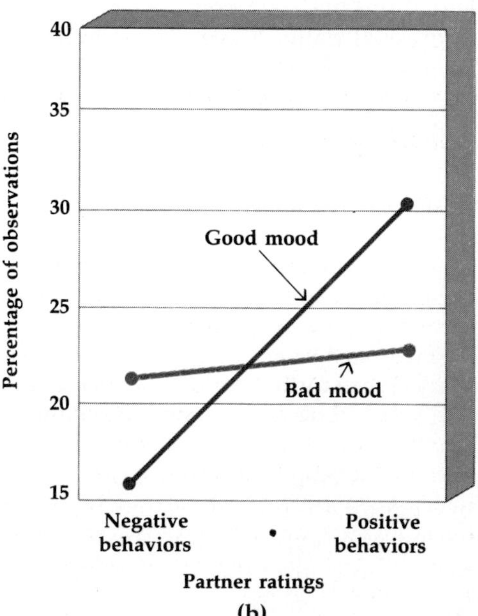

Figure 16-5 *A happy or depressed mood strongly influences people's rating of both (a) their own and (b) others' behavior. In a recent experiment, those in a hypnotically induced good mood detected many more positive than negative behaviors. The reverse was true for those in a bad mood.*

Lewinsohn concluded that depression is often brought on by aversive experiences—losing one's job, being criticized, suffering marital discord, and so forth. When unable to cope with such stresses, people tend to become self-focused (Pyszczynski & Greenberg, 1985). Their brooding over their problems may produce self-blame and a depressed mood, which in turn triggers all the other cognitive and behavioral symptoms of depression. Moreover, being withdrawn, passive, and complaining tends to elicit more social rejection. In one study, researchers Stephen Strack and James Coyne (1983) observed that "depressed persons induced hostility, depression, and anxiety in others and got rejected. Their guesses that they were not accepted were not a matter of cognitive distortion." In everyday life, the spouse may threaten to leave or the boss may begin to question the person's competence.

"Man never reasons so much and becomes so introspective as when he suffers, since he is anxious to get at the cause of his sufferings."
Luigi Pirandello,
Six Characters in Search of an Author, 1922

Lewinsohn believes that a vicious cycle of depression can help fit together the pieces of the depression puzzle: (1) the negative experiences that trigger (2) the self-preoccupation and self-blame that create (3) the depressed mood that drastically changes (4) the way the person thinks and acts, which, in turn, fuels (back to 1) more negative experiences (Figure 16-6). On the brighter side, one can break the cycle of depression at any of these points—by engaging in more pleasant activities and more competent behavior, by turning one's attention outward, by moving to a different environment, or by reversing one's self-blame and negative attributions. The fact that there are several points at which the cycle can be broken helps explain why several different therapy methods have been found effective and why depression is usually of relatively short duration.

It also explains why human beings are not necessarily defeated by depression, poison though it is to the human spirit. Winston Churchill called it a "black dog" that periodically hounded him. Poet Emily Dickinson was so afraid of bursting into tears that she spent much of her adult life in seclusion (Patterson, 1951). Abraham Lincoln was so withdrawn and brooding as a young man that his friends feared he might take his own life (Kline, 1974). Yet, as each of these lives remind us, people can and do struggle out of depression and regain their capacity to love, to work, and even to succeed at the highest levels.

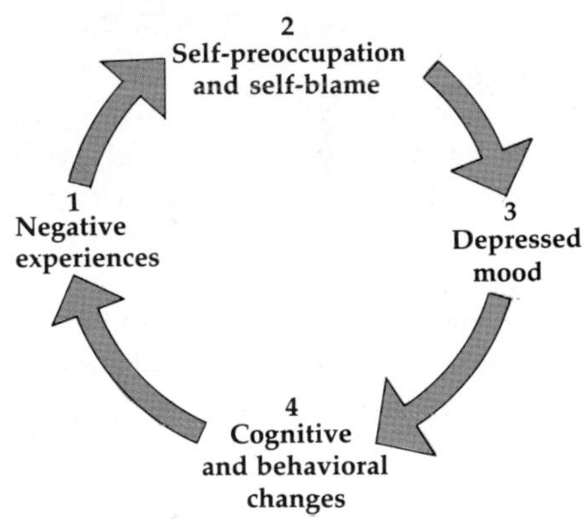

Figure 16-6 *The vicious cycle of depression.*

Loneliness

Loneliness—the painful awareness that one's social relationships are deficient—is both a cause of depression and a problem in itself. The deficiency stems from a mismatch between one's social contacts and one's desire for contact. Thus, one person may feel lonely when isolated, while another may feel lonely in a crowd (Peplau & Perlman, 1982).

College students commonly experience one or more of four types of loneliness (Beck & Young, 1978). To be lonely is to feel *excluded* from a group you would like to belong to; to feel *unloved* and uncared about by those around you; to feel *constricted* and unable to share your private concerns with anyone; or to feel *alienated,* or different from, those in your community. Like depressed people, lonely people tend to blame themselves, attributing their deficient social relationships to their own inadequacies (Anderson & others, 1983). There may be a basis for this self-blame: Chronically lonely people tend to be shy, self-conscious, and lacking in self-esteem. They often find it hard to introduce themselves, make phone calls, and participate in groups (Rook, 1984). In addition, their belief in their social unworthiness tends to restrict them from taking steps that would reduce their loneliness. Thus it seems that many of the factors that work to create and maintain depression can also produce loneliness.

SCHIZOPHRENIC DISORDERS

The odds are 1 in 100 that a given individual will become schizophrenic. Those who do join the millions who have suffered one of humanity's most dreaded disorders. It is a ***psychotic disorder,*** a disorder in which a person loses contact with reality by experiencing grossly irrational ideas and distorted perceptions. Schizophrenia is a devastating ailment that typically strikes an adolescent or young adult (it affects the two sexes about equally). Although it tends to be diagnosed more frequently in the lower socioeconomic classes, it knows no national boundaries (World Health Organization, 1979).

Symptoms of Schizophrenia

Schizophrenia literally translated means "split mind." The split is not a Dr. Jekyll and Mr. Hyde type of multiple-personality split, but rather a split from reality that shows itself in disorganized thinking, disturbed perceptions, and inappropriate emotions and actions.

Disorganized Thinking

Imagine trying to communicate with a young woman, Sylvia Frumkin, whose thoughts spill out in no logical order. Her biographer, Susan Sheehan (1982, p. 25), caught her saying aloud to no one in particular,

> "This morning, when I was at Hillside [Hospital], I was making a movie. I was surrounded by movie stars. The X-ray technician was Peter Lawford. The security guard was Don Knotts. That Indian doctor in Building 40 was Lou Costello. I'm Mary Poppins. Is this room painted blue to get me upset? My grandmother died four weeks after my eighteenth birthday." Miss Frumkin laughed.

As this strange monologue illustrates, the schizophrenic's thinking is fragmented, bizarre, and distorted by false beliefs, called ***delusions*** ("I'm Mary Poppins"). The jumping from one idea to another may even occur within sentences, creating a sort of "word salad," as in the case of the young man who begged for "a little more allegro in the treatment," and who suggested that "liberationary movement with a view to the widening of the horizon," will "ergo extort some wit in lectures."

The causes of schizophrenia are not well understood. However, many psychologists believe that the disorganized thoughts arise from a breakdown in the normal human capacity for selective attention. As we noted in Chapter 7, "Perception," we normally have a remarkable capacity for selective attention—for, say, giving our undivided attention to one voice at a party while filtering out all the other sensory stimuli. Schizophrenics seem to have impaired attention (Gjerde, 1983). Thus, they are easily distracted by an irrelevant stimulus or an extraneous part of the preceding thought. As one former schizophrenic patient recalled, "What had happened to me in Toronto was a breakdown in the filter, and a hodge-podge of unrelated stimuli were distracting me from things which should have had my undivided attention" (MacDonald, 1960, p. 218).

Disturbed Perceptions

The schizophrenic's experience of the world is altered. Minute stimuli, such as the grooves on a brick or the inflections of a voice, may distract attention, disrupting the person's perception of the whole scene or of the speaker's meaning. Worse, the person may perceive things that are not there.

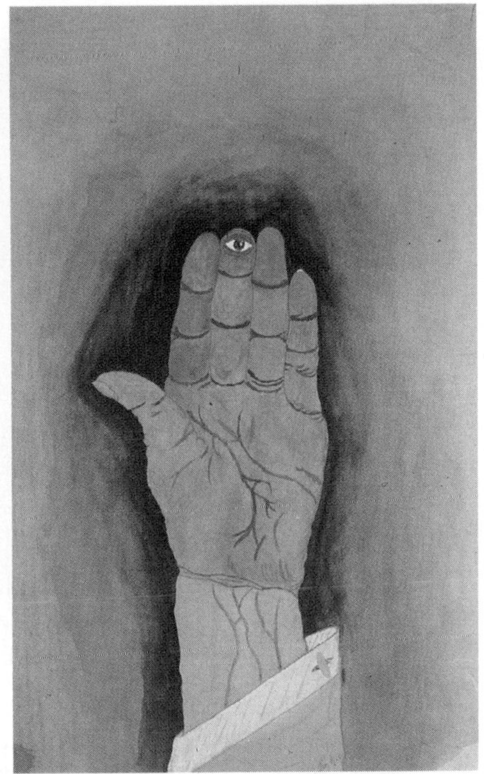

In reviewing a showing of works by mentally ill artists like those above, poet John Ashbery wrote: "The lure of the work is strong, but so is the terror of the unanswerable riddles it proposes."

Hallucinations (sensory experiences without sensory stimulation) are most commonly auditory. The person may hear voices that seem to come from outside the head and which make insulting statements or give orders. The voices may, for example, tell the patient that she is bad or that he must burn himself with a cigarette lighter. Less commonly, people may see, feel, taste, or smell things that are not there. Such hallucinations have been likened to dreams breaking into waking consciousness. The unreal has become real, and the resulting perceptions are at best bizarre and at worst terrifying.

Inappropriate Emotions and Actions

The emotions of people with schizophrenia are often utterly inappropriate to what they have said or heard. Sylvia Frumkin's emotions seemed split off from reality; she laughed after recalling her grandmother's death. On other occasions, she would become angry for no apparent reason or cry when others would laugh. In other cases, schizophrenics sometimes lapse into a flat, zombie-like state of emotionless apathy.

Motor behavior also tends to be inappropriate. The person may perform senseless repetitive acts, such as rocking or rubbing an arm for hours on end, or may remain motionless.

Needless to say, disorganized thinking, disturbed perceptions, and inappropriate emotions and actions disrupt normal social relationships. During their worst periods, schizophrenics often live in a private inner world, preoccupied with illogical ideas and unreal images. Indeed, some schizophrenics remain socially withdrawn and isolated throughout much of their lives.

Types of Schizophrenia

We have described schizophrenia as if it were a single disorder. Actually, it is a cluster of disorders that have common features but also some distinguishing symptoms. For example, some schizophrenic patients are disorganized and deluded in their talk, others are mute and rigid. The distinc-

Schizophrenics during their worst periods often withdraw into an inner world of bizarre thoughts and disturbed perceptions. Their inappropriate behaviors demonstrate their loss of contact with reality.

tions among the schizophrenic disorders listed in Table 16-1 are hazy. Nevertheless, we should not think of schizophrenia simplistically, as one disorder for which there is one set of causes.

Table 16-1 **Types of schizophrenia**

Type	Characteristics
Disorganized	Incoherent speech and inappropriate, often silly, emotion. The individual may be extremely withdrawn and behavior may include odd grimaces and mannerisms.
Catatonic	Bizarre physical movements, ranging from motionless stupor to violent hyperactivity and sometimes alternating between these two extremes.
Paranoid	Delusions of persecution or grandeur. The individual may trust no one and may be anxious or angry about supposed tormentors.
Undifferentiated	Delusions, hallucinations, and incoherence typical of schizophrenia; however, the individual does not neatly fit any of the other types.

Sometimes, as in the case of Sylvia Frumkin, schizophrenia develops gradually, emerging from a long history of social inadequacy (which partially explains why those predisposed to schizophrenia often end up in the lower socioeconomic levels, or even as homeless street people). At other times, it appears more suddenly, seemingly as a reaction to stress. For example, shortly after his parents split up, and after his girlfriend took off with another man and his father became "outlandishly famous," Mark Vonnegut (1975), son of the writer Kurt Vonnegut, suffered a schizophrenic disorder. There is a rule of thumb that holds true across the world (World Health Organization, 1979): The more rapidly the disorder develops and the better the person's prior adjustment, the brighter the chances for recovery. After his schizophrenic condition lifted, Mark Vonnegut was able to enter medical school (Gorman, 1984).

Understanding Schizophrenia

Schizophrenia is not only the most dreaded psychological disorder but also the most heavily researched. Some of the most important new discoveries have linked schizophrenia with biological factors.

Biochemical Factors

The idea that biochemical imbalances might underlie schizophrenia has intrigued scientists for a long while. After all, strange behaviors have been known to be caused by chemicals. The saying "mad as a hatter" refers to the experience of British hatmakers who, it was later discovered, were being slowly poisoned as they moistened the brims of mercury-laden felt hats with their lips (Smith, 1983). Other chemicals, such as LSD, are known to create hallucinations. Such discoveries have increased the hope that a biochemical key to schizophrenia might be found.

The search has turned up many leads, some of which have turned out to be false. One researcher may discover an abnormality in the blood or urine of a group of schizophrenics. Upon further investigation the abnormality may turn out to be a product of the hospital diet, or perhaps a *consequence* of the disorder itself or its treatment with drugs.

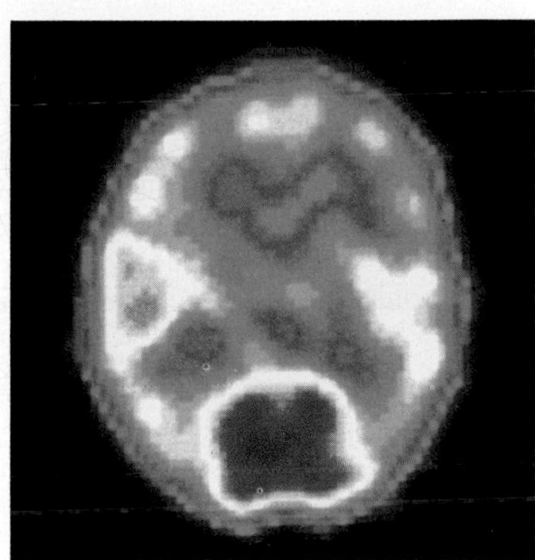

Large green areas near the top of this PET scan of a schizophrenic patient's brain indicate abnormally low levels of metabolism in the frontal lobes.

Nevertheless, the process of debate and testing by which science sifts truth from falsehood has identified neurotransmitter abnormalities that seem involved in some types of schizophrenia. For example, when the brain tissue of schizophrenic patients is examined after death, it has been found to have a higher than normal density of receptors for the neurotransmitter ***dopamine*** (Seeman & others, 1984). Moreover, drugs that block receptors for dopamine often alleviate schizophrenic symptoms; drugs that increase dopamine levels sometimes exacerbate schizophrenic symptoms (S. Snyder, 1984b). One speculation is that the schizophrenics' dopamine overactivity may be what makes them overreactive to (and distracted by) irrelevant external and internal stimuli.

Modern techniques of scanning the brain have revealed that many chronic schizophrenics have a detectable brain abnormality, such as a shrinkage of cerebral tissue or an abnormal pattern of brain metabolism (Seidman, 1983). Patients with diminished brain tissue tend also to have less of an enzyme that converts dopamine to norepinephrine, thereby providing another hint that excess dopamine may be linked with schizophrenia (van Kammen & others, 1983).

Genetic Factors

Naturally, scientists wonder whether the biochemical abnormalities associated with schizophrenia are inherited. The evidence strongly suggests that there is a genetic predisposition to schizophrenia. The 100 to 1 odds against any person's being diagnosed schizophrenic rise to 10 to 1 among those who have a schizophrenic sibling or parent, and 50–50 among those who have an identical twin who has been diagnosed schizophrenic (Figure 16-7). Moreover, although there are only a dozen relevant cases, it appears that an identical twin of a schizophrenic is about as likely to become schizophrenic whether reared with or apart from the schizophrenic twin. Adoption studies also suggest a genetic link (Faraone & Tsuang, 1985). Children of nonschizophrenics who are adopted by someone who becomes schizophrenic are unlikely to "catch" the disorder; but those adopted by nonschizophrenics do suffer an elevated risk of developing the disorder if they have a biological parent who is schizophrenic.

"It is a common observation that men born of parents that are sometimes wont to be mad, will be obnoxious to the same disease."
Thomas Willis, 1685

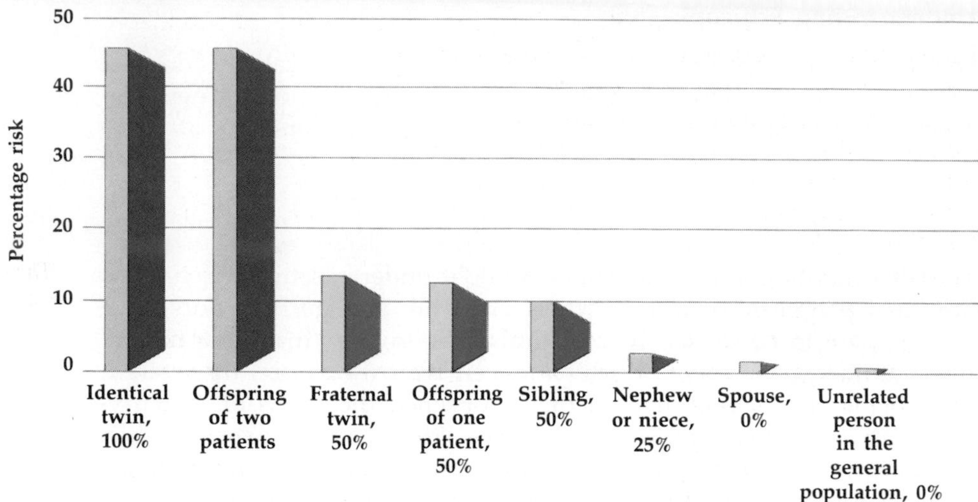

Figure 16-7 *The lifetime risks of being diagnosed schizophrenic are linked with one's genetic relatedness to someone already found to be schizophrenic.*

All in all, a genetic contribution to schizophrenia seems indisputable. Still, the genetic role is not so straightforward as it is in the inheritance of tongue-rolling ability, for example. After all, half the identical twins whose twins are schizophrenics do *not* develop the disorder. Thus, behavior geneticists Susan Nicol and Irvin Gottesman (1983) believe that some people "have a genetic predisposition to the disorder but that this predisposition by itself is not sufficient for the development of schizophrenia."

Psychological Factors

If, by themselves, genetic factors do not cause schizophrenia, neither do psychological factors. Nicol and Gottesman reported that "no environmental causes have been discovered that will invariably, or even with moderate probability, produce schizophrenia in persons who are not related to a schizophrenic."

Nevertheless, if genes predispose some people to *react* to particular experiences by developing a schizophrenic disorder, then there must be identifiable triggering experiences. Researchers have asked: Could schizophrenia be brought on by stress, such as that experienced by Mark Vonnegut? Could it be initiated by difficulties in family communications?

The odds of all four identical quadruplets being diagnosed as schizophrenic are 1 in 2 billion. But Nora, Iris, Myra, and Hester Genain, shown here at their 51st birthday party, were. Problems for the sisters began in high school. Since then they have been in and out of hospitals. Of course, these women share not only identical genes but also similar environments, and have done so from the moment of conception.

The answer to each is perhaps. The psychological triggers of schizophrenia have proved somewhat elusive (partly because they may vary with the type of schizophrenic disorder and whether it is a slow-developing, chronic schizophrenia, or a more sudden reaction to stress). It is true that schizophrenic young people tend to have disturbed communications with their parents; but is this a cause or a result of their disorder? It is true that stressful experiences, biochemical abnormalities, and schizophrenic symptoms often occur together; but since the traffic between brain biochemistry and psychological experiences is two-way, cause and effect are difficult to sort out.

"The cause is hidden. The effect is known."
Ovid, 43 B.C.–A.D. 17

In hopes of identifying the psychological triggers of schizophrenia, several investigators are now following "high risk" children, such as those born to a schizophrenic parent, as they grow and develop (Watt & others, 1984). By comparing the experiences of those who become schizophrenic with the experiences of high- and low-risk children who do not, these researchers hope to spot the early warning signs of schizophrenia and the environments that are most likely to worsen the condition. Preliminary results indicate that children who become schizophrenic are more likely than those who do not to have a mother whose schizophrenia was severe and long-lasting, to have had complications at birth, to have been separated from their parents, and to have created disturbances in school.

Most of us can relate to the ups and downs of the affective disorders. With the strange thoughts, perceptions, and behaviors of the schizophrenic we find it much harder to identify. Sometimes our thoughts do jump around, but we do not talk nonsensically. Occasionally we feel unjustly suspicious of someone, but we do not fear that the world is plotting against us. Often our visual perceptions are distorted, but rarely do we see things that are not there. We have felt regret after laughing at someone's misfortune, but generally we do not giggle in response to bad news. From time to time we just want to be alone, but we do not live in social isolation. However, millions of people across the world do talk strangely, suffer delusions of persecution, hear nonexistent voices, see things that are not there, giggle and cry at inappropriate times, or withdraw into their imaginary private world. So long as this is true the quest to solve the cruel puzzle of schizophrenia will continue.

PERSONALITY DISORDERS

If the medical model makes the most sense when considering the schizophrenic disorders, it probably makes the least sense when considering maladaptive personality traits. And that is why DSM-III groups ***personality disorders*** separately from those we have so far considered. Personality disorders are character problems that sometimes coexist with one of the other disorders we have discussed, but that need not involve any apparent anxiety, depression, or loss of contact with reality.

For society, the most troubling of these disorders is the ***antisocial personality*** disorder. The person (formerly called a sociopath or a psychopath) is typically a man whose lack of conscience appears before age 15, with lying, stealing, fighting, truancy, or unrestrained sexual behavior. In adulthood, additional problems may include the inability to keep a job, irresponsible marital and parental behavior, and a record of assaults and other criminal behaviors. When the antisocial personality combines a keen intelligence with remorseless amorality, the result may be a charming and clever con artist.

Does a full moon trigger "madness" in some people? James Rotton and I. W. Kelley (1985) examined data from 37 studies that related lunar phase to crime, homicides, crisis calls, and mental hospital admissions. Their conclusion: There is virtually no evidence of "moon madness."

Most convicted criminals have exhibited antisocial behavior, but few fit the description of antisocial personality. For example, most criminals show some responsible concern for their friends and family members; the antisocial personality seems to have feeling for no one and to fear almost nothing. They do not accept rules, maintain enduring relationships, or honor financial obligations. In extreme cases, the results can be tragic. Henry Lee Lucas reported that at age 13 he strangled a woman who refused him sex. He admits to having bludgeoned, suffocated, stabbed, shot, or mutilated some 360 women, men, and children over the ensuing 32 years; nearly half the killings have been verified. During the last 6 years of his reign of terror, Lucas teamed with Elwood Toole, who slaughtered about 50 people whom he "didn't think was worth living anyhow." It ended when Lucas confessed to stabbing and dismembering his 15-year-old common-law wife, who was Toole's niece.

The antisocial personality expresses little remorse over violating others' rights. "Once I've done a crime, I just forget it," said Lucas. Toole was equally matter of fact: "I think of killing like smoking a cigarette, like another habit" (Darrach & Norris, 1984).

As with depression and schizophrenia, the antisocial personality is apparently woven of biological and psychological strands. Researchers have found that when antisocial persons await electric shocks or loud noises, they show much less autonomic nervous system arousal than do normal people (Hare, 1975). Such fearlessness may be genetically predisposed. Although most convicted criminals would not be diagnosed as antisocial personalities, some are, and so it is intriguing that the biological children of convicted criminals are more likely than other children to commit property crimes—even if adopted at an early age by noncriminal parents (Mednick & others, 1984; see Figure 16-8). The hope is that if children at greater risk for criminal behavior could be identified, perhaps with the aid of biological tests, then maybe they could be guided toward occupations that have the element of excitement that such people often crave.

Experience forms the other strand. If reared without consistent parental warmth and involvement, a child is less likely to develop internal moral standards. Thus, even if some people are indeed genetically predisposed to be more fearless than others, their experiences will influence whether they become, say, a cool test pilot, a war hero, or a cool and cunning criminal (Mednick, 1985).

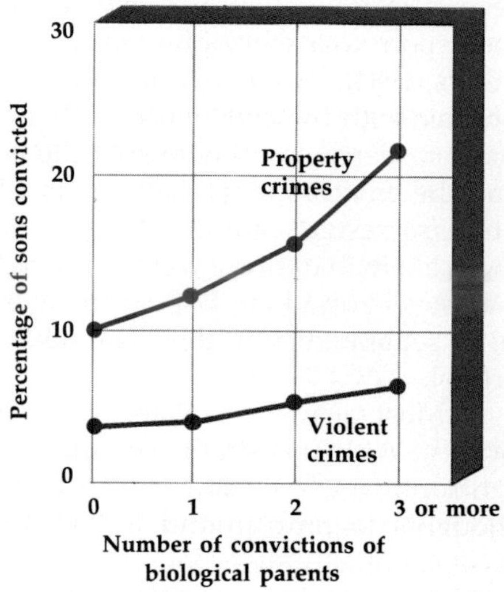

Percentage of sons convicted
30
20
10
0
Property crimes
Violent crimes
0 1 2 3 or more
Number of convictions of biological parents

Figure 16-8 *Genetic influence on criminal convictions. Court data from 14,427 adoptees (who grew up in the homes of parents without criminal records) and their biological parents reveal a significant correlation between the number of the biological parents' criminal convictions and those of their sons for property crimes.*

SHOULD PEOPLE BE LABELED? THE POWER OF PRECONCEPTIONS

As we noted earlier, the practice of attaching diagnostic labels to people has provoked controversy. With broad categories (such as the distinction between the affective and schizophrenic disorders) one psychiatrist's or psychologist's diagnoses will, more often than not, agree with another's. It is with the more specific diagnoses (such as disorganized versus undifferentiated schizophrenia) that the labels are applied less reliably. Critics say that the labels are at best arbitrary and at worst a value judgment that, thanks to the medical model, masquerades as science.

Despite the uncertainty of diagnostic labels, most clinicians believe that classification helps in describing, treating, and researching the causes of disorders. The critics respond that these benefits come at a cost. Once a

"There is a purpose to psychiatric diagnosis. It is to enable mental health professionals to (a) communicate with each other about the subject matter of their concern, (b) comprehend the pathological processes involved in psychiatric illness, and (c) control psychiatric outcomes."
Robert L. Spitzer (1975)

diagnostic label is attached to someone, we are almost sure to see the person differently (Farina, 1982). Labels create preconceptions that, as we have seen in earlier chapters, can bias our perceptions and interpretations.

In the most controversial demonstration of the biasing power of diagnostic labels, David Rosenhan (1973) and seven of his friends and Stanford University colleagues went to mental hospital admissions offices, complaining of "hearing voices" that were saying "empty," "hollow," and "thud." Apart from this complaint and giving false names and occupations, they truthfully answered all questions. All eight were diagnosed as psychotic, seven of them schizophrenic.

"One of the unpardonable sins, in the eyes of most people, is for a man to go about unlabelled. The world regards such a person as the police do an unmuzzled dog, not under proper control."
T. H. Huxley,
Evolution and Ethics, 1893

That these actually normal people were misdiagnosed is not surprising. As one psychiatrist noted, if someone swallowed some blood, went to an emergency room, and spit it up, would we fault the doctor for diagnosing a bleeding ulcer? More startling was the fact that although the "patients" exhibited no further symptoms after being admitted, the clinicians were able to "discover" the causes of their disorders after analyzing their (quite normal) life histories. One person was said to be reacting to mixed emotions regarding his parents. Furthermore, before being released (an average of 19 days later) the "patients' " normal behaviors, such as note-taking, were often overlooked or misinterpreted as symptoms of their disorder.

Other studies confirm that a label can affect what we see in someone. In several studies, Ellen Langer and her colleagues (1974, 1980) had people evaluate someone they thought was either normal (such as a job applicant) or out of the ordinary (such as a psychiatric patient or a cancer patient). In each experiment, all subjects were shown the identical videotape. Nevertheless, interviewers who carried no special label were perceived as normal people, while those who had been labeled were much more likely to be perceived by lay people as "different from most people," or by the therapists who thought they were evaluating a patient as "frightened of his own aggressive impulses," "passive, dependent type," and so forth. Thus, while a label can serve a purpose, it can, as Rosenhan discovered, have "a life and an influence of its own."

Labels can also affect people's self-images and stigmatize them in others' eyes. Senator Thomas Eagleton experienced this when, in 1972, he was dumped as the U.S. Democratic Party's vice-presidential candidate after it was discovered that he had been treated for being (gasp) depressed. The same stigma was revealed when a female associate of psychologist Stewart Page (1977) called 180 people in Toronto who had advertised furnished rooms for rent. Sometimes she merely asked if the room was still available, and the answer was nearly always yes. At other times, when she said that she was about to be released from a mental hospital, the answer 3 times out of 4 was no (as it was, incidentally, when she said she was calling for her brother who was about to be released from jail). When a sample of those who answered no was called by a second person who simply asked if the rooms were still available, the advertisers nearly always revealed that indeed they still were.

We need not romanticize psychological disorders to be encouraged by the fact that not only Thomas Eagleton but many others before him—including Leonardo da Vinci, Isaac Newton, and Leo Tolstoy—have endured psychological difficulties while pursuing brilliant careers. One needs only talk to the many families that have been plunged into bewilderment, fear, and sorrow to realize that the suffering is real. But, as we will see in the next chapter, so is the hope.

"Where there's life, there's hope."
Cicero,
Ad Atticum, 49 B.C.

SUMMING UP

PERSPECTIVES ON PSYCHOLOGICAL DISORDERS

Defining Psychological Disorders The line between normality and abnormality is usually drawn based on a variety of criteria, such as how atypical, undesirable, maladaptive, and unjustifiable a person's behavior is. Insanity, on the other hand, is a legal term that is now applied in rare cases where defendants are judged not to have known that what they were doing was wrong.

Understanding Psychological Disorders The medical model's assumption that psychological disorders are mental illnesses has displaced earlier views that demons and evil spirits were to blame. However, critics question the medical model's association of psychological disorders with physical sicknesses.

Classifying Psychological Disorders Many psychiatrists and psychologists believe that naming and describing psychological disorders facilitates treatment and research. In the United States the third edition of the *Diagnostic and Statistical Manual of Mental Disorders (DSM-III)* is the authoritative classification scheme.

ANXIETY DISORDERS

Persons suffering an anxiety disorder may for no apparent reason feel uncontrollably tense and uneasy (generalized anxiety disorder), or irrationally afraid of a specific object or situation (phobic disorder), or troubled by repetitive thoughts and actions (obsessive-compulsive disorder).

SOMATOFORM DISORDERS

The somatoform disorders involve a somatic (bodily) symptom—a physiologically unexplained but genuinely felt ailment. Of these, Freud was particularly fascinated by conversion disorders, in which anxiety seemed to be converted to a symptom that had no physiological basis. In our day, hypochondriasis (interpreting one's normal sensations as symptoms of a dreaded disease) is much more common.

DISSOCIATIVE DISORDERS

Under stress a person's conscious awareness will sometimes become dissociated, or separated, from previous memories, thoughts, and feelings. Dissociative amnesia usually involves selective forgetting in response to stress. Fugue involves forgetting one's identity and fleeing one's home. But most mysterious of all dissociative disorders are cases of multiple personality in which a person has two or more distinct personalities, with the original typically unaware of the other.

AFFECTIVE DISORDERS

Major Depression In major depression, the person descends into deep unhappiness, lethargy, and feelings of worthlessness for more than 2 weeks, before rebounding to normality.

Bipolar Disorder In the less common bipolar disorder, the person alternates between the hopelessness and lethargy of depression and the hyperactive, wildly optimistic, impulsive phase of mania.

Explaining Depression Current research on depression is vigorously exploring (1) genetic predispositions and neurotransmitter abnormalities, and (2) the self-defeating beliefs, learned helplessness, negative attributions, and aversive experiences that are linked with depression.

SCHIZOPHRENIC DISORDERS

Symptoms of Schizophrenia Schizophrenia shows itself in disordered thinking (nonsensical talk and delusions, which may stem from a breakdown of selective attention), disturbed perceptions (including hallucinations), and inappropriate emotions and actions.

Types of Schizophrenia Schizophrenia is actually a set of disorders (classified as disorganized, catatonic, paranoid, and undifferentiated) that emerge gradually from a long history of social inadequacy (in which case the outlook is dim), or suddenly in reaction to stress (in which case the prospects for recovery are brighter).

Understanding Schizophrenia As in the case of depression, researchers have identified biochemical abnormalities (such as in the neurotransmitter dopamine) that seem linked with certain forms of schizophrenia. Twin and adoption studies also point to a genetic predisposition that, in conjunction with certain environmental factors (which are not as yet well understood), may bring about a schizophrenic disorder.

PERSONALITY DISORDERS

Personality disorders are enduring, maladaptive personality traits. For society, the most troubling of these is the conscienceless, remorseless antisocial personality. The fearlessness that characterizes such persons appears to have both genetic and environmental roots.

SHOULD PEOPLE BE LABELED? THE POWER OF PRECONCEPTIONS

Critics of diagnostic classification point out that for the benefits of labeling people we pay a price. Labels create preconceptions that (1) bias our perceptions of people's past and present behavior, and (2) unfairly stigmatize people.

TERMS AND CONCEPTS TO REMEMBER

Affective Disorders Psychological disorders characterized by emotional extremes. See *major depression* and *bipolar disorder*.

Amnesia Loss of memory. Psychogenic amnesia, a dissociative disorder, is selective memory loss often brought on by extreme stress.

Anorexia Nervosa A disorder in which a person (usually an adolescent female) loses 25 percent or more of normal weight yet, still feeling fat, continues to starve.

Antisocial Personality A personality disorder in which the person (usually a male) exhibits a lack of conscience for wrongdoing, even toward friends and family members. May be aggressive and ruthless or a clever con artist.

Anxiety Disorders Psychological disorders characterized by distressing, persistent anxiety. See *generalized anxiety disorder*, *phobic disorders*, and *obsessive-compulsive disorder*.

Bipolar Disorder An affective disorder in which the person alternates between the hopelessness and lethargy of depression and the overexcited, hyperactive, wildly optimistic state of mania.

Bulimia A disorder characterized by "binge-purge" eating, in which repeated episodes of overeating, usually of high caloric foods, are followed by vomiting or laxative use.

Conversion Disorder A somatoform disorder in which a person experiences genuine physical symptoms for which no physiological basis can be found.

Delusions False beliefs, often of persecution or grandeur, that may accompany psychotic disorders.

Dissociative Disorders Anxiety disorders in which conscious awareness becomes separated (dissociated) from previous memories, thoughts, and feelings. See *amnesia, fugue,* and *multiple personality.*

Dopamine A neurotransmitter that appears to be overly active in some schizophrenic patients.

DSM-III The American Psychiatric Association's *Diagnostic and Statistical Manual of Mental Disorders,* third edition, a widely used system for classifying psychological disorders.

Fugue A dissociative disorder in which amnesia is accompanied by physical flight from one's home and identity.

Generalized Anxiety Disorder An anxiety disorder in which a person is continually tense, apprehensive, and experiencing autonomic nervous system arousal.

Hypochondriasis A somatoform disorder in which a person misinterprets normal physical sensations as symptoms of a disease.

Insanity A legal term for someone who has committed a crime but is judged not to have understood at the time of the crime that the act was wrong.

Major Depression An affective disorder in which a person experiences two or more weeks of depressed moods, feelings of worthlessness, and lethargy.

Mania An overexcited, hyperactive, wildly optimistic state.

Medical Model The concept that diseases have physical causes and that they can be treated and, in most cases, cured. When applied to psychological disorders, it sees them as mental illnesses to be diagnosed on the basis of their symptoms and cured through therapy, which may include treatment in a psychiatric hospital.

Multiple Personality Disorder A rare dissociative disorder in which a person exhibits two or more distinct and alternating personalities.

Neurotic Disorders Psychological disorders that are usually distressing, but allow one to think rationally and function socially. The neurotic disorders are usually viewed as ways of dealing with anxiety. See *anxiety disorders, somatoform disorders,* and *dissociative disorders.*

Obsessive-Compulsive Disorder An anxiety disorder in which a person is troubled by unwanted repetitive thoughts (obsessions) or actions (compulsions).

Panic Attack An episode of intense dread in which for a number of minutes a person experiences terror and accompanying chest pain, choking, or other frightening sensations.

Personality Disorders Psychological disorders characterized by enduring, maladaptive character traits. See *antisocial personality.*

Phobic Disorder An anxiety disorder in which a person is troubled by a persistent, irrational fear of a specific object or situation.

Psychological Disorder A psychological problem that is typically defined on the basis of atypical, undesirable, maladaptive, and unjustifiable behavior.

Psychotic Disorder A psychological disorder in which a person loses contact with reality, experiencing irrational ideas and distorted perceptions.

Schizophrenia A group of psychotic disorders characterized by disorganized thinking, disturbed perceptions, and inappropriate emotions and actions.

Somatoform Disorders Neurotic disorders in which the symptoms take a somatic (bodily) form without apparent physical cause. See *conversion disorder* and *hypochondriasis.*

FOR FURTHER READING

Diagnostic and statistical manual of mental disorders (3rd ed., 1980). Washington, DC: American Psychiatric Association.

Provides the most widely accepted definitions and descriptions of the categories of psychological disorder, including those described in this chapter.

Neale, J. M., Oltmann, T. F., & Davison, G. C. (1982). *Case studies in abnormal psychology.* New York: Wiley.

Describes the development and treatment of cases of psychological disorder, including cases of depression, school phobia, bulimia, and psychosexual disorders.

Sheehan, S. (1982). *Is there no place on earth for me?* Boston: Houghton-Mifflin.

The Pulitzer Prize–winning true story of "Sylvia Frumkin" and her transformation from a highly intelligent grade-school student into a schizophrenic who spent much of her subsequent 17 years in mental institutions. Sylvia's story is told by a writer who followed her in and out of mental hospitals, talking with, observing, and recording her.

Sizemore, C. C., & Pittillo, E. S. (1977). *I'm Eve.* New York: Doubleday.

The autobiography of Chris Sizemore, the multiple personality case on whom the movie The Three Faces of Eve *was based. Eventually, Eve expressed not just three, but twenty-two different personalities, before integrating them into the person she is today.*

Spitzer, R. L., Sokol, A. E., Gibbon, M., & Williams, J. B. W. (1981). *DSM-III case book: A learning companion to the diagnostic and statistical manual of mental disorders (3rd ed.).* Washington, D.C.: American Psychiatric Association.

Further information can be found in textbooks on psychological disorders, several of which are entitled *Abnormal psychology.*

Musée Rodin

Auguste Rodin *Jean de Fiennes*
(detail of *The Burghers of Calais*)

THE PSYCHOLOGICAL THERAPIES

Psychoanalysis
Aims
Methods

Humanistic Therapies
Person-Centered Therapy
Gestalt Therapy
Humanistic Growth Groups

Behavior Therapies
Classical Conditioning Therapies
Operant Conditioning Therapies
Cognitive-Behavior Therapies

Evaluating Psychotherapies
Is Psychotherapy Effective?
Therapy's Effectiveness with Varied People and Problems
Relative Effectiveness of Different Therapies
Commonalities among Psychotherapies

THE BIOMEDICAL THERAPIES

Psychosurgery

Electroconvulsive Therapy

Drug Therapies
Antipsychotic Drugs
Antianxiety Drugs
Antidepressant Drugs

Aerobic Exercise

TREATING THE SOCIAL ROOTS OF PSYCHOLOGICAL DISORDERS

Family Therapies

Preventive Mental Health

CHAPTER 17

Therapy

To judge from the history of attempts to treat psychological disorders, it would seem that our species has found its own problems mystifying. In the 2200 years since Eratosthenes correctly estimated the earth's circumference, we humans have charted the heavens, explored the solar system, reconstructed the basic history of life on earth, cracked the genetic code, and eliminated or found cures for all sorts of diseases. Meanwhile, we have treated psychological disorders with a bewildering variety of harsh and gentle methods: by cutting holes in the head, and by giving warm baths and massages; by restraining, bleeding, or "beating the devil" out of people, and by placing them in sunny, serene environments; by administering drugs and electric shocks, and by talking—talking about childhood experiences, about current feelings, about maladaptive thoughts and behaviors. We can now state with certainty the chemical composition of Jupiter's atmosphere, but when it comes to understanding and treating what is closer to home—the psychological disorders described in Chapter 16—we still are only beginning to make real progress.

Treatment of mental disorders in the eighteenth century. (a) William Hogarth's (1697–1764) famous engraving of St. Mary's of Bethlehem hospital in London (commonly called Bedlam) makes the most of the dramatic aspects of mental illness but is far from an accurate portrayal of the squalor and wretchedness that prevailed in the asylums in the eighteenth century. The insane and feeble-minded were considered to exist at the level of animals. Hospitals were unheated and basic human amenities were neglected. (b) This chair was designed by Benjamin Rush (1746–1813) "for the benefit of maniacal patients." Rush, considered by many the father of American psychiatry, believed that the mentally ill required humanitarian care to regain their sensibilities.

(a)

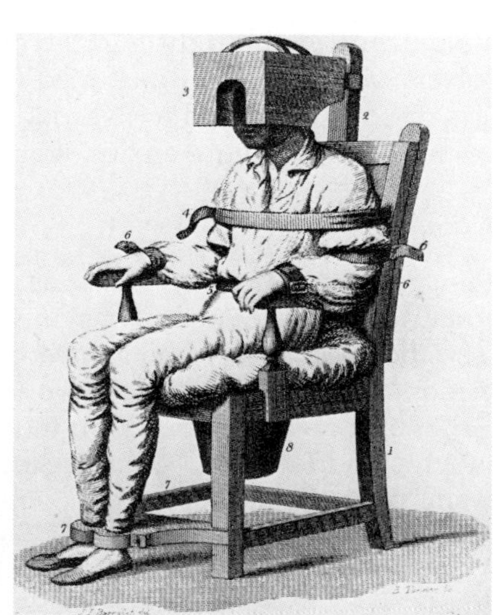

(b)

A catalog of all the therapies that have been tried at one time or another would have two main sections: the psychological therapies (therapies that involve an interaction between a trained professional and a client with a problem) and the biomedical therapies (therapies that alter the brain's structure or functioning). Although surefire "remedies" for most psychological disorders do not exist, current psychological and biomedical therapies are, as we will see, sometimes effective.

THE PSYCHOLOGICAL THERAPIES

The most common psychological form of therapy is ***psychotherapy,*** "a planned, emotionally charged confiding interaction between a trained, socially sanctioned healer and a sufferer" (Frank, 1982). From among the some 200 types of psychotherapy (Pines, 1982), we will consider several of the most influential. Although all the therapies we will consider are distinguishable in their pure forms, in practice, half of all psychotherapists describe themselves as ***eclectic,*** as using a blend of therapies (Smith, 1982). Depending on the client and the problem, an eclectic therapist will use or mix a variety of techniques.

Later, we will ask how successful each technique is and what common threads run through them all. But first, let us consider the basic aims and techniques of each therapy on its own terms. The major therapies are built upon familiar foundations—the psychoanalytic, humanistic, and social-cognitive perspectives on personality considered in Chapter 15.

Psychoanalysis

Although there are few today who practice therapy as Sigmund Freud envisioned it, his psychoanalytic techniques for treating psychological disorders warrant our attention. ***Psychoanalysis*** is part of our modern vocabulary and its assumptions influence many other therapies.

Aims

Psychoanalysis assumes that psychological problems are fueled by unconscious impulses and conflicts, many of which develop and are repressed in childhood. Psychoanalysis aims to bring these repressed feelings into conscious awareness where they can be dealt with. By gradually gaining conscious insight into the origins of the disorder, the person in analysis works through the buried feelings. This releases the energy that was previously devoted to neurotic conflicts, allowing it to be redirected toward healthier, more anxiety-free living.

Methods

When Freud discarded hypnosis as an effective therapeutic technique, he turned to free association. Imagine yourself as a patient using the free association technique: The analyst invites you to relax in a comfortable position, perhaps by lying on a couch. He or she will probably sit out of your line of vision, helping you to focus your attention on your internal thoughts and feelings. Beginning perhaps with a childhood memory, a dream, or a recent experience, you state aloud whatever comes to your mind from moment to moment. It sounds easy, but soon you become aware of how often you edit your thoughts as you speak, by omitting material that seems trivial, irrelevant, or shameful. Even in the relatively safe presence of the analyst, you may pause momentarily before uttering

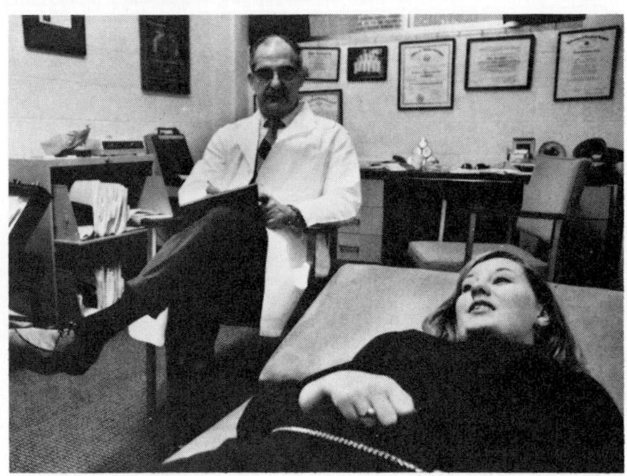

In this classical Freudian setting, the psychoanalyst sits out of view of the patient on the couch.

an embarrassing thought or you may change the subject to something less threatening, and sometimes your mind may seem to go blank or you may find yourself unable to remember important details.

To the psychoanalyst, these blocks in the flow of one's free associations are ***resistances.*** They hint that anxiety lurks and that sensitive material is being blocked from consciousness. The analyst will want to explore these sensitive areas, first by making you aware of your resistances, and later by helping you to interpret their underlying meaning. The analyst's ***interpretations***—suggestions of hidden feelings and conflicts—are considered an important avenue to insight. Through them you may become aware of what you are avoiding, and you may discover what your resistances mean and how they fit with other pieces of your psychological puzzle.

In addition to resistances, Freud believed that another clue to repressed impulses is the *latent content* of our dreams (see Chapter 8, "States of Consciousness"). Thus, after inviting you to report a dream, the analyst may try to interpret its hidden meaning, thereby adding yet another piece to your developing picture of yourself.

After many such sessions you will likely have disclosed more of yourself to your analyst than you have ever revealed to anyone. Because psychoanalytic theory emphasizes the formative power of childhood experiences, much of what you reveal will pertain to your childhood. You will also probably find yourself experiencing strong positive or negative feelings for your analyst, feelings that express the dependency or mingled love and anger that you earlier experienced toward family members or other important people in your life. When this happens, Freud would say that you are actually transferring to the analyst your strongest feelings from those other relationships. This transfer of feelings, called ***transference,*** is believed to expose long repressed feelings, giving you a belated chance to work them through with your analyst's help. By examining your feelings toward the analyst you may also gain insight into your current relationships with others.

Psychoanalysis is susceptible to criticism. Critics say that, like the psychoanalytic theory of personality, its after-the-fact interpretations are hard to disprove. If, in response to the analyst's suggested interpretation, you say, "Yes! I see now," your acceptance confirms the analyst's interpretation. If you emphatically say, "No! That doesn't ring true," your denial may be taken to reveal more resistance, which would also confirm the interpretation. Although psychoanalysts acknowledge that their interpretations cannot be proven or disproven, they insist that interpretations may nevertheless be helpful to patients.

Second, traditional psychoanalysis is a long, hard, expensive process. Although Freud did not intend psychoanalysis to be lengthy, it generally requires well over a year of several sessions a week with a highly trained and well-paid analyst. Only those with a high income or an unusually generous insurance policy can afford such treatment.

Although therapists trained in psychoanalysis are relatively few in number, many more are influenced by its assumptions. The psychoanalytic influence can be seen in any therapist who tries to understand patients' current symptoms by exploring their childhood experiences, who probes for suppressed emotion-laden information, and who seeks to help people gain insight into the unconscious roots of problems and to work through newly resurrected feelings. Although influenced by psychoanalysis, these therapists may talk to people face-to-face (rather than out of the line of vision) once a week (rather than several times weekly) for but a few weeks or months (rather than several years). One such therapist is David Malan, who in the following session with a depressed woman seeks to help her gain insight into the source of her problems. Note how Malan interprets the woman's earlier remarks and suggests that the woman is reenacting her characteristic emotions in her relationship with him (1978, pp. 133–134):

Malan: *I get the feeling that you're the sort of person who needs to keep active. If you don't keep active, then something goes wrong. Is that true?*

Patient: *Yes.*

Malan: *I get a second feeling about you and that is that you must, underneath all this, have an awful lot of very strong and upsetting feelings. Somehow they're there but you aren't really quite in touch with them. Isn't this right? I feel you've been like that as long as you can remember.*

Patient: *For quite a few years, whenever I really sat down and thought about it I got depressed, so I tried not to think about it.*

Malan: *You see, you've established a pattern, haven't you? You're even like that here with me, because in spite of the fact that you're in some trouble and you feel that the bottom is falling out of your world, the way you're telling me this is just as if there wasn't anything wrong.*

Although in this therapy session the couch has disappeared, the influence of psychoanalytic theory probably has not, especially if the therapist probes for the origin of the patient's symptoms by analyzing suppressed information from her past.

Humanistic Therapies

As we noted in Chapter 15, the humanistic perspective emphasizes people's inherent potential for self-fulfillment. Not surprisingly, then, humanistically oriented therapists attempt to facilitate self-fulfillment by helping people grow in self-awareness and self-acceptance. Unlike psychoanalysts, humanistic therapists tend to focus on:

the present instead of the past

becoming aware of feelings as they occur rather than achieving insights into the origins of the feelings

conscious rather than unconscious material

taking immediate responsibility for one's feelings and actions rather than uncovering the hidden obstacles to doing so

promoting growth and fulfillment instead of curing illness.

Person-Centered Therapy

The best known and most widely used humanistic therapy is an outgrowth of Carl Rogers' (1961, 1980) person-centered perspective on personality. Because the therapist seeks to focus on the person's own conscious self-perceptions rather than the therapist's interpretations, the therapy is called ***person-centered*** (or, as Rogers formerly called it, *client-centered).* Because the therapist listens without judgment or interpretation, rather than directing the client toward certain insights, this therapy is also called nondirective therapy.

Carl Rogers, in the center, actively listening to a client during a group therapy session.

Believing that people already possess within themselves the resources for growth, Rogers encourages therapists to exhibit a *genuineness, acceptance,* and *empathy* that he believes enable clients to accept themselves and fulfill their potential (see Chapter 15). When therapists drop their facades and genuinely express their true feelings, when they enable their clients to feel unconditionally accepted, and when they empathically sense and reflect their clients' feelings, the clients may grow in their self-understanding and self-acceptance. Rogers (1980, p. 10) explains:

> Hearing has consequences. When I truly hear a person and the meanings that are important to him at that moment, hearing not simply his words, but him, and when I let him know that I have heard his own private personal meanings, many things happen. There is first of all a grateful look. He feels released. He wants to tell me more about his world. He surges forth in a new sense of freedom. He becomes more open to the process of change.

"It takes a great man to make a good listener."
Sir Arthur Helps,
Brevia, 1870

I have often noticed that the more deeply I hear the meanings of the person, the more there is that happens. Almost always, when a person realizes he has been deeply heard, his eyes moisten. I think in some real sense he is weeping for joy. It is as though he were saying, "Thank God, somebody heard me. Someone knows what it's like to be me."

Rogers' technique of ***active listening***—by echoing, restating, and clarifying what the person has said and acknowledging the feelings expressed—has become an accepted part of counseling practices in many schools, colleges, and clinics. The counselor listens attentively and interrupts only to restate in other words what the client seems to be saying, to indicate acceptance of what the client is expressing, or to ask for clarification. In fact, the listening technique is so easily described (though not so easily practiced) that computer scientist Joseph Weizenbaum developed a delightful computer program named ELIZA that simulates a Rogerian counselor. A few moments ago I (DGM) sat before a computer terminal and had the following conversation with ELIZA:

"We have two ears and one mouth that we may listen the more and talk the less."
Zeno, 335–263 B.C.
Diogenes Laertius

ELIZA: *How do you do. Please state your problem.*

DGM: *Hi, I guess I am feeling just a little nervous.*

ELIZA: *How long have you been feeling a little nervous?*

DGM: *I suppose that when I am writing I am always a little anxious.*

ELIZA: *Can you think of a specific example?*

DGM: *Well, I'm wondering whether students will find this stuff as interesting as I do.*

ELIZA: *Why do you believe it isn't normal to be wondering whether students will find this stuff as interesting as you do?*

DGM: *Maybe it is normal. I guess every author must feel the same. . . .*

ELIZA: *What are your feelings now?*

DGM: *Glad that you are willing to listen.*

ELIZA: *Why would you confide in someone who is willing to listen?*

DGM: *Sometimes it just helps to talk things over.*

ELIZA: *What does that suggest to you?*

DGM: *Perhaps that I should share my feelings more openly.*

ELIZA: *Your feelings more openly.*

DGM: *Yes.*

ELIZA: *I understand, please go on.*

DGM: *Do you understand?*

ELIZA: *Oh, I do understand at times.*

Although ELIZA is infinitely patient and nonjudgmental, she does not understand; she is nothing more than what Weizenbaum programmed—a parody of a nondirective, person-centered counselor. Actual counseling requires what the computer lacks—a sensitivity to meaning and an ability to clarify by reflecting meanings in *different* words. Compare Eliza's conversation with me to Carl Rogers' interaction with a quiet, troubled 28-year-old male client (Meador & Rogers, 1984, p. 167):

Client: *I just ain't no good to nobody, never was, and never will be.*

Rogers: *Feeling that now, hm? That you're just no good to yourself, no good to anybody. Never will be any good to anybody. Just that you're completely worthless, huh?—Those really are lousy feelings. Just feel that you're no good at all, hm?*

Client: *Yeah. (Muttering in low, discouraged voice) That's what this guy I went to town with just the other day told me.*

Rogers: *This guy that you went to town with really told you that you were no good? Is that what you're saying? Did I get that right?*

Client: M-hm.

Rogers: I guess the meaning of that if I get it right is that here's somebody that—meant something to you and what does he think of you? Why, he's told you that he thinks you're no good at all. And that just really knocks the props out from under you. (Client weeps quietly.) It just brings the tears. (Silence of 20 seconds)

Client: (Rather defiantly) I don't care though.

Rogers: You tell yourself you don't care at all, but somehow I guess some part of you cares because some part of you weeps over it.

In person-centered therapy, the person seeking help finds in the therapist an understanding and accepting listener.

As this brief therapy excerpt illustrates, the person-centered counselor seeks to provide a psychological mirror that helps clients to see themselves more clearly. But can a therapist be a perfect mirror, without selecting and interpreting what is reflected? Rogers concedes that there is no way to be totally nondirective but that the most important contribution the therapist can make is to accept and understand the client. In this accepting environment people can come to accept even the ugly or unwanted parts of themselves and feel valued and whole.

Gestalt Therapy

Another influential humanistic therapy, developed by Frederick (Fritz) Perls (1969), joins (1) the psychoanalytic emphasis on bringing unconscious feelings and conflicts into awareness with (2) the humanistic emphasis on getting in touch with oneself and taking responsibility for oneself in the present. Perls' ***Gestalt*** (meaning "whole") ***therapy*** aims to make people whole by breaking through their defenses and helping them tune into and express their moment to moment feelings.

"All therapy that has to be done can only be done in the now. . . . Nothing exists except in the now."
Frederick Perls (1970)

Eavesdropping on a Gestalt therapy session, we might hear the therapist using any one of several techniques for getting people to express their real feelings and to "own responsibility" for them. One way is to train people to speak in the first person (Passons, 1975, p. 79):

Recall from Chapter 11 the power of language to influence thinking: Words shape thoughts.

Client: When you go skiing you feel healthy and vigorous. You have this sense of excitement.

Therapist: Sue, try saying the same thing only substituting the word "I" for "you."

Client: Why?

Therapist: Because I believe you're saying something about yourself except you're not sounding that way.

Client: When I'm skiing I feel healthy and excited.

Therapist: Do you hear the difference?

Client: Yes. The second one is what I really meant.

To get people to take responsibility for their feelings, the Gestalt therapist might get people to change their verbs—to say "I want" instead of "I need," "I choose to" instead of "I have to," and "I won't" instead of "I can't" (Passons, 1975, p. 82):

Client: Every day I just sit there and feel like a stooge. I just can't speak up in that class.

Therapist: You say you can't.

Client: That's right. I've tried and I know I should, I mean I know the stuff, that's not the problem. I just can't get the words out.

Therapist: Try saying "I won't talk" instead of "I can't talk."

Client: I won't talk in that class.

Therapist: Let yourself feel how you are refusing to talk.

Client: *I guess I am holding myself back a little.*

Therapist: *What are your objections to speaking up?*

Client: *Well, everyone else in there seems to be talking just to talk. I don't like doing that.*

Gestalt therapists also capitalize on the power of actions to affect thoughts and feelings (see Chapter 19, "Social Influence"). The therapist may ask people to role-play different aspects of their relationships, or to act out suppressed feelings. The ultimate goal—to become better aware of and able to express one's own feelings—exemplifies the humanistic value of being true to oneself, a value that some critics believe promotes self-centeredness. This value is epitomized in Perls' Gestalt credo (1972, p. 70):

I do my thing, and you do your thing.
I am not in this world to live up to your expectations.
And you are not in this world to live up to mine.
You are you and I am I,
And if by chance we find each other, it's beautiful.
If not, it can't be helped.

At this human sensitivity center, instructors demonstrate a technique for group members to actively show their support for one another. This young woman places her trust in the group and falls forward into the arms of the others, who support her. The atmosphere established encourages the participants to trust one another emotionally as well as physically.

Humanistic Growth Groups

Most of the therapies we are considering in this chapter may also occur in therapist-led groups of roughly eight to ten people. Group therapy saves therapists' time and clients' money. More importantly, the social context allows people to test their old and new behaviors on others and to discover that other people have problems similar to their own. As you have perhaps experienced, it can be a relief to find that you are not alone—to learn that others, despite their smooth exteriors, share your feelings of loneliness, inadequacy, or anger.

It's not always true that "misery loves company," but as often happens in group therapy, it helps to realize that others' fears of disapproval and rejection are much like our own.

One popular form of group experience for those not seriously disturbed began as sensitivity training groups ("T-groups" for short) in which teachers, executives, and other presumably nondisturbed people practiced ways of relating to one another more sensitively and openly. In groups of twelve to twenty that met for limited periods of time, people were encouraged to be less inhibited and defensive in their interactions with others. Before long, Carl Rogers (1970) and others were offering

encounter groups—groups whose emotion-laden experiences were characterized by honesty and openness—to hundreds of thousands of people. Although encounter groups are not as popular today as they were a decade ago, they influenced various sorts of self-help groups—for substance abusers, divorced people, the bereaved, and for those who are simply seeking personal growth.

The purpose of encounter groups is not only to provide a short-term experience of psychological intimacy, but to help people increase their self-awareness and learn to communicate more effectively—to talk straight and to listen empathically. As an encounter group begins, people are typically hesitant and sometimes frustrated at the leader's lack of direction. Gradually, they begin to reveal their feelings toward people outside the group, and then toward others within the group. As trust grows, people offer one another feedback of the sort they seldom receive in polite, reserved society, and frequently they discover a warmth and closeness not found in the bustle of everyday life.

At this high school–sponsored retreat, by sharing, the participants became more aware of themselves, their feelings, and the feelings of others.

It sounds wonderful. Is it? To judge from the testimonials of many participants, the answer is yes. "My relations with my family, friends, and co-workers are more honest and I express my likes and dislikes and true feelings more openly," one participant reported to Rogers. "It has opened up infinite possibilities for me in my relationship to myself and to everyone dear to me. I feel truly alive," said another. To judge from the questionnaire reports of broader samples of encounter participants, the experience is generally recalled as positive. To judge from the behavior of people back home after the experience, the benefits are more modest. Moreover, if a group or its leader aggressively invades one's privacy or attacks one's behavior (which a well-trained professional leader does not), self-esteem can be lowered (Lieberman & others, 1973). Candor usually helps, but sometimes hurts.

"Encounter groups show a modest positive impact, an impact much less than has been portrayed by their supporters and an impact significantly lower than participants' view of their own change would lead one to assume."
Morton Lieberman, Irvin Yalom, and Matthew Miles (1973, p. 130)

Behavior Therapies

So far, all the therapies we have considered assume that psychological problems diminish as self-awareness grows. When the psychoanalyst helps people gain insight into their unresolved and unconscious tensions, or when the humanistic therapist enables people to get in touch with their feelings, symptoms are expected to subside. ***Behavior therapists***—therapists who practice one of several therapeutic techniques derived from research on learning and cognition—doubt that self-awareness is the key. You can, for example, become aware of why you are highly anxious during exams and still be anxious.

Instead of trying to alleviate distressing symptoms by resolving a presumed underlying problem, behavior therapists assume that the symptoms *are* the problems. Symptoms such as phobias, sexual dysfunctions, or depression are behaviors that, like other behaviors, are a product of learning, they maintain. Thus the key to symptom relief is to eliminate the problem thoughts and maladaptive behaviors and replace them with more constructive ways of thinking and acting. The aim of behavior therapy, then, is usually not to change the person's personality but to relieve a specific troubling symptom.

Classical Conditioning Therapies

One cluster of behavior therapies derives from principles developed in Pavlov's classic experiments on the conditioning of dogs. As Pavlov and others demonstrated, various behaviors and emotions could be acquired through classical conditioning (see Chapter 9, "Learning"). If a maladaptive symptom, such as fear of elevators, is assumed to be a conditioned response to the stimulus of being in an enclosed space, then by applying extinction principles, the fear response can be unlearned. Even better, by using ***counterconditioning,*** the stimulus could be paired with a new response that is incompatible with fear. If an adaptive, relaxed response could be repeatedly paired with the enclosed space of the elevator, the fear response would be displaced. Among the several counterconditioning techniques are systematic desensitization and aversive conditioning.

Systematic Desensitization Picture this scene reported in 1924 by Mary Cover Jones, an associate of the behaviorist John B. Watson. Three-year-old Peter is woefully afraid of various objects, including animals such as rabbits and rats. (Unlike Little Albert's laboratory-conditioned fear of white rats described in Chapter 9, Peter's fears arose naturally at home and are more intense.) Jones's solution is to replace the fear with a conditioned response that is incompatible with fear. The response she repeatedly pairs with a fear-evoking rabbit is the pleasurable, relaxed response associated with eating. As the hungry child begins eating his mid-afternoon meal, Jones introduces a caged rabbit on the other side of the huge room. Peter hardly notices as he eagerly munches his crackers and milk. On succeeding days, the rabbit is gradually moved closer and closer. Within 2 months, Peter not only tolerates the rabbit in his lap, but he strokes it with one hand while he eats with the other. Moreover, his fear of other furry objects subsides as well, having been "countered" or replaced by a relaxed state that cannot coexist with fear (Fisher, 1984; Jones, 1924).

Unfortunately for those who might have been helped by her counterconditioning procedures, Jones's story of Peter and the rabbit did not immediately become part of psychology's lore. It was not until more than 30 years later that her technique was refined by psychiatrist Joseph Wolpe (1958, 1982) into what has become the most widely used method of behavior therapy: ***systematic desensitization.*** Wolpe assumed, as did Jones, that you cannot simultaneously be anxious and relaxed. Therefore, if you can repeatedly relax when faced with anxiety-provoking stimuli, you will gradually eliminate your anxiety. The trick is to proceed gradually.

Let us see how this might work with a common phobia—fear of public speaking. If you were troubled by this fear, a behavior therapist would first ask your help in constructing a hierarchy of anxiety-triggering speaking situations. Your anxiety hierarchy might range from mildly anxiety-provoking situations, such as speaking up in a small social group, to panic-provoking situations such as having to address a large audience.

Then the therapist would train you in relaxation. You learn to relax one muscle group after another, until you achieve a drowsy state of complete relaxation and blissful comfort. Then, with your eyes closed, the therapist asks you to imagine a situation listed on your hierarchy that is mildly anxiety-arousing. Perhaps you are having coffee with a group of your friends, and you are deciding whether or not to speak up. If imagining the scene causes you to feel any anxiety at all you signal your tension by raising your finger, and the therapist instructs you to switch off the mental image and go back to deep relaxation. This scene is imagined over and over until you can feel completely relaxed while imagining it, with no trace of anxiety. Gradually but systematically over several therapy sessions, the therapist progresses up your anxiety hierarchy, using the relaxed state to desensitize you to each imagined situation. The therapist may then instruct you to practice the imagined behaviors in actual situations, beginning with relatively easy tasks and gradually moving to more anxiety-filled ones (see Figure 17-1). Conquering your anxiety in an actual situation, not just in your imagination, can raise your feelings of self-efficacy. Eventually, you may be able to actually speak in public without fear.

Figure 17-1 *Systematic desensitization of a phobia. Beverly, who is terribly afraid of spiders, is gradually able to relax—as shown by her decreasing pulse rate—first at the sight of a spider, then in the presence of a toy spider, a dead spider, and a live one.*

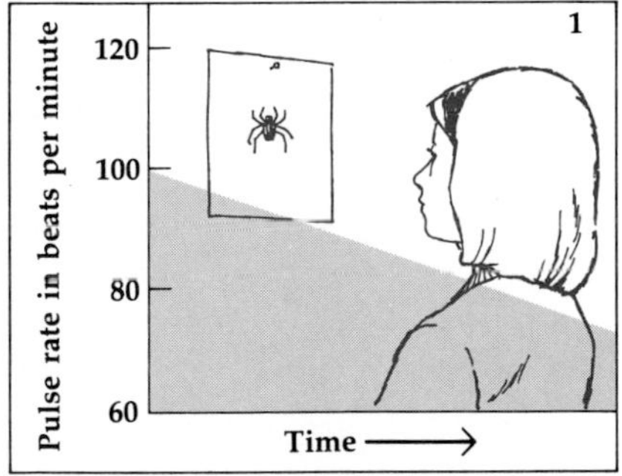

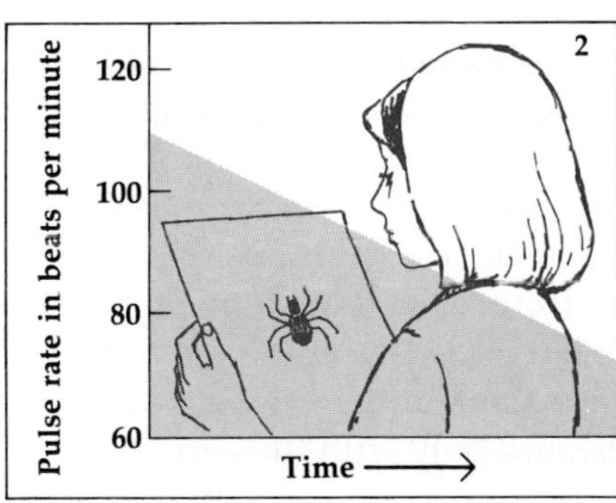

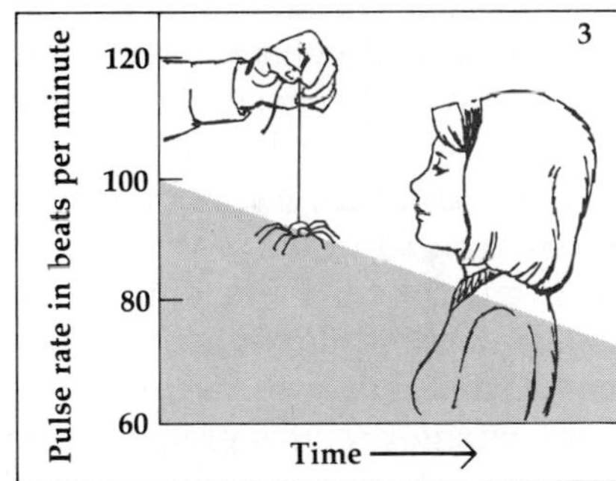

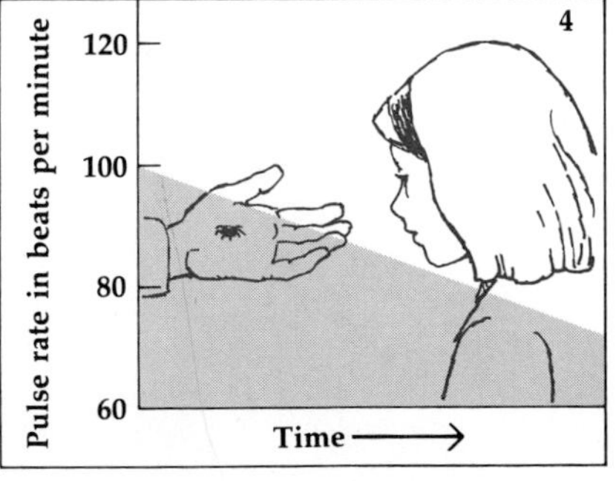

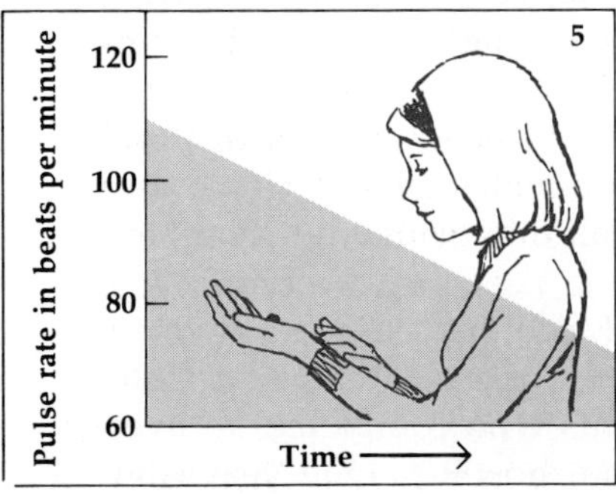

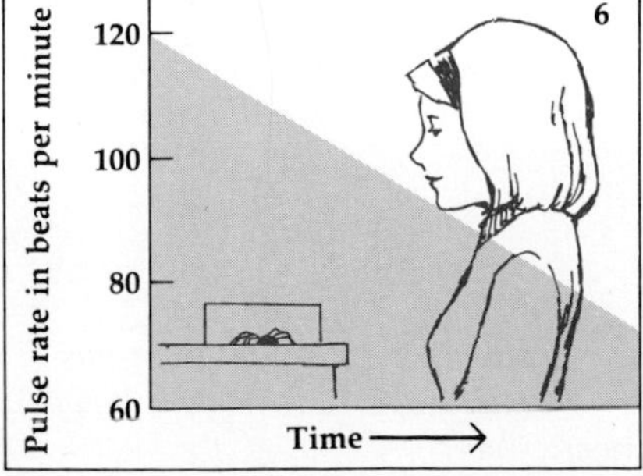

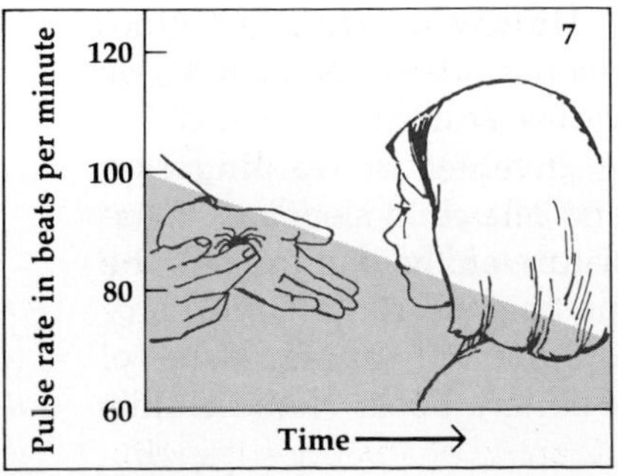

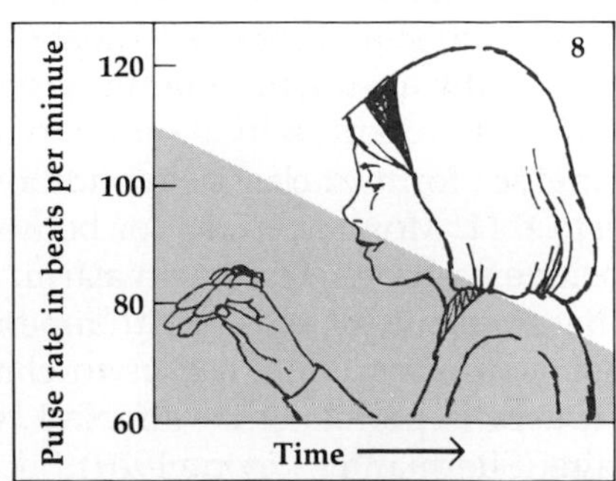

Systematic desensitization is sometimes combined with other techniques. With phobias, desensitization techniques may be supplemented by having someone model appropriate behavior in a fear-arousing situation. For example, if you were afraid of snakes, you would first observe someone handling a snake and then would be coaxed in gradual steps to approach, touch, and handle it yourself (Bandura & others, 1969). By applying this principle of observational learning, therapists have helped people overcome disruptive fears of snakes, spiders, and dogs.

Notice that the systematic desensitization procedure makes no attempt to help you achieve insight into the underlying cause of the fear. If you are afraid of heights, the therapist will not be particularly concerned with the first time you experienced this fear or what may have triggered it. Nor do behavior therapists worry that if your fear of heights is eliminated an underlying problem may still remain and be expressed now as, say, a fear of elevators. On the contrary, they argue, overcoming maladaptive symptoms can help people to feel better about themselves in general and to begin acting in ways that bring greater life satisfaction (Bandura, 1978).

Aversive Conditioning *Aversive conditioning* is the reverse of systematic desensitization. In systematically desensitizing a patient, the therapist seeks to substitute a positive (relaxed) response for a negative (fearful) response to a neutral stimulus. In aversive conditioning, the therapist attempts to substitute a negative (aversive) response for a positive response to an attractive but harmful stimulus. The procedure is simple: It associates unwanted behavior with unpleasant experiences, thus eliminating the behavior. For example, in treating an alcoholic, aversion therapists administer a drug that produces violent nausea when alcohol is consumed. By linking the drinking of alcohol with violent nausea, therapists seek to transform the alcoholic's reaction to alcohol from positive to negative. Similarly, by giving child molesters electric shocks as they view photos of nude children, aversion therapists have tried to eliminate the molesters' sexual response to children. Because this therapy involves an unpleasant experience, it is practiced sparingly and only with the consent of the patient.

Does it work? In the short run it may. But, as we saw in Chapter 9, the problem is that conditioning is influenced by cognition. People know that outside the therapist's office they can drink without fear of nausea or engage in sexually deviant behavior without fear of shock. The person's ability to discriminate between the situation in which the aversive conditioning occurs and all other situations can limit the treatment's long-term effectiveness.

Nevertheless, aversive conditioning of alcoholics has recently enjoyed something of a revival. For example, Arthur Wiens and Carol Menustik (1983) studied 685 alcoholic patients who completed an aversion therapy program at a Portland, Oregon, hospital. One year later, after returning for several booster treatments of alcohol-sickness pairings, 63 percent were still successfully abstaining. Three years later, one-third remained totally abstinent, a hefty improvement on the 7 percent 4-year abstinence rate reported in a summary of earlier studies.

A milder form of classical conditioning, invented by learning psychologist O. H. Mowrer, exists for bedwetters. The child sleeps on a liquid-sensitive pad connected to an alarm. Moisture on the pad triggers the alarm that awakens the child. With repetitions, this association of urinary relaxation with awakening serves to eliminate the bedwetting. Usually, the treatment is permanently effective, providing a boost to the child's self-image (Sherman & Levin, 1979).

What might a psychoanalyst say about this therapy for bedwetting? How might a behavior therapist reply?

Operant Conditioning Therapies

As we saw in Chapter 9, voluntary behaviors are strongly influenced by their consequences. This simple fact enables behavior therapists to influence behavior by controlling its consequences. They reinforce desired behaviors, while withholding reinforcement for undesired behaviors. Such applications of operant conditioning to solve specific behavior problems are sometimes called ***behavior modification,*** a therapy that has raised hopes for some of the most hopeless cases. Retarded children have been taught to care for themselves, withdrawn children have been induced to interact, and schizophrenics have been enabled to behave more rationally.

If this child completes his work before the timer goes off, he will be rewarded with one of the tokens in the cup on the desk—tokens he can later exchange for special privileges. This form of behavior modification is effective in overcoming specific behavior problems.

The rewards vary. With some people the reinforcing power of attention or praise is sufficient. With others, a more concrete reward such as food is required. In institutional settings, a ***token economy*** is sometimes established. When people display appropriate behavior, such as getting out of bed, dressing, washing, eating, talking coherently, cleaning up their rooms, or playing cooperatively, they receive a token of some sort, such as a plastic coin (Kazdin, 1982). The accumulated tokens can later be exchanged for various rewards, such as candy, television watching, trips to town, or better living quarters. Tokens can also be used to shape behavior in the step-by-step manner described on p. 228. Token economies have been successfully applied in various settings (classrooms, hospitals, and homes for the delinquent) and with various populations (disturbed children, the mentally retarded, schizophrenic patients).

Critics of behavior modification express two main concerns. The first is practical: What happens when the reinforcements are terminated, as when the person leaves the institution? Might the person have become so dependent on the extrinsic rewards that the appropriate behaviors quickly disappear? To increase the chance that new desirable behaviors will endure, behavior therapists may attempt to wean patients from the token rewards, to shift them toward rewards (such as social approval) that are typical of life outside the clinical environment, and to train them to engage in behaviors that have intrinsic rewards. As a withdrawn person becomes more socially competent, for example, the intrinsic satisfactions of social interaction may help to maintain the behavior. If the behavior change is to persist, note motivation researchers Edward Deci and Richard Ryan (1985), the person must come to feel not externally manipulated by the therapist's rewards but intrinsically motivated.

The second concern is ethical: Is it right for one human to control another? Those who set up token economics must first deprive people of something they desire (but do not actually need for survival) and then decide which behaviors will be rewarded. To the critics, the whole behavior modification process has a totalitarian taint. Advocates of behavior modification reply that many uses of behavior modification have as their goal increased *self*-control rather than control by others (see Chapter 9), that treatment with positive rewards is more humane than the punitive treatment such people might otherwise receive, and that the right to effective treatment and to the hope for a better life justifies a temporary deprivation of certain privileges.

Cognitive-Behavior Therapies

We have seen how behavior therapies are used in the treatment of specific fears and problem behaviors. But how do behavior therapies deal with unfocused anxiety or major depression? (It is difficult to make a hierarchy of anxiety-triggering situations when the anxiety is unfocused.) The "cognitive revolution" that has so changed psychology during the last two decades has influenced behavior therapists as well, especially in treating these less clearly defined psychological problems.

Cognitive-behavior therapies assume that our feelings and responses to events are strongly influenced by our patterns of thought (see Figure 17-2). For example, as we noted in the last chapter's discussion of depression, self-blaming thoughts and negative attributions are an integral part of the vicious cycle of depression. And if our characteristic thinking patterns are learned, then—this is the behavioral aspect of cognitive-behavior therapy—they can be relearned. Thus, cognitive therapists try in various ways to teach people new, more constructive ways of thinking.

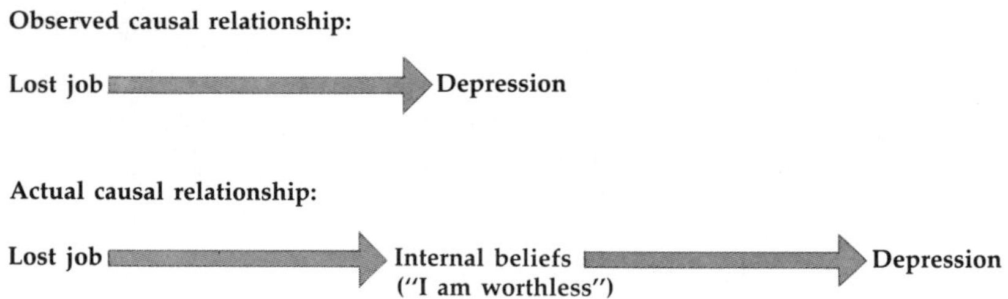

Figure 17-2 *A cognitive perspective on psychological disorders. The person's emotional reactions are produced not directly by the event, but by the person's thoughts and attributions in response to the event.*

Rational-Emotive Therapy According to Albert Ellis (1984), the creator of ***rational-emotive therapy,*** one cause of many problems is irrational thinking. For example, he describes (p. 198) a disturbed woman who

> does not merely believe it is *undesirable* if her love partner is rejecting. She tends to believe, also, that (1) it is *awful;* (2) she *cannot stand* it; (3) she *should not,* must not be rejected; (4) she will *never* be accepted by any desirable partner; (5) she is a *worthless person* because one lover has rejected her; and (6) she *deserves to be damned* for being so worthless. Such common covert hypotheses are nonsensical. . . . They can be easily elicited and demolished by any scientist worth his or her salt; and the rational-emotive therapist is exactly that: an exposing and nonsense-annihilating scientist.

Does this sound like the opposite of Carl Rogers' warm, caring, reflective acceptance of his clients' feelings? It very nearly is. Ellis intends to "make mincemeat" of people's illogical ideas—that we must be loved by everyone, that we must be thoroughly competent and successful at everything, that it is a disaster when things do not go as we wish. Change people's thinking by revealing the "absurdity" of their self-defeating ideas, he believes, and you will change their self-defeating feelings and actions. Let's eavesdrop as Ellis exhibits his bold style with a 25-year-old female client (1984, p. 219):

Ellis: *The same crap! It's always the same crap. Now if you would look at the crap—instead of "Oh, how stupid I am! He hates me! I think I'll kill myself!"—then you'd get better right away.*

Client: *You've been listening! (laughs)*

Ellis: *Listening to what?*

Client: *(laughs) Those wild statements in my mind, like that, that I make.*

Ellis: *That's right! Because I know that you have to make those statements—because I have a good* theory. *And according to my theory, people couldn't get upset* unless *they made those nutty statements to themselves. . . . Even if I loved you madly, the next person you talk to is likely to hate you. So I like brown eyes and he likes blue eyes, or something. So you're then dead! Because you really think: "I've got to be* accepted! *I've got to act intelligently!" Well, why?*

Client: *(very soberly and reflectively) True.*

Ellis: *You see?*

Client: *Yes.*

Ellis: *Now, if you will learn that lesson, then you've had a very valuable session. Because you* don't *have to upset yourself. As I said before: if I thought you were the worst [expletive] who ever existed, well that's my* opinion. *And I'm entitled to it. But does it make you a turd?*

Client: *(reflective silence)*

Ellis: Does *it?*

Client: *No.*

Ellis: What *makes you a turd?*

Client: Thinking *that you are.*

Ellis: *That's right! Your* belief *that you are. That's the only thing that could ever do it. And you never have to believe that. See? You control your thinking. I control my thinking—*my *belief about you. But you don't have to be affected by that. You* always *control what you think.*

Mini-Debate

Values in Psychotherapy

To what extent do therapists' personal attitudes, beliefs, and values influence their advice to and interactions with clients? What values prevail in psychotherapy and what values should prevail? Two sharply contrasting positions are offered by psychotherapists Allen Bergin (coeditor of the *Handbook of Psychotherapy and Behavior Change*) and Albert Ellis (rational-emotive therapist).

Allen Bergin

Values are an inevitable and pervasive part of psychotherapy. To define mental health one must assume a standard of what is better or worse. Yet as professionals, we sometimes follow the leaders of our profession without recognizing that, under the guise of professionalism and science, we are purveying our own personal value systems. If we are unable to face our own values openly, it means we are unable to face ourselves. Since we expect our clients to examine their perceptions and value constructs, we ought to do likewise. ***(Continued on next page.)***

Albert Ellis

Bergin makes many points with which I, as a clinician and a nondogmatic atheist, can heartily agree. His theses that values are a pervasive part of psychotherapy and that mental health professionals' values tend to exclude religious values are probably valid.

My objection is that Bergin does not properly represent the views of nondogmatic atheistic clinicians like myself who tend to believe that human disturbance largely springs from absolutistic thinking—from dogmatism, inflexibility, and devout shoulds, oughts, and musts—and

The dominant values in psychotherapy can be contrasted with those of a theistic approach that roots values in faith in God. The prevailing clinical-humanistic values assume that a) because humans are supreme, the individual self should be liberated from external authority, b) self-expression and self-gratification are to be encouraged, c) self-worth is defined through relationships with others, and d) meaning and purpose are derived from one's own reason and intellect. By contrast, theistic values assume that a) because God is supreme, humility and the acceptance of divine authority are virtues, b) self-control and committed love and self-sacrifice are to be encouraged, c) self-worth is defined through relationship with God, and d) meaning and purpose are derived from spiritual insight.

Drawing from my own religious values, I offer some testable hypotheses: 1. Religious communities that provide both a belief structure and a network of loving support should manifest lower rates of emotional disorder. 2. Those who endorse high standards of impulse control will suffer lower than average rates of alcoholism, addiction, divorce, and emotional instability. 3. Infidelity to any interpersonal commitment, especially marriage, leads to harmful consequences. 4. Teaching clients love, commitment, service, and sacrifice for others will help heal interpersonal difficulties and reduce intrapsychic distress. 5. Improving male commitment, caring, and responsibility in families will reduce marital and familial conflict and associated psychological disorders.

that extreme religiosity is essentially emotional disturbance. I assume that a) no one and nothing is supreme, b) relationships with others do not define self-worth (nothing does—self-acceptance can be had for the asking), c) self-gratification is encouraged with mutually chosen partners, with or without long-term responsibilities, and d) meaning is derived from personal desire and validated by test and by reason.

I therefore offer the following alternative hypotheses: 1) That devout, orthodox, or dogmatic religion is significantly correlated with emotional disturbance, because devoutly religious persons tend to be inflexible, closed, intolerant, and unchanging. 2) The elegant therapeutic solution to emotional problems is to be quite unreligious and have no degree of dogmatic faith that is unfounded or unfoundable in fact. 3) There is no intrinsic connection between religion and morality, and one can be a highly moral atheist or a distinctly immoral religionist (or vice versa). 4) Unequivocal and eternal fidelity to any interpersonal commitment, especially marriage, leads to harmful consequences. 5) Teaching clients unselective, universal, and unequivocal love, commitment, service, and sacrifice for others will help sabotage interpersonal relations and increase intrapsychic distress.

Source: Adapted, with permission, from an exchange in the *Journal of Consulting and Clinical Psychology,* 1980, Vol. 48, pp. 102–103, 635, 637–638.

Cognitive Therapy for Depression Like Ellis, cognitively oriented therapist Aaron Beck was originally trained in Freudian techniques. As Beck analyzed his depressed patients' dreams, negative themes such as loss, rejection, and abandonment seemed to recur and to extend into their waking thoughts. So in his form of cognitive therapy, Beck and his colleagues (1979) seek to reverse clients' negative beliefs about themselves, their situations, and their futures. Although Beck shares with Ellis the goal of getting depressed people to take off the dark-colored glasses through which they view life, his technique is a gentler questioning that aims to help people discover their irrationalities (Beck & others, 1979, pp. 145–146):

Patient: *I agree with the descriptions of me but I guess I don't agree that the way I think makes me depressed.*

Therapist: *How do you understand it?*

Patient: *I get depressed when things go wrong. Like when I fail a test.*

Therapist: *How can failing a test make you depressed?*

Patient: *Well, if I fail I'll never get into law school.*

Therapist: *So failing the test means a lot to you. But if failing a test could drive people into clinical depression, wouldn't you expect everyone who failed the test to have a depression? . . . Did everyone who failed get depressed enough to require treatment?*

Patient: *No, but it depends on how important the test was to the person.*

Therapist: *Right, and who decides the importance?*

Patient: *I do.*

Therapist: *And so, what we have to examine is your way of viewing the test (or the way that you* think *about the test) and how it affects your chances of getting into law school. Do you agree?*

Patient: *Right.*

Therapist: *Do you agree that the way you interpret the results of the test will affect you? You might feel depressed, you might have trouble sleeping, not feel like eating, and you might even wonder if you should drop out of the course.*

Patient: *I have been thinking that I wasn't going to make it. Yes, I agree.*

Therapist: *Now what did failing mean?*

Patient: *(tearful) That I couldn't get into law school.*

Therapist: *And what does that mean to you?*

Patient: *That I'm just not smart enough.*

Therapist: *Anything else?*

Patient: *That I can never be happy.*

Therapist: *And how do these* thoughts *make you feel?*

Patient: *Very unhappy.*

Therapist: *So it is the meaning of failing a test that makes you very unhappy. In fact, believing that you can never be happy is a powerful factor in producing unhappiness. So, you get yourself into a trap—by definition, failure to get into law school equals "I can never be happy."*

GUILT DAY AT SHEA

A new variation of cognitive therapy, called "attributional style therapy," builds upon the finding (described on pp. 445–446) that depressed people often attribute their failures to themselves and their successes to external circumstances, whereas nondepressed people tend to take credit for their successes and blame circumstances when things go wrong. In one attempt to teach depressed people to change their typical attributions, Mary Anne Layden (1982) first explained to them the advantages of making attributions more like those of the typical nondepressed person. Then, after administering a questionnaire and assigning a variety of tasks, she helped the depressed people to see how they typically interpret success and failure. Finally, she instructed each person in keeping a diary of daily successes and failures, making special note of how they contributed to their own successes and of external reasons for their failures. When retested after a month of this attributional retraining (and compared with a control group of untreated depressed people), the experimental group's self-esteem had risen significantly and their attributional style had become more like that of nondepressed people. And the more their attributional style had improved, the more their depression was alleviated.

Donald Meichenbaum (1977) similarly advocates training people to think more adaptively. His "self-instructional training" helps people to identify and change their maladaptive statements. Because we often think in words, getting people to change what they say to themselves is an effective way to change their thinking (Dush & others, 1983). For example, perhaps you can identify with the anxious students who before an exam make matters worse with self-defeating thoughts: "This exam is probably going to be impossible. All these other students seem so relaxed and self-confident. I wish I were better prepared. Oh no, here I go again. I'm so nervous I'll forget everything." To change such negative patterns, Meichenbaum trains people to restructure the way they think in stressful situations. Sometimes it may be enough simply to say more positive things to oneself: "Relax. The exam may be hard, but it will be hard for everyone else, too. I studied harder than most people. Besides, I don't need a perfect score to get a good grade."

Each of these cognitive therapies combines attempts to reverse irrational, self-defeating thinking with more behaviorally oriented practice in new ways of talking and acting and with other standard behavioral techniques such as desensitization. Although they are therefore called *cognitive-behavior* therapies, therapists debate whether treatment successes are due more to the cognitive or the behavioral component (Latimer & Sweet, 1984).

Evaluating Psychotherapies

Several times each month, Ann Landers advises letter writers to get themselves to a mental health professional for psychological repair. One response concludes by urging the writer "not to give up. Hang in there until you find someone [a psychotherapist] who fills the bill. It's worth the effort." The same day's second letter writer is advised, "There are many excellent mental health facilities in your city. I urge you to make an appointment at once" (Farina & Fisher, 1982).

Many people apparently share Ann Landers' confidence in the effectiveness of psychotherapy. Between 1955 and 1980 the number of Americans who had ever been in contact with a mental health practitioner reportedly increased tenfold, from 1 percent to 10 percent (Klerman, 1983). Prior to mid-century, psychiatrists were the main providers of professional mental health treatment. Since then the demand has been growing faster than the psychiatric profession and most psychotherapy is now done by clinical psychologists; clinical social workers; pastoral, marital, and school counselors; and psychiatric nurses. And in the United States alone, the annual mental health bill exceeds $15 billion (Pines, 1982).

Is the faith that Ann Landers and millions of other people place in psychotherapy justified? To pose the question as government and private health-insurance programs do, is psychotherapy effective?

Is Psychotherapy Effective?

The question, though simply put, is not simply answered. For one thing, measuring effectiveness is not like taking temperature readings on a thermometer. If you and I were to undergo psychotherapy, how would we gauge its effectiveness? In terms of how we feel about our progress? How our therapist feels about it? How our friends and family feel about it? How another clinician would independently judge us? How our behavior has changed?

"Therapists are not in agreement as to their goals or aims. . . . They are not in agreement as to what constitutes a successful outcome. They cannot agree as to what constitutes a failure."
Carl Rogers

Clients' Perceptions If clients' testimonials were the only measure, we could strongly affirm the healing power of psychotherapy. In the more than two dozen available studies of consumer satisfaction with psychotherapy, 3 out of 4 clients report themselves satisfied and 1 in 2 say they are "very satisfied" (Lebow, 1982). We have their word for it—and who should know better?

We should not dismiss these testimonials lightly. If after entering therapy because they were suffering, people leave feeling better about themselves, that is not inconsequential. But there are several reasons why testimonials do not persuade skeptics. For one thing, clients may have a need to believe the therapy was worth the effort. To admit that one continued investing time and money in something that was doing no good is like admitting that one continued to have one's car serviced by a mechanic who never fixed it. For another, clients generally like their therapists and speak kindly of them. Even if the clients' problems remain, say the therapy critics, "they work hard to find something positive to say. The therapist had been very understanding, the client had gained a new perspective, he learned to communicate better, his mind was eased, anything at all so as not to have to say treatment was a failure" (Zilbergeld, 1983, p. 117).

"If it is illusion to which I owe the health I believe I enjoy, I humbly entreat the experts who see so clearly not to destroy it."
Testimony of a satisfied patient to the Benjamin Franklin Commission investigating mesmerism

What is more, there is ample evidence that testimonials can be misleading. Despite tributes by encounter group participants to their newfound openness and sensitivity, researchers have found that these self-perceptions "are rarely reflected in significant changes in behavior or interpersonal effectiveness in the work environment" (Chemers & Fiedler, 1978).

Consider a massive experiment with over 500 Massachusetts boys, ages 5 to 13 years, many of whom seemed bound for delinquency. By the toss of a coin, half the boys were assigned to a treatment program for 5 years: They were visited twice a month by counselors, they were involved in community programs such as Boy Scouts, and, as the need arose, they received academic tutoring, medical attention, and family assistance. By 1979, some 30 years after the end of the program, Joan McCord (1978, 1979) managed to locate 97 percent of the participants and to assess the impact of the treatment by questionnaire and by check of public records from courts, mental hospitals, and other sources.

Assessing the treatment program with client testimonials yielded encouraging results. Many of the men offered glowing reports. Some even noted that had it not been for their counselors, "I would probably be in jail," "My life would have gone the other way," or "I think I would have ended up in a life of crime." The court records offered apparent support for these testimonials. Even among the "difficult" boys in the program, 66 percent had no official juvenile crime record.

But for every boy who was counseled in this "Cambridge-Somerville Youth Study," as the project is called, there was a similar boy in the control group of this experiment who was not. McCord tracked down these untreated people, too, and found that of these predelinquent boys, 70 percent had no juvenile record. Moreover, on some measures, such as a record of having committed a second crime, alcoholic tendencies, death rate, and job satisfaction, the treated men exhibited slightly *more* problems. The glowing testimonials of those treated had been deceiving. Perhaps, McCord speculated, the intervention had created a dependency, or maybe it had generated such high expectations that greater frustration was experienced later, or perhaps it had led the boys to view themselves as requiring help.

Clinicians' Perceptions If clinicians' perceptions accurately reflected their own therapeutic effectiveness, we would have even more reason to celebrate. Case studies of successful treatment abound. Furthermore, every therapist treasures compliments from clients as they say goodbye, and from satisfied former clients. The problem is that clients tend to justify their entering psychotherapy by emphasizing their woes, to justify their leaving therapy by emphasizing their well-being, and to stay in touch only if they are satisfied. Therapists are aware of failures, but many of these are the failures of other therapists—therapists whose clients, sometimes having experienced only temporary relief, are now seeking a new therapist for their recurring problems. Thus the same person, with the same recurring difficulty—the same old weight problem, depression, or marital difficulty—may represent "success" stories in several therapists' files.

Outcome Research Psychologists have therefore turned to controlled research studies in hopes of better assessing the effectiveness of psychotherapy. The opening volley in what has become a spirited debate over such research was fired by British psychologist Hans Eysenck (1952). After summarizing the data available from studies of eclectic psychotherapy, he concluded that after undergoing psychotherapy approximately two-thirds of those suffering neurotic disorders had improved markedly. To this day, no one disputes that optimistic estimate.

So why are we still debating psychotherapy's healing power? Because Eysenck also reported a similar improvement rate among *untreated* neurotic persons, such as those who were on waiting lists. With or without psychotherapy, he said, roughly two-thirds improved noticeably. The avalanche of criticism prompted by Eysenck's analysis revealed some shortcomings in his work. For one thing, those in the untreated control group were not exactly comparable to those who were treated. When clinical researchers Allen Bergin and Michael Lambert (1978) reanalyzed Eysenck's data, they found that the ***spontaneous remission*** rate (the rate of improvement without treatment) was actually 43 percent. (Even this rate of spontaneous remissions is heartening evidence of the capacity of human beings to overcome their miseries.)

"Fortunately, [psycho]analysis is not the only way to resolve inner conflicts. Life itself still remains a very effective therapist."
Karen Horney,
Our Inner Conflicts, 1945

Despite its weaknesses, Eysenck's paper was a historic prod. It raised such questions as: How can we objectively measure the effectiveness of psychotherapy? What types of people and problems are most likely to be helped, and by what type of psychotherapy? The questions have both academic and personal relevance. If you or someone you care about suffers a psychological disorder, how likely is it that psychotherapy will help? And how great might you expect the dividends to be?

In 1952, Eysenck could find only twenty-four studies of psychotherapy outcomes to analyze. Today, there are hundreds. In the best of these studies, people on a waiting list for therapy are randomly assigned to different treatments or to no treatment. Afterward, all of the people are evaluated using tests and the reports of their close associates or those of psychologists who are "blind" as to whether therapy was given. The results of such studies are being digested by a new technique called ***meta-analysis,*** a procedure for statistically combining the results of many different studies.

In the first reported meta-analysis of psychotherapy outcome studies, Mary Lee Smith, Gene Glass, and Thomas Miller (1980) combined the results of 475 investigations. For psychotherapists, the welcome result was that "The evidence overwhelmingly supports the efficacy of psychotherapy" (p. 183). Figure 17-3 depicts their finding—that the average therapy client ends up better off than 80 percent of the untreated individuals on waiting lists. While the claim is more modest than first appears—50 percent of the untreated people also are better off than the average untreated person—Smith and her collaborators concluded that: "Psychotherapy benefits people of all ages as reliably as schooling educates them, medicine cures them, or business turns a profit" (p. 183).

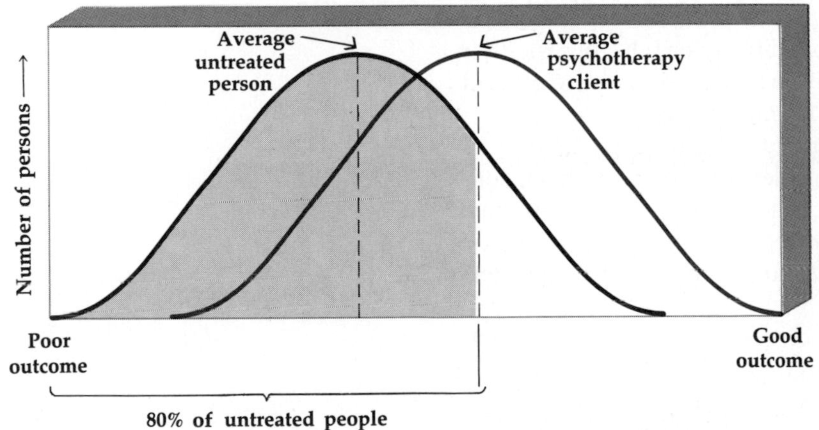

Figure 17-3 *The two normal distribution curves show the improvement of untreated people (black curve) and psychotherapy clients (red curve), based on data from 475 cases. The outcome for the average therapy client surpasses that for 80 percent of the untreated people.*

So, while extravagant claims that psychotherapy can transform one's personality seem unwarranted, Eysenck's extreme pessimism also seems unwarranted. On the average, psychotherapy is somewhat effective. But note that "on the average" refers to no one therapy in particular. It is like saying "surgery is somewhat effective," or like reassuring lung cancer patients that "on the average," medical treatment of health problems is effective. What people want to know is not the effectiveness of therapy in general, but the effectiveness of particular treatments for their particular problems.

"Man can't help hoping, even if he is a scientist. He can only hope more accurately."
Karl Menninger,
Love Against Hate, 1959

Therapy's Effectiveness with Varied People and Problems.

As veteran clinical researcher Hans Strupp (1984) explains, "*Under appropriate circumstances* psychotherapy has a great deal to offer. Such circumstances prevail when the 'right' patient meets the 'right' therapist." But who is the "right" patient?

Strupp says that those most likely to benefit are sufficiently uncomfortable to desire change, are able to step back and examine themselves, and are reasonably mature and in control of themselves: "When these preconditions are not met or are only partially met (which is typically the case), psychotherapy faces an uphill battle."

Certain problems also seem more amenable to change. In general, the best results are obtained when the problem is clear-cut and specific (Singer, 1981). Those who suffer fears and phobias, who are impeded by a lack of assertiveness, or who are frustrated by premature ejaculation or orgasmic dysfunction can hope for improvement. Those who have been chronically schizophrenic, who lack the ability to control some impulse, or who wish their sexual orientation changed, are less likely to benefit from psychotherapy (Zilbergeld, 1983).

Relative Effectiveness of Different Therapies

Those who are considering therapy will want to know not only whether psychotherapy is likely to be effective for their problem but *which* psychotherapy will be most effective. The meta-analysis conducted by Mary Lee Smith and her colleagues (1977, 1980) enabled them to compare the effectiveness of different therapies. What do you suppose they found? Did one therapeutic technique get the best results? Did people benefit more from group or individual therapy? From sustained or short-term therapy? From therapy with experienced or novice therapists?

Despite claims of superiority by advocates of different therapies, Smith's comparison of the therapies revealed no clear winner. No one type of therapy proved consistently superior. Moreover—and more astonishing—it seemed to make no discernible difference whether the therapy was group or individual, whether many or few sessions were offered, or how well-trained and experienced the therapist was.

Some therapies may yet prove superior for treating particular disorders, however. With specific behavior problems such as phobias, compulsions, or sexual dysfunctions, the conditioning therapies have achieved especially favorable results; with depression, the cognitive-behavior therapies have been especially successful (Frank, 1982; Giles, 1983; Shapiro & Shapiro, 1982).

Given the roughly 200 psychological disorders defined in DSM-III, the questions that remain for future research are almost limitless: What specific therapeutic techniques are helpful with what problems for what types of people under what conditions? As answers become available, hopes grow that it may be possible to integrate different therapies and to guide people toward therapies that are likely to be most effective for them (Goldfried, 1980, 1982).

Commonalities among Psychotherapies

Although the search to find the "best" therapy for the particular disorder will go on for a long while, the search may turn out to be unnecessary. Some clinicians now believe that there is a reason why no one therapeutic method seems to be generally superior or inferior to another: because, despite their apparent differences, their healing powers derive from their underlying commonalities.

Jerome Frank (1982) and Marvin Goldfried (Goldfried & Padawer, 1982), two psychologists who have studied the common ingredients of different therapies, suggest that all therapies offer the following:

Hope for Demoralized People People who seek therapy typically are anxious, depressed, or lacking in self-esteem and feeling incompetent to turn things around. What any therapy offers is an expectation that things can and will get better. Quite apart from the particular therapeutic technique, this belief may itself be sufficient to promote improved morale, new feelings of self-efficacy, and diminished symptoms (Prioleau & others, 1983). This effect of a person's belief in a treatment is called a ***placebo***

effect. As we saw in Chapter 8, a placebo is a treatment, often used as a control treatment in drug experiments, that has no actual effect apart from a person's believing it does.

The finding that placebo-treated people improve more than do untreated people, and nearly as much as those receiving actual psychotherapy, does not mean the psychotherapies are ineffective, only that part of the reason they help seems to be the hope that they offer. In their individual ways, each therapy may harness the person's own healing powers. And this, says Jerome Frank, helps us understand why all sorts of treatments—including some folk healing rites and medical practices now known to be powerless apart from the patient's belief—may in their own time and place produce cures.

"There are in every great, rich city a number of persons, who are never in health, because they are fond of medicines, and always taking them whereby they derange the natural functions, and hurt their constitution. If these people can be persuaded to forbear their drugs, in expectation of being cured by only the physician's finger, or an iron rod pointing at them, they may possibly find good effects, though they mistake the cause."
Benjamin Franklin, 1781

A New Perspective on Oneself and the World Every therapy offers people a plausible explanation of their symptoms and an alternative way of looking at themselves or responding to their worlds. Each also offers new learning experiences that help people to change their views of themselves.

An Empathic, Trusting, Caring Relationship To say that all therapies are about equally effective is not to say that all *therapists* are equally effective. Regardless of their therapeutic technique, effective therapists seem to be empathic people who can understand another's experience; whose care and concern are felt by the client; and whose respectful listening, reassurance, and advice earn the client's trust and respect (Strupp, 1984).

Effective therapists are those capable of forming a bond of trust with their clients, whether they be adults or children.

This seems to be supported by an important result, drawn from a meta-analysis of thirty-nine studies that compared treatment offered by professional therapists with the help offered by lay people—friendly professors, people who have had a few hours' training in empathic listening skills, college students who are being supervised by a professional clinician. The result? The "paraprofessionals," as these people are called, typically proved as effective as the professionals with whom they were compared (Berman & Norton, 1985; Hattie & others, 1984). Although most of the behavior problems they treated were mild, the trained paraprofessionals seemed as effective as professionals even when dealing with more disturbed adults, such as those who were seriously depressed.

Self-help groups, like this one for widows and widowers, often are started by a person who has experienced a tragedy—a serious illness or accident, loss of a spouse or a child, a problem with drinking or drugs—and who believes that by mutual sharing and support such traumas can be eased. These types of groups provide therapy for many who would not seek or could not afford professional help.

To review, what have we learned about the effectiveness of psychotherapy? People who seek help usually improve. So do many of those who do not receive psychotherapy, and that perhaps is a tribute to our human resourcefulness and to our capacity to care for one another. Nevertheless, though it appears not to matter much which type of therapy is practiced, nor how much is received, nor how experienced the therapist is, those who receive at least some therapy often improve more than those who receive none. Especially likely to improve are mature, articulate people with specific behavior problems. Part of what all therapies offer is hope and an empathic, caring relationship. That may explain why for mild problems, at least, the sympathy and friendly counsel of paraprofessionals are so often as helpful as professional psychotherapy. And that may also be why those who are supported by close relationships—who enjoy the fellowship and friendship of caring people—are less likely to need or seek therapy (Frank, 1982; O'Connor & Brown, 1984).

"I believe we are entering an era in which the claims and aspirations of psychotherapy will become more circumscribed and more focused. It may also spell a return to greater modesty, from which we should never have departed."
Hans Strupp

THE BIOMEDICAL THERAPIES

Psychotherapy is one major way of dealing with psychological disorders. The other is to alter the brain's functioning—by disconnecting its circuits through psychosurgery, by overloading its circuits with electroconvulsive shock, or by altering its electrochemical transmissions with drugs.

Psychosurgery

Because its effects are irreversible, ***psychosurgery***—surgery that removes or destroys brain tissue in an effort to change behavior—is the most drastic biomedical intervention. In the 1930s, Portugese physician Egas Moniz developed an operation that came to be called a ***lobotomy.*** Moniz found that when he surgically cut the nerves that connect the frontal lobes with the emotion-controlling centers of the inner brain, uncontrollably emotional and violent patients were calmed. During the 1940s and

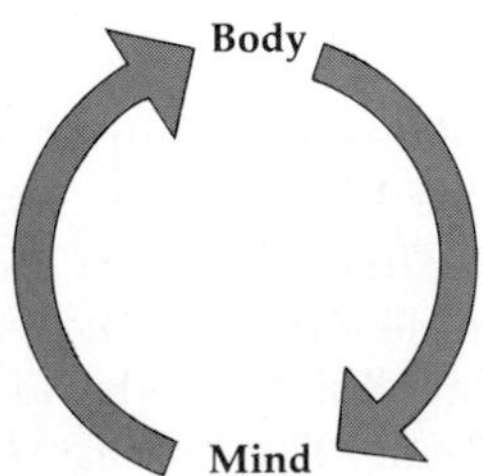

The biomedical therapies are based upon the belief that mind and body are a unity: affect one and you likely will affect the other.

1950s literally tens of thousands of severely disturbed people were "lobotomized," and Moniz was honored with a Nobel Prize.

Although the intention was simply to disconnect emotion from thought, the effect was often more drastic; it produced a permanently lethargic, immature personality. When during the 1950s calming drugs became readily available, psychosurgery was largely abandoned. Today, psychosurgery is used only in extreme cases. For example, if a patient suffers uncontrollable seizures, surgeons can deactivate the specific nerve clusters that cause the convulsions (Valenstein, 1980). Even such apparently beneficial operations are irreversible, however, and so are used only as a last resort.

Electroconvulsive Therapy

A less drastic manipulation of the brain occurs with the still widely practiced use of ***electroconvulsive therapy (ECT).*** When first introduced in 1938, the wide-awake patient would be strapped to a table and jolted with roughly 100 volts of electricity to the brain, producing bone-rattling convulsions and momentary unconsciousness. Today, the procedure is much less terrifying and is used only with severely depressed patients (having been found to be ineffective in treating other disorders such as schizophrenia). The patient is first given a general anesthetic and a muscle relaxant. Then the shock is administered to the soundly sleeping patient for a fraction of a second, causing a minute or so of convulsions. Within 30 minutes the patient awakens and remembers nothing of the treatment.

The medical use of electricity is actually an ancient practice. The Roman Emperor Claudius (10 B.C.–A.D. 54) was treated for headaches by pressing electric eels to his temples.

Although some patients complain of temporary memory loss, after three such treatments a week for 2 to 4 weeks, depressed people often improve markedly and without discernible brain damage (Scovern & Kilmann, 1980; Weiner, 1984). "A miracle had happened in two weeks," reported noted research psychologist Norman Endler (1982) after ECT alleviated his deep depression. A 1985 panel of the National Institutes of Health reports that for others the effect may be less than a miracle, but still an effective treatment for severe depression that has not responded to drug therapy (Kolata, 1985b). Thus, during the 1980s the use of ECT has been on the rise.

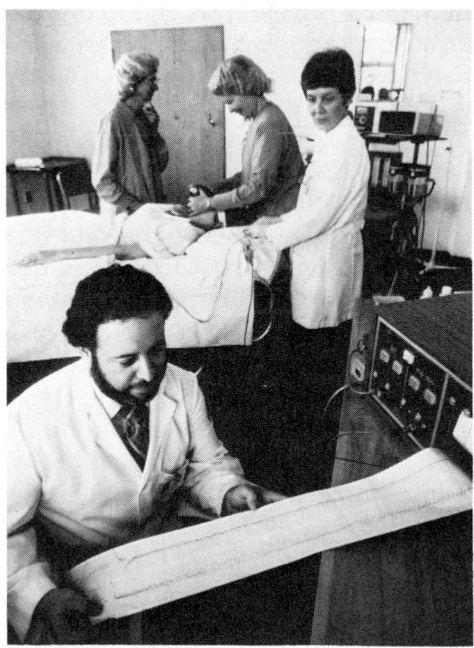

Electroconvulsive therapy is a controversial treatment that may provide relief from depression.

How does it work? After 45 years of use, the process remains a mystery. ECT has so many effects on the brain, endocrine glands, and muscles that the difficulty lies in discerning which changes are linked to its antidepressant effect and which are irrelevant. One possible explanation is that it triggers increased release of norepinephrine, the neurotransmitter that elevates arousal and mood and seems in short supply during depression. Another is that depression is linked with the overactivity of certain brain areas and that these may become less active as the brain reacts against the hyperactivity of the shock-induced seizure (Sackheim, 1985).

Although ECT is believed to have saved thousands from suicide and is now used on some 80,000 Americans a year (Sackheim, 1985), its Frankenstein-like image continues. No matter how impressive the results, the idea of shocking people into convulsions does seem barbaric to many of us, especially given our ignorance about why ECT works. (In 1982, the voters of Berkeley, California banned its use within their city, a vote that was later overturned in court.) Nevertheless, for the present, ECT remains in the minds of many psychiatrists and patients a lesser evil than the misery, anguish, and risk of suicide that are associated with severe depression.

Drug Therapies

By far the most widely used biomedical treatments are the drug therapies. Introduced in the 1950s, they have reduced the need for psychosurgery and in many cases have reduced the need for hospitalization. New discoveries in ***psychopharmacology*** (the study of the effect of drugs on mind and behavior) have revolutionized the treatment of severely disordered people, enabling thousands to be liberated from confinement in mental hospitals (Figure 17-4). (For others—those still unable to care for themselves—release from hospitals has meant not liberation but hunger and homelessness [Cordes, 1985].)

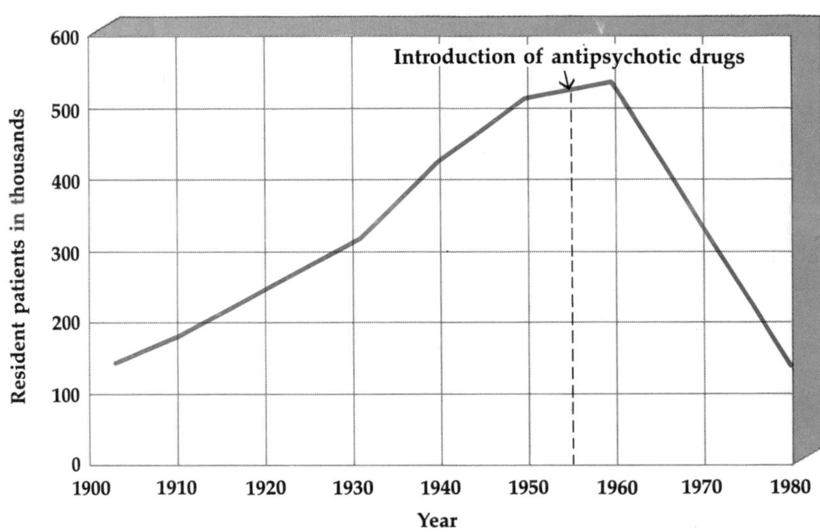

Figure 17-4 *The emptying of America's mental hospitals. After the widespread introduction of antipsychotic drugs, starting in about 1955, the number of residents in state and county mental hospitals began to decline and has been dropping sharply ever since. The new drugs and efforts to "normalize" patients' environments were primarily responsible, but concerns about the involuntary hospitalization of patients have also had an effect. This rush to "deinstitutionalize" the mentally ill has unfortunately left many people who are ill-equipped to care for themselves homeless on our city streets.*

With almost any new treatment, there is initially a wave of enthusiasm as many people recover. But that enthusiasm often diminishes after researchers subtract (1) the rate of normal recovery among untreated persons, and (2) that due to the placebo effect, which arises from expectations of improvement on the part of patients and staff alike. So, to evaluate the effectiveness of a drug, researchers use a ***double-blind*** experiment. Half the patients are given the drug, the other half a similar-appearing placebo. Neither the patients nor the staff knows whether a given patient has received the drug or placebo; both groups are "blind." In double-blind studies, several categories of drugs have been found useful for treatment of psychological disorders.

Antipsychotic Drugs

The revolution in drug therapy for psychological disorders began when it was accidentally discovered that certain drugs, which were being used for other medical purposes, also served to calm psychotic patients. For example, many schizophrenics, especially those experiencing auditory hallucinations and paranoia, seem to be helped by antipsychotic drugs that dampen their responsiveness to irrelevant stimuli (Figure 17-5). The drug molecules, which are similar to molecules of the neurotransmitter dopamine, occupy receptor sites for dopamine, thus blocking its activity and decreasing its production (Pickar & others, 1984). This finding that antipsychotic drugs block dopamine receptors reinforces an idea noted in Chapter 16 that, as psychopharmacologist Solomon Snyder (1984b) put it, "dopamine systems in the brain are closely related to whatever is fundamentally abnormal in schizophrenic brains—either an excess of dopamine formation or perhaps a supersensitivity of dopamine receptors."

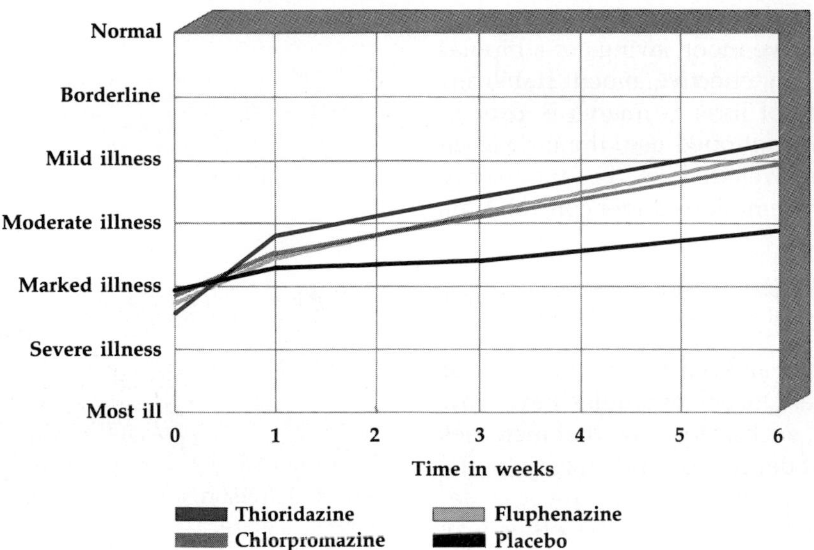

Figure 17-5 *A double-blind study comparing the improvement of schizophrenic patients who received placebos to the improvement of those who received one of three related antipsychotic drugs.*

The antipsychotics are powerful drugs that can have side effects similar to the tremors and muscular coordination problems of Parkinson's disease (Kaplan & Sadock, 1981). Thus, the trick with every drug and every patient is to tread the fine line between relieving the symptoms and causing unpleasant side effects by carefully monitoring the dosage and its effects. In this way, and with the help of supportive people, hundreds of thousands of schizophrenic patients who had been consigned to the back wards of mental hospitals have been able to return to jobs and to near-normal lives.

Antianxiety Drugs

Antianxiety drugs, such as Valium and Librium, are among the most heavily prescribed drugs. In 1984, American druggists filled 25 million prescriptions for Valium, which is now also sold under its generic name, diazepam. Like alcohol, these drugs depress central nervous system activity. Because they seem to reduce tension and anxiety without causing excessive sleepiness, they have been prescribed even for minor emotional stresses. Sometimes, too, an antianxiety drug used in combination with other therapy can help a person learn to cope successfully with fear-arousing situations. Calmed with the help of a drug, the person may be able to face anxiety-triggering stimuli and so learn to lessen the anxiety response.

The criticism sometimes made of the behavior therapies—that they reduce symptoms without resolving underlying problems—has been made of antianxiety drugs, which, unlike the behavior therapies, may be used as a continuing treatment. Routinely "popping a Valium" at the first sign of tension can eventually produce psychological dependence on the drug. Also, apart from its temporary calming effect, a recent study of Valium users suggests that the drug does less to reduce ongoing anxiety than its users believe (Caplan & others, 1984). When one's anxiety level is high it tends to come down within a few weeks, but this occurs as quickly for those not using Valium as for those who are.

Antidepressant Drugs

If the antianxiety drugs can be said to calm anxious people down, the antidepressants could be said to lift up the mood of depressed people. These drugs apparently increase the release of the neurotransmitters such as norepinephrine that are thought to be scarce during depression.

For those suffering the manic-depressive mood swings of a bipolar disorder, the chemical ***lithium*** is often an effective mood stabilizer. Within 2 weeks after beginning daily use of lithium, mania is usually controlled (Kaplan & Sadock, 1981). With continued use, the emotional highs and lows are typically somewhat leveled. Like the antianxiety drugs, the antidepressants are used to bring emotions under control, thus facilitating the process of psychotherapy.

Aerobic Exercise

The newest form of therapy is the least risky and most natural of all, and its side effects are almost entirely positive. Dozens of studies have now linked ***aerobic exercise*** (sustained exercise, such as jogging, that increases heart and lung fitness) with lower levels of depression and anxiety. Some studies simply report that people who exercise regularly are less depressed than those who do not. But when we say this the other way around—people who are more depressed seem not to be very physically active—we see that it is not clear which is the cause and which the effect.

"A strong body makes the mind strong."
Thomas Jefferson,
Letter to Peter Carr, 1785

This ambiguity is resolved by new experiments that have randomly assigned depressed or anxious people to aerobic exercise treatments or to other treatments. In one experiment (that was briefly introduced on p. 14), Lisa McCann and David Holmes (1984) assigned one-third of a group of mildly depressed women students to a program of aerobic dancing and running, another third to a placebo treatment of relaxation exercises, and the remaining third to a no-treatment control condition. As Figure 17-6 illustrates, when the students' self-reported depression levels were reassessed 5 and 10 weeks later, the aerobic exercise group had become less depressed, while the other two groups had changed less.

It remains for future research to determine the necessary "dosage levels" for desirable effects (will jogging 4 miles a day accomplish more than 2 miles three times a week?), to ascertain whether aerobic exercise can also help *prevent* depression and anxiety, and to specify more clearly why aerobic exercise affects our psychological state. For instance, does vigorous exercise trigger increased production of mood-boosting neurotransmitters such as norepinephrine or the endorphins? Does exercise burn off anxiety-creating biochemicals such as lactic acid? Do the emotional benefits occur as side effects of increased muscle relaxation and sounder sleep? Do a sense of accomplishment and an improved physique contribute to the emotional benefits? These and other possibilities have been suggested (Ledwidge, 1980; Mihevic, 1982).

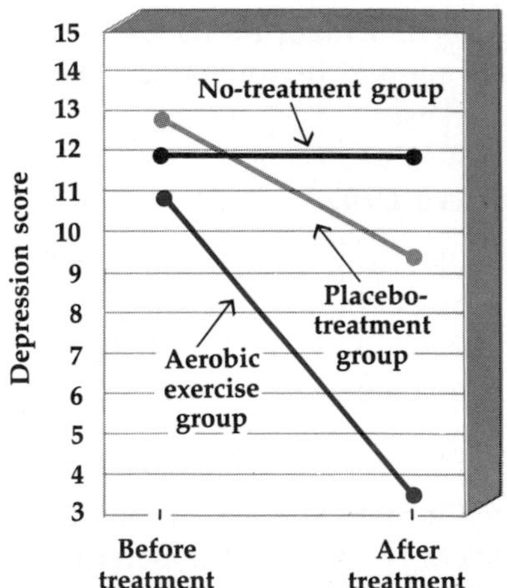

Figure 17-6 *Aerobic exercise and depression. Mildly depressed college students who participated in an aerobic exercise program experienced markedly reduced depression compared to those assigned to a placebo treatment of relaxation exercises or no treatment.*

TREATING THE SOCIAL ROOTS OF PSYCHOLOGICAL DISORDERS

Both the psychotherapies and the biomedical therapies locate psychological disorders within individuals and thus seek to remedy them by changing individuals. Thus we infer that people who act cruelly must be cruel people and that people who act "crazy" must be "sick." We attach labels to such people, thereby distinguishing them from the rest of us "normal" people. It follows, then, that we try to treat "abnormal" people by giving them insight into their problems, by changing their thinking, or by controlling them with drugs.

However, there is another way to view many psychological disorders—as an understandable response to a disturbed and stressful society. According to this view, it is not just the individual who needs treatment, but also the social context in which the individual acts. The idea is that many of these problems do not suddenly spring up in an individual but develop from the person's history of stressful experiences in a particular environment.

Family Therapies

The fundamental assumption of ***family therapy*** is that no one is an island. Because we live and grow in relationship to others, especially our families, our problem behaviors can often be understood as our responses to others and as our attempts to influence them. Consequently, family therapists attempt to heal broken family relationships by opening up communication within the family and by helping family members to discover new ways of resolving conflicts. Family therapist Virginia Satir (1967, pp. 98–100) illustrates the process:

> ***Therapist:*** *As far as you know, have you ever been in that same spot before, that is, were you puzzled by something Alice said or did?*
>
> ***Husband:*** *Hell, yes, lots of times.*
>
> ***Therapist:*** *Have you ever told Alice you were puzzled when you were?*
>
> ***Wife:*** *He never says anything.*
>
> ***Therapist:*** *(smiling, to Alice) Just a minute, Alice, let me hear what Ralph's idea is of what he does. Ralph, how do you think you have let Alice know when you are puzzled?*
>
> ***Husband:*** *I think she knows.*
>
> ***Therapist:*** *Well, let's see. Suppose you ask Alice if she knows.*
>
> ***Husband:*** *This is silly.*
>
> ***Therapist:*** *(smiling) I suppose it might seem so in this situation, because Alice is right here and certainly has heard what your question is. She knows what it is. I have the suspicion, though, that neither you nor Alice are very sure about what the other expects, and I think you have not developed ways to find out. Alice, let's go back to when I commented on Ralph's wrinkled brow. Did you happen to notice it, too?*
>
> ***Wife:*** *(complaining) Yes, he always looks like that.*
>
> ***Therapist:*** *What kind of message did you get from that wrinkled brow?*
>
> ***Wife:*** *He don't want to be here. He don't care. He never talks. Just looks at television or he isn't home.*
>
> ***Therapist:*** *I'm curious. Do you mean that when Ralph has a wrinkled brow that you take this as Ralph's way of saying, "I don't love you, Alice. I don't care about you, Alice"?*
>
> ***Wife:*** *(exasperated and tearfully) I don't know.*
>
> ***Therapist:*** *Well, maybe the two of you have not yet worked out crystal-clear ways of giving your love and value messages to each other. Everyone needs crystal-clear ways of giving their value messages. (To son) What do you know, Jim, about how you give your value messages to your parents?*
>
> ***Son:*** *I don't know what you mean.*
>
> ***Therapist:*** *Well, how do you let your mother, for instance, know that you like her, when you are feeling that way. Everyone feels different ways at different times. When you are feeling glad your mother is around, how do you let her know?*
>
> ***Son:*** *I do what she tells me to do. Work and stuff. . . .*

Therapist: *Let's check this out and see if you are perceiving clearly. Do you, Alice, get a love message from Jim when he works around the house?*

Wife: *I s'pose—he doesn't do very much.*

Therapist: *So from where you sit, Alice, you don't get many love messages from Jim. Tell me, Alice, does Jim have any other ways . . . that say to you he is glad you are around?*

Wife: *(softly) The other day he told me I looked nice.*

Crisis intervention centers like this one provide immediate short-term help for those who during a period of severe stress are unable to cope. While providing reassurance, the therapist works with the client to alleviate the problem, involving other agencies or family members when their help is needed.

Preventive Mental Health

Some therapists look beyond the family to the even larger social context in which both families and individuals act. These concerns can be illustrated in a story about someone who rescues a drowning person from a river. Having successfully administered first aid, the rescuer spots another struggling person and pulls her out, too. After a half dozen repetitions of this, the rescuer suddenly turns and starts running away while yet another person is seen floundering. "Aren't you going to rescue that fellow?" asks a bystander. "Heck no," the rescuer replies. "I'm going upstream to find what's pushing all these people in." Preventive mental health is upstream work. It seeks to prevent psychological casualties by identifying and alleviating the conditions that cause them. George Albee (1982), a past president of the American Psychological Association, contends that there is abundant evidence that poverty, meaningless work, constant criticism, unemployment, racism, and sexism undermine people's senses of competence, personal control, and self-esteem, thereby increasing their risk of psychological disorders. Those who care about preventing psychological casualties should therefore support programs that alleviate poverty and other demoralizing situations: "Everything aimed at improving the human condition, at making life more fulfilling and meaningful, may be considered part of primary prevention of mental or emotional disturbance" (Kessler & Albee, 1975, p. 557).

SUMMING UP

THE PSYCHOLOGICAL THERAPIES

The major psychotherapies are derived from the familiar psychoanalytic, humanistic, and cognitive-learning perspectives on personality.

Psychoanalysis The goal of psychoanalysts is to help people gain insight into the unconscious origins of their disorders and to work through the accompanying feelings. To do so, they draw upon techniques such as free association and the interpretation of resistances, dreams, and the transference to the therapist of long repressed feelings. Like psychoanalytic theory, psychoanalysis is criticized for its after-the-fact interpretations and for being time-consuming and costly. Although traditional psychoanalysis is not practiced widely, its influence can be seen in therapists who explore childhood experiences, who assume that defense mechanisms suppress emotion-laden information, and who seek to help their clients achieve insight into the roots of their problems.

Humanistic Therapies Unlike psychoanalysts, humanistic therapists tend to focus on clients' current, conscious feelings and on their taking responsibility for their own growth. Carl Rogers, in his person-centered therapy, uses active listening to express genuineness, acceptance, and empathy. With Gestalt therapy, Fritz Perls sought to break down people's defenses and to make them accept responsibility for their feelings. Many therapeutic techniques can also be applied in group therapy, as in the application of humanistic principles within encounter groups.

Behavior Therapies Behavior therapists worry less about promoting self-awareness and more about directly modifying problem behaviors. Thus they may countercondition behaviors through systematic desensitization or aversive conditioning. Or they may apply operant conditioning principles with behavior modification techniques such as token economies. The newer cognitive-behavior therapies, such as Ellis's rational-emotive therapy, Beck's cognitive therapy for depression, and Meichenbaum's self-instructional training, all aim to change self-defeating thinking by training people to look at themselves in new, more positive ways.

Evaluating Psychotherapies Because the positive testimonials of clients and therapists cannot prove that therapy is actually effective, psychologists have conducted hundreds of studies of the outcomes of psychotherapy. These studies indicate that (1) people who remain untreated often improve (a phenomenon called spontaneous remission); (2) those who receive psychotherapy tend to improve somewhat more, regardless of what kind of therapy they receive and for how long; (3) mature, articulate people with specific behavior problems often receive the greatest benefits from therapy; but (4) placebo treatments or the sympathy and friendly counsel of paraprofessionals also tend to produce more improvement than occurs with untreated people.

THE BIOMEDICAL THERAPIES

Although radical, irreversible psychosurgery procedures, such as lobotomy, are now seldom used, the controversial but sometimes mysteriously effective procedure of electroconvulsive therapy (ECT) still is. But far more widely used are the antipsychotic, antianxiety, and antidepressant drugs. Aerobic exercise also appears to help alleviate high levels of depression or anxiety.

TREATING THE SOCIAL ROOTS OF PSYCHOLOGICAL DISORDERS

Rather than locating psychological problems within individuals, family therapists treat the family relationships out of which they believe problem behaviors arise. Psychologists concerned with preventive mental health argue that many psychological disorders could be prevented by changing oppressive, esteem-destroying environments.

TERMS AND CONCEPTS TO REMEMBER

Active Listening Empathic listening in which the listener echoes, restates, and clarifies. A feature of Rogers' person-centered therapy.

Aerobic Exercise Sustained exercise that increases heart and lung fitness; often helps to alleviate depression and anxiety.

Aversive Conditioning A type of counterconditioning that associates an unpleasant state (such as nausea) with an unwanted behavior (such as drinking alcohol).

Behavior Modification The application of operant conditioning principles to the modification of human behavior. (Behavior modification is also sometimes used as a synonym for behavior therapy.)

Behavior Therapy Therapy that applies learning principles to the elimination of unwanted behaviors.

Cognitive-Behavior Therapy Therapy that teaches people new, more adaptive ways of thinking and acting; based on the assumption that thoughts intervene between events and our emotional reactions.

Counterconditioning A behavior therapy procedure that conditions new responses to stimuli that trigger unwanted behaviors; based on classical conditioning. See also *systematic desensitization* and *aversive conditioning*.

Double-blind Procedure An experimental procedure in which both the patient and the staff are ignorant (blind) as to whether the patient has received the treatment or a placebo. Commonly used in drug evaluation studies.

Eclectic Selecting what appears to be the best of various theories and methods; eclectic therapists draw techniques from the various forms of therapy, depending on the problems encountered.

Electroconvulsive Therapy (ECT) A biomedical therapy sometimes used with severely depressed patients in which a brief electric current is sent through the brain, producing a minute or so of convulsions followed by a period of relief from depression.

Encounter Groups Gatherings of 12 to 20 people whose emotion-laden group experiences are characterized by honesty and openness, through which the participants hope to grow in self-awareness and social sensitivity.

Family Therapy Therapy that treats individuals as part of a family system in which unwanted behaviors may be engendered by or directed at other family members, and that encourages family members to heal relationships and improve communication.

Gestalt Therapy A therapy developed by Fritz Perls that combines the psychoanalytic emphasis on bringing to awareness unconscious feelings and the humanistic emphasis on getting in touch with oneself; aims to help people become more aware of and able to express their moment-to-moment feelings.

Interpretation In psychoanalysis, the analyst's assisting the patient to note and understand resistances and other significant behaviors in order to promote insight.

Lithium A chemical that provides an effective drug therapy for the mood swings of bipolar (manic-depressive) disorders.

Lobotomy A no-longer-used psychosurgical procedure to calm uncontrollably emotional or violent patients in which the nerves that connect the frontal lobes to the emotion-controlling centers of the inner brain are cut. Also called frontal (or prefrontal) lobotomy.

Meta-analysis A procedure for statistically combining the results of many different studies.

Person-Centered Therapy Carl Rogers' humanistic therapy, in which the therapist attempts to facilitate clients' growth by offering genuineness, acceptance, and empathy.

Placebo Effect The beneficial effect of a person's *expecting* that a treatment will be therapeutic. A placebo is a neutral treatment (such as an inactive pill) that may nevertheless promote healing because of the hope and confidence placed in it.

Psychoanalysis Sigmund Freud's therapy technique, in which the patient's free associations, resistances, dreams, and transferences—and the therapist's interpretations of them—are the means by which previously repressed feelings are released and the patient gains insight into them.

Psychopharmacology The study of the effects of drugs on mind and behavior.

Psychosurgery Surgery that removes or destroys brain tissue in an effort to change behavior.

Psychotherapy A planned, emotionally charged, confiding interaction between a trained, socially approved healer and someone who suffers a psychological difficulty.

Rational-Emotive Therapy A type of cognitive-behavior therapy developed by Albert Ellis that vigorously challenges people's illogical, self-defeating thinking.

Resistance In psychoanalysis, the blocking from consciousness of anxiety-laden material.

Spontaneous Remission Improvement without treatment. In psychotherapy, symptom relief without psychotherapy.

Systematic Desensitization A type of counterconditioning that associates a pleasant, relaxed state with gradually increasing anxiety-triggering stimuli. Commonly used to treat phobias.

Token Economy An operant conditioning procedure in which a token of some sort, which can later be exchanged for various privileges or treats, is given as a reward for desired behavior.

Transference In psychoanalysis, the patient's transfer to the analyst of emotions linked with other relationships (such as love or hatred for a parent).

FOR FURTHER READING

Corsini, R. J. (Ed.) (1984). *Current psychotherapies* (3rd ed.). Itasca, IL: Peacock.

Prominent therapists of various persuasions describe their techniques of psychotherapy in their own words.

Endler, N. S. (1982). *Holiday of darkness.* New York: Wiley.

A psychologist's account of his own struggle with depression. Discusses various attempts at treatment, including electroconvulsive therapy.

Garfield, S. L., & Bergin, A. E. (Eds.) (1986). *Handbook of psychotherapy and behavior change* (3rd ed.). New York: Wiley.

An authoritative source of research information. Contains expertly written chapters on every major therapeutic approach and on scientific issues regarding psychotherapy.

Zilbergeld, B. (1983). *The shrinking of America: Myths of psychological change.* Boston: Little, Brown.

One clinical psychologist's analysis of psychotherapy and its limits. Challenges myths about the need for and practicality of personal change and reassures readers about accepting their own uniqueness.

Michael O'Brien

STRESS AND ILLNESS

What Is Stress?
The Stress Response System
Stressful Life Events

Stress and Heart Disease

Stress and Resistance to Disease
Stress and the Immune System
Stress and Cancer
The Conditioning of the Immune Response

PAIN AND ITS CONTROL

What Is Pain?

Pain Control

REACTIONS TO ILLNESS

Am I Sick? Noticing and Explaining Symptoms

Seeking Treatment

The Patient Role

Patient Adherence to Treatment

HEALTH PROMOTION

Consumption
Nutrition and Behavior
Smoking

Stress Management
Exercise
Biofeedback
Relaxation
Social Support

CHAPTER 18

Health

No one needs to be told that psychological stress can trigger physical reactions. Nervous about an important exam, we feel butterflies in the stomach. Anxious over a public speaking assignment, we make frequent trips to the bathroom. Smoldering over a conflict with a family member, we develop a splitting headache. If the stress is prolonged, it may also bring on (in those who are physiologically predisposed) a skin rash, an asthma attack, or an ulcer.

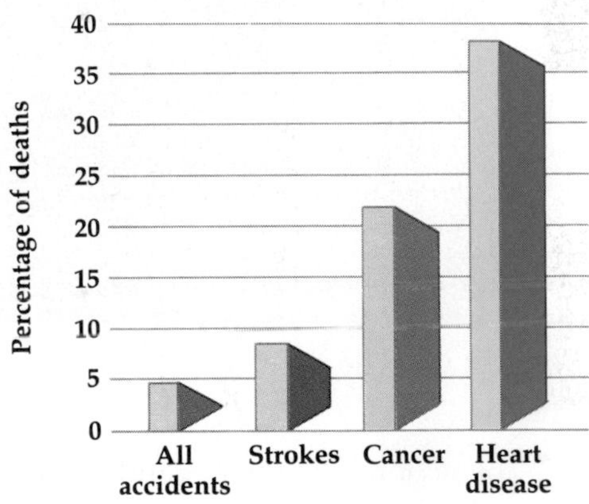

Figure 18-1 *The four leading causes of death are all strongly influenced by people's behavior—by their patterns of consumption, their reactions to stress, and their health-related behaviors.*

Many people are less aware, however, that their own behavior has a direct influence on whether they will become victims of one of the four leading causes of serious illness and death in the United States today (Figure 18-1). In fact, according to the National Academy of Science's Institute of Medicine (1982), half the mortality from the ten leading causes of death in the United States can be traced to people's behavior—to cigarette smoking, excessive alcohol consumption, maladaptive responses to stress, nonadherence to doctor's orders, insufficient exercise, use of illicit drugs, and poor nutrition. If we could understand and modify the behavioral sources of serious illness, we could alleviate a vast amount of human suffering and almost certainly increase life expectancy. In response to these concerns, behavioral and medical knowledge relevant to health and disease are now being integrated into the new interdisciplinary field of ***behavioral medicine*** (Miller, 1983a).

Research psychologist Gary Schwartz (1982, 1983) contrasts traditional efforts to link specific diseases to single causes (specific genes, germs, or emotions) with the "systems theory" perspective of behavioral medicine. The systems are biological, psychological, even sociological. Your body organs, for example, are part of a larger system—you—and you are a part of a number of your community groups—your family, your school, and so forth. Your organs, in turn, are composed of subsystems—cells, which are composed of biochemicals, which are composed of atoms, and so forth. So virtually every system is both a component of larger systems and composed of smaller systems. Instead of assuming that illnesses have either a physical or a psychological cause, systems theorists view the body as a whole system whose functioning is influenced by the larger systems of which it is a part and the smaller systems

"The past decade has ushered in a shift of almost revolutionary proportions in the study of health and disease. Today the purely biological model of disease based on the concept of 'one germ, one disease, one therapy' is seen as too simplistic. A more complex and holistic model is gaining ground, one that directs attention to interactions among social and psychological as well as biological factors."
John B. Jemmott III and Steven E. Locke (1984)

of which it is composed. Your illness or well-being depends on the interaction of all these interdependent systems (as studied by physiologists, nutritionists, psychologists, and sociologists, among others).

The new field of ***health psychology*** is a subfield of psychology that provides psychology's contribution to behavioral medicine. One indicator of health psychology's explosive growth is the number of psychologists working in medical schools. In 1953, there were 255; by the 1980s, there were several thousand (Matarazzo & others, 1981).

"Health has its science as well as disease."
Elizabeth Blackwell,
Medicine as a Profession for Women, 1860

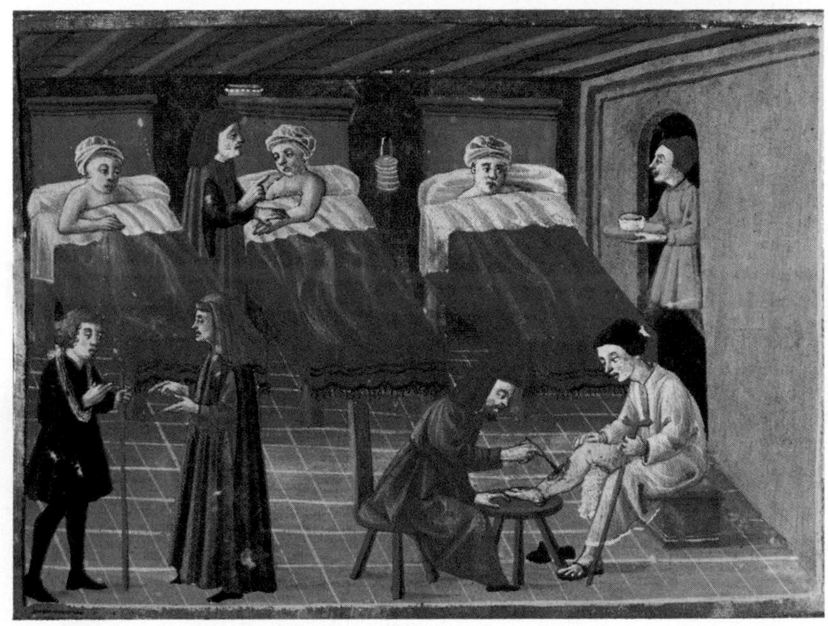

Many of the germ-caused diseases that were treated in this medieval hospital are no longer with us. Modern physicians instead must frequently face the consequences of our life-styles or behavior.

Behavioral medicine and health psychology are recent developments in the rapidly evolving history of modern medicine. Little more than a century ago, after certain diseases such as anthrax were found to be caused by bacteria, germ theory—the idea that infectious organisms cause disease—revolutionized medicine. By the middle of this century we were enjoying the benefits of pasteurization, purification, and insect-control measures to prevent disease-causing organisms from reaching us, and we had immunizations and antibiotic drugs to protect us in case they did. Thanks to germ theory, the once-leading causes of death—influenza, pneumonia, diphtheria, tuberculosis, and intestinal infections—are no longer potent threats to those who enjoy modern health care (Surgeon General, 1979).

With these battles against germ-caused disease largely won, attention is now being turned toward the "diseases of civilization" that are not caused by germs. These are the diseases that arise partly from our interaction with our physical and social environments—from the food we eat and air we breathe, the amount we exercise, and the emotions we experience. Unlike infectious diseases, those linked with modern life-styles resist medical cures. Thus, behavioral medicine focuses not so much on surgery for diseased hearts as on ways to prevent heart disease.

It is in this historical context that health psychology's key issues, and this chapter's questions, arise: Are our emotions and our responses to stressful events linked with heart disease, strokes, and even our susceptibility to diseases? What causes pain, and how might we reduce it?

"We have grown accustomed to the idea that we become sick, and doctors make us well. In all too many cases, however, the truth is that we make ourselves sick, and the doctors can do little or nothing to make us better."
Ian Robertson (in press)

How do people decide whether they are sick, and what steps can be taken to facilitate their treatment? What life-style changes would promote good health and feelings of well-being?

STRESS AND ILLNESS

Walking along the path toward his Rocky Mountain campsite, Karl hears a rustle in the grass off to his left. His muscles tense, his adrenaline flows, his heart pounds as he glimpses a rattlesnake slithering toward him. His body is mobilized to fight or flee. Flee he does, racing to the security of his camp, where his muscles gradually relax and his breathing eases.

Karen leaves her suburban apartment and, delayed by road construction, arrives at the parking lot of the commuter train station just in time to see the 8:05 pull away. Catching the next train, she arrives in the city late and elbows her way through the pedestrians at rush hour. Arriving at her bank office, she apologizes to her first client, who is wondering where she has been and is irritated that his quarterly investment report is not ready. She attempts to mollify him, and only when he has gone does she notice her own pent-up emotion—her tense muscles, gritted teeth, and churning stomach.

Karl's response to stress was a lifesaver. Karen's, if chronic, could increase her risk of heart disease and high blood pressure and make her more vulnerable to a variety of stress-linked illnesses. Moreover, feeling the pressures, she might sleep and exercise less, and smoke and drink more, further endangering her long-term health.

According to the American Academy of Family Physicians, two-thirds of office visits to family doctors are prompted by symptoms related to stress (Wallis, 1983).

What Is Stress?

Stress is a slippery concept. It is sometimes used to describe threats and challenges ("Karen was facing considerable stress"), and sometimes to describe our responses to challenges ("When Karl saw the rattler he experienced acute stress"). To encompass both meanings, we can define ***stress*** as the whole process by which environmental events, called *stressors*, threaten or challenge us (Gatchel & Baum, 1983). Such challenges can have positive effects, by arousing and motivating us, or harmful effects, when distress is severe or prolonged.

Tragedies, like the destruction of this couple's house by a tornado, can cause stress. So too can joyous events, like the birth of a baby.

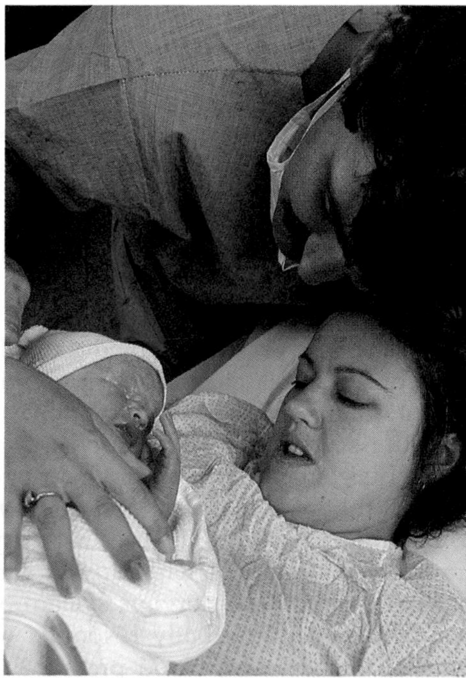

The researchers' hunch had paid off: The mind alone can alter blood cholesterol level and clotting time.

The stage was thus set for what was to become their classic 9-year study of more than 3000 healthy men, 35 to 59 years of age. At the start of the study, each was interviewed for 15 minutes about his work and eating habits, and his patterns of talking and thinking were noted. Half the men—those who seemed most competitive, hard-driving, impatient, time-conscious, supermotivated, verbally aggressive, and easily angered—were called ***Type A.*** The other half—those who were more easygoing—were called ***Type B.*** Which do you suppose were most coronary-prone? By the time the study was complete, 257 of these men had suffered heart attacks, 178 of whom were Type A. Compared to the Type B men, the Type A's were twice as vulnerable. Moreover, not one of the "pure" Type B's—the most mellow and laid back of the group—had suffered a heart attack.

As with all such classifications, people vary along a continuum from "pure" Type A to "pure" Type B.

As often happens in science, this discovery provoked enormous public interest; millions of people have by now analyzed themselves and labeled their friends with the aid of such newspaper and magazine checklists as the one in Figure 18-6. But after the honeymoon period, in which an exciting discovery is typically seen as definitive and revolutionary, other researchers begin the necessary labor of inspecting, replicating, and refining the findings. Some studies, such as one that interviewed and then studied 1600 Framingham, Massachusetts, residents over 8 years, confirmed that, for women as well as men, Type A behavior is a risk factor comparable to smoking (Baker & others, 1984; Haynes & others, 1980). Other studies produced more ambiguous results.

**Self-evaluation:
Which type are you?**

	Type A		Type B
1.	Very competitive	1.	Noncompetitive
2.	Always on the go, in a hurry	2.	Relaxed, in control
3.	Hard-driving	3.	Easygoing
4.	Demands perfection	4.	Understanding, forgiving
5.	Ambitious, wants quick promotions	5.	Confident and happy in job
6.	Is a "workaholic" —even at play	6.	Enjoys leisure and weekends

Figure 18-6 *One of the many questionnaires found in the popular press for evaluating whether your behavior patterns are more those of a Type A or Type B personality.*

These mixed findings led investigators to ask which specific components of the Type A cluster of traits are most predictive of coronary disease and heart attacks. Is it the Type A person's time urgency? Competitiveness? Irritability? Their investigations revealed that heart disease is linked not so much with a fast-paced, time-conscious life-style or with high ambitions as with an aggressively reactive temperament (Chesney, 1984; Dembroski & others, 1985; Spielberger & others, 1984). Especially among middle-aged and younger adults, those who react with anger over little things are the most coronary-prone. Rage "seems to lash back and strike us in the heart muscle," report Charles Spielberger and Perry London (1982). Such people often are verbally assertive as well; if you pause in the middle of a sentence, they may jump in and finish it for you.

"The fire you kindle for your enemy often burns you more than him."
Chinese proverb

Why are anger-prone Type A people more prone to heart disease? There are at least two possibilities: First, such individuals tend to smoke more, sleep less, and drink less milk and more caffeinated drinks (Hicks & others, 1982, 1983), behaviors that may contribute to coronary risk. Second, their temperament seems to contribute directly to heart disease. In relaxed situations, their hormonal secretions, pulse rate, and blood pressure are no different from those of Type B persons. But when harassed, given a difficult challenge, or threatened with a loss of freedom and control, Type A individuals are more physiologically reactive (Krantz & Manuck, 1984). For example, when Redford Williams and his associates (1982) asked Duke University males to repeatedly subtract 13, beginning with 7683 (and with a prize to go to the fastest), the Type A students' stress hormone levels rose at least twice as high as the levels of their Type B classmates. These hormones are believed to accelerate the buildup of plaques (scarlike masses formed by cholesterol deposits) on the artery walls, producing atherosclerosis, or "hardening" of the arteries. People who inwardly boil when criticized or evaluated unfairly also are prone to hypertension, a risk factor for heart attacks (see Figure 18-7).

These findings suggest that during the course of a day the reactive Type A individuals are more often "combat ready." In such times, their blood flow is redistributed to the muscles and away from internal organs such as the liver (which removes cholesterol and fat from the blood). Thus, they may have heightened levels of blood cholesterol and fat, which later get deposited around the heart. In such ways, the hearts and minds of Type A people interact.

"At ten-thirty, you have an appointment to get even with Ward Ingram. At twelve, you're going to get even with Holus Wentworth at lunch. At three, you're getting even with the Pro-Tech Company at their annual meeting. And at five you're going to get even with Fred Benton over drinks."

"My tongue will tell the anger of my heart,
Or else my heart, concealing it, will break."
William Shakespeare,
The Taming of the Shrew, 1594

The Anger-in Scale

Directions: For each item circle the number which seems to best describe how you *generally* act or feel when you are *angry* or *furious.*

When angry or furious, . . .	Almost never	Sometimes	Often	Almost always
I keep things in	1	2	3	4
I pout or sulk	1	2	3	4
I withdraw from people	1	2	3	4
I boil inside, but I don't show it	1	2	3	4
I tend to harbor grudges that I don't tell anyone about	1	2	3	4
I am secretly quite critical of others	1	2	3	4
I am angrier than I am willing to admit	1	2	3	4
I am irritated a great deal more than people are aware of	1	2	3	4

Scoring: Add up the points (1–4) for each item to get your total "anger-in" score, somewhere between 8 and 32. Most American college students tested by Charles Spielberger score between 10 and 18. High school students tend to score higher.

Source: The Anger-In Scale is a subscale of the Anger Expression Scale. Copyright © 1982 by C. D. Spielberger, E. H. Johnson, and G. A. Jacobs. Reprinted with permission.

Figure 18-7 *People who suppress their anger (as measured by a high score on the anger-in scale to the left) tend to have higher blood pressure than those who do not. Each data point on this graph (from Spielberger & others, 1985) represents approximately 100 high school students.*

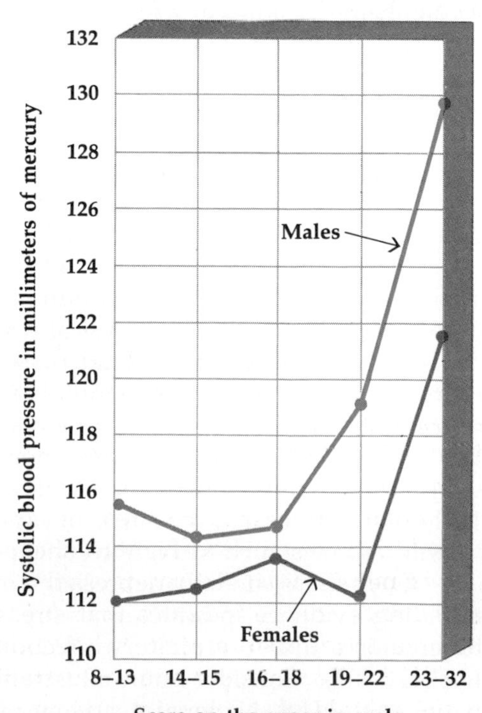

Stress and Resistance to Disease

Not so long ago, "psychosomatic" was the word used to describe psychologically caused physical symptoms. To some people, the word implied that the symptoms were not real—they were "merely" psychosomatic. To avoid such connotations, and to describe better the genuine physiological effects of psychological states, most experts today refer instead to ***psychophysiological*** ("mind-body") ***illnesses.*** These illnesses, which include certain forms of hypertension, ulcers, and headaches, are not triggered by any known physical disorder but instead seem linked to stress. Chronic stress produces not only cardiovascular changes in people with reactive temperaments, but other physiological changes as well. In one person, prolonged resentment, anger, or anxiety may stimulate an outpouring of digestive acids beyond what is needed for digestion. If prolonged, the lining of the stomach or small intestine may be eaten away in spots, creating ulcers. Another person under stress may retain excess sodium and fluids, which along with constriction of the arteries' muscle walls would contribute to increased blood pressure (Light & others, 1983). If the stress is continual, the elevated blood pressure may develop into chronic hypertension, putting the person at greater risk for a stroke or for heart or kidney failure.

When organic causes of illness are unknown, we must be careful not merely to invent psychological explanations. Before the germ that causes tuberculosis was discovered, personality explanations of TB were popular (Sontag, 1978).

Stress and the Immune System

Perhaps the strongest indication that psychophysiological ailments are real and not faked or imagined comes from dozens of new experiments that link the nervous and endocrine systems with the body's immune system—its mechanisms for fighting disease. The immune system is a complex surveillance system that defends the body by recognizing and removing bacteria, viruses, and other foreign substances (Pomerleau & Rodin, in press). It includes two types of white blood cells called ***lymphocytes.*** The B lymphocytes form in the bone marrow and release antibodies that fight bacterial infections; the T lymphocytes form in the spleen and other lymphatic tissue and, among other duties, attack cancer cells, viruses, and foreign substances such as organ transplants. These and other elements of the immune system must be delicately regulated, so that the lymphocytes are mobilized in response to infectious bacteria and viruses, and then suppressed once their job is done, in order to prevent their attacking the body's own tissues. If the immune system becomes subdued, we become vulnerable to infections and malignancy—the problems that plague victims of Acquired Immune Deficiency Syndrome (AIDS). If unrestrained, the overzealous immune system may destroy some healthy cells, causing such problems as arthritis.

"Each patient carries his own doctor inside him."
Albert Schweitzer, 1875–1965

The rapid increase in numbers of those identified as having AIDS and the deadly nature of this disease of the immune system have generated enormous public interest and public fear.

Age, nutrition, genetics, body temperature—and, we now know, stress—can all influence the immune system's activity. In laboratory experiments, animals that are physically restrained, given unavoidable electric shocks, or subjected to loud noises or crowded conditions become more susceptible to disease (Jemmott & Locke, 1984). These experiments reveal one further reason for the stress-disease connection: Increases in the stress hormones epinephrine, norepinephrine, and cortisol help to suppress the proliferation of disease-fighting lymphocyte cells (Marx, 1985). For this reason, the stress of capture can reduce disease resistance in wild animals such as bighorn sheep.

Does stress similarly depress the human immune system? The accumulating evidence indicates that stress lowers the body's resistance to tuberculosis, upper respiratory infections, and other diseases (Jemmott & Locke, 1984). Consider some illustrative findings: A 1984 report by a panel of the U.S. National Academy of Sciences indicated that the grief and depression that frequently follow the death of a spouse can have physiological counterparts—not only increased risk of a heart attack or stroke but also depressed protection against disease by the immune system's lymphocytes. In three separate Skylab missions, the immune systems of the astronauts showed reduced effectiveness immediately after the excitement of reentry and splashdown (Kimzey, 1975; Kimzey & others, 1976). Other studies confirm that students' disease-fighting mechanisms tend to weaken during high-stress times, such as exam weeks (Jemmott & Locke, 1984).

Stress and Cancer

Even more provocative—and controversial—are new findings that link stress to cancer. Several investigators have reported that states of depression, helplessness, or bereavement are sometimes followed by the appearance of cancer a year or so later (Sklar & Anisman, 1981). For example, cancer appears more often than usual among those who are widowed, divorced, or separated. One study of the husbands of women with terminal breast cancer pinpointed a possible reason; during the first 2 months after the death of their wives, the bereaved men's lymphocyte responses dropped (Schleifer & others, 1979). What is more, there are indications that cancer patients who bottle up their negative emotions have less chance of survival than those who are able to express their anger.

To understand better the stress-cancer link, experimenters have inoculated rodents with tumor cells or given them carcinogens. Those that are also exposed to uncontrollable stress, such as inescapable shocks, are less resistant to cancer (Sklar & Anisman, 1981). Because their immune systems are weakened, their tumors develop sooner and grow larger.

It is important not to overstate the link between emotions and cancer. Researcher Alan Justice (1985) explains that stress does not cause cancer but rather affects its growth by weakening the body's natural defenses against a few malignant cells. One danger in publicizing such reports is that some patients may blame themselves for their cancer—"If only I had been more expressive, relaxed, hopeful." Although, as we will see, there are some things we can do to control our experiences of stress, temperament is partly inherited (Matthews & others, 1984; see also pp. 112–113). As Reinhold Niebuhr advised, we therefore do well to accept those things about ourselves that we cannot change, to change those things that we can, and to use wisdom in discerning the difference.

The Conditioning of the Immune Response

A hay fever sufferer sees the flower on the restaurant table and, not realizing it is plastic, begins to sneeze. Such experiences hint that stress is not the sole psychological influence upon the body's ailments; simple conditioning, generalized to similar stimuli, may be an added influence. Could this be true of the immune system as well? Can immune functioning be conditioned?

Psychologist Robert Ader together with immunologist Nicholas Cohen (1984) discovered that the answer is yes. Ader came upon this discovery while researching taste aversion in rats. He had paired the rats' drinking of saccharin-sweetened water with injections of a drug that caused stomachaches. Not surprisingly, the rats developed a taste aversion for sweetened water, an aversion the experimenter could extinguish only after force-feeding the rats with sweetened water alone for several days. About 40 days after the experiment, some of the animals unexpectedly died. Ader subsequently learned that the stomachache-producing drug given to the rats in the experiment was known to suppress immune functioning. As he reports, "It dawned on me that at the same time we were conditioning an aversion to saccharin, we might be inadvertently conditioning a suppression of immune response" (quoted by Anderson, 1982). Further experiments confirmed that animals indeed could be conditioned to suppress their own immune systems by associating the taste of saccharin (the conditioned stimulus) with the physiological effects of the drug (the unconditioned stimulus).

If it is possible to condition a suppression of the immune system, might it also be possible to condition an enhancement of it? Might this be one way in which placebos promote healing? Research now underway may soon answer such questions and may also identify the precise effects of particular stressors on specific aspects of immune functioning.

For now, we view the toll that stress sometimes takes on our disease resistance as a price we pay for the adaptive benefits of the stress response. Stress, as we noted earlier, invigorates our lives by arousing and motivating us. The unstressed life is not worth living, or at least would not be very challenging or productive. Expending our resources in fighting or fleeing an external challenge also aids our immediate survival; but it may do so at the cost of a diminished preparedness to fight internal challenges to the body's health. Later, we will consider stress management techniques that can help minimize the costs.

The Ethics of Animal Research

Each year, nearly 20 million animals are used in scientific research, 90 percent of them rats and mice, along with tens of thousands of dogs, cats, and monkeys. Throughout this book we have seen dozens of examples of psychologists using animals—to understand better:

- **the workings of the brain**
- **the effects of isolation and abuse on infant development**
- **the mechanisms by which the visual cortex organizes neural impulses into a perceived image**
- **the rudiments of learning and memory**
- **basic emotions and motives**
- **the influence of genes and environment on every sort of behavior**
- **the effects of stress on disease and immunity**

"Were it not for behavioral research with animals we would be without critical information about the emotional, social, and intellectual development of children; language systems that enable profoundly retarded children to communicate; the use of biofeedback techniques for the control of hypertension and hypotension; methods for reduction of pain in humans and nonhumans; conditioned taste aversion in the treatment of cancer patients; treatment of eating disorders; and improved captive breeding for endangered species."
Michael S. Pallak (1984)
Executive Officer, American Psychological Association

All told, about 8 percent of the studies compiled by *Psychological Abstracts* use animals, and about 10 percent of these animal studies involve electric shock (Coile & Miller, 1984; Cunningham, 1984).

During the 1980s, a growing animal rights movement has protested the use of animals in psychological, biological, and medical research. To rally support for a protest at the 1984 American Psychological Association convention, Mobilization for Animals, a network of 400 animal protection organizations, declared that in psychological experiments animals are shocked "until they lose the ability to even scream in pain," "deprived of food and water to suffer and die slowly from hunger and thirst," "put in total isolation chambers until they are driven insane or even die, from despair and terror," and made "the victims of extreme pain and stress, inflicted upon them out of idle curiosity."

"The greatness of a nation can be judged by the way its animals are treated."
Mahatma Gandhi, 1869–1948

After analyzing every animal research article published in the American Psychological Association journals during the preceding 5 years, psychologists Caroline Coile and Neal Miller (1984) found not one study in which any of these allegations was true. Even when shock was used, it usually was of a mild intensity that humans can easily endure on their fingers. Moreover, say researchers, animals have been an essential part of the experiments that led to the development of insulin for diabetes, vaccines to prevent polio and other diseases, and various surgical and transplant procedures. Current research on the two big killers—heart disease and cancer—would be seriously hampered without animals. Does anyone who cares about the millions of people who are alive thanks to animal research wish that the advice of the president of the American Anti-Vivisection Society had been heeded: that animals should not be used in an experiment if the experiment "is not for the benefit of the animals involved" (Goodman, 1982)? And would we really wish to deprive ourselves of the knowledge, gleaned from psychological research with animals, that has led to new methods of training retarded children, treating disturbed people, and controlling stress-related discomfort and disease? Psychologist Miller's (1983b) answer is unhesitating: "I believe that to prevent, cripple, or needlessly complicate the research that can relieve animal and human suffering is profoundly inhuman, cruel, and immoral."

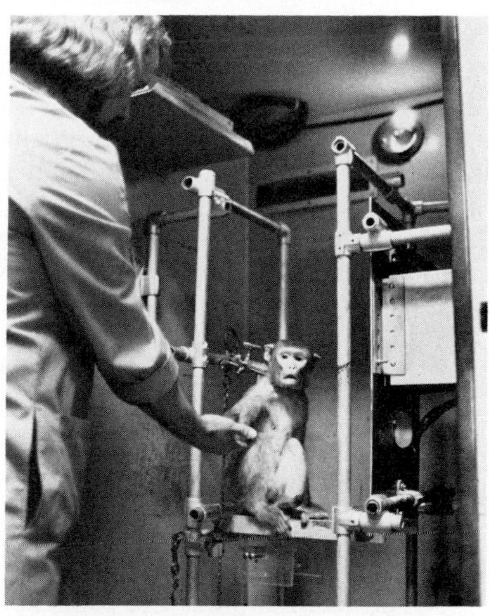

Is it right that animals be used to advance our understanding of how humans function? For animal-rights activists, no purpose justifies hurting or frightening an animal. However, most psychologists and medical researchers believe that animal research is necessary and ethically justified so long as strict standards for the animals' care are observed and no unnecessary pain is inflicted.

Out of such heated debate, two issues emerge. The basic one is whether it is right to place the well-being of humans above that of animals. Is it right that a baboon die in hopes that a child who receives its heart might live? In experiments on stress and cancer, is it right that mice get tumors so that people might not? Defenders of research on animals argue that anyone who has eaten a hamburger, tolerated hunting and fishing, or supported the extermination of pests that destroy crops or carry plague has already agreed that, yes, it is sometimes permissible to sacrifice animals for the sake of human well-being.

Assuming that human life is given first priority, the second issue is what priority should be given to the well-being of animals? With what safeguards should they be protected? Scientific researchers generally agree that pointless exploitation of animals is *not* justified. They may stop short of agreeing with Michael Fox, the scientific director of the Humane Society of the United States, that scientists "have no God-given right to inflict pain on animals" (Fields, 1984). But most researchers today believe that the needless suffering of animals is inexcusable and they welcome periodic required inspections of their laboratories. Indeed, many researchers study animals in the conviction that animals are worthy of study for their own sake. More than that, psychological research has helped improve the care of zoo animals (see p. 67), and, by demonstrating our behavioral kinship with animals, has served to increase our empathy for them. At its best, a psychology that is concerned for humans and sensitive to animals can serve the welfare of both.

PAIN AND ITS CONTROL

Pain is the body's way of telling us that something has gone wrong. It draws our attention to a burn, a break, or a rupture, and tells us to change our behavior immediately. The few people who are born without the ability to feel pain may experience severe injury without ever being alerted by pain's danger signals.

"When belly with bad pains doth swell,
It matters nought what else goes well."
Sadi, *The Gulistan*, 1258

At the other end of the spectrum from those who feel no pain are the many more people who endure chronic pain. The suffering of people with persistent or recurring backaches, arthritis, headaches, and cancer-related pain gives a special impetus to finding the answers to two questions: What is pain? How might it be controlled?

What Is Pain?

Although we may not know much about what pain is, we do know some things about what pain is not. Pain is not only a property of the senses—of the region where we feel the pain—but of the brain as well. People who have had limbs amputated may feel pain in their nonexistent limbs. These "phantom limb sensations" indicate that with pain, as with vision, the brain can interpret incoming neural activity as something it is not. To use an analogy from the philosopher René Descartes (1596–1650), a flame at the toe may pull a cord that rings a bell in the brain; but the same bell can be rung by pulling the cord up near the bell (Figure 18-8).

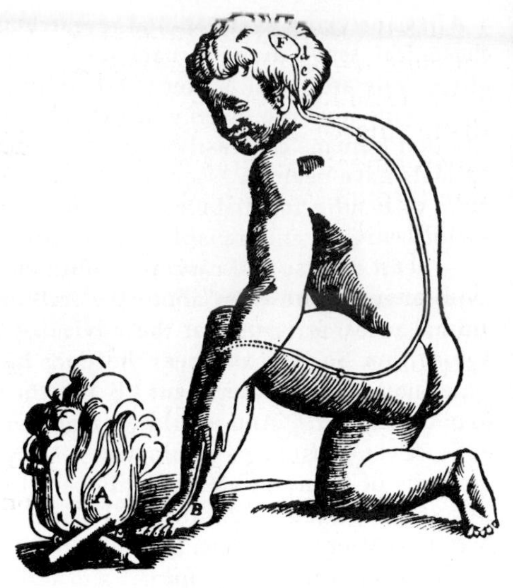

Figure 18-8 *René Descartes' mechanical pain response.*

Unlike vision, however, the pain system is not located in a simple neural "cord" running from a sensing device to a definable spot in the brain. Moreover, there is no one type of stimulus, such as light, that triggers pain, and no special receptors, such as the rods and cones of the retina, for pain. At lower intensities, the stimuli that result in pain cause other sensations, including warmth or coolness, smoothness or roughness.

Although no theory of pain explains all the available findings, psychologist Ronald Melzack and biologist Patrick Wall's (1965) ***gate-control theory*** remains the most useful model. Melzack and Wall believe that the spinal cord contains a sort of neurological "gate" that either blocks or allows pain signals to pass on to the brain. The spinal cord contains small-diameter nerve fibers that conduct impulses rapidly, and larger fibers that conduct more slowly. When tissue is injured, the activation of the small-diameter fibers opens the neural gate, and you feel pain. Activity in the large fibers tends to close the gate, turning pain off. Thus, one method of treating chronic pain has been to stimulate (either electrically, by massage, or even by acupuncture) "gate-closing" activity in the large neural fibers. An arthritis patient, for example, may wear in a normally painful area a small portable electrical stimulation unit that replaces the pain with a vibrating sensation (Murphy, 1982).

Melzack and Wall believe that the gate can be closed not only by stimulation of nerves that compete with those that carry the pain signals, but also by the kind of information that comes down from the brain. These brain-to-spinal cord messages help explain some striking psychological influences on pain. A football player or soldier may suffer an injury yet feel no pain until off the football field or battlefield. When we are not attending to pain signals, our experience of pain may be greatly diminished. Additionally, pain can stimulate release of the painkilling endorphins (see p. 32).

"Pain is increased by attending to it."
Charles Darwin,
The Expression of Emotion in Man and Animals, 1872

Pain Control

If pain is both a physical and a psychological phenomenon, then it should be treatable through physical and psychological therapies. Depending on the type of symptoms, pain control clinics select one or more therapies from a list that includes drugs, surgery, acupuncture, electrical stimulation, massage, exercise, hypnosis, relaxation training, and thought distraction (Leepson, 1983).

The widely practiced Lamaze method of prepared childbirth combines several of these pain control techniques, including relaxation (through deep breathing and muscle relaxation), distraction (through focusing attention on, say, a pleasant photograph), and counterstimulation (through gentle massage). After Everett Worthington and his colleagues (1983) gave women training in the use of such techniques, the women could more easily tolerate the pain of having their hand in ice water. The women's pain tolerance was even greater when they were encouraged by a trusted "coach," as Lamaze-trained women are by their husbands or an intimate friend during childbirth. Other studies, too, have used the ice water technique for measuring pain tolerance. These studies confirm that distracting people with pleasant images ("think of a warm, comfortable environment") or drawing their attention away from the painful stimulation ("count backward by 3s") increases their pain tolerance (McCaul & Malott, 1984).

The same principles operate in everyday health-care situations. A well-trained nurse will engage needle-shy patients with distracting chatter and may ask them to look away as the needle is inserted. For hospitalized patients, a pleasing window view of natural vegetation may have a similarly relaxing and distracting effect. In examining the records of one Pennsylvania hospital, Roger Ulrich (1984) discovered that gall bladder surgery patients assigned to rooms that looked out on trees required less pain medication and had shorter stays than did those assigned identical rooms that overlooked a brick wall.

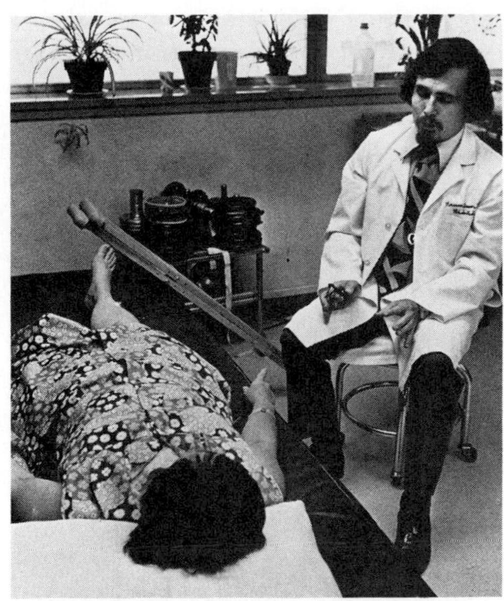

This woman, whose leg had to be amputated due to cancer, is being trained through relaxation psychology to be less mindful of "phantom pains"—pains that feel as if they are located in the missing limb.

REACTIONS TO ILLNESS

In a perfect world, everyone would correctly interpret pain's danger signals—whether routine aches and pains or symptoms of serious illness—and, when appropriate, would promptly seek treatment and comply with doctor's orders. At each step in the decision scheme of Figure 18-9, people would behave rationally: first, by noticing and determining the seriousness of their symptoms; second, by seeking care when needed; third, by responding wisely to treatment regimens. Of course, they do not. To find out why, health psychologists are studying people's reactions at each of these three stages.

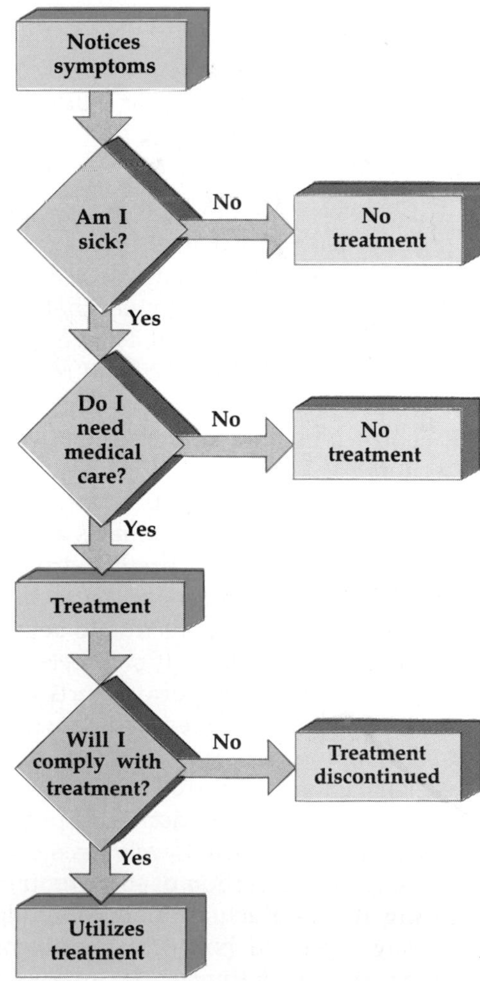

Figure 18-9 *The three stages of the decision to seek and to comply with medical treatment.*

Am I Sick? Noticing and Explaining Symptoms

The typical complaints of college students include headache, stomachache, nasal congestion, sore muscles, ringing in the ears, excess perspiration, cold hands, racing heart, dizziness, stiff joints, and diarrhea or constipation. In fact, the chances are good that you have recently experienced one or more of these symptoms, to at least a slight degree (Pennebaker, 1982). Such symptoms require your interpretation. Are you coming down with the flu or a cold? Or is the symptom not worthy of your attention?

With more serious aches and pains the questions become more significant. Is your stubbed toe bruised or broken? Is your abdominal pain caused by indigestion or a ruptured appendix? Is the chest pain a muscle spasm or a heart attack? Is the small lump a meaningless cyst or a tumor? What factors influence whether we notice and how we explain such symptoms?

Noticing and interpreting our body's signals is like noticing and interpreting the noises of our car. Unless the signals are loud and clear, we often miss them (Pennebaker, 1982). Most of us cannot tell whether our car needs an oil change merely by listening to its engine. Similarly, most of us are not very good at diagnosing our physical state by estimating our blood pressure, heart rate, skin temperature, or blood-sugar level. The early signs of many illnesses, including cancer and heart disease, are subtle and often go unnoticed. Half or more of heart attack victims die before seeking and receiving medical help (DiMatteo & Friedman, 1982).

As the discussion of sensation in Chapter 6 explained, our ability to attend consciously to different inputs is limited. We can attend selectively to one thing—say, one voice at a party—at a time. Thus, if the external environment commands our attention, our internal cues do not. When students in one experiment were working comfortably on an arithmetic task, they were less likely to notice bursts of air on their forearms (Pennebaker & Brittingham, 1982). Students in another experiment who jogged through a beautiful wooded environment ran faster than when running the same distance around a track, apparently because they were less aware of their fatigue (Pennebaker & Lightner, 1980) (see Figure 18-10). In general, we are more likely to notice symptoms, such as fatigue, when in quiet, boring environments than when our minds are engaged.

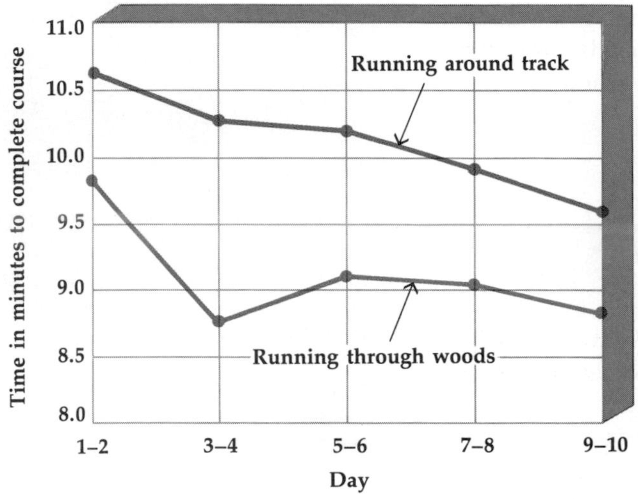

Figure 18-10 *Joggers run faster when distracted from their fatigue by the beauty of a course in the woods than when running the same distance around a track.*

Once we notice symptoms, we tend to interpret them according to culturally defined schemas. Pressured medical students not only commonly experience a variety of stress-related symptoms, they also are learning new disease schemas that can explain their symptoms. Once they form an idea ("Might I have a slight case of pneumonia?"), they become more likely to notice and remember sensory information that fits the schema. (As you have perhaps already discovered, psychology students are vulnerable to the same effect as they read about psychological disorders.)

Recall from Chapter 11 the powerful phenomenon of "confirmation bias"—a tendency to register information that fits our preconceptions.

Researchers Diane Ruble and Jeanne Brooks-Gunn (1979) suggest that women who believe females are more depressed, irritable, and uncomfortable during their premenstrual and menstrual phases tend to notice and remember instances that confirm their beliefs. If a woman feels tense the day her period is due to begin, she may attribute the tension to the premenstrual phase. If she feels similarly tense 2 weeks later or not tense the day her next period starts, she may be less likely to notice and remember these instances, which would tend to *dis*confirm the premenstrual symptom schema. Without discounting the reality of the severe menstrual cramps endured by some women, research generally indicates that most women's emotions and physical symptoms are not so strongly related to the menstrual cycle as is commonly believed. Moreover, contrary to the presumption of some employers, women's physical and mental skills do not fluctuate noticeably with their menstrual cycles.

In the nineteenth century, some doctors insisted that during "the temporary insanity of menstruation no mental activity can be carried out." Harvard University apparently was not sure about this, for in 1875 it sponsored an essay contest, "Do women require mental and bodily rest during menstruation?"
Beatrice S. Levin (1980)

Given both a boring external environment and a handy disease schema for interpreting weak internal signals, people sometimes incorrectly attribute stress-related symptoms to a disease. The result can be a "mass psychogenic illness." In one Southern textile mill, several workers

"When a man can't explain a woman's actions, the first thing he thinks about is the condition of her uterus."
Clare Booth Luce,
Slam the Door Softly, 1970

fell ill at the peak of the production season and attributed their various symptoms to the bite of a mysterious "June bug" (Kerckhoff & Back, 1968). Soon, other workers noticed that they, too, had symptoms, and before long the factory had to be closed because of the "epidemic." An investigation revealed that not only was there no "June bug," there was no epidemic of any sort, apart from the epidemic misinterpretation of life's normal aches and pains.

Taken together, all these examples indicate that people's sensitivity in noticing and interpreting bodily symptoms varies along a continuum from a life-threatening failure to notice serious illness to hypochondriasis—the persistent conviction of being ill. Contrary to the common belief that elderly people tend to overreport medical complaints, Paul Costa and Robert McCrae (1985) found that, although the elderly have more health complaints, these occur only if and when their health actually deteriorates.

Seeking Treatment

Once people notice a symptom and interpret it as possibly serious, the decision to seek medical care is influenced by a variety of factors. For example, if they believe their symptoms have a physical rather than a psychological cause, they are more likely to seek treatment (Bishop, 1984b). If, on the other hand, they feel embarrassed about their ailment, if they think the likely benefits of medical attention or counseling not worth the anticipated cost and inconvenience, or if they dread and want to avoid a potentially devastating diagnosis, they may delay seeking help.

The U.S. National Center for Health Statistics reports a gender difference in medical treatment: Women report more symptoms, visit physicians more often, and use more prescription and nonprescription drugs. Are women more often sick? Actually, men have higher diagnosed rates of hypertension, ulcers, and cancer and have shorter life expectancies (Pennebaker, 1982). This finding suggests several possibilities: Perhaps males are more focused on the external environment and are less attentive to their internal state. Or perhaps they perceive as many symptoms but are more reluctant to admit "weakness" and seek help (Bishop, 1984a).

The Patient Role

Approaching the hospital, Maria anxiously wonders whether a woman in her seventies should really be having heart surgery. After filling out admissions papers, she is given the standard hospital gown to wear and put in a sterile room with three other patients. From time to time—she can never predict when—nurses and technicians come in to stick her with a needle or cart her off for a test. Many of the staff members talk to her in ways she is unaccustomed to, as if she were a child. "Climb up on this table, dear," the x-ray technician orders, "so we can have a little look inside your tummy." With visits by friends and family members prohibited during some hours, and occurring unpredictably during others, Maria feels no more control over her social contacts than over her hospital regimen.

Certainly, Maria's experience does not describe that of patients in all hospitals. But it is typical enough to draw the attention of psychologists to people's reactions to a loss of control in such settings. Losing control over what you do and what others do to you can make unpleasant events profoundly stressful (Pomerleau & Rodin, in press). For example, an "executive" rat that can switch off electric shocks it receives (see Figure 18-11) is not likely to develop ulcers. An electrically yoked "subordinate" rat that receives these same shocks in a nearby cage is more vulnerable to ulcers (Weiss, 1977) and to depressed immune responses (Laudenslager & Reite, 1984).

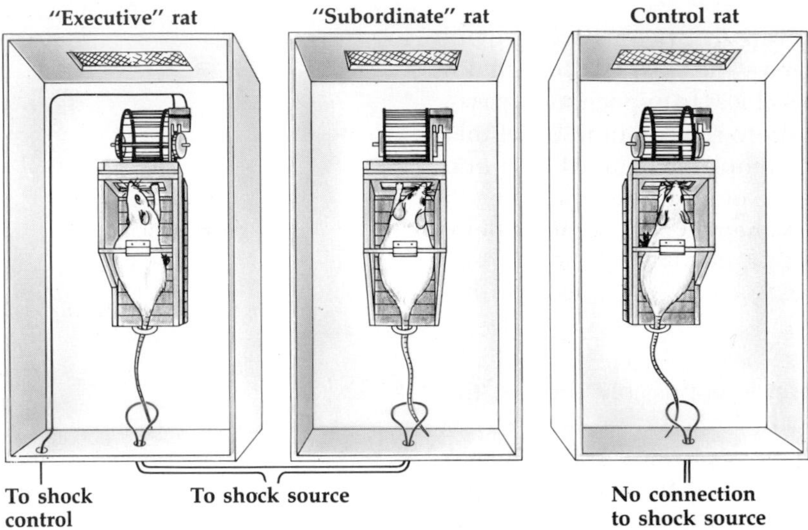

Figure 18-11 *The health consequences of a loss of control. The animal at left can switch off the tail shock by turning the wheel. Because it has control over the shock, it is no more likely to develop ulcers than the unshocked control rat at right. The yoked animal in the center receives the identical shocks, but because it has no control over the shock it is more likely to develop ulcers.*

Similar findings have been obtained with humans: People who experience a loss of perceived control over their lives are more likely to suffer ill health. Elderly people who are placed in nursing homes without their consent and who lose control over their surroundings tend to decline more rapidly and die sooner than those who help decide their placement, who are given more control over their activities, and who are taught more effective ways of coping (Rodin, 1983). Executives who fall ill after facing high stress tend to be less confident and vigorous in their approach to life than their hardier colleagues who do not become ill when facing similar stresses (Kobasa, 1979). On the other hand, those who can meet stress with what Israeli sociologist Aaron Antonovsky (1979) called a "sense of coherence"—a confidence that things are predictable and will work out reasonably well—tend to be *less* vulnerable to disease or death after facing enormous stress. Whether they achieve their sense of coherence through a confidence in their own efforts ("I am in control") or through a faith in the merciful power of experts or of God ("things are under control"), they are spared the sense of hopelessness that accompanies the belief that things are out of control. For example, Antonovsky reported that when American Indian tribes and South African Bantu natives were uprooted from their homelands and transferred to strange places, they lost their "sense of coherence," and in many cases their physical health as well.

Does the finding that rats tormented by uncontrollable shock are more ulcer-prone seem like common sense? An earlier finding for a time suggested the opposite conclusion—that "executive" animals were more ulcer-prone. This finding, too, seemed commonsensical, until a flaw was discovered in the original experiment, and new research revealed that animals in control actually are less *ulcer-prone.*

Why does loss of control sometimes lead to health problems? Animal studies indicate—and human studies confirm—that losing control triggers an outpouring of stress hormones. When rats cannot control the shock or when humans feel helpless to control their environments, cortisol levels rise higher and immune responses drop (Rodin, 1983). Those who adopt what psychologist Shelley Taylor (1979) called the ***good-patient role*** may also suffer loss of control and the ill effects of stress. "Good" patients are cooperative, unquestioning, and undemanding. But such "good" behavior may be bad for the patient, especially if the docile patient is actually feeling helpless, anxious, and depressed. Those who

Losing a leg due to cancer might slow others down, but not Ted Kennedy, Jr. His sense of control over his life is obvious in his numerous athletic and philanthropic activities.

instead adopt the more uncooperative, complaining, demanding ***bad-patient role*** may not be much better off, because as we have seen, anger and hostility also can have harmful consequences. On a happier note, some researchers have found that the stress experienced by both the helpless "good" patient and the angry "bad" patient can be lessened by making patients more active participants in their treatment (Pomerleau & Rodin, in press).

The stress of undergoing medical procedures can be lessened in another way: by providing patients with realistic information well in advance of medical treatments. Imagine that you have just been admitted to the hospital and that tomorrow you will be undergoing surgery. Should the doctor offer you kind-hearted reassurances that "it really won't be so bad"? Or should the doctor instead let you know just how it is going to hurt afterwards, so you can prepare yourself to cope with it and not be surprised when it *does* hurt? Several studies indicate that realistic information before surgery, together with instruction on how to cope with discomfort, serves to reduce patients' distress later (Janis, 1983) (see Figure 18-12). When patients know that things are going according to plan, they may be less anxious, and when they are less anxious, they are better able to cope with discomfort. As a patient in one of these experiments explained, "I knew there might be some bad pains, so when my side started to ache, I told myself that this didn't mean anything had gone wrong" (Janis, 1969, p. 98).

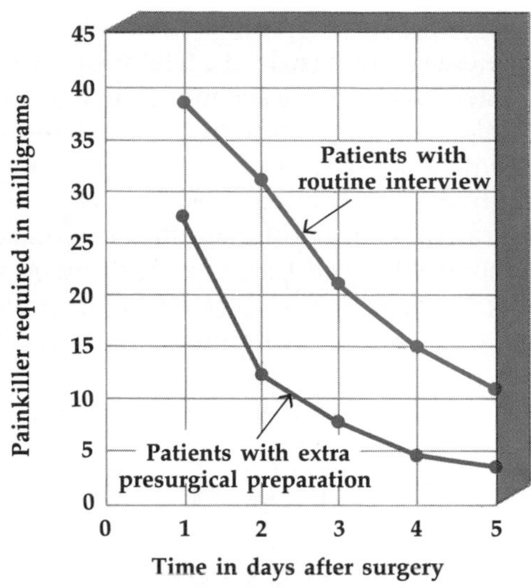

Figure 18-12 *Surgery patients who were fully informed about the consequences of abdominal surgery and how to cope with them required less painkilling morphine after the surgery than patients not so informed.*

Patient Adherence to Treatment

Until recently, it was widely assumed that patients did as instructed. The doctor orders; the patient dutifully obeys. Then, between 1974 and 1977, a flood of 250 research studies revealed that as many as half of all patients fail to follow their doctors' recommendations (Adler & Stone, 1984). Patients discontinue taking their prescribed medications, ignore suggestions for more healthful life-styles, and fail to report recurrences of symptoms. Of those discovered to have dangerously high blood pressure, only about half follow the advice to seek treatment and only about half of these adhere to the treatment regimen (Leventhal & others, 1984).

Such findings have stimulated social psychologists to apply their understanding of social influence to the doctor-patient relationship (DiMatteo & Friedman, 1982). As we will see in our next chapter, "Social Influence," people in experiments will comply with direct orders even to the point of giving others supposedly painful electric shocks. Yet, once patients are away from their doctors' surveillance, they may fail to comply even with orders to take pills that will prevent their going blind. Why? And how might physicians more effectively influence their patients?

As Chapter 19 will explain, many factors affect one person's influence, including the person's credibility, attractiveness, and effectiveness in communicating. These factors also affect doctors' influence on their patients. For example, the doctor-patient studies revealed that surprising numbers of patients simply did not understand their illnesses or the doctors' treatment instructions. Patients told to take a prescription "as needed for water retention" sometimes understand this to mean they should take the pill when they need to retain water (Mazullo & others, 1974). When information is presented vividly and in language the patients can understand, with easy-to-follow written instructions, compliance increases (Gatchel & Baum, 1983). Patients' adherence to treatment instructions also improves when they have a warm relationship with their doctor and when they are involved in planning their own regimen (Janis, 1982).

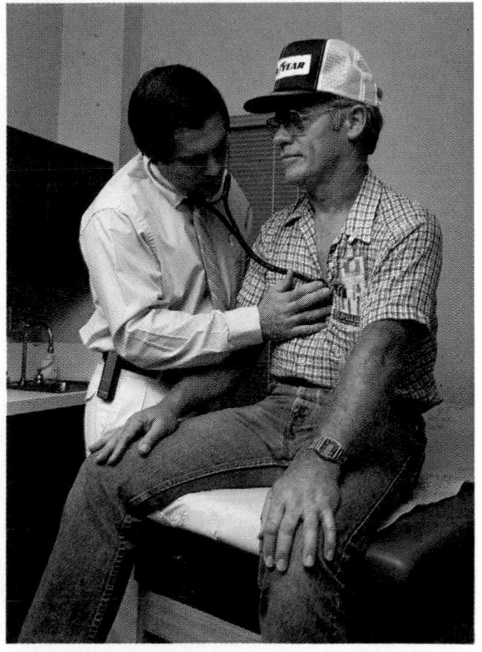

What health psychologists have learned about the factors that affect patients' decisions to comply with treatment regimens suggests that the physician's communicating skills are extremely important, perhaps as important as their diagnostic skills.

Patients may understand that their behavior is harmful, yet, when the delayed rewards of a healthful life-style must compete with the immediate discomfort or inconvenience of giving up smoking, of exercising, or of flossing one's teeth, the immediate consequences often win out. Recall from Chapter 9, "Learning," that immediate reinforcements are more effective than delayed ones. One can *know* that in the long run smoking is harmful and hardly worth the pleasure it provides, yet continue to smoke. One can *know* that high blood pressure is dangerous, yet ignore the problem. Thus, to be effective, strategies for increasing patients' compliance should create immediate incentives for compliant behavior.

HEALTH PROMOTION

Traditionally, people have looked to medicine only for diagnosis and treatment of disease. That, say advocates of behavioral medicine, is like seeking out a mechanic after you have ignored your car's maintenance. Now that in affluent societies most of the major infectious diseases have been conquered and many of the remaining medical problems have been shown to be the by-products of harmful behaviors, attention is being focused on ways to *prevent* illness and enhance wellness.

The recognition that many illnesses are linked to aspects of our modern life-style—the way we cope with stress, the foods we eat, the amount we exercise—has stimulated new interest in more healthful living.

Most health care administrators want to provide the best possible care at the lowest possible cost. Let's suppose that we have $100 million to spend on health protection. Where should we spend it to save the most lives? By comparing the cost of a preventive measure per life saved, we can estimate the cost-effectiveness of different preventive measures. For example, it has been estimated that decreasing the concentration of benzene in the air of paint factories to 0.2 parts per million would cost $3.5 million per life saved. Automobile airbags cost less than $300,000 for every life saved (Graham & Vaupel, 1981). Although researchers are only beginning to compute the cost-effectiveness of health-promotion programs (see Kaplan, 1984), many are optimistic that it will cost far less to prevent certain diseases by creating programs for modifying people's personal habits than it now costs to treat those diseases.

Consumption

Nutrition and Behavior

Is the way you feel and act affected by what you eat? The discovery that specific neurotransmitters affect emotion and behavior has fueled speculation that certain foods, which provide the biochemical building blocks for those neurotransmitters, may affect mood and behavior. For example, the body synthesizes the neurotransmitter serotonin from the amino acid tryptophan. Several studies have found that high-carbohydrate foods (such as bread and potatoes) increase the relative amount of tryptophan in the blood, which serves to raise the level of serotonin, which facilitates feeling relaxed, sleepy, and less sensitive to pain (Kolata, 1982). When we instead desire food for thought, a low-carbohydrate, high-protein meal seems to improve concentration and alertness.

Other nutritional issues are now the subject of vigorous research and debate. Are children and prisoners calmed by a low-sugar diet? Some researchers now doubt this folk wisdom (Brody, 1984). Do diets high in cholesterol literally eat your heart out? Researchers now debate this (Kaplan, 1984), although men with high cholesterol levels who take a cholesterol-reducing drug are indeed less likely to suffer heart disease (Kolata, 1984). What are the links between diet and high blood pressure? New findings indicate that hypertensive people tend to have not only higher-than-normal salt intake, but also lower-than-normal calcium intake (Feinleib & others, 1984; McCarron & others, 1984). As researchers clarify the precise interplay among diet, behavior, and health, psychologists will be challenged to persuade people to adopt healthier eating behaviors.

Such persuasion may not be easy. People tend to see themselves as relatively invulnerable to health problems, especially ones that could arise from their own actions (Weinstein, 1984). In fact, for most health behaviors—reducing consumption of alcoholic beverages, avoiding sweets and cholesterol, and so forth—they think they are living a more healthful life than others. The individuals who do admit to a risk-increasing behavior often do not admit that their behavior actually makes them more vulnerable to illness or injury. Smokers, for example, may claim that their exercise counteracts the negative effects of the cigarettes.

Smoking

There is much less debate about the effects of alcohol and cigarette consumption. Alcohol abuse is linked with traffic deaths, homicide, liver disease, and various forms of cancer. In the United States, the economic costs of alcohol abuse are well in excess of $40 billion annually (Miller, 1983a). Smoking is even more destructive. The U.S. Public Health Service (1980, p. 7) declared it to be "clearly the largest preventable cause of illness and premature death." Because 30 percent of all U.S. cancer deaths and 30 percent or more of deaths caused by heart disease are linked with cigarette smoking, the elimination of the habit would do more to increase life expectancy than any other preventive measure (Surgeon General, 1983). This reality has prompted psychologists to study the factors that influence people to start smoking, the rewards that maintain smoking, and the effectiveness of efforts to stop or prevent smoking.

When and Why Do People Start Smoking? Smoking most often begins during early adolescence and is especially common among those whose friends, parents, and siblings are smokers (Chassin & others, 1984). Teenage smokers tend to be perceived by other teenagers as tough, precocious, and sociable (Barton & others, 1982). Such findings can be explained by social-cognitive theory, the theory that explains behavior partly in terms of the models we imitate and the powerful influence of immediate social rewards. Self-conscious adolescents, who tend to see the world as their audience, may therefore begin smoking in imitation of a tough, cool model and in order to receive the rewards of social acceptance from their peers.

For early adolescents, the decision to smoke is usually influenced by a need for acceptance by their peers and by a desire to project the images they see in cigarette ads.

Why Do People Continue Smoking? Most adults who smoke cigarettes would rather not, and have at some time tried to stop. Why do they fail? The social and psychological influences that help initiate smoking seem less important in maintaining it. Continuing to smoke seems more linked to smoking's physiological reinforcers. Recall from Chapter 9 that a negative reinforcer is one that terminates an aversive state. The habit is so hard to break because the craving, hunger, and irritability that accompany nicotine withdrawal are aversive states that can be relieved by a negatively reinforcing cigarette. After an hour or a day without smoking, the habitual smoker finds a cigarette reinforcing. In fact, if given low-nicotine cigarettes, the smoker will smoke more of them in order to maintain a roughly constant level of nicotine in the blood.

Behavioral medicine researchers Ovide and Cynthia Pomerleau (1984) reported that smoking may also function as a positive reinforcer. It not only allows the smoker to escape the discomfort of withdrawal but also produces intrinsically pleasurable states. Nicotine triggers the release of epinephrine and norepinephrine, which in turn diminish appetite and boost alertness and mental efficiency. More important, nicotine also stimulates the central nervous system to release acetylcholine and beta-endorphin, neurotransmitters that serve to calm anxiety and reduce sensitivity to pain.

These positive rewards of smoking, when combined with the relief smoking provides from the unpleasantness of withdrawal, keep people smoking even when they wish they could stop, even when they know that they are committing "slow-motion suicide."

How Effective Are Programs to Stop Smoking? Efforts to help people stop smoking have used a variety of techniques, including public health warnings, counseling, drug treatments, hypnosis, aversive conditioning (by having people smoke rapidly until they cannot tolerate another cigarette), behavior modification, cognitive therapy, and group support. The bad news is that although such treatments are often effective in the short run, all but one-third to one-quarter of the participants eventually return to the habit (Pomerleau & Rodin, in press).

Better news comes from a Surgeon General's report (1983) indicating that among all American men there were in 1980 roughly as many former smokers (30 percent) as people who had never smoked (32 percent) (see Figure 18-13). (Because fewer women have ever started smoking, there are fewer former smokers among women—16 percent.) If these data have a familiar ring, recall (from Chapter 13, "Motivation") that weight-reduction programs tend to be (1) effective in the short run, (2) ineffective in the long run, but that (3) a surprising number of people were at one time much heavier than they are now. Perhaps weight-reduction and smoking-treatment programs attract the people least able to succeed on their own. Although smoking-treatment programs have enjoyed somewhat more success than weight-reduction programs, most people who quit smoking do it on their own, often after repeated attempts to stop.

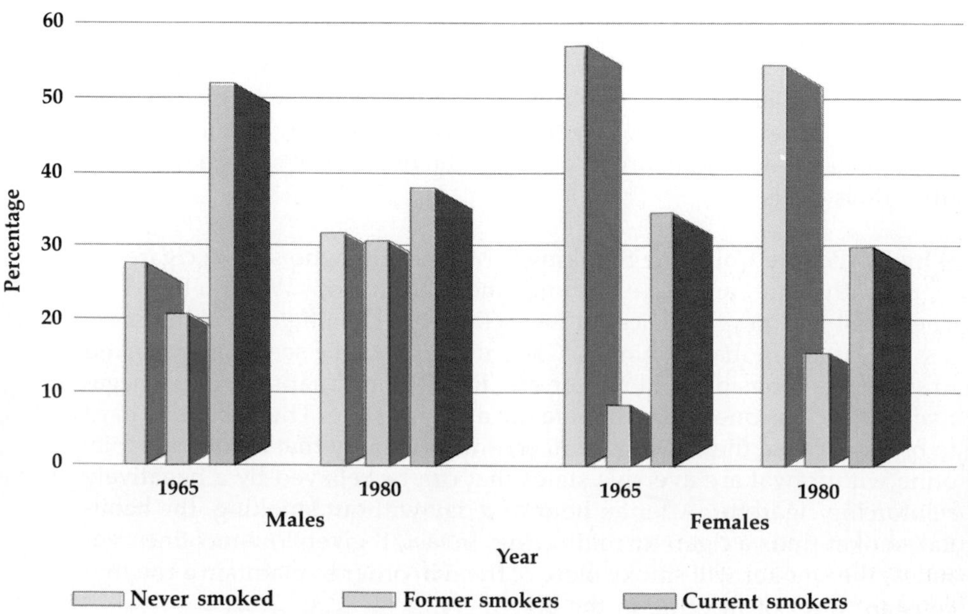

Figure 18-13 *The proportion of adults who are former smokers has increased since the 1964 Surgeon General's report linking smoking to health risks. However, one-third of adults still smoke, most of whom would like to quit.*

Thanks partly to the doubling of the number of former smokers between 1965 and 1980 in the United States, the proportion of male smokers has dropped from 52 to 38 percent and the proportion of female smokers has declined from 34 to 30 percent (Figure 18-13). Because of this decrease (and because of such factors as improved medical care), the coronary heart disease death rate has declined during these years by almost 30 percent.

How Might We Prevent Smoking? It is vastly easier never to begin smoking than to stop, once addicted. Drawing upon social psychological analyses of why youngsters begin smoking, several research teams have devised strategies for interrupting the behavior pattern that leads to smoking (Evans & others, 1984; Murray & others, 1984). In one such study, a research team led by Alfred McAlister (1980) had high school students prepare seventh graders to resist peer pressures to smoke. The seventh graders were taught to respond to ads implying that liberated women smoke by observing, "She's not really liberated if she is hooked on tobacco." They also role-played being called a chicken for not trying a cigarette and responding with statements like, "I'd be a real chicken if I smoked just to impress you." After several such sessions during the seventh and eighth grades, these students were half as likely to begin smoking as were students at a sister junior high school where the students' parents had an identical smoking rate (see Figure 18-14). This experiment and several others like it suggest curricular programs that individual teachers could implement easily, inexpensively, and with hope of significant reduction in future smoking rates.

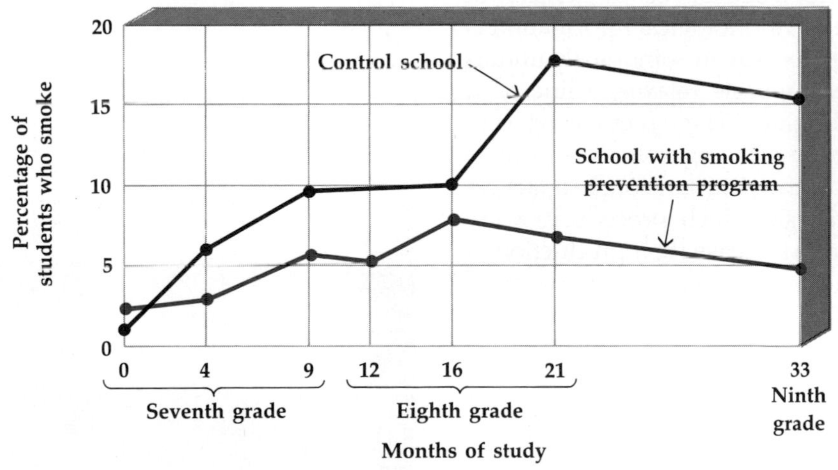

Figure 18-14 *Junior high school students who experienced a smoking prevention program that prepared them to cope with smoking ads and peer pressures were much less likely to begin smoking than were students at a matched control school.*

Stress Management

The growing realization that stress experiences are linked with heart disease, lowered immunity, chronic pain, and other bodily ailments has brought about a variety of new community and corporate stress-management programs. These commonly include not only nutrition education and smoking-cessation techniques, but also training in exercise and relaxation.

Exercise

As we noted in Chapter 17, "Therapy," recent research reveals that aerobic exercise can help reduce depression and anxiety. Sustained exercise can also help control some of the physical effects of stress, by lowering blood pressure and strengthening the heart (Roviario & others, 1984).

Moreover, several industrial health-promotion studies (for example, Naditch, 1985) have also revealed that employees who exercise regularly have significantly lower medical claims than do sedentary employees.

One explanation for this exercise-health correlation is that exercise promotes health. What would be another?

Like weight-reduction and smoking-cessation programs, exercise programs have been more noteworthy for their short-term rather than long-term effects; within 6 months or so many of the participants return to their old ways (Oldbridge, 1982). Once again, the challenge facing health psychologists is to design health-promotion programs that will have more enduring success.

Drawing by Park; © 1985 The New Yorker

Biofeedback

As we noted earlier, most of us are unaware from moment to moment of our blood pressure, heart rate, skin temperature, etc., and we certainly do not presume ourselves able to control them voluntarily. They are, after all, controlled by the autonomic ("involuntary") nervous system. Thus when some psychologists started experimenting with ways to train people to bring their internal functioning under conscious control, many of their colleagues thought them foolhardy. Then, in the late 1960s, some ingenious experiments by respected psychologists such as Neal Miller revealed that, if given pleasurable brain stimulation when they increased or decreased their heart rate, rats could learn to control their heartbeats. Later research revealed that even paralyzed humans (who could not use their skeletal muscles) could learn to control their blood pressure (Miller & Brucker, 1979).

Miller had used ***biofeedback,*** a system for electronically recording, amplifying, and feeding back information regarding a subtle physiological response. In the example of Figure 18-15, a sensor records tension in the forehead muscle of a headache sufferer. This biological information is processed by a computer and fed back to the person in some easily understood image. For example, as the forehead muscle relaxes, a line on a screen may go down or a light may grow brighter. The patient's task is to learn to control the line or the light, thereby learning voluntary control over the physiological state and the accompanying tension headaches. Biofeedback researchers and practitioners using such procedures were soon reporting that people could be trained to increase their production of alpha brain waves, warm their hands, and lower their blood pressure—all signs of a more relaxed state.

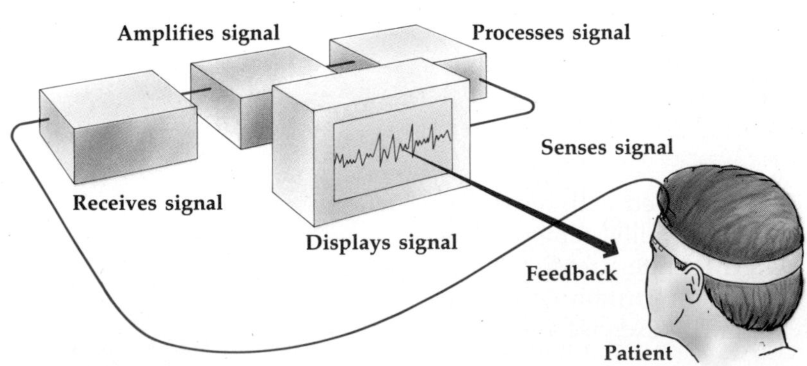

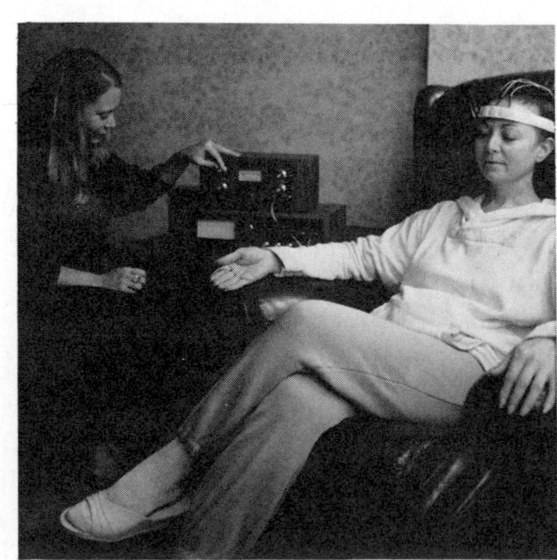

Figure 18-15 *Biofeedback systems such as this one, which records tension in the forehead muscle of a headache sufferer, allow people to monitor one or another of their subtle physiological responses in an attempt to modify that response.*

As often happens following a new scientific discovery, the initial skepticism about biofeedback soon was transformed into popular hopes for a revolution in people's abilities to treat their own stress-related disorders. A 1971 *Saturday Review* magazine article proclaimed that biofeedback research was "convincingly demonstrating that it may be possible to learn personal mastery over the functions of our visceral organs—the heart, liver, kidneys, intestines, glands, and blood vessels—in the same specific way that we learn to manipulate our fingers to play Chopin or our legs to kick a field goal" (Collier, 1971).

A decade later, as researchers stepped back to assess the results of hundreds of biofeedback experiments, the initial expectations seemed overblown and oversold (Miller, 1985). During biofeedback training, people do enjoy a calm, tranquil experience—but this results mostly from other accompanying factors such as restricted sensory input (Plotkin, 1979). Biofeedback does enable some people to gain somewhat greater control over their finger temperature, forehead-muscle tension, and chronic pain (King & Montgomery, 1980; Qualls & Sheehan, 1981; Turk & others, 1979), but other, simpler, methods of relaxation—for which no expensive equipment is required—produce many of the same benefits.

Today, biofeedback is often used in combination with other techniques in helping patients to control the physical symptoms of stress (Miller, 1983a). For example, a hypertension program at the Menninger Foundation in Kansas places patients on a drug that reduces their blood pressure, and then introduces biofeedback in an effort to wean them from the medication while maintaining or further lowering their blood pressure. With the aid of biofeedback, 65 percent of patients treated between 1975 and 1983 were successfully weaned from the medication (Fahrion & others, in press).

Relaxation

If relaxation is an important component of biofeedback, then might relaxation exercises provide an even more natural antidote to stress? Cardiologist Herbert Benson (1975, 1982, 1984) became intrigued with this possibility when he found that experienced meditators were able to decrease blood pressure, heart rate, and oxygen consumption and raise fingertip temperatures. The essence of their "relaxation response," as he called it, can be experienced by following a few simple steps: Assume a comfortable position, close your eyes and relax your muscles from foot to face, concentrate on a single word or phrase, and cast off other thoughts as you repeat this phrase for 10 or 20 minutes. The phrase may be a word, such as "one," or perhaps a prayer, such as "Lord, have mercy." By setting aside a quiet time or two each day—periods of what Chapter 7, "Perception," called sensory restriction—many people report enjoying tranquillity and inward stillness.

If Type A heart attack victims could be taught to relax, might their risk of another attack be reduced? Might the management of one's emotions do as much as controlled exercise and an altered diet to prevent heart attacks? To find out, Meyer Friedman and his colleagues randomly assigned hundreds of middle-aged heart attack survivors in San Francisco to one of two groups: The first group received standard advice from cardiologists concerning medications and eating and exercise habits; the second group received similar advice plus continuing counseling regarding how to slow down and relax—by walking, talking, and eating more slowly, smiling at others and laughing at themselves, admitting mistakes, taking time to enjoy life, and renewing their religious faith. As Figure 18-16 indicates, over the ensuing 3 years the second group experienced half as many heart attacks as the first. This, wrote the exuberant Friedman, is "a spectacular reduction in their cardiac recurrence rate. No drug, food, or exercise program ever devised, not even a coronary bypass surgical program, could match the protection against recurrent heart attacks" (Friedman & Ulmer, 1984, p. 141).

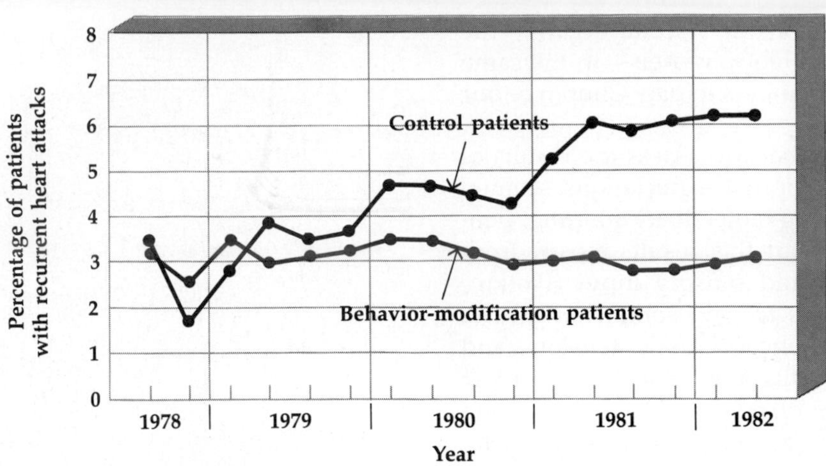

Figure 18-16 *In the San Francisco Recurrent Coronary Prevention Project, heart attack survivors who received counseling aimed at modifying their Type A behavior suffered fewer heart attacks than those in the control group who received only counseling from a cardiologist.*

It remains for other researchers to do the painstaking work of identifying which of Friedman's dozens of Type A reduction drills are actually beneficial. Even while Friedman was collecting his data, other investigators were at work studying specific stress buffers. For example, laughter seems to work in ways similar to exercise—it arouses us and then leaves us feeling more relaxed (Robinson, 1983). This may help explain the findings of Rod Martin and Herbert Lefcourt (1984) that people who laugh readily and have a sense of humor are less disturbed by stressful life events. So there is reason to suspect that, indeed, he who laughs, lasts.

"A cheerful heart is a good medicine, but a downcast spirit dries up the bones."
Proverbs 17:22

Social Support

Yet another stress buffer is the support enjoyed by those who are upheld by close relationships with friends, kin, or fellow members of close-knit religious or other organizations. People who enjoy such relationships—who are married or who have strong social and community ties—are less likely to die prematurely from various diseases than those with few social ties (Cohen & Syme, 1985). In one study, in which nearly 3000 Michigan residents were interviewed, given medical exams, and then restudied 10 years later, those who had few supportive social relationships were more likely to have died (House, 1984). This was especially true of men, and the higher death rate among those more isolated was not attributable to age or preexisting health problems. There are several possible explanations for this link between social support and health: Perhaps sick people are more socially isolated; perhaps people with strong, positive social ties have less stress with which to cope; perhaps social support helps reduce the trauma of stressful life events.

The accumulating evidence indicates that, although the conflicts associated with close relationships can actually be a source of stress when external stresses are low, such relationships help to buffer major stresses such as unemployment, surgery, or bereavement (Cohen & Syme, 1985). Why do you think this is so? As yet, the answer is not entirely clear (Jung, 1984). But social support seems to provide help in evaluating and dealing with a stressful event and a boost to our threatened self-esteem (Cohen & Wills, 1985). Wounded by a social rejection or the loss of a job, the reassurances of an intimate friend may be good medicine. Social support may be most helpful when it reduces our anxiety and when we interpret it not as meaning that we are weak and pathetic but that we are likable, loved, valued, and part of a caring group (Brehm, 1985).

Another significant aspect of close relationships is the opportunity they provide to confide painful feelings. In one study, health psychologists James Pennebaker and Robin O'Heeron (1984) contacted the surviving spouses of people who had committed suicide or died in car accidents. Those who bore their grief alone had more health problems than those who were open about their grief. In a simulated confessional, Pennebaker asked volunteers to share with an experimenter, who was hidden behind a screen, some upsetting events that had been preying on their minds. Before their confession, some were asked to describe a trivial event without yet divulging the troubling thoughts. Physiological measures revealed that their bodies were tense, and became relaxed only later when they confided their turmoil. Even writing about personal traumas in a nightly diary, as volunteers in another experiment did, resulted in fewer health problems during the ensuing 6 months (Pennebaker & Beall, 1984). As one subject explained, "Although I have not talked with anyone about what I wrote, I was finally able to deal with it, work through the pain instead of trying to block it out. Now it doesn't hurt to think about it."

Those who do not share their grief more often later experience the added suffering of illness.

Sometimes suppressed traumas eat away at us for months or years. When Pennebaker surveyed more than 700 undergraduate women, he found that about 1 in 12 reported a traumatic sexual experience in childhood. Compared with women who had experienced nonsexual traumas, such as parental death or divorce, the sexually abused women, especially those who had kept their secret to themselves, acknowledged more health problems, such as headaches and stomach ailments. So it seems that, if we can overcome the barriers of our own shyness, pride, and fears, our friends or family can indeed be good medicine.

SUMMING UP

With the conquering of many of the major infectious diseases, people's behaviors and stress responses have come to be recognized as major influences upon health and disease. Health psychology and the interdisciplinary field of behavioral medicine provide new avenues for the prevention and treatment of illness. Among their concerns are the effects of stress, the control of pain, the seeking of treatment, the adherence to health-enhancing regimens, and the promotion of healthier ways of living.

STRESS AND ILLNESS

What Is Stress? Stress, the process by which events challenge or threaten us, was conceptualized by Walter Cannon as a "fight or flight" system and by Hans Selye as a three-stage (alarm/resistance/exhaustion) general adaptation syndrome. Modern research on stress has assessed the health consequences of cataclysmic events, significant life changes, and daily hassles.

Stress and Heart Disease Coronary heart disease, the number one cause of death in the United States, has been linked with a competitive, hard-driving, impatient, and (especially) anger-prone Type A personality. Under stress, the body of a more reactive, Type A person secretes more of the "stress hormones" that are believed to accelerate the buildup of plaques on the heart's artery walls.

Stress and Resistance to Disease In addition to contributing to heart disease and a variety of psychophysiological illnesses, stress can suppress the immune system, making a person more vulnerable to infections and malignancy. New experiments indicate that the immune system's responses can be influenced by conditioning.

PAIN AND ITS CONTROL

Although pain is a vital danger signal, the suffering of those who experience chronic pain has prompted the search for the secrets of pain and its control.

What Is Pain? Although we are a long way from a complete understanding of the mysteries of pain, one useful theory has proposed that the spinal cord has a gate that either permits pain signals traveling up small nerve fibers to reach the brain or prevents their passage.

Pain Control Because pain is both a physiological and a psychological phenomenon, its treatment can be through a combination of biomedical and psychological means, including drugs, surgery, acupuncture, massage, electrical stimulation, exercise, hypnosis, relaxation, and thought distraction.

REACTIONS TO ILLNESS

Am I Sick? Noticing and Explaining Symptoms Our body provides us with a variety of ambiguous signals. If they catch our attention, we often interpret them according to our learned schemas.

Seeking Treatment If the symptoms seem to fit one of our disease schemas, we must decide, based on anticipated costs and benefits, whether medical care is warranted.

The Patient Role Feelings of loss of control—a common experience of those who adopt the good-patient role—can have the effect of triggering an outpouring of stress hormones, which can be as bad for the good patient as is hostility for those who adopt the bad-patient role. Realistic information before stressful medical procedures, plus advice on how to cope, helps patients to endure medical trauma more effectively.

Patient Adherence to Treatment The realization that patients often ignore doctors' instructions has stimulated social psychologists to study ways to increase patients' compliance. The personal characteristics of the physician, the nature of the physician's communication, and the immediate incentives for adhering to or discontinuing treatment regimens are the most important influences on the patient's behavior.

HEALTH PROMOTION

Everyone agrees that it is far better to prevent illness than to treat it once it occurs. What steps can be taken to prevent illness and promote wellness?

Consumption Researchers are now exploring how specific foods, by providing the building blocks for specific neurotransmitters, can affect mood and behavior. The largest preventable cause of death is cigarette smoking, a fact that has prompted psychologists to study the social influences that motivate adolescents to start smoking, the negative and positive reinforcers that maintain the habit once established, and possible ways of stopping and preventing smoking.

Stress Management Among the components of stress management programs are training in exercise, biofeedback, and relaxation. Although the degree of mind control over the body gained through biofeedback has fallen short of early expectations, biofeedback has become one accepted method for helping people control ailments such as tension headaches and high blood pressure. Simple relaxation exercises accomplish some of the same benefits. Moreover, counseling Type A heart attack survivors to slow down and relax has helped them lower their rate of recurring attacks. A sense of humor and social support also help to buffer the impact of stress.

TERMS AND CONCEPTS TO REMEMBER

Bad-Patient Role Uncooperative, complaining, demanding patient behavior.

Behavioral Medicine An interdisciplinary field that integrates and applies behavioral and medical knowledge to health and disease.

Biofeedback A system for electronically recording, amplifying, and feeding back information regarding a subtle physiological state.

Coronary Heart Disease The narrowing of the vessels that nourish the heart muscle; the number one cause of death in the United States today.

Gate-Control Theory Melzack and Wall's theory that the spinal cord contains a neurological "gate" that blocks or allows pain signals to pass on to the brain; the "gate" is opened by the activity of pain signals traveling up small nerve fibers and closed by activity in larger fibers or by information coming from the brain.

General Adaptation Syndrome Selye's concept of the body's adaptive response to stress as composed of three stages—alarm, resistance, exhaustion.

Good-Patient Role Cooperative, unquestioning, undemanding patient behavior, sometimes exhibited by anxious, helpless, depressed patients.

Health Psychology A subfield of psychology that provides psychology's contribution to behavioral medicine.

Lymphocytes The two types of white blood cells that are part of the body's immune system—the first (B lymphocytes) form in the bone marrow and release infection-fighting antibodies that fight bacterial infections, and the second (the T lymphocytes) form in the thymus and, among other duties, attack cancer cells, viruses, and foreign substances.

Psychophysiological Illness Literally, mind-body illness; any illness, such as certain forms of hypertension, ulcers, and headaches, that is not caused by any known physical disorder, but instead seems linked with stress.

Stress The whole process by which environmental events, called stressors, threaten or challenge us.

Type A Friedman and Rosenman's conception of behavior—competitive, hard-driving, impatient, verbally aggressive, easily angered—that is associated with increased incidence of coronary heart disease.

Type B Friedman and Rosenman's conception of an easygoing person who is less susceptible than the Type A person to coronary heart disease.

FOR FURTHER READING

Benson, H., & Proctor, W. (1984). *Beyond the relaxation response: How to harness the healing power of your personal beliefs.* New York: Times Books.

A physician's advice on how to relax, manage stress, and harness your body's healing powers.

Friedman, M., & Ulmer, D. (1984). *Treating Type A behavior—and your heart.* New York: Knopf.

An easy-to-read book that summarizes the results of a massive experiment in heart attack prevention and offers advice on how life-style changes can help minimize one's risk of heart attack.

Gatchel, R. J., & Baum, A. (1983). *An introduction to health psychology.* Reading, MA: Addison-Wesley.

A short textbook introduction to research on psychological factors in health.

Handbook of psychology and health (Vols. 1 to 4) (1982–1984). Hillsdale, NJ: Erlbaum.

Authoritative reviews of research in health psychology contributed by leading researchers.

Lazarus, R. S., & Folkman, S. (1984). *Stress, appraisal, and coping.* New York: Springer.

A comprehensive and scholarly analysis of stress—what it is and how we react to it.

Taylor, S. E. (1985). *Introduction to health psychology.* New York: Random House.

An overview of the psychology of health by a leading researcher.

Collection of Kimiko and John Powers

Red Grooms *Maine Room,* 1965

PART SEVEN

SOCIAL PSYCHOLOGY

Social psychologists study interpersonal behavior—how we relate to one another. They investigate the origins and consequences of attitudes and beliefs, conformity and independence, love and hate. Chapter 19, "Social Influence," examines the social forces that influence our willingness to comply, our openness to persuasion, and our behavior in groups. Chapter 20, "Social Relations," explores the crucial human processes of hurting and helping, prejudice and attraction, conflict and peacemaking.

Harry Callahan *Providence, 1966*

CHAPTER 19

Social Influence

Social psychology's great lesson—the enormous power of social influences on our decisions, beliefs, attitudes, and actions—is difficult to appreciate fully. But consider some illustrative phenomena.

Suggestibility: Suicides, bomb threats, hijackings, and UFO sightings have a curious tendency to come in waves. One well-publicized incident—the suicide of a famous movie star—can inspire imitation. And as we will see, copycat perceptions and actions are *not* restricted to crazy people. Laughter, even canned laughter, is contagious. Bartenders and beggars know to "seed" their tip or money cups with money supposedly left by others.

Role playing: A group of decent young men volunteered to spend time in a simulated prison devised by psychologist Philip Zimbardo (1972). Some were randomly designated as guards. They were given uniforms, billy clubs, and whistles, and were instructed to enforce certain rules. The remainder became prisoners, locked in barren cells and forced to wear humiliating outfits. After a day or two of "playing" their roles, the young men became caught up in the situation. The guards devised cruel and degrading routines, and one by one the prisoners either broke down, rebelled, or became passively resigned. Meanwhile, outside the laboratory, another group of men was being trained by the military junta then in power in Greece to become torturers (Goleman, 1985). The men's indoctrination into cruelty occurred in small steps. First, the trainee would stand guard outside the interrogation and torture cells. Then he would stand guard inside. Only then was he ready to become actively involved in the questioning and cruelty.

Persuasion: In late October of 1980, U.S. presidential candidate Ronald Reagan trailed incumbent Jimmy Carter by 8 percentage points in the Gallup Poll. On November 4, after a 2-week media blitz and a presidential debate, Reagan, "the great persuader," emerged victorious by a stunning 10 percentage points. The Reagan landslide made many people wonder what qualities made Ronald Reagan so persuasive? And his audience so persuadable?

Group influence: One of the first major decisions President John F. Kennedy and his bright and loyal advisers had to make was whether to approve a Central Intelligence Agency plan to invade Cuba. The group's high morale seemed to foster a sense that the plan couldn't help but succeed. No one spoke sharply against the idea, so everyone assumed there was consensus support for the plan, which was then implemented. When the small band of U.S.-trained and -supplied Cuban refugee invaders was easily captured and soon linked to the American government, Kennedy wondered aloud, "How could we have been so stupid?"

These actual happenings illustrate some of the intriguing effects of social influence. Before examining these phenomena, let's first consider the extent to which people recognize social psychology's great lesson and attribute others' behavior to social influences.

EXPLAINING OUR OWN AND OTHERS' BEHAVIOR

When visiting another culture, we are sometimes struck by how much "they" think and act differently than "we" do. A Westerner in China may at first be puzzled when the gracious performer claps while being applauded. To a Latin American dinner guest, his North American hosts may seem curiously uptight about his not having arrived on time. A preppy in a punk setting, a small town student at an urban university, and a Methodist in a Roman Catholic mass may feel like fish out of their cultural waters.

When we find ourselves among people whose customs we do not understand, we notice and try to explain how they differ from us. We may be struck by how alike "they all" are. For example, we may stereotype the Japanese as polite, the students at Medfield College as party types, New Yorkers as aggressive. Within our own familiar environment, where we hardly notice accepted behaviors and beliefs, we are more aware of differences among individuals. We notice that "Jack is shy, Julie is outgoing," thereby attributing Jack's and Julie's behaviors to their personal dispositions. Such ***attributions*** (explanations for behavior) are sometimes valid; in earlier chapters we saw that individuals do have enduring personality traits. However, we too easily underestimate the extent to which people's actions are influenced by their situations.

This underappreciation of social influences is called the ***fundamental attribution error.*** An experiment by David Napolitan and George Goethals (1979) illustrates this tendency to underestimate social forces. The researchers had individual Williams College students talk with a young woman who acted either aloof and critical or warm and friendly. Half the students were told beforehand that her behavior would be spontaneous. The other half were told the truth—that for the purposes of the experiment she had been instructed to *act* friendly (or unfriendly). What effect do you suppose this information had?

People see themselves acting differently in different situations, and so are aware that their behavior depends on the situation in which they find themselves. Observers may see a particular person in but one type of situation, and infer that that person's behavior is a reflection of his or her inner traits. Most of Rock Hudson's public were unaware that his heterosexual movie persona was just that—a role.

The students disregarded it. If she acted friendly, they inferred that she really was a warm person; if she acted unfriendly, they inferred she really was a cold person. In other words, they attributed her behavior to her personal disposition, *even if told that she was merely acting that way for purposes of the experiment.*

My students and I sometimes do the same when observing class debates. We know that the debaters' positions, pro or con, have been assigned by the toss of a coin; we have no way of even guessing their actual opinions. Yet we often attribute their remarks to their actual feelings, believing that their attitudes really correspond to what they are saying. The debaters, on the other hand, are keenly aware that their position on the issue is externally compelled.

You, too, likely have experienced the fundamental attribution error. In judging, say, whether your psychology instructor is shy or outgoing, you perhaps have inferred from your experience in class that he or she has an outgoing personality. But, you know your instructor only from the classroom, a situation that demands social interaction and public speaking. The instructor, on the other hand, observes his or her own behavior in many different situations—in the classroom, in meetings, at home, and so forth—and so might say, "Me outgoing? It all depends on the situation. When I'm in class or with good friends, yes, I'm outgoing. But at conventions and meetings I'm really rather shy."

So, when explaining *our own* behavior we are usually sensitive to how our behavior depends on the changing situations that we encounter. When explaining *others'* behavior, particularly after observing them in but one type of situation, we often commit the fundamental attribution error by leaping to unwarranted conclusions about their traits. We therefore often miss the great lesson of social psychology—that behavior is a product not only of the person, but also of the ways in which we are influenced by others.

Recall from Chapter 15 that personality psychologists study the enduring, inner determinants of behavior that help to explain why in a given situation different people act differently. Social psychologists study the social influences that help explain why a person will act differently in different situations.

Who or What Is to Blame? A Question of Attribution

How do you explain poverty or unemployment? Researchers in Britain, India, Australia, and the United States (Furnham, 1982; Pandey & others, 1982; Wagstaff, 1983) have found that political conservatives tend to attribute these and other social problems to the personal dispositions of the poor and unemployed themselves: "People generally get what they deserve; thus the types of people who don't work or have much money are usually lazy and undeserving." Political liberals are less likely to attribute responsibility to the dispositions of people in disadvantaged groups and more likely to blame past and current situations: "If you or I were to experience and live with the same overcrowding, poor education, and discrimination, would we be any better off than they are?"

As this illustrates, the attributions we make to explain behavior—to individuals' dispositions or to their situations—have important practical consequences.

CONFORMITY AND COMPLIANCE

From our observations of people in different cultures and environments we know that social influences are important. But what are these influences? How do they operate? To find out, social psychologists often create laboratory simulations of everyday social situations. In the miniature social world of the experiment, researchers will vary just one or two factors at a time—while holding all others constant—to pinpoint how these changes affect us. This strategy of experimentation is roughly comparable to what aeronautical engineers do when they construct a wind tunnel, a simplified reality in which they can vary wind conditions and study their precise effects on wing structures. Let's see how social psychologists have done this by imagining ourselves as participants in some classic experiments.

Self-Justifying Our Actions: Cognitive Dissonance Theory

One way to explain the effect of actions on attitudes is to note how strongly motivated we are to justify our actions. We want to relieve the discomfort we feel when our behavior differs noticeably from what we think and feel. This is the implication of ***cognitive dissonance theory*** (Cooper & Fazio, 1984). The theory was developed by Leon Festinger when he wondered why people living just outside an earthquake disaster zone in India spread rumors of disasters yet to come. Festinger suspected that the rumors served to justify the anxieties the villagers, having witnessed the nearby devastation, were already feeling. Generalizing from this case, he proposed that people tend to make their view of the world fit with how they have responded.

To put it as the theory does, dissonance is the tension we feel when two of our thoughts (cognitions) are psychologically inconsistent. If we feel one way but act in another and are aware of the discrepancy and the potential consequences of our action, then we experience cognitive dissonance. Dissonance, like hunger, motivates its own reduction. The theory therefore offers an intriguing prediction: If you can get people to choose to behave in a way that is contrary to their usual attitudes, they will feel the discomfort of cognitive dissonance. This discomfort can be reduced by bringing their attitude more into line with what they have done. "If I chose to do it," they might rationalize, "it must be worth doing." (On the other hand, dissonance will be minimal if they cannot foresee the consequences of their actions, or if they feel their action was coerced and thus not their responsibility.)

The theory has been confirmed by many experiments in which people are either coaxed or forced into complying with some disagreeable request. See if you can guess the results of one such study, conducted by Robert Croyle and Joel Cooper (1983) with Princeton University men, all of whom had indicated they were opposed to the banning of alcohol from the Princeton campus. Supposedly to provide information to a committee that was studying the issue, some were asked to write forcefully all the arguments they could think of in *support* of the ban. Half of these writers were first reminded that their participation in the research was "completely voluntary"; the other half were merely ordered to begin writing the arguments. Afterward, Croyle and Cooper had the men again indicate their actual attitude. As Figure 19-6 indicates, after writing the arguments, the men were more sympathetic to the ban, especially if they could not easily attribute their behavior to the experimenter's coercion. If you argue for a point without feeling coerced, you are likely to see more clearly the rationale for it.

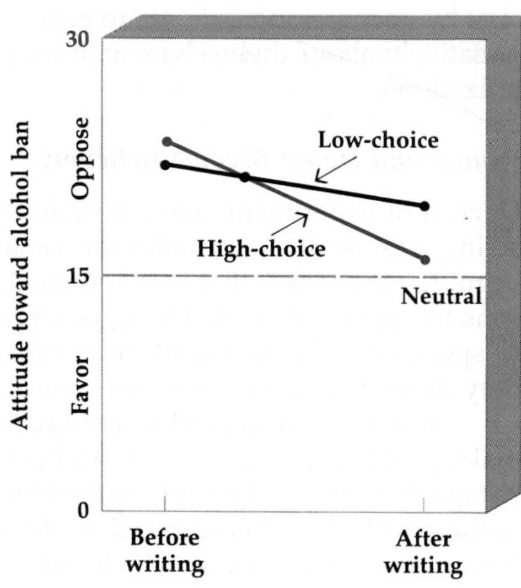

Figure 19-6 *Cognitive dissonance theory predicts that when we act contrary to our prevailing attitudes and cannot attribute our actions to coercion, we experience dissonance, which can be reduced by coming to believe in what we have done. Princeton men who felt responsible (high-choice) for essays they had written in support of a drinking ban became more sympathetic to the ban, despite having originally opposed the ban.*

Inferring Our Attitudes: Self-Perception Theory

Cognitive dissonance theory assumes that our need to maintain a consistent and positive self-image motivates us to adopt attitudes that justify our actions and decisions. ***Self-perception theory*** assumes no such motive. It simply suggests that when our attitudes are unclear to us, we observe our actions and then infer our attitudes.

When Daryl Bem (1972) proposed this theory, he assumed that we make inferences about our own attitudes much as we infer others' attitudes. Were we to see someone freely volunteer to write arguments in opposition to a drinking ban, we would infer that the person probably is opposed to the ban. Were we to see someone forced to write arguments opposing the ban, we would be less likely to make such an inference. Perhaps before writing the anti-alcohol arguments many of the Princeton men were not sure how they felt, so they inferred their attitudes from

"I can watch myself and my actions, just like an outsider."
Anne Frank,
The Diary of a Young Girl, 1947

what they wrote. And so it goes as we observe our own behavior. What we freely say and do can be self-revealing. As we noted in Chapter 14, "Emotion," even observing our own facial expressions can help us to surmise what our feelings are.

Self-perception theory also helps explain the overjustification effect described on p. 236. Recall that promising people a reward for doing what they already enjoy can lead them to infer that their behavior is due to the reward, thus undermining their intrinsic enjoyment. Dissonance theory cannot explain this phenomenon: When an already justifiable activity is *overjustified* by the promise of added reward, there is no cause for dissonance because the person is not doing anything that is contrary to his or her prevailing attitudes.

The debate over these and other explanations of the attitudes-follow-behavior principle has inspired hundreds of experiments that have shown the conditions under which dissonance and self-perception processes operate. To summarize the findings, it seems that dissonance theory best explains what happens when our actions openly contradict our well-defined previous attitudes: We feel tension that is measurable as physiological arousal and we reduce it by adjusting our attitudes. When we are unsure of our attitudes we may, as self-perception theory suggests, simply infer them by observing our uncoerced actions. As often happens in science, the two theories each provide a partial explanation of a complex reality.

PERSUASION

Does the attitudes-follow-behavior principle explain important instances of change in people's attitudes? To some extent, yes. The "brainwashing" that American prisoners of war underwent during the Korean war appears to have been partly an aftereffect of behaviors they had agreed to perform. The typical prisoner would first be asked to write only a trivial statement such as "the United States is not perfect." Then the ante would be upped; the man might be asked to list some flaws in American democracy and culture and to sign his name. Later, the prisoner might be asked to expand his ideas into an essay or speech. Aware that his behavior had not been brutally coerced and that his statements were being shown to others, the prisoner's attitudes would often shift toward consistency with his actions (Schein, 1956). Likewise, in the years immediately following the introduction of school desegregation and the passage of the U.S. Civil Rights Act of 1964, white Americans expressed diminishing racial prejudice. And as Americans in different regions came to act more alike—thanks to more uniform national standards against discrimination—they began to think more alike (Myers, 1983). Behavior can affect attitudes, sometimes turning prisoners into collaborators and enemies into friends.

"Gentlemen, *please*! I'm sure we can all agree that both the rowing machine *and* the stationary bicycle have a place in any serious program of cardiovascular exercise."

But change does occur by other means as well. The physical fitness movement, for example, has convinced many people to change their habits. As we noted in the last chapter, 30 percent of adults are now ex-smokers and many formerly sedentary people are now regularly jogging, biking, or swimming. Thanks to effective persuasion, people sometimes adopt new behaviors.

"A man should never be ashamed to own that he has been in the wrong, which is but saying, in other words, that he is wiser today than he was yesterday."
Jonathan Swift,
Thoughts on Various Subjects, 1711

What makes for effective persuasion? If you want to communicate your beliefs more effectively, sell a product or idea, or simply sharpen your awareness of the persuasion techniques advertisers and others use to influence you, what should you know? Social psychologists have broken down the process of persuasion into four elements: the communicator, the message, the medium, and the audience; or *who* says *what* by *what means* to *whom*.

Who Says? The Communicator

In the 1920s, Edward Bernays, an enterprising public relations expert working for the American Tobacco Company, was asked to convince American women, few of whom smoked, that smoking was acceptable (Cunningham, 1983). His strategy: to present examples of attractive or respectable women smokers. Bernays hired models to smoke in the lobby of New York's Waldorf-Astoria Hotel and persuaded debutantes to smoke while walking in the New York City Easter Parade. Magazine advertisements began to portray enviable women smoking cigarettes and stage and screen stars attesting to the pleasures of smoking. By the 1940s, the number of women smokers was rising dramatically.

What makes for an effective communicator? As Bernays recognized, *attractiveness* is important, especially on matters of personal preference rather than fact. In preferences that have to do with life-style, tastes, and values, an appealing source—one who is physically attractive or whose characteristics are similar to those of the audience—is most persuasive.

On matters of fact, the *credibility* of the source becomes more important. Credible sources are those perceived as both expert and trustworthy. Experimenters have found that these perceived qualities can be enhanced by looking the listener straight in the eye, by talking fairly rapidly, and by arguing against one's self-interest or expected beliefs. In one study, researchers Wendy Wood and Alice Eagly (1981) found that university students were persuaded more by antipornography arguments attributed to someone generally opposed to censorship than by arguments attributed to someone who favored censorship. When the anticensorship source argued an unexpected position, such as a ban, people attributed his message to compelling evidence rather than to his personal bias.

Our responsiveness to a frank appeal, to a trustworthy look directed exclusively at us, to a well-known, physically attractive individual—all these and more go into making this an effective advertisement.

What Is Said? The Message

Is a message more persuasive when it differs from the audience's existing opinions by a great deal or by only a little? Experiments suggest that highly credible sources effect greater opinion change when they argue a relatively extreme position rather than a moderate one. Less credible people may be discredited when they take extreme positions, and so are more effective when they advocate points of view closer to those of the audience.

Should a message argue your side only, or also acknowledge and refute the opposing position? Researchers report that it depends on the listeners. If the audience already tends to agree with the message and is unlikely ever to hear the opposing one, then a one-sided appeal will be most persuasive. To persuade more sophisticated and well-informed audiences, however, speakers need to address the opposing arguments.

If both sides of an issue are presented, does the side going first or second have the advantage? Often, the side going first has an edge, especially when the first speaker can affect how people interpret what the second speaker says. But if a time gap separates the two presentations and if a decision is made immediately after hearing them, the second side is more likely to have the advantage. Thus, salespeople often get good results when their presentation occurs just before the customer's decision is made.

Is a tightly reasoned message more powerful than one that arouses emotion? It would be nice if the answer were simple, but here, too, the human reality is complex. The answer depends on the interaction of reason and emotion with other factors, including the listener's expectations and knowledge. For example, people who are both informed and concerned about the topic tend to respond thoughtfully to the accuracy and logic of the presentation. And as we saw earlier in this chapter, attitudes that we consciously examine tend to be long lasting and to guide our behavior. People who are less well informed or concerned are persuaded more effectively by emotional factors. They tend to form attitudes based on their response to the appeal of the communicator or to emotional associations with the message (Petty & others, 1983).

Heartrending images, like this photo of a child in an Ethiopian refugee camp, and rousing appeals by well-known entertainers, moved many people who had been vaguely aware of the long-existing drought and famine in Africa to contribute desperately needed millions for famine relief. This supports findings that those who are less concerned or informed about an issue are more responsive to a vivid emotional message or one delivered by an appealing communicator.

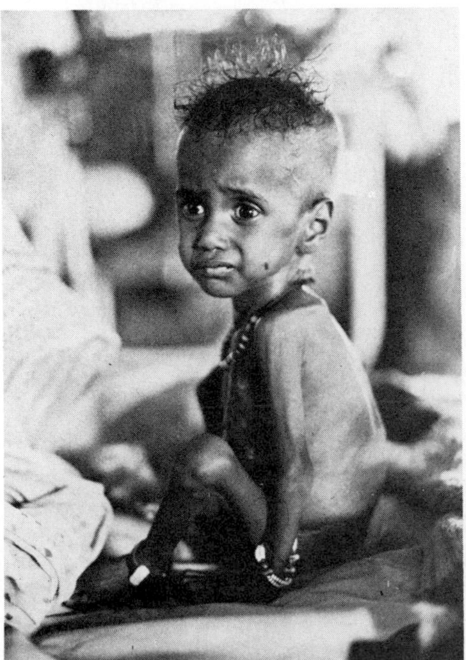

Evidence that emotional factors are important for persuasion comes from a variety of studies. Associating a message with the good feelings we have while eating, drinking, or listening to music can make it more convincing (which is perhaps why so many business deals are made over lunch). Messages that arouse fear can also be effective. Such messages are often vivid, and, as we noted in Chapter 11, "Thinking and Language," vivid information tends to be more available to memory than that which is matter-of-fact. When various teams of researchers sampled the audience of 100 million Americans before and again several weeks after the telecast of the 1983 nuclear-war film, "The Day After," they found that concern over nuclear war had risen (Oskamp & others, 1985; Schofield & Pavelchak, 1985). When it comes to memory and persuasion, an emotional picture can indeed be worth a thousand words.

By What Means? The Medium

Which media are the most effective for changing attitudes, the mass media and direct mail or face-to-face appeals? If you are campaigning for a cause or a candidate, do you spend your time more effectively by leaving leaflets at many houses or by going to fewer houses and taking the time to talk with people?

On relatively minor or unfamiliar issues, the mass media and mailings can be a powerful tool. Advertisers can more easily persuade us to choose one brand of aspirin over another chemically identical brand than to change our basic values. Although the Reagan triumph over the incumbent Carter demonstrated that people can sometimes be persuaded to change their leanings in an important election, they can be more easily persuaded to choose one unknown candidate over another for a less important office, such as water commissioner.

"And now a message of importance to those of you who have been giving serious thought to the purchase of a new tube of toothpaste."

Generally, face-to-face appeals are even more persuasive than media appeals and mailings. This was demonstrated three decades ago in Ann Arbor, Michigan, where citizens intending to vote against a revision of the city charter were split into three groups (Eldersveld & Dodge, 1954). Of those exposed only to mass media advertisements for the charter revision, 19 percent voted for it when election day came. Of those who received four mailings supporting the revision, 45 percent voted for it. Of those personally visited and appealed to face-to-face, 75 percent were persuaded to cast their votes for it.

To Whom? The Audience

The final ingredient in our recipe for persuasion is the audience. The ultimate determinant of persuasion is not the message itself but what thoughts it triggers. When a message seems important to its listeners, they will not just soak it up, they will internally agree or counterargue. In his *Pensées,* French philosopher and mathematician Blaise Pascal more than 300 years ago anticipated the findings of many recent experiments on persuasion: "People are usually more convinced by reasons they discover themselves than by those found by others."

In an extensive series of experiments, Richard Petty and John Cacioppo (1986) found that a message that evokes the desired thoughts is even more persuasive when techniques are used to make the audience think about it. Asking rhetorical questions is one such technique. For example, Ronald Reagan's closing question to viewers at the end of his 1980 debate with President Carter—"Are you better off than you were four years ago?"—enhanced his message by creating the desired thoughts in the voters' minds.

The audience's personal characteristics also affect their openness to persuasion. People whose opinions are not strongly defined are, quite naturally, more open to persuasion than those whose opinions are well-informed. Thus, political canvassers are advised not to linger in conversation with people who either strongly favor or strongly oppose their candidate or cause, and to focus their energies instead on those in the middle. Because many of their opinions are not yet well-defined, teenagers and young adults seem to be good candidates for persuasion. When researchers have surveyed and resurveyed the social attitudes of groups of younger and older people over several years, they generally find that the younger people's attitudes have changed more (Sears, 1979). For this reason, the influences that people subject themselves to during these years—the peers they spend time with; the schools they attend; the media they read, hear, and watch; the groups they join—can have a lasting impact.

Aspiring politicians quickly learn to make the most of their campaigning time by focusing their energies on uncommitted citizens.

GROUP INFLUENCE

How do the groups we belong to affect our behavior? Social psychologists have explored this question by studying the influences operating in the simplest of groups—one person in the presence of another—and the more complex interaction within larger groups, such as families, athletic teams, and decision-making committees.

Individual Behavior in the Presence of Others

Social Facilitation

The simplest of all social-psychological questions was appropriately one of the first: How are we influenced by the mere presence of others—by people either watching us or joining us in such activities as jogging or solving puzzles? Having noticed that cyclists' racing times were faster when they cycled with others, Norman Triplett (1898) guessed that the presence of others boosts performance. To test his hypothesis, Triplett had adolescents wind a fishing reel as rapidly as possible. He discovered that they wound faster in the presence of a ***coactor*** (someone who worked simultaneously on the same task) than they did alone. The phenomenon Triplett observed is called ***social facilitation***—the tendency to perform simple tasks better when others are present. Mysteriously, later studies found the opposite effect: On such tasks as learning nonsense syllables or solving complex multiplication problems, people did less well when observers or coactors were present.

Two hundred and forty studies and nearly 24,000 subjects later, the mystery is nearly solved (Bond & Titus, 1983). The Sherlock Holmes in this scientific story was social psychologist Robert Zajonc (pronounced ZY-ence). Wondering why the presence of others would sometimes boost and sometimes hurt task performance, Zajonc (1965) recalled a basic principle of experimental psychology (see p. 370): On easy tasks (such as unscrambling the anagram *irlg*), highly anxious people outperform relaxed subjects. On difficult tasks, however, anxious people do less well. In other words, arousal enhances the most likely response—the correct one on an easy task, the incorrect one on a difficult task. If people also get anxious or aroused when performing such tasks in the presence of others, reasoned Zajonc, then easy tasks should become easier and difficult tasks harder.

A variety of carefully controlled laboratory studies have confirmed Zajonc's hunch. When observed by others, people do sometimes get

Performers, whether amateur or professional, often find they are only really "on" before an audience. The presence of onlookers inspires them to turn in a better performance. This reinforces the idea (discussed in Chapter 14) that emotional arousal leads to better performance on well-learned tasks.

aroused (Geen & Gange, 1983; Moore & Baron, 1983), and they do perform easy tasks (such as winding fishing reels) more quickly and complex tasks (such as complicated multiplication problems) more slowly and less accurately. The effect is small but is sometimes noticeable in everyday activities. For example, James Michaels and his associates (1982) found that expert pool players in the Virginia Polytechnic Institute student union (having made 71 percent of their shots while being unobtrusively observed) made 80 percent when four people came up to watch them. Poor shooters (having made 36 percent of their shots) made only 25 percent when watched. The moral: What you do well, you are likely to do even better in front of an audience. What you find difficult may seem impossible when others are watching.

Social Loafing

Perhaps you noted that the social-facilitation experiments evaluate people's *individual* efforts, from winding fishing reels to shooting pool. What about situations that require a team effort in order to achieve a common goal? In a team tug-of-war, for example, do you suppose each person would exert more, less, or the same effort as that expended in a tug-of-war between two people?

To find out, Alan Ingham and his fellow researchers (1974) asked blindfolded University of Massachusetts students to "pull as hard as you can" on a rope. When the students were fooled into believing that three others behind them were also pulling, they pulled only 82 percent as hard as when they knew they were pulling alone.

Bibb Latané (1981) and his colleagues call this diminished effort by those submerged in a group the ***social loafing*** effect. Social loafing has now been demonstrated on various tasks and in several cultures, including the United States, India, Thailand, Japan, and Taiwan (Gabrenya & others, 1983). In some experiments, blindfolded subjects seated in a group are asked to clap or shout as loud as they can while listening over headphones to the sound of loud clapping or shouting. When told they are doing it with others, they produce about one-third less noise than when they think their individual effort is identifiable.

How do we explain social loafing? First, people acting in a group are less accountable and therefore less worried about what others think. Second, they may view their contribution as dispensable (Kerr & Bruun, 1983). And, as many organization leaders know, if group members share equally in the benefits of a group, regardless of how much they contribute to it, they may slack off and "free ride" on the other group members' efforts.

People who anonymously pool their efforts toward a group goal tend to "free ride" on the group by exerting less effort than when they are individually accountable for attaining the goal.

Deindividuation

We have seen that the presence of others can arouse people (the social facilitation experiments) or can diminish their feelings of responsibility (the social loafing experiments). Sometimes the presence of others both arouses people *and* diminishes their sense of responsibility, causing unrestrained behavior ranging from food throwing in the dining hall or screaming at a basketball referee to vandalism or riots. Such abandonment of normal restraints to the power of the group is called ***deindividuation.*** To be deindividuated is to become less self-conscious and more uninhibited in a group situation.

Deindividuation often occurs when participating in a group activity makes people feel aroused, distracted, and anonymous. Rioters, made faceless by the mob, feel free to vandalize. In one experiment with New York University women, those dressed in depersonalizing Ku Klux Klan–style hoods (Figure 19-7) delivered twice as much electric shock to a victim as did women who were identifiable (Zimbardo, 1970). (The "victim" did not actually receive the shocks.) Similarly, tribal warriors who depersonalize themselves with face paints or masks are more likely than those with exposed faces—and identities—to kill, torture, or mutilate their captured enemies (Watson, 1973). Whether in a mob, at a rock concert, at a party, or at worship, to lose one's self-consciousness (to become deindividuated) is to become more responsive to social cues and—for better or for worse—to become caught up in the group experience.

Figure 19-7 *In one experiment on the effects of deindividuation, subjects made anonymous by wearing Ku Klux Klan–style hoods delivered more electric shock to victims than did identifiable subjects.*

Crowding

Sometimes the density of other people (the number of people per unit of space) becomes so great that we feel crowded. If someone invades our ***personal space***—the buffer zone we like to maintain around our bodies—we may become uncomfortable. We are especially likely to feel crowded if we feel constrained and if we sense that we lack control. In one experiment, Judith Rodin and her fellow researchers (1978) jockeyed elevator passengers to a position either away from or in front of the elevator controls. When upon leaving the elevator the passengers were approached to complete a survey on elevator design, those who had stood away from the controls reported feeling more crowded.

Do these people know each other well or not? Their animated conversation seems to indicate they do. But the manner in which she hugs herself and so defends her personal space and he hesitates about coming closer indicate just the opposite.

Experimenters have sometimes found that density amplifies people's reactions. For example, friendly people who sit close are liked even more, and unfriendly people are liked even less (Schiffenbauer & Schiavo, 1976; Storms & Thomas, 1977). Density has a funny effect, too: Comedy records that seem somewhat humorous to those in a large, uncrowded room seem even funnier to those in a small, densely packed room (Aiello & others, 1983; Freedman & Perlick, 1979).

Why? Perhaps we are more aware of and responsive to others' reactions when they are close. Or perhaps, as the social-facilitation experiments suggest, being more aroused when others are nearby intensifies our reactions.

If, indeed, conditions of high density are arousing, do people who have lived many years in crowded conditions suffer ill effects? It is true that densely populated urban areas have higher rates of crime and mental disorder than do small towns. But the greater incidence could be due to other factors, such as lower levels of income and education and higher noise levels in these areas. Needed is a self-contained physical environment in which the population density varies over time. In such an environment would behavior and health problems rise and fall with changes in population density?

Researchers Verne Cox, Paul Paulus, and Garvin McCain (1984) identified one such environment: prisons. They analyzed the records for four state prison systems and discovered that when a prison's population goes up, so do its rates of death, suicide, disciplinary infraction, and psychiatric commitment. Such problems occur more often in prisons with large populations than in prisons with fewer inmates. Moreover, the more inmates a prison houses in a cell (and therefore the less privacy it provides) the greater the problems it will encounter. Even blood pressure and illness complaints are higher among inmates living under crowded prison conditions (Figure 19-8).

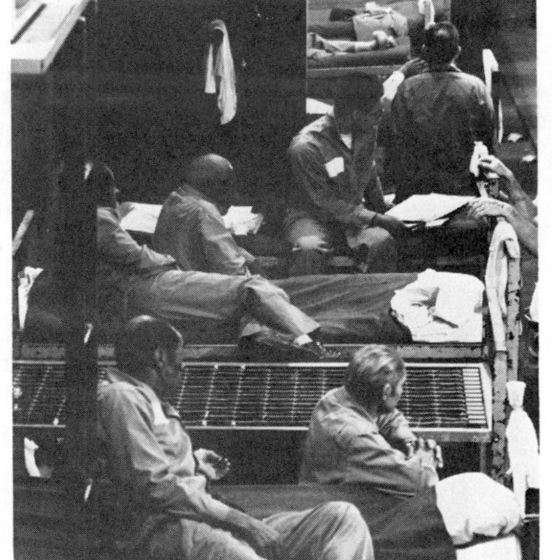

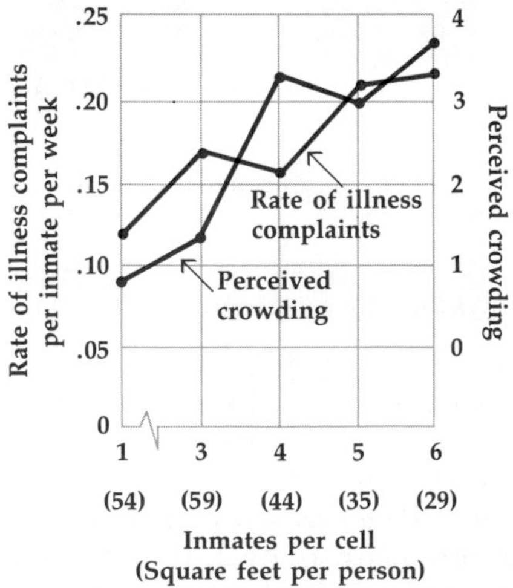

Figure 19-8 *Studies of prison records clearly show the ill effects of crowding: greater incidence of death, suicide, disciplinary infraction, and psychiatric commitment. In one study, inmates living six per cell felt much more crowded and experienced more illness than those in individual cells.*

Effects of Group Interaction

We have examined the conditions under which the presence of others can fuel mob violence and enhance humor; make easy tasks easier and difficult tasks harder; tempt people to free-ride on the efforts of others and motivate them to jog faster. Research on the effects of group interaction also yields mixed findings.

Group Polarization

Educational researchers have long been intrigued by a peculiar phenomenon: With time, initial differences between college-student groups often become accentuated. If the freshmen at College X are more intellectually oriented than those at College Y, this difference is likely to become more pronounced by their senior year. If the attitudes of people who join fraternities and sororities differ from those of people who do not, this attitude gap will likely grow as the two groups progress through college (Wilson & others, 1975).

Why? Might discussion among like-minded people strengthen their shared attitudes? Dozens of experiments indicate that group interaction does have a polarizing effect—it enhances each group's prevailing tendency. This ***group polarization*** phenomenon is commonly observed when people within the group discuss statements that most of them favor or oppose. For example, Serge Moscovici and Marisa Zavalloni (1969) found that group discussion strengthened French students' initially positive attitudes toward their premier and negative attitudes toward Americans. And George Bishop and I (Myers & Bishop, 1970) discovered that when groups of highly prejudiced high-school students discussed racial issues their opinions became even more prejudiced, and those of low-prejudice groups became even less so (Figure 19-9). In the laboratory, as in life, discussion tended to accentuate the initial leanings within each group.

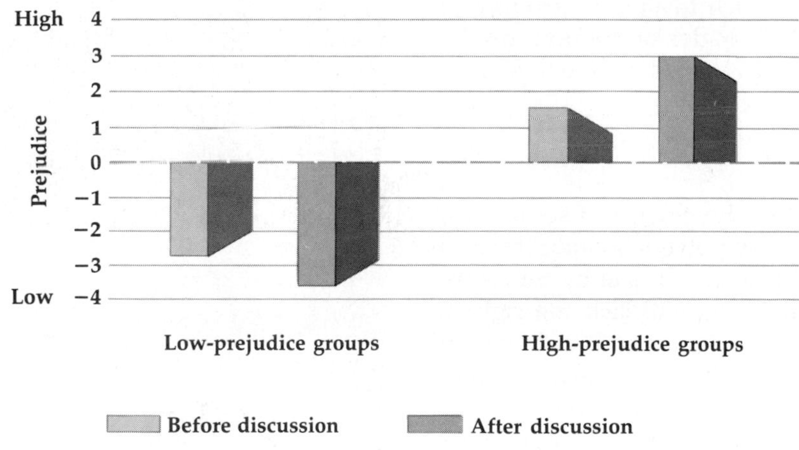

Figure 19-9 *If a group is like-minded, discussion strengthens its prevailing opinions. Talking over racial issues increased prejudice in a high-prejudice group of high school students and decreased it in a low-prejudice group.*

Groupthink

Does the polarization that often occurs when like-minded people talk together ever distort important group decisions? Social psychologist Irving Janis thought so when he first read historian Arthur M. Schlesinger Jr.'s account of how President John Kennedy and his advisers blundered into the ill-fated Bay of Pigs invasion—sending 1400 CIA-trained Cuban exiles into Cuba to overthrow the Castro government. As Janis (1982a) studied the decision-making procedures that led to the fiasco, he discovered that, in the interest of group harmony, dissenting views had been suppressed. Because the Kennedy group wanted to maintain their high morale, the members felt pressured not to speak unless in favor of the emerging plan, especially after the President had indicated his enthusiasm for it. The net effect was that the group convinced itself that the plan was both moral and foolproof. To describe this harmonious but unrealistic type of group thinking, Janis coined the term ***groupthink.***

"One's impulse to blow the whistle on this nonsense was simply undone by the circumstances of the discussion."
Arthur M. Schlesinger, Jr. (1965, p. 255)

This group, whose harmonious but unrealistic thinking led to the disastrous Bay of Pigs invasion, was responsible for the plan that effectively prevented the Soviets from installing missiles in Cuba. One key difference in the processes by which these two group decisions were made was the sense members had of whether dissenting opinions were welcome.

As Janis examined other historical fiascos—the failure to anticipate the attack on Pearl Harbor, the escalation of the Vietnam war, the Watergate cover-up—he uncovered more and more evidence that groupthink is fed by such psychological processes as conformity, self-justification, and group polarization. Yet he was also aware of experiments indicating that to solve some types of problems, two heads are indeed better than one. So he studied instances in which American presidents and their advisers made good decisions collectively. Examples were the Truman administration's formulation of the Marshall Plan for getting Europe back on its feet after World War II and the Kennedy administration's actions to keep the Soviets from installing missiles in Cuba. In such instances, groupthink was prevented by a leader who welcomed all shades of opinion, invited experts' critiques of developing plans, or even assigned people to identify possible problems.

Minority Influence

Throughout this chapter we have emphasized the powers of social influence. Let us close with the reminder that these powers include the individual's power to influence groups. Social history is made by minorities that sway majorities. Were it not, women would still lack the right to vote, communism would not have spread beyond the minds of Marx and Engels, and Christianity would be a small Middle Eastern sect. Technological history is similarly made by innovative minorities. Railroads were first viewed as a nonsensical idea and farmers feared that their noise would prevent hens from laying eggs. Robert Fulton's steamboat—"Fulton's Folly"—was greeted with derision: "Never did a single encouraging remark, a bright hope, a warm wish, cross my path." Much the same reaction greeted the printing press, telegraph, incandescent lamp, and typewriter (Cantril & Bumstead, 1960).

To understand better how minorities sway majorities, social psychologists in Europe have exposed people to groups in which an individual or two consistently express a controversial attitude or an unusual perceptual judgment (like calling a bluish slide green). One repeated finding of this research is that a minority voice (especially a minority of more than one person) that unswervingly holds to its position is far more successful in swaying the majority than is a minority that waffles. Holding consistently to a minority opinion will not make you popular, but it may make you influential, especially if your self-confidence stimulates the others to consider why you react as you do. Although people often comply publicly with the majority view, they may privately develop sympathy with the minority view. So even when a minority's influence is not yet

"If the single man plant himself indomitably on his instincts, and there abide, the huge world will come round to him."
Ralph Waldo Emerson,
Addresses and Lectures, 1849

visible, it may be persuading some members of the majority to rethink their views (Maass & Clark, 1984).

The social influence principles of this chapter can help us to understand how people are persuaded to buy certain products, vote for particular candidates, or join religious cults. The combined powers of social pressure, behavioral commitments, persuasion, and group influence are indeed enormous. But so are the powers of the person. We choose or create many of the situations that influence us. We also reassert our sense of freedom and uniqueness when we feel it threatened. And our minority opinions can move majorities.

Finally, we do well to remember that explaining *why* someone has adopted a particular belief says nothing about the belief's truth or falsity. To know why someone does or does not believe that jogging benefits health does not tell us whether jogging is, in fact, beneficial. To know why one person is a devout religious believer and another a nonbeliever does not tell us whether God, in fact, exists. So let no one say to you, and do not say to anyone, "Your convictions are silly. You believe them because of social influence." The second statement may be true, but it can never justify the first.

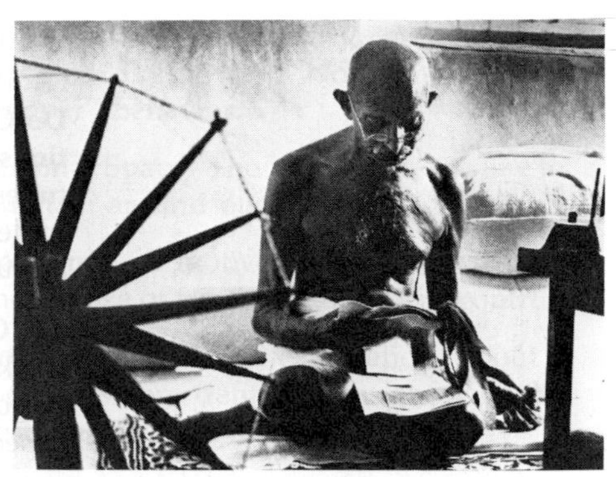

As the life of Mahatma Gandhi (1869–1948) powerfully testifies, a consistent and persistent minority voice can sometimes sway the majority. Gandhi was often villified and imprisoned. But his appeals and fasts on behalf of nonviolence in the struggle for India's independence eventually won that independence peacefully.

SUMMING UP

Social psychology's great lesson is that our behavior is powerfully influenced by social situations as well as by personal dispositions.

EXPLAINING OUR OWN AND OTHERS' BEHAVIOR

Because we need to explain people's behavior, we generally attribute it either to internal disposition or to external situations. In accounting for others' actions, we tend to underestimate social influences, thus committing the fundamental attribution error. When we explain our own behavior, however, we more often point to the situation and not to ourselves.

CONFORMITY AND COMPLIANCE

Suggestibility As the pioneering studies by Sherif demonstrated, when we are not sure about our judgments, we are likely to adjust them toward the assumed group standard.

Group Pressure and Conformity Solomon Asch and others found that under certain conditions people will conform to a group's judgment even when it clearly is incorrect.

Obedience In Milgram's famous experiments, people who were torn between obeying the experimenter and responding to another's pleas usually chose to obey orders, even though obedience supposedly meant harming another person.

Lessons from the Conformity and Compliance Studies These classic experiments demonstrate the potency of social forces, and they indicate that we may conform either to gain or protect social approval (normative social influence) or because we accept the information that others provide (informational social influence).

Personal Control and Social Control People also select and are part of many of the situations that influence them. If not intimidated, they will react against the pressures of social control that constrain their freedom and that reduce their sense of uniqueness.

Abbas *Wall Paintings by Keith Haring*

CHAPTER 20

Social Relations

Keith Haring *Untitled,* 1985

"We cannot live for ourselves alone," remarked the novelist Herman Melville, for "our lives are connected by a thousand invisible threads." These connecting threads may strain with tension, vibrate with joy, or lie peacefully calm. In our day-to-day relations with one another we sometimes harm and sometimes help, we sometimes feel dislike and sometimes feel love, we are sometimes in conflict and sometimes at peace.

In this concluding chapter we will look at these two-sided aspects of social relations—at aggression and altruism, prejudice and attraction, conflict and peacemaking. Why and when do we respond in such ways? And what steps might we take to transform the closed fists of aggression, prejudice, and conflict into the open arms of altruism, attraction, and peace?

AGGRESSION

Aggressive behavior, as we noted in our earlier discussion of gender differences, is behavior that intends to hurt or destroy. The assertive salesperson who is irritatingly persistent and the dentist who makes you wince are not displaying aggression. The person who passes along a vicious rumor about you and the attacker who flattens you, are. Aggression is any physical or verbal behavior intended to hurt, whether done out of hostility (as when someone attacks another in fury) or as a calculated means to an end (as when a "hit man" calmly mugs or murders another for pay). Some of the 19,000 murders and 685,000 assaults committed in the United States during 1984 (Federal Bureau of Investigation, 1985) were cool, calculated acts; more were hostile outbursts.

Time and again, we have seen that behavior emerges from the interaction of nature and nurture, and research on aggression is a helpful reminder of that theme. For a gun to fire, the trigger must be pulled, but with some guns, as with some people, the trigger pulls more easily. Let us look first at biological factors that influence the trigger's threshold for firing, and then at psychological factors that pull or restrain the trigger finger.

The Biology of Aggression

Is Aggression an Instinctive Drive?

According to one view, argued by both Sigmund Freud and the animal behavior theorist Konrad Lorenz, our species is like an active volcano with a potential to erupt in aggression. Freud thought that along with positive survival instincts, we harbor a self-destructive drive, a "death instinct," that is usually redirected toward others as aggression. Lorenz believed that in humans and other animals aggressive energy wells up instinctively from within until released by appropriate stimuli or inhibited by gestures of submission. But we have now armed our "fighting instinct" with weapons that cause injury and death to unseen victims miles away, victims unable to inhibit their attackers with white flags or hands held high as they did in the days of hand-to-hand combat. How, then, should we keep the human volcano from erupting? One way, said Freud and Lorenz, is to drain off its pent-up energy in safe activities ranging from painting to competitive sports that express the aggression symbolically.

These photos from Vietnam are poignant testimony to the horrors of modern warfare. Has our inventiveness for new and more deadly weapons outstripped our ability to inhibit our aggressive impulses, leaving us an endangered species?

How do today's research psychologists view this idea that aggression is an instinctive drive? Not very favorably. For one thing, to "explain" aggression (or any other human behavior) by calling it an instinct is usually no explanation at all. Some behaviors, the nest building of birds, for instance, do qualify as *instinctive*—as unlearned behavior patterns that characterize a whole species. But most human behaviors do not. The gentle Tasaday tribe in the Philippines exhibits virtually no physical aggression and apparently has no word for war; the Yanomamo Indians of South America, on the other hand, are perpetually warring. Because aggressiveness varies so widely from culture to culture and person to person, it can hardly be said to be an unlearned characteristic of our species. Moreover, the reasoning that attributes human behavior to instinct is often circular: "Why do people act violently?" "Because of their aggression instinct." "How do you know that?" "Well, just look at all their aggressive acts."

Physiological Influences on Aggression

Although aggression may not be an instinctive drive, our aggressive reactions to certain events in our environment are biologically influenced. External stimuli influence our behaviors by operating through our biological system. Our *genes* design our individual *nervous systems,* which are *biochemically* influenced. Thus we can look for physiological influences on the way stimuli elicit aggressive behavior at each of these three levels.

Genetic Influences Many strains of animals have been bred for aggressiveness: sometimes for sport, sometimes for research. Finnish psychologist Kirsti Lagerspetz (1979) showed just how powerful these genetic controls of aggressiveness can be. She took a group of normal mice and bred the most aggressive with one another and the least aggressive with one another. After repeating this for another twenty-five generations, she had a group of vicious mice that would attack immediately when put together and a group of docile mice that, no matter what she did to them, would refrain from fighting. Such experiments suggest that these individual temperamental differences have a genetic basis.

Neural Influences According to aggression researcher Kenneth Moyer (1983) there is "abundant evidence" that animal and human brains have neural systems that, when stimulated, produce aggressive behavior. Drawing from research on brain stimulation, Moyer described provocative findings to support his claim:

> A gentle, nonpredatory cat lives harmoniously with a rat until one day a specific spot in its hypothalamus is stimulated via an implanted electrode. Immediately, the cat attacks its cage-mate and kills it precisely as would a wild, predatory cat, by biting through the spinal cord at the neck.
>
> A small, submissive male monkey is placed in a cage with a larger, dominant male and its female partner. When stimulated in a specific spot in the hypothalamus, the smaller monkey vigorously attacks the dominant male, and, after a number of repetitions, the dominant male becomes the submissive one.
>
> A kindly, mild-mannered woman has an electrode implanted deep in her brain's limbic system (in the amygdala) by neurosurgeons who are seeking to diagnose a disorder. Because the brain has no sensory receptors, she cannot feel any stimulation. But her behavior is revealing. At the flick of a switch she snarls orders to "Take my blood pressure. Take it now," and then stands up and begins to strike the doctor.
>
> The domineering, aggressive leader of a monkey colony has a radio-controlled electrode implanted in an area of his neural system that, when stimulated, inhibits aggression. When the button activating this electrode is placed in the colony's cage, one small monkey learns to push it every time the boss becomes threatening, thereby calming him down.

Biochemical Influences Neural systems that activate and inhibit aggression are influenced in turn by hormones and other substances in the blood. The aggressive behavior of animals can be manipulated by changing their levels of the male sex hormone testosterone (Moyer, 1983). A raging bull will become a gentle Ferdinand when its testosterone level is reduced through castration. The same occurs with castrated mice. But if the mice are then injected with testosterone they will again become aggressive. As we noted in Chapter 13, "Motivation," humans are less sensitive to hormonal changes; nevertheless, drugs that diminish testosterone levels have sometimes been found to subdue the aggressive tendencies of violent males.

Alcohol has repeatedly been found to diminish restraints against aggressive responses to provocation (Taylor, 1983). Police data and prison surveys confirm the link between alcohol and aggression. One study of state prisoners by the U.S. Bureau of Justice Statistics reported "an alcohol problem of staggering size." When interviewed, one-fourth of 12,000 inmates acknowledged drinking heavily just before committing their crimes (Rosewicz, 1983). As we noted in Chapter 8, "States of Consciousness," alcohol's effects can be psychological (a consequence of people's beliefs about its effects) as well as physiological.

"He that is naturally addicted to Anger, let him Abstain from Wine; for it is but adding Fire to Fire."
Seneca,
De Ira, A.D. 49

A 1985 riot at a soccer game in Brussels left 38 dead and 437 injured after English fans, aroused by the competition, provoked by the Italian fans, and loaded with alcohol, lost all restraint and attacked the Italians, who upon retreating were crushed against a wall.

The Psychology of Aggression

So far we have seen that genetic, neural, and biochemical factors influence the ease with which the aggression trigger is pulled. But what kind of events lead to the trigger being pulled, and how does learning buffer or amplify these events?

Aversive Events

Although suffering may sometimes build character, it may also bring out the worst in us. Studies in which animals or humans are subjected to a variety of unpleasant experiences reveal that those who are made miserable often make others miserable as well (Berkowitz, 1983).

Initially, investigators found that being frustrated in an attempt to achieve some goal increased people's readiness to behave aggressively. This observation led to the ***frustration-aggression theory:*** Frustration creates anger, which may provoke aggression. When later it was realized that a variety of other unpleasant events—physical pain and personal insults, for example—also trigger aggression, social psychologists saw that frustrations are simply instances of aversive events. Foul odors, hot temperatures, cigarette smoke, and a host of other aversive stimuli can also lead people to react with hostility (Figure 20-1).

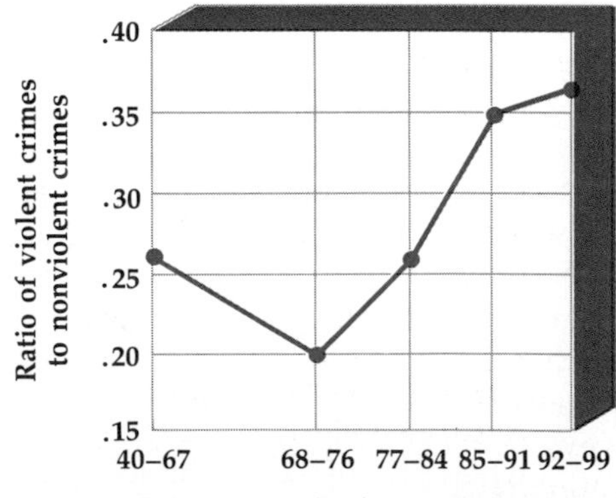

Figure 20-1 *Uncomfortable heat can elicit and heighten aggressive reactions. On days when the weather was hot in Houston, Texas, between 1980 and 1982, the number and (shown here) proportion of violent crimes rose. This finding is consistent with those from laboratory experiments in which people working in a hot room reacted to provocations with greater hostility.*

This confrontation is not just the result of a near collision, but also of each driver's belief that the other is at fault.

Whether we actually respond aggressively to aversive stimulation depends partly on our interpretation of it. Imagine that, as you are walking along a noisy sidewalk, someone comes out from a doorway and trips you with a stick. You fall, are bruised, and rise in anger to discover you tripped over the cane of a now-dismayed blind person. Instantly your urge to say or do something hurtful is transformed into a reaction of sympathy. As we noted in Chapter 14, "Emotion," thinking affects emotion—our interpretation of our arousal influences the emotion we feel.

Learning to Express and Inhibit Aggression

Aggression may be a natural response to aversive events, especially when the aggression trigger is biologically sensitized. But natural reactions can be altered by learning. Animals naturally eat when hungry, but if appropriately rewarded or punished, they can be taught to either overeat or to starve. Our reactions, too, are more likely to be aggressive in situations where experience has taught us that aggression pays, and less likely to be aggressive in situations where such behavior has been punished or unrewarded.

Aggressive behavior can be learned either through direct rewards (as when animals, having fought successfully, obtain food or mates and so become increasingly ferocious) or through observation (see Chapter 9, "Learning"). Children who grow up observing physically aggressive models in their family, their culture, and the mass media often imitate the behaviors they see. To Leonard Eron and Rowell Huesmann (1984), these ways of learning aggression suggested three ways in which it might be counteracted.

The recent glorification of the Vietnam war has yielded a new hero for children—the angry but patriotic Rambo. By observing such aggressive models, children can readily learn aggressive methods of coping with conflict.

First, we could teach young children how to interpret media violence. Studies in six nations indicate that children under 12 are more susceptible than older age groups to the influence of violent television models. Despairing that the TV networks would ever "face the facts and change their programming," Eron and Huesmann taught 170 young children in suburban Chicago that television portrays the world unrealistically, that aggression is not so common or effective as it appears on TV, and that such behavior is wrong. When restudied 2 years later, these children were found to be less influenced by viewing violence than were untrained children.

Second, the family and other social institutions could use the power of rewards to socialize boys to be more like girls. As Eron and Huesmann explained,

> if we want to reduce the level of aggression in society, we should also discourage boys from aggression very early on in life and reward them for other behaviors. In other words, we should socialize boys more in the manner that we have been socializing girls. . . .Boys should be . . . encouraged to develop socially positive qualities like tenderness, sensitivity to feelings, nurturance, cooperativeness, and empathy. Such prosocial behaviors and attitudes are incompatible with aggressive behaviors.

"Women's liberation is the liberation of the feminine in the man and the masculine in the woman."
Corita Kent, 1974

Third, we could teach better parenting skills. Studies by Gerald Patterson and his associates (1982) suggested that parents of delinquent youngsters tend to be unaware of their children's whereabouts, to not discipline their children effectively for antisocial behavior, and to rely on spankings and beatings (thereby modeling the use of aggression as a method of dealing with problems). Once established, aggressive behavior patterns are difficult to modify. Patterson therefore recommends using teachers' and parents' reports to identify children who seem headed for delinquency and then to teach the parents how to monitor their children's behavior, to punish antisocial behavior consistently but nonphysically, and to reinforce positive behavior.

We have seen that aggression is triggered by aversive events but that the effect of such events is influenced by one's physiology and learning. Let us now consider in more depth one way in which aggressive behavior can be learned.

If aggression is learned, what steps might be taken to counteract aggressive tendencies?

Mass Media Violence

Fairport, New York: After the violent Vietnam war movie *The Deer Hunter* was telecast, high school student Christopher Mahan put a bullet in his father's handgun, spun the barrel, pulled the trigger, and killed himself, becoming the thirty-fifth person known to have lost while reenacting the movie's climactic game of Russian roulette (Radecki, 1984).

Ingham County, Michigan: After robbing a gas station and driving the attendant to a remote rural location, Peter Grenier (1984) decided to give himself an extra hour of getaway time by simply knocking the attendant out—as he had seen it done hundreds of times on TV, leaving nothing more than a lump on the head. "If all those characters on television could engage so easily in such activities, I reckoned there must be something wrong with me if I could not," he later reported. When he did so, what he experienced was not the "painless operation" he had witnessed on television, but rather, he later wrote, "a nauseating sound of crushed and mushy flesh as the gun butt smashed into the attendant's head and bore through to a solid bone surface, lubricated by the flow of warm blood."

Joyce, Washington: Eugene Pyles picked up a teenage girl in the early afternoon, drove her to a remote area, and then raped and stabbed her. He returned and smashed her head with a rock. Miraculously, she survived, crawled out, and was discovered. When Pyles was arrested later that evening, his motel room was found to contain a cache of pornographic magazines and videos depicting violent sexual acts against women.

These actual cases are, of course, exceptional, but they make us wonder: Do prime-time crime and pornography influence as well as entertain us? The accumulated research on television and behavior and a new generation of experiments on the effects of pornography provide some tentative answers.

Television and Aggression The undisputed facts are these: In 1983, the average American household had its TV set on 7 hours a day (Figure 20-2), and the average household member watched TV for about 4 of those hours. Prime-time programs offer about five violent acts per hour, the average cartoon, three to four times more. Thus, during the first 18 years, most children spend more time watching television than they spend in school, and during their impressionable elementary and junior high school years, they will view some 13,000 murders.

Does viewing such acts actually cause some people to commit them? With fewer than 100 independent studies of television viewing and aggression, the answer is still disputed (Freedman, 1984). But as the National Institute of Mental Health indicated in 1982 in its summary of *Television and Behavior,* "The consensus among most of the research community is that violence on television does lead to aggressive behavior by children and teenagers who watch the programs."

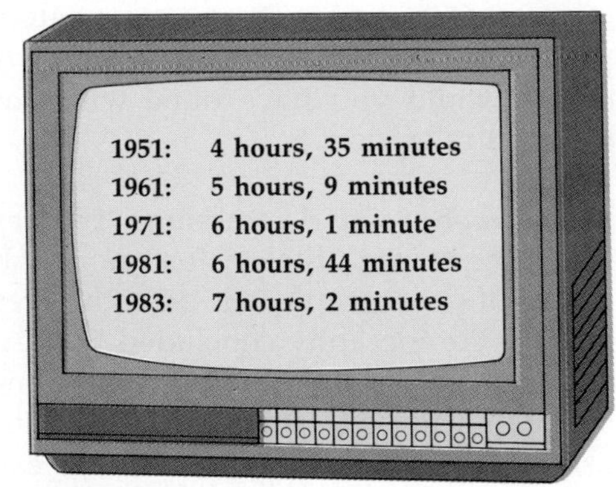

Figure 20-2 *Our growing appetite for TV can be seen in the not so gradual increase in the number of hours between 1951 and 1983 that the average American household has had its set on per day. As TV leaves less and less time for other social activities, what will be its effects?*

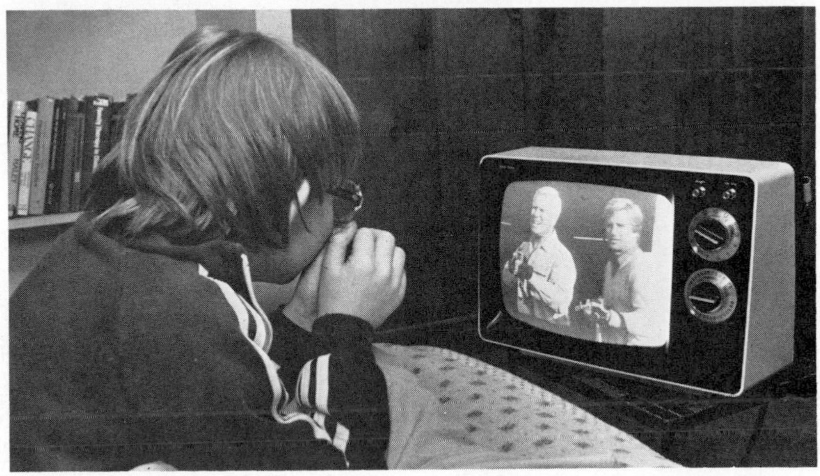

Most researchers believe that children's behaviors and attitudes can be affected by the several thousand aggressive acts they view each year on television.

This near consensus emerges from both correlational and experimental studies. Correlational studies have established a link between the amount of TV violence young children watch and their combativeness as teenagers and young adults (Eron & Huesmann, 1984). Critics respond that the link between violence-viewing and aggressiveness is modest. They also argue that, despite efforts to extract the effects of other factors that are linked with both TV viewing and aggression (such as poverty), these studies have not proven that the viewing of violence actually *causes* aggression (Freedman, 1984).

Experimenters have tried to find a causal factor in this correlation by exposing some viewers to an episode of violence and others to entertaining nonviolence. More often than not, those exposed to cruelty are later more likely to commit a hurtful act. The effect seems to be due to a combination of factors—to having been aroused by the excitement of violence, to the erosion of one's inhibitions against such acts, and to imitation.

Television has other effects as well. Prolonged viewing seems to desensitize viewers to cruelty; those who have viewed violence tend to be more indifferent to it when later viewing a brawl, whether on TV or in real life (Berkowitz, 1984). Television's unreal world—in which acts of assault greatly outnumber acts of affection—can also affect our thinking about the real world; those who have watched a great deal of fictional crime on television tend to perceive the world as more dangerous (Singer & others, 1984). But TV's greatest effect may stem from what it displaces. Children and adults who spend 4 hours a day watching television spend 4 fewer hours in other activities—talking, sleeping, studying, playing, reading, listening to the radio, communal activities, and so forth. (What would you have done with your extra time if you had never watched television?)

"When the TV set is on, it freezes everybody. Everything that used to go on between people—the games, the arguments, the emotional scenes out of which personality and ability develop—is stopped."
Urie Bronfenbrenner (1983)

Pornography and Aggression The research techniques developed to study the effects of television are now being used in new studies of the effects of pornography. In 1970, the President's Commission on Obscenity and Pornography concluded that exposure to pornography (explicit depictions of sexual activity) had no measurable influence on antisocial behavior. Fifteen years later, a new national commission has been established, and if the findings of recent experiments are any indication, its conclusions will differ. They will differ because pornography itself has changed (Malamuth & Donnerstein, 1984) and is now conveniently available through cable television, home video systems, and America's 20,000 adults-only bookstores (Galloway, 1984). Having followed the evolution of film pornography, from nudity to explicit sex to violent sex, the head of the British film review board expressed alarm that rape is treated increasingly not as a "reprehensible crime" but as "an erotic spectacle." "A strange myth has grown up . . . that rape is really not so bad, that it may even be a form of liberation for the victim, who may be getting what she secretly desires . . ." (Lord Harlech, quoted by Penrod & Linz, 1984).

New experiments on the effects of viewing pornography, and the increasing availability of hard-core and violent pornography, have raised concerns about society's acceptance of pornography's images of women.

In less graphic form, the same falsehood can be found on TV and in romantic novels. One such novel in my local public library depicts a woman, Shanna, struggling to resist her attacker. Notice how the author caters to and reinforces the myth that women enjoy being aggressively overpowered (Woodiwiss, 1977, pp. 154–155):

> "Go away!" she sobbed. "Let me be! What can I say that will convince you that I want no part of you? I hate you! I despise you! I cannot stand the sight of you!" . . .
>
> Shanna began to struggle, and he clasped his arms about her holding her close, smothering her movements in an embrace of steel. Sobbing, Shanna pushed in vain against his chest. Her head tipped backward with her effort, and his mouth crushed down upon hers. In the way of love, rage was

> transformed into passion. Shanna's arms slipped upward about his neck and were locked in a frantic embrace. Her lips twisted against his, and the full heat of her hunger flooded him until his mind reeled with the frenzy of her answer. He had expected a fight and instead found the fury of a consuming desire sweet on her lips, warm in her mouth, stirring as the quick thrust of her tongue met his own.

To examine the effects of viewing erotic depictions (with or without violence), researchers have conducted experiments in which they first exposed young adults to such scenes and then provided them with an opportunity to indicate their attitudes or to deliver what they think is electric shock to someone who has provoked them. These experiments, especially those involving sexual violence, reveal that exposure to pornography creates:

a change in attitudes, especially an increased acceptance of rape myths (the ideas that women enjoy rape and invite it), a diminished sense that rape is a serious crime, and other attitudes characteristic of rapists

an increased willingness of male viewers to say that they might commit a sexual assault if they knew they would escape punishment

actual increases in men's aggressive behavior against women in laboratory settings

In one such study, Edward Donnerstein and Daniel Linz (1984) exposed University of Wisconsin men to sexually violent "slasher" movies, such as *Texas Chainsaw Massacre.* After watching one slasher movie a day for 5 days, the men no longer found the violent scenes as offensive as they had at first. And they were more likely than men who had not seen the films to judge the victim in a reenacted rape trial as worthless and her injury as not severe. (After such experiments, the participants are given an extensive reeducation to resensitize them to the actual horror of sexual violence.)

Dolf Zillmann and Jennings Bryant (1984) observed a similar result when they showed forty male and forty female undergraduates either three or six brief, sexually explicit films a week for 6 weeks. A control group of men and women were shown nonsexual films during the same 6-week period. Three weeks later, all three groups read a newspaper report of a man who had been convicted of raping a hitchhiker but had not yet been sentenced. When asked to suggest an appropriate prison term, those in the massive exposure group (six sexually explicit films a week) recommended sentences half as long as the control group (see Figure 20-3). In a follow-up study, Zillmann (1985) found that men and women who were massively exposed to pornography became more accepting not only of premarital and extramarital sexual behavior but also of women's sexual submission to men.

The trivialization of rape and the acceptance of promiscuity and male sexual dominance are not the only effects of viewing pornography. Zillmann also reports that those whom he massively exposed to sexually explicit films later offered greatly increased estimates of the normality of various sexual practices, such as marital unfaithfulness and group sex. (Notice how the effect of television viewing is paralleled by this finding: those who have watched a great deal of fictional sex tend to perceive the world as more sexual.) Moreover, Zillmann (1985) reports that pornography exposure "produces a powerful effect: It generates sexual discontent" and dissatisfaction with one's intimate partner. (Perhaps you can speculate why.) Finally, the experiments suggest that viewing pornography may foster an appetite for more and stronger pornography. This is

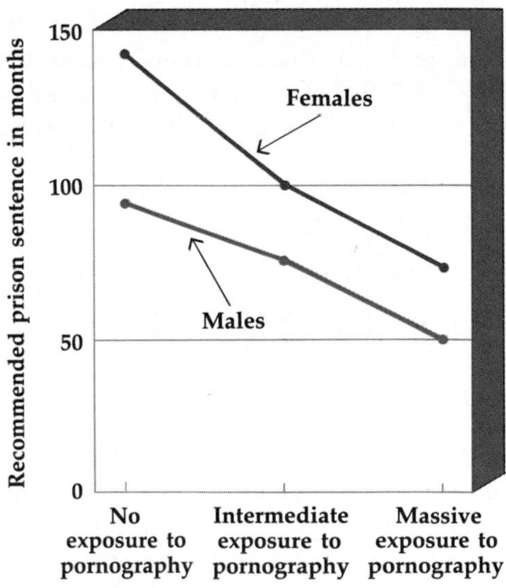

Figure 20-3 *The effects of exposure to pornography on tolerance of sexual violence can be seen in a study in which for 6 weeks, groups of subjects viewed either nonsexual films or three or six brief sexually explicit films a week. Those more massively exposed to pornography recommended shorter prison sentences for a convicted rapist.*

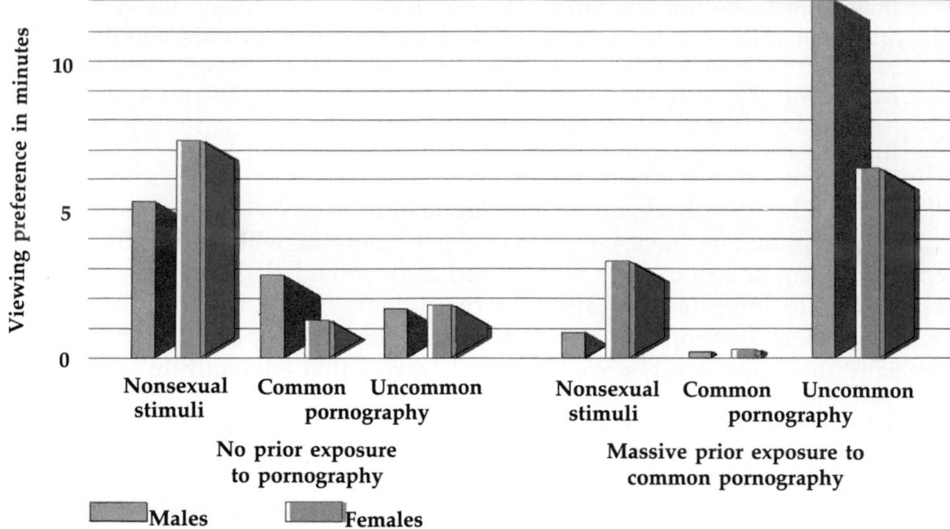

Figure 20-4 *A study similar to that in Figure 20-3 examined the effects of exposure to pornography on later appetite for pornography. For six weeks, subjects either viewed nonsexual films or films of "common" pornography in which strangers met and were instantly overcome by urges to engage in various sexual behaviors. Two weeks later, all were given opportunities to privately view videotapes of their choice. Those who had viewed pornography now preferred to view stronger forms of "uncommon" pornography, depicting bondage, sadomasochism, or bestiality.*

because viewers who are initially repulsed become desensitized and more accepting and will often then, as Figure 20-4 indicates, "graduate" to new forms of pornography.

These experimental studies are complemented by correlational studies of pornography and aggression in everyday life. John Court (1984) reported that in the United States, and across the world, the incidence of reported rapes rose sharply during the 1960s and 1970s as pornography became much more available. Countries and areas where pornography has been controlled have tended not to experience this steep rise in reported rapes. And where laws regulating pornography have suddenly changed, rape rates have changed, too. For example, in Hawaii the number of reported rapes rose by 900 percent between 1960 and 1974, then dropped when restraints on pornography were temporarily imposed, then rose again when the restraints were lifted (see Figure 20-5).

"If we value interpersonal sensitivity and sound human relationships in which sexuality has a vital part, if we value the nuclear family and the institution of marriage, and if we care to see women as equals rather than as servants to men's sexual imagination, pornography has demonstrable effects that are somewhat less than wonderful."
Dolf Zillmann (1985)

Figure 20-5 *As can be noted from this graph of reported rapes in Hawaii from 1960 to 1978, during a 2-year period when pornography was restricted, a downturn in reported rapes occurred.*

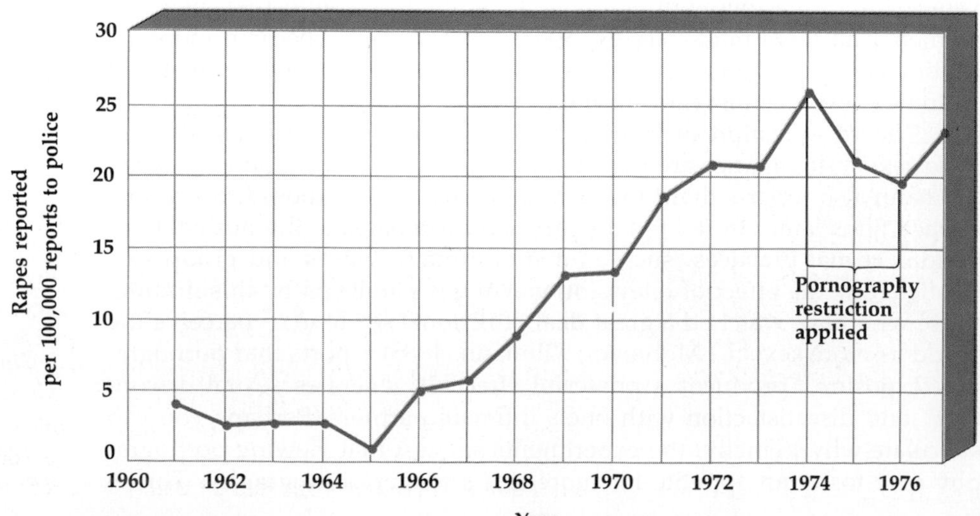

In another correlational study, Larry Baron and Murray Straus (1984) determined the per capita sales rates of eight sexually explicit magazines *(Chic, Club, Forum, Gallery, Genesis, Hustler, Oui,* and *Playboy)* for each of the fifty states. When this indicator of the availability of "soft-core" pornography was correlated with the rate of reported rapes in each state, a positive relationship was found—the higher the sales rate, the higher was the state's rape rate. For example, among the fifty states, Alaska ranked first in sexually explicit magazine sales and first in rape; Nevada was number two on both measures. Of course, the correlation does not prove that magazine sales are causing the high rape rates in states such as Alaska and Nevada. But the correlation held even when the researchers controlled for the effect of other factors, such as the population percentage of young males in each state.

We must be careful not to oversimplify the complex causes of violent crime. Murders and assaults were common before television, and rape predated pornographic books and movies. Such crimes also result from other influences, such as whether the abusers were themselves the victims of child abuse.

Still, for those concerned about sexual violence and the suffering it inflicts, the results are sobering. If the last half-hour was typical, four distraught American women have just called police departments or visited hospital emergency rooms to report having been raped (Federal Bureau of Investigation, 1984). Surveys of both women and men suggest that unreported rapes outnumber those reported, and that most unreported rapes are committed not by pathological strangers but by acquaintances or dates (DiVasto & others, 1984; Rapaport & Burkhart, 1984). In one recent survey of college women, one-half reported having suffered some form of sexual assault while on a date, and one-fifth said they had been raped (Sandberg & others, 1985). Men who have raped, or who indicate that they might, tend to have the sort of attitudes toward women that pornography cultivates (Briere & Malamuth, 1983). They are more likely to believe the misconception that females provoke rape and that, as the *Penthouse* adviser has written, "When she says no, it may well mean yes." Thankfully, most such men do not rape. But enough do, and enough more engage in sexual harassment of women, that the control of pornography is an issue that sparks continued debate.

"Judges usually do not exonerate robbers who complain that their victims provoked them by wearing jewelry or living in nice houses."
Carol Tavris and Carole Wade (1984)

Mini-Debate
Should Pornography Be Controlled?

Susan Brownmiller, a founder of Women Against Pornography and author of *Against Our Will: Men, Women, and Rape:* YES

Pornography is propaganda against women, and propaganda is a very powerful spur to action—think of the anti-Semitic propaganda in Hitler's Germany. In an age when women are putting forward their aspirations toward equality in a healthy, positive way, pornography is working to increase hostility toward women, and therefore to increase tensions between the sexes. I find this unbearable; and I don't think there's any danger that if

Aryeh Neier, former national executive director of the American Civil Liberties Union, currently vice chair of Helsinki Watch and Americas Watch: NO

Two weeks ago, in a displaced-persons camp in El Salvador, I talked to a group of women, every one of whom had been raped; some told me of friends who had been killed after they were raped. Pornography was not a factor. There isn't any pornography in El Salvador. . . .

That a majority of the people in a given community say they don't want to hear or see something is no legal basis for suppressing it. You could suppress virtually

we limit pornography we will eventually ban *Leaves of Grass* or *Ulysses* or even Henry Miller's *Tropic of Cancer.* Those battles were fought and won a long time ago. . . .

I don't want to spend my time fighting against pornography. I would much rather be gardening, or writing my books. But someone has to do it, and feminists have brought new ideas to the struggle. Someone has to make society recognize that pornography is a problem—that it is in fact anti-female propaganda that presents a distorted picture of female sexuality. We've got to do something about it. The question is, how do we do it while protecting our important right of free speech? One way to start is by restricting the public display of pornography. And restricting public display obviously means restricting public access.

anything if all you had to do was submit it to a vote. But our Constitution says that "Congress shall make no law"—that is, the democratic process shall not be a basis for prohibiting speech or expression. . . .

One has to ask a simple question of those who favor censorship: What do you regard as an intellectually honest method of distinguishing between material you find offensive and other forms of expression? We need a persuasive argument that regulating pornography would not at the same time allow the regulation of other forms of communication. . . .

Source: Excerpted from "Forum on pornography," *Harper's Magazine,* pp. 31–45, November 1984.

ALTRUISM

Altruism—unselfish regard for the welfare of others—became a major concern of social psychologists after Kitty Genovese, walking from a train station parking lot to her nearby Queens, New York apartment at 3:20 a.m. on March 13, 1964 was murdered by a knife-wielding stalker. "Oh, my God, he stabbed me!," she screamed into the early morning stillness. "Please help me!" Windows opened and lights went on as thirty-eight of her neighbors heard her screams. One couple pulled up chairs to the window and turned out the light to see better. Her attacker at first fled, then returned to stab her eight more times and sexually molest her. Not until he departed for good did anyone so much as call the police. It was then 3:50 a.m.

The stabbing of Kitty Genovese, in full view of thirty-eight of her neighbors who did not respond to her cries for help, stimulated research into why bystanders often do not become involved when an emergency occurs in public.

The incident is not isolated. A 20-year-old Trenton, New Jersey woman was raped in full view of twenty-five employees of a nearby roofing company. They watched intently, but not one answered her screams for help. Later one workman explained, "We thought, well, if we went up there, it might turn out to be her boyfriend or something like that" (Shotland & Goodstein, 1984).

Could these reactions be typical? Harold Takooshian and Herzel Bodinger (1982) wondered. So they asked volunteers from a social psychology class, most of whom had been victims of street crime, to simulate the burglary of a parked car (which was actually a volunteer's car). In full view of passersby, the "burglar" would inspect a row of parked cars in a Manhattan business district, spend a minute forcing open the door of one with a coat hanger, remove a large valuable object such as a fur coat, relock the car, and hurry away.

Expecting that they would be apprehended, the "burglars" understandably felt queasy; their hands shook, and they felt a desire to quit the experiment (despite having full identification and proof of ownership).

In one of Takooshian and Bodinger's experiments, a "suspect" breaks into a car and walks away with a fur coat, while bystanders either ignore or merely watch the event. This was the typical reaction in several cities.

After 214 such "burglaries," their fears were allayed. Of the more than 3000 passersby, many paused to stop, stare, or snicker, and some even offered to help, but only six, three of them police officers, raised any question about the activity. The "break-ins" were restaged in seventeen other U.S. and Canadian cities. In these the bystanders were somewhat more likely to intervene than in New York. Still, 9 times out of 10, the "burglars" were unchallenged.

Bystander Intervention

Reflecting on the Genovese murder, most commentators lamented the bystanders' "apathy" and "indifference." Rather than blaming these people, social psychologists John Darley and Bibb Latané instead attributed the bystanders' inaction to an important situational factor—the presence of others. Given the right circumstances, they suspected, most of us might behave like the witnesses to the Genovese murder.

To test this assumption, they and others staged emergencies under various conditions. Most of these experiments confirm the ***bystander effect:*** Any given bystander is less likely to give aid if other bystanders are present.

"Probably no single incident has caused social psychologists to pay as much attention to an aspect of social behavior as Kitty Genovese's murder."

R. Lance Shotland (1984)

Often we walk by derelicts on our city streets. We wonder, "Are they drunk or on drugs or are they sick?" "Will they be abusive?" "What can I do for them, anyway?" Despite these questions, which help to excuse our inaction, sometimes we stop to try to help. What prompts us to do so in one instance and not in others?

Darley and Latané assembled their findings into a decision sequence: We will help if and only if the situation enables us first to *notice* the incident, then to *interpret* it correctly, and finally to *assume responsibility* for helping (Figure 20-6). At each step the presence of other bystanders can turn people away from the path that leads to helping. In laboratory experiments and in street situations such as the car break-ins, people in groups of strangers are more likely than solitary individuals to keep their eyes on what they are doing or where they are going and thus not notice an unusual situation. Some who did notice the car entry—and observed the blasé reaction of the other passersby—interpreted the situation as a locked-out car owner.

But sometimes, as with the Genovese murder, the emergency is unambiguous and people still fail to respond. The witnesses looking out through their windows both noticed the incident and correctly interpreted the emergency but failed to assume responsibility. To explore why, Darley and Latané (1968b) simulated a physical emergency. They had university students, each in a separate cubicle in the laboratory, participate in a discussion over an intercom in which only the person whose microphone was switched on could be heard. When his turn came, one student (actually an accomplice of the experimenters) was heard being overwhelmed by an epileptic seizure and calling for help. As Figure 20-7 indicates, those led to believe they were the only listener—and therefore bearing total responsibility to help—usually helped. Those who thought there were four other listeners were more likely to react as did Kitty Genovese's neighbors.

In hundreds of additional experiments psychologists have studied other influences upon bystanders' willingness to relay an emergency phone call, to aid a stranded motorist, to donate blood, to pick up dropped books, to contribute money, to give time to someone. For example, Latané, James Dabbs (1975), and 145 collaborators took 1497 elevator rides in three American cities and "accidentally" dropped coins or pencils in the presence of 4813 fellow passengers. Women coin-droppers received help more often than men—a finding often reported by other researchers (Renner & Eagly, 1984). But the major finding was the bystander effect: When one other person was on the elevator, those who dropped the coins were helped 40 percent of the time. With six passengers, help came less than 20 percent of the time.

From their observations of tens of thousands of such acts, and tens of thousands of failures to help, altruism researchers have discerned some patterns. The odds of our helping someone are best when:

We have just observed someone else being helpful.

We are not in a hurry.

The recipient appears to need and deserve help.

The recipient is similar to ourselves.

We are feeling guilty (and therefore needing to restore our self-image).

We are focused on others and not self-preoccupied.

We are in a good mood.

This last result, that happy people are helpful people, is one of the most consistent findings in all psychology. No matter how people are put in a good mood—whether by having been made to feel successful and intelligent, by thinking happy thoughts, by finding money, or even by

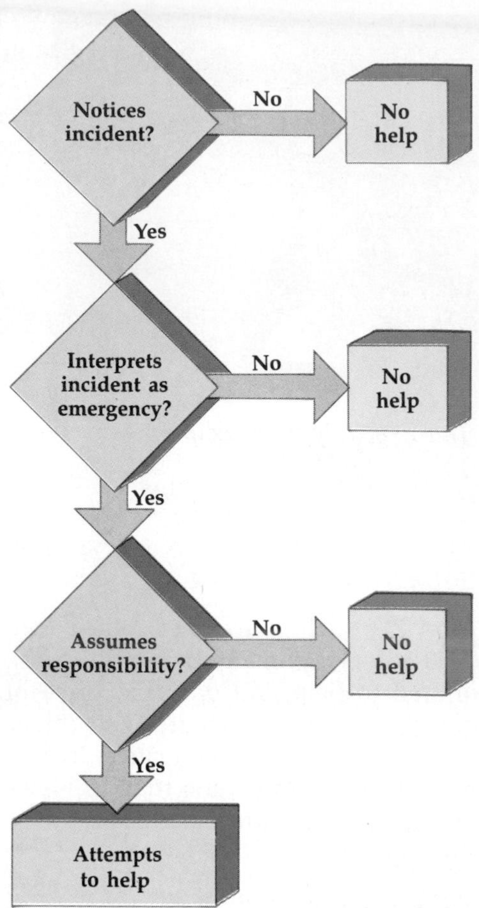

Figure 20-6 *The decision-making process for bystander intervention.*

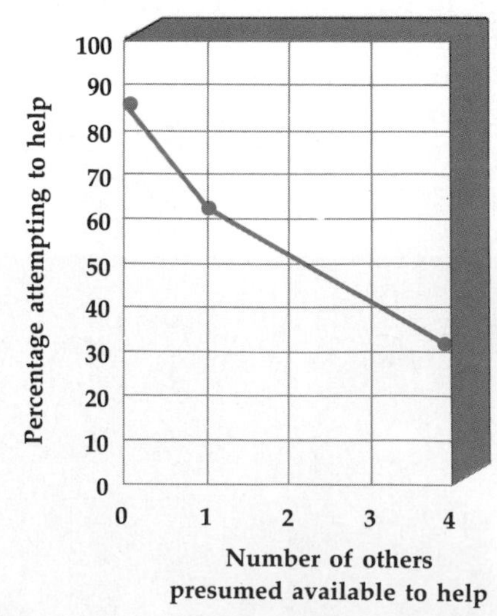

Figure 20-7 *When people who overheard an epileptic seizure victim calling for help thought they alone heard the plea, they usually helped. But when they thought four others were hearing it too, only 31 percent responded.*

receiving a posthypnotic suggestion—they become more generous, more eager to help. As you may recall from Chapter 10's discussion of state-dependent memory, being in a good mood (or any other mood state) tends to trigger memories of things previously associated with that mood. When happy, we may therefore tend to recall happy events, to think happy thoughts, to see ourselves as competent and caring, and to act accordingly.

Why Do We Help?

To answer the question "Why do we help?," we need to examine both the psychological and the biological dimensions of altruism.

The Psychology of Helping

One widely held view is that at the basis of all human interactions is the goal of maximizing our rewards and minimizing our costs. Economic theorists call it cost-benefit analysis, philosophers call it utilitarianism, and social psychologists call it social exchange theory. As we exchange either material or social goods, we weigh costs and benefits. For example, if you are pondering whether to donate blood, you may weigh the costs of donating (the time, discomfort, and anxiety) against the benefits (the reduced guilt, the social approval, the good feelings). If the anticipated rewards of helping exceed the anticipated costs, you are likely to help.

What motivates these volunteers—preparing and distributing free food, assisting in a hospital, taking an orphan to a ballgame—to help? Whatever it is, if the rewards, whether psychic or social, aren't greater than the costs, these volunteers aren't likely to continue. Fortunately, most people who do "get involved" find it very rewarding.

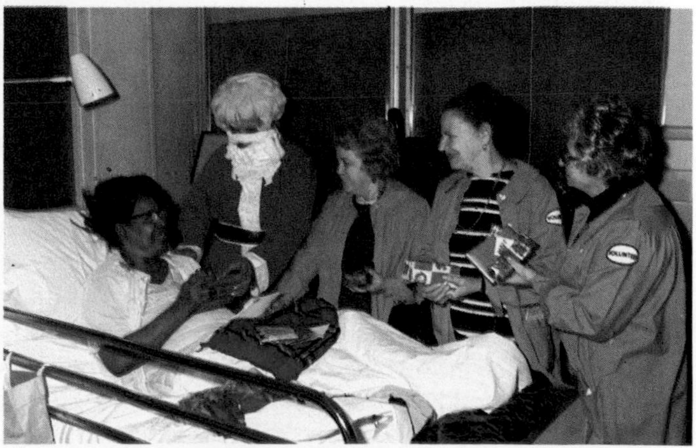

This *social exchange theory* (that our social behavior is an exchange process the goal of which is to maximize rewards and minimize costs) helps to explain why we are most likely to help those whose approval we desire, who can reciprocate favors in the future, or whose suffering causes us to feel distress (Myers, 1983). In such cases, the subtle, perhaps unconscious, calculations of costs and benefits motivate us to give aid.

Perhaps you are wondering, "Doesn't social exchange theory suggest that helping is not truly altruistic, but is rather a disguised form of selfishness?" If we helped merely to feel good, the answer might be yes. However, many humans of all ages exhibit a natural empathy for others—they feel distress when they observe someone in distress and they feel genuine pleasure in giving of themselves (Batson, 1985). There is a difference between helping in order to feel good, and feeling good about having helped.

But social exchange is not the whole story. Social norms prescribe how we ought to behave, often to our mutual benefit. Through socialization, we learn the "reciprocity norm," which tells us to return help, not harm, to those who have helped us. It tells us that, over time, in our relations with someone of similar status we should give (in favors, gifts, or social invitations) about as much as we receive. And with young children, the disabled, and other people whose dependence on us prevents their giving as much as they receive, we also learn to apply a "social responsibility norm"—to help those who need our help, even if the costs outweigh the benefits.

The Biology of Helping

Are these altruistic psychological processes predisposed by our genes? Sociobiologists suspect that they are. As we saw in Chapter 2, "Biological Roots of Behavior," sociobiologists use the principles of natural selection to study social behavior. Their main assumption is that any behavior tendency that helps perpetuate our genes should tend to be selected in the competition for gene survival. Self-sacrifice is generally *not* favored, because those who give their lives for another are less likely to leave descendants who will perpetuate their "unselfish" genes.

Sociobiologists remind us, however, that some forms of altruism do help to perpetuate our genes. Devotion to our children—the carriers of our genes—is the most obvious example. Natural selection predisposes parents to care deeply about the welfare and survival of their children, by feeling distress when they are distressed. Empathy is usually felt toward other relatives, too, in proportion to their genetic closeness, sociobiologists believe. People also empathize with strangers who are similar to themselves. In experiments, strangers perceived as similar are offered more help and friendship than those perceived as dissimilar (Rushton & others, 1984).

That we may be genetically biased to behave altruistically toward our kin and toward similar strangers (in order to enhance the survival of our mutually shared genes) is a mixed blessing. Writes sociobiologist E. O. Wilson (1978, p. 167): "Altruism based on kin selection is the enemy of civilization. If human beings are to a large extent guided . . . to favor their own relatives and tribe, only a limited amount of global harmony is possible."

Social psychologist Daniel Batson (1983) notes that religion has sometimes accentuated this division of people into the believers within the group (for whom concern is felt) and the "heathens" on the outside (who are regarded with contempt). Nevertheless, Batson believes that the religious themes of "brotherly love" toward the entire human "family," the "children of God," serve to extend family-linked altruism beyond one's immediate biological relatives. And there is some evidence that devotion to such religious precepts does indeed correlate with long-term altruism. For example, among Americans whom George Gallup (1984) classified as "highly spiritually committed," 46 percent said they were presently working among the poor, the infirm, or the elderly—significantly more than the corresponding altruism reported by those classified as "moderately committed" (36 percent), "moderately uncommitted" (28 percent), or "highly uncommitted" (22 percent).

Evidence of at least a limited form of genetically programmed altruism comes from instances of altruism among insects and animals. The clearest case of altruistic species behavior is the self-sacrifice of worker ants, honeybees, and termites, all of whom are sterile. The altruistic worker bee that gives its life by stinging an intruder is helping to perpetuate its genes, which are transmitted by the queen bee, whose genes are identical to the worker's. Cases of individual altruistic acts among higher animals, however, are perhaps more to the point. Porpoises, for example, have been observed to cooperate in giving aid to an injured porpoise (Hebb, 1980; see Figure 20-8). Consider, too, an act by Washoe, one of the first chimps to receive language training. One day Washoe observed another chimp, Cindy, leap an electric fence that ringed their island compound. Cindy landed in the water, came to the surface, thrashed, and went under. Washoe immediately leaped the electric fence and reached out to Cindy with one hand while holding the grass at the water's edge with the other. When Cindy resurfaced, Washoe grabbed and pulled her to safety, and then sat with her, rescuer and rescued. "Washoe's act gave me a new perspective on chimpanzees," reported her caretaker, Roger Fouts (1984). "I was impressed with her heroism in risking her life on the slippery banks. She cared about someone in trouble; someone she didn't even know that well."

It would be naive to think that such devotion to others is common among animals or humans. Moreover, in humans it is social learning, not genetics, that provides the norms of reciprocity and social responsibility, the imitation of altruistic models, and our concept of the universal kinship of the human family. Transmitted culture helps make genuine altruism possible. To strangers in great need, people will sometimes give blood, food, and money, asking nothing in return. The heroes among us have risked loss of life in doing so. On a hillside in Jerusalem, 800 trees form a line, The Avenue of the Righteous (Hellman, 1980). Beneath each is a plaque bearing the name of a European Christian who, during the Holocaust, gave refuge to one or more Jews. These people knew that if the refugees were discovered, both host and refugee would suffer a common fate—and many did.

"Human history can be viewed as a slowly dawning awareness that we are members of a larger group. Initially our loyalties were to ourselves and our immediate family, next, to bands of wandering hunter-gatherers, then to tribes, small settlements, city-states, nations. We have broadened the circle of those we love. We have now organized what are modestly described as super-powers, which include groups of people from divergent ethnic and cultural backgrounds working in some sense together—surely a humanizing and character-building experience. If we are to survive, our loyalties must be broadened further, to include the whole human community, the entire planet Earth."
Carl Sagan (1980, p. 339)

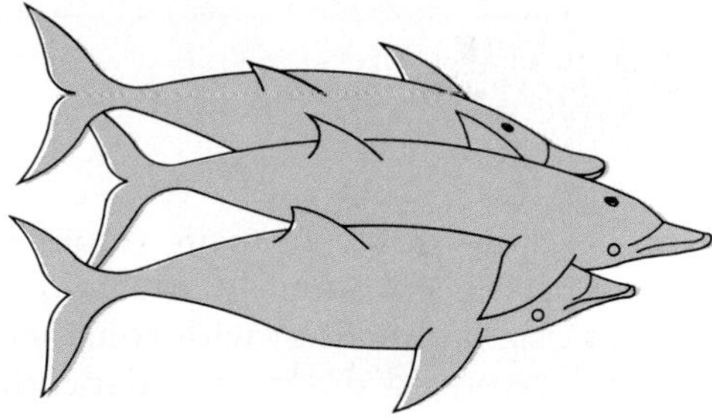

Figure 20-8 *Porpoises have been observed to cooperate to aid an injured porpoise.*

PREJUDICE

Prejudice means prejudgment. It is an unjustifiable and usually negative attitude toward a group and its members. Like all attitudes, prejudice is a mixture of beliefs (called ***stereotypes***) and feelings. These prejudiced beliefs and feelings may then predispose discriminatory actions. To generalize that overweight people are gluttonous is to stereotype; to feel contempt for an overweight person is to be prejudiced; to avoid hiring or dating such a person is to discriminate.

Prejudice can be assessed by noting what people say and do. To judge by what Americans say, attitudes regarding blacks and women have improved since the 1940s (see Figure 20-9). Americans have achieved a virtual national consensus that white and black children should not be sent to separate schools and that there should be "equal pay for women and men when they are doing the same job."

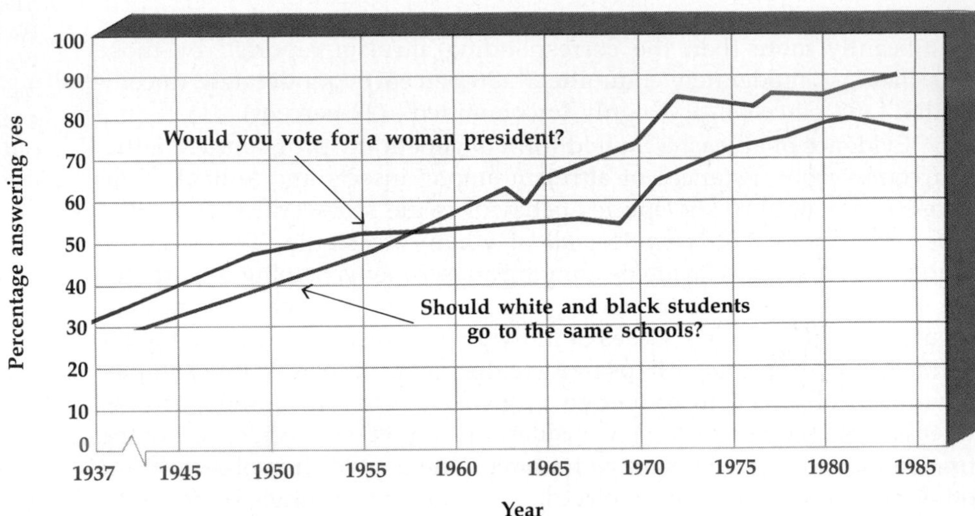

Figure 20-9 *The nearly unanimous expressed attitudes of Americans in the 1980s to the questions above seem to indicate a tremendous reduction in racial and gender prejudice. But if our actions are to be judged, many subtle forms of prejudice still abound. (Responses to the racial question are from whites only.)*

Despite this consensus, more subtle forms of prejudice persist. Many people still admit to discomfort at socially intimate relations (such as dancing and dating) with someone of a different race. Behaviors are often interpreted differently, depending on race. In one experiment, a white man shoving a black tended to be perceived by whites as "horsing around," while the same behavior by the black toward the white was more likely to be seen as "violent" (Duncan, 1976). Moreover, people tend to choose for friends and neighbors those of their own race (Schofield, 1982). Techniques for measuring subtle forms of gender prejudice also reveal a lingering but potentially potent bias in people's beliefs, feelings, and actions regarding women. Perhaps the least subtle of these is the hope of most prospective parents that their first child will be a boy.

The fact that prejudice can change suggests that it can be learned and unlearned as situations change. Prejudice is fed by a complex of social, emotional, and cognitive factors.

Social Roots of Prejudice

Once established, prejudice is largely maintained by its own inertia—by conformity to established norms of prejudice and by the support prejudice finds in the media, in schools, and in other institutions. But how does prejudice arise in the first place?

Social Inequalities

If some people have money, power, and prestige and others do not, the "haves" are likely to develop attitudes regarding the "have nots" that justify and help preserve the status difference. Slaves are perceived as being lazy and irresponsible—the very traits that will justify enslaving them. Women are seen as weak, emotional, and fit for the menial tasks they often perform. Prejudice rationalizes inequalities.

"Prejudice is never easy unless it can pass itself off for reason."
William Hazlitt,
On Prejudice, 1839

Discrimination can lead to increased prejudice by the reactions it provokes in its victims. In his classic book *The Nature of Prejudice*, Gordon Allport showed how being a victim of discrimination can trigger either

Often groups preserve their social status by rationalizing the validity of the prejudicial social system underlying it. This is true in both India and South Africa. Although the Indian caste system, which is closely intertwined with Hindu religion, was officially abolished in 1949, in rural areas it still dominates the lives of millions of Indians. The outcastes shown here are often called untouchables because even to be touched by their shadows is a form of pollution. The South Africa social system, whose purpose is to maintain white supremacy, is still rigorously enforced by the apartheid laws, as shown by the separate "public conveniences" for Europeans and non-Europeans. The plight of this refugee Vietnamese fisherman whose fishing boat has been burned is also the result of prejudice, that which arises from our bias toward our own group and our distorted perceptions of other groups.

self-blame and self-deprecation or anger and rebellion. Either reaction may create new grounds for prejudice; in the classic "blame the victim" manner, the victims' plight is turned against them. For example, if the circumstances of ghetto life breed a higher crime rate, the higher crime rate can then be used to justify continuing the discrimination that has helped to create it.

We and They: Ingroup and Outgroup

The social definition of who we are—our race, sex, and group memberships—also indicates who we are not. The circle that defines and includes "us" excludes "them." And, mysteriously, the very act of being put in a group tends to trigger an ***ingroup bias***—a tendency to favor one's own group.

British psychologist Henri Tajfel (1982) conducted a series of studies showing that ingroup bias occurs even when the we-they distinction is trivial. In the initial experiment, boys sat together in groups of eight and watched dots flash on a screen. After individually guessing how many had flashed on each slide, four of the boys were together taken aside and told that they tended to overestimate. The other four were told that they tended to underestimate. Later, each of the eight boys was given some money to divide between two of the other boys, one a fellow overestimator (or underestimator), the other not. It wasn't much to respond to, but it was enough; the boys gave more money to those who were labeled as they were. In this experiment—and in later ones with people of varying ages, sexes, and nationalities—temporarily forming people into inconsequential groups was enough to evoke favoritism toward the members of their own group (Wilder, 1981).

"I'm surprised, Marty. I thought you were one of us."

Emotional Roots of Prejudice

Prejudice can spring from the passions of the heart as well as the rationalizations of the mind. For one thing, prejudice may express anger. When things go wrong, it is convenient to find someone to blame. Evidence for this ***scapegoat theory*** of prejudice comes from surveys of economically frustrated people, who exhibit heightened prejudice, and from experiments in which people who are temporarily frustrated express intensified prejudice. As Nazi leader Hermann Rausching once explained, "If the Jew did not exist, we should have to invent him" (quoted by Koltz, 1983).

"If the Tiber reaches the walls, if the Nile does not rise to the fields, if the sky doesn't move or the earth does, if there is famine, if there is plague, the cry is at once: 'The Christians to the lion!'"
Tertullian,
Apologeticus, A.D. 197

"I blame everything on the Russians,
except for the few things, Stacey, I blame on you."

Despised outgroups not only provide a handy target for anger but also boost self-esteem. To see ourselves as high in status, it helps to have others to look down on. For this reason, we may sometimes feel a twinge of pleasure at the misfortune of a rival. In experiments, students who have just experienced failure or who are made to feel insecure are more likely to disparage a rival school or another person's work (Amabile & Glazebrook, 1982; Cialdini & Richardson, 1980). More generally, people who have difficulty accepting themselves tend to be less affirming of others (see p. 415).

Cognitive Roots of Prejudice

So far, we have noted some of the social and emotional roots of prejudice. Recent research on how we process information suggests another root: Stereotyped beliefs may be a natural by-product of our normal ways of cognitively simplifying our complex worlds—by organizing items into categories and generalizing from memorable cases.

Categorization

One way we simplify our worlds is to categorize things. A chemist classifies molecules as organic and inorganic. A mental health professional classifies people's psychological disorders by types. Such categories help organize our thoughts and speed our thinking.

But we pay a price for categorizing things and people into groups. We tend to overestimate the similarity of people within groups other than our own. "They," the members of some other group, seem to look and act alike, but "we" are diverse (Taylor, 1981). To us on the outside, the members of fraternity X are jocks, those in fraternity Y are intellectuals; those within each fraternity see much more diversity among its members.

A similar stereotype appears in people's simplified judgments of the past (Silka, 1983). "Last winter was warm, the winter before was cold," a person may think, "but this winter the temperatures are up and down." "Last year's basketball team was pretty consistent, but this year's team has hot and cold streaks." The past is uniform, the present seems more variable.

Vivid Cases

As noted in Chapter 11, "Thinking and Language," we tend to judge the frequency of events in terms of instances that readily come to mind. If asked whether blacks can run faster than whites, many whites may think of Jesse Owens, Carl Lewis, and other black speedsters and may overgeneralize from such vivid but exceptional cases that "Yes, blacks seem to be faster."

That we do tend to overgeneralize from vivid, memorable cases has been verified in experiments by Myron Rothbart and his colleagues (1978). In one, University of Oregon students were divided into two groups, each of which was shown a list of fifty men, ten of whom had committed crimes. The ten criminals in the first group's list had committed nonviolent crimes such as forgery. Those in the second group's list had committed violent crimes, such as rape. When both groups were tested for recall and asked how many men on their list had committed any sort of crime, the group with violent criminals on their list significantly overestimated the actual number. Vivid cases, being readily available to memory, powerfully influence the generalizations we make.

The Just-World Phenomenon

Earlier we noted that oppressors tend to justify their acts by blaming their victims. Impartial observers also tend to blame victims, by assuming that the world is just and that people therefore get what they deserve. In laboratory experiments, merely observing someone receive painful shocks led many viewers to think less of the victim (Lerner, 1980). This ***just-world phenomenon*** is reflected in an idea we commonly teach our children—that good is rewarded and evil punished. Therefore, those who are rewarded must be good, and those who suffer (often those who are poor, sick, or have been abused) must deserve their fate. As one German civilian remarked after being shown the concentration camp at Bergen-Belsen at the close of World War II, "What terrible criminals these prisoners must have been to receive such treatment."

The Cognitive Consequences of Stereotypes

Like other forms of prejudgment, prejudices are schemas that influence what we notice, interpret, and remember. If told that a friendly person they are about to meet is unfriendly, people may treat the person with kid gloves and then reflect that it was their gentle handling that led the "unfriendly" person to act so well (Ickes & others, 1982).

In one of his last research projects, Stanley Milgram (1984) demonstrated the biasing power of preconceptions by creating "cyranoids"—people who (like a character under the influence of Cyrano de Bergerac in the play of the same name) echo someone else's thoughts. In his experiment, Milgram transmitted his thoughts to such a speaker through a wireless radio receiver in the ear. In one experiment, high school teachers were invited to interview 11- and 12-year-old boys, each of whom echoed whatever 50-year-old Milgram said. Without realizing it, the teachers were actually talking to one of America's most brilliant scholars, who was literally speaking through the mouths of sixth and seventh graders. The teachers were asked to probe the limits of each child's knowledge in science, literature, and current events "so that you would be able to recommend a grade level for each subject."

Although the teachers were impressed with the children and recognized that they were above average, their impressions were constrained by their preconceptions. As Milgram noted:

> The opinions teachers formed of our child cyranoids depended as much on the teacher as on the child, and the questions asked and avoided. Teachers varied in how they approached their questions, the best of them allowing the cyranoids' responses to guide their interview, the worst never seeing beyond the possibilities of an average 11-year-old.
>
> Moreover, we see how general preconceptions did not allow the teachers to get anywhere near the appropriate grade level of the cyranoid in some subjects. After all, to assign a Ph.D. to a 10th grade class of social studies does no great honor to his Harvard degree. . . . As the source, I was hoping they would ask the cyranoid about Freud, Jung, Adler or at least Darwin and Wittgenstein, but some teachers stuck to fractions and parts of speech.

We see then that prejudice not only is nurtured by its social, emotional, and cognitive roots but also bears cognitive fruits. Our preconceived ideas about people bias the impressions we form of them. To believe is to see.

ATTRACTION

Pause a moment and think about two people—one a close friend, the other someone who either now or in the past has stirred you to feel romantic love. What factors led you into these close relationships?

We endlessly wonder what makes our affections flourish and fade and how we can win the affection of others. In literature, song lyrics, and social commentary we can find a variety of possible explanations. Do birds of a feather flock together, or do opposites attract? Does familiarity breed contempt or liking? Does absence make the heart grow fonder, or is out of sight out of mind? To these questions, social-psychological studies suggest some answers.

"Love comes in at the eye."
William Butler Yeats,
A Drinking Song, 1909

Liking

What is the psychological chemistry that binds two people together in a friendship so deep that it helps them cope with all their other relationships? More simply, what factors help predict whether two people will become friends?

Proximity

Before they become deep, friendships must first be initiated. And proximity—geographical nearness—is perhaps the most powerful predictor of friendship. (Proximity also provides opportunities for assaults, rapes, and murders. But more often it triggers liking.) Study after study reveals that people are most likely to like, and even to marry, those who have lived in the same neighborhood, had a nearby dorm room or apartment, worked in the same office, or even shared the same parking lot. Classroom seating charts also help determine friendship patterns. Though it may seem like a trivial factor, chances are that physical proximity contributed to the development of your close relationships.

The Dan Rather we know and like is at the top. But, if asked, Dan Rather would probably prefer the self he sees in the mirror every day (bottom).

Why is proximity so conducive to liking? Obviously, part of the answer is the greater availability of those we run into often. But there is more to it than that. For one thing, being repeatedly exposed to novel stimuli—whether they be Chinese characters, nonsense syllables, musical selections, geometric figures, or human faces—increases our liking for such stimuli (Moreland & Zajonc, 1982). Within certain limits, familiarity breeds not contempt but fondness.

This ***mere exposure effect,*** the finding that exposure breeds liking, applies even to our view of ourselves. Have you ever noticed that in pictures you never look quite right? An experiment by Theodore Mita and his colleagues (1977) with women at the University of Wisconsin, Milwaukee, revealed why. They photographed each woman, then showed her and a close friend the actual picture along with the mirror image of it. Most of the friends preferred the actual photo, which portrayed the face as *they* had been repeatedly exposed to it; most of the subjects, however, preferred their mirror image photo—which is the way *they* were used to seeing themselves.

Physical Attractiveness

Once proximity has brought you into contact with someone, what most affects your first impressions: the person's sincerity? intelligence? personality? Hundreds of experiments reveal that it is likely to be something more superficial: appearance.

For people taught that "beauty is only skin deep" and that "appearances can be deceiving," the power of physical attractiveness is unnerving. In one early study, Elaine Hatfield and her co-workers (Walster & others, 1966) randomly matched University of Minnesota freshmen for a "Welcome Week" dance. All were given a battery of personality and aptitude tests. On the night of the blind date, the couples danced and talked for more than 2 hours, and then took a brief intermission to evaluate their dates. What determined whether they liked each other? So far as the researchers could determine, only one thing mattered: physical attractiveness (which had been rated by the researchers beforehand). Both the men and the women liked good-looking dates best.

Subsequent studies revealed that people's rated physical attractiveness is linked with their dating frequency, their feelings of popularity, and the impressions others form of their personalities. Attractive people, including children and those of one's sex, are perceived as happier, more sensitive, more successful, and more socially skilled (Hatfield and Sprecher, 1986). Not surprisingly, attractive people are also more likely to make a favorable impression on potential employers (Cash & Janda, 1984).

"Personal beauty is a greater recommendation than any letter of introduction."
Aristotle,
Apothogems, 330 B.C.

Dating and married couples tend to be matched in attractiveness or, if unmatched, the less attractive member often has compensating assets. The same holds true for friends.

If looks matter, who dates and marries those who are less attractive? They tend to match up with people who are about as attractive as they are (McKillip & Riedel, 1983; Murstein, 1976). In cases where partners are noticeably unequal in attractiveness, the less attractive person often has compensating assets, such as greater wealth or status (Berscheid & others, 1973). This helps explain why beautiful young women often marry men whose social status is higher than their own (Elder, 1969).

That looks matter may seem unfair and unenlightened. Two thousand years ago the Roman statesman Cicero felt the same way: "The final good and the supreme duty of the wise man is to resist appearance." Cicero might be reassured by two other findings.

First, people's attractiveness is surprisingly unrelated to their self-esteem (Major & others, 1984). One reason may be that few people view themselves as very unattractive. (Thanks, perhaps, to the mere exposure effect, most of us have become accustomed to our face.) Another reason is that strikingly attractive people are sometimes suspicious that the praise they receive may be simply a reaction to their looks; when less attractive people are praised for their work, they are less likely to discount it as flattery. In fact, attraction researcher Ellen Berscheid (1981) reported that those who have improved their appearance by cosmetic surgery are often disturbed to discover the extent to which this influences how people react to them.

"The thin, narrow-shouldered ectomorph who was yesterday's spinster librarian is today's high fashion model; the plump and buxom endomorph who was a Victorian romantic ideal today is eating cottage cheese and grapefruit, and weighing in every Tuesday at Weight Watchers."

Phyllis Bronstein-Burrows (1981)

Cicero might also find comfort in knowing that the perception of attractiveness is a relative judgment. It is relative not only to one's time and place and to the standards of beauty to which one has been socialized but also to our feelings about the person. In a Rodgers and Hammerstein musical, Prince Charming asks Cinderella, "Do I love you because you are beautiful, or are you beautiful because I love you?" Chances are it is both. As we discover someone's similarities to us, see them again and again, and come to like them, their physical imperfections usually grow less noticeable and their attractiveness grows more apparent (Beaman & Klentz, 1983; Gross & Crofton, 1977). E.T. is as ugly as Darth Vader, until you get to know him.

"If Jack's in love, he's no judge of Jill's beauty."

Benjamin Franklin, 1748

These beauties from around the world illustrate differing cultures' ideas of what is attractive.

Similarity

Let us say that proximity has brought you into contact with someone and that your appearance has helped make a sufficiently favorable first impression to create opportunities for future impressions. As you now get to know one another better, what will influence whether acquaintanceship develops into friendship? For example, is attraction more likely if you are opposites or if you are birds of a feather?

Among social psychologists there is consensus: Birds who flock together are usually of a feather. Friends and couples are far more likely than randomly paired people to share common attitudes, beliefs, and interests (or, for that matter, age, religion, race, education, intelligence, smoking behavior, and economic status). Moreover, the greater the similarity, the more likely the relationship is to endure (Byrne, 1971). We not only tend to assume that recognizably familiar people are similar to us (Judd & others, 1983; Moreland & Zajonc, 1982), we also tend to like people to the extent that their attitudes are similar to our own. Those we perceive as similar to us we also see as embodying our ideals, for which we then love and admire them (Wetzel & Insko, 1982).

Proximity, attractiveness, and similarity, however, are not the only determinants of liking. We tend to like those who like us, especially when we are experiencing a wounded self-image. We respond this way because flattery is rewarding, so long as we do not attribute the flattery to an ulterior motive. Indeed, a simple reward theory of attraction—that we will like those whose behavior is rewarding to us and that we will continue relationships that offer more rewards than costs—can, in hindsight, explain all the findings we have so far considered. When a person lives or works in close proximity with someone else, it costs less time and effort to enjoy the friendship's benefits. Attractive people are aesthetically pleasing, and we suspect that they offer other desirable traits as well. Those with similar views reward us by validating our own ideals.

Loving

Occasionally, people progress from initial impressions to friendship to the more intense, complex, and mysterious state of love. Elaine Hatfield and William Walster (1978) distinguish two types of love: the temporary state of romantic love and the more enduring "companionate" love.

Romantic Love

Romantic love is a passionate state of intense absorption in another. Noting that emotional arousal is a key ingredient of romantic love, Hatfield and Walster suggest that the *two-factor theory of emotion* (see pp. 387–388) can help us understand it. The theory assumes that emotions have two ingredients—physical arousal plus a cognitive label—and that arousal from any source can therefore be steered into one emotion or another, depending on how we interpret and label the arousal.

Laboratory experiments have supported this theory. College men were first aroused by viewing erotic materials, being frightened, running in place, or listening to humorous or repulsive monologues. They were then introduced to an attractive woman or asked to rate their girlfriends. Compared with men who were not initially aroused, those who were stirred up were likely to attribute some of their arousal to the woman or girlfriend and to report more positive feelings toward her (Carducci & others, 1978; Dermer & Pyszczynski, 1978; Kight & White, 1984; White & others, 1981). Outside the laboratory, Donald Dutton and Arthur Aron (1974) staked out two bridges across British Columbia's rocky Capilano River. One was a swaying footbridge, 230 feet above the rocks, the other a low, solid bridge. An attractive young female accomplice intercepted men coming off each bridge, sought their help in filling out a short questionnaire, and then offered her phone number in case they wanted to hear more about her project. Far more of those who had just crossed the high bridge—with pounding hearts—accepted the number and did later call her.

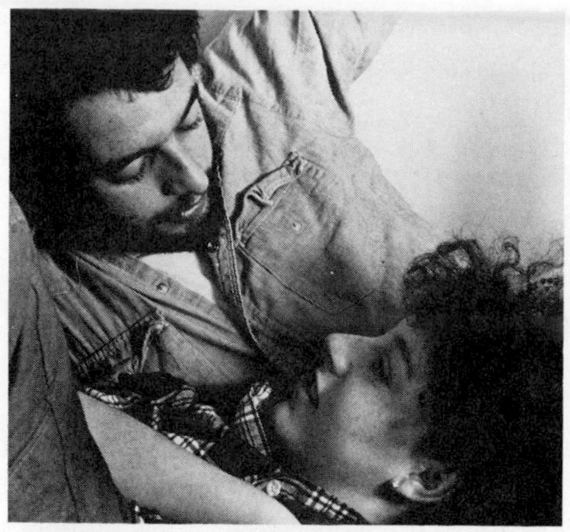

The quality of love changes as a relationship matures from passionate absorption to deep, affectionate attachment.

Companionate Love

The fires of passionate, romantic love burn hot, and then, in a relationship that endures, usually cool to a warm afterglow that Hatfield calls ***companionate love***—a deep, affectionate attachment. As a marriage proceeds, the initial elation of romantic love usually subsides (though it may rebound after the children leave home—Hatfield & others, 1984; Mathes & Wise, 1983). And although the affection of companionate love may also dwindle as a relationship ages, under favorable circumstances it deepens.

But what are favorable circumstances? One key to a gratifying and enduring relationship is ***equity:*** Both partners receive in proportion to what they contribute. If both contribute and enjoy benefits and if decision-making power is shared, the chances for sustained and satisfying companionate love are good (Gray-Little & Burks, 1983; Matthews & Clark, 1982). Indeed, one recent study suggested that equitable giving and receiving—mutually sharing oneself and one's possessions, giving and getting emotional support, promoting and caring about one another's welfare—are at the core of every type of loving relationship, whether with a lover, a parent or child, or an intimate friend (Sternberg & Grajek, 1984).

"When two people are under the influence of the most violent, most insane, most delusive, and most transient of passions, they are required to swear that they will remain in that excited, abnormal, and exhausting condition continuously until death do them part."
George Bernard Shaw
Man and Superman, Maxims for Revolutionists, 1903

CONFLICT AND PEACEMAKING

Conflict, a perceived incompatibility of actions or goals, is an almost inevitable part of social relations. When two people are deeply involved with each other, their needs and desires will occasionally clash. If managed well, such occasions provide opportunities for improved relations, by identifying and eliminating irritations. If not, they can bring out the worst in us. Our human capacity for destructive aggression and mean-spirited prejudice makes conflicts potentially dangerous—whether between individuals (a married couple, roommates, parents and child), between groups (blacks and whites, labor and management, teachers and students), or between nations (Israel and Syria, Iran and Iraq, the United States and the U.S.S.R.).

What triggers conflict? And what steps can be taken to resolve conflict peacefully, to the mutual satisfaction of both parties?

"The natural forces which are the causes of war are human passions which it lies in our power to change."
Ellen Key,
War, Peace, and the Future, 1916

Conflict

The elements of conflict are much the same for situations involving individuals, groups, or nations. So to examine these elements let us focus on one situation—the international tension that has fueled the nuclear arms race. Writing on the prevention of nuclear holocaust, psychologist M. Brewster Smith (1982) noted that

> all other questions of human value and social controversy are dwarfed in comparison. If psychology as a science and profession is to be concerned with the promotion of human welfare, if indeed it is to persist as a science, there must be surviving human beings!

The closeness of the minute hand to midnight on the "Doomsday Clock" symbolizes how close the editors of the Bulletin of the Atomic Scientists *believe the world is to nuclear war. In 1984, the editors, after consultation with a committee of forty-seven world-renowned scientists, advanced the clock to 3 minutes to midnight—the closest the world is believed to have been to nuclear holocaust since 1953.*

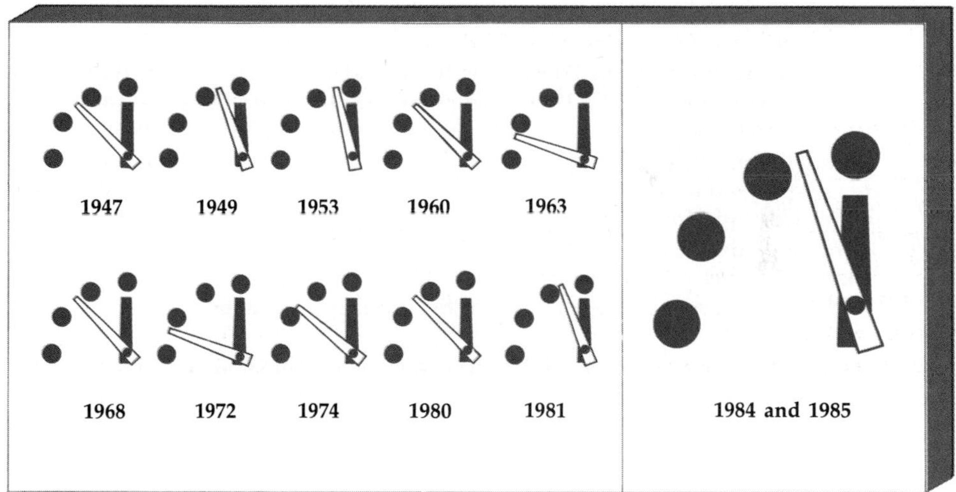

International conflict springs from tensions between people with differing histories, ideologies, and economies. To understand why every thinking person dreads nuclear war while most technological states plan for it, we need the insights of many disciplines. Psychology can contribute by helping us to understand how, as the United Nations Educational, Scientific, and Cultural Organization (UNESCO) motto declares, "wars begin in the minds of men."

When psychiatrist Robert Jay Lifton (1982) went to Hiroshima in 1962 to study the psychological aftereffects of the dropping of the atomic bomb, he encountered an emotional defense process that he called "psychic numbing." The survivors "saw people dying around them, they knew they were dying, they knew something horrible was happening, but they suddenly ceased to feel, underwent what one woman writer described as a 'paralysis of the mind.' " Lifton now believes that psychic numbing occurs in the minds of all those who today collaborate to plan, produce, and prepare to use such bombs and in the minds of many more

"My God, what have we done!"
Robert A. Lewis, co-pilot of the B-29 *Enola Gay,* August 7, 1945, as he watched the blast created by the atom bomb which his plane had just dropped on Hiroshima

of us who cannot imagine what nuclear war would be like, or do not wish to think about it. One way to "break out of the numbing," Lifton urges, is to be mindful of the truth, as told by sober voices (see "To End Psychic Numbing—American Leaders Look at the Arms Race").

To End Psychic Numbing—American Leaders Look at the Arms Race

Mark O. Hatfield, U.S. Senator from Oregon

We must, for a change, address the causes of violence and war. . . . The world spends $17 billion for arms every two weeks. With $17 billion, we could feed every hungry person, clothe every cold person, house everyone, and provide medical assistance for each person in the world for one year. The cost of one-half day of armament could eradicate malaria from the face of the earth.

The cost of one modern-day tank could provide 1,000 classrooms for 30,000 students. The costs of one modern fighter aircraft could provide 40,000 village pharmacies to meet part of the health needs of the people of the world.

An address, "Nuclear Arms: Fear, Faith, and the Future"

Carl Sagan, scientist and author

The conventional bombs of World War II were called blockbusters. Filled with twenty tons of TNT, they could destroy a city block. All the bombs dropped on all the cities in World War II amounted to some two million tons, two megatons, of TNT—Coventry and Rotterdam, Dresden and Tokyo, all the death that rained from the skies between 1939 and 1945: a hundred thousand blockbusters, two megatons. By the late twentieth century, two megatons was the energy released in the explosion of a single more or less humdrum thermonuclear bomb: one bomb with the destructive force of the Second World War. But there are tens of thousands of nuclear weapons. . . . a blockbuster for every family on the planet, a World War II every second for the length of a lazy afternoon. . . .

How would we explain the global arms race to a dispassionate extraterrestrial observer? How would we justify the most recent destabilizing developments of killer-satellites, particle beam weapons, lasers, neutron bombs, cruise missiles, and the proposed conversion of areas the size of modest countries to the enterprise of hiding each intercontinental ballistic missile among hundreds of decoys? Would we argue that ten thousand targeted nuclear warheads are likely to enhance the prospects for our survival? What account would we give of our stewardship of the planet Earth?

***Cosmos* (1980, pp. 320–321, 329)**

Paul Warnke, former director, U.S. Arms Control and Disarmament Agency

Mutually assured destruction isn't a theory. It's a fact. . . . The fact is that if one side attacks the other with nuclear weapons, both sides will be destroyed, and you can't get away from that.

"Nuclear Strategy: A Guide for the Beginner," PBS *Nova*, December 13, 1983

President Dwight D. Eisenhower

People in the long run are going to do more to promote peace than our governments. Indeed, I think that people want peace so much that one of these days governments had better get out of their way and let them have it.

A 1959 speech

National Conference of Catholic Bishops

> **The evil of the proliferation of nuclear arms becomes more evident every day to all people. No one is exempt from their danger. If ridding the world of the weapons of war could be done easily, the whole human race would do it gladly tomorrow. Shall we shrink from the task because it is so hard?**
>
> ***The Challenge of Peace,* 1983**

Social psychologists believe that many conflicts arise from a destructive social process by which even well-meaning persons become enmeshed in a web of hostilities that no one really wants. Psychologist Morton Deutsch (1983) has identified several elements of such "malignant social processes." Let's consider two: social traps and mirror-image perceptions.

Social Traps

In some situations, we can contribute to our collective betterment by pursuing our own self-interest. As the eighteenth century capitalist economist Adam Smith wrote in *The Wealth of Nations,* "It is not from the benevolence of the butcher, the brewer, or the baker, that we expect our dinner, but from their regard to their own interest." In other situations, however, self-serving behavior can be collectively destructive.

Consider the simple matrix in Figure 20-10, one similar to those used in experiments with thousands of people. Pretend that you are person 1, and that you and person 2 will each receive the amount of money indicated after separately choosing either A or B. (You might invite someone to look at the matrix and take the role of person 2.) Which do you choose—A or B?

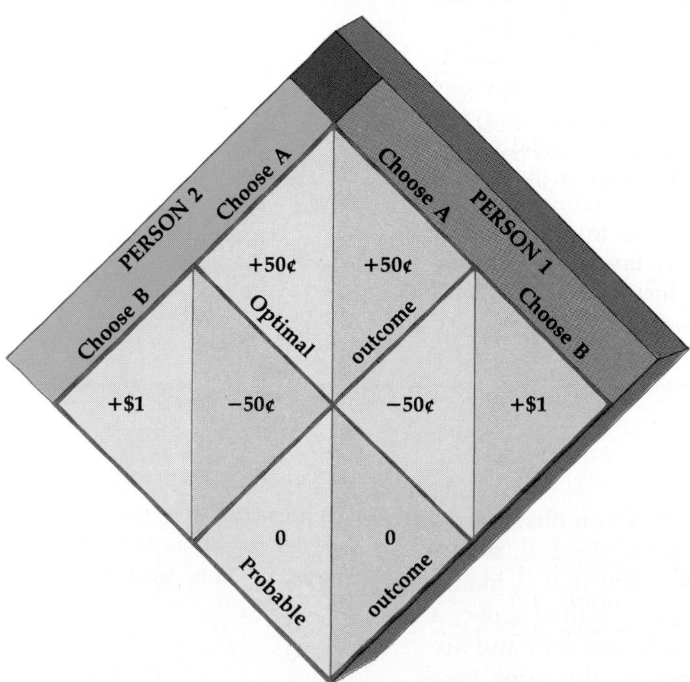

Figure 20-10 *By pursuing our best interests and not trusting others, we can end up losers. To illustrate this, play the game to the left. The tan triangles indicate the outcomes for person 1, which depend on the choices made by both persons. If you were person 1, would you choose A or B? (This game is called a "non-zero-sum game," because the outcomes need not sum to zero; both sides can win or both can lose.)*

Games such as this expose what underlies many a conflict. Each party in our matrix is caught in a dilemma. As you perhaps noticed, you and the other person mutually benefit if you both choose A (and make 50 cents) rather than both choosing B (and making nothing). However, if you study the matrix, you will realize that no matter what the other person does, you are better off choosing B. (Note that if person 2 chooses A, you make $1 by choosing B, but only 50 cents by choosing A; if person 2 chooses B, you lose nothing by choosing B but lose 50 cents by choosing A.) Moreover, you know that the other person may similarly realize that no matter what you do, he or she does better by choosing B. Hence, the malignant ***social trap:*** If you both pursue your self-interest, you both end up with nothing instead of 50 cents. It is a maddening predicament. Yet most people, pursuing their self-interest and mistrusting one another, fall into the trap.

The Commons Dilemma

Another social trap is what ecologist Garret Hardin (1968) calls the "tragedy of the commons." The "commons" refers to the grazing pasture that was once maintained at the center of many rural communities and to which all the town's residents had rights. If 100 farmers surround a commons that is capable of sustaining 100 cows, and each grazes one cow, then the pasture is fully used without being overgrazed.

The commons could as well be air, water, food, whales, or any shared but limited resource. If all restrain their use of the resource, it replenishes itself as fast as it is harvested, and there continues to be enough for all. But imagine a farmer who reasons, "If I put a second cow in the pasture, I'll double my milk production, minus the small cost I'll pay for the one percent overgrazing of the meadow." The farmer adds a second cow, and so does each of his neighbors, reasoning the same way. The result is the tragedy of the commons.

The tragedy is replayed in many real-life situations in which people are caught in dilemmas that pit their individual interests against their communal well-being. Each may reason that the personal benefits of polluting the environment or consuming more natural resources outweigh the costs, because the costs are diffused across everyone. The individual polluter may correctly reason that "It would cost me lots of money to buy expensive pollution controls. And, besides, by itself my pollution has negligible effects." For example, "My car's defective exhaust system doesn't noticeably harm the air in my city." But if everyone reasons the same way, the collective result is environmentally devastating.

The dilemma challenges us to find ways of reconciling our right to pursue our personal well-being with our responsibility to remember the well-being of all. Psychologists are therefore exploring ways to induce people to cooperate for their mutual betterment—through agreed-upon regulations, through better communication with one another, and through attempts to increase each person's feelings of responsibility (Dawes, 1980; Linder, 1982).

The arms race can be understood as a social trap. To an observer, it defies logic. The leaders of both the United States and the U.S.S.R. recognize, as President Eisenhower once said, that "Every gun that is made, every warship launched, every rocket fired signifies, in the final sense, a theft from those who hunger and are not fed, those who are cold and are not clothed." Yet, to both countries' mutual detriment, the arms race

"I can calculate the motions of the heavenly bodies, but not the madness of people."
Sir Isaac Newton, 1642–1727

accelerates. The matrix helps us understand why (Figure 20-11). Strategists in each nation figure that if the other nation is arming, then so must we; a military buildup is the only way to avoid the disaster that might come if they secretly arm while we disarm. Indeed, in laboratory simulations of the arms race, those who play a pacifistic strategy of unconditional disarmament are usually exploited (Reychler, 1979).

To many people, the arms race defies logic.

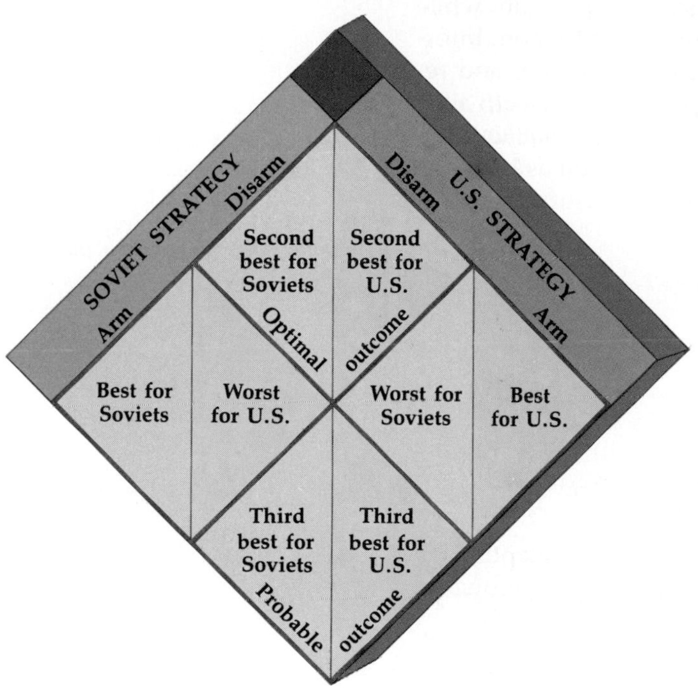

Figure 20-11 *In trying to control the arms race, when America and Russia each protect their self-interest and distrust the other, the result is mutually defeating.*

Mirror-Image Perceptions

The following words, reported by the Associated Press, could have originated with the leader of either the United States or the U.S.S.R. Guess who was speaking:

> [The President/Premier] acknowledged that [Washington's/the Kremlin's] military might had grown in the last decade, but said the [United States/Soviet Union] had been compelled to strengthen itself because of the "feverish [U.S.S.R./U.S.] effort to establish bases near [American/Soviet] territory" and to counter "the [U.S.S.R./U.S.] military superiority for which [Moscow/Washington] is now pining so much."

The words were those of the Soviet leader. But if you imagine President Reagan saying them, they sound familiar. Indeed, psychologists (such as Ralph White, 1984) and political scientists (such as Robert Jervis, 1976) have noted a curious tendency for those in conflict to form diabolical images of each other. These distorted images are so similar that they are called ***mirror images:*** as we see them—as untrustworthy and evil-intentioned—so they see us. Thus, during the 1980s, the American government has viewed the Communist support of guerrillas trying to overthrow the government of El Salvador as evidence of an "evil empire" at work. Meanwhile, the Soviets have seen the American support of guerrillas trying to overthrow the government of Nicaragua as the work of "imperialist warmongers." Such mirror-image perceptions extend to the arms race: "Our nuclear weapons are defensive," each nation declares. "And

"Why do you see the speck that is in your brother's eye, but do not notice the log that is in your own eye?"
Jesus,
The Gospel According to Luke 6:41–42

unlike those who build aggressive weapons in hopes of dominating us and who propose arms control for propaganda purposes, we really desire peace."

Elsewhere in this book, and especially in the preceding chapter, we considered the psychological roots of such biased thinking. The *self-serving bias* leads people to accept credit for their good deeds and to shuck the blame for, or to *self-justify*, their bad deeds. Although both nations admit to a buildup of military forces, the *fundamental attribution error* leads each to see the other's actions as arising from its aggressive disposition, while its own buildup is explained as a necessary response to a situation. Information about one another's actions is then filtered, interpreted, and remembered to fit preconceived *stereotypes*. Group interaction with like-minded others may *polarize* these tendencies, leading to a *groupthink* tendency to see one's own group as moral and one's opposition as less than fully human, with motives and behaviors which fully justify whatever one does to retaliate.

"If real peace is to exist, it must exist along with men's ambitions, their pride, and their hatreds."
Richard M. Nixon,
Real Peace: A Strategy for the West, 1984

Conflict Resolution

Come, my friends,
'Tis not too late to seek
a newer world.

Alfred, Lord Tennyson

Although conflicts are easily ignited by social traps and misperceptions, it is possible for acts of retaliation to be replaced by gestures of reconciliation. Such transformations are most likely in situations characterized by cooperation, communication, and conciliation.

Cooperation

Would it help to put two conflicting parties into close contact, where they might get to know and like one another? It depends. When the contact is noncompetitive between people of equal status, it may indeed help. Initially prejudiced co-workers of different races have, in such circumstances, learned to accept one another (Pettigrew, 1969). However, sometimes mere contact is not enough. In most desegregated junior high schools, whites and blacks resegregate themselves in the lunchrooms and on the school grounds (Schofield, 1982).

Nor was contact enough to defuse the intense conflict that developed when Muzafer Sherif (1966) placed twenty-two Oklahoma City boys in two separate areas within a Boy Scout camp and then put the two groups through a series of competitive activities, with prizes going to the victors. Before long, each group became intensely proud of itself and hostile to the "sneaky," "smart-alecky" "stinkers" in the other group. Dining hall garbage-throwing wars broke out, cabins were ransacked, and fistfights had to be broken up by members of the camp staff. When brought together, the two groups avoided talking to one another, except to threaten and taunt.

Nevertheless, within a few more days, Sherif managed to transform these young enemies into jovial comrades. He did so by giving all twenty-two boys some ***superordinate goals,*** shared goals that overrode their differences and required their cooperation. A disruption of the camp water supply necessitated all the boys' working together to restore water. The opportunity to rent a movie required pooling their combined resources. A stalled truck was restarted by all the boys pulling and pushing together to get it moving. Having used isolation and competition to make strangers into enemies, Sherif used shared predicaments and goals to reconcile them as friends. Thus Sherif showed that what reduces conflict is not contact itself but cooperative contact.

During the 1970s, several teams of educational researchers simultaneously had an idea: If successful, cooperative contacts between members of rival groups encourage more positive attitudes, could this principle be applied in desegregated schools? Could one promote interracial friendships by replacing competitive classroom situations with cooperative ones? Their hunch—now confirmed in many experiments—was that the principle would work (Maruyama & others, 1984). Those who work and play together in interracial projects and on athletic teams are more likely to feel friendly toward those of the other race. So are those who engage in cooperative learning activities within the classroom by participating in interracial groups in which everyone is able to make a valuable contribution. So encouraging were the results that more than 14,000 teachers have already introduced interracial cooperative learning into their classrooms (Cook, 1984).

Cooperative efforts to achieve superordinate goals break down barriers between people.

The power of cooperative activity to make friends of former enemies has led psychologists to urge that opportunities for international exchange and cooperation be increased (Klineberg, 1984). As we engage in mutually beneficial trade, as we come to recognize our common fate on this fragile spaceship Earth, and as we become better aware that our hopes and fears are shared, we can begin changing some of the negative attitudes that contribute to international conflict.

Communication

In the conflict games we considered earlier, people unable to communicate with one another usually became distrustful and felt compelled to arm themselves as a defense against exploitation. If allowed to communicate—to discuss the dilemma they shared and to negotiate a commitment to cooperate—cooperation usually rose (Jorgenson & Papciak, 1981).

"You cannot shake hands with a clenched fist."
Indira Gandhi, 1971

When conflicts are intense, a third-party mediator—a marriage counselor, a labor mediator, a diplomat—may facilitate communication (Pruitt, 1981). Mediators help each party to voice, and in the process to understand, the other's views. Such understanding is most needed, yet least likely, in times of crisis (Tetlock, 1983a, 1983b). When conflicts grow more intense, our images of one another become more distorted and oversimplified, and communication becomes more difficult.

"The time of flight between Cairo and Jerusalem is short. But the distance between them was, until yesterday, quite large."
Menachim Begin, addressing the Knesset, November 21, 1977

When in 1977 after 29 years of hostilities, President Anwar el-Sadat—shown here shaking hands with Menachem Begin—visited Israel in a dramatic gesture for peace, the world was taken by surprise. By his courageous act, he began a dialogue that eventually won a generous peace treaty that greatly benefitted his country.

Conciliation

If tension and suspicion run high, cooperation and communication become impossible. Each party is likely to threaten, coerce, or retaliate—the very actions that worsen the conflict. Both parties recognize that appeasement through unconditional cooperation is both politically naive and likely to invite exploitation.

Under such conditions, is there an alternative to war or surrender? Social psychologist Charles Osgood (1962, 1980) advocates a strategy of *G*raduated and *R*eciprocated *I*nitiatives in *T*ension-reduction, nicknamed ***GRIT.*** In applying GRIT, one side announces its intent to reduce tensions and then initiates one or more small, conciliatory acts. Without weakening its retaliatory capability, this modest beginning opens the door for reciprocation by the enemy. Should the enemy respond with hostility, this would be reciprocated in kind, as would any conciliatory response. In laboratory experiments, GRIT is the most effective strategy known for increasing trust and cooperation (Lindskold & others, 1978, 1983). Even in times of intense personal conflict, when communication is nonexistent, a small conciliatory gesture—a smile, a touch, a small apology—may be all that is needed for both people to begin edging down the tension ladder to a safer rung where mutual understanding can begin.

"The 'madness' that is carrying the world closer and closer to nuclear war has at its core a psychological explanation: . . . Each side imagines that it faces an inherently, implacably aggressive enemy when actually it faces an enemy as fearful as itself—an enemy driven mainly by fear to do the things that lead to war."
Ralph K. White,
Fearful Warriors: A Psychological Profile of U.S.–Soviet Relations, 1984

The closest thing to a conscious application of GRIT to international relations was the "Kennedy experiment," in which President John F. Kennedy in 1963 proclaimed "A Strategy for Peace," announcing that as a gesture of conciliation the United States was stopping all atmospheric nuclear tests (Etzioni, 1967). This offer initiated a series of reciprocated conciliatory acts that culminated in an atmospheric test-ban treaty that has endured to the present.

"It is . . . our intention to challenge the Soviet Union, not to an arms race, but to a peace race; to advance step by step, stage by stage, until general and completed disarmament has actually been achieved."
John F. Kennedy, 1962

By the mid-1980s, the U.S. nuclear capability included thirty strategic submarines, each capable of destroying 160 Soviet cities, to say nothing of the cruise missiles, intermediate-range missiles, ICBMs, aircraft, and the newer weapons now on the drawing board (Sagan, 1984). The Soviets have a huge stockpile of various weapons of their own that are similarly targeted at the United States. If either nation, without sacrificing its retaliatory capability, were to give up some small part of its overkill capability as a gesture of conciliation, might it again be possible to evoke a series of reciprocated conciliatory acts?

"When a person or a society or, as in this case, a whole planet is embarked on a self-destructive and ultimately suicidal course, the first order of business is a decision to reverse course."
Jonathan Schell,
The Abolition, 1984

The answer is debated, and we must be careful not to oversimplify complex questions of diplomatic and military policy. But neither should we ignore their psychological components. Because of its hostile tendencies and prejudiced perceptions, our endangered species teeters at the edge of failure. Within the last hundredth of a percent of the lifetime of our species, we have equipped ourselves with the power to exterminate ourselves. After passing the baton of life from generation to generation across ages of time, the biggest question about our social relations lies before us: Will we act to preserve the world so that the baton can be handed on to our children and our children's children?

"But can they save themselves?"

SUMMING UP

We have considered both undesirable and desirable social relations: aggression and altruism, prejudice and attraction, conflict and peacemaking.

AGGRESSION

The Biology of Aggression Aggressive behavior, like all behavior, is a product of both nature and nurture. Although the idea that aggression is an instinctive drive is no longer accepted, there is ample evidence that aggressiveness is genetically influenced, that certain areas of the brain, when stimulated, activate or inhibit aggression, and that these areas are biochemically influenced.

The Psychology of Aggression A variety of aversive events are known to heighten people's hostility. Such stimuli are especially likely to trigger aggression in those who have been rewarded for aggression or have observed role models portraying it positively. Violent television and pornographic films present numerous aggressive models. Viewers of such media are somewhat more likely, when provoked, to behave aggressively, and they tend to become desensitized to the cruelties depicted.

ALTRUISM

Bystander Intervention In response to incidents of bystander nonintervention in crisis situations, social psychologists undertook experiments that revealed a bystander effect—any given bystander is less likely to help if others are present. This is especially true in situations where the presence of others inhibits one's noticing the event, interpreting it as an emergency, or assuming responsibility for helping. Other factors, such as mood, also influence willingness to help someone in distress.

Why Do We Help? Both psychological and biological explanations have been offered. Social-exchange theory proposes that our social behaviors—even our helpful acts—are based on calculations, often unconscious, designed to maximize our rewards (which may include our own good feelings) and minimize our costs. Our helping is also affected by social norms, which prescribe reciprocating the help we ourselves receive and being socially responsible toward those in need. Sociobiologists suggest that such psychological processes may be undergirded by a genetic predisposition to preserve our own genes—through reciprocal helpfulness and through devotion to those, such as our kin, with whom we share genes.

PREJUDICE

Prejudice is an unjustifiable attitude toward a group or its members that usually is supported by stereotyped beliefs. Although overt prejudice against racial minorities and women has declined in the United States since the 1940s, subtle prejudice yet lives. Such prejudice arises from an interplay of social, emotional, and cognitive factors.

Social Roots of Prejudice Prejudice often arises as those who enjoy social and economic superiority justify the status quo. Even the temporary assignment of people to groups can trigger an ingroup bias. Once established, the inertia of conformity helps to maintain prejudice.

Emotional Roots of Prejudice Prejudice may also serve the emotional functions of draining off the anger brought about by frustration and of boosting self-esteem.

Cognitive Roots of Prejudice Newer research reveals how our ways of processing information—for example, by characterizing people by the groups they belong to or by noticing and remembering vivid cases—work to create stereotypes.

ATTRACTION

Liking Three factors are known to influence our liking for one another. Geographical proximity is conducive to attraction, partly because mere exposure to novel stimuli tends to enhance liking. Physical attractiveness influences both social opportunities and the way one is perceived. As acquaintanceship moves toward friendship, similarity of attitudes and interests greatly increases liking.

Loving Romantic love can be viewed as a temporary aroused state that we cognitively label as love. The strong affection of companionate love is enhanced by an equitable relationship.

CONFLICT AND PEACEMAKING

Conflict Conflicts often arise from a malignant social process that includes social traps, in which each party, by protecting and pursuing its self-interest, creates a result that no one wants. The vicious spiral of conflict both feeds and is fed by distorted mirror-image perceptions, in which each party views itself as moral and the other as untrustworthy and evil-intentioned.

Conflict Resolution Enemies sometimes become friends, especially when the circumstances favor cooperation toward superordinate goals, communication that facilitates understanding, and reciprocated conciliatory gestures.

TERMS AND CONCEPTS TO REMEMBER

Altruism Unselfish regard for the welfare of others.

Bystander Effect The tendency for any given bystander to be less likely to give aid if other bystanders are present.

Companionate Love The deep affectionate attachment we feel for those with whom our lives are intertwined.

Conflict A perceived incompatibility of actions or goals.

Equity A condition in which people receive from a relationship in proportion to what they contribute to it.

Frustration-Aggression Theory The theory that frustration—the blocking of an attempt to achieve some goal—creates anger which can provoke aggression.

GRIT *G*raduated and *R*eciprocated *I*nitiatives in *T*ension-reduction—a strategy designed to decrease international tensions.

Ingroup Bias The tendency to favor one's own group.

Just-World Phenomenon The tendency of people to believe the world is just and that people therefore get what they deserve and deserve what they get.

Mere Exposure Effect The phenomenon that repeated exposure to novel stimuli increases liking.

Mirror-Image Perceptions Distinct but similar views of one another often held by parties in conflict; each views itself as moral and peace-loving and the other as evil and aggressive.

Prejudice An unjustifiable attitude toward a group and its members.

Romantic Love The passionate state of intense absorption we feel for another.

Scapegoat Theory The theory that prejudice provides frustrated people with an outlet for their anger.

Social Exchange Theory The theory that our social behavior is an exchange process the aim of which is to maximize rewards and minimize costs.

Social Traps Situations in which two parties, by each rationally pursuing their self-interest, become caught in mutually destructive behavior.

Stereotype A generalized (often overgeneralized) belief about a group of people.

Superordinate Goals Shared goals that override differences among people and require their cooperation.

FOR FURTHER READING

Aronson, E. (1984). *The social animal* (4th ed.). New York: Freeman.

A delightful, witty, overview of social psychology.

Brehm, S.S. (1985). *Intimate relationships.* New York: Random House.

Draws on social, clinical, and developmental psychology in describing the life cycle of close relationships, from acquaintance to intimacy and sometimes to breakup. Discusses ways to improve intimate relationships.

Frank, J.D. (1982). *Sanity and survival in the nuclear age: Psychological aspects of war and peace.* New York: Random House.

A reissuance with a new introduction of Frank's classic and insightful book on the psychology of why people and nations fight and prepare for war, and what steps might be taken toward peace.

Hatfield, E., & Walster, G.W. (1978). *A new look at love.* Reading, MA: Addison-Wesley.

A scientific look at romantic love—how it develops, how long it lasts, the pain it causes. Case histories, questionnaires, and sometimes surprising findings make this a hard book to put down.

Liebert, R.M., Sprafkin, J.N., & Davidson, E.S. (1982). *The early window: Effects of television on children and youth* (2nd ed.). New York: Pergamon Press.

A comprehensive and well-written analysis of television's effects on children. Discusses antisocial behavior, sexual behavior, commercials, and portrayals of minorities and women.

White, R.K. (1984). *Fearful warriors: A psychological profile of U.S.-Soviet relations.* New York: Free Press.

A compelling analysis of how Americans and Soviets perceive each other, and why predictable misperceptions are endangering the world.

DESCRIBING DATA

Distributions

Central Tendencies

Variation

Correlation

GENERALIZING FROM INSTANCES

Populations and Samples

Principle 1: Representative Samples Are Better Than Biased Samples

Principle 2: Random Sequences May Not Look Random

Principle 3: More Cases Are Better Than Fewer

Principle 4: Less Variable Observations Are Better Than More Variable

Testing Differences

APPENDIX A

Statistical Reasoning in Everyday Life

"Statistical thinking will one day be as necessary for efficient citizenship," H. G. Wells once wrote, "as the ability to read and write." If by statistical thinking he meant not a technical knowledge of how to compute statistics but rather an understanding of the principles of statistical reasoning, then that day has arrived.

Virtually every college—including yours, I would wager—requires its psychology majors to study statistics. Statistics are to a research psychologist what a microscope is to a biologist or a telescope is to an astronomer. All three are tools that help us to see and interpret what the unaided eye might miss. That is why, if you become a psychology major, you will surely be taught how to see data through the lens of statistics.

The chances, however, are that you will not major in psychology. For you, my aim in this appendix is to suggest how you can use the power of statistical reasoning in your own everyday thinking to help you to organize and interpret the events you observe, to generalize from instances more realistically, and to improve your reasoning skills. First I will introduce you to a few basic statistical concepts and formulas. If you are not mathematically inclined, stay with me, rereading where necessary. I think you will be amazed at how easy it is.

DESCRIBING DATA

Both researchers and lay people often make observations or obtain data that must be organized and interpreted.

> In trying to predict which applicants will be most likely to succeed at her school, Laura, a college admissions officer, sorts through grades, aptitude scores, biographical statements, and letters of recommendation.
>
> To decide in which of his region's small towns there is more poverty, Andrew, a government official, gathers figures indicating the residents' incomes.

> To keep track of his progress, Peter, the punter on his college football team, carefully monitors the distance and consistency of his punts.

Let's see how these three people might go about their tasks.

Distributions

Consider first some of the ways these people might organize and describe the raw information available to them. If Laura wants to gain a sense of the past academic performance of her pool of applicants, she could thumb through their files and form some impressions. But she realizes that there is too much information to remember. Moreover, she knows that impressions are influenced by the information most available to memory, which tends to be the vivid or extreme instances (recall the "availability heuristic" introduced in Chapter 11, "Thinking and Language"). So instead of trusting her impressions, she begins by organizing the applicants' high school grade point averages (GPAs) into a ***frequency distribution.*** To do this, she breaks the entire range of scores into equal intervals and then counts the number of scores falling into each interval. Table A-1 presents a frequency distribution of the actual high school GPAs of fifty randomly selected sophomores at my own institution (whom we will use for several examples).

To make the general picture easier to see, Laura puts this distribution into the form of a graph called a ***histogram*** (Figure A-1), in which the frequency of GPAs within a particular interval is represented as a bar. This also helps Laura to see about where any particular student falls relative to the others. Any student's ranking may be expressed more exactly as a ***percentile rank,*** which is simply the percentage of scores that the student's score exceeds. Thus a student whose percentile rank is 99 has a GPA which exceeds that of 99 percent of the students. (Note that you can never achieve a percentile rank of 100; you can never exceed 100 percent of the people because you are one of them.)

Take care when reading statistical graphs: Depending on what people want to emphasize, they can visually make a difference seem small or big. For example, Laura could present the high school GPAs of the men and women among the students we sampled to look slightly different or greatly different (Figure A-2a and b), depending on whether she stretches or shrinks the vertical dimension. The moral: Always read the units on the vertical axis.

Table A-1 **Frequency distribution of high school GPAs of fifty college sophomores**

Interval	Number of persons in interval
3.51–4.00	19
3.01–3.50	13
2.51–3.00	14
2.01–2.50	4

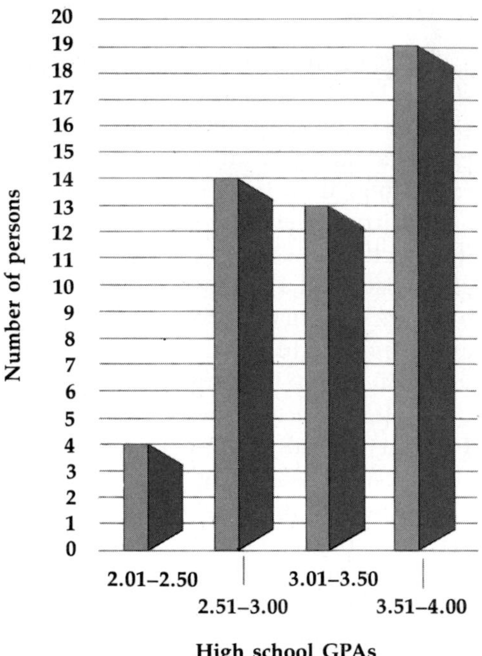

Figure A-1 *A histogram of the frequency distribution in Table A-1 of the high school GPAs of fifty college sophomores.*

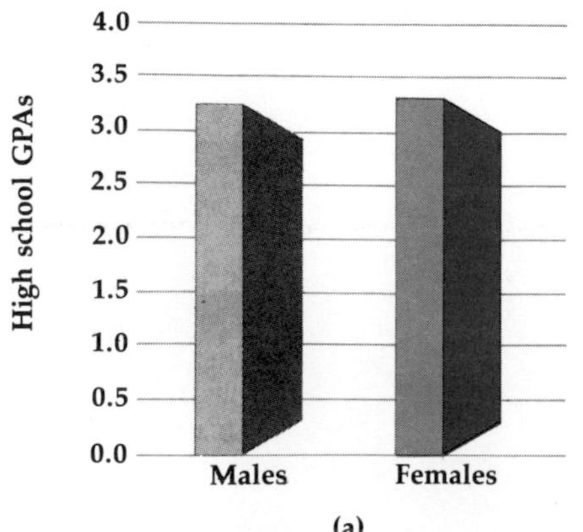

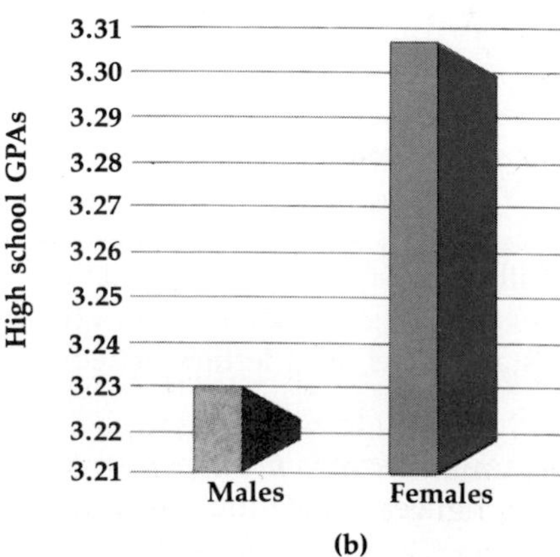

Figure A-2 *Two histograms comparing the average high school GPAs of males and females in a sample of fifty college sophomores. Notice how a difference in the vertical dimension of the two graphs can make this difference seem either (a) small or (b) large.*

Florence Nightingale: Pioneer in the Use of Statistics

Florence Nightingale (1820–1910)

Florence Nightingale (1820–1910) is remembered as a pioneer nurse and hospital reformer. Less well known is her equally pioneering use of statistics to persuade people of the facts. In advocating medical reform, Nightingale became a promoter of statistical description. She developed a uniform procedure by which hospitals reported statistical information. She invented the pie chart, in which proportions are represented as wedges in a circular diagram. And she struggled to get the student of statistics introduced into higher education.

One of Nightingale's analyses compared the peacetime death rates of British soldiers and civilians. She discovered and depicted the fact that the soldiers living in barracks under unhealthy conditions were twice as likely to die as civilians of the same age and sex (Figure A-3). She then used her statistics to persuade the Queen and Prime Minister to establish a Royal Commission on the Health of the Army. It is just as criminal, she wrote, for the army to have a mortality of twenty per thousand "as it would be to take 1,100 men per annum out upon Salisbury Plain and shoot them." (The 1100 represented 20 per thousand of an enlisted force of 55,000.)

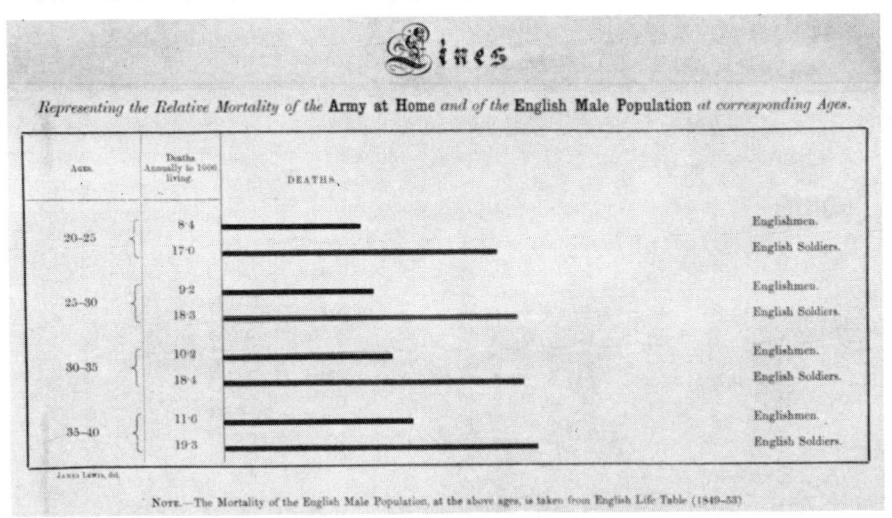

Figure A-3 *Florence Nightingale's histogram comparing peacetime death rates of English soldiers and civilian males illustrates her innovative approach to the presentation of statistics.*

I. Bernard Cohen (1984) reports that "Nightingale's commitment to statistics transcended her interest in health care reform, and it was closely tied to her religious convictions. To her, laws governing social phenomena, 'the laws of our moral progress,' were God's laws, to be revealed by statistics."

Central Tendencies

Now let's see how Andrew, the government official, might describe the incomes earned by the residents in each of his small towns. To simplify things, he might boil the distribution of incomes for a town down to a single "central tendency" that represents a typical income. What measure of central tendency he chooses can make a considerable difference.

The simplest of these, the ***mode,*** is the most frequently occurring score. The most commonly reported, the arithmetic average or ***mean,*** is the total sum of all the scores divided by the number of scores. The ***median*** is the midmost score, the one for which half the scores are above it and half below (the one at the 50th percentile). The confusion that can be created by not understanding the meaning of these measures can be illustrated quite easily. Recently, my wife and I had dinner with three other couples. I suppose you could say that we four couples were a very affluent group, since we had an average or *mean* net worth of over $100 million each. But then again, you might say we were a middle income group, since we had a median net worth of around $100,000. (Most of us had a net worth of about $100,000 but one of the dinner couples had a net worth of $500 million.)

Among the families in the first town Andrew studies, suppose that the mean annual income is $19,000 and that in the second town is only $13,000. At first, Andrew might assume there are more families in poverty in the second town. But as Figure A-4 indicates, the first town, which has a few wealthy employers and quite a few poorly paid employees, actually has many families struggling to live on less than $10,000.

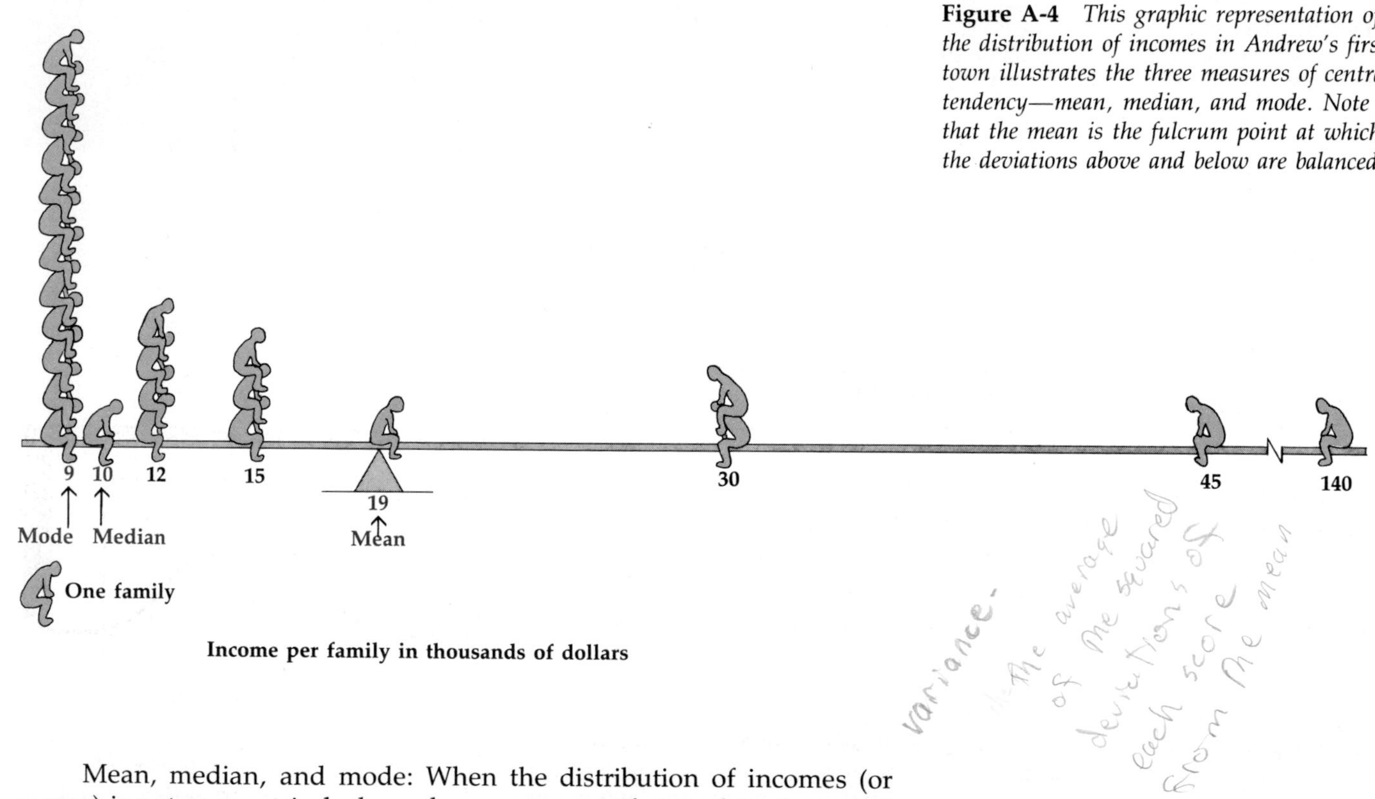

Figure A-4 *This graphic representation of the distribution of incomes in Andrew's first town illustrates the three measures of central tendency—mean, median, and mode. Note that the mean is the fulcrum point at which the deviations above and below are balanced.*

Mean, median, and mode: When the distribution of incomes (or scores) is not symmetrical, these three measures of central tendency tell different stories. When the mean is biased by a relatively few extreme scores, the median is a more appropriate estimate of the central tendency. The moral: Always consider which measure of central tendency is actually being reported and whether a relative few scores might be distorting this statistic.

In Brazil, the mean income in 1981 was $2220; the median income was $291. What does this tell you about the distribution of Brazil's incomes?

Variation

It is also useful to know if the data—the scores—tend to be similar or widely spread out. The ***range*** of scores—the gap between the lowest and highest—provides only a crude estimate of variation, because one extreme score in an otherwise uniform group will create a large range. If in a small class, all the scores on an exam were between 70 and 80, except for one person who scored 20, the range of 60 (80 − 20 = 60) would mislead us about the actual amount of variation. (Question: Would the mean or median score better indicate how most people in the class did?)

The more standard measure of how much scores vary, or deviate, from one another is easily remembered as the ***standard deviation.*** Although this measure, like the range, is also influenced by extreme scores, it is a better gauge of whether scores are packed together or dispersed because it uses information from each score. The standard deviation is important, yet simple to compute. You (1) calculate the deviation between each score and the mean, (2) square these deviations, (3) sum these squared deviations and divide by the number of scores to find the average squared deviation, and (4) find the square root of this average.

It sounds complicated, but it's not. As an example, take our punter, Peter. He does not trust his gut-level impression of how consistent his punting is. After his college's first football game, Peter therefore calculates the standard deviation for his four punts:

Punting distance	Deviation from mean (40 yards)	Deviation squared
36	−4	16
38	−2	4
41	+1	1
45	+5	25
Mean = 160/4 = 40		Sum of (deviations)^2 = 46

Thus,

$$\text{Standard deviation} = \sqrt{\frac{\text{Sum of (deviations)}^2}{\text{Number of scores}}} = \sqrt{46/4} = 3.4 \text{ yards.}$$

To grasp the meaning of this statistic, Peter would need to understand how scores tend to be distributed. It is a convenient fact of nature that large amounts of data—of heights, weights, IQ scores, grades, punt distances, and so forth—often form a roughly symmetrical, bell-shaped distribution, with most cases falling near the mean and fewer cases near the extremes. This bell-shaped distribution is so normal that the curve it forms is called the ***normal curve.*** As Figure A-5 indicates, a useful property of the normal curve is that roughly 68 percent of the cases fall within 1 standard deviation on either side of the mean—in Peter's case within 3.4 yards of his 40-yard average. Ninety-five percent fall within 2 standard deviations. Thus, as we noted in Chapter 12, "Intelligence," about 68 percent of people will score within 15 IQ points (1 standard deviation) of 100 on a standardized IQ test and 95 percent will score within 30 points (2 standard deviations).

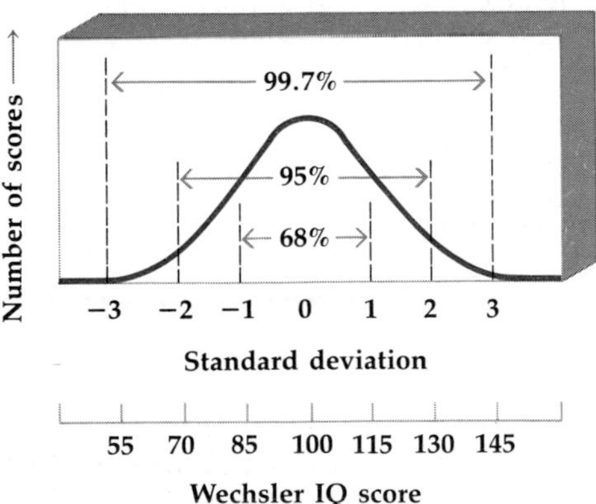

Figure A-5 *The normal curve. Data are often distributed in a normal or bell-shaped curve with 68 percent of the cases falling within 1 standard deviation of the mean and 95 percent within 2 standard deviations. For example, on an IQ test, such as the WAIS, the mean is assigned a score of 100; 68 percent of the scores fall within 15 points above and below 100 and 95 percent within 30 points above and below 100.*

Correlation

In this book we have often asked how much one thing is related to another—how closely related the personality scores of twins are to one another, how well IQ scores predict school grades, how closely stress experiences are linked with disease. To get a feel for whether one set of scores is related to a second set we can once again begin visually, with a graph called a ***scatterplot.*** For example, Figure A-6a depicts the actual relationship between SAT scores and college freshman GPAs among the fifty actual students we met earlier. Each point represents these two numbers for one student. Figure A-6b is a scatterplot of the relationship between these students' high school and college freshman GPAs.

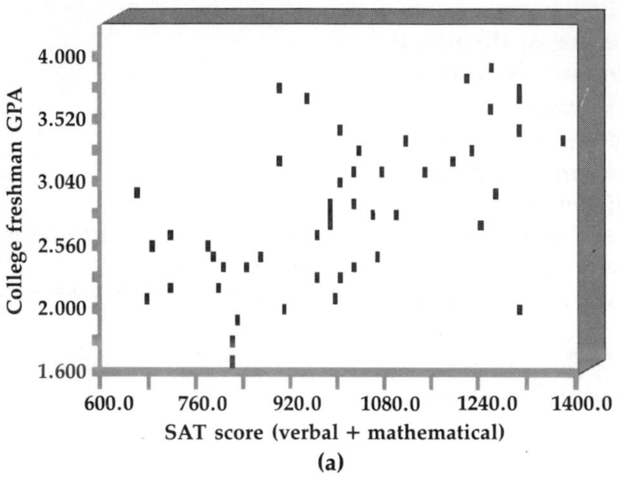

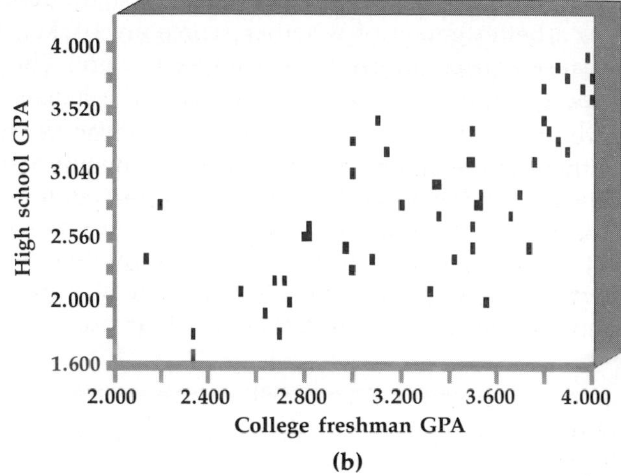

Figure A-6 *Computer-generated scatterplots (a) of the relationship between total SAT scores (verbal and mathematical) and college freshman GPAs and (b) of the relationship between high school and college freshman GPAs of fifty college sophmores. Note that each of the points (shown as short dashes) represents one student's data.*

The ***correlation coefficient*** provides a statistical measure of how strongly related any two sets of scores are. It can range from +1.00 (see Figure A-7a), which means that one set of scores increases in direct proportion to the other, through 0.00, meaning that the scores are not related at all, to −1.00 (see Figure A-7b), which indicates that one set of scores goes up precisely as the other goes down. (Note that a negative correlation need not be a weak correlation; a weak correlation is one that expresses a relationship near zero.) Now look again at Figure A-6a and b: Do the correlations look to be on the positive or negative side of zero?

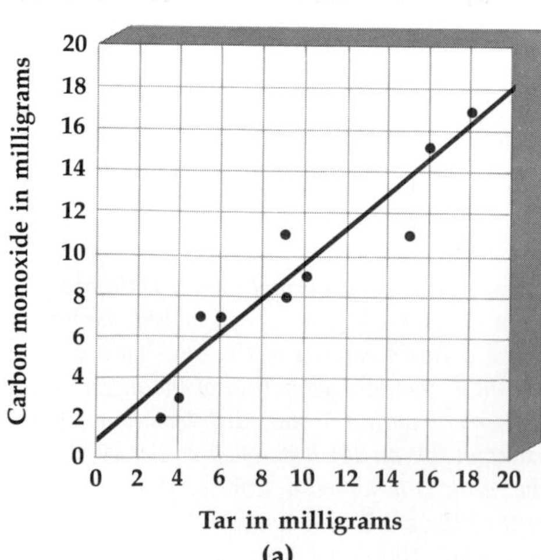

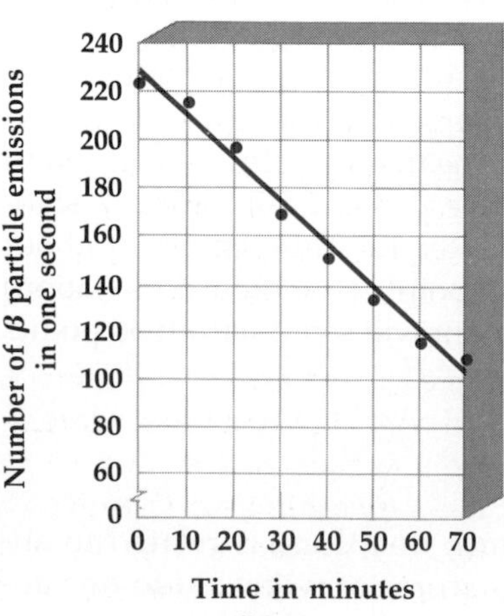

Figure A-7 *Scatterplots showing a strong positive and a strong negative correlation. (a) Measurements of ten brands of king-sized cigarettes revealed a +.94 correlation coefficient between number of milligrams of tar and number of milligrams of carbon monoxide per cigarette. (b) Measurements of a radioactive substance made every 10 minutes showed a −.99 correlation coefficient between radioactive emissions per second and time elapsed. For clarity, in each case the line depicting the relationship between the two sets of data has been shown.*

The upward slope of the cluster of points as one moves to the right indicates that the two sets of scores are tending to rise together, which means the correlations are positive (+.59 for the SAT–college freshman GPA relationship and a stronger +.72 for the high school GPA–college freshman GPA relationship). As SAT scores and, especially, high school grades go up, so do college grades. (The GPA-GPA relationship, incidentally, illustrates the common finding that the best predictor of people's future behavior is usually their behavior in similar situations in the past. This, however, is not to say people cannot and do not change.)

I said at the beginning that statistics help us to see what the naked eye sometimes misses. To demonstrate this to yourself, first try to determine what, if any, relationship exists between two sets of scores not organized into a scatterplot. Elaine wonders whether men's height is related to their temperament. She measures the height of twenty men, has someone else independently assess their temperament (from 0, calm and placid, to 100, highly reactive), and obtains the data in Table A-2.

Table A-2 **Height and temperament of twenty men**

Subject	Height in inches	Temperament
1	80	75
2	63	66
3	61	60
4	79	90
5	74	60
6	69	42
7	62	42
8	75	60
9	77	81
10	60	39
11	64	48
12	76	69
13	71	72
14	66	57
15	73	63
16	70	75
17	63	30
18	71	30
19	68	84
20	70	39

Can you tell, with all the relevant data in front of you, whether there is (1) a positive correlation between height and reactive temperament, (2) very little or no correlation, or (3) a negative correlation?

Comparing the columns in Table A-2, you can probably detect very little relationship between height and temperament. In fact, the correlation in this imaginary example is a moderately positive +.57 (as you could begin to see if you made a scatterplot of the data). If we fail to see a relationship when the data are presented as systematically as this, how much less likely are we to notice them in everyday life. To see what is right in front of us, we need the statistical microscope.

But we also sometimes "see" relationships that do not exist. This tendency to perceive a correlation where there is none is called ***illusory correlation.*** When we believe a relationship exists between two things, we are likely to notice and recall instances that confirm rather than disconfirm our belief. In one experiment, a group of people were shown the results of a hypothetical 50-day cloud-seeding experiment (Ward & Jenkins, 1965). They were told for each of the 50 days whether the clouds had been seeded or not and whether it had rained or had not. The "results" given were random; they showed no relationship between rainfall and cloud seeding. Nevertheless, the subjects typically were convinced—in conformity with what they already believed—that they really had observed a positive relationship between cloud seeding and rain.

Because we are especially sensitive to dramatic or unusual events, the occurrence of two such events in sequence—say a premonition of an unlikely phone call followed by the call—is likely to be noticed and remembered. When the call does not follow the premonition, we are less likely to take note of that fact and remember it. And when we notice and remember only the vivid (but random) events we may forget they are random and see them as correlated. The moral: Beware—we can easily be deceived into missing what is there and seeing what is not. Although the correlation coefficient may tell us nothing about cause and effect (recall Chapter 1), it does help us to see the world more clearly—by revealing the actual extent to which events are related.

The phenomenon of illusory correlation can feed another illusion—that chance events are subject to our personal control. Gamblers, remembering their lucky rolls, may come to believe that they can influence the roll of the dice by doing what they did then—breathing on the dice or throwing softly for low numbers and hard for high numbers. The illusion that uncontrollable events are correlated with our actions is also fed by a statistical phenomenon called ***regression toward the average.*** Average results are more typical than extreme results. Thus after an unusual event, things tend to return toward their average level. Extraordinary happenings tend to be followed by more ordinary happenings. Basketball players who make or miss all their shots in the first half of the game are likely to "regress" (fall back) to their more usual performance during the second half. Students who score much lower or higher on an exam than they usually do are likely, when retested, to regress toward their average. The unusual ESP subject who defies chance when first tested, seems to lose the "psychic powers" when retested (a phenomenon that parapsychologists have called the "decline effect").

The point may seem obvious, yet we regularly miss it, and instead attribute what may be a normal statistical regression to something we have done. If, after doing miserably on the first test, we stop reading the chapter summaries before reading the chapters and then do better on the second test, we may attribute our improvement to the new study technique. If, after a sudden crime wave, the town government initiates a "stop crime" drive and then notes with relief that the crime rate has returned to normal, the drive may appear to have had more impact than it actually did. Coaches who yell at their players after an unusually bad first half may, after the next half, feel rewarded for having done so.

On the other hand, scientists who win Nobel Prizes often thereafter have diminished accomplishments, leading some to wonder whether winning the Nobel hinders creativity. Likewise, some people believe there is a "*Sports Illustrated* jinx"—that athletes whose peak performances get them on the magazine cover will often then suffer a decline in their performance. In each case, it is possible that a genuine effect occurred. But it is also possible that all these cases represent nothing more than the phenomenon of behavior regressing from the unusual to the more usual. The failure to recognize this is the source of many superstitions and ineffective practices. Indeed, when day-to-day behavior has a substantial element of chance fluctuation, we may observe that others' behavior improves (regresses toward average) after we criticize them for a very bad performance and worsens (regresses toward average) after we warmly praise them for an exceptionally fine performance. Ironically, then, regression toward the average operates in such a way that we sometimes feel rewarded for having punished others and punished for having rewarded them (Tversky & Kahneman, 1974). The moral: When it is a statistical likelihood that a behavior will return to normal, there is no need to invent fancy explanations for why it does.

"Once you become sensitized to it, you see regression everywhere."
Daniel Kahneman (1985)

GENERALIZING FROM INSTANCES

So far we have seen how statistical reasoning can help us to digest and describe information more accurately. Statistical reasoning can also help us in a second important way—to make correct leaps from our sample of information to what is generally true. From the friendliness of the people a prospective student meets during a visit to campus, how much has the student learned about the overall friendliness of the campus? From the male-female GPA difference among the fifty students Laura sampled, can we infer that females on this campus generally received better grades? If Peter's first game punts were a representative sample of his punt distances, how much might we expect his punting average to vary from game to game? Again, to understand the practical lessons, we must first understand a few basic statistical concepts.

Populations and Samples

A ***population*** is the whole group we are interested in, of which the cases we observe are but a sample. For convenience, we often limit our observations to a small sample of cases and then generalize to the population from which the sample was drawn. We meet a few members of a group and infer from them what the whole group is like. We observe the weather during a week-long visit to Seattle and then tell our friends about the climate there. What principles can guide us in generalizing from instances?

Principle 1: Representative Samples Are Better Than Biased Samples

It is often tempting to overgeneralize from highly select samples. For example, we can delude ourselves about the actual difference between two groups when we compare people drawn from the extremes. When the Olympic finalists in any sport are all of one race (in the 1984 men's Olympic competition, blacks in the 100-meter dash, whites in the 400-meter freestyle swim), how much does this tell us about the general abilities of the different races? As you can see from the hypothetical illustration in Figure A-8, even if the Olympic finalists are all members of Race B, knowing that any individual is a member of Race A or Race B tells you virtually nothing about that person's running abilities. The same is true when the superstars in some nonathletic pursuit come mostly from a given race, culture, or gender.

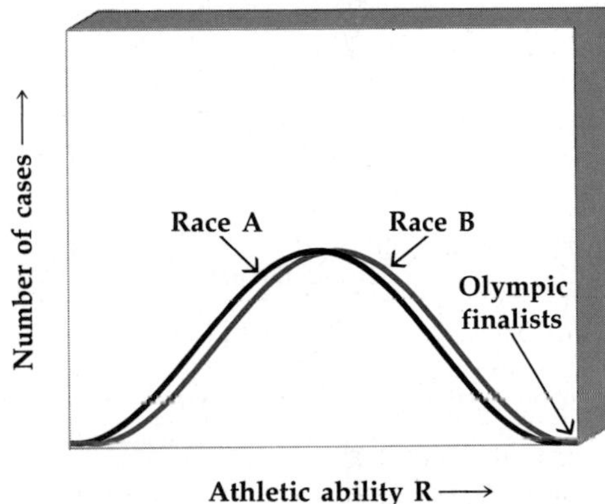

Figure A-8 *Hypothetical normal curves for athletic ability R for two races. As you can see, sampling from the extremes is not the best basis for inferring general racial differences.*

Though it seems obvious, this lesson is often missed in everyday life (Nisbett & Ross, 1980). Given a statistical summary of student evaluations of Professor Zeno's class plus the more vivid comments of two irate students, the administrator's impression may be as much influenced by the unhappy two as by the generally favorable sample of the many. Driving into Chicago from the South, many people see miles of tenement housing near the highway and think, "What an ugly city this is." Standing in the checkout line at the supermarket, George sees the woman in front of him pay with food stamps and then drive away in a Cadillac. "What an easy life these welfare bums have!" he later tells his friends. In each case, the nearly irresistible temptation is to generalize from a few unrepresentative but vivid cases. The moral: The best basis for generalizing is not from the vivid though exceptional cases one finds at the extremes but from a representative sample of cases.

Principle 2: Random Sequences May Not Look Random

As we noted in Chapter 1, gathering a *random* sample—one in which each person in the population has an equal chance of being selected—is a formal technique for making the sample representative. As chance would have it, though, random sequences often do not look random. If someone were to flip a coin six times, would one of these sequences of heads (H) and tails (T) be more likely than the other two: HHHTTT or HTTHTH or HHHHHH? Daniel Kahneman and Amos Tversky (1972) reported that most people believe that HTTHTH and its mirror image are the most likely random sequences. Actually, all possible sequences are equally likely (or, you might say, equally unlikely). A bridge or poker hand in which all the cards were of one suit would seem extraordinary; actually it would be no more or less so than any other given hand of cards.

This failure to recognize random, coincidental occurrences for what they are can predispose people to seek extraordinary explanations for ordinary events.

When You're Hot You're Hot? Random Sequences That Don't Look Random

Every basketball player and fan "knows" that players have hot and cold streaks. Players who have the hot hand can't seem to miss while those having a cold night can't find the center of the hoop. When Amos Tversky (1985), Robert Vallone, and Thomas Gilovich interviewed team members of the Philadelphia 76ers, the players estimated they were about 25 percent more likely to make a shot after a basket than after a miss. Of course: When you're hot you're hot.

The only trouble was, it wasn't true. When Tversky and his collaborators studied detailed game shooting records, they found that the 76ers—and the Boston Celtics, the New Jersey Nets, and the New York Knicks—were no more likely to score after a basket than after a miss. Why, then, do players and fans alike believe in the hot hand phenomenon? Because, Tversky pointed out, in any series of twenty flips of a coin—or twenty shots by a 50 percent shooter—there is a 50-50 chance of four heads (or baskets) in a row and it is quite possible that one person out of five will have a streak of five or six. Players and fans notice these random streaks and so form the myth that "when you're hot you're hot."

Imagine that one warm spring day 4000 college students gather for a coin-tossing contest.[1] Their task is to flip heads. On the first toss, 2000 students do so and advance to the second round. As you might expect, about 1000 of these progress to a third round, 500 to a fourth, 250 to a fifth, 125 to a sixth, 62 to a seventh, 31 to an eighth, 15 to a ninth, and 8 amazing individuals, having flipped heads nine times in a row with great displays of concentration and effort, advance to the tenth round.

By now, the crowd of losers is in awestruck silence as these expert coin-tossers display their amazing ability. The finalists are the center of celebration and adulation. The proceedings are temporarily halted so that a panel of impartial scientists can be called in to observe and document the incredible abilities of these gifted individuals. Alas, in the next few tosses they each freeze up and lose their coin-tossing gift (they regress to normal). "But of course," their admirers surmise, "successful coin tossing is a highly sensitive skill, and the tense, pressured atmosphere created by the scientific scrutiny has disrupted their fragile gift."

The moral: By chance, strange-seeming events must occasionally be expected; it is normal for some events to stray from the hump of the normal distribution.

Principle 3: More Cases Are Better Than Fewer

I have seen it happen: An eager high school senior visits two campuses, each for a day. At the first, the student randomly selects three classes and discovers each instructor to be witty and engaging. At the next campus, the three instructors sampled seem uninspired. Returning home, the student tells friends what "great teachers" there were at the first school, and what "bores" the faculty were at the second school. Again, we know it but we ignore it: Small samples provide a less reliable estimate of the average than do large samples. The proportion of heads in samples of 10 coin tosses varies more than in samples of 100 tosses.

[1]This example was inspired by economist Burton Malkiel's book, *A Random Walk Down Wall Street* (New York: Norton, 1981).

We can actually estimate the reliability of an observed average, given the number and variability of the scores on which the average is based. Without describing this computational procedure, we can state the principle that it illustrates: *averages based on more cases are more reliable* (less variable) than averages based on but a few cases. Knowing this, maybe you will reason differently than did the University of Michigan introductory psychology students to whom Christopher Jepson, David Krantz, and Richard Nisbett (1983) gave the following problem:

> The registrar's office at the University of Michigan has found that there are usually about 100 students in Arts and Sciences who have a 4.00 GPA at the end of their first term at the University. However, only about 10–15 students graduate with a 4.00 GPA. What do you think is the most likely explanation for the fact that there are more 4.00 GPAs after one term than at graduation?

Most students invented plausible causes for the GPA drop, such as, "Students tend to work harder at the beginning of their college careers and not as hard toward the end." Fewer than a third clearly recognized the statistical phenomenon at work: Averages based on fewer courses are more variable. This guarantees a greater number of extremely low and high GPAs.

Principle 4: Less Variable Observations Are Better Than More Variable

Averages derived from scores with low variability (such as among Peter's punts, which varied by only 9 yards) tend to be more reliable than averages based on more diverse scores. If Peter's four punts had ranged from 20 to 60 yards, we should be less confident that his 40-yard average would be close to the average of his next four punts.

Intuitively, you know this to be the case. Surely you would respond much as did the students in another experiment by Nisbett and his colleagues (1983) if asked to "Imagine that you are an explorer who has landed on a little known island in the Southeastern Pacific." You encounter three natives, each of whom is obese and brown-skinned. What percent of all the natives on the island do you expect to be obese? Brown-skinned? Knowing that body weight within a geographical group tends to be more variable than skin color, the students in the experiment were much more likely to infer that all the people on the island were brown than obese.

Well and good. The problem comes when forming impressions of groups that we falsely assume to be relatively homogeneous, such as unfamiliar "outgroups." As demonstrated in numerous experiments, we tend to perceive such groups as more homogeneous than groups we know well. With this in mind, put yourself in the place of the Princeton students to whom George Quattrone and Edward Jones (1980) showed a videotape of a subject who was said to attend either Princeton or Rutgers and who either chose to wait alone or with others for an experiment to begin. When asked to guess what percentage of the other subjects in the experiment chose to wait alone, the Princeton students were much more willing to generalize from the single case when the supposed subject came from the other school. For example, if the videotaped subject chose to wait with others and was said to be from Rutgers, then the Princeton viewers formed a sociable impression of Rutgers students. (Rutgers students were similarly more likely to overgeneralize from the behavior of a supposed Princeton student than from the behavior of a fellow Rutgers student.) The moral: less variable observations do indeed provide a better basis for generalizing; but often we misperceive people in other groups as more uniform than they are.

Testing Differences

We have seen that we can have more confidence in generalizing from samples that are: (1) representative of the population we wish to study; (2) larger rather than smaller, and (3) less rather than more variable. These principles extend to our making inferences about differences between groups. When can we reliably generalize from a difference we have observed—say, from that between the male and female grade point averages in Figure 4-2 to the whole campus population of males and females?

There are tests of ***statistical significance*** that estimate the reliability of observed differences. You needn't understand their computations to understand their logic: When averages from two samples are each judged to be reliable estimates of their populations (as when each is based on a large number of observations that have a small standard deviation), then the difference observed between them is more likely to be reliable. When the difference between the two averages is large, we have even more confidence that the difference between the two samples reflects a real population difference. In short, to the extent that the sample averages are reliable and the difference between them is large, then we can say (as psychologists often do) that the difference is "statistically significant," which simply means that the difference very likely reflects a real difference and is not due to chance variation in and between the samples.

When reading about research, you should bear in mind that, given large or homogeneous enough samples, a difference between them may be "significant" yet unimportant. For example, when comparing the IQs among several hundred thousand firstborn and later-born individuals, there is a "highly significant"—but very small—tendency for firstborn individuals within a family to have higher average scores than their later-born siblings (by a single IQ point or two—Zajonc & Markus, 1975). To repeat, "statistical significance" does not equal importance; rather, it means the results are not likely to be due to chance.

Equipped with these basic statistical tools, we can see more clearly what we might otherwise miss or misinterpret and we can generalize more validly from the instances we observe. Indeed, when we understand and use the principles of statistics, we think more rationally. This may require training and practice, acknowledges a new report of the Project on Redefining the Meaning and Purpose of Baccalaureate Degrees (1985), but in a college education there are few higher priorities:

> "If anything is paid attention to in our colleges and universities, thinking must be it. Unfortunately, thinking can be lazy. It can be sloppy. It can be reactive rather than active. It can be inert. It can be fooled, misled, bullied. . . . Students possess great untrained and untapped capacities for logical thinking, critical analysis, and inquiry, but these are capacities that are not spontaneous: they grow out of wise instruction, experience, encouragement, correction, and constant use."

TERMS AND CONCEPTS TO REMEMBER

Correlation Coefficient A measure of the direction and extent of relationship between two sets of scores. Scores with a positive relationship (such as high school and college GPAs) tend to go up and down together. (Also called the coefficient of correlation.)

Frequency Distribution A listing of the number of individual scores occurring within each equal size interval into which the range of scores has been divided.

Histogram A bar graph that depicts a frequency distribution.

Illusory Correlation The perception of a relationship where none exists or of a stronger relationship than actually exists.

Mean The arithmetic average of a distribution, obtained by adding the scores and dividing by their number.

Median The middle score in a distribution, with half the scores above and half below.

Mode The most frequently occurring score in a distribution.

Normal Curve (or **Normal Distribution**) A symmetrical, bell-shaped curve that describes the distribution of many physical and psychological attributes, with most scores falling near the mean (68 percent within 1 standard deviation of it) and fewer and fewer near the extremes.

Percentile Rank The percentage of the scores in a distribution that a given score exceeds.

Population All the cases in a total group, from which samples may be drawn for study.

Range The difference between the highest and lowest scores in a distribution.

Regression Toward the Average The tendency for extreme or unusual scores to fall back ("regress") toward the average.

Scatterplot A graphed cluster of dots, each dot representing the values of two variables (such as a student's high school and college GPAs). The shape of the cluster suggests the nature and degree of relationship between the two variables. (Also called a scattergram or scatter diagram.)

Standard Deviation A measure of variability, defined as the square root of the average squared deviation of scores from the mean.

Statistical Significance A statistical statement of how small the likelihood is that an obtained result occurred by chance.

FOR FURTHER READING

Huff, D. (1954). *How to lie with statistics.* New York: Norton.

A delightful, easy-to-read little book on the uses and abuses of statistics. Its real message is how to see through the deceptions in the ways people present statistics.

Nisbett, R., & Ross, L. (1980). *Human inference: Strategies and shortcomings in social judgments.* Englewood Cliffs, NJ: Prentice Hall.

This provocative and playful book, written by two prominent social psychologists, reveals the pitfalls created by common failures to use principles of statistical reasoning. Recommended reading for anyone who wishes to think more rationally.

Shaughnessy, J. J., & Zechmeister, E. B. (1985). *Research methods in psychology.* New York: Knopf.

An excellent and gentle introduction to the basic methods and statistical procedures used by psychologists, and to how our everyday use of them can sharpen our reasoning.

APPENDIX B

Specialties in Psychology's Major Fields

SYSTEMS, METHODOLOGIES, AND ISSUES

History and Systems of Psychology
General theories
Experimentation and Observation and Experimental Design
Psychometrics
Test theory and scale analysis
Test construction and validation
Survey theory and methodology
Statistics
Models and Mathematical Models
Factor Analysis and Related Techniques
Computer Applications and Programming
Systems analysis
Artificial intelligence
Apparatus/Equipment
Operations Research
Professional Issues in Psychology
Human resources
Training
Employment and activities
Psychology and social problems
Program Evaluation

EXPERIMENTAL PSYCHOLOGY (Human and Animal)

Learning/Learning Theory
Avoidance and escape
Conditioning
Discrimination
Punishment and extinction
Reinforcement
Verbal learning
Verbal behavior
Sensory and Perceptual Processes
Audition
Chemical senses
Somesthesia
Vision
Intersensory perception (time, space, and illusion)
Sensory adaptation
Sensory-motor interactions
Altered states of consciousness
Biofeedback
Experimental Analysis of Behavior
Personality and experimental psychopathology
Behavior Modification
Operant Behavior/Conditioning

Motivation and Emotion
Memory
Thinking Processes
Decision and Choice Behavior
Attention, Expectancy, and Set
Motor Performance
Reaction Time
Comparative Psychology
Natural Observation
Instincts
Early Experience
Social and Sexual Behavior
Environmental Effects
Hypnosis and Suggestibility
Sleep, Fatigue, and Dreams

PHYSIOLOGICAL PSYCHOLOGY

Neurology
Neuroanatomy
Neurophysiology
Neuropsychology
Sensory Physiology
Brain function
Brain Lesions
Brain damage
Brain Stimulation, Chemical
Brain Stimulation, Electrical
Electrical Activity
Biofeedback
Biochemistry
Drug effects—human
Drug effects—animal
Hormones
Cardiovascular Processes
Gastrointestinal Processes and Nutrition
Environment and Stress
Behavior Genetics
Motivation and Emotion
Personality Correlates
Sexual Physiology
Electrophysical Psychology
Psychophysiology

DEVELOPMENTAL PSYCHOLOGY (Life-Span)

Infancy
Childhood
Perception
Learning
Concepts and language
Abilities
Emotional development
Motivational development
Personality
Social behavior
Parent-child and family relations
Child abuse
Physical/motor development
Children's literature and art
Basic reading processes
Adolescence
Adulthood
Aging
Developmental Theory and Methodology
Development of the Mentally Retarded
Development of the Physically Handicapped
Development of the blind
Development of the deaf
Thanatology
Cognition

PERSONALITY PSYCHOLOGY

Personality Theory
Personality Traits and Processes
Behavior correlates
Culture and personality
Creativity
Intelligence and Measurement of Intelligence
Individual Differences
Personality Measurement
Inventories and rating scales
Projective techniques
Rorschach tests
Personality Assessment
Social Learning and Personality
Self-concept and role-concept learning

SOCIAL PSYCHOLOGY

Interpersonal Processes
Influence and communication
Interpersonal relations
Social perception and motivation
Aggression

Intra- and Inter-Group Processes
Group conflict and attitudes
Influence and communication
Group decision-making and performance
Group structure
Leadership
T-groups/sensitivity/encounter

Communication
Mass media communication
Language
Nonverbal and paraverbal communication

Attitudes and Opinions
Formation and change
Influence and behavior
Survey and measurement
Attribution theory

Values and Moral Behavior

Alcohol Use

Drug Use

Smoking

Sexual Behavior
Birth control
Sexual life-styles
Sex roles and differences

Human Ecology

Psychology and the Arts

Culture and Social Processes
Ethnology
Socioeconomic structure and roles
Religion
Cross-cultural comparison
Family
Social change and programs
Crime reduction

Psychology of Ethnic Groups

Social Psychology of Education

Social Psychology of Science

Deviant Behavior

CLINICAL PSYCHOLOGY

Psychotherapy
Client-therapist interaction
Behavior and conditioning therapy
Group therapy
Drug therapy
Hypnotherapy
Special and adjunctive therapy
Adolescent therapy
Gestalt therapy
Individual and group therapy
Behavior modification
Primal therapy
Adlerian therapy
Applied behavior analysis
Bioenergetic therapy
Biofeedback
Existential therapy
Feminist therapy
Jungian therapy
Psychodrama
Rational-emotive therapy
Reichian therapy
Sex/marital therapy
Transactional therapy
Transpersonal therapy
Multimodal therapy

Clinical Child Psychology
Childhood disorders
Assessment
Family therapy
Art/play therapy
Institutions and programs
Child therapy
Autism
Learning disabilities
Parent education

Psychoanalysis
Psychoanalytic theory

Psychodiagnosis

Psychopathology

Behavior and Mental Disorders
Alcoholism
Crime
Drug abuse
Sexual inadequacy and dysfunction
Juvenile delinquency
Neurosis and emotional disorder
Pyschosis
Schizophrenia
Suicide
Psychopathic and character disorders
Obesity/aphagia

Neurological Disorder
Brain damage
Epilepsy
Clinical neuropsychology

Mentally Retarded
Learning and motor ability
Training and vocational rehabilitation

Speech Disorder

Psychosomatic Disorder

Medical Psychology

Gerontology

Clinical Community Services

Hospital Care and Institutionalization

Applied Clinical Research

Reading Disorders

Physically Handicapped
Disabled
Blind
Deaf
Death and Dying
Program Evaluation

COMMUNITY PSYCHOLOGY

Community Mental Health
Family therapy
Crisis intervention and therapy
Day hospital practices
Small-group processes
Mental health services
Community mental health consultation
Community mental health services planning
Community mental health administration
Community Development
Community leadership
Manpower training (nonprofessional)
Community organization
Social-policy analysis
Social-program planning
Community advocacy
Research and Training in Community Psychology
Counselor Education
Rehabilitation Administration

COUNSELING PSYCHOLOGY

(see also School and Industrial Psychology)

General Counseling
Rehabilitation counseling
Vocational counseling
Educational counseling
Employee counseling
Marriage and family counseling
Personal or adjustment counseling
Pastoral counseling
Counseling, disabled and handicapped
Counseling, employment
Counseling Methods and Processes
Individual and group counseling
Testing
Diagnosis and assessment
Psychotherapy
Test Validation and Counseling Effectiveness
Counseling Theory
Counseling Education

SCHOOL PSYCHOLOGY

(see also Counseling Psychology)

School Counseling
Behavior problems
Emotional adjustment
Learning difficulties
Physically handicapped
Gifted children
Preschool children
Methods and Processes
Testing
Diagnosis and assessment
Therapeutic processes
Student-teacher relationship
Parent-child relationship
Child Growth and Development
Administration of Psychological Services
School Organization and Administration
Psychoeducational Diagnosis

EDUCATIONAL PSYCHOLOGY

School Learning, Theory and Processes
Teacher Selection and Training
Teaching Methods
Teaching machines
Programmed instruction
Teaching aids
Special Education
Disadvantaged
Gifted
Emotionally disturbed
Mentally deficient
Physically handicapped
Preschool Education and Day Care
Curriculum Development and Evaluation
Special Programs (Compensatory, Remedial)

Educational Measurement and Evaluation
- *Intelligence*
- *Aptitude and adjustment*
- *Readiness*
- *School learning achievement*

Educational Research
Educational Technology
College/University Teaching
Continuing/Adult Education

ENGINEERING PSYCHOLOGY

Work Performance and Schedules
- *Stress factors (fatigue, monotony)*
- *Work performance improvement (time and motion study)*
- *Accident prevention, safety*

Work Environments
- *Lighting and atmosphere*
- *Noise and vibration*
- *Special environments (space, underwater)*

Man-Machine Systems (Analysis and Design)
- *Human factors*
- *Displays and controls*
- *Equipment design*
- *Instructional materials and training*

INDUSTRIAL AND ORGANIZATIONAL PSYCHOLOGY

(see also Counseling Psychology)

Personnel
- *Selection and placement*
- *Career development and training*
- *Performance evaluation*
- *Job satisfaction, morale, and attitudes*
- *Retirement*

Management and Organization
- *Organizational behavior*
- *Labor-management relations*
- *Position and task analysis*
- *Compensation*
- *Human relations*
- *Organization development*

Employee/Vocational Counseling
Environment and Quality of Life

CONSUMER PSYCHOLOGY

Consumer Behavior
- *Attitudes and attitude change*
- *Behavior and attitude models*
- *Group influences*
- *Decision processes*

Advertising and Advertising Effectiveness
- *Perception and cognition*
- *Motivational and emotional factors*

Product and Packaging Design
Consumer Surveys
Market Analysis
Consumerism

OTHER PSYCHOLOGICAL SPECIALTIES

Architectural Psychology
Correctional Psychology
Environmental Psychology
Existential Psychology
Forensic Psychology
General Psychology
Gestalt Psychology
Humanistic Psychology
Mathematical Psychology
Military Psychology
Parapsychology
Pastoral Psychology
Pediatric Psychology
Phenomenological Psychology
Philosophical Psychology
Political Psychology
Population Psychology
Professional Psychology
Program Evaluation
Psychoanalysis
Psychobiology
Psycholinguistics
Psychology of Women
Psychometrics
Psychopathology
Psychopharmacology
Psychophysics
Psychotherapy
Rehabilitation Psychology

(APA Directory Survey)

References

Aarons, L. (1976). Sleep-assisted instruction. *Psychological Bulletin, 83,* 1–40.

Abrams, D. B., & Wilson, G. T. (1983). Alcohol, sexual arousal, and self-control. *Journal of Personality and Social Psychology, 45,* 188–198.

Abramson, L. Y., Seligman, M. E. P., & Teasdale, J. D. (1978). Learned helplessness in humans: Critique and reformation. *Journal of Abnormal Psychology, 87,* 49–74.

Adams, D. B., Gold, A. R., & Burt, A. D. (1978). Rise in female-initiated sexual activity at ovulation. *New England Journal of Medicine, 299,* 1145–1150.

Adams, P. R., & Adams, G. R. (1984). Mount Saint Helens's ashfall: Evidence for a disaster stress reaction. *American Psychologist, 39,* 252–260.

Ader, R., & Cohen, N. (1984). Behavior and the immune system. In W. D. Gentry (Ed.), *Handbook of Behavioral Medicine.* New York: Guilford Press.

Adler, N., & Stone, G. (1984). Psychology and the health system. In J. Ruffini (Ed.), *Advances in medical social science.* New York: Gordon & Breach.

Aiello, J. R., Thompson, D. E., & Brodzinsky, D. M. (1983). How funny is crowding anyway? Effects of room size, group size, and the introduction of humor. *Basic and Applied Social Psychology, 4,* 193–207.

Ainsworth, M. D. S. (1979). Infant-mother attachment. *American Psychologist, 34,* 932–937.

Alba, J. W., & Hasher, L. (1983). Is memory schematic? *Psychological Bulletin, 93,* 203–231.

Albee, G. W. (1982). Preventing psychopathology and promoting human potential. *American Psychologist, 37,* 1043–1050.

Allen, M. (1983). Models of hemispheric specialization. *Psychological Bulletin, 93,* 73–104.

Allen, M. G. (1976). Twin studies of affective illness. *Archives of General Psychiatry, 33,* 1476–1478.

Allison, R. B. (1984). Difficulties diagnosing the multiple personality syndrome in a death penalty case. *International Journal of Clinical and Experimental Hypnosis, 32,* 102–117.

Alloy, L. B., & Abramson, L. Y. (1979). Judgment of contingency in depressed and nondepressed students: Sadder but wiser? *Journal of Experimental Psychology: General, 108,* 441–485.

Allport, G. W. (1943). The ego in contemporary psychology. *Psychological Review, 50,* 451–478.

Allport, G. W. (1967). Gordon W. Allport. In E. G. Boring & G. Lindzey (Eds.), *A history of psychology in autobiography* (Vol. V). New York: Appleton-Century-Crofts.

Allport, G. W., & Odbert, H. S. (1936). Trait-names: A psycho-lexical study. *Psychological Monographs, 47,* (1).

Altus, W. D. (1966). Birth order and its sequelae. *Science, 151,* 44–49.

Amabile, T. M. (1983a). Brilliant but cruel: Perceptions of negative evaluators. *Journal of Experimental Social Psychology, 19,* 146–156.

Amabile, T. M. (1983b). *The social psychology of creativity.* New York: Springer-Verlag.

Amabile, T. M. (1985). Motivation and creativity: Effects of motivational orientation on creative writers. *Journal of Personality and Social Psychology, 48,* 393–399.

Amabile, T. M., & Glazebrook, A. H. (1982). A negativity bias in interpersonal evaluation. *Journal of Experimental Social Psychology, 18,* 1–22.

American Council on Education (1983, July 15). National ed debate neglects adult learner, advocate says. *Higher Education and National Affairs,* p. 3.

American Psychiatric Association (1980a). *Diagnostic and statistical manual of mental disorders* (3rd ed.). Washington, DC: American Psychiatric Association.

American Psychological Association (1980b). John Garcia. *American Psychologist, 35,* 37–43.

Anastasi, A. (1982). *Psychological testing.* New York: Macmillan.

Anderson, A. (1982, December). How the mind heals. *Psychology Today,* pp. 51–56.

Anderson, B. L. (1983). Primary orgasmic dysfunction: Diagnostic considerations and review of treatment. *Psychological Bulletin, 93,* 105–136.

Anderson, C. A., & Anderson, D. C. (1984). Ambient temperature and violent crime: Tests of the linear and curvilinear hypotheses. *Journal of Personality and Social Psychology, 46,* 91–97.

Anderson, C. A., Horowitz, L. M., & French, R. D. (1983). Attributional style of lonely and depressed people.

Journal of Personality and Social Psychology, 45, 127–136.

Anderson, C. A., Lepper, M. R., & Ross, L. (1980). Perserverance of social theories: The role of explanation in the persistence of discredited information. *Journal of Personality and Social Psychology, 39,* 1037–1049.

Anderson, J. R. (1983). Retrieval of information from long-term memory. *Science, 220,* 25–30.

Andrews, K. H., & Kandel, D. B. (1979). Attitude and behavior: A specification of the contingent consistency hypothesis. *American Sociological Review, 44,* 298–310.

Antill, J. K. (1983). Sex role complementarity versus similarity in married couples. *Journal of Personality and Social Psychology, 45,* 145–155.

Antonovsky, A. (1979). *Health, stress, and coping.* San Francisco: Jossey-Bass.

Arendt, H. (1963). *Eichmann in Jerusalem: A report on the banality of evil.* New York: Viking Press.

Ariès, P. (1962). In R. Baldick (Trans.), *Centuries of childhood: A social history of family life.* New York: Knopf.

Arnold, A. P. (1980). Sexual differences in the brain. *American Scientist, 68,* 165–173.

Asch, S. E. (1955). Opinions and social pressure. *Scientific American, 193,* 31–35.

Associated Press (1983, March 12). Leaks fought with lie tests. *Holland Sentinel,* p. 1.

Astin, G. R., & Garber, H. (1982). *The rise and fall of national test scores.* New York: Academic Press.

Astin, A. W., & Panos, R. J. (1969). *The educational and vocational development of college students.* Washington, DC: American Council on Education.

Averill, J. R. (1969). Autonomic response patterns during sadness and mirth. *Psychophysiology, 5,* 399–414.

Averill, J. R. (1983). Studies on anger and aggression: Implications for theories of emotion. *American Psychologist, 38,* 1145–1160.

Ax, A. F. (1953). The physiological differentiation of fear and anger in humans. *Psychosomatic Medicine, 15,* 433–442.

Axelrod, J., & Reisine, T. D. (1984). Stress hormones: Their interaction and regulation. *Science, 224,* 452–459.

Azuma, H. (1984). Secondary control as a heterogeneous category. *American Psychologist, 39,* 970–971.

Bachman, J. G., O'Malley, P. M., & Johnston, L. D. (1984). Drug use among young adults: The impacts of role status and social environment. *Journal of Personality and Social Psychology, 47,* 629–645.

Backus, J. (1977). *The acoustical foundations of music* (2nd ed.). New York: Norton.

Baddeley, A. D. (1982). *Your memory: A user's guide.* New York: Macmillan.

Badenhoop, M. S. & Johansen, M. K. (1980). Do reentry women have special needs? *Psychology of Women Quarterly, 4,* 591–595.

Bahrick, H. P. (1984a). Memory and people. In J. Harris (Ed.), *Everyday memory, actions, and absentmindedness.* Orlando, FL: Academic Press.

Bahrick, H. P. (1984b). Semantic memory content in permastore: 50 years of memory for Spanish learned in school. *Journal of Experimental Psychology: General, 113,* 1–29.

Bahrick, H. P., Bahrick, P. O., & Wittlinger, R. P. (1975). Fifty years of memory for names and faces: A cross-sectional approach. *Journal of Experimental Psychology: General, 104,* 54–75.

Bailey, R. E., & Bailey, M. B. (1980). A view from outside the Skinner box. *American Psychologist, 35,* 942–946.

Baker, L. J., Dearborn, M., Hastings, J. E., & Hamberger, K. (1984). Type A behavior in women: A review. *Health Psychology, 3,* 477–497.

Ball, W., & Tronick, E. (1971). Infant responses to impending collision: Optical and real. *Science, 171,* 818–820.

Baltes, P. (1983, August). *New perspectives on the development of intelligence.* Paper presented at the meeting of the American Psychological Association, Anaheim, CA.

Bandura, A. (1977). *Social learning theory.* Englewood Cliffs, NJ: Prentice-Hall.

Bandura, A. (1978). The self system in reciprocal determinism. *American Psychologist, 33,* 344–358.

Bandura, A. (1982). The psychology of chance encounters and life paths. *American Psychologist, 37,* 747–755.

Bandura, A. (1983). Temporal dynamics and decomposition of reciprocal determinism: A reply to Phillips and Orton. *Psychological Review, 90,* 166–170.

Bandura, A. (1986). *Social foundations of thought and action: A social-cognitive theory.* Englewood Cliffs, NJ: Prentice-Hall.

Bandura, A., Blanchard, E. B., & Ritter, B. (1969). Relative efficacy of desensitization and modeling approaches for inducing behavioral, affective, and attitudinal changes. *Journal of Personality and Social Psychology, 13,* 173–199.

Bandura, A., Ross, D., & Ross, S. A. (1961). Transmission of aggression through imitation of aggressive models. *Journal of Abnormal and Social Psychology, 63,* 575–582.

Barash, D. (1979). *The whisperings within.* New York: Harper & Row.

Barber, T. X., Spanos, N. P., & Chaves, J. F. (1974). *Hypnosis, imagination and human potentialities.* New York: Pergamon.

Barlow, H. B. (1972). Single units and sensations: A neuron doctrine for perceptual psychology? *Perception, 1,* 371–394.

Baron, J. (1985). *Rationality and intelligence.* New York: Cambridge University Press.

Baron, L., & Straus, M. A. (1984). Sexual stratification, pornography, and rape in the United States. In N. M. Malamuth & E. Donnerstein (Eds.), *Pornography and sexual aggression.* Orlando, FL: Academic Press.

Barton, J., & Chassin, L., Presson, C. C., & Sherman, S. J. (1982). Social image factors as motivators of smoking initiation in early and middle adolescence. *Child Development, 53,* 1499–1511.

Batson, C. D. (1983). Sociobiology and the role of religion in promoting prosocial behavior: An alternative view. *Journal of Personality and Social Psychology, 45,* 1380–1385.

Batson, C. D. (1985). *Prosocial motiva-*

tion: Is it ever altruistic? Unpublished manuscript, University of Kansas, Lawrence.

Baucom, D. H., & Danker-Brown, P. (1984). Sex role identity and sex-stereotyped tasks in the development of learned helplessness in women. *Journal of Personality and Social Psychology, 46,* 422–430.

Baumeister, R. F. (1985, April). The championship choke. *Psychology Today,* pp. 48–52.

Baumrind, D. (1967). The development of instrumental competence through socialization. In A. D. Pick (Ed.), *Minnesota symposium on child psychology* (Vol. 7). Minneapolis: University of Minnesota Press.

Baumrind, D. (1982). Adolescent sexuality: Comment on Williams' and Silka's comments on Baumrind. *American Psychologist, 37,* 1402–1403.

Baumrind, D. (1983). Rejoinder to Lewis's reinterpretation of parental firm control effects: Are authoritative families really harmonious? *Psychological Bulletin, 94,* 132–142.

Baumrind, D. (1984). *A developmental perspective on adolescent drug use.* Unpublished manuscript, University of California, Berkeley.

Beaman, A. L., & Klentz, B. (1983). The supposed physical attractiveness bias against supporters of the women's movement: A meta-analysis. *Personality and Social Psychology Bulletin, 9,* 544–550.

Beck, A. T. (1982). *Depression: Clinical, experimental, and theoretical aspects.* New York: Harper & Row.

Beck, A. T., & Young, J. E. (1978, September). College blues. *Psychology Today,* pp. 80–92.

Beck, A. T., Rush, A. J., Shaw, B. F., & Emery, G. (1979). *Cognitive therapy of depression.* New York: Guilford Press.

Becklen, R., & Cervone, D. (1983). Selective looking and the noticing of unexpected events. *Memory and Cognition, 11,* 601–608.

Behavior Today Staff (1984, November 26). Canada: Recent study shows decline in marijuana use among teenagers. *Behavior Today,* pp. 7–8.

Bekesy, G. von. (1957, August). The ear. *Scientific American,* pp. 66–78.

Bell, A. P. (1982, November/December). Sexual preference: A postscript. (SIECUS Report, *11,* No. 2) *Church and Society,* pp. 34–37.

Bell, A. P., Weinberg, M. S., & Hammersmith, S. K. (1981). *Sexual preference: Its development in men and women.* Bloomington: Indiana University Press.

Bem, D. (1984). Quoted in the *Skeptical Inquirer, 8,* 194.

Bem, D. J. (1972). Self-perception theory. In L. Berkowitz (Ed.), *Advances in experimental social psychology* (Vol. 6). New York: Academic Press.

Bem, D. J. (1983). Further *deja vu* in the search for cross-situational consistency: A response to Mischel and Peake. *Psychological Review, 90,* 390–393.

Bem, D. J., & Allen, A. (1974). On predicting some of the people some of the time: The search for cross-situational consistencies in behavior. *Psychological Review, 81,* 506–520.

Bem, S. L. (1985). Androgeny and gender schema theory: A conceptual and empirical integration. *Nebraska Symposium on Motivation, 32,* 179–226.

Benbow, C. P., & Stanley, J. C. (1980). Sex differences in mathematical ability: Fact or artifact? *Science, 210,* 1262–1264.

Benbow, C. P., & Stanley, J. C. (1983). Sex differences in mathematical reasoning ability: More facts. *Science, 222,* 1029–1031.

Bennett, T. L. (1983). *Introduction to physiological psychology.* Monterey, CA: Brooks/Cole.

Benson, H., & Klipper, M. Z. (1976). *The relaxation response.* New York: Morrow.

Benson, H., Lehmann, J. W., Malhotra, M. S., Goldman, R. F., Hopkins, J., & Epstein, M. D. (1982). Body temperature changes during the practice of g Tum-mo yoga. *Nature, 295,* 234–236.

Benson, H., & Proctor, W. (1984). *Beyond the relaxation response: How to harness the healing power of your personal beliefs.* New York: Times Books.

Bergin, A. E., & Lambert, M. J. (1978). The evaluation of therapeutic outcomes. In S. L. Garfield & A. E. Bergin (Eds.), *Handbook of psychotherapy and behavior change: An empirical analysis* (2nd ed.). New York: Wiley.

Berkowitz, L. (1983). Aversively stimulated aggression: Some parallels and differences in research with animals and humans. *American Psychologist, 38,* 1135–1144.

Berkowitz, L. (1984). Some effects of thoughts on anti- and prosocial influences of media events: A cognitive-neoassociation analysis. *Psychological Bulletin, 95,* 410–427.

Berman, J. S., & Norton, N. C. (1985). Does professional training make a therapist more effective? *Psychological Bulletin, 98,* 401–407.

Berman, P. W. (1980). Are women more responsive than men to the young? A review of developmental and situational variables. *Psychological Bulletin 88,* 668–695.

Berscheid, E. (1981). An overview of the psychological effects of physical attractiveness and some comments upon the psychological effects of knowledge of the effects of physical attractiveness. In G. W. Lucker, K. Ribbens, & J. A. McNamara (Eds.), *Psychological aspects of facial form* (Craniofacial growth series). Ann Arbor: Center for Human Growth and Development, University of Michigan.

Berscheid, E., Walster (Hatfield), E., & Bohrnstedt, G. (1973, November). The body image report. *Psychology Today,* pp. 119–131.

Best, J. A., & Suedfeld, P. (1982). Restricted environmental stimulation therapy and behavioral self-management in smoking cessation. *Journal of Applied Social Psychology, 12,* 408–419.

Binet, A., & Simon, T. (1905; reprinted 1916). New methods for the diagnosis of the intellectual level of subnormals. In A. Binet & T. Simon, *The development of intelligence in children.* Baltimore: Williams & Wilkins.

Birren, J. E., Cunningham, W. R., & Yamamoto, K. (1983). Psychology of adult development and aging. *Annual Review of Psychology, 34,* 543–575.

Bishop, G. D. (1984a). Gender, role, and illness behavior in a military population. *Health Psychology, 3,* 519–534.

Bishop, G. D. (1984b, August). *Lay conceptions of physical symptoms.* Paper presented at the meeting of the American Psychological Association, Toronto, Canada.

Bishop, G. D., & Converse, S. A. (in press). Illness representations: A prototype. *Health Psychology.*

Bishop, G. D., McMahon, S., Grotzinger, R., Cavazos, L., Briede, C., Wood, R., Wodkins, M., Rodriguez, L., & Doyle, D. (1985, August). *Disease prototypes: Speed of processing and associations.* Paper presented at the meeting of the American Psychological Association, Los Angeles.

Bjork, R. A. (1978). The updating of human memory. In G. H. Bower (Ed.), *The psychology of learning and motivation* (Vol. 12). New York: Academic Press.

Blake, C., & Cohen, H. (1985, May). A meta-analysis of sex differences in moral development. *Resources in Education,* Document ED251749.

Blakemore, C., & Cooper, G. F. (1970). Development of the brain depends on the visual environment. *Nature, 228,* 477–478.

Blasi, A. (1980). Bridging moral cognition and moral action: A critical review of the literature. *Psychological Bulletin, 88,* 1–45.

Block, J. (1981). Some enduring and consequential structures of personality. In A. I. Rabin (Ed.), *Further explorations in personality.* New York: Wiley.

Bloom, B. J. (1964). *Stability and change in human characteristics.* New York: Wiley.

Bond, C. F., & Titus, L. J. (1983). Social facilitation: A meta-analysis of 241 studies. *Psychological Bulletin, 94,* 265–292.

Bootzin, R. R., & Acocella, J. R. (1984). *Abnormal psychology: Current perspectives* (4th ed.). New York: Random House.

Borgida, E., & Nisbett, R. E. (1977). The differential impact of abstract vs. concrete information on decisions. *Journal of Applied Social Psychology, 7,* 258–271.

Boring, E. G. (1930). A new ambiguous figure. *American Journal of Psychology, 42,* 444–445.

Boswell, J. (1980). *Christianity, social tolerance, and homosexuality.* Chicago: University of Chicago Press.

Bouchard, T. (1981, December 6). Interview on *Nova: Twins* [program broadcast by the Public Broadcasting Service].

Bouchard, T. J., Jr. (1982). Twins—Nature's twice told tale. In *1983 Yearbook of science and the future.* Chicago: Encyclopaedia Britannica.

Bouchard, T. J., Jr. (1984). Twins reared together and apart: What they tell us about human diversity. In S. W. Fox (Ed.), *Individuality and determinism.* New York: Plenum Press.

Bouchard, T. J., Jr., & McGue, M. (1981). Familial studies of intelligence: A review. *Science, 212,* 1055–1059.

Bower, G. (1981, June). Mood and memory. *Psychology Today,* pp. 60–69.

Bower, G. H., & Clark, M. C. (1969). Narrative stories as mediators for serial learning. *Psychonomic Science, 14,* 181–182.

Bower, G. H., Clark, M. C., Lesgold, A. M., & Winzenz, D. (1969). Hierarchical retrieval schemes in recall of categorized word lists. *Journal of Verbal Learning and Verbal Behavior, 8,* 323–343.

Bower, T. G. R. (1974). *Development in infancy.* San Francisco: Freeman.

Bower, T. G. R. (1977). *A primer of infant development.* San Francisco: Freeman.

Bowers, K. S. (1983). *Hypnosis for the seriously curious.* New York: Norton.

Bowers, K. S. (1984). Hypnosis. In N. Endler & J. M. Hunt (Eds.), *Personality and behavioral disorders* (2nd ed.). New York: Wiley.

Bowers, P. G., & Bowers, K. S. (1979). Hypnosis and creativity: A theoretical and empirical rapprochement. In E. Fromm & R. E. Shor (Eds.), *Hypnosis: Developments in research and new perspectives.* New York: Aldine.

Bowlby, J. (1973). *Separation: Anxiety and anger.* New York: Basic Books.

Boynton, R. M. (1979). *Human color vision.* New York: Holt, Rinehart & Winston.

Bradley, D. R., Dumais, S. T., & Petry, H. M. (1976). Reply to Cavonius. *Nature, 261,* 78.

Bransford, J. D., & Johnson, M. K. (1972). Contextual prerequisites for understanding: Some investigations of comprehension and recall. *Journal of Verbal Learning and Verbal Behavior, 11,* 717–726.

Bray, G. A. (1969). Effect of caloric restriction on energy expenditure in obese patients. *Lancet, 2,* 397–398.

Brehm, S. (1985). *Social support processes: Problems, perspectives, and a social psychological approach.* Unpublished manuscript, University of Kansas, Lawrence.

Brehm, S., & Brehm, J. W. (1981). *Psychological reactance: A theory of freedom and control.* New York: Academic Press.

Breland, K., & Breland, M. (1961). The misbehavior of organisms. *American Psychologist, 16,* 661–664.

Brewer, W. F. (1977). Memory for the pragmatic implications of sentences. *Memory & Cognition, 5,* 673–678.

Brickman, P., Coates, D., & Janoff-Bulman, R. J. (1978). Lottery winners and accident victims: Is happiness relative? *Journal of Personality and Social Psychology, 36,* 917–927.

Briere, J., & Malamuth, N. M. (1983). Self-reported likelihood of sexually aggressive behavior: Attitudinal versus sexual explanations. *Journal of Research in Personality, 17,* 315–323.

Broadbent, D. E. (1978). The current state of noise research: Reply to Poulton. *Psychological Bulletin, 85,* 1052–1067.

Brockner, J., & Hulton, A. J. B. (1978). How to reverse the vicious cycle of low self-esteem: The importance of attentional focus. *Journal of Experimental Social Psychology, 14,* 564–578.

Brody, J. E. (1984, December 4). Diet therapy for behavior is criticized as premature. *The New York Times,* pp. C1, C15

Bronfenbrenner, U. (1983, January). Quoted by E. H. Methvin in TV violence: The shocking new evidence. *Reader's Digest,* pp. 49–53.

Bronstein-Burrows, P. (1981, August). *Introductory psychology: A course in the psychology of both sexes.* Paper presented at the meeting of the American Psychological Association, Los Angeles, CA.

Brooks-Gunn, J., & Petersen, A. C. (1983). *Girls at puberty: Biological and psychosocial perspectives.* New York: Plenum Press.

Brown, E. L., & Deffenbacher, K. (1979). *Perception and the senses.* New York: Oxford University Press.

Brown, R. (1965). *Social psychology.* New York: Free Press.

Buck, R. (1984). *The communication of emotion.* New York: Guilford Press.

Bugelski, B. R. (1968). Images as mediators in one-trial paired-associate learning. II: Self-timing in successive lists. *Journal of Experimental Psychology, 77,* 328–334.

Bugelski, B. R., Kidd, E., & Segmen, J. (1968). Image as a mediator in one-trial paired-associate learning. *Journal of Experimental Psychology, 76,* 69–73.

Bureau of the Census (1982). *Statistical abstract of the United States 1982–1983.* Washington, DC: U.S. Government Printing Office.

Burns, D. D. (1980). *Feeling good: The new mood therapy.* New York: Signet.

Buss, A. H., & Plomin, R. A. (1975). *A temperamental theory of personality development.* London: Wiley.

Buss, D. M., Block, J. H., & Block, J. (1980). Preschool activity level: Personality correlates and developmental implications. *Child Development, 51,* 401–408.

Butler, R. A. (1954, February). Curiosity in monkeys. *Scientific American,* pp. 70–75.

Byrne, D. (1971). *The attraction paradigm.* New York: Academic Press.

Byrne, D. (1982). Predicting human sexual behavior. In A. G. Kraut, *The G. Stanley Hall Lecture Series* (Vol. 2). Washington, DC: American Psychological Association.

Cacioppo, J. T., & Petty, R. E. (1984). The need for cognition: Relationship to attitudinal processes. In R. P. McGlynn, J. H. Harvey, J. E. Maddux, & C. D. Stoltenberg (Eds.), *Social perception in clinical and counseling psychology.* Lubbock: Texas Tech University Press.

Cajal, R. Y. (1917). *Recollections of my life.* Cited by M. Jacobson (1970), *Developmental neurobiology.* New York: Holt, Rinehart, & Winston.

Cameron, P., & Biber, H. (1973). Sexual thought throughout the life-span. *Gerontologist, 13,* 144–147.

Campbell, B. A., & Coulter, X. (1976). The ontogenesis of learning and memory. In M. R. Rosenzweig & E. L. Bennet (Eds.), *Neural mechanisms of learning and memory,* pp. 209–235. Cambridge, MA: MIT Press.

Campbell, D. T., & Specht, J. C. (1985). Altruism: Biology, culture, and religion. *Journal of Social and Clinical Psychology. 3*(1), 33–42.

Campbell, S. (1982–1983, Winter). The 'monster' tree-trunk of Loch Ness. *Skeptical Inquirer,* pp. 42–46.

Cannon, W. B. (1929). *Bodily changes in pain, hunger, fear, and rage.* New York: Branford.

Cannon, W. B., & Washburn, A. (1912). An explanation of hunger. *American Journal of Physiology, 29,* 441–454.

Cantril, H., & Bumstead, C. H. (1960). *Reflections on the human venture.* New York: New York University Press.

Caplan, R. D., Abbey, A., Abramis, D. J., Andrews, F. M., Conway, T. L., & French, J. R. P., Jr. (1984). *Tranquillizer use and well-being: A longitudinal study of social and psychological effects.* Ann Arbor: Institute for Social Research, University of Michigan.

Carducci, B. J., Cosby, P. C., & Ward, C. D. (1978). Sexual arousal and interpersonal evaluations. *Journal of Experimental Social Psychology, 14,* 449–457.

Carey, S. (1977). The child as word learner. In M. Halle, J. Bresman, & G. A. Miller (Eds.), *Linguistic theory and psychological reality.* Cambridge, MA: MIT Press.

Carroll, J. B. (1982). The measurement of intelligence. In R. J. Sternberg (Ed.), *Handbook of human intelligence.* New York: Cambridge University Press.

Carter-Saltzman, L. (1980). Biological and sociocultural effects on handedness: Comparison between biological and adoptive families. *Science, 209,* 1263–1265.

Carver, C. S., & Ganellen, R. J. (1983). Depression and components of self-punitiveness: High standards, self-criticism, and overgeneralization. *Journal of Abnormal Psychology, 92,* 330–337.

Cash, T., & Janda, L. H. (1984, December). The eye of the beholder. *Psychology Today,* pp. 46–52.

Cattell, R. B. (1973, July). Personality pinned down. *Psychology Today,* pp. 40–46.

Center for Disease Control (1983). Behavioral risk factor prevalence surveys—United States. Reported in *Behavior Today Newsletter,* October 29, 1984, p. 7.

Cerella, J. (1985). Information processing rates in the elderly. *Psychological Bulletin, 98,* 67–83.

Charny, I. W. (1982). *How can we commit the unthinkable? Genocide: The human cancer.* Boulder, CO: Westview Press.

Chase, M. H., & Morales, F. R. (1983). Subthreshold excitatory activity and motoneuron discharge during REM periods of active sleep. *Science, 221,* 1195–1198.

Chase, W. G., & Simon, H. A. (1973). Perception in chess. *Cognitive Psychology, 4,* 55–81.

Chassin, L., Presson, C. C., Sherman, S. J., Corty, E., & Olshavsky, R. W. (1984). Predicting the onset of cigarette smoking in adolescents: A longitudinal study. *Journal of Applied Social Psychology, 14,* 224–243.

Chemers, M. M., & Fiedler, F. E. (1978). The effectiveness of leadership training: A reply to Argyris. *American Psychologist, 33,* 391–392.

Chesney, M. A. (1984, August). *Behavioral factors in coronary heart disease separating benign from malignant.* Paper presented at the meeting of the American Psychological Association, Toronto, Canada.

Chi, M. T. H. (1976). Short-term memory limitations in children: Capacity or processing deficits. *Memory & Cognition, 4,* 559–572.

Chomsky, N. (1959). Review of B. F. Skinner's *Verbal behavior. Language, 35,* 26–58.

Chomsky, N. (1972). *Language and mind.* New York: Harcourt Brace Jovanovich.

Chomsky, N. (1975). *Reflections on language.* New York: Pantheon.

Cialdini, R. B., & Carpenter, K. (1981). The availability heuristic: Does imagining make it so? In P. H. Reingen & A. G. Woodside (Eds.), *Buyer-seller interactions: Empirical issues and normative issues*. Chicago: American Marketing Association.

Cialdini, R. B., & Richardson, K. D. (1980). Two indirect tactics of image management: Basking and blasting. *Journal of Personality and Social Psychology, 39*, 406–415.

Clausen, J. A. (1975). The social meaning of differential physical and sexual maturation. In S. E. Dragastin & G. H. Elder, Jr. (Eds.), *Life cycle*. New York: Wiley.

Cohen, I. B. (1984, March). Florence Nightingale. *Scientific American*, pp. 128–137.

Cohen, S., Evans, G., Krantz, D., & Stokols, D. (1980). Physiological, motivational and cognitive effects of aircraft noise on children: Moving from the laboratory to the field. *American Psychologist, 35*, 231–243.

Cohen, S., & Hoberman, H. M. (1983). Positive events and social supports as buffers of life change stress. *Journal of Applied Social Psychology, 13*, 99–125.

Cohen, S., & Syme, S. L. (Eds.). (1985). *Social support and health*. Orlando, FL: Academic Press.

Cohen, S., & Wills, T. A. (1985). Stress, social support, and the buffering hypothesis. *Psychological Bulletin, 98*, 310–357.

Coile, D. C., & Miller, N. E. (1984). How radical animal activists try to mislead humane people. *American Psychologist, 39*, 700–701.

Coleman, J. C. (1980). *The nature of adolescence*. London: Methuen.

Coleman, L. M., & Antonucci, T. C. (in press). Impact of work on women at midlife. *Developmental Psychology, 19*.

Coles, R. (1973, February 22). Shrinking history, Part I. *New York Review of Books*, pp. 15–21.

Coles, R. (1973, March 8). Shrinking history, Part II. *New York Review of Books*, pp. 25–29.

Collier, B. L. (1971, April 10). Brain power: The case for bio-feedback training. *Saturday Review*, pp. 10–13, 58.

Collins, A. M., & Quillian, M. R. (1969). Retrieval time from semantic memory. *Journal of Verbal Learning and Verbal Behavior, 8*, 240–247.

Collins, R. C. (1983, Summer). Head start: An update on program effects. *Newsletter, Society for Research in Child Development*, pp. 1–2.

Collins, R. C. (1984, April). *Head start: A review of research with implications for practice in early childhood education*. Paper presented at the meeting of the American Education Research Association, New Orleans, LA.

Colombo, J. (1982). The critical period concept: Research, methodology, and theoretical issues. *Psychological Bulletin, 91*, 260–275.

Condon, W. S., & Sander, L. (1974). Neonate movement is synchronized with adult speech: Interactional participation and language acquisition. *Science, 183*, 99–101.

Condry, J., & Condry, S. (1976). Sex differences: A study in the eye of the beholder. *Child Development, 47*, 812–819.

Conel, J. L. (1939–1963). *The postnatal development of the human cerebral cortex* (Vols. I–VI). Cambridge, MA: Harvard University Press.

Conway, M., & Ross, M. (1984). Getting what you want by revising what you had. *Journal of Personality and Social Psychology, 47*, 738–748.

Cook, S. W. (1984). The 1954 social science statement and school desegregation—A reply to Gerard. *American Psychologist, 39*, 819–832.

Cooper, J., & Fazio, R. H. (1984). A new look at dissonance theory. In L. Berkowitz (Ed.), *Advances in experimental social psychology* (Vol. 17). Orlando, FL: Academic Press.

Cooper, W. H. (1983). An achievement motivation nomological network. *Journal of Personality and Social Psychology, 44*, 841–861.

Coopersmith, S. (1967). *The antecedents of self-esteem*. San Francisco: Freeman.

Cordes, C. (1985, April). A step back. *APA Monitor*, pp. 12–14.

Coren, S., & Girgus, J. S. (1978). *Seeing is deceiving: The psychology of visual illusions*. Hillsdale, NJ: Erlbaum.

Coren, S., Porac, C., & Ward, L. M. (1984). *Sensation and perception* (2nd ed.). Orlando, FL: Academic Press.

Cornelius, R. R., & Averill, J. R (1983). Sex differences in fear of spiders. *Journal of Personality and Social Psychology, 45*, 377–383.

Costa, P. T., Jr., & McCrae, R. R. (1980). Still stable after all these years: Personality as a key to some issues in adulthood and old age. In P. B. Baltes & O. Brim, Jr. (Eds.), *Life-span development and behavior* (Vol. 3). New York: Academic Press.

Costa, P. T., Jr., & McCrae, R. R. (1985). Hypochondriasis, neuroticism, and aging: When are somatic complaints unfounded? *American Psychologist, 40*, 19–28.

Cotman, C. W., & Nieto-Sampedro, M. (1982). Brain function, synapse renewal, and plasticity. *Annual Review of Psychology, 33*, 371–401.

Court, J. H. (1984). Sex and violence: A ripple effect. In N. M. Malamuth & E. Donnerstein (Eds.), *Pornography and sexual aggression*. Orlando, FL: Academic Press.

Cowart, B. J. (1981). Development of taste perception in humans: Sensitivity and preference throughout the life span. *Psychological Bulletin, 90*, 43–73.

Cox, V. C., Paulus, P. B., & McCain, G. (1984). Prison crowding research: The relevance for prison housing standards and a general approach regarding crowding phenomena. *American Psychologist, 39*, 1148–1160.

Coyle, J. T., Price, D. L., & DeLong, M. R. (1983). Alzheimer's disease: A disorder of cortical cholinergic innervation. *Science, 219*, 1184–1190.

Coyne, J. C., & Gotlib, I. H. (1983). The role of cognition in depression: A critical appraisal. *Psychological Bulletin, 94*, 472–505.

Craik, F. I. M. (1977). Age differences in human memory. In J. E. Birren & K. W. Schaie (Eds.), *Handbook of the psychology of aging*. New York: Van Nostrand Reinhold.

Craik, F. I. M., & Tulving, E. (1975). Depth of processing and the retention of words in episodic memory. *Journal of Experimental Psychology: General, 104*, 268–294.

Craik, F. I. M., & Watkins, M. J. (1973). The role of rehearsal in short-term memory. *Journal of Verbal Learning and Verbal Behavior, 12,* 599–607.

Crandall, J. E. (1984). Social interest as a moderator of life stress. *Journal of Personality and Social Psychology, 47,* 164–174.

Crocker, J., & Schwartz, I. (1985). Effects of self-esteem on prejudice and ingroup favoritism in a minimal intergroup situation. *Personality and Social Psychology Bulletin, 11*(4).

Crombie, A. C. (1964, May). Early concepts of the senses and the mind. *Scientific American,* pp. 108–116.

Croyle, R. T., & Cooper, J. (1983). Dissonance arousal: Physiological evidence. *Journal of Personality and Social Psychology, 45,* 782–791.

Csikszentmihalyi, M. (1975). *Beyond boredom and anxiety.* San Francisco: Jossey-Bass.

Cummings, N. A. (1979). Turning bread into stones: Our modern antimiracle. *American Psychologist, 34,* 1119–1129.

Cunningham, S. (1983, November). Not such a long way, baby: Women and cigarette ads. *APA Monitor,* p. 15.

Cunningham, S. (1984, October). Animal issues explored peacefully. *APA Monitor,* pp. 1, 14.

Curtiss, S. (1977). *Genie: A psycholinguistic study of a modern-day "wild child."* New York: Academic Press.

Damon, W., & Hart, D. (1982). The development of self-understanding from infancy through adolescence. *Child Development, 53,* 841–864.

Darley, J. (1983, October). *Self-esteem and social comparison.* Paper presented to the meeting of the Society for Experimental Social Psychology, Pittsburgh, PA.

Darley, J. M., & Latané, B. (1968a). Bystander intervention in emergencies: Diffusion of responsibility. *Journal of Personality and Social Psychology, 8,* 377–383.

Darley, J. M., & Latané, B. (1968b, December). When will people help in a crisis? *Psychology Today,* pp. 54–57, 70–71.

Darley, J. M., Seligman, C., & Becker, L. J. (1979, April). The lesson of twin rivers: Feedback works. *Psychology Today,* pp. 16, 23–24.

Darrach, B., & Norris, J. (1984, August). An American tragedy. *Life,* pp. 58–74.

Davis, H. P., & Squire, L. R. (1984). Protein synthesis and memory: A review. *Psychological Bulletin, 96,* 518–559.

Davis, J. M. (1980). Antipsychotic drugs. In H. I. Kaplan, A. M. Freedman, & B. J. Sadock (Eds.), *Comprehensive textbook of psychiatry/III.* Baltimore: Williams & Wilkins.

Dawes, R. M. (1980). Social dilemmas. *Annual Review of Psychology, 31,* 169–193.

Deci, E. L. (1984, April 4). Personal communication.

Deci, E. L. (1980). *The psychology of self-determination.* Lexington, MA: Lexington Books.

Deci, E. L., & Ryan, R. M. (1985). *Intrinsic motivation and self-determination in human behavior.* New York: Plenum Press.

Delgado, J. M. R. (1969). *Physical control of the mind: Toward a psychocivilized society.* New York: Harper & Row.

Dembroski, T. M., MacDougall, J. M., Williams, B., & Haney, T. L. (1985). Components of Type A, hostility, and anger-in: Relationship to angiographic findings. *Psychosomatic Medicine, 47,* 219–233.

Dement, W. (1978). *Some must watch while some must sleep.* New York: Norton.

Dement, W. C., & Wolpert, E. A. (1958). The relation of eye movements, body mobility, and external stimuli to dream content. *Journal of Experimental Psychology, 55,* 543–553.

Dennis, W. (1940). Does culture appreciably affect patterns of infant behavior? *Journal of Social Psychology, 12,* 305–317.

Denney, N. W. (1982). Aging and cognitive changes. In B. B. Wolman (Ed.), *Handbook of developmental psychology.* Englewood Cliffs, NJ: Prentice-Hall.

De Paulo, B. M., Zuckerman, M., & Rosenthal, R. (1980). Humans as lie detectors. *Journal of Communication, 30*(2), 129–139.

Dermer, M., & Pyszczynski, T. A. (1978). Effects of erotica upon men's loving and liking responses for women they love. *Journal of Personality and Social Psychology, 36,* 1302–1309.

Dermer, M., Cohen, S. J., Jacobsen, E., & Anderson, E. A. (1979). Evaluative judgments of aspects of life as a function of vicarious exposure to hedonic extremes. *Journal of Personality and Social Psychology, 37,* 247–260.

Descartes, R. (1642; reprinted in 1955). In *The philosophical works of Descartes* (Vol. I, p. 192). Mineola, NY: Dover.

Detterman, D. K., & Sternberg, R. J. (Eds.) (1982). *How and how much can intelligence be increased?* Norwood, NJ: Ablex.

Deutsch, J. A. (1972, July). Brain reward: ESP and ecstasy. *Psychology Today,* pp. 46–48.

Deutsch, M. (1983). The prevention of World War III: A psychological perspective. *Journal of Political Psychology, 4,* 3–31.

DeValois, R. L., & DeValois, K. K. (1975). Neural coding of color. In E. C. Carterette & M. P. Friedman (Eds.), *Handbook of perception: Vol. V. Seeing.* New York: Academic Press.

DeValois, R. L., & DeValois, K. K. (1980). Spatial vision. *Annual Review of Psychology, 31,* 309–341.

Diagnostic and Statistical Manual of Mental Disorders (3rd ed.) (1980). Washington, DC: American Psychiatric Association.

Diamond, M. C. (1978). The aging brain: Some enlightening and optimistic results. *American Scientist, 66,* 66–71.

Dickie, J. R. (1986). Interrelationships within the mother-father-infant triad. In F. Pedersen & P. Berman (Eds.), *Men's transition to parenthood.* Hillsdale, NJ: Erlbaum.

Dickie, J. R., Ludwig, T. L., & Blauw, D. (1979). Life satisfaction among institutionalized and non-institutionalized older adults. *Psychological Reports, 44,* 807–810.

Dickson, D. H., & Kelly, I. W. (1985). The "Barnum effect" in personality assessment: A review of the literature. *Psychological Reports, 57,* 367–382.

Diener, E. (1984). Subjective well-being. *Psychological Bulletin, 95,* 542–575.

Dietz, W. H., Jr., & Gortmaker, S. L. (1985). Do we fatten our children at the television set? Obesity and television viewing in children and adolescents. *Pediatrics, 75,* 807–812.

DiMatteo, M. R., & Friedman, H. S. (1982). *Social psychology and medicine.* Cambridge, MA: Oelgeschlager, Gunn, & Hain.

DiVasto, P. V., Kaufman, A., Rosner, L., Jackson, R., Christy, J., Pearson, S., & Burgett, T. (1984). The prevalence of sexually stressful events among females in the general population. *Archives of Sexual Behavior, 13,* 59–67.

Doerner, W. R. (1985, July 8). To America with skills. *Time,* pp. 42, 44.

Dohrenwend, B., Pearlin, L., Clayton, P., Hamburg, B., Dohrenwend, B., Riley, M., & Rose, R. (1982). Report on stress and life events. In G. R. Elliott & C. Eisdorfer (Eds.), *Stress and human health: Analysis and implications of research* (A study by the Institute of Medicine/National Academy of Sciences). New York: Springer.

Dohrenwend, B. (1980). *Mental illness in The United States: Epidemiological estimates.* New York: Praeger.

Dolezal, H. (1982). *Living in a world transformed.* New York: Academic Press.

Donaldson, M. (1979, March). The mismatch between school and children's minds. *Human Nature,* pp. 60–67.

Donnelly, F. K. (1983, Spring). *People's Almanac* predictions: Retrospective check of accuracy. *Skeptical Inquirer,* pp. 48–52.

Donnerstein, E., & Linz, D. (1984, January). Sexual violence in the media: A warning. *Psychology Today,* pp. 14–15.

Doty, R. L., Shaman, P., Applebaum, S. L., Giberson, R., Siksorski, L., & Rosenberg, L. (1984). Smell identification ability: Changes with age. *Science, 226,* 1441–1443.

Drucker, P. F. (1982, December). A conversation with Peter F. Drucker. *Psychology Today,* pp. 60–67.

Duncan, B. L. (1976). Differential social perception and attribution of intergroup violence: Testing the lower limits of stereotyping of blacks. *Journal of Personality and Social Psychology, 34,* 590–598.

Duncan, G. J. (1984). *Years of poverty, years of plenty.* Ann Arbor: Institute for Social Research, University of Michigan.

Duncker, K. (1945). On problem solving. *Psychological Monographs, 58* (Whole no. 270).

Dush, D. M., Hirt, M. L., & Schroeder, H. (1983). Self-statement modification with adults: A meta-analysis. *Psychological Bulletin, 94,* 408–422.

Dutton, D. G., & Aron, A. P. (1974). Some evidence for heightened sexual attraction under conditions of high anxiety. *Journal of Personality and Social Psychology, 30,* 510–517.

Dweck, C. S., & Elliott, E. S. (1983). In P. Mussen & E. M. Hetherington (Eds.), *Handbook of child psychology* (Vol. IV). New York: Wiley.

Dywan, J., & Bowers, K. (1983). The use of hypnosis to enhance recall. *Science, 222,* 184–185.

Ebbesen, E. B., Duncan, B., & Konecni, V. J. (1975). Effects of content of verbal aggression on future verbal aggression: A field experiment. *Journal of Experimental Social Psychology, 11,* 192–204.

Ebbinghaus, H. (1885). *Uber das Gedachtnis.* Leipzig: Duncker & Humblot. Cited in R. Klatzky (1980), *Human memory: Structures and processes.* San Francisco: Freeman.

Eckenrode, J. (1984). Impact of chronic and acute stressors on daily reports of mood. *Journal of Personality and Social Psychology, 46,* 907–918.

Eckert, E. D., Heston, L. L., Bouchard, T. J., Jr. (1981). MZ twins reared apart: Preliminary findings of psychiatric disturbances and traits. In L. Gedda, P. Paris, & W. D. Nance, (Eds.), *Twin research; Vol. 3. Pt. B: Intelligence, personality, and development.* New York: Alan Liss.

Edwards, C. P. (1981). The comparative study of the development of moral judgement and reasoning. In R. H. Munroe, R. L. Munroe, & B. B. Whiting (Eds.), *Handbook of cross-cultural human development.* New York: Garland STMP Press.

Edwards, C. P. (1982). Moral development in comparative cultural perspective. In D. A. Wagner & H. W. Stevenson (Eds.), *Cultural perspectives on child development.* San Francisco: Freeman.

Egbert, L. D., Battit, G. E., Welch, C. E., & Bartlett, M. K. (1964). Reduction of postoperative pain by encouragement and instruction of patients. *New England Journal of Medicine, 270,* 825–827.

Ehrhardt, A., & Money, J. (1967). Progestin-induced hermaphroditism: IQ and psycho-sexual identity in a study of ten girls. *Journal of Sex Research, 3,* 83–100.

Eibl-Eibesfeldt, I. (1971). *Love and hate: The natural history of behavior patterns.* New York: Holt, Rinehart & Winston.

Eich, J. E. (1980). The cue-dependent nature of state-dependent retrieval. *Memory and Cognition, 8,* 157–173.

Eisenberg, N., & Lennon, R. (1983). Sex differences in empathy and related capacities. *Psychological Bulletin, 94,* 100–131.

Ekman, P. (1975, September). Face muscles talk every language. *Psychology Today,* pp. 35–39.

Ekman, P. (1985). *Telling lies: Clues to deceit in the marketplace, politics, and marriage.* New York: Norton.

Ekman, P., & Friesen, W. V. (1975). *Unmasking the face.* Englewood Cliffs, NJ: Prentice-Hall.

Ekman, P., Levenson, R. W., & Friesen, W. V. (1983). Autonomic nervous system activity distinguishes among emotions. *Science, 221,* 1208–1210.

Elder, G. H., Jr. (1969). Appearance and education in marriage mobility. *American Sociological Review, 34,* 519–533.

Eldersveld, S. J., & Dodge, R. W. (1954). Personal contact or mail propaganda? An experiment in voting turnout and attitude change. In D. Katz, D. Cartwright, S. Eldersveld, & A. M. Lee (Eds.), *Public opinion and propaganda.* New York: Dryden Press.

Ellis, A. (1984). Rational-emotive therapy (3rd ed.). In R. J. Corsini (Ed.), *Current psychotherapies.* Itasca, IL: Peacock.

Emler, N., Renwick, S., & Malone, B. (1983). The relationship between moral reasoning and political orientation. *Journal of Personality and Social Psychology, 45,* 1073–1080.

Empson, J. A. C., & Clarke, P. R. F. (1970). Rapid eye movements and remembering. *Nature, 227,* 287–288.

Endler, N. S. (1982). *Holiday of darkness: A psychologist's personal journey out of his depression.* New York: Wiley.

Ennis, R. H. (1982). Children's ability to handle Piaget's propositional logic: A conceptual critique. In S. Modgil & C. Modgil (Eds.), *Jean Piaget: Consensus and controversy.* New York: Praeger.

Epstein, R., Kirshnit, C. E., Lanza, R. P., & Rubin, L. C. (1984). "Insight" in the pigeon: Antecedents and determinants of an intelligent performance. *Nature, 308,* 61–62.

Epstein, S. (1983a). Aggregation and beyond: Some basic issues on the prediction of behavior. *Journal of Personality, 51,* 360–392.

Epstein, S. (1983b). The stability of behavior across time and situations. In R. Zucker, J. Aronoff, & A. I. Rabin (Eds.), *Personality and the prediction of behavior.* San Diego: Academic Press.

Epstein, S. (1984). Controversial issues in emotions. In P. Shaver (Ed.), *Review of Personality and Social Psychology.* Beverly Hills, CA: Sage.

Ericsson, K. A., & Chase, W. G. (1982). Exceptional memory. *American Scientist, 70,* 607–615.

Erikson, E. H. (1963). *Childhood and society.* New York: Norton.

Erikson, E. H. (1968). *Identity: Youth and crisis.* New York: Norton.

Erikson, E. H. (1983, June). A conversation with Erikson (by E. Hall). *Psychology Today,* pp. 22–30.

Eron, L. D., & Huesmann, L. R. (1984). The control of aggressive behavior by changes in attitudes, values and the conditions of learning. In R. J. Blanchard & C. Blanchard (Eds.), *Advances in the study of aggression* (Vol. 1). Orlando, FL: Academic Press.

Etzioni, A. (1967). The Kennedy experiment. *The Western Political Quarterly, 20,* 361–380.

Evans, R. I., Raines, B. E., & Hanselka, L. (1984). Developing data-based communications in social psychological research: Adolescent smoking prevention. *Journal of Applied Social Psychology, 14,* 289–295.

Eysenck, H. (1963). The validity of questionnaire and rating assessments of extraversion and neuroticism, and their factorial stability. *British Journal of Psychology, 54,* 51–62.

Eysenck, H. (1982). *A model for intelligence.* Berlin: Springer-Verlag.

Eysenck, H. J. (1952). The effects of psychotherapy: An evaluation. *Journal of Consulting Psychology, 16,* 319–324.

Eysenck, H. J. (1981). *A model for personality.* Berlin: Springer-Verlag.

Eysenck, H. J. (1981). *The intelligence controversy: H. J. Eysenck vs. Leon Kamin.* New York: Wiley.

Eysenck, H. J., Wakefield, J. A., Jr., & Friedman, A. F. (1983). Diagnosis and clinical assessment: The DSM-III. *Annual Review of Psychology, 34,* 167–193.

Fagan, J. F. (1984). The intelligent infant: Theoretical implications. *Intelligence, 8,* 1–9.

Fahrion, S. L., Norris, P., Green, A., & Green, E. (in press). The biobehavioral treatment of essential hypertension: A single group outcome study. *Biofeedback and Self-Regulation.*

Fallon, A. E., & Rozin, P. (1985). Sex differences in perceptions of desirable body shape. *Journal of Abnormal Psychology, 94,* 102–105.

Fancher, R. E. (1979). *Pioneers of psychology.* New York: Norton.

Fantz, R. L. (1961, May). The origin of form perception. *Scientific American,* pp. 66–72.

Farina, A. (1982). The stigma of mental disorders. In A. G. Miller (Ed.), *In the eye of the beholder.* New York: Praeger.

Farina, A., & Fisher, J. D. (1982). Beliefs about mental disorders: Findings and implications. In G. Weary & H. L. Mirels (Eds.), *Integrations of clinical and social psychology.* New York: Oxford University Press.

Faraone, S. V., & Tsuang, M. T. (1985). Quantitative models of the genetic transmission of schizophrenia. *Psychological Bulletin, 98*(1) 41–66.

Farrell, P. A., Gates, W. K., Maksud, M. G., & Morgan, W. P. (1982). Increases in plasma beta-endorphin/beta-lipotropin immunoreactivity after treadmill running in humans. *Journal of Applied Physiology, 52,* 1245–1249.

Fazio, R. H. (1986). How do attitudes guide behavior? In R. M. Sorrentino & E. T. Higgins (Eds.), *The handbook of motivation and cognition: Foundations of social behavior.* New York: Guilford Press.

Fechner, G. (1860). Cited in O. Zangwill (1974), Consciousness and the cerebral hemispheres. In S. Dimond and G. Beaumont (Eds.), *Hemispheric function in the human brain.* New York: Halsted Press.

Feder, H. H. (1984). Hormones and sexual behavior. *Annual Review of Psychology, 35,* 165–200.

Federal Bureau of Investigation (1984). *Uniform crime reports for the United States.* Washington, DC: Government Printing Office.

Federal Bureau of Investigation (1985). *Uniform crime reports for the United States,* pp. 6, 21. Washington, DC: U.S. Government Printing Office.

Feinleib, M., Lenfant, C., & Miller, S. A. (1984). Hypertension and calcium. *Science, 226,* 384–385.

Fichten, C. S. (1984). See it from my point of view: Videotape and attributions in happy and distressed couples. *Journal of Social and Clinical Psychology, 2,* 125–142.

Field, T. M., Woodson, R., Greenberg, R., & Cohen, D. (1982). Discrimination and imitation of facial expressions by neonates. *Science, 218,* 179–181.

Fields, C. M. (1984, September 5). Psychologists emphasize their commitment to humane use of animals in research. *Chronicle of Higher Education,* pp. 5, 12.

Findley, M. J., & Cooper, H. M. (1983). Locus of control and academic achievement: A literature review. *Journal of Personality and Social Psychology, 44,* 419–427.

Finucci, J. M., & Childs, B. (1981). Are there really more dyslexic boys than girls? In A. Ansara, N. Geschwind, A. Galaburda, M. Albert, & N. Gartrell (Eds.), *Sex differences in dyslexia.* Townson, MD: The Orton Dyslexia Society.

Fischhoff, B. (1982). Debiasing. In D. Kahneman, P. Slovic, & A. Tversky (Eds.), *Judgment under uncertainty: Heuristics and biases.* New York: Cambridge University Press.

Fischhoff, B., & Beyth, R. (1975). "I knew it would happen": Remembered probabilities of once-future things. *Organizational Behavior and Human Performance, 13,* 1–16.

Fischhoff, B., Slovic, P., & Lichtenstein, S. (1977). Knowing with certainty: The appropriateness of extreme confidence. *Journal of Experimental Psychology: Human Perception and Performance, 3,* 552–564.

Fisher, H. T. (1984). Little Albert and Little Peter. *Bulletin of the British Psychological Society, 37,* 269.

Flanagan, J. C. (1947). Scientific development of the use of human resources: Progress in the Army Air Forces. *Science, 105,* 57–60.

Flavell, J. H. (1982). On cognitive development. *Child Development, 53,* 1–10.

Floderus-Myrhed, B., Pedersen, N., & Rasmuson, I. (1980). Assessment of heritability for personality, based on a short-form of the Eysenck Personality Inventory: A study of 12,898 twin pairs. *Behavior Genetics, 10,* 153–162.

Flynn, J. R. (1984a). Personal communication.

Flynn, J. R. (1984b). The mean IQ of Americans: Massive gains 1932 to 1978. *Psychological Bulletin, 95,* 29–51.

Ford, C. S., & Beach, F. A. (1951). *Patterns of sexual behavior.* New York: Harper & Row.

Forer, B. R. (1949). The fallacy of personal validation: A classroom demonstration of gullibility. *Journal of Abnormal and Social Psychology, 44,* 118–123.

Forgas, J. P., Bower, G. H., & Krantz, S. E. (1984). The influence of mood on perceptions of social interactions. *Journal of Experimental Social Psychology, 20,* 497–513.

Fouts, R. S. (1984, November). *Friends of Washoe letter.* Central Washington University, Ellensburg, WA.

Fouts, R. S., Fouts, D. H., & Schoenfeld, D. J. (1984). Sign language conversational interaction between chimpanzees. *Sign Language Studies, 42,* 1–12.

Fowler, C. A., Wolford, G., Slade, R., & Tassinary, L. (1981). Lexical access with and without awareness. *Journal of Experimental Psychology: General, 110,* 341–362.

Fowler, M. J., Sullivan, M. J., & Ekstrand, B. R. (1973). Sleep and memory. *Science, 179,* 302–304.

Fox, J. L. (1984). The brain's dynamic way of keeping in touch. *Science, 225,* 820–821.

Fozard, J. L., & Popkin, S. J. (1978). Optimizing adult development: Ends and means of an applied psychology of aging. *American Psychologist, 33,* 975–989.

Frank, J. D. (1982). Therapeutic components shared by all psychotherapies. In J. H. Harvey & M. M. Parks (Eds.), *The Master Lecture Series: Vol. 1. Psychotherapy research and behavior change.* Washington, DC: American Psychological Association.

Frazier, K. (1984–1985). Gallup youth poll finds high belief in ESP, astrology. *The Skeptical Inquirer, 9,* 113–114.

Freedman, D. G. (1979). *Human sociobiology: A holistic approach.* New York: Free Press.

Freedman, J. L. (1984). Effect of television violence on aggressiveness. *Psychological Bulletin, 96,* 227–246.

Freedman, J. L., & Perlick, D. (1979). Crowding, contagion, and laughter. *Journal of Experimental Social Psychology, 15,* 295–303.

Freud, S. (1888–1939; reprinted 1963). In J. Strachey (Ed. & trans.), *The standard edition of the complete psychological works of Sigmund Freud.* London: Hogarth Press.

Freud, S. (1935; reprinted 1960). *A general introduction to psychoanalysis.* New York: Washington Square Press.

Friedman, M., & Ulmer, D. (1984). *Treating Type A behavior—And your heart.* New York: Knopf.

Frieze, I. H., Parsons, J. E., Johnson, P. B., Ruble, D. N., & Zellman, G. L. (1978). *Women and sex roles: A social psychological perspective.* New York: Norton.

Fritsch, G., & Hitzig, E. (1870; reprinted 1960). On the electrical excitability of the cerebrum. In G. Von Bonin (Trans.), *Some papers on the cerebral cortex.* Springfield, IL: Charles C Thomas.

Frodi, A., Macaulay, J., & Thome, P. R. (1977). Are women always less aggressive than men? A review of the experimental literature. *Psychological Bulletin, 84,* 634–660.

Fromkin, V., & Rodman, R. (1983). *An introduction to language* (3rd ed.). New York: Holt, Rinehart & Winston.

Furnham, A. (1982). Explanations for unemployment in Britain. *European Journal of Social Psychology, 12,* 335–352.

Gabrenya, W. K., Jr., Latané, B., & Wang, Y-E. (1983). Social loafing in cross-cultural perspective. *Journal of Cross-Cultural Psychology, 14,* 368–384.

Gabrielli, W. F., Jr., & Hutchings, B. (1984). Genetic influences in criminal convictions: Evidence from an adoption cohort. *Science, 224,* 891–894.

Galanter, E. (1962). Contemporary psychophysics. In R. Brown, E. Galanter, E. H. Hess, & G. Mandler (Eds.), *New directions in psychology.* New York: Holt, Rinehart & Winston.

Gallatin, J. (1980). Political thinking in adolescence. In J. Adelson (Ed.), *Handbook of adolescent psychology.* New York: Wiley.

Galloway, J. L. (1984, June 4). Crackdown on pornography—A no-win battle. *U.S. News & World Report,* pp. 84–85.

Gallup Poll (1978). Reported in Princeton Religion Research Center, *Emerging Trends, 1*(3).

Gallup, G. G., Jr. (1979). Self-awareness in primates. *American Scientist, 67,* 417–421.

Gallup, G. G., Jr. (1982). *Adventures in immortality.* New York: McGraw-Hill.

Gallup, G. G., Jr. (1984, March). Religion in America. *The Gallup Report,* No. 222.

Gallup Report (1984, August/September). Women in politics, pp. 2–14.

Galton, F. (1892). *Hereditary genius.* (2nd ed.). London: Macmillan.

Gardner, H. (1982). *Developmental psychology.* Boston: Little, Brown.

Gardner, H. (1983). *Frames of mind: The theory of multiple intelligences.* New York: Basic Books.

Gardner, H. & Dudai, Y. (1985). Biology and giftedness (Report of a workshop of the Social Science Research Council Committee on Development, Giftedness, and the Learning Process). *Items, 39* (1–2), 1–6.

Gardner, M. (1983, Summer). Lessons of a landmark PK hoax. *Skeptical Inquirer,* pp. 16–19.

Gardner, R. A., & Gardner, B. I. (1969). Teaching sign language to a chimpanzee. *Science, 165,* 664–672.

Gartrell, N. K. (1982). Hormones and homosexuality. In W. Paul, J. D. Weinrich, J. C. Gonsiorek, & M. E. Hotvedt (Eds.), *Homosexuality: Social, psychological, and biological issues.* Beverly Hills, CA: Sage.

Gatchel, R. J., & Baum, A. (1983). *An introduction to health psychology.* Reading, MA: Addison-Wesley.

Gazzaniga, M. S. (1967, August). The split brain in man. *Scientific American,* pp. 24–29.

Gazzaniga, M. S. (1983). Right hemisphere language following brain bisection: A 20-year perspective. *American Psychologist, 38,* 525–537.

Gazzaniga, M. S. (1984). Right hemisphere language: Remaining problems. *American Psychologist, 39,* 1494–1495.

Geen, R. G. (1984). Human motivation: New perspectives on old problems. In A. M. Rogers & C. J. Scheirer (Eds.), *The G. Stanley Hall Lecture Series* (Vol. 4). Washington, DC: American Psychological Association.

Geen, R. G., & Gange, J. J. (1983). Social facilitation: Drive theory and beyond. In H. H. Blumberg, A. P. Hare, V. Kent, & M. Davies (Eds.), *Small groups and social interaction* (Vol. 1). New York: Wiley.

Geen, R. G., & Quanty, M. B. (1977). The catharsis of aggression: An evaluation of a hypothesis. In L. Berkowitz (Ed.), *Advances in experimental social psychology* (Vol. 10). New York: Academic Press.

Geiwitz, J. (1980). *Psychology: Looking at ourselves* (2nd ed.). Boston: Little, Brown.

Geldard, F. A. (1972). *The human senses* (2nd ed.). New York: Wiley.

Gelman, R. (1979). Preschool thought. *American Psychologist, 34,* 900–905.

Gerard, R. W. (1953, September). What is memory? *Scientific American,* pp. 118–126.

Gergen, K. J. (1965). The effects of interaction goals and personalistic feedback on the presentation of self. *Journal of Personality and Social Psychology, 1,* 413–424.

Geschwind, N. (1979, September). Specializations of the human brain. *Scientific American,* pp. 180–199.

Geschwind, N., & Behan, P. O. (1984). Laterality, hormones, and immunity. In N. Geschwind & A. M. Galaburda (Eds.), *Cerebral dominance: The biological foundations.* Cambridge, MA: Harvard University Press.

Giambra, L. M. (1974). Daydreaming across the life span: Late adolescent to senior citizen. *Aging and Human Development, 5,* 115–140.

Gibson, E. J., & Walk, R. D. (1960, April). The "visual cliff." *Scientific American,* pp. 64–71.

Gibson, J. J. (1950). *The perception of the visual world.* Boston: Houghton Mifflin.

Giles, T. R. (1983). Probable superiority of behavioral interventions—II: Empirical status of the equivalence of therapies hypothesis. *Journal of Behavior Therapy and Experimental Psychiatry, 14,* 189–196.

Gilligan, C. (1982). *In a different voice: Psychological theory and women's development.* Cambridge, MA: Harvard University Press.

Gilling, D. & Brightwell, R. (1982). *The human brain.* New York: Facts on File.

Gjerde, P. F. (1983). Attentional capacity dysfunction and arousal in schizophrenia. *Psychological Bulletin, 93,* 57–72.

Gladue, B. A., Green, R., & Hellman, R. E. (1984). Neuroendocrine response to estrogen and sexual orientation. *Science, 225,* 1496–1499.

Glass, D. C., & Singer, J. E. (1972). *Urban stress.* New York: Academic Press.

Glick, I. O., Weiss, R. S., & Parkes, C. M. (1974). *The first year of bereavement.* New York: Wiley.

Godden, D. R., & Baddeley, A. D. (1975). Context-dependent memory in two natural environments: On land and underwater. *British Journal of Psychology, 66,* 325–331.

Goldberg, S. (1983). Parent-infant bonding: Another look. *Child Development, 54,* 1355–1382.

Goldfried, M. R. (1980). Toward the delineation of therapeutic change principles. *American Psychologist, 35,* 991–999.

Goldfried, M. R. (1982). On the history of therapeutic integration. *Behavior Therapy, 13,* 572–593.

Goldfried, M. R., & Padawer, W. (1982). Current status and future directions in psychotherapy. In M. R. Goldfried (Ed.), *Converging themes in psychotherapy: Trends in psychodynamic, humanistic, and behavioral practice.* New York: Springer.

Goldsmith, H. H. (1983). Genetic influences on personality from infancy to adulthood. *Child Development, 54,* 331–355.

Goleman, D. (1980, February). 1,528 little geniuses and how they grew. *Psychology Today,* pp. 28–53.

Goleman, D. (1985a, May 14). The torturer's mind: Complex view emerges. *The New York Times,* pp. C1, C5.

Goleman, D. (1985b, May 21). New focus on multiple personality. *The New York Times,* pp. C1, C6.

Golub, S. (1983). *Menarche: The transition from girl to woman.* Lexington, MA: Lexington Books.

Gonsiorek, J. C. (1982). Summary and conclusions. In W. Paul, J. D. Weinrich, J. C. Gonsiorek, & M. E. Hotvedt (Eds.), *Homosexuality: Social, psychological, and biological issues.* Beverly Hills, CA: Sage.

Goodman, W. (1982, August 9). Of

mice, monkeys and men. *Newsweek*, p. 61.

Gorman, M. E. (1984). Using the *Eden Express* to teach introductory psychology. *Teaching of Psychology, 11,* 39–40.

Gormezano, I., & Kehoe, E. J. (1975). Classical conditioning: Some methodological-conceptual issues. In W. K. Estes (Ed.), *Handbook of learning and cognitive processes: Vol. 2. Conditioning and behavior theory.* Hillsdale, NJ: Erlbaum.

Gould, J. L., & Gould, C. G. (1981, May). The instinct to learn. *Science 81,* 44–50.

Gould, R. L. (1978). *Transformations: Growth and change in adult life.* New York: Simon & Schuster.

Gould, S. J. (1981). *The mismeasure of man.* New York: Norton.

Gould, S. J. (1983, June 30). Genes on the brain. *New York Review of Books,* pp. 5, 6, 8, 10.

Graef, R., Csikszentmihalyi, M., & Gianinno, S. M. (1983). Measuring intrinsic motivation in everyday life. *Leisure Studies, 2,* 155–168.

Graham, J. D., & Vaupel, J. W. (1981). The value of life: What difference does it make? *Risk Analysis, 1,* 89–95.

Gray-Little, B., & Burks, N. (1983). Power and satisfaction in marriage: A review and critique. *Psychological Bulletin, 93,* 513–538.

Green, K. (1985). Personal communication, providing data from American Council on Education, U.C.L.A. annual survey.

Greenough, W. T., & Green, E. J. (1981). Experience and the changing brain. In J. L. McGaugh, J. G. March, & S. B. Kiesler (Eds.), *Aging: Biology and behavior.* New York: Academic Press.

Greenspan, E. (1983, August 28). Conditioning athletes' minds. *New York Times Magazine,* pp. 32–35.

Greenwald, A. (1984, June 12). Quoted by D. Goleman, A bias puts self at center of everything. *The New York Times,* pp. C1, C4.

Greenwald, A. G. (1975). Significance, nonsignificance, and interpretation of an ESP experiment. *Journal of Experimental Social Psychology, 11,* 180–191.

Greenwald, A. G., & Pratkanis, A. R. (1984). The self. In R. S. Wyer, & T. K. Srull (Eds.), *Handbook of social cognition.* Hillsdale, NJ: Erlbaum.

Greer, G. (1984, April). The uses of chastity and other paths to sexual pleasures. *MS,* pp. 53–60, 96.

Gregory, R. L. (1968, November). Visual illusions. *Scientific American,* pp. 66–76.

Gregory, R. L. (1978). *Eye and brain: The psychology of seeing* (3rd ed.). New York: McGraw-Hill.

Greif, E. B., & Ulman, K. J. (1982). The psychological impact of menarche on early adolescent females: A review of the literature. *Child Development, 53,* 1413–1430.

Grenier, P. L. (1984, April 8). On smashing the human skull: A convicted felon examines TV's part in a long obsession with violence. *Grand Rapids Press,* p. C1.

Griffin, D. R. (1984). Animal thinking. *American Scientist, 72,* 456–464.

Grobstein, C. (1979, June). External human fertilization. *Scientific American,* pp. 57–67.

Gross, A. E., & Crofton, C. (1977). What is good is beautiful. *Sociometry, 40,* 85–90.

Gross, A. E., & Fleming, I. (1982). Twenty years of deception in social psychology. *Personality and Social Psychology Bulletin, 8,* 402–408.

Grossman, S. P. (1979). The biology of motivation. *Annual Review of Psychology, 30,* 209–242.

Gruder, C. L. (1977). Choice of comparison persons in evaluating oneself. In J. M. Suls & R. L. Miller (Eds.), *Social comparison processes.* New York: Hemisphere.

Gulevich, G., Dement, W., & Johnson, L. (1966). Psychiatric and EEG observations on a case of prolonged (264 hours) wakefulness. *Archives of General Psychiatry, 15,* 29–35.

Gustavson, C. R., Garcia, J., Hankins, W. G., & Rusiniak, K. W. (1974). Coyote predation control by aversive conditioning. *Science, 184,* 581–583.

Gutierres, S. E., Kenrick, D. T., & Goldberg, L. (1985, May). *Adverse influence on exposure to popular erotica: Effects on judgments of others and judgments of one's spouse.* Paper presented at the meeting of the Midwestern Psychological Association, Chicago, IL.

Gutmann, D. (1977). The cross-cultural perspective: Notes toward a comparative psychology of aging. In J. E. Birren & K. Warner Schaie (Eds.), *Handbook of the psychology of aging.* New York: Van Nostrand Reinhold.

Guttentag, M., & Secord, P. F. (1983). *Too many women? The sex ratio question.* Beverly Hills, CA: Sage.

Haber, R. N. (1970, May). How we remember what we see. *Scientific American,* pp. 104–112.

Hall, C. S. (1984). "A ubiquitous sex difference in dreams" revisited. *Journal of Personality and Social Psychology, 46,* 1109–1117.

Hall, C. S., & Lindzey, G. (1978). *Theories of personality* (2nd ed.). New York: Wiley.

Hall, C. S., & Van de Castle, R. L. (1966). *The content analysis of dreams.* New York: Appleton-Century-Crofts.

Hall, C. S., Dornhoff, W., Blick, K. A., & Weesner, K. E. (1982). The dreams of college men and women in 1950 and 1980: A comparison of dream contents and sex differences. *Sleep, 5,* 188–194.

Hall, G. S. (1904). *Adolescence: Its psychology and its relations to physiology, anthropology, sex, crime, religion and education* (Vol. I). New York: Appleton-Century-Crofts.

Halpern, D. (1984). *Thought and knowledge: An introduction to critical thinking.* Hillsdale, NJ: Erlbaum.

Hamill, R., Wilson, T. D., & Nisbett, R. E. (1980). Insensitivity to sample bias: Generalizing from atypical cases. *Journal of Personality and Social Psychology, 39,* 578–589.

Hammersmith, S. K. (1982, August). *Sexual preference: An empirical study from the Alfred C. Kinsey Institute for Sex Research.* Paper presented at the meeting of the American Psychological Association, Washington, D.C.

Hans, V. P., & Slater, D. (1983). John Hinckley, Jr. and the insanity defense: The public's verdict. *Public Opinion Quarterly, 47,* 202–212.

Hansel, C. E. M. (1980). *ESP and parapsychology: A critical reevaluation.* Buffalo, NY: Prometheus.

Hardin, G. (1968). The tragedy of the commons. *Science, 162,* 1243–1248.

Hardyck, C. & Petrinovich, L. F. (1977). Left-handedness. *Psychological Bulletin, 84,* 385–404.

Hare, R. D. (1975). Psychophysiological studies of psychopathy. In D. C. Fowles (Ed.), *Clinical applications of psychophysiology.* New York: Columbia University Press.

Harlow, H. F., Harlow, M. K., & Suomi, S. J. (1971). From thought to therapy: Lessons from a primate laboratory. *American Scientist, 59,* 538–549.

Harre, R., & Lamb, R. (1983). *The encyclopedic dictionary of psychology.* Cambridge, MA: MIT Press.

Harris, B. (1979). Whatever happened to Little Albert? *American Psychologist, 34,* 151–160.

Harris, L. J. (1978). Sex differences in spatial ability: Possible environmental, genetic, and neurological factors. In M. Kinsbourne (Ed.), *The asymmetrical function of the brain.* New York: Cambridge University Press.

Hartmann, E. (1981, April). The strangest sleep disorder. *Psychology Today,* pp. 14, 16, 18.

Hartshorne, H., & May, M. A. (1928a). *Studies in the nature of character* (Vol. 1). New York: Macmillan.

Hartshorne, H., & May, M. A. (1928b). *Studies in deceit.* New York: Macmillan.

Hasher, L., & Zacks, R. T. (1979). Automatic and effortful processes in memory. *Journal of Experimental Psychology: General, 108,* 356–388.

Hatfield, E., & Sprecher, S. (1986). *Mirror, mirror . . . The importance of looks in everyday life.* Albany: State University of New York Press.

Hatfield, E., Traupmann, J., & Sprecher, S. (1984). Older women's perceptions of their intimate relationships. *Journal of Social and Clinical Psychology, 2,* 108–124.

Hatfield, E., & Walster, G. W. (1978). *A new look at love.* Reading, MA: Addison-Wesley.

Hathaway, S. R. (1960). *An MMPI Handbook* (Vol. 1, Foreword). Minneapolis: University of Minnesota Press. (Revised edition, 1972)

Hattie, J. A., Sharpley, C. F., & Rogers, H. J. (1984). Comparative effectiveness of professional and paraprofessional helpers. *Psychological Bulletin, 95,* 534–541.

Hayes, C. (1951). *The ape in our house.* New York: Harper & Row.

Hayes, J. R. (1981). *The complete problem solver.* Philadelphia: Franklin Institute Press.

Haynes, S. G., Feinleib, M., & Kannel, W. B. (1980). The relationships of psychosocial factors to coronary disease in the Framingham Study. III. Eight-year incidence of coronary heart disease. *American Journal of Epidemiology, 111,* 37–58.

Hebb, D. O. (1980). *Essay on mind.* Hillsdale, NJ: Erlbaum.

Heiman, J. R. (1975, April). The physiology of erotica: Women's sexual arousal. *Psychology Today,* 90–94.

Hellman, P. (1980). *Avenue of the righteous of nations.* New York: Atheneum.

Herman, C. P., & Mack, D. (1975). Restrained and unrestrained eating. *Journal of Personality, 43,* 647–660.

Herman, C. P., Olmsted, M. P., & Polivy, J. (1983). Obesity, externality, and susceptibility to social influence: An integrated analysis. *Journal of Personality and Social Psychology, 45,* 926–934.

Herman, C. P., & Polivy, J. (1980). Restrained eating. In A. J. Stunkard (Ed.), *Obesity.* Philadelphia: Saunders.

Heron, W. (1957, January). The pathology of boredom. *Scientific American,* pp. 52–56.

Herzog, A. R., Rogers, W. L., & Woodworth, J. (1982). *Subjective well-being among different age groups.* Ann Arbor: Institute for Social Research, University of Michigan.

Hess, E. H. (1956, July). Space perception in the chick. *Scientific American,* pp. 71–80.

Hetherington, E. M. (1979). Divorce: A child's perspective. *American Psychologist, 34,* 851–858.

Hewitt, J. K. (1984). Normal components of personality variation. *Journal of Personality and Social Psychology, 47,* 671–675.

Hicks, R. A., & Gaus, W. (1983). Type A-Type B behavior and daily milk consumption in college students. *Bulletin of the Psychonomic Society, 21,* 259.

Hicks, R. A., Kilcourse, J., & Sinnott, M. A. (1983). Type A-B behavior and caffeine use in college students. *Psychological Reports, 52,* 338.

Hicks, R. A., & Pellegrini, R. J. (1982). Sleep problems and Type A-B behavior in college students. *Psychological Reports, 51,* 196.

Hilgard, E. R. (1977). *Divided consciousness: Multiple controls in human thought and action.* New York: Wiley.

Hilgard, E. R. (1983, August). *Dissociation theory and hypnosis.* Paper presented at the meeting of the American Psychological Association, Anaheim, CA.

Hinde, R. A. (1984). Why do the sexes behave differently in close relationships? *Journal of Social and Personal Relationships, 1,* 471–501.

Hines, M. (1982). Prenatal gonadal hormones and sex differences in human behavior. *Psychological Bulletin, 92,* 56–80.

Hintzman, D. L. (1978). *The psychology of learning and memory.* San Francisco: Freeman.

Hobson, J. A. (1980, May/June). Quoted by Kiester, E., Jr., Images of the night. *Science 80,* pp. 36–43.

Hohmann, G. W. (1966). Some effects of spinal cord lesions on experienced emotional feelings. *Psychophysiology, 3,* 143–156.

Hokanson, J. E., & Edelman, R. (1966). Effects of three social responses on vascular processes. *Journal of Personality and Social Psychology, 3,* 442–447.

Holden, C. (1980a). Identical twins reared apart. *Science, 207,* 1323–1325.

Holden, C. (1980b, November). Twins reunited. *Science 80,* pp. 55–59.

Holden C. (1985, January). Genes, personality, and alcoholism. *Psychology Today,* pp. 38–44.

Holmes, D. S. (1978). Projection as a defense mechanism. *Psychological Bulletin, 85,* 677–688.

Holmes, D. S. (1981). Existence of classical projection and the stress-reducing function of attributive projection: A reply to Sherwood. *Psychological Bulletin, 90,* 460–466.

Holmes, D. S. (1984). Meditation and somatic arousal reduction: A review of the experimental evidence. *American Psychologist, 39,* 1–10.

Holmes, D. S. (1985). To meditate or rest? The answer is rest. *American Psychologist, 40,* 728–731.

Holmes, T. H., & Rahe, R. H. (1967). The social readjustment rating scale. *Journal of Psychosomatic Research, 11,* 213–218.

Hooykaas, R. (1972). *Religion and the rise of modern science.* Grand Rapids, MI: Eerdmans.

Horn, J. L. (1970). Organization of data on life-span development of human abilities. In L. R. Goulet & P. Baltes (Eds.), *Life-span developmental psychology: Research and theory.* New York: Academic Press.

Horn, J. L. (1982). The aging of human abilities. In J. Wolman (Ed.), *Handbook of developmental psychology.* Englewood Cliffs, NJ: Prentice-Hall.

Horn, J. M. (1982). Unwelcome environmentalism? *Contemporary Psychology, 27,* 117–118.

Horner, M. S. (1972). Toward an understanding of achievement-related conflicts in women. *Journal of Social Issues, 28*(2), 157–175.

House, J. S. (1984, Autumn). Social support. *ISR Newsletter,* pp. 5–6.

Hubel, D. H. (1979, September). The brain. *Scientific American,* pp. 45–53.

Hubel, D. H., & Wiesel, T. N. (1979, September). Brain mechanisms of vision. *Scientific American,* pp. 150–162.

Huesmann, L. R., Eron, L. D., Lefkowitz, M. M., & Walder, L. O. (1984). Stability of aggression over time and generations. *Developmental Psychology, 20,* 1120–1134.

Hunt, E. (1983). On the nature of intelligence. *Science, 219,* 141–146.

Hunt, J. M. (1982). Toward equalizing the developmental opportunities of infants and preschool children. *Journal of Social Issues, 38*(4), 163–191.

Hunt, M. (1974). *Sexual behavior in the 1970s.* Chicago: Playboy Press.

Hunt, M. (1982a). *The universe within.* New York: Simon and Schuster.

Hunt, M. (1982b, September 12). Research through deception. *The New York Times Magazine,* pp. 66–67, 138–143.

Hyde, J. S. (1981). How large are cognitive gender differences? A meta-analysis using w^2 and *d. American Psychologist, 36,* 892–901.

Hyde, J. S. (1983, November). *Bem's gender schema theory.* Paper presented at GLCA Women's Studies Conference, Rochester, IN.

Hyde, J. S. (1984a, July). Children's understanding of sexist language. *Developmental Psychology, 20*(4), 697–706.

Hyde, J. S. (1984b). How large are cognitive gender differences in aggression? A developmental meta-analysis. *Developmental Psychology, 20,* 722–736.

Hyde, J. S. (1986). *Understanding human sexuality* (3rd. ed.). New York: McGraw-Hill.

Hyman, R. (1981). Cold reading: How to convince strangers that you know all about them. In K. Frazier (Ed.), *Paranormal borderlands of science.* Buffalo, NY: Prometheus.

ISR Newsletter (1982, Winter). *Women's well-being at midlife.* Ann Arbor: Institute for Social Research, University of Michigan, pp. 5–6.

ISR Newsletter (1983, Fall). *Teenage drug use. Ann Arbor:* Institute for Social Research, University of Michigan, p. 3.

Ickes, W., Patterson, M. L., Rajecki, D. W., & Tanford, S. (1982). Behavioral and cognitive consequences of reciprocal versus compensatory responses to preinteraction expectancies. *Social Cognition, 1,* 160–190.

Ingham, A. G., Levinger, G., Graves, J., & Peckham, V. (1974). The Ringelmann effect: Studies of group size and group performance. *Journal of Experimental Social Psychology, 10,* 371–384.

Inglis, J., & Lawson, J. S. (1982). Sex differences in the functional asymmetry of the damaged brain. *Behavioral and Brain Sciences, 5,* 307–309.

Inhelder, B., & Piaget, J. (1958). *The growth of logical thinking.* New York: Basic.

Insel, P. M., & Roth, W. T. (1976). *Health in a changing society.* Palo Alto, CA: Mayfield.

Institute of Medicine (1982). *Health and behavior: Frontiers of research in the biobehavioral sciences.* Washington, DC: National Academy Press.

Isen, A. M., & Means, B. (1983). The influence of positive affect on decision-making strategy. *Social Cognition, 2,* 28–31.

Istvan, J. & Matarazzo, J. D. (1984). Tobacco, alcohol, and caffeine use: A review of their interrelationships. *Psychological Bulletin, 95,* 301–326.

Izard, C. E. (1977). *Human emotions.* New York: Plenum Press.

Izard, C. E. (1982). The psychology of emotion comes of age on the coattails of Darwin. *Contemporary Psychology, 27,* 426–429.

Jacklin, C. N., & Maccoby, E. E. (1978). Social behavior at 33 months in same-sex and mixed-sex dyads. *Child Development, 27,* 239–247.

James W. (1890). *The principles of psychology* (Vol. 2). New York: Holt.

James W. (1902; reprinted 1958). *Varieties of religious experience.* New York: Mentor Books.

Janis, I. L. (1969). *Stress and frustration.* New York: Harcourt Brace Jovanovich.

Janis, I. L. (1982a). *Groupthink: Psychological studies of policy decisions and fiascoes.* Boston: Houghton Mifflin.

Janis, I. L. (Ed.) (1982b). *Counseling on personal decisions: Theory and research on short-term helping relationships.* New Haven: Yale University Press.

Janis, I. L. (1983). Stress inoculation in health care: Theory and research. In D. Meichenbaum & M. E. Jaremko (Eds.), *Stress reeducation and prevention.* New York: Plenum Press.

Jarvik, L. F. (1975). Thoughts on the psychobiology of aging. *American Psychologist, 30,* 576–583.

Jaynes, J. (1976). *The origin of consciousness in the breakdown of the bicameral mind.* Boston: Houghton Mifflin.

Jeffery, R. W., & Wing, R. R. (1983). Recidivism and self-cure of smoking and obesity: Data from population studies. *American Psychologist, 38,* 852.

Jemmott, J. B., III, & Locke, S. E. (1984). Psychosocial factors, immunologic mediation, and human susceptibility to infectious diseases: How much do we know? *Psychological Bulletin, 95,* 78–108.

Jenkins, J. G., & Dallenbach, K. M. (1924). Obliviscence during sleep and waking. *American Journal of Psychology, 35,* 605–612.

Jenni, D. A., & Jenni, M. A. (1976). Carrying behavior in humans: Analysis of sex differences. *Science, 194,* 859–860.

Jensen, A. R. (1980). *Bias in mental testing.* New York: The Free Press.

Jensen, A. R. (1983, August). *The nature of the black-white difference on various psychometric tests: Spearman's hypothesis.* Paper presented at the meeting of the American Psychological Association, Anaheim, CA.

Jensen, A. R. (1984, March). Political ideologies and educational research. *Phi Delta Kappan,* pp. 460–462.

Jepson, C., Krantz, D. H., & Nisbett, R. E. (1983). Inductive reasoning: Competence or skill. *The Behavioral and Brain Sciences, 3,* 494–501.

Jervis, R. (1976). *Perception and misperception in international politics.* Princeton: Princeton University Press.

Jervis, R. (1985, April 2). Quoted by D. Goleman, Political forces come under new scrutiny of psychology. *The New York Times,* pp. C1, C4.

Johnson, D., & Drenick, E. J. (1977). Therapeutic fasting in morbid obesity. Long-term follow-up. *Archives of Internal Medicine, 137,* 1381–1382.

Johnson, E. J., & Tversky, A. (1983). Affect, generalization, and the perception of risk. *Journal of Personality and Social Psychology, 45,* 20–31.

Johnston, L. D., O'Malley, P. M., & Bachman, J. G. (1985). *Use of licit and illicit drugs by America's high school students 1975–1984.* Rockville, MD: Superintendent of Documents: National Institute on Drug Abuse, U. S. Department of Health and Human Services (No. ADM 85-1394).

Jones, L. V. (1984). White-black achievement differences: The narrowing gap. *American Psychologist, 39,* 1207–1213.

Jones, M. C. (1924). A laboratory study of fear: The case of Peter. *Journal of Genetic Psychology, 31,* 308–315.

Jones, M. C. (1957). The later careers of boys who were early or late maturing. *Child Development, 28,* 113–128.

Jones, W. H., Carpenter, B. N., & Quintana, D. (1985). Personality and interpersonal predictors of loneliness in two cultures. *Journal of Personality and Social Psychology, 48,* 1503–1511.

Jones, W. H., Russell, D. W., & Nickel, T. W. (1977). Belief in the paranormal scale: An objective instrument to measure belief in magical phenomena and causes (Ms. No. 1577). *JSAS Catalog of Selected Documents in Psychology, 7,* 100.

Jorgenson, D. O., & Papciak, A. S. (1981). The effects of communication, resource feedback, and identifiability on behavior in a simulated commons. *Journal of Experimental Social Psychology, 17,* 373–385.

Judd, C. M., Kenny, D. A., & Krosnick, J. A. (1983). Judging the positions of political candidates: Models of assimilation and contrast. *Journal of Personality and Social Psychology, 44,* 952–963.

Jung, C. (1933). *Modern man in search of a soul.* New York: Harcourt Brace Jovanovich.

Jung, J. (1984). Social support and its relation to health: A critical evaluation. *Basic and Applied Social Psychology, 5,* 143–169.

Justice, A. (1985). Review of the effects of stress on cancer in laboratory animals: Importance of time of stress application and type of tumor. *Psychological Bulletin, 98,* 108–138.

Kagan, J. (1976). Emergent themes in human development. *American Scientist, 64,* 186–196.

Kagan, J. (1978, January). The baby's elastic mind. *Human Nature,* pp. 66–73.

Kagan, J. (1979, April). Growing by leaps: The form of early development. *The Sciences,* pp. 6–9, 23.

Kagan, J. (1982, July). The fearful child's hidden talents (interview with E. Hall). *Psychology Today,* pp. 50–59.

Kahneman, D. (1973). *Attention and effort.* Englewood Cliffs, NJ: Prentice-Hall.

Kahneman, D. (1985, June). Quoted by K. McKean, Decisions, decisions. *Discover,* pp. 22–31.

Kahneman, D., Slovic, P., & Tversky, A. (Eds.) (1982). *Judgment under uncertainty: Heuristics and biases.* New York: Cambridge University Press.

Kahneman, D., & Tversky, A. (1972). Subjective probability: A judgment of representativeness. *Cognitive Psychology, 3,* 430–454.

Kahneman, D., & Tversky, A. (1979). Intuitive prediction: Biases and corrective procedures. *Management Science, 12,* 313–327.

Kahnenan, D., & Tverksy, A. (1984). Choices, values, and frames. *American Psychologist, 39,* 341–350.

Kandel, E. R., & Schwartz, J. H. (1982). Molecular biology of learning: Modulation of transmitter release. *Science, 218,* 433–443.

Kaplan, H. I., & Saddock, B. J. (1981). *Modern synopsis of comprehensive textbook of psychiatry* (3rd ed.). Baltimore: Williams & Wilkins.

Kaplan, H. S. (1979). *Disorders of sexual desire.* New York: Brunner/Mazel.

Kaplan, R. M. (1984). The connection between clinical health promotion and health status: A critical overview. *American Psychologist, 39,* 755–765.

Karacan, I. Aslan, C., & Hirshkowitz, M. (1983). Erectile mechanisms in man. *Science, 220,* 1080–1082.

Kastenbaum, R., & Costa, P. T. (1977). Psychological perspectives on death. *Annual Review of Psychology, 28,* 225–249.

Kaufman, L. (1979). *Perception: The world transformed.* New York: Oxford University Press.

Kazdin, A. E. (1982). The token economy: A decade later. *Journal of Applied Behavior Analysis, 15,* 431–445.

Keesey, R. E. (1978). Set-points and body weight regulation. *Psychiatric Clinics of North America, 1,* 523–543.

Keesey, R. E., & Corbett, S. W. (1983). Metabolic defense of the body weight set-point. In A. J. Stunkard & E. Stellar (Eds.), *Eating and its disorders.* New York: Raven Press.

Kelley, K., & Byrne, D. (1983). Assessment of sexual responding: Arousal, affect, and behavior. In J. Cacioppo & R. Petty (Eds.), *Social psychophysiology.* New York: Guilford Press.

Kelling, S. T., & Halpern, B. P. (1983). Taste flashes: Reaction times, intensity, and quality. *Science, 219,* 412–414.

Kellogg, W. N., & Kellogg, L. A. (1933). *The ape and the child.* New York: McGraw-Hill.

Kelly, E. L. (1955). Consistency of the adult personality. *American Psychologist, 10,* 659–681.

Kelly, E. L., & Fiske, D. W. (1951). *The prediction of performance in clinical psychology.* Ann Arbor: University of Michigan Press.

Kempe, R. S., & Kempe, C. C. (1978). *Child abuse.* Cambridge, MA: Harvard University Press.

Kennedy, E. M. (1984). The challenges before us. *American Psychologist, 39,* 62–66.

Kennell, J. N., & Klaus, M. (1982). *Parent-infant bonding.* St. Louis: C. V. Mosby.

Kenrick, D. T., & Gutierres, S. E. (1980). Contrast effects and judgments of physical attractiveness: When beauty becomes a social problem. *Journal of Personality and Social Psychology, 38,* 131–140.

Kenrick, D. T., & Stringfield, D. O. (1980). Personality traits and the eye of the beholder: Crossing some traditional philosophical boundaries in the search for consistency in all of the people. *Psychological Review, 87,* 88–104.

Kenrick, D. T., & Trost, M. R. (in press). A biosocial model of heterosexual relationships. In D. Byrne & K. Kelly (Eds.), *Males, females, and sexuality.* Albany: State University of New York Press.

Kerckhoff, A., & Back, K. (1968). *The June bug: A study of hysterical contagion.* New York: Appleton-Century-Crofts.

Kerr, N. L., & Bruun, S. E. (1983). Dispensability of member effort and group motivation losses: Free-rider effects. *Journal of Personality and Social Psychology, 44,* 78–94.

Kessler, M., & Albee, G. (1975). Primary prevention. *Annual Review of Psychology, 26,* 557–591.

Kett, J. F. (1977). *Rites of passage: Adolescence in America, 1790 to the present.* New York: Basic Books.

Keys, A., Brozek, J., Henschel, A., Mickelsen, O., & Taylor, H. L. (1950). *The biology of human starvation.* Minneapolis: University of Minnesota Press.

Kihlstrom, J. (1985). Hypnosis. *Annual Review of Psychology, 36,* 385–418.

Kimble, G. A. (1956). *Principles of general psychology.* New York: Ronald Press.

Kimble, G. A. (1981). Biological and cognitive constraints on learning. In L. T. Benjamin, Jr. (Ed.), *The G. Stanley Hall Lecture Series* (Vol. 1). Washington, DC: American Psychological Association.

Kimura, D. (1973, March). The asymmetry of the human brain. *Scientific American,* pp. 70–78.

Kimura, D., & Harshman, R. A. (1984). Sex differences in brain organization for verbal and non-verbal functions. In G. J. deVries, J. P. C. deBruin, M. B. M. Uylings, & M. A. Corner (Eds.), *Progress in Brain Research* (Vol. 61, pp. 423–441). Amsterdam: Elsevier Biomedical Press.

Kimzey, S. L. (1975). The effects of extended spaceflight on hematologic and immunologic systems. *Journal of the American Medical Women's Association, 30*(5), 218–232.

Kimzey, S. L., Johnson, P. C., Ritzman, S. E., & Mengel, C. E. (1976, April). Hematology and immunology studies: The second manned Skylab mission. *Aviation, Space, and Environmental Medicine,* pp. 383–390.

King, N. J., & Montgomery, R. B. (1980). Biofeedback-induced control of human peripheral temperature: A critical review of the literature. *Psychological Bulletin, 88,* 738–752.

Kinsey, A. C., Pomeroy, W., & Martin, C. (1948). *Sexual behavior in the human male.* Philadelphia: Saunders.

Kinsey, A. C., Pomeroy, W., Martin, C., & Gebhard, P. (1953). *Sexual behavior in the human female.* Philadelphia: Saunders.

Klaus, M. (1982, January/February). Quoted by R. Restak, Newborn knowledge. *Science 82,* pp. 58–65.

Kleinmuntz, B., & Szucko, J. J. (1984). A field study of the fallability of polygraph lie detection. *Nature, 308,* 449–450.

Kleitman, N. (1960, November). Patterns of dreaming. *Scientific American,* pp. 82–88.

Klerman, G. L. (1983). The efficacy of psychotherapy as the basis for public policy. *American Psychologist, 38,* 929–934.

Kline, D., & Schieber, F. (1985). Vision and aging. In J. E. Birren & K. W. Schaie (Eds.), *Handbook of the psychology of aging.* New York: Van Nostrand Reinhold.

Kline, N. S. (1974). *From sad to glad.* New York: Ballantine Books.

Klineberg, O. (1938). Emotional expression in Chinese literature. *Journal of Abnormal and Social Psychology, 33,* 517–520.

Klineberg, O. (1984). Public opinion and nuclear war. *American Psychologist, 39,* 1245–1253.

Kluckhohn, C., & Murray, H. A. (1956). Personality formation: The determinants. In C. Kluckhohn, H. A. Murray, & D. Schneider (Eds.), *Personality in nature, society, and culture* (2nd ed.). New York: Knopf.

Kluver, H., & Bucy, P. C. (1939). Preliminary analysis of functions of the temporal lobes in monkeys. *Archives of Neurology and Psychiatry, 42,* 979–1000.

Kobasa, S. C. (1979). Stressful life events, personality, and health: An inquiry into hardiness. *Journal of Personality and Social Psychology, 37,* 1–11.

Kohlberg, L. (1966). A cognitive-developmental analysis of children's sex-role concepts and attitudes. In E. E. Maccoby (Ed.), *The development of sex differences.* Stanford, CA: Stanford University Press.

Kohlberg, L. (1981). *The philosophy of moral development: Essays on moral development* (Vol. I). San Franscisco: Harper & Row.

Kohlberg, L. (1984). *The psychology of moral development: Essays on moral development* (Vol. II). San Francisco: Harper & Row.

Kohler, I. (1962, May). Experiments with goggles. *Scientific American*, pp. 62–72.

Köhler, W. (1925; reprinted 1957). *The mentality of apes.* London: Pelican.

Kolata, G. (1982). Food affects human behavior. *Science, 218,* 1209–1210.

Kolata, G. (1983). Brain-grafting work shows promise. *Science, 221,* 1277.

Kolata, G. (1984). Lowered cholesterol decreases heart disease. *Science, 223,* 381–382.

Kolata, G. (1985a). Obesity declared a disease. *Science, 227,* 1019–1020.

Kolata, G. (1985b). A guarded endorsement for shock therapy. *Science, 228,* 1510–1511.

Kolers, P. A. (1975). Specificity of operations in sentence recognition. *Cognitive Psychology, 7,* 289–306.

Koltz, C. (1983, December). Scapegoating. *Psychology Today,* pp. 68–69.

Korte, C. (1980). Urban-nonurban differences in social behavior and social psychological models of urban impact. *Journal of Social Issues, 36,* 29–51.

Krafft-Ebing, R. von (1886; reprinted 1892). In C. G. Chaddock (Trans.), *Psychopathia sexualis.* Philadelphia: F. A. Davis.

Krantz, D. S., Grunberg, N. E., & Baum, A. (1985). Health psychology. *Annual Review of Psychology, 36,* 349–383.

Krantz, D. S., & Manuck, S. B. (1984). Acute psychophysiologic reactivity and risk of cardiovascular disease: A review and methodologic critique. *Psychological Bulletin, 96,* 435–464.

Kubler-Ross, E. (1969). *On death and dying.* New York: Macmillan.

Kulik, J. A., Bangert-Drowns, R. L., & Kulik, C-L. C. (1984). Effectiveness of coaching for aptitude tests. *Psychological Bulletin, 95,* 179–188.

Kulik, J. A., Kulik, C. C., & Cohen, P. A. (1980). Effectiveness of computer-based college teaching: A meta-analysis of findings. *Review of Educational Research, 50,* 525–544.

Kulik, J. A., Kulik, C. C., & Gangert-Drowns, R. L. (1985). Effectiveness of computer-based education in elementary schools. *Computers in Human Behavior, 1,* 59–74.

Kunst-Wilson, W. R., & Zajonc, R. B. (1980). Affective discrimination of stimuli that cannot be recognized. *Science, 207,* 557–558.

Kurtz, P. (1983, Spring). Stars, planets, and people. *The Skeptical Inquirer,* pp. 65–68.

Kurzweil, R. (1985). What is artificial intelligence anyway? *American Scientist, 73,* 258–264.

Labbe, R., Firl, A., Jr., Mufson, E. J., & Stein, D. G. (1983). Fetal brain transplants: Reduction of cognitive deficits in rats with frontal cortex lesions. *Science, 221,* 470–472.

Labouvie-Vief, G., & Schell, D. A. (1982). Learning and memory in later life. In B. B. Wolman (Ed.), *Handbook of developmental psychology.* Englewood Cliffs, NJ: Prentice-Hall.

Ladd, G. T. (1887). *Elements of physiological psychology.* New York: Scribner's.

Lagerspetz, K. (1979). Modification of aggressiveness in mice. In S. Feshbach & A. Fraczek (Eds.), *Aggression & behavior change: Biological & social processes.* New York: Praeger.

Lagerweij, E., Nelis, P. C., van Ree, J. M., & Wiegant, V. M. (1984). The twitch in horses: A variant of acupuncture. *Science, 225,* 1172–1174.

Laird, J. D. (1974). Self-attribution of emotion: The effects of expressive behavior on the quality of emotional experience. *Journal of Personality and Social Psychology, 29,* 475–486.

Laird, J. D. (1984). The real role of facial response in the experience of emotion: A reply to Tourangeau and Ellsworth, and others. *Journal of Personality and Social Psychology, 47,* 909–917.

Lamb, M. (1979, June 17). Quoted by G. Collins, A new look at life with father. *New York Times Magazine,* pp. 30–31, 48–52, 65.

Lamb, M. (1982, April). Second thoughts on first touch. *Psychology Today,* pp. 9–11.

Lamb, M. E., Thompson, R. A., Gardner, W. P., Charnov, E. L., & Estes, D. (1984). Security of infantile attachment as assessed by the "strange situation": Its study and biological interpretation. *Behavioral and Brain Sciences, 7,* 127–171.

Lancioni, G. (1980). Infant operant conditioning and its implications for early intervention. *Psychological Bulletin, 88,* 516–534.

Langer, E., & Abelson, R. P. (1974). A patient by any other name . . .: Clinician group differences in labeling bias. *Journal of Consulting and Clinical Psychology, 42,* 4 9.

Langer, E., & Imber, L. (1980). The role of mindlessness in the perception of deviance. *Journal of Personality and Social Psychology, 39,* 360–367.

Langer, E. J. (1983). *The psychology of control.* Beverly Hills, CA: Sage.

Langone, J. (1981, February). Girth of a nation. *Discover,* pp. 56–60.

Larrance, D. T., & Twentyman, C. T. (1983). Maternal attributions and child abuse. *Journal of Abnormal Psychology, 92,* 449–457.

Larson, R. (1978). Thirty years of research on the subjective well-being of older Americans. *Journal of Gerontology, 33,* 109–125.

Lashley, K. S. (1950). In search of the engram. In *Symposium of the Society for Experimental Biology* (Vol. 4). New York: Cambridge University Press.

Latané, B. (1981). The psychology of social impact. *American Psychologist, 36,* 343–356.

Latané, B., Dabbs, J. M., Jr. (1975). Sex, group size and helping in three cities. *Sociometry, 38,* 180–194.

Latimer, P. R., & Sweet, A. A. (1984). Cognitive versus behavioral procedures in cognitive-behavior therapy: A critical review of the evidence. *Journal of Behavior Therapy and Experimental Psychiatry, 15,* 9–22.

Laudenslager, M. L., & Reite, M. L. (1984). Losses and separations: Immunological consequences and health implications. *Review of Personality and Social Psychology, 5,* 285–312.

Laurence, J-R., & Perry, C. (1983). Hypnotically created memory among highly hypnotizable subjects. *Science, 222,* 523–524.

Layden, M. A. (1982). Attributional therapy. In C. Antaki & C. Brewin (Eds.), *Attributions and psychological change: Applications of attributional theories to clinical and educational practice.* London: Academic Press.

Layton, B. D., & Turnbull, B. (1975). Belief, evaluation, and performance on an ESP task. *Journal of Experimental Social Psychology, 11,* 166–179.

Lazarus, R. S. (1982). Thoughts on the relations between emotion and cognition. *American Psychologist, 37,* 1019–1024.

Lazarus, R. S. (1984). On the primacy of cognition. *American Psychologist, 39,* 124–129.

Lazarus, R. S., & Folkman, S. (1984). *Stress, appraisal, and coping.* New York: Springer.

Lebow, J. (1982). Consumer satisfaction with mental health treatment. *Psychological Bulletin, 91,* 244–259.

Ledwidge, B. (1980). Run for your mind: Aerobic exercise as a means of alleviating anxiety and depression. *Canadian Journal of Behavioural Science, 13,* 126–140.

Leepson, M. (1983, May 27). Chronic pain: The hidden epidemic. *Editorial Research Reports, 1*(20). (Published by Congressional Quarterly, Inc.)

Lefcourt, H. H. (1982). *Locus of control: Current trends in theory and research.* Hillsdale, NJ: Erlbaum.

Lehman, D. R., Wortman, C. B., & Williams, A. F. (1985). *Long-term effects of losing a spouse or child in a motor vehicle crash.* Unpublished manuscript, Institute for Social Research, University of Michigan, Ann Arbor.

Lenneberg, E. H. (1967). *Biological foundations of language.* New York: Wiley.

Lepper, M. R. (1982, August). *Microcomputers in education: Motivational and social issues.* Paper presented at the meeting of the American Psychological Association, Washington, DC.

Lepper, M. R., & Greene, D. (Eds.) (1979). *The hidden costs of reward.* Hillsdale, NJ: Erlbaum.

Lerner, M. J. (1980). *The belief in a just world: A fundamental delusion.* New York: Plenum Press.

Lerner, R. M. (1983, August). *Children and adolescents as producers of their own development: The sample case of temperament.* Paper presented at the meeting of the American Psychological Association, Anaheim, CA.

Lettvin, J. Y., Maturana, H. R., McCulloch, W. S., & Pitts, W. H. (1959). What the frog's eye tells the frog's brain. *Proceedings of the Institute of Radio Engineers, 47,* 1940–1951.

Leventhal, H., Meyer, D., & Nerenz, D. (1980). The common sense representation of illness danger. In S. Rachman (Ed.), *Medical psychology* (Vol. II). Oxford, England: Pergamon Press.

Leventhal, H., Zimmerman, R., & Gutmann, M. (1984). Compliance: A self-regulation perspective. In D. Gentry (Ed.), *Handbook of behavioral medicine.* New York: Guilford Press.

Levin, B. S. (1980). *Women and medicine.* Metuchen, NJ: Scarecrow Press.

Levinson, D. J., Darow, C. N., Klein, E. B., Levinson, M. H., & McKee, B. (1978). *The seasons of a man's life.* New York: Knopf.

Levy, J. (1978). Lateral differences in the human brain in cognition and behavioral control. In P. Buser & A. Rougeul-Buser (Eds.), *Cerebral correlates of conscious experience.* N.Y.: Elsevier.

Levy, J. (1980). Varieties of human brain organization and the human social system. *Zygon, 15,* 351–375.

Levy, J. (1983). Language, cognition, and the right hemisphere: A response to Gazzaniga. *American Psychologist, 38,* 538–541.

Levy, J. (1985, May). Right brain, left brain: Fact and fiction. *Psychology Today,* pp. 38–44.

Lewinsohn, P. M., Hoberman, H., Teri, L., & Hautzinger, M. (1985). An integrative theory of depression. In S. Reiss & R. Bootzin (Eds.), *Theoretical issues in behavior therapy.* Orlando, FL: Academic Press.

Lewinsohn, P. M., Mischel, W., Chaplin, W., & Barton, R. (1980). Social competence and depression: The role of illusory self-perceptions. *Journal of Abnormal Psychology, 89,* 203–212.

Lewis, C. C. (1981). The effects of parental firm control: A reinterpretation of findings. *Psychological Bulletin, 90,* 547–563.

Lewis, C. S. (1968). *Christian reflections.* Grand Rapids, MI: Eerdmans.

Lewontin, R. (1976). Race and intelligence. In N. J. Block & G. Dworkin (Eds.), *The IQ controversy: Critical readings.* New York: Pantheon.

Lewontin, R. (1982). *Human diversity.* San Francisco: Freeman.

Lieberman, M. A., Yalom, I. D., & Miles, M. B. (1973). *Encounter groups: First facts.* New York: Basic Books.

Lifton, R. J. (1982). Beyond nuclear numbing: A call to teach and learn. In *Proceedings of the Symposium on the Role of the Academy in Addressing the Issues of Nuclear War.* Geneva, NY: Hobart and William Smith Colleges.

Light, K. C., Koepke, J. P., Obrist, P. A., & Willis, P. W., Jr. (1983). Psychological stress induces sodium and fluid retention in men at high risk for hypertension. *Science, 220,* 429–431.

Linder, D. (1982). Social trap analogs: The tragedy of the commons in the laboratory. In V. J. Derlega & J. Grzelak (Ed.), *Cooperative and helping behavior: Theories and research.* New York: Academic Press.

Lindskold, S. (1978). Trust development, the GRIT proposal, and the effects of conciliatory acts on conflict and cooperation. *Psychological Bulletin, 85,* 772–793.

Lindskold, S., Walters, P. S., & Koutsourais, H. (1983). Cooperators, competitors, and response to GRIT. *Journal of Conflict Resolution, 27,* 521–532.

Lindzey, G., Hall, C. S., & Thompson, R. F. (1978). *Psychology.* New York: Worth.

Linn, M. C., & Peterson, A. C. (1986). Meta-analyses of gender differences in spatial ability. In J. Hyde & M. Linn (Eds.), *The psychology of gender: Advances through meta-analysis.* Baltimore: Johns Hopkins University Press.

Linn, R. L. (1982). Ability testing: Individual differences, prediction, and differential prediction. In A. K. Wigdor & W. R. Garner (Eds.), *Ability testing: Uses, consequences, and controversies* (Part II). Washington, DC: National Academy Press.

Livson, F. B. (1976, October). Coming together in the middle years: A longitudinal study of sex role convergence. In B. F. Turner (Chair), *The double standard of aging: A question of sex differences.* Symposium conducted at the Annual Scientific Meeting of the Gerontological Society, New York, NY.

Locke, E. A., Shaw, K. N., Saari, L. M., & Latham, G. P. (1981). Goal setting and task performance: 1969–1980. *Psychological Bulletin, 90,* 125–152.

Locke, J. (1690; reprinted 1964). *An essay concerning human understanding.* New York: Meridian.

Loehlin, J. C. (1983). John Locke and behavior genetics. *Behavior Genetics, 13,* 117–121.

Loehlin, J. C., Horn, J. M., & Willerman, L. (1981). Personality resemblance in adoptive families. *Behavior Genetics, 11,* 309–330.

Loehlin, J. C., Lindzey, G., & Spuhler, J. N. (1975). *Race differences in intelligence.* San Francisco: Freeman.

Loehlin, J. C., & Nichols, R. C. (1976). *Heredity, environment, and personality.* Austin: University of Texas Press.

Loehlin, J. C., Willerman, L., & Horn, J. M. (1982). Personality resemblances between unwed mothers and their adopted-away offspring. *Journal of Personality and Social Psychology, 42,* 1089–1099.

Loehlin, J. C., Willerman, L., & Horn, J. M. (1985). Personality resemblances in adoptive families when the children are late-adolescent or adult. *Journal of Personality and Social Psychology, 48,* 376–392.

Loftus, E. F. (1979). The malleability of human memory. *American Scientist, 67,* 313–320.

Loftus, E. F. (1980). *Memory: Surprising new insights into how we remember and why we forget.* Reading, MA: Addison-Wesley.

Loftus, E. F. (1983). Misfortunes of memory. *Philosophical Transactions. Royal Society of London. Series B. Biological Sciences, 302,* 413–421.

Loftus, E. F., & Loftus, G. R. (1980). On the permanence of stored information in the human brain. *American Psychologist, 35,* 409–420.

Loftus, E. F., & Palmer, J. C. (1973). Reconstruction of automobile destruction: An example of the interaction between language and memory. *Journal of Verbal Learning and Verbal Behavior, 13,* 585–589.

London, P. (1970). The rescuers: Motivational hypotheses about Christians who saved Jews from the Nazis. In J. Macaulay & L. Berkowitz (Eds.), *Altruism and helping behavior.* New York: Academic Press.

LoPiccolo, J. (1983). Challenges to sex therapy. In C. M. Davis (Ed.), *Challenges in sexual science: Current theoretical issues and research advances.* Philadelphia: Society for Scientific Study of Sex.

Lord, C. G., Lepper, M. R., & Preston, E. (1984). Considering the opposite: A corrective strategy for social judgement. *Journal of Personality and Social Psychology, 47,* 1231–1247.

Lord, C. G., Ross, L., & Lepper, M. (1979). Biased assimilation and attitude polarization: The effects of prior theories on subsequently considered evidence. *Journal of Personality and Social Psychology, 37,* 2098–2109.

Lorenz, K. (1937). The companion in the bird's world. *Auk, 54,* 245–273.

Lorenz, K. (1966). *On aggression.* London: Metheun.

Lowenthal, M. F., Thurnher, M., Chiriboga, D., Beefon, D., Gigy, L., Lurie, E., Pierce, R., Spence, D., & Weiss, L. (1975). *Four stages of life.* San Francisco: Jossey-Bass.

Lubin, B., Larsen, R. M., & Matarazzo, J. D. (1984). Patterns of psychological test usage in the United States: 1935–1982. *American Psychologist, 39,* 451–454.

Luchins, A. S. (1946). Classroom experiments on mental set. *American Journal of Psychology, 59,* 295–298.

Lumsden, C. J., & Wilson, E. O. (1983). *Promethean fire: Reflections on the origin of mind.* Cambridge, MA: Harvard University Press.

Luria, A. M. (1968). In L. Solotaroff (Trans.), *The mind of a mnemonist.* New York: Basic Books.

Lykken, D. T. (1979). The detection of deception. *Psychological Bulletin, 86,* 47–53.

Lykken, D. T. (1981). *A tremor in the blood: Uses and abuses of the lie detector.* New York: McGraw-Hill.

Lykken, D. T. (1982, September). Fearlessness: Its carefree charm and deadly risks. *Psychology Today,* pp. 20–28.

Lykken, D. T. (1983, April). Polygraph prejudice. *APA Monitor,* p. 4.

Lynch, G., & Baudry, M. (1984). The biochemistry of memory: A new and specific hypothesis. *Science, 224,* 1057–1064.

Lynn, R. (1982). I.Q. in Japan and the United States shows a growing disparity. *Nature, 297,* 222–223.

Lynn, R. (1983). Lynn replies. *Nature, 306,* 292.

Maass, A., & Clark, R. D., III. (1984). Hidden impact of minorities: Fifteen years of minority influence research. *Psychological Bulletin, 95,* 428–450.

Maccoby, E. (1980). *Social development: Psychological growth and the parent-child relationship.* New York: Harcourt Brace Jovanovich.

MacDonald, N. (1960). Living with schizophrenia. *Canadian Medical Association Journal, 82,* 218–221.

MacFarlane, A. (1978, February). What a baby knows. *Human Nature,* pp. 74–81.

Macfarlane, J. W. (1964). Perspectives on personality consistency and change from the guidance study. *Vita Humana, 7,* 115–126.

MacKay, D. G. (1983). Prescriptive grammar and the pronoun problem. In B. Thorne, C. Kramarae, & N. Henley (Eds.), *Language, gender and society.* Rowley, MA: Newbury House.

Mackenzie, B. (1984). Explaining race differences in IQ: The logic, the methodology, and the evidence. *American Psychologist, 39,* 1214–1233.

MacKinnon, D. W. (1982, August). *Environments that favor creativity.* The Henry A. Murray Award Address presented at the meeting of the American Psychological Association, Washington, DC.

MacKinnon, D. W., & Hall, W. B. (1972). Intelligence and creativity. *Preceedings, XVIIth International Congress of Applied Psychology* (Vol. 2, pp. 1883–1888). Brussels: Editest.

Magoun, H. W. (1963). *The waking brain.* Springfield, IL: Charles C Thomas.

Maital, S. (1982). *Minds, markets, and money: Psychological foundations of economic behavior.* New York: Basic Books.

Major, B., Carrington, P. I., & Carnevale, P. J. D. (1984). Physical attractiveness and self-esteem: Attribution for praise from an other-sex evaluator. *Personality and Social Psychology Bulletin, 10,* 43–50.

Malamuth, N., & Donnerstein, E. (Eds.) (1984). *Pornography and sexual aggression.* Orlando, FL: Academic Press.

Malan, D. H. (1978). "The case of the secretary with the violent father." In H. Davanloo (Ed.), *Basic principles and techniques in short-term dynamic psychotherapy.* New York: Spectrum.

Malone, T. W., & Lepper, M. R. (in press). Making learning fun: A taxonomy of intrinsic motivations for learning. In R. E. Snow & M. J. Farr (Eds.), *Aptitude, learning, and instruction: III. Cognitive and affective process analysis.* Hillsdale, NJ: Erlbaum.

Mandel, D. (1983, March 13). One man's holocaust: Part II. The story of David Mandel's journey through hell as told to David Kagan. *Wonderland Magazine* (Grand Rapids Press), pp. 2–7.

Mandler, G. (1984). *Mind and body: Psychology of emotion and stress.* New York: Norton.

Marcel, A. (1983). Conscious and unconscious perception: Experiments on visual masking and word recognition. *Cognitive Psychology, 15,* 197–237.

Mark, V., & Ervin, F. (1970). *Violence and the brain.* New York: Harper & Row.

Marler, P. (1970). A comparative approach to vocal learning: Song development in white-crowned sparrows. *Journal of Comparative and Physiological Psychology Monograph, 71,* 1–25.

Marsh, H. W., & Parker, J. W. (1984). Determinants of student self-concept: Is it better to be a relatively large fish in a small pond even if you don't learn to swim as well? *Journal of Personality and Social Psychology, 47,* 213–231.

Marshall, D. S. (1971). Sexual behavior on Mangaia. In D. S. Marshall & R. C. Suggs (Eds.), *Human sexual behavior.* New York: Basic Books.

Martin, B. (1982). Families at work: Strengths and strains *Research Report* (Wellesley College Center for Research on Women), 2, 3–4.

Martin, D. J., Abramson, L. Y., & Alloy, L. B. (1984). Illusion of control for self and others in depressed and nondepressed college students. *Journal of Personality and Social Psychology, 46,* 125–136.

Martin, R. A., & Lefcourt, H. M. (1984). Sense of humor as a moderator of the relation between stressors and moods. *Journal of Personality and Social Psychology, 45,* 1313–1324.

Martyna, W. (1978). What does "he" mean? Use of generic masculine. *Journal of Communication, 28*(1), 131–138.

Maruyama, G., Johnson, R., & Johnson, D. (1984). Effects of cooperative learning: A meta-analysis. In N. Miller & M. B. Brewer, *Groups in contact: The psychology of desegregation.* Orlando, FL: Academic Press.

Marx, J. L. (1982). How the brain controls birdsong. *Science, 217,* 1125–1126.

Marx, J. L. (1985). The immune system "belongs in the body." *Science, 227,* 1190–1192.

Maslow, A. (1968). *Toward a psychology of being* (2nd ed.). Princeton, NJ: Van Nostrand Reinhold.

Maslow, A. H. (1970). *Motivation and personality* (2nd ed.). New York: Harper & Row.

Mason, J. W. (1975). A historical view of the stress field. *Journal of Human Stress, 1*(2), 22–36.

Masters, W. H., & Johnson, V. E. (1966). *Human sexual response.* Boston: Little, Brown.

Matarazzo, J. D. (1982). Behavioral health's challenge to academic, scientific, and professional psychology. *American Psychologist, 37,* 1–14.

Matarazzo, J. D. (1983). Computerized psychological testing. *Science, 221,* 323.

Matarazzo, J. D., Carmody, T. P., & Gentry, W. D. (1981). Psychologists on the faculties of United States schools of medicine: Past, present and possible future. *Clinical Psychology Review, 1,* 293–317.

Mathes, E. W., & Wise, P. S. (1983). Romantic love and the ravages of time. *Psychological Reports, 53,* 839–846.

Matthews, C., & Clark, R. D., III (1982). Marital satisfaction: A validation approach. *Basic and Applied Social Psychology, 3,* 169–186.

Matthews, K. A., Roseman, R. H., Dembroski, T. M., Harris, E. L., & MacDougall, J. M. (1984). Familial resemblance in components of the Type A behavior pattern: A reanalysis of the California Type A twin study. *Psychosomatic Medicine, 46,* 512–522.

May, R. (1982). The problem of evil: An open letter to Carl Rogers. *Journal of Humanistic Psychology, 22,* 10–21.

Mayo, C., & Henley, N. M. (1981). *Gender and nonverbal behavior.* New York: Springer-Verlag.

Mazullo, J., Lasagna, L., & Grinar, P. (1974). Variations in interpretation of prescription instructions. *Journal of the American Medical Association, 227,* 929–931.

McAlister, A., Perry, C., Killen, J., Slinkard, L. A., & Maccoby, N. (1980). Pilot study of smoking, alcohol and drug abuse prevention. *American Journal of Public Health, 70,* 719–721.

McBurney, D. H., & Collings, V. B. (1984). *Introduction to sensation perception* (2nd ed.). Englewood Cliffs, NJ: Prentice-Hall.

McBurney, D. H., & Gent, J. F. (1979). On the nature of taste qualities. *Psychological Bulletin, 86,* 151–167.

McCall, R. B. (1981). Early predictors of later IQ: The search continues. *Intelligence, 5,* 141–147.

McCall, R. B., Appelbaum, M. I., & Hogarty, P. S. (1973). Developmental changes in mental performance. *Mono-*

graphs of the Society for Research in Child Development, 38(3, Serial No. 150).

McCann, I. L., & Holmes, D. S. (1984). Influence of aerobic exercise on depression. *Journal of Personality and Social Psychology, 46,* 1142–1147.

McCarley, R. W., & Hobson, E. (1981). REM sleep dreams and the activation-synthesis hypothesis. *American Journal of Psychiatry, 138,* 904–912.

McCarron, D. A., Morris, C. D., Henry, H. J., & Stanton, J. L. (1984). Blood pressure and nutrient intake in the United States. *Science, 225,* 1392–1398.

McCaul, K. D., & Malott, J. M. (1984). Distraction and coping with pain. *Psychological Bulletin, 95,* 516–533.

McClelland, D. C. (1978). Managing motivation to expand human freedom. *American Psychologist, 33,* 201–210.

McClenon, J. (1982). A survey of elite scientists: Their attitudes toward ESP and parapsychology. *Journal of Parapsychology, 46,* 127–152.

McConnell, J. V. (1977). *Understanding human behavior* (2nd ed.). New York: Holt, Rinehart & Winston.

McCord, J. (1978). A thirty-year follow up on treatment effects. *American Psychologist, 33,* 284–289.

McCord, J. (1979). Following up on Cambridge-Somerville. *American Psychologist, 34,* 727.

McCrae, R. R. (1984). Situational determinants of coping responses: Loss, threat, and challenge. *Journal of Personality and Social Psychology, 46,* 919–928.

McCrae, R., & Costa, P. T., Jr. (1982). Self-concept and the stability of personality: Cross-sectional comparisons of self-reports and ratings. *Journal of Personality and Social Psychology, 43,* 1282–1292.

McGaugh, J. L. (1983). Preserving the presence of the past: Hormonal influences on memory storage. *American Psychologist, 38,* 161–174.

McGhee, P. E. (1976). Children's appreciation of humor: A test of the cognitive congruency principle. *Child Development, 47,* 420–426.

McGlone, J. (in press). The neuropsychology of sex differences in human brain organization. In G. Goldstein & R. Tarter (Eds.), *Advances in clinical neuropsychology* (Vol. III). New York: Plenum Press.

McGrath, E. (1983, March 28). Confucian work ethic. *Time,* p. 52.

McGrath, M. J., & Cohen, D. G. (1978). REM sleep facilitation of adaptive waking behavior: A review of the literature. *Psychological Bulletin, 85,* 24–57.

McGuiness, D., & Pribram, K. (1978). The origins of sensory bias in the development of gender differences in perception and cognition. In M. Bortner (Ed.), *Cognitive growth and development: Essays in honor of Herbert G. Birch.* New York: Brunner/Mazel. Cited by D. Goleman in Special abilities of the sexes: Do they begin in the brain? *Psychology Today,* November 1978, pp. 48–59, 120.

McHugh, P. R., & Moran, T. H. (1978). Accuracy of the regulation of caloric ingestion in the rhesus monkey. *American Journal of Physiology, 235,* R29–34.

McKillip, J., & Riedel, S. L. (1983). External validity of matching on physical attractiveness for same and opposite sex couples. *Journal of Applied Social Psychology, 1,* 328–337.

Meador, B. D., & Rogers, C. R. (1984). Person-centered therapy. In R. J. Corsini (Ed.), *Current psychotherapies* (3rd ed.). Itasca, IL: Peacock.

Medawar, P. (1982). *Pluto's republic.* New York: Oxford University Press.

Mednick, S. (1985, March). Crime in the family tree. *Psychology Today,* pp. 58–61.

Mednick, S. A., Gabrielli, W. F., Jr., & Hutchings, B. (1984). Genetic influences in criminal convictions: Evidence from an adoption cohort. *Science, 224,* 891–894.

Meichenbaum, D. (1977). *Cognitive-behavior modification: An integrative approach.* New York: Plenum Press.

Meltzoff, A. N., & Moore, M. K. (1977). Imitation of facial and manual gestures by human neonates. *Science, 198,* 75–78.

Melzack, R., & Wall, P. D. (1965). Pain mechanisms: A new theory. *Science, 150,* 971–979.

Merton, R. K. (1938; reprinted 1970). *Science, technology and society in seventeenth-century England.* New York: Fertig.

Merton, R. K., & Kitt, A. S. (1950). Contributions to the theory of reference group behavior. In R. K. Merton & P. F. Lazarsfeld (Eds.), *Continuities in social research: Studies in the scope and method of the American soldier.* Glencoe, IL: Free Press.

Messenger, J. C. (1971). Sex and repression in an Irish folk community. In D. S. Marshall & R. C. Suggs (Eds.), *Human sexual behavior.* New York: Basic Books.

Messick, S., & Jungeblut, A. (1981). Time and method in coaching for the SAT. *Psychological Bulletin, 89,* 191–216.

Meyer, A. (1982, June). Do lie detectors lie? *Science 82,* pp. 24–26.

Meyer-Bahlburg, H. F. L. (1980). Sexuality in early adolescence. In B. B. Wolman & J. Money (Eds.), *Handbook of human sexuality.* Englewood Cliffs, NJ: Prentice-Hall.

Michaels, J. W., Bloomel, J. M., Brocato, R. M., Linkous, R. A., & Rowe, J. S. (1982). Social facilitation and inhibition in a natural setting. *Replications in Social Psychology, 2,* 21–24.

Michel, G. F. (1981). Right-handedness: A consequence of infant supine head-orientation preference? *Science, 212,* 685–687.

Mihevic, P. M. (1982). Anxiety, depression, and exercise. *Quest, 33,* 140–153.

Milgram, S. (1974). *Obedience to authority.* New York: Harper & Row.

Milgram, S. (1984, August). *Cyranoids.* Paper presented at the meeting of the American Psychological Association, Toronto, Canada.

Miller, G. A. (1956). The magical number seven, plus or minus two: Some limits on our capacity for processing information. *Psychological Review, 63,* 81–97.

Miller, G. A. (1962). *Psychology: The science of mental life.* New York: Harper & Row.

Miller, J. G. (1984). Culture and the development of everyday social explanation. *Journal of Personality and Social Psychology, 46,* 961–978.

Miller, L. L., & Branconnier, R. J. (1983). Cannabis: Effects on memory and the cholinergic limbic system. *Psychological Bulletin, 93,* 441–456.

Miller, N. E. (1983a). Behavioral medicine: Symbiosis between laboratory and clinic. *Annual Review of Psychology, 34,* 1–31.

Miller, N. E. (1983b, August). Value and ethics of research on animals. Paper presented at the meeting of the American Psychological Association, Anaheim, CA.

Miller, N. E. (1985, February). Rx: biofeedback. *Psychology Today,* pp. 54–59.

Miller, N. E., & Brucker, B. S. (1979). A learned visceral response apparently independent of skeletal ones in patients paralyzed by spinal lesions. In N. Birbaumer & H. D. Kimmel (Eds.), *Biofeedback and self-regulation.* Hillsdale, NJ: Erlbaum.

Miller, N., & Maruyama, G. (1976). Ordinal position and peer popularity. *Journal of Personality and Social Psychology, 33,* 123–131.

Mills, M., & Melhuish, E. (1974). Recognition of mother's voice in early infancy. *Nature, 252,* 123–124.

Mineka, S., & Suomi, S. J. (1978). Social separation in monkeys. *Psychological Bulletin, 85,* 1376–1400.

Mischel, W. (1968). *Personality and assessment.* New York: Wiley.

Mischel, W. (1981). Current issues and challenges in personality. In L. T. Benjamin, Jr. (Ed.), *The G. Stanley Hall Lecture Series* (Vol. 1). Washington, DC: American Psychological Association.

Mischel, W. (1984). Convergences and challenges in the search for consistency. *American Psychologist, 39,* 351–364.

Mita, T. H., Dermer, M., & Knight, J. (1977). Reversed facial images and the mere-exposure hypothesis. *Journal of Personality and Social Psychology, 35,* 597–601.

Money, J., Berlin, F. S., Falck, A., & Stein, M. (1983). *Antiandrogenic and counseling treatment of sex offenders.* Baltimore: Department of Psychiatry and Behavioral Sciences, The Johns Hopkins University School of Medicine.

Money, J., Hampson, J. G., & Hampson, J. L. (1957). Imprinting and the establishment of gender role. *AMA Archives of Neurology and Psychiatry, 77,* 333–336.

Monohan, J. (1983). *Predicting violent behavior: An assessment of clinical techniques.* Beverly Hills, CA: Sage.

Moody, R. (1976). *Life after life.* Harrisburg, PA: Stackpole Books.

Mook, D. G. (1983). In defense of external invalidity. *American Psychologist, 38,* 379–387.

Moore, D. L., & Baron, R. S. (1983). Social facilitation: A physiological analysis. In J. T. Cacioppo & R. Petty (Eds.), *Social psychophysiology.* New York: Guilford Press.

Moore, T. E. (1982). Subliminal advertising: What you see is what you get. *Journal of Marketing, 46,* 38–47.

Moreland, R. L., & Zajonc, R. B. (1982). Exposure effects in person perception: Familiarity, similarity, and attraction. *Journal of Experimental Social Psychology, 18,* 395–415.

Morgan, A. H., & Hilgard, E. R. (1971). Age differences in susceptibility to hypnosis. *International Journal of Clinical and Experimental Hypnosis, 21,* 78–95.

Morgan, A. H., Johnson, D. L., & Hilgard, E. R. (1974). The stability of hypnotic susceptibility: A longitudinal study. *International Journal of Clinical and Experimental Hypnosis, 22,* 249–257.

Morris, N. M., & Udry, J. R. (1978). Pheromonal influences on human sexual behavior: An experimental search. *Journal of Biosocial Science, 10,* 147–157.

Moruzzi, G. & Magoun, H. W. (1949). Brain stem reticular formation and activation of the EEG. *Electroencephalography and Clinical Neurophysiology, 1,* 455–473.

Moscovici, S., & Zavalloni, M. (1969). The group as a polarizer of attitudes. *Journal of Personality and Social Psychology, 12,* 124–135.

Moss, H. A., Susman, E. J. (1980). Longitudinal study of personality development. In O. G. Brim, Jr. & J. Kagan (Eds.), *Constancy and change in human development.* Cambridge, MA: Harvard University Press.

Moyer, K. E. (1983). The physiology of motivation: Aggression as a model. In C. J. Scheier & A. M. Rogers (Eds.), *G. Stanley Hall Lecture Series* (Vol. 3). Washington, DC: American Psychological Association.

Murphy, E. A. (1982). Muddling, meddling, and modeling. In V. E. Anderson, W. A. Hauser, J. K. Penry, & C. F. Sing (Eds.), *Genetic basis of the epilepsies.* New York: Raven Press.

Murphy, T. N. (1982). Pain: Its assessment and management. In R. J. Gatchel, A. Baum & J. E. Singer (Eds.), *Handbook of psychology and health: Vol I. Clinical psychology and behavioral medicine: Overlapping disciplines.* Hillsdale, NJ: Erlbaum.

Murray, D. M., Johnson, C. A., Luepker, R. V., Mittelmark, M. B. (1984). The prevention of cigarette smoking in children: A comparison of four strategies. *Journal of Applied Social Psychology, 14,* 274–288.

Murray, H. (1938). *Explorations in personality.* New York: Oxford University Press.

Murray, H. A. (1933). The effect of fear upon estimates of the maliciousness of other personalities. *Journal of Social Psychology, 4,* 310–329.

Murray, H. A., & Wheeler, D. R. (1937). A note on the possible clairvoyance of dreams. *Journal of Psychology, 3,* 309–313.

Murstein, B. I. (1976). *Who will marry whom.* New York: Springer.

Myers, B. J. (1984a). Mother-infant bonding: The status of the critical period hypothesis. *Developmental Review, 4,* 240–274.

Myers, B. J. (1984b). Mother-infant bonding: Rejoinder to Kennell and Klaus. *Developmental Review, 4,* 283–288.

Myers, D. G. (1983). *Social psychology.* New York: McGraw-Hill.

Myers, D. G., & Bishop, G. D. (1970). Discussion effects on racial attitudes. *Science, 169,* 778–779.

Myers, J. K., Weissman, M. M., Tischler, G. L., Holzer, C. E., III, Leaf, P. J., Orvaschel, H., Anthony, J. C., Boyd, J. H., Burke, J. D., Kramer, M., & Stoltzman, R. (1984). Six-month prevalence of psychiatric disorders in three communities. *Archives of General Psychiatry, 41,* 959–967.

Naditch, M. P. (1985). STAYWELL: Evolution of a behavioral medicine program in industry. In M. F. Cataldo & T. Coates (Eds.), *Behavioral medicine in industry.* Orlando, FL: Academic Press.

Napolitan, D. A., & Goethals, G. R. (1979). The attribution of friendliness. *Journal of Experimental Social Psychology, 15,* 105–113.

National Academy of Sciences, Institute of Medicine (1982). *Marijuana and health.* Washington, DC: National Academic Press.

National Center for Education Statistics (1982). *Digest of education statistics 1982.* Washington, DC.

Neisser, U. (1979). The control of information pickup in selective looking. In A. D. Pick (Ed.), *Perception and its development: A tribute to Eleanor J. Gibson.* Hillsdale, NJ: Erlbaum.

Neisser, U. (1981). John Dean's memory: A case study. *Cognition, 9,* 1–22.

Neisser, U. (1982). Memorists. In U. Neisser (Ed.), *Memory observed: Remembering in natural contexts.* San Francisco: Freeman.

Neisser, U. (1984). The role of invariant structures in the control of movement. In M. Frese & J. Sabini (Eds.), *Goal directed behavior: The concept of action in psychology.* Hillsdale, NJ: Erlbaum.

Nelson, K. (1973). Structure and strategy in learning to talk. *Monographs of the Society for Research in Child Development, 38*(1 & 2, Serial No. 149).

Nelson, K. (1981). Individual differences in language development: Implications for development and language. *Developmental Psychology, 17,* 170–187.

Neugarten, B. L. (1974). The roles we play. In American Medical Association, *Quality of Life: The Middle Years.* Acton, MA: Publishing Sciences Group.

Neugarten, B. L. (1979). Time, age and the life cycle. *American Journal of Psychiatry, 136,* 887–894.

Neugarten, B. L. (1980, February). Must everything be a midlife crisis? *Prime Time,* pp. 45–48.

Neugarten, B. L., Wood, V., Kraines, R. J., & Loomis, B. (1963). Women's attitudes toward the menopause. *Vita Humana, 6,* 140–151.

Newcomb, M. D., & Bentler, P. M. (1981). Marital breakdown. In S. Duck & R. Gilmour (Eds.), *Personal relationships: Vol. 3. Personal relationships in disorder.* London: Academic Press.

Newell, A., & Simon, H. A. (1972). *Human problem solving.* Englewood Cliffs, NJ: Prentice-Hall.

Newman, B. (1982). Mid-life development. In B. B. Wolman (Ed.), *Handbook of developmental psychology.* Englewood Cliffs, NJ: Prentice-Hall.

Newman, J., & Layton, B. D. (1984). Overjustification: A self-perception perspective. *Personality and Social Psychology Bulletin, 10,* 419–425.

Newton, N., & Modahl, C. (1978, March). Pregnancy: The closest human relationship. *Human Nature,* pp. 40–56.

Nichols, R. C. (1978). Twin studies of ability, personality and interests. *Homo, 29,* 158–173.

Nickerson, R. S., & Adams, M. J. (1979). Long-term memory for a common object. *Cognitive Psychology, 11,* 287–307.

Nicol, S. E., & Gottesman, I. I. (1983). Clues to the genetics and neurobiology of schizophrenia. *American Scientist, 71,* 398–404.

Nisbett, R. E., & Borgida, E. (1975). Attribution and the psychology of prediction. *Journal of Personality and Social Psychology, 32,* 932–943.

Nisbett, R. E., Krantz, D. H., Jepson, C., & Kunda, Z. (1983). The use of statistical heuristics in everyday inductive reasoning. *Psychological Review, 90,* 339–363.

Nisbett, R., & Ross, L. (1980). *Human inference: Strategies and shortcomings of social judgment.* Englewood Cliffs, NJ: Prentice-Hall.

O'Connor, P., & Brown, G. W. (1984). Supportive relationships: Fact or fancy? *Journal of Social and Personal Relationships, 1,* 159–175.

Office of Technology Assessment (1983). *Scientific validity of polygraph testing: A research review and evaluation—A technical memorandum.* (OTA-TM-H-15). Washington, DC: U.S. Congress, Office of Technology Assessment.

Oldbridge, N. B. (1982). Compliance and exercise in primary and secondary prevention of coronary heart disease: A review. *Preventive Medicine, 11,* 56–70.

Olds, J. (1958). Self-stimulation of the brain. *Science, 127,* 315–324.

Olds, J. (1975). Mapping the mind onto the brain. In F. G. Worden, J. P. Swazey, & G. Adelman (Eds.), *The neurosciences: Paths of discovery.* Cambridge, MA: MIT Press.

Olds, J., & Milner, P. (1954). Positive reinforcement produced by electrical stimulation of the septal area and other regions of rat brain. *Journal of Comparative and Physiological Psychology, 47,* 419–427.

O'Malley, P. M., & Bachman, J. G. (1983). Self-esteem: Change and stability between ages 13 and 23. *Developmental Psychology, 19,* 257–268.

Opton, E., Jr. (1979, December). A psychologist takes a closer look at the recent landmark Larry P. opinion. *American Psychological Association Monitor,* pp. 1, 4.

Orne, M. T. (1982, April 28). Affidavit submitted to State of Pennsylvania.

Orne, M. T. (1984, August). *Compliance, responsibility, and fantasy in hypnotic responding.* Paper presented at the meeting of the American Psychological Association, Toronto, Canada.

Orne, M. T., Dinges, D. F., & Orne, E. C. (1984). On the differential diagnosis of multiple personality in the forensic context. *International Journal of Clinical and Experimental Hypnosis, 32,* 118–169.

Orne, M. T., & Evans, F. J. (1965). Social control in the psychological experiment: Antisocial behavior and hypnosis. *Journal of Personality and Social Psychology, 1,* 189–200.

Ornstein, R. (1978, May). The split and whole brain. *Human Nature,* 76–83.

Osgood, C. E. (1962). *An alternative to war or surrender.* Urbana: University of Illinois Press.

Osgood, C. E. (1980). GRIT: *A strategy for survival in mankind's nuclear age?* Paper presented at the Pugwash Conference on New Directions in Disarmament, Racine, WI.

Osherson, D. N., & Markman, E. (1974–1975). Language and the ability to evaluate contradictions and tautologies. *Cognition, 3,* 213–226.

Oskamp, S., King, J. C., Burn, S. M., Konrad, A. M., Pollard, J. A., & White, M. A. (1985). The media and nuclear war: Fallout from TV's "The Day After." In S. Oskamp (Ed.), *Applied Social Psychology Annual* (Vol. 6). Beverly Hills, CA: Sage.

OSS Assessment Staff (1948). *The assessment of men.* New York: Rinehart.

Page, S. (1977). Effects of the mental illness label in attempts to obtain accommodation. *Canadian Journal of Behavioral Science, 9,* 84–90.

Paivio, A. (1971). *Imagery and verbal processes.* New York: Holt, Rinehart & Winston.

Palladino, J. J., & Carducci, B. J. (1983, March). *"Things that go bump in the night": Students' knowledge of sleep and dreams.* Paper presented at the meeting of the Southeastern Psychological Association, Atlanta, GA.

Pallak, M. S. (1984). Animals in research. *Science, 226,* 114.

Palmblad, J., Petrini, B., Wasserman, J., & Akerstedt, T. (1979). Lymphocyte and granulocyte reactions during sleep deprivation. *Psychosomatic Medicine, 41,* 273–278.

Palmore, E. B. (1981). The facts on aging quiz: Part two. *The Gerontologist, 21,* 431–437.

Palumbo, S. R. (1978). *Dreaming and memory: A new information-processing model.* New York: Basic Books.

Pandey, J., Sinha, Y., Prakash, A., & Tripathi, R. C. (1982). Right-left political ideologies and attribution of the causes of poverty. *European Journal of Social Psychology, 12,* 327–331.

Panksepp, J. (1982). Toward a general psychobiological theory of emotions. *Behavioral and Brain Sciences, 5,* 407–467.

Parke, R. D. (1981). *Fathers.* Cambridge, MA: Harvard University Press.

Parke, R. D. (1974). Rules, roles, and resistance to deviation: Recent advances in punishment, discipline, and self-control. In A. Pick (Ed.), *Symposia of child psychology* (Vol. 8). Minneapolis: University of Minnesota Press.

Parlee, M. B. (1983). Menstrual rhythms in sensory processes: A review of fluctuations in vision, olfaction, audition, taste, and touch. *Psychological Bulletin, 93,* 539–548.

Passons, W. R. (1975). *Gestalt approaches to counseling.* New York: Holt, Rinehart & Winston.

Patterson, F. (1978, October). Conversations with a gorilla. *National Geographic,* pp. 438–465.

Patterson, G. R., Chamberlain, P., & Reid, J. B. (1982). A comparative evaluation of parent training procedures. *Behavior Therapy, 13,* 638–650.

Patterson, R. (1951). *The riddle of Emily Dickinson.* Boston: Houghton Mifflin.

Pavlov, I. P. (1927). In G. V. Anrep (Trans.), *Conditioned reflexes.* London: Oxford University Press.

Pekkanen, J. (1982, June). Why do we sleep? *Science, 82,* p. 86.

Penfield, W. (1969). Consciousness, memory, and man's conditioned reflexes. In K. Pigram (Ed.), *On the biology of learning.* New York: Harcourt, Brace & World.

Penfield, W. (1975). *The mystery of the mind.* Princeton: Princeton University Press.

Pennebaker, J. W. (1982). *The psychology of physical symptoms.* New York: Springer-Verlag.

Pennebaker, J. W., & Beall, S. (1984). *Cognitive, emotional, and physiological components of confiding: Behavioral inhibition and disease.* Unpublished manuscript, Southern Methodist University, Dallas, TX.

Pennebaker, J. W., & Brittingham, G. L. (1982). Environmental and sensory cues affecting the perception of physical symptoms. In A. Baum & J. Singer (Eds.), *Advances in environmental psychology* (Vol. 4). Hillsdale, NJ: Erlbaum.

Pennebaker, J. W., & Lightner, J. M. (1980). Competition of internal and external information in an exercise setting. *Journal of Personality and Social Psychology, 39,* 165–174.

Pennebaker, J. W., & O'Heeron, R. C. (1984). Confiding in others and illness rate among spouses of suicide and accidental death victims. *Journal of Abnormal Psychology, 93,* 473–476.

Penrod, S., & Linz, D. (1984). Using psychological research on violent pornography to inform legal change. In N. Malamuth & E. Donnerstein (Eds.), *Pornography and sexual aggression.* Orlando, FL: Academic Press.

Peplau, L. A. (1982). Research on homosexual couples: An overview. *Journal of Homosexuality, 8*(2), 3–8.

Peplau, L. A., & Perlman, D. (1982). *Loneliness: A sourcebook of current theory, research and therapy.* New York: Wiley.

Perlmutter, M. (1983). Learning and memory through adulthood. In M. W. Riley, B. B. Hess, & K. Bond (Eds.), *Aging in society: Selected reviews of recent research.* Hillsdale, NJ: Erlbaum.

Perls, F. (1972). Gestalt therapy [interview]. In A. Bry (Ed.), *Inside psychotherapy.* New York: Basic Books.

Perls, F. S. (1969). *Ego, hunger and aggression: The beginning of Gestalt therapy.* New York: Random House.

Perls, F. S. (1970). Four lectures. In J. Fagan & I. L. Shepherd, *Gestalt therapy now.* Palo Alto, CA: Science and Behavior Books.

Pert, C. B., & Snyder, S. H. (1973). Opiate receptor: Demonstration in nervous tissue. *Science, 179,* 1011–1014.

Peters, T. J., & Waterman, R. H., Jr. (1982). *In search of excellence: Lessons from America's best-run companies.* New York: Harper & Row.

Peterson, L. R., & Peterson, M. J. (1959). Short-term retention of individual verbal items. *Journal of Experimental Psychology, 58,* 193–198.

Peterson, R. (1978). Review of the Rorschach. In O. K. Buros (Ed.), *The eighth mental measurements yearbook* (Vol. I). Highland Park, NJ: Gryphon Press.

Pettigrew, T. F. (1969). Racially separate or together? *Journal of Social Issues, 25,* 43–69.

Petty, R. E., & Cacioppo, J. T. (1986). The elaboration likelihood model of persuasion. In L. Berkowitz (Ed.), *Advances in experimental social psychology* (Vol. 19). Orlando, FL: Academic Press.

Petty, R. E., Cacioppo, J. T., & Schu-

mann, D. (1983). Central and peripheral routes to advertising effectiveness: The moderating role of involvement. *Journal of Consumer Research, 10,* 135–146.

Pfeiffer, E. (1977). Sexual behavior in old age. In E. W. Busse & E. Pfeiffer (Eds.), *Behavior and adaptation in late life* (2nd ed.). Boston: Little, Brown.

Phelps, M. E., & Mazziotta, J. C. (1985). Positron emission tomography: Human brain function and biochemistry. *Science, 228,* 799–809.

Phillips, D. P. (1974). The influence of suggestion on suicide: Substantive and theoretical implications of the Werther effect. *American Sociological Review, 39,* 340–354.

Phillips, D. P. (1982). The impact of fictional television stories on U.S. adult fatalities: New evidence on the effect of the mass media on violence. *American Journal of Sociology, 87,* 1340–1359.

Phillips, D. P. (1985). Natural experiments on the effects of mass media violence on fatal aggression: Strengths and weaknesses of a new approach. In L. Berkowitz. (Ed.), *Advances in experimental social psychology* (Vol. 19). Orlando, FL: Academic Press.

Phillips, J. L. (1969). *Origins of intellect: Piaget's theory.* San Francisco: Freeman.

Piaget, J. (1930). *The child's conception of physical causality.* London: Routledge & Kegan Paul.

Piaget, J. (1932). *The moral judgement of the child.* New York: Harcourt, Brace & World.

Piaget, J. (1970). Piaget's theory. In P. H. Mussen (Ed.), *Carmichael's manual of child psychology* (Vol. 1). New York: Wiley.

Piaget, J. (1972). Intellectual evolution from adolescence to adulthood. *Human Development, 15,* 1–12.

Pickar, D., Labarca, R., Linnoila, M., Roy, A., Hommer, D., Everett, D., & Payl, S. M. (1984). Neuroleptic-induced decrease in plasma homovanillic acid and antipsychotic activity in schizophrenic patients. *Science, 225,* 954–957.

Piliavin, J. A., Callero, P. L., & Evans, D. E. (1982). Addiction to altruism? Opponent-process theory and habitual blood donation. *Journal of Personality and Social Psychology, 43,* 1200–1213.

Pines, M. (1982, May 4). Movement grows to create guidelines for mental therapy. *New York Times,* p. C1.

Pirke, K. M., Kockott, G., & Dittmar, F. (1974). Psychosexual stimulation and plasma testosterone in man. *Archives of Sexual Behavior,* 3(6), 577–584.

Pittman, T. S., Davey, M. E., Alafat, K. A., Vetherill, K. V., & Kramer, N. A. (1980). Informational versus controlling verbal rewards. *Personality and Social Psychology Bulletin, 6,* 228–233.

Pleck, J. (1981). *Three conceptual issues in research on male roles.* Working paper no. 98, Wellesley College Center for Research on Women, Wellesley, MA.

Plomin, R. (1982). Childhood temperament. In B. Lahey & A. Kazdin (Eds.), *Advances in clinical child psychology* (Vol. 6). New York: Plenum Press.

Plomin, R. (1984). Behavior genetics. In D. K. Detterman (Ed.), *Current topics in human intelligence: Research methodology.* Norwood, NJ: Ablex.

Plomin, R., & DeFries, J. C. (1980). Genetics and intelligence: Recent data. *Intelligence, 4,* 15–24.

Plotkin, W. B. (1979). The alpha experience revisited: Biofeedback in the transformation of psychological state. *Psychological Bulletin, 86,* 1132–1148.

Polivy, J., & Herman, C. P. (1985). Dieting and binging: A causal analysis. *American Psychologist, 40,* 193–201.

Pomerleau, O. F., & Pomerleau, C. S. (1984). Neuroregulators and the reinforcement of smoking: Towards a biobehavioral explanation. *Neuroscience and Biobehavioral Reviews, 8,* 503–513.

Pomerleau, O. F., & Rodin, J. (in press). Behavioral medicine and health psychology. In S. L. Garfield & A. E. Bergin (Eds.), *Handbook of psychotherapy and behavior change* (3rd ed.). New York: Wiley.

Porter, P. B. (1954). Another puzzle picture. *American Journal of Psychology, 67,* 550–551.

Powell, M. C., & Fazio, R. H. (1984). Attitude accessibility as a function of repeated attitudinal expression. *Personality and Social Psychology Bulletin, 10,* 139–148.

Premack, D. (1983). The codes of man and beasts. *The Behavioral and Brain Sciences, 6,* 125–167.

Prioleau, L., Murdock, M., & Brody, N. (1983). An analysis of psychotherapy versus placebo studies. *The Behavioral and Brain Sciences, 6,* 275–310.

Pritchard, R. M. (1961, June). Stabilized images on the retina. *Scientific American,* pp. 72–78.

Project on Redefining the Meaning and Purpose of Baccalaureate Degrees (1985). *Integrity in the College Curriculum.* Washington, D.C.: Association of American Colleges.

Pruitt, D. G. (1981). *Negotiation behavior.* New York: Academic Press.

Psychic Abscam (1983, March). *Discover,* p. 10.

Public Opinion (1978, September/October). New women's roles welcomed, p. 36.

Public Opinion (1980, December/January). Women in the 70's, p. 33.

Public Opinion (1984, August/September). Phears and phobias, p. 32.

Pyszczynski, T., & Greenberg, J. (1985). Depression and preference for self-focusing stimuli after success and failure. *Journal of Personality and Social Psychology, 49,* 1066–1075.

Qualls, P. J., & Sheehan, P. W. (1981). Electromyograph biofeedback as a relaxation technique: A critical appraisal and reassessment. *Psychological Bulletin, 90,* 21–42.

Quasha, S. (1980). *Albert Einstein: An intimate portrait.* New York: Forest.

Quattrone, G. A., & Jones, E. E. (1980). The perception of variability within in-groups and out-groups: Implications for the law of small numbers. *Journal of Personality and Social Psychology, 38,* 141–152.

Racial gap in SAT scores. (1982, October 18). *Newsweek,* p. 110.

Radecki, T. (1984). Deerhunter continues to kill, 35th victim—31 dead. *NCTV News,* 5(3–4), 3.

Randi, J. (1983a, Summer). The Project Alpha experiment: Part 1. The first two years. *Skeptical Inquirer,* pp. 24–33.

Randi, J. (1983b, Fall). The Project Alpha experiment: Part 2. Beyond the laboratory. *Skeptical Inquirer*, pp. 36–45.

Rapaport, K., & Burkhart, B. R. (1984). Personality and attitudinal characteristics of sexually coercive college males. *Journal of Abnormal Psychology, 93*, 216–221.

Raskin, D. C., & Podlesny, J. A. (1979). Truth and deception: A reply to Lykken. *Psychological Bulletin, 86*, 54–59.

Razran, G. H. S. (1940). Conditioned response changes in rating and appraising sociopolitical solutions. *Psychological Bulletin, 37*, 481.

Reagan, N., & Libby, B. (1980). *Nancy*. New York: Morrow.

Reason, J., & Mycielska, K. (1982). *Absent-minded? The psychology of mental lapses and everyday errors*. Englewood Cliffs, NJ: Prentice-Hall.

Redican, W. K., & Taube, D. M. (1981). Male parental care in monkeys and apes. In M. E. Lamb (Ed.), *The role of the father in child development*. New York: Wiley.

Regier, D. A., Myers, J. K., Kramer, M., Robins, L. N., Blazer, D. G., Hough, R. L., Eaton, W. W., & Locke, B. Z. (1984, October). The NIMH epidemiologic catchment area program: historical contact, major objectives, and study population characteristics. *Archives of General Psychiatry, 41*(10), 934–941.

Reich, W. (1983, January 30). The world of Soviet psychiatry. *New York Times Magazine*, pp. 20–26, 48.

Reisenzein, R. (1983). The Schachter theory of emotion: Two decades later. *Psychological Bulletin, 94*, 239–264.

Reiser, M. (1982). *Police psychology*. Los Angeles: LEHI.

Renner, P., & Eagly, A. (1984, May). Meta-analysis of gender differences in helping behavior. Paper presented at the meeting of the Midwestern Psychological Association, Chicago, IL.

Rescorla, R. A., & Wagner, A. R. (1972). A theory of Pavlovian conditioning: Variations in the effectiveness of reinforcement and nonreinforcement. In A. H. Black & W. F. Perokasy (Eds.), *Classical conditioning II: Current theory*. N.Y.: Appleton-Century-Crofts.

Reychler, L. (1979). The effectiveness of a pacifist strategy in conflict resolution. *Journal of Conflict Resolution, 23*, 228–260.

Reynolds, D. K. (1982). *The quiet therapies*. Honolulu: University of Hawaii Press.

Rheingold, H. L. (1985). Development as the acquisition of familiarity. *Annual Review of Psychology, 36*, 1–17.

Rice, M. E., & Grusec, J. E. (1975). Saying and doing: Effects on observer performance. *Journal of Personality and Social Psychology, 32*, 584–593.

Ridenour, M. (1982). Infant walkers: Developmental tool or inherent danger. *Perceptual and Motor Skills, 55*, 1201–1202.

Rieff, P. (1979). *Freud: The mind of a moralist* (3rd ed.). Chicago: University of Chicago Press.

Riggs, L. A. (1975). Visual acuity. In C. H. Graham (Ed.), *Vision and visual perception*. New York: Wiley.

Ring, K. (1980). *Life at death: A scientific investigation of the near-death experience*. New York: Coward, McCann & Geoghegan.

Robertson, I. (in press). *Sociology* (3rd ed.). New York: Worth.

Robins, L. N., Helzer, J. E., Weissman, M. M., Orvaschel, H., Gruenberg, E., Burke, J. D., Jr., & Regier, D. A. (1984). Lifetime prevalence of specific psychiatric disorders in three sites. *Archives of General Psychiatry, 41*, 949–958.

Robinson, D. N. (1981). *An intellectual history of psychology* (rev. ed.). New York: Macmillan.

Robinson, F. P. (1970). *Effective study*. New York: Harper & Row.

Robinson, V. M. (1983). Humor and health. In P. E. McGhee & J. H. Goldstein (Eds.), *Handbook of humor research: Vol. II. Applied studies*. New York: Springer-Verlag.

Roche, A. F. (1979). Secular trends in stature, weight, and maturation. *Monographs of the Society for Research in Child Development, 44* (Serial No. 179, pp. 3–27).

Rodin, J. (1979, December). *Obesity theory and behavior therapy: An uneasy couple?* Paper presented at the meeting of the Association for the Advancement of Behavior Therapy, San Francisco, CA.

Rodin, J. (1981). Current status of the internal-external hypothesis for obesity. *American Psychologist, 36*, 361–372.

Rodin, J. (1983, April). *Aging, control and health*. Paper presented at the meeting of the Eastern Psychological Association, Philadelphia, PA.

Rodin, J. (1984, December). A sense of control [interview]. *Psychology Today*, pp. 38–45.

Rodin, J. (1985). Insulin levels, hunger and food intake: An example of feedback loops in body weight regulation. *Health Psychology, 4*, 1–18.

Rodin, J., Silberstein, S., & Striegel-Moore, R. (1984). Women and weight: A normative discontent. *The Nebraska Symposium on Motivation*. Lincoln: The University of Nebraska Press.

Rodin, J., & Slochower, J. (1976). Externality in the nonobese: Effects of environmental responsiveness on weight. *Journal of Personality and Social Psychology, 33*, 338–344.

Rodin, J., Solomon, S. K., & Metcalf, J. (1978). Role of control in mediating perceptions of density. *Journal of Personality and Social Psychology, 36*, 988–999.

Rogers, C. R. (1958). Reinhold Niebuhr's *The self and the dramas of history:* A criticism. *Pastoral Psychology, 9*, 15–17.

Rogers, C. R. (1961). *On becoming a person: A therapist's view of psychotherapy*. Boston: Houghton Mifflin.

Rogers, C. R. (1970). *Carl Rogers on encounter groups*. New York: Harper & Row.

Rogers, C. R. (1980). *A way of being*. Boston: Houghton Mifflin.

Rogers, C. R. (1981, Summer). Notes on Rollo May. *Perspectives, 2*(1), p. 16.

Rollins, B. C., & Galligan, R. (1978). The developing child and marital satisfaction of parents. In R. M. Lerner & G. B. Spanier (Eds.), *Child influences on marital and family interaction: A life-span perspective*. New York: Academic Press.

Rook, K. S. (1984). Promoting social bonding: Strategies for helping the lonely and socially isolated. *American Psychologist, 39*, 1389–1407.

Roper Organization (1979). *The 1980 Virginia Slims American women's opinion poll.* New York: Philip Morris USA.

Rosch, E. (1974). Linguistic relativity. In A. Silverstein (Ed.), *Human communication: Theoretical perspectives.* New York: Halsted Press.

Rosch, E. (1977). Human categorization. In N. Warren (Ed.), *Studies in cross-cultural psychology* (Vol. 1). London: Academic Press.

Rosch, E. (1978). Principles of categorization. In E. Rosch & B. L. Lloyd (Eds.), *Cognition and categorization.* Hillsdale, NJ: Erlbaum.

Rose, G. A., & Williams, R. T. (1961). Metabolic studies on large and small eaters. *British Journal of Nutrition, 1,* 1–9.

Rose, R. J., Harris, E. L., Christian, J. C., & Nance, W. E. (1979). Genetic variance in nonverbal intelligence: Data from the kinships of identical twins. *Science, 205,* 1153–1155.

Rosenhan, D. L. (1970). The natural socialization of altruistic autonomy. In J. Macaulay & L. Berkowitz (Eds.), *Altruism and helping behavior.* New York: Academic Press.

Rosenhan, D. L. (1973). On being sane in insane places. *Science, 179,* 250–258.

Rosenhan, D. L. (1983a). Psychological abnormality and law. In C. J. Scheirer & B. C. Hammonds (Eds.), *The master lecture series: Vol. 2. Psychology and the law.* Washington, DC: American Psychological Association.

Rosenhan, D. L. (1983b, August). *Psychological realities and judicial policy.* Paper presented at the meeting of the American Psychological Association, Anaheim, CA.

Rosenthal, R., Hall, J. A., Archer, D., DiMatteo, M. R., & Rogers, P. L. (1979). The PONS test: Measuring sensitivity to nonverbal cues. In S. Weitz (Ed.), *Nonverbal communication* (2nd ed.). New York: Oxford University Press.

Rosenzweig, M. R. (1984a). Experience, memory, and the brain. *American Psychologist, 39,* 365–376.

Rosenzweig, M. R. (1984b). U.S. psychology and world psychology. *American Psychologist, 39,* 877–884.

Rosenzweig, M. R., Bennett, E. L., & Diamond, M. C. (1972, February). Brain changes in response to experience. *Scientific American,* 22–29.

Rosewicz, B. (1983, January 31). Study finds grim link between liquor and crime: Figures far worse than officials expected. *Detroit Free Press,* pp. 1A, 4A.

Ross, H. (1975, June 19). Mist, murk, and visual perception. *New Scientist,* pp. 658–660.

Ross, M., McFarland, C., & Fletcher, G. J. O. (1981). The effect of attitude on the recall of personal histories. *Journal of Personality and Social Psychology, 40,* 627–634.

Rossi, A. (1978, June). The biosocial side of parenthood. *Human Nature,* pp. 72–79.

Rossi, P. J. (1968). Adaptation and negative aftereffect to lateral optical displacement in newly hatched chicks. *Science, 160,* 430–432.

Rothbart, M., Fulero, S., Jensen, C., Howard, J., & Birrell, P. (1978). From individual to group impressions: Availability heuristics in stereotype formation. *Journal of Experimental Social Psychology, 14,* 237–255.

Rotton, J., & Kelly, I. W. (1985). Much ado about the full moon: A meta-analysis of lunar-lunacy research. *Psychological Bulletin, 97,* 286–306.

Roviaro, S., Holmes, D. S., & Holmsten, R. D. (1984). Influence of a cardiac rehabilitation program on the cardiovascular, psychological, and social functioning of cardiac patients. *Journal of Behavioral Medicine, 7,* 61–81.

Roy, M. (1977). A current survey of 150 cases. In M. Roy (Ed.), *Battered Women.* New York: Van Nostrand.

Rubin, J. Z., Provenzano, F. J., & Luria, Z. (1974). The eye of the beholder: Parents' views on sex of newborns. *American Journal of Orthopsychiatry, 44,* 512–519.

Rubin, L. B. (1979). *Women of a certain age: The midlife search for self.* New York: Harper & Row.

Rubin, R. T., Reinisch, J. M., & Haskett, R. F. (1980). Postnatal gonadal steroid effects on human behavior. *Science, 211,* 1318–1324.

Ruble, D. N., & Brooks-Gunn, J. (1979). Menstrual symptoms: A social cognition analysis. *Journal of Behavioral Medicine, 2,* 171–194.

Rumbaugh, D. (1977). *Language learning by a chimpanzee: The Lana project.* New York: Academic Press.

Rumbaugh, D. M. (1985). Comparative psychology: Patterns in adaptation. In A. M. Rogers & C. J. Scheirer (Eds.), *The G. Stanley Hall Lecture Series* (Vol. 5). Washington, DC: American Psychological Association.

Rumbaugh, D. M., & Savage-Rumbaugh, S. (1978). Chimpanzee language research: Status and potential. *Behavior Research Methods & Instrumentation, 10,* 119–131.

Rushton, J. P. (1975). Generosity in children: Immediate and long-term effects of modeling, preaching, and moral judgment. *Journal of Personality and Social Psychology, 31,* 459–466.

Rushton, J. P., Russell, R. J. H., & Wells, P. A. (1984). Genetic similarity theory: Beyond kin selection. *Behavior Genetics, 14,* 179–193.

Rutter, M. (1979). Maternal deprivation, 1972–1978: New findings, new concepts, new approaches. *Child Development, 50,* 283–305.

Ryan, E. D. (1980). Attribution, intrinsic motivation, and athletics: A replication and extension. In C. H. Nadeau, W. R. Halliwell, K. M. Newell, & G. C. Roberts (Eds.), *Psychology of motor behavior and sport—1979.* Champaign, IL: Human Kinetics Press.

Sabom, M. (1982). *Recollections of death: A medical investigation.* New York: Harper & Row.

Sackeim, H. A., Gur, R. C., & Saucy, M. C. (1978). Emotions are expressed more intensely on the left side of the face. *Science, 202,* 434–436.

Sackheim, J. A. (1985, June). The case for ECT. *Psychology Today,* pp. 36–40.

Safer, M. A., Tharps, Q. J., Jackson, T. C., & Leventhal, H. (1979). Determinants of three stages of delay in seeking care at a medical clinic. *Medical Care, 17*(1), 11–28.

Sagan, C. (1979a). *Broca's brain.* New York: Random House.

Sagan, C. (1979b). *Dragons of Eden.* New York: Random House.

Sagan, C. (1980). *Cosmos.* New York: Random House.

Sagan, C. (1984, September 30). We can prevent nuclear winter. *Parade Magazine* [unnumbered pages].

Sandberg, G. G., Jackson, T. L., & Petretic-Jackson, P. (1985, May). *Sexual aggression and courtship violence in dating relationships.* Paper presented at the meeting of the Midwestern Psychological Association, Chicago, IL.

Sarason, I. G. (1984). Stress, anxiety, and cognitive interference: Reactions to tests. *Journal of Personality and Social Psychology, 46,* 929–938.

Satir, V. (1967). *Conjoint family therapy.* Palo Alto, CA: Science and Behavior Books.

Savage-Rumbaugh, E. S., Rumbaugh, D. M., & Boysen, S. (1978). Symbolic communication between two chimpanzees (*Pan troglodytes*). *Science, 201,* 641–644.

Sayre, R. F. (1979). The parents' last lessons. In D. D. Van Tassel (Ed.), *Aging, death, and the completion of being.* Philadelphia: University of Pennsylvania Press.

Scanzoni, J. (1981, August 12–19). Family: Crisis or change? *Christian Century,* pp. 794–799.

Scanzoni, L. D., & Scanzoni, J. (1981). *Men, women, and change: A sociology of marriage and family.* New York: McGraw-Hill.

Scarr, S. (1982). Development is internally guided, not determined. *Contemporary Psychology, 27,* 852–853.

Scarr, S. (1984, May). What's a parent to do? [Conversation with E. Hall.] *Psychology Today,* pp. 58–63.

Scarr, S., & McCartney, K. (1983). How people make their own environments: A theory of genotype → environment effects. *Child Development, 54,* 424–435.

Scarr, S., Pakstis, A. J., Katz, S. H., & Barker, W. B. (1977). The absence of a relationship between degree of white ancestry and intellectual skills within a black population. *Human Genetics, 39,* 69–86.

Scarr, S., Webber, P. L., Weinberg, R. A., & Wittig, M. A. (1981). Personality resemblance among adolescents and their parents in biologically related and adoptive families. *Journal of Personality and Social Psychology, 40,* 885–898.

Scarr, S., & Weinberg, R. A. (1976). IQ test performance of black children adopted by white families. *American Psychologist, 31,* 726–739.

Scarr, S., & Weinberg, R. A. (1983). The Minnesota adoption studies: Genetic differences and malleability. *Child Development, 54,* 260–267.

Schachter, S. (1982). Recidivism and self-cure of smoking and obesity. *American Psychologist, 37,* 436–444.

Schachter, S., & Singer, J. E. (1962). Cognitive, social and physiological determinants of emotional state. *Psychological Review, 69,* 379–399.

Schaie, K. W., & Geiwitz, J. (1982). *Adult development and aging.* Boston: Little, Brown.

Schaie, K. W., & Strother, C. R. (1968). A cross-sequential study of age changes in cognitive behavior. *Psychological Bulletin, 70,* 671–680.

Scheerer, M. (1963, April). Problem solving. *Scientific American,* pp. 118–128.

Schein, E. H. (1956). The Chinese indoctrination program for prisoners of war: A study of attempted brainwashing. *Psychiatry, 19,* 149–172.

Schiele, B. C., & Brozek, J. (1956). "Experimental neurosis" resulting from semistarvation in man. In G. S. Welsh & W. G. Dahlstrom (Eds.), *Basic reading on the MMPI in psychology and medicine.* Minneapolis: University of Minnesota Press.

Schiffenbauer, A., & Schiavo, R. S. (1976). Physical distance and attraction: An intensification effect. *Journal of Experimental Social Psychology, 12,* 274–282.

Schleifer, S. J., Keller, S. E., McKegney, F. P., & Stein, M. (1979, March). *The influence of stress and other psychosocial factors on human immunity.* Paper presented at the 36th Annual Meeting of the American Psychosomatic Society, Dallas, TX.

Schlenker, B. R., & Miller, R. S. (1977a). Egocentrism in groups: Self-serving biases or logical information processing? *Journal of Personality and Social Psychology, 35,* 755–764.

Schlenker, B. R., & Miller, R. S. (1977b). Group cohesiveness as a determinant of egocentric perceptions in cooperative groups. *Human Relations, 30,* 1039–1055.

Schlesier-Stropp, B. (1984). Bulimia: A review of the literature. *Psychological Bulletin, 95,* 247–257.

Schlesinger, A. M., Jr. (1965). *A thousand days.* Boston: Houghton Mifflin.

Schmeck, H. M., Jr. (1985, January). By training the brain, scientists find links to immune disease. *New York Times,* pp. K15–K16.

Schnaper, N. (1980). Comments germane to the paper entitled "The reality of death experiences" by Ernst Rodin. *Journal of Nervous and Mental Disease, 168,* 268–270.

Schneider, W., & Shiffrin, R. M. (1977). Controlled and automatic human information processing: I. Detection, search, and attention. *Psychological Review, 84,* 1–66.

Schnitzer, B. (1984, May). Repunctuated message. *Games,* pp. 57, 62.

Schofield, J. (1982). *Black and white in school.* New York: Praeger.

Schofield, J., & Pavelchak, M. (1985). The day after: The impact of a media event. *American Psychologist, 40,* 542–548.

Schonfield, D., & Robertson, B. A. (1966). Memory storage and aging. *Canadian Journal of Psychology, 20,* 228–236.

Schroeder, D. H., & Costa, P. T., Jr. (1984). Influence of life event stress on physical illness: Substantive effects or methodological flaws? *Journal of Personality and Social Psychology, 46,* 853–863.

Schwartz, B. (1984). *Psychology of learning and behavior* (2nd ed.). New York: Norton.

Schwartz, G. E. (1982). Testing the biopsychosocial model: The ultimate challenge facing behavioral medicine? *Journal of Consulting and Clinical Psychology, 50,* 1040–1053.

Schwartz, G. E. (1983). Disregulation

theory and disease: Applications to the repression/cerebral disconnection/cardiovascular disorder hypothesis. *International Review of Applied Psychology, 32,* 95–118.

Schwarz, N., & Clore, G. L. (1983). Mood, misattribution, and judgments of well-being: Informative and directive functions of affective states. *Journal of Personality and Social Psychology, 45,* 513–523.

Scovern, A. W., & Kilmann, P. R. (1980). Status of electroconvulsive therapy: Review of the outcome literature. *Psychological Bulletin, 87,* 260–303.

Scribner, S. (1977). Modes of thinking and ways of speaking: Culture and logic reconsidered. In P. N. Johnson-Laird & P. C. Wason (Eds.), *Thinking: Readings in cognitive science.* New York: Cambridge University Press.

Seamon, J. G., Brody, N., & Kauff, D. M. (1983). Affective discrimination of stimuli that are not recognized: Effects of shadowing, masking, and cerebral laterality. *Journal of Experimental Psychology: Learning, Memory, and Cognition, 9,* 544–555.

Sears, D. O. (1979, May 3–5). *Life stage effects upon attitude change, especially among the elderly.* Paper presented at the Workshop on the Elderly of the Future, Committee on Aging, National Research Council, Annapolis, MD.

Seeman, P., Ulpian, C., Bergeron, C., Riederer, P., Jellinger, K., Gabriel, E., Reynolds, G. P., & Tourtellotte, W. W. (1984). Bimodal distribution of dopamine receptor densities in brains of schizophrenics. *Science, 225,* 728–731.

Seidman, L. J. (1983). Schizophrenia and brain dysfunction: An integration of recent neurodiagnostic findings. *Psychological Bulletin, 94,* 195–238.

Seligman, M. E. P. (1974, May). Submissive death: Giving up on life. *Psychology Today,* pp. 80–85.

Seligman, M. E. P. (1975). *Helplessness: On depression, development and death.* San Francisco: Freeman.

Selye, H. (1936). A syndrome produced by diverse nocuous agents. *Nature, 138,* 32.

Selye, H. (1976). *The stress of life.* New York: McGraw-Hill.

Senden, M. von (1932; reprinted 1960). In P. Heath (Trans.), *Space and sight: The perception of space and shape in the congenitally blind before and after operation.* Glencoe, IL: Free Press.

Shaffer, L. F. (1947). Fear and courage in aerial combat. *Journal of Consulting Psychology, 11,* 137–143.

Shapiro, C. M., Bortz, R., Mitchell, D., Bartel, P., & Jooste, P. (1981). Slow-wave sleep: A recovery period after exercise. *Science, 214,* 1253–1254.

Shapiro, D. A., & Shapiro, D. (1982). Meta-analysis of comparative therapy outcome studies: A replication and refinement. *Psychological Bulletin, 92,* 581–604.

Shaughnessy, J. J., & Zechmeister, E. B. (1979, November). *Memory-monitoring accuracy: The role of the distribution of retrieval attempts and study opportunities.* Paper presented at the 20th Annual Meeting of the Psychonomic Society, Phoenix, AZ.

Sheehan, S. (1982). *Is there no place on earth for me?* Boston: Houghton Mifflin.

Sheldon, W. H. (1954). *Atlas of man: A guide for somatotyping the adult male of all ages.* New York: Harper & Row.

Shepard, R. N. (1981). Psychophysical complementarity. In M. Kubovy & J. R. Pomerantz (Eds.), *Perceptual organization* (pp. 279–341). Hillsdale, NJ: Erlbaum.

Sheperd-Look, D. L. (1982). Sex differentiation and the development of sex roles. In B. B. Wolman (Ed.), *Handbook of developmental psychology.* Englewood Cliffs, NJ: Prentice-Hall.

Sherif, M. (1937). An experimental approach to the study of attitudes. *Sociometry, 1,* 90–98.

Sherif, M. (1966). *In common predicament: Social psychology of intergroup conflict and cooperation.* Boston: Houghton Mifflin.

Sherif, M., & Sherif, C. W. (1969). *Social psychology.* New York: Harper & Row.

Sherman, A. R., & Levin, M. P. (1979). *In vivo* therapies for compulsive habits, sexual difficulties, and severe adjustment problems. In A. P. Goldstein & F. H. Kanfer (Eds.), *Maximizing treatment gains: Transfer enhancement in psychotherapy.* New York: Academic Press.

Shettleworth, S. J. (1973). Food reinforcement and the organization of behavior in golden hamsters. In R. A. Hinde & J. Stevenson-Hinde (Eds.), *Constraints on learning.* London: Academic Press.

Shiffrin, R. M., & Schneider, W. (1977). Controlled and automatic human information processing: II. Perceptual learning, automatic attending, and a general theory. *Psychological Review, 84,* 127–190.

Shostrom, E. L. (1966). *EITS Manual for the Personal Orientation Inventory.* San Diego: Educational and Industrial Testing Service.

Shotland, R. L. (1984, March 12). Quoted by Maureen Dowd, 20 years after the murder of Kitty Genovese, the question remains: Why? *The New York Times,* p. B1.

Shotland, R. L., & Goodstein, L. I. (1984). The role of bystanders in crime control. *Journal of Social Issues, 40,* 9–26.

Shweder, R. A. (1982). Liberalism as destiny. *Contemporary Psychology, 27,* 421–424.

Siebenhaler, J. B., & Caldwell, D. K. (1956). Cooperation among adult dolphins. *Journal of Mammalogy, 37,* 126–128.

Siegel, L. S., & Hodkin, B. (1982). The garden path to the understanding of cognitive development: Has Piaget led us into the poison ivy? In S. Modgil & C. Modgil (Eds.), *Jean Piaget: Consensus and controversy.* New York: Praeger.

Siegel, R. K. (1977, October). Hallucinations. *Scientific American,* pp. 132–140.

Siegel, R. K. (1980). The psychology of life after death. *American Psychologist, 35,* 911–931.

Siegel, R. K. Quoted by J. Hooper (1982, October), Mind tripping. *Omni,* pp. 72–82, 159–160.

Siegel, R. K. (1984, March 15). Personal communication.

Silka, L. (1983). "You just can't count on things anymore": Perceptions of increased variability in the present. *Personality and Social Psychology Bulletin, 9,* 621–628.

Silver, M., & Geller, D. (1978). On the irrelevance of evil: The organization and individual action. *Journal of Social Issues, 34,* 125–136.

Singer, J. L. (1975). Navigating the stream of consciousness: Research in daydreaming and related inner experience. *American Psychologist, 30,* 727–738.

Singer, J. L. (1976, July). Fantasy: The foundation of serenity. *Psychology Today,* pp. 32–37.

Singer, J. L. (1981). Clinical intervention: New developments in methods and evaluation. In L. T. Benjamin, Jr. (Ed.), *The G. Stanley Hall Lecture Series,* (Vol. 1). Washington, DC: American Psychological Association.

Singer, J. L., Singer, D. G., & Rapaczynski, W. S. (1984). Family patterns and television viewing as predictors of children's beliefs and aggression. *Journal of Communication, 34*(2), 73–89.

Six, B., & Krahe, B. (1984). Implicit psychologists' estimates of attitude-behaviour consistencies. *European Journal of Social Psychology, 14,* 79–86.

Sjostrom, L. (1980). Fat cells and bodyweight. In A. J. Stunkard (Ed.), *Obesity.* Philadelphia: Saunders.

Skeels, H. M. (1966). Adult status of children with contrasting early life experiences: A follow-up study. *Monographs of the Society for Research in Child Development, 31* (Serial No. 105).

Skinner, B. F. (1956). A case history in scientific method. *American Psychologist, 11,* 221–233.

Skinner, B. F. (1957). *Verbal behavior.* Englewood Cliffs, NJ: Prentice-Hall.

Skinner, B. F. (1961, November). Teaching machines. *Scientific American,* pp. 91–102.

Skinner, B. F. (1983, September). Origins of a behaviorist. *Psychology Today,* pp. 22–33.

Skinner, B. F. (1984). The shame of American education. *American Psychologist, 39,* 947–954.

Skinner, B. F. (1985). *Cognitive science and behaviorism.* Unpublished manuscript, Harvard University, Cambridge, MA.

Sklar, L. S., & Anisman, H. (1981). Stress and cancer. *Psychological Bulletin, 89,* 369–406.

Sladek, Jr., R., & Gash, D. M. (Eds.) (1984). *Neural transplants: Development and function.* New York: Plenum Press.

Slovic, P., & Fischhoff, B. (1977). On the psychology of experimental surprises. *Journal of Experimental Psychology: Human Perception and Performance, 3,* 544–551.

Slovic, P., Fischhoff, B., & Lichtenstein, S. (1985). Regulation of risk: A psychological perspective. In R. Noll (Ed.), *Social science and regulatory policy.* Berkley, CA: University of California Press.

Smith, A. (1983, April 26). Personal communication.

Smith, A., & Sugar, O. (1975). Development of above normal language and intelligence 21 years after left hemispherectomy. *Neurology, 25,* 813–818.

Smith, D. (1982). Trends in counseling and psychotherapy. *American Psychologist, 37,* 802–809.

Smith, D., & Kraft, W. A. (1983). DSM-III: Do psychologists really want an alternative? *American Psychologist, 38,* 777–785.

Smith, M. B. (1978). Psychology and values. *Journal of Social Issues, 34,* 181–199.

Smith, M. B. (1982, August). *Psychologists and peace.* Paper presented at the meeting of the American Psychological Association, Washington, DC.

Smith, M. C. (1983). Hypnotic memory enhancement of witnesses: Does it work? *Psychological Bulletin, 94,* 387–407.

Smith, M. L., & Glass, G. V. (1977). Meta-analysis of psychotherapy outcome studies. *American Psychologist, 32,* 752–760.

Smith, M. L., Glass, G. V., & Miller, R. L. (1980). *The benefits of psychotherapy.* Baltimore: Johns Hopkins Press.

Smith, P. K., & Daglish, L. (1977). Sex differences in parent and infant behavior in the home. *Child Development, 48,* 1250–1254.

Smith, R. J. (1984). Polygraph tests: Dubious validity. *Science, 224,* 1217.

Smith, T. W. (1979). Happiness: Time trends, seasonal variations, intersurvey differences, and other mysteries. *Social Psychology Quarterly, 42,* 18–30.

Snarey, J. R. (1985). Cross-cultural universality of social-moral development: A critical review of Kohlbergian research. *Psychological Bulletin, 97,* 202–233.

Snyder, C. R., & Fromkin, H. (1980). Uniqueness: The human pursuit of difference. New York: Plenum Press.

Snyder, C. R., Shenkel, R. J., & Lowry, C. R. (1977). Acceptance of personality interpretations: The "Barnum effect" and beyond. *Journal of Consulting and Clinical Psychology, 45,* 104–114.

Snyder, M. (1983). The influence of individuals on situations: Implications for understanding the links between personality and social behavior. *Journal of Personality, 51,* 497–516.

Snyder, M., Tanke, E. D., & Berscheid, E. (1977). Social perception and interpersonal behavior: On the self-fulfilling nature of social stereotypes. *Journal of Personality and Social Psychology, 35,* 656–666.

Snyder, S. H. (1984a, September). Neurosciences: An integrative discipline. *Science, 225,* 1255–1257.

Snyder, S. H. (1984b, November). Medicated minds. *Science 84,* pp. 141–142.

Sokoll, G. R., & Mynatt, C. R. (1984, May). *Arousal and free throw shooting.* Paper presented at the meeting of the Midwestern Psychological Association, Chicago, IL.

Solomon, R. L. (1980). The opponent-process theory of acquired motivation: The costs of pleasure and the benefits of pain. *American Psychologist, 35,* 691–712.

Solomon, R. L., Kamin, L. J., & Wynne, L. C. (1953). Traumatic avoidance learning: The outcomes of several extinction procedures with dogs. *Journal of Abnormal and Social Psychology, 48,* 291–302.

Sontag, S. (1978). *Illness as metaphor.* New York: Farrar, Straus, & Giroux.

Sontag, S. (1982). The double standard of aging. In L. R. Allman & D. T. Jaffe (Eds.), *Readings in adult psychology.* New York: Harper & Row.

Spanos, N. P. (1982). A social psychological approach to hypnotic behavior. In G. Weary & H. L. Mirels (Eds.), *Inte-*

grations of clinical and social psychology (pp. 231–271). New York: Oxford.

Spanos, N. P. (1984, August). *Disavowed responsibility for action: Demonic possession, hypnosis, and multiple personality.* Paper presented to the meeting of the American Psychological Association, Toronto, Canada.

Spanos, N. P., Radtke, L., Bertrand, L. D. (1985). Hypnotic amnesia as a strategic enactment: Breaching amnesia in highly susceptible subjects. *Journal of Personality and Social Psychology, 47,* 1155–1169.

Spence, J. T., & Helmreich, R. L. (1983). Achievement-related motives and behavior. In J. T. Spence (Ed.), *Achievement and achievement motives: Psychological and sociological approaches.* New York: Freeman.

Sperling, G. (1960). The information available in brief visual presentations. *Psychological Monographs, 74* (Whole No. 498).

Sperry, R. W. (1956, May). The eye and the brain. *Scientific American,* pp. 48–52.

Sperry, R. W. (1964). *Problems outstanding in the evolution of brain function.* James Arthur Lecture, American Museum of Natural History, New York. Cited by R. Ornstein (1977), *The psychology of consciousness* (2nd ed., p. 29) New York: Harcourt Brace Jovanovich.

Sperry, R. W. (1968). Hemisphere deconnection and unity in conscious awareness. *American Psychologist, 23,* 723–733.

Sperry, R. W. (1982). Some effects of disconnecting the cerebral hemispheres. *Science, 217,* 1223–1226.

Sperry, R. W. (1983, August). [Interview] *Omni,* pp. 69–75, 98, 100.

Spezzano, C. (1981, May). Prenatal psychology: Pregnant with questions. *Psychology Today,* pp. 49–57.

Spielberger, C., & London, P. (1982). Rage boomerangs. *American Health, 1,* 52–56.

Spielberger, C. D., Johnson, E. H., Russell, S. F., Crane, R. J., Jacobs, G. A., & Worden, T. J. (1985). The experience and expression of anger. In M. A. Chesney, S. E. Goldston, & R. H. Rosenman (Eds.), *Anger and hostility in behavioral medicine.* New York: Hemisphere/McGraw-Hill.

Spiess, W. F. J., Greer, J. H., & O'Donohue, W. T. (1984). Premature ejaculation: Investigation of factors in ejaculatory latency. *Journal of Abnormal Psychology, 93,* 242–245.

Spitzer, L. (1983). *The effects of type of sugar ingested on subsequent eating behavior.* Unpublished doctoral dissertation, Yale University, New Haven, CT.

Spitzer, R. L. (1975). On pseudoscience in science, logic in remission, and psychiatric diagnosis: A critique of Rosenhan's "On being sane in insane places." *Journal of Abnormal Psychology, 84,* 442–452.

Spitzer, R. L., Skokol, A. E., Gibbon, M., & Williams, J. B. W. (1981). *DSM-III case book: A learning companion to the diagnostic and statistical manual of mental disorders* (3rd ed.). Washington, DC: American Psychiatric Association.

Springer, S. P., & Deutsch, G. (1985). *Left brain, right brain.* San Francisco: W. H. Freeman.

Squire, L. R. (1982). The neuropsychology of human memory. *Annual Review of Neuroscience, 5,* 241–273.

Sroufe, L. A. (1978, October). Attachment and the roots of competence. *Human Nature, 1*(10), 50–57.

Sroufe, L. A., Fox, N. E., & Pancake, V. R. (1983). Attachment and dependency in developmental perspective. *Child Development, 54,* 1615–1627.

Stapp, J., & Fulcher, R. (1983). The employment of APA members: 1982. *American Psychologist, 38,* 1298–1320.

Steele, C. M., Critchlow, B., & Liu, T. J. (1985). Alcohol and social behavior II: The helpful drunkard. *Journal of Personality and Social Psychology, 48,* 35–46.

Steele, C. M., & Southwick, L. (1985). Alcohol and social behavior I: The psychology of drunken excess. *Journal of Personality and Social Psychology, 48,* 18–34.

Stengel, E. (1981). Suicide. In *The new encyclopaedia britannica, macropaedia* (Vol. 17, pp. 777–782). Chicago: Encyclopaedia Britannica.

Sternberg, R. J. (1982). Reasoning, problem solving, and intelligence. In R. J. Sternberg (Ed.), *Handbook of human intelligence.* New York: Cambridge University Press.

Sternberg, R. J. (1984). Testing intelligence without IQ tests. *Phi Delta Kappan, 65*(10), 694–698.

Sternberg, R. J., & Grajek, S. (1984). The nature of love. *Journal of Personality and Social Psychology, 47,* 312–329.

Sternberg, R. J., & Salter, W. (1982). Conceptions of intelligence. In R. J. Sternberg (Ed.), *Handbook of human intelligence.* New York: Cambridge University Press.

Stevenson, H. W. (1983). *Making the grade: School achievement in Japan, Taiwan, and the United States.* Stanford, CA: Center for Advanced Study in the Behavioral Sciences (Annual Report).

Stone, A. A., & Neale, J. M. (1984). Effects of severe daily events on mood. *Journal of Personality and Social Psychology, 46,* 137–144.

Storms, M. D. (1980). Theories of sexual orientation. *Journal of Personality and Social Psychology, 38,* 783–792.

Storms, M. D. (1981). A theory of erotic orientation development. *Psychological Review, 88,* 340–353.

Storms, M. D. (1983). *Development of sexual orientation.* Washington, DC: Office of Social and Ethical Responsibility, American Psychological Association.

Storms, M. D., & Thomas, G. C. (1977). Reactions to physical closeness. *Journal of Personality and Social Psychology, 35,* 412–418.

Strack, S., & Coyne, J. C. (1983). Social confirmation of dysphoria: Shared and private reactions to depression. *Journal of Personality and Social Psychology, 44,* 798–806.

Stratton, G. M. (1896). Some preliminary experiments on vision without inversion of the retinal image. *Psychological Review, 3,* 611–617.

Stratton, G. M. (1917). The mnemonic feat of the "Shass Pollak." *Psychological Review, 24,* 244–247.

Straub, R. O., Seidenberg, M. S., Bever, T. G., & Terrace, H. S. (1979). Serial learning in the pigeon. *Journal of the Experimental Analysis of Behavior, 32,* 137–148.

Strauss, M. A., & Gelles, R. J. (1980). *Behind closed doors: Violence in the American family.* New York: Anchor/Doubleday.

Strentz, H. (1984, December 25). The road to imbecility. *Cleveland Plain Dealer,* p. B23.

Stroop, J. R. (1935). Studies of interference in serial verbal reactions. *Journal of Experimental Psychology, 18,* 643–662.

Stroup, A. L., & Manderscheid, R. W. (1984). *The development of the state mental system in the United States: 1840–1980.* Unpublished manuscript, Division of Biometry and Epidemiology, National Institute of Mental Health, Rockville, MD.

Strupp, H. H. (1982). The outcome problem in psychotherapy: Contemporary perspectives. In J. H. Harvey & M. M. Parks (Eds.), *The master lecture series: Vol. 1. Psychotherapy research and behavior change.* Washington, DC: American Psychological Association.

Strupp, H. H. (1984). Psychotherapy research: Reflections on my career and the state of the art. *Journal of Social and Clinical Psychology, 2,* 3–24.

Stuss, D. T., & Benson, D. F. (1984). Neuropsychological studies of the frontal lobes. *Psychological Bulletin, 95,* 3–28.

Suedfeld, P. (1975). The benefits of boredom: Sensory deprivation reconsidered. *American Scientist, 63,* 60–69.

Suedfeld, P. (1980). *Restricted environmental stimulation: Research and clinical applications.* New York: Wiley.

Suedfeld, P., & Kristeller, J. L. (1982). Stimulus reduction as a technique in health psychology. *Health Psychology, 1,* 337–357.

Suls, J. M., & Tesch, F. (1978). Students' preferences for information about their test performance: A social comparison study. *Journal of Experimental Social Psychology, 8,* 189–197.

Suomi, S. J. (1983). Social development in rhesus monkeys: Consideration of individual differences. In A. Oliverio & M. Zappella (Eds.), *The behavior of human infants.* New York: Plenum Press.

Super, C. M. (1981). Behavioral development in infancy. In R. H. Munroe, R. L. Munroe, & B. B. Whiting (Eds.), *Handbook of cross-cultural human development.* New York: Garland STMP Press.

Surgeon General. (1979). *Healthy people.* Washington, DC: Government Printing Office.

Surgeon General. (1983). *The health consequences of smoking: Cardiovascular disease.* Washington, DC: Government Printing Office.

Swann, W. B., Jr., & Miller, L. C. (1982). Why never forgetting a face matters: Visual imagery and social memory. *Journal of Personality and Social Psychology, 43,* 475–480.

Szasz, T. (1984). *The therapeutic state: Psychiatry in the mirror of current events.* Buffalo, NY: Prometheus.

Tajfel, H. (Ed.) (1982). *Social identity and intergroup relations.* New York: Cambridge University Press.

Takooshian, H., & Bodinger, H. (1982). Bystander indifference to street crime. In L. Savitz & N. Johnston (Eds.), *Contemporary criminology.* New York: Wiley.

Tanford, S., & Penrod, S. (1984). Social influence model: A formal integration of research on majority and minority influence processes. *Psychological Bulletin, 95,* 189–225.

Tanner, J. M. (1978). *Fetus into man: Physical growth from conception to maturity.* Cambridge, MA: Harvard University Press.

Tart, C. T. (1983). *The Open Mind, 1*(1), 6.

Tavris, C. (1982, November). Anger defused. *Psychology Today,* pp. 25–35.

Tavris, C., & Wade, C. (1984). *The longest war: Sex differences in perspective* (2nd ed.). San Diego: Harcourt Brace Jovanovich.

Taylor, M. C., & Hall, J. A. (1982). Psychological androgyny: Theories, methods and conclusions. *Psychological Bulletin, 92,* 347–366.

Taylor, S. E. (1979). Hospital patient behavior: Reactance, helplessness, or control? *Journal of Social Issues, 35,* 156–184.

Taylor, S. E. (1981). A categorization approach to stereotyping. In D. L. Hamilton (Ed.), *Cognitive processes in stereotyping and intergroup behavior.* Hillsdale, NJ: Erlbaum.

Taylor, S. P. (1983). Alcohol and human physical aggression. *Aggression, 2,* 77–101.

Taylor, S. P., & Leonard, K. E. (1983). Alcohol and human physical aggression. In R. Geen & E. Donnerstein (Eds.), *Aggression: Theoretical and empirical reviews* (Vol. 1). New York: Academic Press.

Teevan, R. C., & McGhee, P. E. (1972). Childhood development of fear of failure motivation. *Journal of Personality and Social Psychology, 21,* 345–348.

Teghtsoonian, R. (1971). On the exponents of Stevens' Law and the constant in Ekman's Law. *Psychology Review, 78,* 71–80.

Telch, M. J., Killen, J. D., McAlister, A. L., Perry, C. L., & Maccoby, N. (1982). Long-term follow-up of a pilot project on smoking prevention with adolescents. *Journal of Behavioral Medicine, 5,* 1–7.

Terman, L. M. (1916). *The measurement of intelligence.* Boston: Houghton Mifflin.

Terrace, H. S. (1979, November). How Nim Chimpsky changed my mind. *Psychology Today,* pp. 65–76.

Tetlock, P. E. (1983a). Policy-makers' images of international conflict. *Journal of Social Issues, 39*(1), 67–86.

Tetlock, P. E. (1983b). Psychological research on foreign policy: A methodological overview. In L. Wheeler & P. Shaver (Eds.), *Review of personality and social psychology* (Vol. 4). Beverly Hills, CA: Sage.

Teuber, M. L. (1974, July). Sources of ambiguity in the prints of Maurits C. Escher. *Scientific American,* pp. 90–104.

Thomas, A., & Chess, S. (1977). *Temperament and development.* New York: Brunner-Mazel.

Thomas, A., & Chess, S. (1981). The role of temperament in the contributions of individuals to their development. In R. M. Lerner & N. A. Bush-Rossnagel (Eds.), *Individuals as producers of their own development: A life-span perspective.* New York: Academic Press.

Thomas, A., & Chess, S. (1984). Genesis and evolution of behavioral disorders: From infancy to early adult life. *American Journal of Psychiatry, 141,* 1–9.

Thompson, J. K., Jarvie, G. J., Lahey, B. B., & Cureton, K. J. (1982). Exercise and obesity: Etiology, physiology, and intervention. *Psychological Bulletin, 91,* 55–79.

Thorndike, R. L., & Hagen, E. P. (1977). *Measurement and evaluation in psychology and education* (4th ed.). New York: Wiley.

Tierney, J. (1982, June). Doctor, is this man dangerous? *Science 82,* pp. 28–31.

Tinbergen, N. (1951). *The study of instinct.* Oxford: Clarendon.

Tisdell, P. (1983, September). Mixed messages. *Science 83,* pp. 84–85.

Tolman, E. C. (1948). Cognitive maps in rats and men. *Psychological Review, 55,* 189–208.

Tolman, E. C., & Honzik, C. H. (1930). Introduction and removal of reward, and maze performance in rats. *University of California publications in psychology, 4,* 257–275.

Triandis, H. C. (1980). Preface. In H. C. Triandis & W. W. Lambert (Eds.), *Handbook of cross-cultural psychology* (Vol. 1). Boston: Allyn & Bacon.

Triplett, N. (1898). The dynamogenic factors in pacemaking and competition. *American Journal of Psychology, 9,* 507–533.

True, R. M. (1949). Experimental control in hypnotic age regression states. *Science, 110,* 583–584.

Trueblood, D. E. (1983). *Quarterly Yoke Letter, 25*(4), p. 2.

Tryon, R. C. (1940). Genetic differences in maze-learning ability in rats. In *Thirty-ninth yearbook of the National Society for the Study of Education. Intelligence: Its nature and nurture. Part I. Comparative and critical exposition.* Bloomington, IL: Public School Publishing.

Tsang, Y. C. (1938). Hunger motivation in gastrectomized rats. *Journal of Comparative Psychology, 26,* 1–17.

Tucker, D. M. (1981). Lateral brain function, emotion, and conceptualization. *Psychological Bulletin, 89,* 19–46.

Tucker L. A. (1983). Muscular strength and mental health. *Journal of Personality and Social Psychology, 45,* 1355–1360.

Turk, D. C., Meichenbaum, D. H., & Berman, W. H. (1979). Application of biofeedback for the regulation of pain: A critical review. *Psychological Bulletin, 86,* 1322–1338.

Turner, B. F. (1982). Sex-related differences in aging. In B. B. Wolman (Ed.), *Handbook of developmental psychology.* Englewood Cliffs, NJ: Prentice-Hall.

Turner, S. M., Beidel, D. C., & Nathan, R. S. (1985). Biological factors in obsessive-compulsive disorders. *Psychological Bulletin, 97,* 430–450.

Tversky, A. (1985, June). Quoted by K. McKean, Decisions, decisions. *Discover,* pp. 22–31.

Tversky, A., & Kahneman, D. (1974). Judgment under uncertainty: Heuristics and biases. *Science, 185,* 1124–1131.

Tversky, A., & Kahneman, D. (1980). Causal schemas in judgments under uncertainty. In M. Fishbein (Ed.), *Progress in social psychology.* Hillsdale, NJ: Erlbaum.

Tversky, A., & Kahneman, D. (1983). Extensional versus intuitive reasoning: The conjunction fallacy in probability judgement. *Psychological Review, 90,* 293–315.

Ulrich, R. S. (1984). View through a window may influence recovery from surgery. *Science, 224,* 420–421.

Underwood, B. J. (1957). Interference and forgetting. *Psychological Review, 64,* 49–60.

Unger, R. K. (1979). Toward a redefinition of sex and gender. *American Psychologist, 34,* 1085–1094.

United Nations (1980). *Demographic yearbook.* New York.

U.S. Congress, Office of Technology Assessment (1983, November). *Scientific validity of polygraph testing: A research review and evaluation—A technical memorandum,* p. 4. Washington, DC: U.S. Government Printing Office.

U.S. Department of Health and Human Services (1983a, September/October). *Smoking and health bulletin.* Washington, DC: U.S. Government Printing Office.

U.S. Department of Health and Human Services (1983b). *Vital and health statistics* (Series 11, No. 230, pp. 4–5). Washington, DC: U.S. Government Printing Office.

U.S. Public Health Service (1980). *Smoking, tobacco & health: A fact book.* Washington, DC: U.S. Government Printing Office.

Valenstein, E. S. (1980). *The psychosurgery debate.* San Francisco: Freeman.

Vaillant, G. E. (1977). *Adaption to life.* Boston: Little, Brown.

Vance, E. B., & Wagner, N. N. (1976). Written descriptions of orgasm: A study of sex differences. *Archives of Sexual Behavior, 5,* 87–98.

Vandenberg, S. G., & Kuse, A. R. (1978). Mental rotations, a group test of three-dimensional spatial visualization. *Perceptual and Motor Skills, 47,* 599–604.

Van Dyke, C., & Byck, R. (1982, March). Cocaine. *Scientific American,* pp. 128–141.

van Kammen, D. P., Mann, L. S., Sternberg, D. E., Scheinin, M., Ninan, P. T., Marder, S. R., van Kammen, W. B., Rieder, R. O., & Linnoila, M. (1983). Dopamine-B-hydroxylase activity and homovanillic acid in spinal fluid of schizophrenics with brain atrophy. *Science, 220,* 974–977.

Van Leeuwen, M. S. (1978). A cross-cultural examination of psychological differentiation in males and females. *International Journal of Psychology, 13,* 87–122.

Van Leeuwen, M. S. (1982). I.Q.ism and the just society: Historical background. *Journal of the American Scientific Affiliation, 34,* 193–201.

VanTassel-Baska, J. (1983). Profiles of precocity: The 1982 Midwest Talent Search finalists. *Gifted Child Quarterly, 27,* 139–145.

Vaughn, K. B., & Lanzetta, J. T. (1981). The effect of modification of expressive displays on vicarious emotional arousal. *Journal of Experimental Social Psychology, 17,* 16–30.

Vernon, P. A. (1983). Speed of information processing and general intelligence. *Intelligence, 7,* 53–70.

Von Frisch, K. (1974). Decoding the language of the bee. *Science, 185,* 663–668.

Vonnegut, M. (1975). *The Eden express:*

A personal account of schizophrenia. New York: Praeger.

Waber, D. (1976). Sex differences in cognition: A function of maturation rate? *Science, 192,* 572–573.

Waddington, C. H. (1962). *New patterns in genetics and development.* New York: Columbia University Press.

Wagner, R. K., & Sternberg, R. J. (1985). Practical intelligence in real-world pursuits: The role of tacit knowledge. *Journal of Personality and Social Psychology, 49*(2), 436–458.

Wagstaff, G. F. (1983). Attitudes to poverty, the Protestant ethic, and political affiliation: A preliminary investigation. *Social Behavior and Personality, 11,* 45–47.

Wallace, R. K., & Benson, H. (1972, February). The physiology of meditation. *Scientific American,* pp. 84–90.

Wallach, M. A., & Wallach, L. (1983). *Psychology's sanction for selfishness: The error of egoism in theory and therapy.* New York: Freeman.

Wallach, M. A., & Wallach, L. (1985, February). How psychology sanctions the cult of the self. *Washington Monthly,* pp. 46–56.

Walling, W. H. (1912). *Sexology.* Philadelphia: Puritan.

Wallis, C. (1983, June 6). Stress: Can we cope? *Time,* pp. 48–54.

Walster (Hatfield), E., Aronson, V., Abrahams, D., & Rottman, L. (1966). Importance of physical attractiveness in dating behavior. *Journal of Personality and Social Psychology, 4,* 508–516.

Walster, E. H., & Walster, G. W. (1978). *A new look at love.* Reading, MA: Addison-Wesley.

Ward, W. C., & Jenkins, H. M. (1965). The display of information and the judgment of contingency. *Canadian Journal of Psychology, 19,* 231–241.

Wason, P. C. (1981). The importance of cognitive illusions. *The Behavioral and Brain Sciences, 4,* 356.

Wason, P. C., & Johnson-Laird, P. N. (Eds.) (1968). *Thinking and reasoning.* Baltimore: Penguin.

Wass, H., Christian, M., Myers, J., & Murphey, M. (1978–1979). Similarities and dissimilarities in attitudes toward death in a population of older persons. *Omega, 9,* 337–354.

Waterman, A. S., Geary, P. S., & Waterman, C. K. (1974). A longitudinal study of changes in ego identity status during the freshman to the senior year in college. *Developmental Psychology, 10,* 387–392.

Watkins, J. G. (1984). The Bianchi (L.A. Hillside Strangler) case: Sociopath or multiple personality? *International Journal of Clinical and Experimental Hypnosis, 32,* 67–101.

Watkins, L. R., & Mayer, D. J. (1982). Organization of endogenous opiate and nonopiate pain control systems. *Science, 216,* 1185–1192.

Watkins, P., & Soledad, G. (1979). *My life with Charles Manson.* New York: Bantam.

Watson, J. B. (1913). Psychology as the behaviorist views it. *Psychological Review, 20,* 158–177.

Watson, J. B. (1930). *Behaviorism.* Chicago, IL: University of Chicago Press (Revised ed.)

Watson, J. B., & Rayner, R. (1920). Conditioned emotional reactions. *Journal of Experimental Psychology, 3,* 1–14.

Watson, R. I. (1978). *The great psychologists* (4th ed.). Philadelphia: Lippincott.

Watson, R. I., Jr. (1973). Investigation into deindividuation using a cross-cultural survey technique. *Journal of Personality and Social Psychology, 25,* 342–345.

Watt, N., Anthony, J., Wynne, L., & Rolf, J. (1984). *Children at risk for schizophrenia: A longitudinal perspective.* New York: Cambridge University Press.

Weaver, J. B., Masland, J. L., & Zillmann, D. (1984). Effect of erotica on young men's aesthetic perception of their female sexual partners. *Perceptual and Motor Skills, 58,* 929–930.

Webb, W. B. (1981). The return of consciousness. In L. T. Benjamin, Jr. (Ed.), *The G. Stanley Hall Lecture Series* (Vol. 1). Washington, DC: American Psychological Association.

Webb, W. B. (1982a). Sleep and biological rhythms. In W. B. Webb (Ed.), *Biological rhythms, sleep, and performance* (pp. 87–110). Chichester, England: Wiley.

Webb, W. B. (1982b). Sleep and dreaming. In *Encyclopedia of Science and Technology* (pp. 470–474). New York: McGraw-Hill.

Webb, W. B., & Campbell, S. S. (1983). Relationships in sleep characteristics of identical and fraternal twins. *Archives of General Psychiatry, 40,* 1093–1095.

Webb, W. G. (1979). Are short and long sleepers different? *Psychological Reports, 44,* 259–264.

Weber, A. M., & Bradshaw, J. L. (1981). Levy and Reid's neurological model in relation to writing hand/posture. An evaluation. *Psychological Bulletin, 90,* 74–88.

Wechsler, D. (1972). "Hold" and "Don't Hold" tests. In S. M. Chown (Ed.), *Human aging.* New York: Penguin.

Weinberg, M. S., & Williams, C. (1974). *Male homosexuals: Their problems and adaptations.* New York: Oxford University Press.

Weinberg, R. S. (1981). The relationship between mental preparation and motor performance: a review and critique. *Quest, 33,* 195–213.

Weinberger, N. M., Gold, P. E., & Sternberg, D. B. (1984). Epinephrine enables Pavlovian fear conditioning under anesthesia. *Science, 223,* 605–607.

Weiner, R. D. (1984). Does electroconvulsive therapy cause brain damage? *The Behavioral and Brain Sciences, 7,* 1–53.

Weingartner, H., Rudorfer, M. V., Buchsbaum, M. S., & Linnoila, M. (1983). Effects of serotonin on memory impairments produced by ethanol. *Science, 221,* 472–473.

Weinstein, N. D. (1984). Why it won't happen to me: Perceptions of risk factors and susceptibility. *Health Psychology, 3,* 431–457.

Weiskrantz, L., & Warrington, L. (1979). Conditioning in amnesic patients. *Neuropsychologia, 17,* 187–194.

Weiss, J. M. (1977). Psychological and behavioral influences on gastrointestinal lesions in animal models. In J. D. Maser & M. E. P. Seligman (Eds.), *Psychopathology: Experimental models.* San Francisco: Freeman.

Weisz, J. R., Rothbaum, F. M., &

Blackburn, T. C. (1984). Standing out and standing in: The psychology of control in America and Japan. *American Psychologist, 39,* 955–969.

Wells, C. (1983, March). Teaching the brain new tricks. *Esquire,* pp. 49–57.

Wells, G. L. (1981). Lay analyses of causal forces on behavior. In J. Harvey (Ed.), *Cognition, social behavior and the environment.* Hillsdale, NJ. Erlbaum.

Wetzel, C. G., & Insko, C. A. (1982). The similarity-attraction relationship: Is there an ideal one? *Journal of Experimental Social Psychology, 18,* 253–276.

WGBH (1983, March 22). *Fat chance in a thin world.* Transcript of *Nova* PBS program. (Available from WGBH, 125 Western Avenue, Boston, Mass. 02134).

Wheeler, D. D., & Janis, I. L. (1980). *A practical guide for making decisions.* New York: Free Press.

White, G. L., Fishbein, S., & Rutsein, J. (1981). Passionate love and the misattribution of arousal. *Journal of Personality and Social Psychology, 41,* 56–62.

White, G. L., & Kight, T. D. (1984). Misattribution of arousal and attraction: Effects of salience of explanations for arousal. *Journal of Experimental Social Psychology, 20,* 55–64.

White, R. K. (1984). *Fearful warriors: A psychological profile of U.S.-Soviet Relations.* New York: Free Press.

Whorf, B. L. (1956). Science and linguistics. In J. B. Carroll (Ed.), *Language, thought, and reality: Selected writings of Benjamin Lee Whorf.* Cambridge, MA: MIT Press.

Wickelgren, W. A. (1977). *Learning and memory.* Englewood Cliffs, NJ: Prentice-Hall.

Wicker, A. W. (1971). An examination of the "other variables" explanation of attitude-behavior inconsistency. *Journal of Personality and Social Psychology, 19,* 18–30.

Wiens, A. N., & Menustik, C. E. (1983). Treatment outcome and patient characteristics in an aversion therapy program for alcoholism. *American Psychologist, 38,* 1089–1096.

Wiesel, T. N. (1982). Postnatal development of the visual cortex and the influence of environment. *Nature, 299,* 583–591.

Wigdor, A. K., & Garner, W. R. (1982). *Ability testing: Uses, consequences, and controversies.* Washington, DC: National Academic Press.

Wilder, D. A. (1981). Perceiving persons as a group: Categorization and intergroup relations. In D. L. Hamilton (Ed.), *Cognitive processes in stereotyping and intergroup behavior.* Hillsdale, NJ: Erlbaum.

Williams, D. (1984, April 23). A formula for success. *Newsweek,* pp. 77–78.

Williams, J. E., & Best, D. L. (1982). *Measuring sex stereotypes.* Beverly Hills, CA: Sage.

Williams, R. B., Jr., Lane, J. D., Kuhn, C. M., Melosh, W., White, A. D., & Schanberg, S. M. (1982). Type A behavior and elevated physiological and neuroendocrine responses to cognitive tasks. *Science, 218,* 438–485.

Wills, T. A. (1981). Downward comparison principles in social psychology. *Psychological Bulletin, 90,* 245–271.

Wilson, E. O. (1978). *On human nature.* Cambridge, MA: Harvard University Press.

Wilson, R. C., Gaft, J. G., Dienst, E. R., Wood, L., & Bavry, J. L. (1975). *College professors and their impact on students.* New York: Wiley.

Wilson, R. S. (1978). Synchronies in mental development: An epigenetic perspective. *Science, 202,* 939–948.

Wilson, W. R. (1979). Feeling more than we can know: Exposure effects without learning. *Journal of Personality and Social Psychology, 37,* 811–821.

Wing, R. R., & Jeffery, R. W. (1979). Outpatient treatments of obesity: A comparison of methodology and clinical results. *International Journal of Obesity, 3,* 261–279.

Wolpe, J. (1958). *Psychotherapy by reciprocal inhibition.* Stanford, CA: Stanford University Press.

Wolpe, J. (1982). *The practice of behavior therapy.* New York: Pergamon.

Wood, W., & Eagly, A. H. (1981). Stages in the analysis of persuasive messages: The role of causal attributions and message comprehension. *Journal of Personality and Social Psychology, 40,* 246–259.

Woodiwiss, K. E. (1977). *Shanna.* New York: Avon Books.

Woodruff, D. (1977). Can you live to be one hundred? New York: Chatham Square.

Woodruff, D. S. (1983). A review of aging and cognitive processes. *Research on Aging, 5,* 139–153.

Woods, N. F., Dery, G. K., & Most, A. (1983). Recollections of menarche, current menstrual attitudes, and premenstrual symptoms. In S. Golub (Ed.), *Menarche: The transition from girl to woman.* Lexington, MA: Lexington Books.

Wooley, S., & Wooley, O. (1973). Salivation to the sight and thought of food: A new measure of appetite. *Psychosomatic Medicine, 35,* 136.

Wooley, S., & Wooley, O. (1983). Should obesity be treated at all? *Psychiatric Annals, 13:*11, 884–885, 888.

Wooley, S. C., Wooley, O. W., & Dyrenforth, S. R. (1979). Theoretical, practical, and social issues in behavioral treatments of obesity. *Journal of Applied Behavior Analysis, 12,* 3–25.

World Health Organization (1979). *Schizophrenia: An international follow-up study.* Chicester, England: Wiley.

Worthington, E. L., Jr., Martin, G. A., Shumate, M., & Carpenter, J. (1983). The effect of brief Lamaze training and social encouragement on pain endurance in a cold pressor tank. *Journal of Applied Social Psychology, 13,* 223–233.

Wright, J. D. (1978). Are working women really more satisfied? Evidence from several national surveys. *Journal of Marriage and the Family, 40,* 301–313.

Wyman, A. (1983, October 25). Animal talk: Instinct or intelligence? *Detroit Free Press,* pp. 1B, 2B.

Yarnell, P. R., & Lynch, S. (1970, April 25). Retrograde memory immediately after concussion. *Lancet,* pp. 863–865.

Yarrow, L. J., Goodwin, M. S., Manheimer, H., & Milowe, I. D. (1973). Infancy experience and cognitive and personality development at ten years. In L. J. Stone, H. T. Smith, & L. B. Murphy (Eds.), *The competent infant.* New York: Basic Books.

Zaidel, E. (1983). A response to Gazzaniga: Language in the right hemisphere. *American Psychologist, 38,* 542–546.

Zajonc, R. B. (1965). Social facilitation. *Science, 149,* 269–274.

Zajonc, R. B. (1980). Feeling and thinking: Preferences need no inferences. *American Psychologist, 35,* 151–175.

Zajonc, R. B. (1984). On the primacy of affect. *American Psychologist, 39,* 117–123.

Zajonc, R. B. Quoted by D. Goleman (1984, July 22), Rethinking I.Q. tests and their value. *The New York Times,* p. D22.

Zajonc, R. B. (1985). Emotion and facial efference: A theory reclaimed. *Science, 228,* 15–21.

Zajonc, R. B., & Markus, G. B. (1975). Birth order and intellectual development. *Psychological Review, 82,* 74–88.

Zanna, M. P., & Pack, S. J. (1975). On the self-fulfilling nature of apparent sex differences in behavior. *Journal of Experimental Social Psychology, 11,* 583–591.

Zelnick, M., & Kim, Y. J. (1982). Sex education and its association with teenage sexual activity, pregnancy, and contraceptive use. *Family Planning Perspectives, 14*(3).

Zigler, E., & Berman, W. (1983). Discerning the future of early childhood intervention. *American Psychologist, 38,* 894–906.

Zilbergeld, B. (1983). *The shrinking of America: Myths of psychological change.* Boston: Little, Brown.

Zillmann, D. (1979). *Hostility and aggression.* Hillsdale, NJ: Erlbaum.

Zillmann, D., & Bryant, J. (1984). Effects of massive exposure to pornography. In N. Malamuth & E. Donnerstein (Eds.), *Pornography and sexual aggression.* Orlando, FL· Academic Press.

Zimbardo, P. G. (1970). The human choice: Individuation, reason, and order versus deindividuation, impulse, and chaos. In W. J. Arnold & D. Levine (Eds.), *Nebraska Symposium on Motivation, 1969.* Lincoln: University of Nebraska Press.

Zimbardo, P. G. (1972, April). Pathology of imprisonment. *Society,* pp. 4–8.

Glossary

Absolute Threshold The minimum stimulation that a subject can detect 50 percent of the time. (p. 140)

Accommodation The process by which the lens of the eye changes shape to focus the image of near or distant objects on the retina. (p. 145)

Accommodation Adaptation of one's current understandings (schemas) to incorporate new information. (p. 71)

Acetylcholine (a-seat-el-KO-leen) **(ACh)** A neurotransmitter that, among its functions, triggers muscle contraction. (p. 31)

Achievement Tests Tests designed to assess what a person has already learned. (p. 306)

Acoustic Encoding The encoding of sound, especially the sound of words. (p. 247)

Acquisition The initial stage of classical conditioning during which a response to a neutral stimulus is established and gradually strengthened. (p. 222)

Active Listening Empathic listening in which the listener echoes, restates, and clarifies. A feature of Rogers' person-centered therapy. (p. 466)

Acuity The sharpness of sight. (p. 149)

Adaptation-Level Phenomenon The tendency for our judgments (of sounds, of lights, of income, and so forth) to be relative to a neutral "adaptation level" that is defined by our prior experience. (p. 382)

Addiction A physical dependence or need for a drug, with accompanying withdrawal symptoms if discontinued. (p. 206)

Adolescence The period from puberty to independent adulthood; in industrialized nations roughly the teen years. (p. 89)

Adrenal (a-DREEN-el) **Glands** A pair of endocrine glands atop the kidneys. The adrenals secrete the hormones epinephrine (adrenaline) and norepinephrine (noradrenaline), which help to arouse the body in times of stress. (p. 52)

Aerial Perspective A monocular cue for perceiving distance; distant objects appear less distinct than nearby objects. (p. 171)

Aerobic Exercise Sustained exercise that increases heart and lung fitness; often helps to alleviate depression and anxiety. (p. 488)

Affective Disorders Psychological disorders characterized by emotional extremes. See *major depression* and *bipolar disorder*. (p. 441)

Age Regression In hypnosis, the supposed reliving of earlier experiences, such as in early childhood; has been found to be greatly susceptible to false recollections. (p. 201)

Aggression Physical or verbal behavior intended to hurt someone. (p. 121)

Algorithm A methodical, logical rule or procedure for solving a particular problem. May be contrasted with the more efficient, but also more error-prone use of *heuristics*. (p. 273)

All-or-None-Response The principle that, like a gun, at any moment a neuron either fires or does not. (p. 30)

Alpha Waves The relatively slow brain waves of a relaxed but awake state. (p. 192)

Altruism Unselfish regard for the welfare of others. (p. 566)

Amnesia Loss of memory. Psychogenic amnesia, a dissociative disorder, is selective memory loss often brought on by extreme stress. (p. 439)

Amphetamines Drugs that stimulate neural activity, causing speeded-up body functions and associated energy and mood changes. (p. 209)

Amygdala (a-MIG-dull-a) A neural center in the limbic system that is linked to emotion. (p. 37)

Anal Stage The second of Freud's psychosexual stages, during which pleasure is focused on bowel and bladder elimination and retention. (p. 398)

Androgyny (*andros,* man, + *gyne,* woman) Possession of both masculine and feminine psychological traits. (p. 133)

Anorexia Nervosa A disorder in which a person (usually an adolescent female) loses 25 percent or more of normal weight yet, still feeling fat, continues to starve. (p. 437)

Antisocial Personality A personality disorder in which the person (usually a male) exhibits a lack of conscience for wrongdoing, even toward friends and family members. May be aggressive and ruthless or a clever con artist. (p. 453)

Anxiety Disorders Psychological disorders characterized by distressing, persistent anxiety. See *generalized anxiety disorder, phobic disorders,* and *obsessive-compulsive disorder.* (p. 433)

Aphasia Impairment of language, usually caused by left hemisphere damage either to Broca's area (impairing speaking) or to Wernicke's area (impairing understanding). (p. 42)

Aptitute Tests Aptitude is the capacity to learn. Thus aptitude tests are designed to predict a person's future performance. (p. 306)

Artificial Intelligence (AI) The science of making computers do things that appear intelligent; includes both practical applications (chess playing robots, expert systems) and theoretically inspired efforts at modeling thinking. (p. 285)

Assimilation Interpretation of one's experience in terms of one's existing schemas. (p. 71)

Association Areas Poorly understood brain areas that are involved not in primary motor or sensory functions, but rather in higher mental functions such as learning, remembering, thinking, and speaking. (p. 41)

Attachment An emotional tie with another person; evidenced in children by their seeking closeness to the caregiver and their showing distress on separation. (p. 73)

Attitude Beliefs and feelings that may predispose us to respond in particular ways to objects, people, and events. (p. 537)

Attribution A causal explanation for someone's behavior, such as an explanation in terms of the situation or the person's disposition. (p. 528)

Audition The sense of hearing. (p. 152)

Automatic Processing Effortless encoding of incidental information, such as space, time, and frequency, and of well-learned information, such as word meanings; not under conscious control. (p. 247)

Autonomic (awt-uh-NAHM-ik) **Nervous System** The part of the peripheral nervous system that controls the glands and the muscles of the internal organs (such as the heart). Its sympathetic division arouses; its parasympathetic division calms. (p. 27)

Availability Heuristic Judges the likelihood of things in terms of their availability in memory; if instances of something come readily to mind (perhaps because of their vividness), we presume the thing to be more likely. (p. 279)

Aversive Conditioning A type of counterconditioning that associates an unpleasant state (such as nausea) with an unwanted behavior (such as drinking alcohol). (p. 472)

Avoidance Learning Learning to avoid an aversive stimulus or to prevent it from occurring. (p. 231)

Axon The part of a neuron through which messages are sent to other neurons or to muscles or glands. (p. 29)

Babbling Stage The stage in speech development, beginning at about 3 or 4 months, in which the infant spontaneously utters a variety of sounds (which at first are unrelated to the household language). (p. 288)

Bad-Patient Role Uncooperative, complaining, demanding patient behavior. (p. 513)

Barnum Effect The tendency to accept as valid descriptions of one's personality that are generally true of everyone (such as those found in astrology books). (p. 420)

Basic Trust According to Erik Erikson, a sense that the world is predictable and trustworthy; said to be formed during infancy by experiences with responsive caregivers. (p. 77)

Behavior Modification The application of operant conditioning principles to the modification of human behavior. (Behavior modification is also sometimes used as a synonym for *behavior therapy.*) (p. 473)

Behavior Therapy Therapy that applies learning principles to the elimination of unwanted behaviors. (p. 473)

Behavioral Medicine An interdisciplinary field that integrates and applies behavioral and medical knowledge to health and disease. (p. 495)

Behavioral Perspective Emphasizes environmental influences upon observable behaviors. (p. 7)

Behaviorism The view that psychology should (1) be an objective science, that (2) studies only overt behavior without reference to mental processes.

Belief Perseverance Clinging to one's initial conceptions after the basis on which they were formed has been discredited. (p. 282)

Binocular Cues Depth cues that depend on the use of two eyes. (p. 170)

Biofeedback A system for electronically recording, amplifying, and feeding back information regarding a subtle physiological state. (p. 518)

Biological Perspective Emphasizes the influences of heredity and physiology upon our emotions, memories, and sensory experiences. (p. 7)

Bipolar Disorder An affective disorder in which the person alternates between the hopelessness and lethargy of depression and the overexcited, hyperactive, wildly optimistic state of mania. (p. 441)

Blind Spot The insensitive area of the retina (without rods and cones) where the optic nerve leaves the eye. (p. 145)

Brainstem The central core of the brain, beginning where the spinal cord swells as it enters the skull. (p. 36)

Brightness The psychological dimension of color (its brilliance) that is determined mostly by the intensity of light, but also by its nearness to the middle of the visible spectrum. (p. 145)

Broca's Area An area of the left frontal lobe that directs the muscle movements involved in speech. (p. 42)

Bulimia A disorder characterized by "binge-purge" eating, in which repeated episodes of overeating, usually of high caloric foods, are followed by vomiting or laxative use. (p. 437)

Bystander Effect The tendency for any given bystander to be less likely to give aid if other bystanders are present. (p. 567)

CAT (Computerized Axial Tomograph) A three-dimensional X-ray photograph of a body structure such as the brain, which can reveal hidden damage or disease.

Cannon-Bard Theory The theory that an emotion-arousing stimulus simultaneously triggers (1) physiological responses, and (2) the subjective experience of emotion. (p. 386)

Case Study An observational technique in which one person is studied in depth. (p. 10)

Catharsis Emotional release. In psychology, the catharsis hypothesis maintains that aggressive urges are relieved by "releasing" aggressive energy (through action or fantasy). (p. 379)

Central Nervous System (CNS) The brain and spinal cord. (p. 27)

Cerebellum (sehr-uh-BELL-um) The "little brain" attached to the rear of the brainstem that helps to coordinate voluntary movement and balance. (p. 36)

Cerebral (seh-REE-bruhl) **Cortex** The intricate fabric of interconnected neural cells that covers the cerebral hemispheres; the body's ultimate control and information-processing center. (p. 38)

Chromosomes Threadlike structures that contain the genes. A human cell has 23 pairs of chromosomes, one member of each pair coming from each parent. (p. 53)

Chunking Organization of items into familiar or manageable units. (p. 252)

Circadian Rhythm Regular bodily rhythms (for example, of temperature and wakefulness) that occur on a 24-hour schedule. (p. 191)

Classical Conditioning A type of learning in which a neutral stimulus, after being paired with an unconditioned stimulus, begins to trigger a response similar to that normally triggered by the unconditioned stimulus. (Also known as Pavlovian or respondent conditioning.) (p. 220)

Clinical Psychology A branch of psychology, usually practiced by people with a Ph.D. degree, involving the assessment and treatment of those with psychological disorders. (p. 7)

Closure The perceptual tendency to fill in gaps, thus enabling one to perceive disconnected parts as a whole object. (p. 169)

Coactors People who are simultaneously at work on the same noncompetitive task. (p. 545)

Cochlea (COCK-lee-a) A coiled, bony, fluid-filled tube in the inner ear in which sound waves trigger nerve impulses. (p. 153)

Cocktail Party Effect The ability to attend selectively to but one voice among many. (p. 178)

Cognition All the mental activities associated with thinking and knowing. (p. 69)

Cognitive Dissonance The discomfort (dissonance) we feel when two of our thoughts (cognitions) are inconsistent, as when we are aware that we have chosen to act in a manner that contradicts our attitudes. (p. 540)

Cognitive Map A mental representation of the layout of one's environment. For example, once they have learned a maze, rats act as if they have acquired a cognitive map of the maze. (p. 235)

Cognitive Perspective Emphsizes how the mind processes and retains information. (p. 8)

Cognitive-Behavior Therapy Therapy that teaches people new, more adaptive ways of thinking and acting; based on the assumption that thoughts intervene between events and our emotional reactions. (p. 474)

Collective Unconscious Carl Jung's concept of memory traces from our species' history. (p. 401)

Color Constancy Perceiving familiar objects as having consistent color, even if their actual color is altered by changing illumination. (p. 174)

Companionate Love The deep affectionate attachment we feel for those with whom our lives are intertwined. (p. 580)

Complexity The mixture of different wavelengths of light or sound. Complexity determines the saturation of light and the timbre of sounds (low complexity = purity). (p. 145)

Computer Assisted Instruction (CAI) Computer tutored teaching featuring self-paced, individualized instruction and immediate feedback. (p. 234)

Concept A mental grouping of similar things, events, and people. (p. 270)

Concrete Operational Stage In Piaget's theory, the stage of cognitive development (from about 7 to 12 years of age) during which children acquire the mental operations that enable them to think logically about concrete events. (pp. 70, 81)

Conditioned Response (CR) In classical conditioning, the learned response to a conditioned stimulus. (p. 221)

Conditioned Stimulus (CS) In classical conditioning, an originally neutral stimulus that, after association with an unconditioned stimulus, comes to trigger a conditioned response. (p. 221)

Conduction Deafness Hearing loss caused by damage to the mechanical system that conducts sound waves to the cochlea. (p. 155)

Cones Receptor cells concentrated near the center of the retina that operate in daylight. The cones detect fine detail and give rise to color sensations. (p. 145)

Confirmation Bias A tendency to search for information that confirms one's preconceptions. (p. 273)

Conflict A perceived incompatibility of actions or goals. (p. 580)

Conformity Adjusting one's behavior or thinking to coincide with an assumed group standard. (p. 530)

Consciousness Selective attention to ongoing perceptions, thoughts, and feelings. (p. 189)

Conservation The principle (which Piaget believed comes to be understood during the concrete operational period) that properties such as mass, volume, and number remain the same despite changes in the appearance of objects. (p. 81)

Content Validity The extent to which a test samples the very behavior that is of interest (such as a driving test that samples driving tasks). (p. 313)

Continuity A perceptual tendency to group stimuli into smooth, continuous patterns. (p. 169)

Continuous Reinforcement Reinforcing a response every time it occurs. (p. 229)

Control Condition The condition of an experiment in which the experimental treatment of interest is absent; serves as a comparison for evaluating the effect of the treatment. (p. 13)

Convergence A binocular depth cue; the extent to which the eyes converge inward when looking at an object. (p. 170)

Conversion Disorder A somatoform disorder in which a person experiences genuine physical symptoms for which no physiological basis can be found. (p. 438)

Coronary Heart Disease The narrowing of the vessels that nourish the heart muscle; the number one cause of death in the United States today. (p. 501)

Corpus Callosum (kah-LOW-sum) The largest bundle of nerve fibers connecting and carrying messages between the two brain hemispheres. (p. 44)

Correlation A statistical index that indicates the extent to which two things vary together and thus how well one measure can be predicted from knowing the other. (p. 11)

Correlation Coefficient A measure of the direction and extent of relationship between two sets of scores. Scores with a positive relationship (such high school and college GPAs) tend to go up and down together. (Also called the coefficient of correlation.) (p. 598)

Counterconditioning A behavior therapy that conditions new responses to stimuli that trigger unwanted behaviors; based on classical conditioning. See also *systematic desensitization* and *aversive conditioning*. (p. 470)

Creativity The ability to produce ideas that are both novel and valuable. (p. 321)

Criterion The behavior (such as obtained college grades) that a test (such as the SAT) is designed to predict; thus the measure used in defining whether the test has predictive validity. (p. 314)

Critical Period A restricted period of development during which an organism is especially susceptible to certain influences, such as the formation of attachments or the learning of language. (p. 73)

Cross-sectional Study A study in which different population groups (for example, people of different ages) are tested or observed at a given period in time. (p. 106)

Crystallized Intelligence One's accumulated information and verbal skills; tends to increase with age. (p. 108)

DNA (Deoxyribonucleic Acid) The complex molecules that contain the genetic information in cells. (p. 53)

DSM-III The American Psychiatric Association's *Diagnostic and Statistical Manual of Mental Disorders*, third edition, a widely used system for classifying psychological disorders. (p. 432)

Decay Theory The idea that the physical memory trace fades with time, causing forgetting. (p. 261)

Decibel A unit of measure that specifies sound intensity. (p. 156)

Deductive Reasoning The deriving of conclusions, given certain assumptions. (p. 282)

Defense Mechanisms In psychoanalytic theory, the ego's methods of reducing anxiety by unconsciously distorting reality. (p. 399)

Deindividuation The loss of self-awareness and self-restraint that can occur in group situations that foster anonymity and distract attention away from oneself. (p. 547)

Delta Waves The large, slow brain waves associated with deep sleep. (p. 193)

Delusions False beliefs, often of persecution or grandeur, that may accompany psychotic disorders. (p. 448)

Dendrite The bushy, branching extensions of a neuron that conduct impulses toward the cell body. (p. 29)

Dependent Variable The variable that is being measured; in an experiment, the variable that may change in response to manipulations of the independent variable. (p. 13)

Depressants Drugs (such as alcohol, barbituates, and opiates) that reduce neural activity and slow down body functions. (p. 206)

Depth Perception The ability to see objects in three dimensions although the images that strike the retinas are two-dimensional. (p. 170)

Developmental Psychology The study of the process of physical, cognitive, and social changes throughout the life cycle. (p. 6)

Difference Threshold The minimum difference in stimulation that a subject can detect 50 percent of the time. We experience the difference threshold as a just noticeable difference (jnd). (p. 143)

Discrimination The ability to distinguish between a conditioned stimulus and similar stimuli that do not signal an unconditioned stimulus. (p. 223)

Displacement The shifting of one's impulses toward a more acceptable or less threatening object or person, as when redirecting anger toward a safer outlet. (p. 400)

Dissociation A split in consciousness, allowing some thoughts and behaviors to occur simultaneously with others. (p. 205)

Dissociative Disorders Anxiety disorders in which conscious awareness becomes separated (dissociated) from previous memories, thoughts, and feelings. See *amnesia*, *fugue*, and *multiple personality*. (p. 439)

Dopamine A neurotransmitter that appears to be overly active in some schizophrenic patients. (p. 451)

Double-blind Procedure An experimental procedure in which both the patient and the staff are ignorant (blind) as to whether the patient has received the treatment or a placebo. Commonly used in drug evaluation studies. (p. 486)

Down's Syndrome A condition of retardation and associated physical disorders caused by an extra chromosome in one's genetic makeup. (p. 320)

Drive An aroused state that typically arises from an underlying need. (p. 339)

Drive-Reduction Theory The theory that the purpose of motivated behavior is to reduce drives. (p. 339)

Dualism The presumption that mind and body are two distinct entities that interact with each other. (p. 212)

Echoic Memory A momentary sensory memory of auditory stimuli; if attention is elsewhere, sounds and words can still be recalled within 3 or 4 seconds. (p. 246)

Eclectic Selecting what appears to be the best of various theories and methods; eclectic therapists draw techniques from the various forms of therapy, depending on the problems encountered. (p. 462)

Effortful Processing Encoding that requires attention and effort; influenced by practice and motivation. (p. 247)

Ego The largely conscious executive part of personality that, according to Freud, mediates between the demands of the id and superego and the reality of the external world. (p. 398)

Egocentrism In Piaget's theory, the inability of the preoperational child to take another's point of view. (p. 80)

Electroconvulsive Therapy (ECT) A biomedical therapy sometimes used with severely depressed patients in which a brief electric current is sent through the brain, producing a minute or so of convulsions followed by a period of relief from depression. (p. 485)

Electroencephalogram (EEG) An amplified recording of the waves of electrical activity that sweep across the brain's surface. These waves are measured by placing electrodes on the scalp. (p. 34)

Embryo The early developmental stage of an organism after fertilization; in human development, the prenatal stage from about 2 weeks to 2 months. (p. 65)

Emotion A response of the whole organism, involving (1) physical arousal, (2) expressive reactions, and (3) conscious experience. (p. 369)

Empathy To be able to understand and feel what another feels. (p. 122)

Empirically Derived Test An inventory (such as the MMPI) that is developed by testing a pool of items and then selecting those that differentiate groups of interest. (p. 407)

Empiricism The view that ideas and perceptions are learned through experience. (p. 167)

Encoding The process of getting information into the memory system, for example by extracting meaning. (p. 245)

Encounter Groups Gatherings of 12 to 20 people whose emotion-laden group experiences are characterized by honesty and openness, through which the participants hope to grow in self-awareness and social sensitivity. (p. 469)

Endocrine (EN-duh-krin) **System** The body's chemical communication system; a set of glands that secrete hormones into the bloodstream. (p. 52)

Endorphins (EN-dor-fins) "Morphine within"—natural, opiatelike neurotransmitters linked to pain control and pleasure. (p. 32)

Equilibrium The sense of body movement and position, including the sense of balance. (p. 159)

Equity A condition in which people receive from a relationship in proportion to what they contribute to it. (p. 580)

Escape Learning Learning to terminate an aversive stimulus. (p. 231)

Estrogen A sex hormone, secreted in greater amounts by females than males. In nonhuman female mammals, estrogen levels peak during ovulation, triggering sexual receptivity. (p. 354)

Excitement Phase The first phase of the sexual response cycle, in which the genital areas become somewhat engorged with blood. (p. 353)

Experiment A research method in which the investigator manipulates one or more independent variables to observe their effect upon some behavior (the *dependent variable*) while controlling other relevant factors. (p. 12)

Experimental Condition The condition of an experiment in which subjects are exposed to the treatment, that is, to the independent variable. (p. 13)

Experimental Psychology A branch of psychology that uses experimental methods to discover principles of behavior, such as those underlying sensation and perception, learning and memory, motivation and emotion. (p. 7)

External Locus of Control The belief that one's fate is determined by chance or outside forces that are beyond one's control. (p. 418)

Extinction The fading of a response when a conditioned stimulus is not followed by an unconditioned stimulus or when a response is not reinforced. (p. 223)

Extrasensory Perception (ESP) The controversial claim that valid perceptions of the environment can occur apart from sensory input. Said to include telepathy, clairvoyance, and precognition. (p. 181)

Extrinsic Motivation A desire to perform a behavior due to rewards or threats of punishment. (p. 362)

Factor Analysis A statistical procedure that identifies clusters of related items (called factors) on a test; used to identify different dimensions of performance that underlie one's total score. (p. 317)

Family Therapy Therapy that treats individuals as part of a family system in which unwanted behaviors may be engendered by or directed at other family members, and that encourages family members to heal relationships and improve communication. (p. 489)

Farsightedness A condition in which faraway objects are seen clearly, but near objects are blurred because the lens focuses the image behind the retina. (p. 149)

Feature Detectors Nerve cells in the brain that respond to specific features of the stimulus, such as movement or shape. (p. 147)

Fetus The developing human organism from 8 weeks after conception to birth. (p. 66)

Figure-Ground The organization of the visual field into objects (the figure) that stand out from the background (the ground). (p. 168)

Fixation According to Freud, a lingering focus of pleasure-seeking energies at an earlier psychosexual stage. (p. 399)

Fixation The inability to take a new perspective on a problem. (p. 275)

Fixed-Interval Schedule In operant conditioning, a schedule of reinforcement in which a response is reinforced only after a specified time interval has elapsed. (p. 230)

Fixed-Ratio Schedule In operant conditioning, a schedule of reinforcement in which a response is reinforced only after a specified number of responses. (p. 230)

Fluid Intelligence One's ability to reason abstractly; tends to decrease after early adulthood. (p. 108)

Formal Operational Stage In Piaget's theory, the stage of cognitive development (normally beginning about age 12) during which people learn to reason abstractly and think hypothetically. (pp. 70, 92)

Framing The way an issue to be decided is posed; can significantly affect judgments. (p. 281)

Fraternal Twins Twins who develop from separate eggs and sperm cells, thus ordinary brothers and sisters who happen to be born only moments apart. (p. 54)

Free Association A psychoanalytic method of exploring the unconscious in which the person relaxes and says whatever comes to mind, no matter how trivial or embarrassing. (p. 397)

Frequency Distribution A listing of the number of individual scores occurring within each equal size interval into which the range of scores has been divided. (p. 594)

Frequency Theory In hearing, the theory that the rate of pulses traveling up the auditory nerve matches the frequency of a tone, thus enabling us to sense its pitch. (p. 153)

Frontal Lobes The portion of the cerebral cortex lying behind the forehead; directs speaking and muscle movements and is involved in making plans and judgments. (p. 39)

Frustration-Aggression Theory The theory that frustration—the blocking of an attempt to achieve some goal—creates anger which can provoke aggression. (p. 558)

Fugue A dissociative disorder in which amnesia is accompanied by physical flight from one's home and identity. (p. 439)

Functional Fixedness The tendency to think of things only in terms of their usual functions; an impediment to problem solving. (p. 276)

Fundamental Attribution Error The tendency for observers to underestimate the impact of the situation and overestimate the impact of inner dispositions upon another's behavior. (p. 528)

GRIT *G*raduated and *R*eciprocated *I*nitiatives in *T*ension-reduction—a strategy designed to decrease international tensions. (p. 588)

Gate-Control Theory Melzack and Wall's theory that the spinal cord contains a neurological "gate" that blocks or allows pain signals to pass on to the brain; the "gate" is opened by the activity of pain signals traveling up small nerve fibers and closed by activity in larger fibers or by information coming from the brain. (p. 508)

Gender Identity One's sense of being a male or a female. Note: One's gender identity is distinct from one's sexual orientation and from the strength of one's *gender-typing*. (p. 119)

Gender Role A set of expected behaviors for males and for females. (p. 131)

Gender Schema Theory The theory that the process of gender-typing is explained by children's developing schemas for maleness and femaleness, the content of which is determined by social learning. (p. 130)

Gender-Typing The extent to which a male displays traditionally masculine traits or a female displays traditionally feminine traits. (p. 129)

General Adaptation Syndrome Selye's concept of the body's adaptive response to stress as composed of three stages—alarm, resistance, exhaustion. (p. 498)

General Intelligence (g) A general underlying intelligence factor that was believed by Spearman and others to be measured by every task on an intelligence test. (p. 317)

Generalization The tendency, once a response has been conditioned, for stimuli similar to the conditioned stimulus to evoke the response. (p. 223)

Generalized Anxiety Disorder An anxiety disorder in which a person is continually tense, apprehensive, and experiencing autonomic nervous system arousal. (p. 433)

Generativity In Erikson's theory, the impulse to be productive, such as by raising children and through creative work. (p. 100)

Genes The basic units of heredity that make up the chromosomes. A segment of DNA capable of synthesizing a protein. (p. 23)

Genital Stage The final of Freud's psychosexual stages, beginning in puberty, during which pleasure is sought through sexual contact with others. (p. 399)

Gestalt An organized whole. Gestalt psychologists emphasize our tendency to integrate pieces of information into meaningful wholes. (p. 167)

Gestalt Therapy A therapy developed by Fritz Perls that combines the psychoanalytic emphasis on bringing to awareness unconscious feelings and the humanistic emphasis on getting in touch with oneself; aims to help people become more aware of and able to express their moment-to-moment feelings. (p. 467)

Glucose The form of sugar that circulates in the blood and provides the major source of energy for body tissues. (p. 343)

Good-Patient Role Cooperative, unquestioning, undemanding patient behavior, sometimes exhibited by anxious, helpless, depressed patients. (p. 512)

Grammar A system of rules that enables us to use our language to speak to and understand others. (p. 288)

Group Polarization The enhancement of a group's prevailing tendencies through discussion. (p. 549)

Grouping The tendency, emphasized by the Gestalt psychologists, to organize stimuli into coherent groups. (p. 169)

Groupthink The mode of thinking that occurs when the desire for harmony in a decision-making group overrides a realistic appraisal of alternatives. (p. 549)

Guilty Knowledge Test A lie detection procedure that assesses a suspect's responses to details of a crime known only to the guilty person. (p. 373)

Hallucinations False sensory experiences, such as seeing something in the absence of any external visual stimulus. (p. 192)

Hallucinogens Psychedelic ("mind-manifesting") drugs, such as LSD, that distort perceptions and evoke sensory images in the absence of sensory input. (p. 206)

Health Psychology A subfield of psychology that provides psychology's contribution to behavioral medicine. (p. 496)

Heritability The extent to which differences in a trait can be attributed to genes. Heritability of a trait may vary, depending on the populations and environments studied. (p. 54)

Heuristic A rule-of-thumb strategy that enables efficient judgments and problem solutions. (p. 273)

Hidden Observer Hilgard's term describing a hypnotized subject's awareness of experiences, such as pain, that go unreported during hypnosis. (p. 205)

Hierarchy of Needs Maslow's pyramid of human needs, beginning at the base with physiological needs that must first be satisfied before higher-level safety needs and then psychological needs become active. (p. 341)

Histogram A bar graph that depicts a frequency distribution. (p. 594)

Homeostasis A tendency to maintain a balanced or constant internal state; refers especially to the body's tendency to maintain an optimum internal state for functioning. (p. 340)

Hormones Chemical messengers manufactured by the endocrine glands and sent through the bloodstream. (p. 52)

Hospice An organization that in special facilities and in people's own homes supports dying people and their families (p. 110)

Hue The dimension of color that we know as the color names (blue, green, and so forth) and that is determined by the wavelength of light. (p. 144)

Humanistic Perspective Emphasizes people's capacities for choice and growth; studies people's subjective experiences. (p. 7)

Hypnosis A temporary state of heightened suggestibility in which some people narrow their focus of attention and experience imaginary happenings as if they were real. (p. 199)

Hypochondriasis A somatoform disorder in which a person misinterprets normal physical sensations as symptoms of a disease. (p. 439)

Hypothalamus A neural structure lying below (hypo) the thalamus that directs several maintenance activities (eating, drinking, body temperature), helps govern the endocrine system via the pituitary gland, and is linked to emotion and reward. (p. 37)

Hypothesis A testable proposition, often derived from a theory. (p. 10)

Hypothesis Testing A problem-solving process in which a tentative assumption is made about how to solve the problem and then tested to see if it works. (p. 272)

I-Knew-It-All-Along Phenomenon The tendency to exaggerate one's ability to have foreseen how something turned out, *after* learning the outcome. (Also known as the hindsight bias.) (p. 17)

Iconic Memory A momentary sensory memory of visual stimuli; a photographic or picture image memory lasting no more than a second or so. (p. 246)

Id The instinctual drives that, according to Freud, supply psychic energy to personality. (p. 398)

Identical Twins Twins that develop from a single fertilized egg that splits in two, creating two genetic replicas. (Also called monozygotic twins.) (p. 54)

Identification Freud's term for the presumed process by which a child adopts the characteristics of the same-sex parent. More generally, the process by which people associate themselves with and copy the behavior of significant others. (pp. 129, 399)

Identity One's sense of who one is. According to Erikson, the adolescent task is to form a sense of self by integrating one's various roles. (p. 96)

Idiot Savant A retarded person who possesses an amazing specific skill, such as in computation or drawing. (p. 317)

Illusory Correlation The perception of a relationship where none exists or of a stronger relationship than actually exists. (p. 599)

Imagery Mental pictures. A powerful aid to memory, especially when combined with the encoding of meaning. (p. 250)

Imprinting The process by which certain birds and mammals form attachments during a critical period early in life. (p. 75)

Incentives Positive or negative environmental stimuli that motivate behavior. Incentives are the external "pull" of motivation. (p. 340)

Independent Variable The experimental factor, the variable whose effect is being studied. In an experiment, the independent variable is the variable manipulated by the investigator. (p. 13)

Inductive Reasoning The inferring of a general truth from particular examples. (p. 282)

Informational Social Influence Conformity resulting from accepting others' opinions about reality. (p. 532)

Ingroup Bias The tendency to favor one's own group. (p. 573)

Inner Ear The innermost part of the ear, containing the cochlea, semicircular canals, and vestibular sacs. (p. 153)

Insanity A legal term for someone who has committed a crime but is judged not to have understood at the time of the crime that the act was wrong. (p. 429)

Insight A sudden and often novel realization of the solution to a problem; contrasts with trial-and-error solutions. (p. 276)

Insomnia Difficulty in falling or staying asleep. (p. 194)

Instinct A behavior that is rigidly patterned, characteristic of a whole species, and unlearned. (p. 339)

Insulin A hormone that, among its effects, helps body tissues convert blood glucose into stored fat. (p. 343)

Integrity In Erikson's theory, the positive outcome of later life: A nondespairing sense that one's life was meaningful and worthwhile. (pp. 108–109)

Intelligence The capacity for goal-directed adaptive behavior (behavior that successfully meets challenges and achieves its aims). Involves the abilities to profit from experience, solve problems, reason, remember, and so forth. (p. 315)

Intelligence Quotient (IQ) An intelligence measure that was originally defined as the ratio of mental age to chronological age multiplied by 100 (thus IQ = MA/CA × 100). Contemporary tests compute IQ by giving the average performance for a given age a score of 100, with other IQ scores defined in terms of their deviation from the average. (p. 304)

Intensity The amount of energy in a light or sound wave. (p. 145)

Interaction Effect The result in which the effect of one factor depends on the level of another. (p. 363)

Internal Locus of Control The belief that one can control one's own fate. (p. 418)

Interneurons Central nervous system neurons that intervene between the sensory inputs and motor outputs. (p. 28)

Interpretation In psychoanalysis, the analyst's assisting of the patient to note and understand resistances and other significant behaviors in order to promote insight. (p. 463)

Intrinsic Motivation Desire to perform a behavior for its own sake and to be effective. (p. 362)

Iris A ring of tissue that forms the colored portion of the eye around the pupil and controls the size of the pupil opening. (p. 145)

James-Lange Theory The theory stating that to experience emotion is to be aware of one's physiological responses to emotion-arousing stimuli. (p. 386)

Just Noticeable Difference See *Difference Threshold.*

Just-World Phenomenon The tendency of people to believe the world is just and that people therefore get what they deserve and deserve what they get. (p. 575)

Kinesthesis The system for sensing the position and movement of muscles, tendons, and joints. (p. 158)

LSD (Lysergic Acid Diethylamide) A powerful hallucinogenic drug, also known as "acid." (p. 209)

Latency Period The fourth of Freud's psychosexual stages, from about age 6 to puberty, during which sexual impulses are repressed. (p. 399)

Latent Content According to Freud, the underlying but censored meaning of a dream (as distinct from its manifest content). Freud believed that a dream's latent content serves a safety valve function. (p. 196)

Latent Learning Learning that occurs but is not apparent until there is an incentive to demonstrate it. (p. 236)

Lateral Hypothalamus (LH) The side areas of the hypothalamus that, when stimulated, trigger eating and, when destroyed, cause an animal to stop eating. (p. 343)

Learned Helplessness A condition of passive resignation that is learned when an animal or human has been unable to avoid repeated aversive events. (p. 419)

Learning A change in an organism, due to experience, which can affect the organism's behavior. (p. 219)

Lens The transparent structure behind the pupil that changes shape to focus images on the retina. (p. 145)

Lesion (LEE-zhuhn) Tissue destruction. A brain lesion is naturally or experimentally caused destruction of brain tissue. (p. 33)

Limbic System A doughnut-shaped system of neural structures at the border of the brainstem and cerebral hemispheres; associated with emotions such as fear and aggression and drives such as those for food and sex. (p. 37)

Linear Perspective A monocular cue for perceiving distance; we perceive the convergence of what we know to be parallel lines as indicating increasing distance. (p. 172)

Linguistic Relativity Whorf's hypothesis that language determines the way we think. (p. 294)

Lithium A chemical that provides an effective drug therapy for the mood swings of bipolar (manic-depressive) disorders. (p. 488)

Lobotomy A no-longer-used psychosurgical procedure to calm uncontrollably emotional or violent patients in which the nerves that connect the frontal lobes to the emotion-controlling centers of the inner brain are cut. Also called frontal (or prefrontal) lobotomy. (p. 484)

Long-term Memory A relatively permanent and limitless component of the memory system. (p. 247)

Longitudinal Study Research in which the same people are restudied at different points in time. (p. 107)

Lymphocytes The two types of white blood cells that are part of the body's immune system—the first (B lymphocytes) form in the bone marrow and release infection-fighting antibodies that fight bacterial infections and the second (the T lymphocytes) form in the thymus and, among other duties, attack cancer cells, viruses, and foreign substances. (p. 504)

Major Depression An affective disorder in which a person experiences two or more weeks of depressed moods, feelings of worthlessness, and lethargy. (p. 441)

Mania An overexcited, hyperactive, wildly optimistic state. (p. 441)

Manifest Content According to Freud, the remembered story line of a dream (as distinct from its latent content). (p. 196)

Maturation Biological growth processes that, relatively uninfluenced by experience, enable orderly changes in behavior. (p. 64)

Mean The arithmetic average of a distribution, obtained by adding the scores and dividing by their number. (p. 596)

Median The middle score in a distribution, with half the scores above and half below. (p. 596)

Medical Model The conception that diseases have physical causes and that they can be treated and, in most cases, cured. When applied to psychological disorders, it sees them as mental illnesses to be diagnosed on the basis of their symptoms and cured through therapy, which may include treatment in a psychiatric hospital. (p. 431)

Medulla (muh-DUL-uh) The lowest part of the brainstem; controls heartbeat and breathing. (p. 36)

Memory The persistence of learning over time. (p. 243)

Menarche (meh-NAR-key) The first menstrual period. (p. 90)

Menopause The cessation of menstruation. Also used loosely to refer to the biological and psychological changes during the several years of declining ability to reproduce. (p. 99)

Mental Age A measure of intelligence test performance devised by Binet; the chronological age that most typically corresponds to a given level of performance. Thus a child who does as well as the average 8-year-old is said to have a mental age of 8. (p. 304)

Mental Retardation A condition of low IQ (such as below 70) plus difficulty adapting to the demands of life; varies from mild to profound. (p. 320)

Mental Set A tendency to approach a problem in a particular way, especially a way that has been successful in the past but may or may not be helpful in solving a new problem. (p. 275)

Mere Exposure Effect The phenomenon that repeated exposure to novel stimuli increases liking. (p. 577)

Meta-analysis A procedure for statistically combining the results of many different studies. (p. 481)

Metabolic Rate The body's rate of energy expenditure. (p. 346)

Middle Ear The chamber between the eardrum and cochlea containing three tiny bones (hammer, anvil, and stirrups) that concentrate the vibrations of the eardrum on the cochlea. (p. 153)

Minnesota Multiphasic Personality Inventory (MMPI) The most widely researched and used of all personality inventories, containing ten scales of clinical dimensions and other validity scales and subscales. (p. 407)

Mirror-Image Perceptions Distinct but similar views of one another often held by parties in conflict; each views itself as moral and peace-loving and the other as evil and aggressive. (p. 585)

Mnemonics (ni-MON-iks) Memory aids, especially those techniques that employ vivid imagery and devices for organization. (p. 251)

Mode The most frequently occurring score in a distribution. (p. 596)

Monism The presumption that mind and body are different aspects of the same thing. (p. 212)

Monocular Cues Depth cues available to either eye alone. (p. 170)

Morphemes The smallest speech units that carry meaning; may be words or parts of words (such as a prefix). (p. 288)

Motivation The forces that energize and direct behavior. (p. 337)

Motor Cortex An area at the rear of the frontal lobes that controls voluntary movements. (p. 40)

Motor Neurons The neurons that carry outgoing information from the central nervous system to the muscles and glands. (p. 28)

Multiple Personality Disorder A rare dissociative disorder in which a person exhibits two or more distinct and alternating personalities. (p. 440)

Narcolepsy A sleep disorder characterized by uncontrollable sleep attacks in which the sufferer lapses directly into REM sleep, often at inopportune times. (p. 195)

Nativism The view that important aspects of perception are innate, and thus do not have to be learned through experience. (p. 167)

Natural Selection The process by which evolution favors organisms that, within a particular environment, are genetically best equipped to survive and reproduce. (p. 24)

Naturalistic Observation Observing and recording behavior in naturally occurring situations, without trying to manipulate and control the situation. (p. 11)

Nature-Nurture Debate The long-standing controversy over the relative contributions of heredity and experience to psychological traits. (p. 53)

Near-Death Experience An altered state of consciousness reported after a close brush with death (such as through cardiac arrest); often similar to drug-induced hallucinations. (p. 211)

Nearsightedness A condition in which nearby objects are seen clearly, but distant objects are blurred because the lens focuses the image in front of the retina. (p. 149)

Need A deprivation that usually triggers a drive to reduce or eliminate itself. (p. 339)

Need for Achievement A desire for significant accomplishment; for mastery of things, people, or ideas; for rapidly attaining a high standard. (p. 361)

Negative Reinforcer The withdrawal of an aversive stimulus, such as shock; as with all reinforcers, negative reinforcers strengthen behaviors that trigger them. (p. 229)

Nerve Deafness Hearing loss caused by damage to the cochlea's receptor cells or to the auditory nerves. (p. 155)

Nervous System The body's electrochemical communication system, consisting of all the nerve cells of the peripheral and central nervous systems. (p. 23)

Neuron A nerve cell; the basic building block of the nervous system. (p. 27)

Neurotic Disorders Psychological disorders that are usually distressing, but allow one to think rationally and function socially. The neurotic disorders are usually viewed as ways of dealing with anxiety. See *anxiety disorders, somatoform disorders,* and *dissociative disorders.* (p. 433)

Neurotransmitters Chemical messengers that traverse the synapses between neurons. When released by the sending neuron, neurotransmitters travel across the synapse and bind to receptor sites on the receiving neuron, thereby influencing whether it will fire. (p. 31)

Night Terrors A sleep disorder characterized by high arousal and an appearance of being terrified; unlike nightmares, night terrors occur during Stage 4 sleep, within 2 or 3 hours of falling asleep, and are seldom remembered. (p. 195)

Normal Curve (or **Normal Distribution**) The symmetrical, bell-shaped curve that describes the distribution of many physical and psychological attributes (including IQ scores), with most scores falling near the mean (68 percent within 1 standard deviation) and fewer and fewer near the extremes. (pp. 311, 597)

Normative Social Influence Conformity resulting from a person's desire to gain approval or avoid disapproval. (p. 532)

Norms Understood rules for accepted and expected behavior. Norms prescribe "proper" behavior. (p. 532)

Obesity Having a surplus of body fat. Obesity is not defined simply as weighing more than normal, which may also be caused by large muscle mass. (p. 344)

Object Permanence The awareness that things continue to exist even when not perceived. (p. 72)

Observational Learning Learning by observing and imitating the behavior of others. (p. 237)

Obsessive-Compulsive Disorder An anxiety disorder in which a person is troubled by unwanted repetitive thoughts (obsessions) or actions (compulsions). (p. 433)

Occipital (ahk-SIP-uht-uhl) **Lobes** The portion of the cerebral cortex lying at the back of the head, including the visual areas, each of which receives visual information, primarily from the opposite eye. (p. 39)

Oedipus Complex According to Freud, the 3- to 5- or 6-year-old child's sexual desires toward the parent of the other sex and feelings of jealousy and hatred for the rival parent of the same sex. (p. 399)

One-Word Stage The stage in speech development, from about age 1 to 2 years, during which a child speaks mostly in single words. (p. 289)

Operant Behavior Behavior that operates upon the environment to produce consequences. (p. 227)

Operant Conditioning A type of learning in which behavior is strengthened if followed by reinforcement, or suppressed if followed by punishment. (p. 220)

Opiates Opium and its derivatives, such as morphine and heroin, which depress neural activity, temporarily alleviating pain and anxiety. (p. 208)

Opponent-Process Theory In visual sensation, the theory that color vision depends on pairs of opposing retinal processes (red-green, yellow-blue, and white-black). For example, some cells are stimulated by green and inhibited by red, while others are stimulated by red and inhibited by green. (p. 151)

Opponent-Process Theory The theory that every emotion triggers an opposing emotion that fights it and lingers after the first emotion is extinguished. (p. 384)

Optic Nerve The nerve that carries neural impulses from the eye to the brain. (p. 145)

Oral Stage The first of Freud's psychosexual stages, during which pleasure centers on the mouth. (p. 398)

Orgasm An intense sensation experienced at the peak of the sexual response cycle; involves rhythmic muscle contractions, increases in breathing, pulse, and blood pressure rates, and pleasurable feelings of sexual release. (p. 353)

Overconfidence Phenomenon The tendency to be more confident than correct—to overestimate the accuracy of one's beliefs and judgments. (p. 280)

Overjustification Effect The effect of being promised a reward for doing what one already likes doing: The person may now see the reward, rather than intrinsic interest, as the motivation for performing the task. (p. 236)

Overlap A monocular cue for perceiving distance; nearby objects partially block our view of more distant objects. (Also called interposition, because nearby objects are interposed between our eyes and more distant objects.) (p. 171)

Ovum The female reproductive cell, which after fertilization develops into a new individual. (p. 65)

PET Scan (Positron Emission Tomograph) A visual display of brain activity that detects where a radioactive sugar goes while the brain performs a given task. (p. 34)

Panic Attack An episode of intense dread in which for a number of minutes a person experiences terror and accompanying chest pain, choking, or other frightening sensations. (p. 434)

Parapsychology The study of paranormal phenomena such as ESP. (p. 181)

Parasympathetic Nervous System The division of the autonomic nervous system that calms the body, conserving its energy. (p. 28)

Parietal (puh-RYE-uht-uhl) **Lobes** The portion of the cerebral cortex lying atop the head and toward the rear; includes the somatosensory cortex. (p. 39)

Partial Reinforcement Reinforcing a response only part of the time; results in less rapid acquisition of response but much greater resistance to extinction than does continuous reinforcement. (p. 229)

Percentile Rank The percentage of the scores in a distribution that a given score exceeds. (p. 594)

Perception The process of organizing and interpreting sensory information, enabling us to recognize meaningful objects and events. (p. 140)

Perceptual Adaptation In vision, the ability to adjust to an artificially displaced or even inverted visual world. (p. 177)

Perceptual Set A mental predisposition to perceive one thing and not another. (p. 179)

Peripheral Nervous System (PNS) The part of the nervous system that lies outside of the central nervous system. It consists of the sensory neurons, which carry messages to the central nervous system from the body's sense receptors, and motor neurons, which carry messages from the central nervous system to the muscles and glands. (p. 27)

Person-Centered Therapy Carl Rogers' humanistic therapy, in which the therapist attempts to facilitate clients' growth by offering genuineness, acceptance, and empathy. (p. 465)

Personal Control People's perception that they can control their environment. (p. 418)

Personal Space The buffer zone we like to maintain around our bodies. (p. 547)

Personality An individual's relatively distinctive and consistent pattern of thinking, feeling, and acting. (p. 395)

Personality Disorders Psychological disorders characterized by enduring, maladaptive character traits. See *antisocial personality*. (p. 453)

Personality Inventories Questionnaires (often with true-false or agree-disagree items) on which people report their customary feelings and behaviors; used to assess personality traits. (p. 407)

Personality Psychology A branch of psychology that studies how individuals are influenced by relatively enduring inner factors. (p. 7)

Phallic Stage The third of Freud's psychosexual stages, during which the pleasure zone is the genitals and sexual feelings arise toward the parent of the other sex. (p. 398)

Phobic Disorder An anxiety disorder in which a person is troubled by a persistent, irrational fear of a specific object or situation. (p. 433)

Phonemes A language's smallest distinctive sound units. (p. 287)

Phrenology A discarded nineteenth-century theory that the conformation of the skull reveals one's abilities and character. (p. 23)

Physiological Psychology A branch of psychology concerned with the links between biology and behavior. (p. 6)

Pituitary Gland The endocrine system's master gland. Under the influence of the hypothalamus, the pituitary regulates growth and controls other endocrine glands. (p. 52)

Place Theory In hearing, the theory that links the pitch we hear with the place where the cochlea's membrane is stimulated. (p. 153)

Placebo An inert substance that may, in an experiment, be administered in place of an active drug; it may trigger the effects that the user believes the actual drug has. (p. 209)

Placebo Effect The beneficial effect of a person's *expecting* that a treatment will be therapeutic. A placebo is a neutral treatment (such as an inactive pill) that may nevertheless promote healing because of the hope and confidence placed in it. (pp. 482–483)

Plasticity The brain's capacity for modification, as evident in brain reorganization following damage (especially in children) and in experiments on the effects of experience on brain development. (p. 51)

Plateau Phase The second phase of the sexual response cycle, occurring just before orgasm, in which excitement peaks and blood pressure rates continue to rise. (p. 353)

Pleasure Principle The id's demand for immediate gratification. (p. 398)

Polygraph A machine, commonly used in attempts to detect lies, that measures several of the physiological responses that accompany emotion (such as perspiration, heart rate, and breathing changes). (p. 372)

Population All the cases in a total group, from which samples may be drawn for study. (p. 601)

Positive Reinforcer A rewarding stimulus, such as food, which, when presented after a response, strengthens the response. (p. 228)

Posthypnotic Amnesia A condition, sometimes suggested during hypnosis, in which a subject appears unable to recall what happened during hypnosis. Recall may, however, be established if a prearranged signal is given to remember. (p. 199)

Posthypnotic Suggestion A suggestion made during a hypnotic session that is to be carried out afterward when the subject is no longer hypnotized; it is used by some clinicians as a boost to controlling undesired symptoms and behaviors. (p. 202)

Preconscious The region of the unconscious that, according to Freud, contains nonthreatening material that can be retrieved into conscious awareness. (p. 396)

Predictive Validity The success with which a test predicts the behavior it is designed to predict; assessed by computing the correlation between test scores and the criterion behavior. (p. 314)

Prejudice An unjustifiable attitude toward a group and its members. (p. 571)

Preoperational Stage In Piaget's theory, the stage (from about 2 to 6 years of age) during which the child learns to use language but does not yet comprehend the mental operations of concrete logic. (pp. 70, 81)

Primary Reinforcer An innately reinforcing stimulus, such as one that satisfies a biological need. (p. 229)

Primary Sex Characteristics The body structures that enable reproduction. (p. 90)

Proactive Interference The disrupting effect of prior learning on the recall of new information. (p. 262)

Projection In psychoanalytic theory, the defense mechanism by which people disguise threatening impulses by imputing them to others. (p. 400)

Projective Tests Personality tests, such as the Rorschach and TAT, that provide ambiguous stimuli designed to trigger projection of one's inner dynamics. (p. 401)

Prosocial Behavior Positive, constructive, helpful behavior. The opposite of antisocial behavior. (p. 238)

Prototype The best example of a category; matching new items to the prototype provides a quick and easy method for including items in a category (for example, comparing feathered creatures to a prototypical bird such as a robin). (p. 271)

Proximity A perceptual tendency to group together things that are near each other. (p. 169)

Psychiatry A branch of medicine, practiced by physicians with an M.D. degree, and sometimes involving medical (for example, drug) treatments as well as psychological assistance. (p. 7)

Psychoactive Drugs Drugs that alter mood and perceptions. (p. 205)

Psychoanalysis Freud's therapy technique in which the patient's free associations, resistances, dreams, and transferences—and the therapist's interpretations of them—are the means by which previously repressed feelings are released and the patient gains insight into them. Freud's psychoanalytic theory of personality sought to explain what he observed during psychoanalysis. (pp. 397, 462)

Psychoanalytic Perspective Builds on Freud's ideas that behavior arises from unconscious drives and conflicts, some of which may stem from childhood experiences. (p. 7)

Psychological Dependence A psychological need to use a drug, such as to relieve stress. (p. 206)

Psychological Disorder A psychological problem that is typically defined on the basis of atypical, undesirable, maladaptive, and unjustifiable behavior. (p. 429)

Psychology The science of behavior and mental processes. (p. 5)

Psychopharmacology The study of the effects of drugs on mind and behavior. (p. 486)

Psychophysiological Illness Literally, mind-body illness; any illness, such as certain forms of hypertension, ulcers, and headaches, that is not caused by any known physical disorder but instead seems linked with stress. (p. 504)

Psychosexual Stages The developmental stages (oral, anal, phallic, latency, genital) during which, according to Freud, the id's pleasure-seeking energies are focused on different erogenous zones. (p. 398)

Psychosurgery Surgery that removes or destroys brain tissue in an effort to change behavior. (p. 484)

Psychotherapy A planned, emotionally charged, confiding interaction between a trained, socially approved healer and someone who suffers a psychological difficulty. (p. 462)

Psychotic Disorder A psychological disorder in which a person loses contact with reality, experiencing irrational ideas and distorted perceptions. (p. 448)

Puberty The early adolescent period during which growth surges and sexual maturity develops. (p. 90)

Punishment An aversive stimulus that, when presented, suppresses prior behavior. (p. 231)

Pupil The adjustable opening in the center of the eye through which light enters. (p. 145)

REM Rebound The tendency for REM sleep to increase following REM sleep deprivation (created by repeated awakenings during REM sleep). (p. 198)

REM Sleep Rapid eye movement, a recurring sleep stage during which vivid dreams commonly occur. Also known as paradoxical sleep, because the muscles are relaxed (except for minor twitches) but the brain and eyes are active. (p. 193)

Random Assignment Assigning subjects to experimental and control conditions by chance, thus minimizing preexisting differences between those assigned to the different groups. (p. 13)

Random Sample A sample that is representative of some larger group because every person has an equal chance of being included. (p. 11)

Range The difference between the highest and lowest scores in a distribution. (p. 596)

Rational-Emotive Therapy A type of cognitive-behavior therapy developed by Albert Ellis that vigorously challenges people's illogical, self-defeating thinking. (p. 474)

Rationalization In psychoanalytic theory, a defense mechanism in which self-justifying explanations are offered in place of the real, more threatening, unconscious reasons for one's actions. (p. 400)

Reactance A motive to protect or restore one's sense of freedom from social control. (p. 536)

Reaction Formation In psychoanalytic theory, the ego's unconscious switching of unacceptable impulses into their opposites. Thus people may express feelings that are the opposite of their anxiety-arousing unconscious feelings. (p. 400)

Reality Principle The ego's tendency to satisfy the id's desires in ways that will realistically bring pleasure rather than pain. (p. 398)

Recall A measure of memory in which the person must reproduce information learned earlier. (p. 256)

Reciprocal Determinism The two-way influences among personal factors, environmental factors, and behavior. (p. 417)

Recognition A measure of memory in which the person need only identify items previously learned, as on a multiple-choice test. (p. 256)

Reflex A simple, automatic, inborn response to a sensory input, such as the knee-jerk response. (p. 29)

Refractory Period A resting period after orgasm during which a male cannot be aroused to another orgasm. (p. 353)

Regression In psychoanalytic theory, an individual's retreat, when faced with anxiety, to an earlier, more comfortable stage of development. (p. 400)

Regression Toward the Average The tendency for extreme or unusual scores to fall back ("regress") toward the average. (p. 599)

Rehearsal The conscious repetition of information, either simply to maintain information in consciousness or to encode it for storage. (p. 248)

Reification To regard an abstract concept (such as giftedness) as if it were a real, concrete thing. (p. 315)

Reinforcement In operant conditioning, any event that increases the likelihood of a response that it follows. (p. 228)

Relative Deprivation The sense that one is worse off relative to those with whom one compares oneself. (p. 382)

Relative Height A monocular cue for perceiving distance; we perceive higher objects as farther away. (p. 172)

Relative Motion A monocular cue for perceiving distance; when we move, objects at different distances change their relative positions in our visual image, with those closest moving most. (Also called motion parallax.) (p. 172)

Relative Size A monocular cue for perceiving distance; when two objects are assumed to be the same size, the one that produces the smaller image appears to be more distant. (p. 171)

Relearning A measure of memory that assesses the amount of time saved when relearning previously learned information. (p. 256)

Reliability The extent to which a test yields consistent results (as assessed by the consistency of scores on two halves of the test, on alternate forms of the test, or on retesting). See *split-half* and *test-retest reliability*. (p. 312)

Replication Repeating the essence of an experiment with different subjects to see whether the basic finding is repeatable. (p. 15)

Representativeness Heuristic Judging the likelihood of things in terms of how well they seem to represent, or match, particular prototypes; may lead one to ignore other relevant information. (p. 278)

Repression In psychoanalytic theory, the basic defense mechanism that banishes anxiety-arousing thoughts and feelings from consciousness. (p. 400)

Resistance In psychoanalysis, the blocking from consciousness of anxiety-laden material. (p. 463)

Resolution Phase The last phase in the sexual response cycle, during which the body gradually returns to its unaroused state. (p. 353)

Respondent Behavior Behavior that

occurs as an automatic response to some stimulus. (p. 227)

Reticular Activating System A nerve network in the brainstem that plays an important role in controlling arousal and attention. (p. 36)

Retina The light-sensitive inner surface of the eye, containing the receptor rods and cones plus layers of neurons that begin the processing of visual information. (p. 145)

Retinal Disparity A binocular cue for perceiving depth; the more the disparity (difference) between the retinal images of an object in each of our eyes, the closer to us the object is. (Also called binocular disparity.) (p. 170)

Retrieval The process of getting information out of memory storage. (p. 245)

Retroactive Interference The disrupting effect of new learning on the recall of old information. (p. 262)

Rods Retinal receptors that detect black, white, and gray, especially in peripheral and nighttime vision. (p. 145)

Role A set of social expectations about a social position, defining how those in the position ought to behave. (p. 538)

Romantic Love The passionate state of intense absorption we feel for another. (p. 580)

Rooting Reflex A baby's tendency, when touched on the cheek, to open the mouth and search for the nipple. (p. 67)

Rorschach A projective test designed by Hermann Rorschach that uses people's interpretations of inkblots in an attempt to identify their projected feelings. (p. 402)

Saturation The purity of color, which is greater when complexity (the number of other wavelengths mixed in) is low. (p. 145)

Scapegoat Theory The theory that prejudice provides frustrated people with an outlet for their anger. (p. 574)

Scatterplot A graphed cluster of dots, each dot representing the values of two variables (such as a student's high school and college GPAs). The shape of the cluster suggests the nature and degree of relationship between the two variables. (Also called a scattergram or scatter diagram.) (p. 598)

Schema A concept or framework that organizes and interprets information. (p. 71)

Schizophrenia A group of psychotic disorders characterized by disorganized thinking, disturbed perceptions, and inappropriate emotions and actions. (p. 448)

Secondary Reinforcer A conditioned reinforcer; a stimulus that acquires its reinforcing power by association with another reinforcer, such as a primary reinforcer. (p. 229)

Secondary Sex Characteristics Nonreproductive sexual characteristics such as female breasts, male voice quality, and body hair. (p. 90)

Selective Breeding A technique useful for studying genetic influences in which animals that display a particular trait are mated and those among their descendants that best express this trait are selected for further mating. If a trait is genetically influenced, continued selection should produce animals that strongly exhibit that trait. (p. 54)

Self-Actualization According to Maslow, the final psychological need that arises when basic physical and psychological needs are met; the process of fulfilling one's potential as one achieves qualities such as self-acceptance, spontaneity, love, mastery, and creativity. (p. 411)

Self-Concept All our thoughts and feelings about ourselves in answer to the question, "Who am I?" (p. 412)

Self-Esteem One's feelings of high or low self-worth. (p. 415)

Self-Perception Theory The theory that when we are unsure of our attitudes we infer them much as an outside observer would, by looking at our behavior and the circumstances under which it occurs. (p. 540)

Self-Serving Bias The bias of perceiving oneself favorably. (p. 416)

Semantic Encoding The encoding of meaning, including the meaning of words. (p. 247)

Semantics The study of meaning, as derived from morphemes, words, and sentences. (p. 288)

Semicircular Canals Three curved, fluid-filled structures of the inner ear with receptors that detect body motion. (p. 159)

Sensation The process by which certain stimulus energies are detected and experienced. (p. 140)

Sensorimotor Stage In Piaget's theory, the stage (from birth to about 2 years of age) during which infants know the world mostly in terms of their sensory impressions and motor activities. (pp. 70, 72)

Sensory Adaptation Diminished sensitivity with constant stimulation. (p. 143)

Sensory Interaction The principle that one sense may influence another, as when the smell of food influences its taste. (p. 157)

Sensory Neurons Neurons that carry incoming information from the body's sense receptors to the central nervous system. (p. 28)

Serial Position Effect The tendency for our recall of the items in a list to depend on their position. For example, when immediately recalling the items in any order, the last and first items are most easily recalled. (p. 249)

Set Point The point at which an individual's weight "thermostat" is set. When the body falls below this weight, changes in hunger and metabolic rate act to restore the lost weight. (p. 343)

Sexual Dysfunction Problems that consistently impair sexual functioning. (p. 359)

Sexual Orientation One's sexual attraction toward and responsiveness to erotic stimuli associated with members of either one's own sex (homosexual orientation) or the other sex (heterosexual orientation). (p. 356)

Shape Constancy Perceiving familiar objects as having a constant shape, even while their retinal image changes with viewing angle. (p. 172)

Shaping A procedure in operant conditioning that starts with some existing behavior and reinforces closer and closer approximations to a desired behavior. (p. 228)

Short-term Memory A component of memory that holds few items briefly, such as the seven digits of a phone number while dialing. (p. 247)

Signal Detection Theory A theory that assumes that there is no single absolute threshold, because the detection of a weak signal depends partly on a person's experience, expectations, and motivation. (p. 141)

Similarity A perceptual tendency to group together similar elements. (p. 169)

Size Constancy Perceiving an object as having a constant size, despite variations in its retinal image. (p. 173)

Skinner Box An operant conditioning chamber, containing a bar or key that an animal can manipulate to obtain a food or water reinforcer and devices to record the animal's rate of bar pressing or key pecking. (p. 228)

Sleep Apnea A sleep disorder characterized by temporary cessation of breathing when the person is asleep, and consequent momentary reawakenings. (p. 195)

Sleep Spindles Rhythmic bursts of brain activity occurring during Stage 2 sleep. (p. 192)

Social Clock The culturally preferred timing of social events dictating when one should, for example, leave home, marry, have children, and retire. (p. 101)

Social-Cognitive Perspective Applies principles of social learning and cognition to personality. (p. 417)

Social Exchange Theory The theory that our social behavior is an exchange process, the aim of which is to maximize rewards and minimize costs. (p. 570)

Social Facilitation The tendency to perform simple tasks better or faster when others are present. (p. 545)

Social Loafing The tendency for people to exert less effort when they are pooling their efforts toward a common goal than when individually accountable. (p. 546)

Social Psychology The study of how people influence and relate to one another. (p. 7)

Social Traps Situations in which two parties, by each rationally pursuing their self-interest, become caught in mutually destructive behavior. (p. 584)

Sociobiology The study of the evolution of social behavior using the principles of natural selection. Social behaviors that are heritable and that contribute to the preservation and spread of one's genes are presumed to be favored by natural selection. (p. 25)

Somatic (so-MAT-ic) **Nervous System** The division of the peripheral nervous system that receives information from various sense receptors and that controls the skeletal muscles. (p. 27)

Somatoform Disorders Neurotic disorders in which the symptoms take a somatic (bodily) form without apparent physical cause. See *conversion disorder* and *hypochondriasis*. (p. 438)

Somatosensory Cortex The area at the front of the parietal lobes that registers and processes body sensations. (p. 41)

Split-Brain A condition in which the two hemispheres are isolated by cutting the connecting fibers between them (mainly those of the corpus callosum). (p. 45)

Split-half Reliability A measure of the internal consistency of a test; typically assessed by correlating total scores obtained on the odd and even items. (p. 313)

Spontaneous Recovery The reappearance, after a rest period, of an extinguished conditioned response. (p. 223)

Spontaneous Remission Improvement without treatment. In psychotherapy, symptom relief without psychotherapy. (p. 480)

SQ3R An acronym for Survey, Question, Read, Review, Recite—a method of study. (p. 265)

Standard Deviation A measure of variability, defined as the square root of the average squared deviation of scores from the mean. (p. 597)

Standardization Defining meaningful scores by comparison with the performance of a representative "standardization group" that has been pretested. (p. 310)

Stanford-Binet The widely used American revision (by Terman at Stanford University) of Binet's original intelligence test. (p. 304)

State-Dependent Memory The tendency to recall information best when in the same emotional or physiological state as when the information was learned. (p. 257)

Statistical Significance A statistical statement of how small the likelihood is that an obtained result occurred by chance. (p. 604)

Stereotype A generalized (often overgeneralized) belief about a group of people. (p. 571)

Stimulants Drugs (such as caffeine, nicotine, and the more powerful amphetamines and cocaine) that excite neural activity and arouse body functions. (p. 206)

Storage The maintenance of encoded information over time. (p. 245)

Stranger Anxiety The fear of strangers that infants commonly display for a few months beginning at about 8 months of age. (p. 72)

Stress The whole process by which environmental events, called stressors, threaten or challenge us. (p. 497)

Sublimation In psychoanalytic theory, the defense mechanism by which people rechannel their unacceptable impulses into socially approved activities. (p. 400)

Subliminal Below threshold. (p. 141)

Successive Approximations In operant conditioning, the small steps by which some existing behavior is shaped toward a desired behavior. (p. 228)

Superego The part of personality that, according to Freud, represents internalized ideals, thus providing standards for judgment (conscience) and for future aspirations. (p. 398)

Superordinate Goals Shared goals that override differences among people and require their cooperation. (p. 586)

Survey Ascertaining the self-reported attitudes or behaviors of people by questioning a representative (random) sample of them. (p. 10)

Syllogism An argument in which two presumably true statements, called premises, lead to a third statement, the conclusion; the basis of formal deductive reasoning. (p. 283)

Sympathetic Nervous System The division of the autonomic nervous system that arouses the body, mobilizing its energy in stressful situations. (p. 27)

Synapse (SIN-aps) The junction between the axon tip of the sending neuron and the dendrite or cell body of the receiving neuron. (p. 31)

Syntax Rules for combining words into grammatically correct sentences. (p. 288)

Systematic Desensitization A type of counterconditioning that associates a pleasant, relaxed state with gradually increasing anxiety-triggering stimuli. Commonly used to treat phobias. (p. 470)

THC (Delta-9-Tetrahydrocannabinol) The active ingredient in marijuana that triggers a variety of effects, including mild hallucinations. (p. 210)

Telegraphic Speech An early speech stage in which the child speaks like a telegram—using mostly nouns and verbs and omitting prepositions and other auxiliary words. (p. 289)

Temperament One's characteristic emotional reactivity and intensity. (p. 112)

Temporal Lobes The portion of the cerebral cortex lying roughly above the ears, including the auditory areas, each of which receives auditory information, primarily from the opposite ear. (p. 39)

Teratogens Agents, such as chemicals and viruses, that sometimes cross the placenta from mother to fetus, causing harm. (p. 66)

Test-Retest Reliability A measure of the consistency of test scores obtained by retesting people. (p. 313)

Testosterone The most important of the male sex hormones (androgens). Both males and females have it, but the additional testosterone in males stimulates the growth of the male sex organs before birth and the development of the male sex characteristics during puberty. (p. 126)

Texture Gradient A monocular cue for perceiving distance; a gradual change to a less distinct texture suggests increasing distance. (p. 17)

Thalamus (THALL-uh-muss) The brain's sensory switchboard. Located atop the brainstem, the thalamus directs messages to the brain's sensory receiving areas and transmits replies to the cerebellum and medulla. (p. 36)

Theory An integrated set of principles that organizes, predicts, and explains observations. (p. 9)

Threshold The level of stimulation required to trigger a response. (p. 30)

Timbre The tone color of a sound that distinguishes it from other sounds of the same pitch and loudness. (p. 152)

Token Economy An operant conditioning procedure in which a token of some sort, which can later be exchanged for various privileges or treats, is given as a reward for desired behavior. (p. 473)

Tolerance Requiring larger and larger doses before experiencing a drug's effect, or a diminishing of the drug's effect with regular use of the same dose. (p. 206)

Traits Our predispositions to behave in given ways, measured by personality inventories. (p. 406)

Trait Perspective Describes personality in terms of scores on various scales, each of which represents a personality dimension. (p. 405)

Transduction Conversion of one form of energy into another. In sensation, the transforming of stimulus energies into neural firings. (p. 144)

Transference In psychoanalysis, the patient's transfer to the analyst of emotions linked with other relationships (such as love or hatred for a parent). (p. 463)

Trial and Error A problem-solving process in which one solution after another is tried until success is achieved. (p. 272)

Two-Factor Theory The theory that to experience emotion one must (1) be physically aroused and (2) cognitively label the arousal. (p. 387)

Two-Word Stage The stage in speech development, beginning about age 2, during which a child speaks mostly two-word utterances. (p. 289)

Type A Friedman and Rosenman's conception of behavior—competitive, hard-driving, impatient, verbally aggressive, easily angered—that is associated with increased incidence of coronary heart disease. (p. 502)

Type B Friedman and Rosenman's conception of an easygoing person who is less susceptible than the Type A person to coronary heart disease (p. 502)

Unconditional Positive Regard According to Rogers, an attitude of total acceptance toward another person. (p. 412)

Unconditioned Response (UCR) In classical conditioning, the unlearned response to an unconditioned stimulus. (p. 221)

Unconditioned Stimulus (UCS) In classical conditioning, a stimulus that naturally triggers a response without conditioning. (p. 221)

Unconscious According to Freud, a reservoir of mostly unacceptable thoughts, wishes, feelings, and memories. According to contemporary research psychologists, information processing of which we are unaware. (p. 396)

Validity The extent to which a test measures or predicts what it is supposed to measure (or predict). (See also *content validity* and *predictive validity*.) (p. 313)

Variable-Interval Schedule In operant conditioning, a schedule of reinforcement in which a response is reinforced after unpredictable time intervals. (p. 230)

Variable-Ratio Schedule In operant conditioning, a schedule of reinforcement in which a response is reinforced after an unpredictable number of responses. (p. 230)

Ventromedial Hypothalamus (VMH) The bottom and middle areas of the hypothalamus that, when stimulated, trigger the cessation of eating and, when destroyed, cause an animal to overeat. (p. 343)

Vestibular Sacs Two structures of the inner ear with receptors that provide the sense of upright body position. (p. 159)

Visual Cliff A laboratory device for testing depth perception. (p. 170)

Visual Encoding The encoding of picture images. (p. 246)

Wavelength The distance from the peak of one light or sound wave to the peak of the next. Waves vary from long and slow to short and fast. (p. 144)

Weber's Law The principle that two stimuli must differ by a constant minimum percentage (rather than a constant amount) for their difference to be perceived. (p. 143)

Weschler Adult Intelligence Scale (WAIS) The most widely used intelligence test; contains a variety of verbal and nonverbal (performance) subtests. (p. 307)

Wernicke's Area An area of the left hemisphere involved in language comprehension. (p. 42)

Whiteness Constancy Perceiving objects as having consistent whiteness even when their illumination varies. (p. 174)

Withdrawal The distressing physical and psychological symptoms that follow the discontinued use of certain drugs. (p. 206)

X Sex Chromosome The chromosome (from the father) that, when paired with the mother's X sex chromosome, will produce a female. (p. 65)

Y Sex Chromosome The chromosome (which only comes from the father) that, when paired with an X sex chromosome from the mother, will produce a male. (p. 65)

Yerkes-Dodson Law The principle that, in general, moderate arousal enables optimal performance. But for different tasks the optimal level of arousal varies; the easier the task, the higher the optimum arousal. (p. 370)

Young-Helmholtz Three-Color Theory The theory that the retina contains three different color receptors—one most sensitive to red, one to green, one to blue—which in combination can produce the perception of any color. (p. 151)

Zygote The one-celled organism created by the union of sperm and ovum. (p. 65)

Illustration Credits

Part I Courtesy of Christopher Meatyard

Chapter 1 Photo by Victor Arnolds, Courtesy of Galerie Barbara Farber, Amsterdam

Chapter 2 from *Brancusi, Photographer*, Agrinde Publications, Ltd., New York.

Part II © Aperture, Inc., from *Dorothea Lange: Photographs of a Lifetime*, Aperture, New York, 1982.

Chapter 3 (*top*) Scala/Art Resource; (*bottom*) The Museum of Modern Art

Chapter 4 Scala/Art Resource

Chapter 5 (*top*) ©1970 Imogen Cunningham Trust; (*bottom*) Courtesy Pennsylvania Academy of the Fine Arts

Part III © Charles Harbutt/Archive Pictures

Chapter 6 Courtesy of Christopher Meatyard

Chapter 7 (*top*) © Robert Doisneau/Photo Researchers; (*bottom*) © Zeke Berman 1982

Chapter 8 Photo by eeva-inkeri, Courtesy of Paula Cooper Gallery, New York

Part IV © David Hockney 1983

Chapter 9 (*top*) Alfred Eisenstaedt, LIFE Magazine © 1963 Time Inc.; (*bottom*) © 1984 Bill Witt

Chapter 10 (*left page*) © W. Eugene Smith; (*right page*) Berenice Abbott/Courtesy of Commerce Graphics Ltd., Inc.

Chapter 12 (*top*) © Werner Bischof/Magnum Photos; (*bottom*) Photo by Robert E. Mates, Courtesy of the Solomon R. Guggenheim Museum

Part V © Aperture, Inc., from *William Klein: An Aperture Monograph*, Aperture, New York, 1981.

Chapter 13 Courtesy of The Henry Moore Foundation

Chapter 14 (*left page*) from *Brancusi, Photographer*, Agrinde Publications Ltd., New York; (*right page*) © Georgeann Packard 1985

Part VI Andre Kertesz/Archive Pictures

Chapter 16 (*left page*) Scala/Art Resource; (*right page*) © Algimantas Kezys/Click, Chicago

Chapter 18 © Michael O'Brien/Archive Pictures

Part VII Photo by Marc Schuman

Chapter 19 © Aperture, Inc., from *Callahan*, Aperture, New York, 1976.

Chapter 20 (*left page*) © Abbas/Magnum Photos; (*right page*) Photo by Ivan Dalla Tana, Courtesy of Tony Shafrazi Gallery

Chapter 1

p. 5 Wundt, Hall, James, Thorndike, Freud, Binet, Watson: Brown Brothers; Ebbinghaus, Dix: The Bettmann Archive; Pavlov: Sovfoto; Washburn: National Library of Medicine

p. 6 © Marcia Weinstein

p. 7 © Ken Karp

p. 8 © Martin M. Rotker/Taurus Photos

p. 10 © Peter Menzel 1983/Stock, Boston

p. 11 © Jeff Foott/Bruce Coleman Inc.

p. 12 © Hazel Hankin 1980

p. 13 © Historical Pictures Service

p. 14 © Enrico Ferorelli/DOT

p. 16 © Fred Bavendam/Peter Arnold, Inc.

Chapter 2

p. 23 The Bettmann Archive

Figure 2–1 © M. W. E. Tweedie/Bruce Coleman Inc.

p. 25 (*left*) © Tony Brandenburg/Bruce Coleman Inc.; (*right*) © Peter Vandermark/Stock, Boston

p. 26 (*top row, left to right*) © David Austen/Stock, Boston; © Owen Franken/Stock, Boston; © Ira Kirschenbaum/Stock, Boston; © Owen Franken/Stock, Boston; (*bottom row, left to right*) © Owen Franken/Stock, Boston; © Owen Franken/Stock, Boston; © Owen Franken/Stock, Boston; © Owen Franken/Stock, Boston

p. 32 © Ira Berger 1981/Woodfin Camp & Associates

p. 33 Musée Dupuytren, Paris

Figure 2–7 © Ken Karp

Figure 2–8 © Kevin Byron/Bruce Coleman Inc.

Figure 2–9 Courtesy of Drs. Michael Phelps and John Mazziota, U.C.L.A. School of Medicine

p. 37 © Frank Siteman 1981/Taurus Photos

Figure 2–11 Adapted from M. S. Gazzaniga and others, *Functional neuroscience*, p. 278. Copyright © 1979 by Harper & Row, Publishers. Reprinted by permission.

p. 39 AP/Wide World Photos

p. 41 Courtesy of Drs. Michael Phelps and John Mazziota, U.C.L.A. School of Medicine

Figure 2–14 S. Rose, *The conscious brain*. Copyright © 1983 by Alfred A. Knopf, Inc. Reprinted by permission of the publisher.

p. 42 The Warren Anatomical Museum, Harvard Medical School

Figure 2–15 N. Geschwind, "Specializations of the human brain," *Scientific American*, Sept. 1979, pp. 180–199. Copyright © 1979 by Scientific American, Inc. All rights reserved.

Figure 2–19 M. S. Gazzaniga, "Right hemisphere language following brain bisection: A 20-year perspective." *American Psychologist*, 1983, *38*, 525–537. Copyright © 1983 by the American Psychological Association. Reprinted by permission of the author.

Figure 2–20 J. Jaynes, *The origin of consciousness in the breakdown of the bicameral mind*. Copyright © 1976 by J. Jaynes. Reprinted by permission of Houghton Mifflin Company.

Figure 2–21 (*left*) © Ira Wyman; (*right*) R. Labbe, A. Firl, Jr., E.J. Mufson, D.G. Stein, "Fetal brain transplants: Reduction of cognitive deficits in rats with frontal cortex lesions." *Science*, 1983, *221*, 470–472. Copyright © 1983 by the American Association for the Advancement of Science.

p. 54 (*top*) © Mark Sherman/Bruce Coleman Inc.; (*bottom*) © Cecile Brunswick/Peter Arnold, Inc.

Figure 2–24 © Lenore Weber/Taurus Photos

Chapter 3

p. 63 (*both*) © William Hubbell 1984/ Woodfin Camp & Associates

Figure 3–1 Adapted from C. H. Waddington, *New patterns in genetics and development*. New York: Columbia University Press, 1962.

p. 64 © Eric Kroll 1984/Taurus Photos

Figure 3–2 (*top*) © Per Sundström/Gamma-Liaison; (a–d) Dr. Landrum B. Shettles

p. 66 © Mimi Cotter/Int'l. Stock Photo

Figure 3–3 J. L. Conel, *The postnatal development of the human cerebral cortex* (Vols. 1–VI). Cambridge, MA: Harvard University Press, 1939–1963. Reprinted by permission.

Figure 3–4 M. R. Rosenzweig, E. L. Bennett, and M. C. Diamond, "Brain changes in response to experience." *Scientific American*, Feb. 1972, 22–29. Copyright © 1972 by Scientific American, Inc. All rights reserved.

p. 67 © Jason Laure/Woodfin Camp & Associates

Figure 3–5 Adapted from W. K. Frankenburg and J. B. Dodds, "The Denver developmental screening test." *Journal of Pediatrics*, 1967, *71*(2), 181–191.

p. 68 © Jason Laure 1984/Woodfin Cam. & Associates

p. 69 (*top*) © Joel Gordon 1975; (*bottom*) © Randy Matusow/Monkmeyer Press Photo Service

Figure 3–6 © Peter Menzel 1984/Stock, Boston

Figure 3–7 © Elizabeth Crews

p. 71 © Bill Anderson/Monkmeyer Press Photo Service

Figure 3–8 Matthäus Merian, *Landscape-Head*

p. 72 (*left*) Pierre Dupuis, *Still Life with Grapes*, c. 1650, Louvre, Paris. Photo: Scala/ Art Resource; (*right*) Gino Severini, *The Basket of Fruit*, 1919, Private Collection, Florence. Photo: Scala/Art Resource

Figure 3–9 © Hazel Hankin

p. 73 © Hazel Hankin 1981

p. 74 © Erika Stone/Peter Arnold, Inc.

Figure 3–10 University of Wisconsin Primate Laboratory

p. 75 (*bottom*) Thomas McAvoy, LIFE Magazine © 1955 Time Inc.

p. 76 (*top*) © Peter Menzel 1982/Stock, Boston; (*bottom*) Mary Cassatt, *Mother and Child*, c.1900, oil on canvas, 39 ⅝ × 32⅛", Gift of Alexander Stewart. The Art Institute of Chicago. All rights reserved.

Figure 3–11 University of Wisconsin Primate Laboratory

p. 77 © Mark Antman/The Image Works

Figure 3-12 University of Wisconsin Primate Laboratory

Figure 3–13 J. Kagan, "Emergent themes in human development." *American Scientist*, 1976, *64*, 186–196. Reprinted by permission of *American Scientist*, journal of Sigma XI.

p. 79 William Hogarth, *The Price Family*, 1735. Photo: The Bettmann Archive

Figure 3–14 © Mimi Forsyth/Monkmeyer Press Photo Service

p. 82 (*top left*) © Michael Weisbrot and family/Stock, Boston; (*top right*) © Alice Kandell/ Kay Reese & Associates; (*bottom*) © Elizabeth Crews

p. 83 © Owen Franken/Stock, Boston

p. 84 © James Carroll

Chapter 4

p. 89 The Bettmann Archive

Figure 4–1 J. M. Tanner, *Fetus into man: Physical growth from conception to maturity*. Cambridge, MA: Harvard University Press, 1978. Reprinted by permission.

p. 91 © Donald Dietz 1980/Stock, Boston

p. 92 © Paul S. Conklin

p. 93 © Owen Franken/Stock, Boston

p. 95 AP/Wide World Photos

p. 96 (*top*) © Hazel Hankin 1985; (*bottom left*) © Marion Bernstein; (*bottom right*) © Rae Russel 1981/Int'l. Stock Photo

p. 97 © Sybil Shelton/Peter Arnold, Inc.

Figure 4–3 Adapted from P. M. Insel and W. T. Roth, *Health in a changing society*, p. 98. Palo Alto, CA: Mayfield Publishing Co., 1976. Reprinted by permission.

p. 99 © Heinz Kluetmeier/Sports Illustrated

Figure 4–4 D. Schonfield and B. A. Robertson, "Memory storage and aging." *Canadian Journal of Psychology*, 1966, *20*, 228–236. Copyright © 1966, Canadian Psychological Association. Reprinted by permission.

p. 100 © Laimute E. Druskis 1979/Taurus Photos

Figure 4–5 D. J. Levinson, C.N. Darow, E.B. Klein, M.H. Levinson, and B. McKee, *The seasons of a man's life*. Copyright © 1978 by Alfred A. Knopf, Inc. Reprinted by permission of the publisher.

p. 101 (*left*) © Elizabeth Crews; (*right*) © Michael Habicht/Taurus Photos

p. 102 © Ken Karp

p. 103 (*left*) © Sybil Shelton/Monkmeyer Press Photo Service; (*top center*) © Eric Kroll 1978/Taurus Photos; (*top right*) © Bob Hahn/ Taurus Photos; (*bottom center*) © Michael Habicht/Taurus Photos; (*bottom right*) © Richard Wood 1984/Taurus Photos

Figure 4–7 Lou Harris, *Aging in the 80's: America in transition*, November 1981. Courtesy of The National Council on Aging, Inc.

Figure 4–8 Adapted from R. L. Doty and others, "Smell identification ability: Changes with age." *Science*, 1984, *226*, 1441–1443. Copyright © 1984 by the American Association for the Advancement of Science.

Figure 4–9 J. Geiwitz, *Psychology: Looking at ourselves*. Copyright © 1980 by Little, Brown and Co. Reprinted by permission of the publisher.

Figure 4–10 K. W. Schaie and C. R. Strother, "A cross-sequential study of age changes in cognitive behavior." *Psychological Bulletin*, 1968, *70*, 671–680. Copyright © 1968 by the American Psychological Association. Reprinted by permission of the author.

p. 107 © Sybil Shelton/Monkmeyer Press Photo Service

p. 108 © Ken Karp

Figure 4–11 Data from survey by Audits and Surveys for the Merit Report, January 17–20, 1983. Reprinted by permission of *Public Opinion*, August/September 1984.

p. 109 © Anthony Suau 1985/Black Star

p. 110 © Ken Karp

p. 111 (*both*) © Enrico Ferorelli/DOT

p. 112 © Alice Kandell/Kay Reese & Associates

p. 113 © Doris Pinney

p. 114 © Michael Malyszko 1979/Stock, Boston

Chapter 5

p. 120 © Sylvia Johnson 1980/Woodfin Camp & Associates

p. 121 (*top*) © John Dominis/Wheeler Pictures; (*bottom*) © Shirley Zeiberg 1985/Taurus Photos

p. 122 © Frank Siteman/Stock, Boston

Figure 5–1 Adapted from J. S. Hyde, "How large are cognitive gender differences? A meta-analysis using w^2 and *d*." *American Psychologist*, 1981, *36*, 892–901. Copyright © 1981 by the American Psychological Association. Reprinted by permission of the author.

Figure 5–2 Adapted from J. S. Hyde, "How large are cognitive gender differences? A meta-analysis using w^2 and *d*." *American Psychologist*, 1981, *36*, 892–901. Copyright © 1981 by the American Psychological Association. Reprinted by permission of the author.

p. 123 S. G. Vandenberg and A. R. Kuse, "Mental rotations, a group test of three-dimensional spatial visualization." *Perceptual and Motor Skills*, 1978, *47*, 599–604. Reprinted with permission of authors and publisher.

Figure 5–3 Adapted from C. N. Jacklin and E. E. Maccoby, "Social behavior at 33 months in same-sex and mixed-sex dyads." *Child Development*, 1978, *27*, 239–247. Copyright © 1978 by The Society for Research in Child Development.

p. 124 © Sybil Shelton/Monkmeyer Press Photo Service.

p. 125 (*both*) The Bettmann Archive

Figure 5–4 D. A. Jenni and M. A. Jenni, "Carrying behavior in humans: Analysis of sex differences." *Science*, 19 November 1976, *194*, 859–860. Copyright © 1976 by the American Association for the Advancement of Science.

p. 128 © L. I. T. Rhodes/Taurus Photos

p. 129 (*left*) © Frank Siteman 1983/Stock, Boston; (*right*) © J. Berndt/Stock, Boston

p. 130 (*top*) © Erika Stone 1979; (*bottom*) © Elizabeth V. Gemmette

p. 133 (*top*) © Alan Carey/The Image Works; (*center*) © G. Cloyd/Taurus Photos; (*bottom*) Movie Still Archives

p. 134 (*left*) © Hazel Hankin/Stock, Boston; (*right*) © Cary Wolinsky/Stock, Boston

Chapter 6

Figure 6–1 P. B. Porter, "Another puzzle picture." *American Journal of Psychology*, 1954, *67*, 550–551. Copyright © 1954 by the Board of Trustees and the University of Illinois.

p. 142 (*left*) © Pam Hasegawa/Taurus Photos; (*right*) © Marcia Weinstein

p. 147 © E. R. Lewis

Figure 6–8 Fritz Goro, LIFE Magazine © 1971 Time Inc.

Figure 6–9 Adapted from J. P. Frisby, *Seeing: Illusion, brain and mind*, p. 157. New York: Oxford University Press, 1980. Reprinted by permission of the publisher.

Figure 6–10 (*all*) © Susan T. McElhinney/American Image, Inc.

Figure 6–11 © Joel Gordon 1985

Figure 6–12 R. M. Pritchard, "Stabilized images on the retina." *Scientific American*, June 1961, 72–78. Copyright © 1961 by Scientific American, Inc. All rights reserved.

Figure 6–13 Fritz Goro, LIFE Magazine © 1944 Time Inc.

Figure 6–17 E. G. Wever, *Theory of hearing*. New York: Wiley, 1949. Reprinted by permission.

p. 156 Robert Preston, Courtesy of J. E. Hawkins, Kresge Hearing Research Institute, The University of Michigan Medical School

p. 158 (*top*) © Mary Bloom 1981/Peter Arnold, Inc.; (*bottom*) © Bill Luster/Sports Illustrated

p. 159 (*top*) © Charles Gupton 1984/Stock, Boston; (*bottom*) Yale Joel, LIFE Magazine © 1958 Time Inc.

Chapter 7

p. 166 (*center*) AP/Wide World Photos; (*bottom*) Photos courtesy Helen E. Ross from H. E. Ross, "Mist, murk and visual perception." *New Scientist*, 1975, *66*, 658–660.

Figure 7–1 D. R. Bradley and others, "Reply to Cavonius." *Nature*, 1976, *261*, 78. Reprinted by permission of Macmillan Journals Ltd.

Figure 7–2 D.R. Bradley and others, "Reply to Cavonius." *Nature*, 1976, *261*, 78. Reprinted by permission of Macmillan Journals Ltd.

Figure 7–3 Kaiser Porcelain Ltd.

Figure 7–4 © M.C. Escher Heirs, c/o Cordon Art, Baarn, Holland; photo by D. James Dee, courtesy Vorpal Galleries: New York, San Francisco, Laguna Beach.

Figure 7–5 Walter Wick

Figure 7–6 (a) D. H. McBurney and V. B. Collings, *Introduction to sensation/perception* (2nd ed.). Adapted by permission of Prentice-Hall, Inc., Englewood Cliffs, NJ, 1984; (b) © Martin Rogers 1984/Stock, Boston

Figure 7–7 J. R. Eyerman, LIFE Magazine © 1952, 1980 Time Inc.

p. 171 (*top*) © Joel Gordon 1980; (*bottom*) © Joel Gordon 1982

p. 172 (*top*) © Frank Siteman 1984/Taurus Photos; (*bottom*) © Joel Gordon 1980

Figure 7–8 (a) *Wine Harvest, Tomb of Night*/Scala, Art Resource; (b) Canaletto, detail from *Il Canale Grande e Palazzo Bembo*, 1730–1731. Woburn Abbey, Collection of the Duke of Bedford/Scala, Art Resource

Figure 7–9 E. J. Gibson and R. D. Walk, The "visual cliff." *Scientific American*, April 1950, p. 170. Copyright © 1950 by Scientific American, Inc. All rights reserved.

p. 173 (a) R. N. Shepard, "Psychophysical complementarity." In M. Kubovy and J. R. Pomerantz (Eds.), *Perceptual organization*, pp. 279–341. Copyright © 1981 by Lawrence Erlbaum Associates, Inc., Hillsdale, NJ. (b) Coren and others, *Sensation and perception*, p. 400. Orlando, FL: Academic Press, Inc., 1984. Reprinted by permission of Harcourt Brace Jovanovich, Inc.

Figure 7–10 J. J. Gibson, *The perception of the visual world*. Copyright © 1950 by Houghton Mifflin Company. Reprinted by permission.

Figure 7–11 Courtesy Weidenfeld & Nicholson Ltd.

Figure 7–12 © J. Alan Cash

Figure 7–15 C. Blakemore and G. F. Cooper, "Development of the brain depends on the visual environment." *Nature*, 1970, *228*, 447–478. Reprinted by permission of Macmillan Journals Ltd.

Figure 7–16 (a) Wallace Kirkland; (b) Eckhard H. Hess

p. 177 Courtesy Hubert Dolezal from Dolezal, *Living in a World Transformed*. New York: Academic Press, 1982.

p. 178 © Joel Gordon 1981

Figure 7–17 U. Neisser, "The control of information pickup in selective looking." In A. D. Pick (Ed.), *Perception and its development: A tribute to Eleanor J. Gibson*. Copyright © 1979 by Laurence Erlbaum Associates, Inc., Hillsdale, NJ.

Figure 7–18 Adapted from R. W. Leeper, "A study of a neglected portion of the field of learning: The development of sensory organization." *Journal of Genetic Psychology*, 1935, *46*, 41–75. Reprinted by permission of the Helen Dwight Reid Educational Foundation. Copyright © 1935 by Heldref Publications, Washington, D.C.

Figure 7–19 Courtesy Dr. Peter Thompson, York University

Figure 7–20 © Frank Searle, photo supplied by Steuart Campbell

Figure 7–22 S. Coren, C. Porac and L. M. Ward, *Sensation and perception* (2nd ed.), p. 490. Orlando, FL: Academic Press, 1984. Reprinted by permission of Harcourt Brace Jovanovich, Inc.

p. 180 Adapted from R. L. Gregory and E. H. Gombrich (Eds.), *Illusion in nature and art*. Copyright © 1973 by C. Blakemore, J. D. Deregowski, E. H. Gombrich, R. L. Gregory, H. P. Hinton, R. Primrose. New York: Charles Scribner's Sons, 1974. Reprinted by permission of Charles Scribner's Sons and Duckworth.

p. 181 Walter Wick

p. 182 © Billy E. Barnes

p. 183 © Dana Fineman/Sygma

Chapter 8

p. 190 (*top*) © Gregory Edwards 1982/Int'l Stock Photo; (*bottom*) André Derain, *La Tasse de Thé*, 1935, Gallery of Modern Art, Paris/ SEF, Art Resource

p. 190 (*both*) © Michal Heron 1981

Figure 8–1 W. Dement, *Some must watch while some must sleep*. New York: W. W. Norton & Company, Inc., 1978. Reprinted by permission of The Portable Stanford, Stanford Alumni Association.

Figure 8–2 W. Dement, *Some must watch while some must sleep*. New York: W. W. Norton & Company, Inc., 1978. Reprinted by permission of The Portable Stanford, Stanford Alumni Association.

Figure 8–3 R. D. Cartwright, *A primer on sleep and dreaming*, Fig. 1.6. Reading, MA: Addison-Wesley, 1978. Reprinted by permission.

Figure 8–4 R. L. Van de Castle, *The psychology of dreaming*. Morristown, NJ: General Learning Press, 1971. Copyright © 1971 General Learning Corporation.

p. 195 © Phototake

p. 197 (*top*) © Peter Angelo Simon/Phototake; (*bottom*) Paul Klee, *The Mount of the Sacred Cat*, 1923, Private Collection/Giraudon, Art Resource

Figure 8–5 H. P. Roffwarg, J. N. Muzio, and W. C. Dement, "Ontogenetic Development of the Human Sleep-Dream Cycle." *Science*, 1966, *37*(9), 604–619. Copyright © 1966 by the American Association for the Advancement of Science.

p. 198 © Charles E. Schmidt/Taurus Photos

p. 199 © Mimi Forsyth/Monkmeyer Press Photo Service

Figure 8–6 A. H. Morgan and E. R. Hilgard, "Age differences in susceptibility to hypnosis." *International Journal of Clinical and Experimental Hypnosis*, 1971, *21*, 78–95.

p. 203 © Jim Anderson/Woodfin Camp & Associates

p. 205 Courtesy News and Publications Service, Stanford University

p. 208 (*left*) © Charles Gatewood/Stock, Boston; (*right*) Courtesy The Advertising Council, Inc.

Figure 8–8 Ronald K. Siegel, P.O. Box 84358, VA Branch, Los Angeles, CA 90073.

p. 210 © Marcia Weinstein

Figure 8–9 Ronald K. Siegel, P.O. Box 84358, VA Branch, Los Angeles, CA 90073.

Chapter 9

p. 220 © Mike Mazzaschi/Stock, Boston

p. 221 Sovfoto

Figure 9–1 H. E. Garrett, *Great experiments in psychology*. New York: Appleton-Century-Crofts, 1951. Reprinted by permission.

Figure 9–4 Data from I. P. Pavlov. In G. P. Anrep (Trans.), *Conditioned reflexes*, p. 185. London: Oxford University Press, 1927. Reprinted by permission of the publisher.

p. 224 Brown Brothers

p. 226 © Ed Cesar/National Audubon Society, Photo Researchers

p. 227 © Ken Karp

Figure 9–5 (a) © Sybil Shelton/Monkmeyer Press Photo Service; (b) Courtesy Gerbrands Corp.

p. 228 © Jean-Claude Lejeune/Stock, Boston

p. 229 © Hazel Hankin

p. 231 (*bottom*) After photograph by Philip G. Zimbardo, Stanford University

p.230 © Jack Prelutsky/Stock, Boston

Figure 9–6 B. F. Skinner, "Teaching machines." *Scientific American*, November 1961, pp. 91–102. Copyright © 1961 by Scientific American, Inc. All rights reserved.

p. 231 © Billy E. Barnes/Stock, Boston

p. 233 © Bohdan Hrynewych/Stock, Boston

p. 235 © Joe McNally/Wheeler Pictures

Figure 9–7 E. C. Tolman and C. H. Honzik, "Introduction and removal of reward, and maze performance in rats." *University of California publications in psychology*, 1930, *4*, 257–275. Reprinted by permission of the University of California Press.

p. 237 (*left*) © Zig Leszczynski/Animals Animals; (*right*) Courtesy Animal Behavior Enterprises

p. 238 Courtesy News and Publications Service, Stanford University

Chapter 10

p. 245 AP/Wide World Photos

Figure 10–3 L. R. Peterson and M. J. Peterson, "Short-term retention of individual verbal items." *Journal of Experimental Psychology*, 1959, *58*, 193–198. Copyright © 1959 by the American Psychological Association. Reprinted by permission of the authors.

Figure 10–4 Data from H. Ebbinghaus, 1885. Graph from A. D. Baddeley, *Your memory: A user's guide*. Copyright © 1982 by Macmillan Publishing Co., Inc. Reprinted by permission.

Figure 10–5 F. I. M. Craik and M. J. Watkins, "The role of rehearsal in short-term memory." *Journal of Verbal Learning and Verbal Behavior*, 1973, *12*, 599–607.

Figure 10–6 F. I. M. Craik and E. Tulving, "Depth of processing and the retention of words in episodic memory." *Journal of Experimental Psychology: General*, 1975, *104*, 268–294. Copyright © 1975 by the American Psychological Association. Reprinted by permission of the authors

Figure 10–7 (*top*) AP/Wide World Photos; (*bottom*) *Physics and Society*, October 1983, *12*(4). Reprinted by permission.

Figure 10–8 G. H. Bower and M. C. Clark, "Narrative stories as mediators for serial learning." *Psychonomic Science*, 1969, *14*, 181–182. Copyright © 1969, G. H. Bower and M. C. Clark. Reprinted by permission of the Psychonomic Society.

Figure 10–9 D. L. Hintzman, *The psychology of learning and memory*. Copyright © 1978 by W. H. Freeman and Company. All rights reserved.

Figure 10–11 G. H. Bower and others, "Hierarchical retrieval schemes in recall of categorized word lists." *Journal of Verbal Learning and Verbal Behavior*, 1969, *8*, 323–343.

p. 255 © Nubar Alexanian

p. 256 © Bob Sacha 1983/Phototake

Figure 10–12 Adapted from D. R. Godden and A. D. Baddeley, "Context-dependent memory in two natural environments: On land and underwater." *British Journal of Psychology*, 1975, *66*, 325–331. Reprinted by permission of the British Psychological Society.

Figure 10–13 G. Bower, "Mood and Memory". *Psychology Today*, June 1981, pp. 60–69. Reprinted with permission of *Psychology Today* Magazine. Copyright © 1981 by the American Psychological Association.

Figure 10–14 E. F. Loftus, "The malleability of human memory." *American Scientist*, 1979, *67*, 313–320. Reprinted by permission of *American Scientist, Journal of Sigma XI.*

Figure 10–16 R. S. Nickerson and M. J. Adams, "Long-term memory for a common object." *Cognitive Psychology*, 1979, *11*, 287–307.

Figure 10–17 Adapted from H. Ebbinghaus, *Über das Gedächtnis*. Leipzig: Duncker, 1885. Cited in R. Klatsky, *Human memory: Structures and processes*. Copyright © 1980 by W. H. Freeman and Company. All rights reserved.

Figure 10–18 Adapted from H. P. Bahrick, "Semantic memory content in permastore: 50 years of memory for Spanish learned in school." *Journal of Experimental Psychology: General*, 1984, *113*, 1–29.

Figures 10–19 J. G. Jenkins and K. M. Dallenbach, "Obliviscence during sleep and waking." *American Journal of Psychology*, 1924, *35*, 605–612. Copyright © 1924 by the Board of Trustees and the University of Illinois.

p. 264 © Bohdan Hrynewych/Stock, Boston

Chapter 11

Figure 11–1 Adapted from A. M. Collins and M. R. Quillian, "Retrieval time from semantic memory." *Journal of Verbal Learning and Verbal Behavior*, 1969, *8*, 240–247.

p. 272 (*all*) © Stephen Green-Armytage 1984

p. 273 © Laimute E. Druskis/Taurus Photos

Figure 11–3 M. Scheerer, "Problem solving." *Scientific American*, April 1963, pp. 118–128. Copyright © 1963 by Scientific American, Inc. All rights reserved.

Figure 11–4 Adapted from A. S. Luchins, "Classroom experiments on mental set." *American Journal of Psychology*, 1946, *59*, 295–298. Copyright © 1946 by the Board of Trustees and the University of Illinois.

Figure 11–5 K. Duncker, "On problem solving."*Psychological Monographs*, 1945, *58*, (Whole no. 270). Copyright © 1945 by the American Psychological Association. Reprinted by permission.

Figure 11–6 M. Scheerer, "Problem solving." *Scientific American*, April 1963, pp. 118–128. Copyright © 1963 by Scientific American, Inc. All rights reserved.

Figure 11–7 Adapted from A. S. Luchins, "Classroom experiments on mental set." *American Journal of Psychology*, 1946, *59*, 295–298. Copyright © 1946 by the Board of Trustees and the University of Illinois.

Figure 11–8 K. Duncker, "On problem solving." *Psychological Monographs*, 1945, *58* (Whole no. 270). Copyright © 1945 by the American Psychological Association. Reprinted by permission.

Figure 11–9 Yerkes Regional Primate Research Center of Emory University

Figure 11–10 Norman Baxley © DISCOVER Magazine 1984, Time Inc.

Figure 11–11 D. D. Wheeler and I. L. Janis, *A practical guide for making decisions*. Copyright © 1950 by The Free Press, a division of Macmillan Publishing Co., Inc.

p. 282 © Peter Vandermark/Stock, Boston

p. 283 © Harvey Eisner/Taurus Photos

p. 282 (*top*) © Tim Kelly; (*bottom*) © Dick Durrance 1982/Woodfin Camp & Associates

p. 287 © Marc & Evelyne Bernheim/Woodfin Camp & Associates

p. 289 © Joel Gordon 1977

Figure 11–12 K. von Frisch, "Decoding the language of the bee." *Science*, 1974, *185*, 663–668. Copyright © 1974 by the Nobel Foundation.

p. 291 W. N. Kellogg and L. A. Kellogg, *The Ape and the Child*. New York: McGraw-Hill, 1933.

p. 292 (*top*) Courtesy Friends of Washoe, Central Washington University; (*center*) Yerkes Regional Primate Research Center of Emory University

p. 294 Yerkes Regional Primate Research Center of Emory University

Chapter 12

p. 303 National Library of Medicine

p. 304 Brown Brothers

p. 305 (*top*) © Mimi Forsyth/Monkmeyer Press Photo Service: (*bottom*) Courtesy News and Publications Service, Stanford University

p. 306 Brown Brothers

p. 307 (*left*) © John Holland/Stock, Boston; (*center, bottom*) © Mimi Forsyth/Monkmeyer Press Photo Service

Figure 12–1 A. L. Thorndike and E. P. Hagen, *Measurement and evaluation in psychology and education*. New York: Macmillan, 1977 (formerly a John Wiley & Sons, Inc., title). Reprinted with permission of Macmillan Publishing Company.

Figure 12–1 (*photo*) © Paula Wright/Animals Animals

Figure 12–2 Sample SAT questions from *10 SATs*. College Entrance Examination Board, 1983. © 1983 Educational Testing Service, Princeton, NJ. Reprinted by permission.

Figure 12–3 From the Differential Aptitude Test, Forms V & W. Copyright © 1982, 1972 by The Psychological Corporation. All rights reserved. Reprinted by permission.

Figure 12–6 Data from The College Board. Figure from *The Chronicle of Higher Education*, September 26, 1984, Vol. XXIX, No. 5.

p. 312 © Mimi Forsyth/Monkmeyer Press Photo Service

p. 316 (*top*) © Georg Gerster 1975/Rapho, Photo Researchers; (*bottom*) © Hope Alexander 1978/Woodfin Camp & Associates

Figure 12–7 From L. Selfe, *Nadia*. New York: Academic Press, 1979.

p. 320 (*top*) © Susan Lapides 1981/Design Conceptions; (*bottom*) © Bohdan Hrynewych/Stock, Boston

Figure 12–8 T. J. Bouchard, Jr., "Twins—Nature's twicetold tale." In *1983 Yearbook of Science and the Future*. Chicago: Encyclopedia Britannica, 1982.

Figure 12–9 Data summarized by T. J. Bouchard, Jr. and M. McGue, "Familial studies of intelligence: A review." *Science*, 1981, *212*, 1055–1059. Copyright © 1981 by the American Association for the Advancement of Science.

Figure 12–10 Courtesy J. McVicker Hunt

Figure 12–11 R. Plomin and J. C. DeFries, "Genetics and intelligence: Recent data." *Intelligence*, 1980, *4*, p. 22, Fig. 1. Copyright © 1980 by Ablex Publishing Corp. Reprinted by permission of the publisher.

p. 327 © Peter Dublin/Stock, Boston

Figure 12–12 R. Lewontin, "Race and intelligence." In N. J. Block and G. Dworken (Eds.), *The IQ controversy: Critical readings*. Copyright © 1976 by Pantheon Books. Reprinted by permission.

p. 329 © Alec Duncan/Taurus Photos

p. 330 (*top*) © Charles Gatewood/The Image Works; (*bottom*) © Erika Stone 1983/Peter Arnold, Inc.

Chapter 13

p. 338 Courtesy Hope College, Holland, Michigan

p. 341 (*left*) © Eric Simmons/Stock, Boston; (*right*) © B. I. Ullmann/Taurus Photos

Figure 13–2 A. H. Maslow, *Motivation and personality* (2nd ed.). Copyright © 1970 by Harper & Row, Publishers. Reprinted by permission.

Figure 13–3 Wallace Kirkland, LIFE Magazine © 1945 Time Inc.

Figure 13–4 Adapted from W. B. Cannon, *Bodily changes in pain, hunger, fear, and rage*. New York: Branford, 1929.

Figure 13–5 Richard Howard © DISCOVER Magazine 1981, Time Inc.

p. 344 © Freda Leinwand/Monkmeyer Press Photo Service

p. 345 (*top*) © Joel Gordon 1980; (*center*) © Susan Lapides 1984/Design Conceptions; (*bottom*) © Lincoln Russell/Stock, Boston

Figure 13–6 G. A. Bray, "Effect of caloric restriction on energy expenditure in obese patients." *Lancet*, 1969, *2*, 397–398. Reprinted by permission.

Figure 13–7 Adapted from D. Johnson and E. J. Drenick, "Therapeutic fasting in morbid obesity. Long-term follow-up." *Archives of Internal Medicine*, 1977, *137*, 1381–1382. Reprinted by permission of the American Medical Association.

Figure 13–8 W. H. Dietz, Jr. and S. L. Gortmaker, "Do we fatten our children at the television set? Obesity and television viewing in children and adolescents." *Pediatrics*, 1985, *75*, 807–812. Reproduced by permission.

p. 349 Courtesy Yale University

Figure 13–9 C. P. Herman and D. Mack, "Restrained and unrestrained eating." *Journal of Personality*, 1975, *43*(4), 647–660. Copyright © 1975 Duke University Press.

p. 350 (*left*) © Owen Franken/Stock, Boston; (*right*) © Enrico Ferorelli/DOT

p. 351 (*top*) © Fulvio Eccardi/Bruce Coleman Inc.; (*bottom*) © Shirley Zeiberg

Figure 13–10 W. H. Masters and V. E. Johnson, *Human sexual response*. Copyright © 1966 by Little, Brown and Co. Reprinted by permission of the publisher.

p. 355 © Joel Gordon 1983

Figures 13–11 Adapted from D. Byrne, "Predicting human sexual behavior." In A. G. Kraut, *The G. Stanley Hall Lecture Series* (Vol. 2). Copyright © 1982 by the American Psychological Association. Reprinted by permission of the author.

p. 357 (*top*) © Barbara Alper/Stock, Boston; (*bottom*) © Joel Gordon 1980

p. 358 Courtesy S.U.N.Y., Albany

p. 359 © Susan Lapides 1982/Design Conceptions

p. 360 (*top*) University of Wisconsin Primate Laboratory; (*bottom*) © George Bellerose/ Stock, Boston

Figure 13–12 David C. McClelland and others, *The achievement motive*, Appleton-Century-Crofts, Inc., 1953. Reprinted with permission of Irvington Publishers, Inc., New York.

p. 362 © Enrico Ferorelli/DOT

Figure 13–13 J. T. Spence and R. L. Helmreich, "Achievement-related motives and behavior." In J. T. Spence (Ed.), *Achievement and achievement motives: Psychological and sociological approaches*. Copyright © 1983 by W. H. Freeman and Company. All rights reserved.

p. 364 © Alan Carey/The Image Works

Chapter 14

p. 370 © Ed Lettau/Photo Researchers

Figure 14–2 (a) © Chicago Tribune 1985; (b) Courtesy David Raskin, University of Utah, as shown in *Science '82*, June, pp. 24-27.

Figure 14–3 B. Kleinmuntz and J. J. Szucko, "A field study of the fallability of polygraph lie detection." *Nature*, 1984, *308*, 449–450. Reprinted by permission of Macmillan Journals, Ltd.

p. 374 (*left*) © Joel Gordon 1982; (*center*) © Laimute E. Druskis/Taurus Photos; (*right*) © Joel Gordon 1978; (*bottom*) © Eric Kroll/ Taurus Photos

Figure 14–4 Courtesy Dr. Paul Ekman, from P. Ekman and W. V. Friesen, *Unmasking the face*, reprint edition. Palo Alto, CA: Consulting Psychologists Press, 1984.

p. 375 © Benjamin F. Boblett 1985

Figure 14–5 Courtesy Dr. Paul Ekman, University of California at San Francisco

p. 376 Courtesy Carroll Izard, University of Delaware

p. 378 AP/Wide World Photos

p. 379 AP/Wide World Photos

Figure 14–7 Higher Education Research Institute, UCLA

Figure 14–8 T. W. Smith, "Happiness: Time trends, seasonal variations, intersurvey differences, and other mysteries." *Social Psychology Quarterly*, 1979, *42*, 18–30. Reprinted by permission of the American Sociological Association.

Figure 14–9 Roper report 84–1, December 3–10, 1983. Reprinted by permission of *Public Opinion*, August/September 1984, p. 25.

p. 383 (*left*) © Jerry Howard/Positive Images; (*top center*) © Charles Gupton/ Stock, Boston; (*bottom center*) © Nubar Alexanian/Stock, Boston; (*top right*) © Nicholas Sapieha/Stock, Boston; (*bottom right*) © Charles Gupton/Stock, Boston

Figure 14–10 Adapted from R. L. Solomon, "The opponent-process theory of acquired motivation: The costs of pleasure and the benefits of pain." *American Psychologist*, 1980, *35*, 691–712. Copyright © 1980 by the American Psychological Association. Reprinted by permission of the author.

Chapter 15

p. 396 Brown Brothers

p. 398 Movie Still Archives

Figure 15–1 © Sing–Si Schwartz/Kay Reese & Associates

Figure 15–2 © Sepp Seitz 1982/Woodfin Camp & Associates

p. 405 (*top*) © Michal Heron 1983/Woodfin Camp & Associates; (*bottom*) © Robert A. Isaacs/Photo Researchers

Figure 15–3 H. Eysenck, "The validity of questionnaire and rating assessments of extraversion and neuroticism, and their factorial stability." *British Journal of Psychology*, 1963, *54*, 51–62. Reprinted by permission of the British Psychological Society.

Figure 15–5 B. C. Schiele and J. Brozek, "Experimental neuroses" resulting from semistarvation in man. In G. S. Welsh and W. G. Dahlstrom (Eds.), *Basic reading on the MMPI in psychology and medicine*. Copyright © 1956 by the University of Minnesota Press.

p. 409 © Dan Brinzac/Peter Arnold, Inc.

p. 411 Ted Polumbaum, LIFE Magazine © 1968 Time Inc.

p. 412 © Gale Zucker/Stock, Boston

p.414 (*left*) Michael Rougier, LIFE Magazine © 1966 Time Inc.; (*right*) Alfred Eisenstaedt, LIFE Magazine © Time Inc.

Figure 15–6 Adapted from A. Bandura, "The self system in reciprocal determinism." *American Psychologist*, 1978, *33*, 344–358. Copyright © 1978 by the American Psychological Association. Adapted by permission of the author.

p. 418 © Frank Siteman/Taurus Photos

p. 419 (*left*) © Jean-Pierre Ragot/Stock, Boston; (*right*) © Paul S. Conklin/Monkmeyer Press Photo Service

Chapter 16

p. 429 AP/Wide World Photos

Figure 16–1 Courtesy Department of Library Services, American Museum of Natural History

p. 431 © Michael D. Sullivan

Figure 16–2 Roper report 84–3, February 11–25, 1984. Reprinted by permission of *Public Opinion*, August/September 1984.

p. 435 (*left*) © Hugh Rogers/Monkmeyer Press Photo Service; (*right*) © Peter Menzel/ Stock, Boston

p. 437 AP/Wide World Photos

Figure 16–3 A. E. Fallon and P. Rozin, "Sex differences in perceptions of desirable body shape." *Journal of Abnormal Psychology*, 1985, *94*, 102–105. Copyright © 1985 by the American Psychological Association. Reprinted by permission of the author.

p. 440 AP/Wide World Photos

p. 441 © Norman Hurst/Stock, Boston

p. 442 (*left*) AP/Wide World Photos; (*right*) © Van Bucher/Photo Researchers

p. 445 Courtesy of Drs. Michael Phelps and John Mazziota, U.C.L.A. School of Medicine

Figure 16–5 J. P. Forgas and others, "The influence of mood on perceptions of social interactions." *Journal of Experimental Social Psychology*, 1984, *20*, 497–513. Orlando, FL: Academic Press, Journals Division, 1984.

Figure 16–6 Adapted from Lewinsohn and others, "An integrative theory of depression." In S. Reiss and R. Bootzin (Eds.), *Theoretical issues in behavior therapy*. Orlando, FL: Academic Press, 1985.

p. 449 (*left*) August Natterer, *Witch's Head*, The Prinzhorn Collection, University of Heidelberg; (*right*) Berthold L., *Untitled*, The Prinzhorn Collection, University of Heidelberg. Photos: Krannert Museum, University of Illinois at Urbana

p. 450 © Raymond Depardon/Magnum Photos

p. 451 Courtesy Brookhaven National Laboratory, N.Y.U. Medical Center

Figure 16–7 S. E. Nicol and I. I. Gottesman, "Clues to the genetics and neurobiology of schizophrenia." *American Scientist*, 1983, *71*, 398–404. Reprinted by permission of *American Scientist*, journal of Sigma XI.

p. 452 National Institute of Mental Health

Figure 16–8 S. A. Mednick and others, "Genetic influences in criminal convictions: Evidence from an adoption cohort." *Science*, 1984, *224*, 891–894. Copyright © 1984 by the American Association for the Advancement of Science.

Chapter 17

p. 461 (*left*) William Hogarth, *Bethlem Royal Hospital*/Art Resource; (*right*) Snark, Art Resource

p. 463 © Van Bucher/Photo Researchers

p. 464 © Ken Karp

p. 465 Michael Rougier, LIFE Magazine © 1966 Time Inc.

p. 467 © Michael Weisbrot and family/ Stock, Boston

p. 468 (*top*) © Watriss-Baldwin 1982/ Woodfin Camp & Associates; (*bottom*) © Ken Karp

p. 469 © Sepp Seitz 1978/Woodfin Camp & Associates

Figure 17–1 D. Gilling and R. Brightwell, *The human brain*. Copyright © 1982 by D. Gilling and R. Brightwell. Reprinted by permission of Facts on File, Inc.

p. 473 © Sybil Shelton/Peter Arnold, Inc.

Figure 17–2 Adapted from A. Ellis, "Rational-emotive therapy." In R. J. Corsini (Ed.), *Current psychotherapies* (3rd ed.), 1984. Reproduced by permission of the publisher, F. E. Peacock, Inc., Itasca, IL.

p. 475 (*left*) Courtesy Brigham Young University; (*right*) Courtesy Institute for Rational-Emotive Therapy

Figure 17–3 Adapted from M. L. Smith and others, *The benefits of psychotherapy*, p. 88. Baltimore: Johns Hopkins Press, 1980. Reprinted by permission.

p. 483 © Mimi Forsyth/Monkmeyer Press Photo Service

p. 484 © Sybil Shelton/Peter Arnold, Inc.

p. 485 © Will McIntyre/Photo Researchers

Figure 17–4 Data from NIMH; (*photo*) © Judy Sloan 1985/ Gamma-Liaison

Figure 17-5 Data from NIMH—PSC Collaborative Study I

Figure 17–6 Adapted from I. L. McCann and D. S. Holmes, "Influence of aerobic exercise on depression." *Journal of Personality and Social Psychology*, 1984, *46*, 1142-1147. Copyright © 1984 by the American Psychological Association. Reprinted by permission of the authors.

p. 490 © Sybil Shelton/Peter Arnold, Inc.

Chapter 18

p. 496 *Canon of Avicenna Visiting Hospital*, Laurentian Library, Florence/Scala, Art Resource

p. 497 (*left*) © John Troha 1984/Black Star; (*right*) © Nancy Pierce 1984/Black Star

Figure 18–4 Selye's general adaptation syndrome. In T. Cox, *Stress*. Copyright © 1978 by Tom Cox. Reprinted by permission of Macmillan, London and Basingstoke.

Figure 18–5 P. R. Adams and G. R. Adams, "Mount Saint Helens's ashfall: Evidence for a disaster stress reaction." *American Psychologist*, 1984, *29*, 252–260. Copyright © 1984 by the American Psychological Association. Reprinted by permission of the authors.

Table 18–1 Adapted from T. H. Holmes and R. H. Rahe, "The social readjustment rating scale." *Journal of Psychosomatic Research*, 1967, *11*, 213–218. Copyright © 1967 by Pergamon Press, Ltd.

Figure 18–6 From "How to Cope Better with Stress." *Reader's Digest*, March 1984. Copyright © 1984 by the Reader's Digest Association, Inc., and the Campbell's Soup Company. Reprinted with permission.

Figure 18–7 C. D. Spielberger and others, "The experience and expression of anger." In M. A. Chesney, S. E. Goldston, and R. H. Rosenman (Eds.), *Anger and hostility in behavioral medicine*. New York: Hemisphere, 1985.

p. 504 © Christopher Morris 1983/Black Star

p. 507 © Mimi Forsyth/Monkmeyer Press Photo Service

Figure 18–8 Historical Pictures Service

p. 509 © Sam C. Pierson, Jr. 1977/Photo Researchers

Figure 18–9 Adapted from M. A. Safer and others, "Determinants of three stages of delay in seeking care at a medical clinic." *Medical Care*, 1979, *17*(1), 11–28. Reprinted by permission of J. B. Lippincott Co.

Figure 18–10 J. W. Pennebaker and J. M. Lightner, "Competition of internal and external information in an exercise setting." *Journal of Personality and Social Psychology*, 1980, *39*, 165–174. Copyright © 1980 by the American Psychological Association. Reprinted by permission of the author.

Figure 18–10 (*photo*) © Wayne Sproul/Int'l. Stock Photo

Figure 18–11 J. M. Weiss, "Psychological and behavioral influences on gastrointestinal lesions in animal models." In J. D. Maser and M. E. P. Seligman (Eds.), *Psychopathology: Experimental models*. Copyright © 1977 by W. H. Freeman and Company. All rights reserved.

p. 512 © Art Seitz/Gamma-Liaison

Figure 18–12 L. D. Egbert and others, "Reduction of postoperative pain by encouragement and instruction of patients." *New England Journal of Medicine*, 1964, *270*, 825–827. Reprinted by permission.

p. 513 © Phil Huber 1985/Black Star

p. 514 © Jonathan E. Pite/Int'l. Stock Photo

p. 515 © Jean Boughton/Stock, Boston

Figure 18–14 Data from A. McAlister and others, "Pilot study of smoking, alcohol and drug abuse prevention." *American Journal of Public Health*, 1980, *70*, 719–721. Data also from M. J. Telch and others, "Long-term follow-up of a pilot project on smoking prevention with adolescents." *Journal of Behavioral Medicine*, 1982, *5*, 1–7. Reprinted by permission of Plenum Publishing Corporation.

Figure 18–15 (*photo*) © Joel Gordon 1984

Figure 18–16 M. Friedman and D. Ulmer, *Treating type A behavior—and your heart*. New York: Alfred A. Knopf, Inc., 1984. Reprinted by permission.

p. 521 Vincent Van Gogh, *Treurende Man*, 1890, Rijksmuseum Kröller-Müller, Otterlo, The Netherlands

Chapter 19

p. 528 Movie Still Archives

Figure 19–1 Data from M. Sherif and C. W. Sherif, *Social Psychology*. Copyright © 1969 by Harper & Row, Publishers. Reprinted by permission.

Figure 19–2 D. P. Phillips, "The influence of suggestion on suicide: Substantive and theoretical implications of the Werther effect." *American Sociological Review*, 1974, *39*, 340–354. Reprinted by permission of the American Sociological Association.

Figure 19–3 S. E. Asch, "Opinions and social pressure." *Scientific American*, November 1955, pp. 31–35. Copyright © 1955 by Scientific American, Inc. All rights reserved.

p. 533 (*top*) © Eiji Miyazawa/Black Star; (*bottom*) Courtesy Graduate School and University Center of the City University of New York

Figure 19–4 Data from S. Milgram, *Obedience to authority*, p. 35. Copyright © 1974 by Harper & Row, Publishers. Reprinted by permission.

p. 538 © Andy Levin 1980/Black Star

p. 539 (*both*) © Mimi Forsyth/Monkmeyer Press Photo Service

Figure 19–6 R. T. Croyle and J. Cooper, "Dissonance arousal: Physiological evidence." *Journal of Personality and Social Psychology*, 1983, *45*, 782–791. Copyright © 1983 by the American Psychological Association. Reprinted by permission of the author.

p. 542 © 1985 AT&T Communications

p. 543 (*left*) AP/Wide World Photos; (*right*) © Anthony Suau 1985/Black Star

p. 545 (*top*) © Mimi Forsyth/Monkmeyer Press Photo Service; (*bottom*) © Martha Cooper/Peter Arnold, Inc.

p. 546 Courtesy The Henry Ford Museum, Dearborn, Michigan

Figure 19–7 Courtesy Philip G. Zimbardo, Stanford University

p. 548 © Joel Gordon 1978

Figure 19–8 (*photo*) © Bill Powers 1981/ Frost Publishing Co.

Figure 19–8 V. C. Cox and others, "Prison crowding research: The relevance for prison housing standards and a general approach regarding crowding phenomena." *American Psychologist*, 1984, *39*, 1148–1160. Copyright © 1984 by the American Psychological Association. Reprinted by permission of the author.

Figure 19–9 Data from D. G. Myers and G. D. Bishop, "Discussion effects on racial attitudes." *Science*, 1970, *169*, 778–779. Copyright © 1970 by the American Association for the Advancement of Science.

p. 550 UPI/Bettmann Newsphotos

p. 551 Margaret Bourke-White, LIFE Magazine © 1946 Time Inc.

Chapter 20

p. 556 (*both*) © Bill Strode 1980/Woodfin Camp & Associates

p. 558 © Photo-News/Gamma Liaison

Figure 20–1 C. A. Anderson and D. C. Anderson, "Ambient temperature and violent crime: Tests of the linear and curvilinear hypotheses." *Journal of Personality and Social Psychology*, 1984, *46*, 91–97. Copyright © 1984 by the American Psychological Association. Reprinted by permission of the author.

p. 559 (*top*) © Serge de Sazo/Rapho, Photo Researchers; (*bottom*) © Ralph Lewin Studio 1985

p. 560 © Hugh Rogers/Monkmeyer Press Photo Service

Figure 20–2 Data from A. C. Nielson Co.

p. 561 © Mark Antman/The Image Works

p. 562 (*left*) © Summer Productions/Taurus Photos

Figure 20–3 Data from D. Zillmann and J. Bryant, "Effects of massive exposure to pornography." In N. M. Malamuth and E. Donnerstein (Eds.), *Pornography and sexual aggression*. Orlando, FL: Academic Press, 1984.

Figure 20–4 D. Zillmann, "Effects of repeated exposure to nonviolent pornography." Testimony to the Attorney General's Commission on Pornography, September 11, 1985, Houston, TX.

Figure 20–5 J. H. Court, "Sex and violence: A ripple effect." In N. M. Malamuth and E. Donnerstein (Eds.), *Pornography and sexual aggression*. Orlando, FL: Academic Press, 1984.

p. 565 (*left*) © Nancy Crampton 1984; (*right*) Courtesy Americas Watch

p. 566 AP/Wide World Photos

p. 567 (*top*) © Michael Abramson/Gamma-Liaison; (*bottom left*) © Christopher Morrow 1982/Black Star; (*bottom right*) © Trevor Ferrel/Gamma-Liaison

Figure 20–6 Adapted from J. M. Darley and B. Latané, "Bystander intervention in emergencies: Diffusion of responsibility." *Journal of Personality and Social Psychology*, 1968, *8*, 377–383. Copyright © 1968 by the American Psychological Association. Reprinted by permission of the author.

Figure 20–7 Data from J. M. Darley and B. Latané, "When will people help in a crisis?" *Psychology Today*, December 1968, pp. 54–57, 70–71. Reprinted by permission of *Psychology Today* magazine. Copyright © 1968 by the American Psychological Association.

p. 569 (*top left*) © Bill Stanton 1983/Int'l. Stock Photo; (*top right*) © Joseph Nettis 1982/Photo Researchers; (*bottom left*) © Scott Thode/Int'l. Stock Photo; (*bottom right*) © Martin M. Rotker/Taurus Photos

Figure 20–8 J. B. Siebenaler and D. K. Caldwell, "Cooperation among adult dolphins." *Journal of Mammalogy*, 1956, *37*, 126–128.

Figure 20–9 (*racial prejudice curve*) Data from *Public Opinion*, October/November 1984, p. 15, the National Opinion Research Center; (*gender prejudice curve*) Data from Gallup Report 228/229, August/September 1984, p. 13. Reprinted by permission.

p. 573 (*top left*) © Eddie Adams/Gamma-Liaison; (*top right*) © Mark Peters 1985/Black Star; (*bottom*) © Shelly Katz 1985/Black Star

p. 576 © Randy Matusow/Monkmeyer Press Photo Service

p. 577 © Carl Mydans 1983/Black Star

p. 578 (*left*) © Lenore Weber/Taurus Photos; (*center*) © Lenore Weber/Taurus Photos; (*top right*) © Andy Levin 1982/Black Star; (*bottom right*) © Andy Levin 1982/Black Star

p. 579 (*top row, left to right*) © Fred Ward/Black Star; © George Holton 1973/Photo Researchers; © Nik Wheeler 1982/Black Star; © Nik Wheeler 1980/Black Star; (*bottom*) © O. P. Sharma/Taurus Photos

p. 580 (*top*) © Joel Gordon 1980; (*bottom*) © Joel Gordon 1983

p. 585 (*photo*) © Scott Thode/Int'l. Stock Photo

p. 585 Reprinted by permission of the *Bulletin of Atomic Scientists*, a magazine of science and world affairs. Copyright © 1947 by the Educational Foundation for Nuclear Science, Chicago.

p. 587 © James Carroll

p. 588 © Tom Keller/Gamma-Liaison

Appendix A

p. 595 The Bettmann Archive

Figure A–3 Tom Pantages, Courtesy Widener Library, Harvard University

Figure A–7 Courtesy of Elliot A. Tanis, Hope College, Holland, Michigan

Name Index

Subject Index